ADVANCED
ACCOUNTING

ELEVENTH EDITION

ADVANCED
ACCOUNTING

Floyd A. Beams
Virginia Polytechnic Institute
and State University

Joseph H. Anthony
Michigan State University

Bruce Bettinghaus
Grand Valley State University

Kenneth A. Smith
University of Washington

PEARSON

Boston Columbus Indianapolis New York San Francisco Upper Saddle River
Amsterdam Cape Town Dubai London Madrid Milan Munich Paris Montréal Toronto
Delhi Mexico City São Paulo Sydney Hong Kong Seoul Singapore Taipei Tokyo

Editorial Director: Sally Yagan
Editor in Chief: Donna Battista
Director of Editorial Services: Ashley Santora
Senior Editorial Project Manager: Karen Kirincich
Director of Marketing: Patrice Jones
Marketing Assistant: Ian Gold
Senior Managing Editor: Cindy Zonneveld
Production Project Manager: Carol O'Rourke
Senior Art Director: Jonathan Boylan
Interior Design: Jonathan Boylan
Cover Designer: Jonathan Boylan
Composition: PreMediaGlobal
Full-Service Project Management: Kristy Zamagni
Senior Operations Specialist: Diane Peirano
Printer/Binder: Edwards Brothers
Cover Printer: Demand Production Center
Typeface:10/12 Times

Credits and acknowledgments borrowed from other sources and reproduced, with permission, in this textbook appear on appropriate page within text.

Microsoft® and Windows® are registered trademarks of the Microsoft Corporation in the U.S.A. and other countries. Screen shots and icons reprinted with permission from the Microsoft Corporation. This book is not sponsored or endorsed by or affiliated with the Microsoft Corporation.

CIP data is on file at the Library of Congress.

Prentice Hall
is an imprint of

www.pearsonhighered.com

10 9 8 7 6 5 4 3 2 1
ISBN 13: 978-0-13-256896-8
ISBN 10:   0-13-256896-9

ABOUT THE AUTHORS

FLOYD A. BEAMS, PH.D., authored the first edition of *Advanced Accounting* in 1979 and actively revised his text through the next six revisions and twenty-one years while maintaining an active professional and academic career at Virginia Tech where he rose to the rank of Professor, retiring in 1995.

Beams earned his B.S. and M.A. degrees from the University of Nebraska, and a Ph.D. from the University of Illinois. He published actively in journals including *The Accounting Review*, *Journal of Accounting, Auditing and Finance, Journal of Accountancy, The Atlantic Economic Review, Management Accounting*, and others. He was a member of the American Accounting Association and the Institute of Management Accountants and served on committees for both organizations. Beams was honored with the National Association of Accounts' Lybrand Bronze Medal Award for outstanding contribution to accounting literature, the Distinguished Career in Accounting award from the Virginia Society of CPAs, and the Virginia Outstanding Accounting Educator award from the Carman G. Blough student chapter of the Institute of Management Accountants. Professor Beams passed away three years ago; however, we continue to honor his contribution to the field, and salute the impact he had on this volume.

JOSEPH H. ANTHONY, PH.D., joined the Michigan State University faculty in 1983 and is an Associate Professor of Accounting at the Eli Broad College of Business. He earned his B.A. in 1971 and his M.S. in 1974, both awarded by Pennsylvania State University, and he earned his Ph.D. from The Ohio State University in 1984. He is a Certified Public Accountant, and is a member of the American Accounting Association, American Institute of Certified Public Accountants, American Finance Association, and Canadian Academic Accounting Association. He has been recognized as a Lilly Foundation Faculty Teaching Fellow and as the MSU Accounting Department's Outstanding Teacher in 1998–99 and in 2010–2011.

Anthony teaches a variety of courses, including undergraduate introductory, intermediate, and advanced financial accounting. He also teaches financial accounting theory and financial statement analysis at the master's level, as well as financial accounting courses in Executive MBA programs, and a doctoral seminar in financial accounting and capital markets research. He co-authored an introductory financial accounting textbook.

Anthony's research interests include financial statement analysis, corporate reporting, and the impact of accounting information in the securities markets. He has published a number of articles in leading accounting and finance journals, including *The Journal of Accounting & Economics, The Journal of Finance, Contemporary Accounting Research, The Journal of Accounting, Auditing, & Finance*, and *Accounting Horizons*.

BRUCE BETTINGHAUS, PH.D., is an Assistant Professor of Accounting in the School of Accounting in The Seidman College of Business at Grand Valley State University. His teaching experience includes corporate governance and accounting ethics, as well as accounting theory and financial reporting for both undergraduates and graduate classes. He earned his Ph.D at Penn State University and his B.B.A. at Grand Valley State University. Bruce has also served on the faculties of the University of Missouri and Michigan State University. He has been recognized for high quality teaching at both Penn State and Michigan State universities. His research interests focus on governance and financial reporting for public firms. He has published articles in *The International Journal of Accounting* and *The Journal of Corporate Accounting and Finance*.

KENNETH A. SMITH, PH.D., is a Senior Lecturer in the Evans School of Public Affairs at the University of Washington. He earned his Ph.D. from the University of Missouri, his M.B.A. from Ball State University and his B.A. in Accounting from Anderson University (IN). He is a Certified Public Accountant. Smith's research interests include government accounting and budgeting, non-profit financial management, non-financial performance reporting and information systems in government and non-profit organizations. He has published articles in such journals as *Accounting Horizons, Journal of Government Financial Management, Public Performance & Management Review, Nonprofit and Voluntary Sector Quarterly, International Public Management Journal, Government Finance Review*, and *Strategic Finance*.

Smith's professional activities include membership in the American Accounting Association, the Association of Government Accountants, the Government Finance Officers Association, the Institute of Internal Auditors, and the Institute of Management Accountants. He serves on the Steering Committee for the Public Performance Measurement Reporting Network and as the Executive Director for the Oregon Public Performance Measurement Association.

BRIEF
CONTENTS

Preface xvii

CHAPTER 1
Business Combinations 1

CHAPTER 2
Stock Investments—Investor Accounting
and Reporting 27

CHAPTER 3
An Introduction to Consolidated Financial Statements 63

CHAPTER 4
Consolidation Techniques and Procedures 99

CHAPTER 5
Intercompany Profit Transactions—Inventories 145

CHAPTER 6
Intercompany Profit Transactions—Plant Assets 185

CHAPTER 7
Intercompany Profit Transactions—Bonds 219

CHAPTER 8
Consolidations—Changes in Ownership Interests 247

CHAPTER 9
Indirect and Mutual Holdings 279

CHAPTER 10
Subsidiary Preferred Stock, Consolidated Earnings per
Share, and Consolidated Income Taxation 315

CHAPTER 11
Consolidation Theories, Push-Down Accounting, and
Corporate Joint Ventures 369

CHAPTER 12
Derivatives and Foreign Currency: Concepts and Common
Transactions 409

CHAPTER 13
Accounting for Derivatives and Hedging Activities 429

CHAPTER 14
Foreign Currency Financial Statements 463

CHAPTER 15
Segment and Interim Financial Reporting 497

CHAPTER 16
Partnerships—Formation, Operations, and Changes
in Ownership Interests 525

CHAPTER 17
Partnership Liquidation 561

CHAPTER 18
Corporate Liquidations and Reorganizations 591

CHAPTER 19
An Introduction to Accounting for State and Local
Governmental Units 625

CHAPTER 20
Accounting for State and Local Governmental
Units—Governmental Funds 663

CHAPTER 21
Accounting for State and Local Governmental
Units—Proprietary and Fiduciary Funds 711

CHAPTER 22
Accounting for Not-for-Profit Organizations 737

CHAPTER 23
Estates and Trusts 775

Glossary G-1

Index I-1

CONTENTS

Preface xvii

CHAPTER 1
Business Combinations   1

Reasons for Business Combinations   2
Antitrust Considerations   3
Legal Form of Business Combinations   4
Accounting Concept of Business Combinations   4
Accounting for Combinations as Acquisitions   6
Disclosure Requirements   15
The Sarbanes-Oxley Act   17
Electronic Supplement to Chapter 1 ES1

CHAPTER 2
Stock Investments—Investor Accounting and Reporting   27

Accounting for Stock Investments   27
Equity Method—a One-Line Consolidation   31
Investment in a Step-by-Step Acquisition   39
Sale of an Equity Interest   39
Stock Purchases Directly from the Investee   40
Investee Corporation with Preferred Stock   40
Extraordinary Items and other Considerations   41
Disclosures for Equity Investees   42
Testing Goodwill for Impairment   44

CHAPTER 3
An Introduction to Consolidated Financial Statements   63

Business Combinations Consummated through Stock Acquisitions   63
Consolidated Balance Sheet at Date of Acquisition   68
Consolidated Balance Sheets after Acquisition   72
Assigning Excess to Identifiable Net Assets and Goodwill   74
Consolidated Income Statement   80
Push-Down Accounting   81
Preparing a Consolidated Balance Sheet Worksheet   83
Electronic Supplement to Chapter 3 ES3

CHAPTER **4**

Consolidation Techniques and Procedures   **99**

Consolidation under the Equity Method   99

Locating Errors   106

Excess Assigned to Identifiable Net Assets   106

Consolidated Statement of Cash Flows   112

Preparing a Consolidation Worksheet   117

Electronic Supplement to Chapter 4 ES4

CHAPTER **5**

Intercompany Profit Transactions—Inventories   **145**

Intercompany Inventory Transactions   146

Downstream and Upstream Sales   150

Unrealized Profits from Downstream Sales   153

Unrealized Profits from Upstream Sales   156

Consolidation Example—Intercompany Profits from Downstream Sales   158

Consolidation Example—Intercompany Profits from Upstream Sales   161

Electronic Supplement to Chapter 5 ES5

CHAPTER **6**

Intercompany Profit Transactions—Plant Assets   **185**

Intercompany Profits on Nondepreciable Plant Assets   185

Intercompany Profits on Depreciable Plant Assets   190

Plant Assets Sold at Other than Fair Value   198

Consolidation Example—Upstream and Downstream Sales of Plant Assets   199

Inventory Purchased for Use as Operating Assets   202

Electronic Supplement to Chapter 6 ES6

CHAPTER **7**

Intercompany Profit Transactions—Bonds   **219**

Intercompany Bond Transactions   219

Constructive Gains and Losses on Intercompany Bonds   220

Parent Bonds Purchased by Subsidiary   222

Subsidiary Bonds Purchased by Parent   228

Electronic Supplement to Chapter 7 ES7

CHAPTER **8**

Consolidations—Changes in Ownership Interests   **247**

Acquisitions During an Accounting Period   247

Piecemeal Acquisitions   251

Sale of Ownership Interests   253

Changes in Ownership Interests from Subsidiary Stock Transactions   258

Stock Dividends and Stock Splits by a Subsidiary   262

CHAPTER **9**

Indirect and Mutual Holdings   **279**

Affiliation Structures   279

Indirect Holdings—Father-Son-Grandson Structure   281

Indirect Holdings—Connecting Affiliates Structure   285

Mutual Holdings—Parent Stock Held by Subsidiary   289

Subsidiary Stock Mutually-Held   298

CHAPTER 10

Subsidiary Preferred Stock, Consolidated Earnings per Share, and Consolidated Income Taxation   315

Subsidiaries with Preferred Stock Outstanding   315

Parent and Consolidated Earnings Per Share   322

Subsidiary with Convertible Preferred Stock   324

Subsidiary with Options and Convertible Bonds   325

Income Taxes of Consolidated Entities   326

Income Tax Allocation   328

Separate-Company Tax Returns with Intercompany Gain   330

Effect of Consolidated and Separate-Company Tax Returns on Consolidation Procedures   334

Business Combinations   341

Financial Statement Disclosures for Income Taxes   346

Electronic Supplement to Chapter 10 ES10

CHAPTER 11

Consolidation Theories, Push-Down Accounting, and Corporate Joint Ventures   369

Comparison of Consolidation Theories   370

Illustration—Consolidation Under Parent-Company and Entity Theories   372

Push-Down Accounting and Other Basis Considerations   381

Joint Ventures   388

Accounting for Variable Interest Entities   391

CHAPTER 12

Derivatives and Foreign Currency: Concepts and Common Transactions   409

Derivatives   409

Foreign Exchange Concepts and Definitions   414

Foreign Currency Transactions Other than Forward Contracts   416

CHAPTER 13

Accounting for Derivatives and Hedging Activities   429

Accounting for Derivative Instruments and Hedging Activities   429

Accounting for Hedge Contracts: Illustrations of Cash Flow and Fair Value Hedge Accounting Using Interest Rate Swaps   439

Foreign Currency Derivatives and Hedging Activities   443

CHAPTER 14

Foreign Currency Financial Statements   463

Objectives of Translation and the Functional Currency Concept   463

Application of the Functional Currency Concept   465

Illustration: Translation   469

Illustration: Remeasurement   475

Hedging a Net Investment in a Foreign Entity   479

CHAPTER 15
Segment and Interim Financial Reporting   497

Segment Reporting   497

Interim Financial Reporting   504

Guidelines for Preparing Interim Statements   506

CHAPTER 16
Partnerships—Formation, Operations, and Changes in Ownership Interests   525

Nature of Partnerships   525

Initial Investments in a Partnership   526

Additional Investments and Withdrawals   528

Partnership Operations   529

Profit and Loss Sharing Agreements   530

Changes in Partnership Interests   536

Purchase of an Interest from Existing Partners   537

Investing in an Existing Partnership   539

Dissociation of a Continuing Partnership Through Death or Retirement   542

Limited Partnerships   544

CHAPTER 17
Partnership Liquidation   561

The Liquidation Process   561

Safe Payments to Partners   565

Installment Liquidations   567

Cash Distribution Plans   573

Insolvent Partners and Partnerships   576

CHAPTER 18
Corporate Liquidations and Reorganizations   591

Bankruptcy Reform Act of 1978   591

Liquidation   594

Illustration of a Liquidation Case   596

Reorganization   603

Financial Reporting During Reorganization   607

Financial Reporting for the Emerging Company   608

Illustration of Reorganization Case   610

CHAPTER 19
An Introduction to Accounting for State and Local Governmental Units   625

Historical Development of Accounting Principles for State and
    Local Governmental Units   625

Overview of Basic Governmental Accounting Models and Principles   627

The Financial Reporting Entity   638

Comprehensive Annual Financial Report   639

CHAPTER 20

Accounting for State and Local Governmental Units—Governmental Funds   663

Recent Changes to Governmental Fund Accounting   663

The General Fund   664

Accounting for the General Fund   664

Permanent Funds   677

Capital Projects Funds   678

Special Assessment Activities   683

Debt Service Funds   683

Governmental Fund Financial Statements   685

Preparing the Government-Wide Financial Statements   688

CHAPTER 21

Accounting for State and Local Governmental Units—Proprietary and Fiduciary Funds   711

Proprietary Funds   711

Internal Service Funds   712

Enterprise Funds   715

Proprietary Fund Financial Statements   718

Fiduciary Funds   722

Preparing the Government-Wide Financial Statements   727

Required Proprietary Fund Note Disclosures   727

CHAPTER 22

Accounting for Not-for-Profit Organizations   737

The Nature of Not-for-Profit Organizations   737

Not-for-Profit Accounting Principles   738

Voluntary Health and Welfare Organizations   743

"Other" Not-for-Profit Organizations   749

Nongovernmental Not-for-Profit Hospitals and Other Health Care Organizations   750

Private Not-for-Profit Colleges and Universities   755

CHAPTER 23

Estates and Trusts   775

Creation of an Estate   775

Probate Proceedings   776

Administration of the Estate   776

Accounting for the Estate   777

Illustration of Estate Accounting   778

Accounting for Trusts   782

Estate Taxation   783

Glossary   G-1

Index   I-1

PREFACE

NEW TO THIS EDITION

Important changes in the 11th edition of *Advanced Accounting* include the following:

- The text has been rewritten to align with the *Financial Accounting Standards Board Accounting Standards Codification*.
- The entire text has been revised to remove constant references to official reporting standards from the body of the text itself. The text now provides references to a listing of official pronouncements at the end of each chapter. Text length is reduced and rendered much more readable for the students.
- Former Chapters 12 and 13 have now been expanded to include an additional chapter, Chapter 14. These chapters cover accounting for derivatives and foreign currency transactions and translations, and have been substantially revised, rewritten, and expanded. This will allow students to better understand these complex and important topics.
- All chapters have been updated to include coverage of the latest international reporting standards and issues, where appropriate. As U.S. and international reporting standards move toward greater harmonization, the international coverage continues to expand in the 11th edition.
- Chapters 1 through 11 have been updated to reflect the most recent Financial Accounting Standards Board (FASB) statements and interpretations related to consolidated financial reporting, including accounting for variable-interest entities. Fair-value accounting has been added to all appropriate sections of the text.
- The governmental and not-for-profit chapters have been updated to include all standards through *GASB No. 59*. These chapters have also been enhanced with illustrations of the financial statements from Golden, Colorado. Coverage now includes service efforts and accomplishments, as well as post-employment benefits other than pensions. Chapter 20 includes an exhibit with t-accounts to help students follow the governmental fund transactions and their financial statement impact.
- Chapter 23 coverage of fiduciary accounting for estates and trusts has been revised and updated to reflect current taxation of these entities. Assignment materials have been added to enhance student learning.

This 11th edition of *Advanced Accounting* is designed for undergraduate and graduate students majoring in accounting. This edition includes twenty-three chapters designed for financial accounting courses beyond the intermediate level. Although this text is primarily intended for accounting students, it is also useful for accounting practitioners interested in preparation or analysis of consolidated financial statements, accounting for derivative securities, and governmental and not-for-profit accounting and reporting. This 11th edition has been thoroughly updated to reflect recent business developments, as well as changes in accounting standards and regulatory requirements.

This comprehensive textbook addresses the practical financial reporting problems encountered in consolidated financial statements, goodwill, other intangible assets, and derivative securities. The text also includes coverage of foreign currency transactions and translations, partnerships, corporate liquidations and reorganizations, governmental accounting and reporting, not-for-profit accounting, and estates and trusts.

An important feature of the 11th edition is the continued student orientation, which has been further enhanced with this edition. This 11th edition strives to maintain an interesting and readable text for the students. The focus on the complete equity method is maintained to allow students to focus on accounting concepts rather than bookkeeping techniques in learning the consolidation materials. This edition also maintains the reference text quality of prior editions through the use of electronic supplements to the consolidation chapters provided on the Web site that accompanies this text, at www.pearsonhighered.com/beams. The presentation of consolidation materials highlights working paper–only entries with shading and presents working papers on single upright pages. All chapters include excerpts from the popular business press and references to familiar real-world companies, institutions, and events. This book uses examples from annual reports of well-known companies and governmental and not-for-profit institutions to illustrate key concepts and maintain student interest. Assignment materials include adapted items from past CPA examinations and have been updated and expanded to maintain close alignment with coverage of the chapter concepts. Assignments have been updated to include additional research cases and simulation-type problems. This edition maintains identification of names of parent and subsidiary companies beginning with P and S, allowing immediate identification. It also maintains parenthetical notation in journal entries to clearly indicate the direction and types of accounts affected by the transactions. The 11th edition retains the use of learning objectives throughout all chapters to allow students to better focus study time on the most important concepts.

ORGANIZATION OF THIS BOOK

Chapters 1 through 11 cover business combinations, the equity and cost methods of accounting for investments in common stock, and consolidated financial statements. This emphasizes the importance of business combinations and consolidations in advanced accounting courses as well as in financial accounting and reporting practices.

Accounting and reporting standards for acquisition-method business combinations are introduced in Chapter 1. Chapter 1 also provides necessary background material on the form and economic impact of business combinations. Chapter 2 introduces the complete equity method of accounting as a one-line consolidation, and this approach is integrated throughout subsequent chapters on consolidations. This approach permits alternate computations for such key concepts as consolidated net income and consolidated retained earnings, and it helps instructors explain the objectives of consolidation procedures. The alternative computational approaches also assist students by providing a check figure for their logic on these key concepts.

The one-line consolidation is maintained as the standard for a parent company in accounting for investments in its subsidiaries. Procedures for situations in which the parent company uses the cost method or an incomplete equity method to account for investments in subsidiaries are covered in electronic supplements to the chapters, which are available at the *Advanced Accounting* Web site, www.pearsonhighered.com/beams. The supplements include assignment materials for these alternative methods so that students can be prepared for consolidation assignments, regardless of the method used by the parent company.

Chapter 3 introduces the preparation of consolidated financial statements. Students learn how to record the fair values of the subsidiary's identifiable net assets and implied goodwill. Chapter 4 continues consolidations coverage, introducing working paper techniques and procedures. The text emphasizes the three-section, vertical financial statement working paper approach throughout, but Chapter 4 also offers a trial balance approach in the appendix. The standard employed throughout the consolidation chapters is working papers for a parent company that uses the complete equity method of accounting (i.e., one-line consolidations) for investments in subsidiaries.

Chapters 5 through 7 cover intercompany transactions in inventories, plant assets, and bonds. The Appendix to Chapter 5 reviews SEC accounting requirements.

Chapter 8 discusses changes in the level of subsidiary ownership, and Chapter 9 introduces more complex affiliation structures. Chapter 10 covers several consolidation-related topics: subsidiary preferred stock, consolidated earnings per share, and income taxation for consolidated business entities. The electronic supplement to Chapter 10 covers branch accounting. Chapter 11 is a theory chapter that discusses alternative consolidation theories, push-down accounting, leveraged buyouts, corporate joint ventures, and key concepts related to accounting and reporting by variable interest entities. The electronic supplement to Chapter 11 presents current cost implications for consolidated financial reporting. Chapters 9 through 11 cover specialized topics and have been written as stand-alone materials. Coverage of these chapters is not necessary for assignment of subsequent text chapters.

Business enterprises become more global in nature with each passing day. Survival of a modern business depends upon access to foreign markets, suppliers, and capital. Some of the unique challenges of international business and financial reporting are covered in Chapters 12 and 13. These chapters, covering accounting for derivatives and foreign currency transactions and translations, have been substantially revised and rewritten. The concepts and the accounting for derivatives are now separated. Chapter 12 covers the concepts and common transactions for derivatives and foreign currency. Chapter 13 covers accounting for derivative and hedging activities. Coverage includes import and export activities and forward or similar contracts used to hedge against potential exchange losses. Chapter 14 focuses on preparation of consolidated financial statements for foreign subsidiaries. This chapter includes translation and remeasurement of foreign-entity financial statements, one-line consolidation of equity method investees, consolidation of foreign subsidiaries for financial reporting purposes, and the combination of foreign branch operations.

Chapter 15 introduces topics of segment reporting under *FASB ASC Topic 280*, as well as interim financial reporting issues. Partnership accounting and reporting are covered in Chapters 16 and 17. Chapter 18 discusses accounting and reporting procedures related to corporate liquidations and reorganizations.

Chapters 19 through 21 provide an introduction to governmental accounting, and Chapter 22 introduces accounting for voluntary health and welfare organizations, hospitals, and colleges and universities. These chapters are completely updated through *GASB Statement No. 59*, and provide students with a good grasp of key concepts and procedures related to not-for-profit accounting.

Finally, Chapter 23 provides coverage of fiduciary accounting and reporting for estates and trusts.

CUSTOMIZING THIS TEXT

You can easily customize this text via Pearson Learning Solutions. Pearson Learning Solutions offers you the flexibility to select specific chapters from this text to create a customized book that exactly fits your course needs. When you customize your book will have the chapters in the order that matches your syllabus, with sequential pagination. All cross-references to other chapters will be removed. You even have the option to add your own material or third-party content!

To receive your free evaluation copy or build your book online, visit *www.pearsoncustom.com,* contact your Pearson representative, or contact us directly at Pearson Custom Publishing, e-mail dbase.pub@pearsoncustom.com; phone 800-777-6872. You can expect your evaluation copy to arrive within 7 to 10 business days.

INSTRUCTORS' RESOURCES

The supplements that accompany this text are available for instructors only to download at our Instructor Resource Center, at *www.pearsonhighered.com/irc*. Resources include the following:

- **Solutions manual:** Prepared by the authors, the solutions manual includes updated answers to questions, and solutions to exercises and problems. Solutions to assignment materials included in the electronic supplements are also included. Solutions are provided in electronic format, making electronic classroom display easier for instructors. All solutions have been accuracy-checked to maintain high-quality work.
- **Instructor's manual:** The instructor's manual contains comprehensive outlines of all chapters, class illustrations, descriptions for all exercises and problems (including estimated times for completion), and brief outlines of new standards set apart for easy review.

- **Test item file:** This file includes test questions in true/false, multiple-choice, short-answer, and problem formats. Solutions to all test items are also included.
- **PowerPoint presentation:** A ready-to-use PowerPoint slideshow designed for classroom presentation is available. Instructors can use it as-is or edit content to fit particular classroom needs.

STUDENT RESOURCES

To access the student download Web site, visit www.pearsonhighered.com/beams. This Web site includes the electronic supplements for certain chapters, spreadsheet templates, and PowerPoint presentations by chapter.

ACKNOWLEDGMENTS

Many people have made valuable contributions to this 11th edition of *Advanced Accounting*, and we are pleased to recognize their contributions. We are indebted to the many users of prior editions for their helpful comments and constructive criticisms. We also acknowledge the help and encouragement that we received from students at Grand Valley State, Michigan State, and University of Washington, who, often unknowingly, participated in class testing of various sections of the manuscript.

We want to thank our faculty colleagues for the understanding and support that have made 11 editions of *Advanced Accounting* possible.

A special thank you to Carolyn Streuly for her many hours of hard work and continued dedication to the project.

The following accuracy checkers and supplements authors whose contributions we appreciate—Jeanne David, University Detroit Mercy; Linda Hajec, Penn State-Erie, The Behrend College; Sheila Handy, East Stroudsburg University.

We would like to thank the members of the Prentice Hall book team for their hard work and dedication: Sally Yagan, Vice President, Editorial Director; Donna Battista, Editor in Chief; Karen Kirincich, Senior Project Manager; Carol O'Rourke, Production Project Manager. Kristy Zamagni, Project Manager, PreMedia Global.

Our thanks to the reviewers who helped to shape this 11th edition:

Marie Archambault, Marshall University

Ron R. Barniv, Kent State University

Nat Briscoe, Northwestern State University

Michael Brown, Tabor School of Business

Susan Cain, Southern Oregon University

Kerry Calnan, Elmus College

Eric Carlsen, Kean University

Gregory Cermignano, Widener University

Lawrence Clark, Clemson University

Penny Clayton, Drury University

Lynn Clements, Florida Southern College

David Dahlberg, The College of St. Catherine

Patricia Davis, Keystone College

David Doyon, Southern New Hampshire University

John Dupuy, Southwestern College

Thomas Edmonds, Regis University

Charles Fazzi, Saint Vincent College

Roger Flint, Oklahoma Baptist University

Margaret Garnsey, Siena College

Sheri Geddes, Andrews University

Gary Gibson, Lindsey Wilson College

Bonnie Givens, Avila University

Steve Hall, University of Nebraska at Kearney

Matthew Henry, University of Arkansas at Pine Bluff

Judith Harris, Nova Southeastern University

Joyce Hicks, Saint Mary's College

Marianne James, California State University, Los Angeles

Patricia Johnson, Canisius College

Stephen Kerr, Hendrix College

Thomas Largay, Thomas College

Stephani Mason, Hunter College

Mike Metzcar, Indiana Wesleyan University

Dianne R. Morrison, University of Wisconsin, La Crosse

David O'Dell, McPherson College

Bruce Oliver, Rochester Institute of Technology

Pamela Ondeck, University of Pittsburgh at Greensburg

Anne Oppegard, Augustana College

Larry Ozzello, University of Wisconsin, Eau Claire

Glenda Partridge, Spring Hill College

Thomas Purcell, Creighton University

Abe Qastin, Lakeland College

Donna Randolph, National American University

Frederick Richardson, Virginia Tech

John Rossi, Moravian College

Angela Sandberg, Jacksonville State University

Mary Jane Sauceda, University of Texas at Brownville and Texas Southmost College

John Schatzel, Stonehill College

Michael Schoderbeck, Rutgers University

Joann Segovia, Minnesota State University, Moorhead

Stanley Self, East Texas Baptist University

Ray Slager, Calvin College

Duane Smith, Brescia University

Keith Smith, George Washington University

Kimberly Smith, County College of Morris

Pam Smith, Northern Illinois University

Jeffrey Spear, Houghton College

Catherine Staples, Randolph-Macon College

Natalie Strouse, Notre Dame College

Zane Swanson, Emporia State University

Anthony Tanzola, Holy Family University

Christine Todd, Colorado State University, Pueblo

Ron Twedt, Concordia College

Barbara Uliss, Metropolitan State College of Denver

Joan Van Hise, Fairfield University

Dan Weiss, Tel Aviv University, Faculty of Management

Stephen Wheeler, Eberhardt School of Business

Deborah Williams, West Virginia State University

H. James Williams, Grand Valley State University

Joe Wilson, Muskingum College

Alex Yen, Suffolk University

Sung Wook Yoon, California State University, Northridge

Suzanne Alonso Wright, Penn State

Ronald Zhao, Monmouth University

ADVANCED
ACCOUNTING

1 CHAPTER

Business Combinations

- On December 31, 2008, *Wells Fargo & Company* acquired all of the outstanding shares of *Wachovia Corporation* for $23.1 billion, making Wells Fargo one of the largest U.S. commercial banks.
- In October 2001, *Chevron* and *Texaco* announced completion of their merger agreement valued in excess of $30 billion. In 1998, gasoline-producing rivals *Exxon* and *Mobil* merged to form *ExxonMobil* Corporation in a deal valued at $80 billion.
- *Bank of America* acquired *FleetBoston Financial Corporation* for $47 billion in 2004 and followed up with a purchase of *MBNA Corporation* for $35 billion in 2005.
- In November 2006, *Freeport-McMoRan Copper & Gold* acquired rival copper producer *Phelps Dodge* for $25.9 billion.

Welcome to the world of business combinations. The 1990s witnessed a period of unparalleled growth in merger and acquisition activities in both the United States and in international markets (often referred to as *merger mania*), and the trend continues.

Merger activities slowed with the stock market downturn in 2001, and again during the financial crisis of 2008, but when the market recovers, the pace picks up. The following firms announced combinations in December 2004. *Symantec* (manufacturer of the Norton antivirus software) acquired *Veritas Software* for $13.5 billion. *Oracle Corporation* acquired *People-Soft, Inc.*, for $10.3 billion. *Johnson & Johnson* acquired *Guidant* for $25.4 billion. Guidant produces pacemakers, defibrillators, heart stents, and other medical devices. In July 2010, insurer *Aon* announced that it had agreed to acquire human resources consultant *Hewitt Associates* for $4.9 billion in cash and stock, and *GM* announced that it would acquire *AmeriCredit* for $3.5 billion.

Firms strive to produce economic value added for shareholders. Related to this strategy, expansion has long been regarded as a proper goal of business entities. A business may choose to expand either internally (building its own facilities) or externally (acquiring control of other firms in business combinations). The focus in this chapter will be on why firms often prefer external over internal expansion options and how financial reporting reflects the outcome of these activities.

In general terms, **business combinations** unite previously separate business entities. The overriding objective of business combinations must be increasing profitability; however, many firms can become more efficient by horizontally or vertically integrating operations or by diversifying their risks through conglomerate operations.

Horizontal integration is the combination of firms in the same business lines and markets. The business combinations of Chevron and Texaco, Exxon and Mobil, and Wells Fargo and Wachovia

NOTE 27: OPERATING SEGMENTS

Revenues (in millions)

	Total Revenues		
	2009	2008	2007
Energy Infrastructure	$ 37,134	$ 38,571	$ 30,698
Technology Infrastructure	42,474	46,316	42,801
NBC Universal	15,436	16,969	15,416
Capital Finance	50,622	67,008	66,301
Consumer & Industrial	9,703	11,737	12,663
Corporate items and eliminations	1,414	1,914	4,609
Total	$156,783	$182,515	$172,488

The note goes on to provide similar detailed breakdown of intersegment revenues; external revenues; assets; property, plant, and equipment additions; depreciation and amortization; interest and other financial charges; and the provision for income taxes.

are examples of horizontal integration. The past 15 years have witnessed significant consolidation activity in banking and other industries. *Kimberly-Clark* acquired *Scott Paper*, creating a consumer paper and related products giant. Paint manufacturers *Sherwin-Williams* and *Pratt and Lambert* combined in a $400 million deal. *Delta Air Lines* took control of its rival *Northwest Air Lines* in 2008 at a cost of $3.353 billion.

Vertical integration is the combination of firms with operations in different, but successive, stages of production or distribution, or both. In June 2004, *Briggs & Stratton Corporation* announced an agreement to acquire *Simplicity Manufacturing, Inc.*, for $227.5 million. Briggs & Stratton is the world's largest producer of small gasoline-powered engines, whereas Simplicity is a leader in design, manufacture, and marketing of premium commercial and consumer lawn-and-garden equipment. In March 2007, *CVS Corporation* and *Caremark Rx, Inc.*, merged to form *CVS/Caremark Corporation* in a deal valued at $26 billion. The deal joined the nation's largest pharmacy chain with one of the leading healthcare/pharmaceuticals service companies.

Conglomeration is the combination of firms with unrelated and diverse products or service functions, or both. Firms may diversify to reduce the risk associated with a particular line of business or to even out cyclical earnings, such as might occur in a utility's acquisition of a manufacturing company. Several utilities combined with telephone companies after the 1996 Telecommunications Act allowed utilities to enter the telephone business. For example, in November 1997, *Texas Utilities Company* acquired *Lufkin-Conroe Communications Company*, a local-exchange telephone company, to diversify into a communications business. The early 1990s saw tobacco maker *Phillip Morris Company* acquire food producer *Kraft* in a combination that included over $11 billion of recorded goodwill alone. Although all of us have probably purchased a light bulb manufactured by **General Electric Company**, the scope of the firm's operations goes well beyond that household product. Exhibit 1-1 excerpts Note 27 from General Electric's 2009 annual report on its major operating segments.

LEARNING OBJECTIVE **1**

REASONS FOR BUSINESS COMBINATIONS

If expansion is a proper goal of business enterprise, why would a business expand through combination rather than by building new facilities? Among the many possible reasons are the following:

> **Cost Advantage.** It is frequently less expensive for a firm to obtain needed facilities through combination than through development. This is particularly true in periods of inflation. Reduction of the total cost for research and development activities was a prime motivation in *AT&T's* acquisition of *NCR*.

> **Lower Risk.** The purchase of established product lines and markets is usually less risky than developing new products and markets. The risk is especially low when the goal is diversification. Scientists may discover that a certain product provides an environmental or health hazard. A single-product, non-diversified firm may

be forced into bankruptcy by such a discovery, while a multiproduct, diversified company is more likely to survive. For companies in industries already plagued with excess manufacturing capacity, business combinations may be the only way to grow. When *Toys R Us* decided to diversify its operations to include baby furnishings and other related products, it purchased retail chain *Baby Superstore*.

Fewer Operating Delays. Plant facilities acquired in a business combination are operative and already meet environmental and other governmental regulations. The time to market is critical, especially in the technology industry. Firms constructing new facilities can expect numerous delays in construction, as well as in getting the necessary governmental approval to commence operations. Environmental impact studies alone can take months or even years to complete.

Avoidance of Takeovers. Many companies combine to avoid being acquired themselves. Smaller companies tend to be more vulnerable to corporate takeovers; therefore, many of them adopt aggressive buyer strategies to defend against takeover attempts by other companies.

Acquisition of Intangible Assets. Business combinations bring together both intangible and tangible resources. The acquisition of patents, mineral rights, research, customer databases, or management expertise may be a primary motivating factor in a business combination. When *IBM* purchased *Lotus Development Corporation,* $1.84 billion of the total cost of $3.2 billion was allocated to research and development in process.

Other Reasons. Firms may choose a business combination over other forms of expansion for business tax advantages (for example, tax-loss carryforwards), for personal income and estate-tax advantages, or for personal reasons. One of several motivating factors in the combination of *Wheeling-Pittsburgh Steel*, a subsidiary of *WHX*, and *Handy & Harman* was Handy & Harman's overfunded pension plan, which virtually eliminated Wheeling-Pittsburgh Steel's unfunded pension liability. The egos of company management and takeover specialists may also play an important role in some business combinations.

ANTITRUST CONSIDERATIONS

Federal antitrust laws prohibit business combinations that restrain trade or impair competition. The U.S. Department of Justice and the Federal Trade Commission (FTC) have primary responsibility for enforcing federal antitrust laws. For example, in 1997 the FTC blocked *Staples's* proposed $4.3 billion acquisition of *Office Depot*, arguing in federal court that the takeover would be anticompetitive.

In 2004, the FTC conditionally approved *Sanofi-Synthelabo SA's* $64 billion takeover of *Aventis SA*, creating the world's third-largest drug manufacturer. Sanofi agreed to sell certain assets and royalty rights in overlapping markets in order to gain approval of the acquisition.

Business combinations in particular industries are subject to review by additional federal agencies. The Federal Reserve Board reviews bank mergers, the Department of Transportation scrutinizes mergers of companies under its jurisdiction, the Department of Energy has jurisdiction over some electric utility mergers, and the Federal Communications Commission (FCC) rules on the transfer of communication licenses. After the Justice Department cleared a $23 billion merger between *Bell Atlantic Corporation* and *Nynex Corporation*, the merger was delayed by the FCC because of its concern that consumers would be deprived of competition. The FCC later approved the merger. Such disputes are settled in federal courts.

In addition to federal antitrust laws, most states have some type of statutory takeover regulations. Some states try to prevent or delay hostile takeovers of the business enterprises incorporated within their borders. On the other hand, some states have passed antitrust exemption laws to protect hospitals from antitrust laws when they pursue cooperative projects.

Interpretations of antitrust laws vary from one administration to another, from department to department, and from state to state. Even the same department under the same administration can change its mind. A completed business combination can be re-examined by the FTC at any time. Deregulation in the banking, telecommunication, and utility industries permits business combinations that once would have been forbidden. In 1997, the Justice Department and the FTC jointly issued new guidelines for evaluating proposed business combinations that allow companies to argue that cost savings or better products could offset potential anticompetitive effects of a merger.

LEARNING
OBJECTIVE **2**

LEGAL FORM OF BUSINESS COMBINATIONS

Business combination is a general term that encompasses all forms of combining previously separate business entities. Such combinations are **acquisitions** when one corporation acquires the productive assets of another business entity and integrates those assets into its own operations. Business combinations are also acquisitions when one corporation obtains operating control over the productive facilities of another entity by acquiring a majority of its outstanding voting stock. The acquired company need not be dissolved; that is, the acquired company does not have to go out of existence.

The terms **merger** and **consolidation** are often used as synonyms for acquisitions. However, legally and in accounting there is a difference. A merger entails the dissolution of all but one of the business entities involved. A consolidation entails the dissolution of all the business entities involved and the formation of a new corporation.

A *merger* occurs when one corporation takes over all the operations of another business entity and that entity is dissolved. For example, Company A purchases the assets of Company B directly from Company B for cash, other assets, or Company A securities (stocks, bonds, or notes). This business combination is an acquisition, but it is not a merger unless Company B goes out of existence. Alternatively, Company A may purchase the stock of Company B directly from Company B's stockholders for cash, other assets, or Company A securities. This acquisition will give Company A operating control over Company B's assets. It will not give Company A legal ownership of the assets unless it acquires all the stock of Company B and elects to dissolve Company B (again, a merger).

A *consolidation* occurs when a new corporation is formed to take over the assets and operations of two or more separate business entities and dissolves the previously separate entities. For example, Company D, a newly formed corporation, may acquire the net assets of Companies E and F by issuing stock directly to Companies E and F. In this case, Companies E and F may continue to hold Company D stock for the benefit of their stockholders (an acquisition), or they may distribute the Company D stock to their stockholders and go out of existence (a consolidation). In either case, Company D acquires ownership of the assets of Companies E and F.

Alternatively, Company D could issue its stock directly to the stockholders of Companies E and F in exchange for a majority of their shares. In this case, Company D controls the assets of Company E and Company F, but it does not obtain legal title unless Companies E and F are dissolved. Company D must acquire all the stock of Companies E and F and dissolve those companies if their business combination is to be a consolidation. If Companies E and F are not dissolved, Company D will operate as a holding company, and Companies E and F will be its subsidiaries.

Future references in this chapter will use the term *merger* in the technical sense of a business combination in which all but one of the combining companies go out of existence. Similarly, the term *consolidation* will be used in its technical sense to refer to a business combination in which all the combining companies are dissolved and a new corporation is formed to take over their net assets. *Consolidation* is also used in accounting to refer to the accounting process of combining parent and subsidiary financial statements, such as in the expressions "principles of consolidation," "consolidation procedures," and "consolidated financial statements." In future chapters, the meanings of the terms will depend on the context in which they are found.

Mergers and consolidations do not present special accounting problems or issues after the initial combination, apart from those discussed in intermediate accounting texts. This is because only one legal and accounting entity survives in a merger or consolidation.

ACCOUNTING CONCEPT OF BUSINESS COMBINATIONS

GAAP defines the accounting concept of a business combination as:

> *A transaction or other event in which an acquirer obtains control of one or more businesses. Transactions sometimes referred to as true mergers or mergers of equals also are business combinations.*[1]

Note that the accounting concept of a business combination emphasizes the creation of a single entity and the independence of the combining companies before their union. Although one or more of the companies may lose its separate legal identity, dissolution of the legal entities is not necessary within the accounting concept.

Previously separate businesses are brought together into one entity when their business resources and operations come under the control of a single management team. Such control within one business entity is established in business combinations in which:

1. One or more corporations become subsidiaries.
2. One company transfers its net assets to another, or
3. Each company transfers its net assets to a newly formed corporation.

A corporation becomes a **subsidiary** when another corporation acquires a majority (more than 50 percent) of its outstanding voting stock. Thus, one corporation need not acquire all of the stock of another corporation to consummate a business combination. In business combinations in which less than 100 percent of the voting stock of other combining companies is acquired, the combining companies necessarily retain separate legal identities and separate accounting records even though they have become one entity for financial reporting purposes.

Business combinations in which one company transfers its net assets to another can be consummated in a variety of ways, but the acquiring company must acquire substantially all the net assets in any case. Alternatively, each combining company can transfer its net assets to a newly-formed corporation. Because the newly-formed corporation has no net assets of its own, it issues its stock to the other combining companies or to their stockholders or owners.

A Brief Background on Accounting for Business Combinations

Accounting for business combinations is one of the most important and interesting topics of accounting theory and practice. At the same time, it is complex and controversial. Business combinations involve financial transactions of enormous magnitudes, business empires, success stories and personal fortunes, executive genius, and management fiascos. By their nature, they affect the fate of entire companies. Each is unique and must be evaluated in terms of its economic substance, irrespective of its legal form.

Historically, much of the controversy concerning accounting requirements for business combinations involved the **pooling of interests method**, which became generally accepted in 1950. Although there are conceptual difficulties with the pooling method, the underlying problem that arose was the introduction of alternative methods of accounting for business combinations (pooling versus purchase). Numerous financial interests are involved in a business combination, and alternate accounting procedures may not be neutral with respect to different interests. That is, the individual financial interests and the final plan of combination may be affected by the method of accounting.

Until 2001, accounting requirements for business combinations recognized both the pooling and purchase methods of accounting for business combinations. In August 1999, the FASB issued a report supporting its proposed decision to eliminate pooling. Principal reasons cited included the following:

- Pooling provides less relevant information to statement users.
- Pooling ignores economic value exchanged in the transaction and makes subsequent performance evaluation impossible.
- Comparing firms using the alternative methods is difficult for investors.

Pooling creates these problems because it uses historical book values to record combinations, rather than recognizing fair values of net assets at the transaction date. Generally accepted accounting principles (GAAP) generally require recording asset acquisitions at fair values.

Further, the FASB believed that the economic notion of a pooling of interests rarely exists in business combinations. More realistically, virtually all combinations are acquisitions, in which one firm gains control over another.

GAAP eliminated the pooling of interests method of accounting for all transactions initiated after June 30, 2001.[2] Combinations initiated subsequent to that date must use the acquisition method. Because the new standard prohibited the use of the pooling method only for combinations initiated after the issuance of the revised standard, prior combinations accounted for under the pooling of interests method were grandfathered; that is, both the acquisition and pooling methods continue to exist as acceptable financial reporting practices for past business combinations.

Therefore, one cannot ignore the conditions for reporting requirements under the pooling approach. On the other hand, because no new poolings are permitted, this discussion focuses on the acquisition method. More detailed coverage of the pooling of interests method is relegated to *Electronic Supplements* on the *Advanced Accounting* Web site.

INTERNATIONAL ACCOUNTING Elimination of pooling made GAAP more consistent with international accounting standards. Most major economies prohibit the use of the pooling method to account for business combinations. International Financial Reporting Standards (IFRS) require business combinations to be accounted for using the purchase method, and specifically prohibit the pooling of interests method. In introducing the new standard, International Accounting Standards Board (IASB) Chairman Sir David Tweedie noted:

> *Accounting for business combinations diverged substantially across jurisdictions. IFRS 3 marks a significant step toward high quality standards in business combination accounting, and in ultimately achieving international convergence in this area.*[3]

Accounting for business combinations was a major joint project between the FASB and IASB. As a result, accounting in this area is now generally consistent between GAAP and IFRS. Some differences remain, and we will point them out in later chapters as appropriate.

ACCOUNTING FOR COMBINATIONS AS ACQUISITIONS

LEARNING OBJECTIVE **3**

GAAP requires that all business combinations initiated after December 15, 2008, be accounted for as acquisitions.[4] The **acquisition method** follows the same GAAP for recording a business combination as we follow in recording the purchase of other assets and the incurrence of liabilities. We record the combination using the fair value principle. In other words, we measure the cost to the purchasing entity of acquiring another company in a business combination by the amount of cash disbursed or by the fair value of other assets distributed or securities issued.

We expense the direct costs of a business combination (such as accounting, legal, consulting, and finders' fees) other than those for the registration or issuance of equity securities. We charge registration and issuance costs of equity securities issued in a combination against the fair value of securities issued, usually as a reduction of additional paid-in capital. We expense indirect costs such as management salaries, depreciation, and rent under the acquisition method. We also expense indirect costs incurred to close duplicate facilities.

NOTE TO THE STUDENT

The topics covered in this text are sometimes complex and involve detailed exhibits and illustrative examples. Understanding the exhibits and illustrations is an integral part of the learning experience, and you should study them in conjunction with the related text. Carefully review the exhibits as they are introduced in the text. Exhibits and illustrations are designed to provide essential information and explanations for understanding the concepts presented.

Understanding the financial statement impact of complex business transactions is an important element in the study of advanced financial accounting topics. To assist you in this learning endeavor, this book depicts journal entries that include the types of accounts being affected and the directional impact of the event. Conventions used throughout the text are as follows: A parenthetical reference added to each account affected by a journal entry indicates the type of account and the effect of the entry. For example, an increase in accounts receivable, an asset account, is denoted as "Accounts receivable (+A)." A decrease in this account is denoted as "Accounts receivable (−A)." The symbol (A) stands for assets, (L) for liabilities, (SE) for stockholders' equity accounts, (R) for revenues, (E) for expenses, (Ga) for gains, and (Lo) for losses.

To illustrate, assume that Pop Corporation issues 100,000 shares of $10 par common stock for the net assets of Son Corporation in a business combination on July 1, 2011. The market price of Pop common stock on this date is $16 per share. Additional direct costs of the business combination consist of Securities and Exchange Commission (SEC) fees of $5,000, accountants' fees in connection with the SEC registration statement of $10,000, costs for printing and issuing the common stock certificates of $25,000, and finder's and consultants' fees of $80,000.

Pop records the issuance of the 100,000 shares on its books as follows (in thousands):

Investment in Son (+A)	1,600	
Common stock, $10 par (+SE)		1,000
Additional paid-in capital (+SE)		600

To record issuance of 100,000 shares of $10 par
common stock with a market price of $16 per share
in a business combination with Son Corporation.

Pop records additional direct costs of the business combination as follows:

Investment expense (E, –SE)	80	
Additional paid-in capital (–SE)	40	
Cash (or other net assets) (–A)		120

To record additional direct costs of combining with Son
Corporation: $80,000 for finder's and consultants' fees
and $40,000 for registering and issuing equity securities.

We treat registration and issuance costs of $40,000 as a reduction of the fair value of the stock issued and charge these costs to Additional paid-in capital. We expense other direct costs of the business combination ($80,000). The total cost to Pop of acquiring Son is $1,600,000, the amount entered in the Investment in Son account.

We accumulate the total cost incurred in purchasing another company in a single investment account, regardless of whether the other combining company is dissolved or the combining companies continue to operate in a parent–subsidiary relationship. If we dissolve Son Corporation, we record its identifiable net assets on Pop's books at fair value, and record any excess of investment cost over fair value of net assets as goodwill. In this case, we allocate the balance recorded in the Investment in Son account by means of an entry on Pop's books. Such an entry might appear as follows:

Receivables (+A)	XXX	
Inventories (+A)	XXX	
Plant assets (+A)	XXX	
Goodwill (+A)	XXX	
Accounts payable (+L)		XXX
Notes payable (+L)		XXX
Investment in Son (–A)		1,600

To record allocation of the $1,600,000 cost of acquiring
Son Corporation to identifiable net assets according to
their fair values and to goodwill.

If we dissolve Son Corporation, we formally retire the Son Corporation shares. The former Son shareholders are now shareholders of Pop.

If Pop and Son Corporations operate as parent company and subsidiary, Pop will not record the entry to allocate the Investment in Son balance. Instead, Pop will account for its investment in

Son by means of the Investment in Son account, and we will make the assignment of fair values to identifiable net assets required in the consolidation process.

Because of the additional complications of accounting for parent–subsidiary operations, the remainder of this chapter is limited to business combinations in which a single acquiring entity receives the net assets of the other combining companies. Subsequent chapters cover parent-subsidiary operations and the preparation of consolidated financial statements.

Recording Fair Values in an Acquisition

LEARNING OBJECTIVE 4

The first step in recording an acquisition is to determine the fair values of all identifiable tangible and intangible assets acquired and liabilities assumed in the combination. This can be a monumental task, but much of the work is done before and during the negotiating process for the proposed merger. Companies generally retain independent appraisers and valuation experts to determine fair values. GAAP provides guidance on the determination of fair values. There are three levels of reliability for fair value estimates.[5] Level 1 is fair value based on established market prices. Level 2 uses the present value of estimated future cash flows, discounted based on an observable measure such as the prime interest rate. Level 3 includes other internally-derived estimations. Throughout this text, we will assume that total fair value is equal to the total market value, unless otherwise noted.

We record identifiable assets acquired, liabilities assumed and any noncontrolling interest using fair values at the acquisition date. We determine fair values for all identifiable assets and liabilities, regardless of whether they are recorded on the books of the acquired company. For example, an acquired company may have expensed the costs of developing patents, blueprints, formulas, and the like. However, we assign fair values to such identifiable intangible assets of an acquired company in a business combination accounted for as an acquisition.[6]

Assets acquired and liabilities assumed in a business combination that arise from contingencies should be recognized at fair value if fair value can be reasonably estimated. If fair value of such an asset or liability cannot be reasonably estimated, the asset or liability should be recognized in accordance with general FASB guidelines to *account for contingencies*, and *reasonable estimation of the amount of a loss*. It is expected that most litigation contingencies assumed in an acquisition will be recognized only if a loss is probable and the amount of the loss can be reasonably estimated.[7]

There are few exceptions to the use of fair value to record assets acquired and liabilities assumed in an acquisition. Deferred tax assets and liabilities arising in a combination, pensions and other employee benefits, and leases should be accounted for in accordance with normal guidance for these items.[8]

We assign no value to the goodwill recorded on the books of an acquired subsidiary because such goodwill is an unidentifiable asset and because we value the goodwill resulting from the business combination directly:[9]

> *The acquirer shall recognize goodwill as of the acquisition date, measured as the excess of (a) over (b):*
>
> **a.** *The aggregate of the following:*
>   **1.** *The consideration transferred measured in accordance with this Section, which generally requires acquisition-date fair value (see paragraph 805-30-30-7)*
>   **2.** *The fair value of any noncontrolling interest in the acquiree*
>   **3.** *In a business combination achieved in stages, the acquisition-date fair value of the acquirer's previously held equity interest in the acquiree.*
> **b.** *The net of the acquisition-date [fair value] amounts of the identifiable assets acquired and the liabilities assumed measured in accordance with this Topic.*

RECOGNITION AND MEASUREMENT OF OTHER INTANGIBLE ASSETS GAAP[10] clarifies the recognition of intangible assets in business combinations under the acquisition method. Firms should recognize intangibles separate from goodwill only if they fall into one of two categories.

Recognizable intangibles must meet either a separability criterion or a contractual–legal criterion.

GAAP defines intangible assets as either current or noncurrent assets (excluding financial instruments) that lack physical substance. Per GAAP:

> *The acquirer shall recognize separately from goodwill the identifiable intangible assets acquired in a business combination. An intangible asset is identifiable if it meets either the separability criterion or the contractual-legal criterion described in the definition of identifiable.*
>
> *The separability criterion means that an acquired intangible asset is capable of being separated or divided from the acquiree and sold, transferred, licensed, rented, or exchanged, either individually or together with a related contract, identifiable asset, or liability. An intangible asset that the acquirer would be able to sell, license, or otherwise exchange for something else of value meets the separability criterion even if the acquirer does not intend to sell, license, or otherwise exchange it. …*
>
> *An acquired intangible asset meets the separability criterion if there is evidence of exchange transactions for that type of asset or an asset of a similar type, even if those transactions are infrequent and regardless of whether the acquirer is involved in them. …*
>
> *An intangible asset that is not individually separable from the acquiree or combined entity meets the separability criterion if it is separable in combination with a related contract, identifiable asset, or liability.*[11]

Intangible assets that are not separable should be included in goodwill. For example, acquired firms will have a valuable employee workforce in place, but this asset cannot be recognized as an intangible asset separately from goodwill. GAAP (reproduced in part in Exhibit 1-2) provides more detailed discussion and an illustrative list of intangible assets that firms can recognize separately from goodwill.

CONTINGENT CONSIDERATION IN AN ACQUISITION Some business combinations provide for additional payments to the previous stockholders of the acquired company, contingent on future events or transactions. The contingent consideration may include the distribution of cash or other assets or the issuance of debt or equity securities.

Contingent consideration in an acquisition must be measured and recorded at fair value as of the acquisition date as part of the consideration transferred in the acquisition. In practice, this requires the acquirer to estimate the amount of consideration it will be liable for when the contingency is resolved in the future.

The contingent consideration can be classified as equity or as a liability. An acquirer may agree to issue additional shares of stock to the acquiree if the acquiree meets an earnings goal in the future. Then, the contingent consideration is in the form of equity. At the date of acquisition, the Investment and Paid-in Capital accounts are increased by the fair value of the contingent consideration. Alternatively, an acquirer may agree to pay additional cash to the acquiree if the acquiree meets an earnings goal in the future. Then, the contingent consideration is in the form of a liability. At the date of the acquisition, the Investment and Liability accounts are increased by the fair value of the contingent consideration.

The accounting treatment of subsequent changes in the fair value of the contingent consideration depends on whether the contingent consideration is classified as equity or as a liability. If the contingent consideration is in the form of equity, the acquirer does not remeasure the fair value of the contingency at each reporting date until the contingency is resolved. When the contingency is settled, the change in fair value is reflected in the equity accounts. If the contingent consideration is in the form of a liability, the acquirer measures the fair value of the contingency at each reporting date until the contingency is resolved. Changes in the fair value

EXHIBIT 1-2

Intangible Assets that are Identifiable[13]

The following guidance presents examples of identifiable intangible assets acquired in a business combination. Some of the examples may have characteristics of assets other than intangible assets. The acquirer should account for those assets in accordance with their substance. The examples are not intended to be all-inclusive.

Intangible assets designated with the symbol # are those that arise from contractual or other legal rights. Those designated with the symbol * do not arise from contractual or other legal rights but are separable. Intangible assets designated with the symbol # might also be separable, but separability is not a necessary condition for an asset to meet the contractual-legal criterion.

Marketing-Related Intangible Assets

a. Trademarks, trade names, service marks, collective marks, certification marks #

b. Trade dress (unique color, shape, package design) #

c. Newspaper mastheads #

d. Internet domain names #

e. Noncompetition agreements #

Customer-Related Intangible Assets

a. Customer lists *

b. Order or production backlog #

c. Customer contracts and related customer relationships #

d. Noncontractual customer relationships *

Artistic-Related Intangible Assets

a. Plays, operas, ballets #

b. Books, magazines, newspapers, other literary works #

c. Musical works such as compositions, song lyrics, advertising jingles #

d. Pictures, photographs #

e. Video and audiovisual material, including motion pictures or films, music videos, television programs #

Contract-Based Intangible Assets

a. Licensing, royalty, standstill agreements #

b. Advertising, construction, management, service or supply contracts #

c. Lease agreements (whether the acquiree is the lessee or the lessor) #

d. Construction permits #

e. Franchise agreements #

f. Operating and broadcast rights #

g. Servicing contracts such as mortgage servicing contracts #

h. Employment contracts #

i. Use rights such as drilling, water, air, timber cutting, and route authorities #

Technology-Based Intangible Assets

a. Patented technology #

b. Computer software and mask works #

c. Unpatented technology *

d. Databases, including title plants *

of the contingent consideration are reported as a gain or loss in earnings, and the liability is also adjusted.[12]

COST AND FAIR VALUE COMPARED After assigning fair values to all identifiable assets acquired and liabilities assumed, we compare the investment cost with the total fair value of identifiable assets less liabilities. If the investment cost exceeds net fair value, we first assign it to identifiable net assets according to their fair values and then assign the excess to goodwill.

In some business combinations, the total fair value of identifiable assets acquired over liabilities assumed may exceed the cost of the acquired company. GAAP[14] offers accounting procedures to dispose of the excess fair value in this situation. The gain from such a *bargain purchase* is recognized as an ordinary gain by the acquirer.

Illustration of an Acquisition

Pit Corporation acquires the net assets of Sad Company in a combination consummated on December 27, 2011. Sad Company is dissolved. The assets and liabilities of Sad Company on this date, at their book values and at fair values, are as follows (in thousands):

	Book Value	Fair Value
Assets		
Cash	$ 50	$ 50
Net receivables	150	140
Inventories	200	250
Land	50	100
Buildings—net	300	500
Equipment—net	250	350
Patents	—	50
Total assets	$1,000	$1,440
Liabilities		
Accounts payable	$ 60	$ 60
Notes payable	150	135
Other liabilities	40	45
Total liabilities	$ 250	$ 240
Net assets	$ 750	$1,200

CASE 1: GOODWILL

Pit Corporation pays $400,000 cash and issues 50,000 shares of Pit Corporation $10 par common stock with a market value of $20 per share for the net assets of Sad Company. The following entries record the business combination on the books of Pit Corporation on December 27, 2011.

Investment in Sad Company (+A)	1,400	
Cash (−A)		400
Common stock, $10 par (+SE)		500
Additional paid-in capital (+SE)		500

To record issuance of 50,000 shares of $10 par common stock plus $400,000 cash in a business combination with Sad Company.

Cash (+A)	50	
Net receivables (+A)	140	
Inventories (+A)	250	
Land (+A)	100	
Buildings (+A)	500	
Equipment (+A)	350	
Patents (+A)	50	
Goodwill (+A)	200	
Accounts payable (+L)		60
Notes payable (+L)		135
Other liabilities (+L)		45
Investment in Sad Company (−A)		1,400

To assign the cost of Sad Company to identifiable assets acquired and liabilities assumed on the basis of their fair values and to goodwill.

We assign the amounts to the assets and liabilities based on fair values, except for goodwill. We determine goodwill by subtracting the $1,200,000 fair value of identifiable net assets acquired from the $1,400,000 purchase price for Sad Company's net assets.

CASE 2: FAIR VALUE EXCEEDS INVESTMENT COST (BARGAIN PURCHASE)

Pit Corporation issues 40,000 shares of its $10 par common stock with a market value of $20 per share, and it also gives a 10 percent, five-year note payable for $200,000 for the net assets of Sad Company. Pit's books record the Pit/Sad business combination on December 27, 2011, with the following journal entries:

Investment in Sad Company (+A)	1,000	
Common stock, $10 par (+SE)		400
Additional paid-in capital (+SE)		400
10% Note payable (+L)		200

To record issuance of 40,00 0 shares of $10 par common stock
plus a $200,000, 10% note in a business combination with
Sad Company.

Cash (+A)	50	
Net receivables (+A)	140	
Inventories (+A)	250	
Land (+A)	100	
Buildings (+A)	500	
Equipment (+A)	350	
Patents (+A)	50	
Accounts payable (+L)		60
Notes payable (+L)		135
Other liabilities (+L)		45
Investment in Sad Company (−A)		1,000
Gain from bargain purchase (Ga, +SE)		200

To assign the cost of Sad Company to identifiable assets
acquired and liabilities assumed on the basis of their fair
values and to recognize the gain from a bargain purchase.

We assign fair values to the individual asset and liability accounts in this entry in accordance with GAAP provisions for an acquisition.[15] The $1,200,000 fair value of the identifiable net assets acquired exceeds the $1,000,000 purchase price by $200,000, so Pit recognizes a $200,000 gain from a bargain purchase.

Bargain purchases are infrequent, but may occur even for very large corporations. Two notable transactions related to the sub-prime mortgage crisis in U.S. financial markets were reported in the *Wall Street Journal* in early 2008. "***Bank of America*** offered an all-stock deal valued at $4 billion for ***Countrywide*** – a fraction of the company's $24 billion market value a year ago. Pushed to the brink of collapse by the mortgage crisis, ***Bear Stearns Cos.*** agreed – after prodding by the federal government – to be sold to ***J.P. Morgan Chase & Co.*** for the fire-sale price of $2 a share in stock, or about $236 million. Bear Stearns had a stock-market value of about $3.5 billion as of Friday – and was worth $20 billion in January 2007."

The Goodwill Controversy

GAAP[16] defines *goodwill* as the excess of the investment cost over the fair value of net assets received. Theoretically, it is a measure of the present value of the combined company's projected future excess earnings over the normal earnings of a similar business. Estimating it requires considerable speculation. Therefore, the amount that we generally capitalize as goodwill is the portion of the purchase price left over after all other identifiable tangible and intangible assets and liabilities have been valued. Errors in the valuation of other assets will affect the amount capitalized as goodwill.

Under current GAAP, goodwill is not amortized. There are also income tax controversies relating to goodwill. In some cases, firms can deduct goodwill amortization for tax purposes over a 15-year period.

INTERNATIONAL ACCOUNTING FOR GOODWILL   U.S. companies had long complained that the accounting rule for amortizing goodwill put them at a disadvantage in competing against foreign companies for merger partners. Some countries, for example, permit the immediate write-off of goodwill to stockholders' equity. Even though the balance sheet of the combined company may show negative net worth, the company can begin showing income from the merged operations immediately. Current GAAP alleviates these competitive disadvantages.

Companies in most other industrial countries historically capitalized and amortized goodwill acquired in business combinations. The amortization periods vary. For instance, prior to adoption of IFRS, the maximum amortization period in Australia and Sweden was 20 years; in Japan, it was 5 years. Some countries permit deducting goodwill amortization for tax purposes, making short amortization periods popular.

The North American Free Trade Agreement (NAFTA) increased trade and investments between Canada, Mexico, and the United States and also increased the need for the harmonization of accounting standards. The standard-setting bodies of the three trading partners are looking at ways to narrow the differences in accounting standards. Canadian companies no longer amortize goodwill. Canadian GAAP for goodwill is now consistent with the revised U.S. standards. Mexican companies amortize intangibles over the period benefited, not to exceed 20 years. Negative goodwill from business combinations of Mexican companies is reported as a component of stockholders' equity and is not amortized.

The IASB is successor to the International Accounting Standards Committee (IASC), a private-sector organization formed in 1973 to develop international accounting standards and promote harmonization of accounting standards worldwide. Under current IASB rules, goodwill and other intangible assets having indeterminate lives are no longer amortized but are tested for value impairment. Impairment tests are conducted annually, or more frequently if circumstances indicate a possible impairment. Firms may not reverse previously-recognized impairment losses for goodwill. These revisions make the IASB rules consistent with both U.S. and Canadian GAAP. Although accounting organizations from all over the world are members, the IASB does not have the authority to require compliance. However, this situation is changing rapidly. The European Union requires IFRS in the financial reporting of all listed firms beginning in 2005. Many other countries are replacing, or considering replacing, their own GAAP with IFRS.

Both the IASB and FASB are working to eliminate differences in accounting for business combinations under IFRS and GAAP. Recently, FASB revised its standards for purchased in-process research and development to harmonize with IFRS requirements. GAAP requires purchased in-process research and development to be capitalized until the research and development phase is complete or the project is abandoned. IFRS also requires capitalization of these costs as a separate and identifiable asset. Under GAAP, this asset will be classified as an intangible asset with an indefinite life and thus will not be amortized.

Current GAAP for business combinations are the result of a joint project with the IASB. The IASB issued a revision of *IFRS 3* at the same time FASB revised the standards on business combinations. Some differences still remain. For example, the FASB requires an acquirer to measure the noncontrolling interest in the acquiree at its fair value, while the IASB permits acquirers to record noncontrolling interests at either fair value or a proportionate share of the acquiree's identifiable net assets.

Current GAAP for Goodwill and Other Intangible Assets

GAAP dramatically changed accounting for goodwill in 2001.[17] GAAP maintained the basic computation of goodwill, but the revised standards mitigate many of the previous controversies.

Current GAAP provides clarification and more detailed guidance on when previously unrecorded intangibles should be recognized as assets, which can affect the amount of goodwill that firms recognize.

Under current GAAP,[18] firms record goodwill but do *not* amortize it. Instead, GAAP requires that firms periodically assess goodwill for impairment in its value. An impairment occurs when the recorded value of goodwill is greater than its fair value. We calculate the fair value of goodwill in a manner similar to the original calculation at the date of the acquisition. Should such impairment occur, firms will write down goodwill to a new estimated amount and will record an offsetting loss in calculating net income for the period.

Further goodwill amortization is not permitted, and firms may not write goodwill back up to reverse the impact of prior-period amortization charges.

Firms no longer amortize goodwill or other intangible assets that have indefinite useful lives. Instead, firms will periodically review these assets (at least annually) and adjust for value impairment. GAAP provides detailed guidance for determining and measuring impairment of goodwill and other intangible assets.

GAAP also defines the reporting entity in accounting for intangible assets. Under prior rules, firms treated the acquired entity as a stand-alone reporting entity. GAAP now recognizes that many acquirees are integrated into the operations of the acquirer. GAAP treats goodwill and other intangible assets as assets of the business reporting unit, which is discussed in more detail in a later chapter on segment reporting. A reporting unit is a component of a business for which discrete financial information is available and its operating results are regularly reviewed by management.

Firms report intangible assets, other than those acquired in business combinations, based on their fair value at the acquisition date. Firms allocate the cost of a group of assets acquired (which may include both tangible and intangible assets) to the individual assets based on relative fair values and "shall not give rise to goodwill."

GAAP is specific on accounting for internally developed intangible assets:[19]

> *Costs of internally developing, maintaining, or restoring intangible assets that are not specifically identifiable, that have indeterminate lives, or that are inherent in a continuing business and related to the entity as a whole, shall be recognized as an expense when incurred.*

RECOGNIZING AND MEASURING IMPAIRMENT LOSSES The goodwill impairment test is a two-step process.[20] Firms first compare carrying values (book values) to fair values at the business reporting unit level. Carrying value includes the goodwill amount. If fair value is less than the carrying amount, then firms proceed to the second step, measurement of the impairment loss.

The second step requires a comparison of the carrying amount of goodwill to its implied fair value. Firms should again make this comparison at the business reporting unit level. If the carrying amount exceeds the implied fair value of the goodwill, the firm must recognize an impairment loss for the difference. The loss amount cannot exceed the carrying amount of the goodwill. Firms cannot reverse previously-recognized impairment losses.

Firms should determine the implied fair value of goodwill in the same manner used to originally record the goodwill at the business combination date. Firms allocate the fair value of the reporting unit to all identifiable assets and liabilities as if they purchased the unit on the measurement date. Any excess fair value is the implied fair value of goodwill.

Fair value of assets and liabilities is the value at which they could be sold, incurred, or settled in a current arm's-length transaction. GAAP considers quoted market prices as the best indicators of fair values, although these are often unavailable. When market prices are unavailable, firms may determine fair values using market prices of similar assets and liabilities or other commonly used valuation techniques. For example, firms may employ present value techniques to value estimated future cash flows or earnings. Firms may also employ techniques based on multiples of earnings or revenues.

Firms should conduct the impairment test for goodwill at least annually. GAAP[21] requires more-frequent impairment testing if any of the following events occurs:

a. *A significant adverse change in legal factors or in the business climate*

b. *An adverse action or assessment by a regulator*

c. *Unanticipated competition*

d. *A loss of key personnel*

e. *A more-likely-than-not expectation that a reporting unit or a significant portion of a reporting unit will be sold or otherwise disposed of*

f. *The testing for recoverability under the Impairment or Disposal of Long-Lived Assets Subsections of Subtopic 360-10 of a significant asset group within a reporting unit*

g. *Recognition of a goodwill impairment loss in the financial statements of a subsidiary that is a component of a reporting unit*

The goodwill impairment testing is complex and may have significant financial statement impact. An entire industry has sprung up to assist companies in making goodwill valuations.

AMORTIZATION VERSUS NON-AMORTIZATION Firms must amortize intangibles with a definite useful life over that life. GAAP defines *useful life* as estimated useful life to the reporting entity. The method of amortization should reflect the expected pattern of consumption of the economic benefits of the intangible. If firms cannot determine a pattern, then they should use straight-line amortization.

If intangibles with an indefinite life later have a life that can be estimated, they should be amortized at that point. Firms should periodically review intangibles that are not being amortized for possible impairment loss.

DISCLOSURE REQUIREMENTS

GAAP requires significant disclosures about a business combination. FASB SFAS No. 141(R) requires specific disclosures that are categorized by: (1) disclosures for the reporting period that includes a business combination, (2) disclosures when a business combination occurs after a reporting period ends, but before issuance of the financial statements, (3) disclosures about provisional amounts related to the business combination and (4) disclosures about adjustments related to business combinations.

The specific information that must be disclosed in the financial statements for the period in which a business combination occurs can be categorized as follows:

1. General information about the business combination such as the name of the acquired company, a description of the acquired company, the acquisition date, the portion of the acquired company's voting stock acquired, the acquirer's reasons for the acquisition and the manner the acquirer obtained control of the acquiree;

2. Information about goodwill or a gain from a bargain purchase that results from the business combination;

3. Nature, terms and fair value of consideration transferred in a business combination;

4. Details about specific assets acquired, liabilities assumed and any noncontrolling interest recognized in connection with the business combination;

5. Reduction in acquirer's pre-existing deferred tax asset valuation allowance due to the business combination;

6. Information about transactions with the acquiree accounted for separately from the business combination;

7. Details about step acquisitions;

8. If the acquirer is a public company, additional disclosures are required such as pro forma information.

GAAP[22] requires firms to report material aggregate amounts of goodwill as a separate balance sheet line item. Likewise, firms must show goodwill impairment losses separately in the income statement, as a component of income from continuing operations (unless the impairment relates to discontinued operations). GAAP also provides increased disclosure requirements for intangible assets (which are reproduced in Exhibit 1-3).

Before completing the chapter, let's take a look at a summary example of required disclosures from a real-world company. In November 2009, *AT&T* completed its acquisition of

EXHIBIT 1-3

Intangible Assets Disclosure Requirements[23]

Source: FASB Statement No. 142, pp. 16–17. [1]

For intangible assets acquired either individually or as part of a group of assets (in either an asset acquisition or business combination), all of the following information shall be disclosed in the notes to financial statements in the period of acquisition:

a. For intangible assets subject to amortization, all of the following:
1. The total amount assigned and the amount assigned to any major intangible asset class
2. The amount of any significant residual value, in total and by major intangible asset class
3. The weighted-average amortization period, in total and by major intangible asset class

b. For intangible assets not subject to amortization, the total amount assigned and the amount assigned to any major intangible asset class.

c. The amount of research and development assets acquired in a transaction other than a business combination and written off in the period and the line item in the income statement in which the amounts written off are aggregated.

d. For intangible assets with renewal or extension terms, the weighted-average period before the next renewal or extension (both explicit and implicit), by major intangible asset class.

This information also shall be disclosed separately for each material business combination or in the aggregate for individually immaterial business combinations that are material collectively if the aggregate fair values of intangible assets acquired, other than goodwill, are significant.

The following information shall be disclosed in the financial statements or the notes to financial statements for each period for which a statement of financial position is presented:

a. For intangible assets subject to amortization, all of the following:
1. The gross carrying amount and accumulated amortization, in total and by major intangible asset class
2. The aggregate amortization expense for the period
3. The estimated aggregate amortization expense for each of the five succeeding fiscal years

b. For intangible assets not subject to amortization, the total carrying amount and the carrying amount for each major intangible asset class

c. The entity's accounting policy on the treatment of costs incurred to renew or extend the term of a recognized intangible asset

d. For intangible assets that have been renewed or extended in the period for which a statement of financial position is presented, both of the following:
1. For entities that capitalize renewal or extension costs, the total amount of costs incurred in the period to renew or extend the term of a recognized intangible asset, by major intangible asset class
2. The weighted-average period before the next renewal or extension (both explicit and implicit), by major intangible asset class.

For each impairment loss recognized related to an intangible asset, all of the following information shall be disclosed in the notes to financial statements that include the period in which the impairment loss is recognized:

a. A description of the impaired intangible asset and the facts and circumstances leading to the impairment

b. The amount of the impairment loss and the method for determining fair value

c. The caption in the income statement or the statement of activities in which the impairment loss is aggregated

d. If applicable, the segment in which the impaired intangible asset is reported under Topic 280

EXHIBIT 1-4

Note 2. Acquisitions, Dispositions, and Other Adjustments

Source: Excerpt from *AT&T* 2009 Annual Report.

ACQUISITIONS (IN MILLIONS OF DOLLARS)

Centennial In November 2009, we acquired the assets of Centennial, a regional provider of wireless and wired communications services with approximately 865,000 customers as of December 31, 2009. Total consideration of $2,961 included $955 in cash for the redemption of Centennial's outstanding common stock and liquidation of outstanding stock options and $2,006 for our acquisition of Centennial's outstanding debt (including liabilities related to assets subject to sale, as discussed below), of which we repaid $1,957 after closing in 2009. The preliminary fair value measurement of Centennial's net assets at the acquisition date resulted in the recognition of $1,276 of goodwill, $647 of spectrum licenses, and $273 of customer lists and other intangible assets for the Wireless segment. The Wireline segment added $339 of goodwill and $174 of customer lists and other intangible assets from the acquisition. The acquisition of Centennial impacted our Wireless and Wireline segments, and we have included Centennial's operations in our consolidated results since the acquisition date. As the value of certain assets and liabilities are preliminary in nature, they are subject to adjustment as additional information is obtained about the facts and circumstances that existed at the acquisition date. When the valuation is final, any changes to the preliminary valuation of acquired assets and liabilities could result in adjustments to identified intangibles and goodwill. See Notes 6 and 8 for additional information regarding the impact of the Centennial acquisition on our goodwill and other intangibles and our long-term debt repayment for 2009.

Centennial. AT&T was primarily interested in getting access to Centennial's 865,000 customers. Exhibit 1-4 provides excerpts of Note 2 from AT&T's 2009 annual report related to this acquisition. Note, in particular, that $2.196 billion of the $2.961 billion price tag relates to purchased intangible assets. AT&T allocates $1.276 billion to goodwill and another $647 million to spectrum licenses for the Wireless segment. Note too, AT&T's explicit recognition of the uncertainty involved in estimation of assets and liabilities and the likelihood of future adjustments.

THE SARBANES-OXLEY ACT

You have likely heard about Sarbanes-Oxley and are wondering why we haven't mentioned it yet. The financial collapse of *Enron Corporation* and *WorldCom* (among others) and the demise of public accounting firm *Arthur Andersen and Company* spurred Congress to initiate legislation intended to prevent future financial reporting and auditing abuse. The result was the *Sarbanes-Oxley Act of 2002* (SOX). For the most part, the rules focus on corporate governance, auditing, and internal-control issues, rather than the details of financial reporting and statement presentation that are the topic of this text. However, you should recognize that the law will impact all of the types of companies that we study. Here are a few of the important areas covered by SOX:

- Establishes the independent Public Company Accounting Oversight Board (PCAOB) to regulate the accounting and auditing profession
- Requires greater independence of auditors and clients, including restrictions on the types of consulting and advisory services provided by auditors to their clients
- Requires greater independence and oversight responsibilities for corporate boards of directors, especially for members of audit committees
- Requires management (CEO and CFO) certification of financial statements and internal controls
- Requires independent auditor review and attestation on management's internal-control assessments
- Increases disclosures about off–balance sheet arrangements and contractual obligations
- Increases types of items requiring disclosure on Form 8-K and shortens the filing period

Enforcement of Sarbanes-Oxley is under the jurisdiction of the Securities and Exchange Commission. The SEC treats violations of SOX or rules of the PCAOB the same as violations of the Securities Exchange Act of 1934. Congress also increased the SEC's budget to permit improved review and enforcement activities. SEC enforcement actions and investigations have increased considerably since the Enron collapse. One example is *Krispy Kreme Doughnuts, Inc.* A January 4, 2005, press

MANAGEMENT'S RESPONSIBILITY FOR FINACIAL STATEMENTS TO THE STOCKHOLDERS OF CHEVRON CORPORATION

Management of Chevron is responsible for preparing the accompanying Consolidated Financial Statements and the related information appearing in this report. The statements were prepared in accordance with accounting principles generally accepted in the United States of America and fairly represent the transactions and financial position of the company. The financial statements include amounts that are based on management's best estimates and judgment.

As stated in its report included herein, the independent registered public accounting firm of PricewaterhouseCoopers LLP has audited the company's consolidated financial statements in accordance with the standards of the Public Company Accounting Oversight Board (United States).

The Board of Directors of Chevron has an Audit Committee composed of directors who are not officers or employees of the company. The Audit Committee meets regularly with members of management, the internal auditors and the independent registered public accounting firm to review accounting, internal control, auditing and financial reporting matters. Both the internal auditors and the independent registered public accounting firm have free and direct access to the Audit Committee without the presence of management.

MANAGEMENT'S REPORT ON INTERNAL CONTROL OVER FINANCIAL REPORTING

The company's management is responsible for establishing and maintaining adequate internal control over financial reporting, as such term is defined in Exchange Act Rule 13a–15(f). The company's management, including the Chief Executive Officer and Chief Financial Officer, conducted an evaluation of the effectiveness of its internal control over financial reporting based on the *Internal Control—Integrated Framework* issued by the Committee of Sponsoring Organizations of the Treadway Commission. Based on the results of this evaluation, the company's management concluded that internal control over financial reporting was effective as of December 31, 2009.

The effectiveness of the company's internal control over financial reporting as of December 31, 2009, has been audited by PricewaterhouseCoopers LLP, an independent registered public accounting firm, as stated in its report included herein.

JOHN S. WATSON
Chairman of the Board
and Chief Executive Officer

PATRICIA E. YARRINGTON
Vice President
and Chief Financial Officer

MARK A. HUMPHREY
Vice President
and Comptroller

February 25, 2010

release on the company's Web site announced that earnings for fiscal 2004 and the last three quarters were being restated. Apparently the company did not make as much "dough" as originally reported. Pre-tax income was reduced by between $6.2 million and $8.1 million. Another example appeared in a *Reuters Limited* story on January 6, 2005, which noted that former directors of **WorldCom** agreed to a $54 million settlement in a class-action lawsuit brought by investors. This included $18 million from personal funds, with the remainder being covered by insurance.

Exhibit 1-5 provides an example of the required management responsibilities under SOX from the 2009 annual report of Chevron Corporation (p. 49). Notice that management's statement reads much like a traditional independent auditor's report. Management takes responsibility for preparation of the financial reports, explicitly notes compliance with GAAP, and declares amounts to be fairly presented. Management also takes explicit responsibility for designing and maintaining internal controls. Finally, the statement indicates the composition and functioning of the Audit Committee, which is designed to comply with SOX requirements. The statement is signed by the CEO, CFO, and comptroller of the company.

We will note other relevant material from Sarbanes-Oxley throughout the text, as applicable. For example, transactions with related parties and variable interest entities are included in Chapter 11.

SUMMARY

A business combination occurs when two or more separate businesses join into a single accounting entity. All combinations initiated after December 15, 2008, must be accounted for as acquisitions. Acquisition accounting requires the recording of assets acquired and liabilities assumed at their fair values at the date of the combination.

The illustrations in this chapter are for business combinations in which there is only one surviving entity. Later chapters cover accounting for parent–subsidiary operations in which more than one of the combining companies continue to exist as separate legal entities.

QUESTIONS

1. What is the accounting concept of a business combination?

2. Is dissolution of all but one of the separate legal entities necessary in order to have a business combination? Explain.

3. What are the legal distinctions between a business combination, a merger, and a consolidation?

4. When does goodwill result from a business combination? How does goodwill affect reported net income after a business combination?

5. What is a bargain purchase? Describe the accounting procedures necessary to record and account for a bargain purchase.

EXERCISES

E 1-1
General questions

1. A business combination in which a new corporation is formed to take over the assets and operations of two or more separate business entities, with the previously separate entities being dissolved, is a/an:
   a Consolidation
   b Merger
   c Pooling of interests
   d Acquisition

2. In a business combination, the direct costs of registering and issuing equity securities are:
   a Added to the parent/investor company's investment account
   b Charged against other paid-in capital of the combined entity
   c Deducted from income in the period of combination
   d None of the above

3. An excess of the fair value of net assets acquired in a business combination over the price paid is:
   a Reported as a gain from a bargain purchase
   b Applied to a reduction of noncash assets before negative goodwill may be reported
   c Applied to reduce noncurrent assets other than marketable securities to zero before negative goodwill may be reported
   d Applied to reduce goodwill to zero before negative goodwill may be reported

4. Cork Corporation acquires Dart Corporation in a business combination. Which of the following would be excluded from the process of assigning fair values to assets and liabilities for purposes of recording the acquisition? (Assume Dart Corporation is dissolved.)
   a Patents developed by Dart because the costs were expensed under GAAP
   b Dart's mortgage payable because it is fully secured by land that has a market value far in excess of the mortgage
   c An asset or liability amount for over- or underfunding of Dart's defined-benefit pension plan
   d None of the above

E 1-2
[Based on AICPA] General problems

1. Pat Corporation paid $100,000 cash for the net assets of Sag Company, which consisted of the following:

	Book Value	Fair Value
Current assets	$ 40,000	$ 56,000
Plant and equipment	160,000	220,000
Liabilities assumed	(40,000)	(36,000)
	$160,000	$240,000

Assume Sag Company is dissolved. The plant and equipment acquired in this business combination should be recorded at:
   a $220,000
   b $200,000
   c $183,332
   d $180,000

2. On April 1, Par Company paid $1,600,000 for all the issued and outstanding common stock of Son Corporation in a transaction properly accounted for as an acquisition. Son Corporation is dissolved. The recorded assets and liabilities of Son Corporation on April 1 follow:

Cash	$160,000
Inventory	480,000
Property and equipment (net of	
accumulated depreciation of $640,000)	960,000
Liabilities	(360,000)

On April 1, it was determined that the inventory of Son had a fair value of $380,000 and the property and equipment (net) had a fair value of $1,120,000. What is the amount of goodwill resulting from the acquisition?

a *0*

b *$100,000*

c *$300,000*

d *$360,000*

E 1-3

Prepare stockholders' equity section

The stockholders' equities of Pal Corporation and Sip Corporation at January 1 were as follows (in thousands):

	Pal	Sip
Capital stock, $10 par	$3,000	$1,600
Other paid-in capital	400	800
Retained earnings	1,200	600
Stockholders' equity	$4,600	$3,000

On January 2, Pal issued 300,000 of its shares with a market value of $20 per share for all of Sip's shares, and Sip was dissolved. On the same day, Pal paid $10,000 to register and issue the shares and $20,000 for other direct costs of combination.

REQUIRED: Prepare the stockholders' equity section of Pal Corporation's balance sheet immediately after the acquisition on January 2. (Hint: Prepare the journal entry.)

E 1-4

Journal entries to record an acquisition

Pan Company issued 480,000 shares of $10 par common stock with a fair value of $10,200,000 for all the voting common stock of Set Company. In addition, Pan incurred the following costs:

Legal fees to arrange the business combination	$100,000
Cost of SEC registration, including accounting	
and legal fees	48,000
Cost of printing and issuing net stock certificates	12,000
Indirect costs of combining, including allocated	
overhead and executive salaries	80,000

Immediately before the acquisition in which Set Company was dissolved, Set's assets and equities were as follows (in thousands):

	Book Value	Fair Value
Current assets	$4,000	$4,400
Plant assets	6000	8,800
Liabilities	1,200	1,200
Common stock	8,000	
Retained earnings	800	

REQUIRED: Prepare all journal entries on Pan's books to record the acquisition.

E 1-5

Journal entries to record an acquisition with direct costs and fair value/book value differences

On January 1, Pan Corporation pays $400,000 cash and also issues 36,000 shares of $10 par common stock with a market value of $660,000 for all the outstanding common shares of Sis Corporation. In addition, Pan pays $60,000 for registering and issuing the 36,000 shares and $140,000 for the other direct costs of the business combination, in which Sis Corporation is dissolved. Summary balance sheet information for the companies immediately before the merger is as follows (in thousands):

	Pan Book Value	Sis Book Value	Sis Fair Value
Cash	$700	$ 80	$ 80
Inventories	240	160	200
Other current assets	60	40	40
Plant assets—net	520	360	560
Total assets	$1,520	$640	$880
Current liabilities	$320	$ 60	$ 60
Other liabilities	160	100	80
Common stock, $10 par	840	400	
Retained earnings	200	80	
Total liabilities and owners' equity	$1,520	$640	

REQUIRED: Prepare all journal entries on Pan's books to account for the acquisition.

PROBLEMS

P 1-1

Prepare balance sheet after acquisition

Comparative balance sheets for Pin and San Corporations at December 31, 2010, are as follows (in thousands):

	Pin	San
Current assets	$ 520	$ 240
Land	200	400
Buildings—net	1,200	400
Equipment—net	880	960
Total assets	$2,800	$2,000
Current liabilities	$ 200	$ 240
Capital stock, $10 par	2,000	800
Additional paid-in capital	200	560
Retained earnings	400	400
Total equities	$2,800	$2,000

On January 2, 2011, Pin issues 60,000 shares of its stock with a market value of $40 per share for all the outstanding shares of San Corporation in an acquisition. San is dissolved. The recorded book values reflect fair values, except for the buildings of Pin, which have a fair value of $1,600,000, and the current assets of San, which have a fair value of $400,000.

Pin pays the following expenses in connection with the business combination:

Costs of registering and issuing securities	$60,000
Other direct costs of combination	100,000

REQUIRED: Prepare the balance sheet of Pin Corporation immediately after the acquisition.

P 1-2
Prepare balance sheet after an acquisition

On January 2, 2011, Pet Corporation enters into a business combination with Sea Corporation in which Sea is dissolved. Pet pays $1,650,000 for Sea, the consideration consisting of 66,000 shares of Pet $10 par common stock with a market value of $25 per share. In addition, Pet pays the following expenses in cash at the time of the merger:

Finders' fee	$ 70,000
Accounting and legal fees	130,000
Registration and issuance costs of securities	80,000
	$280,000

Balance sheet and fair value information for the two companies on December 31, 2010, immediately before the merger, is as follows (in thousands):

	Pet Book Value	Sea Book Value	Sea Fair Value
Cash	$ 300	$ 60	$ 60
Accounts receivable—net	460	100	80
Inventories	1,040	160	240
Land	800	200	300
Buildings—net	2,000	400	600
Equipment—net	1,000	600	500
Total assets	$5,600	$1,520	$1,780
Accounts payable	$ 600	$ 80	$ 80
Note payable	1,200	400	360
Capital stock, $10 par	1,600	600	
Other paid-in capital	1,200	100	
Retained earnings	1,000	340	
Total liabilities and owners' equity	$5,600	$1,520	

REQUIRED: Prepare a balance sheet for Pet Corporation as of January 2, 2011, immediately after the merger, assuming the merger is treated as an acquisition.

P 1-3
Journal entries and balance sheet for an acquisition

On January 2, 2011, Par Corporation issues its own $10 par common stock for all the outstanding stock of Sin Corporation in an acquisition. Sin is dissolved. In addition, Par pays $40,000 for registering and issuing securities and $60,000 for other costs of combination. The market price of Par's stock on January 2, 2011, is $60 per share. Relevant balance sheet information for Par and Sin Corporations on December 31, 2010, just before the combination, is as follows (in thousands):

	Par Historical Cost	Sin Historical Cost	Sin Fair Value
Cash	$ 240	$ 20	$ 20
Inventories	100	60	120
Other current assets	200	180	200
Land	160	40	200
Plant and equipment—net	1,300	400	700
Total assets	$ 2,000	$700	$1,240
Liabilities	$ 400	$ 100	$ 100
Capital stock, $10 par	1,000	200	
Additional paid-in capital	400	100	
Retained earnings	200	300	
Total liabilities and owners' equity	$2,000	$700	

REQUIRED

1. Assume that Par issues 25,000 shares of its stock for all of Sin's outstanding shares.
   a. Prepare journal entries to record the acquisition of Sin.
   b. Prepare a balance sheet for Par Corporation immediately after the acquisition.

2. Assume that Par issues 15,000 shares of its stock for all of Sin's outstanding shares.
   a. Prepare journal entries to record the acquisition of Sin.
   b. Prepare a balance sheet for Par Corporation immediately after the acquisition.

P 1-4
Allocation schedule and balance sheet

The balance sheets of Pub Corporation and Sun Corporation at December 31, 2010, are summarized with fair value information as follows (in thousands):

	Pub Corporation		Sun Corporation	
	Book Value	Fair Value	Book Value	Fair Value
Assets				
Cash	$115	$115	$ 10	$ 10
Receivables—net	40	40	20	20
Inventories	120	150	50	30
Land	45	100	30	100
Buildings—net	200	300	100	150
Equipment—net	180	245	90	150
Total assets	$700	$950	$300	$460
Equities				
Accounts payable	$ 90	$ 90	$ 30	$ 30
Other liabilities	100	90	60	70
Capital stock, $10 par	300		100	
Other paid-in capital	100		80	
Retained earnings	110		30	
Total equities	$700		$300	

On January 1, 2011, Pub Corporation acquired all of Sun's outstanding stock for $300,000. Pub paid $100,000 cash and issued a five-year, 12 percent note for the balance. Sun was dissolved.

REQUIRED

1. Prepare a schedule to show how the investment cost is allocated to identifiable assets and liabilities.

2. Prepare a balance sheet for Pub Corporation on January 1, 2011, immediately after the acquisition.

P 1-5
Journal entries and balance sheet for an acquisition

Pat Corporation paid $5,000,000 for Saw Corporation's voting common stock on January 2, 2011, and Saw was dissolved. The purchase price consisted of 100,000 shares of Pat's common stock with a market value of $4,000,000, plus $1,000,000 cash. In addition, Pat paid $100,000 for registering and issuing the 100,000 shares of common stock and $200,000 for other costs of combination. Balance sheet information for the companies immediately before the acquisition is summarized as follows (in thousands):

	Pat	Saw	
	Book Value	Book Value	Fair Value
Cash	$ 6,000	$ 480	$ 480
Accounts receivable—net	2,600	720	720
Notes receivable—net	3,000	600	600
Inventories	5,000	840	1,000
Other current assets	1,400	360	400
Land	4,000	200	400
Buildings—net	18,000	1,200	2,400
Equipment—net	20,000	1,600	1,200
Total assets	$60,000	$6,000	$7,200
Accounts payable	$ 2,000	$ 600	$ 600
Mortgage payable—10%	10,000	1,400	1,200
Capital stock, $10 par	20,000	2,000	
Other paid-in capital	16,000	1,200	
Retained earnings	12,000	800	
Total equities	$60,000	$6,000	

REQUIRED

1. Prepare journal entries for Pat Corporation to record its acquisition of Saw Corporation, including all allocations to individual asset and liability accounts.

2. Prepare a balance sheet for Pat Corporation on January 2, 2011, immediately after the acquisition and dissolution of Saw.

INTERNET ASSIGNMENT

1. What can you learn about business combinations from the Internet? Visit the Web sites of at least three major publicly traded companies. Review their recent annual reports for evidence of significant merger and acquisition activities over the past three years. Answer the following questions for each company.

   a. What information is provided about recent merger activity?

   b. What was the cost of the company's most significant acquisition? How was that cost allocated? What amount of goodwill was recorded?

   c. What was the business strategy motivation underlying the merger activity?

   d. How were major acquisitions financed (e.g., common stock, preferred stock, cash, debt securities, or some combination thereof)?

2. For one of your chosen firms, review the company's Form 10-K. You may find a direct link on the company Web site, or you can view the filing by visiting the SEC's EDGAR Web site. What additional information about merger activity do you find in the Form 10-K that was not available in the company's annual report?

RESEARCH CASE: IF YOU CAN'T BEAT 'EM, BUY 'EM

Assume that Wal-Mart decided to acquire major retailing rival Target Corporation on January 31, 2010. Target's fiscal year ended on January 30, 2010, but you may assume that the year ends are identical to keep the calculations simpler. Visit the two firms' Web sites to acquire their annual reports on this date (Wal-Mart lists this as the 2010 annual report, while Target lists this as a 2009 annual report).

Assumptions:

Wal-Mart issued 1 billion shares of $.10 par value common stock to acquire 100% of Target's outstanding common shares.

Wal-Mart stock had a fair market value of $50 per share on this date.

Fair values of all assets and liabilities are equal to book values, except as noted.

- Inventories were undervalued by 10 percent.

- Property and equipment were undervalued by 20 percent, except construction in progress, where book value equaled fair value.

REQUIRED

1. Prepare all the journal entries on Wal-Mart's books to account for the acquisition of Target. Assume Target's Accumulated Other Comprehensive Loss of $581 million is also acquired. Assume Target is dissolved.

2. Prepare the balance sheet of Wal-Mart Corporation immediately after the acquisition of Target.

REFERENCES TO THE AUTHORITATIVE LITERATURE

[1] FASB ASC 805-10. Originally *Statement of Financial Accounting Standards No. 141(R).* "Business Combinations." Norwalk, CT: Financial Accounting Standards Board, 2007.

[2] FASB ASC 805. Originally *Statement of Financial Accounting Standards No. 141(R).* "Business Combinations." Norwalk, CT: Financial Accounting Standards Board, 2007.

[3] IFRS 3. "Business Combinations." London, UK: International Accounting Standards Board, 2004.

[4] FASB ASC 810-10-5-2. Originally *Statement of Financial Accounting Standards No. 141(R).* "Business Combinations." Norwalk, CT: Financial Accounting Standards Board, 2007.

[5] FASB ASC 820-10. Originally *Statement of Financial Accounting Standards No. 157.* "Fair Value Measurements." Norwalk. CT: Financial Accounting Standards Board, 2006.

[6] FASB ASC 750-10. *Statement of Financial Accounting Standards No. 2.* "Accounting for Research and Development Costs." Stamford, CT: Financial Accounting Standards Board, 1974.

[7] FASB ASC 450. *Statement of Financial Accounting Standards No. 5.* "Accounting for Contingencies." Stamford, CT: Financial Accounting Standards Board, 1975.

[8] FASB ASC 740. *Statement of Financial Accounting Standards No. 109.* "Accounting for Income Taxes." Norwalk, CT: Financial Accounting Standards Board, 1992 and FASB Interpretation No. 48. "Accounting for Uncertainty in Income Taxes." Norwalk, CT: Financial Accounting Standards Board, 2006.

[9] FASB ASC 715 and 84010-25. Originally *Statement of Financial Accounting Standards No. 158.* "Employers' Accounting for Defined Benefit Pension and Other Postretirement Plans—An amendment *of FASB Statements No 87, 88, 106, and 132R.*" Norwalk, CT: Financial Accounting Standards Board, 2006.

[10] FASB ASC 805-20-25. Originally *Statement of Financial Accounting Standards No. 141(R).* "Business Combinations." Norwalk, CT: Financial Accounting Standards Board, 2007.

[11] FASB ASC 805-20-55-11 through 55-38. Originally *Statement of Financial Accounting Standards No. 141(R).* "Business Combinations." Appendix A. Norwalk, CT: Financial Accounting Standards Board, 2007.

[12] FASB ASC 805-30-25-5 through 25-7. Originally *Statement of Financial Accounting Standards No. 141(R).* "Business Combinations." Norwalk, CT: Financial Accounting Standards Board, 2007.

[13] FASB ASC 805-20-55-11through 55-38. Originally *Statement of Financial Accounting Standards No. 141(R).* "Business Combinations." Norwalk, CT: Financial Accounting Standards Board, 2007.

[14] FASB ASC 805-30-25-2. Originally *Statement of Financial Accounting Standards No. 141(R).* "Business Combinations." Norwalk, CT: Financial Accounting Standards Board, 2007.

[15] FASB ASC 805. Originally *Statement of Financial Accounting Standards No. 141(R).* "Business Combinations." Norwalk, CT: Financial Accounting Standards Board, 2007.

[16] FASB ASC 350-20-35-1. Originally *Statement of Financial Accounting Standards No. 142. "Goodwill and Other Intangible Assets."* Stamford, CT: Financial Accounting Standards Board, 2001.

[17] FASB ASC 350-20. Originally *Statement of Financial Accounting Standards No. 142. "Goodwill and Other Intangible Assets."* Stamford, CT: Financial Accounting Standards Board, 2001.

[18] FASB ASC 350-20-35. Originally *Statement of Financial Accounting Standards No. 142. "Goodwill and Other Intangible Assets."* Stamford, CT: Financial Accounting Standards Board, 2001.

[19] FASB ASC 350-20-35-3. Originally *Statement of Financial Accounting Standards No. 142. "Goodwill and Other Intangible Assets."* Stamford, CT: Financial Accounting Standards Board, 2001.

[20] FASB ASC 350-20-35. Originally *Statement of Financial Accounting Standards No. 142. "Goodwill and Other Intangible Assets."* Stamford, CT: Financial Accounting Standards Board, 2001.

[21] FASB ASC 350-20-35-30. Originally *Statement of Financial Accounting Standards No. 142. "Goodwill and Other Intangible Assets."* Stamford, CT: Financial Accounting Standards Board, 2001.

[22] FASB ASC 350-20-35. Originally *Statement of Financial Accounting Standards No. 142. "Goodwill and Other Intangible Assets."* Stamford, CT: Financial Accounting Standards Board, 2001.

[23] FASB ASC 350-20-35. Originally *Statement of Financial Accounting Standards No. 142. "Goodwill and Other Intangible Assets."* Stamford, CT: Financial Accounting Standards Board, 2001.

2 CHAPTER

Stock Investments—Investor Accounting and Reporting

C hapter 1 illustrated business combinations in which one surviving entity received the net assets of other combining companies. A single legal and accounting entity, with one record-keeping system, integrated the net assets and operations of all combining companies. In Chapter 1, we recorded the business combination in an investment account and immediately eliminated the account through allocation to individual asset and liability accounts.

Chapter 2 focuses on equity investments in which the investor maintains the investment account on a continuous basis. It includes accounting for investments under the fair value/ cost (fair value for marketable securities and cost for nonmarketable securities) method, in which the investor does not have the ability to influence the activities of the investee, as well as accounting under the equity method, in which the investor can exercise significant influence over the investee's operations. GAAP generally prescribes equity method accounting for investments that represent a 20 percent ownership through a 50 percent ownership in the investee.

Investors also use the equity method for internal parent-company accounting for investments in subsidiaries. This situation arises when the investor controls the operating, investing, and financing decisions of the investee through ownership of more than 50 percent of the voting stock of the investee as the result of a business combination in which one or more companies became subsidiaries. For financial-reporting purposes, such combinations result in the preparation of consolidated financial statements.

This chapter covers parent-company accounting for its subsidiaries under the acquisition method, but it does *not* cover consolidated financial statements. Consolidated financial statements for parent and subsidiary companies appear in Chapter 3 and subsequent chapters.

LEARNING OBJECTIVES

1 Recognize investors' varying levels of influence or control, based on the level of stock ownership.

2 Anticipate how accounting adjusts to reflect the economics underlying varying levels of investor influence.

3 Apply the fair value/cost and equity methods of accounting for stock investments.

4 Identify factors beyond stock ownership that affect an investor's ability to exert influence or control over an investee.

5 Apply the equity method to stock investments.

6 Learn how to test goodwill for impairment.

ACCOUNTING FOR STOCK INVESTMENTS

LEARNING OBJECTIVE 1

GAAP for recording common stock acquisitions requires that the investor record the investment at its cost (which is equal to its fair value at acquisition). The basic guidelines measure investment costs by including cash disbursed; the fair value of other assets given or securities issued; and additional direct costs of obtaining the investment, other than the costs of registering and issuing equity securities, which GAAP charges to additional paid-in capital.

One of the two basic methods of accounting for common stock investments generally applies— the **fair value (cost) method**[1] or the **equity method**.[2]

Concepts Underlying Fair Value/Cost and Equity Methods

Under the fair value/cost method, we record investments in common stock at cost and report dividends received as dividend income. There is an exception. Dividends received in excess of the investor's share of earnings after the stock is acquired are considered returns of capital (or liquidating dividends) and recorded as reductions in the investment account. We classify equity securities that have a readily determinable fair value as either trading securities (securities bought and held principally for the purpose of resale in the near term) or available-for-sale securities (investments not classified as trading securities).[3]

Both classifications use fair values to report the investments at the end of each reporting period and report realized gains, losses, and dividends in net income. GAAP also includes unrealized gains and losses (changes in fair value) from the trading-securities classification in net income. However, we report unrealized gains and losses from the available-for-sale securities classification at a net amount as a separate line item under other comprehensive income. GAAP allows other comprehensive income to be reported either on the income statement, as[4] a separate statement of comprehensive income, or in a statement of changes in equity. These amounts accumulate in the equity section of the balance sheet in the account titled *Accumulated other comprehensive income.* This treatment does not apply to investments in equity securities accounted for under the equity method or to investments in consolidated subsidiaries.[5]

The equity method of accounting is essentially accrual accounting for equity investments that enable the investor to exercise significant influence over the investee. Under the equity method, we record the investments at cost and adjust for earnings, losses, and dividends. The investor reports its share of the investee's earnings as investment income and its share of the investee's losses as investment loss. We increase the investment account for investment income and decrease it for investment losses. Dividends received from investees are disinvestments under the equity method, and they are recorded as decreases in the investment account. Thus, investment income under the equity method reflects the investor's share of the net income of the investee, and the investment account reflects the investor's share of the investee's net assets.

We account for an investment in voting stock that gives the investor the ability to exercise significant influence over the financial and operating policies of the investee using the equity method of accounting. GAAP requires the equity method of accounting for an investment in common stock by an investor whose investment in common stock gives it the ability to exercise significant influence over operating and financial policies of an investee even though the investor holds 50 percent or less of the voting shares.[6]

GAAP bases the ability to exert significant influence on a 20 percent ownership test:

> *An investment (direct or indirect) of 20 percent or more of the voting stock of an investee shall lead to a presumption that in the absence of predominant evidence to the contrary an investor has the ability to exercise significant influence over an investee. Conversely, an investment of less than 20 percent of the voting stock of an investee shall lead to a presumption that an investor does not have the ability to exercise significant influence unless such ability can be demonstrated.[7]*

An investor may be able to exert significant influence over its investee with an investment interest of less than 20 percent, according to GAAP. The following statement from *AT&T Inc.'s* 2009 annual report (p. 73) provides an example of the exception:

> *As of December 31, 2009, our investments in equity affiliates included an 9.8% interest in Telefonos de Mexico, S.A. de C.V. (Telmex), Mexico's national telecommunications company, and an 8.8 percent interest in America Movil S.A. de C.V. (America Movil), primarily a wireless provider in Mexico, with telecommunications investments in the United States and Latin America.*

GAAP[8] cites (1) opposition by the investee that challenges the investor's influence, (2) surrender of significant stockholder rights by agreement between the investor and investee,

(3) concentration of majority ownership in another group rather than the investor, (4) inadequate or untimely information to apply the equity method, and (5) failure to obtain representation on the investee's board of directors as indicators of an investor's inability to exercise significant influence. Application of the equity method is discontinued when the investor's share of losses reduces the carrying amount of the investment to zero.

The equity method of accounting is important for several reasons. First, these investments represent a significant component of total assets, net income, or both for some firms. Second, corporate joint ventures and other special-purpose entities widely use the equity method. Third, the equity method is used in the discussion of the preparation of consolidated financial statements in later chapters.

Many well known firms report using the equity method for investments in other companies. *Microsoft Corporation* discloses equity and other investments of $4.933 billion (6.3 percent of total assets) in its 2009 Annual Report. *AT&T* reports investments in equity method affiliates of $2.921 billion in its 2009 Annual Report. Net income was $12.843 billion in 2009, including $734 million from these equity method investments. *Dow Chemical's* 2009 Annual Report discloses equity method investments of $3.224 billion (4.9 percent of total assets) and income from those investments of $630 million (93.2 percent of net income).

A parent may use the equity method to account for its investments even though the financial statements of the subsidiaries are subsequently included in the consolidated financial statements for the parent and its subsidiaries. In other words, the parent maintains the "investment in subsidiary account" by taking up its share of the subsidiary's income and reducing the investment account for its share of subsidiary dividends declared. Under the equity method, the parent's investment income and parent's share of consolidated net income are equal. The consolidated income statement reflects the income of the parent and its subsidiaries as a single economic entity.

GAAP requires that all majority-owned subsidiaries be consolidated, except when control does not lie with the majority interests. Examples of control of a subsidiary not resting with the parent include a subsidiary in legal reorganization or in bankruptcy, or a subsidiary operating under severe foreign-exchange restrictions or other governmentally imposed uncertainties.[9] An investment in an unconsolidated subsidiary is reported in the parent's financial statements by either the fair value/cost or the equity method. Chapter 3 discusses situations in which certain subsidiaries should not be consolidated.

Accounting Procedures Under the Fair Value/Cost and Equity Methods

LEARNING OBJECTIVE **2**

Assume that Pil Company acquires 2,000 of the 10,000 outstanding shares of Sud Corporation at $50 per share on July 1. Assume the book value and fair value of Sud's assets and liabilities are equal. Further, the cash paid equals 20 percent of the fair value of Sud's net assets. Sud's net income for the fiscal year ending December 31 is $50,000, and dividends of $20,000 are paid on November 1. If there is evidence of an inability to exercise significant influence, Pil should apply the fair value/cost method, revaluing the investment account to fair market value at the end of the accounting period. Otherwise, the equity method is required. Accounting by Pil under the two methods is as follows:

Entry on July 1 to Record the Investment:

Fair Value/Cost Method		*Equity Method*	
Investment in Sud (+A) 100,000		Investment in Sud (+A) 100,000	
Cash (−A)	100,000	Cash (−A)	100,000

Entry on November 1 to Record Dividends:

Fair Value/Cost Method		*Equity Method*	
Cash (+A) 4,000		Cash (+A) 4,000	
Dividend income (R, +SE) 4,000		Investment in Sud (−A)	4,000

Entry on December 31 to Recognize Earnings:

Fair Value/Cost Method		*Equity Method*	
None (Assume that the stock is either nonmarketable or has a market price = $50 per share so that no revaluing is needed.)		Investment in Sud (+A) 5,000	
		Income from Sud (R, +SE)	5,000
		($50,000 × 1/2 year × 20%)	

Under the fair value/cost method, Pil recognizes income of $4,000 and reports its investment in Sud at its $100,000 cost at December 31. Under the equity method, Pil recognizes $5,000 in income and reports the investment in Sud at $101,000 at December 31. Here is a summary of Pil's equity method investment account activity:

July 1	Initial cost	$100,000
November 1	Dividends received	(4,000)
December 31	Recognize 20% of Sud's net income for 1/2 year	5,000
December 31	Ending balance	$101,000

The entries to illustrate the fair value/cost method reflect the usual situation in which the investor records dividend income equal to dividends actually received. An exception arises when dividends received exceed the investor's share of earnings after the investment has been acquired. From the investor's point of view, the excess dividends since acquisition of the investment are a return of capital, or liquidating dividends. For example, if Sud's net income for the year had been $30,000, Pil's share would have been $3,000 ($30,000 × 1/2 year × 20%). The $4,000 dividend received exceeds the $3,000 equity in Sud's income, so the $1,000 excess would be considered a return of capital and credited to the Investment in Sud account. Assuming that Pil records the $4,000 cash received on November 1 as dividend income, a year-end entry to adjust dividend income and the investment account is needed. The investor would record as follows:

Dividend income (−R,−SE)	1,000	
Investment in Sud (−A)		1,000
To adjust dividend income and investment accounts for dividends received in excess of earnings.		

This entry reduces dividend income to Pil's $3,000 share of income earned after July 1 and reduces the investment in Sud to $99,000, the new fair value/cost basis for the investment. If, after the liquidating dividend, the stock (classified as an available-for-sale security) had a fair value of $120,000 at December 31, then another entry would be required to increase the investment to its fair value:

Allowance to adjust available-for-sale securities to market value (+A)	21,000	
Unrealized gain on available-for-sale securities (+SE)		21,000

The unrealized gain on available-for-sale securities would be included in reporting other comprehensive income for the period.

Economic Consequences of Using the Fair Value/Cost and Equity Methods

LEARNING OBJECTIVE **3**

The different methods of accounting (fair value/cost and equity) result in different investment amounts in the balance sheet of the investor and different income amounts in the income statement. When the investor can significantly influence or control the operations of the investee, including dividend declarations, the fair value/cost method is unacceptable. By influencing or controlling investee dividend decisions, the investor is able to manipulate its reported investment income. The possibility of income manipulation does not exist when the financial statements of a parent company/investor are consolidated with the statements of a subsidiary/investee because the consolidated statements are the same, regardless of which method of accounting is used.

Although the equity method is not a substitute for consolidation, the income reported by a parent in its separate income statement under the equity method of accounting is generally the same as the parent's share of consolidated net income reported in consolidated financial statements for a parent and its subsidiary.

EQUITY METHOD—A ONE-LINE CONSOLIDATION

The equity method of accounting is often called a **one-line consolidation**. The name comes about because the investment is reported in a single amount on one line of the investor's balance sheet, and investment income is reported in a single amount on one line of the investor's income statement (except when the investee has extraordinary or other "below-the-line" items that require separate disclosure). "One-line consolidation" also means that a parent-company/investor's income and stockholders' equity are the same when a subsidiary company/investee is accounted for under a complete and correct application of the equity method and when the financial statements of a parent and subsidiary are consolidated. Consolidated financial statements show the same income and the same net assets but include the details of revenues and expenses and assets and liabilities.

The equity method creates many complexities; in fact, it requires the same computational complexities encountered in preparing consolidated financial statements. For this reason, the equity method is the standard of parent-company accounting for subsidiaries, and the one-line consolidation is integrated throughout the consolidation chapters of this book. This parallel one-line consolidation/consolidation coverage permits you to check your work just as practitioners do, by making alternative computations of such key financial statement items as consolidated net income and consolidated retained earnings.

Basic accounting procedures for applying the equity method are the same whether the investor has the ability to exercise significant influence over the investee (20 percent to 50 percent ownership) or the ability to control the investee (more than 50 percent ownership). This is important because investments of more than 50 percent are business combinations and require preparation of consolidated financial statements. Thus, the accounting principles that apply to the acquisition method of accounting for business combinations also apply to accounting for investments of 50 percent or greater under the equity method. The difference between the way combination provisions are applied in this chapter and the way they are applied in Chapter 1 arises because:

1. Both the investor and investee continue to exist as separate legal entities with their own accounting systems (an acquisition).
2. The equity method applies to only one of the entities—the investor.
3. The investor's equity interest may range from 20 percent to 100 percent.

Equity Investments at Acquisition[1]

Equity investments in voting common stock of other entities measure the investment cost by the cash disbursed or the fair value of other assets distributed or securities issued. Similarly, we charge direct costs of registering and issuing equity securities against additional paid-in capital, and we expense other direct costs of acquisition. We enter the total investment cost in an investment account under the one-line consolidation concept.

Assume that Payne Company purchases 30 percent of Sloan Company's outstanding voting common stock on January 1 from existing stockholders for $2,000,000 cash plus 200,000 shares of Payne Company $10 par common stock with a market value of $15 per share. Additional cash costs of the equity interest consist of $50,000 for registration of the shares and $100,000 for

[1]GAAP differs in equity method accounting for 20 to 50 percent ownership versus ownership greater than 50 percent which will require preparation of consolidated financial statements. Our remaining discussion of equity method accounting focuses on application of the acquisition method for investments greater than 50 percent owned, except where otherwise noted.

LEARNING OBJECTIVE 4

consulting and advisory fees. Payne Company records these events with the following journal entries (in thousands):

January 1

Investment in Sloan (+A)	5,000	
Common stock (+SE)		2,000
Additional paid-in capital (+SE)		1,000
Cash (−A)		2,000

To record acquisition of a 30% equity investment in Sloan Company.

January 1

Investment expense (E,−SE)	100	
Additional paid-in capital (−SE)	50	
Cash (−A)		150

To record additional direct costs of purchasing the 30% equity
  interest in Sloan.

Under a one-line consolidation, these entries can be made without knowledge of book value or fair value of Sloan Company's assets and liabilities.

LEARNING
OBJECTIVE 5

Assignment of Excess Investment Cost over Underlying Book Value of Equity

Information regarding the individual assets and liabilities of Sloan Company at the time of the purchase is important because subsequent accounting under the equity method requires accounting for any differences between the investment cost and the underlying book value of equity in the net assets of the investee.

Assume that the following book value and fair value information for Sloan Company at January 1 is available (in thousands):

	Book Value	Fair Value
Cash	$ 1,500	$ 1,500
Receivables—net	2,200	2,200
Inventories	3,000	4,000
Other current assets	3,300	3,100
Equipment—net	5,000	8,000
Total assets	$15,000	$18,800
Accounts payable	$ 1,000	$ 1,000
Note payable, due in five years	2,000	1,800
Common stock	10,000	
Retained earnings	2,000	
Total liabilities and stockholders' equity	$15,000	

The underlying book value of equity in the net assets of Sloan Company is $3,600,000 (30 percent of the $12,000,000 book value of Sloan Company's net assets), and the difference between the investment cost and the underlying book value of equity is $1,400,000. The investor assigns this difference to identifiable assets and liabilities based on fair values and assigns the remaining difference to goodwill. Exhibit 2-1 illustrates the assignment to identifiable net assets and goodwill.

Payne Company does not record separately the asset and liability information given in Exhibit 2-1. The $1,400,000 excess of cost over the underlying book value of equity is already reflected in Payne's Investment in Sloan account. Under the equity method of accounting, we eliminate this difference by periodic charges (debits) and credits to income from the investment and by equal charges or credits to the investment account. Thus, the original difference between investment cost and book value acquired disappears over the remaining lives of identifiable assets and liabilities. Exceptions arise for land, goodwill, and intangible assets having an indefinite life, which are not amortized under GAAP.

We determined the $200,000 assigned to goodwill in Exhibit 2-1 as a remainder of the total excess of cost over book value acquired ($1,400,000) over amounts assigned to identifiable assets

PAYNE COMPANY AND ITS 30%-OWNED EQUITY INVESTEE, SLOAN COMPANY (IN THOUSANDS)					
Investment in Sloan					$5,000
Book value of the interest acquired (30% × $12,000,000 equity of Sloan)					(3,600)
Total excess of cost over book value acquired					$1,400
Assignment to Identifiable Net Assets and Goodwill					
	Fair Value	−	Book Value	×	% Interest Acquired	=	Amount Assigned
Inventories	$4,000		$3,000		30%		$ 300
Other current assets	3,100		3,300		30		(60)
Equipment	8,000		5,000		30		900
Note payable	1,800		2,000		30		60
Total assigned to identifiable net assets							1,200
Remainder assigned to goodwill							200
Total excess of cost over book value acquired							$1,400

EXHIBIT 2-1

Schedule for Allocating the Excess of Investment Cost (Fair Value) over the Book Value of the Interest Acquired

and liabilities ($1,200,000). However, we can also compute the goodwill amount as the excess of the investment cost of $5,000,000 over the $4,800,000 fair value of Sloan's net assets acquired (30 × $16,000,000). We consider the difference as goodwill if it cannot be related to identifiable assets and liabilities.

Recall from our discussion in Chapter 1 that, under current GAAP, firms do not amortize goodwill and other intangible assets that have an indefinite life. Instead, we review such assets for impairment on a periodic basis. We write down these assets when impairment losses become evident.

The same procedure also applies to investments that will be reported under equity method accounting. However, the impairment test differs. When evaluating an equity method investment for impairment, we recognize impairment losses in the value of the investment as a whole.[10]

Accounting for Excess of Investment Cost over Book Value

Assume that Sloan pays dividends of $1,000,000 on July 1 and reports net income of $3,000,000 for the year. The excess cost over book value is amortized as follows:

	Amortization Rates
Excess allocated to:	
Inventories—sold in the current year	100%
Other current assets—disposed of in the current year	100%
Equipment—depreciated over 20 years	5%
Note payable—due in 5 years	20%

Payne makes the following entries under a one-line consolidation to record its dividends and income from Sloan (in thousands):

July 1

Cash (+A)	300	
Investment in Sloan (−A)		300
To record dividends received from Sloan ($1,000,000 × 30%).		

December 31

Investment in Sloan (+A)	900	
Income from Sloan (R,+SE)		900
To record equity in income of Sloan ($3,000,000 × 30%).		

December 31

Income from Sloan (−R, −SE)	300	
Investment in Sloan (−A)		300

    To record write-off of excess allocated to inventory items that were sold in the current year.

December 31

Investment in Sloan (+A)	60	
Income from Sloan (R, +SE)		60

    To record income credit for overvalued other current assets disposed of in the current year.

December 31

Income from Sloan (−R, −SE)	45	
Investment in Sloan (−A)		45

    To record depreciation on excess allocated to undervalued equipment with a 20-year remaining useful life ($900,000 ÷ 20).

December 31

Income from Sloan (−R, −SE)	12	
Investment in Sloan (−A)		12

    To amortize the excess allocated to the overvalued note payable over the remaining life of the note ($60,000 ÷ 5 years).

The last five journal entries involve the income and investment accounts, so Payne could record its income from Sloan in a single entry at December 31, as follows:

Investment in Sloan (+A)	603	
Income from Sloan (R, +SE)		603

To record equity income from 30% investment in Sloan calculated as follows:

Equity in Sloan's reported income ($3,000,000 × 30%)	$900
Amortization of excess cost over book value:	
Inventories sold in the current year ($300,000 × 100%)	(300)
Other current assets sold in the current year ($60,000 x 100%)	60
Equipment ($900,000 × 5%) depreciation rate	(45)
Note payable ($60,000 × 20%) amortization rate	(12)
Total investment income from Sloan	$603

Payne reports its investment in Sloan at December 31 on one line of its balance sheet at $5,303,000 (see the following summary) and its income from Sloan at $603,000 on one line of its income statement. Sloan's book value of net assets (stockholders' equity) increased by $2,000,000 to $14,000,000, and Payne's share of this underlying equity is 30 percent, or $4,200,000. The $1,103,000 difference between the investment balance and the underlying book value of equity at December 31 represents the unamortized excess of investment cost over book value acquired. Confirm this amount by subtracting the $297,000 net amortization from the original excess of $1,400,000.

Here is a summary of Payne's equity method investment account activity:

January 1	Initial cost	$5,000,000
July 1	Dividends received	(300,000)
December 31	Recognize 30% of Sloan's net income	900,000
December 31	Write off excess allocated to inventory	(300,000)
December 31	Record income from Sloan's overvalued current assets sold in the current year	60,000
December 31	Additional equipment depreciation	(45,000)
December 31	Amortize note payable excess	(12,000)
December 31	Ending balance	$5,303,000

When the full $1,400,000 excess has been amortized (or written off as an impairment loss in the case of goodwill), the investment balance will equal its underlying book value, which is 30 percent of the stockholders' equity of Sloan. A summary of these observations follows (in thousands):

	Stockholders' Equity of Sloan (A)	Underlying Equity (30% of Sloan's Equity) (B)	Investment in Sloan Account Balance (C)	Unamortized Cost/Book Value (C − B)
January 1	$12,000	$3,600	$5,000	$1,400
Dividends, July	(1,000)	(300)	(300)	—
Income	3,000	900	900	—
Amortization	—	—	(297)	(297)
December 31	$14,000	$4,200	$5,303	$1,103

Excess of Book Value over Cost

The book value of the interest acquired in an investee may be greater than the investment cost or fair value. This indicates that the identifiable net assets of the investee are overvalued or that the interest was acquired at a bargain price. The bargain purchase amount is recorded as an ordinary gain as explained in Chapter 1.

To illustrate, assume that Post Corporation purchases 50 percent of the outstanding voting common stock of Taylor Corporation on January 1 for $40,000 in cash. A summary of the changes in Taylor's stockholders' equity during the year appears as follows (in thousands):

Stockholders' equity January 1	$100
Add: Income	20
Deduct: Dividends paid July 1	(5)
Stockholders' equity December 31	$115

The $10,000 excess of book value acquired over investment cost ($100,000 × 50%) −$40,000 was due to inventory items and equipment that were overvalued on Taylor's books. Taylor's January 1 inventory was overvalued by $2,000 and was sold in December. The remaining $18,000 overvaluation related to equipment with a 10-year remaining useful life from January 1. No goodwill results because the $40,000 cost is equal to the fair value of the net assets acquired (50% × $80,000).

The assignment of the difference between book value acquired and investment cost is as follows (in thousands):

Cost of the investment in Taylor	$ 40
Less: Underlying book value of Post's 50% interest in Taylor ($100,000 stockholders' equity × 50%)	(50)
Excess book value over cost	$(10)
Excess assigned to:	
Inventories ($2,000 overvaluation × 50% owned)	$ (1)
Equipment ($18,000 overvaluation × 50% owned)	(9)
Excess book value over cost	$(10)

Journal entries to account for Post Corporation's investment in Taylor are as follows:

January 1

Investment in Taylor (+A)	40	
Cash (−A)		40
To record purchase of 50% of Taylor's outstanding voting stock.		

July 1

Cash (+A)	2.5	
Investment in Taylor (−A)		2.5
To record dividends received (5,000 × 50%) .		

December 31

Investment in Taylor (+A)   10

    Income from Taylor (R, +SE)   10

    To recognize equity in the income of Taylor (20,000 × 50%) .

December 31

Investment in Taylor (+A)   1.9

    Income from Taylor (R, +SE)   1.9

    To amortize excess of book value over investment cost assigned to:

Inventory (1,000 × 100%)	$1.0
Equipment (9,000 × 10%)	.9
Total	$1.9

Because assets were purchased at less than book value, Post reports investment income from Taylor of $11,900 ($10,000+$1,900) and an Investment in Taylor balance at December 31 of $49,400. Amortization of the excess of book value over investment cost increases Post's Investment in Taylor balance by $1,900 during the year.

Here is a summary of the equity method investment account activity:

January 1	Initial cost	$40,000
July 1	Dividends received	(2,500)
December 31	Recognize 50% of Taylor's net income	10,000
December 31	Amortization of excess of book value over investment cost	1,900
December 31	Ending balance	$49,400

Bargain Purchase

Assume that Post Corporation also acquires a 25 percent interest in Saxon Corporation for $110,000 on January 1, at which time Saxon's net assets consist of the following (in thousands):

	Book Value	Fair Value	Excess Fair Value
Inventories	$240	$260	$20
Other current assets	100	100	
Equipment—net	50	50	
Buildings—net	140	200	60
	530	610	
Less: Liabilities	130	130	
Net assets	$400	$480	$80

Saxon's net income and dividends for the year are $60,000 and $40,000, respectively. The undervalued inventory items were sold during the year, and the undervalued buildings had a four-year remaining useful life when Post acquired its 25 percent interest. Exhibit 2-2 illustrates the assignment of the excess cost over book value.

EXHIBIT 2-2

Schedule for Allocating the Excess of Investment Cost (Fair Value) over the Book Value of the Interest Acquired

POST CORPORATION AND ITS 25%-OWNED EQUITY INVESTEE, SAXON CORPORATION (IN THOUSANDS)			
Investment cost			$110
Book value acquired ($400,000 × 25%)			(100)
Excess cost over book value acquired			$ 10
	Assignment to Fair Value	Negative Excess	Final Assignment
Inventory ($20,000 × 25%)	$ 5		$ 5
Buildings—net ($60,000 × 25%)	15		15
Gain from bargain purchase		$10	(10)
Excess	$20	$ 0	$10

In reviewing Exhibit 2-2, notice that the excess cost over book value is first assigned to fair values of identifiable net assets. Because the fair value of the net assets acquired exceeds the cost of the investment, the difference is a bargain purchase gain. This bargain purchase gain is recognized as an ordinary gain on the books of the investor.

Journal entries for Post to account for its investment in Saxon follow:

January 1

Investment in Saxon (+A)	120	
Cash (−A)		110
Gain on bargain purchase (Ga,+SE)		10
To record purchase of a 25% interest in Saxon's voting stock.		

Throughout the year

Cash (+A)	10	
Investment in Saxon (−A)		10
To record dividends received ($40,000 × 25%) .		

December 31

Investment in Saxon (+A)	6.25	
Income from Saxon (R,+SE)		6.25
To recognize investment income from Saxon computed as follows:		

25% of Saxon's $60,000 net income	$15,000
Excess allocated to inventories	(5,000)
Excess allocated to buildings ($15,000 ÷ 4 years)	(3,750)
	$ 6,250

Post Corporation's investment in Saxon balance at December 31 is $116,250, and the underlying book value of the investment is $105,000 ($420,000 × 25%) on that same date. The $11,250 difference is due to the $11,250 unamortized excess assigned to buildings.

Interim Acquisitions of Investment Interest

Accounting for equity investments becomes more specific when the firm makes acquisitions within an accounting period (interim acquisitions). Additional computations determine the underlying equity at the time of acquisition and the investment income for the year. We compute stockholders' equity of the investee by adding income earned since the last statement date to the date of purchase to the beginning stockholders' equity and subtracting dividends declared date of purchase. In accounting for interim acquisitions, we assume that income of the investee is earned proportionately throughout the year unless there is evidence to the contrary.

Assume that Petron Corporation acquires 40 percent of the voting common stock of Fair Company for $80,000 on October 1. Fair's net assets (owners' equity) at January 1 are $150,000, and it reports net income of $25,000 for the year ended December 31 and declares $15,000 dividends on July 1. The book values of Fair's assets and liabilities are equal to fair values on October 1, except for a building worth $60,000 and recorded at $40,000. The building has a 20-year remaining useful life from October 1. GAAP requires application of the equity method and assignment of any difference between investment cost and book value acquired first to identifiable assets and liabilities and then to goodwill.

The excess of Petron's investment cost over book value of its 40 percent interest in Fair is computed and assigned to identifiable assets and goodwill, as shown in Exhibit 2-3.

EXHIBIT 2-3		
Schedule for Allocating the Excess of Investment Fair Value over Book Value		

PETRON CORPORATION AND ITS 40%-OWNED EQUITY INVESTEE, FAIR CORPORATION		
Investment cost		$80,000
Less: Share of Fair equity on October 1		
Beginning equity	$150,000	
Add: Income to October 1	18,750	
Less: Dividends	(15,000)	
	153,750	
Times: Interest purchased	40%	(61,500)
Excess cost over book value		$18,500
Excess assigned to: Buildings [($60,000 − $40,000) × 40%]		$ 8,000
Goodwill (remainder)		10,500
Excess cost over book value		$18,500

Journal entries on Petron's books to account for the 40 percent equity interest in Fair for the current year are as follows (in thousands):

October 1

Investment in Fair (+A)	80	
Cash (−A)		80

To record acquisition of 40% of Fair's voting stock.

December 31

Investment in Fair (+A)	2.5	
Income from Fair (R, +SE)		2.5

To record equity in Fair's income
(40% × $25,000 × 1/4 year)

December 31

Income from Fair (−R, −SE)	.1	
Investment in Fair (−A)		.1

To record amortization of excess of cost over book value
  allocated to the undervalued building
($8,000 ÷ 20 years) × 1/4 year.

At December 31, after the entries are posted, Petron's Investment in Fair account will have a balance of $82,400 ($80,000 cost +$2,400 income). This investment account balance is $18,400 more than the $64,000 underlying book value of Petron's interest in Fair on that date (40% × $160,000). The $18,400 consists of the original excess cost over book value of $18,500 less the $100 amortized in the current year.

Here is a summary of Petron's equity method Investment in Fair account activity:

October 1	Initial cost	$80,000
December 31	Recognize 40% of Fair's net income for 1/4 year	2,500
December 31	Amortization of excess of cost over book value for 1/4 year	(100)
December 31	Ending balance	$82,400

Notice that we do not recognize 40 percent of the dividends declared and paid by Fair in this example. The dividends were paid on July 1, prior to Petron's investment. Under the equity method, investors recognize dividends received, not their proportional share of total dividends declared and/or paid. Of course, if the investment is owned for the entire year, these amounts will be the same.

INVESTMENT IN A STEP-BY-STEP ACQUISITION

An investor may acquire significant influence over the operating and financial policies of an investee in a series of stock acquisitions, rather than in a single purchase. For example, the investor may acquire a 10 percent interest in an investee and later acquire another 10 percent interest. We account for the original 10 percent interest by the fair value/cost method until we reach a 20 percent interest. Then we adopt the equity method and adjust the investment and retained earnings accounts retroactively.

Assume that Hop Corporation acquires a 10 percent interest in Skip Corporation for $750,000 on January 2, 2011, and another 10 percent interest for $850,000 on January 2, 2012. The stockholders' equity of Skip Corporation on the dates of these acquisitions is as follows (in thousands):

	January 2, 2011	January 2, 2012
Capital stock	$5,000	$5,000
Retained earnings	2,000	2,500
Total stockholders' equity	$7,000	$7,500

Hop Corporation is not able to relate the excess of investment cost over book value to identifiable net assets. Accordingly, the excess of cost over book value from each of the acquisitions is goodwill.

On January 2, 2012, when the second 10 percent is acquired, Hop Corporation adopts the equity method of accounting for its 20 percent interest. This requires converting the carrying value of the original 10 percent interest from its $750,000 cost to its correct carrying value on an equity basis. The entry to adjust the investment account of Hop Corporation is as follows (in thousands):

January 2, 2012

Investment in Skip (+A)	50	
Retained earnings (+SE)		50

To adjust the Investment in Skip account from a cost
   to an equity basis as follows: Share of Skip's retained
   earnings increase during 2011 of $50,000 [$500,000 × 10%
   interest held during the year] equals the retroactive adjustment
   from accounting change of $50,000.

Skip's $500,000 retained earnings increase for 2011 represents its income less dividends for 2011. Hop reports its share of dividends received from Skip as income under the cost method; therefore, Hop's income for 2011 under the equity method is greater by 10 percent of Skip's retained earnings increase for 2011.

Changes in the cost, equity, and consolidation methods of accounting for subsidiaries and investments are changes in the reporting entity that require restatement of prior-period financial statements if the effect is material.[11]

SALE OF AN EQUITY INTEREST

When an investor sells a portion of an equity investment that reduces its interest in the investee to below 20 percent or to less than a level necessary to exercise significant influence, the equity method of accounting is no longer appropriate for the remaining interest. We account for the investment under the fair value/cost method from this time forward, and the investment account balance after the sale becomes the new basis. We require no other adjustment, and the investor accounts for the investment under the fair value/cost method in the usual manner. Gain or loss from the equity interest sold is the difference between the selling price and the book value of the equity interest immediately before the sale.

To illustrate, Leigh Industries acquires 320,000 shares (a 40 percent interest) in Sergio Corporation on January 1, 2011, for $580,000. Sergio's stockholders' equity is $1,200,000, and the book values of its assets and liabilities equal their fair values. Leigh accounts for its investment in Sergio under the equity method during the years 2011 through 2012. At December 31, 2012, the balance of the investment account is $700,000, equal to 40 percent of Sergio's $1,500,000 stockholders' equity plus $100,000 goodwill.

On January 1, 2013, Leigh sells 80 percent of its holdings in Sergio (256,000 shares) for $600,000, reducing its interest in Sergio to 8 percent (40% $\times$ 20%). The book value of the interest sold is $560,000, or 80 percent of the $700,000 balance of the Investment in Sergio account. Leigh recognizes a gain on the sale of its interest in Sergio of $40,000 ($600,000 selling price less $560,000 book value of the interest sold). The balance of the Investment in Sergio account after the sale is $140,000 ($700,000 less $560,000 interest sold). Leigh determines that it can no longer exercise significant influence over Sergio, and accordingly, it switches to the fair value/cost method and accounts for its investment with the $140,000 balance becoming the new basis of the investment.[12]

STOCK PURCHASES DIRECTLY FROM THE INVESTEE

We have assumed up to now that the investor purchased its shares from existing stockholders of the investee. In that situation, the interest acquired was equal to the shares acquired divided by the investee's outstanding shares. If an investor purchases shares directly from the issuing corporation, however, we determine the investor's interest by the shares acquired divided by the shares outstanding after the investee issues the new shares.

Assume that Karl Corporation purchases 20,000 shares of previously unissued common stock directly from Master Corporation for $450,000 on January 1, 2011. Master's stockholders' equity at December 31, 2010, consists of $200,000 of $10 par common stock and $150,000 retained earnings.

We compute Karl's 50 percent interest in Master as follows:

A	Shares purchased by Karl		20,000 shares
B	Shares outstanding after new shares are issued:		
	Outstanding December 31, 2010	20,000	
	Issued to Karl	20,000	40,000 shares
	Karl's interest in Master: A/B = 50%		

The book value of the interest acquired by Karl is $400,000, which is determined by multiplying the 50 percent interest acquired by Master's $800,000 stockholders' equity immediately after the issuance of the additional 20,000 shares. Computations are as follows:

Master's stockholders' equity before issuance ($200,000 capital stock + $150,000 retained earnings)	$350,000
Sale of 20,000 shares to Karl	450,000
Master's stockholders' equity after issuance	800,000
Karl's percentage ownership	50%
Book value acquired by Karl	$400,000

INVESTEE CORPORATION WITH PREFERRED STOCK

The equity method applies to investments in common stock, and some adjustments in applying the equity method are necessary when an investee has preferred as well as common stock outstanding. These adjustments require the following:

1. Allocation of the investee corporation's stockholders' equity into preferred and common equity components upon acquisition in order to determine the book value of the common stock investment

2. Allocation of the investee's net income into preferred and common income components to determine the investor's share of the investee's income to common stockholders

Assume that Tech Corporation's stockholders' equity is $6,000,000 at the beginning of the year and $6,500,000 at the end of the year. Its net income and dividends for the year are $700,000 and $200,000, respectively.

(Amounts in thousands)	January 1	December 31
10% cumulative preferred stock, $100 par	$1,000	$1,000
Common stock, $10 par	3,000	3,000
Other paid-in capital	500	500
Retained earnings	1,500	2,000
	$6,000	$6,500

If Monet Corporation pays $2,500,000 on January 2 for 40 percent of Tech's outstanding common stock, the investment is evaluated as follows (in thousands):

Cost of 40% common interest in Tech		$2,500
Book value (and fair value) acquired:		
Stockholders' equity of Tech	$6,000	
Less: Preferred stockholders' equity	1,000	
Common stockholders' equity	5,000	
Percent acquired	40%	2,000
Goodwill		$ 500

The equity of preferred stockholders is equal to the par value of outstanding preferred stock, increased by the greater of any call or liquidating premium and by preferred dividends in arrears.

Monet's income from Tech for the year from its 40 percent interest is computed as follows (in thousands):

Tech's net income	$700
Less: Preferred income ($1,000,000 × 10%)	100
Income to common	$600
Share of Tech's common income ($600,000 × 40%)	240

GAAP provides that when an investee has cumulative preferred stock outstanding, an investor in common stock computes its share of earnings or losses after deducting preferred dividends, whether or not preferred dividends are declared. Additional coverage of accounting matters related to investees with preferred stock outstanding is provided in Chapter 10.

EXTRAORDINARY ITEMS AND OTHER CONSIDERATIONS

In accounting for an investment under the equity method, the investor reports its share of the ordinary income of an investee on one line of its income statement. However, the one-line consolidation does not apply to the reporting of investment income when the investee corporation's income includes extraordinary items. In this case, the investment income must be separated into its ordinary and extraordinary components and reported accordingly.

Assume that Carl Corporation owns 40 percent of the outstanding stock of Home Corporation and that Home's income consists of the following (in thousands):

Income from continuing operations before extraordinary item	$500
Extraordinary item—casualty loss (less applicable income taxes of $25,000)	(50)
Net income	$450

Carl records its investment income from Home as follows:

Investment in Home (+A)	180	
Casualty loss—Home (E,−SE)	20	
Income from Home (R,+SE)		200
To record investment income from Home.		

Carl reports the $200,000 income from Home as investment income and reports the $20,000 casualty loss along with any extraordinary items that Carl may have had during the year. A gain or loss on an investee's disposal of a segment of a business would be treated similarly.

Other Requirements of the Equity Method

In reporting its share of earnings and losses of an investee under the equity method, an investor must eliminate the effect of profits and losses on transactions between the investor and investee until they are realized. This means adjusting the investment and investment income accounts as we have illustrated to amortize over- or under valued identifiable net assets. Transactions of an investee that change the investor's share of the net assets of the investee also require adjustments under the equity method of accounting. These and other complexities of the equity method are covered in subsequent chapters, along with related consolidation procedures. Chapter 10 covers preferred stock, earnings per share, and income tax considerations.

DISCLOSURES FOR EQUITY INVESTEES

The extent to which separate disclosure should be provided for equity investments depends on the significance (materiality) of such investments to the financial position and results of operations of the investor. If equity investments are significant, the investor should disclose the following information, parenthetically or in financial statement notes or schedules:

1. The name of each investee and percentage of ownership in common stock
2. The accounting policies of the investor with respect to investments in common stock

EXHIBIT 2-4

The Dow Chemical Company and Subsidiaries Notes to the Consolidated Financial Statements

NOTE H—NONCONSOLIDATED AFFILIATES AND RELATED COMPANY TRANSACTIONS (EXCERPT)

Dow's principal nonconsolidated affiliates and the Company's direct or indirect ownership interest for each at December 31, 2009, 2008 and 2007 are shown below:

PRINCIPAL NONCONSOLIDATED AFFILIATES AT DECEMBER 31

	Ownership Interest		
	2009	*2008*	*2007*
Americas Styrenics LLC	50%	50%	—
Compañía Mega S. A.	28%	28%	28%
Dow Corning Corporation	50%	50%	50%
EQUATE Petrochemical Company K.S.C.	42.5%	42.5%	42.5%
Equipolymers	50%	50%	50%
The Kuwait Olefins Company K.S.C.	42.5%	42.5%	42.5%
MEGlobal	50%	50%	50%
The OPTIMAL Group:			
OPTIMAL Chemicals (Malaysia) Sdn Bhd	—	50%	50%
OPTIMAL Glycols (Malaysia) Sdn Bhd	—	50%	50%
OPTIMAL Olefins (Malaysia) Sdn Bhd	—	23.75%	23.75%
The SCG-Dow Group:			
Pacific Plastics (Thailand) Limited	—	—	49%
Siam Polyethylene Company Limited	49%	49%	49%
Siam Polystyrene Company Limited	50%	50%	49%
Siam Styrene Monomer Co., Ltd.	50%	50%	49%
Siam Synthetic Latex Company Limited	50%	50%	49%
Univation Technologies LLC	50%	50%	50%

On September 30, 2009, the Company completed the sale of its ownership interest in the OPTIMAL Group of companies, see Note E.

The Company's investment in its principal nonconsolidated affiliates was $2,359 million at December 31, 2009, and $2,439 million at December 31, 2008. Equity earnings from these companies were $587 million in 2009, $824 million in 2008 and $1,072 million in 2007. The summarized financial information presented below represents the combined accounts (at 100 percent) of the principal nonconsolidated affiliates.

SUMMARIZED BALANCE SHEET INFORMATION AT DECEMBER 31

In millions	2009	2008
Current assets	$ 6,916	$ 6,391
Noncurrent assets	14,538	14,226
Total assets	$21,454	$20,617
Current liabilities	$ 4,147	$ 3,644
Noncurrent liabilities	10,504	9,876
Total liabilities	$14,651	$13,520

SUMMARIZED INCOME STATEMENT INFORMATION

In millions	2009(1)	2008(2)	2007
Sales	$12,590	$15,508	$13,884
Gross profit	$ 2,910	$ 4,064	$ 3,492
Net income	$ 1,281	$ 1,940	$ 2,451

1. The summarized income statement information for 2009 includes the results for the OPTIMAL Group of companies from January 1, 2009 through September 30, 2009 (see Note E).
2. The summarized income statement information for 2008 includes the results for Americas Styrenics LLC from May 1, 2008 through December 31, 2008.

The Company has service agreements with some of these entities, including contracts to manage the operations of manufacturing sites and the construction of new facilities; licensing and technology agreements; and marketing, sales, purchase and lease agreements.

Excess ethylene glycol produced in Dow's plants in the United States and Europe is sold to MEGlobal and represented 1 percent of total net sales in 2009 (2 percent of total net sales in 2008 and 2007). The impact of these sales to MEGlobal by operating segment is summarized below:

IMPACT OF SALES TO MEGLOBAL BY OPERATING SEGMENT

Percent of segment sales	2009	2008	2007
Basic Chemicals	11%	14%	21%
Hydrocarbons and Energy	4%	3%	4%

Overall, transactions with other nonconsolidated affiliates and balances due to and due from these entities were not material to the consolidated financial statements.

3. The difference, if any, between the amount at which an investment is carried and the amount of underlying equity in net assets, including the accounting treatment of the difference[13]

Additional disclosures for material equity investments include the aggregate value of each identified investment for which quoted market prices are available and summarized information regarding the assets, liabilities, and results of operations of the investees. An excerpt from The *Dow Chemical Company and Subsidiaries' 2009* annual report is presented in Exhibit 2-4 to illustrate the disclosure requirements. Financial information is separately presented for all significant equity investees as a group. Dow includes its share of the underlying net assets of these investees as "Investments" in the balance sheet and includes its share of the investees' net income in the income statement as "Equity in income of investees." The operating-activities section of Dow's consolidated statement of cash flows shows both "Equity in income of investees" and "Cash distributions from equity investees" as adjustments to net income.

Related-Party Transactions

There is no presumption of arm's-length bargaining between related parties. GAAP identifies material transactions between affiliated companies as related-party transactions requiring financial statements disclosure.[14] Related-party transactions arise when one of the transacting parties has the ability to influence significantly the operations of the other. The required disclosures include the following:

1. The nature of the relationship
2. A description of the transaction
3. The dollar amounts of the transaction and any change from the previous period in the method used to establish the terms of the transaction for each income statement presented
4. Amounts due to or due from related parties at the balance sheet date for each balance sheet presented

Exhibit 2-4 summarizes Dow's related-party transactions disclosures.

Exhibit 2-5 illustrates related-party disclosures for affiliated companies for *Chevron Corporation*. Note 7 to Chevron's 2009 annual report identifies *Tengizchevroil* as a major equity method affiliate. Chevron's 2009 balance sheet lists "Investments and advances" totaling $21.158 billion (12.85 percent of total consolidated assets).

<table>
<tr><td>LEARNING
OBJECTIVE **6**</td></tr>
</table>

TESTING GOODWILL FOR IMPAIRMENT

Chapter 1 introduced the rules for goodwill and other intangible assets. This section provides additional discussion and examples of impairment tests.

Goodwill and certain other intangible assets having an indefinite useful life are not amortized. Recorded intangible assets having a definite useful life continue to be amortized over that life. If an intangible asset has a definite, but unknown, useful life, firms should amortize over the best estimate of useful life.

Those intangibles (including goodwill) having an indefinite life are not amortized, but are subject to annual review and testing for impairment. The focus here is impairment testing and reporting for goodwill.

Time Warner, Inc. (formerly *AOL Time Warner*) provides an example of significant goodwill and intangible asset impairment write-offs. In its 2003 annual report, the consolidated income statement includes "Impairment of goodwill and other intangible assets" of $318 million in calculating income from operations. This amount pales in comparison to the 2002 amounts. Operating income for 2002 included an impairment loss for goodwill and intangibles of $44.039 billion. Net income for 2002 included an additional cumulative effect of accounting changes of $(54.235) billion, due mostly to goodwill write-offs, and this number is net of tax.

Add up the numbers and you discover that total goodwill impairments (including the discontinued operations) were $98.884 billion in 2002, and an additional $1.418 billion in 2003. The note for 2002 also discloses an $853 million impairment write-off for brands and trademarks for the Music segment. To put this in perspective, Time Warner's total assets at December 31, 2001, were $208.5 billion; the impairment write-offs in 2002 represent almost 50% of that amount. Time Warner points out, correctly, that these are noncash charges; however, this is still a lot of shareholder value wiped off the books.

EXHIBIT 2-5

Related-Party
Disclosures for
Affiliates

CHEVRON CORPORATION 2009 ANNUAL REPORT NOTE 12: INVESTMENTS AND ADVANCES (PARTIAL) (IN MILLIONS OF DOLLARS)

Other Information "Sales and other operating revenues" on the Consolidated Statement of Income includes $10,391, $15,390 and $11,555 with affiliated companies for 2009, 2008 and 2007, respectively. "Purchased crude oil and products" includes $4,631, $6,850 and $5,464 with affiliated companies for 2009, 2008 and 2007, respectively.

"Accounts and notes receivable" on the Consolidated Balance Sheet includes $1,125 and $701 due from affiliated companies at December 31, 2009 and 2008, respectively. "Accounts payable" includes $345 and $289 due to affiliated companies at December 31, 2009 and 2008, respectively.

EXHIBIT 2-6

Excerpts from Citigroup
Inc. 2008 Annual Report
(pp. 166–167)

19. GOODWILL AND INTANGIBLE ASSETS

...Goodwill impairment testing is performed at a level below the business segments (referred to as a reporting unit). Changes in the management structure in 2008 resulted in the creation of new business segments. As a result, commencing with the third quarter of 2008, the Company identified new reporting units as required under SFAS No. 142, *Goodwill and Other Intangible Assets* (SFAS 142). Goodwill affected by the reorganization has been reallocated from seven reporting units to ten, using a relative fair-value approach. Subsequent to the reorganization, goodwill was reallocated to disposals and tested for impairment under the new reporting units....

The results of the first step of the impairment test showed no indication of impairment in any of the reporting units at any of the periods except December 31, 2008 and, accordingly, the Company did not perform the second step of the impairment test, except for the test performed as of December 31, 2008. As of December 31, 2008, there was an indication of impairment in the *North America Consumer Banking, Latin America consumer Banking and EMEA Consumer Banking* reporting units and, accordingly, the second step of testing was performed on these reporting units.

Based on the results of the second step of testing, the Company recorded a $9.6 billion pretax ($8.7 billion after tax) goodwill impairment charge in the fourth quarter of 2008, representing the entire amount of goodwill allocated to these reporting units. The primary cause for the goodwill impairment in the above reporting units was the rapid deterioration in the financial markets, as well as in the global economic outlook particularly during the period beginning mid-November through year end 2008....

Exhibit 2-6 provides a more recent example of goodwill impairment charges for **Citigroup Inc.** in 2008.

Time Warner was not alone in taking large goodwill and intangible asset impairment charges. **MCI, Inc.,** (formerly **WorldCom**) reported $5.7 billion in impairment charges in 2001 and an additional $400 million in 2002. **Corning's** 2002 annual report included a $294 million after-tax impairment charge for goodwill related to its telecommunications reporting unit. **E.I. Du Pont De Nemours** included a charge of $2.9 billion for the cumulative effect of adoption of the new goodwill impairment standard in its 2002 annual report. **Dillard's, Inc.,** the department store chain, reported a $530 million impairment charge in 2002. **Intel Corporation's** 2002 impairment loss was $617 million.

Recognizing and Measuring Impairment Losses

The goodwill impairment test is a two-step process.[15] Firms must first compare carrying values (book values) to fair values of all assets and liabilities at the business-reporting-unit level. Carrying value includes the goodwill amount. For purposes of applying the standard, GAAP[16] defines the reporting unit as an operating segment or one level below an operating segment. The definition of business reporting units is discussed in a later chapter on segment reporting.

If the reporting unit's fair value exceeds its carrying value, goodwill is unimpaired. No further action is needed.

If fair value is less than the carrying amount, then firms proceed to step 2, measurement and recognition of the impairment loss. Step 2 requires a comparison of the carrying amount of goodwill to its implied fair value. Firms should again make this comparison at the business-reporting-unit level. If the carrying amount exceeds the implied fair value of the goodwill, the firm must recognize an impairment loss for the difference. The loss amount cannot exceed the carrying amount of the goodwill. Firms cannot reverse previously recognized impairment losses.

Implied Fair Value of Goodwill

Firms should determine the implied fair value of goodwill in the same manner used to originally record the goodwill at the business combination date. Firms allocate the fair value of the reporting unit to all identifiable assets and liabilities, as if they had purchased the unit on the measurement date. Any excess fair value is the implied fair value of goodwill.

Assume that Paul Corporation owns 80% of Surly Corporation, which qualifies as a business reporting unit. The consolidated balance sheet carries goodwill of $6.3 million related to the investment in Surly. Paul would assess the implied fair value of goodwill as follows.

Paul first estimates that if it purchased its investment in Surly today, the total fair value of Surly would be $36.25 million, based on current market prices for Surly's shares. Paul allocates the total fair value to the identifiable assets and liabilities of Surly as shown (figures are in millions):

	Book Value	Fair Value
Current assets	$11.10	$12.85
Property, plant, and equipment	45.00	48.00
Patents	4.00	5.40
Current liabilities	(9.00)	(9.00)
Long-term liabilities	(26.00)	(26.00)
Net	$25.10	$31.25
Total fair value		36.25
Implied fair value of Goodwill		$ 5.00

The fair value of Surly's identifiable assets and liabilities is $31.25 million. Therefore, goodwill has an implied fair value of $5 million ($36.25 million less $31.25 million). Notice that goodwill applies to the entire business reporting unit.

Because the current carrying value for goodwill is $6.3 million and its implied fair value is only $5 million, Paul must record a goodwill impairment loss of $1.3 million. The carrying value of goodwill is adjusted to $5 million for purposes of future impairment testing. (If the carrying value for goodwill had been less than $5 million, no impairment loss would have been recognized.)

Determining the Fair Value of the Reporting Unit

Fair values of assets and liabilities are the amounts at which they could be exchanged in an arm's-length transaction. Therefore, the fair value of a reporting unit is the amount for which it could be purchased or sold in a current transaction. The previous example assumed that a current quoted market price was available for Surly's shares. GAAP considers current market prices (in an active market) to be the most reliable indicator of fair value for a reporting unit.

Of course, these values will not always be available. If Paul owned 100% of Surly's common stock, there would be no active market for Surly's shares. The same situation holds if Surly's shares are not publicly traded. In these cases GAAP suggests estimating fair values by using prices for similar assets and liabilities or by applying other valuation techniques. For example, Paul might estimate future cash flows from Surly's operations and apply present value techniques to estimate the value of the reporting unit. Paul might also employ earnings or revenue multiples techniques to estimate the fair value of Surly.

Firms must conduct the impairment test for goodwill at least annually. GAAP requires more-frequent impairment testing if any of the following events occurs:

- Significant adverse changes in legal factors or business climate
- Adverse regulatory actions or assessments
- New and unanticipated competition
- Loss of key personnel
- A more-likely-than-not expectation that a reporting unit or a significant portion of a reporting unit will be sold or disposed of
- Testing for the recoverability of a significant asset group within a reporting unit
- Recognition of a goodwill impairment loss of a subsidiary that is a component of the reporting unit[17]

Fair Value Option for Equity Method Investments

Historically, equity method investments were not adjusted for changes in fair market value, but GAAP[18] now provides firms with an option to record equity method investments at fair value. The option may be elected on an investment-by-investment basis. Firms taking the fair value option would calculate fair values using methods described above. The option must continue as long as the investment is owned. Fair value is recalculated annually. Changes in fair value are reflected in the investor's net income, and the offsetting cumulative amount will be recorded in a valuation allowance.[19]

Assume that Boron Corporation purchased a 30% interest in Digby Company on July 1. Applying the equity procedures described previously, Boron's investment account has a balance of $202,000 on December 31. Boron elects the fair value option for this investment. Based on market prices, Digby Company is valued at $700,000 on December 31. Therefore, the fair value of Boron's 30% interest is $210,000. Boron would record the following adjusting entry:

Allowance to adjust equity method		
Investment to fair value (+A)	8,000	
Unrealized holding gain on equity method investment (Ga, +SE)		8,000

Under GAAP, investors must separately disclose equity method investments using the fair value option.

Reporting and Disclosures

GAAP requires firms to report material aggregate amounts of goodwill as a separate line item on the balance sheet. Likewise, firms must show goodwill impairment losses separately in the income statement, as a component of income from continuing operations (unless the impairment relates to discontinued operations). Goodwill impairments from discontinued operations should be reported separately (net of income tax effects) in the discontinued operations section of the income statement.

Equity Method Investments

The previous discussion on goodwill impairment applies only to goodwill arising from business combinations (i.e., a parent company acquires a controlling interest in a subsidiary). Impairment testing also applies to goodwill reflected in investments reported under the equity method of accounting when the investor has a noncontrolling interest.

Once again, the rules eliminate periodic amortization of goodwill, replacing that treatment with periodic tests for impairment. However, impairment tests for equity method investments do not follow the same guidelines. Impairment tests for equity method investments are performed based on fair value versus book value of the investment taken as a whole. An impairment loss may be recognized for the equity method investment as a whole. Goodwill arising from an equity method investment is not separately tested for impairment.

Potential Problems

The GAAP rules are straightforward in concept, but practical application may be difficult, especially in those cases in which quoted market prices are unavailable to value business reporting units. Alternative valuation methods are highly subjective.

The rules also pose considerable problems for auditors. Fair value estimations are very difficult to verify objectively. Auditors may also be faced with earnings-management issues for some clients. If a firm chooses to take a big bath by writing off large amounts of goodwill, the conservative nature of financial reporting makes it difficult to challenge managers' estimates.

SUMMARY

Exhibit 2-7 is a flowchart summary of accounting procedures for business investments. Investments in the voting common stock of an investee are accounted for under the fair value/cost method if the investment does not give the investor an ability to exercise significant influence over the investee. Otherwise, investors should normally use the equity method (a one-line consolidation). In the absence of evidence to the contrary, a 20 percent-ownership test determines whether the investor has significant influence over the investee.

The equity method is referred to as a one-line consolidation because its application produces the same net income and stockholders' equity for the investor as would result from consolidation of the financial statements of the investor and investee corporations. Under the one-line consolidation, the investment is reflected in a single amount on one line of the investor's balance sheet, and the investor reports income from the investee on one line of the investor's income statement, except when the investee's income includes extraordinary items or discontinued operations.

As you can see in the flow chart in Exhibit 2-7, the equity method can be used to account for investments that follow the acquisition method for business combinations. The flow chart also indicates that consolidated statements are generally required for investments in excess of 50 percent of the voting stock of the investee and that the one-line consolidation (equity method) is used in reporting investments of 20 percent to 50 percent in the investor's financial statements.

| NOTE TO THE STUDENT

In solving problems in the areas of business combinations, equity investments, and consolidations, we frequently must make assumptions about the nature of the difference between investment cost (fair value) and book value of the net assets acquired, the timing of income earned within an accounting period, the period in which inventory items affecting intercompany investments are sold, and the source from which an equity interest is acquired. In the absence of evidence to the contrary, you should make the following assumptions:

1. An excess of investment cost (fair value) over book value of the net assets acquired is goodwill.
2. Goodwill is not amortized.
3. Income is earned evenly throughout each accounting period.
4. Inventory items on hand at the end of an accounting period are sold in the immediately succeeding fiscal period.
5. An equity interest is purchased from the stockholders of the investee rather than directly from the investee (that is, the total outstanding stock of the investee does not change).

QUESTIONS

1. How are the accounts of investor and investee companies affected when the investor acquires stock from stockholders of the investee (for example, a New York Stock Exchange purchase)? Does this differ if the investor acquires previously unissued stock directly from the investee?

2. Should goodwill arising from an equity investment of more than 20 percent be recorded separately on the books of the investor? Explain.

3. Under the fair value/cost method of accounting for stock investments, an investor records dividends received from earnings accumulated after the investment is acquired as dividend income. How does an investor treat dividends received from earnings accumulated before an investment is acquired?

4. Describe the equity method of accounting.

5. Why is the equity method referred to as a "one-line consolidation"?

6. Is there a difference between the amount of a parent's net income under the equity method and the consolidated net income for the same parent and its subsidiaries?

7. What is the difference in reporting income from a subsidiary in the parent's separate income statement and in consolidated financial statements?

8. Cite the conditions under which you would expect the balance of an equity investment account on a balance sheet date subsequent to acquisition to be equal to the underlying book value represented by that investment.

9. What accounting procedures or adjustments are necessary when an investor uses the cost method of accounting for an investment in common stock and later increases the investment such that the equity method is required?

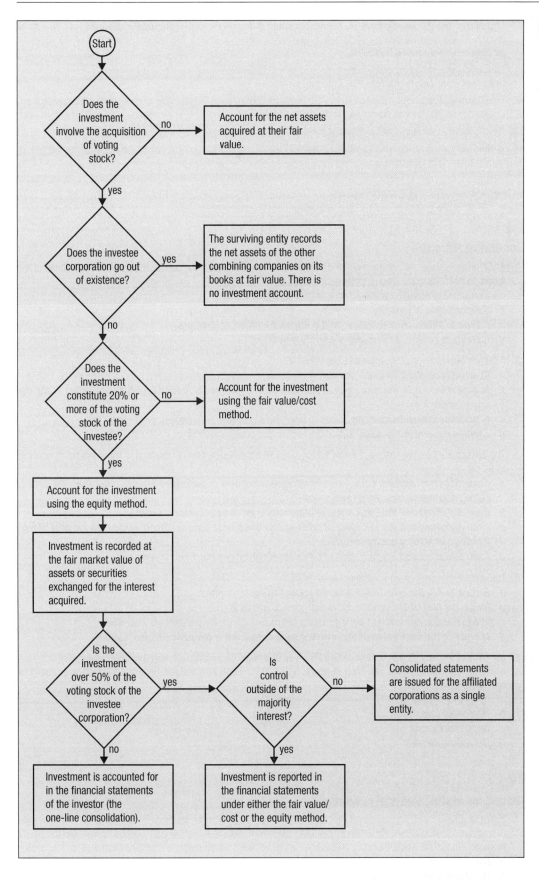

EXHIBIT 2-7

**Accounting for
Equity Investments
Generally**

10. Ordinarily, the income from an investment accounted for by the equity method is reported on one line of the investor's income statement. When would more than one line of the income statement of the investor be required to report such income?

11. Describe the accounting adjustments needed when a 25 percent equity interest in an investee is decreased to a 15 percent equity interest.

12. Does cumulative preferred stock in the capital structure of an investee affect the way that an investor accounts for its 30 percent common stock interest? Explain.

13. Briefly outline the steps to calculate a goodwill impairment loss.

14. Is there any difference in computing goodwill impairment losses for a controlled subsidiary versus an equity method investment?

EXERCISES

E 2-1

General questions

1. GAAP provides indicators of an investor's inability to exercise significant influence over an investee. Which of the following is *not* included among those indicators?
   a *Surrender of significant stockholder rights by agreement*
   b *Concentration of majority ownership*
   c *Failure to obtain representation on the investee's board of directors*
   d *Inability to control the investee's operating policies*

2. A 20 percent common stock interest in an investee:
   a *Must be accounted for under the equity method*
   b *Is accounted for by the cost method because over 20 percent is required for the application of the equity method*
   c *Is presumptive evidence of an ability to exercise significant influence over the investee*
   d *Enables the investor to apply either the cost or the equity method*

3. The cost of a 25 percent interest in the voting stock of an investee that is recorded in the investment account includes:
   a *Cash disbursed and the book value of other assets given or securities issued, other than the cost of registering and issuing equity securities*
   b *Cash disbursed and the book value of other assets given or securities issued*
   c *Cash disbursed and the fair value of other assets given or securities issued, other than the cost of registering and issuing equity securities*
   d *Cash disbursed and the fair value of other assets given or securities issued*

4. The underlying equity of an investment at acquisition:
   a *Is recorded in the investment account under the equity method*
   b *Minus the cost of the investment is assigned to goodwill*
   c *Is equal to the fair value of the investee's net assets times the percentage acquired*
   d *Is equal to the book value of the investee's net assets times the percentage acquired*

5. Jar Corporation is a 25 percent-owned equity investee of Mar Corporation. During the current year, Mar receives $12,000 in dividends from Jar. How does the $12,000 dividend affect Mar's financial position and results of operations?
   a *Increases assets*
   b *Decreases investment*
   c *Increases income*
   d *Decreases income*

E 2-2

[Based on AICPA] General problems

1. Invest Company owns 30 percent of Ali Corporation. During the year, Ali had net earnings of $200,000 and paid dividends of $18,000. Invest mistakenly recorded these transactions using the cost method rather than the equity method. What effect would this have on the investment account, net earnings, and retained earnings, respectively?
   a *Understate, overstate, overstate*
   b *Overstate, understate, understate*
   c *Overstate, overstate, overstate*
   d *Understate, understate, understate*

2. A corporation exercises control over an affiliate in which it holds a 25 percent common stock interest. If its affiliate completed a fiscal year profitably but paid *no* dividends, how would this affect the investor?

   a **Result in an increased current ratio**

   b **Result in increased earnings per share**

   c **Increase several turnover ratios**

   d **Decrease book value per share**

3. An investor uses the cost method to account for an investment in common stock. A portion of the dividends received this year were in excess of the investor's share of investee's earnings after the date of the investment. The amount of dividends revenue that should be reported in the investor's income statement for this year would be:

   a **Zero**

   b **The total amount of dividends received this year**

   c **The portion of the dividends received this year that were in excess of the investor's share of investee's earnings after the date of investment**

   d **The portion of the dividends received this year that were not in excess of the investor's share of investee's earnings after the date of investment**

4. On January 1, Gar Company paid $600,000 for 20,000 shares of Med Company's common stock, which represents a 15 percent investment in Med. Gar does not have the ability to exercise significant influence over Med. Med declared and paid a dividend of $2 per share to its stockholders during the year. Med reported net income of $520,000 for the year ended December 31. The balance in Gar's balance sheet account "Investment in Med Company" at December 31 should be

   a **$560,000**

   b **$600,000**

   c **$638,000**

   d **$678,000**

5. On January 2, 2011, Two Corporation bought 15 percent of Zef Corporation's capital stock for $30,000. Two accounts for this investment by the cost method. Zef's net income for the years ended December 31, 2011, and December 31, 2012, were $10,000 and $50,000, respectively. During 2012 Zef declared a dividend of $70,000. No dividends were declared in 2011. How much should Two show on its 2012 income statement as income from this investment?

   a **$1,575**

   b **$7,500**

   c **$9,000**

   d **$10,500**

6. Par purchased 10 percent of Tot Company's 100,000 shares of common stock on January 2 for $100,000. On December 31, Par purchased an additional 20,000 shares of Tot for $300,000. There was no goodwill as a result of either acquisition, and Tot had not issued any additional stock during the year. Tot reported earnings of $600,000 for the year. What amount should Par report in its December 31 balance sheet as investment in Tot?

   a **$340,000**

   b **$400,000**

   c **$460,000**

   d **$580,000**

7. On January 1, Pin purchased 10 percent of Ion Company's common stock. Pin purchased additional shares, bringing its ownership up to 40 percent of Ion's common stock outstanding, on August 1. During October, Ion declared and paid a cash dividend on all of its outstanding common stock. How much income from the Ion investment should Pin's income statement report for the year ended December 31?

   a **10 percent of Ion's income for January 1 to July 31, plus 40 percent of Ion's income for August 1 to December 31**

   b **40 percent of Ion's income for August 1 to December 31 only**

   c **40 percent of Ion's income**

   d **Amount equal to dividends received from Ion**

8. On January 2, Ken Company purchased a 30 percent interest in Pod Company for $250,000. On this date, the book value of Pod's stockholders' equity was $500,000. The carrying amounts of Pod's identifiable net assets approximated fair values, except for land, whose fair value exceeded its carrying amount by $200,000. Pod reported net income of $100,000 and paid no dividends. Ken accounts for this investment using the equity method. In its December 31 balance sheet, what amount should Ken report for this investment?

   a **$210,000**

   b **$220,000**

   c **$270,000**

   d **$280,000**

E 2-3

Calculate percentage ownership and goodwill on investment acquired directly from investee

Tre Corporation's stockholders' equity at December 31 consisted of the following (in thousands):

Capital stock, $10 par, 60,000 shares issued and outstanding	$ 600
Additional paid-in capital	150
Retained earnings	250
Total stockholders' equity	$1,000

On January 1, 2011, Bow Corporation purchased 20,000 previously unissued shares of Tre stock directly from Tre for $500,000.

REQUIRED

1. Calculate Bow Corporation's percentage ownership in Tre.

2. Determine the goodwill from Bow's investment in Tre. Assume the book value of all identifiable assets and liabilities equals the fair value.

E 2-4

Calculate income for a midyear investment

Car Corporation pays $600,000 for a 30 percent interest in Med Corporation on July 1, 2011, when the book value of Med's identifiable net assets equals fair value. Information relating to Med follows (in thousands):

	December 31, 2010	December 31, 2011
Capital stock, $1 par	$ 600	$ 600
Retained earnings	400	500
Total stockholders' equity	$1,000	$1,100
Med's net income earned evenly throughout 2011		$200
Med's dividends for 2011 (paid $50,000 on March 1 and $50,000 on September 1)		$100

REQUIRED: Calculate Car's income from Med for 2011.

E 2-5

Calculate income and investment balance allocation of excess to undervalued assets

Dok Company acquired a 30 percent interest in Oak on January 1 for $2,000,000 cash. Assume the cost of the investment equals the fair value of Oak's net assets. Dok assigned the $500,000 fair value over book value of the interest acquired to the following assets:

Inventories	$100,000 (sold in the current year)
Building	$200,000 (4-year remaining life at January 1)
Goodwill	$200,000

During the year Oak reported net income of $800,000 and paid $200,000 dividends.

REQUIRED

1. Determine Dok's income from Oak.

2. Determine the December 31 balance of the Investment in Oak account.

E 2-6

Journal entry to record income from investee with loss from discontinued operations

Man Corporation purchased a 40 percent interest in Nib Corporation for $1,000,000 on January 1, at book value, when Nibs's assets and liabilities were recorded at their fair values. During the year, Nib reported net income of $600,000 as follows (in thousands):

Income from continuing operations	$700
Less: Loss from discontinued operations	100
Net income	$600

REQUIRED: Prepare the journal entry on Man's books to recognize income from the investment in Nib for the year.

E 2-7
General problems

1. On January 3, 2011, Han Company purchases a 15 percent interest in Ben Corporation's common stock for $50,000 cash. Han accounts for the investment using the cost method. Ben's net income for 2011 is $20,000, but it declares no dividends. In 2012, Ben's net income is $80,000, and it declares dividends of $120,000. What is the correct balance of Han's Investment in Ben account at December 31, 2012?

   a $47,000
   b $50,000
   c $62,000
   d $65,000

2. Sew Corporation's stockholders' equity at December 31, 2011, follows (in thousands):

Capital stock, $100 par	$3,000
Additional paid-in capital	500
Retained earnings	500
Total stockholders' equity	$4,000

   On January 3, 2012, Sew sells 10,000 shares of previously unissued $100 par common stock to Pan Corporation for $1,400,000. On this date the recorded book values of Sew's assets and liabilities equal their fair values. Goodwill from Pan's investment in Sew at the date of purchase is:

   a $0
   b $50,000
   c $300,000
   d $400,000

3. On January 1, Leg Company paid $300,000 for a 20 percent interest in Moe Corporation's voting common stock, at which time Moe's stockholders' equity consisted of $600,000 capital stock and $400,000 retained earnings. Leg was not able to exercise any influence over the operations of Moe and accounted for its investment in Moe using the cost method. During the year, Moe had net income of $200,000 and paid dividends of $150,000. The balance of Leg's Investment in Moe account at December 31 is:

   a $330,000
   b $310,000
   c $307,500
   d $300,000

4. Jot Corporation owns a 40 percent interest in Kaz Products acquired several years ago at book value. Kaz's income statement contains the following information (in thousands):

Income before extraordinary item	$200
Extraordinary loss	50
Net income	$150

   Jot should report income from Kaz in its income from continuing operations at:

   a $20,000
   b $60,000
   c $80,000
   d $100,000

E 2-8
Calculate investment balance four years after acquisition

Ray Corporation owns a 40 percent interest in the outstanding common stock of Ton Corporation, having acquired its interest for $2,400,000 on January 1, 2011, when Ton's stockholders' equity was $4,000,000. The fair value/book value differential was allocated to inventories that were undervalued by $100,000 and sold in 2011, to equipment with a four-year remaining life that was undervalued by $200,000, and to goodwill for the remainder.

The balance of Ton's stockholders' equity at December 31, 2016, is $5,500,000, and all changes therein are the result of income earned and dividends paid.

REQUIRED: Determine the balance of Ray's investment in Ton at December 31, 2016.

E 2-9

Calculate income and investment balance when investee capital structure includes preferred stock

Run Company had net income of $400,000 and paid dividends of $200,000 during 2012. Run's stockholders' equity on December 31, 2011, and December 31, 2012, is summarized as follows (in thousands):

	December 31, 2011	December 31, 2012
10% cumulative preferred stock, $100 par	$ 300	$ 300
Common stock, $1 par	1,000	1,000
Additional paid-in capital	2,200	2,200
Retained earnings	500	700
Stockholders' equity	$4,000	$4,200

On January 2, 2012, Nic Corporation purchased 300,000 common shares of Run at $4 per share and also paid $50,000 direct costs of acquiring the investment.

REQUIRED: Determine (1) Nic's income from Run for 2012 and (2) the balance of the investment in the Run account at December 31, 2012.

E 2-10

Calculate income and investment balance for midyear investment

Arb Corporation acquired 25 percent of Tee Corporation's outstanding common stock on October 1, for $600,000. A summary of Tee's adjusted trial balances on this date and at December 31 follows (in thousands):

	December 31	October 1
Debits		
Current assets	$ 500	$ 250
Plant assets—net	1,500	1,550
Expenses (including cost of goods sold)	800	600
Dividends (paid in July)	200	200
	$3,000	$2,600
Credits		
Current liabilities	$ 300	$ 200
Capital stock (no change during the year)	1,000	1,000
Retained earnings January 1	500	500
Sales	1,200	900
	$3,000	$2,600

Arb uses the equity method of accounting. No information is available concerning the fair values of Tee's assets and liabilities.

REQUIRED

1. Determine Arb's investment income from Tee Corporation for the year ended December 31.
2. Compute the correct balance of Arb's investment in Tee account at December 31.

E 2-11

Adjust investment account and determine income when additional investment qualifies for equity method of accounting

Summary balance sheet and income information for Pim Company for two years is as follows (in thousands):

	January 1, 2011	December 31, 2011	December 31, 2012
Current assets	$ 50	$ 60	$ 75
Plant assets	200	240	250
	$250	$300	$325
Liabilities	$ 40	$ 50	$50
Capital stock	150	150	150
Retained earnings	60	100	$125
	$250	$300	$325

	2011	2012
Net income	$100	$ 50
Dividends	60	25

On January 2, 2011, Pim Corporation purchases 10 percent of Fed Company for $25,000 cash, and it accounts for its investment (classified as an available-for-sale security) in Fed using the fair value method. On December 31, 2011, the fair value of all of Fed's stock is $500,000. On January 2, 2012, Pim purchases an additional 10 percent interest in Fed stock for $50,000 and adopts the equity method to account for the investment. The fair values of Fed's assets and liabilities were equal to book values as of the time of both stock purchases.

REQUIRED

1. Prepare a journal entry to adjust the Investment in Fed account to an equity basis on January 2, 2012.

2. Determine Pim's income from Fed for 2012.

E 2-12

Journal entries (investment in previously unissued stock)

The stockholders' equity of Tal Corporation at December 31, 2011, was $380,000, consisting of the following (in thousands):

Capital stock, $10 par (24,000 shares outstanding)	$240
Additional paid-in capital	60
Retained earnings	80
Total stockholders' equity	$380

On January 1, 2012, Tal Corporation, which was in a tight working capital position, sold 12,000 shares of previously unissued stock to Riv Corporation for $250,000. All of Tal's identifiable assets and liabilities were recorded at fair values on this date except for a building with a 10-year remaining useful life that was undervalued by $60,000. During 2012, Tal Corporation reported net income of $120,000 and paid dividends of $90,000.

REQUIRED: Prepare all journal entries necessary for Riv Corporation to account for its investment in Tal for 2012.

E 2-13

Prepare journal entries and income statement, and determine investment account balance

BIP Corporation paid $390,000 for a 30 percent interest in Cow Corporation on December 31, 2011, when Cow's equity consisted of $1,000,000 capital stock and $400,000 retained earnings. The price paid by BIP reflected the fact that Cow's inventory (on a FIFO basis) was overvalued by $100,000. The overvalued inventory items were sold in 2012.
    During 2012 Cow paid dividends of $200,000 and reported income as follows (in thousands):

Income before extraordinary items	$340
Extraordinary loss (net of tax effect)	40
Net income	$300

REQUIRED

1. Prepare all journal entries necessary to account for BIP's investment in Cow for 2012.

2. Determine the correct balance of BIP's Investment in Cow account at December 31, 2012.

3. Assume that BIP's net income for 2012 consists of $2,000,000 sales, $1,400,000 expenses, and its investment income from Cow. Prepare an income statement for BIP Corporation for 2012.

E 2-14

Calculate income and investment account balance (investee has preferred stock)

Val Corporation paid $290,000 for 40 percent of the outstanding common stock of Wat Corporation on January 2, 2012. During 2012, Wat paid dividends of $48,000 and reported net income of $108,000. A summary of Wat's stockholders' equity at December 31, 2011 and 2012, follows (in thousands):

December 31,	2011	2012
8% cumulative preferred stock, $100 par	$100	$100
Common stock, $10 par	300	300
Premium on preferred stock	10	10
Other paid-in capital	90	90
Retained earnings	100	160
Total stockholders' equity	$600	$660

REQUIRED: Calculate Val Corporation's income from Wat for 2012 and its Investment in Wat account balance at December 31, 2012. Assume the book value of all assets and liabilities equals the fair value.

E 2-15

Goodwill impairment

Par Corporation recorded goodwill in the amount of $100,000 in its acquisition of Sel Company in 2011. Par paid a total of $350,000 to acquire Sel. In preparing its 2012 financial statements, Par estimates that identifiable net assets still have a fair value of $250,000, but the total fair value of Sel is now $320,000. Calculate the implied value of goodwill at December 31, 2012, and indicate how the change in value (if any) will affect Par's 2012 income statement.

E 2-16

Goodwill impairment

Flash, Inc. has two primary business reporting units: Alfa and Beta. In preparing its 2012 financial statements, Flash conducts an annual impairment review of goodwill. Alfa has recorded goodwill of $35,000 that has an estimated fair value of $30,000. Beta has recorded goodwill of $65,000 that has an estimated fair value of $80,000. What amount of impairment loss, if any, must Flash report in its 2012 income statement? Where in the income statement should this appear?

PROBLEMS

P 2-1

Computations for a midyear purchase (investee has an extraordinary gain)

Rit Corporation paid $1,372,000 for a 30 percent interest in Tel Corporation's outstanding voting stock on April 1, 2011. At December 31, 2010, Tel had net assets of $4,000,000 and only common stock outstanding. During 2011, Tel declared and paid dividends of $80,000 each quarter on March 15, June 15, September 15, and December 15 ($320,000 in total). At April 1, 2011, the book value of assets and liabilities equals the fair value. Tel's 2011 income was reported as follows:

Income before extraordinary item	$480,000
Extraordinary gain, December 2011	160,000
Net income	$640,000

REQUIRED: Determine the following items for Rit:

1. Goodwill from the investment in Tel
2. Income from Tel for 2011
3. Investment in Tel account balance at December 31, 2011
4. Rit's equity in Tel's net assets at December 31, 2011
5. The amount of extraordinary gain that Rit will show on its 2011 income statement

P 2-2

Journal entries for midyear investment (cost and equity methods)

Put Company paid $220,000 for an 80% interest in Sel Company on July 1, 2011, when Sel Company had total equity of $110,000. Sel Company reported earnings of $10,000 for 2011 and declared dividends of $8,000 on November 1, 2011.

REQUIRED: Give the entries to record these facts on the books of Put Company:

1. Assuming that Put Company uses the cost method of accounting for its subsidiaries.
2. Assuming that Put Company uses the equity method of accounting for its subsidiaries. (Any difference between investment cost and book value acquired is to be assigned to equipment and amortized over a 10-year period.)

P 2-3

Computations for investee when excess allocated to inventories, building, and goodwill

Vat Company acquired a 30 percent interest in the voting stock of Zel Company for $331,000 on January 1, 2011, when Zel's stockholders' equity consisted of capital stock of $600,000 and retained earnings of

$400,000. At the time of Vat's investment, Zel's assets and liabilities were recorded at their fair values, except for inventories that were undervalued by $30,000 and a building with a 10-year remaining useful life that was overvalued by $60,000. Zel has income for 2011 of $100,000 and pays dividends of $50,000. Assume undervalued inventories are sold in 2011.

REQUIRED

1. Compute Vat's income from Zel for 2011.
2. What is the balance of Vat's Investment in Zel account at December 31, 2011?
3. What is Vat's share of Zel's recorded net assets at December 31, 2011?

P 2-4

Journal entries for midyear investment (excess allocated to land, equipment, and goodwill)

Jack Corporation paid $380,000 for 40 percent of Jill Corporation's outstanding voting common stock on July 1, 2011. Jill's stockholders' equity on January 1, 2011, was $500,000, consisting of $300,000 capital stock and $200,000 retained earnings.

During 2011, Jill had net income of $100,000, and on November 1, 2011, Jill declared dividends of $50,000.

Jill's assets and liabilities were stated at fair values on July 1, 2011, except for land that was undervalued by $30,000 and equipment with a five-year remaining useful life that was undervalued by $50,000.

REQUIRED: Prepare all the journal entries (other than closing entries) on the books of Jack Corporation during 2011 to account for the investment in Jill.

P 2-5

Prepare an allocation schedule, compute income and the investment balance

Quake Corporation paid $1,680,000 for a 30 percent interest in Tremor Corporation's outstanding voting stock on January 1, 2011. The book values and fair values of Tremor's assets and liabilities on January 1, along with amortization data, are as follows (in thousands):

	Book Value	Fair Value
Cash	$ 400	$ 400
Accounts receivable—net	700	700
Inventories (sold in 2011)	1,000	1,200
Other current assets	200	200
Land	900	1,700
Buildings—net (10-year remaining life)	1,500	2,000
Equipment—net (7-year remaining life)	1,200	500
Total assets	$5,900	$6,700
Accounts payable	$ 800	$ 800
Other current liabilities	200	200
Bonds payable (due January 1, 2016)	1,000	1,100
Capital stock, $10 par	3,000	
Retained earnings	900	
Total equities	$5,900	

Tremor Corporation reported net income of $1,200,000 for 2011 and paid dividends of $600,000.

REQUIRED

1. Prepare a schedule to allocate the investment fair values/book value differentials relating to Quake's investment in Tremor.
2. Calculate Quake's income from Tremor for 2011.
3. Determine the balance of Quake's Investment in Tremor account at December 31, 2011.

P 2-6

Computations for a midyear acquisition

Pal Corporation purchased for cash 6,000 shares of voting common stock of Sap Corporation at $16 per share on July 1, 2011. On this date, Sap's equity consisted of $100,000 of $10 par capital stock, $20,000 retained earnings from prior periods, and $10,000 current earnings (for one-half of 2011).

Sap's income for 2011 was $20,000, and it paid dividends of $12,000 on November 1, 2011.

All of Sap's assets and liabilities had book values equal to fair values at July 1, 2011, and any differences between investment cost and book value acquired should be assigned to equipment and amortized over a 10-year period.

REQUIRED: Compute the correct amounts for each of the following items using the equity method of accounting for Pal's investment:

1. Pal's income from its investment in Sap for the year ended December 31, 2011.

2. The balance of Pal's Investment in Sap account at December 31, 2011.

(Note: Assumptions on page 46 are needed for this problem.)

P 2-7

Partial income statement with an extraordinary item

Dil Corporation acquired 30 percent of the voting stock of Lar Company at book value on July 1, 2011. During 2013, Lar paid dividends of $160,000 and reported income of $500,000 as follows:

Income before extraordinary item	$300,000
Extraordinary gain (tax credit from operating loss carryforward)	200,000
Net income	$500,000

REQUIRED: Show how Dil's income from Lar should be reported for 2013 by means of a partial income statement for Dil Corporation.

P 2-8

Computations and journal entries with excess of book value over fair value

Jen Corporation became a subsidiary of Laura Corporation on July 1, 2011, when Laura paid $1,980,000 cash for 90 percent of Jen's outstanding common stock. The price paid by Laura reflected the fact that Jen's inventories were undervalued by $50,000 and its plant assets were overvalued by $500,000. Jen sold the undervalued inventory items during 2011 but continues to hold the overvalued plant assets that had a remaining useful life of nine years from July 1, 2011.

During the years 2011 through 2013, Jen's paid-in capital consisted of $1,500,000 capital stock and $500,000 additional paid-in capital. Jen's retained earnings statements for 2011, 2012, and 2013 were as follows (in thousands):

	Year Ended December 31, 2011	Year Ended December 31, 2012	Year Ended December 31, 2013
Retained earnings January 1	$525	$600	$700
Add: Net income	250	300	200
Deduct: Dividends (declared in December)	(175)	(200)	(150)
Retained earnings December 31	$600	$700	$750

Laura uses the equity method in accounting for its investment in Jen.

REQUIRED

1. Compute Laura Corporation's income from its investment in Jen for 2011.

2. Determine the balance of Laura Corporation's Investment in Jen account at December 31, 2012.

3. Prepare the journal entries for Laura to account for its investment in Jen for 2013.

P 2-9

Prepare allocation schedules under different stock price assumptions (bargain purchase)

Tricia Corporation exchanged 40,000 previously unissued no par common shares for a 40 percent interest in Lisa Corporation on January 1, 2011. The assets and liabilities of Lisa on that date (after the exchange) were as follows (in thousands):

	Book Value	Fair Value
Cash	$ 200	$ 200
Accounts receivable—net	400	400
Inventories	1,000	1,200
Land	200	600
Buildings—net	1,200	800
Equipment—net	800	1,000
Total assets	$3,800	$4,200
Liabilities	$1,800	$1,800
Capital stock	1,400	
Retained earnings	600	
Total equities	$3,800	

The direct cost of issuing the shares of stock was $20,000, and other direct costs of combination were $80,000.

REQUIRED

1. Assume that the January 1, 2011, market price for Tricia's shares is $24 per share. Prepare a schedule to allocate the investment cost/book value differentials.

2. Assume that the January 1, 2011, market price for Tricia's shares is $16 per share. Prepare a schedule to allocate the investment cost/book value differentials. Assume that other direct costs were $0.

P 2-10

Computations for a piecemeal acquisition

Fred Corporation made three investments in Prima during 2011 and 2012, as follows:

Date Acquired	Shares Acquired	Cost
July 1, 2011	3,000	$ 48,750
January 1, 2012	6,000	99,000
October 1, 2012	9,000	162,000

Prima's stockholders' equity on January 1, 2011, consisted of 20,000 shares of $10 par common stock and retained earnings of $100,000. Fred's intention was to buy a controlling interest in Prima, so it never considered its investment in Prima as a trading security. Prima stock had a market value of $16.50 on December 31, 2011, and $19.00 on December 31, 2012.

Prima had net income of $40,000 and $60,000 in 2011 and 2012, respectively, and paid dividends of $15,000 on May 1 and November 1, 2011 and 2012 ($60,000 total for the two years).

Fred Corporation accounts for its investment in Prima using the equity method. It does not amortize differences between investment cost and book value acquired.

REQUIRED: Compute the following amounts:

1. Fred's income from its investment in Prima for 2011

2. The balance of Fred's Investment in Prima account at December 31, 2011

3. Fred's income from its investments in Prima for 2012

4. The balance of Fred's Investment in Prima account at December 31, 2012

P 2-11

Computations and a correcting entry (errors)

Pat Corporation purchased 40 percent of the voting stock of Sue Corporation on July 1, 2011, for $300,000. On that date, Sue's stockholders' equity consisted of capital stock of $500,000, retained earnings of $150,000, and current earnings (just half of 2011) of $50,000. Income is earned proportionately throughout each year.

The Investment in Sue account of Pat Corporation and the retained earnings account of Sue Corporation for 2011 through 2014 are summarized as follows (in thousands):

RETAINED EARNINGS (SUE)

Dividends November 1, 2011	$40	Balance January 1, 2011	$150
Dividends November 1, 2012	40	Earnings 2011	100
Dividends November 1, 2013	50	Earnings 2012	80
Dividends November 1, 2014	50	Earnings 2013	130
		Earnings 2014	120

INVESTMENT IN SUE (PAT)

Investment July 1, 2011 40%	$300	Dividends 2011	$16
Income 2011	40	Dividends 2012	16
Income 2012	32	Dividends 2013	20
Income 2013	52	Dividends 2014	20
Income 2014	48		

REQUIRED

1. Determine the correct amount of the investment in Sue that should appear in Pat's December 31, 2014, balance sheet. Assume any difference between investment cost and book value acquired is due to a building with a 10-year remaining life.

2. Prepare any journal entry (entries) on Pat's books to bring the Investment in Sue account up to date on December 31, 2014, assuming that the books have not been closed at year-end 2014.

P 2-12

Allocation schedule and computations (excess cost over fair value)

John Corporation acquired a 70 percent interest in Jojo Corporation on April 1, 2011, when it purchased 14,000 of Jojo's 20,000 outstanding shares in the open market at $13 per share. Additional costs of acquiring the shares consisted of $10,000 legal and consulting fees. Jojo Corporation's balance sheets on January 1 and April 1, 2011, are summarized as follows (in thousands):

	January 1 (per books)	April 1 (per books)	April 1 (fair values)
Cash	$ 40	$ 45	$ 45
Inventories	35	60	50
Other current assets	25	20	20
Land	30	30	50
Equipment—net	100	95	135
Total assets	$230	$250	$300
Accounts payable	$ 45	$ 40	$ 40
Other liabilities	15	20	20
Capital stock, $5 par	100	100	
Retained earnings January 1	70	70	
Current earnings		20	
Total liabilities and equity	$230	$250	

ADDITIONAL INFORMATION

1. The overvalued inventory items were sold in September 2011.

2. The undervalued items of equipment had a remaining useful life of four years on April 1, 2011.

3. Jojo's net income for 2011 was $80,000 ($60,000 from April to December 31, 2011).

4. On December 1, 2011, Jojo declared dividends of $2 per share, payable on January 10, 2012.

5. Any unidentified assets of Jojo are not amortized.

REQUIRED

1. Prepare a schedule showing how the difference between John's investment cost and book value acquired should be allocated to identifiable and/or unidentifiable assets.

2. Calculate John's investment income from Jojo for 2011.

3. Determine the correct balance of John's Investment in Jojo account at December 31, 2011.

COCA-COLA: A CASE STUDY ON THE EQUITY METHOD

Coca-Cola lists significant equity method investments on its balance sheet. Visit Coca-Cola's web site and obtain the 2009 annual report. Review Coke's 2009 annual report and answer the following questions:

1. What are Coke's major equity method investments? Prepare a brief summary.
2. What amount of income does Coke report on these investments, and how significant are those amounts to Coke's overall profitability?
3. Compare and summarize reported income amounts between 2008 and 2009. Can you account for the change?
4. What type of intercompany transactions does Coke engage in with its equity method affiliates? You may focus on transactions with the largest equity affiliate—Coca-Cola Enterprises, Inc.
5. Refer to Note 4. Can you explain how Coke recognizes gains and losses when its equity method affiliates sell shares of common stock to the public?

INTERNET ASSIGNMENT

Visit the Ford Motor Company Web site and review Ford's 2009 annual report. You will note that Ford makes numerous investments in other companies. Prepare a brief summary of intercompany investments included by Ford (you will want to look at the financial statements and the notes).

a. Does Ford report any investments carried as trading securities, available-for-sale securities, or held-to-maturity securities? If so, summarize their significance to both the balance sheet and income statement.
b. Does Ford report any investments carried under the equity method? If so, summarize their significance to both the balance sheet and income statement. What additional disclosures, if any, are made concerning equity method investments?
c. Did Ford realize any gains or losses from security sales during 2009?
d. Has Ford tested for goodwill impairment during 2009? Did Ford experience an impairment during 2009?

REFERENCES TO THE AUTHORITATIVE LITERATURE

[1] FASB ASC 320-10. Originally *Statement of Financial Accounting Standards No. 115*. "Accounting for Certain Investments in Debt and Equity Securities." Norwalk, CT: Financial Accounting Standards Board, 1993.

[2] FASB ASC 323-10. Originally *Accounting Principles Board Opinion No. 18*. "The Equity Method of Accounting for Investments in Common Stock." New York: American Institute of Certified Public Accountants, 1971.

[3] FASB ASC 320-10-35-1. Originally *Statement of Financial Accounting Standards No. 115*. "Accounting for Certain Investments in Debt and Equity Securities." Norwalk, CT: Financial Accounting Standards Board, 1993.

[4] FASB ASC 220-10-45-8. Originally *Statement of Financial Accounting Standards No. 130*. "Reporting Comprehensive Income." Stamford, CT: Financial Accounting Standards Board, 1997.

[5] FASB ASC 220. Originally *Statement of Financial Accounting Standards No. 115*. "Accounting for Certain Investments in Debt and Equity Securities." Norwalk, CT: Financial Accounting Standards Board, 1993.

[6] FASB ASC 323-10-15-3. Originally *Accounting Principles Board Opinion No. 18*. "The Equity Method of Accounting for Investments in Common Stock." New York: American Institute of Certified Public Accountants, 1971.

[7] FASB ASC 325. Originally *Accounting Principles Board Opinion No. 18.* "The Equity Method of Accounting for Investments in Common Stock." New York: American Institute of Certified Public Accountants, 1971.

[8] FASB ASC 323-10-15-10. Originally *FASB Interpretation No. 35.* "Criteria for Applying the Equity Method of Accounting for Investments in Common Stock." An Interpretation of *APB Opinion No. 18.* Stamford, CT: Financial Accounting Standards Board, May 1981.

[9] FASB ASC 323-10-15. Originally *Accounting Principles Board Opinion No. 18.* "The Equity Method of Accounting for Investments in Common Stock." New York: American Institute of Certified Public Accountants, 1971.

[10] FASB ASC 350-20-35. Originally *Statement of Financial Accounting Standards No. 142.* "Goodwill and Other Intangible Assets." Stamford, CT: Financial Accounting Standards Board, 2001.

[11] FASB ASC 250-10-45. Originally *Statement of Financial Accounting Standards No. 154.* "Accounting Changes and Error Correction." Norwalk, CT: Financial Accounting Standards Board, 2005.

[12] FASB ASC 320-10-30-4. Originally *Statement of Financial Accounting Standards No. 115.* "Accounting for Certain Investments in Debt and Equity Securities." Norwalk, CT: Financial Accounting Standards Board, 1993.

[13] FASB ASC 323-10-50. Originally *Accounting Principles Board Opinion No. 18.* "The Equity Method of Accounting for Investments in Common Stock." New York: American Institute of Certified Public Accountants, 1971.

[14] FASB ASC 850-10-50-5. Originally *Statement of Financial Accounting Standards No. 57.* "Related Party Disclosures." Norwalk, CT: Financial Accounting Standards Board, 1982.

[15] FASB ASC 350-20-35-4 through 35-13. Originally *Statement of Financial Accounting Standards No. 142.* "Goodwill and Other Intangible Assets." Stamford, CT: Financial Accounting Standards Board, 2001.

[16] FASB ASC 280-10-55-47. Originally *Statement of Financial Accounting Standards No. 131.* "Disclosures About Segments of an Enterprise and Related Information." Stamford, CT: Financial Accounting Standards Board, 1997.

[17] FASB ASC 350-20-35-30. Originally *Statement of Financial Accounting Standards No. 121.* "Accounting for the Impairment of Long-lived Assets and for long-lived Assets to be Disposed Of." Stamford, CT: Financial Accounting Standards Board, 1995.

[18] FASB ASC 825-10-25. Originally *Statement of Financial Accounting Standards No. 159.* "The Fair Value Option for Financial Assets and Financial Liabilities (Including an Amendment of FASB Statement No. 115)." Norwalk, CT: Financial Accounting Standards Board, 2007.

[19] FASB ASC 820-10-05. Originally *Statement of Financial Accounting Standards No. 157.* "Fair Value Measurements." Norwalk, CT: Financial Accounting Standards Board, 2006.

3 CHAPTER

An Introduction to Consolidated Financial Statements

LEARNING OBJECTIVES

1 Recognize the benefits and limitations of consolidated financial statements.

2 Understand requirements for including a subsidiary in consolidated financial statements.

3 Apply consolidation concepts to parent company recording of an investment in a subsidiary company at the date of acquisition.

4 Record the fair value of the subsidiary at the date of acquisition.

5 Learn the concept of non-controlling interest when a parent company acquires less than 100 percent of a subsidiary's outstanding common stock.

6 Prepare consolidated balance sheets subsequent to the acquisition date, including preparation of eliminating entries.

7 Amortize the excess of the fair value over the book value in periods subsequent to the acquisition.

8 Apply the concepts underlying preparation of a consolidated income statement.

9 **For the Students:** Create an electronic spreadsheet to prepare a consolidated balance sheet.

This chapter contains material necessary for understanding consolidated financial statements and provides an overview of the procedures necessary to the consolidation process. The acquisition method of accounting for business combinations is applied in the chapter. (Pooled subsidiaries are covered on the *Advanced Accounting* Web site). We assume the parent company/investor uses the complete equity method of accounting for subsidiary investments. Further discussions of business combinations in this book assume acquisition accounting.

Required consolidated financial statements include a consolidated balance sheet; a consolidated income statement; a consolidated retained earnings statement, or consolidated statement of changes in stockholders' equity; and a consolidated statement of cash flows.[1] The consolidated balance sheet and consolidated income and retained earnings statements in this chapter are prepared from the separate financial statements of the parent company and its subsidiaries. We prepare the consolidated statement of cash flows (introduced in Chapter 4) from consolidated income statements and consolidated balance sheets.

BUSINESS COMBINATIONS CONSUMMATED THROUGH STOCK ACQUISITIONS

LEARNING OBJECTIVE **1**

The accounting concept of a business combination under GAAP [2] includes combinations in which one or more companies become subsidiaries of a parent corporation. A corporation becomes a subsidiary when another corporation acquires a controlling interest in its outstanding voting stock. Ordinarily, one company gains control of another directly by acquiring a majority (more than 50 percent) of its voting stock. An investor may also gain control through indirect stock ownership, which is covered in Chapter 9 of this book. Until then, assume that direct ownership of a majority of the voting stock is required for control and to have a parent–subsidiary relationship.

Once a parent–subsidiary relationship is established, the purchase of additional subsidiary stock is not a business combination. In other words, separate entities can combine only once. Increasing a controlling interest is the same as simply making an additional investment. Under GAAP [3], acquisition of additional subsidiary stock is recorded by increasing the investment account and reducing the noncontrolling interest, based on the carrying amount of the noncontrolling interest at the additional acquisition date. (The increase in the investment account presumes that the fair value of the subsidiary increases after the additional investment.) Any

---

[1]GAAP [1] also requires a statement of comprehensive income. We ignore that statement, except in instances where it is particularly relevant to the material being discussed.

difference between the acquisition price and the carrying amount of the noncontrolling interest plus the increase in the investment account is an adjustment to additional paid-in capital of the parent company.

The Reporting Entity

A business combination brings two previously separate corporations under the control of a single management team (the officers and directors of the parent). Although both corporations continue to exist as separate legal entities, the acquisition creates a new reporting entity that encompasses all operations controlled by the management of the parent.

When an investment in voting stock creates a parent–subsidiary relationship, the purchasing entity (parent) and the entity acquired (subsidiary) continue to function as separate entities and maintain accounting records on a separate basis. Separate parent and subsidiary financial statements are converted into consolidated financial statements that reflect the financial position and the results of operations of the combined entity. The new reporting entity is responsible for reporting to the stockholders and creditors of the parent and to other interested parties.

This chapter introduces combining the separate accounting records of the parent and subsidiary into a more meaningful set of consolidated financial statements for the reporting entity. As you continue through the remaining chapters on acquisitions, you may at times feel that companies maintain separate legal entities and accounting systems only to make life difficult for advanced accounting students. In fact, there are sound business reasons for keeping these separate identities.

A parent may acquire a subsidiary in a very different industry from its own as a means of diversifying its overall business risk. In such cases, the management experience and skills required in the subsidiary's line of business are already in place and are preserved within the separate entity. Further, the subsidiary may have established supply-chain and distribution systems very different from its parent's. The subsidiary also may have established customer loyalties, which are easier to maintain with a separate identity.

Brand names and trademarks associated with the subsidiary represent extremely valuable intangible assets. If **Goodyear** were to purchase the **Coca-Cola Company** or **PepsiCo**, it likely would not be a great strategic move to rename it as **Goodyear Tire and Cola!**

There are also compelling legal reasons for maintaining separate identities. In a typical investment, the parent buys the common stock of the subsidiary. Under the U.S. legal system, stockholders enjoy limited legal liability. If a major lawsuit against a subsidiary results in a significant loss (e.g., from an environmental catastrophe involving the subsidiary), the parent cannot be held accountable for more than the loss of its investment.

The Parent–Subsidiary Relationship

We presume that a corporation that owns more than 50 percent of the voting stock of another corporation controls that corporation through its stock ownership, and a parent–subsidiary relationship exists between the two corporations. When parent–subsidiary relationships exist, the companies are affiliated. Often the term **affiliate** is used to mean subsidiary, and the two terms are used interchangeably in this book. In many annual reports, however, the term *affiliate* is used to include all investments accounted for by the equity method. The following excerpt from the **Deere & Company** 2009 annual report (p. 27) is an example of this latter usage of the term *affiliate*: "Deere & Company records its investment in each unconsolidated affiliated company (generally 20 to 50 percent ownership) at its related equity in the net assets of such affiliate."

Exhibit 3-1 illustrates an affiliation structure with two subsidiaries, with Percy Company owning 90 percent of the voting stock of San Del Corporation and 80 percent of the voting stock of Saltz Corporation. Percy Company owns 90 percent of the voting stock of San Del, and stockholders outside the affiliation structure own the other 10 percent. These outside stockholders are the noncontrolling stockholders, and their interest is referred to as a **noncontrolling interest**.[2] Outside stockholders have a 20 percent noncontrolling interest in Saltz Corporation.

---

[2]GAAP prefers the term *noncontrolling interest* to minority interest. [4] Some companies retain the more-traditional *minority interest* designation in their annual reports, but we use *noncontrolling* throughout this text.

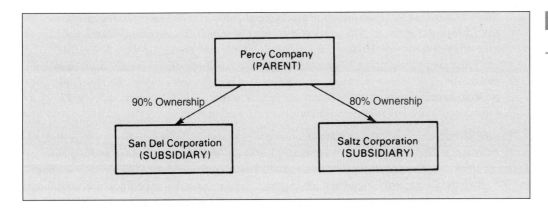

EXHIBIT 3-1

Affiliation Structure

Percy Company and each of its subsidiaries are separate legal entities that maintain separate accounting records. In its separate records, Percy Company uses the equity method described in Chapter 2 to account for its investments in San Del and Saltz Corporations. For reporting purposes, however, the equity method of reporting usually does not result in the most meaningful financial statements. This is so because the parent, through its stock ownership, is able to elect subsidiary directors and control subsidiary decisions, including dividend declarations. Although affiliated companies are separate legal entities, there is really only one economic entity because all resources are under control of a single management—the directors and officers of the parent.

Under GAAP [5]:

> *The purpose of consolidated financial statements is to present, primarily for the benefit of the owners and creditors of the parent company, the results of operations and the financial position of a parent and all its subsidiaries as if the consolidated group were a single economic entity. There is a presumption that consolidated financial statements are more meaningful than separate financial statements and that they are usually necessary for a fair presentation when one of the entities in the consolidated group directly or indirectly has a controlling financial interest in the other entities.*

Consolidated statements are intended primarily for the parent's investors, rather than for the noncontrolling stockholders and subsidiary creditors. The subsidiary, as a separate legal entity, continues to report the results of its own operations to the noncontrolling shareholders.

Consolidation Policy

Consolidated financial statements provide much information that is not included in the separate statements of the parent, and are usually required for fair presentation of the financial position and results of operations for a group of affiliated companies. The usual condition for consolidation is ownership of more than 50 percent of the voting stock of another company. Under current GAAP [6], a subsidiary can be excluded from consolidation in some situations: (1) when control does not rest with the majority owner, (2) formation of joint ventures, (3) the acquisition of an asset or group of assets that does not constitute a business, (4) a combination between entities under common control, and (5) a combination between not-for-profit entities or the acquisition of a for-profit business by a not-for-profit entity. Control does not rest with the majority owner if the subsidiary is in legal reorganization or bankruptcy or is operating under severe foreign-exchange restrictions, controls, or other governmentally-imposed uncertainties.

The *Anheuser-Busch Companies* 2006 annual report (p. 50) provides an example of exclusions in which the majority owner lacks the ability to control the subsidiary companies.

Note 2. International Equity Investments (Partial)

Grupo Modelo

Anheuser-Busch owns a 35.12 percent direct interest in Grupo Modelo, S.A.B. de C.V. (Modelo), Mexico's largest brewer and producer of the Corona brand, and a 23.25 percent direct interest in Modelo's operating subsidiary Diblo, S.A. de C.V. (Diblo).

The company's direct investments in Modelo and Diblo give Anheuser-Busch an effective (direct and indirect) 50.2 percent equity interest in Diblo. Anheuser-Busch holds nine of 19 positions on Modelo's board of directors (with the Controlling Shareholders Trust holding the other 10 positions) and also has membership on the audit committee. Anheuser-Busch does not have voting or other effective control of either Diblo or Modelo and consequently accounts for its investments using the equity method. The total cost of the company's investments was $1.6 billion.

The FASB has long considered a consolidation policy based on financial control, rather than majority ownership. The FASB issued *Preliminary Views on Major Issues Related to Consolidation Policy* in 1994 and an exposure draft, "Consolidated Financial Statements: Policy and Procedures," in 1995. Both the *Preliminary Views* and the exposure draft proposed that a corporation consolidate all entities that it controls unless control is temporary at the time the business becomes a subsidiary. Control of an entity was defined as power over its assets. During the deliberations of the exposure draft, the board was asked to further define control and to clarify the presumption of control. Other questions about when a subsidiary should be consolidated arose during the redeliberations: Should the parent receive some level of benefits? Should a level of ownership be required? Eventually, the board agreed that a consolidation policy should include both control and benefits.[3]

More recent FASB pronouncements have refined, but not finally resolved, the issue of financial control. An amendment in 2007 [7], applies the concept of financial control, rather than a simple majority ownership of a subsidiary's outstanding voting shares. An earlier amendment in 2003 provides other evidence of financial control that may result in consolidating a less-than-50 percent-owned subsidiary. We discuss this topic in Chapter 11.

DISCLOSURE OF CONSOLIDATION POLICIES   GAAP [8] requires a description of significant accounting policies for financial reporting and traditionally, consolidation-policy disclosures were among the most frequent of all policy disclosures. Consolidation-policy disclosures are needed to report exceptions (e.g., inability to control) to the required consolidation of all majority-owned subsidiaries. In addition, GAAP requires an extensive list of disclosures. Disclosures are required for:

1. the reporting period that includes a business combination
   a. general information about the business combination such as name of target and acquisition date
   b. information about goodwill or bargain purchase gain
   c. nature, terms and fair value of consideration transferred
   d. details about specific assets, liabilities and any noncontrolling interest
   e. reduction in buyer's pre-existing deferred tax asset valuation allowance
   f. information about transactions accounted for separately from the business combination
   g. information about step acquisitions

2. a business combination that occurs after the reporting period but before the financial statements are issued

3. provisional amounts related to business combinations

4. adjustments related to business combinations.

The SEC requires publicly held companies to report their consolidation policies under Regulation S-X, Rule 3A-03 [9]. Consolidation policy is usually presented under a heading such as "principles of consolidation" or "basis of consolidation." The *GE* 2009 annual report contains a typical "principles of consolidation" policy note:

Our financial statements consolidate all of our affiliates—entities that we control, most often because we hold a majority voting interest. Associated companies are entities that we do not control but over which we have significant influence, most often

---

[3]Financial Accounting Series, *Status Report 295*, November 26, 1997.

because we hold a voting interest of 20 percent to 50 percent. Results of associated companies are presented on a one-line basis. Investments in and advances to associated companies are presented on a one-line basis in the caption "All other assets" in our Statement of Financial Position, net of allowance for losses that represents our best estimate of probable losses inherent in such assets.

Parent and Subsidiary with Different Fiscal Periods

When the fiscal periods of the parent and its subsidiaries differ, we prepare consolidated statements for and as of the end of the parent's fiscal period. If the difference in fiscal periods is not in excess of three months, it usually is acceptable to use the subsidiary's statements for its fiscal year for consolidation purposes, with disclosure of the effect of intervening events which materially affect the financial position or results of operations. Otherwise, the statements of the subsidiary should be adjusted so that they correspond as closely as possible to the fiscal period of the parent company. *Abbott Laboratories* 2009 annual report (p. 43) includes the following explanation of its fiscal year ending December 31, 2009:

> *The accounts of foreign subsidiaries are consolidated as of November 30, due to the time needed to consolidate these subsidiaries. In December 2009, a foreign subsidiary acquired certain technology that was accounted for as acquired in-process research and development. This transaction was recorded in 2009 due to the significance of the amount. No other events occurred related to these foreign subsidiaries in December 2009, 2008 and 2007 that materially affected the financial position, results of operations or cash flows.*

Financing the Acquisition

There are many avenues available for financing an acquisition. As students, you are well aware that sufficient cash isn't always available for the things you'd like to buy; companies face the same problem in making significant purchases. The investor may pay cash, sell shares of authorized but previously unissued common stock, issue preferred shares, sell debt securities (bonds), or utilize some combination of these financial instruments.

Prior to 2001, firms often exchanged shares of common stock in order to qualify for the pooling of interests method of accounting for the combination. Poolings are no longer permitted under GAAP. [10]

The financing decision can be important strategically. Common shares are accompanied by voting rights, and an especially large acquisition may cost management its voting control. Nonvoting preferred shares or other financing alternatives are useful in cases in which keeping voting control is an important consideration.

Compaq Computer Corporation's 2000 annual report (p. 52) provides some interesting examples:

Note 3. Acquisitions and Divestitures (Partial)

In August 1999, Compaq sold an 81.5 percent equity interest in AltaVista for approximately 38 million CMGI common shares, CMGI preferred shares convertible into 3.6 million CMGI common shares and a $220 million three-year note receivable. In October 1999, CMGI converted the CMGI preferred shares held by Compaq into 3.6 million CMGI common shares. The CMGI common shares acquired by Compaq in this transaction carry certain restrictions whereby Compaq may not sell more than 50 percent (20.8 million) of such shares prior to August 2001.

In June 1998, Compaq consummated its acquisition of Digital for an aggregate purchase price of $9.1 billion. The purchase price consisted of approximately $4.5 billion in cash, the issuance of approximately 141 million shares of Compaq common stock valued at approximately $4.3 billion and the issuance of approximately 25 million options to purchase Compaq common stock valued at approximately $249 million.

LEARNING
OBJECTIVE 3

CONSOLIDATED BALANCE SHEET AT DATE OF ACQUISITION

A consolidated entity is a fictitious (conceptual) reporting entity. It is based on the assumption that the separate legal and accounting entities of a parent and its subsidiaries can be combined into a single meaningful set of financial statements for external reporting purposes. Note that the consolidated entity does not have transactions and does not maintain a consolidated ledger of accounts.

LEARNING
OBJECTIVE 4

Parent Acquires 100 Percent of Subsidiary at Book Value

Exhibit 3-2 shows the basic differences between separate-company and consolidated balance sheets. Pen Corporation acquires 100 percent of Sel Corporation at its book value and fair value of $40,000 in an acquisition on January 1, 2011. Exhibit 3-2 shows the balance sheets prepared immediately after the investment. Pen's "Investment in Sel" appears in the separate balance sheet of Pen, but not in the consolidated balance sheet for Pen and Subsidiary. When preparing the balance sheet, we eliminate the Investment in Sel account (Pen's books) and the stockholders' equity accounts (Sel's books) because they are reciprocal—both representing the net assets of Sel at January 1, 2011. We combine the nonreciprocal accounts of Pen and Sel and include them in the consolidated balance sheet of Pen Corporation and Subsidiary. Note that the consolidated balance sheet is not merely a summation of account balances of the affiliates. We eliminate reciprocal accounts in the process of consolidation and combine only nonreciprocal accounts. The capital stock that appears in a consolidated balance sheet is the capital stock of the parent, and the consolidated retained earnings are the retained earnings of the parent company.

EXHIBIT 3-2

100 Percent Ownership acquired at Book Value (Equal to Fair Value)

(in thousands)	Separate Balance Sheets		Consolidated Balance Sheet: Pen and Subsidiary
	Pen	Sel	
Assets			
Current assets			
Cash	$ 20	$10	$ 30
Other current assets	45	15	60
Total current assets	65	25	90
Plant assets	75	45	120
Less: Accumulated depreciation	(15)	(5)	(20)
Total plant assets	60	40	100
Investment in Sel—100%	40	—	—
Total assets	$165	$65	$190
Liabilities and Stockholders' Equity			
Current liabilities			
Accounts payable	$ 20	$15	$ 35
Other current liabilities	25	10	35
Total current liabilities	45	25	70
Stockholders' equity			
Capital stock	100	30	100
Retained earnings	20	10	20
Total stockholders' equity	120	40	120
Total liabilities and stockholders' equity	$165	$65	$190

Parent Acquires 100 Percent of Subsidiary—With Goodwill

Exhibit 3-2 presented the consolidated balance sheet prepared for a parent company that acquired all the stock of Sel Corporation at book value. If, instead, Pen acquires all of Sel's stock for $50,000, there will be a $10,000 excess of investment cost over book value acquired ($50,000 investment cost less $40,000 stockholders' equity of Sel). The $10,000 appears in the consolidated balance sheet at acquisition as an asset of $10,000. In the absence of evidence that identifiable net assets are undervalued, this asset is assumed to be goodwill. Exhibit 3-3 illustrates procedures for preparing a consolidated balance sheet for Pen Corporation, assuming that Pen pays $50,000 for the outstanding stock of Sel.

We need only one workpaper entry to consolidate the balance sheets of Pen and Sel at acquisition. Take a few minutes to review the format of the workpaper in Exhibit 3-3. The first two columns provide information from the separate balance sheets of Pen and Sel. The third column records adjustments and eliminations, subdivided into debits and credits. The last column presents the totals that will appear in the consolidated balance sheet. We calculate amounts in the Consolidated Balance Sheet column by adding together amounts from the first two columns and then adding or subtracting the adjustments and eliminations, as appropriate. This basic workpaper format is used throughout the discussions of acquisitions and preparation of consolidated financial statements in this book. The elimination entry is reproduced in general journal form for convenient reference:

a	Capital stock—Sel (–SE)	30	
	Retained earnings—Sel (–SE)	10	
	Goodwill (+A)	10	
	Investment in Sel (–A)		50
	To eliminate reciprocal investment and equity accounts and to assign the excess of investment cost (fair value) over book value to goodwill.		

Entries such as those shown in Exhibit 3-3 are only workpaper adjustments and eliminations and *are not recorded in the accounts of the parent or subsidiary corporations*. The entries will never be journalized or posted. Their only purpose is to facilitate completion of the workpapers to consolidate a parent and subsidiary at and for the period ended on a particular date. In this book, workpaper entries are shaded in blue to avoid confusing them with actual journal entries that are recorded in the accounts of the parent and subsidiary companies.

In future periods, the difference between the investment account balance and the subsidiary equity will decline *if, and only if, goodwill is written down due to impairment*.

Parent Acquires 90 Percent of Subsidiary—With Goodwill

LEARNING OBJECTIVE **5**

Assume that instead of acquiring all of Sel's outstanding stock, Pen acquires 90 percent of it for $45,000. GAAP requires the acquisition method to record business combinations and subsequent issuance of consolidated financial statements. Essentially, the acquisition method uses the entity theory of consolidations. Under the acquisition method, all assets and liabilities of the subsidiary are reported using 100 percent of fair values at the combination date, based on the price paid by the parent for its controlling interest, even when the parent acquires less than a 100 percent interest. Thus, both the controlling and noncontrolling interests will be reported based on fair values at the acquisition date.[4] GAAP provides guidance for measuring fair values. [11] Fair values are not recalculated at future reporting dates, with two exceptions. Impairments of assets must be recorded, including goodwill impairments. In addition, financial assets and liabilities may be revalued under GAAP [12], but this revaluation is optional.

There are also two major exceptions to the initial recording of fair values for assets and liabilities. Deferred tax assets and liabilities and employee benefit amounts will be recorded at book values consistent with existing GAAP standards (presumably already recorded by the subsidiary). However, recognize that since the subsidiary is recorded at its fair value, differences in fair values and book values of these accounts are reflected in goodwill. They are not separately identified.

---

[4]GAAP requires measurement of noncontrolling interests at fair values. The IASB [13] will permit acquirers either fair value or measurement of the proportional interest in the fair value of the subsidiary's net assets for each acquisition.

EXHIBIT 3-3

100 Percent Ownership,
Cost (Fair Value)
$10,000 Greater
Than Book Value

PEN CORPORATION AND SUBSIDIARY
CONSOLIDATED BALANCE SHEET WORKPAPERS
JANUARY 1, 2011 (IN THOUSANDS)

	Pen	100% Sel	Adjustments and Eliminations		Consolidated Balance Sheet
			Debits	Credits	
Assets					
Cash	$ 10	$10			$ 20
Other current assets	45	15			60
Plant assets	75	45			120
Accumulated depreciation	(15)	(5)			(20)
Investment in Sel	50			a 50	
Goodwill			a 10		10
Total assets	$165	$65			$190
Liabilities and Equity					
Accounts payable	$ 20	$15			$ 35
Other current liabilities	25	10			35
Capital stock—Pen	100				100
Retained earnings—Pen	20				20
Capital stock—Sel		30	a 30		
Retained earnings—Sel		10	a 10		
Total liabilities and stockholders' equity	$165	$65			$190

a. To eliminate reciprocal investment and equity accounts and to assign the excess of investment cost (fair value) over book value to goodwill.

We can assume that the acquisition is an "arm's-length" transaction. Pen paid $45,000 for a 90 percent interest. This implies that the total fair value of Sel is $50,000 ($45,000 / 90 percent). In this case, the excess of total fair value over book value of Sel's net identifiable assets and liabilities is $10,000, and there is a noncontrolling interest of $5,000 (10 percent of the $50,000 fair value of Sel's equity). The $10,000 excess of fair value over book value is goodwill. The workpapers in Exhibit 3-4 illustrate procedures for preparing the consolidated balance sheet for Pen and Sel under the 90 percent ownership assumption.

Workpaper entry a eliminates the reciprocal accounts of Pen and Sel and recognizes goodwill and the noncontrolling interest in Sel at the date of acquisition:

a	Capital stock—Sel (–SE)	30	
	Retained earnings—Sel (–SE)	10	
	Goodwill (+A)	10	
	Investment in Sel (–A)		45
	Noncontrolling interest (+SE)		5

To eliminate reciprocal investment and equity balances, to assign the $10,000 excess of investment fair value ($50,000) over book value ($40,000) to goodwill, and to recognize a $5,000 noncontrolling interest in the net assets of Sel ($50,000 equity × 10% noncontrolling interest).

Noncontrolling Interest

We include all assets and liabilities of the subsidiary in the consolidated balance sheet and record the noncontrolling interest's share of subsidiary net assets based on fair values separately in stockholders' equity.

EXHIBIT 3-4

90 Percent Ownership,
Fair Value Greater than
Book Value

PEN CORPORATION AND SUBSIDIARY
CONSOLIDATED BALANCE SHEET WORKPAPERS
JANUARY 1, 2011 (IN THOUSANDS)

| | Pen | 90% Sel | Adjustments and Eliminations | | Consolidated Balance Sheet |
			Debits	Credits	
Assets					
Cash	$ 15	$10			$ 25
Other current assets	45	15			60
Plant assets	75	45			120
Accumulated depreciation	(15)	(5)			(20)
Investment in Sel	45			a 45	
Goodwill			a 10		10
Total assets	$165	$65			$195
Liabilities and Equity					
Accounts payable	$ 20	$15			$ 35
Other current liabilities	25	10			35
Capital stock—Pen	100				100
Retained earnings—Pen	20				20
Capital stock—Sel		30	a 30		
Retained earnings—Sel		10	a 10		
	$165	$65			
Noncontrolling interest				a 5	5
Total liabilities and stockholders' equity					$195

a. To eliminate reciprocal investment and equity balances, assign the $10,000 excess of investment fair value ($50,000) over book value ($40,000) to goodwill, and recognize a $5,000 noncontrolling interest in the fair value of net assets of Sel ($50,000 equity × 10% noncontrolling interest).

Workpapers provide the basis of preparing formal financial statements, and the question arises about how the $5,000 noncontrolling interest that appears in Exhibit 3-4 would be reported in a formal balance sheet. Historically, practice varied with respect to classification. The noncontrolling interest in subsidiaries was generally shown in a single amount in the liability section of the consolidated balance sheet, frequently under the heading of noncurrent liabilities. Conceptually, the classification of noncontrolling stockholder interests as liabilities was inconsistent because the interests of noncontrolling stockholders represent equity investments in the subsidiary net assets by stockholders outside the affiliation structure.

Current GAAP requires:

- A noncontrolling interest in a subsidiary should be displayed and labeled in the consolidated balance sheet as a separate component of equity.
- Income attributable to the noncontrolling interest is not an expense or a loss but a deduction from consolidated net income to compute income attributable to the controlling interest.
- Both components of consolidated net income (net income attributable to noncontrolling interest and net income attributable to controlling interest) should be disclosed on the face of the consolidated income statement. [14]

CONSOLIDATED BALANCE SHEETS AFTER ACQUISITION

The account balances of both parent and subsidiary change to reflect their separate operations after the parent–subsidiary relationship has been established. Subsequently, we make additional adjustments to eliminate other reciprocal balances. If a consolidated balance sheet is prepared between the date a subsidiary declares and the date it pays dividends, the parent's books will show a dividend receivable account that is the reciprocal of a dividends payable account on the books of the subsidiary. Such balances do not represent amounts receivable or payable outside the affiliated group; therefore, they must be reciprocals that we eliminate in preparing consolidated statements. We also eliminate other intercompany receivables and payables, such as accounts receivable and accounts payable, in preparing consolidated statements.

The balance sheets of Pen and Sel Corporations at December 31, 2011, one year after acquisition, contain the following (in thousands):

	Pen	Sel
Cash	$ 27.4	$15
Dividends receivable	9	—
Other current assets	41	28
Plant assets	75	45
Accumulated depreciation	(20)	(8)
Investment in Sel (90%)	54	—
Total assets	$186.4	$80
Accounts payable	$ 30	$15
Dividends payable	—	10
Other current liabilities	20	5
Capital stock	100	30
Retained earnings	36.4	20
Total equities	$186.4	$80

Assumptions

1. Pen acquired a 90 percent interest in Sel for $45,000 on January 1, 2011, when Sel's stockholders' equity at book value was $40,000 (see Exhibit 3-4).

2. The accounts payable of Sel include $5,000 owed to Pen.

3. During 2011 Sel had income of $20,000 and declared $10,000 in dividends.

Exhibit 3-5 presents consolidated balance sheet workpapers reflecting this information. We determine the balance in the Investment in Sel account at December 31, 2011, using the equity method of accounting. Calculations of the December 31, 2011, investment account balance are as follows:

Original investment January 1, 2011	$45,000
Add: 90% of Sel's $20,000 net income for 2011	18,000
Deduct: 90% of Sel's $10,000 dividends for 2011	(9,000)
Investment account balance December 31, 2011	$54,000

Even though the amounts involved are different, the *process* of consolidating balance sheets after acquisition is basically the same as at acquisition. In all cases, we eliminate the amount of the subsidiary investment account and the equity accounts of the subsidiary. We enter the excess of fair value over book value (goodwill in this illustration) in the workpapers during the process of eliminating reciprocal investment and equity balances. Goodwill does not appear on the books of the parent; we add it to the asset listing when preparing the workpapers. The noncontrolling interest is equal to the percentage of noncontrolling ownership times the fair value of the equity of the subsidiary at the balance sheet date. Consolidated retained earnings equal the parent company's retained earnings.

The workpaper entries necessary to consolidate the balance sheets of Pen and Sel are reproduced in general journal form for convenient reference:

PEN CORPORATION AND SUBSIDIARY
CONSOLIDATED BALANCE SHEET WORKPAPERS
DECEMBER 31, 2011 (IN THOUSANDS)

	Pen	90% Sel	Adjustments and Eliminations Debits	Credits	Consolidated Balance Sheet
Assets					
Cash	$ 27.4	$15			$ 42.4
Dividends receivable	9			b 9	
Other current assets	41	28		c 5	64
Plant assets	75	45			120
Accumulated depreciation	(20)	(8)			(28)
Investment in Sel	54			a 54	
Goodwill			a 10		10
Total assets	$186.4	$80			$208.4
Liabilities and Equity					
Accounts payable	$ 30	$15	c 5		$ 40
Dividends payable		10	b 9		1
Other current liabilities	20	5			25
Capital stock—Pen	100				100
Retained earnings—Pen	36.4				36.4
Capital stock—Sel		30	a 30		
Retained earnings—Sel		20	a 20		
	$186.4	$80			
Noncontrolling interest				a 6	6
Total liabilities and stockholders' equity					$208.4

a. To eliminate reciprocal investment and equity balances, record goodwill, and enter the noncontrolling interest ($60,000 × 10%).

b. To eliminate reciprocal dividends receivable and payable amounts (90 percent of $10,000 dividends payable of Sel).

c. To eliminate intercompany accounts receivable and accounts payable.

a	Capital stock—Sel (–SE)	30	
	Retained earnings—Sel (–SE)	20	
	Goodwill (+A)	10	
	Investment in Sel (–A)		54
	Noncontrolling interest (+SE)		6

To eliminate reciprocal investment and equity balances, record goodwill, and enter the noncontrolling interest ($60,000 × 10%).

b	Dividends payable (–L)	9	
	Dividends receivable (–A)		9

To eliminate reciprocal dividends receivable and payable amounts (90% of $10,000 dividends payable of Sel).

c	Accounts payable (–L)	5	
	Other current assets (–A)		5

To eliminate intercompany accounts receivable and accounts payable.

ASSIGNING EXCESS TO IDENTIFIABLE NET ASSETS AND GOODWILL

We assigned the excess of fair value over the book value in the Pen–Sel illustration to goodwill. An underlying assumption of that assignment of the excess is that the book values and fair values of identifiable assets and liabilities are equal. When the evidence indicates that fair values exceed book values or book values exceed fair values, however, we assign the excess accordingly.

Effect of Assignment on Consolidated Balance Sheet at Acquisition

The separate books of the affiliated companies do not record fair value/book value differentials in acquisitions that create parent–subsidiary relationships. We use workpaper procedures to adjust subsidiary book values to reflect the fair value/book value differentials. The adjusted amounts appear in the consolidated balance sheet. We determine the amount of the adjustment to individual assets and liabilities using the one-line consolidation approach presented in Chapter 2.

On December 31, 2011, Pil purchases 90 percent of Sad Corporation's outstanding voting common stock directly from Sad Corporation's stockholders for $5,200,000 cash plus 100,000 shares of Pil Corporation $10 par common stock with a market value of $5,000,000. Additional costs of combination are $200,000. Pil pays these additional costs in cash. Pil and Sad must continue to operate as parent company and subsidiary because 10 percent of Sad's shares are outstanding and held by noncontrolling stockholders. We expense the $200,000 costs in recording the investment.

Comparative book value and fair value information for Pil and Sad immediately before the acquisition on December 31, 2011, appears in Exhibit 3-6. Pil records the acquisition on its books with the following journal entries in thousands:

Investment in Sad (+A)	10,200	
Common stock (+SE)		1,000
Additional paid-in capital (+SE)		4,000
Cash (−A)		5,200
To record acquisition of 90% of Sad Corporation's		
outstanding stock for $5,200,000 in cash and 100,000		
shares of Pil common stock with a value of $5,000,000.		
Investment expense (E, −SE)	200	
Cash (−A)		200
To record additional costs of combining with Sad.		

These are the only entries on Pil's books necessary to record the combination of Pil and Sad. Sad records no entries because Pil acquired its 90 percent interest directly from Sad's stockholders. We do not use the balance sheet information given in Exhibit 3-6 in recording the acquisition on Pil's books; we use it in preparing the consolidated balance sheet for the combined entity immediately after the acquisition.

Recording the Fair Value/Book Value Differential We determine the adjustments necessary to combine the balance sheets of parent and subsidiary corporations by *assigning* the difference between fair value and book value to undervalued or overalued identifiable assets and liabilities and any remainder to goodwill. The schedule in Exhibit 3-7 illustrates the adjustment necessary to consolidate the balance sheets of Pil and Sad at December 31, 2011.

Although we do not use the book values of assets and liabilities in determining fair values for individual assets and liabilities (these are usually determined by management), we use book values in the mechanical process of combining the balance sheets of parent and subsidiary.

The underlying book value of Sad Corporation is $5,900,000 (as shown in Exhibit 3-7), and the excess of fair value over book value is $5,433,000. We assign this excess first to the identifiable assets and liabilities and then assign the remainder to goodwill. The amounts assigned to identifiable assets and liabilities are for 100 percent of the fair value and book value difference. The other 10 percent interest in Sad's identifiable net assets relates to the interests of noncontrolling stockholders adjusted to their fair values on the basis of the price paid by Pil for its 90 percent interest.[5]

Workpaper Procedures to Enter Allocations in Consolidated Balance Sheet We incorporate the excess fair value over book value as determined in Exhibit 3-7 into a consolidated balance

---

[5]Revaluation of all assets and liabilities of a subsidiary on the basis of the price paid by the parent for its controlling interest is supported by the entity theory of consolidation. Entity theory is covered in more detail in Chapter 11.

(in thousands)	Pil Corporation		Sad Corporation	
	Per Books	Fair Values	Per Books	Fair Values
Assets				
Cash	$ 6,600	$ 6,600	$ 200	$ 200
Receivables—net	700	700	300	300
Inventories	900	1,200	500	600
Other current assets	600	800	400	400
Land	1,200	11,200	600	800
Buildings—net	8,000	15,000	4,000	5,000
Equipment—net	7,000	9,000	2,000	1,700
Total assets	$25,000	$44,500	$8,000	$9,000
Liabilities and Equity				
Accounts payable	$ 2,000	$ 2,000	$ 700	$ 700
Notes payable	3,700	3,500	1,400	1,300
Common stock, $10 par	10,000		4,000	
Additional paid-in capital	5,000		1,000	
Retained earnings	4,300		900	
Total liabilities and stockholders'equity	$25,000		$8,000	

EXHIBIT 3-6

Preacquisition Book and Fair Value Balance Sheets

PIL CORPORATION AND ITS 90%-OWNED SUBSIDIARY, SAD CORPORATION (IN THOUSANDS)

Fair value (purchase price) of 90% interest acquired		$ 10,200
Implied fair value of Sad ($10,200 / 90%)		$ 11,333
Book value of Sad's net assets		(5,900)
Total excess of fair value over book value		$ 5,433

Allocation to Identifiable Assets and Liabilities

	Fair Value	Book Value	Excess Allocated
Inventories	$ 600	$ 500	$ 100
Land	800	600	200
Buildings	5,000	4,000	1,000
Equipment	1,700	2,000	(300)
Notes payable	1,300	1,400	100
Total allocated to identifiable net assets			$ 1,100
Remainder allocated to goodwill			4,333
Total excess of fair value over book value			$ 5,433

EXHIBIT 3-7

Schedule for Allocating the excess of Investment Fair Value over the Book Value

sheet through workpaper procedures. Exhibit 3-8 illustrates these procedures for Pil and Sad as of the date of their affiliation.

The consolidated balance sheet workpapers show two workpaper entries for the consolidation. Entry a in general journal form follows:

a	Unamortized excess (+A)	5,433	
	Common stock, $10 par—Sad (–SE)	4,000	
	Additional paid-in capital—Sad (–SE)	1,000	
	Retained earnings—Sad (–SE)	900	
	Investment in Sad (–A)		10,200
	Noncontrolling interest—10% (+SE)		1,133

EXHIBIT 3-8

90 Percent Ownership, Excess Allocated to Identifiable Net Assets and Goodwill

PIL CORPORATION AND SUBSIDIARY
CONSOLIDATED BALANCE SHEET WORKPAPERS
AFTER COMBINATION ON DECEMBER 31, 2011
(IN THOUSANDS)

	Pil	90% Sad	Adjustments and Eliminations Debits	Adjustments and Eliminations Credits	Consolidated Balance Sheet
Assets					
Cash	$ 1,200	$ 200			$ 1,400
Receivables—net	700	300			1,000
Inventories	900	500	b 100		1,500
Other current assets	600	400			1,000
Land	1,200	600	b 200		2,000
Buildings—net	8,000	4,000	b 1,000		13,000
Equipment—net	7,000	2,000		b 300	8,700
Investment in Sad	10,200			a 10,200	
Goodwill			b 4,333		4,333
Unamortized excess			a 5,433	b 5,433	
Total assets	$29,800	$8,000			$32,933
Liabilities and Equity					
Accounts payable	$ 2,000	$ 700			$ 2,700
Notes payable	3,700	1,400	b 100		5,000
Common stock—Pil	11,000				11,000
Additional paid-in capital—Pil	9,000				9,000
Retained earnings—Pil	4,100				4,100
Common stock—Sad		4,000	a 4,000		
Additional paid-in capital—Sad		1,000	a 1,000		
Retained earnings—Sad		900	a 900		
	$29,800	$8,000			
Noncontrolling interest				a 1,133	1,133
Total liabilities and stockholders' equity					$32,933

a. To eliminate reciprocal subsidiary investment and equity balances, establish noncontrolling interest, and enter the unamortized excess.
b. To allocate the unamortized excess to identifiable assets, liabilities, and goodwill.

This workpaper entry eliminates reciprocal investment in Sad and stockholders' equity amounts of Sad, establishes the noncontrolling interest in Sad, and enters the total unamortized excess from Exhibit 3-7.

A second workpaper entry assigns the unamortized excess to individual assets and liabilities and to goodwill:

b			
	Inventories (+A)	100	
	Land (+A)	200	
	Buildings—net (+A)	1,000	
	Goodwill (+A)	4,333	
	Notes payable (–L)	100	
	Equipment—net (–A)		300
	Unamortized excess (–A)		5,433

We add a step and employ an unamortized excess account to simplify workpaper entries when assigning the fair value/book value differential to numerous asset and liability accounts. We skip this step when assigning the total excess to goodwill, as in Exhibit 3-4 and Exhibit 3-5. Workpaper entries a and b enter debits and credits equal to the unamortized excess, so the account has no final effect on the consolidated balance sheet.

We combine debit and credit workpaper amounts with the line items shown in the separate statements of Pil and Sad to produce the amounts shown in the Consolidated Balance Sheet column. Sad is a partially owned subsidiary, but we record its assets and liabilities in the consolidated balance sheet at 100 percent of their fair values.

Effect of Amortization on Consolidated Balance Sheet After Acquisition

LEARNING OBJECTIVE 7

The effect of amortizing the $5,433,000 excess on the December 31, 2012, consolidated balance sheet is based on the following assumptions about the operations of Pil and Sad during 2012 and about the relevant amortization periods of the assets and liabilities to which we allocate the excess in Exhibit 3-7. These assumptions are as follows:

Income for 2012

Sad's net income	$ 800,000
Pil's income excluding income from Sad	2,523,500

Dividends Paid in 2012

Sad	$ 300,000
Pil	1,500,000

Amortization of Excess

Undervalued inventories—sold in 2012
Undervalued land—still held by Sad; no amortization
Undervalued buildings—useful life 40 years from January 1, 2012
Overvalued equipment—useful life 5 years from January 1, 2012
Overvalued notes payable—retired in 2012
Goodwill—no amortization

At December 31, 2012, Pil's Investment in Sad account has a balance of $10,501,500, consisting of the original $10,200,000 cost, increased by $571,500 investment income from Sad and decreased by $270,000 dividends received from Sad. Pil's income from Sad for 2012 is calculated under a one-line consolidation as follows:

Using an equity method perspective, we calculate Pil's income from Sad as follows:

90% of Sad's reported net income ($800,000)		$720,000
Add: Pil's 90% share of amortization on overvalued equipment (($300,000/5 years) × 90%)		54,000
Deduct: Amortization of Pil's share of excess allocated to:		
Inventories (sold in 2012) ($100,000 × 90%)	$90,000	
Land	—	
Buildings (($1,000,000/40 years) × 90%)	22,500	
Notes payable (retired in 2012) ($100,000 × 90%)	90,000	(202,500)
Income from Sad		$571,500

Alternatively, we can calculate income from Sad as 90 percent of Sad's "adjusted" net income:

Sad's net income		$800,000
Add: Amortization of overvalued equipment ($300,000/5 years)		60,000
Deduct: Amortization of excess allocated to:		
Inventories (sold in 2012)	$100,000	
Land	—	
Buildings ($1,000,000/40 years)	25,000	
Notes payable (retired in 2012)	100,000	(225,000)
Sad's adjusted net income		$635,000
90% of Sad's adjusted net income		$571,500

We can also verify the noncontrolling interest at December 31, 2012, as follows:

Noncontrolling interest at December 31, 2011	$1,133,000
Add: 10% of Sad's 2012 net income	80,000
Less: 10% of 2012 amortization of excess fair value	(16,500)
Less: 10% of 2012 dividends	(30,000)
Noncontrolling interest at December 31, 2012	$1,166,500

Pil's net income for 2012 is $3,095,000, consisting of income from its own operations of $2,523,500, plus $571,500 income from Sad. Sad's stockholders equity increased $500,000 during 2012, from $5,900,000 to $6,400,000. Pil's retained earnings increased $1,795,000, from $4,100,000 at December 31, 2011, to $5,895,000 at December 31, 2012. Pil's retained earnings decreased from $4,300,000 to $4,100,000 at the acquisition date due to the expensing of the costs of the combination. We reflect this information in consolidated balance sheet workpapers for Pil and Subsidiary at December 31, 2012, in Exhibit 3-9.

We reproduce the workpaper entries as follows:

a	**Common stock—Sad (–SE)**	**4,000**	
	Additional paid-in capital—Sad (–SE)	**1,000**	
	Retained earnings—Sad (–SE)	**1,400**	
	Unamortized excess (+A)	**5,268**	
	Investment in Sad (–A)		**10,501.5**
	Noncontrolling interest (+SE)		**1,166.5**
	To eliminate reciprocal subsidiary investment and equity accounts, establish noncontrolling interest, and enter the unamortized excess.		
b	**Land (+A)**	**200**	
	Buildings—net (+A)	**975**	
	Goodwill (+A)	**4,333**	
	Equipment—net (–A)		**240**
	Unamortized excess (–A)		**5,268**
	To assign the unamortized excess to identifiable assets and goodwill.		

The differences in the adjustments and eliminations in Exhibit 3-8 and Exhibit 3-9 result from changes that occurred between December 31, 2011, when the investment was acquired, and December 31, 2012, when the investment had been held for one year. The following schedule provides the basis for the workpaper entries that appear in Exhibit 3-9.

	Unamortized Excess December 31, 2011	Amortization	Unamortized Excess December 31, 2012
Inventories	$ 100,000	$100,000	$ —
Land	200,000	—	200,000
Buildings—net	1,000,000	25,000	975,000
Equipment—net	(300,000)	(60,000)	(240,000)*
Notes payable	100,000	100,000	—
Goodwill	4,333,000	—	4,333,000
	$5,433,000	$165,000	$5,268,000

*Excess book value over fair value.

**PIL CORPORATION AND SUBSIDIARY
CONSOLIDATED BALANCE SHEET WORKPAPERS
ON DECEMBER 31, 2012 (IN THOUSANDS)**

	Pil	90% Sad	Adjustments and Eliminations Debits	Credits	Consolidated Balance Sheet
Assets					
Cash	$ 253.5	$ 100			$ 353.5
Receivables—net	540	200			740
Inventories	1,300	600			1,900
Other current assets	800	500			1,300
Land	1,200	600	b 200		2,000
Buildings—net	9,500	3,800	b 975		14,275
Equipment—net	8,000	1,800		b 240	9,560
Investment in Sad	10,501.5			a 10,501.5	
Goodwill			b 4,333		4,333
Unamortized excess			a 5,268	b 5,268	
Total assets	$32,095	$7,600			$34,461.5
Liabilities and Equity					
Accounts payable	$ 2,300	$1,200			$ 3,500
Notes payable	4,000				4,000
Common stock—Pil	11,000				11,000
Additional paid-in capital—Pil	8,900				8,900
Retained earnings—Pil	5,895				5,895
Common stock—Sad		4,000	a 4,000		
Additional paid-in capital—Sad		1,000	a 1,000		
Retained earnings—Sad		1,400	a 1,400		
	$32,095	$7,600			
Noncontrolling Interest				a 1,166.5	1,166.5
Total liabilities and stockholders' equity					$34,461.5

a To eliminate reciprocal subsidiary investment and equity balances, establish noncontrolling interest, and enter the unamortized excess.
b To allocate the unamortized excess to identifiable assets and goodwill.

The following summarizes the transactions recorded by Pil in its Investment in Sad account:

Initial cost—December 31, 2011	$10,200,000
90% of Sad's 2012 net income	720,000
90% of Sad's 2012 dividends	(270,000)
Amortization of the fair value/book value differential (90% × 165,000)	(148,500)
Balance—December 31, 2012	$10,501,500

The consolidated balance sheet workpaper adjustments in Exhibit 3-9 show elimination of reciprocal stockholders' equity and Investment in Sad balances. This elimination, entry a, involves debits to Sad's stockholders' equity accounts of $6,400,000, a credit to the noncontrolling interest in Sad of $1,166,500, and a credit to the Investment in Sad account of $10,501,500. The difference between these debits and credits totals $5,268,000, representing the unamortized excess of investment fair value over book value acquired on December 31, 2012, and we enter it in the workpapers as unamortized excess.

The undervalued inventory items and the overvalued notes payable on Sad's books at December 31, 2011, were fully amortized in 2012 (the inventory was sold and the notes payable were retired); therefore, these items do not require balance sheet adjustments at December 31, 2012. We enter the remaining items—land, $200,000; buildings, $975,000; equipment, $240,000 (overvaluation); and goodwill, $4,333,000 (which account for the $5,268,000 unamortized excess)—in the consolidated balance sheet workpapers through workpaper entry b, which assigns the unamortized excess as of the balance sheet date. Technically, the workpaper entries shown in Exhibit 3-9 are combination adjustment and elimination entries, because we eliminate the Investment in Sad and stockholders' equity accounts of Sad, reclassify the noncontrolling interest into a single amount representing 10 percent of the fair value of Sad's stockholders' equity, and adjust the asset accounts.

<table>
<tr><td>LEARNING
OBJECTIVE **8**</td></tr>
</table>

CONSOLIDATED INCOME STATEMENT

Exhibit 3-10 presents comparative separate-company and consolidated income and retained earnings statements for Pil Corporation and Subsidiary. These statements reflect the previous assumptions and amounts that were used in preparing the consolidated balance sheet workpapers for Pil and Sad. Detailed revenue and expense items have been added to illustrate the consolidated income statement, but all assumptions and amounts are completely compatible with those already introduced. Adjustments and elimination entries have not been included in the illustration. These entries are covered extensively in Chapter 4.

The difference between a consolidated income statement and an unconsolidated income statement of the parent company lies in the detail presented. You can see this in Exhibit 3-10 by comparing the separate income statement of Pil with the consolidated income statement of Pil and Subsidiary. Under GAAP [15], consolidated net income is the net income of the consolidated group. The consolidated income statement must clearly separate income attributable to the controlling and noncontrolling interests. Throughout the remainder of this text, we label these as the controlling and noncontrolling interest shares of net income.

Pil's separate income statement shows the revenues and expenses from Pil's own operations plus its investment income from Sad.[6] By contrast, the consolidated income statement column shows the revenues and expenses of both Sad and Pil but does not show the investment income from Sad. The $571,500 investment income is excluded because the consolidated income statement includes the detailed revenues ($2,200,000), expenses ($1,400,000), net amortization of the excess ($165,000), and the noncontrolling interest ($63,500) that account for the investment income.

We reflect the net amortization in the consolidated income statement by increasing cost of goods sold for the $100,000 undervalued inventories that were sold in 2012, increasing depreciation expense on undervalued buildings for the $25,000 amortization on the excess allocated to buildings, decreasing depreciation expense on equipment for the $60,000 amortization of the excess allocated to overvalued equipment, and increasing interest expense for the $100,000 allocated to overvalued notes payable that were retired in 2012.

Consolidated income statements, like consolidated balance sheets, are more than summations of the income accounts of the affiliates. A summation of all income statement items for Pil and Sad would result in a combined income figure of $3,895,000, whereas consolidated net income is only $3,158,500. The $736,500 difference between these two amounts lies in the investment income of $571,500 and the $165,000 amortization.

---

[6]A parent's income from subsidiary investments is referred to as income from subsidiary, equity in subsidiary earnings, investment income from subsidiary, or other descriptive captions.

PIL AND SAD CORPORATIONS
SEPARATE COMPANY AND CONSOLIDATED STATEMENTS
OF INCOME AND RETAINED EARNINGS
FOR THE YEAR ENDED DECEMBER 31, 2012 (IN THOUSANDS)

EXHIBIT 3-10

Separate Company and Consolidated Income and Retained Earnings Statements

	Separate Company		
	Pil	Sad	Consolidated
Sales	$9,523.5	$2,200	$11,723.5
Investment income from Sad	571.5		
Total revenue	10,095	2,200	11,723.5
Less: Operating expenses Cost of sales	4,000	700	4,800
Depreciation expense—buildings	200	80	305
Depreciation expense—equipment	700	360	1,000
Other expenses	1,800	120	1,920
Total operating expense	6,700	1,260	8,025
Operating income	3,395	940	3,698.5
Nonoperating item: Interest expense	300	140	540
Net income	**$3,095**	**$ 800**	
Consolidated net income			3,158.5
Less: Noncontrolling interest share			63.5
Controlling interest share			**$ 3,095**
Retained earnings December 31, 2011	4,300	900	4,300
	7,395	1,700	7,395
Deduct: Dividends	1,500	300	1,500
Retained earnings December 31, 2012	$5,895	$1,400	$ 5,895

Note that consolidated net income represents income to the stockholders of the consolidated group. Income of noncontrolling stockholders is a deduction in the determination of income of the controlling shareholders.

If the parent sells merchandise to its subsidiary, or vice versa, there will be intercompany purchases and sales on the separate books of the parent and its subsidiary. Intercompany purchases and sales balances are reciprocals that must be eliminated in preparing consolidated income statements because they do not represent purchases and sales to parties outside the consolidated entity. Intercompany inventory transactions are discussed in greater detail in Chapter 5. Adjustments for intercompany sales and purchases reduce revenue (sales) and expenses (cost of goods sold) by the same amount and therefore have no effect on consolidated net income. Reciprocal rent income and expense amounts are likewise eliminated without affecting consolidated net income.

Observe that Pil's separate retained earnings are identical to consolidated retained earnings. As expected, the $5,895,000 ending consolidated retained earnings in Exhibit 3-10 is the same amount that appears in the consolidated balance sheet for Pil and Subsidiary at December 31, 2012 (see Exhibit 3-9).

PUSH-DOWN ACCOUNTING

In the Pil and Sad illustration, we recorded the investment on the books of Pil at cost and assign the purchase price to identifiable assets and liabilities and goodwill through workpaper adjusting entries. In some instances, the assignment of the purchase price may be recorded in the subsidiary accounts—in other words, pushed down to the subsidiary records. **Push-down accounting** is the process of recording the effects of the purchase price assignment directly on the books of the subsidiary. Push-down accounting affects the books of the subsidiary and separate subsidiary financial statements. It does not alter consolidated financial statements and, in fact, simplifies the consolidation process. The SEC requires push-down accounting for SEC filings when a subsidiary is substantially wholly owned (approximately 90 percent) with no publicly-held debt or preferred stock outstanding.

Pac Corporation gives 5,000 shares of Pac $10 par common stock and $100,000 cash for all the capital stock of Sim Company, a closely held company, on January 3, 2011. At this time, Pac's stock is quoted on a national exchange at $55 a share. We summarize Sim's balance sheet and fair value information on January 3 as follows (in thousands):

	Book Value	Fair Value
Cash	$ 30	$ 30
Accounts receivable—net	90	90
Inventories	130	150
Land	30	70
Buildings—net	150	130
Equipment—net	80	120
Total assets	$510	$590
Current liabilities	$100	$100
Long-term debt	150	150
Capital stock, $10 par	150	
Retained earnings	110	
Total liabilities and stockholders' equity	$510	

Under push-down accounting, Pac records its investment in Sim in the usual manner:

Investment in Sim (+A)	375	
Cash (−A)		100
Capital stock, $10 par (+SE)		50
Additional paid-in capital (+SE)		225
To record acquisition of Sim Company.		

An entry must also be made on Sim's books on January 3 to record the new asset bases, including goodwill, in its accounts. Because Sim is considered similar to a new entity, it also has to reclassify retained earnings. Sim makes the following entry to record the push-down values:

Inventories (+A)	20	
Land (+A)	40	
Equipment—net (+A)	40	
Goodwill (+A)	35	
Retained earnings (−SE)	110	
Building—net (−A)		20
Push-down capital (+SE)		225

Sim (the subsidiary) records this entry on its separate accounting records when using push-down accounting.

A separate balance sheet prepared for Sim Company immediately after the business combination on January 3 includes the following accounts and amounts (in thousands):

Cash	$ 30
Accounts receivable—net	90
Inventories	150
Land	70
Buildings—net	130
Equipment—net	120
Goodwill	35
Total assets	$625
Current liabilities	$100
Long-term debt	150
Capital stock, $10 par	150
Push-down capital	225
Total liabilities and stockholders' equity	$625

EXHIBIT 3-11

Worksheet for Consolidated Balance Sheet

PARENT CORPORATION AND SUBSIDIARY
CONSOLIDATED BALANCE SHEET WORKPAPER
DECEMBER 31, 2011

(in thousands)	Parent	Subsidiary	Adjustments and Eliminations Debits	Credits	Consolidated Balance Sheet
Cash	420	200			=B7+C7+D7–E7
Receivables—net	500	1,300			=B8+C8+D8–E8
Inventories	3,500	500			=B9+C9+D9–E9
Land	1,500	2,000			=B10+C10+D10–E10
Equipment—net	6,000	1,000			=B11+C11+D11–E11
Investment in Subsidiary	4,590				=B12+C12+D12–E12
					=B13+C13+D13–E13
Total assets	=SUM(B7:B13)	=SUM(C7:C13)			=SUM(F7:F13)
Accounts payable	4,100	800			=B15+C15–D15+E15
Dividends payable	600	100			=B16+C16–D16+E16
Capital stock	10,000	3,000			=B17+C17–D17+E17
Retained earnings	1,810	1,100			=B18+C18–D18+E18
Total equities	=SUM(B15:B18)	=SUM(C15:C18)			
					=SUM(F15:F21)
			=SUM(D7:D22)	=SUM(E7:E22)	

In consolidating the balance sheets of Pac and Sim at January 3, 2011, after the push-down entries are made on Sim's books, we eliminate the investment in Sim account on Pac's books against Sim's capital stock and push-down capital and combine the other accounts.

PREPARING A CONSOLIDATED BALANCE SHEET WORKSHEET

LEARNING OBJECTIVE 9

In this section you will learn how to set up a worksheet to prepare a consolidated balance sheet. Refer to Exhibit 3-11. We have two columns to record the balance sheet information for a parent company and (in our example) a 90 percent-owned subsidiary company. The numbers in these two columns are simply copied from the individual-company balance sheets. We include two columns to record the debits and credits for consolidation adjustments and eliminations. The final column provides calculations of the correct consolidated balance sheet totals.

Exhibit 3-11 shows spreadsheet formulae used in preparing the worksheet. Notice that most of these can be input using the COPY command *available in the spreadsheet software*. In the first two columns, total assets and total equities are simple summations of the relevant balances. The adjustments and eliminations columns each contain a single summation formula for the column totals. This is useful in verifying the equality of debits and credits—that in other words, you have not made any errors in posting your consolidation entries.

There are lots of formulae in the consolidated balance sheet column, but again most of these can be entered with the COPY command. Let's look at the formula for Cash (=B7+C7+D7–E7). We simply sum parent-company cash plus subsidiary-company cash and then make any needed adjustments and eliminations. Notice that cash has a normal debit balance, so we add the debit adjustments (+D7) and subtract credits (–E7) to arrive at the consolidated total. We can copy our formula for all accounts having normal debit balances (i.e., all assets).

Now let's review the formula for Accounts payable (=B15+C15−D15+E15). We sum parent-company accounts payable plus subsidiary-company accounts payable and then make adjustments and eliminations. Notice that accounts payable has a normal credit balance, so we subtract debit adjustments (−D15) and add credits (+E15) to arrive at the consolidated total. We can copy our formula for all accounts having normal credit balances (i.e., all liabilities and equities).

We will discuss the completion of the worksheet by working through a sample problem. Separate company balance sheets for Parent Corporation and Subsidiary Company at December 31, 2011, are summarized as follows (in thousands):

	Parent Corporation	Subsidiary Company
Cash	$ 420	$ 200
Receivables—net	500	1,300
Inventories	3,500	500
Land	1,500	2,000
Equipment—net	6,000	1,000
Investment in Subsidiary	4,590	
Total assets	$16,510	$5,000
Accounts payable	$ 4,100	$ 800
Dividends payable	600	100
Capital stock	10,000	3,000
Retained earnings	1,810	1,100
Total equities	$16,510	$5,000

Parent Corporation acquired 90 percent of the outstanding voting shares of Subsidiary Company for $4,500,000 on January 1, 2011, when Subsidiary's stockholders' equity was $4,000,000. All of the assets and liabilities of Subsidiary were recorded at their fair values (equal to book values) when Parent acquired its 90 percent interest. During 2011, Subsidiary reported net income of $200,000 and declared a dividend of $100,000. The dividend remained unpaid on December 31. Because the fair value of Parent's 90 percent interest is $4,500,000, the implied total fair value of the subsidiary is $5,000,000 on the acquisition date. Because subsidiary book value equals $4,000,000, goodwill must be $1,000,000.

We enter the data into our worksheet in Exhibit 3-11. We record balance sheet amounts picked up from the parent and the subsidiary. Total assets and total equities are simple summation functions. Next, we will review the required consolidation adjustments and eliminations. We provide a separate Exhibit 3-12 to show the final worksheet, after posting the adjustments and eliminations. This is simply Exhibit 3-11 updated to reflect the entries that follow. Notice too, that we have added some new accounts. We create noncontrolling interest and goodwill and copy the relevant formulae. The first workpaper entry in Exhibit 3-12 is the following:

a	Capital stock (−SE)	3,000	
	Retained earnings (−SE)	1,100	
	Goodwill (+A)	1,000	
	Investment in Subsidiary (−A)		4,590
	Noncontrolling interest (+SE)		510
	To enter goodwill and the noncontrolling interest and to eliminate subsidiary capital accounts and the parent-company investment account.		

Here is a journal entry for workpaper entry b for Exhibit 3-12:

b	Dividends payable (−L)	90	
	Receivables—net (−A)		90
	To eliminate the intercompany receivable and payable for dividends.		

Our spreadsheet formulae compute the consolidated totals for us in the final column, completing the worksheet. Practice creating the spreadsheet for a few problems to be certain you understand the mechanics. However, you will not need to create your own spreadsheet for all problem assignments.

EXHIBIT 3-12

Final Worksheet

PARENT CORPORATION AND SUBSIDIARY
CONSOLIDATED BALANCE SHEET WORKPAPER
DECEMBER 31, 2011

(in thousands)	Parent	Subsidiary	Adjustments and Eliminations Debits	Adjustments and Eliminations Credits	Consolidated Balance Sheet
Cash	420	200			620
Receivables—net	500	1,300		b 90	1,710
Inventories	3,500	500			4,000
Land	1,500	2,000			3,500
Equipment—net	6,000	1,000			7,000
Investment in Subsidiary	4,590			a 4,590	0
Goodwill	___	___	a 1,000		1,000
Total assets	16,510	5,000			17,830
Accounts payable	4,100	800			4,900
Dividends payable	600	100	b 90		610
Capital stock	10,000	3,000	a 3,000		10,000
Retained earnings	1,810	1,100	a 1,100		1,810
Total equities	16,510	5,000			
Noncontrolling interest				a 510	510
					17,830
			5,190	5,190	

We eliminate the drudgery, and allow you to focus on learning the concepts, by providing spreadsheet templates for many assignments on the *Advanced Accounting* Web site. An icon in the assignment material indicates the availability of a template. The templates include the data for the parent and subsidiary companies and the formulae for calculating the consolidated balances.

SUMMARY

GAAP usually requires consolidated financial statements for the fair presentation of financial position and the results of operations of a parent company and its subsidiaries. Consolidated financial statements are not merely summations of parent-company and subsidiary financial statement items. Consolidated statements eliminate reciprocal amounts and combine and include only nonreciprocal amounts. We eliminate the investment in subsidiary and the subsidiary stockholders' equity accounts in the preparation of consolidated financial statements because they are reciprocal, both representing the net assets of the subsidiary. Sales and borrowing transactions between parent and subsidiaries also give rise to reciprocal amounts that we eliminate in the consolidating process.

The stockholders' equity amounts that appear in the consolidated balance sheet are those of the parent company, except for the equity of noncontrolling stockholders, which we report as a separate item within consolidated stockholders' equity. Consolidated net income is a measurement of income to the stockholders of the consolidated group. Incomes accruing to the benefit of controlling and noncontrolling stockholders are components of consolidated net income. Parent-company net income and retained earnings are equal to the controlling share of net income and consolidated retained earnings, respectively.

QUESTIONS

1. When does a corporation become a subsidiary of another corporation?
2. In allocating the excess of investment fair value over book value of a subsidiary, are the amounts allocated to identifiable assets and liabilities (land and notes payable, for example) recorded separately in the accounts of the parent? Explain.
3. If the fair value of a subsidiary's land was $100,000 and its book value was $90,000 when the parent acquired its 100 percent interest for cash, at what amount would the land be included in the consolidated balance sheet immediately after the acquisition? Would your answer be different if the parent had acquired an 80 percent interest?
4. Define or explain the terms *parent company*, *subsidiary company*, *affiliates*, and *associates*.
5. What is a noncontrolling interest?
6. Describe the circumstances under which the accounts of a subsidiary would not be included in the consolidated financial statements.
7. Who are the primary users for which consolidated financial statements are intended?
8. What amount of capital stock is reported in a consolidated balance sheet?
9. In what general ledger would you expect to find the account "goodwill from consolidation"?
10. How should the parent's investment in subsidiary account be classified in a consolidated balance sheet? In the parent's separate balance sheet?
11. Name some reciprocal accounts that might be found in the separate records of a parent and its subsidiaries.
12. Why are reciprocal amounts eliminated in preparing consolidated financial statements?
13. How does the stockholders' equity of the parent that uses the equity method of accounting differ from the consolidated stockholders' equity of the parent and its subsidiaries?
14. Is there a difference in the amounts reported in the statement of retained earnings of a parent that uses the equity method of accounting and the amounts that appear in the consolidated retained earnings statement?
15. Is noncontrolling interest share an expense? Explain.
16. Describe how total noncontrolling interest at the end of an accounting period is determined.
17. What special procedures are required to consolidate the statements of a parent that reports on a calendar-year basis and a subsidiary whose fiscal year ends on October 31?
18. Does the acquisition of shares held by noncontrolling shareholders constitute a business combination?

NOTE: Don't forget the assumptions on page 46 when working exercises and problems in this chapter.

EXERCISES

E 3-1 General questions

1. A 75 percent-owned subsidiary should not be consolidated when:
   a. Its operations are dissimilar from those of the parent company
   b. Control of the subsidiary does not lie with the parent company
   c. There is a dominant noncontrolling interest in the subsidiary
   d. Management feels that consolidation would not provide the most meaningful financial statements

2. An 80 percent owned subsidiary that cannot be consolidated must be accounted for:
   a. Under the equity method
   b. Under the cost method
   c. Under the equity method if the parent exercises significant influence over the subsidiary
   d. At market value if the subsidiary is in bankruptcy

3. Consolidated statements for Por Corporation and its 60 percent-owned investee, Spy Company, will not be prepared under current GAAP if:
   a. The fiscal periods of Por and Spy are more than three months apart
   b. Por is a major manufacturing company and Spy is an insurance company
   c. Spy is a foreign company
   d. This is a combination of companies formerly under common control

4. Par Industries owns 7,000,000 shares of Sub Corporation's outstanding common stock (a 70 percent interest). The remaining 3,000,000 outstanding common shares of Sub are held by Ott Insurance Company. On Par Industries' consolidated financial statements, Ott Insurance Company is considered:

   a. *An investee*
   b. *An associated company*
   c. *An affiliated company*
   d. *A noncontrolling interest*

5. On January 1, Paxton Company purchased 75 percent of the outstanding shares of Salem Company at a cost exceeding the book value and fair value of Salem's net assets. Using the following notations, describe the amount at which the plant assets will appear in a consolidated balance sheet of Paxton Company and Subsidiary prepared immediately after the acquisition:

   P_{bv} = book value of Paxton's plant assets
   P_{fv} = fair value of Paxton's plant assets
   S_{bv} = book value of Salem's plant assets
   S_{fv} = fair value of Salem's plant assets

   a. $P_{bv} + S_{bv} \pm (S_{fv} - S_{bv})$
   b. $P_{bv} + 0.75(S_{bv}) \pm 0.75(S_{fv} - S_{bv})$
   c. $P_{bv} + 0.75(S_{fv})$
   d. $P_{bv} + S_{bv} \pm 0.75(S_{fv} - S_{bv})$

E 3-2

General questions

1. Under GAAP, a parent company should exclude a subsidiary from consolidation if:
   a. *It measures income from the subsidiary under the equity method*
   b. *The subsidiary is in a regulated industry*
   c. *The subsidiary is a foreign entity whose books are recorded in a foreign currency*
   d. *The parent and the subsidiary were under common control*

2. The FASB's primary motivation for requiring consolidation of all majority-owned subsidiaries was to:
   a. *Ensure disclosure of all loss contingencies*
   b. *Prevent the use of off–balance sheet financing*
   c. *Improve comparability of the statements of cash flows*
   d. *Establish criteria for exclusion of finance and insurance subsidiaries from consolidation*

3. Parent-company and consolidated financial statement amounts would not be the same for:
   a. *Capital stock*
   b. *Retained earnings*
   c. *Investments in unconsolidated subsidiaries*
   d. *Investments in consolidated subsidiaries*

4. Noncontrolling interest, as it appears in a consolidated balance sheet, refers to:
   a. *Owners of less than 50 percent of the parent company's stock*
   b. *Parent's interest in subsidiary companies*
   c. *Interest expense on subsidiary's bonds payable*
   d. *Equity in the subsidiary's net assets held by stockholders other than the parent*

5. Pat Corporation acquired an 80 percent interest in Sal Corporation on January 1, 2011, and issued consolidated financial statements at and for the year ended December 31, 2011. Pat and Sal had issued separate-company financial statements in 2010.
   a. *The change in reporting entity is reported by restating the financial statements of all prior periods presented as consolidated statements.*
   b. *The cumulative effect of the change in reporting entity is shown in a separate category of the income statement net of tax.*
   c. *The income effect of the error is charged or credited directly to beginning retained earnings.*
   d. *The income effect of the accounting change is spread over the current and future periods.*

6. The noncontrolling interest share that appears in the consolidated income statement is computed as follows:
   a. *Consolidated net income is multiplied by the noncontrolling interest percentage.*
   b. *The subsidiary's income less amortization of fair/book value differentials is multiplied by the noncontrolling interest percentage.*
   c. *Subsidiary net income is subtracted from consolidated net income.*
   d. *Subsidiary income determined for consolidated statement purposes is multiplied by the noncontrolling interest percentage.*

7. The retained earnings that appear on the consolidated balance sheet of a parent company and its 60 percent-owned subsidiary are:

   a. *The parent company's retained earnings plus 100 percent of the subsidiary's retained earnings*

   b. *The parent company's retained earnings plus 60 percent of the subsidiary's retained earnings*

   c. *The parent company's retained earnings*

   d. *Pooled retained earnings*

E 3-3

[Based on AICPA] General problems

1. Cobb Company's current receivables from affiliated companies at December 31, 2011, are (1) a $75,000 cash advance to Hill Corporation (Cobb owns 30 percent of the voting stock of Hill and accounts for the investment by the equity method), (2) a receivable of $260,000 from Vick Corporation for administrative and selling services (Vick is 100 percent owned by Cobb and is included in Cobb's consolidated financial statements), and (3) a receivable of $200,000 from Ward Corporation for merchandise sales on credit (Ward is a 90 percent-owned, unconsolidated subsidiary of Cobb accounted for by the equity method). In the current assets section of its December 31, 2011, consolidated balance sheet, Cobb should report accounts receivable from investees in the amount of:

   a. *$180,000*

   b. *$255,000*

   c. *$275,000*

   d. *$535,000*

Use the following information in answering questions 2 and 3.

On January 1, 2011, Pow Corporation purchased all of Sap Corporation's common stock for $2,400,000. On that date, the fair values of Sap's assets and liabilities equaled their carrying amounts of $2,640,000 and $640,000, respectively. Pow's policy is to amortize intangibles other than goodwill over 10 years. During 2011, Sap paid cash dividends of $40,000.

Selected information from the separate balance sheets and income statements of Pow and Sap as of December 31, 2011, and for the year then ended follows (in thousands):

	Pow	Sap
Balance Sheet Accounts		
Investment in subsidiary	$2,640	—
Retained earnings	2,480	$ 1,120
Total stockholders' equity	5,240	2,240
Income Statement Accounts		
Operating income	$ 840	$ 400
Equity in earnings of Sap	280	—
Net income	800	280

2. In Pow's 2011 consolidated income statement, what amount should be reported for amortization of goodwill?

   a. *$0*

   b. *$24,000*

   c. *$36,000*

   d. *$40,000*

3. In Pow's December 31, 2011, consolidated balance sheet, what amount should be reported as total retained earnings?

   a. *$2,480,000*

   b. *$2,720,000*

   c. *$2,760,000*

   d. *$3,600,000*

4. Pop Corporation has several subsidiaries that are included in its consolidated financial statements. In its December 31, 2011, trial balance, Pop had the following intercompany balances before eliminations:

	Debit	Credit
Current receivable due from Sin Co.	$ 64,000	
Noncurrent receivable from Sin	228,000	
Cash advance from Sun Corp.	12,000	
Cash advance from Sit Co.		$ 30,000
Intercompany payable to Sit		202,000

In its December 31, 2011, consolidated balance sheet, what amount should Pop report as intercompany receivables?

a. $304,000

b. $292,000

c. $72,000

d. $0

E 3-4

Correction of consolidated net income

Pin Corporation paid $1,800,000 for a 90 percent interest in San Corporation on January 1, 2011; San's total book value was $1,800,000. The excess was allocated as follows: $60,000 to undervalued equipment with a three-year remaining useful life and $140,000 to goodwill. The income statements of Pin and San for 2011 are summarized as follows (in thousands):

	Pin	San
Sales	$4,000	$1,600
Income from San	180	
Cost of sales	(2,000)	(800)
Depreciation expense	(400)	(240)
Other expenses	(800)	(360)
Net income	$ 980	$ 200

REQUIRED

1. Calculate the goodwill that should appear in the consolidated balance sheet of Pin and Subsidiary at December 31, 2011.

2. Calculate consolidated net income for 2011.

E 3-5

Disclosure of consolidated dividends

On December 31, 2011, the separate-company financial statements for Pan Corporation and its 70 percent-owned subsidiary, Sad Corporation, had the following account balances related to dividends (in thousands):

	Pan	Sad
Dividends for 2011	$1,200	$800
Dividends payable at December 31, 2011	600	200

REQUIRED

1. At what amount will dividends be shown in the consolidated retained earnings statement?

2. At what amount should dividends payable be shown in the consolidated balance sheet?

E 3-6

Prepare journal entries and balance sheet under push-down accounting

Book values and fair values of Sli Corporation's assets and liabilities on December 31, 2010, are as follows (in thousands):

	Book Value	Fair Value
Cash	$ 140	$ 140
Accounts receivable—net	160	160
Inventories	160	200
Land	300	400
Buildings—net	700	1,000
Equipment—net	440	600
	$1,900	$2,500
Accounts payable	$ 200	$ 200
Note payable	280	300
Capital stock	1,000	
Retained earnings	420	
	$1,900	

On January 1, 2011, Por Corporation acquires all of Sli's capital stock for $2,500,000 cash. The acquisition is recorded using push-down accounting.

REQUIRED

1. Prepare the January 1 journal entry on Sli's books to record push-down values.

2. Prepare a balance sheet for Sli Corporation immediately after the acquisition on January 1 under push-down accounting.

E 3-7

Prepare consolidated income statements with and without fair value/book value differentials

Summary income statement information for Pas Corporation and its 70 percent-owned subsidiary, Sit, for the year 2012 is as follows (in thousands):

	Pas	Sit
Sales	$2,000	$ 800
Income from Sit	98	—
Cost of sales	(1,200)	(400)
Depreciation expense	(100)	(80)
Other expenses	(398)	(180)
Net income	$ 400	$ 140

REQUIRED:

1. Assume that Pas acquired its 70 percent interest in Sit at book value on January 1, 2011, when the fair value of Sits' assets and liabilities were equal to recorded book values. There were no intercompany transactions during 2011 and 2012. Prepare a consolidated income statement for Pas Corporation and Subsidiary for 2012.

2. Assume that Pas acquired its 70 percent interest in Sit on January 1, 2011, for $280,000. $60,000 *was allocated* to a reduction of overvalued equipment with a five-year remaining useful life and the remainder was allocated to goodwill. Sit's book value was $320,000. There were no intercompany transactions during 2011 and 2012. Prepare a consolidated income statement for Pas Corporation and Subsidiary for 2012.

E 3-8

Calculate consolidated balance sheet amounts with goodwill and noncontrolling interest

Pob Corporation acquired an 80 percent interest in Sof Corporation on January 2, 2011, for $1,400,000. On this date the capital stock and retained earnings of the two companies were as follows (in thousands):

	Pob	Sof
Capital stock	$3,600	$1,000
Retained earnings	1,600	200

The assets and liabilities of Sof were stated at fair values equal to book values when Pob acquired its 80 percent interest. Pob uses the equity method to account for its investment in Sof.

Net income and dividends for 2011 for the affiliated companies were as follows:

	Pob	Sof
Net income	$600	$180
Dividends declared	360	100
Dividends payable December 31, 2011	180	50

REQUIRED: Calculate the amounts at which the following items should appear in the consolidated balance sheet on December 31, 2011.

1. Capital stock

2. Goodwill

3. Consolidated retained earnings

4. Noncontrolling interest

5. Dividends payable

E 3-9

Prepare stockholders' equity section of consolidated balance sheet one year after acquisition

Pas and Sal Corporations' balance sheets at December 31, 2010, are summarized as follows (in thousands):

	Pas	Sal
Cash	$510	$120
Other assets	400	350
Total assets	$910	$470
Liabilities	$140	$ 70
Capital stock, par $10	600	350
Additional paid-in capital	100	30
Retained earnings	70	20
Total equities	$910	$470

Pas acquired 80 percent of the voting stock of Sal on January 2, 2011, at a cost of $320,000. The fair values of Sal's net assets were equal to book values on January 2, 2011.

During 2011, Pas reported earnings of $110,000, including income from Sal of $32,000, and paid dividends of $50,000. Sal's earnings for 2011 were $40,000 and its dividends were $30,000.

REQUIRED: Prepare the stockholders' equity section of the December 31, 2011, consolidated balance sheet for Pas Corporation and Subsidiary.

E 3-10

Prepare consolidated income statement three years after acquisition

Comparative income statements of Pek Corporation and Slo Corporation for the year ended December 31, 2013, are as follows (in thousands):

	Pek	Slo
Sales	$3,200	$1,000
Income from Slo	261	—
Total revenue	3,461	1,000
Less: Cost of goods sold	1,800	400
Operating expenses	800	300
Total expenses	2,600	700
Net income	$ 861	$ 300

ADDITIONAL INFORMATION

1. Slo is a 90 percent-owned subsidiary of Pek, acquired by Pek for $1,620,000 on January 1, 2011, when Slo's stockholders' equity at book value was $1,400,000.

2. The excess of the cost of Pek's investment in Slo over book value acquired was allocated $60,000 to undervalued inventories that were sold in 2011, $40,000 to undervalued equipment with a four-year remaining useful life, and the remainder to goodwill.

REQUIRED: Prepare a consolidated income statement for Pek Corporation and Subsidiary for the year ended December 31, 2013.

PROBLEMS

P 3-1

Prepare a consolidated balance sheet at acquisition and compute consolidated net income one year later

On December 31, 2011, Pen Corporation purchased 80 percent of the stock of Sut Company at book value. The data reported on their separate balance sheets immediately after the acquisition follow. At December 31, 2011, Pen Corporation owes Sut $10,000 on accounts payable. (All amounts are in thousands.)

	Pen	Sut
Assets		
Cash	$ 64	$ 36
Accounts receivable	90	68
Inventories	286	112
Investment in Sut	400	
Equipment—net	760	350
	$1,600	$566
Liabilities and Stockholders' Equity		
Accounts payable	$ 80	$ 66
Common stock, $20 par	920	300
Retained earnings	600	200
	$1,600	$566

REQUIRED

1. Prepare a consolidated balance sheet for Pen Corporation and Subsidiary at December 31, 2011.

2. Compute consolidated net income for 2012 assuming that Pen Corporation reported separate income of $340,000 and Sut Company reported net income of $180,000. (Separate incomes does *not* include income from the investment in Sut.)

P 3-2

Allocation schedule for fair value/book value differential and consolidated balance sheet at acquisition

Par Corporation acquired 70 percent of the outstanding common stock of Set Corporation on January 1, 2011, for $350,000 cash. Immediately after this acquisition the balance sheet information for the two companies was as follows (in thousands):

		Set	
	Par Book Value	**Book Value**	**Fair Value**
Assets			
Cash	$ 70	$ 40	$ 40
Receivables—net	160	60	60
Inventories	140	60	100
Land	200	100	120
Buildings—net	220	140	180
Equipment—net	160	80	60
Investment in Set	350	—	—
Total assets	$1,300	$480	$560
Liabilities and Stockholders' Equity			
Accounts payable	$ 180	$160	$160
Other liabilities	20	100	80
Capital stock, $20 par	1,000	200	
Retained earnings	100	20	
Total equities	$1,300	$480	

REQUIRED

1. Prepare a schedule to allocate the difference between the fair value of the investment in Set and the book value of the interest to identifiable and unidentifiable net assets.

2. Prepare a consolidated balance sheet for Par Corporation and Subsidiary at January 1, 2011.

P 3-3 Prepare allocation schedule with book value greater than fair value

PJ Corporation pays $5,400,000 for an 80 percent interest in Sof Corporation on January 1, 2011, at which time the book value and fair value of Sof's net assets are as follows (in thousands):

	Book Value	Fair Value
Current assets	$2,000	$3,000
Equipment—net	4,000	6,000
Other plant assets—net	2,000	2,000
Liabilities	(3,000)	(3,000)
Net assets	$5,000	$8,000

REQUIRED: Prepare a schedule to allocate the fair value/book value differentials to Sof's net assets.

P 3-4

Given separate and consolidated balance sheets, reconstruct the schedule to allocate the fair value/book value differential

Pam Corporation purchased a block of Sap Company common stock for $520,000 cash on January 1, 2011. Separate-company and consolidated balance sheets prepared immediately after the acquisition are summarized as follows (in thousands):

Pam Corporation and Subsidiary Consolidated Balance Sheet at January 1, 2011

	Pam	Sap	Consolidated
Assets			
Current assets	$ 380	$200	$ 580
Investment in Sap	520	—	—
Plant assets—net	1,100	400	1,520
Goodwill	—	—	110
Total assets	$2,000	$600	$2,210
Equities			
Liabilities	$ 800	$ 80	$ 880
Capital stock, $20 par	1,000	400	1,000
Retained earnings	200	120	200
Noncontrolling interest	—	—	130
Total equities	$2,000	$600	$2,210

REQUIRED: Reconstruct the schedule to allocate the fair value/book value differential from Pam's investment in Sap.

P 3-5

Prepare a consolidated balance sheet one year after acquisition

Adjusted trial balances for Pal and Sor Corporations at December 31, 2011, are as follows (in thousands):

	Pal	Sor
Debits		
Current assets	$ 480	$ 200
Plant assets—net	1,000	600
Investment in Sor	840	—
Cost of sales	600	600
Other expenses	200	100
Dividends	100	—
	$3,220	$1,500

(continued)

	Pal	Sor
Credits		
Liabilities	$ 900	$ 420
Capital stock	600	100
Retained earnings	680	180
Sales	1,000	800
Income from Sor	40	—
	$3,220	$1,500

Pal purchased all the stock of Sor for $800,000 cash on January 1, 2011, when Sor's stockholders' equity consisted of $100,000 capital stock and $180,000 retained earnings. Sor's assets and liabilities were fairly valued except for inventory that was undervalued by $40,000 and sold in 2011, and plant assets that were undervalued by $80,000 and had a remaining useful life of four years from the date of the acquisition.

REQUIRED: Prepare a consolidated balance sheet for Pal Corporation and Subsidiary at December 31, 2011.

P 3-6
Consolidated balance sheet workpapers with goodwill and dividends

Per Corporation paid $900,000 cash for 90 percent of Sim Corporation's common stock on January 1, 2011, when Sim had $600,000 capital stock and $200,000 retained earnings. The book values of Sim's assets and liabilities were equal to fair values. During 2011, Sim reported net income of $40,000 and declared $20,000 in dividends on December 31. Balance sheets for Per and Sim at December 31, 2011, are as follows (in thousands):

	Per	Sim
Assets		
Cash	$ 84	$ 40
Receivables—net	100	260
Inventories	700	100
Land	300	400
Equipment—net	1,200	200
Investment in Sim	918	—
	$3,302	$1,000
Equities		
Accounts payable	$ 820	$ 160
Dividends payable	120	20
Capital stock	2,000	600
Retained earnings	362	220
	$3,302	$1,000

REQUIRED: Prepare consolidated balance sheet workpapers for Per Corporation and Subsidiary for December 31, 2011.

P 3-7
Calculate items that may appear in consolidated statements two years after acquisition

Por Corporation acquired 80 percent of the outstanding stock of Sle Corporation for $560,000 cash on January 3, 2011, on which date Sle's stockholders' equity consisted of capital stock of $400,000 and retained earnings of $100,000.

There were no changes in the outstanding stock of either corporation during 2011 and 2012. At December 31, 2012, the adjusted trial balances of Por and Sle are as follows (in thousands):

	Por	Sle
Debits		
Current assets	$ 408	$ 150
Plant assets—net	800	600
Investment in Sle—80%	680	—
Cost of goods sold	500	240
Other expenses	100	60
Dividends	120	50
	$2,608	$1,100
Credits		
Current liabilities	$ 324	$ 100
Capital stock	1,000	400
Retained earnings	404	200
Sales	800	400
Income from Sle	80	—
	$2,608	$1,100

ADDITIONAL INFORMATION

1. All of Sle's assets and liabilities were recorded at fair values equal to book values on January 3, 2011.

2. The current liabilities of Sle at December 31, 2012, include dividends payable of $20,000.

REQUIRED: Determine the amounts that should appear in the consolidated statements of Por Corporation and Subsidiary at December 31, 2012, for each of the following:

1. Noncontrolling interest share
2. Current assets
3. Income from Sle
4. Capital stock
5. Investment in Sle

6. Excess of investment fair value over book value
7. Consolidated net income for the year ended December 31, 2012
8. Consolidated retained earnings, December 31, 2011
9. Consolidated retained earnings, December 31, 2012
10. Noncontrolling interest, December 31, 2012

P 3-8

[Based on AICPA] Prepare journal entries to account for investments, and compute noncontrolling interest, consolidated retained earnings, and investment balances

On January 1, 2011, Pod Corporation made the following investments:

1. Acquired for cash, 80 percent of the outstanding common stock of Saw Corporation at $140 per share. The stockholders' equity of Saw on January 1, 2011, consisted of the following:

Common stock, par value $100	$100,000
Retained earnings	40,000

2. Acquired for cash, 70 percent of the outstanding common stock of Sun Corporation at $80 per share. The stockholders' equity of Sun on January 1, 2011, consisted of the following:

Common stock, par value $40	$120,000
Capital in excess of par value	40,000
Retained earnings	80,000

3. After these investments were made, Pod was able to exercise control over the operations of both companies.

   An analysis of the retained earnings of each company for 2011 is as follows:

	Pod	Saw	Sun
Balance January 1	$480,000	$40,000	$80,000
Net income (loss)	209,200	72,000	(24,000)
Cash dividends paid	(80,000)	(32,000)	(18,000)
Balance December 31	$609,200	$80,000	$38,000

REQUIRED

1. What entries should have been made on the books of Pod during 2011 to record the following?

   a. Investments in subsidiaries
   b. Subsidiary dividends received
   c. Parent's share of subsidiary income or loss

2. Compute the amount of noncontrolling interest in each subsidiary's stockholders' equity at December 31, 2011.

3. What amount should be reported as consolidated retained earnings of Pod Corporation and subsidiaries as of December 31, 2011?

4. Compute the correct balances of Pod's Investment in Saw and Investment in Sun accounts at December 31, 2011, before consolidation.

P 3-9

Consolidated balance sheet workpapers (excess allocated to equipment and goodwill)

Pan Corporation purchased 90 percent of Son Corporation's outstanding stock for $7,200,000 cash on January 1, 2011, when Son's stockholders' equity consisted of $4,000,000 capital stock and $1,400,000 retained earnings. The excess was allocated $1,600,000 to undervalued equipment with an eight-year remaining useful life and $1,000,000 to goodwill. Son's net income and dividends for 2011 were $1,000,000 and $400,000, respectively. Comparative balance sheet data for Pan and Son Corporations at December 31, 2011, are as follows (in thousands):

	Pan	Son
Cash	$ 600	$ 400
Receivables—net	1,200	800
Dividends receivable	180	—
Inventory	1,400	1,200
Land	1,200	1,400
Buildings—net	4,000	2,000
Equipment—net	3,000	1,600
Investment in Son	7,560	—
	$19,140	$7,400
Accounts payable	$ 600	$1,200
Dividends payable	1,000	200
Capital stock	14,000	4,000
Retained earnings	3,540	2,000
	$19,140	$7,400

REQUIRED: Prepare consolidated balance sheet workpapers for Pan Corporation and Subsidiary on December 31, 2011.

P 3-10

Calculate investment cost and account balances from a consolidated balance sheet four years after acquisition

The consolidated balance sheet of Pan Corporation and its 80 percent subsidiary, Sun Corporation, contains the following items on December 31, 2015 (in thousands):

Cash	$ 40
Inventories	384
Other current assets	140
Plant assets—net	540
Goodwill	120
	$1,224
Liabilities	$ 240
Capital stock	800
Retained earnings	60
Noncontrolling interests	124
	$1,224

Pan Corporation uses the equity method of accounting for its investment in Sun. Sun Corporation stock was acquired by Pan on January 1, 2011, when Sun's capital stock was $400,000 and its retained earnings were $40,000. The fair values of Sun's net assets were equal to book values on January 1, 2011, and there have been no changes in outstanding stock of either Pan or Sun since January 1, 2011.

REQUIRED: Determine the following:

1. The purchase price of Pan's investment in Sun stock on January 1, 2011.

2. The total of Sun's stockholders' equity on December 31, 2015.

3. The balance of Pan's Investment in Sun account at December 31, 2015.

4. The balances of Pan's Retained earnings and Capital stock accounts on December 31, 2015.

P 3-11

Consolidated balance sheet workpapers (fair value/book value differentials and noncontrolling interest)

Pop Corporation acquired a 70 percent interest in Stu Corporation on January 1, 2011, for $1,400,000, when Stu's stockholders' equity consisted of $1,000,000 capital stock and $600,000 retained earnings. On this date, the book value of Stu's assets and liabilities was equal to the fair value, except for inventories that were undervalued by $40,000 and sold in 2011, and plant assets that were undervalued by $160,000 and had a remaining useful life of eight years from January 1. Stu's net income and dividends for 2011 were $140,000 and $20,000, respectively.

Separate-company balance sheet information for Pop and Stu Corporations at December 31, 2011, follows (in thousands):

	Pop	Stu
Cash	$ 120	$ 40
Accounts receivable—customers	880	400
Accounts receivable from Pop	—	20
Dividends receivable	14	—
Inventories	1,000	640
Land	200	300
Plant assets—net	1,400	700
Investment in Stu	1,442	—
	$5,056	$2,100
Accounts payable—suppliers	$ 600	$ 160
Accounts payable to Stu	20	—
Dividends payable	80	20
Long-term debt	1,200	200
Capital stock	2,000	1,000
Retained earnings	1,156	720
	$5,056	$2,100

REQUIRED: Prepare consolidated balance sheet workpapers for Pop Corporation and Subsidiary at December 31, 2011.

P 3-12

Calculate separate company and consolidated statement items given investment account for three years

A summary of changes in Pen Corporation's Investment in Sam account from January 1, 2011, to December 31, 2013, follows (in thousands):

INVESTMENT IN SAM (80%)

January 1, 2011	$1,520		
Income—2011	128	Dividends—2011	$ 64
2012	160	2012	80
2013	192	2013	96
		to balance	1,760
	$2,000		$2,000
December 31, 2013			
Balance forward	$1,760		

ADDITIONAL INFORMATION

1. Pen acquired its 80 percent interest in Sam Corporation when Sam had capital stock of $1,200,000 and retained earnings of $600,000.

2. Dividends declared by Sam Corporation in each of the years 2011, 2012, and 2013 were equal to 50 percent of Sam Corporation's reported net income.

3. Sam Corporation's assets and liabilities were stated at fair values equal to book values on January 1, 2011.

REQUIRED: Compute the following amounts:

1. Sam Corporation's dividends declared in 2012

2. Sam Corporation's net income for 2012

3. Goodwill at December 31, 2012

4. Noncontrolling interest share for 2013

5. Noncontrolling interest at December 31, 2013

6. Consolidated net income for 2013, assuming that Pen's separate income for 2013 is $560,000, without investment income from Sam

INTERNET ASSIGNMENT

Visit the Web site of *Delta Airlines* and obtain the 2009 annual report. Summarize the disclosures made concerning the merger with *Northwest Airlines*.

REFERENCES TO THE AUTHORITATIVE LITERATURE

[1] FASB ASC 220. Originally *Statement of Financial Accounting Standards No. 130.* "Reporting Comprehensive Income." Stamford, CT: Financial Accounting Standards Board, 1997.

[2] FASB ASC 805. Originally *Statement of Financial Accounting Standards No. 141(R).* "Business Combinations." Norwalk, CT: Financial Accounting Standards Board, 2007.

[3] FASB ASC 810-10-65. Originally *Statement of Financial Accounting Standards No. 160.* "Noncontrolling Interests." Norwalk, CT: Financial Accounting Standards Board, 2007 (paragraph 34).

[4] FASB ASC 810-10-65. Originally *Statement of Financial Accounting Standards No. 141(R).* "Business Combinations." Norwalk, CT: Financial Accounting Standards Board, 2007.

[5] FASB ASC 810-10-10-1. Originally *Statement of Financial Accounting Standards No. 160.* "Noncontrolling Interests." Norwalk, CT: Financial Accounting Standards Board, 2007.

[6] FASB ASC 810-10-45. Originally *Statement of Financial Accounting Standards No. 94.* "Consolidation of All Majority-Owned Subsidiaries." Stamford CT: Financial Accounting Standards Board, 1987.

[7] FASB ASC 810-10-15. Originally *Statement of Financial Accounting Standards No. 160.* "Noncontrolling Interests." Norwalk, CT: Financial Accounting Standards Board, 2007.

[8] FASB ASC 235-10-05-2. Originally APB Opinion No. 22. "Disclosure of Accounting Policies." New York: American Institute of Certified Public Accountants, 1972.

[9] FASB ASC 810-10-50. Originally *Statement of Financial Accounting Standards No. 160.* "Noncontrolling Interests." Norwalk, CT: Financial Accounting Standards Board, 2007.

[10] FASB ASC 805-10-15. Originally *Statement of Financial Accounting Standards No. 141(R).* "Business Combinations." Norwalk, CT: Financial Accounting Standards Board, 2007.

[11] FASB ASC 820-10-05. Originally *Statement of Financial Accounting Standards No. 157.* "Fair Value Measurements." Norwalk, CT: Financial Accounting Standards Board, 2006.

[12] FASB ASC 825-10-05. *Statement of Financial Accounting Standards No. 159.* "The Fair Value Option for Financial Assets and Financial Liabilities (Including an Amendment of FASB Statement No. 115)." Norwalk, CT: Financial Accounting Standards Board, 2007.

[13] IASB IAS 27 "Consolidated and Separate Financial Statements." London, UK: International Accounting Standards Board, 2008.

[14] FASB ASC 805-10. Originally *Statement of Financial Accounting Standards No. 160.* "Noncontrolling Interests." Norwalk, CT: Financial Accounting Standards Board, 2007.

[15] FASB ASC 810-10-65. Originally *Statement of Financial Accounting Standards No. 160.* "Noncontrolling Interests." Norwalk, CT: Financial Accounting Standards Board, 2007.

4 CHAPTER

Consolidation Techniques and Procedures

This chapter examines procedures for consolidating the financial statements of parent and subsidiary companies. Some differences in the consolidation process result from different methods of parent-company accounting for subsidiary investments. Consolidation workpapers for a parent company/investor that uses the complete equity method of accounting are illustrated in the chapter to set the standard for good consolidation procedures. Illustrations for an incomplete equity method and the cost method of parent-company accounting are presented in the electronic supplement on the *Advanced Accounting* Web site. The chapter examines additional complexities that arise from errors and omissions in the separate-company records and detailed recording of fair values of a subsidiary's net assets. The appendix to the chapter also illustrates the trial balance workpaper format, which is an alternative to the financial statement format used in other sections of the chapter.

Chapter 3 presented the balance sheet workpaper used to organize the information needed for consolidated balance sheets. By contrast, this chapter presents a workpaper that develops the information needed for consolidated balance sheets and income and retained earnings statements. A consolidated statement of cash flows is illustrated in a later section of this chapter.

LEARNING OBJECTIVES

1 Prepare consolidation workpaper for the year of acquisition when the parent uses the complete equity method to account for its investment in a subsidiary.

2 Prepare consolidation workpaper for the years subsequent to acquisition.

3 Locate errors in consolidation workpaper.

4 Assign fair value to identifiable net assets.

5 Apply concepts to prepare a consolidated statement of cash flows.

6 **For the Students:** Create an electronic spreadsheet to prepare a consolidation workpaper.

7 Appendix: Understand the alternative trial balance consolidation workpaper format.

8 Electronic supplement: Understand differences in consolidation workpaper techniques when the parent company uses either an incomplete equity method or the cost method.

CONSOLIDATION UNDER THE EQUITY METHOD

The following example of a parent that uses the complete equity method of accounting for its subsidiary explains basic procedures used to consolidate the financial statements of affiliated companies.

LEARNING OBJECTIVE **1**

Equity Method—Year of Acquisition

Pep Corporation pays $88,000 for 80 percent of the outstanding voting stock of Sap Corporation on January 1, 2011, when Sap Corporation's stockholders' equity consists of $60,000 capital stock and $30,000 retained earnings. This implies that the total fair value of Sap is $110,000 ($88,000 ÷ 80%). We assign the $20,000 excess fair value to previously unrecorded patents with a 10-year amortization period. Sap's net income and dividends are as follows:

	2011	2012
Net income	$25,000	$30,000
Dividends	15,000	15,000

Financial statements for Pep and Sap Corporations for 2011 are presented in the first two columns of Exhibit 4-1. Pep's $18,400 income from Sap for 2011 consists of 80 percent of Sap's $25,000 net income for 2011 less $1,600 [($20,000 ÷ 10 yrs.) × 80%] patent amortization. Its

EXHIBIT 4-1

Equity Method—
Workpaper for Year
of Acquisition

PEP CORPORATION AND SUBSIDIARY CONSOLIDATION WORKPAPER FOR THE YEAR ENDED DECEMBER 31, 2011 (IN THOUSANDS)

	Pep	80% Sap	Adjustments and Eliminations Debits	Adjustments and Eliminations Credits	Consolidated Statements
Income Statement Revenue	$ 250	$ 65			$315
Income from Sap	18.4		a 18.4		
Expenses	(200)	(40)	d 2		(242)
Noncontrolling interest share ($23,000 × 20%)			b 4.6		(4.6)
Controlling share of net income	**$ 68.4**	**$ 25**			**$ 68.4**
Retained Earnings Statement Retained earnings—Pep	$ 5				$ 5
Retained earnings—Sap		$ 30	c 30		
Add: Controlling share of net income	**68.4**	**25**			**68.4**
Deduct: Dividends	(30)	(15)		a 12	
				b 3	(30)
Retained earnings— December 31	**$ 43.4**	**$ 40**			**$ 43.4**
Balance Sheet Cash	$ 39	$10			$ 49
Other current assets	90	50			140
Investment in Sap	94.4			a 6.4	
				c 88	
Plant and equipment	300	100			400
Accumulated depreciation	(50)	(30)			(80)
Patents			c 20	d 2	18
	$ 473.4	$130			$527
Liabilities	$ 80	$ 30			$110
Capital stock	350	60	c 60		350
Retained earnings	**43.4**	**40**			**43.4**
	$ 473.4	$130			
Noncontrolling interest January 1 ($110,000 fair value × 20%)				c 22	
Noncontrolling interest December 31				b 1.6	23.6
			135	135	$527

$94,400 investment in Sap account at December 31, 2011, consists of $88,000 investment cost plus $18,400 income from Sap, less $12,000 dividends received from Sap during 2011.

Numerous consolidation approaches and any number of different adjustment and elimination combinations will result in correct amounts for the consolidated financial statements. The adjustment and elimination entries that appear in the workpapers *do not affect the general ledger accounts of either the parent or its subsidiaries*. Adjusting or eliminating accounts or balances simply means that the amounts listed in the separate-company columns of the workpapers are either (1) adjusted before inclusion in the consolidated statement column or (2) eliminated and do not appear in the consolidated statement column. A single workpaper entry often adjusts some items and eliminates others. Labeling the workpaper entries as either adjusting or eliminating entries is not important. It is important that you understand the consolidation process and develop your workpaper skills.

Take a few minutes to review the consolidation workpaper in Exhibit 4-1. This format is used extensively throughout the chapters on consolidated financial statements. The worksheet rows for controlling share of consolidated net income and ending retained earnings are in boldface to highlight that we do not make adjustments or eliminations directly on these lines. We do this because consolidated net income consists of consolidated revenues less consolidated expenses, and if we require adjustments, they will be made to the individual revenue and expense accounts, not directly to net income.

Similarly, the consolidated balance sheet reflects consolidated retained earnings. We calculate the balance sheet amount for consolidated retained earnings as follows:

Beginning consolidated retained earnings
Plus: Controlling share of consolidated net income
(or minus a controlling share of consolidated net loss)
Less: Parent-company dividends
Ending consolidated retained earnings

In our workpaper format, we carry the controlling share of net income line down to the *Retained Earnings* section of the worksheet without further adjustment. We similarly carry the ending retained earnings row down to the *Balance Sheet* section, again without further adjustments or eliminations. Notice too that each row in the workpaper generates the consolidated amounts by adding together the parent and subsidiary account balances and then adding or subtracting the adjustments and eliminations as appropriate.

Parent retained earnings under the complete equity method of accounting is equal to consolidated retained earnings. Because Pep Corporation (Exhibit 4-1) correctly applies the equity method, its net income of $68,400 equals its controlling share of consolidated net income. Its beginning and ending retained earnings balances equal the $5,000 and $43,400 consolidated retained earnings amounts, respectively.

The first workpaper entry in Exhibit 4-1 is as follows:

a	**Income from Sap (– R, –SE)**	18,400	
	Dividends (+SE)		12,000
	Investment in Sap (–A)		6,400
	To eliminate income and dividends from Sap and return the investment account to its beginning-of-the-period balance.		

Recall that throughout the consolidation coverage in this text workpaper entries are shaded to avoid confusion with journal entries that are recorded by parents and subsidiaries. We eliminate investment income because the consolidated income statement shows the details of revenues and expenses rather than the one-line consolidation reflected in the Income from Sap account. We eliminate dividends received from Sap because they are mere transfers within the consolidated entity for which we prepare the consolidated statements.

The difference between income from a subsidiary recognized on the books of the parent and dividends received represents the change in the investment account for the period. The $6,400 credit to the Investment in Sap account reduces that account to its $88,000 beginning-of-the-period balance and thereby establishes reciprocity between the investment in Sap and Sap's stockholders' equity at January 1, 2011.

Here is a journal entry for workpaper entry b from Exhibit 4-1:

b	Noncontrolling interest share (−SE)	4,600	
	Dividends (+SE)		3,000
	Noncontrolling interest (+SE)		1,600
	To enter noncontrolling interest share of subsidiary income and dividends.		

Entry b incorporates the noncontrolling interest in a subsidiary's net income and the noncontrolling interest's share of dividends declared by the subsidiary directly into the consolidation workpaper. This approach explains all noncontrolling interest components through consolidation workpaper entries.

The portion of a subsidiary's net income not accruing to the parent is referred to as *noncontrolling interest share* throughout this text. Minority interest (income or expense) is the more-traditional term still sometimes found in published financial statements.

In this book, the term *noncontrolling interest* is used to reflect the balance sheet amount. Note that often noncontrolling interest or noncontrolling interest share does not appear in published, consolidated balance sheets or income statements because the amounts are immaterial.

GAAP recommends noncontrolling interest as better reflecting the complexities of the modern business world. Many firms create *special purpose entities* (SPEs), not surprisingly created for a special business purpose. For example, SPEs may be created to facilitate leasing activities, loan securitizations, research and development activities, hedging transactions, or other business arrangements. SPEs gained fame (or infamy) with **Enron Corporation**, which used these as a vehicle to set up energy futures trading and related business ventures. By excluding such ventures from consolidation, Enron was able to keep billions of dollars of debt off its balance sheet, hiding significant business risk from investors.

GAAP clarifies rules defining a *variable interest entity* as a subset of SPEs which should be included in preparing consolidated financial statements. Under GAAP, "the usual condition for a controlling financial interest is ownership of a majority voting interest." GAAP further clarifies, adding: "However, application of the majority voting interest requirement to certain types of entities may not identify the party with a controlling financial interest because the controlling financial interest may be achieved through arrangements that do not involve voting interests."[1] It is possible to achieve financial control of an entity with only a small equity voting interest through other contractual arrangements[1]. Chapter 11 discusses variable interest entities in greater detail. These voting, non–majority control situations are consistent with the GAAP preference for the controlling and noncontrolling, versus majority and minority interests, terminology.

Workpaper entry c in journal entry form is as follows:

c	Retained earnings—Sap (beginning) (−SE)	30,000	
	Capital stock—Sap (−SE)	60,000	
	Patents (+A)	20,000	
	Investment in Sap (−A)		88,000
	Noncontrolling interest (+SE)		22,000
	To eliminate reciprocal equity and investment balances, establish beginning noncontrolling interest, and enter unamortized patents.		

This entry eliminates reciprocal investment and equity balances, enters the unamortized patents as of the beginning of the year, and constructs beginning noncontrolling interest ($110,000 × 20%) at fair value as a separate item. Observe that entry c eliminates reciprocal investment and equity balances as of the beginning of the period and enters noncontrolling interest as of the same date. Therefore, the patents portion of the entry is also a beginning-of-the-period unamortized amount.

Many accountants prefer to eliminate only the parent's percentage of the capital stock and retained earnings of the subsidiary and to transfer the amount not eliminated directly to the noncontrolling interest. Although the difference is solely a matter of preference, the approach used

---

[1]For example, if an acquirer becomes the primary beneficiary in a variable interest entity.

here emphasizes that we eliminate all the individual stockholders' equity accounts of a subsidiary in the process of consolidation.

Entry d in the workpapers of Exhibit 4-1 enters the current year's patent amortization as an expense of the consolidated entity and reduces unamortized patents from its $20,000 unamortized balance at January 1 to its $18,000 amortized balance at December 31, 2011.

d	Expenses (E, –SE)	2,000	
	Patents (–A)		2,000
	To enter current amortization of patents.		

We need this workpaper entry to adjust consolidated expenses even though Pep amortized patents on its separate books under the equity method. Pep reflects amortization of the patents in its Income from Sap account, and workpaper entry a eliminated that account for consolidation purposes in order to disaggregate the revenue and expense components in reporting consolidated income.

Sequence of Workpaper Entries

The sequence of the workpaper entries in Exhibit 4-1 is both logical and necessary. Entry a adjusts the investment in Sap for changes during 2011, and entry c eliminates the investment in Sap after adjustment to its beginning-of-the-period balance in entry a. Entry c also enters unamortized patents in the workpaper as of the beginning of the period. Subsequently, entry d amortizes the patents for the current period and reduces the asset patents to its amortized amount at the balance sheet date. As we encounter additional complexities of consolidation, the sequence of workpaper adjustments and eliminations expands to the following:

1. Adjustments for errors and omissions in the separate parent and subsidiary statements

2. Adjustments to eliminate intercompany profits and losses

3. Adjustments to eliminate income and dividends from subsidiary and adjust the investment in subsidiary to its beginning-of-the-period balance

4. Adjustment to record the noncontrolling interest in subsidiary's earnings and dividends

5. Eliminations of reciprocal investment in subsidiary and subsidiary equity balances

6. Allocation and amortization of fair value differentials (from step 5)

7. Elimination of other reciprocal balances (intercompany receivables and payables, revenues and expenses, and so on)

Although other sequences of workpaper entries may be adequate in a given consolidation, the sequence just presented will always work. You should learn it and apply it throughout your study of consolidations.

We compute the noncontrolling interest reflected in the consolidated balance sheet as beginning noncontrolling interest plus noncontrolling interest share less noncontrolling interest dividends. If ownership in a subsidiary increases during a period, the noncontrolling interest computation will reflect the noncontrolling interest at the balance sheet date, with noncontrolling interest share and dividends also reflecting the ending noncontrolling interest percentages. Note that the noncontrolling interest reflects fair value.

Note that we always eliminate the investment in subsidiary balances when a subsidiary is consolidated. Although the investment in subsidiary account may be adjusted to establish reciprocity, it never appears in a consolidated balance sheet. Likewise, we always eliminate investment income from consolidated subsidiaries. We compute consolidated net income by deducting consolidated expenses from consolidated revenues. It is *not* determined by adjusting the separate net incomes of parent and subsidiary. We then allocate consolidated net income into the shares attributable to the controlling (parent) and noncontrolling interests.

Capital stock and other paid-in capital accounts appearing in a consolidated balance sheet are those of the parent. Under GAAP [2] the noncontrolling interest must be reported as a component of consolidated stockholders' equity.

Equity Method—Year Subsequent to Acquisition

Pep Corporation maintains its 80 percent ownership interest in Sap throughout 2012, recording income from Sap of $22,400 for the year (80 percent of Sap's $30,000 net income less $2,000 patents amortization). At December 31, 2012, Pep's Investment in Sap account has a balance of $104,800, determined as follows:

Investment cost January 1, 2011	$ 88,000
Income from Sap—2011	18,400
Dividends from Sap—2011	−12,000
Investment in Sap December 31, 2011	94,400
Income from Sap—2012	22,400
Dividends from Sap—2012	−12,000
Investment in Sap December 31, 2012	$104,800

The only intercompany transaction between Pep and Sap during 2012 was a $10,000 non-interest-bearing loan to Sap during the third quarter of the year.

Consolidation workpapers for Pep Corporation and Subsidiary for 2012 are presented in Exhibit 4-2.

There were no errors or omissions or intercompany profits relating to the consolidation, so the first workpaper entry is to eliminate income and dividends from Sap as follows:

a	Income from Sap (−R, −SE)	22,400	
	Dividends (+SE)		12,000
	Investment in Sap (−A)		10,400
	To eliminate income and dividends from Sap and return the investment account to its beginning-of-the-period balance.		

This entry adjusts the Investment in Sap account to its $94,400 December 31, 2011, balance and establishes reciprocity with Sap's stockholders' equity at December 31, 2011.

Entry b incorporates the noncontrolling interest in Sap's net income and the noncontrolling share of Sap's dividends:

b	Noncontrolling interest share (−SE)	5,600	
	Dividends (+SE)		3,000
	Noncontrolling interest (+SE)		2,600
	To enter noncontrolling interest share of subsidiary income and dividends.		

Entry c eliminates Investment in Sap and stockholders' equity of Sap as follows:

c	Retained earnings—Sap (−SE)	40,000	
	Capital stock—Sap (−SE)	60,000	
	Patents (+A)	18,000	
	Investment in Sap (−A)		94,400
	Noncontrolling interest (+SE)		23,600
	To eliminate reciprocal investment and equity balances, establish beginning noncontrolling interest, and enter unamortized patents.		

Entry c eliminates the Investment in Sap and stockholders' equity of Sap amounts at December 31, 2011, and enters the noncontrolling interest at December 31, 2011; therefore, the $18,000 investment's fair value difference reflects unamortized patents at December 31, 2011. Entry d amortizes this amount to the $16,000 balance at December 31, 2012:

d	Expenses (E, −SE)	2,000	
	Patents (−A)		2,000
	To enter current amortization.		

PEP CORPORATION AND SUBSIDIARY CONSOLIDATION WORKPAPER FOR THE YEAR ENDED DECEMBER 31, 2012 (IN THOUSANDS)			Adjustments and Eliminations		Consolidated Statements
	Pep	80% Sap	Debits	Credits	
Income Statement Revenue	$300	$ 75			$375
Income from Sap	22.4		a 22.4		
Expenses	(244)	(45)	d 2		(291)
Noncontrolling interest share ($28,000 × 20%)			b 5.6		(5.6)
Controlling share of Net income	**$ 78.4**	**$ 30**			**$ 78.4**
Retained Earnings Statement Retained earnings—Pep	$ 43.4				$ 43.4
Retained earnings—Sap		$ 40	c 40		
Add: Controlling share of Net income	78.4	30			78.4
Deduct: Dividends	(45)	(15)		a 12 b 3	(45)
Retained earnings— December 31	**$ 76.8**	**$ 55**			**$ 76.8**
Balance Sheet Cash	$ 45	$ 20			$ 65
Note receivable—Sap	10			e 10	
Other current assets	97	70			167
Investment in Sap	104.8			a 10.4 c 94.4	
Plant and equipment	300	100			400
Accumulated depreciation	(60)	(40)			(100)
Patents			c 18	d 2	16
	$496.8	$150			$548
Note payable—Pep		$ 10	e 10		
Liabilities	$ 70	25			$ 95
Capital stock	350	60	c 60		350
Retained earnings	76.8	55			76.8
	$496.8	$150			
Noncontrolling interest January 1 ($118,000 × 20%)				c 23.6	
Noncontrolling interest December 31				b 2.6	26.2
			158	158	$548

EXHIBIT 4-2

Equity Method— Workpaper for Year Subsequent to Acquisition

The final workpaper entry eliminates intercompany notes payable and notes receivable balances because the amounts are not assets and liabilities of the consolidated entity:

e	Note payable—Pep (–L)	10,000	
	Note receivable—Sap (–A)		10,000
	To eliminate reciprocal receivable and payable balances.		

The intercompany loan was not interest bearing, so the note receivable and the note payable are the only reciprocal balances created by the intercompany transaction. We would need additional eliminations for reciprocal interest income and interest expense and interest receivable and interest payable balances if the intercompany loan had been interest bearing.

Compare the consolidation workpaper of Exhibit 4-2 with that of Exhibit 4-1. Notice that the December 31, 2011, noncontrolling interest from Exhibit 4-1 is the beginning noncontrolling interest in Exhibit 4-2. Note that the unamortized patents amount in the consolidated balance sheet of Exhibit 4-1 is the beginning-of-the-period unamortized patents in Exhibit 4-2.

LOCATING ERRORS

LEARNING OBJECTIVE **3**

The last part of a consolidation workpaper to be completed is the consolidated balance sheet section. Most errors made in consolidating the financial statements will show up when the consolidated balance sheet does not balance. If the consolidated balance sheet fails to balance after recomputing totals, we should then check individual items to ensure that all items have been included. Omissions involving the noncontrolling interest share in the consolidated income statement and noncontrolling interest equity in the consolidated balance sheet occur frequently because these items do not appear on the separate-company statements. We check the equality of debits and credits in the workpaper entries by totaling the adjustment and elimination columns. Although proper coding of each workpaper entry minimizes this type of error, many accountants prefer to total the adjustment and elimination columns as a regular workpaper procedure.

EXCESS ASSIGNED TO IDENTIFIABLE NET ASSETS

LEARNING OBJECTIVE **4**

GAAP [3] requires firms to provide at least summary disclosures regarding the allocation of the purchase price of an acquired subsidiary, especially as related to acquired goodwill and other intangible assets. GAAP specifically requires firms to disclose, in the year of acquisition, the fair value of the acquired enterprise, a condensed balance sheet showing amounts assigned to major classes of assets and liabilities, the amounts of purchased research and development in process acquired, and total amounts assigned to major intangible asset categories. GAAP [4] further requires that the amount of goodwill be shown as a separate balance sheet line item (assuming it is material). Firms must also disclose material noncontrolling interests on the balance sheet and report noncontrolling interests' share of consolidated net income.

For example, **Walt Disney Company's** 2009 annual report discloses goodwill of $21.7 billion and other intangible assets of $2.2 billion on its balance sheet. The balance sheet also itemizes minority interest of $1.7 billion. In 2009, **GE** reported $65.6 billion of goodwill and $11.9 billion of other intangible assets. The separate listing of goodwill versus other intangible assets reflects new disclosure requirements for these assets under GAAP. [5]

The discussions thus far assume that firms assign any excess fair value either to previously unrecorded patents or to goodwill. Consolidation workpaper procedures for allocating an excess to specific assets and liabilities are similar to those illustrated for patents. The workpaper entries are more complex, however, because they affect more accounts and require additional allocation, amortization, and depreciation schemes. We illustrate these additional workpaper complexities here for Pat Corporation and its 90 percent-owned subsidiary, Sol Corporation.

Pat acquired its equity interest in Sol on December 31, 2011, for $360,000 cash, when Sol's stockholders' equity consisted of $200,000 capital stock and $50,000 retained earnings. This price implies a total fair value of $400,000 for Sol ($360,000 ÷ 90%). On the date that Sol became a subsidiary of Pat, the following assets of Sol had book values different from their fair values (amounts in thousands):

	Fair Value	Book Value	Undervaluation (Overvaluation)
Inventories	$ 60	$ 50	$ 10
Land	60	30	30
Buildings—net	180	100	80
Equipment—net	70	90	(20)
	$370	$270	$100

Based on this information, Pat assigns the $150,000 excess fair value to identifiable assets and goodwill, as shown in the following schedule:

	Undervaluation (Overvaluation)	Excess Allocation	Amortization Period
Inventories	$10	$ 10	Sold in 2012
Land	30	30	None
Buildings—net	80	80	20 years
Equipment—net	(20)	(20)	10 years
Goodwill—remainder		50	None
		$150	

The schedule also shows the amortization periods assigned to the undervalued and overvalued assets.

Consolidation at Acquisition

Exhibit 4-3 shows a consolidated balance sheet workpaper for Pat Corporation and Subsidiary immediately after the business combination on December 31, 2011. The excess fair value allocation is reasonably complex, so we use an unamortized excess account in the workpaper.

The first workpaper entry eliminates reciprocal Investment in Sol and stockholders' equity accounts of Sol, enters the 10 percent noncontrolling interest in Sol (based on fair value), and debits the unamortized excess account for the $150,000 excess fair value over book value. A second workpaper entry assigns the excess to identifiable net assets and goodwill. The amounts assigned in the second workpaper entry are the original amounts because Pat and Sol are being consolidated immediately after the acquisition.

Consolidation After Acquisition

Sol reports $60,000 net income for 2012 and declares dividends of $10,000 on June 1 and December 1 ($20,000 total for 2012). Sol pays the June 1 dividend on July 1, but the December 1 dividend remains unpaid at December 31, 2012. During 2012, Sol sells the undervalued inventory items, but the undervalued land and buildings and overvalued equipment are still in use by Sol at December 31, 2012. On the date of acquisition, the buildings had a remaining useful life of 20 years, and the equipment, 10 years.

During 2012, Sol borrows $20,000 from Pat on a non-interest-bearing note. Sol repays the note on December 30, but the repayment check to Pat was in transit and was not reflected in Pat's separate balance sheet at December 31, 2012.

EXHIBIT 4-3

Consolidation at
Acquisition

PAT CORPORATION AND SUBSIDIARY CONSOLIDATED BALANCE SHEET WORKPAPER ON DECEMBER 31, 2011 (IN THOUSANDS)

	Pat	90% Sol	Adjustments and Eliminations		Consolidated Balance Sheet
			Debits	Credits	
Assets					
Cash	$ 25	$ 5			$ 30
Receivables—net	90	25			115
Inventories	80	50	b 10		140
Land	60	30	b 30		120
Buildings—net	200	100	b 80		380
Equipment—net	135	90		b 20	205
Investment in Sol	360			a 360	
Goodwill			b 50		50
Unamortized excess			a 150	b 150	
Totals	$950	$300			$1,040
Liabilities and Equity					
Accounts payable	$130	$ 50			$ 180
Capital stock—Pat	700				700
Retained earnings—Pat	120				120
Capital stock—Sol		200	a 200		
Retained earnings—Sol		50	a 50		
Noncontrolling interest				a 40	40
Totals	$950	$300	570	570	$1,040

Pat made the following journal entries in 2012 to account for its investment in Sol:

July 1

Cash (+A)	9,000	
Investment in Sol (−A)		9,000

To record dividends from Sol ($10,000 × 90%).

December 31

Investment in Sol (+A)	43,200	
Income from Sol (R, + SE)		43,200

To record investment income from Sol, determined as follows:

Sol's net income	$60,000
Amortization of excess assigned to:	
Inventories (100% recognized)	−10,000
Buildings ($80,000 ÷ 20 years)	−4,000
Equipment ($20,000 ÷ 10 years)	+ 2,000
Adjusted Income from Sol for 2012	$48,000
Pat's Share ($48,000 × 90%)	$43,200

These entries show that Pat has used a one-line consolidation in accounting for its $43,200 income from Sol for 2012, but it has failed to recognize Sol's December 1 dividend declaration. Accordingly, Pat has overstated its investment in Sol at December 31, 2012, by $9,000 (90 percent of Sol's $10,000 December 1 dividend declaration). The consolidation workpaper for Pat and Subsidiary for 2012 in Exhibit 4-4 shows Pat's investment in Sol at $394,200 ($360,000 cost plus

PAT CORPORATION AND SUBSIDIARY CONSOLIDATION WORKPAPER FOR THE YEAR ENDED DECEMBER 31, 2012 (IN THOUSANDS)

EXHIBIT 4-4

Consolidation One Year After Acquisition

	Pat	90% Sol	Adjustments and Eliminations Debits	Adjustments and Eliminations Credits	Consolidated Statements
Income Statement					
Sales	$ 900	$300			$1,200
Income from Sol	43.2		c 43.2		
Cost of goods sold	(600)	(150)	f 10		(760)
Operating expenses	(190)	(90)	g 4	h 2	(282)
Noncontrolling interest share ($48,000 × 10%)			d 4.8		(4.8)
Controlling share of Net income	**$ 153.2**	**$ 60**			**$ 153.2**
Retained Earnings Statement					
Retained earnings—Pat	$ 120				$ 120
Retained earnings—Sol		$ 50	e 50		
Controlling share of Net income	153.2	60			153.2
Dividends	(100)	(20)		c 18	(100)
				d 2	
Retained earnings—December 31	**$ 173.2**	**$ 90**			**$ 173.2**
Balance Sheet					
Cash	$ 13	$ 15	b 20		$ 48
Accounts receivable—net	76	25			101
Note receivable—Sol	20			b 20	
Inventories	90	60			150
Land	60	30	f 30		120
Buildings—net	190	110	f 80	g 4	376
Equipment—net	150	120	h 2	f 20	252
Investment in Sol	394.2			a 9	
				c 25.2	
				e 360	
Dividends receivable			a 9	i 9	
Goodwill			f 50		50
Unamortized excess			e150	f150	
	$ 993.2	$360			$1,097
Accounts payable	$ 120	$ 60			$ 180
Dividends payable		10	i 9		1
Capital stock	700	200	e 200		700
Retained earnings	173.2	90			173.2
	$993.2	$360			
Noncontrolling interest January 1				e 40	
Noncontrolling interest December 31				d 2.8	42.8
			662	662	$1,097

$43,200 income less $9,000 dividends received), whereas the correct amount is $385,200. The overstatement is corrected in workpaper entry a of Exhibit 4-4:

a	Dividends receivable (+A)	9,000	
	Investment in Sol (−A)		9,000
	To correct investment balance for unrecorded dividends receivable.		

This entry is different from previous workpaper entries because it represents a real adjustment that should also be recorded on Pat's books.

Workpaper entry b adjusts for the $20,000 cash in transit from Sol to Pat at December 31, 2012:

b	Cash (+A)	20,000	
	Note receivable—Sol (−A)		20,000
	To enter receipt of intercompany note receivable.		

Workpaper entry b is also a real adjustment. Pat records this entry on its separate books, as well as in the consolidation workpaper. If Pat fails to record entries a and b as correcting entries on its separate books, it will record them in the normal course of events in 2013 when Pat receives the $9,000 dividend and the $20,000 note repayment checks from Sol. It is important that we always review year-end transactions between affiliates to make sure that both parent and subsidiary records properly reflect these events.

Entry c eliminates the income from Sol and 90 percent of Sol's dividends, and it adjusts the Investment in Sol account to its $360,000 beginning-of-the-period balance. Entry d incorporates the noncontrolling interest in Sol's net income and the noncontrolling share of Sol's dividends. Entry e eliminates the reciprocal Investment in Sol account and the stockholders' equity accounts of Sol, records the 10 percent noncontrolling interest at the beginning of the period, and enters the $150,000 unamortized excess:

c	Income from Sol (−R, −SE)	43,200	
	Dividends (+SE)		18,000
	Investment in Sol (−A)		25,200
	To eliminate income and dividends of Sol and return Investment account to beginning-of-the-period balance.		
d	Noncontrolling interest share (−SE)	4,800	
	Dividends (+SE)		2,000
	Noncontrolling interest (+SE)		2,800
	To enter noncontrolling interest share of subsidiary income and dividends.		
e	Retained earnings—Sol (−SE)	50,000	
	Capital stock—Sol (−SE)	200,000	
	Unamortized excess (+A)	150,000	
	Investment in Sol (−A)		360,000
	Noncontrolling interest—January 1 (+SE)		40,000
	To eliminate reciprocal investment and equity amounts, establish beginning noncontrolling interest, and enter unamortized excess.		

We assign the unamortized excess entered in workpaper entry e to identifiable assets and goodwill as of December 31, 2011, in entry f and amortize it in entries g and h. It is convenient to prepare a schedule to support these allocations and amortizations in preparing the workpaper entries and to provide documentation for subsequent consolidations:

	Unamortized Excess December 31, 2011	Amortization 2012	Unamortized Excess December 31, 2012
Inventories	$ 10,000	$10,000	$ —
Land	30,000	—	30,000
Buildings—net	80,000	4,000	76,000
Equipment—net	(20,000)	(2,000)	(18,000)
Goodwill	50,000	—	50,000
	$150,000	$12,000	$138,000

With the exception of the $10,000 excess assigned to cost of goods sold, the allocation in workpaper entry f of Exhibit 4-4 is the same as the allocation in workpaper entry b in the consolidated balance sheet workpapers of Exhibit 4-3. We assign the $10,000 excess assigned to inventories to cost of goods sold because the related undervalued inventories from December 31, 2011, were sold in 2012, thus increasing cost of goods sold in the 2012 consolidated income statement. We journalize workpaper entry f as follows:

f	Cost of goods sold (E, –SE)	10,000	
	Land (+A)	30,000	
	Building—net (+A)	80,000	
	Goodwill (+A)	50,000	
	Equipment—net (–A)		20,000
	Unamortized excess (–A)		150,000
	To assign unamortized excess to identifiable assets and goodwill.		

Workpaper entries g and h are necessary to increase operating expenses for depreciation on the $80,000 excess assigned to undervalued buildings and to decrease operating expenses for excessive depreciation on the $20,000 assigned to overvalued equipment. Entry g for recording depreciation on the excess assigned to buildings is procedurally the same as the adjustment for patents shown previously, except that we credit buildings—net of depreciation. We can also show the credit to accumulated depreciation. The $2,000 debit to equipment—net and credit to operating expenses in workpaper entry h corrects for excessive depreciation on the overvalued equipment. Procedurally, this adjustment is the exact opposite of entry g, which corrects for underdepreciation on the buildings:

g	Operating expenses (E, –SE)	4,000	
	Buildings—net (–A)		4,000
	To enter current depreciation on excess assigned to buildings.		
h	Equipment—net (+A)	2,000	
	Operating expenses (–E, + SE)		2,000
	To adjust current depreciation for excess assigned to reduce equipment.		

Workpaper entry i eliminates reciprocal dividends payable and dividends receivable amounts:

i	Dividends payable (–L)	9,000	
	Dividends receivable (–A)		9,000
	To eliminate reciprocal receivables and payables.		

The $1,000 dividends payable of Sol that is not eliminated belongs to the noncontrolling interest. We include it among consolidated liabilities because it represents an amount payable outside the consolidated entity.

LEARNING
OBJECTIVE 5

CONSOLIDATED STATEMENT OF CASH FLOWS

We prepare the consolidated statement of cash flows (SCF) from consolidated income statements and consolidated balance sheets, rather than from the separate parent and subsidiary statements. With minor exceptions, the preparation of a consolidated SCF involves the same analysis and procedures that are used in preparing the SCF for separate entities.

Exhibit 4-5 presents consolidated balance sheets at December 31, 2011 and 2012, and the 2012 consolidated income statement for Pol Corporation and its 80 percent-owned subsidiary, Sed Corporation. We use consolidated balance sheets at the beginning and end of the year to calculate the year's changes, which must be explained in the SCF. Other information pertinent to the preparation of Pol's consolidated SCF is as follows:

1. During 2012, Sed sold land that cost $20,000 to outside entities for $10,000 cash.
2. Pol issued a $300,000, two-year note on January 8, 2012, for new equipment.
3. Patents amortization from the Pol-Sed business combination is $10,000 per year.
4. Pol received $10,000 in dividends from its investments in equity investees.
5. Changes in plant assets not explained above are due to provisions for depreciation.

We prepare the SCF using a single concept: cash and cash equivalents. GAAP permits two presentations for reporting net cash flows from operations. The indirect method begins with the controlling share of consolidated net income and includes adjustments for items not providing or using cash to arrive at net cash flows from operations. The direct method offsets cash received from customers and investment income against cash paid to suppliers, employees, governmental units, and so on to arrive at net cash flows from operations. Although the GAAP has expressed a preference for the direct method of reporting net cash flows from operations [6] , most companies present a statement of cash flows using the indirect method.

EXHIBIT 4-5

Consolidated Balance
Sheets and Income
Statement for Pol and
Subsidiary

POL CORPORATION AND SUBSIDIARY COMPARATIVE BALANCE SHEETS AT DECEMBER 31 (IN THOUSANDS)

	2012	2011	Year's Change: Increase (Decrease)
Cash	$ 255	$ 180	$ 75
Accounts receivable—net	375	270	105
Inventories	250	205	45
Equity investments	100	95	5
Land	80	100	(20)
Buildings—net	200	220	(20)
Equipment—net	800	600	200
Patents	90	100	(10)
	$2,150	$1,770	$380
Accounts payable	$ 250	270	$(20)
Dividends payable	20	20	—
Note payable due 2014	300	—	300
Common stock	500	500	—
Other paid-in capital	300	300	—
Retained earnings	670	600	70
Noncontrolling interest—20%	110	80	30
	$2,150	$1,770	$380

CONSOLIDATED INCOME STATEMENT FOR THE YEAR ENDED DECEMBER 31, 2012

Sales			$750
Income from equity investees			15
Total revenue			765
Less expenses:			
Cost of goods sold		$ 300	
Depreciation expense		120	
Patents amortization		10	
Wages and salaries		54	
Other operating expenses		47	
Interest expense		24	
Loss on sale of land		10	(565)
Total consolidated income			200
Less: Noncontrolling interest share			(50)
Controlling share of consolidated net income			150
Consolidated retained earnings January 1			600
Less: Cash dividends paid			(80)
Consolidated Retained Earnings December 31			$670

EXHIBIT 4-5

Consolidated Balance Sheets and Income Statement for Pol and Subsidiary (*Continued*)

POL CORPORATION AND SUBSIDIARY CONSOLIDATED STATEMENT OF CASH FLOWS FOR THE YEAR ENDED DECEMBER 31, 2012 (IN THOUSANDS)

Cash Flows from Operating Activities		
Controlling share of consolidated net income		$150
Adjustments to reconcile controlling share of consolidated net income to net cash provided by operating activities:		
Noncontrolling interest share	$ 50	
Undistributed income—equity investees	(5)	
Loss on sale of land	10	
Depreciation on equipment	100	
Depreciation on buildings	20	
Amortization of patents	10	
Increase in accounts receivable	(105)	
Increase in inventories	(45)	
Decrease in accounts payable	(20)	15
Net cash flows from operating activities		165
Cash Flows from Investing Activities		
Proceeds from sale of land	$ 10	
Net cash flows from investing activities		10
Cash Flows from Financing Activities		
Payment of cash dividends—controlling interest	$ (80)	
Payment of cash dividends—noncontrolling interest	(20)	
Net cash flows from financing activities		(100)
Increase in cash for 2012		75
Cash on January 1, 2012		180
Cash on December 31, 2012		$255
Listing of Noncash Investing and Financing Activities		
Equipment Purchased for $300,000 by Issuing a two-year note payable		

EXHIBIT 4-6

Consolidated Statement of Cash Flows—Indirect Method

Consolidated Statement of Cash Flows—Indirect Method

Exhibit 4-6 presents a consolidated SCF for Pol Corporation and Subsidiary under the indirect method. This statement is based on the consolidated balance sheet changes and the 2012 consolidated income statement that appear in Exhibit 4-5 for Pol Corporation and Subsidiary. Exhibit 4-7 presents a statement of cash flows worksheet that organizes the information for statement preparation using the schedule approach. We prepare the consolidated SCF directly from the Cash Flow from Operations, Cash Flow—Investing Activities, and Cash Flow—Financing Activities columns of the worksheet in Exhibit 4-7.

Noncontrolling interest share of consolidated net income is an increase in the cash flow from operating activities because noncontrolling interest share increases consolidated assets and liabilities in exactly the same manner as consolidated net income. Similarly, we deduct noncontrolling interest dividends in reporting the cash flows from financing activities.

EXHIBIT 4-7

Worksheet for Consolidated SCF—Indirect Method

POL CORPORATION AND SUBSIDIARY WORKPAPERS FOR THE STATEMENT OF CASH FLOWS (INDIRECT METHOD) FOR THE YEAR ENDED DECEMBER 31, 2012 (IN THOUSANDS)

	Year's Change	Reconciling Items		Cash Flow from Operations	Cash Flow—Investing Activities	Cash Flow—Financing Activities
		Debit	Credit			
Asset Changes						
Cash	75					
Accounts receivable—net	105		k 105			
Inventories	45		l 45			
Equity investments	5		e 5			
Land	(20)	f 20				
Buildings—net	(20)	i 20				
Equipment—net*	200	h 100	g 300			
Patents	(10)	j 10				
Total asset changes	380					
Equity Changes						
Accounts payable	(20)		m 20			
Dividends payable	0					
Note payable due 2014*	300	g 300				
Common stock	0					
Other paid-in capital	0					
Retained earnings	70	a 150	b 80			
Noncontrolling interest	30	c 50	d 20			
Total equity changes	380					
Controlling share of consolidated net income			a 150	150		
Noncontrolling interest share			c 50	50		
Income—equity investees		e 5		(5)		
Loss of sale of land			f 10	10		
Depreciation on equipment			h 100	100		
Depreciation on buildings			i 20	20		
Amortization of patents			j 10	10		
Increase in accounts receivable		k 105		(105)		
Increase in inventories		l 45		(45)		
Decrease in accounts payable		m 20		(20)		
Proceeds from sale of land			f 10		10	
Payment of dividends—controlling		b 80				(80)
Payment of dividends—noncontrolling		d 20				(20)
		925	925	165	10	(100)
Cash flows from operations				$165		
Cash flows from investing activities				10		
Cash flows from financing activities				(100)		
Increase in cash for 2012 = cash change above				$ 75		

*Noncash investing and financing transaction: equipment purchased for $300,000 by issuing a two-year note payable.

Income and Dividends from Investees Under the Indirect and Direct Methods

Income from equity investees is an item that requires special attention in the consolidated SCF when using the indirect method. Income from equity investees increases income without increasing cash because the investment account reflects the increase. Conversely, dividends received from equity investees increase cash but do not affect income because the investment account reflects the decrease.

We deduct (or add) the net amount of these items from controlling share of net income in the Cash Flows from Operating Activities section of the SCF under the indirect method. We add an excess of dividends received over equity income. We would deduct an excess of equity income over dividends received. We simply report dividends received from equity investees as cash inflows from operating activities when using the direct method to prepare the SCF.

Consolidated Statement of Cash Flows—Direct Method

Exhibit 4-8 presents a consolidated SCF for Pol Corporation and Subsidiary under the direct method. This statement is identical to the one presented in Exhibit 4-6, except for cash flows from operating activities. Under the direct method, we convert the consolidated income statement items

POL CORPORATION AND SUBSIDIARY CONSOLIDATED STATEMENT OF CASH FLOWS FOR THE YEAR ENDED DECEMBER 31, 2012 (IN THOUSANDS)		
Cash Flows from Operating Activities		
Cash received from customers		$645
Dividends received from equity investees		10
Less: Cash paid to suppliers	$ 365	
Cash paid to employees	54	
Paid for other operating items	47	
Cash paid for interest expense	24	(490)
Net cash flows from operating activities		165
Cash Flows from Investing Activities		
Proceeds from sale of land	$ 10	
Net cash flows from investing activities		10
Cash Flows from Financing Activities		
Payment of cash dividends—controlling interests	$ (80)	
Payment of cash dividends—noncontrolling interests	(20)	
Net cash flows from financing activities		(100)
Increase in cash for 2012		75
Cash on January 1, 2012		180
Cash on December 31, 2012		$255
Listing of Noncash Investment and Financing Activities		
Equipment was purchased for $300,000 through the issuance of a two-year note payable		
Reconciliation of Controlling share of Consolidated Net Income to Net Cash from operating activities		
Controlling share of consolidated net income		$150
Adjustments to reconcile controlling share of consolidated net income to net cash provided by operating activities:		
Noncontrolling interest share	$ 50	
Undistributed income—equity investees	(5)	
Loss on sale of land	10	
Depreciation on equipment	100	
Depreciation on buildings	20	
Amortization of patents	10	
Increase in accounts receivable	(105)	
Increase in inventories	(45)	
Decrease in accounts payable	(20)	15
Net cash flows from operating activities		$165

EXHIBIT 4-8

Consolidated Statement of Cash Flows—Direct Method

that involve cash flows from the accrual to the cash basis, and we explain those items that do not involve cash in notes or schedules supporting the cash flow statement. Exhibit 4-9 shows a worksheet that organizes information for a consolidated statement of cash flows under the direct method. We prepare the SCF from the last three columns of the worksheet.

If you compare the cash flow statements in Exhibits 4-6 and 4-8, you should observe that the cash flows from investing and financing activities are identical. The significant differences lie in the presentation of cash flows from operating activities and the additional schedule to reconcile the controlling share of consolidated net income to net cash flows from operating activities under the

---

EXHIBIT 4-9

Worksheet for Consolidated SCF—Direct Method

POL CORPORATION AND SUBSIDIARY WORKPAPERS FOR THE STATEMENT OF CASH FLOWS (DIRECT METHOD) FOR THE YEAR ENDED DECEMBER 31, 2012 (IN THOUSANDS)

	Year's Change	Reconciling Items Debit	Reconciling Items Credit	Cash Flow from Operations	Cash Flow— Investing Activities	Cash Flow— Financing Activities
Asset Changes						
Cash	75					
Accounts receivable—net	105		a 105			
Inventories	45		c 45			
Equity investments	5		b 5			
Land	(20)	h 20				
Buildings—net	(20)	f 20				
Equipment—net*	200	e 100	d 300			
Patents	(10)	g 10				
Total asset changes	380					
Equity Changes						
Accounts payable	(20)		c 20			
Dividends payable	0					
Note payable due 2014*	300	d 300				
Common stock	0					
Other paid-in capital	0					
Retained earnings**	70					
Noncontrolling interest	30	i 50	j 20			
Total equity changes	380					
*Retained Earnings Changes***						
Sales	750	a 105		645		
Income—equity investees	15	b 5		10		
Cost of goods sold	(300)	c 65		(365)		
Depreciation on equipment	(100)		e 100			
Depreciation on buildings	(20)		f 20			
Patents amortization	(10)		g 10			
Wages and salaries	(54)			(54)		
Other operating expenses	(47)			(47)		
Interest expense	(24)			(24)		
Loss on sale of land	(10)		h 10			
Noncontrolling interest share	(50)		i 50			
Dividends paid by Pol	(80)		k 80			
Change in retained earnings	70					
Payment of dividends—controlling		k 80				(80)
Payment of dividends—noncontrolling		j 20				(20)
Proceeds from the land sale			h 10		10	
		775	775	165	10	(100)

*Noncash investing and financing transaction: equipment purchased for $300,000 by issuing a two-year note payable.
**Retained earnings changes replace the retained earnings account for reconciling purposes.

direct method. Although the presentation in Exhibit 4-8 under the direct method may be less familiar, it is somewhat easier to interpret.

PREPARING A CONSOLIDATION WORKSHEET

LEARNING
OBJECTIVE 6

In this section you will learn how to set up a three-part worksheet to prepare a consolidated income statement, retained earnings statement, and balance sheet. This worksheet follows the same basic pattern as that described in Chapter 3 to prepare a consolidated balance sheet at acquisition. Refer to Exhibit 4-10. We have two columns to record trial balance information for a parent and (in our example) a 70 percent-owned subsidiary. Most of the numbers in these two columns are simply copied from the individual company trial balances. Note that we record 100 percent of amounts from the subsidiary, even though the parent owns only 70 percent of the common stock. We will adjust for the 30 percent of the subsidiary not controlled by the parent (the noncontrolling interest) in computing our consolidated totals. We include two columns to record

EXHIBIT 4-10

Preparing a Complete Consolidation Worksheet

PARENT AND SUBSIDIARY CONSOLIDATION WORKSHEET FOR THE YEAR ENDED DECEMBER 31, 2011

(in thousands)	Parent	70% Subsidiary	Adjustments & Eliminations		Consolidated Statements
			Debits	Credits	
Income Statement					
Sales					$= B6 + C6 - D6 + E6$
Income from Subsidiary					$= B7 + C7 - D7 + E7$
Cost of goods sold					$= B8 + C8 - D8 + E8$
Operating expenses					$= B9 + C9 - D9 + E9$
Noncontrolling interest share					$= B10 + C10 - D10 + E10$
Controlling share of net income	$= SUM(B6 : B10)$	$= SUM(C6 : C10)$			$= SUM(F5:F10)$
Retained Earnings Statement					
Retained earnings—Parent					$= B13 + C13\text{-}D13 + E13$
Retained earnings—Subsidiary					$= B14 + C14\text{-}D14 + E14$
Controlling share of net income	$= B11$	$= C11$			$= F11$
Dividends					$= B16 + C16 - D16 + E16 - D17 + E17$
Ret earnings—ending	$= SUM(B13 : B16)$	$= SUM(C13 : C16)$			$= SUM(F13:F17)$
Balance Sheet					
Cash					$= B20 + C20 + D20 - E20$
Receivables—net					$= B21 + C21 + D21 - E21$
Inventories					$= B22 + C22 + D22 - E22$
Plant & equipment—net					$= B23 + C23 + D23 - E23$
Investment in Subsidiary					$= B24 + C24 + D24 - E24 + D25\text{-}E25$
					$= B26 + C26 + D26 - E26$
Total assets	$= SUM(B20 : B26)$	$= SUM(C20 : C26)$			$= SUM(F20:F26)$
Accounts payable					$= B28 + C28 - D28 + E28$
Other liabilities					$= B29 + C29 - D29 + E29$
Capital stock, $10 par					$= B30 + C30 - D30 + E30$
Other paid-in capital					$= B31 + C31 - D31 + E31$
Retained earnings	$= B18$	$= C18$			$= F18$
Total equities	$= SUM(B28 : B32)$	$= SUM(C28 : C32)$			
Noncontrolling interest					$= B34 + C34 - D34 + E34 - D35 + E35$
			$= SUM(D6 : D35)$	$= SUM(E6 : E35)$	$= SUM(F28:F35)$

the debits and credits for consolidation adjustments and eliminations. The final column provides calculations of the correct consolidated financial statement balances. Vertically, we divide the worksheet into three separate parts for the three financial statements we want to prepare. Notice the bold-faced items: **controlling share of net income**, **retained earnings (ending)**, **total assets**, and **total equities**. No amounts are input for these items. They are either calculated or are carried forward from a previous part of the worksheet.

Exhibit 4-10 shows spreadsheet formulae used in preparing the worksheet. Notice that most of these can be input using the COPY command available in the spreadsheet software. In the first two columns, controlling share of net income, retained earnings—ending, total assets, and total equities are simple summations of the relevant balances. Notice, too, that controlling share of net income in the retained earnings section of the worksheet and retained earnings in the balance sheet section are simple amount carryforwards from the income statement and retained earnings sections, respectively. The adjustments and eliminations columns each contain a single summation formula for the column totals. This is useful in verifying the equality of debits and credits (in other words, that you have not made any errors in posting your consolidation entries).

There are lots of formulae in the final consolidated statements column, but again most of these can be entered with the COPY command. As in the first two columns, controlling share of net income, retained earnings—ending, total assets, and total equities are simple summations of the relevant balances, and controlling share of net income in the retained earnings section and retained earnings in the balance sheet section are simply amount carryforwards from the income statement and retained earnings sections, respectively. Let's look at the formula for Sales (= B6 + C6 − D6 + E6). We simply sum parent-company sales plus subsidiary-company sales and then make any needed adjustments and eliminations. Notice that sales has a normal credit balance, so we subtract the debit adjustments (−D6) and add credits (+E6) to arrive at the consolidated total. We can simply copy our formula for all accounts having normal credit balances (i.e., revenues, liabilities, and equities).

We keep the same basic formula for cost of goods sold and any other expenses in the income statement portion of the worksheet. We do so because we enter the expenses as negative amounts.

If you look to the balance sheet section, our formula for consolidated cash (= B20 + C20 + D20 − E20) reflects the fact that cash has a normal debit balance that is increased by debit adjustments and decreased by credits. Formulae for the remaining asset balances are entered using the COPY command. Before leaving Exhibit 4-10, pay attention to the formula for the investment in subsidiary. This is a bit longer than the cash formula, and it simply illustrates how to adjust the formula when we have multiple debit and credit adjustments to the same account.

We will discuss the completion of the worksheet by working through a sample problem. Separate-company trial balances for Parent Corporation and Subsidiary Company at December 31, 2011, are summarized as follows (in thousands):

	Parent Corporation	Subsidiary Company
Sales	$3,100	$1,000
Income from Subsidiary	105	—
Accounts payable	300	180
Other liabilities	200	120
Capital stock, $10 par	1,500	500
Other paid-in capital	200	40
Retained earnings—January 1	650	110
	$6,055	$1,950
Cash	$ 455	$ 150
Accounts receivable—net	600	300
Cost of sales	2,000	650
Dividends	300	100
Inventory	240	200
Investment in Subsidiary—70%	490	—
Operating expenses	770	200
Plant & equipment—net	1,200	350
	$6,055	$1,950

Parent Corporation acquired 70 percent of the outstanding voting shares of Subsidiary Company for $455,000 on January 1, 2011, when Subsidiary's stockholders' equity at book value was $650,000. Note that the acquisition price implies that the total fair value of the subsidiary is

EXHIBIT 4-11

Building the Worksheet

PARENT AND SUBSIDIARY CONSOLIDATION WORKSHEET FOR THE YEAR ENDED DECEMBER 31, 2011 (IN THOUSANDS)

	Parent	70% Subsidiary	Adjustments & Eliminations Debits	Adjustments & Eliminations Credits	Consolidated Statements*
Income Statement					
Sales	3,100	1,000			4,100
Income from Subsidiary	105				105
Cost of goods sold	(2,000)	(650)			(2,650)
Operating expenses	(770)	(200)			(970)
Net income	435	150			585
Retained Earnings Statement					
Retained earnings—Parent	650				650
Retained earnings—Subsidiary		110			110
Net income	435	150			585
Dividends	(300)	(100)			(400)
Ret earnings—ending	785	160			945
Balance Sheet					
Cash	455	150			605
Accounts receivable—net	600	300			900
Inventories	240	200			440
Plant & equipment—net	1,200	350			1,550
Investment in Subsidiary	490				490
					0
Total assets	2,985	1,000			3,985
Accounts payable	300	180			480
Other liabilities	200	120			320
Capital stock, $10 par	1,500	500			2,000
Other paid-in capital	200	40			240
Retained earnings	785	160			945
Total equities	2,985	1,000			
					3,985

* Note the Consolidated statements column is before adjustments and eliminations.

$650,000 ($455,000 ÷ 70%). All of the assets and liabilities of Subsidiary were stated at fair values (equal to book values) when Parent acquired its 70 percent interest.

We enter the data into our worksheet in Exhibit 4-11. Exhibit 4-11 is our template worksheet from Exhibit 4-10, but we have added the example data in columns one and two. We begin with the income statement accounts. Note that we record revenues as positive amounts and expenses as negatives. Net income is then a simple summation of revenues and expenses. We carry the calculated Net income down to the *Retained Earnings* section of the worksheet with no further adjustment required.

Beginning-of-the-year retained earnings amounts come from the Parent and Subsidiary trial balances. We record dividends as negative amounts because they reduce retained earnings. Ending retained earnings is now a simple summation. We carry the calculated ending retained earnings down to the *Balance Sheet* section of the worksheet with no further adjustment required.

We record balance sheet amounts picked up from the Parent and Subsidiary trial balances. Notice that we record assets, liabilities, and equities as positive amounts. Total assets and total equities are simple summation functions.

Parent's $105,000 income from Subsidiary for 2011 consists of 70 percent of Subsidiary's $150,000 net income for 2011. Its $490,000 Investment in Subsidiary account balance at December 31, 2011, consists of the $455,000 investment cost plus $105,000 income from Subsidiary, less $70,000 dividends received from Subsidiary during 2011.

In our workpaper format, we carry the controlling share of net income line down to the retained earnings section of the worksheet without any further adjustment. We similarly carry the ending retained earnings row down to the balance sheet section, again without further adjustments or eliminations. Notice, too, that each row in the workpaper generates the consolidated amounts by adding together the Parent and Subsidiary account balances and then adding or subtracting the adjustments and eliminations as appropriate.

Finally, we are going to review the required consolidation adjustments and eliminations. We provide a separate Exhibit 4-12 to show the final consolidation worksheet, after posting the adjustments and eliminations. This is simply Exhibit 4-11, updated to reflect the entries that follow. Notice, too, that we have added some new accounts. We create noncontrolling interest share in the income statement section and noncontrolling interest in the balance sheet section and copy the relevant formulae for expense accounts and liabilities. The first workpaper entry in Exhibit 4-12 is the following:

a	Income from Subsidiary (−R, −SE)	105,000	
	Dividends (+SE)		70,000
	Investment in Subsidiary (−A)		35,000
	To eliminate income and dividends from subsidiary and return the investment account to its beginning-of-the-period balance.		

The difference between income from a subsidiary recognized on the books of the parent and the dividends received represents the change in the investment account for the period. The $35,000 credit to the Investment in Subsidiary account reduces that account to its $455,000 beginning-of-the-period balance and thereby establishes reciprocity between the Investment in Subsidiary and Subsidiary's stockholders' equity at January 1, 2011.

Here is a journal entry for workpaper entry b for Exhibit 4-12:

b	Noncontrolling interest share (−SE)	45,000	
	Dividends (+SE)		30,000
	Noncontrolling interest (+SE)		15,000
	To enter noncontrolling interest share of Subsidiary income and dividends.		

Entry b incorporates the noncontrolling interest in a Subsidiary's net income and the noncontrolling interest's share of dividends declared by Subsidiary directly into the consolidation workpapers.

Workpaper entry c in journal entry form is as follows:

c	Retained earnings—Sub. (beginning) (−SE)	110,000	
	Capital stock—Subsidiary (−SE)	500,000	
	Other paid in capital—Subsidiary (−SE)	40,000	
	Investment in Subsidiary (−A)		455,000
	Noncontrolling interest (+SE)		195,000
	To eliminate reciprocal equity and investment balances, and establish beginning noncontrolling interest.		

This entry eliminates reciprocal investment and equity balances, enters the unamortized excess of investment fair value over book value acquired as of the beginning of the year (zero in this example), and constructs beginning noncontrolling interest ($650,000 × 30 percent) as a separate item. Observe that entry c eliminates reciprocal investment and equity balances as of the beginning of the period and enters noncontrolling interest as of the same date.

Parent retained earnings under the complete equity method of accounting are equal to consolidated retained earnings. Because Parent correctly applies the equity method, its net income of $435,000 equals the controlling share of consolidated net income. Its beginning and ending retained earnings balances equal the $650,000 and $785,000 consolidated retained earnings amounts, respectively.

Our spreadsheet formulae compute the final consolidated statement totals for us in the final column. The worksheet is complete. You may want to practice creating the worksheet for a few problems to be certain you understand the mechanics. However, you will not need to create your

EXHIBIT 4-12

Completing the Worksheet

PARENT CORPORATION AND SUBSIDIARY CONSOLIDATION WORKSHEET FOR THE YEAR ENDED DECEMBER 31, 2011 (IN THOUSANDS)

	Parent	70% Subsidiary	Adjustments & Eliminations		Consolidated Statements
			Debits	Credits	
Income Statement					
Sales	3,100	1,000			4,100
Income from Subsidiary	105		a 105		0
Cost of goods sold	(2,000)	(650)			(2,650)
Operating expenses	(770)	(200)			(970)
Noncontrolling interest share			b 45		(45)
Controlling share of net income	435	150			435
Retained Earnings Statement					
Retained earnings—Parent	650				650
Retained earnings—Subsidiary		110	c 110		0
Controlling share of Net income	435	150			435
Dividends	(300)	(100)		a 70	
				b 30	(300)
Ret earnings—ending	785	160			785
Balance Sheet					
Cash	455	150			605
Receivables—net	600	300			900
Inventories	240	200			440
Plant & equipment—net	1,200	350			1,550
Investment in Subsidiary	490			a 35	0
				c 455	
Total assets	2,985	1,000			3,495
Accounts payable	300	180			480
Other liabilities	200	120			320
Capital stock, $10 par	1,500	500	c 500		1,500
Other paid-in capital	200	40	c 40		200
Retained earnings	785	160			785
Total equities	2,985	1,000			
Noncontrolling interest				c 195	210
				b 15	
			800	800	3,495

own worksheet for all problem assignments. We eliminate the mechanical drudgery, and allow you to focus on learning the advanced accounting concepts, by providing worksheet templates for many assignments. An icon in the assignment material indicates the availability of a template. The templates already include the data from the problem for the parent and subsidiary and the formulae for calculating consolidated balances. You can find the templates on the *Advanced Accounting* Web site.

SUMMARY

Workpapers are prepared to produce meaningful financial reports for a consolidated business entity. Preparation of meaningful consolidated financial statements is the objective. The workpapers are tools for organizing and manipulating data. If you clearly understand the objective, you can determine the proper amounts for the consolidated statements without preparing the workpapers.

Throughout the chapter it was assumed that the parent uses the complete equity method to account for its investment in the subsidiary. Alternative methods of parent accounting and necessary revisions to the eliminations and adjustments are discussed on the *Advanced Accounting* Web site.

The consolidated statement of cash flows can be prepared from the consolidated balance sheets and income statements.

QUESTIONS

1. If a parent in accounting for its subsidiary amortizes patents on its separate books, why do we include an adjustment for patents amortization in the consolidation workpaper?

2. How is noncontrolling interest share entered in consolidation workpapers?

3. How are the workpaper procedures for the investment in subsidiary, income from subsidiary, and subsidiary's stockholders' equity accounts alike?

4. If a parent uses the equity method but does not amortize the difference between fair value and book value on its separate books, its net income and retained earnings will not equal its share of consolidated net income and consolidated retained earnings. How does this affect consolidation workpaper procedures?

5. Are workpaper adjustments and eliminations entered on the parent's books? The subsidiary's books? Explain.

6. The financial statement and trial balance workpaper approaches illustrated in the chapter generate comparable information, so why learn both approaches?

7. In what way do the adjustment and elimination entries for consolidation workpapers differ for the financial statement and trial balance approaches?

8. When is it necessary to adjust the parent's retained earnings account in the preparation of consolidation workpapers? In answering this question, explain the relationship between parent retained earnings and consolidated retained earnings.

9. What approach would you use to check the accuracy of the consolidated retained earnings and noncontrolling interest amounts that appear in the balance sheet section of completed consolidation workpapers?

10. Explain why noncontrolling interest share is added to the controlling share of consolidated net income in determining cash flows from operating activities.

11. Controlling share of consolidated net income is a measurement of income to the stockholders of the parent, but does a change in cash as reflected in a statement of cash flows also relate to other stockholders of the parent?

EXERCISES

E 4-1 General questions

1. Workpaper entries normally:
   a   Are posted to the general ledger accounts of one or more of the affiliates
   b   Are posted to the general ledger accounts only when the financial statement approach is used
   c   Are posted to the general ledger accounts only when the trial balance approach is used
   d   Do not affect the general ledger accounts of any of the affiliates

2. Workpaper techniques assume that nominal accounts are:
   a   Open when the financial statement approach is used
   b   Open when the trial balance approach is used
   c   Open in all cases
   d   Closed

3. Most errors made in consolidating financial statements will appear when:
   a   The consolidated balance sheet does not balance
   b   Consolidated net income does not equal parent net income
   c   The retained earnings amount on the balance sheet does not equal the amount on the retained earnings statement
   d   Adjustment and elimination column totals do not equal

4. Net income on consolidation workpapers is:
   a   Adjusted when the parent uses the cost method
   b   Adjusted when the parent uses the equity method
   c   Adjusted in all cases
   d   Not an account balance and not subject to adjustment

5. On consolidation workpapers, individual stockholders' equity accounts of a subsidiary are:

   a   *Added to parent stockholders' equity accounts*
   b   *Eliminated*
   c   *Eliminated only to the extent of noncontrolling interest*
   d   *Eliminated to the extent of the parent's interest*

6. On consolidation workpapers, investment income from a subsidiary is:

   a   *Added to the investment account*
   b   *Added to the parent's beginning retained earnings*
   c   *Allocated between controlling and noncontrolling stockholders*
   d   *Eliminated*

7. On consolidation workpapers, the investment in subsidiary account balances are:

   a   *Allocated between controlling and noncontrolling interests*
   b   *Always eliminated*
   c   *Carried forward to the consolidated balance sheet*
   d   *Eliminated when the financial statement approach is used*

8. On consolidation workpapers, the controlling share of consolidated net income is determined by:

   a   *Adding net income of the parent and subsidiary*
   b   *Deducting consolidated expenses and noncontrolling interest share from consolidated revenues*
   c   *Making adjustments to the parent's income*
   d   *Subtracting noncontrolling interest share from parent net income*

9. On consolidation workpapers, consolidated ending retained earnings is determined by:

   a   *Adding beginning consolidated retained earnings and the controlling share of consolidated net income and subtracting parent dividends*
   b   *Adding end-of-the-period retained earnings of the affiliates*
   c   *Adjusting beginning parent retained earnings for subsidiary profits and dividends*
   d   *Adjusting the parent's retained earnings account balance*

10. Under the trial balance approach to consolidation workpapers, which of the following is used?

   a   *Unadjusted trial balances*
   b   *Adjusted trial balances*
   c   *Postclosing trial balances*
   d   *Either a or b, depending on the circumstances*

E 4-2 Consolidated statement items with equity method

Pan Corporation purchased 80 percent of the outstanding voting common stock of Sal Corporation on January 2, 2011, for $600,000 cash. Sal's balance sheets on this date and on December 31, 2011, are as follows:

SAL CORPORATION BALANCE SHEETS

	January 2	December 31
Inventory	$100,000	$ 40,000
Other current assets	100,000	160,000
Plant assets—net	400,000	440,000
Total assets	$600,000	$640,000
Liabilities	$100,000	$120,000
Capital stock	300,000	300,000
Retained earnings	200,000	220,000
Total equities	$600,000	$640,000

ADDITIONAL INFORMATION

1. Pan uses the equity method of accounting for its investment in Sal.

2. Sal's 2011 net income and dividends were $140,000 and $120,000, respectively.

3. Sal's inventory, which was sold in 2011, was undervalued by $25,000 at January 2, 2011.

REQUIRED

1. What is Pan's income from Sal for 2011?

2. What is the noncontrolling interest share for 2011?

3. What is the total noncontrolling interest at December 31, 2011?

4. What will be the balance of Pan's Investment in Sal account at December 31, 2011, if investment income from Sal is $100,000? *Ignore* your answer to 1.

5. What is consolidated net income for Pan Corporation and Subsidiary if Pan's net income for 2011 is $360,400? (Assume investment income from subsidiary is $100,000, and it is included in the $360,400.)

E 4-3

General problems

1. Peg Corporation owns a 70 percent interest in San Corporation, acquired several years ago at book value. On December 31, 2011, San mailed a check for $20,000 to Peg in part payment of a $40,000 account with Peg. Peg had not received the check when its books were closed on December 31. Peg Corporation had accounts receivable of $300,000 (including the $40,000 from San), and San had accounts receivable at $440,000 at year-end. In the consolidated balance sheet of Peg Corporation and Subsidiary at December 31, 2011, accounts receivable will be shown at what amount?

   Use the following information in answering questions 2 and 3.

   Pim Corporation purchased a 70 percent interest in Sar Corporation on January 1, 2011, for $28,000, when Sar's stockholders' equity consisted of $6,000 common stock, $20,000 additional paid-in capital, and $4,000 retained earnings. Income and dividend information for Sar is as follows:

	2011	2012	2013
Net income (or loss)	$2,000	$400	$(1,000)
Dividends	800	200	—

2. Pim reported income of $24,000 for 2013. This does not include income from Sar. What is consolidated net income for 2013?

3. What is Pim's Investment in Sar balance at December 31, 2013, under the equity method?

E 4-4

Equity method

The stockholder's equity accounts of Pen Corporation and Sin Corporation at December 31, 2010, were as follows (in thousands):

	Pen Corporation	Sin Corporation
Capital stock	$1,200	$500
Retained earnings	500	100
Total	$1,700	$600

On January 1, 2011, Pen Corporation acquired an 80 percent interest in Sin Corporation for $580,000. The excess fair value was due to Sin Corporation's equipment being undervalued by $50,000 and unrecorded patents. The undervalued equipment had a 5-year remaining useful life when Pen acquired its interest. Patents are amortized over 10 years.

The income and dividends of Pen and Sin are as follows:

	Pen 2011	Pen 2012	Sin 2011	Sin 2012
Net income	$340	$350	$120	$150
Dividends	240	250	80	90

REQUIRED: Assume that Pen Corporation uses the equity method of accounting for its investment in Sin.

1. Determine consolidated net income for Pen Corporation and Subsidiary for 2011.

2. Compute the balance of Pen's Investment in Sin account at December 31, 2011.

3. Compute noncontrolling interest share for 2011.

4. Compute noncontrolling interest at December 31, 2012.

E 4-5
General questions on statement of cash flows

1. In preparing a statement of cash flows, the cost of acquiring a subsidiary is reported:
a As an operating activity under the direct method
b As an operating activity under the indirect method
c As an investing activity
d As a financing activity

2. In computing cash flows from operating activities under the direct method, the following item is an addition:
a Cash dividends from equity investees
b Collection of principal on a loan made to a subsidiary
c Noncontrolling interest dividends
d Noncontrolling interest share

3. In computing cash flows from operating activities under the indirect method, the following item is an addition to the controlling share of consolidated net income:
a Noncontrolling interest dividends
b Noncontrolling interest share
c Income from equity investees in excess of dividends received
d Write-off of negative goodwill

4. In computing cash flows from operating activities under the direct method, the following item is an addition:
a Sales
b Noncontrolling interest share
c Cash received from customers
d Depreciation expense

5. Dividends paid as presented in a consolidated cash flow statement are:
a Parent dividends
b Subsidiary dividends
c Parent and subsidiary dividends
d Parent and noncontrolling interest dividends

E 4-6
Prepare cash flows from operating activities section

Information needed to prepare the Cash Flow from Operating Activities section of Par Corporation's consolidated statement of cash flows is included in the following list:

Amortization of patents	$ 16,000
Consolidated net income	150,000
Decrease in accounts payable	20,000
Depreciation expense	120,000
Increase in accounts receivable	105,000
Increase in inventories	45,000
Loss on sale of land	100,000
Noncontrolling interest share	50,000
Noncontrolling interest dividends	24,000
Undistributed income of equity investees	5,000

REQUIRED: Prepare the Cash Flows from Operating Activities section of Par's consolidated statement of cash flows under the indirect method.

E 4-7

Prepare cash flows from operating activities section

The information needed to prepare the Cash Flow from Operating Activities section of Pro Corporation's consolidated statement of cash flows is included in the following list:

Cash received from customers	$322,500
Cash paid to suppliers	182,500
Cash paid to employees	27,000
Cash paid for other operating items	23,500
Cash paid for interest expense	12,000
Cash proceeds from sale of land	60,000
Noncontrolling interest dividends	10,000
Dividends received from equity investees	7,000

REQUIRED: Prepare the Cash Flows from Operating Activities section of Pro's consolidated statement of cash flows under the direct method.

PROBLEMS

P 4-1

Calculations five years after acquisition

Pea Corporation purchased 75 percent of the outstanding voting stock of Sen Corporation for $2,400,000 on January 1, 2011. Sen's stockholders' equity on this date consisted of the following (in thousands):

Capital stock, $10 par	$1,000
Additional paid-in capital	600
Retained earnings December 31, 2010	800
Total stockholders' equity	$2,400

The excess fair value of the net assets acquired was assigned 10 percent to undervalued inventory (sold in 2011), 40 percent to undervalued plant assets with a remaining useful life of eight years, and 50 percent to goodwill.

Comparative trial balances of Pea Corporation and Sen Corporation at December 31, 2015, are as follows:

	Pea	Sen
Other assets—net	$3,765	$2,600
Investment in Sen—75%	2,340	—
Expenses (including cost of sales)	3,185	600
Dividends	500	200
	$9,790	$3,400
Capital stock, $10 par	$3,000	$1,000
Additional paid-in capital	850	600
Retained earnings	1,670	800
Sales	4,000	1,000
Income from Sen	270	—
	$9,790	$3,400

REQUIRED: Determine the amounts that would appear in the consolidated financial statements of Pea Corporation and Subsidiary for each of the following items:

1. Goodwill at December 31, 2015
2. Noncontrolling interest share for 2015
3. Consolidated retained earnings at December 31, 2014
4. Consolidated retained earnings at December 31, 2015
5. Consolidated net income for 2015
6. Noncontrolling interest at December 31, 2014
7. Noncontrolling interest at December 31, 2015

P 4-2
Workpapers and financial statements in year of acquisition

Pal Corporation acquired 70 percent of the outstanding voting stock of Sal Corporation for $91,000 cash on January 1, 2011, when Sal's stockholders' equity was $130,000. All the assets and liabilities of Sal were stated at fair values (equal to book values) when Pal acquired its 70 percent interest.

Financial statements of the two corporations at and for the year ended December 31, 2011, are summarized as follows (in thousands):

	Pal	Sal
Combined Income and Retained Earnings		
Statements for the Year Ended December 31		
Sales	$620	$200
Income from Sal	21	—
Cost of Goods Sold	(400)	(130)
Operating expenses	(154)	(40)
Net income	87	30
Add: Retained earnings January 1	130	22
Deduct: Dividends	(60)	(20)
Retained earnings December 31	$157	$ 32
Balance Sheet at December 31		
Cash	$ 91	$ 30
Receivables—net	120	60
Inventories	48	40
Plant and equipment—net	240	70
Investment in Sal	98	—
Total assets	$597	$200
Accounts payable	$ 60	$ 36
Other liabilities	40	24
Capital stock, $10 par	300	100
Other paid-in capital	40	8
Retained earnings	157	32
Total equities	$597	$200

REQUIRED

1. Prepare consolidation workpapers for Pal Corporation and Subsidiary for 2011.

2. Prepare a consolidated income statement and a consolidated balance sheet for Pal Corporation and Subsidiary.

P 4-3
Workpapers in year of acquisition (goodwill and intercompany transactions)

Pan Corporation acquired a 75 percent interest in Saf Corporation on January 1, 2011. Financial statements of Pan and Saf Corporations for the year 2011 are as follows (in thousands):

	Pan	Saf
Combined Income and Retained Earnings		
Statements for the Year Ended December 31		
Sales	$800	$200
Income from Saf	27.6	—
Cost of sales	(500)	(100)
Other expenses	(194)	(52)
Net income	133.6	48
Add: Retained earnings January 1	360	68
Deduct: Dividends	(100)	(32)
Retained earnings December 31	$393.6	$ 84

	Pan	Saf
Balance Sheet at December 31		
Cash	$ 106	$ 30
Accounts receivable—net	172	40
Dividends receivable from Saf	12	—
Inventories	190	20
Note receivable from Pan	—	10
Land	130	60
Buildings—net	340	160
Equipment—net	260	100
Investment in Saf	363.6	—
Total assets	$1,573.6	$420
Accounts payable	$ 170	$ 20
Note payable to Saf	10	—
Dividends payable	—	16
Capital stock, $10 par	1,000	300
Retained earnings	393.6	84
Total equities	$1,573.6	$420

REQUIRED: Prepare consolidation workpapers for Pan Corporation and Subsidiary for the year ended December 31, 2011. Only the information provided in the financial statements is available; accordingly, your solution will require some standard assumptions. Saf owned unrecorded patents having a fair value of $112,000, and a useful life of 10 years.

P 4-4
Consolidation workpapers from separate financial statements

Pal Corporation acquired a 75 percent interest in Sun Corporation on January 1, 2011, for $360,000 in cash. Financial statements of Pal and Sun Corporations for 2011 are as follows (in thousands):

	Pal	Sun
Combined Income and Retained Earnings Statements for the Year Ended December 31		
Sales	$800	$200
Income from Sun	36	—
Cost of sales	(500)	(100)
Other expenses	(194)	(52)
Net income	142	48
Add: Retained earnings January 1	360	68
Deduct: Dividends	(100)	(32)
Retained earnings December 31	$402	$ 84
Balance Sheet at December 31		
Cash	$ 118	$ 30
Accounts receivable—net	160	40
Dividends receivable from Sun	12	—
Inventories	190	20
Note receivable from Pal	—	10
Land	130	60
Buildings—net	340	160
Equipment—net	260	100
Investment in Sun	372	—
Total assets	$1,582	$420
Accounts payable	$ 170	$ 20
Note payable to Sun	10	—
Dividends payable	—	16
Capital stock, $10 par	1,000	300
Retained earnings	402	84
Total equities	$1,582	$420

REQUIRED: Prepare consolidation workpapers for Pal Corporation and Subsidiary for the year ended December 31, 2011. Only the information provided in the financial statements is available; accordingly, your solution will require some standard assumptions.

P 4-5
Workpapers in year of acquisition (excess assigned to inventory, building, equipment, patents and goodwill)

Par Corporation acquired a 70 percent interest in Sul Corporation's outstanding voting common stock on January 1, 2011, for $490,000 cash. The stockholders' equity (book value) of Sul on this date consisted of $500,000 capital stock and $100,000 retained earnings. The differences between the fair value of Sul and the book value of Sul were assigned $5,000 to Sul's undervalued inventory, $14,000 to undervalued buildings, $21,000 to undervalued equipment, and $40,000 to previously unrecorded patents. Any remaining excess is goodwill.

The undervalued inventory items were sold during 2011, and the undervalued buildings and equipment had remaining useful lives of seven years and three years, respectively. The patents have a 40-year life. Depreciation is straight line.

At December 31, 2011, Sul's accounts payable include $10,000 owed to Par. This $10,000 account payable is due on January 15, 2012. Separate financial statements for Par and Sul for 2011 are summarized as follows (in thousands):

	Par	Sul
Combined Income and Retained Earnings		
Statements for the Year Ended December 31		
Sales	$ 800	$700
Income from Sul	59.5	—
Cost of sales	(300)	(400)
Depreciation expense	(154)	(60)
Other expenses	(160)	(140)
Net income	245.5	100
Add: Retained earnings January 1	300	100
Deduct: Dividends	(200)	(50)
Retained earnings December 31	$ 345.5	$150
Balance Sheet at December 31		
Cash	$ 86	$ 60
Accounts receivable—net	100	70
Dividends receivable	14	—
Inventories	150	100
Other current assets	70	30
Land	50	100
Buildings—net	140	160
Equipment—net	570	330
Investment in Sul	514.5	—
Total assets	$1,694.5	$850
Accounts payable	$ 200	$ 85
Dividends payable	100	20
Other liabilities	49	95
Capital stock, $10 par	1,000	500
Retained earnings	345.5	150
Total equities	$1,694.5	$850

REQUIRED: Prepare consolidation workpapers for Par Corporation and Subsidiary for the year ended December 31, 2011. Use an unamortized excess account.

P 4-6

Workpapers (determine ownership interest, year after acquisition, excess assigned to land and patents)

Separate company financial statements for Pen Corporation and its subsidiary, Syn Company, at and for the year ended December 31, 2012, are summarized as follows (in thousands):

	Pen	Syn
Combined Income and Retained Earnings Statements for the Year Ended December 31		
Sales	$400	$100
Income from Syn	18	—
Cost of sales	(250)	(50)
Expenses	(100.6)	(26)
Net income	67.4	24
Add: Retained earnings January 1	177	34
Deduct: Dividends	(50)	(16)
Retained earnings December 31	$194.4	$ 42
Balance Sheet at December 31		
Cash	$ 18	$ 15
Accounts receivable—net	80	20
Dividends receivable from Syn	7.2	—
Note receivable from Pen	—	5
Inventory	95	10
Investment in Syn	219.6	—
Land	65	30
Buildings—net	170	80
Equipment—net	130	50
Total assets	$784.8	$210
Accounts payable	$ 85.4	$ 10
Note payable to Syn	5	—
Dividends payable	—	8
Capital stock, $10 par	500	150
Retained earnings	194.4	42
Total equities	$784.8	$210

ADDITIONAL INFORMATION

1. Pen Corporation acquired 13,500 shares of Syn Company stock for $15 per share on January 1, 2011, when Syn's stockholders' equity consisted of $150,000 capital stock and $15,000 retained earnings.

2. Syn Company's land was undervalued when Pen acquired its interest, and accordingly, $20,000 of the fair value/book value differential was assigned to land. Any remaining differential is assigned to unrecorded patents with a 10-year remaining life.

3. Syn Company owes Pen $5,000 on account, and Pen owes Syn $5,000 on a note payable.

REQUIRED: Prepare consolidated workpapers for Pen Corporation and Subsidiary for the year ended December 31, 2012.

P 4-7

Workpapers (year of acquisition, excess assigned to inventory, building equipment, and goodwill, intercompany balances)

Par Corporation acquired a 70 percent interest in Sol Corporation's outstanding voting common stock on January 1, 2011, for $490,000 cash. The stockholders' equity of Sol on this date consisted of $500,000 capital stock and $100,000 retained earnings. The difference between the fair value of Sol and the underlying equity acquired in Sol was assigned $5,000 to Sol's undervalued inventory, $14,000 to undervalued buildings, $21,000 to undervalued equipment, and $60,000 to goodwill.

The undervalued inventory items were sold during 2011, and the undervalued buildings and equipment had remaining useful lives of seven years and three years, respectively. Depreciation is straight line.

At December 31, 2011, Sol's accounts payable include $10,000 owed to Par. This $10,000 account payable is due on January 15, 2012. Par sold equipment with a book value of $15,000 for $25,000 on June 1, 2011. This is not an intercompany sale transaction. Separate financial statements for Par and Sol for 2011 are summarized as follows (in thousands):

	Par	Sol
Combined Income and Retained Earnings Statements for the Year Ended December 31		
Sales	$ 800	$700
Income from Sol	60.2	—
Gain on equipment	10	—
Cost of sales	(300)	(400)
Depreciation expense	(155)	(60)
Other expenses	(160)	(140)
Net income	255.2	100
Add: Retained earnings January 1	300	100
Deduct: Dividends	(200)	(50)
Retained earnings December 31	$ 355.2	$150
Balance Sheet at December 31		
Cash	$ 96	$ 60
Accounts receivable—net	100	70
Dividends receivable	14	—
Inventories	150	100
Other current assets	70	30
Land	50	100
Buildings—net	140	160
Equipment—net	570	330
Investment in Sol	515.2	—
Total assets	$1,705.2	$850
Accounts payable	$ 200	$ 85
Dividends payable	100	20
Other liabilities	50	95
Capital stock, $10 par	1,000	500
Retained earnings	355.2	150
Total equities	$1,705.2	$850

REQUIRED: Prepare consolidation workpapers for Par Corporation and Sol for the year ended December 31, 2011. Use an unamortized excess account.

P 4-8
Workpapers (excess assigned to land and goodwill)

Separate-company financial statements for Pun Corporation and its subsidiary, Son Company, at and for the year ended December 31, 2012, are summarized as follows (in thousands):

	Pun	Son
Combined Income and Retained Earnings Statement for the Year Ended December 31		
Sales	$400	$100
Income from Son	21.6	—
Cost of sales	(250)	(50)
Expenses	(100.6)	(26)
Net income	71	24
Add: Retained earnings January 1	181	34
Deduct: Dividends	(50)	(16)
Retained earnings December 31	$202	$ 42

	Pun	Son
Balance Sheet at December 31		
Cash	$ 18	$ 15
Accounts receivable—net	80	20
Dividends receivable from Son	7.2	—
Note receivable from Pun	—	5
Inventory	95	10
Investment in Son	226.8	—
Land	65	30
Buildings—net	170	80
Equipment—net	130	50
Total assets	$792	$210
Accounts payable	$ 85	$ 10
Note payable to Son	5	—
Dividends payable	—	8
Capital stock, $10 par	500	150
Retained earnings	202	42
Total equities	$792	$210

ADDITIONAL INFORMATION

1. Pun Corporation acquired 13,500 shares of Son Company stock for $15 per share on January 1, 2011, when Son's stockholders' equity consisted of $150,000 capital stock and $15,000 retained earnings.

2. Son Company's land was undervalued when Pun acquired its interest, and accordingly, $20,000 of the fair value/book value differential was assigned to land. Any remaining differential is goodwill.

3. Son Company owes Pun $5,000 on account, and Pun owes Son $5,000 on a note payable.

REQUIRED: Prepare consolidation workpapers for Pun Corporation and Subsidiary for the year ended December 31, 2012.

P 4-9
Workpapers (year of acquisition, excess assigned to inventory, equipment and patents, intercompany transactions)

Pas Corporation acquired 80 percent of Sel Corporation's common stock on January 1, 2011, for $210,000 cash. The stockholders' equity of Sel at this time consisted of $150,000 capital stock and $50,000 retained earnings. The difference between the fair value of Sel and the underlying equity acquired in Sel was due to a $12,500 undervaluation of Sel's inventory, a $25,000 undervaluation of Sel's equipment, and unrecorded patents with a 20-year life.

The undervalued inventory items were sold by Sel during 2011, and the undervalued equipment had a remaining useful life of five years. Straight-line depreciation is used.

Sel owed Pas $4,000 on accounts payable at December 31, 2011.

The separate financial statements of Pas and Sel Corporations at and for the year ended December 31, 2011, are as follows (in thousands):

	Pas	Sel
Combined Income and Retained Earnings		
Statements for the Year Ended December 31		
Sales	$200	$110
Income from Sel	17	—
Cost of sales	(80)	(40)
Depreciation expense	(40)	(20)
Other expenses	(25.5)	(10)
Net income	71.5	40
Add: Retained earnings January 1	75	50
Deduct: Dividends	(40)	(20)
Retained earnings December 31	$106.5	$ 70

	Pas	Sel
Balance Sheet at December 31		
Cash	$ 29.5	$ 30
Trade receivables—net	28	40
Dividends receivable	8	—
Inventories	40	30
Land	15	30
Buildings—net	65	70
Equipment—net	200	100
Investment in Sel	211	—
Total assets	$596.5	$300
Accounts payable	$ 40	$ 50
Dividends payable	100	10
Other liabilities	50	20
Capital stock, $10 par	300	150
Retained earnings	106.5	70
Total equities	$596.5	$300

REQUIRED: Prepare consolidation workpapers for Pas Corporation and Subsidiary at and for the year ended December 31, 2011.

P 4-10
Workpapers (year of acquisition, fair value/book value differentials, intercompany balances)

Pik Corporation acquired 80 percent of Sel Corporation's common stock on January 1, 2011, for $210,000 cash. The stockholders' equity of Sel at this time consisted of $150,000 capital stock and $50,000 retained earnings. The difference between the fair value of Sel and the underlying equity acquired in Sel was due to a $12,500 undervaluation of Sel's inventory, a $25,000 undervaluation of Sel's equipment, and goodwill.

The undervalued inventory items were sold by Sel during 2011, and the undervalued equipment had a remaining useful life of five years. Straight-line depreciation is used.

Sel owed Pik $4,000 on accounts payable at December 31, 2011.

The separate financial statements of Pik and Sel Corporations at and for the year ended December 31, 2011, are as follows (in thousands):

	Pik	Sel
Combined Income and Retained Earnings		
Statements for the Year Ended December 31		
Sales	$200	$110
Income from Sel	18	—
Cost of sales	(80)	(40)
Depreciation expense	(40)	(20)
Other expenses	(25.5)	(10)
Net income	72.5	40
Add: Retained earnings January 1	75	50
Deduct: Dividends	(40)	(20)
Retained earnings December 31	$107.5	$ 70
Balance Sheet at December 31		
Cash	$ 29.5	$ 30
Trade receivables—net	28	40
Dividends receivable	8	—
Inventories	40	30
Land	15	30
Buildings—net	65	70
Equipment—net	200	100
Investment in Sel	212	—
Total assets	$597.5	$300

	Pik	Sel
Accounts payable	$ 40	$ 50
Dividends payable	100	10
Other liabilities	50	20
Capital stock, $10 par	300	150
Retained earnings	107.5	70
Total equities	$597.5	$300

REQUIRED: Prepare consolidation workpapers for Pik Corporation and Sel at and for the year ended December 31, 2011.

P 4-11
Balance sheet (four years after acquisition, fair value/book value differentials)

Pil Corporation paid $170,000 for an 80 percent interest in Stu Corporation on December 31, 2011, when Stu's stockholders' equity consisted of $100,000 capital stock and $50,000 retained earnings. A summary of the changes in Pil's Investment in Stu account from December 31, 2011, to December 31, 2015, follows:

Investment cost December 31, 2011		$170,000
Increases		
80% of Stu's net income 2012 through 2015		112,000
		282,000
Decreases		
80% of Stu's dividends 2012 through 2015	$56,000	
80% of Amortization of excess fair value over book value:		
Assigned to inventories, $8,750 (sold in 2012)	7,000	
Assigned to plant assets, $22,500 (depreciated over a nine-year period) 2012 through 2015	8,000	
Assigned to patents, $31,250 (amortized over a five-year period) 2012 through 2015	20,000	91,000
Investment balance December 31, 2015		$191,000

Financial statements for Pil and Stu at and for the year ended December 31, 2015, are summarized as follows (in thousands):

	Pil	Stu
Combined Income and Retained Earnings Statements for the Year Ended December 31		
Sales	$300	$200
Income from Stu	25	—
Cost of sales	(180)	(140)
Other expenses	(50)	(20)
Net income	95	40
Add: Retained earnings January 1	255	100
Deduct: Dividends	(50)	(20)
Retained earnings December 31	$300	$120
Balance Sheet at December 31		
Cash	$ 41	$ 35
Trade receivables—net	60	55
Dividends receivable	8	—
Advance to Stu	25	—
Inventories	125	35
Plant assets—net	300	175
Investment in Stu	191	—
Total assets	$750	$300

	Pil	Stu
Accounts payable	$ 50	$ 45
Dividends payable	—	10
Advance from Pil	—	25
Capital stock	400	100
Retained earnings	300	120
Total equities	$750	$300

ADDITIONAL INFORMATION

1. The accounts payable of Stu at December 31, 2015, include $5,000 owed to Pil.

2. Pil advanced $25,000 to Stu during 2013. This advance is still outstanding.

3. Half of Stu's 2015 dividends will be paid in January 2016.

REQUIRED: Prepare workpapers to consolidate the balance sheets only of Pil and Stu Corporations at December 31, 2015.

P 4-12
Workpapers (two years after acquisition, fair value/book differentials, adjustments)

Pat Corporation acquired an 80 percent interest in Sci Corporation for $480,000 on January 1, 2011, when Sci's stockholders' equity consisted of $400,000 capital stock and $50,000 retained earnings. The excess fair value over book value acquired was assigned to plant assets that were undervalued by $100,000 and to goodwill. The undervalued plant assets had a four-year useful life.

ADDITIONAL INFORMATION

1. Pat's account receivable includes $10,000 owed by Sci.

2. Sci mailed its check for $40,000 to Pat on December 30, 2012, in settlement of the advance.

3. A $20,000 dividend was declared by Sci on December 30, 2012, but was not recorded by Pat.

4. Financial statements for Pat and Sci Corporations for 2012 follow (in thousands):

	Pat	Sci
Statements of Income and Retained Earnings for the Year Ended December 31		
Sales	$1,800	$600
Income from Sci	76	—
Cost of sales	(1,200)	(300)
Operating expenses	(380)	(180)
Net Income	296	120
Add: Retained earnings January 1	244	100
Less: Dividends	(200)	(40)
Retained earnings December 31	$ 340	$180
Balance Sheet at December 31		
Cash	$ 12	$ 30
Accounts receivable—net	52	40
Inventories	164	120
Advance to Sci	40	—
Other current assets	160	10
Land	320	60
Plant assets—net	680	460
Investment in Sci	560	—
Total assets	$1,988	$720

	Pat	Sci
Accounts payable	$ 48	$ 30
Dividends payable	—	20
Other liabilities	200	90
Capital stock	1,400	400
Retained earnings	340	180
Total liabilities and stockholders' equity	$1,988	$720

REQUIRED: Prepare consolidation workpapers for Pat Corporation and Subsidiary for 2012.

P 4-13

[Appendix] Workpapers for two successive years (equity method misapplied in second year)

Comparative adjusted trial balances for Ply Corporation and Ski Corporation are given here. Ply Corporation acquired an 80 percent interest in Ski Corporation on January 1, 2011, for $80,000 cash. Except for inventory items that were undervalued by $1,000 and equipment that was undervalued by $4,000, all of Ski's identifiable assets and liabilities were stated at their fair values on December 31, 2010. The remaining excess was assigned to previously-unrecorded intangibles, which had a 40-year remaining life.

Ski Corporation sold the undervalued inventory items during 2011 but continues to own the equipment, which had a four-year remaining useful life as of December 31, 2010. (All amounts are in thousands.)

	December 31, 2010		December 31, 2011		December 31, 2012	
	Ply	**Ski**	**Ply**	**Ski**	**Ply**	**Ski**
Cash	$100	$ 30	$ 24.7	$ 15	$ 26.7	$ 20
Trade receivables—net	30	15	25	20	45	30
Dividends receivable	—	—	4	—	4	—
Inventories	50	20	40	30	40	30
Plant and equipment—net	90	60	100	55	95	60
Investment in Ski	—	—	86.3	—	94.3	—
Cost of sales	100	40	105	35	110	35
Operating expenses	20	30	35	30	30	35
Dividends	10	5	10	5	15	10
	$400	$200	$430	$190	$460	$220
Accounts payable	$ 30	$ 35	$ 20.7	$ 15	$ 17.7	$ 25
Dividends payable	10	—	9	5	6	5
Capital stock	100	40	100	40	100	40
Other paid-in capital	60	20	60	20	60	20
Retained earnings	50	25	70	30	90.3	40
Sales	150	80	160	80	170	90
Income from Ski	—	—	10.3	—	16	—
	$400	$200	$430	$190	$460	$220

REQUIRED: Prepare consolidation workpapers for Ply Corporation and Subsidiary for 2011 and 2012 using the financial statement approach. (*Hint:* Ply Corporation's accountant applied the equity method correctly for 2011 but misapplied the equity method for 2012.)

P 4-14

[Appendix] Investment account analysis and trial balance workpapers

Pep Company paid $99,000 for a 90 percent interest in Sim on January 5, 2011, when Sim's capital stock was $60,000 and its retained earnings $20,000. Trial balances for the companies at December 31, 2014, are as follows (in thousands):

	Pep	**Sim**
Cash	$ 11	$ 15
Accounts receivable	15	25
Plant assets	220	180
Investment in Sim	136.8	—
Cost of goods sold	50	30
Operating expenses	25	40
Dividends	20	10
	$477.8	$300
Accumulated depreciation	$ 90	$ 50
Liabilities	80	30
Capital stock	100	60
Paid-in excess	20	—
Retained earnings	71.6	70
Sales	100	90
Income from Sim	16.2	—
	$477.8	$300

The excess fair value over book value acquired was assigned $10,000 to undervalued inventory items that were sold in 2011 and the remainder to patents having a remaining useful life of 10 years from January 1, 2011.

REQUIRED

1. Summarize the changes in Pep Company's Investment in Sim account from January 5, 2011, through December 31, 2014.

2. Prepare consolidation workpapers for Pep Company and Sim for 2014 using the trial balance approach for your workpapers.

P 4-15
[Appendix] Trial balance workpapers and financial statements in year of acquisition

Peg Corporation owns 90 percent of the voting stock of Sup Corporation and 25 percent of the voting stock of Ell Corporation.

The 90 percent interest in Sup was acquired for $18,000 cash on January 1, 2011, when Sup's stockholders' equity was $20,000 ($18,000 capital stock and $2,000 retained earnings).

Peg's 25 percent interest in Ell was purchased for $7,000 cash on July 1, 2011, when Ell's stockholders' equity was $24,000 ($15,000 capital stock, $6,000 retained earnings, and $3,000 current earnings—first half of 2010).

The difference between fair value and book value is due to unrecorded patents and is amortized over 10 years.

Adjusted trial balances of the three associated companies at December 31, 2011, are as follows:

	Peg	**Sup**	**Ell**
Cash	$ 18,950	$ 4,000	$ 1,000
Other current assets	40,000	11,000	10,000
Plant assets—net	120,000	14,000	20,000
Investment in Sup—90 percent	19,800	—	—
Investment in Ell—25%	6,450	—	—
Cost of sales	60,000	16,000	15,000
Other expenses	25,000	7,000	9,000
Dividends (paid in November)	10,000	3,000	5,000
Total Debits	$300,200	$55,000	$60,000

	Peg	Sup	Ell
Current liabilities	$ 25,000	$ 7,000	$ 9,000
Capital stock	150,000	18,000	15,000
Retained earnings	20,000	2,000	6,000
Sales	100,000	28,000	30,000
Income from Sup	4,500	—	—
Income from Ell	700	—	—
Total credits	$300,200	$55,000	$60,000

REQUIRED

1. Reconstruct the journal entries that were made by Peg Corporation during 2011 to account for its investments in Sup and Ell Corporations.

2. Prepare an income statement, a retained earnings statement, and a balance sheet for Peg Corporation for December 31, 2011.

3. Prepare consolidation workpapers (trial balance format) for Peg and Subsidiaries for 2011.

4. Prepare consolidated financial statements other than the cash flows statement for Peg Corporation and Subsidiaries for the year ended December 31, 2011.

P 4-16
Prepare cash flows from operating activities section (direct method)

The accountant for Pil Corporation collected the following information that he thought might be useful in the preparation of the company's consolidated statement of cash flows (in thousands):

Cash paid for purchase of equipment	$ 270
Cash paid for other expenses	450
Cash paid to suppliers	630
Cash received from customers	1,600
Cash received from sale of land	500
Cash received from treasury stock sold	400
Dividends from equity investees	40
Dividends paid to noncontrolling stockholders	20
Dividends paid to Pil's stockholders	50
Gain on sale of land	200
Income from equity investees	80
Interest received from short-term loan	5
Noncontrolling interest share	45

REQUIRED: Prepare the Cash Flows from Operating Activities section of the consolidated statement of cash flows for Pil Corporation and Subsidiaries using the *direct method* of presentation.

P 4-17
Prepare consolidated statement of cash flows using the direct method or indirect method

Comparative consolidated financial statements for Pes Corporation and its 90 percent-owned subsidiary, Sun Corporation, at and for the years ended December 31 are as follows:

**PES CORPORATION AND SUBSIDIARY COMPARATIVE
CONSOLIDATED FINANCIAL STATEMENTS**

	Year 2011	Year 2010	2011–2010
Income and Retained Earnings Statements for the Year			*Change*
Sales	$ 675	$600	$ 75
Cost of sales	(350)	(324.5)	(25.5)
Depreciation expense	(51)	(51)	0
Other operating expenses	(139)	(120.5)	(18.5)
Noncontrolling interest share	(5)	(4)	(1)

Controlling share of income	130	100	30
Add: Beginning retained earnings	190	130	60
Less: Dividends	(40)	(40)	0
Ending Retained Earnings	$ 280	$190	$ 90

Balance Sheets at December 31

Assets			
Cash	$ 55.5	$ 65	$ (9.5)
Accounts receivable—net	85	80	5
Inventories	140	120	20
Other current assets	100	81	19
Plant and equipment—net	674	600	74
Patents	19	19.5	(.5)
Total assets	$1,073.5	$965.5	$108
Equities			
Accounts payable	$ 85	$ 63	$ 22
Dividends payable	21	17	4
Long-term liabilities	35	46	(11)
Capital stock	500	500	0
Other paid-in capital	120	120	0
Retained earnings	280	190	90
Noncontrolling interest—10%	32.5	29.5	3
Total equities	$1,073.5	$965.5	$108

REQUIRED: Prepare a consolidated statement of cash flows for Pes Corporation and Subsidiary for the year ended December 31, 2011, using either the indirect method or the direct method. All changes in plant assets are due to asset acquisitions and depreciation. Sun's net income and dividends for 2011 are $50,000 and $20,000, respectively.

P 4-18
[Based on AICPA] Prepare consolidated statement of cash flows

The consolidated workpaper balances of Puh, Inc., and its subsidiary, Sto Corporation, as of December 31 are as follows (in thousands):

	2011	2010	Net Change Increase (Decrease)
Assets			
Cash	$ 313	$ 195	$118
Marketable equity securities at cost (MES)	175	175	—
Allowance to reduce MES to market	(13)	(24)	11
Accounts receivable—net	418	440	(22)
Inventories	595	525	70
Land	385	170	215
Plant and equipment	755	690	65
Accumulated depreciation	(199)	(145)	(54)
Patents—net	57	60	(3)
Total assets	$2,486	$2,086	$400
Liabilities and Stockholders' Equity			
Note payable, current portion	$ 150	$ 150	$ —
Accounts and accrued payables	595	474	121
Note payable, long-term portion	300	450	(150)
Deferred income taxes	44	32	12
Noncontrolling interest in Sto	179	161	18
Common stock—$10 par	580	480	100
Additional paid-in capital	303	180	123
Retained earnings	335	195	140
Treasury stock at cost	—	(36)	36
Total equities	$2,486	$2,086	$400

ADDITIONAL INFORMATION

1. On January 20, 2011, Puh issued 10,000 shares of its common stock for land having a fair value of $215,000.

2. On February 5, 2011, Puh reissued all of its treasury stock for $44,000.

3. On May 15, 2011, Puh paid a cash dividend of $58,000 on its common stock.

4. On August 8, 2011, equipment was purchased for $127,000.

5. On September 30, 2011, equipment was sold for $40,000. The equipment cost $62,000 and had a carrying amount of $34,000 on the date of sale.

6. On December 15, 2011, Sto Corporation paid a cash dividend of $15,000 on its common stock.

7. Deferred income taxes represent temporary differences relating to the use of accelerated depreciation methods for income tax reporting and the straight-line method for financial reporting.

8. Controlling share of net income for 2011 was $198,000. Sto's net income was $110,000.

9. Puh owns 70 percent of its subsidiary, Sto Corporation. There was no change in the ownership interest in Sto during 2010 and 2011. There were no intercompany transactions other than the dividend paid to Puh by its subsidiary.

REQUIRED: Prepare a consolidated statement of cash flows for Puh and Subsidiary for the year ended December 31, 2011. Use the *indirect method*.

P 4-19
Prepare consolidated statement of cash flows using either the direct or indirect method

Comparative consolidated financial statements for Pil Corporation and its 80 percent-owned subsidiary at and for the years ended December 31 are summarized as follows:

PIL CORPORATION AND SUBSIDIARY COMPARATIVE CONSOLIDATED FINANCIAL STATEMENTS AT AND FOR THE YEAR ENDED DECEMBER 31 (IN THOUSANDS)

	Year 2011	Year 2010	Year's Change 2011–2010
Income and Retained Earnings			
Sales	$2,600	$2,400	$200
Income—equity investees	60	50	10
Cost of sales	(1,450)	(1,408)	(42)
Depreciation expense	(200)	(150)	(50)
Other operating expenses	(470)	(462)	(8)
Noncontrolling interest share	(40)	(30)	(10)
Controlling share of income	500	400	100
Retained earnings, January 1	1,000	700	300
Dividends	(150)	(100)	(50)
Retained earnings, December 31	$1,350	$1,000	$350
Balance Sheet			
Cash	$ 430	$ 360	70
Accounts receivable—net	750	540	210
Inventories	700	700	0
Plant and equipment—net	1,800	1,500	300
Equity investments	430	400	30
Patents	190	200	(10)
Total assets	$4,300	$3,700	$600
Accounts payable	$ 492	$ 475	$ 17
Dividends payable	38	25	13
Long-term note payable	600	400	200
Capital stock	1,000	1,000	0
Other paid-in capital	600	600	0
Retained earnings	1,350	1,000	350
Noncontrolling interest—20%	220	200	20
Total equities	$4,300	$3,700	$600

REQUIRED: Prepare a consolidated statement of cash flows for Pil Corporation and Subsidiary for the year ended December 31, 2011. Assume that all changes in plant assets are due to asset acquisitions and depreciation. Income and dividends from 20 percent- to 50 percent-owned investees for 2011 were $60,000 and $30,000, respectively. Pil's only subsidiary reported $200,000 net income for 2011 and declared $100,000 in dividends during the year. Patent amortization for 2011 is $10,000.

INTERNET ASSIGNMENT

Delta Airlines completed a merger with *Northwest Airlines* in 2008. Visit Delta's Web site and download a copy of its 2009 annual report. Review the financial statements and accompanying notes for evidence of current and past acquisition activities.

   a. What amounts does Delta report for goodwill and other intangible assets at December 31, 2009?
   b. Summarize Delta's intangible assets from recent acquisitions.
   c. Briefly summarize Delta's amortization policies related to intangible assets. What accounting methods and lives are assigned to the assets?
   d. Does Delta report material balance sheet or income statement amounts for noncontrolling interests in 2009?

APPENDIX

Trial Balance Workpaper Format

LEARNING OBJECTIVE **7**

The main text of Chapter 4 discusses preparation of consolidated statements using a workpaper format called the financial statement approach. This appendix presents an alternative workpaper format using parent- and subsidiary-company trial balances.

The trial balance approach to consolidation workpapers brings together the adjusted trial balances for affiliated companies. Both the financial statement approach and the trial balance approach generate the same information, so the selection is based on user preference. If completed financial statements are available, the financial statement approach is easier to use because it provides measurements of parent and subsidiary income, retained earnings, assets, and equities that are needed in the consolidating process. If the accountant is given adjusted trial balances to consolidate, the trial balance approach may be more convenient.

Workpaper entries illustrated in this chapter are designed for convenient switching between the financial statement and trial balance approaches for consolidation workpapers. Recall that we adjust or eliminate account balances. Net income is not an account balance, so it is not subject to adjustment. We assume all nominal accounts are open to permit adjustment. The only retained earnings amount that appears in an adjusted trial balance is the beginning retained earnings amount. Therefore, the adjustments and eliminations are exactly the same whether we use the trial balance approach or the financial statement approach. This is so because we are working with beginning retained earnings and adjusting actual account balances.

Consolidation Example—Trial Balance Format and Equity Method

Exhibit 4-13 illustrates consolidation workpapers using the trial balance format for Pib Corporation and its 90 percent-owned subsidiary, Sad Corporation. Pib acquired its interest in Sad on January 1, 2011, at a price $14,000 in excess of Sad's total $40,000 book value, and it assigned the excess to patents with a 10-year amortization period.

EXHIBIT 4-13

Trial Balance Approach for Workpapers

PIB CORPORATION AND SUBSIDIARY CONSOLIDATION WORKPAPER FOR THE YEAR ENDED DECEMBER 31, 2012 (IN THOUSANDS)

	Pib	90% Sad	Adjustments and Eliminations		Income Statement	Retained Earnings	Balance Sheet
Debits							
Cash	$ 6.8	$ 20					$ 26.8
Accounts receivable	30	15		f 5			40
Inventories	50	25					75
Plant and equipment	75	45					120
Investment in Sad	68.4			b 7.2			
				d 61.2			
Cost of goods sold	80	30		a 14	$(96)		
Operating expenses	19.6	20	e 2		(41.6)		
Dividends	15	10		b 9		$(15)	
				c 1			
Patents			d 18	e 2			16
	$344.8	$165					$277.8
Credits							
Accumulated depreciation	$ 25	$ 11					$ 36
Accounts payable	45	34	f 5				74
Common stock	100	30	d 30				100
Retained earnings	38.6	20	d 20			38.6	
Sales	120	70	a 14		176		
Income from Sad	16.2		b 16.2				
	$344.8	$165					
Noncontrolling interest January 1				d 6.8			
Noncontrolling Interest Share ($18,000 × 10%)			c 1.8		(1.8)		
Controlling share of Consolidated net income					$36.6	36.6	
Consolidated retained earnings December 31						$ 60.2	60.2
Noncontrolling interest December 31 (6.8 + .8)				c 0.8			7.6
			107	107			$277.8

A summary of changes in Pib's Investment in Sad account from the date of acquisition to December 31, 2012, the report date, is as follows:

Investment cost January 1, 2011	$54,000
Add: Income—2011 (90% of Sad's $10,000 net income less $2,000 amortization of patents)	7,200
Investment balance December 31, 2011	61,200
Add: Income—2012 (90% of Sad's $20,000 net income less $2,000 amortization of patents)	16,200
Deduct: Dividends received from Sad (90% × $10,000)	–9,000
Investment balance December 31, 2012	$68,400

The workpapers presented in Exhibit 4-13 reflect the additional assumptions that Pib sold merchandise to Sad during 2012 for $14,000, and that, as of December 31, 2012, Sad owed Pib $5,000 from the sale. Sad sold the merchandise to its customers, so the consolidated entity realized all profit from the sale during 2012.

Separate adjusted trial balances are presented in the first two columns of Exhibit 4-13. As shown in the exhibit, debit-balance accounts are presented first and totaled, and credit-balance accounts are presented and totaled below the debit-balance accounts. Separate lines are added at the bottom of the list of accounts for Noncontrolling Interest Beginning of Year, Noncontrolling Interest Share, and Noncontrolling Interest End of Year.

The workpaper entries to prepare consolidated financial statements using the trial balance are the same as those for the financial statement approach. However, we classify the accounts in a trial balance according to their debit and credit balances, so the locations of the accounts vary from those found in the financial statement format. Also, the trial balance includes only beginning-of-the-period retained earnings amounts.

Workpaper entries to consolidate the trial balances of Pib and Subsidiary at December 31, 2012, are as follows:

a	Sales (–R, –SE)	14,000	
	Cost of goods sold (–E, + SE)		14,000
	To eliminate reciprocal sales and cost of sales from intercompany purchases.		
b	Income from Sad (–R, –SE)	16,200	
	Dividends (+SE)		9,000
	Investment in Sad (–A)		7,200
	To eliminate income and dividends from Sad and adjust the investment account to its beginning-of-the-year amount.		
c	Noncontrolling interest share (–SE)	1,800	
	Dividends (+SE)		1,000
	Noncontrolling interest (+SE)		800
	To enter noncontrolling interest share of subsidiary income and dividends.		
d	Common stock—Sad (–SE)	30,000	
	Retained earnings—Sad (–SE)	20,000	
	Patents (+A)	18,000	
	Investment in Sad (–A)		61,200
	Noncontrolling interest (10%) (+SE)		6,800
	To eliminate reciprocal investment in Sad and equity amounts of Sad, record beginning noncontrolling interest, and enter unamortized patents.		
e	Operating expenses (E, –SE)	2,000	
	Patents (–A)		2,000
	To record current amortization of patents as an expense.		
f	Accounts payable (–L)	5,000	
	Accounts receivable (–A)		5,000
	To eliminate reciprocal accounts payable and receivable balances.		

After entering all adjustments and eliminations in the workpapers, we carry items not eliminated to the Income Statement, Retained Earnings Statement, or Balance Sheet columns. Next, we take noncontrolling interest share from entry c and include it in the Income Statement column as a deduction.

Here we can see an inconvenience of the trial balance workpaper approach. We must compute Sad's $20,000 net income from the revenue and expense data and adjust for the patent amortization of $2,000 before multiplying by the noncontrolling interest percentage. We computed noncontrolling interest share directly when we used the financial statement workpaper approach.

We total the Consolidated Income Statement column and carry the total to the Consolidated Retained Earnings Statement column. We calculate noncontrolling interest at December 31 (6.8 + .8 = 7.6). We next total the consolidated Retained Earnings Statement column and carry that total to the consolidated Balance Sheet column. Finally, we total the consolidated Balance Sheet debits and credits and complete the workpaper. We prepare the consolidated financial statements directly from the consolidated Income Statement, consolidated Retained Earnings Statement, and consolidated Balance Sheet columns.

REFERENCES TO THE AUTHORITATIVE LITERATURE

[1] FASB ASC 810-10-05, ASC 810-10-15. Originally *FASB Interpretation No. 46 (Revised)*. "Consolidation of Variable Interest Entities: An Interpretation of ARB No 51." Norwalk, CT: Financial Accounting Standards Board, December 2003.

[2] FASB ASC 810-10-05. Originally *Statement of Financial Accounting Standards No. 141(R)*. "Business Combinations." Norwalk, CT: Financial Accounting Standards Board, 2007.

[3] FASB ASC 805-10-55-25. Originally *Statement of Financial Accounting Standards No. 141(R)*. "Business Combinations." Norwalk, CT: Financial Accounting Standards Board, 2007.

[4] FASB ASC 350-10-05. Originally *Statement of Financial Accounting Standards No. 142*. "Goodwill and Other Intangible Assets." Stamford, CT: Financial Accounting Standards Board, 2001.

[5] FASB ASC 350-10-05. Originally *Statement of Financial Accounting Standards No. 142*. "Goodwill and Other Intangible Assets." Stamford, CT: Financial Accounting Standards Board, 2001.

[6] FASB ASC 230-10-45-25. Originally *Statement of Financial Accounting Standards No. 95*. "Statement of Cash Flows." Stamford, CT: Financial Accounting Standards Board, 1987.

5 CHAPTER

Intercompany Profit Transactions—Inventories

W e prepare consolidated statements to show the financial position and the results of operations of two or more affiliates as if they were one entity. Therefore, we eliminate the effects of transactions between the affiliates (referred to as *intercompany transactions*) from consolidated financial statements.

Intercompany transactions may result in reciprocal account balances on the books of the affiliates. For example, intercompany sales transactions produce reciprocal sales and purchases (or cost of goods sold) balances, as well as reciprocal balances for accounts receivable and accounts payable. Intercompany loan transactions produce reciprocal notes receivable and payable balances, as well as reciprocal interest income and expense balances. These intercompany transactions are intracompany transactions from the viewpoint of the consolidated entity; therefore, we eliminate their effects in the consolidation process.

GAAP concisely summarizes consolidation procedures:

> *In the preparation of consolidated financial statements, intercompany balances and transactions shall be eliminated. This includes intercompany open account balances, security holdings, sales and purchases, interest, dividends, etc. As consolidated financial statements are based on the assumption that they represent the financial position and operating results of a single economic entity, such statements should not include gain or loss on transactions among the entities in the consolidated group. Accordingly, any intercompany income or loss on assets remaining within the consolidated group shall be eliminated; the concept usually applied for this purpose is profit or loss.* [1]

The reason we eliminate intercompany profits and losses is that the management of the parent controls all intercompany transactions, including authorization and pricing, without arm's-length bargaining between the affiliates. In eliminating the effect of intercompany profits and losses from consolidated statements, however, the issue is not whether the intercompany transactions were or were not at arm's length. *The objective is to show the income and financial position of the consolidated entity as they would have appeared if the intercompany transactions had never taken place*, irrespective of the amounts involved in such transactions. The same reasoning applies to the measurement of the investment account and investment income under a one-line consolidation. In the case of a one-line consolidation, however, evidence that intercompany transactions were not at arm's length may necessitate additional adjustments for fair presentation of the parent's income and financial position in separate parent financial statements. [2]

LEARNING OBJECTIVES

1 Understand the impact of intercompany profit in inventories on preparing consolidation workpapers.

2 Apply the concepts of upstream versus downstream inventory transfers.

3 Defer unrealized inventory profits remaining in the ending inventory.

4 Recognize realized, previously deferred inventory profits in the beginning inventory.

5 Adjust calculations of noncontrolling interest amounts in the presence of intercompany inventory profits.

6 Electronic supplement: Understand differences in consolidation workpaper techniques related to intercompany inventory profits when the parent company uses either an incomplete equity method or the cost method.

Most intercompany transactions creating gains and losses can be grouped as inventory items, plant assets, and bonds. Consolidation procedures for inventory items are discussed in this chapter, and those for plant assets and bonds are covered in subsequent chapters. Although the discussion and illustrations in this chapter relate to intercompany profit situations, the examples also provide a basis for analyzing and accounting for intercompany losses. Tax considerations are covered in Chapter 10.

LEARNING OBJECTIVE **1**

INTERCOMPANY INVENTORY TRANSACTIONS

Firms recognize revenue when it is realized, that is, when it is earned. For revenue to be earned from the viewpoint of the consolidated entity, there must be a sale to outside entities. Revenue on sales between affiliates cannot be recognized until merchandise is sold outside of the consolidated entity. No consolidated income results from transfers between affiliates. The sale of inventory items by one company to an affiliate produces reciprocal sales and purchases accounts when the purchaser has a periodic inventory system, and reciprocal sales and cost of goods sold accounts when the purchaser uses a perpetual inventory system. We eliminate reciprocal sales and cost of goods sold (or purchases) amounts in preparing a consolidated income statement in order to report sales and cost of goods sold for the consolidated entity; eliminating equal sales and cost of goods sold has no effect on consolidated net income.

As mentioned in Chapter 1, vertical integration of operating activities is often a prime motivation for business combinations. **Walt Disney's** 2009 annual report makes some related disclosures in *Note 1, Segments*. Here we find that the studio entertainment segment generated intersegment revenues of $120 million. Disney does not offer any evidence about how they price these intersegment transfers, but they eliminate them in consolidation.

Segment information presented in the **The Coca-Cola Company and Subsidiaries** 2009 annual report (p. 120) discloses elimination of intersegment sales of $1.85 billion. Similarly, **Chevron Corporation** discloses elimination of intersegment sales of $30.4 billion (2009 annual report, p. 49).

Elimination of Intercompany Purchases and Sales

We eliminate intercompany sales and purchases (or cost of goods sold) in the consolidation process in order to report consolidated sales and purchases (or cost of goods sold) at amounts purchased from and sold to outside entities. When a periodic inventory system is used, the workpaper entry to eliminate intercompany sales and purchases is simply a debit to sales and a credit to purchases. The workpaper elimination under a perpetual inventory system (used throughout this book) is a debit to sales and a credit to cost of goods sold. The reason is that a perpetual inventory system includes intercompany purchases in a separate cost of goods sold account of the purchasing affiliate when it is sold to outside third parties. These observations are illustrated for Pin Corporation and its subsidiary, Sep Corporation.

Pin Corporation formed a subsidiary, Sep Corporation, in 2011 to retail a special line of Pin's merchandise. All Sep's purchases are made from Pin Corporation at 20 percent above Pin's cost. During 2011, Pin sold merchandise that cost $20,000 to Sep for $24,000, and Sep sold all the merchandise to its customers for $30,000. Both Pin and Sep record journal entries relating to the merchandise on their separate books, as follows:

PIN'S BOOKS

Inventory (+A)	20,000	
Accounts payable (+L)		20,000
To record purchases on account from other entities.		
Accounts receivable—Sep (+A)	24,000	
Sales (R, +SE)		24,000
To record intercompany sales to Sep.		
Cost of sales (E, −SE)	20,000	
Inventory (−A)		20,000
To record cost of sales to Sep.		

SEP'S BOOKS

Inventory (+A)	24,000	
Accounts payable—Pin (+L)		24,000
To record intercompany purchases from Pin.		
Accounts receivable (+A)	30,000	
Sales (R, +SE)		30,000
To record sales to customers outside the consolidated entity.		
Cost of sales (E, −SE)	24,000	
Inventory (−A)		24,000
To record cost of sales to customers.		

At year-end 2011, Pin's sales include $24,000 sold to Sep, and its cost of sales includes the $20,000 cost of merchandise transferred to Sep. Sep's sales consist of $30,000 in merchandise sold to other entities, and its cost of sales consists of the $24,000 transfer price from Pin. Pin and Sep are considered one entity for reporting purposes, so combined sales and cost of sales are overstated by $24,000. We eliminate that overstatement in the consolidation workpapers, where measurements for consolidated sales and cost of sales are finalized. The workpaper elimination is as follows:

	Pin	100% Sep	Adjustments and Eliminations		Consolidated
Sales	$24,000	$30,000	a 24,000		$30,000
Cost of sales	20,000	24,000		a 24,000	20,000
Gross profit	$ 4,000	$ 6,000			$10,000

The workpaper elimination has no effect on consolidated net income because it eliminates equal sales and cost of sales amounts, and combined gross profit equals consolidated gross profit. However, the elimination is necessary to reflect merchandising activity accurately for the consolidated entity that purchased merchandise for $20,000 (Pin) and sold it for $30,000 (Sep). The fact that Pin's separate records include $4,000 gross profit on the merchandise and Sep's records show $6,000 is irrelevant in reporting the consolidated results of operations. In addition to eliminating intercompany profit items, it is necessary to eliminate intercompany receivables and payables in consolidation.

Elimination of Unrealized Profit in Ending Inventory

The consolidated entity realizes and recognizes the full amount of intercompany profit on sales between affiliates in the period in which the merchandise is resold to outside entities. Until reselling the merchandise, any profit or loss on intercompany sales is unrealized, and we must eliminate its effect in the consolidation process. The *ending inventory of the purchasing affiliate* reflects any unrealized profit or loss on intercompany sales because that inventory reflects the intercompany transfer price rather than cost to the consolidated entity. The elimination is a debit to cost of goods sold and a credit to the ending inventory for the amount of unrealized profit. The credit reduces the inventory to its cost basis to the consolidated entity; and the debit to cost of goods sold increases cost of goods sold to its cost basis. These relationships are illustrated by continuing the Pin and Sep example for 2012.

During 2012 Pin sold merchandise that cost $30,000 to Sep for $36,000, and Sep sold all but $6,000 of this merchandise to its customers for $37,500. Journal entries relating to the merchandise transferred intercompany during 2012 are as follows:

PIN'S BOOKS

Inventory (+A)	30,000	
Accounts payable (+L)		30,000
To record purchase on account from other entities.		
Accounts receivable—Sep (+A)	36,000	
Sales (R, +SE)		36,000
To record intercompany sales to Sep.		
Cost of sales (E, −SE)	30,000	
Inventory (−A)		30,000
To record cost of sales to Sep.		

SEP'S BOOKS

Inventory (+A)	36,000	
Accounts payable—Pin (+L)		36,000
To record intercompany purchases from Pin.		
Accounts receivable (+A)	37,500	
Sales (R, +SE)		37,500
To record sales to customers outside the consolidated entity.		
Cost of sales (E, −SE)	30,000	
Inventory (−A)		30,000
To record cost of sales to outside entities.		

Pin's sales for 2012 include $36,000 sold to Sep, and its cost of sales reflects the $30,000 cost of merchandise transferred to Sep. Sep's $37,500 sales for 2012 consist of merchandise acquired from Pin, and its $30,000 cost of sales equals 5/6, or $30,000/$36,000, of the $36,000 transfer price of merchandise acquired from Pin. The remaining merchandise acquired from Pin in 2012 stays in Sep's December 31, 2012, inventory at the $6,000 transfer price, which includes $1,000 unrealized profit.

WORKPAPER ENTRIES The consolidated entity views this as an intercompany transfer of merchandise that cost $30,000:

- $25,000 (or 5/6) of this merchandise was then sold to outside entities for $37,500.
- $5,000 (or 1/6) remains in inventory at year-end.
- The consolidated entity realizes a gross profit of $12,500.

We accomplish these consolidated results through workpaper entries that eliminate the effects of the intercompany transactions from sales, cost of sales, and inventory. Although a single entry can be made to reduce combined sales by $36,000, combined cost of sales by $35,000, and inventory by $1,000, two entries are ordinarily used in order to separate the elimination of intercompany sales and cost of sales from the elimination (deferral) of unrealized profit.

The eliminations follow:

	Pin	Sep	Adjustments and Eliminations	Consolidated
Income Statement				
Sales	$36,000	$37,500	a 36,000	$37,500
Cost of sales	30,000	30,000	b 1,000 a 36,000	25,000
Gross profit	$ 6,000	$ 7,500		$12,500
Balance Sheet				
Inventory		$ 6,000	b 1,000	$ 5,000

The first entry eliminates intercompany sales and cost of sales, journalized as follows:

a **Sales (−R, −SE)**	**36,000**	
Cost of sales (−E, +SE)		**36,000**
To eliminate intercompany sales and cost of sales.		

This entry is procedurally the same as the one made in 2011 to eliminate intercompany cost of sales and sales.

A secondary entry defers the $1,000 intercompany profit that remains unrealized ($13,500 combined gross profit − $12,500 consolidated gross profit) and reduces the ending inventory from $6,000 to its $5,000 cost to the consolidated entity:

b **Cost of sales (E, −SE)**	**1,000**	
Inventory (−A)		**1,000**
To eliminate intercompany profit from cost of sales and inventory.		

The debit to cost of sales reduces profit by increasing consolidated cost of sales, and the credit reduces the valuation of inventory for consolidated statement purposes from the intercompany transfer price to cost. From the viewpoint of the consolidated entity, Sep overstated its ending inventory by the $1,000 unrealized profit. An overstated ending inventory understates cost of sales and overstates gross profit, so we correct the error with entry b, which increases (debits) cost of sales and decreases (credits) the overstated ending inventory. This elimination reduces consolidated gross profit by $1,000 (income effect) and consolidated ending inventory by $1,000 (balance sheet effect).

These two workpaper entries should be learned at this time because they are always the same, regardless of additional complexities to be introduced later.

EQUITY METHOD On December 31, 2012, Pin computes its investment income in the usual manner, except that Pin defers $1,000 intercompany profit. Pin's one-line consolidation entry reduces income from Sep by the $1,000 unrealized profit in the ending inventory and accordingly reduces the Investment in Sep account by $1,000.

Recognition of Unrealized Profit in Beginning Inventory

Unrealized profit in an ending inventory is realized for consolidated statement purposes when the merchandise is sold outside the consolidated entity. Ordinarily, realization occurs in the immediately succeeding fiscal period, so firms simply defer recognition for consolidated statement purposes until the following year. Recognition of the previously unrealized profit requires a workpaper credit to cost of goods sold because the amount of the beginning inventory is reflected in cost of goods sold when the perpetual system is used. The direction of the sale, noncontrolling ownership percentage, and parent method of accounting for the subsidiary may complicate the related workpaper debits. These complications do not affect consolidated gross profit, however, and we extend the previous example to reflect 2013 operations for Pin and Sep.

During 2013, Pin Corporation sold merchandise that cost $40,000 to Sep for $48,000, and Sep sold 75 percent of the merchandise for $45,000. Sep also sold the items in the beginning inventory with a transfer price of $6,000 to its customers for $7,500. Journal entries relating to the merchandise transferred intercompany follow:

PIN'S BOOKS

Inventory (+A)	40,000	
Accounts payable (+L)		40,000
To record purchase on account from other entities.		
Accounts receivable—Sep (+A)	48,000	
Sales (R, +SE)		48,000
To record intercompany sales to Sep.		
Cost of sales (E, −SE)	40,000	
Inventory (−A)		40,000
To record cost of sales to Sep.		

Sep's Books

Inventory (+A)	48,000	
Accounts payable—Pin (+L)		48,000
To record intercompany purchases from Pin.		
Accounts receivable (+A)	52,500	
Sales (R, +SE)		52,500
To record sales of $45,000 and $7,500 to outside entities.		
Cost of sales (E, −SE)	42,000	
Inventory (−A)		42,000
To record cost of sales ($48,000 transfer price × 75% sold) and $6,000 from beginning inventory.		

Sep sold 75 percent of the merchandise purchased from Pin, so its ending inventory in 2013 is $12,000 ($48,000 × 25%), and that inventory includes $2,000 unrealized profit [$12,000−($12,000/1.2 transfer price)].

WORKPAPER ENTRIES From the viewpoint of the consolidated entity, merchandise that cost $40,000 was transferred intercompany:

- $30,000 of this merchandise, plus $5,000 beginning inventory, was sold for $52,500.
- $10,000 remained in inventory at year-end 2013.
- The consolidated entity realized a gross profit of $17,500.

The workpapers that eliminate the effects of intercompany transactions from sales, cost of sales, and inventory reflect these consolidated results. Three workpaper entries eliminate intercompany cost of sales and sales, recognize previously deferred profit from beginning inventory, and defer unrealized profit in the ending inventory, as follows:

	Pin	Sep	Adjustments and Eliminations		Consolidated
Income Statement					
Sales	$48,000	$52,500	a 48,000		$52,500
Cost of sales	40,000	42,000	c 2,000	a 48,000	
				b 1,000	35,000
Gross profit	$ 8,000	$10,500			$17,500
Balance Sheet					
Inventory		$12,000		c 2,000	$10,000
Investment in Sep	XXX			b 1,000	

Journal entries to eliminate the effects of intercompany transactions between Pin and Sep for 2013 follow:

a	Sales (−R, −SE)	48,000	
	Cost of sales (−E, +SE)		48,000
	To eliminate intercompany cost of sales and sales.		
b	Investment in Sep (+A)	1,000	
	Cost of sales (−E, +SE)		1,000
	To recognize previously deferred profit from beginning inventory.		
c	Cost of sales (E, −SE)	2,000	
	Inventory (−A)		2,000
	To defer unrealized profit in ending inventory.		

Workpaper entries a and c are procedurally the same as the entries for 2012. Their purpose is to eliminate intercompany cost of sales and sales and defer unrealized profit in the ending inventory. From the consolidated viewpoint, the $1,000 overstated beginning inventory overstates cost of sales in 2013. Entry b recognizes previously deferred profit from 2012 by reducing consolidated cost of sales and thereby increasing consolidated gross profit. (Note, of course, that entry b is made only in those cases in which the inventory has subsequently been sold to a customer outside the consolidated entity.) The related debit to the Investment in Sep account adjusts for the one-line consolidation entry that reduced the Investment in Sep account in 2012 to defer unrealized profit in the ending inventory of that year. Although the credit side of this entry is always the same, additional complexities sometimes arise with the debit side of the entry.

The Pin–Sep example illustrates the effects of intercompany inventory transactions on consolidated sales, cost of sales, and gross profit, and these effects are always the same. But the example did not cover the effects of intercompany inventory transactions on noncontrolling interest computations or on parent accounting under the equity method. These ramifications are discussed and illustrated next.

DOWNSTREAM AND UPSTREAM SALES

LEARNING OBJECTIVE 2

A **downstream sale** is a sale by a parent to a subsidiary, and a sale by a subsidiary to its parent is an **upstream sale**. The upstream and downstream designations relate to the usual diagram of affiliation structures that places the parent at the top. Thus, sales from top to bottom are downstream, and sales from bottom to top are upstream.

Consolidated statements eliminate reciprocal sales and cost of goods sold amounts regardless of whether the sales are upstream or downstream. We also eliminate any unrealized gross profit in ending inventory in its entirety for both downstream and upstream sales. However, the effect of unrealized profits in ending inventory on separate parent statements (as investor) and on consolidated financial statements (which show income to the controlling and noncontrolling stockholders) is determined by both the direction of the intercompany sales activity and the percentage ownership of the subsidiary, except for 100 percent-owned subsidiaries that have no noncontrolling ownership.

In the case of downstream sales, the parent's separate income includes the full amount of any unrealized profit (included in its sales and cost of sales accounts), and the subsidiary's income is unaffected. When sales are upstream, the subsidiary's net income includes the full amount of any unrealized profit (included in its sales and cost of sales accounts), and the parent's separate income is unaffected. The consolidation process eliminates the full amount of intercompany sales and cost of sales, regardless of whether the sales are downstream or upstream. However, the noncontrolling interest share *may be affected* if the subsidiary's net income includes unrealized profit (the upstream situation). It *is not affected* if the parent's separate income includes unrealized profit (the downstream situation) because the noncontrolling shareholders have an interest only in the income of the subsidiary. When subsidiary net income is overstated (from the viewpoint of the consolidated entity) because it includes unrealized profit, the income allocated to noncontrolling interests should be based on the *realized income of the subsidiary*. A subsidiary's realized income is its reported net income adjusted for intercompany profits from upstream sales.

Noncontrolling interest share *may be affected* by unrealized profit from upstream sales because accounting standards are not definitive with respect to the computation. GAAP provides that elimination of intercompany profit or loss may be allocated proportionately between controlling and noncontrolling interests but does not require such allocation [3]. The alternative to allocation is to eliminate intercompany profits and losses from upstream sales in the same manner as for downstream sales, debiting (crediting) the full amount of unrealized gain (loss) to the parent's income.

The approach that allocates unrealized profits and losses from upstream sales proportionately between noncontrolling and controlling interests is conceptually superior because it applies the viewpoint of the consolidated entity consistently to both controlling and noncontrolling interests. That is, both controlling share of consolidated income and noncontrolling interest share are computed on the basis of income that is realized from the viewpoint of the consolidated entity. In addition, material amounts of unrealized profits and losses from upstream sales may be allocated between controlling and noncontrolling interests in accounting practice. *Accordingly, unrealized profits and losses from upstream sales are allocated proportionately between consolidated net income (controlling interests) and noncontrolling interest share (noncontrolling interests) throughout this book.* Using the same allocation approach in accounting for the parent/investor's interest under the equity method accomplishes a consistent treatment between consolidation procedures and equity method accounting (the one-line consolidation).

Downstream and Upstream Effects on Income Computations

Assume that the separate incomes of a parent and its 80 percent-owned subsidiary for 2011 are as follows (in thousands):

	Parent	**Subsidiary**
Sales	$600	$300
Cost of sales	300	180
Gross profit	300	120
Expenses	100	70
Parent's separate income	$200	
Subsidiary's net income		$ 50

Intercompany sales during the year are $100,000, and the December 31, 2011, inventory includes $20,000 unrealized profit.

NONCONTROLLING INTEREST SHARE COMPUTATION If the intercompany sales are downstream, the parent's sales and cost of sales accounts reflect the $20,000 unrealized profit, and the subsidiary's

EXHIBIT 5-1

Consolidated Income
Effect of Downstream
and Upstream Sales

PARENT CORPORATION AND SUBSIDIARY CONSOLIDATED INCOME STATEMENT (IN THOUSANDS) FOR THE YEAR ENDED DECEMBER 31, 2011

	Downstream Sales	Upstream Sales
Sales ($900 − $100)	$800	$800
Cost of sales (480 + $20 − $100)	400	400
Gross profit	400	400
Expenses ($100 + $70)	170	170
Consolidated net income	$230	$230
Less: Noncontrolling interest share	10	6
Controlling interest share of consolidated net income	$220	$224

$50,000 net income is equal to its realized income. In this case the noncontrolling interest share computation is unaffected by the intercompany transactions and is computed as

$$\$50,000 \text{ net income of subsidiary} \times 20\% = \underline{\underline{\$10,000}}$$

If the intercompany sales are upstream, the subsidiary's sales and cost of sales accounts reflect the $20,000 unrealized profit, and the subsidiary's realized income is $30,000. In this case the non-controlling interest share computation is

$$(\$50,000 \text{ net income of subsidiary} - \$20,000 \text{ unrealized}) \times 20\% = \underline{\underline{\$6,000}}$$

CONSOLIDATED NET INCOME COMPUTATION Exhibit 5-1 shows comparative consolidated income statements for the parent and its 80 percent-owned subsidiary under the two assumptions. In examining the exhibit, note that the only difference in the computation of controlling interest share of consolidated net income under the two assumptions lies in the computation of noncontrolling interest share. This is so because the eliminations for intercompany cost of sales and sales and intercompany inventory profits are the same regardless of whether the sales are downstream or upstream. Parent net income under the equity method is equal to the controlling share of consolidated net income, so the approach used in computing income from subsidiary must be consistent with the approach used in determining consolidated net income. For downstream sales, the full amount of unrealized profit is charged against the income from subsidiary, but for upstream sales, only the parent's proportionate share is charged against its investment income from subsidiary. Computations are as follows (in thousands):

	Downstream	Upstream
Parent's separate income	$200	$200
Add: Income from subsidiary		
Downstream		
Equity in subsidiary's reported income less unrealized profit [($50,000 × 80%) − $20,000]	20	
Upstream		
Equity in subsidiary realized income [($50,000 − $20,000) × 80%]		24
Parent net income	$220	$224

Recognize that affiliates may engage in simultaneous upstream and downstream inventory transactions. In such cases, it is necessary to eliminate both the upstream and downstream sales/cost of sales. These transactions do not simply offset one another, due to the deferral of unrealized intercompany inventory profits.

For example, assume that the parent sells $100,000 of inventory to its wholly-owned subsidiary at a profit of $20,000. The entire inventory remains unsold at year-end. The subsidiary company likewise sells $100,000 of inventory to the parent, including an identical intercompany inventory profit of $20,000. This inventory also remains unsold at year-end.

We could simply assume that the two transactions are offsetting. However, this would distort both the consolidated balance sheet and income statement. The combined parent and subsidiary balance sheets include the inventory at the total intercompany transfer price of $200,000. However, $40,000 of this total is intercompany profit. The correct consolidated balance sheet inventory should be the cost of $160,000.

We would also overstate consolidated net income by $40,000. The intercompany profit must be deferred until the affiliates realize the gains through sales to parties outside the consolidated entity.

We can avoid these misstatements only if we separately eliminate the effects of all upstream and downstream transactions. Notice that intercompany inventory transactions provide a convenient means of managing reported consolidated net income if the impact of simultaneous upstream and downstream sales is not properly eliminated.

UNREALIZED PROFITS FROM DOWNSTREAM SALES

LEARNING OBJECTIVE **3**

Sales by a parent to its subsidiaries increase parent sales, cost of goods sold, and gross profit but do not affect the income of subsidiaries until the merchandise is resold to outside parties. The full amount of gross profit on merchandise sold downstream and remaining in subsidiary inventories increases parent income, so the full amount must be eliminated from the parent's income statement under the equity method of accounting. Consistent with the one-line consolidation concept, this is done by reducing investment income and the investment account. Consolidated financial statements eliminate unrealized gross profit by increasing consolidated cost of goods sold and reducing merchandise inventory to its cost basis to the consolidated entity. The overstatement of the ending inventory from the consolidated viewpoint understates consolidated cost of goods sold.

Deferral of Intercompany Profit in Period of Intercompany Sale

The following example illustrates the deferral of unrealized profits on downstream sales. Pot Corporation owns 90 percent of the voting stock of Sot Corporation. Separate income statements of Pot and Sot for 2011, before consideration of unrealized profits, are as follows (in thousands):

	Pot	Sot
Sales	$100	$50
Cost of goods sold	60	35
Gross profit	40	15
Expenses	15	5
Operating income	25	10
Income from Sot	9	—
Net income	$ 34	$10

Pot's sales include $15,000 to Sot at a profit of $6,250, and Sot's December 31, 2011, inventory includes 40 percent of the merchandise from the intercompany transaction. Pot's operating income reflects the $2,500 unrealized profit in Sot's inventory ($6,000 transfer price less $3,500 cost). On its separate books, Pot records its share of Sot's income and defers recognition of the unrealized profit with the following entries:

Investment in Sot (+A)	9,000	
Income from Sot (R, +SE)		9,000
To record share of Sot's income.		
Income from Sot (−R, −SE)	2,500	
Investment in Sot (−A)		2,500
To eliminate unrealized profit on sales to Sot.		

The second entry on Pot's books reduces Pot's income from Sot from $9,000 to $6,500. Reciprocal sales and cost of goods sold, as well as all unrealized profit, must be eliminated in consolidated financial statements. These adjustments are shown in the partial workpaper in Exhibit 5-2.

EXHIBIT 5-2

Inventory Profit on Downstream Sales in Year of Intercompany Sales

POT AND SUBSIDIARY, SOT, PARTIAL WORKPAPER FOR THE YEAR ENDED DECEMBER 31, 2011 (IN THOUSANDS)

	Pot	90% Sot	Adjustments and Eliminations Debits	Adjustments and Eliminations Credits	Consolidated Statements
Income Statement Sales	$100	$50	a 15		$135
Income from Sot	6.5		c 6.5		
Cost of goods sold	(60)	(35)	b 2.5	a 15	(82.5)
Expenses	(15)	(5)			(20)
Consolidated net income					$ 32.5
Noncontrolling interest share ($10,000 × 10%)					(1)
Controlling interest share	$ 31.5	$10			$ 31.5
Balance Sheet Inventory		$ 6		b 2.5	$ 3.5
Investment in Sot	XXX			c 6.5	

a Eliminates reciprocal sales and cost of goods sold.
b Adjusts cost of goods sold and ending inventory to a cost basis to the consolidated entity.
c Eliminates investment income and adjusts the Investment in Sot account to the January 1, 2011, balance.

Entry a deducts the full amount of intercompany sales from sales and cost of goods sold. Entry b then corrects cost of goods sold for the unrealized profit at year-end and reduces the inventory to its cost basis to the consolidated entity. Note that entries a and b are equivalent to a single debit to sales for $15,000, a credit to cost of goods sold for $12,500, and a credit to inventory for $2,500.

In examining Exhibit 5-2, observe that Pot's net income on an equity basis is equal to the controlling share of consolidated net income. This equality would not have occurred without the equity method journal entry that reduced Pot's income from $34,000 to $31,500. The $1,000 noncontrolling interest share shown in Exhibit 5-2 is not affected by the unrealized profit on Pot's sales because noncontrolling stockholders share only in subsidiary profit and Sot's reported income for 2011 (equal to its realized income) is unaffected by the unrealized profit in its ending inventory.

LEARNING OBJECTIVE 4

Recognition of Intercompany Profit upon Sale to Outside Entities

Now assume that the merchandise acquired from Pot during 2011 is sold by Sot during 2012, and there are no intercompany transactions between Pot and Sot during 2012. Separate income statements for 2012 before consideration of the $2,500 unrealized profit in Sot's beginning inventory are as follows (in thousands):

	Pot	Sot
Sales	$120	$60
Cost of goods sold	80	40
Gross profit	40	20
Expenses	20	5
Operating income	20	15
Income from Sot	13.5	—
Net income	$ 33.5	$15

Pot's operating income for 2012 is unaffected by the unrealized profit in Sot's December 31, 2011, inventory. But Sot's 2012 profit is affected because the $2,500 overstatement of Sot's beginning inventory overstates cost of goods sold from a consolidated viewpoint. From Pot's viewpoint, the unrealized profit from 2011 is realized in 2012, and its investment income is recorded and adjusted as follows:

Investment in Sot (+A)	13,500	
Income from Sot (R, +SE)		13,500
To record investment income from Sot.		
Investment in Sot (+A)	2,500	
Income from Sot (R, +SE)		2,500
To record realization of profit from 2011 intercompany sales to Sot.		

The last entry increases Pot's investment from $13,500 to $16,000 and Pot's net income from $33,500 to $36,000. The partial workpaper for Pot and Sot for 2012 reflects the adjusted amounts as shown in Exhibit 5-3.

In examining Exhibit 5-3, note that entry a debits the Investment in Sot account and credits cost of goods sold for $2,500. The beginning inventory of Sot has already been closed to cost of goods sold under a perpetual inventory system, so the inventory cannot be adjusted. The adjustment to the investment account is necessary to increase the investment account at the beginning of the year to reflect realization during 2012 of the unrealized profit that was deferred at the end of 2011. *This adjustment reestablishes reciprocity between the investment balance at January 1, 2012, and the subsidiary equity account at the same date. It is important to record this adjustment before eliminating reciprocal investment and equity balances.* The computation of noncontrolling interest share in Exhibit 5-3 is unaffected because the sales are downstream.

Unrealized inventory profits in consolidated financial statements are self-correcting over any two accounting periods and are subject to the same type of analysis as inventory errors. Total consolidated net income for Pot and Sot for 2011 and 2012 is unaffected by the $2,500 deferral in 2011 and recognition in 2012. The significance of the adjustments lies in the accurate statement of the consolidated income for each period.

EXHIBIT 5-3

Inventory Profit on Downstream Sales in Year After Intercompany Sales

POT AND SUBSIDIARY, SOT, PARTIAL WORKPAPER FOR THE YEAR ENDED DECEMBER 31, 2012 (IN THOUSANDS)

	Pot	90% Sot	Adjustments and Eliminations Debits	Adjustments and Eliminations Credits	Consolidated Statements
Income Statement					
Sales	$120	$60			$180
Income from Sot	16		b 16		
Cost of goods sold	(80)	(40)		a 2.5	(117.5)
Expenses	(20)	(5)			(25)
Consolidated net income					$37.5
Noncontrolling interest share ($15,000 × 10%)					(1.5)
Controlling interest share	$ 36	$15			$ 36
Balance Sheet					
Investment in Sot	XXX		a 2.5	b 16	

a Adjusts cost of goods sold to a cost basis and adjusts the Investment in Sot account balance to reestablish reciprocity with the beginning subsidiary equity accounts.

b Eliminates investment income and adjusts the Investment in Sot account to the January 1, 2012, balance.

UNREALIZED PROFITS FROM UPSTREAM SALES

Sales by a subsidiary to its parent increase the sales, cost of goods sold, and gross profit of the subsidiary, but they do not affect the operating income of the parent until the merchandise is resold by the parent to outside entities. The parent's net income is affected in the year of transfer from the subsidiary, however, because the parent recognizes its share of the subsidiary's income on an equity basis. If the selling subsidiary is a 100 percent-owned affiliate, the parent defers 100 percent of any unrealized profit in the year of intercompany sale. If the subsidiary is a partially owned affiliate, the parent defers only its proportionate share of the unrealized subsidiary profit.

LEARNING OBJECTIVE **5**

Deferral of Intercompany Profit in Period of Intercompany Sale

Assume that Sal Corporation (subsidiary) sells merchandise that it purchased for $7,500 to Par Corporation (parent) for $20,000 during 2011 and that Par Corporation sold 60 percent of the merchandise to outsiders during the year for $15,000. At year-end the unrealized inventory profit is $5,000 (cost $3,000, but included in Par's inventory at $8,000). If Sal reports net income of $50,000 for 2011, Par recognizes its proportionate share as shown in Exhibit 5-4. The exhibit compares parent-company accounting for a one-line consolidation of a 100 percent-owned subsidiary and a 75 percent-owned subsidiary.

As the illustration shows, if Par records 100 percent of Sal's income under the equity method, it must eliminate 100 percent of any unrealized profit included in that income. However, if Par records only 75 percent of Sal's income under the equity method, it must eliminate only 75 percent of any unrealized profit included in Sal's income. In both cases, Par eliminates all the unrealized profit from its income and investment accounts.

The elimination of unrealized inventory profits from upstream sales in consolidated financial statements results in the elimination of 100 percent of all unrealized inventory profits from consolidated sales and cost of goods sold accounts. However, because the controlling share of consolidated net income is a measurement of income to the stockholders of the parent, noncontrolling interest share is reduced for its proportionate share of any unrealized profit of the subsidiary. This requires deducting the noncontrolling interest's share of unrealized profits from the noncontrolling interest's share of the subsidiary's reported net income. Thus, the effect on consolidated net income of unrealized profits from upstream sales is the same as the effect on parent income under the equity method of accounting.

Exhibit 5-5 illustrates partial consolidation workpapers for Par Corporation and its 75 percent-owned subsidiary, Sal Corporation. Although the amounts for sales, cost of goods sold, and expenses are presented without explanation, the data provided are consistent with previous assumptions for Par and Sal Corporations.

EXHIBIT 5-4

Entries for a One-Line Consolidation on the Books of Par

Part A
If Sal Is a 100%-Owned Subsidiary

Investment in Sal (+A)	50,000	
Income from Sal (R, +SE)		50,000
To record 100% of Sal's reported income as income from subsidiary.		
Income from Sal (−R, −SE)	5,000	
Investment in Sal (−A)		5,000
To defer 100% of the unrealized inventory profits reported by Sal until realized.		

A single entry for $45,000 [($50,000 − $5,000) × 100%] is equally acceptable.

Part B
If Sal Is a 75%-Owned Subsidiary

Investment in Sal (+A)	37,500	
Income from Sal (R, +SE)		37,500
To record 75% of Sal's reported income as income from subsidiary.		
Income from Sal (−R, −SE)	3,750	
Investment in Sal (−A)		3,750
To defer 75% of the unrealized inventory profits reported by Sal until realized.		

A single entry for $33,750 [($50,000 − $5,000) × 75%] is equally acceptable.

	Par	75% Sal	Adjustments and Eliminations		Consolidated Statements
			Debits	Credits	
Income Statement					
Sales	$250	$150	a 20		$380
Income from Sal	33.75		c 33.75		
Cost of goods sold	(100)	(80)	b 5	a 20	(165)
Expenses	(50)	(20)			(70)
Consolidated net income					$145
Noncontrolling interest share [($50,000 − $5,000) × 25%]					(11.25)
Controlling interest share	$133.75	$ 50			$133.75
Balance Sheet					
Inventory	$ 8			b 5	
Investment in Sal	XXX			c 33.75	

PAR AND SUBSIDIARY, SAL, PARTIAL WORKPAPER FOR THE YEAR ENDED DECEMBER 31, 2011 (IN THOUSANDS)

a Eliminates reciprocal sales and cost of goods sold.
b Adjusts cost of goods sold and ending inventory to a cost basis to the consolidated entity.
c Eliminates investment income and adjusts the Investment in Sal account to the January 1, 2011, balance.

EXHIBIT 5-5

Inventory Profit on Upstream Sales in Year of Intercompany Sales

Part B of Exhibit 5-4 explains the $33,750 income from Sal that appears in Par's separate income statement in Exhibit 5-5. Noncontrolling interest share is computed by subtracting unrealized profit from Sal's reported income and multiplying by the noncontrolling interest percentage. Failure to adjust the noncontrolling interest share for unrealized profit will result in a lack of equality between parent net income on an equity basis and the controlling share of consolidated net income. This potential problem is, of course, absent in the case of a 100 percent-owned subsidiary because there is no noncontrolling interest.

Recognition of Intercompany Profit upon Sale to Outside Entities

The effect of unrealized profits in a beginning inventory on parent and consolidated net incomes is just the opposite of the effect of unrealized profits in an ending inventory. That is, the relationship between unrealized profits in ending inventories (year of intercompany sale) and consolidated net income is direct, whereas the relationship between unrealized profit in beginning inventories (year of sale to outside entities) and consolidated net income is inverse. This is illustrated by continuing the Par and Sal example to show realization during 2012 of the $5,000 unrealized profit in the December 31, 2011, inventories. Assume that there are no intercompany transactions between Par and Sal during 2012, that Sal is a 75 percent-owned subsidiary of Par, and that Sal reports income of $60,000 for 2012. Par records its share of Sal's income under the equity method as follows:

Investment in Sal (+A)	45,000	
Income from Sal (R, +SE)		45,000
To record 75% of Sal's reported income as income		
from subsidiary.		
Investment in Sal (+A)	3,750	
Income from Sal (R, +SE)		3,750
To record realization during 2012 of 75% of the $5,000		
unrealized inventory profits of Sal from 2011.		

EXHIBIT 5-6

Inventory Profit on
Upstream Sales in Year
After Intercompany
Sales

PAR AND SUBSIDIARY, SAL, PARTIAL WORKPAPER FOR THE YEAR ENDED DECEMBER 31, 2012 (IN THOUSANDS)

	Par	75% Sal	Adjustments and Eliminations Debits	Adjustments and Eliminations Credits	Consolidated Statements
Income Statement Sales	$275	$160			$435
Income from Sal	48.75		b 48.75		
Cost of goods sold	(120)	(85)		a 5	(200)
Expenses	(60)	(15)			(75)
Consolidated net income					$160
Noncontrolling interest share [($60,000 + $5,000) × 25%]					(16.25)
Controlling interest share	$143.75	$ 60			$143.75
Balance Sheet Investment in Sal	XXX		a 3.75	b 48.75	
Noncontrolling interest: January 1, 2012			a 1.25		

a Adjusts cost of goods sold to a cost basis and adjusts the Investment in Sal account balance to reestablish reciprocity with the beginning subsidiary equity accounts.
b Eliminates investment income and adjusts the Investment in Sal account to the January 1, 2012, balance.

Exhibit 5-6 illustrates consolidation procedures for unrealized profits in beginning inventories from upstream sales for Par and Subsidiary. Several of the items in Exhibit 5-6 differ from those for upstream sales with unrealized profit in the ending inventory (Exhibit 5-5). In particular, cost of goods sold is overstated (because of the overstated beginning inventory) and requires a worksheet adjustment to reduce it to its cost basis. This is shown in entry a, which also adjusts the investment account and beginning noncontrolling interest. *Consolidated statements require the allocation between the investment balance (75 percent) and the noncontrolling interest (25 percent) for unrealized profits in beginning inventories from upstream sales to correct for prior-year effects on the investment account and the noncontrolling interest.*

CONSOLIDATION EXAMPLE—INTERCOMPANY PROFITS FROM DOWNSTREAM SALES

Say Corporation is a 90 percent-owned subsidiary of Pak Corporation, acquired for $94,500 cash on July 1, 2011, when Say's net assets consisted of $100,000 capital stock and $5,000 retained earnings. The cost of Pak's 90 percent interest in Say was equal to book value and fair value of the interest acquired ($105,000 × 90 percent), and accordingly, no allocation to identifiable and unidentifiable assets was necessary.

Pak sells inventory items to Say on a regular basis, and the intercompany transaction data for 2014 are as follows:

Sales to Say in 2014 (cost $15,000), selling price	$20,000
Unrealized profit in Say's inventory at December 31, 2013 (inventory was sold during 2014)	2,000
Unrealized profit in Say's inventory at December 31, 2014	2,500
Say's accounts payable to Pak at December 31, 2014	10,000

Equity Method

At December 31, 2013, Pak's Investment in Say account had a balance of $128,500. This balance consisted of Pak's 90 percent equity in Say's $145,000 net assets on that date less $2,000 unrealized profit in Say's December 31, 2013, inventory.

During 2014, Pak made the following entries on its books for its investment in Say under the equity method:

Cash (+A)	9,000	
Investment in Say (−A)		9,000
To record dividends from Say ($10,000 × 90%).		
Investment in Say (+A)	26,500	
Income from Say (R, +SE)		26,500
To record income from Say for 2014 computed as follows:		
Equity in Say's net income ($30,000 × 90%)		$27,000
Add: 2013 inventory profit recognized in 2014		2,000
Less: 2014 inventory profit deferred at year-end		−2,500
		$26,500

The intercompany sales that led to the unrealized inventory profits were downstream, so we recognize the full amount of profit deferred in 2013 in 2014, and the full amount of the unrealized inventory profit originating in 2014 is deferred at December 31, 2014. Pak's Investment in Say account increased from $128,500 at January 1, 2014, to $146,000 at December 31, 2014, the entire change consisting of $26,500 income less $9,000 dividends for the year. Exhibit 5-7 shows these amounts in the separate-company columns of the consolidation workpaper for Pak Corporation and Subsidiary for the year ended December 31, 2014.

The entries in Exhibit 5-7 are presented in journal form as follows:

a	Sales (−R, −SE)	20,000	
	Cost of goods sold (−E, +SE)		20,000
	To eliminate intercompany sales and related cost of goods sold amounts.		
b	Investment in Say (+A)	2,000	
	Cost of goods sold (−E, +SE)		2,000
	To adjust cost of goods sold and the beginning investment balance for unrealized profits in the beginning inventory.		
c	Cost of goods sold (E, −SE)	2,500	
	Inventory (−A)		2,500
	To eliminate unrealized profits in the ending inventory and to increase cost of goods sold to the consolidated entity.		
d	Income from Say (−R, −SE)	26,500	
	Dividends (+SE)		9,000
	Investment in Say (−A)		17,500
	To eliminate the investment income and 90 percent of the dividends of Say and to reduce the investment account to its beginning-of-the-period balance, plus the $2,000 from entry b.		
e	Noncontrolling interest share (−SE)	3,000	
	Dividends (+SE)		1,000
	Noncontrolling interest (+SE)		2,000
	To enter noncontrolling interest share of subsidiary income and dividends.		
f	Capital stock—Say (−SE)	100,000	
	Retained earnings—Say (−SE)	45,000	
	Investment in Say (−A)		130,500
	Noncontrolling interest (+SE)		14,500
	To eliminate reciprocal investment and equity balances and record beginning noncontrolling interest.		
g	Accounts payable (−L)	10,000	
	Accounts receivable (−A)		10,000
	To eliminate reciprocal payables and receivables from intercompany sales.		

EXHIBIT 5-7

Intercompany Profits
on Downstream Sales—
Equity Method

PAK CORPORATION AND SUBSIDIARY CONSOLIDATION WORKPAPER FOR THE YEAR ENDED DECEMBER 31, 2014 (IN THOUSANDS)

	Pak	90% Say	Adjustments and Eliminations Debits	Adjustments and Eliminations Credits	Consolidated Statements
Income Statement Net sales	$1,000	$300	a 20		$1,280
Income from Say	26.5		d 26.5		
Cost of goods sold	(550)	(200)	c 2.5	a 20 b 2	(730.5)
Other expenses	(350)	(70)			(420)
Consolidated net income					129.5
Noncontrolling interest share ($30,000 × 10%)			e 3		(3)
Controlling share of net income	**$ 126.5**	**$ 30**			**$ 126.5**
Retained Earnings Statement Retained earnings—Pak	$ 194				$ 194
Retained earnings—Say		$ 45	f 45		
Controlling share of net income	**126.5**	**30**			**126.5**
Dividends	(50)	(10)		d 9 e 1	(50)
Retained earnings—December 31	**$ 270.5**	**$ 65**			**$ 270.5**
Balance Sheet Cash	$ 30	$ 5			$ 35
Accounts receivable	70	20		g 10	80
Inventory	90	45		c 2.5	132.5
Other current assets	64	10			74
Plant and equipment	800	120			920
Investment in Say	146		b 2	d 17.5 f 130.5	
	$1,200	$200			$1,241.5
Accounts payable	$ 80	$ 15	g 10		$ 85
Other liabilities	49.5	20			69.5
Capital stock	800	100	f 100		800
Retained earnings	**270.5**	**65**			**270.5**
	$1,200	$200			
Noncontrolling interest January 1				f 14.5	
Noncontrolling interest December 31				e 2	16.5
					$1,241.5

In examining the workpaper of Pak Corporation and Subsidiary in Exhibit 5-7, note that Pak's net income ($126,500) is equal to the controlling share of consolidated net income, and Pak's retained earnings amount ($270,500) equals consolidated retained earnings. These equalities are expected from a correct application of the equity method of accounting. The sales that gave rise to the intercompany profits in Say's inventories were downstream, so neither beginning noncontrolling interest ($14,500) nor noncontrolling interest share ($3,000) was affected by the intercompany transactions.

CONSOLIDATION EXAMPLE—INTERCOMPANY PROFITS FROM UPSTREAM SALES

Sit Corporation is an 80 percent-owned subsidiary of Poh Corporation, acquired for $480,000 on January 2, 2011, when Sit's stockholders' equity consisted of $500,000 capital stock and $100,000 retained earnings. The investment cost was equal to the book value and fair value of Sit's net assets acquired, so no fair value/book value differential resulted from the acquisition.

Sit Corporation sells inventory items to Poh Corporation on a regular basis. The intercompany transaction data for 2012 are as follows:

Sales to Poh in 2012	$300,000
Unrealized profit in Poh's inventory, December 31, 2011 (inventory was sold during 2012)	40,000
Unrealized profit in Poh's inventory, December 31, 2012	30,000
Intercompany accounts receivable and payable at December 31, 2012	50,000

Equity Method

At December 31, 2011, Poh's Investment in Sit account had a balance of $568,000, consisting of $600,000 underlying equity in Sit's net assets ($750,000 × 80%) less 80 percent of the $40,000 unrealized profit in Poh's December 31, 2011, inventory from upstream sales. During 2012, Poh made the following entries to account for its investment in Sit under the equity method:

Cash (+A)	40,000	
Investment in Sit (−A)		40,000
To record dividends from Sit ($50,000 × 80%).		
Investment in Sit (+A)	88,000	
Income from Sit (R, +SE)		88,000
To record income from Sit for 2012, computed as follows:		
Equity in Sit's net income ($100,000 × 80%)		$80,000
Add: 80% of $40,000 unrealized profit deferred in 2011		32,000
Less: 80% of $30,000 unrealized profit at December 31, 2012		−24,000
		$88,000

The intercompany sales that led to the unrealized inventory profits in 2011 and 2012 were upstream, and, accordingly, only 80 percent of the $40,000 unrealized profit from 2011 is recognized by Poh in 2012. Similarly, only 80 percent of the $30,000 unrealized profit from 2012 sales is deferred by Poh at December 31, 2012. Poh's Investment in Sit account was increased by the $88,000 income from Sit during 2012 and decreased by $40,000 dividends received from Sit. Thus, the $568,000 Investment in Sit account at December 31, 2011, increased to $616,000 at December 31, 2012. These amounts, combined with other compatible information to provide complete separate-company financial statements, are shown in the separate-company columns of the consolidation workpaper for Poh Corporation and Subsidiary in Exhibit 5-8.

EXHIBIT 5-8

Intercompany Profits on
Upstream Sales—Equity
Method

POH CORPORATION AND SUBSIDIARY CONSOLIDATION WORKPAPER FOR THE YEAR ENDED DECEMBER 31, 2012 (IN THOUSANDS)

	Poh	80% Sit	Adjustments and Eliminations Debits	Adjustments and Eliminations Credits	Consolidated Statements
Income Statement Sales	$3,000	$1,500	a 300		$4,200
Income from Sit	88		d 88		
Cost of goods sold	(2,000)	(1,000)	c 30	a 300 b 40	(2,690)
Other expenses	(588)	(400)			(988)
Consolidated net income					522
Noncontrolling interest share*			e 22		(22)
Controlling share of Net income	**$ 500**	**$ 100**			**$ 500**
Retained Earnings Statement Retained earnings—Poh	$1,000				$1,000
Retained earnings—Sit		$ 250	f 250		
Add: Controlling share of Net income	**500**	**100**			**500**
Deduct: Dividends	(400)	(50)		d 40 e 10	(400)
Retained earnings—December 31	**$1,100**	**$ 300**			**$1,100**
Balance Sheet Cash	$ 200	$ 50			$ 250
Accounts receivable	700	100		g 50	750
Inventory	1,100	200		c 30	1,270
Other current assets	384	150			534
Plant and equipment—net	2,000	500			2,500
Investment in Sit	616		b 32	d 48 f 600	
	$5,000	$1,000			$5,304
Accounts payable	$ 500	150	g 50		$ 600
Other liabilities	400	50			450
Capital stock	3,000	500	f 500		3,000
Retained earnings	**1,100**	**300**			**1,100**
	$5,000	$1,000			
Noncontrolling interest January 1			b 8	f 150	
Noncontrolling interest December 31				e 12	154
					$5,304

* Noncontrolling interest share ($100,000 + $40,000 − $30,000) × 20% = $22,000

The entries in Exhibit 5-8 appear below in journal form for convenient reference:

a	Sales (−R, −SE)	300,000	
	Cost of goods sold (−E, +SE)		300,000
	To eliminate reciprocal sales and cost of goods sold amounts.		
b	Investment in Sit (+A)	32,000	
	Noncontrolling interest (−SE)	8,000	
	Cost of goods sold (−E, +SE)		40,000
	To adjust cost of goods sold for unrealized profit in beginning inventory and to allocate the unrealized profit 80% to the parent's investment account and 20% to noncontrolling interest.		
c	Cost of goods sold (E, −SE)	30,000	
	Inventory (−A)		30,000
	To eliminate unrealized profit from ending inventory and increase cost of goods sold.		
d	Income from Sit (−R, −SE)	88,000	
	Dividends (+SE)		40,000
	Investment in Sit (−A)		48,000
	To eliminate investment income and 80% of the dividends by Sit and to reduce the investment account to its beginning balance.		
e	Noncontrolling interest share (−SE)	22,000	
	Dividends (+SE)		10,000
	Noncontrolling interest (+SE)		12,000
	To enter noncontrolling interest share of subsidiary income and dividends.		
f	Retained earnings—Sit (−SE)	250,000	
	Capital stock—Sit (−SE)	500,000	
	Investment in Sit (−A)		600,000
	Noncontrolling interest (+SE)		150,000
	To eliminate reciprocal investment and equity balances and to enter beginning noncontrolling interest.		
g	Accounts payable (−L)	50,000	
	Accounts receivable (−A)		50,000
	To eliminate reciprocal accounts receivable and payable.		

The consolidation workpaper entries shown in Exhibit 5-8 are similar to those in the Pak–Say illustration. Only entry b, which allocates the unrealized profit in Poh's beginning inventory between investment in Sit (80%) and noncontrolling interest (20%), differs significantly. Allocation is necessary because the unrealized profit arises from an upstream sale and was included in Sit's reported income for 2011. Poh's share of the $40,000 unrealized profit is only 80 percent. The other 20 percent relates to noncontrolling interests, and, accordingly, the $8,000 debit is necessary to reduce beginning noncontrolling interest from $150,000 (20% of Sit's reported equity of $750,000) to $142,000— 20 percent of Sit's realized equity of $710,000 ($750,000 − $40,000) at December 31, 2011.

NONCONTROLLING INTEREST In computing noncontrolling interest share for 2012, it is necessary to adjust Sit's reported net income for unrealized profits before multiplying by the noncontrolling interest percentage. The computation is:

Reported net income of Sit	$100,000
Add: Inventory profits from 2011 realized in 2012	+ 40,000
Deduct: Unrealized inventory profits at December 31, 2012	(30,000)
Sit's realized income for 2012	110,000
Noncontrolling interest percentage	20%
Noncontrolling interest share	$ 22,000

The $154,000 noncontrolling interest at December 31, 2012, is determined in the workpapers by adding noncontrolling interest share of $22,000 to beginning noncontrolling interest of $142,000 and subtracting noncontrolling interest dividends. An alternative computation that may be used as a check is to deduct unrealized profit in the December 31, 2012, inventory from Sit's equity at December 31, 2012, and multiply the resulting realized equity of Sit by the 20 percent noncontrolling interest [($800,000 − $30,000) × 20% = $154,000]. The advantage of this approach is that only unrealized profits at the balance sheet date need to be considered in the computation.

SUMMARY

Intercompany sales and purchases of inventory items result in reciprocal sales and cost of goods sold amounts that do not reflect merchandising activity of the consolidated entity. These intercompany transactions also give rise to unrealized intercompany profits. The consolidated entity defers recognition of these profits until they can be realized by subsequent sales to parties outside the consolidated entity.

The direction of intercompany sales is important, except for consolidated companies with only 100 percent-owned subsidiaries. We deduct the full amount of the unrealized intercompany profit from downstream sales against parent and consolidated net income. In the case of upstream sales, however, we deduct unrealized profits from consolidated net income and noncontrolling interest share on the basis of controlling and noncontrolling ownership. Intercompany profits that are deferred in one period are subsequently recognized in the period in which the related inventory items are sold to nonaffiliated entities. Exhibit 5-9 presents a summary illustration of the effect of intercompany profit eliminations on parent and consolidated net income.

Under the assumption that Parent(P) sells to Subsidiary(S), P's net income and the controlling share of consolidated net income are exactly the same as if the sales had never taken place. In that case, P's separate income would have been $95,000 ($100,000 + $5,000 − $10,000), and P's income from S would have been $45,000 ($50,000 × 90%), for a total of $140,000. Under the assumption that S sells to P, P's net income and the controlling share of consolidated net income are exactly the same as if the intercompany sales had never taken place. In that case, P's income would have been $100,000 (as given), and S's net income would have been $45,000 ($50,000 + $5,000 − $10,000).

EXHIBIT 5-9

Summary Illustration—
Unrealized Inventory
Profits

Assumptions

1. Parent company's income, excluding income from subsidiary, is $100,000.
2. 90%-owned subsidiary reports net income of $50,000.
3. Unrealized profit in beginning inventory is $5,000. (Sold in current year.)
4. Unrealized profit in ending inventory is $10,000.

	Downstream: Assume That P Sells to S	Upstream: Assume That S Sells to P
P's Net Income—Equity Method		
P's separate income	$100,000	$100,000
P's share of S's reported net income:		
($50,000 × 90%)	45,000	45,000
Add: Unrealized profit in beginning inventory:		
($5,000 × 100%)	5,000	
($5,000 × 90%)		4,500
Deduct: Unrealized profit in ending inventory:		
($10,000 × 100%)	(10,000)	
($10,000 × 90%)		(9,000)
P's net income	$140,000	$140,500
Controlling share of Consolidated Net Income		
P's separate income plus S's net income	$150,000	$150,000
Adjustments for unrealized profits:		
Beginning inventory ($5,000 × 100%)	5,000	5,000
Ending inventory ($10,000 × 100%)	(10,000)	(10,000)
Total realized income	145,000	145,000
Less: Noncontrolling interest share:		
($50,000 × 10%)	(5,000)	
($50,000 + $5,000—$10,000) × 10%		(4,500)
Controlling share of consolidated net income	$140,000	$140,500

P's $100,000 separate income plus P's income from S of $40,500 ($45,000 × 90%) is equal to P's net income and the controlling share of consolidated net income.

QUESTIONS

1. The effect of unrealized profits and losses on sales between affiliated companies is eliminated in preparing consolidated financial statements. When are profits and losses on such sales realized for consolidated statement purposes?

2. In eliminating unrealized profit on intercompany sales of inventory items, should gross profit or net profit be eliminated?

3. Is the amount of intercompany profit to be eliminated from consolidated financial statements affected by the existence of a noncontrolling interest? Explain.

4. What effect does the elimination of intercompany sales and cost of goods sold have on consolidated net income?

5. What effect does the elimination of intercompany accounts receivable and accounts payable have on consolidated working capital?

6. Explain the designations *upstream sales* and *downstream sales*. Of what significance are these designations in computing parent and consolidated net income?

7. Would failure to eliminate unrealized profit in inventories at December 31, 2011, have any effect on consolidated net income in 2012? 2013?

8. Under what circumstances is noncontrolling interest share affected by intercompany sales activity?

9. How does a parent adjust its investment income for unrealized profit on sales it makes to its subsidiaries (a) in the year of the sale and (b) in the year in which the subsidiaries sell the related merchandise to outsiders?

10. How is the combined cost of goods sold affected by unrealized profit in (a) the beginning inventory of the subsidiary and (b) the ending inventory of the subsidiary?

11. Is the effect of unrealized profit on consolidated cost of goods sold influenced by (a) the existence of a noncontrolling interest and (b) the direction of intercompany sales?

12. Unrealized profit in the ending inventory is eliminated in consolidation workpapers by increasing cost of sales and decreasing the inventory account. How is unrealized profit in the beginning inventory reflected in the consolidation workpapers?

13. Describe the computation of noncontrolling interest share in a year in which there is unrealized inventory profit from upstream sales in both the beginning and ending inventories of the parent.

14. Consolidation workpaper procedures are usually based on the assumption that any unrealized profit in the beginning inventory of one year is realized through sales in the following year. If the related merchandise is not sold in the succeeding period, would the assumption result in an incorrect measurement of consolidated net income?

NOTE: Don't forget the assumptions on page 46 when working exercises and problems in this chapter.

EXERCISES

E 5-1 General Questions

1. Intercompany profit elimination entries in consolidation workpapers are prepared in order to:
   a *Nullify the effect of intercompany transactions on consolidated statements*
   b *Defer intercompany profit until realized*
   c *Allocate unrealized profits between controlling and noncontrolling interests*
   d *Reduce consolidated income*

2. The direction of intercompany sales (upstream or downstream) does not affect consolidation workpaper procedures when the intercompany sales between affiliates are made:
   a *At fair value*
   b *Above market value*
   c *At book value*
   d *To a 100 percent-owned subsidiary*

3. Pet Corporation sells inventory items for $500,000 to Sen Corporation, its 80 percent-owned subsidiary. The consolidated workpaper entry to eliminate the effect of this intercompany sale will include a debit to sales for:
   a *$500,000*
   b *$400,000*
   c *The amount remaining in Sen's ending inventory*
   d *80 percent of the amount remaining in Sen's ending inventory*

4. Sar Corporation, a 90 percent-owned subsidiary of Pan Corporation, buys half of its raw materials from Pan. The transfer price is exactly the same price as Sar pays to buy identical raw materials from outside suppliers and the same price as Pan sells the materials to unrelated customers. In preparing consolidated statements for Pan Corporation and Subsidiary:

 a *The intercompany transactions can be ignored because the transfer price represents arm's-length bargaining*

 b *Any unrealized profit from intercompany sales remaining in Pan's ending inventory must be offset against the unrealized profit in Pan's beginning inventory*

 c *Any unrealized profit on the intercompany transactions in Sar's ending inventory is eliminated in its entirety*

 d *Only 90 percent of any unrealized profit on the intercompany transactions in Sar's ending inventory is eliminated*

5. Pit Corporation sells an inventory item to its subsidiary, Sin Company, to be used as a plant asset by Sin. The workpaper entry to eliminate intercompany profits in the year of sale will *not* include:

 a *A debit to sales*

 b *A credit to cost of sales*

 c *A credit to inventories*

 d *A credit to plant assets*

6. Sel Corporation regularly sells inventory items to its parent, Pul Corporation. In preparing the consolidated income statement, which of the following items would *not* be affected by the direction (upstream or downstream) of these intercompany sales?

 a *Consolidated gross profit*

 b *Noncontrolling interest share*

 c *Controlling interest share of consolidated net income*

 d *Consolidated retained earnings*

7. Pen Corporation regularly sells inventory items to its subsidiary, Shu Corporation. If unrealized profits in Shu's 2011 year-end inventory exceed the unrealized profits in its 2012 year-end inventory:

 a *Combined cost of sales will be greater than consolidated cost of sales in 2011*

 b *Combined cost of sales will be less than consolidated cost of sales in 2011*

 c *Combined gross profit will be greater than consolidated gross profit in 2011*

 d *Combined sales will be less than consolidated sales in 2011*

8. Spa Corporation is a 90 percent-owned subsidiary of Ply Corporation, acquired on January 1, 2011, at a price equal to book value and fair value. Ply accounts for its investment in Spa using the equity method of accounting. The only intercompany transactions between the two affiliates in 2011 and 2012 are as follows:

2011	Ply sold inventory items that cost $400,000 to Spa for $500,000. One-fourth of this merchandise remains unsold at December 31, 2011
2012	Ply sold inventory items that cost $600,000 to Spa for $750,000. One-third of this merchandise remains unsold at December 31, 2012

At December 31, 2012, Ply's Investment in Spa account:

 a *Will equal its underlying equity in Spa*

 b *Will be $25,000 greater than its underlying equity in Spa*

 c *Will be $50,000 less than its underlying equity in Spa*

 d *Will be $25,000 less than its underlying equity in Spa*

E 5-2

[Based on AICPA] General problems

1. Per, Inc., owns 80 percent of Sen, Inc. During 2011, Per sold goods with a 40 percent gross profit to Sen. Sen sold all of these goods in 2011. For 2011 consolidated financial statements, how should the summation of Per and Sen income statement items be adjusted?

 a *Sales and cost of goods sold should be reduced by the intercompany sales.*

 b *Sales and cost of goods sold should be reduced by 80 percent of the intercompany sales.*

 c *Net income should be reduced by 80 percent of the gross profit on intercompany sales.*

 d *No adjustment is necessary.*

2. Car Company had the following transactions with affiliated parties during 2011.

 ■ Sales of $180,000 to Den, with $60,000 gross profit. Den had $45,000 of this inventory on hand at year-end. Car owns a 15 percent interest in Den and does not exert significant influence.

 ■ Purchases of raw materials totaling $720,000 from Ken Corporation, a wholly owned subsidiary. Ken's gross profit on the sale was $144,000. Car had $180,000 of this inventory remaining on December 31, 2011.

Before eliminating entries, Car had consolidated current assets of $960,000. What amount should Car report in its December 31, 2011, consolidated balance sheet for current assets?

a $960,000
b $951,000
c $924,000
d $303,000

3. Par Corporation owns 80 percent of Sit's common stock. During 2011, Par sold Sit $750,000 of inventory on the same terms as sales made to third parties. Sit sold 100 percent of the inventory purchased from Par in 2011. The following information pertains to Sit's and Par's sales for 2011:

	Par	Sit
Sales	$3,000,000	$2,100,000
Cost of Sales	1,200,000	1,050,000
	$1,800,000	$1,050,000

What amount should Par report as cost of sales in its 2011 consolidated income statement?

a $2,250,000
b $2,040,000
c $1,500,000
d $1,290,000

E 5-3

Downstream sales

1. The separate incomes of Pil Corporation and Sil Corporation, a 100 percent-owned subsidiary of Pil, for 2012 are $2,000,000 and $1,000,000, respectively. Pil sells all of its output to Sil at 150 percent of Pil's cost of production. During 2011 and 2012, Pil's sales to Sil were $9,000,000 and $7,000,000, respectively. Sil's inventory at December 31, 2011, included $3,000,000 of the merchandise acquired from Pil, and its December 31, 2012, inventory included $2,400,000 of such merchandise. Assume Sil sells the inventory purchased from Pil in the following year.

A consolidated income statement for Pil Corporation and Subsidiary for 2012 should show controlling interest share of consolidated net income of:

a $2,200,000
b $2,800,000
c $3,000,000
d $3,200,000

USE THE FOLLOWING INFORMATION IN ANSWERING QUESTIONS 2 AND 3:

Pan Corporation owns 75 percent of the voting common stock of Sat Corporation, acquired at book value during 2011. Selected information from the accounts of Pan and Sat for 2011 are as follows:

	Pan	Sat
Sales	$1,800,000	$1,000,000
Cost of Sales	980,000	380,000

During 2012 Pan sold merchandise to Sat for $100,000, at a gross profit to Pan of $40,000. Half of this merchandise remained in Sat's inventory at December 31, 2012. Sat's December 31, 2011, inventory included unrealized profit of $8,000 on goods acquired from Pan.

---

2. In a consolidated income statement for Pan Corporation and Subsidiary for the year 2012, consolidated sales should be:

a $2,900,000
b $2,800,000
c $2,725,000
d $2,700,000

3. In a consolidated income statement for Pan Corporation and Subsidiary for the year 2012, consolidated cost of sales should be:

a $1,372,000
b $1,360,000
c $1,272,000
d $1,248,000

E 5-4

Upstream sales

Pid Corporation owns an 80 percent interest in Sed Corporation and at December 31, 2011, Pid's investment in Sed on an equity basis was equal to 80 percent of Sed's stockholders' equity. During 2012, Sed sells merchandise to Pid for $200,000, at a gross profit to Sed of $40,000. At December 31, 2012, half of this merchandise is included in Pid's inventory. Separate incomes for Pid and Sed for 2012 are summarized as follows:

	Pid	Sed
Sales	$1,000,000	$600,000
Cost of sales	(500,000)	(400,000)
Gross profit	500,000	200,000
Operating expenses	(250,000)	(80,000)
Separate incomes	$ 250,000	$120,000

1. Pid's income from Sed for 2012 is:
   a $96,000
   b $80,000
   c $76,000
   d $56,000

2. Consolidated cost of sales for 2012 is:
   a $920,000
   b $900,000
   c $880,000
   d $720,000

3. Noncontrolling interest share for 2012 is:
   a $24,000
   b $20,000
   c $8,000
   d $4,000

E 5-5

Upstream sales

Par Corporation owns an 80 percent interest in Sel Corporation acquired several years ago. Sel regularly sells merchandise to its parent at 125 percent of Sel's cost. Gross profit data of Par and Sel for 2012 are as follows:

	Par	Sel
Sales	$1,000,000	$800,000
Cost of goods sold	800,000	640,000
Gross profit	$ 200,000	$160,000

During 2012, Par purchased inventory items from Sel at a transfer price of $400,000. Par's December 31, 2011 and 2012, inventories included goods acquired from Sel of $100,000 and $125,000, respectively. Assume Par sells the inventory purchased from Sel in the following year.

1. Consolidated sales of Par Corporation and Subsidiary for 2012 were:
   a $1,800,000
   b $1,425,000
   c $1,400,000
   d $1,240,000

2. The unrealized profits in the year-end 2011 and 2012 inventories were:
   a $100,000 and $125,000, respectively
   b $80,000 and $100,000, respectively
   c $20,000 and $25,000, respectively
   d $16,000 and $20,000, respectively

3. Consolidated cost of goods sold of Par Corporation and Subsidiary for 2012 was:
   a $1,024,000
   b $1,045,000
   c $1,052,800
   d $1,056,000

E 5-6

Upstream and downstream sales

1. Pat Corporation owns 70 percent of Sue Company's common stock, acquired January 1, 2012. Patents from the investment are being amortized at a rate of $20,000 per year. Sue regularly sells merchandise to Pat at 150 percent of Sue's cost. Pat's December 31, 2012, and 2013 inventories include goods purchased intercompany of $112,500 and $33,000, respectively. The separate incomes (do not include investment income) of Pat and Sue for 2013 are summarized as follows:

	Pat	Sue
Sales	$1,200,000	$800,000
Cost of sales	(600,000)	(500,000)
Other expenses	(400,000)	(100,000)
Separate incomes	$ 200,000	$200,000

Total consolidated income should be allocated to controlling and noncontrolling interest shares in the amounts of:

a **$344,550 and $61,950, respectively**

b **$358,550 and $60,000, respectively**

c **$346,500 and $60,000, respectively**

d **$346,500 and $67,950, respectively**

2. Pac acquired a 60 percent interest in Slo on January 1, 2011, for $360,000, when Slo's net assets had a book value and fair value of $600,000. During 2011, Pac sold inventory items that cost $600,000 to Slo for $800,000, and Slo's inventory at December 31, 2011, included one-fourth of this merchandise. Pac reported separate income from its own operations (excludes investment income) of $300,000, and Slo reported a net loss of $150,000 for 2011. Controlling share of consolidated net income for Pac Corporation and Subsidiary for 2011 is:

a **$260,000**

b **$180,000**

c **$160,000**

d **$100,000**

3. San Corporation, a 75 percent-owned subsidiary of Par Corporation, sells inventory items to its parent at 125 percent of cost. Inventories of the two affiliates for 2011 are as follows:

	Par	San
Beginning inventory	$400,000	$250,000
Ending inventory	500,000	200,000

Par's beginning and ending inventories include merchandise acquired from San of $150,000 and $200,000, respectively, which is sold in the following year. If San reports net income of $300,000 for 2011, Par's income from San will be:

a **$255,000**

b **$217,500**

c **$215,000**

d **$195,000**

E 5-7

Determine consolidated net income with downstream intercompany sales

Pan Corporation owns an 80 percent interest in the common stock of She Corporation, acquired several years ago at book value. Pan regularly sells merchandise to She. Information relevant to the intercompany sales and profits of Pan and She for 2011, 2012, and 2013 is as follows:

	2011	2012	2013
Sales to She	$300,000	$360,000	$600,000
Unrealized profit in She's inventory at December 31	90,000	120,000	60,000
She's separate income	1,500,000	1,650,000	1,425,000
Pan's separate income (does not include investment income)	900,000	1,200,000	1,050,000

REQUIRED: Prepare a schedule showing consolidated net income for each year.

E 5-8

Consolidated income statement with downstream sales

The separate incomes (which do not include investment income) of Pic Corporation and Sil Corporation, its 80 percent-owned subsidiary, for 2011 were determined as follows (in thousands):

	Pic	Sil
Sales	$800	$200
Less: Cost of sales	400	80
Gross profit	400	120
Other expenses	200	60
Separate incomes	$200	$ 60

During 2011, Pic sold merchandise that cost $40,000 to Sil for $80,000, and at December 31, 2011, half of these inventory items remained unsold by Sil.

REQUIRED: Prepare a consolidated income statement for Pic Corporation and Subsidiary for the year ended December 31, 2011.

E 5-9

Compute noncontrolling interest and consolidated cost of sales (upstream sales)

Income statement information for 2011 for Pug Corporation and its 60 percent-owned subsidiary, Sev Corporation, is as follows:

	Pug	Sev
Sales	$900	$350
Cost of sales	400	250
Gross profit	500	100
Operating expenses	250	50
Sev's net income		$ 50
Pug's separate income	$250	

Intercompany sales for 2011 are upstream (from Sev to Pug) and total $100,000. Pug's December 31, 2010, and December 31, 2011, inventories contain unrealized profits of $5,000 and $10,000, respectively.

REQUIRED

1. Compute noncontrolling interest share for 2011.

2. Compute consolidated sales, cost of sales, and total consolidated income for 2011.

E 5-10

Consolidated income statement (upstream sales)

Pap Corporation purchased an 80 percent interest in Sak Corporation for $1,200,000 on January 1, 2012, at which time Sak's stockholders' equity consisted of $1,000,000 common stock and $400,000 retained earnings. The excess fair value over book value was goodwill. Comparative income statements for the two corporations for 2013 are as follows:

	Pap	Sak
Sales	$2,000	$1,000
Income from Sak	224	—
Cost of sales	(800)	(500)
Depreciation expense	(260)	(80)
Other expenses	(180)	(120)
Net income	$ 984	$ 300

Dividends of Pap and Sak for all of 2013 were $600,000 and $200,000, respectively. During 2012 Sak sold inventory items to Pap for $160,000. This merchandise cost Sak $100,000, and one-third of it remained in Pap's December 31, 2012, inventory. During 2013 Sak's sales to Pap were $180,000. This merchandise cost Sak $120,000, and one-half of it remained in Pap's December 31, 2013, inventory.

REQUIRED: Prepare a consolidated income statement for Pap Corporation and Subsidiary for the year ended December 31, 2013.

E 5-11

Upstream sales

On January 1, 2004, Pre Corporation acquired 60 percent of the voting common shares of Sue Corporation at an excess of fair value over book value of $1,000,000. This excess was attributed to plant assets with a remaining useful life of five years. For the year ended December 31, 2011, Sue prepared *condensed* financial statements as follows (in thousands):

Condensed Balance Sheet at December 31, 2011	
Current assets (except inventory)	$ 600
Inventories	300
Plant assets—net	5,000
Total assets	$5,900
Liabilities	$ 400
Capital stock	3,400
Retained earnings	2,100
Total equities	$5,900
Condensed Statement of Income and Retained Earnings	
Sales	$1,000
Cost of sales	(500)
Other expenses	(300)
Net income	200
Add: Retained earnings January 1, 2011	2,000
Less: Dividends	100
Retained earnings December 31, 2011	$2,100

Sue regularly sells inventory items to Pre at a price of 120 percent of cost. In 2010 and 2011, sales from Sue to Pre are as follows:

	2010	2011
Sales at selling price	$840	$960
Inventory unsold by Pre on December 31	120	360

1. Under the equity method, Pre reports investment income from Sue for 2011 of:

a *$120*

b *$96*

c *$80*

d *$104 loss*

2. Noncontrolling interest on December 31, 2011, is:

a *$2,200*

b *$2,184*

c *$2,176*

d *$2,140*

3. On the books of Pre Corporation, the investment account is properly reflected on December 31, 2011, at:

a *$3,240*

b *$3,264*

c *$3,276*

d *Not enough information is given.*

E 5-12

Consolidated income statement (intercompany sales correction)

The consolidated income statement of Pul and Swa for 2011 was as follows (in thousands):

Sales	$2,760
Cost of sales	(1,840)
Operating expenses	(320)
Income to 20 percent noncontrolling interest in Swa	(80)
Consolidated net income	$ 520

After the consolidated income statement was prepared, it was discovered that intercompany sales transactions had not been considered and that unrealized profits had not been eliminated. Information concerning these items follows (in thousands):

	Cost	Selling Price	Unsold at Year-End
2010 Sales—Pul to Swa	$320	$360	25%
2011 Sales—Swa to Pul	180	240	40

REQUIRED: Prepare a corrected consolidated income statement for Pul and Swa for the year ended December 31, 2011.

PROBLEMS

P 5-1

Consolidated income and retained earnings (upstream sales, noncontrolling interest)

Por Corporation acquired its 90 percent interest in Sam Corporation at its book value of $1,800,000 on January 1, 2011, when Sam had capital stock of $1,500,000 and retained earnings of $500,000.

The December 31, 2011 and 2012, inventories of Por included merchandise acquired from Sam of $150,000 and $200,000, respectively. Sam realizes a gross profit of 40 percent on all merchandise sold. During 2011 and 2012, sales by Sam to Por were $300,000 and $400,000, respectively.

Summary adjusted trial balances for Por and Sam at December 31, 2012, follow (in thousands):

	Por	Sam
Cash	$ 500	$ 100
Receivables—net	1,000	250
Inventories	1,200	500
Plant assets—net	1,250	2,400
Investment in Sam—90%	2,178	—
Cost of sales	4,000	1,950
Other expenses	1,700	800
Dividends	500	250
	$12,328	$6,250

	Por	Sam
Accounts payable	$ 750	$ 450
Other liabilities	300	300
Capital stock, $10 par	2,500	1,500
Retained earnings	1,846	750
Sales	6,500	3,250
Income from Sam	432	—
	$12,328	$6,250

REQUIRED: Prepare a combined consolidated income and retained earnings statement for Por Corporation and Subsidiary for the year ended December 31, 2012.

P 5-2

Computations (upstream sales)

Put Corporation acquired a 90 percent interest in Sam Corporation at book value on January 1, 2011. Intercompany purchases and sales and inventory data for 2011, 2012, and 2013, are as follows:

	Sales by Sam to Put	Intercompany Profit in Put's Inventory at December 31
2011	$200,000	$15,000
2012	150,000	12,000
2013	300,000	24,000

Selected data from the financial statements of Put and Sam at and for the year ended December 31, 2013, are as follows:

	Put	Sam
Income Statement		
Sales	$900,000	$600,000
Cost of sales	625,000	300,000
Expenses	225,000	150,000
Income from Sam	124,200	—
Balance Sheet		
Inventory	$150,000	$ 80,000
Retained earnings December 31, 2013	425,000	220,000
Capital stock	500,000	300,000

REQUIRED: Prepare well-organized schedules showing computations for each of the following:

1. Consolidated cost of sales for 2013
2. Noncontrolling interest share for 2013
3. Consolidated net income for 2013
4. Noncontrolling interest at December 31, 2013

P 5-3
Computations (parent buys from one subsidiary and sells to the other)

Pot Company owns controlling interests in San and Tay Corporations, having acquired an 80 percent interest in San in 2011, and a 90 percent interest in Tay on January 1, 2012. Pot's investments in San and Tay were at book value equal to fair value.

Inventories of the affiliated companies at December 31, 2012, and December 31, 2013, were as follows:

	December 31, 2012	December 31, 2013
Pot inventories	$120,000	$108,000
San inventories	77,500	62,500
Tay inventories	48,000	72,000

Pot sells to San at a 25 percent markup based on cost, and Tay sells to Pot at a 20 percent markup based on cost. Pot's beginning and ending inventories for 2013 consisted of 40 percent and 50 percent, respectively, of goods acquired from Tay. All of San's inventories consisted of merchandise acquired from Pot.

REQUIRED

1. Calculate the inventory that should appear in the December 31, 2012, consolidated balance sheet.
2. Calculate the inventory that should appear in the December 31, 2013, consolidated balance sheet.

P 5-4
Computations (upstream and downstream sales)

Comparative income statements of Stu Corporation for the calendar years 2011, 2012, and 2013 are as follows (in thousands):

	2011	2012	2013
Sales	$12,000	$12,750	$14,250
Cost of sales	6,300	6,600	7,500
Gross profit	5,700	6,150	6,750
Operating expenses	4,500	4,800	5,700
Net income	$ 1,200	$ 1,350	$ 1,050

ADDITIONAL INFORMATION

1. Stu was a 75 percent-owned subsidiary of Pli Corporation throughout the 2011–2013 period. Pli's separate income (excludes income from Stu) was $5,400,000, $5,100,000, and $6,000,000 in 2011, 2012, and 2013, respectively. Pli acquired its interest in Stu at its underlying book value, which was equal to fair value on July 1, 2010.

2. Pli sold inventory items to Stu during 2011 at a gross profit to Pli of $600,000. Half the merchandise remained in Stu's inventory at December 31, 2011. Total sales by Pli to Stu in 2011 were $1,500,000. The remaining merchandise was sold by Stu in 2012.

3. Pli's inventory at December 31, 2012, included items acquired from Stu on which Stu made a profit of $300,000. Total sales by Stu to Pli during 2012 were $1,200,000.

4. There were no unrealized profits in the December 31, 2013, inventories of either Stu or Pli.

5. Pli uses the equity method of accounting for its investment in Stu.

REQUIRED

1. Prepare a schedule showing Pli's income from Stu for the years 2011, 2012, and 2013.

2. Compute Pli's net income for the years 2011, 2012, and 2013.

3. Prepare a schedule of consolidated net income for Pli Corporation and Subsidiary for the years 2011, 2012, and 2013, beginning with the separate incomes of the two affiliates and including noncontrolling interest computations.

P 5-5

Workpapers (100 percent owned, downstream sales, year after acquisition)

Pan Corporation acquired 100 percent of Sal Corporation's outstanding voting common stock on January 1, 2011, for $660,000 cash. Sal's stockholders' equity on this date consisted of $300,000 capital stock and $300,000 retained earnings. The difference between the price paid by Pan and the underlying equity acquired in Sal was allocated $30,000 to Sal's undervalued inventory and the remainder to patents with a five-year write-off period. The undervalued inventory items were sold by Sal during 2011.

Pan made sales of $100,000 to Sal at a gross profit of $40,000 during 2011; during 2012, Pan made sales of $120,000 to Sal at a gross profit of $48,000. One-half the 2011 sales were inventoried by Sal at year-end 2011, and one-fourth the 2012 sales were inventoried by Sal at year-end 2012. Sal owed Pan $17,000 on account at December 31, 2012.

The separate financial statements of Pan and Sal Corporations at and for the year ended December 31, 2012, are summarized as follows (in thousands):

	Pan	Sal
Combined Income and Retained Earnings Statements for the Year Ended December 31, 2012		
Sales	$ 800	$400
Income from Sal	102	—
Cost of sales	(400)	(200)
Depreciation expense	(110)	(40)
Other expenses	(192)	(60)
Net income	200	100
Beginning retained earnings	600	380
Less: Dividends	(100)	(50)
Retained earnings December 31, 2012	$ 700	$430
Balance Sheet at December 31, 2012		
Cash	$ 54	$ 37
Receivables—net	90	60
Inventories	100	80
Other assets	70	90
Land	50	50
Buildings—net	200	150
Equipment—net	500	400
Investment in Sal	736	—
Total assets	$1,800	$867

	Pan	Sal
Accounts payable	$ 160	$ 47
Other liabilities	340	90
Common stock, $10 par	600	300
Retained earnings	700	430
Total equities	$1,800	$867

REQUIRED: Prepare workpapers to consolidate the financial statements of Pan Corporation and Subsidiary at and for the year ended December 31, 2012.

P 5-6

Workpapers (noncontrolling interest, downstream sales, year after acquisition)

Pay Corporation acquired a 75 percent interest in Sue Corporation for $600,000 on January 1, 2011, when Sue's equity consisted of $300,000 capital stock and $100,000 retained earnings. The fair values of Sue's assets and liabilities were equal to book values on this date, and goodwill is not amortized. Pay uses the equity method of accounting for Sue.

During 2011, Pay sold inventory items to Sue for $160,000, and at December 31, 2011, Sue's inventory included items on which there were $20,000 unrealized profits. During 2012, Pay sold inventory items to Sue for $260,000, and at December 31, 2012, Sue's inventory included items on which there were $40,000 unrealized profits.

On December 31, 2012, Sue owed Pay $30,000 on account for merchandise purchases. The financial statements of Pay and Sue Corporations at and for the year ended December 31, 2012, are summarized as follows (in thousands):

	Pay	Sue
Combined Income and Retained Earnings Statements for the Year Ended December 31, 2012		
Sales	$ 1,200	$ 800
Income from Sue	205	—
Cost of sales	(540)	(420)
Operating expenses	(290)	(80)
Net income	575	300
Beginning retained earnings	365	180
Deduct: Dividends	(300)	(100)
Retained earnings December 31, 2012	$ 640	$ 380
Balance Sheet at December 31, 2012		
Cash	$ 170	$ 60
Accounts receivable	330	200
Dividends receivable	30	—
Inventories	120	160
Land	160	100
Buildings—net	460	200
Equipment—net	400	280
Investment in Sue	770	—
Total assets	$ 2,440	$1,000
Accounts payable	$ 450	$ 200
Dividends payable	140	40
Other liabilities	310	80
Common stock, $10 par	900	300
Retained earnings	640	380
Total equities	$ 2,440	$1,000

REQUIRED: Prepare consolidation workpapers for Pay Corporation and Subsidiary for the year ended December 31, 2012.

P 5-7

Consolidation workpapers (upstream sales, noncontrolling interest)

Pol Corporation purchased a 90 percent interest in San Corporation on December 31, 2010, for $2,700,000 cash, when San had capital stock of $2,000,000 and retained earnings of $500,000. All San's assets and liabilities were recorded at their fair values when Pol acquired its interest. The excess of fair value over book value is due to previously unrecorded patents and is being amortized over a 10-year period.

The Pol–San affiliation is a vertically integrated merchandising operation, with San selling all of its output to Pol Corporation at 140 percent of its cost. Pol sells the merchandise acquired from San at 150 percent of its purchase price from San. All of Pol's December 31, 2011, and December 31, 2012, inventories of $280,000 and $420,000, respectively, were acquired from San. San's December 31, 2011, and December 31, 2012, inventories were $800,000 each.

Pol's accounts payable at December 31, 2012, includes $100,000 owed to San from 2012 purchases.

Comparative financial statements for Pol Corporation and San Corporation at and for the year ended December 31, 2012, are as follows (in thousands):

	Pol	San
Combined Income and Retained Earnings Statement for the Year Ended December 31, 2012		
Sales	$8,190	$5,600
Income from San	819	—
Cost of sales	(5,460)	(4,000)
Other expenses	(1,544)	(600)
Net income	2,005	1,000
Add: Beginning retained earnings	1,200	700
Deduct: Dividends	(1,000)	(500)
Retained earnings December 31, 2012	$2,205	$1,200
Balance Sheet at December 31, 2012		
Cash	$ 753	$ 500
Inventory	420	800
Other current assets	600	200
Plant assets—net	3,000	3,000
Investment in San	3,132	—
Total assets	$7,905	$4,500
Current liabilities	$1,700	$1,300
Capital stock	4,000	2,000
Retained earnings	2,205	1,200
Total equities	$7,905	$4,500

REQUIRED: Prepare consolidation workpapers for Pol Corporation and Subsidiary for the year ended December 31, 2012.

P 5-8

Consolidated workpapers (downstream sales)

Pan Corporation acquired 100 percent of Sal Corporation's outstanding voting common stock on January 1, 2011, for $660,000 cash. Sal's stockholders' equity on this date consisted of $300,000 capital stock and $300,000 retained earnings. The difference between the fair value of Sal and the underlying equity acquired in Sal was allocated $30,000 to Sal's undervalued inventory and the remainder to goodwill. The undervalued inventory items were sold by Sal during 2011.

Pan made sales of $100,000 to Sal at a gross profit of $40,000 during 2011; during 2012, Pan made sales of $120,000 to Sal at a gross profit of $48,000. One-half the 2011 sales were inventoried by Sal at year-end 2011, and one-fourth the 2012 sales were inventoried by Sal at year-end 2012. Sal owed Pan $17,000 on account at December 31, 2012.

The separate financial statements of Pan and Sal Corporations at and for the year ended December 31, 2012, are summarized as follows:

	Pan	Sal
Combined Income and Retained Earnings Statements for the Year Ended December 31, 2012 (in thousands)		
Sales	$ 800	$400
Income from Sal	108	—
Cost of sales	(400)	(200)
Depreciation expense	(110)	(40)
Other expenses	(192)	(60)
Net income	206	100
Beginning retained earnings	606	380
Less: Dividends	(100)	(50)
Retained earnings December 31, 2012	$ 712	$430
Balance Sheet at December 31, 2012		
Cash	$ 54	$ 37
Receivables—net	90	60
Inventories	100	80
Other assets	70	90
Land	50	50
Buildings—net	200	150
Equipment—net	500	400
Investment in Sal	748	—
Total assets	$1,812	$867
Accounts payable	$ 160	$ 47
Other liabilities	340	90
Common stock, $10 par	600	300
Retained earnings	712	430
Total equities	$1,812	$867

REQUIRED: Prepare workpapers to consolidate the financial statements of Pan Corporation and Subsidiary at and for the year ended December 31, 2012.

P 5-9

Consolidated workpaper (noncontrolling interest, upstream sales, intercompany receivables/payables)

Poe Corporation purchased a 90 percent interest in San Corporation on December 31, 2011, for $2,700,000 cash, when San had capital stock of $2,000,000 and retained earnings of $500,000. All San's assets and liabilities were recorded at fair values when Poe acquired its interest. The excess of fair value over book value is goodwill.

The Poe–San affiliation is a vertically integrated merchandising operation, with San selling all of its output to Poe Corporation at 140 percent of its cost. Poe sells the merchandise acquired from San at 150 percent of its purchase price from San. All of Poe's December 31, 2013, and December 31, 2014, inventories of $280,000 and $420,000, respectively, were acquired from San. San's December 31, 2013, and December 31, 2014, inventories were $800,000 each.

Poe's accounts payable at December 31, 2014, includes $100,000 owed to San from 2014 purchases.

Comparative financial statements for Poe and San Corporations at and for the year ended December 31, 2014, are as follows:

	Poe	San
Combined Income and Retained Earnings Statement for the Year Ended December 31, 2014 (in thousands)		
Sales	$8,190	$5,600
Income from San	864	—
Cost of sales	(5,460)	(4,000)
Other expenses	(1,544)	(600)
Net income	2,050	1,000
Add: Beginning retained earnings	1,250	700
Deduct: Dividends	(1,000)	(500)
Retained earnings December 31, 2014	$2,300	$1,200

	Poe	San
Balance Sheet at December 31, 2014		
Cash	$ 758	$ 500
Inventory	420	800
Other current assets	600	200
Plant assets—net	3,000	3,000
Investment in San	3,222	—
Total assets	$8,000	$4,500
Current liabilities	$1,700	$1,300
Capital stock	4,000	2,000
Retained earnings	2,300	1,200
Total equities	$8,000	$4,500

REQUIRED: Prepare a consolidation workpaper for Poe Corporation and Subsidiary for the year ended December 31, 2014.

INTERNET ASSIGNMENT

Visit *Ford Motor Company's* Web site and download the 2009 annual report. First, review the annual report and summarize any information you find concerning intercompany inventory transfers, or intersegment sales. Prepare a brief summary of your findings.

SEC Influence on Accounting

Accountants recognize the influence of the Securities and Exchange Commission (SEC) on the development of accounting and reporting principles. Congress gave the SEC authority to establish accounting principles when it passed the Securities Exchange Act of 1934, which created the SEC. Initially, Congress assigned the administration of the Securities Act of 1933 to the Federal Trade Commission. But a year later, the 1934 act created the Securities and Exchange Commission and made it responsible for establishing regulations over accounting and auditing matters for firms under its jurisdiction. Thus, the SEC has the authority to prescribe accounting principles for entities that fall under its jurisdiction.[1]

A combination of inadequate regulation of securities at the federal and state levels, the stock market crash of 1929, and the Great Depression of the 1930s contributed to the enactment of new securities legislation in the early 1930s. Similar circumstances surrounding the collapse of **Enron Corporation, WorldCom,** and others led to passage of the Sarbanes-Oxley Act and related legislation in recent years.

THE 1933 SECURITIES ACT

A primary objective of the Securities Act of 1933 was "to provide full and fair disclosure of the character of securities sold in interstate and foreign commerce and the mails, and to prevent fraud in the sale thereof" (Securities Act of 1933). Another objective of the 1933 act was to protect investors against fraud, deceit, and misrepresentation. There have been many amendments, but these objectives still constitute the primary thrust of the 1933 Act.

The Securities Act of 1933 is often called the "Truth in Securities Act." This is because the SEC's objective is to prevent the issuers of securities from disclosing false, incomplete, or otherwise misleading information to prospective buyers of their securities. The SEC emphasizes that its objective is not to pass judgment on the merits of any firm's securities. The SEC imposes severe penalties on firms and individuals that violate its disclosure requirements.

Issuance of Securities in Public Offerings

The Securities Act of 1933 regulates the issuance of specific securities to investors in public offerings. Public offerings of securities must be registered with the SEC and be advertised in a prospectus before being offered for sale to the public.

---

[1]For example, in 1993 the SEC issued *Staff Accounting Bulletin No. 93*, which requires discontinued operations that have not been divested within one year of their measurement dates to be accounted for prospectively as investments held for sale.

EXEMPT SECURITY ISSUES Certain security issuances are exempt from the 1933 Act. A partial list of exempt securities includes those issued by governmental units, not-for-profit organizations, firms in bankruptcy and subject to court order, firms in stock splits or in direct sales to existing shareholders (private placements), and firms issuing intrastate securities with sales limited to residents of that state.

ISSUES OF $5,000,000 OR LESS *Regulation A* provides less-restrictive registration procedures for security issuances not exceeding $5,000,000. Regulation A permits firms to use an *offering circular* rather than the prospectus required for full registration.

THE PROSPECTUS The **prospectus** is a part of the registration statement that provides detailed information about the background of the registrant firm, including its development, its business, and its financial statements. An **offering circular** is like a prospectus but has fewer disclosure requirements. A copy of the prospectus must be presented to prospective buyers before the securities are offered for sale. A **preliminary prospectus** (also known as a *red herring prospectus*) is a communication that identifies the nature of the securities to be issued, states that they have not been approved or disapproved by the SEC, and explains how to obtain the prospectus when it becomes available.

THE SECURITIES EXCHANGE ACT OF 1934

The Securities Exchange Act of 1934 created the Securities and Exchange Commission and gave it authority to administer the 1933 Act as well as to regulate the trading of securities on national exchanges. Subsequently, the 1934 Act was amended to include securities traded in over-the-counter markets, provided that the firms have total assets of more than $10 million and at least 500 stockholders. Firms that want their securities traded on the national exchanges or in over-the-counter markets subject to the net-asset and stockholder limitations must file **registration statements** with the SEC. Form 10 is the primary form used for registering securities on national stock exchanges or in over-the-counter markets. This registration for trading purposes is required in addition to the registration prepared for new security issuances under the 1933 Act.

ADDITIONAL PERIODIC REPORTING REQUIREMENTS Companies covered by the 1934 Act also have periodic reporting responsibilities. These include filing 10-K annual reports, 10-Q quarterly reports, and 8-K current "material event" reports with the SEC. The information in these reports is publicly available so that company officers, directors, and major stockholders (insiders) will not be able to use it to gain an unfair advantage over the investing public. In other words, the objective is to provide full disclosure of all material facts about the company and thereby contribute to a more efficient and ethical securities market.

THE SEC AND NATIONAL EXCHANGES In addition to the registration and periodic reporting rules for publicly traded companies, the Securities Exchange Act contains registration and reporting requirements for the national securities exchanges. The SEC has responsibility for monitoring the activities of the national exchanges and ensuring their compliance with applicable legal provisions. The 1934 Act also gave the SEC broad enforcement powers over stockbrokers and dealers and over accountants involved in SEC work.

THE SARBANES-OXLEY ACT

The passage of Sarbanes-Oxley and related legislation provides the SEC with even broader powers and an increased budget for enforcement activities. SEC inquiries and enforcement actions against public companies have increased substantially since 2000. Many firms, for example, ***Krispy Kreme Doughnuts*** in January 2005, have restated earnings as a result of SEC investigations. Such activity is likely to continue.

Among SEC pronouncements, one of the most far-reaching is *Staff Accounting Bulletin No. 101, Revenue Recognition in Financial Statements*, issued in December 1999. Here the SEC addresses and clarifies revenue recognition issues commonly encountered in the modern and increasingly complex business world. Current common practices of selling bundled products and services and how to separate and recognize the components of revenue in such contracts are some of the SEC's many concerns. *SAB No. 101* represents the SEC's response to a research study on fraudulent reporting practices conducted by the Committee of Sponsoring Organizations (COSO) of the Treadway Commission in March 1999. That report indicated that more than one-half of the reporting frauds reviewed involved overstatement of revenues.

Additional Responsibilities of the SEC

Subsequent to the Securities Exchange Act of 1934, the SEC acquired regulatory and administrative responsibilities under the Public Utilities Holding Company Act of 1935, the Trust Indenture Act of 1939, the Investment Company Act of 1940, the Investment Advisers Act of 1940, the Securities Investor Protection Act of 1970, and the Foreign Corrupt Practices Act of 1977. These acts are listed for identification purposes, but this appendix does not discuss the SEC's responsibility under them.

THE REGISTRATION STATEMENT FOR SECURITY ISSUES

The Securities Act of 1933 requires firms issuing securities to the public to provide full and fair disclosure of all material facts about those securities. The disclosures are provided in a registration statement filed with the SEC at least 20 days before the securities are offered for sale to the public. The SEC may extend the 20-day waiting period if it finds deficient or misleading information in the registration statement. In addition, if a firm files an amendment to the registration statement, the SEC treats the amended statement as a new one for purposes of applying the 20-day rule.

Security Registration

The registration of securities with the SEC is ordinarily a major undertaking for the registrant company. The process includes developing a registration team consisting of financial managers, legal counsel, security underwriters, public accountants, and other professionals as needed. The team plans the registration process in detail, assigns responsibility for each task, coordinates the efforts of all team members, and maintains a viable timetable throughout each phase of the project. Because of its complexity, the coordination of efforts is sometimes referred to as a balancing act.

REGISTERING SECURITIES UNDER THE INTEGRATED DISCLOSURE SYSTEM In 1980 the SEC changed the process of registering securities when it adopted an integrated disclosure system for almost all reports required by the 1933 and 1934 Securities Acts. The integrated system revised the registration forms and streamlined the process for filing with the SEC. As a result, the registration statement is now completed in accordance with instructions for the particular registration form deemed appropriate for a specific registrant company.

For example, Form S-1 is a general form to be used by firms going public (issuing securities to the public for the first time) and by firms that have been SEC registrants for fewer than three years. It is also a default form to be used unless another form is specified. Forms S-2 and S-3 are forms with fewer disclosure requirements than S-1. They are used primarily for registrations of established firms that have been SEC registrants for more than three years and that meet certain other criteria. Form S-4 is used for registering securities issued in a business combination. Firms issuing securities under Regulation A use Form 1-A. A number of other registration forms are applicable to selected types of security issues and firm situations.

THE INTEGRATED DISCLOSURE SYSTEM

The basic regulations of the Securities and Exchange Commission are found in *Regulation S-X*, which prescribes rules for the form and content of financial statements filed with the SEC, and *Regulation S-K*, which covers the nonfinancial statement disclosures of the registration statements and other periodic filings with the SEC. Before the 1980s, the two regulations sometimes had conflicting requirements, and firms often had difficulty in identifying the appropriate rules and procedures for reporting to the SEC.

From 1933 to 1980 the SEC issued numerous *Accounting Series Releases* (ASRs)—official supplements to AICPA and FASB pronouncements—and *Staff Accounting Bulletins* (SABs)—informal interpretations by the SEC staff on GAAP and S-X provisions. The issuance of these ASRs and SABs often increased the difficulty of complying with SEC regulations because their provisions were sometimes inconsistent with GAAP or other SEC regulations.

Codification of SABs and ASRs

In implementing the integrated disclosure system, the SEC issued *SAB No. 40* to codify *SABs 1 through 38*. This was done to revise the content of the SABs to conform to GAAP, to eliminate duplicate material contained in some SABs, and in some cases to recognize FASB pronouncements as meeting the SEC's requirements. The SEC also codified the relevant accounting-related ASRs into *Financial Reporting Release (FRR) No. 1*. Thus, the current series consists of FRRs rather than ASRs.

Objectives of Integrated Disclosure System

The objectives of the integrated disclosure system are to simplify the registration process, to reduce the cost of compliance with SEC regulations, and to improve the quality of information provided to investors and other parties. Under the integrated system, the disclosure included in SEC filings and those distributed to investors via prospectuses, proxy statements, and annual reports are essentially the same.

Standardization of Audited Financial Statements

The integrated disclosure system amended Regulation S-X in order to standardize the financial statement requirements in most SEC filings. For example, Regulation S-X, which prescribes the form and content of financial statements filed with the SEC, was amended in 1992 to conform certain of its accounting and disclosure requirements to those contained in the FASB Standards (now the Codification). This permits the financial statements included in annual reports to shareholders to be the same as those included in the prospectus, the 10-K, and other reports filed with the SEC.

Note that the SEC's proxy rules govern the content of annual reports to shareholders. Under current rules, the content of the annual report to shareholders is the same as in 10-K filings. **Form 10-K** is the general form for the annual report that registrants file with the SEC. It is required to be filed within 90 days after the end of the registrant company's fiscal year. The 10-K report must be signed by the chief executive officer, the chief financial officer, the chief accounting officer, and a majority of the company's board of directors.

Exhibit A-1 summarizes the 10-K disclosures required by the SEC for public companies. As shown in the exhibit, the SEC divides the disclosures into four groups. This is done to distinguish the information required to be disclosed in annual reports to shareholders from the complete 10-K information package required for filings with the SEC. For example, the information included in Part II of the exhibit is primarily accounting information that is required for annual reports filed with the SEC as well as the annual reports distributed to the company's shareholders. The disclosure requirements summarized in Parts I, III, and IV of the exhibit are only required for SEC filings, but they may be included in annual reports to shareholders.

In implementing its integrated disclosure system, the SEC eliminated a number of differences between reports filed with the SEC and those contained in annual reports to shareholders. This permitted public companies to meet many of the SEC filing requirements by reference to disclosures made in the annual reports to shareholders. That is, companies can include copies of their annual shareholder reports in their 10-K filings and satisfy many SEC disclosure requirements with one report. The SEC encourages the incorporation of information by reference to other reports and does not require that information to be duplicated. This "incorporation by reference" ruling resulted in a substantial increase in the size of corporate annual reports and a corresponding decrease in the size of 10-K reports filed with the SEC.

FORM 8-K Form 8-K is a report that requires registrants to inform the SEC about significant changes that take place regarding firm policies or financial condition. Firms must submit the report within 15 days (5 days in some cases) of the occurrence of the event. Items that might be disclosed in Form 8-K include changes in management, major acquisitions or disposals of assets, lawsuits, bankruptcy filings, and unexpected changes in directors.

SUMMARY OF REQUIRED DISCLOSURES UNDER SEC FORM 10-K

Part I

Item 1: Business (nature and history of the business, industry segments, etc.)
Item 2: Properties (location, description, and use of property, etc.)
Item 3: Legal proceedings (details of pending legal proceedings)
Item 4: Voting by security holders (items submitted to shareholders for voting)

Part II

Item 5: Market for common equity (place traded, shares, dividends, etc.)
Item 6: Selected financial data (five-year trend data for net sales, income from continuing operations including EPS, total assets, long-term debt, cash dividends, etc.)
Item 7: Management's discussion and analysis (discussion of the firm's liquidity, capital resources, operations, financial condition, etc.)
Item 8: Financial statements and supplementary data (requirements include audited balance sheets for two years and audited income statements and statements of cash flows for three years; three-year and five-year summaries are required for selected statement items)
Item 9: Changes in accountants and disagreements on accounting matters (changes in accountants and accounting changes, disagreements, disclosures, etc.)

Part III

Item 10: Directors and executive officers (names, ages, positions, etc.)
Item 11: Executive compensation (names, positions, salaries, stock options, etc.)
Item 12: Security ownership of beneficial owners and management (listing of insider owners of securities)
Item 13: Certain relationships (business relations and transactions with management, etc.)

Part IV

Item 14: Exhibits, financial statement schedules, and 8-K reports (supporting schedules of securities, borrowings, subsidiaries, ratios, etc.)

FORM 10-Q Form 10-Q contains quarterly data prepared in accordance with GAAP and must be filed within 45 days of the end of each of the registrant's first three quarters. Chapter 14 of this text describes and illustrates the SEC requirements for quarterly reports. The SEC Web site (www.sec.gov) provides access to details of various SEC forms and filing requirements under the Securities Acts of 1933 and 1934, as well as subsequent legislation. The Web site also provides access to all of the SEC's rules and pronouncements.

SEC DEVELOPMENTS

INTERNATIONAL REGISTRANTS The SEC also regulates international firms that list their shares for trading on U.S. securities exchanges. Historically, the SEC required these firms to either convert to U.S. GAAP or to prepare financial statements in accordance with either their home nation's GAAP or International Financial Reporting Standards (IFRS). Those firms choosing to use non-U.S. GAAP were required to provide supplemental disclosures, notably including a reconciliation of their financial statements to U.S. GAAP. In November 2007, the SEC voted to change the rules for international registrants. The SEC permits these firms to provide IFRS-based financial statements. Reconciliations to U.S. GAAP are no longer necessary if the registrant prepares statements under IFRS.

This change may mark the demise of the FASB. There will likely be a domino effect. U.S. firms with significant international operations are likely to request similar treatment (i.e., preparation of IFRS-based financials), arguing for fairness. If the SEC permits these firms to use IFRS, all U.S. firms are likely to follow suit and request the same option. If these arguments succeed, the FASB may cease to exist or, at a minimum, see a dramatic reduction in its authority. A potential new role for the FASB would be to carve out a subset of IFRS deemed appropriate for U.S. financial reporting. For example, the United States would likely still permit firms to use the LIFO inventory method due to its significant tax ramifications. Most other nations ban LIFO.

REGULATION S The SEC issued **Regulation S** in 1990 to clarify the applicability of U.S. securities laws across national boundaries. Generally, the regulation provides that sales of securities outside the United States are not subject to the 1933 Securities Act. The regulation also provides "safe harbor" rules to exempt any U.S. companies that sell securities offshore from SEC registration requirements.

THE EDGAR SYSTEM The Securities and Exchange Commission introduced a massive new computerized system to facilitate the process of filing, reviewing, and disseminating corporate information to the public in 1984 [*www.sec.gov/edaux/searches.htm*]. **EDGAR** is an abbreviation for the SEC's system, titled Electronic Data Gathering Analysis and Retrieval System. One of the SEC's goals under the integrated disclosure system is to provide investors, analysts, and other interested parties with instant access to corporate information on file with the SEC.

SMALL BUSINESS Although most SEC registrants are large public companies, the capital needs of small business issuers (under $25 million in both revenue and public float) have been addressed by the SEC, and new financial rules for small business enterprises were adopted in 1992 and 1993. Those rules provide new opportunities for small firms to raise capital to start or expand their businesses. Rule 504 relating to certain tax-exempt private offerings was amended to allow issuers other than development-stage enterprises to raise up to $1,000,000 in any 12-month period without registering under the 1933 Securities Act. Also, safe-harbor rules for information or trends and future events that may affect future operating results have been revised.

SUMMARY

This appendix provides an overview of securities legislation related to financial accounting and reporting. It also explains the function of the Securities and Exchange Commission and its authority to prescribe accounting principles. SEC requirements that are relevant to particular topics are integrated into the chapters throughout this book. For example, Chapters 3 and 11 discuss and illustrate the SEC's requirement to push down the purchase price of a subsidiary to the subsidiary's financial statements. Chapter 8 discusses the SEC's position on recognizing gain on a subsidiary's stock sales, and Chapter 14 traces the history of the SEC's efforts in requiring segment disclosures and SEC requirements for interim reports.

REFERENCES TO THE AUTHORITATIVE LITERATURE

[1] FASB ASC 810-10-45-1. Originally *Statement of Financial Accounting Standards No. 160.* "Noncontrolling Interests." Norwalk, CT: Financial Accounting Standards Board, 2007.

[2] FASB ASC 323-10-15. Originally *Accounting Interpretation No. 1 of APB Opinion No. 18.* New York: American Institute of Certified Public Accountants, 1971.

[3] FASB ASC 810-10-45. Originally *Accounting Research Bulletin No. 51.* "Consolidated Financial Statements." New York: American Institute of Certified Public Accountants, 1959.

6 CHAPTER

Intercompany Profit Transactions—Plant Assets

Transactions between affiliates for sales and purchases of plant assets create unrealized profits and losses to the consolidated entity. The consolidated entity eliminates (defers) such profits and losses in reporting the results of operations and its financial position. We also eliminate these in reporting the financial position and results of operations of a parent under the equity method. The adjustments to eliminate the effects of intercompany profits on plant assets are similar to, but not identical with, those for unrealized inventory profits. Unrealized inventory profits self-correct over any two accounting periods, but unrealized profits or losses on plant assets affect the financial statements until the related assets are sold outside the consolidated entity or are exhausted through use by the purchasing affiliate. This chapter covers concepts and procedures for eliminating unrealized profits on plant assets in one-line consolidations under the equity method and in consolidated statements.

INTERCOMPANY PROFITS ON NONDEPRECIABLE PLANT ASSETS

LEARNING OBJECTIVE 1

The transfer of nondepreciable plant assets between affiliates at a price other than book value gives rise to unrealized profit or loss to the consolidated entity. An intercompany gain or loss appears in the income statement of the selling affiliate in the year of sale. However, such gain or loss is unrealized and must be eliminated from investment income in a one-line consolidation by the parent. We also eliminate its effects in preparing consolidated financial statements.

Intercompany transfers of plant assets are much less frequent than intercompany inventory transfers. They most likely occur when mergers are completed, as a part of a reorganization of the combined companies. Note 28 provides segment information in the 2009 annual report of **Ford Motor Company** (p. 160). If we look at total reported revenues by the automotive sector for 2009, we see an elimination of $1.003 billion of intersegment revenues. Ford is not required to break this amount down, but presumably a large part is deferral of unrealized profits on intercompany transfers of inventory and plant assets.

The direction of intercompany sales of plant assets, like intercompany sales of inventory items, is important in evaluating the effect of unrealized profit on parent and consolidated financial statements. Any gain or loss on sales downstream from parent to subsidiary is initially included in parent income and must be eliminated. The amount of elimination is 100 percent, regardless of the noncontrolling interest percentage. Subsidiary accounts include any profit or loss from upstream sales from subsidiary to parent. The parent recognizes only its share of the subsidiary's income, so only the parent's proportionate share of unrealized profits should be eliminated. The effect on consolidated net income is the same as for the parent.

This section of the chapter discusses and illustrates accounting practices for intercompany sales of land, covering both downstream and upstream sales.

Downstream Sale of Land

San Corporation is a 90 percent-owned subsidiary of Pak Corporation, acquired for $270,000 on January 1, 2011. Investment cost was equal to book value and fair value of the interest acquired. San's net income for 2011 was $70,000, and Pak's income, excluding its income from San, was $90,000. Pak's income includes a $10,000 unrealized gain on land that cost $40,000 and was sold to San for $50,000. Accordingly, Pak makes the following entries in accounting for its investment in San at December 31, 2011:

Investment in San (+A)	63,000	
Income from San (R, +SE)		63,000
To record 90% of San's $70,000 reported income.		
Income from San (−R, −SE)	10,000	
Investment in San (−A)		10,000
To eliminate unrealized profit on land sold to San.		

Exhibit 6-1 presents a consolidation workpaper for Pak and Subsidiary for 2011. Separate summary financial statements for Pak and San appear in the first two columns.

Gain on the sale of land should not appear in the consolidated income statement, and the land should be included in the consolidated balance sheet at its cost of $40,000. Entry a eliminates the gain on sale of land and reduces the land account to $40,000—its cost to the consolidated entity. This is the only entry that is significantly different from adjustments and eliminations illustrated in previous chapters.

a **Gain on sale of land (−Ga, −SE)**	**10,000**	
Land (−A)		**10,000**
To eliminate gain on intercompany sale of land and reduce land to its cost basis.		

The overvalued land will continue to appear in the separate balance sheet of San in subsequent years until it is sold outside of the consolidated entity, but the gain on land does not appear in the separate income statements of Pak in subsequent years. Therefore, entry a as shown in Exhibit 6-1 applies only in the year of the intercompany sale.

YEARS SUBSEQUENT TO INTERCOMPANY SALE   Here is the adjustment to reduce land to its cost to the consolidated entity in years subsequent to the year of the intercompany downstream sale:

Investment in San (+A)	**10,000**	
Land (−A)		**10,000**
To reduce land to its cost basis and adjust the investment account to establish		
reciprocity with San's equity accounts at the beginning of the period.		

The debit to the investment account adjusts its balance to establish reciprocity with the subsidiary equity accounts at the beginning of each subsequent period in which the land is held. For example, the investment account balance at December 31, 2011, is $323,000. This is $10,000 less than Pak's underlying equity in San of $333,000 on that date ($370,000 × 90%). The difference arises from the entry on the parent's books to reduce investment income and the investment account for the intercompany profit in the year of sale.

Sale in Subsequent Year to Outside Entity

Assume that San uses the land for four years and sells it for $65,000 in 2015. In the year of sale, San reports a $15,000 gain ($65,000 proceeds less $50,000 cost), but the gain to the consolidated entity is $25,000 ($65,000 proceeds less $40,000 cost to Pak).

PAK CORPORATION AND SUBSIDIARY CONSOLIDATION WORKPAPER FOR THE YEAR ENDED DECEMBER 31, 2011 (IN THOUSANDS)

EXHIBIT 6-1

Intercompany Profit from Downstream Sale of Land

	Pak	90% San	Adjustments and Eliminations Debits	Adjustments and Eliminations Credits	Consolidated Statements
Income Statement Sales	$380	$220			$600
Income from San	53		b 53		
Gain on sale of land	10		a 10		
Expenses (including cost of goods sold)	(300)	(150)			(450)
Noncontrolling interest share ($70,000 × 10%)			c 7		(7)
Controlling Share of Net income	**$143**	**$ 70**			**$143**
Retained Earnings Statement Retained earnings—Pak	207				$207
Retained earnings—San		$100	d 100		
Add: Controlling Share of Net income	143	70			143
Retained earnings—December 31	**$350**	**$170**			**$350**
Balance Sheet Other assets	$477	$350			$827
Land		50		a 10	40
Investment in San	323			b 53 d 270	
	$800	**$400**			**$867**
Liabilities	$ 50	$ 30			$ 80
Capital stock	400	200	d 200		400
Retained earnings	350	170			350
	$800	**$400**			
Noncontrolling interest				c 7 d 30	37
					$867

a Eliminates gain on sale of land and reduces land to a cost basis.
b Eliminates investment income and reduces the investment account to its January 1 balance.
c Records the noncontrolling interest in subsidiary earnings for the current period.
d Eliminates reciprocal equity and investment amounts and establishes beginning noncontrolling interest.

Pak recognizes its gain on the land in 2015 under the equity method by adjusting its investment income. The entry on Pak's books is:

Investment in San (+A)	10,000	
Income from San (R, +SE)		10,000

To recognize previously deferred profit on sale of land to San.

This entry on Pak's books reestablishes equality between the investment account and 90 percent of the equity of San on the same date.

The following workpaper entry adjusts the $15,000 gain to San to the $25,000 consolidated gain on the land:

Investment in San (+A)	**10,000**	
Gain on land (Ga, +SE)		**10,000**
To adjust gain on land to the $25,000 gain to the consolidated entity.		

This entry in the year of sale is almost the same as the entry in each of the years 2012, 2013, and 2014 to eliminate the unrealized profit from the land account. The difference is that the credit is gain because the land no longer appears on the separate books of Pak or San.

Upstream Sale of Land

To illustrate the accounting for upstream sales of nondepreciable plant assets, assume that Pak purchases the land referred to in the previous section during 2011 from its 90 percent-owned affiliate, San. As before, San's net income for 2011 is $70,000, and Pak's income, excluding its income from San, is $90,000. However, the $10,000 unrealized profit on the intercompany sale of land is now reflected in the income of San, rather than Pak. In accounting for its investment in San at year-end 2011, Pak makes the following entries:

Investment in San (+A)	63,000	
Income from San (R, +SE)		63,000
To record 90% of San's reported net income.		
Income from San (−R, −SE)	9,000	
Investment in San (−A)		9,000
To eliminate 90% of the $10,000 unrealized profit on land purchased from San.		

These entries record Pak's investment income for 2011 in the amount of $54,000 ($63,000 − $9,000). Note that the $54,000 investment income consists of 90 percent of San's $60,000 realized income for 2011 ($70,000 reported income less $10,000 unrealized gain on land). Pak's net income for 2011 is $144,000 ($90,000 separate income plus $54,000 investment income), as compared with $143,000 in the case of the downstream sale. The difference lies in the $1,000 unrealized gain attributed to noncontrolling interest and deducted from noncontrolling interest share.

Exhibit 6-2 presents a consolidation workpaper for Pak Corporation and Subsidiary for 2011. The workpaper uses the same information as in Exhibit 6-1 except for minor changes necessary to switch to the upstream sale situation.

The adjustments reflected in the consolidation workpaper in Exhibit 6-2 are the same as those in Exhibit 6-1 except for the amount of entry b, which is $54,000 rather than $53,000 and the amount of entry c, which is discussed below. Entry a eliminates the full amount of the gain on the sale of land and reduces the land to its cost basis to the consolidated entity whether the intercompany sale is upstream or downstream.

Noncontrolling Interest Share   Noncontrolling interest share is $7,000 in Exhibit 6-1 but only $6,000 in Exhibit 6-2. We reduce the noncontrolling interest share with its share of the unrealized gain on San's sale of land to Pak. We do this in the consolidation workpaper by converting San's reported net income into realized income and multiplying by the noncontrolling interest percentage. Thus, the $6,000 noncontrolling interest share is 10 percent of San's $60,000 realized income.

Years Subsequent to Intercompany Sale   While Pak continues to hold the land in subsequent years, consolidation will require an adjusting entry to reduce the land account to its cost basis to the consolidated entity. The entry to eliminate unrealized profit from the land account is:

Investment in San (+A)	**9,000**	
Noncontrolling interest (−SE)	**1,000**	
Land (−A)		**10,000**
To reduce land to its cost basis and adjust the investment account and		
beginning noncontrolling interest to establish reciprocity with San's		
equity accounts at the beginning of the period.		

EXHIBIT 6-2

Intercompany Profit
from Upstream Sale of
Land

PAK CORPORATION AND SUBSIDIARY CONSOLIDATION WORKPAPER FOR THE YEAR ENDED DECEMBER 31, 2011 (IN THOUSANDS)

	Pak	90% San	Adjustments and Eliminations Debits	Adjustments and Eliminations Credits	Consolidated Statements
Income Statement					
Sales	$390	$210			$600
Income from San	54		b 54		
Gain on sale of land		10	a 10		
Expenses (including cost of goods sold)	(300)	(150)			(450)
Noncontrolling interest share [($70,000 − $10,000) × 10%]			c 6		(6)
Controlling share of Net income	**$144**	**$ 70**			**$144**
Retained Earnings Statement Retained earnings—Pak	$207				$207
Retained earnings—San		$100	d 100		
Add: Controlling Share of Net income	144	70			144
Retained earnings—December 31	**$351**	**$170**			**$351**
Balance Sheet Other assets	$427	$400			$827
Land	50			a 10	40
Investment in San	324			b 54 d 270	
	$801	$400			$867
Liabilities	$ 50	$ 30			$ 80
Capital stock	400	200	d 200		400
Retained earnings	351	170			351
	$801	$400			
Noncontrolling interest				c 6 d 30	36
					$867

a Eliminates gain on sale of land and reduces land to a cost basis.
b Eliminates investment income and reduces the investment account to its January 1 balance.
c Records the noncontrolling interest in subsidiary earnings for the current period.
d Eliminates reciprocal equity and investment amounts and establishes beginning noncontrolling interest.

We enter noncontrolling interest in the workpaper at the noncontrolling interest share of *reported* subsidiary equity when reciprocal investment and subsidiary equity accounts are eliminated, so we need the forgoing adjustment to reduce noncontrolling interest to its *realized* amount each time we prepare consolidation workpapers. In other words, this adjustment makes the beginning noncontrolling interest in 2012 equal to ending noncontrolling interest in 2011, and so on.

Sale in Subsequent Year to Outside Entity

Assume that Pak uses the land for four years and sells it for $65,000 in 2015. In the year of sale, Pak will report a $15,000 gain ($65,000 proceeds less $50,000 cost), but the gain to the consolidated entity is $25,000, allocated $24,000 [$15,000 + ($10,000 × 0.9)] to controlling stockholders and $1,000 to noncontrolling stockholders.

Pak adjusts its investment income from San in 2015 with the following entry:

Investment in San (+A)	9,000	
Income from San (R, +SE)		9,000
To recognize previously deferred intercompany profits on land.		

The $15,000 gain on the sale of land plus the $9,000 increase in investment income on Pak's books equals the $24,000 effect on consolidated net income in 2015.

In the consolidation workpaper, the adjustment of the $15,000 gain of Pak to the $25,000 consolidated gain requires the following entry:

Investment in San (+A)	**9,000**	
Noncontrolling interest (− SE)	**1,000**	
Gain on land (Ga, +SE)		**10,000**
To adjust gain on land to the $25,000 gain to the consolidated entity.		

This entry allocates the $10,000 gain between the Investment in San (90%) and noncontrolling interest (10%).

LEARNING OBJECTIVE **2**

INTERCOMPANY PROFITS ON DEPRECIABLE PLANT ASSETS

The accounts of the selling affiliate reflect intercompany sales of plant assets subject to depreciation, depletion, or amortization that result in unrealized gains or losses. Firms must eliminate the effects of these gains and losses from parent and consolidated financial statements until the consolidated entity realizes them *through sale to other entities or through use within the consolidated entity*. The adjustments to eliminate the effects of unrealized gains and losses on parent and consolidated financial statements are more complex than in the case of nondepreciable assets. This additional complexity stems from the depreciation (or depletion or amortization) process that affects parent and consolidated income in each year in which the related assets are held by affiliates.

The discussion of intercompany sales of plant assets in this section is limited to depreciable assets, but the analysis and procedures illustrated apply equally to assets subject to depletion or amortization. Intercompany gains and losses from downstream sales of depreciable plant assets are considered initially, and the upstream-sale situation is covered next.

Downstream Sales of Depreciable Plant Assets

The initial effect of unrealized gains and losses from downstream sales of depreciable assets is the same as for nondepreciable assets. Gains or losses appear in the parent's accounts in the year of sale and must be eliminated by the parent in determining its investment income under the equity method. Similarly, we eliminate such gains or losses from consolidated statements by removing each gain or loss and reducing the plant assets to their depreciated cost to the consolidated entity.

DOWNSTREAM SALE AT THE END OF A YEAR Assume that Per Corporation sells machinery to its 80 percent-owned subsidiary, Sop Corporation, on December 31, 2011. The machinery has an undepreciated cost of $50,000 on this date (cost, $90,000, and accumulated depreciation,

$40,000), and it is sold to Sop for $80,000. Journal entries to record the sale and purchase on Per's and Sop's books are as follows:

PER'S BOOKS		
Cash (+A)	80,000	
Accumulated depreciation (+A)	40,000	
Machinery (−A)		90,000
Gain on sale of machinery (Ga, +SE)		30,000

SOP'S BOOKS		
Machinery (+A)	80,000	
Cash (−A)		80,000

There is an unrealized gain on Per's books at December 31, 2011, and, accordingly, Per adjusts its investment income for 2011 under the equity method for the full amount of the unrealized gain:

Income from Sop (−R, −SE)	30,000	
Investment in Sop (−A)		30,000

The gain on machinery should not appear in the consolidated income statement for 2011, and Per should include the machinery in the consolidated balance sheet at $50,000, its depreciated cost to the consolidated entity. A consolidation adjustment accomplishes this effect:

Gain on sale of machinery (−Ga, −SE)	30,000	
Machinery (−A)		30,000

We could also record this effect by debiting Gain on sale of machinery for $30,000, debiting Machinery for $10,000, and crediting Accumulated depreciation—machinery for $40,000. Conceptually, this entry is superior because it results in reporting plant assets and accumulated depreciation at the amounts that would have been shown if the intercompany sale had not taken place. From a practical viewpoint, however, the additional detail is usually not justified by cost–benefit considerations, because the same net asset amounts are obtained without the additional record-keeping costs. The examples in this book reflect the more practical approach.

No adjustment of the noncontrolling interest is necessary, because the intercompany sale does not affect Sop's income. Note that the analysis up to this point is equivalent to the one for the intercompany sale of land discussed earlier in this chapter.

DOWNSTREAM SALE AT THE BEGINNING OF A YEAR If the sale from Per to Sop had occurred on January 1, 2011, the machinery would have been depreciated by Sop during 2011, and any depreciation on the unrealized gain would be considered a piecemeal recognition of the gain during 2011. Assume that on January 1, 2011, the date of the intercompany sale, the machinery has a five-year remaining useful life and no expected residual value at December 31, 2015. Straight-line depreciation is used. The entries to record the sale and purchase are the same as for the December 31 sale; however, Sop also records depreciation expense of $16,000 for 2011 ($80,000 ÷ 5 years). Of this $16,000 depreciation, $10,000 is based on cost to the consolidated entity ($50,000 cost ÷ 5 years), and $6,000 is based on the $30,000 unrealized gain ($30,000 ÷ 5 years). The $6,000 is considered a piecemeal recognition of one-fifth of the $30,000 unrealized gain on the intercompany transaction. Conceptually, this is equivalent to the sale to other entities of one-fifth of the services remaining in the machinery.[1]

---

[1] We assume that the machine services have entered the cost of goods delivered to customers during the current period. If, instead, they are included in inventory, realization has not yet occurred and appropriate adjustments should be made. This additional refinement is not justified when the amounts involved are immaterial.

In eliminating the effect of the intercompany sale from its Investment in Sop account for 2011, Per Corporation makes the following entries:

Income from Sop (−R, −SE)	30,000	
Investment in Sop (−A)		30,000
Investment in Sop (+A)	6,000	
Income from Sop (R, +SE)		6,000

Thus, elimination of the effect of the intercompany sale reduces Per's investment income in 2011 by $24,000 ($30,000 unrealized gain less $6,000 realized through depreciation). Although Sop's income decreases by the $6,000 excess depreciation during 2011, the $6,000 is considered realized through use, and, accordingly, no adjustment of the noncontrolling interest share is necessary.

LEARNING OBJECTIVE 3

EFFECT OF DOWNSTREAM SALE ON A CONSOLIDATION WORKPAPER A partial consolidation workpaper illustrates the effects of the January 1 intercompany sale of machinery on the consolidated financial statements at December 31, 2011 as follows (in thousands):

	Per	80% Sop	Adjustments and Eliminations		Consolidated Statements
Income Statement					
Gain on sale of machinery	$30		a 30		
Depreciation expense		$16		b 6	$10
Balance Sheet					
Machinery		$80		a 30	$50
Accumulated depreciation		16	b 6		10

The first entry eliminates the $30,000 unrealized gain on machinery and reduces machinery to its cost basis to the consolidated entity at the time of intercompany sale. The second entry reduces depreciation expense and accumulated depreciation in order to adjust these items to the depreciated cost basis to the consolidated entity at December 31, 2011. Noncontrolling interest computations are not affected by the workpaper adjustments because the sale was downstream.

In each of the years 2012 through 2015, Per adjusts its investment income for the piecemeal recognition of the previously unrecognized gain on the machinery with the following entry:

2012, 2013, 2014, and 2015

Investment in Sop (+A)	6,000	
Income from Sop (R, +SE)		6,000

Accordingly, by December 31, 2015, the end of the useful life of the machinery, Per will have recognized the full $30,000 gain as investment income. Its investment account balance will reflect the elimination and piecemeal recognition of the unrealized gain as follows:

Year	Elimination of Gain on Machinery	Piecemeal Recognition of Gain Through Depreciation	Effect on Investment Balance at December 31
2011	$−30,000	$+6,000	$−24,000
2012		+6,000	−18,000
2013		+6,000	−12,000
2014		+6,000	−6,000
2015		+6,000	0

In a consolidation workpaper, it is necessary to establish reciprocity between the investment and subsidiary equity accounts at the beginning of the period before eliminating reciprocal balances.

Thus, we eliminate the effect of the unrealized gain on the December 31, 2011, investment account in the 2012 consolidation workpaper with the following entry:

Investment in Sop (+A)	**24,000**	
Accumulated depreciation (+A)	**6,000**	
Machinery (−A)		**30,000**

The partial consolidation workpaper shown in Exhibit 6-3 for Per and Sop include the entry for 2012. The exhibit shows eliminations for each subsequent year (after 2011) in which the unrealized gain on machinery would require adjustment.

The partial workpaper in Exhibit 6-3 shows two adjustments for each of the years 2012 through 2015. We use two entries for each year to isolate the effect on beginning-of-the-period balances and current-year changes. Current-year changes affect depreciation expense and accumulated depreciation in equal amounts, so the entries can be combined and frequently are combined in subsequent illustrations and in problem solutions.

Upstream Sales of Depreciable Plant Assets

Upstream sales of depreciable assets from a subsidiary to a parent result in unrealized gains or losses in the subsidiary accounts in the year of sale (unless the assets are sold at book values). In computing its investment income in the year of sale, the parent adjusts its share of the reported income of the subsidiary for (1) its share of any unrealized gain on the sale and (2) its share of any piecemeal recognition of such unrealized gain through depreciation.

EFFECT OF UPSTREAM SALE ON THE AFFILIATES' SEPARATE BOOKS The effect of a gain on an upstream sale is illustrated by the following example. Pru Corporation purchases a truck from its 80 percent-owned subsidiary, Sot Corporation, on January 1, 2011. Other information is as follows:

Sot's reported net income for 2011	$50,000
Remaining useful life of the truck at January 1, 2011	3 years
Depreciation method	Straight line
Trade-in value of the truck at December 31, 2013	$ 3,000
Cost of truck to Sot	$14,000
Accumulated depreciation on truck at December 31, 2010	$ 5,000

If Sot sells the truck to Pru for $12,000 cash, Sot and Pru make the following journal entries on their separate books for 2011:

SOT'S BOOKS

January 1 (sale of truck)		
Cash (+A)	12,000	
Accumulated depreciation (+A)	5,000	
Trucks (−A)		14,000
Gain on sale of truck (Ga, +SE)		3,000
To record sale of truck.		

PRU'S BOOKS

January 1 (purchase of truck)		
Trucks (+A)	12,000	
Cash (−A)		12,000
To record purchase of truck.		
December 31 (depreciation expense)		
Depreciation expense (E, −SE)	3,000	
Accumulated depreciation (−A)		3,000
To record depreciation for one year		
[($12,000 − $3,000 scrap) ÷ 3 years]		

(continued)

EXHIBIT 6-3

Downstream Sale of
Depreciable Asset—
Years Subsequent
to Sale

PER CORPORATION AND SUBSIDIARY PARTIAL CONSOLIDATION WORKPAPERS FOR THE YEARS 2012, 2013, 2014, AND 2015 (IN THOUSANDS)

	Per	80% Sop	Adjustments and Eliminations Debits	Credits	Consolidated Statements
2012					
Income Statement					
Depreciation expense		$16		b 6	$10
Balance Sheet—December 31					
Machinery		80		a 30	50
Accumulated depreciation		32	a 6 b 6		20
Investment in Sop	XXX*		a 24		
2013					
Income Statement					
Depreciation expense		$16		b 6	$10
Balance Sheet—December 31					
Machinery		80		a 30	50
Accumulated depreciation		48	a 12 b 6		30
Investment in Sop	XXX*		a 18		
2014					
Income Statement					
Depreciation expense		$16		b 6	$10
Balance Sheet—December 31					
Machinery		80		a 30	50
Accumulated depreciation		64	a 18 b 6		40
Investment in Sop	XXX*		a 12		
2015					
Income Statement					
Depreciation expense		$16		b 6	$10
Balance Sheet—December 31					
Machinery		80		a 30	50
Accumulated depreciation		80	a 24 b 6		50
Investment in Sop	XXX*		a 6		

* Whatever the balance of the investment account, it will be less than the underlying book value of the investment at the beginning of the year by the amount of the unrealized profit.

a Eliminates unrealized profit from machinery and accumulated depreciation as of the beginning of the year and adjusts the Investment in Sop account to establish reciprocity with Sop's equity accounts at the beginning of the period.

b Eliminates the current year's effect of unrealized profit from depreciation expense and accumulated depreciation.

PRU'S BOOKS

December 31 (investment income)

Investment in Sot (+A)	38,400	
Income from Sot (R, +SE)		38,400

To record investment income for 2011 computed as follows:

Share of Sot's reported net income ($50,000 × 80%)	$40,000
Less: Unrealized gain on truck ($3,000 × 80%)	−2,400
Add: Piecemeal recognition of gain	
[($3,000 gain ÷ 3 years) × 80%]	+800
Investment income	$38,400

The deferral of the intercompany gain on the truck decreases Pru's investment income for 2011 by $1,600 (from $40,000 to $38,400). This is 80 percent of the unrealized gain at December 31, 2011 [($3,000 unrealized gain from sale – $1000 piecemeal recognition through depreciation) × 80%]. Pru will recognize the remaining $1,600 during 2012 and 2013 at the rate of $800 per year.

EFFECT OF UPSTREAM SALE ON CONSOLIDATION WORKPAPERS To illustrate the workpaper procedures for Pru and Sot, we include the following investment and equity balances—and changes in them—as additional assumptions:

	Investment in Sot 80%	80% of the Equity of Sot	100% of the Equity of Sot
December 31, 2010	$400,000	$400,000	$500,000
Income—2011	+38,400	+40,000	+50,000
December 31, 2011	438,400	440,000	550,000
Income—2012	+40,800	+40,000	+50,000
December 31, 2012	479,200	480,000	600,000
Income—2013	+40,800	+40,000	+50,000
December 31, 2013	$520,000	$520,000	$650,000

Pru's Investment in Sot account at December 31, 2011, is $1,600 below its underlying book value ($438,400, compared with $440,000), and at December 31, 2012, it is $800 below its underlying book value ($479,200, compared with $480,000). By December 31, 2013, the $3,000 gain on the truck has been realized through depreciation. Pru's share of that gain ($2,400) has been recognized at the rate of $800 per year in 2011, 2012, and 2013. Thus, reciprocity between Pru's investment account and its underlying book value is reestablished at the end of 2013.

A partial consolidation workpaper for 2011, the year of sale, appears next, followed by the workpaper entries in journal form.

2011: Year of Sale (In Thousands)

	Pru	80% Sot	Adjustments and Eliminations Debits	Adjustments and Eliminations Credits	Consolidated Statements
Income Statement					
Income from Sot	$ 38.4		c 38.4		
Gain on sale of truck		$ 3	b 3		
Depreciation expense	3			a 1	$ 2
Noncontrolling interest share			d 9.6		9.6
Balance Sheet					
Trucks	$ 12			b 3	$ 9
Accumulated depreciation	3		a 1		2
Investment in Sot	438.4			c 38.4	
				e 400	
Equity of Sot—January 1		$500	e 500		
Noncontrolling interest				d 9.6	
				e 100	109.6

LEARNING OBJECTIVE 4

a	Accumulated depreciation (+A)	1,000	
	Depreciation expense (−E, +SE)		1,000
	To eliminate the current year's effect of unrealized gain from depreciation accounts.		
b	Gain on sale of truck (−Ga, −SE)	3,000	
	Trucks (−A)		3,000
	To eliminate unrealized gain and to reduce trucks to a cost basis.		
c	Income from Sot (−R, −SE)	38,400	
	Investment in Sot (−A)		38,400
	To eliminate investment income and to adjust the investment account to its beginning-of-the-period balance.		
d	Noncontrolling interest share (−SE)	9,600	
	Noncontrolling interest (+SE)		9,600
	To enter noncontrolling interest share of subsidiary income.		
e	Equity of Sot January 1, 2011 (−SE)	500,000	
	Investment in Sot (−A)		400,000
	Noncontrolling interest January 1, 2011 (+SE)		100,000
	To eliminate reciprocal investment and equity accounts and to establish beginning noncontrolling interest.		

Note that we compute noncontrolling interest share of $9,600 for 2011 as 20 percent of Sot's realized income of $48,000 [($50,000 − $3,000 + $1,000) × 20%].

A partial consolidation workpaper and the workpaper entries in journal form for 2012, the first subsequent year after the upstream sale, are as follows:

2012: First Subsequent Year (In Thousands)

	Pru	80% Sot	Adjustments and Eliminations Debits	Adjustments and Eliminations Credits	Consolidated Statements
Income Statement					
Income from Sot	$ 40.8		c 40.8		
Depreciation expense	3			a 1	$ 2
Noncontrolling interest share			d 10.2		10.2
Balance Sheet					
Trucks	$ 12			b 3	$ 9
Accumulated depreciation	6		a 1 b 1		4
Investment in Sot	479.2		b 1.6	c 40.8 e 440	
Equity of Sot—January 1		$550	e 550		
Noncontrolling interest			b .4	d 10.2 e 110	119.8

a	Accumulated depreciation (+A)	1,000	
	Depreciation expense (−E, +SE)		1,000
	To eliminate the effect of the 2011 unrealized gain from current depreciation accounts.		
b	Accumulated depreciation (+A)	1,000	
	Investment in Sot (+A)	1,600	
	Noncontrolling interest January 1, 2012 (−SE)	400	
	Trucks (−A)		3,000
	To eliminate the effect of 2011 unrealized gain from accumulated depreciation and truck accounts and to assign the unrealized gain of $2,000 at January 1 to the investment account (80%) and noncontrolling interest (20%).		

c Income from Sot (–R, –SE)	40,800	
Investment in Sot (–A)		40,800
To eliminate investment income and to adjust the investment account to its beginning-of-the-period balance.		
d Noncontrolling interest share (–SE)	10,200	
Noncontrolling interest (+SE)		10,200
To enter noncontrolling interest share of subsidiary income.		
e Equity of Sot January 1, 2012 (–SE)	550,000	
Investment in Sot (–A)		440,000
Noncontrolling interest January 1, 2012 (+SE)		110,000
To eliminate reciprocal investment and equity accounts and to establish beginning noncontrolling interest.		

Noncontrolling interest share of $10,200 for 2012 consists of 20 percent of Sot's reported net income of $50,000 plus 20 percent of the $1,000 gain realized through depreciation in 2012. In 2013 the computation of noncontrolling interest share is the same as in 2012.

To explain further, noncontrolling interest share in 2011 (the year of sale) is decreased by $400, the noncontrolling interest's share of the $2,000 gain not realized through depreciation in 2011. The 2011 beginning equity of Sot is not affected by the intercompany sale in 2011, so beginning noncontrolling interest is unaffected and does not require adjustment. Depreciation expense for each of the years 2011, 2012, and 2013 of $3,000 is reduced to $2,000 by a workpaper adjustment of $1,000. The $2,000 depreciation expense that appears in the consolidated income statement is simply one-third of the book value less residual value of the truck at the time of intercompany sale [($9,000 − $3,000) ÷ 3 years].

EFFECT OF UPSTREAM SALE ON SUBSEQUENT YEARS In 2012, the first subsequent year after the intercompany sale, the unrealized gain affects both the beginning investment account and the beginning noncontrolling interest. Entry b allocates the $2,000 unrealized gain 80 percent to the Investment in Sot account and 20 percent to beginning noncontrolling interest. The debit to the Investment in Sot account adjusts for the $1,600 difference between the investment account and 80 percent of Sot's equity at December 31, 2011. The $400 debit to noncontrolling interest is necessary to adjust beginning noncontrolling interest in 2012 to $109,600, equal to the ending noncontrolling interest in 2011.

In the partial consolidation workpaper for 2013, the second subsequent year after the upstream sale, the amounts allocated in entry b are $800 to the investment account and $200 to noncontrolling interest because only $1,000 of the initial $3,000 unrealized gain is unrealized at January 1, 2013. No further adjustments are necessary in 2013 because the full amount of the unrealized gain has been realized through depreciation. Observe that the truck account less accumulated depreciation on the consolidated statements at December 31, 2013, is equal to the $3,000 residual value of the truck on that date (trucks, $9,000, less accumulated depreciation, $6,000).

2013: Second Subsequent Year (In Thousands)

	Pru	80% Sot	Adjustments and Eliminations Debits	Adjustments and Eliminations Credits	Consolidated Statements
Income Statement					
Income from Sot	$ 40.8		c40.8		
Depreciation expense	3			a 1	$ 2
Noncontrolling interest share			d 10.2		10.2
Balance Sheet					
Trucks	$ 12			b 3	$ 9
Accumulated depreciation	9		a 1 b 2		6
Investment in Sot	520		b .8	c 40.8 e 480	
Equity of Sot—January 1		$600	e 600		
Noncontrolling interest			b .2	d 10.2 e 120	130

| a | Accumulated depreciation (+A) | 1,000 | |
| | Depreciation expense (−E, +SE) | | 1,000 |

To eliminate the effect of the 2011 unrealized gain from
current depreciation accounts.

b	Accumulated depreciation (+A)	2,000	
	Investment in Sot (+A)	800	
	Noncontrolling interest January 1, 2013 (−SE)	200	
	Trucks (−A)		3,000

To eliminate the effect of 2011 unrealized gain from
accumulated depreciation and truck accounts and to
assign the unrealized gain of $1,000 at January 1 to the
investment account (80%) and noncontrolling interest (20%).

| c | Income from Sot (−R, −SE) | 40,800 | |
| | Investment in Sot (−A) | | 40,800 |

To eliminate investment income and to adjust the
investment account to its beginning-of-the-period balance.

| d | Noncontrolling interest share (−SE) | 10,200 | |
| | Noncontrolling interest (+SE) | | 10,200 |

To enter noncontrolling interest share of subsidiary
income.

e	Equity of Sot January 1, 2013 (−SE)	600,000	
	Investment in Sot (−A)		480,000
	Noncontrolling interest January 1, 2013 (+SE)		120,000

To eliminate reciprocal investment and equity accounts
and to establish beginning noncontrolling interest.

PLANT ASSETS SOLD AT OTHER THAN FAIR VALUE

An intercompany sale of plant assets at a loss requires special evaluation to make sure that the loss is not one that the seller should have recognized on its separate books prior to the intercompany sale (or in the absence of an intercompany sale). For example, if a parent sells a machine with a book value of $30,000 to its 90 percent-owned subsidiary for $20,000 on January 1, 2011, a question should arise as to the fair value of the asset at the time of sale. If the fair value is in fact $20,000, then the parent should have written the asset down to its $20,000 fair value before the sale and recognized the actual loss on its separate books. If the fair value is $30,000, then the propriety of the parent's action is suspect because the controlling stockholders lose and the noncontrolling stockholders gain on the exchange. Parent officers and directors may be charged with improper stewardship.

Similar suspicions arise if a subsidiary sells an asset to the parent at less than its fair value, because the transaction would have been approved by parent officials who also serve as directors of the subsidiary.

Intercompany sales at prices above fair value also create inequities. The Federal Trade Commission charged **Nynex Corporation** with overcharging its own telephone subsidiaries for equipment, supplies, and services. The telephone companies were fined $1.4 million for passing the costs of the overpayments along to customers.[2]

Consolidation with Loss on Intercompany Sale

Consolidation procedures to eliminate intercompany unrealized losses are essentially the same as those to eliminate unrealized gains. Assume that a machine had a remaining useful life of five years when it was sold on January 1, 2011, to the 90 percent-owned subsidiary for $20,000. The book value was $30,000. The parent has a $10,000 unrealized loss that is recognized on a piecemeal

---

[2] *The Wall Street Journal,* February 21, 1990, p. B8.

basis over five years. If the subsidiary's net income for 2011 is $200,000 and there are no other intercompany transactions, the parent records its income from subsidiary as follows:

Investment in subsidiary (+A)	188,000	
Income from subsidiary (R, +SE)		188,000
To record income for 2011 determined as follows:		
Equity in subsidiary's income ($200,000 × 90%)		$180,000
Add: Unrealized loss on machine		10,000
Less: Piecemeal recognition of loss ($10,000 ÷ 5 years)		(2,000)
		$188,000

Consolidation workpaper entries relating to the intercompany loss for 2011 would be as follows:

Machinery (+A)	**10,000**	
Loss on sale of machinery (−Lo, +SE)		**10,000**
To eliminate unrealized intercompany loss on downstream sale.		
Depreciation expense (E, −SE)	**2,000**	
Accumulated depreciation (−A)		**2,000**
To increase depreciation expense to reflect depreciation on a cost basis.		

In the years 2012 through 2015, the parent's income from subsidiary will be reduced by $2,000 each year under the equity method. Consolidated net income is also reduced by $2,000 each year through entries to eliminate the effect of the intercompany loss. The elimination reduces consolidated income by increasing depreciation expense to a cost basis for consolidated statement purposes. In 2012 the entry would be as follows:

Machinery (+A)	**10,000**	
Depreciation expense (E, −SE)	**2,000**	
Accumulated depreciation (−A)		**4,000**
Investment in subsidiary (−A)		**8,000**
To eliminate the effects of intercompany sale at a loss.		

An upstream sale of plant assets at a loss would be accounted for in similar fashion, except that the intercompany loss and its piecemeal recognition would be allocated proportionately to controlling stockholders and noncontrolling interests.

CONSOLIDATION EXAMPLE—UPSTREAM AND DOWNSTREAM SALES OF PLANT ASSETS

Pan Corporation acquired a 90 percent interest in Sap Corporation at its underlying book value (equal to fair value) of $450,000 on January 3, 2011. Since Pan Corporation acquired its interest in Sap, the two corporations have participated in the following transactions involving plant assets:

1. On July 1, 2011, Pan sold land to Sap at a gain of $5,000. Sap resold the land to outside entities during 2013 at a loss to Sap of $1,000.

2. On January 2, 2012, Sap sold equipment with a five-year remaining useful life to Pan at a gain of $20,000. This equipment was still in use by Pan at December 31, 2013.

3. On January 5, 2013, Pan sold a building to Sap at a gain of $32,000. The remaining useful life of the building on this date was eight years, and Sap still owned the building at December 31, 2013.

Exhibit 6-4 shows comparative financial statements for Pan and Sap Corporations for 2013 in the separate-company columns of the consolidation workpaper.

EXHIBIT 6-4

Intercompany Sales of
Plant Assets—Equity
Method

PAN CORPORATION AND SUBSIDIARY CONSOLIDATION WORKPAPER FOR THE YEAR ENDED DECEMBER 31, 2013 (IN THOUSANDS)

	Pan	90% Sap	Adjustments and Eliminations Debits	Adjustments and Eliminations Credits	Consolidated Statements
Income Statement Sales	$2,000	$700			$2,700
Gain on building	32		c 32		
Gain or (loss) on land		(1)		a 5	4
Income from Sap	52.6		d 52.6		
Cost of goods sold	(1,000)	(320)			(1,320)
Depreciation expense	(108)	(50)		b 4 c 4	(150)
Other expenses	(676.6)	(249)			(925.6)
Noncontrolling interest share			e 8.4		(8.4)
Controlling share of Net income	**$ 300**	**$ 80**			**$ 300**
Retained Earnings Statement Retained earnings—Pan	$ 400				$ 400
Retained earnings—Sap		$200	f 200		
Controlling Share of Net income	300	80			300
Dividends	(200)	(30)		d 27 e 3	(200)
Retained earnings—December 31	**$ 500**	**$250**			**$ 500**
Balance Sheet Cash	$ 131.8	$ 32			$ 163.8
Other current assets	200	150			350
Land	160	40			200
Buildings	500	232		c 32	700
Accumulated depreciation—buildings	(200)	(54)	c 4		(250)
Equipment	620	400		b 20	1,000
Accumulated depreciation—equipment	(258)	(100)	b 8		(350)
Investment in Sap	546.2		a 5 b 14.4	d 25.6 f 540	
	$1,700	$700			$1,813.8
Current liabilities	$ 200	$ 50			$ 250
Capital stock	1,000	400	f 400		1,000
Retained earnings	**500**	**250**			**500**
	$1,700	$700			
Noncontrolling interest			b 1.6	e 5.4 f 60	63.8
					$1,813.8

Equity Method

An examination of the consolidation workpaper in Exhibit 6-4 shows that Pan Corporation uses the equity method. The fact that Pan's net income of $300,000 is equal to the controlling share as well as the equality of Pan's retained earnings and consolidated retained earnings are evidence of the use of the equity method. A reconciliation of Pan's Investment in Sap account at December 31, 2012, and December 31, 2013, follows:

Underlying equity in Sap December 31, 2012	$540,000
($600,000 equity of Sap × 90%)	
Less: Unrealized profit on land	(5,000)
Less: 90% of unrealized profit on equipment ($16,000 × 90%)	(14,400)
Investment in Sap December 31, 2012	520,600
Add: Income from Sap 2013 (90% of Sap's $80,000 net	
income + $5,000 gain on land + $3,600 piecemeal recognition	
of gain on equipment – $28,000 unrealized profit on building)	52,600
Less: Dividends received 2013	(27,000)
Investment in Sap December 31, 2013	$546,200

Pan Corporation sold land to Sap in 2011 at a gain of $5,000. This gain was realized in 2013 when Sap sold the land to another entity. However, Sap sold the land at a $1,000 loss based on the transfer price, and the net result is a $4,000 gain for the consolidated entity during 2013. Workpaper entry a converts the $1,000 loss included in Sap's separate income to a $4,000 consolidated gain:

a	Investment in Sap (+A)	5,000	
	Gain on land (Ga, +SE)		5,000
	To recognize previously deferred gain on land.		

Entry b relates to the $20,000 intercompany profit on Sap's sale of equipment to Pan at the beginning of 2012. The adjustment is:

b	Investment in Sap (+A)	14,400	
	Noncontrolling interest January 1, (−SE)	1,600	
	Accumulated depreciation—equipment (+A)	8,000	
	Depreciation expense (−E, +SE)		4,000
	Equipment (−A)		20,000
	To eliminate unrealized profit on upstream sale of equipment and eliminate current year's effect of unrealized gain from depreciation accounts.		

Depreciation on the unrealized gain is $4,000 per year ($20,000 ÷ 5 years), and the portion unrealized at the beginning of 2013 was $16,000, the original gain less piecemeal recognition of $4,000 through depreciation in 2012. The sale was upstream, so the $16,000 unrealized profit is allocated 90 percent and 10 percent on investment in Sap ($14,400) and beginning noncontrolling interest ($1,600), respectively. The $14,400 is debited to the Investment in Sap account because Pan used the equity method.

Entry c eliminates intercompany profit on the buildings that Pan sold to Sap in 2013 at a gain of $32,000:

c	Gain on buildings (−Ga, −SE)	32,000	
	Accumulated depreciation—buildings (+A)	4,000	
	Buildings (−A)		32,000
	Depreciation expense (−E, +SE)		4,000
	To eliminate unrealized gain on the downstream sale of buildings and eliminate current year's effect of unrealized gain from depreciation accounts.		

The transaction occurred at the beginning of the year, so the sale did not affect prior-period balances. We eliminate the $32,000 gain and reduce buildings to reflect their cost to the consolidated entity. We also eliminate depreciation expense and accumulated depreciation relating to the unrealized gain.

Entry d in the consolidation workpaper eliminates income from Sap and 90 percent of Sap's dividends, and it credits Investment in Sap for the $25,600 difference in order to establish reciprocity between investment and equity accounts at the beginning of the year. Entry f eliminates reciprocal investment and equity accounts and establishes the noncontrolling interest at the beginning of the year:

d	Income from Sap (−R, −SE)	52,600	
	Dividends (+SE)		27,000
	Investment in Sap (−A)		25,600
	To eliminate income and dividends from subsidiary.		
e	Noncontrolling interest share (−SE)	8,400	
	Dividends (+SE)		3,000
	Noncontrolling interest (+SE)		5,400
	To enter noncontrolling interest share of subsidiary income and dividends.		
f	Retained earnings—Sap (−SE)	200,000	
	Capital stock—Sap (−SE)	400,000	
	Investment in Sap (−A)		540,000
	Noncontrolling interest—beginning (+SE)		60,000
	To eliminate reciprocal investment and equity balances and establish noncontrolling interest at beginning of year.		

The $8,400 deduction for noncontrolling interest in the consolidated income statement of Exhibit 6-4 is equal to 10 percent of Sap's reported income for 2013 plus the piecemeal recognition of the gain in 2013 from Sap's sale of equipment to Pan [(80,000 + $4,000) × 10 percent]. At December 31, 2013, the noncontrolling interest's share of the unrealized gain on the equipment is $1,200. This $1,200 is reflected in the $63,800 noncontrolling interest that is shown in the consolidated balance sheet. If the effect of the unrealized gain applicable to noncontrolling interest had not been eliminated, noncontrolling interest in the consolidated balance sheet would be $65,000, 10 percent of Sap's reported equity at December 31, 2013.

INVENTORY PURCHASED FOR USE AS OPERATING ASSETS

Intercompany asset transactions do not always fall neatly into the categories of inventory items or plant assets. For example, inventory items may be sold for use in the operations of an affiliate. In this case, any gross profit on the sale will be realized for consolidated statement purposes as the purchaser depreciates the property.

Assume that Pem Company sells a computer that it manufactures at a cost of $150,000 to Sev Corporation, its 100 percent-owned subsidiary, for $200,000. The computer has a five-year expected useful life, and straight-line depreciation is used. Pem's separate income statement includes $200,000 intercompany sales, but Sev's cost of sales does *not* include intercompany purchases, because the purchase price is reflected in its plant assets, and the $50,000 gross profit is reflected in its equipment account. Workpaper entries to consolidate the financial statements of Pem and Sev in the year of sale are:

Sales (−R, −SE)	200,000	
Cost of sales (−E, +SE)		150,000
Equipment (−A)		50,000
To eliminate intercompany sales and to reduce cost of sales and equipment for the cost and gross profit, respectively.		
Accumulated depreciation (+A)	10,000	
Depreciation expense (−E, +SE)		10,000
To eliminate depreciation on the gross profit from the sale ($50,000 ÷ 5 years).		

Recognition of the remaining $40,000 unrealized profit will occur as Sev depreciates the computer over its remaining four-year useful life. Assuming that Pem adjusts its Investment in Sev account for the unrealized profit on the sale under the equity method, the workpaper entry for the second year will be:

Investment in Sev (+A)	**40,000**	
Accumulated depreciation—equipment (+A)	**20,000**	
Equipment (−A)		**50,000**
Depreciation expense (−E, +SE)		**10,000**
To reduce equipment to its cost basis to the consolidated entity, to eliminate the effects of the intercompany sale from depreciation expense and accumulated depreciation, and to establish reciprocity between beginning-of-the-period equity and investment amounts.		

Workpaper entries for the remaining three years of the computer's useful life will include the same debit and credit items, but the accumulated depreciation debit will increase by $10,000 in each subsequent year to a maximum of $50,000, and the debits to Investment in Sev will decrease by $10,000 in each subsequent year as the gross profit is realized. The credit amounts are the same in each year.

SUMMARY

The effects of intercompany gains and losses on plant assets must be eliminated from consolidated financial statements until the consolidated entity realizes the gains and losses through use or sale of the assets. Realization through use results from the depreciation recorded by the purchaser. Although all unrealized profit must be eliminated from the consolidated statements, we adjust consolidated net income for all unrealized gains and losses in the case of downstream sales. For upstream sales, however, we allocate the total amount of unrealized gains and losses between the controlling and noncontrolling interest shares. One-line consolidation procedures for parent financial statements must be compatible with consolidation procedures in order to maintain the equality of parent income under the equity method and the controlling share of consolidated net income (see Exhibit 6-5).

QUESTIONS

1. What is the objective of eliminating the effects of intercompany sales of plant assets in preparing consolidated financial statements?

2. In accounting for unrealized profits and losses from intercompany sales of plant assets, does it make any difference if the parent is the purchaser or the seller? Would your answer be different if the subsidiary were 100 percent owned?

3. When are unrealized gains and losses from intercompany sales of land realized from the viewpoint of the selling affiliate?

4. How is the computation of noncontrolling interest share affected by downstream sales of land? By upstream sales of land?

5. Consolidation workpaper entries are made to eliminate 100 percent of the unrealized profit from the land account in downstream sales of land. Is 100 percent also eliminated for upstream sales of land?

6. How are unrealized gains and losses from intercompany transactions involving depreciable assets eventually realized?

7. Describe the computation of noncontrolling interest share in the year of an upstream sale of depreciable plant assets.

8. How does a parent eliminate the effects of unrealized gains on intercompany sales of plant assets under the equity method?

9. What is the effect of intercompany sales of plant assets on parent and consolidated net income in years subsequent to the year of sale?

10. Explain the sequence of workpaper adjustments and eliminations for unrealized gains and losses on depreciable plant assets. Is your answer affected by whether the intercompany transaction occurred in the current year or in prior years?

EXHIBIT 6-5

Summary Illustration—
Unrealized Profit from
Plant Assets

Assumptions

1. Parent's(P) net income, excluding income from Subsidiary(S), is $100,000.
2. 90 percent-owned Subsidiary reported net income of $50,000.
3. An intercompany sale of land in the current year resulted in a gain of $5,000.
4. The land is still held within the consolidated entity.

	Downstream	Upstream
	Assume that P sells to S	Assume that S sells to P
P's Net Income—Equity Method		
P's separate income	$100,000	$100,000
P's share of S's reported net income	45,000	45,000
Deduct: Unrealized gain from land		
($5,000 × 100%)	(5,000)	
($5,000 × 90%)		(4,500)
P's Net Income	$140,000	$140,500
Controlling share of Consolidated Net Income		
P's separate income plus S's net income	$150,000	$150,000
Less: Unrealized gain on land	(5,000)	(5,000)
Total realized income	145,000	145,000
Less: Noncontrolling interest share		
($50,000 × 10%)	(5,000)	
($50,000 − $5,000) × 10%		(4,500)
Controlling share of net income	$140,000	$140,500

Note that P's net income and controlling share of consolidated net income are the same as if the intercompany transaction had never taken place. In the downstream example, P's separate income would have been $95,000 ($100,000 − $5,000 gain) without the intercompany transaction, and S's reported income would have remained at $50,000. P's separate income of $95,000 plus P's $45,000 income from S ($50,000 × 90%) equals $140,000.

In the upstream example, P's separate income would have been unchanged at $100,000 in the absence of the intercompany transaction, but S's reported income would have been only $45,000 ($50,000 − $5,000 gain). P's separate income of $100,000 plus P's $40,500 income from S ($45,000 × 90%) equals $140,500. Although helpful in understanding the nature of accounting procedures, these assumptions concerning what the incomes would have been without the intercompany transactions lack economic realism because they ignore the productive use of the land.

EXERCISES

E 6-1 General Questions

Use the following information in answering questions 1 and 2:

Par Company sells land with a book value of $5,000 to Sub Company for $6,000 in 2011. Sub Company holds the land during 2012. Sub Company sells the land for $8,000 to an outside entity in 2013.

1. In 2011 the unrealized gain:

   a *To be eliminated is affected by the noncontrolling interest percentage*

   b *Is initially included in the subsidiary's accounts and must be eliminated from Par Company's income from Sub Company under the equity method*

   c *Is eliminated from consolidated net income by a workpaper entry that includes a credit to the land account for $1,000*

   d *Is eliminated from consolidated net income by a workpaper entry that includes a credit to the land account for $6,000*

2. Which of the following statements is true?

   a *Under the equity method, Par Company's Investment in Sub account will be $1,000 less than its underlying equity in Sub throughout 2012.*

   b *No workpaper adjustments for the land are required in 2012 if Par Company has applied the equity method correctly.*

   c *A workpaper entry debiting gain on sale of land and crediting land will be required each year until the land is sold outside the consolidated entity.*

   d *In 2013, the year of Sub's sale to an outside entity, the workpaper adjustment for the land will include a debit to gain on sale of land for $2,000.*

Use the following information in answering questions 3 and 4:

Pen Corporation sold machinery to its 80 percent-owned subsidiary, Sam Corporation, for $100,000 on December 31, 2011. The cost of the machinery to Pen was $80,000, the book value at the time of sale was $60,000, and the machinery had a remaining useful life of five years.

3. How will the intercompany sale affect Pen's income from Sam and Pen's net income for 2011?

	Pen's Income from Sam	Pen's Net Income
a	No effect	No effect
b	Increased	No effect
c	Decreased	No effect
d	No effect	Decreased

4. How will the consolidated assets and consolidated net income for 2011 be affected by the intercompany sale?

	Consolidated Net Assets	Consolidated Net Income
a	No effect	Decreased
b	Decreased	Decreased
c	Increased	No effect
d	No effect	No effect

E 6-2

Discuss effect of intercompany sale of land

Sam Corporation is a 90 percent-owned subsidiary of Par Corporation, acquired by Par in 2011. During 2014 Par sells land to Sam for $50,000 for which it paid $25,000. Sam owns this land at December 31, 2014.

REQUIRED

1. How and in what amount will the sale of land affect Par's income from Sam and net income for 2014 and the balance of Par's Investment in Sam account on December 31, 2014?

2. How will the consolidated financial statements of Par Corporation and Subsidiary for 2014 be affected by the intercompany sale of land?

3. If Sam still owns the land at December 31, 2015, how will Par's income from Sam and net income for 2015 be affected and what will be the effect on Par's Investment in Sam account on December 31, 2015?

4. If Sam sells the land during 2016 for $50,000, how will Par's income from Sam and total consolidated income for 2016 be affected?

E 6-3

Computations for downstream and upstream sales of land

Sir Corporation is a 90 percent-owned subsidiary of Pit Corporation, acquired several years ago at book value equal to fair value. For 2011 and 2012, Pit and Sir report the following:

	2011	2012
Pit's separate income (excludes income from Sir)	$300,000	$400,000
Sir's Net Income	80,000	60,000

The only intercompany transaction between Pit and Sir during 2011 and 2012 was the January 1, 2011, sale of land. The land had a book value of $20,000 and was sold intercompany for $30,000, its appraised value at the time of sale.

1. Assume that the land was sold by Pit to Sir and that Sir still owns the land at December 31, 2012.
   a Calculate controlling share of consolidated net income for 2011 and 2012.
   b Calculate noncontrolling interest share for 2011 and 2012.

2. Assume that the land was sold by Sir to Pit and Pit still holds the land at December 31, 2012.
   a Calculate controlling share of consolidated net income for 2011 and 2012.
   b Calculate noncontrolling interest share for 2011 and 2012.

E 6-4

Journal entries and consolidated income statement (downstream sale of building)

Sal is a 90 percent-owned subsidiary of Pig Corporation, acquired at book value several years ago. Comparative separate-company income statements for the affiliates for 2011 are as follows:

	Pig Corporation	**Sal Corporation**
Sales	$1,500,000	$700,000
Income from Sal	108,000	—
Gain on building	30,000	—
Income credits	1,638,000	700,000
Cost of sales	1,000,000	400,000
Operating expenses	300,000	150,000
Income debits	1,300,000	550,000
Net income	$ 338,000	$150,000

On January 5, 2011, Pig sold a building with a 10-year remaining useful life to Sal at a gain of $30,000. Sal paid dividends of $100,000 during 2011.

REQUIRED

1. Reconstruct the journal entries made by Pig during 2011 to account for its investment in Sal. Explanations of the journal entries are required.

2. Prepare a consolidated income statement for Pig Corporation and Subsidiary for 2011.

E 6-5

[Based on AICPA] General questions

1. On January 1, 2011, Pan Company sold equipment to its wholly-owned subsidiary, Sun Company, for $1,800,000. The equipment cost Pan $2,000,000. Accumulated depreciation at the time of sale was $500,000. Pan was depreciating the equipment on the straight-line method over 20 years with no salvage value, a procedure that Sun continued. On the consolidated balance sheet at December 31, 2011 the cost and accumulated depreciation, respectively, should be:
   a *$1,500,000 and $600,000*
   b *$1,800,000 and $100,000*
   c *$1,800,000 and $500,000*
   d *$2,000,000 and $600,000*

2. In the preparation of consolidated financial statements, intercompany items for which eliminations will not be made are:
   a *Purchases and sales where the parent employs the equity method*
   b *Receivables and payables where the parent employs the cost method*
   c *Dividends received and paid where the parent employs the equity method*
   d *Dividends receivable and payable where the parent employs the equity method*

3. Pun Corporation owns 100 percent of Sir Corporation's common stock. On January 2, 2011, Pun sold to Sir for $40,000 machinery with a carrying amount of $30,000. Sir is depreciating the acquired machinery over a five-year life by the straight-line method. The net adjustments to compute 2011 and 2012 consolidated income before income tax would be an increase (decrease) of:

	2011	**2012**
a	$ (8,000)	$2,000
b	$ (8,000)	0
c	$(10,000)	$2,000
d	$(10,000)	0

4. Pot Company owns 100 percent of Sal Company. On January 1, 2011, Pot sold Sal delivery equipment at a gain. Pot had owned the equipment for two years and used a five-year straight-line depreciation rate with no residual value. Sal is using a three-year straight-line depreciation rate with no residual value for the

equipment. In the consolidated income statement, Sal's recorded depreciation expense on the equipment for 2011 will be decreased by:

a *20% of the gain on sale*

b *33.33% of the gain on sale*

c *50% of the gain on sale*

d *100% of the gain on sale*

E 6-6

General problems

1. Son Corporation is an 80 percent-owned subsidiary of Pin Corporation. In 2011, Son sold land that cost $15,000 to Pin for $25,000. Pin held the land for eight years before reselling it in 2019 to Roy Company, an unrelated entity, for $55,000. The 2019 consolidated income statement for Pin and its subsidiary, Son, will show a gain on the sale of land of:

   a *$40,000*

   b *$32,000*

   c *$30,000*

   d *$24,000*

2. On January 3, 2011, Pal Corporation sells equipment with a book value of $90,000 to its 100 percent-owned subsidiary, Sat Corporation, for $120,000. The equipment has a remaining useful life of three years with no salvage at the time of transfer. Sat uses the straight-line method of depreciation. As a result of this intercompany transaction, Pal's Investment in Sat account balance at December 31, 2011, will be:

   a *$20,000 greater than its underlying equity interest*

   b *$20,000 less than its underlying equity interest*

   c *$30,000 less than its underlying equity interest*

   d *$10,000 greater than its underlying equity interest*

3. Pen Corporation sells equipment with a book value of $80,000 to Sir Company, its 75 percent-owned subsidiary, for $100,000 on January 1, 2011. Sir determines that the remaining useful life of the equipment is four years and that straight-line depreciation is appropriate. The December 31, 2011, separate financial statements of Pen and Sir show equipment—net of $500,000 and $300,000, respectively. Consolidated equipment—net will be:

   a *$800,000*

   b *$785,000*

   c *$780,000*

   d *$650,000*

4. Par Corporation sold equipment with a remaining three-year useful life and a book value of $14,500 to its 80 percent-owned subsidiary, Sad Corporation, for $16,000 on January 2, 2011. A consolidated workpaper entry on December 31, 2011, to eliminate the unrealized profits from the intercompany sale of equipment will include:

   a *A debit to gain on sale of equipment for $1,000*

   b *A debit to gain on sale of equipment for $1,500*

   c *A credit to depreciation expense for $1,500*

   d *A debit to machinery for $1,500*

5. A subsidiary sells equipment with a four-year remaining useful life to its parent at a $12,000 gain on January 1, 2011. The effect of this intercompany transaction on the parent's investment income from its subsidiary for 2011 will be:

   a *An increase of $12,000 if the subsidiary is 100% owned*

   b *An increase of $9,000 if the subsidiary is 100% owned*

   c *A decrease of $9,000 if the subsidiary is 100% owned*

   d *A decrease of $3,600 if the subsidiary is 60% owned*

6. On January 1, 2011, Sin Corporation, a 60 percent-owned subsidiary of Pot Company, sells a building with a book value of $300,000 to its parent for $350,000. At the time of sale, the building has an estimated remaining life of 10 years with no salvage value. Pot uses straight-line depreciation. If Sin reports net income of $1,000,000 for 2011, noncontrolling interest share will be:

   a *$450,000*

   b *$400,000*

   c *$382,000*

   d *$355,000*

E 6-7

Consolidated income statement (sale of asset sold upstream 2 years earlier)

A summary of the separate income of Pod Corporation and the net income of its 75 percent-owned subsidiary, Sev Corporation, for 2011 is as follows:

	Pod	Sev
Sales	$500,000	$300,000
Gain on sale of machinery	10,000	
Cost of good sold	(200,000)	(130,000)
Depreciation expense	(50,000)	(30,000)
Other expenses	(80,000)	(40,000)
Separate income (excludes investment income)	$180,000	$100,000

Sev Corporation sold machinery with a book value of $40,000 to Pod Corporation for $65,000 on January 2, 2009. At the time of the intercompany sale, the machinery had a remaining useful life of five years. Pod uses straight-line depreciation. Pod used the machinery until December 28, 2011, when it was sold to another entity for $36,000.

REQUIRED: Prepare a consolidated income statement for Pod Corporation and Subsidiary for 2011.

E 6-8

Investment income from 40 percent investee (upstream and downstream sales)

Pep Corporation owns 40 percent of the outstanding voting stock of Sat Corporation, acquired for $100,000 on July 1, 2011, when Sat's common stockholders' equity was $200,000. The excess of investment fair value over book value acquired was due to valuable patents owned by Sat that were expected to give Sat a competitive advantage until July 1, 2016.

Sat's net income for 2011 was $40,000 (for the entire year), and for 2012, Sat's net income was $60,000. Pep's December 31, 2011 and 2012, inventories included unrealized profit on goods acquired from Sat in the amounts of $4,000 and $6,000, respectively. At December 31, 2011, Pep sold land to Sat at a gain of $2,000. This land is still owned by Sat at December 31, 2012.

REQUIRED

1. Compute Pep's investment income from Sat for 2011 on the basis of a one-line consolidation.

2. Compute Pep's investment income from Sat for 2012 on the basis of a one-line consolidation.

E 6-9

Upstream sale of equipment, noncontrolling interest

Pan Corporation has an 80 percent interest in Sip Corporation, its only subsidiary. The 80 percent interest was acquired on July 1, 2011, for $400,000, at which time Sip's equity consisted of $300,000 capital stock and $100,000 retained earnings. The excess of fair value over book value was assigned to buildings with a 20-year remaining useful life.

On December 31, 2013, Sip sold equipment with a remaining useful life of four years to Pan at a gain of $20,000. Pan Corporation had separate income for 2013 of $500,000 and for 2014 of $600,000.

Income and retained earnings data for Sip Corporation for 2013 and 2014 are as follows:

	2013	2014
Retained earnings January 1	$150,000	$200,000
Add: Net income	100,000	110,000
Deduct: Dividends	−50,000	−60,000
Retained earnings December 31	$200,000	$250,000

REQUIRED

1. Compute Pan Corporation's income from Sip, net income, and consolidated net income for each of the years 2013 and 2014.

2. Compute the correct balances of Pan's investment in Sip at December 31, 2013 and 2014, assuming no changes in Sip's outstanding stock since Pan acquired its interest.

E 6-10

Inventory items of parent capitalized by subsidiary

Ped Industries manufactures heavy equipment used in construction and excavation. On January 3, 2011, Ped sold a piece of equipment from its inventory that cost $180,000 to its 60 percent-owned subsidiary, Spa Corporation, at Ped's standard price of twice its cost. Spa is depreciating the equipment over six years using straight-line depreciation and no salvage value.

REQUIRED

1. Determine the net amount at which this equipment will be included in the consolidated balance sheets for Ped Industries and Subsidiary at December 31, 2011 and 2012.

2. Ped accounts for its investment in Spa as a one-line consolidation. Prepare the consolidation workpaper entries related to this intercompany sale that are necessary to consolidate the financial statements of Ped and Spa at December 31, 2011 and 2012.

E 6-11

Consolidated net income (upstream and downstream sales)

Income data from the records of Par Corporation and Sum Corporation, Par's 80 percent-owned subsidiary, for 2011 through 2014 follow (in thousands):

	2011	2012	2013	2014
Par's separate income	$200	$150	$40	$120
Sum's net income	60	70	80	90

Par acquired its interest in Sum on January 1, 2011, at a price of $40,000 less than book value. The $40,000 was assigned to a reduction of plant assets with a remaining useful life of 10 years.

On July 1, 2011, Sum sold land that cost $25,000 to Par for $30,000. This land was resold by Par for $35,000 in 2014.

Par sold machinery to Sum for $100,000 on January 2, 2012. This machinery had a book value of $75,000 at the time of sale and is being depreciated by Sum at the rate of $20,000 per year.

Par's December 31, 2013, inventory included $8,000 unrealized profit on merchandise acquired from Sum during 2013. This merchandise was sold by Par during 2014.

REQUIRED: Prepare a schedule to calculate the consolidated net income of Par Corporation and Subsidiary for each of the years 2011, 2012, 2013, and 2014.

PROBLEMS

P 6-1

Consolidated income statement (incomplete equity method, downstream sales)

The separate income statements of Pea Corporation and its 90 percent-owned subsidiary, Sea Corporation, for 2011 are summarized as follows (in thousands):

	Pea	Sea
Sales	$1,000	$600
Income from Sea	90	—
Gain on equipment	40	—
Cost of sales	(600)	(400)
Other expenses	(200)	(100)
Net income	$ 330	$100

Investigation reveals that the effects of certain intercompany transactions are not included in Pea's income from Sea. Information about those intercompany transactions follows:

1. Inventories—Sales of inventory items from Pea to Sea are summarized as follows:

	2010	2011
Intercompany sales	$100,000	$150,000
Cost of intercompany sales	60,000	90,000
Percentage unsold at year-end	50%	40%

2. Plant assets—Pea sold equipment with a book value of $60,000 to Sea for $100,000 on January 1, 2011. Sea depreciates the equipment on a straight-line basis (no scrap) over a four-year period.

REQUIRED

1. Determine the correct amount of Pea's income from Sea for 2011.

2. Prepare a consolidated income statement for Pea Corporation and Subsidiary for 2011.

P 6-2

Consolidated workpaper (downstream sales, intercompany receivable/ payable)

Sim Corporation, a 90 percent-owned subsidiary of Pal Corporation, was acquired on January 1, 2011, at a price of $45,000 in excess of underlying book value. The excess was due to goodwill. Separate financial statements for Pal and Sim for 2012 follow (amounts in thousands):

	Pal	Sim
Combined Income and Retained Earnings Statement for the Year Ended December 31, 2012		
Sales	$300	$100
Income from Sim	31	—
Gain on sale of equipment	9	—
Cost of sales	(140)	(50)
Operating expenses	(60)	(10)
Net income	140	40
Add: Beginning retained earnings	157	70
Less: Dividends	(60)	(20)
Retained earnings, December 31	$237	$ 90
Balance Sheet at December 31, 2012		
Cash	$100	$ 17
Accounts receivable	90	50
Dividends receivable	9	—
Inventories	20	8
Land	40	15
Buildings—net	135	50
Equipment—net	165	60
Investment in Sim	158	—
Total assets	$717	$200
Accounts payable	$ 98	$ 30
Dividends payable	15	10
Other liabilities	67	20
Capital stock	300	50
Retained earnings	237	90
Total equities	$717	$200

ADDITIONAL INFORMATION

1. Pal sold inventory items to Sim during 2011 and 2012 as follows (in thousands):

	2011	2012
Sales	$30	$20
Cost of sales to Pal	15	10
Unrealized profit at December 31	5	4

2. Pal sold land that cost $7,000 to Sim for $10,000 during 2011. The land is still owned by Sim.

3. In January 2012, Pal sold equipment with a book value of $21,000 to Sim for $30,000. The equipment is being depreciated by Sim over a three-year period using the straight-line method.

4. On December 30, 2012, Sim remitted $2,000 to Pal for merchandise purchases. The remittance was not recorded by Pal until January 5, 2013, and it is not reflected in Pal's financial statements at December 31, 2012.

REQUIRED: Prepare a consolidation workpaper for Pal Corporation and Subsidiary for the year ended December 31, 2012.

P 6-3

Consolidated workpaper (downstream sales, intercompany receivable/ payable)

Pal Corporation acquired a 90 percent interest in Sor Corporation on January 1, 2011, for $270,000, at which time Sor's capital stock and retained earnings were $150,000 and $90,000, respectively. The fair value/book value differential is goodwill. Financial statements for Pal and Sor for 2012 are as follows (in thousands):

	Pal	Sor
Combined Income and Retained Earnings Statement		
for the Year Ended December 31, 2012		
Sales	$ 450	$190
Income from Sor	40	—
Gain on land	5	—
Cost of sales	(200)	(100)
Operating expenses	(113)	(40)
Net income	182	50
Add: Retained earnings January 1	202	120
Less: Dividends	(150)	(20)
Retained earnings, December 31	$ 234	$150
Balance Sheet at December 31, 2012		
Cash	$ 133	$ 14
Accounts receivable	180	100
Dividends receivable	18	—
Inventories	60	36
Land	100	30
Buildings—net	280	80
Machinery—net	330	140
Investment in Sor	303	—
	$1,404	$400
Accounts payable	$ 200	$ 50
Dividends payable	30	20
Other liabilities	140	30
Capital stock	800	150
Retained earnings	234	150
	$1,404	$400

ADDITIONAL INFORMATION

1. Pal sold inventory items to Sor for $60,000 during 2011 and $72,000 during 2012. Sor's inventories at December 31, 2011 and 2012, included unrealized profits of $10,000 and $12,000, respectively.

2. On July 1, 2011, Pal sold machinery with a book value of $28,000 to Sor for $35,000. The machinery had a useful life of 3.5 years at the time of sale, and straight-line depreciation is used.

3. During 2012, Pal sold land with a book value of $15,000 to Sor for $20,000.

4. Pal's accounts receivable on December 31, 2012, includes $10,000 due from Sor.

5. Pal uses the equity method for its 90% interest in Sor.

REQUIRED: Prepare a consolidation workpaper for Pal Corporation and Subsidiary for the year ended December 31, 2012.

P 6-4

Workpaper in year of acquisition (downstream sales)

Par Corporation acquired a 90 percent interest in Sag Corporation's outstanding voting common stock on January 1, 2011, for $630,000 cash. The stockholders' equity of Sag on this date consisted of $500,000 capital stock and $200,000 retained earnings.

The financial statements of Par and Sag at and for the year ended December 31, 2011, are summarized as follows (in thousands):

	Par	Sag
Combined Income and Retained Earnings Statement		
for the Year Ended December 31, 2011		
Sales	$ 700	$ 500
Income from Sag	70	—
Gain on land	—	10
Gain on equipment	20	—
Cost of sales	(300)	(300)
Depreciation expense	(90)	(35)
Other expenses	(200)	(65)
Net income	200	110
Beginning retained earnings	600	200
Dividends	(100)	(50)
Retained earnings December 31	$ 700	$ 260
Balance Sheet at December 31, 2011		
Cash	$ 35	$ 30
Accounts receivable—net	90	110
Inventories	100	80
Other current items	70	40
Land	50	70
Buildings—net	200	150
Equipment—net	500	400
Investment in Sag	655	—
	$1,700	$ 880
Accounts payable	$ 160	$ 50
Other liabilities	340	70
Capital stock, $10 par	500	500
Retained earnings	700	260
	$1,700	$ 880

During 2011, Par made sales of $50,000 to Sag at a gross profit of $15,000. One-third of these sales were inventoried by Sag at year-end. Sag owed Par $10,000 on open account at December 31, 2011.

Sag sold land that cost $20,000 to Par for $30,000 on July 1, 2011. Par still owns the land. On January 1, 2011, Par sold equipment with a book value of $20,000 and a remaining useful life of four years to Sag for $40,000. Sag uses straight-line depreciation and assumes no salvage value on this equipment.

REQUIRED: Prepare a consolidation workpaper for Par and Subsidiary for the year ended December 31, 2011.

P 6-5

Workpaper (downstream sales, two years)

Pal Corporation acquired a 90 percent interest in Sto Corporation on January 1, 2011, for $270,000, at which time Sto's capital stock and retained earnings were $150,000 and $90,000, respectively. The fair value cost/book value differential is due to a patent with a 10-year amortization period. Financial statements for Pal and Sto for 2012 are as follows (in thousands):

	Pal	Sto
Combined Income and Retained Earnings Statement		
for the Year Ended December 31, 2012		
Sales	$ 450	$190
Income from Sto	34.6	—
Gain on land	5	—
Cost of sales	(200)	(100)
Operating expenses	(113)	(40)
Net income	176.6	50
Add: Retained earnings January 1	200	120
Less: Dividends	(150)	(20)
Retained earnings, December 31	$ 226.6	$150

	Pal	Sto
Balance Sheet at December 31, 2012		
Cash	$ 136.4	$ 14
Accounts receivable	180	100
Dividends receivable	18	—
Inventories	60	36
Land	100	30
Buildings—net	280	80
Machinery—net	330	140
Investment in Sto	292.2	—
	$1,396.6	$400
Accounts payable	$ 200	$ 50
Dividends payable	30	20
Other liabilities	140	30
Capital stock	800	150
Retained earnings	226.6	150
	$1,396.6	$400

ADDITIONAL INFORMATION

1. Pal sold inventory to Sto for $60,000 during 2011 and $72,000 during 2012; Sto's inventories at December 31, 2011 and 2012, included unrealized profits of $10,000 and $12,000, respectively.

2. On July 1, 2011, Pal sold machinery with a book value of $28,000 to Sto for $35,000. The machinery had a useful life of 3.5 years at the time of intercompany sale, and straight-line depreciation is used.

3. During 2012, Pal sold land with a book value of $15,000 to Sto for $20,000.

4. Pal's accounts receivable on December 31, 2012, includes $10,000 due from Sto.

5. Pal uses the equity method for its 90 percent interest in Sto.

REQUIRED: Prepare a consolidation workpaper for Pal and Subsidiary for the year ended December 31, 2012.

P 6-6
Workpaper (fair value/book value differential, downstream sales)

Financial statements for Pil and San Corporations for 2011 are as follows (in thousands):

	Pil	San
Combined Income and Retained Earnings Statement		
for the Year Ended December 31, 2011		
Sales	$210	$130
Income from San	31.9	—
Gain on sale of land	—	10
Depreciation expense	(40)	(30)
Other expenses	(110)	(60)
Net income	91.9	50
Add: Beginning retained earnings	140.4	50
Deduct: Dividends	(30)	—
Retained earnings December 31	$202.3	$100
Balance Sheet at December 31, 2011		
Current assets	$200	$170
Plant assets	550	350
Accumulated depreciation	(120)	(70)
Investment in San	322.3	—
Total assets	$952.3	$450
Current liabilities	$150	$ 50
Capital stock	600	300
Retained earnings	202.3	100
Total equities	$952.3	$450

ADDITIONAL INFORMATION

1. Pil acquired an 80 percent interest in San on January 2, 2009, for $290,000, when San's stockholders' equity consisted of $300,000 capital stock and no retained earnings. The excess of investment fair value over book value of the net assets acquired related 50 percent to undervalued inventories (subsequently sold in 2009) and 50 percent to a patent with a 10-year amortization period.

2. San sold equipment to Pil for $25,000 on January 1, 2010, at which time the equipment had a book value of $10,000 and a five-year remaining useful life (included in plant assets in the financial statements).

3. During 2011, San sold land to Pil at a profit of $10,000 (included in plant assets in the financial statements).

4. Pil uses the equity method to accounting for its investment in San.

REQUIRED: Prepare a consolidation workpaper for Pil Corporation and Subsidiary for the year ended December 31, 2011.

P 6-7

Workpaper (downstream and upstream sales)

Pot Corporation acquired all the outstanding stock of Ski Corporation on April 1, 2011, for $15,000,000, when Ski's stockholders' equity consisted of $5,000,000 capital stock and $2,000,000 retained earnings. The price reflected a $500,000 undervaluation of Ski's inventory (sold in 2011) and a $3,500,000 undervaluation of Ski's buildings (remaining useful life seven years from April 1, 2011).

During 2012, Ski sold land that cost $1,000,000 to Pot for $1,500,000. Pot resold the land for $2,200,000 during 2015.

Pot sells inventory items to Ski on a regular basis, as follows (in thousands):

	Sales to Ski	Cost to Pot	Percentage Unsold by Ski at Year End	Percentage Unpaid by Ski at Year End
2011	$ 500	$300	0%	0%
2012	1,000	600	30	50
2013	1,200	720	18	30
2014	1,000	600	25	20
2015	1,500	900	20	20

Ski sold equipment with a book value of $800,000 to Pot on January 3, 2015, for $1,600,000. This equipment had a remaining useful life of four years at the time of sale.

Pot uses the equity method to account for its investment in Ski. The financial statements for Pot and Ski are summarized as follows (in thousands):

	Pot	Ski
Combined Income and Retained Earnings Statement for the Year Ended December 31, 2015		
Sales	$26,000	$11,000
Gain on land	700	—
Gain on equipment	—	800
Income from Ski	1,380	—
Cost of sales	(15,000)	(5,000)
Depreciation expense	(3,700)	(2,000)
Other expenses	(4,280)	(2,800)
Net income	5,100	2,000
Add: Beginning retained earnings	12,375	4,000
Deduct: Dividends	(3,000)	(1,000)
Retained earnings December 31	$14,475	$ 5,000
Balance Sheet at December 31, 2015		
Cash	$ 1,170	$ 500
Accounts receivable—net	2,000	1,500
Inventories	5,000	2,000
Land	4,000	1,000
Buildings—net	15,000	4,000

	Pot	Ski
Equipment—net	10,000	4,000
Investment in Ski	14,405	—
Total assets	$51,575	$13,000
Accounts payable	$ 4,100	$ 1,000
Other liabilities	7,000	2,000
Capital stock	26,000	5,000
Retained earnings	14,475	5,000
Total equities	$51,575	$13,000

REQUIRED: Prepare a consolidation workpaper for Pot Corporation and Subsidiary for the year ended December 31, 2015.

P 6-8

Workpaper (incomplete equity method, upstream sale)

Pic Corporation acquired an 80 percent interest in Sic Company on January 1, 2011, for $136,000, when Sic's capital stock and retained earnings were $100,000 and $70,000, respectively.

At the beginning of 2011, Sic sold a machine to Pic for $10,000. The machine had cost Sic $7,000, had depreciated $2,000 while being used by Sic, and had a remaining useful life of five years from the date of sale.

Trial balances of the two companies on December 31, 2011 and 2012, are as follows (in thousands):

	2011		2012	
	Pic	**Sic**	**Pic**	**Sic**
Debits				
Cash and equivalents	$ 50	$ 30	$ 63	$ 30
Other current assets	130	70	140	80
Plant and equipment	400	200	440	245
Investment in Sic	160	—	192	—
Cost of sales	250	130	260	140
Depreciation expense	50	25	50	25
Other expenses	60	20	55	30
	$1,100	$475	$1,200	$550
Credits				
Accumulated depreciation	$ 150	$ 50	$ 200	$ 75
Liabilities	100	50	48	40
Capital stock	300	100	300	100
Retained earnings	126	70	190	100
Sales	400	200	430	235
Gain on plant asset	—	5	—	—
Income from Sic	24	—	32	—
	$1,100	$475	$1,200	$550

REQUIRED: Prepare consolidation workpapers for Pic Corporation and Subsidiary for the year ended December 31, 2011, and the year ended December 31, 2012.

P 6-9

Workpaper (upstream sales current and previous years)

Par Corporation acquired an 80 percent interest in Sin Corporation on January 1, 2011, for $108,000 cash, when Sin's capital stock was $100,000 and retained earnings were $10,000. The difference between investment fair value and book value acquired is due to a patent being amortized over a 10-year period.

Separate financial statements for Par and Sin on December 31, 2014, are summarized as follows (in thousands):

	Par	Sin
Combined Income and Retained Earnings Statement for the Year Ended December 31, 2014		
Sales	$650	$120
Income from Sin	42	—
Cost of sales	(390)	(40)
Other expenses	(170)	(30)
Net income	132	50
Add: Beginning retained earnings	95.6	20
Deduct: Dividends	(70)	(20)
Retained earnings December 31	$157.6	$ 50
Balance Sheet at December 31, 2014		
Cash	$ 58	$ 20
Accounts receivable	40	20
Inventories	60	35
Plant assets	290	205
Accumulated depreciation	(70)	(100)
Investment in Sin	121.6	—
Total assets	$499.6	$180
Accounts payable	$ 42	$ 30
Capital stock	300	100
Retained earnings	157.6	50
Total equities	$499.6	$180

ADDITIONAL INFORMATION

1. Sin's sales include intercompany sales of $8,000, and Par's December 31, 2014, inventory includes $1,000 profit on goods acquired from Sin. Par's December 31, 2013, inventory contained $2,000 profit on goods acquired from Sin.

2. Par owes Sin $4,000 on account.

3. On January 1, 2013, Sin sold plant assets to Par for $60,000. These assets had a book value of $40,000 on that date and are being depreciated by Par over five years.

4. Park uses the equity method to account for its investment in Sin.

REQUIRED: Prepare a consolidation workpaper for Par Corporation and Subsidiary for 2014.

P 6-10

Consolidation workpaper (upstream sales)

Financial statements for Pal and Sun Corporations for 2011 are as follows (in thousands):

	Pal	Sun
Combined Income and Retained Earnings Statement for the Year Ended December 31, 2011		
Sales	$210	$130
Income from Sun	34.4	—
Gain on sale of land	—	10
Depreciation expense	(40)	(30)
Other expenses	(110)	(60)
Net income	94.4	50
Add: Beginning retained earnings	145.4	50
Deduct: Dividends	(30)	—
Retained earnings December 31	$209.8	$100
Balance Sheet at December 31, 2011		
Current assets	$200	$170
Plant assets	550	350

	Pal	Sun
Accumulated depreciation	(120)	(70)
Investment in Sun	329.8	—
Total assets	$959.8	$450
Current liabilities	$150	$ 50
Capital stock	600	300
Retained earnings	209.8	100
Total equities	$959.8	$450

ADDITIONAL INFORMATION

1. Pal acquired an 80 percent interest in Sun on January 2, 2009, for $290,000, when Sun's stockholders' equity consisted of $300,000 capital stock and no retained earnings. The excess of investment fair value over book value of the net assets acquired related 50 percent to undervalued inventories (subsequently sold in 2009) and 50 percent to goodwill.

2. Sun sold equipment to Pal for $25,000 on January 1, 2010, when the equipment had a book value of $10,000 and a five-year remaining useful life (included in plant assets).

3. During 2011, Sun sold land to Pal at a profit of $10,000 (included in plant assets).

4. Pal uses the equity method to account for its investment in Sun.

REQUIRED: Prepare a consolidation workpaper for Pal and Subsidiary for the year ended December 31, 2011.

P 6-11

Analyze provided separate company and consolidated statements

Separate company and consolidated financial statements for Pop Corporation and its only subsidiary, Sal Corporation, for 2012 are summarized here. Pop acquired its interest in Sal on January 1, 2011, at a price in excess of book value, which was due to an unrecorded patent.

POP CORPORATION AND SUBSIDIARY SEPARATE COMPANY AND CONSOLIDATED FINANCIAL STATEMENTS AT AND FOR THE YEAR ENDED DECEMBER 31, 2012 (IN THOUSANDS)

	Pop	Sal	Consolidated
Income Statement			
Sales	$ 500	$300	$ 716
Income from Sal	17.4	—	—
Gain on equipment	20	—	—
Cost of sales	(200)	(150)	(275)
Depreciation expense	(60)	(40)	(95)
Other expenses	(77)	(60)	(141)
Noncontrolling interest share	—	—	(4.6)
Controlling share of net income	$ 200.4	$ 50	$ 200.4
Retained Earnings			
Retained earnings	$ 250	$120	$ 250
Net income	200.4	50	200.4
Dividends	(100)	(30)	(100)
Retained earnings	$ 350.4	$140	$ 350.4
Balance Sheet			
Cash	$ 21.1	$ 35	$ 56.1
Accounts receivable—net	50	30	70
Dividends receivable	13.5	—	—
Inventories	90	60	136
Other current assets	70	40	110
Land	50	20	70
Buildings—net	100	50	150
Equipment—net	300	265	550

(continued)

	Pop	Sal	Consolidated
Investment in Sal	305.8	—	—
Patents	—	—	32
Total assets	$1,000.4	$500	$1,174.1
Accounts payable	$ 60	$ 50	$ 100
Dividends payable	—	15	1.5
Other liabilities	90	95	185
Capital stock, $10 par	500	200	500
Retained earnings	350.4	140	350.4
Noncontrolling interest December 31, 2012	—	—	37.2
Total equities	$1,000.4	$500	$1,174.1

REQUIRED: Answer the following questions about the financial statements of Pop and Sal.

1. What is Pop's percentage interest in Sal Corporation? Provide a computation to explain your answer.

2. Does Pop use a one-line consolidation in accounting for its investment in Sal? Explain your answer.

3. Were there intercompany sales between Pop and Sal in 2012? If so, show computations.

4. Are there unrealized inventory profits on December 31, 2012? If so, show computations.

5. Provide computations to explain the difference between the combined separate cost of sales and consolidated cost of sales.

6. Explain the difference between combined separate and the consolidated "equipment—net" line item by reconstructing the workpaper entry(s) that was (were) apparently made.

7. Are there intercompany receivables and payables? If so, identify them and state the amounts.

8. Beginning with the noncontrolling interest at January 1, 2012, provide calculations of the $37,200 noncontrolling interest at December 31, 2012.

9. What was the amount of patents at December 31, 2011? Show computations.

10. Provide computations to explain the $305,800 Investment in Sal account balance on December 31, 2012.

INTERNET ASSIGNMENT

Obtain AT&T's 2009 annual report from the company's Web site. Refer to Note 4. What information do you find indicating the amount of intercompany asset transfers during 2009?

7 CHAPTER

Intercompany Profit Transactions—Bonds

C ompanies frequently hold the debt instruments of affiliates and justify such intercompany borrowing and lending activity on the basis of convenience, efficiency, and flexibility. Even though each affiliate is a separate legal entity, the parent is in a position to negotiate all loans between affiliates, and a decision to borrow from or loan directly to affiliates is really only a decision to transfer funds among affiliates. Direct loans among affiliates produce reciprocal receivable and payable accounts for principal and interest, as well as reciprocal income and expense accounts. Companies eliminate these reciprocal accounts in preparing consolidated financial statements because the intercompany receivables and payables do not reflect assets or obligations of the consolidated entity.

Special problems of accounting for intercompany bonds and notes arise when one company purchases the debt instruments of an affiliate from outside entities. Such purchases constitute a retirement of debt from a consolidated viewpoint, even though the debt remains outstanding from the viewpoint of the debtor corporation as a separate legal entity. That is, the issuing affiliate (debtor) accounts for its debt obligations as if they were held by unaffiliated entities, and the purchasing affiliate accounts for its investment in the affiliate's obligations as if they were the obligations of unaffiliated entities. Consolidated statements, however, show the financial position and results of operations as if the issuing corporation had purchased and retired its own debt.

Prior experience teaching this material indicates that students often have difficulty with this chapter due to a lack of familiarity with the basics of accounting for bond transactions. You may want to review the bond accounting information included in the Electronic supplement to Chapter 7 (on the *Advanced Accounting* Web site) before continuing this chapter.

LEARNING OBJECTIVES

1 Differentiate between intercompany receivables and payables, and assets or liabilities of the consolidated reporting entity.

2 Demonstrate how a consolidated reporting entity constructively retires debt.

3 Defer unrealized gains/ losses and later recognize realized gains/losses on bond transfers between parent and subsidiary.

4 Adjust calculation of noncontrolling interest share amounts in the presence of intercompany gains/losses on debt transfers.

5 Electronic supplement: Account for bond transactions by both investors and issuers.

6 Electronic supplement: Understand differences in consolidation techniques for debt transfers when the parent uses either an incomplete equity method or the cost method.

INTERCOMPANY BOND TRANSACTIONS

> LEARNING OBJECTIVE 1

At the time a company issues bonds, its bond liability will reflect the current market rate of interest. However, subsequent changes in the market rate of interest create a disparity between the book value and the market value of that liability. If the market rate of interest increases, the market value of the liability decreases. The gain is *not recognized* on the issuer's books under GAAP. Similarly, a decline in the market rate of interest gives rise to an *unrealized* loss that is *not recognized*. These unrecognized gains and losses are disclosed in the financial statements or footnotes in accordance with GAAP [1]. GAAP offers a fair value option for liabilities, which, if elected, permits recognition of gains and losses due to changes in market values.

A firm can recognize previously unrecognized gains or losses on outstanding bonds by retiring the outstanding bonds. The parent, which controls all debt retirement and other decisions for the consolidated entity, has the following options:

1. The *issuer* (parent or subsidiary) can use its available resources to purchase and *retire its own bonds*.

2. The *issuer* (parent or subsidiary) can borrow money from unaffiliated entities at the market rate of interest and use the proceeds to *retire its own bonds*. (This option constitutes refunding.)

3. The *issuer* can borrow money from an affiliate and use the proceeds to *retire its own bonds*.

4. An *affiliate* (parent or subsidiary) can purchase the bonds of the issuer from outside entities, in which case the bonds are *constructively retired*.

The first three options result in an **actual retirement** of the bonds. The issuer recognizes the previously unrecognized gain or loss in these three situations and includes it appropriately in measuring consolidated net income. The fourth option results in a **constructive retirement**. This means that the bonds are retired for consolidated statement purposes because the bond investment and payable items of the parent and the subsidiary are reciprocals that must be eliminated in consolidation. The difference between the book value of the bond liability and the purchase price of the bond investment is a gain or loss for consolidated statement purposes. It is also a gain or loss for parent accounting under the equity method. The gain or loss is not recognized on the books of the issuer, whose bonds are held as an investment by the purchasing affiliate.

Although the constructive retirement is different in form, the substance of the debt extinguishment is the same as for the other three options from the consolidated viewpoint. The effect of a constructive retirement on consolidated statements is the same as for an actual retirement. The gain or loss on constructive retirement of bonds payable is a gain or loss of the issuer that has been realized by changes in the market rate of interest after the bonds were issued, and it is recognized for consolidated statement purposes when the bonds are repurchased and held within the consolidated entity.

For example, *CARGOTEC* issued a press release on September 24, 2010, announcing a repurchase of EUR 77.8 million in outstanding debt obligations. A similar February 23, 2009, press release from *Pixelworks, Inc.* announced a repurchase of $27 million of its outstanding convertible debt. Prior to 2002, any such gains or losses were reported as extraordinary items under GAAP [2]. Under current GAAP [3], a firm may classify debt extinguishment as extraordinary only if the transaction meets the "unusual and infrequent" criteria for extraordinary item. Most debt extinguishment requires classification as ordinary gains or losses.

CONSTRUCTIVE GAINS AND LOSSES ON INTERCOMPANY BONDS

If the price paid by one affiliate to acquire the debt of another is greater than the book value of the liability (par value plus unamortized premium or less unamortized discount and issuance costs), a constructive loss on the retirement of debt occurs. Alternatively, if the price paid is less than the book value of the debt, a constructive gain results. The gain or loss is referred to as *constructive* because it is a gain or loss that is realized and recognized from the viewpoint of the consolidated entity, but it is not recorded on the separate books of the affiliates at the time of purchase.

Constructive gains and losses on bonds are (1) realized gains and losses from the consolidated viewpoint (2) that arise when a company purchases the bonds of an affiliate (3) from other entities (4) at a price other than the book value of the bonds. No gains or losses result from the purchase of an affiliate's bonds at book value or from direct lending and borrowing between affiliates.

Some accounting theorists argue that constructive gains and losses on intercompany bond transactions should be allocated between the purchasing and issuing affiliates according to the par value of the bonds. For example, if Parent pays $99,000 for $100,000 par of Subsidiary's outstanding bonds with $2,000 unamortized premium, they would allocate the $3,000 constructive gain ($102,000 less $99,000) $1,000 to Parent and $2,000 to Subsidiary. This is known as **par value theory**.

The alternative to the par value theory is **agency theory**, under which the affiliate that purchases the intercompany bonds acts as agent for the issuer, under directions from Parent management. Agency theory assigns the $3,000 constructive gain to the subsidiary (the issuer), and the consolidated statement effect is the same as if the subsidiary had purchased its own bonds for $99,000. Although not supported by a separate theory, constructive gains and losses are sometimes assigned 100 percent to the parent on the basis of expediency. The accounting is less complicated.

Changes in market interest rates generate gains and losses for the issuer, so accounting procedures should assign such gains and losses to the issuer, irrespective of the form of the transaction (direct retirement by the issuer or purchase by an affiliate). Failure to assign the full amount of a constructive gain or loss to the issuer results in recognizing form over substance in debt retirement transactions. The substance of a transaction should be considered over its form (incidentally, this is what consolidation is all about); therefore, the agency theory is conceptually superior, and, accordingly, we assign constructive gains and losses to the issuer in this book.

Most corporate long-term debt is in the form of outstanding bonds, so the analysis in this chapter relates to bonds even though it also applies to other types of debt instruments. Straight-line rather than effective interest amortization of premiums and discounts is used in the illustrations throughout the chapter to make the illustrations easier to follow and to help students learn the concepts involved without the added complexity of effective interest computations. It should be understood that the *effective interest method is generally superior* to the straight-line method.[1] This discussion of intercompany bond transactions among affiliates also applies to investments accounted for under the equity method.

The first illustration in this section assumes that the subsidiary purchases parent bonds (the parent is the issuer) and assigns the constructive gain or loss to the parent. In the second illustration, the parent purchases bonds issued by the subsidiary, and we assign the constructive gain or loss to the subsidiary.

Subsidiary Acquisition of Parent Bonds

LEARNING OBJECTIVE 2

Sun Corporation is an 80 percent-owned affiliate of Pat Corporation, and Pat issues $1,000,000 par of 10 percent, 10-year bonds at par value to the public on December 30, 2010. On December 31, 2011, Sun purchases $100,000 of the bonds for $104,500 in the open market. Sun's purchase results in the constructive retirement of $100,000 of Pat bonds and a constructive loss of $4,500 ($104,500 paid to retire bonds with a book value of $100,000).

Pat adjusts investment income and investment accounts at December 31, 2011 to record the constructive loss under the equity method. The entry on Pat's books is:

Income from Sun (−R, −SE)	4,500	
Investment in Sun (−A)		4,500
To adjust income from Sun for the constructive loss on bonds.		

Without this entry, the income of Pat on an equity basis would not equal its share of consolidated net income.

We charge the $4,500 constructive loss against Pat's share of Sun's reported income because Pat is the issuer. Agency theory assigns the full amount of any constructive gain or loss on bonds to the issuer. The parent is the issuer, so the analysis is similar to one for a downstream sale, and we charge the full amount to Pat.

The $4,500 constructive loss appears in the consolidated income statement of Pat and Subsidiary for 2011, and the 10 percent bond issue is reported at $900,000 in the consolidated balance sheet at December 31, 2011. The following workpaper adjustment accomplishes this:

Loss on constructive retirement of bonds (Lo, −SE)	**4,500**	
10% bonds payable (−L)	**100,000**	
Investment in bonds (−A)		**104,500**
To enter loss and eliminate reciprocal bond investment and liability amounts.		

---

[1]GAAP [4] generally requires the effective interest method of amortization but it does not apply to transactions between parent and subsidiary companies and between subsidiaries of a common parent.

Parent Acquisition of Subsidiary Bonds

Assume that Sun sold $1,000,000 par of 10 percent, 10-year bonds to the public at par on December 30, 2010, and that Pat acquires $100,000 par of these bonds for $104,500 on December 31, 2011, in the open market. The purchase by Pat results in a constructive retirement of $100,000 par of Sun bonds and a constructive loss of $4,500 to the consolidated entity. We assign only 80 percent of the constructive loss to controlling stockholders because the purchase of subsidiary bonds is equivalent to an upstream sale, in which the intercompany transactions affect noncontrolling interest share.

In accounting for its investment in Sun under the equity method, Pat recognizes 80 percent of the constructive loss at December 31, 2011 with the following entry:

Income from Sun (−R, −SE)	3,600	
Investment in Sun (−A)		3,600
Recognize the constructive loss		
on acquisition of Sun's bonds.		

The workpaper adjustment in the year of the intercompany bond purchase is the same as that illustrated for the intercompany purchase of Pat bonds. However, the $3,600 decrease in consolidated net income consists of the $4,500 constructive loss less the $900 noncontrolling interest share of the loss, which reduces noncontrolling interest share.

To summarize, when the parent is the issuer, no allocation of gains and losses from intercompany bond transactions is necessary. When the subsidiary is the issuer, intercompany gains and losses on bonds must be allocated between controlling and noncontrolling interest shares in the consolidated income statement. In a one-line consolidation, the parent company recognizes only its proportionate share of the constructive gain or loss on purchases of bonds issued by a subsidiary.

PARENT BONDS PURCHASED BY SUBSIDIARY

A constructive retirement of parent bonds occurs when an affiliate purchases the outstanding bonds of the parent. The purchaser records the amount paid as an investment in bonds. This is the only entry made by either the purchaser or the issuer at the time of the intercompany purchase. The separate accounts of the affiliates do *not* record any gain or loss that results from the constructive retirement, although it is included in investment income on the parent's books under the equity method. The difference between the bond liability and bond investment accounts on the books of the parent and subsidiary reflects the constructive gain or loss.

To illustrate, assume that Sue is a 70 percent-owned subsidiary of Pam, acquired at a fair value equal to its $6,300,000 book value on December 31, 2011, when Sue had capital stock of $5,000,000 and retained earnings of $4,000,000.

Pam has $10,000,000 par of 10 percent bonds outstanding with a $100,000 unamortized premium on January 2, 2012, at which time Sue purchases $1,000,000 par of these bonds for $950,000 from an investment broker. The purchase results in a constructive retirement of 10 percent of Pam's bonds and a $60,000 constructive gain, computed as follows:

Book value of bonds purchased	$1,010,000
[10% × ($10,000,000 par + $100,000 premium)]	
Purchase price	950,000
Constructive gain on bond retirement	$ 60,000

The only entry Sue makes when purchasing the Pam bonds is:

Investment in Pam bonds (+A)	950,000	
Cash (−A)		950,000
To record acquisition of Pam bonds at 95, and classify as		
a held to maturity investment.		

Equity Method

If we prepare consolidated financial statements immediately after the constructive retirement, the workpaper entry to eliminate the intercompany bond investment and liability balances[2] includes the $60,000 gain as follows:

January 2, 2012		
10% bonds payable (−L)	1,010,000	
Investment in Pam bonds (−A)		950,000
Gain on retirement of bonds (Ga, +SE)		60,000

As a result of this workpaper entry, the Investment in Pam bonds is eliminated, the consolidated income statement reflects the gain and the consolidated balance sheet shows the bond liability to holders outside the consolidated entity at $9,090,000 ($9,000,000 par plus $90,000 unamortized premium).

During 2012, Pam amortizes the bond premium on its books and Sue amortizes the discount on its bond investment. Assuming that interest is paid on January 1 and July 1, that the bonds mature on January 1, 2017 (five years after purchase), and that straight-line amortization is used at year end, Pam amortizes 20 percent of the bond premium annually and Sue amortizes 20 percent of the discount annually as follows:

PAM'S BOOKS

July 1		
Interest expense (E, −SE)	500,000	
Cash (−A)		500,000
($10,000,000 par × 10% × 1/2 year)		

December 31		
Interest expense (E, −SE)	500,000	
Interest payable (+L)		500,000
($10,000,000 par × 10% × 1/2 year)		

December 31		
Bonds payable (−L)	20,000	
Interest expense (−E, +SE)		20,000
($100,000 premium ÷ 5 years)		

SUE'S BOOKS

July 1		
Cash (+A)	50,000	
Interest income (R, +SE)		50,000
($1,000,000 par × 10% × 1/2 year)		

December 31		
Interest receivable (+A)	50,000	
Interest income (R, +SE)		50,000
($1,000,000 par × 10% × 1/2 year)		

December 31		
Investment in Pam bonds (+A)	10,000	
Interest income (R, +SE)		10,000
($50,000 discount ÷ 5 years)		

At December 31, 2012, after posting the foregoing entries, the ledgers of Pam and Sue show the following balances:

Pam's Books	
10 percent bonds payable (including $80,000 unamortized premium)	$10,080,000
Interest expense	980,000
Sue's Books	
Investment in Pam bonds	$ 960,000
Interest income	$ 110,000

---

[2] We employ the net method in accounting for bonds throughout the chapter. We do not separately record premiums and discounts.

The difference between the bond investment ($960,000) and 10 percent of Pam's bond liability ($1,008,000) is now $48,000 rather than $60,000. The reason is that there has been a piecemeal realization and recognition of the constructive gain on the separate books of Pam and Sue. This piecemeal recognition occurred during 2012 as Pam amortized the $2,000 premium and Sue amortized the $10,000 discount on bonds that were constructively retired on January 2, 2012. This difference is reflected in interest expense and income accounts relating to the constructively retired bonds. That is, interest income of $110,000 less 10 percent of $980,000 interest expense equals $12,000, or 20 percent of the original constructive gain. The workpaper entries to eliminate reciprocal bond accounts at December 31, 2012, are:

a	10% bonds payable (−L)	1,008,000	
	Investment in Pam bonds (−A)		960,000
	Gain on retirement of bonds (Ga, +SE)		48,000
b	Interest income (−R, −SE)	110,000	
	Interest expense (−E, +SE)		98,000
	Gain on retirement of bonds (Ga, +SE)		12,000
f	Interest payable (−L)	50,000	
	Interest receivable (−A)		50,000

Because 2012 is the year in which the bonds are constructively retired, the combined gain that is entered by the workpaper entries is $60,000, the original gain. If the workpaper entries were combined, the gain would appear as a single amount. Note that the amount of piecemeal recognition of a constructive gain or loss is always the difference between the intercompany interest expense and income amounts that are eliminated. The fact that the piecemeal recognition was 20 percent of the $60,000 gain is the result of straight-line amortization, a relationship that would not hold under the effective interest method.

The first two columns of the consolidation workpaper in Exhibit 7-1 include financial statements for Pam and Sue. Except for the Investment in Sue and the Income from Sue accounts, the amounts shown reflect all previous assumptions and computations.

We compute Pam's investment income of $202,000 as follows:

70% of Sue's reported income of $220,000	$154,000
Add: Constructive gain on bonds	60,000
	214,000
Less: Piecemeal recognition of constructive gain	
($60,000 ÷ 5 years)	12,000
Income from Sue	$202,000

Separate entries on the books of Pam to record the investment income from Sue under a one-line consolidation are as follows:

Investment in Sue (+A)	154,000	
Income from Sue (R, +SE)		154,000
To record investment income from Sue ($220,000 × 70%).		
Investment in Sue (+A)	60,000	
Income from Sue (R, +SE)		60,000
To adjust income from Sue for 100% of the $60,000 constructive gain on bonds.		
Income from Sue (−R, −SE)	12,000	
Investment in Sue (−A)		12,000
To adjust income from Sue for the piecemeal recognition of the constructive gain on bonds that occurred during 2012. (Either $60,000 gain ÷ 5 years or $110,000 interest income − $98,000 interest expense.)		

We add the $60,000 constructive gain to Pam's share of the reported income of Sue because it is realized from the consolidated viewpoint. We recognize this constructive gain on the books of

EXHIBIT 7-1

Parent-Company Bonds
Held by Subsidiary

PAM CORPORATION AND SUBSIDIARY CONSOLIDATION WORKPAPER FOR THE YEAR ENDED DECEMBER 31, 2012 (IN THOUSANDS)

	Pam	70% Sue	Adjustments and Eliminations Debits	Adjustments and Eliminations Credits	Consolidated Statements
Income Statement					
Sales	$ 4,000	$ 2,000			$ 6,000
Income from Sue	202		c 202		
Gain on retirement of bonds				a 48 b 12	60
Interest income		110	b 110		
Expenses including cost of sales	(1,910)	(1,890)			(3,800)
Interest expense	(980)			b 98	(882)
Noncontrolling interest share ($220 × 30%)			d 66		(66)
Controlling interest share	**$ 1,312**	**$ 220**			**$ 1,312**
Retained Earnings Statement					
Retained earnings—Pam	$ 4,900				$ 4,900
Retained earnings—Sue		$ 4,000	e 4,000		
Add: Controlling interest share	**1,312**	**220**			**1,312**
Retained earnings— December 31	**$ 6,212**	**$ 4,220**			**$ 6,212**
Balance Sheet					
Other assets	$39,880	$19,100			$58,980
Interest receivable		50		f 50	
Investment in Sue	6,502			c 202 e 6,300	
Investment in Pam bonds		960		a 960	
	$46,382	$20,110			$58,980
Other liabilities	$ 9,590	$10,890			$20,480
Interest payable	500		f 50		450
10% bond payable	10,080		a 1,008		9,072
Common stock	20,000	5,000	e 5,000		20,000
Retained earnings	**6,212**	**4,220**			**6,212**
	$46,382	$20,110			
Noncontrolling interest				d 66 e 2,700	2,766
					$58,980

the affiliates as they continue to account for the $1,000,000 par of bonds constructively retired on January 2, 2012.

Pam's investment income for 2012 increases by $48,000 from the constructive retirement of the bonds ($60,000 constructive gain less $12,000 piecemeal recognition of the gain). In the years 2013, 2014, 2015, and 2016, Pam's investment income will be reduced $12,000 each year as the constructive gain is recognized on the books of Pam and Sue. In other words, in addition to recording its share of the reported income of Sue in each of these four years, Pam makes the following entry to adjust its income from Sue for the piecemeal recognition of the constructive gain:

Income from Sue (−R, −SE)	12,000	
Investment in Sue (−A)		12,000

At January 1, 2017, the maturity date of the bonds, the full amount of the constructive gain will have been recognized, and Pam's Investment in Sue account will equal 70 percent of the equity of Sue.

The following workpaper entries consolidate the financial statements of Pam Corporation and Subsidiary at December 31, 2012 (see Exhibit 7-1):

a	**10% bonds payable (−L)**	**1,008,000**	
	Gain on retirement of bonds (Ga, +SE)		**48,000**
	Investment in Pam bonds (−A)		**960,000**
	To enter gain and eliminate reciprocal bond investment and bond liability amounts, including unamortized premium.		
b	**Interest income (−R, −SE)**	**110,000**	
	Interest expense (−E, +SE)		**98,000**
	Gain on retirement of bonds (Ga, +SE)		**12,000**
	To eliminate reciprocal interest income and interest expense amounts.		
c	**Income from Sue (−R, −SE)**	**202,000**	
	Investment in Sue (−A)		**202,000**
	To establish reciprocity, eliminate investment income and adjust the investment account to its beginning of the period balance.		
d	**Noncontrolling interest share (−SE)**	**66,000**	
	Noncontrolling interest (+SE)		**66,000**
	To enter noncontrolling interest share of subsidiary income.		
e	**Retained earnings—Sue (−SE)**	**4,000,000**	
	Common stock—Sue (−SE)	**5,000,000**	
	Investment in Sue (−A)		**6,300,000**
	Noncontrolling interest January 1, 2012 (+SE)		**2,700,000**
	To eliminate reciprocal investment and equity accounts and set up beginning noncontrolling interest.		
f	**Interest payable (−L)**	**50,000**	
	Interest receivable (−A)		**50,000**
	To eliminate reciprocal interest payable and interest receivable amounts.		

The first workpaper entry eliminates 10 percent of Pam's bond liability and 100% of Sue's bond investment and also enters $48,000 of the gain on retirement of bonds. This $48,000 is that part of the $60,000 constructive gain not recognized on the separate books of Pam and Sue as of December 31, 2012.

Entry b eliminates reciprocal interest expense and income. The difference between the interest expense and income amounts represents that part of the constructive gain recognized on the books of Pam and Sue through amortization in 2012. This amount is $12,000 and, when credited to the gain on retirement of bonds, it brings the gain up to the original $60,000. As mentioned earlier, if entries a and b had been combined, we would enter the constructive gain in the workpaper as one amount.

Workpaper entry c eliminates investment income and adjusts the Investment in Sue account to its beginning-of-the-period balance. Entry d enters the noncontrolling interest share of subsidiary net income. Entry e eliminates Pam's Investment in Sue and the equity accounts of Sue and establishes the beginning-of-the-period noncontrolling interest.

Entry f of the consolidation workpaper eliminates reciprocal interest payable and receivable amounts on the intercompany bonds. This results in showing interest payable in the consolidated balance sheet at $450,000, the nominal interest payable for one-half year on the $9,000,000 par of bonds held outside of the consolidated entity. Noncontrolling interest share computations in Exhibit 7-1 are not affected by the intercompany bond holdings. This is because Pam issued the bonds, and the full amount of the constructive gain is assigned to the issuer.

Effect on Consolidated Statements in Subsequent Years

LEARNING
OBJECTIVE **3**

In subsequent years until the actual maturity of the bonds, Pam and Sue continue to account for the bonds on their separate books—reporting interest expense (Pam) of $98,000 and interest income (Sue) of $110,000. The $12,000 difference is recognized on Pam's books as an adjustment of investment income. Consolidated financial statements for 2013 through 2016 eliminate all balances related to the intercompany bonds. Exhibit 7-2 shows the year-end balances related to the intercompany bonds on the books of Pam and Sue.

A single adjusting and eliminating entry in the consolidation workpaper at December 31, 2013, could be used for items relating to the intercompany bonds:

Interest income (−R, −SE)	110,000	
Interest payable (−L)	50,000	
10% bonds payable (−L)	1,006,000	
Interest expense (−E, +SE)		98,000
Interest receivable (−A)		50,000
Investment in Pam bonds (−A)		970,000
Investment in Sue (−A)		48,000

This entry eliminates reciprocal interest income and expense amounts, reciprocal interest receivable and payable amounts, and reciprocal bond investment and liability amounts. We credit the remaining difference of $48,000 to the Investment in Sue account to establish reciprocity between Pam's Investment in Sue and the equity accounts of Sue at the beginning of 2013. This is necessary because Pam increased its investment account in 2012 when it adjusted its investment income account for the constructive gain. In other words, Pam's Investment in Sue account exceeded its underlying book value in Sue by $48,000 at December 31, 2012. The 2013 workpaper entry to adjust the Investment in Sue account establishes reciprocity with the equity accounts of Sue and is entered in the consolidation workpaper before eliminating reciprocal investment and equity amounts.

Similar workpaper adjustments are necessary in 2014, 2015, and 2016. For example, the consolidation workpaper credit to the Investment in Sue account will be $36,000 in 2014, $24,000 in 2015, and $12,000 in 2016.

EXHIBIT 7-2

**Year-End Account
Balances Relating to
Intercompany Bonds**

Pam's Books (in thousands)

	December 31,			
	2013	2014	2015	2016
Interest expense	$ 980	$ 980	$ 980	$ 980
Interest payable	500	500	500	500
Bonds payable	10,060	10,040	10,020	10,000

Sue's Books (in thousands)

	December 31,			
	2013	2014	2015	2016
Interest income	$ 110	$ 110	$ 110	$ 110
Interest receivable	50	50	50	50
Investment in Pam bonds	970	980	990	1,000

SUBSIDIARY BONDS PURCHASED BY PARENT

The illustration in this section is similar to that for Pam and Sue, except that the subsidiary is the issuer and the constructive retirement of bonds results in a loss to the consolidated entity.

Pro Corporation owns 90 percent of the voting common stock of Sky Corporation. Pro purchased its interest in Sky a number of years ago at its book value of $9,225,000. Sky's capital stock was $10,000,000 and its retained earnings were $250,000 on the acquisition date.

At December 31, 2011, Sky had $10,000,000 par of 10 percent bonds outstanding with an unamortized discount of $300,000. The bonds pay interest on January 1 and July 1 of each year, and they mature in five years on January 1, 2017.

On January 2, 2012, Pro purchases 50 percent of Sky's outstanding bonds for $5,150,000 cash and classifies the bonds as a held-to-maturity investment. This is a constructive retirement and results in a loss of $300,000 from the viewpoint of the consolidated entity. The consolidated entity retires a liability of $4,850,000 (50% of the $9,700,000 book value of the bonds) at a cost of $5,150,000. We assign the loss to Sky under the theory that the parent acts as agent for Sky, the issuer, in all intercompany transactions.

During 2012, Sky records interest expense on the bonds of $1,060,000 [($10,000,000 par × 10%) + $60,000 discount amortization]. Of this interest expense, $530,000 relates to the intercompany bonds. Pro records interest income from its investment in bonds during 2012 of $470,000 [($5,000,000 par × 10%) − $30,000 premium amortization]. The $60,000 difference between the interest expense and the income on the intercompany bonds reflects recognition of one-fifth of the constructive loss during 2012. At December 31, 2012, the books of Pro and Sky have not recognized $240,000 of the constructive loss through premium amortization (Pro's books) and discount amortization (Sky's books).

Equity Method

Sky reports net income of $750,000 for 2012, and Pro computes its $459,000 income from Sky as follows:

90% of Sky's $750,000 reported income	$675,000
Deduct: $300,000 constructive loss × 90%	(270,000)
Add: $60,000 recognition of constructive loss × 90%	54,000
Investment income from Sky	$459,000

The journal entries Pro makes to account for its investment in Sky during 2012 follow:

December 31, 2012

Investment in Sky (+A)	675,000	
Income from Sky (R, +SE)		675,000
To record 90% of Sky's reported income for 2012.		

December 31, 2012

Income from Sky (−R, −SE)	270,000	
Investment in Sky (−A)		270,000
To adjust investment income from Sky for 90% of		
the loss on the constructive retirement of Sky's bonds.		
(This entry could be made on January 2, 2012.)		

December 31, 2012

Investment in Sky (+A)	54,000	
Income from Sky (R, +SE)		54,000
To adjust investment income from Sky for 90% of the		
$60,000 piecemeal recognition of the constructive loss		
on Sky bonds during 2012.		

In future years until the bonds mature, Pro computes income from Sky by adding $54,000 annually to its share of the reported income of Sky.

Pro's Investment in Sky account at December 31, 2012, has a balance of $10,584,000. This balance equals the underlying book value of Pro's investment in Sky at January 1, 2012, plus $459,000 investment income from Sky for 2012:

Investment in Sky January 1 ($11,250,000 × 90%)	$10,125,000
Add: Income from Sky	459,000
Investment in Sky December 31	$10,584,000

Exhibit 7-3 presents a consolidated financial statement workpaper for Pro and Subsidiary. The constructive loss of $300,000 on the intercompany bonds appears in the consolidated income statement for 2012. Because $5,000,000 par of Sky bonds have been constructively retired, the consolidated balance sheet reports bonds payable of $4,880,000 ($5,000,000 par less the unamortized discount of $120,000) related to the bonds held outside of the consolidated entity.

EFFECT OF CONSTRUCTIVE LOSS ON NONCONTROLLING INTEREST SHARE AND CONSOLIDATED NET INCOME
Noncontrolling interest share for 2012 is $51,000 [($750,000 − $300,000 + $60,000) × 10%]. We assign the constructive loss to Sky. We charge the noncontrolling interest for 10 percent of the $300,000 constructive loss and credit it for 10 percent of the $60,000 piecemeal recognition of the constructive loss during 2012. Accordingly, noncontrolling interest share for 2012 is 10 percent of Sky's $510,000 realized income, and not 10 percent of Sky's $750,000 reported net income.

The constructive retirement of bonds payable reduces the controlling interest share of consolidated net income for 2012 by $216,000. We reflect this reduction in the consolidated income statement through the inclusion of the $300,000 loss on the constructive retirement of the bonds, elimination of interest income of $470,000 and interest expense of $530,000, and reduction of noncontrolling interest share by $24,000 (from $75,000 based on reported net income of Sky to $51,000 noncontrolling interest share for the year). An analysis of the effect follows:

> LEARNING OBJECTIVE **4**

Controlling Interest Share of Consolidated Net Income—2012

Decreased by:	
Constructive loss	$300,000
Elimination of interest income	470,000
Total decreases	$770,000
Increased by:	
Elimination of interest expense	$530,000
Reduction of noncontrolling interest share ($75,000 − $51,000)	24,000
Total increases	$554,000
Effect on controlling interest share for 2012	$216,000

The reduction of noncontrolling interest share is similar to the reduction of other expenses.

CONSOLIDATION WORKPAPER ENTRIES The entries shown in the consolidation workpaper of Exhibit 7-3 are similar to those in the Pam–Sue illustration in Exhibit 7-1 except for the amounts and the shift to a constructive loss situation. As in the previous illustration, workpaper entries a, b and e are separated for illustrative purposes, but they could be combined into a single entry as follows:

Loss on retirement of bonds (Lo, −SE)	300,000	
Interest payable (−L)	250,000	
Interest income (−R, −SE)	470,000	
10 percent bonds payable (−L)	4,880,000	
Investment in Sky bonds (−A)		5,120,000
Interest receivable (−A)		250,000
Interest expense (−E, +SE)		530,000

EXHIBIT 7-3

Subsidiary Bonds Held
by Parent

PRO CORPORATION AND SUBSIDIARY CONSOLIDATION WORKPAPER FOR THE YEAR ENDED DECEMBER 31, 2012 (IN THOUSANDS)

	Pro	90% Sky	Adjustments and Eliminations Debits	Adjustments and Eliminations Credits	Consolidated Statements
Income Statement Sales	$25,750	$14,250			$40,000
Income from Sky	459		c 459		
Interest income	470		b 470		
Expenses including cost of sales	(21,679)	(12,440)			(34,119)
Interest expense		(1,060)		b 530	(530)
Loss on retirement of bonds			a 240 b 60		(300)
Noncontrolling interest share ($750 − $300 + $60) × 10%			f 51		(51)
Controlling interest share	**$ 5,000**	**$ 750**			**$ 5,000**
Retained Earnings Statement Retained earnings—Pro	$13,000				$13,000
Retained earnings—Sky		$ 1,250	d 1,250		
Add: Controlling interest share	**5,000**	**750**			**5,000**
Retained earnings— December 31	**$18,000**	**$ 2,000**			**$18,000**
Balance Sheet Other assets	$34,046	$25,000			$59,046
Interest receivable	250			e 250	
Investment in Sky	10,584			c 459 d 10,125	
Investment in Sky bonds	5,120			a 5,120	
	$50,000	$25,000			$59,046
Other liabilities	$12,000	$ 2,740			$14,740
Interest payable		500	e 250		250
10% bonds payable		9,760	a 4,880		4,880
Capital stock	20,000	10,000	d 10,000		20,000
Retained earnings	**18,000**	**2,000**			**18,000**
	$50,000	$25,000			
Noncontrolling interest				f 51 d 1,125	1,176
					$59,046

Effect on Consolidated Statements in Subsequent Years

The loss on the retirement of bonds only appears in the consolidated income statement in the year in which we constructively retire the bonds. In subsequent years, we allocate the unrecognized portion of the constructive loss between the investment account (the controlling interest) and noncontrolling interest. For example, the combined workpaper entry to eliminate the bond investment and bonds payable and the interest income and interest expense amounts at December 31, 2013, would be as follows:

Investment in Sky (+A)	216,000	
Noncontrolling interest (−SE)	24,000	
Interest income (−R, −SE)	470,000	
10% bonds payable (−L)	4,910,000	
Investment in Sky bonds (−A)		5,090,000
Interest expense (−E, +SE)		530,000

The assignment of the constructive loss to Sky dictates allocation of the unrecognized loss between the investment in Sky ($216,000) and noncontrolling interest ($24,000). The loss is a subsidiary loss, so noncontrolling interest must share in the loss. In computing noncontrolling interest share for 2013, we add 10 percent of the $60,000 constructive loss recognized in 2013 to the noncontrolling interest share of income reported by Sky. We require this adjustment of noncontrolling interest share each year through 2016. By December 31, 2016, the bond investment will decrease to $5,000,000 through premium amortization, and the intercompany bond liability will increase to $5,000,000 through discount amortization.

The intercompany bond holdings increase the controlling share of consolidated net income by $54,000 each year for 2013 through 2016. Under the equity method, Pro's income from Sky and net income also increase by $54,000 in each of the years. Computations of the controlling share of consolidated net income effect follow:

Controlling Share of Consolidated Net Income—2013 Through 2016

Increased by:	
Elimination of interest expense	$530,000
Decreased by:	
Elimination of interest income	$470,000
Increase in noncontrolling interest share	
($60,000 piecemeal recognition × 10%)	6,000
Total decreases	$476,000
Annual effect on controlling share	$ 54,000

Exhibit 7-4 summarizes the intercompany bond account balances that appear on the books of Pro and Sky at year-end 2013 through 2016. The exhibit also summarizes the required workpaper adjustments to consolidate the financial statements of Pro and Sky for years subsequent to the year of intercompany purchase of Sky bonds. Because the Investment in Sky account is involved, we make the workpaper entries shown in Exhibit 7-4 before eliminating reciprocal investment and subsidiary equity amounts.

The workpaper entries shown in Exhibit 7-4 eliminate those amounts that would have been eliminated from the separate statements of Pro and Sky if the bonds had in fact been retired in 2012. The objective is to produce the consolidated financial statements as if Sky had purchased and retired its own bonds.

EXHIBIT 7-4

Subsidiary Bonds
Held by Parent—Years
Subsequent to Year of
Intercompany Purchase

SUMMARY OF INTERCOMPANY BOND ACCOUNT BALANCES ON SEPARATE BOOKS

December 31,	2013	2014	2015	2016
Pro's Books (in thousands)				
Investment in Sky bonds	$5,090	$5,060	$5,030	$ 5,000
Interest income	470	470	470	470
Interest receivable	250	250	250	250
Sky's Books (in thousands)				
10% bonds payable	$9,820	$9,880	$9,940	$10,000
Interest expense	1,060	1,060	1,060	1,060
Interest payable	500	500	500	500

SUMMARY OF CONSOLIDATION WORKPAPER ADJUSTMENTS

December 31,	2013	2014	2015	2016
Debits				
Investment in Sky (90%)*	$ 216	$ 162	$ 108	$ 54
Noncontrolling interest (10%)*	24	18	12	6
Interest income	470	470	470	470
10% bonds payable**	4,910	4,940	4,970	5,000
Interest payable	250	250	250	250
Credits				
Investment in Sky bonds	5,090	5,060	5,030	5,000
Interest expense**	530	530	530	530
Interest receivable	250	250	250	250

*The unrecognized portion of the constructive loss at the beginning of the year is charged 90 percent to the Investment in Sky account and 10 percent to noncontrolling interest.

**Elimination of 50 percent of Sky's bonds (including 50% of the unamortized discount on the bonds) and 50% of the current interest expense on the bonds.

SUMMARY

Transactions in which one corporation acquires the outstanding bonds of an affiliate on the open market result in constructive gains and losses except when an affiliate purchases bonds at book value. The consolidated entity realizes constructive gains and losses when an affiliate purchases another affiliate's bonds. The constructive gains and losses should be reflected in the income of the parent (under the equity method) and consolidated net income in the year of purchase.

Constructive gains and losses on parent bonds purchased by a subsidiary are similar to unrealized gains and losses on downstream sales and do not require allocation between noncontrolling and controlling interests. However, constructive gains and losses on subsidiary bonds purchased by the parent company should be allocated between the controlling and noncontrolling interests. Constructive gains or losses on intercompany bonds are recognized on the books of the purchaser and issuer as they amortize differences between the book value and par value of bonds.

A summary illustration comparing effects of constructive gains and losses from intercompany bond transactions on parent and consolidated net incomes is presented in Exhibit 7-5.

QUESTIONS

1. What reciprocal accounts arise when one company borrows from an affiliate?
2. Do direct lending and borrowing transactions between affiliates give rise to unrealized gains or losses? To unrecognized gains or losses?

ASSUMPTIONS

1. Parent (P) Company's net income, excluding income from Subsidiary (S), was $100,000 for 2011.
2. 90%-owned Subsidiary reported net income of $50,000 for 2011.
3. $100,000 of 10% bonds payable are outstanding with $6,000 unamortized premium as of January 1, 2011.
4. $50,000 par of the bonds were purchased for $51,500 on January 2, 2011.
5. The bonds mature on January 1, 2014.

	S Acquires P's Bonds (similar to downstream)	P Acquires S's Bonds (similar to upstream)
P's Net Income—Equity Method		
P's separate income	$100,000	$100,000
P's share of S's reported net income	45,000	45,000
Add: Constructive gain on bonds		
($53,000 − $51,500) × 100%	1,500	
($53,000 − $51,500) × 90%		1,350
Deduct: Piecemeal recognition of constructive gain		
($1,500 gain ÷ 3 years) × 100%	(500)	
($1,500 gain ÷ 3 years) × 90%		(450)
P's net income	$146,000	$145,900
Controlling Interest Share of Consolidated Net Income		
P's separate income plus S's net income	$150,000	$150,000
Add: Constructive gain on bonds	1,500	1,500
Eliminate: Interest expense (increase)	4,000	4,000
Interest income (decrease)	(4,500)	(4,500)
Total realized income	151,000	151,000
Less: Noncontrolling interest share		
($50,000 × 10%)	(5,000)	
($50,000 + $1,500 − $500) × 10%		(5,100)
Controlling interest share of consolidated net income	$146,000	$145,900

P's net income and controlling share of consolidated net income of $146,000 when S acquires P's bonds are the same as if the bonds were retired by P at the end of 2011. In that case, P's separate income would have been $101,000 ($100,000 plus $1,000 constructive gain), and S's net income would be unchanged. P's $101,000 plus P's $45,000 share of S's reported net income equals $146,000. An assumption of retirement at year-end is necessary because interest expense of P and interest income of S are both realized and recognized during 2011. The amount of the gain is $1,000 ($1,500 less $500 realized and recognized during the current year).

P's net income and controlling share of consolidated net income of $145,900 when P acquires S's bonds are the same as if the bonds were retired by S at the end of 2011. In that case, P's separate income would be unchanged at $100,000, and S's reported net income would be $51,000 ($50,000 plus $1,000 constructive gain). P's $100,000 separate income plus P's $45,900 share of S's reported income ($51,000 × 90%) equals $145,900. Again, the assumption of retirement at year-end is necessary because interest income of P and interest expense of S are realized and recognized during the current year.

3. What are constructive gains and losses? Describe a transaction having a constructive gain.

4. A company has a $1,000,000 bond issue outstanding with unamortized premium of $10,000 and unamortized issuance cost of $5,300. What is the book value of its liability? If an affiliate purchases half the bonds in the market at 98, what is the gain or loss? Is the gain or loss actual or constructive?

5. Compare a constructive gain on intercompany bonds with an unrealized gain on the intercompany sale of land.

6. Describe the process by which constructive gains on intercompany bonds are realized and recognized on the books of the affiliates. Does recognition of a constructive gain in consolidated financial statements precede or succeed recognition on the books of affiliates?

7. If a subsidiary purchases parent bonds at a price in excess of recorded book value, is the gain or loss attributed to the parent or the subsidiary? Explain.

8. The following information related to intercompany bond holdings was taken from the adjusted trial balances of a parent and its 90 percent-owned subsidiary four years before the bond issue matured:

	Parent	Subsidiary
Investment in S bonds, $50,000 par	$49,000	
Interest receivable	2,500	
Interest expense		$ 9,000
10% bonds payable, $100,000 par		100,000
Bond premium		4,000
Interest income	5,250	
Interest payable		5,000

Construct the consolidation workpaper entries necessary to eliminate reciprocal balances (a) assuming that the parent acquired its intercompany bond investment at the beginning of the current year, and (b) assuming that the parent acquired its intercompany bond investment two years prior to the date of the adjusted trial balance.

9. Prepare a journal entry (or entries) to account for the parent's investment income for the current year if the reported income of its 80 percent-owned subsidiary is $50,000 and the consolidated entity has a $4,000 constructive gain from the subsidiary's acquisition of parent bonds.

10. Calculate the parent's income from its 75 percent-owned subsidiary if the reported net income of the subsidiary for the period is $100,000 and the consolidated entity has a constructive loss of $8,000 from the parent's acquisition of subsidiary bonds.

11. If a parent reports interest expense of $4,300 with respect to bonds held intercompany and the subsidiary reports interest income of $4,500 for the same bonds, (a) Was there a constructive gain or loss on the bonds? (b) Is the gain or loss attributed to the parent or the subsidiary? and (c) What does the $200 difference between interest income and expense represent?

EXERCISES

E 7-1

General questions

1. Which of the following is not a characteristic of a constructive retirement of bonds from an intercompany bond transaction?

  a *Bonds are retired for consolidated statement purposes only.*

  b *The reciprocal intercompany bond investment and liability amounts are eliminated in the consolidation process.*

  c *Any gain or loss from the intercompany bond transaction is recognized on the books of the issuer.*

  d *For consolidated statement purposes, the gain or loss on the constructive retirement of bonds is the difference between the book value of the bond liability and the purchase price of the bond investment.*

2. When bonds are purchased in the market by an affiliate, the book value of the intercompany bond liability is:

  a *The par value of the bonds less unamortized issuance costs and less unamortized discount or plus unamortized premium.*

  b *The par value of the bonds less issuance costs, less unamortized discount or plus unamortized premiums, and less the costs incurred to purchase the bond investment.*

  c *The par value of the bonds.*

  d *The par value of the bonds less the discount or plus the premium at issuance.*

3. Constructive gains and losses:

  a *Arise when one company purchases the bonds of an affiliate or lends money directly to the affiliate to repurchase its own bonds*

  b *Are realized gains and losses from the viewpoint of the issuer affiliate*

  c *Are always assigned to the parent because its management makes the decisions for intercompany transactions*

  d. *Are realized and recognized from the viewpoint of the consolidated entity*

4. Straight-line interest amortization of bond premiums and discounts is used as an expedient in this book. However, the effective interest rate method is generally required under GAAP. When using the effective interest rate method:

  a *The amount of the piecemeal recognition of a constructive gain or loss is the difference between the intercompany interest expense and income that is eliminated.*

  b *The piecemeal recognition of a constructive gain or loss is recorded in the separate accounts of the affiliates.*

c *No piecemeal recognition of the constructive gain or loss is required for consolidated statement purposes.*

d *The issuing and the purchasing affiliates do not amortize the discounts and premiums on their separate books because the bonds are retired.*

E 7-2
General problems

Sow Corporation is a 70 percent-owned subsidiary of Pan Corporation. On January 2, 2011, Sow purchased $600,000 par of Pan's $900,000 outstanding bonds for $602,000 in the bond market. Pan's bonds have an 8 percent interest rate, pay interest on January 1 and July 1, and mature on January 1, 2015. There was $48,000 unamortized premium on the bond issue on January 1, 2011. Assume straight-line amortization.

1. The constructive gain or loss that should appear in the consolidated income statement of Pan Corporation and Subsidiary for 2011 is:

a *$30,000 gain*
b *$46,000 gain*
c *$2,000 loss*
d *$30,000 loss*

2. Interest expense that should appear in the 2011 consolidated income statement for Pan's bond issue is:

a *$28,000*
b *$24,000*
c *$20,800*
d *$20,000*

E 7-3
Constructive gain on purchase of parent bonds

Pal Corporation's long-term debt on January 1, 2011, consists of $400,000 par value of 10 percent bonds payable due on January 1, 2015, with an unamortized discount of $8,000. On January 2, 2011, Sot Corporation, Pal's 90 percent-owned subsidiary, purchased $80,000 par of Pal's 10 percent bonds for $76,000. Interest payment dates are January 1 and July 1, and straight-line amortization is used.

1. On the consolidated income statement of Pal Corporation and Subsidiary for 2011, a gain or loss should be reported in the amount of:

a *$5,600 loss*
b *$4,000 gain*
c *$2,400 gain*
d *$2,000 loss*

2. Bonds payable of Pal less unamortized discount appears in the consolidated balance sheet at December 31, 2011, in the amount of:

a *$392,000*
b *$394,000*
c *$320,000*
d *$315,200*

3. The amount of the constructive gain or loss that is unrecognized on the separate books of Pal and Sot at December 31, 2011, is:

a *$2,400*
b *$2,200*
c *$1,800*
d *$0*

4. Interest expense on Pal bonds appears in the consolidated income statement for 2011 at:

a *$42,000*
b *$40,000*
c *$33,600*
d *$32,000*

5. Consolidated net income for 2012 will be affected by the intercompany bond transactions as follows:

a *Increased by 100% of the constructive gain from 2011*
b *Decreased by 25% of the constructive gain from 2011*
c *Increased by 25% of the constructive loss from 2011*
d *Decreased by (25% × 90%) of the constructive loss from 2011*

E 7-4

Subsidiary purchases parent bonds

Pat Company acquired an 80 percent interest in Sal Company on January 1, 2011, for $400,000 in excess of book value and fair value. On January 1, 2014, Pat had $1,000,000 par, 8 percent bonds outstanding with $40,000 unamortized discount. On January 2, 2014, Sal purchased $400,000 par of Pat's bonds at par. The bonds mature on January 1, 2018, and pay interest on January 1 and July 1. Pat's separate income, not including investment income, for 2014 is $800,000, and Sal's reported net income is $500,000.

REQUIRED: Determine the following:

1. Controlling interest share of consolidated net income for Pat Corporation and Subsidiary for 2014

2. Noncontrolling interest share for 2014

E 7-5

Consolidated income statement (constructive gain on purchase of parent's bonds)

Comparative income statements for Pim Corporation and its 100 percent-owned subsidiary, Sad Corporation, for the year ended December 31, 2019, are summarized as follows:

	Pim	Sad
Sales	$1,000,000	$500,000
Income from Sad	226,000	—
Bond interest income (includes discount amortization)	—	22,000
Cost of sales	(670,000)	(200,000)
Operating expenses	(150,000)	(100,000)
Bond interest expense	(50,000)	—
Net income	$ 356,000	$222,000

Pim purchased its interest in Sad at fair value equal to book value on January 1, 2011. On January 1, 2012, Pim sold $500,000 par of 10 percent, 10-year bonds to the public at par, and on January 2, 2019, Sad purchased $200,000 par of the bonds at 97. The companies use straight-line amortization. There are no other intercompany transactions between the affiliates.

REQUIRED: Prepare a consolidated income statement for Pim Corporation and Subsidiary for the year ended December 31, 2019.

E 7-6

Parent purchases subsidiary bonds

Pat Corporation owns a 70 percent interest in Son Corporation acquired several years ago at book value equal to fair value. On January 1, 2011, Son had outstanding $1,000,000 of 9 percent bonds with a book value of $990,000. On January 2, 2011, Pat purchased $500,000 of Son's 9 percent bonds for $503,000. The bonds are due on January 1, 2015, and pay interest on January 1 and July 1.

REQUIRED

1. Determine the gain or loss on the constructive retirement of Son's bonds.

2. Son reports net income of $14,000 for 2011. Determine Pat's income from Son.

E 7-7

Constructive gain purchase of subsidiary's bonds

Comparative balance sheets of Pit and Sal Corporations at December 31, 2011, follow:

	Pit	Sal
Assets		
Accounts receivable—net	$ 1,024,300	$ 300,000
Interest receivable	10,000	—
Inventories	3,000,000	500,000
Other current assets	98,500	200,000
Plant assets—net	3,840,000	2,500,000
Investment in Sal stock	1,830,800	—
Investment in Sal bonds	196,400	—
Total assets	$10,000,000	$3,500,000

	Pit	Sal
Liabilities and Stockholders' Equity		
Accounts payable	$ 400,000	$ 139,000
Interest payable	—	50,000
10% bonds payable	—	1,036,000
Capital stock	8,000,000	2,000,000
Retained earnings	1,600,000	275,000
Total equities	$10,000,000	$3,500,000

Pit acquired 80 percent of Sal's capital stock for $1,660,000 on January 1, 2009, when Sal's capital stock was $2,000,000 and its retained earnings was $75,000.

On January 2, 2011, Pit acquired $200,000 par of Sal's 10 percent bonds in the bond market for $195,500, on which date the unamortized premium for bonds payable on Sal's books was $45,000. The bonds pay interest on January 1 and July 1 and mature on January 1, 2016. (Assume straight-line amortization.)

1. The gain or loss on the constructive retirement of $200,000 of Sal bonds on January 2, 2011, is reported in the consolidated income statement in the amount of:

  a *$13,500*
  b *$11,500*
  c *$10,500*
  d *$7,000*

2. The portion of the constructive gain or loss on Sal bonds that remains unrecognized on the separate books of Pit and Sal at December 31, 2011, is:

  a *$12,000*
  b *$10,800*
  c *$10,500*
  d *$9,200*

3. Consolidated bonds payable at December 31, 2011, should be reported at:

  a *$1,036,000*
  b *$1,000,000*
  c *$828,800*
  d *$800,000*

E 7-8
Midyear purchase of parent's bonds

The consolidated balance sheet of Par Corporation and Say (its 80 percent-owned subsidiary) at December 31, 2011, includes the following items related to an 8 percent, $1,000,000 outstanding bond issue:

Current Liabilities	
Bond interest payable (6 months' interest due January 1, 2012)	$ 40,000
Long-Term Liabilities	
8% bonds payable (maturity date January 1, 2016, net of $30,000 unamortized discount)	$970,000

Par Corporation is the issuer, and straight-line amortization is applicable. Say purchases $600,000 par of the outstanding bonds of Par on July 2, 2012, for $574,800.

REQUIRED

1. Calculate the following:
  a. The gain or loss on constructive retirement of the bonds
  b. The consolidated bond interest expense for 2012
  c. The consolidated bond liability at December 31, 2012

2. How would the amounts determined in part 1 differ if Par purchased Say's bonds?

E 7-9

Different assumptions for purchase of parent's bonds and subsidiary's bonds

The balance sheets of Pin and Sid Corporations, an 80 percent-owned subsidiary of Pin, at December 31, 2011, are as follows (in thousands):

	Pin	Sid
Assets		
Cash	$ 2,440	$2,500
Accounts receivable—net	3,000	300
Other current assets	8,000	1,200
Plant assets—net	15,000	5,500
Investment in Sid	6,560	—
Total assets	$35,000	$9,500
Liabilities and Stockholders' Equity		
Accounts payable	$ 750	$ 230
Interest payable	250	50
10% bonds payable (due January 1, 2017)	4,900	1,020
Capital stock	25,000	7,000
Retained earnings	4,100	1,200
Total liabilities and stockholders' equity	$35,000	$9,500

The book value of Pin's bonds reflects a $100,000 unamortized discount. The book value of Sid's bonds reflects a $20,000 unamortized premium.

REQUIRED

1. Assume that Sid purchases $2,000,000 par of Pin's bonds for $1,900,000 on January 2, 2012, and that semiannual interest is paid on July 1 and January 1. Determine the amounts at which the following items should appear in the consolidated financial statements of Pin and Sid at and for the year ended December 31, 2012.
   a. Gain or loss on bond retirement
   b. Interest payable
   c. Bonds payable at par value
   d. Investment in Pin bonds

2. Disregard 1 above and assume that Pin purchases $1,000,000 par of Sid's bonds for $1,030,000 on January 2, 2012, and that semiannual interest on the bonds is paid on July 1 and January 1. Determine the amounts at which the following items will appear in the consolidated financial statements of Pin and Sid for the year ended December 31, 2012.
   a. Gain or loss on bond retirement
   b. Interest expense (assume straight-line amortization)
   c. Interest receivable
   d. Bonds payable at book value

E 7-10

Constructive retirement of parent's bonds

Pad Corporation has $2,000,000 of 12 percent bonds outstanding on December 31, 2011, with unamortized premium of $60,000. These bonds pay interest semiannually on July 1 and January 1 and mature on January 1, 2017.

On January 2, 2012, Sal Corporation, an 80 percent-owned subsidiary of Pad, purchases $500,000 par of Pad's outstanding bonds in the market for $490,000.

ADDITIONAL INFORMATION

1. Pad and Sal use the straight-line method of amortization.
2. The financial statements are consolidated.
3. Pad's bonds are the only outstanding bonds of the affiliated companies.
4. Sal's net income for 2012 is $200,000 and for 2013, $300,000.

REQUIRED

1. Compute the constructive gain or loss that will appear in the consolidated income statement for 2012.

2. Prepare a consolidation entry (entries) at December 31, 2012, to eliminate the effect of the intercompany bondholdings.

3. Compute the amounts that will appear in the consolidated income statement for 2013 for the following:
   a. Constructive gain or loss
   b. Noncontrolling interest share
   c. Bond interest expense
   d. Bond interest income

4. Compute the amounts that will appear in the consolidated balance sheet at December 31, 2013, for the following:
   a. Investment in Pad bonds
   b. Book value of bonds payable
   c. Bond interest receivable
   d. Bond interest payable

E 7-11

Consolidated income statement (constructive retirement of all subsidiary bonds)

Comparative income statements for Par Corporation and its 80 percent-owned subsidiary, Saw Corporation, for the year ended December 31, 2012, are summarized as follows:

	Par	Saw
Sales	$1,200,000	$600,000
Income from Saw	260,800	—
Bond interest income (includes discount amortization)	91,000	—
Cost of sales	(750,000)	(200,000)
Operating expenses	(200,000)	(200,000)
Bond interest expense	—	(60,000)
Net income	$ 601,800	$140,000

Par purchased its 80 percent interest in Saw at book value on January 1, 2011, when Saw's assets and liabilities were equal to their fair values.

On January 1, 2012, Par paid $783,000 to purchase all of Saw's $1,000,000, 6 percent outstanding bonds. The bonds were issued at par on January 1, 2010, pay interest semiannually on June 30 and December 31, and mature on December 31, 2018.

REQUIRED: Prepare a consolidated income statement for Par Corporation and Subsidiary for the year ended December 31, 2012.

E 7-12

Computations and entries (parent purchases subsidiary bonds)

Pub Corporation, which owns an 80 percent interest in Sap Corporation, purchases $100,000 of Sap's 8 percent bonds at 106 on July 2, 2011. The bonds pay interest on January 1 and July 1 and mature on July 1, 2014. Pub uses the equity method for its investment in Sap. Selected data from the December 31, 2011, trial balances of the two companies are as follows:

	Pub	Sap
Interest receivable	$ 4,000	$ —
Investment in Sap 8% bonds	105,000	—
Interest payable	—	40,000
8% bonds payable ($1,000,000 par)	—	985,000
Interest income	3,000	—
Interest expense	—	86,000
Gain or loss on retirement of intercompany bonds		

REQUIRED

1. Determine the amounts for each of the foregoing items that will appear in the consolidated financial statements on or for the year ended December 31, 2011.

2. Prepare in general journal form the workpaper adjustments and eliminations related to the foregoing bonds that are required to consolidate the financial statements of Pub and Sap Corporations for the year ended December 31, 2011.

3. Prepare in general journal form the workpaper adjustments and eliminations related to the bonds that are required to consolidate the financial statements of Pub and Sap Corporations for the year ended December 31, 2012.

E 7-13

Computations and entries (constructive gain on purchase of parent bonds)

Pap Corporation acquired an 80 percent interest in Son Corporation at book value equal to fair value on January 1, 2012, at which time Son's capital stock and retained earnings were $100,000 and $40,000, respectively. On January 2, 2013, Son purchased $50,000 par of Pap's 8 percent, $100,000 par bonds for $48,800 three years before maturity. Interest payment dates are January 1 and July 1. During 2013, Son reports interest income of $4,400 from the bonds, and Pap reports interest expense of $8,000.

ADDITIONAL INFORMATION

1. Pap's separate income for 2013 is $200,000.

2. Son's net income for 2013 is $50,000.

3. Pap accounts for its investment by the equity method.

4. Straight-line amortization is applicable.

REQUIRED

1. Determine the gain or loss on the bonds.

2. Prepare the journal entries for Son to account for its bond investment during 2013.

3. Prepare the journal entries for Pap to account for its bonds payable during 2013.

4. Prepare the journal entry for Pap to account for its 80% investment in Son for 2013.

5. Calculate noncontrolling interest share and consolidated net income for 2013.

PROBLEMS

P 7-1

Computations and entries (constructive retirement of parent's bonds)

Partial adjusted trial balances for Pan Corporation and its 90 percent-owned subsidiary, Son Corporation, for the year ended December 31, 2011, are as follows:

	Pan Corporation Debit (Credit)	Son Corporation Debit (Credit)
Interest receivable	$ —	$ 1,000
Investment in Pan bonds	—	52,700
Interest payable	(2,000)	—
8% bonds payable, due April 1, 2014	(98,200)	—
Interest income	—	(2,100)
Interest expense	8,800	—

Son Corporation acquired $50,000 par of Pan bonds on April 2, 2011, for $53,600. The bonds pay interest on April 1 and October 1 and mature on April 1, 2014.

REQUIRED

1. Compute the gain or loss on the bonds that will appear in the 2011 consolidated income statement.

2. Determine the amounts of interest income and expense that will appear in the 2011 consolidated income statement.

3. Determine the amounts of interest receivable and payable that will appear in the December 31, 2011, consolidated balance sheet.

4. Prepare in general journal form the consolidation workpaper entries needed to eliminate the effects of the intercompany bonds for 2011.

P 7-2
Four-year income schedule (several intercompany transactions)

Intercompany transactions between Pew Corporation and Sat Corporation, its 80 percent-owned subsidiary, from January 2011, when Pew acquired its controlling interest, to December 31, 2014, are summarized as follows:

2011	Pew sold inventory items that cost $60,000 to Sat for $80,000. Sat sold $60,000 of these inventory items in 2011 and $20,000 of them in 2012.
2012	Pew sold inventory items that cost $30,000 to Sat for $40,000. All of these items were sold by Sat during 2013.
2013	Sat sold land with a book value of $40,000 to Pew at its fair market value of $55,000. This land is to be used as a future plant site by Pew.
2013	Pew sold equipment with a four-year remaining useful life to Sat on January 1 for $80,000. This equipment had a book value of $50,000 at the time of sale and was still in use by Sat at December 31, 2014.
2014	Sat purchased $100,000 par of Pew's 10% bonds in the bond market for $106,000 on January 2, 2014. These bonds had a book value of $98,000 when acquired by Sat and mature on January 1, 2018.

The separate income of Pew (excludes income from Sat) and the reported net income of Sat for 2011 through 2014 were:

	2011	2012	2013	2014
Separate income of Pew	$500,000	$375,000	$460,000	$510,000
Net income of Sat	100,000	120,000	110,000	120,000

REQUIRED: Compute Pew's net income (and the controlling share of consolidated net income) for each of the years 2011 through 2014. A schedule with columns for each year is suggested as the most efficient approach to solve of this problem. (Use straight-line depreciation and amortization and take a full year's depreciation on the equipment sold to Sat in 2013.)

P 7-3
Workpapers (constructive retirement of bonds, intercompany sales)

Financial statements for Pad Corporation and its 75 percent-owned subsidiary, Sum Corporation, for 2011 are summarized as follows (in thousands):

	Pad	Sum
Combined Income and Retained Earnings Statement		
for the Year Ended December 31, 2011		
Sales	$1,260	$1,000
Gain on land	20	—
Gain on building	40	—
Income from Sum	104	—
Cost of goods sold	(700)	(600)
Depreciation expense	(152)	(80)
Interest expense	(40)	—
Other expenses	(92)	(120)
Net income	440	200
Add: Retained earnings, January 1	300	200
Deduct: Dividends	(320)	(160)
Retained earnings, December 31	$ 420	$ 240

(*continued*)

	Pad	Sum
Balance Sheet at December 31, 2011		
Cash	$ 54	$ 162
Bond interest receivable	—	10
Other receivables—net	80	60
Inventories	160	100
Land	180	140
Buildings—net	300	360
Equipment—net	280	180
Investment in Sum	686	—
Investment in Pad Bonds	—	188
Total assets	$1,740	$1,200
Accounts payable	$ 100	$ 160
Bond interest payable	20	—
10% bonds payable	400	—
Common stock	800	800
Retained earnings	420	240
Total equities	$1,740	$1,200

Pad acquired its interest in Sum at book value during 2008, when the fair values of Sum's assets and liabilities were equal to their recorded book values.

ADDITIONAL INFORMATION

1. Pad uses the equity method for its investment in Sum.

2. Intercompany merchandise sales totalled $100,000 during 2011. All intercompany balances have been paid except for $20,000 in transit at December 31, 2011.

3. Unrealized profits in Sum's inventory of merchandise purchased from Pad were $24,000 on December 31, 2010, and $30,000 on December 31, 2011.

4. Sum sold equipment with a six-year remaining life to Pad on January 3, 2009, at a gain of $48,000. Pad still uses the equipment in its operations.

5. Pad sold land to Sum on July 1, 2011, at a gain of $20,000.

6. Pad sold a building to Sum on July 1, 2011, at a gain of $40,000. The building has a 10-year remaining life and is still used by Sum.

7. Sum purchased $200,000 par value of Pad's 10 percent bonds in the open market for $188,000 plus $10,000 accrued interest on December 31, 2011. Interest is paid semiannually on January 1 and July 1. The bonds mature on December 31, 2016.

REQUIRED: Prepare consolidation workpapers for Pad Corporation and Subsidiary for the year ended December 31, 2011.

P 7-4

Computations of separate and consolidated statements given

Pet Corporation acquired an 80 percent interest in She Corporation on January 1, 2011, for $320,000, at which time She had capital stock of $200,000 outstanding and retained earnings of $100,000. The price paid reflected a $100,000 undervaluation of She's plant and equipment. The plant and equipment had a remaining useful life of eight years when Pet acquired its interest.

Separate and consolidated financial statements for Pet Corporation and its subsidiary, She Corporation, for the year ended December 31, 2013, are as follows:

	Pet	She	Consolidated
Combined Income and Retained Earnings Statement for the Year Ended December 31, 2013			
Sales	$ 180,000	$100,000	$230,000
Income from She	20,000	—	—
Interest income	—	8,000	—
Cost of goods sold	(110,000)	(60,000)	(110,000)
Operating expenses	(30,000)	(18,000)	(58,000)

	Pet	She	Consolidated
Interest expense	(18,000)	—	(9,000)
Loss	—	—	(3,000)
Noncontrolling interest share	—	—	(8,000)
Controlling share of net income	42,000	30,000	42,000
Add: Beginning retained earnings	294,000	135,000	294,000
Deduct: Dividends	(20,000)	(15,000)	(20,000)
Ending retained earnings	$ 316,000	$150,000	$316,000
Balance Sheet at December 31, 2013			
Cash	$ 60,000	$ 26,000	$ 86,000
Accounts receivable	120,000	$ 60,000	165,000
Inventories	100,000	50,000	140,000
Plant and equipment	500,000	200,000	780,000
Accumulated depreciation	(100,000)	(50,000)	(180,000)
Investment in She stock	320,000	—	—
Investment in Pet bonds	—	104,000	—
Total assets	$1,000,000	$390,000	$991,000
Accounts payable	$ 80,000	$ 40,000	$105,000
10% bonds payable	204,000	—	102,000
Common stock	400,000	200,000	400,000
Retained earnings	316,000	150,000	316,000
Noncontrolling interest	—	—	68,000
Total equities	$1,000,000	$390,000	$991,000

She sells merchandise to Pet but never purchases from Pet. On January 1, 2013, She purchased $100,000 par of 10 percent Pet Corporation bonds for $106,000. These bonds mature on December 31, 2015, and She expects to hold the bonds until maturity. Both She and Pet use straight-line amortization. Interest is payable on December 31.

REQUIRED: Show computations for each of the following items:

1. The $3,000 loss in the consolidated income statement
2. The $230,000 consolidated sales
3. Consolidated cost of goods sold of $110,000
4. Intercompany profit in beginning inventories
5. Intercompany profit in ending inventories
6. Consolidated accounts receivable of $165,000
7. Noncontrolling interest share of $8,000 (Hint: The amount $8,000 may be incorrect.)
8. Noncontrolling interest at December 31, 2013
9. Investment in She stock at December 31, 2012
10. Investment income account of $20,000 (Pet's books)

P 7-5

[Based on AICPA] Computations (constructive retirement of subsidiary bonds)

Selected amounts from the separate unconsolidated financial statements of Poe Corporation and its 90 percent-owned subsidiary, Saw Company, at December 31, 2011, are as follows.

	Poe	Saw
Selected Income Statement Amounts		
Sales	$710,000	$530,000
Cost of goods sold	490,000	370,000
Gain on sale of equipment	—	21,000
Earnings from investment in subsidiary	63,000	—
Interest expense	—	16,000
Depreciation	25,000	20,000

(continued)

	Poe	Saw
Selected Balance Sheet Amounts		
Cash	$ 50,000	$ 15,000
Inventories	229,000	150,000
Equipment	440,000	360,000
Accumulated depreciation	(200,000)	(120,000)
Investment in Saw	189,000	—
Investment in bonds	91,000	—
Bonds payable	—	(200,000)
Common stock	(100,000)	(10,000)
Additional paid-in capital	(250,000)	(40,000)
Retained earnings	(402,000)	(140,000)
Selected Statement of Retained Earnings Amounts		
Beginning balance December 31, 2010	$272,000	$100,000
Net income	212,000	70,000
Dividends paid	80,000	30,000

ADDITIONAL INFORMATION

1. On January 2, 2011, Poe purchased 90 percent of Saw's 100,000 outstanding common stock for cash of $153,000. On that date, Saw's stockholders' equity equaled $150,000 and the fair values of Saw's assets and liabilities equaled their carrying amounts. Poe accounted for the combination as an acquisition. The difference between fair value and book value was due to goodwill.

2. On September 4, 2011, Saw paid cash dividends of $30,000.

3. On December 31, 2011, Poe recorded its equity in Saw's earnings.

4. On January 3, 2011, Saw sold equipment with an original cost of $30,000 and a carrying value of $15,000 to Poe for $36,000. The equipment had a remaining life of three years and was depreciated using the straight-line method by both companies.

5. During 2011, Saw sold merchandise to Poe for $60,000, which included a profit of $20,000. At December 31, 2011, half of this merchandise remained in Poe's inventory.

6. On December 31, 2011, Poe paid $91,000 to purchase half of the outstanding bonds issued by Saw. The bonds mature on December 31, 2017, and were originally issued at par. These bonds pay interest annually on December 31 of each year, and the interest was paid to the prior investor immediately before Poe's purchase of the bonds.

REQUIRED: Determine the amounts at which the following items will appear in the consolidated financial statements of Poe Corporation and Subsidiary for the year ended December 31, 2011.

1. Cash

2. Equipment less accumulated depreciation

3. Investment in Saw

4. Bonds payable (net of unamortized discount)

5. Common stock

6. Beginning retained earnings

7. Dividends paid

8. Gain on retirement of bonds

9. Cost of goods sold

10. Interest expense

11. Depreciation expense

P 7-6

Workpapers (constructive retirement of bonds, intercompany sales)

Financial statements for Par Corporation and its 75 percent-owned subsidiary, Sal Corporation, for 2012 are summarized as follows (in thousands):

	Par	Sal
Combined Income and Retained Earnings Statement for the Year Ended December 31, 2012		
Sales	$630	$500
Gain on plant	30	—
Income from Sal	52	—
Cost of goods sold	(350)	(300)
Depreciation expense	(76)	(40)
Interest expense	(20)	—
Other expenses	(46)	(60)
Net income	220	100
Add: Beginning retained earnings	150	100
Deduct: Dividends	(160)	(80)
Retained earnings December 31	$210	$120
Balance Sheet at December 31, 2012		
Cash	$ 27	$ 81
Bond interest receivable	—	5
Other receivables—net	40	30
Inventories	80	50
Land	90	70
Buildings—net	150	180
Equipment—net	140	90
Investment in Sal	343	—
Investment in Par bonds	—	94
Total assets	$870	$600
Accounts payable	$ 50	$ 80
Bond interest payable	10	—
10% bonds payable	200	—
Common stock	400	400
Retained earnings	210	120
Total equities	$870	$600

Par Corporation acquired its interest in Sal at book value during 2009, when the fair values of Sal's assets and liabilities were equal to recorded book values.

ADDITIONAL INFORMATION

1. Par uses the equity method for its investment in Sal.

2. Intercompany sales of merchandise between the two affiliates totalled $50,000 during 2012. All intercompany balances have been paid except for $10,000 in transit from Sal to Par at December 31, 2012.

3. Unrealized profits in Sal's inventories of merchandise acquired from Par were $12,000 at December 31, 2011, and $15,000 at December 31, 2012.

4. Sal sold equipment with a six-year remaining useful life to Par on January 2, 2010, at a gain of $24,000. The equipment is still in use by Par.

5. Par sold a plant to Sal on July 1, 2012. The land was sold at a gain of $10,000 and the building, which had a remaining useful life of 10 years, at a gain of $20,000.

6. Sal purchased $100,000 par of Par 10 percent bonds in the open market for $94,000 plus $5,000 accrued interest on December 31, 2012. Interest is paid semiannually on January 1 and July 1, and the bonds mature on January 1, 2017.

REQUIRED: Prepare a consolidation workpaper for Par Corporation and Subsidiary for the year ended December 31, 2012.

INTERNET ASSIGNMENT

Use an Internet search engine such as Lycos, Google, Yahoo, or any other engine you are familiar with to locate two examples of gains or losses on extinguishment of debt. Briefly summarize the financial statement presentation of the gains or losses and any supplemental disclosures provided by the firms.

REFERENCES TO THE AUTHORITATIVE LITERATURE

[1] FASB ASC 825-10-55-4. Originally *Statement of Financial Accounting Standards No. 157.* "Fair Value Measurements." Norwalk, CT: Financial Accounting Standards Board, 2006.

[2] FASB ASC 470-50-45-1. Originally *Statement of Financial Accounting Standards No. 145*: "Rescission of FASB Statements No. 4, 44, and 64, Amendment of FASB Statement No. 13, and Technical Corrections." Stamford, CT: Financial Accounting Standards Board, 2002.

[3] FASB ASC 225-20-45-2. Originally *Accounting Principles Board Opinion No. 30.* "Reporting the Results of Operations." New York: American Institute of Certified Public Accountants, 1973.

[4] FASB ASC 835-30-15-2. Originally *Accounting Principles Board Opinion No. 21.* "Interest on Receivables and Payables." New York: American Institute of Certified Public Accountants, 1971.

8 CHAPTER

Consolidations—Changes in Ownership Interests

This chapter considers several topics related to changes in parent/investor ownership interests. These topics include parent/investor accounting and consolidation procedures for interim acquisitions of stock, piecemeal acquisitions of a controlling interest, sales of ownership interests, and changes in ownership interests through investee stock issuances and treasury stock transactions.

LEARNING OBJECTIVES

1 Prepare consolidated statements when parent's ownership percentage increases or decreases during the reporting period.

2 Apply consolidation procedures to interim (mid-year) acquisitions.

3 Record subsidiary/investee stock issuances and treasury stock transactions.

ACQUISITIONS DURING AN ACCOUNTING PERIOD

LEARNING OBJECTIVE 1

Previous chapters have illustrated consolidations for subsidiary acquisitions at the beginning of an accounting period. When the parent acquires a subsidiary during an accounting period, some consolidation adjustments have to be made in order to account for the income of the subsidiary that was earned prior to acquisition and included in the purchase price. Such income is referred to as **preacquisition earnings** to distinguish it from income of the consolidated entity. Similarly, **preacquisition dividends** are dividends paid on stock before its acquisition that require additional consolidation adjustments.

Such interim acquisitions are common transactions. For example, in Note 4 (p. 78) in its 2009 annual report, **The Walt Disney Company** discloses the following:

> On August 1, 2007, the Company acquired all of the outstanding shares of **Club Penguin Entertainment, Inc.** (Club Penguin), a Canadian company that operates clubpenguin.com, an online virtual world for children. The purchase price included upfront cash consideration of approximately $350 million and additional consideration of up to $350 million if Club Penguin achieved predefined earnings targets in calendar years 2008 and 2009. ...

The 2009 annual report (p. 68) of **AT&T** discloses the following:

Note 2. Acquisitions, Dispositions, Other Adjustments

Dollars in millions except per share amounts

Acquisitions

Centennial *In November 2009, we acquired the assets of Centennial, a regional provider of wireless and wired communications services with approximately 865,000 customers as of December 31, 2009. Total consideration of $2,961 included $955 in cash for the redemption of Centennial's outstanding common stock and liquidation of outstanding stock options and $2,006 for our acquisition of Centennial's outstanding debt* *(including liabilities related to assets subject to sale, as discussed below), of which we repaid $1,957 after closing in 2009. The preliminary fair value measurement of Centennial's net assets at the acquisition date resulted in the recognition of $1,276 of goodwill, $647 of spectrum licenses, and $273 of customer lists and other intangible assets for the Wireless segment. The Wireline segment added $339 of goodwill and $174 of customer lists and other intangible assets from the acquisition. The acquisition of Centennial impacted our Wireless and Wireline segments, and we have included Centennial's operations in our consolidated results since the acquisition date. As the value of certain assets and liabilities are preliminary in nature, they are subject to adjustment as additional information is obtained about the facts and circumstances that existed at the acquisition date. When the valuation is final, any changes to the preliminary valuation of acquired assets and liabilities could result in adjustments to identified intangibles and goodwill.*

Preacquisition Earnings

Conceptually, we eliminate preacquisition earnings (or *purchased income*) from consolidated income by either of two methods. We could exclude the revenues and expenses of the subsidiary prior to acquisition from consolidated revenues and expenses. Or we could include the revenues and expenses of the subsidiary in the consolidated income statement for the full year and deduct preacquisition income as a separate item.

Assume, for example, that Pat Corporation purchases a 90 percent interest in Sis Company on April 1, 2011, for $213,750. Sis's income, dividends, and equity for 2011 are as follows:

	January 1 to March 31	April 1 to December 31	January 1 to December 31
Income			
Sales	$ 25,000	$ 75,000	$100,000
Cost of sales and expenses	12,500	37,500	50,000
Net income	$ 12,500	$ 37,500	$ 50,000
Dividends	$ 10,000	$ 15,000	$ 25,000
	January 1	**April 1**	**December 31**
Stockholders' Equity			
Capital stock	$200,000	$200,000	$200,000
Retained earnings	35,000	37,500	60,000
Stockholders' equity	$235,000	$237,500	$260,000

Sis's income from January 1 to March 31, is $12,500 ($25,000 sales − $12,500 expenses), and Sis's equity at April 1 is $237,500. Therefore, the book value acquired by Pat (237,500 × 90% interest) is equal to the $213,750 purchase price of Sis stock.

In recording income from its investment in Sis at year-end, Pat makes the following entry:

Investment in Sis (+A)	33,750	
Income from Sis (R, +SE)		33,750

To record income from the last three quarters
of 2011 ($37,500 × 90%).

Recording investment income on an equity basis increases Pat's income by $33,750, so the effect on Pat's controlling share of consolidated net income must also be $33,750. Conceptually, the consolidated income statement is affected as follows:

Sales (last three quarters of 2011)	$75,000
Expenses (last three quarters of 2011)	(37,500)
Noncontrolling interest share (last three quarters of 2011)	(3,750)
Effect on controlling share of consolidated net income	$33,750

This solution poses two practical problems. First, the 10 percent noncontrolling interest share for 2011 is $5,000 for the full year, even though it is only $3,750 for the last nine months. Second, by consolidating revenues and expenses for only nine months of the year, the consolidated income statement does not provide a basis for projecting future annual revenues and expenses for the consolidated entity.

Historically, GAAP [1] held that the most meaningful consolidated income statement presentation results from including the revenues and expenses in the consolidated income statement for the full year and deducting preacquisition income as a separate item. GAAP recommended consolidating subsidiary accounts in the following manner:

Sales (full year)	$100,000
Expenses (full year)	(50,000)
Preacquisition income	(11,250)
Noncontrolling interest share	(5,000)
Effect on controlling share of consolidated net income	$ 33,750

GAAP [2] changed in 2007 indicating that an acquirer purchases control of the assets and assumes the liabilities of a subsidiary at a price that reflects fair values at the combination date. The acquirer does not purchase earnings. Under current GAAP, consolidated net income should only reflect subsidiary earnings subsequent to the acquisition date. Preacquisition earnings should not appear as a reduction of consolidated net income. Under this approach, we essentially close the books of the subsidiary at the acquisition date. So, our Pat Corporation example reverts to the first presentation above under current GAAP, calculating the controlling share of consolidated net income as follows:

Sales (last three quarters of 2011)	$ 75,000
Expenses (last three quarters of 2011)	(37,500)
Noncontrolling interest share (last three quarters of 2011)	(3,750)
Effect on controlling share of consolidated net income	$ 33,750

Preacquisition Dividends

We eliminate dividends paid on stock prior to its acquisition (preacquisition dividends) in the consolidation process because they are not part of the equity acquired. Sis paid $25,000 dividends during 2011, but it paid $10,000 of this amount before the acquisition by Pat. Accordingly, Pat makes the following entry to account for dividends received (after the acquisition):

Cash (+A)	13,500	
Investment in Sis (−A)		13,500
Record dividends received		
from Sis.		

We eliminate preacquisition dividends relating to the 90 percent interest acquired by Pat in the consolidation process along with preacquisition revenues and expenses. We include these eliminations in the workpaper entry that eliminates reciprocal investment in subsidiary and subsidiary equity balances in order to compensate for the fact that subsidiary equity balances are eliminated as of the beginning of the period and the investment account balance is eliminated as of the acquisition date within the period. Sis's allocations of income and dividends are as follows:

	Controlling Interest (Pat)	Noncontrolling Interest (10%)	Preacquisition Eliminations	Total
Sis's net income	$33,750	$3,750	$12,500	$50,000
Sis's dividends	13,500	2,500	9,000	25,000

Consolidation

LEARNING OBJECTIVE **2**

Exhibit 8-1 illustrates consolidation procedures for the mid-year acquisition of the Subsidiary by Pat. The $234,000 Investment in Sis balance in Pat's balance sheet consists of the $213,750 cost plus $33,750 income less $13,500 dividends received. Although other amounts in the statements

EXHIBIT 8-1

Preacquisition
Income and Dividends
in Consolidation
Workpapers

PAT CORPORATION AND SUBSIDIARY CONSOLIDATION WORKPAPER FOR THE YEAR ENDED DECEMBER 31, 2011

	Pat	90% Sis	Adjustments and Eliminations Debits	Adjustments and Eliminations Credits	Consolidated Statements
Income Statement Sales	$300,000	$100,000	b 25,000		$375,000
Income from Sis	33,750		a 33,750		
Expenses including cost of sales	(200,000)	(50,000)		b 12,500	(237,500)
Consolidated net income					137,500
Noncontrolling interest share (10% × $37,500)			c 3,750		(3,750)
Controlling share of Consolidated Net Income	**$133,750**	**$ 50,000**			**$133,750**
Retained Earnings Statement Retained earnings - Pat	$266,250				$266,250
Retained earnings - Sis		$ 35,000	b 35,000		
Controlling share of Consolidated NI	133,750	50,000			133,750
Dividends	(100,000)	(25,000)		a 13,500 b 9,000 c 2,500	(100,000)
Retained earnings — Dec. 31	**$300,000**	**$ 60,000**			**$300,000**
Balance Sheet Other assets	$566,000	$260,000			$826,000
Investment in Sis	234,000			a 20,250 b 213,750	
	$800,000	$260,000			$826,000
Capital stock	$500,000	$200,000	b 200,000		$500,000
Retained earnings	300,000	60,000			300,000
	$800,000	$260,000			
Noncontrolling interest				b 24,750 c 1,250	26,000
					$826,000

of Pat and Sis are introduced for the first time in the consolidation workpapers, they are entirely compatible with previous assumptions and data for Pat and Sis Corporations.

Workpaper entry a eliminates the income from Sis and dividends received from Sis and returns the Investment in Sis account to its $213,750 balance at acquisition on April 1, 2011:

a	Income from Sis (−R, −SE)	33,750	
	Dividends—Sis (+SE)		13,500
	Investment in Sis (−A)		20,250
	To eliminate investment income and the dividends received from Sis and to adjust the investment in Sis to its fair value on April 1, 2011.		

This entry does not reflect new procedures, but we must be careful to eliminate only dividends actually received (90% × $15,000) rather than multiplying the ownership percentage times dividends paid by the subsidiary for the year.

The second workpaper entry in Exhibit 8-1 reflects new workpaper procedures because it contains items from preacquisition sales and cost of sales and expenses and dividends. We journalize it as follows:

b	**Sales (−R, −SE)***	25,000	
	Cost of sales and expenses (−E, +SE)*		12,500
	Capital stock − Sis (−SE)	200,000	
	Retained earnings—Sis (−SE)	35,000	
	Dividends − Sis (+SE)*		9,000
	Investment in Sis (−A)		213,750
	Noncontrolling interest—beginning (+SE)		24,750

To eliminate reciprocal investment and equity balances, preacquisition income, and preacquisition dividends and to record the beginning noncontrolling interest. The * items represent the preacquisition income and dividends. Note that the beginning noncontrolling interest is the amount at the acquisition date. It represents 10% of the January 1 beginning capital stock plus retained earnings, plus the preacquisition earnings [10% × ($200,000 + $35,000 + $12,500)].

c	**Noncontrolling interest share (−SE)**	3,750	
	Dividends − Sis (+SE)		2,500
	Noncontrolling interest (+SE)		1,250

To enter noncontrolling interest share of subsidiary's post-acquisition earnings and dividends.

In cases of *increases* in ownership interests during a period, we compute noncontrolling interest for the noncontrolling shares outstanding at year end. Mid-year acquisitions do not affect consolidation workpapers in subsequent accounting periods.

Sis's 10 percent ending noncontrolling interest at December 31, 2011 (as reported on the balance sheet), is held outside of the consolidated entity for the entire year, so the noncontrolling interest computation is simply 10 percent of Sis's equity at the beginning of the year plus 10 percent of Sis's net income for the year less 10 percent of the dividends declared by Sis during the year.

PIECEMEAL ACQUISITIONS

A corporation may acquire an interest in another corporation in a series of separate stock purchases over a period of time. For example, *USX Corporation's* Note 28 to its 2000 annual report discloses that:

> *On February 7, 2001, Marathon acquired 87 percent of the outstanding common stock of Pennaco Energy, Inc., a natural gas producer. Marathon plans to acquire the remaining Pennaco shares through a merger.*

These **piecemeal acquisitions** require the previously held investment to be remeasured at fair value at the date control of the subsidiary is obtained. Piecemeal acquisitions also increase the details of computing investment income and consolidated net income. This section discusses these details and illustrates accounting for them.

Pod Corporation acquires a 90 percent interest in Sap Corporation in a series of separate stock purchases between July 1 and October 1, 2013. Data concerning the acquisitions and interests acquired are as follows:

Date	Interest Acquired	Investment Cost	Equity at Acquisition Date
July 1	5%	$ 7,000	
August 1	5%	8,000	
October 1	80%	210,000	$220,000

The net identifiable assets of Sap have fair values equal to book values. Any excess of investment cost over fair value/book value is due to goodwill. Pod's acquired interests during July

EXHIBIT 8-2

Piecemeal Acquisition
of a Controlling
Interest

POD CORPORATION AND SUBSIDIARY CONSOLIDATION WORKPAPER FOR THE YEAR ENDED DECEMBER 31, 2013

	Pod	90% Sap	Adjustments and Eliminations Debits	Adjustments and Eliminations Credits	Consolidated Statements
Income Statement Sales	$274,875	$150,000	b 112,500		$ 312,375
Income from Sap	9,000		a 9,000		
Gain from revaluation of investment in Sap	11,250				11,250
Expenses including cost of sales	(220,000)	(110,000)		b 82,500	(247,500)
Consolidated net income					76,125
Noncontrolling interest share (10% × $40,000 × 3/12)			c 1,000		(1,000)
Controlling share of Consolidated Net Income	**$ 75,125**	**$ 40,000**			**$ 75,125**
Retained Earnings Statement Retained earnings—Pod	$221,500				$ 221,500
Retained earnings—Sap		$ 90,000	b 90,000		
Controlling share of Consolidated NI	75,125	40,000			75,125
Retained earnings—Dec. 31	**$296,625**	**$130,000**			**$ 296,625**
Balance Sheet Other assets	$451,375	$300,000			$ 751,375
Investment in Sap	245,250			a 9,000 b 236,250	
Goodwill			b 42,500		42,500
	$696,625	$300,000			$ 793,875
Liabilities	$100,000	$70,000			$ 170,000
Capital stock	300,000	100,000	b 100,000		300,000
Retained earnings	296,625	130,000			296,625
	$696,625	$300,000			
Noncontrolling interest				b 26,250 c 1,000	27,250
					$ 793,875

and August are less than 20 percent, so Pod appropriately records these investments using the cost method. The additional investment on October 1, 2013 increases the investment account balance to $225,000 and increases Pod's ownership interest to 90 percent. An acquisition has now taken place, and Sap must be consolidated. The $210,000 price paid for the 80 percent interest implies a total fair value for Sap of $262,500. The fair value of identifiable net assets is $220,000, implying total goodwill of $42,500 for Sap. The original 10 percent investment must be adjusted to reflect the fair value on October 1, 2013. The fair value of the 10 percent interest is 10% of $262,500. Pod will record a gain from revaluation of the investment in Sap of $11,250. The gain is calculated by $26,250 − ($7,000 + $8,000). October 1 makes this a mid-year acquisition. The consolidated income statement should only include Sap's revenues and expenses for the last three months of 2013. Exhibit 8-2 shows consolidation workpapers for Pod Corporation and Subsidiary for 2013. Additional data, compatible with previous information for the Pod-Sap example, is provided for illustrative purposes. Sap earned income during the year as follows: January 1 through September 30—$30,000 and October 1 through December 31—$10,000.

The workpaper entries are reproduced here for convenient reference:

a	**Income from Sap (−R, −SE)**	9,000	
	Investment in Sap (−A)		9,000

To eliminate investment income and return the investment account to its beginning-of-the-period (i.e., acquisition date) balance.

b	**Sales (−R, −SE)***	112,500	
	Cost of sales and expenses (−E, +SE)*		82,500
	Capital stock – Sap (−SE)	100,000	
	Retained earnings – Sap (−SE)	90,000	
	Goodwill (+A)	42,500	
	Investment in Sap (−A)		236,250
	Noncontrolling interest – beginning (+SE)		26,250

To eliminate reciprocal investment and equity balances, and preacquisition income, and record the beginning noncontrolling interest and goodwill. The * items represent the preacquisition revenues and expenses. Note that the beginning noncontrolling interest is the amount at the acquisition date of October 1, 2013. It represents 10% of the January 1 beginning capital stock plus retained earnings, plus implied goodwill, plus the revenues and expenses prior to the acquisition date. [10% × ($100,000 + $90,000 + $42,500 + $30,000)].

c	**Noncontrolling interest share (−SE)**	1,000	
	Noncontrolling interest (+SE)		1,000

To enter noncontrolling interest share of subsidiary's post-acquisition earnings (10% × $40,000 × 3/12 year).

Except for the adjustment for preacquisition earnings, the consolidation workpaper procedures are equivalent to those used in previous chapters.

SALE OF OWNERSHIP INTERESTS

When an investor sells an ownership interest in an investment, we normally compute a gain or loss on the sale as the difference between the sales proceeds and the carrying value of the investment interest sold. The carrying value of the investment should reflect the equity method when the investor is able to exercise significant influence over the investee. If the investor acquired its interest in several different purchases, the shares sold must be identified with particular acquisitions. This is usually done on the basis of specific identification or the first-in, first-out flow assumption.

GAAP changed the rules for consolidated groups of firms in 2007 [3]. When a parent/investor sells an ownership interest, computation of a gain or loss on the sale is dependent on the nature and size of the transaction. We record a gain or loss only in those cases where the interest sold leads to deconsolidation of a former subsidiary. In other words, gains and losses are only recorded when a parent no longer holds a controlling interest after the sale.

If control is maintained, the sale of subsidiary shares is treated as an equity transaction. No gain or loss is recorded. There will be no recognized changes in recorded amounts for the subsidiary's assets and liabilities.

Both Coke and Pepsi regularly sell (and repurchase) ownership interests in their affiliated bottling companies. *PepsiCo, Inc.,* and Subsidiaries' 1999 annual report includes a $1 billion gain on bottling transactions in calculating its $2.05 billion net income for the year. Similarly, although smaller in amount, the 2006 annual report of the *Coca-Cola Company* and Subsidiaries reveals gains on stock issued by its equity investees in 2004 and 2005. No such gains or losses were included in the 2009 annual reports of the two companies, consistent with the 2007 changes in GAAP.

The following information illustrates sale of ownership interests, both at the beginning of the period and during the period. Sag Corporation is a 90 percent-owned subsidiary of Pan Corporation. Pan's Investment in Sag account at January 1, 2012, has a balance of $288,000, consisting of its underlying equity in Sag plus $18,000 goodwill. (Implied total goodwill of Sag is therefore $20,000.) Sag's stockholders' equity at January 1, 2012, consists of $200,000 capital stock and $100,000 retained earnings. During 2012, Sag reports income of $36,000, earned proportionately throughout the year, and it pays dividends of $20,000 on July 1.

Sale of an Interest at the Beginning of the Period

If Pan sells a 10 percent interest in Sag (one ninth of its holdings) on January 1, 2012, for $40,000, we record no gain or loss on the transaction. Pan still maintains an 80 percent controlling interest in Sag, and the noncontrolling interest increases to 20 percent. Recorded assets and liabilities of Sag, including goodwill, are unaffected. Pan makes the following entry to record the sale:

Cash (+A)	40,000	
Investment in Sag (−A)		32,000
Additional paid-in capital - Pan (+SE)		8,000
To record sale of a 10% interest in Sag.		

The consolidation workpaper entries will increase the noncontrolling interest balance to reflect the transfer from the controlling (parent) to the noncontrolling interest.

During 2012, Pan accounts for its 80 percent interest under the equity method and records income of $28,800 ($36,000 net income of Sag × 80%) and a reduction in its investment account for dividends received. At December 31, 2012, Pan's Investment in Sag account has a balance of $268,800, computed as follows:

Investment balance January 1, 2012	$288,000
Less: Book value of interest sold	32,000
	256,000
Add: Income less dividends ($28,800 − $16,000)	12,800
Investment balance December 31, 2012	$268,800

The investment balance at year-end consists of Pan's underlying equity in Sag of $252,800 ($316,000 × 80%) plus $16,000 goodwill on the 80 percent retained interest. Consolidation workpapers for Pan Corporation and Subsidiary as shown in Exhibit 8-3 illustrate the effect of a decrease in ownership interest on workpaper procedures.

The sale of the interest was at the beginning of the period, so the effect of the sale on consolidation procedures for 2012 is minimal. The workpaper entries from Exhibit 8-3 are in general journal form:

a	Income from Sag (−R, −SE)	28,800	
	Dividends—Sag (+SE)		16,000
	Investment in Sag (−A)		12,800
	To eliminate income and dividends from Sag and return the investment account to its beginning-of-the-period balance after the sale of the 10% interest.		
b	Capital stock—Sag (−SE)	200,000	
	Retained earnings—Sag (−SE)	100,000	
	Goodwill (+A)	20,000	
	Investment in Sag (−A)		256,000
	Noncontrolling interest (20%) (+SE)		64,000
	To eliminate reciprocal investment and equity balances, and to record goodwill and beginning noncontrolling interest.		
c	Noncontrolling interest share (−SE)	7,200	
	Dividends—Sag (+SE)		4,000
	Noncontrolling interest (+SE)		3,200
	To enter noncontrolling interest share of subsidiary income and dividends.		

Workpaper entry a reduces the investment in Sag to its $256,000 beginning balance after sale of the 10 percent interest, and entry b enters goodwill and noncontrolling interest based on amounts immediately after the 10 percent interest was sold. The last entry records the noncontrolling interest share of subsidiary income and dividends.

EXHIBIT 8-3

Sale of a 10% Interest at the Beginning of the Period

PAN CORPORATION AND SUBSIDIARY CONSOLIDATION WORKPAPER FOR THE YEAR ENDED DECEMBER 31, 2012

	Pan	80% Sag	Adjustments and Eliminations Debits	Credits	Consolidated Statements
Income Statement					
Sales	$600,000	$136,000			$736,000
Income from Sag	28,800		a 28,800		
Expenses including cost of sales	(508,800)	(100,000)			(608,800)
Consolidated net income					127,200
Noncontrolling interest share			c 7,200		(7,200)
Controlling share of NI	**$120,000**	**$ 36,000**			**$ 120,000**
Retained Earnings Statement					
Retained earnings—Pan	$210,000				$210,000
Retained earnings—Sag		$100,000	b 100,000		
Controlling share of NI	120,000	36,000			120,000
Dividends	(80,000)	(20,000)		a 16,000 c 4,000	(80,000)
Retained earnings — Dec. 31	**$250,000**	**$116,000**			**$ 250,000**
Balance Sheet					
Other assets	$639,200	$350,000			$989,200
Investment in Sag	268,800			a 12,800 b 256,000	
Goodwill			b 20,000		20,000
	$908,000	$350,000			$1,009,200
Liabilities	$150,000	$34,000			$184,000
Capital stock	500,000	200,000	b 200,000		500,000
Other paid-in capital	8,000				8,000
Retained earnings	250,000	116,000			250,000
	$908,000	$350,000			
Noncontrolling interest				b 64,000 c 3,200	67,200
					$1,009,200

Sale of an Interest During an Accounting Period

If Pan sells the 10 percent interest in Sag on April 1, 2012, for $40,000, the sale may be recorded as of April 1, 2012, or, as an expedient, as of January 1, 2012. Assuming that Pan records the sale as of January 1, 2012, Pan records the $8,000 stockholders' equity effect the same as in the beginning-of-the-year sale situation and makes the same one-line consolidation entries as those illustrated in the earlier example. Consistency with the one-line consolidation requires that we prepare the consolidated financial statements using the same beginning-of-the-period sale assumption. That is, we compute noncontrolling interest share for a 20 percent noncontrolling interest outstanding throughout 2012, and we base beginning and ending noncontrolling interest amounts on a 20 percent noncontrolling interest. This alternative beginning-of-the-period sale assumption affects the parent's controlling share of consolidated net income and any difference in the additional paid-in capital is offset by differences in computing the income from subsidiary under a one-line consolidation and in computing noncontrolling interest share amounts in the consolidated financial statements.[1]

If the sale is recorded as of April 1, 2012, the stockholders' equity effect will be $7,100, computed as:

Selling price of 10% interest		$40,000
Less: Book value of the interest sold:		
Investment balance January 1	$288,000	
Equity in income $36,000 \times 1/4$ year $\times 90\%$	8,100	
	296,100	
Portion of investment sold	$\times 1/9$	32,900
Stockholders' equity effect		$ 7,100

Journal entries on Pan's books during 2012 to account for the 10 percent interest sold and its investment in Sag are as follows:

April 1, 2012

Investment in Sag (+A)	8,100	
Income from Sag (R, +SE)		8,100
To record income for first quarter		
($8,100 equity in income).		
Cash (+A)	40,000	
Investment in Sag (−A)		32,900
Additional paid-in Capital (+SE)		7,100
To record sale of a 10% interest in Sag.		
(See earlier computations.)		

July 1, 2012

Cash (+A)	16,000	
Investment in Sag (−A)		16,000
To record dividends received ($20,000 \times 80\%$).		

December 31, 2012

Investment in Sag (+A)	21,600	
Income from Sag (R, +SE)		21,600
To record income for last three quarters of 2012.		

The income from Sag for 2012 is $29,700, consisting of $8,100 the first quarter and $21,600 the last three quarters. At year-end, the Investment in Sag account has the same $268,800 balance as in the beginning-of-the-period sale illustration, but the balance includes different amounts:

Investment balance January 1	$288,000
Less: Book value of interest sold	32,900
	255,100
Add: Income less dividends	13,700
Investment balance December 31	$268,800

The investment balance at year-end is the same as before because Pan holds the same ownership interest as under the beginning-of-the-year sale assumption. Further, Pan has received the same cash inflow from the investment ($40,000 proceeds from the sale and $16,000 dividends). We explain the effects under the different assumptions as follows:

	Sale at or Assumed at Beginning of Period	Sale Within the Accounting Period
Equity effect on sale of investment	$ 8,000	$ 7,100
Income from Sag	28,800	29,700
Total equity effect	$36,800	$36,800

---

[1] If recorded as of the beginning of the period, we must consider dividends received on the interest sold prior to sale and adjust consolidation procedures accordingly.

EXHIBIT 8-4

Sale of a 10 percent
Interest Within an
Accounting Period

PAN CORPORATION AND SUBSIDIARY CONSOLIDATION WORKPAPER FOR THE YEAR ENDED DECEMBER 31, 2012

	Pan	80% Sag	Adjustments and Eliminations Debits	Credits	Consolidated Statements
Income Statement Sales	$600,000	$136,000			$ 736,000
Income from Sag	29,700		a 29,700		
Expenses including cost of sales	(508,800)	(100,000)			(608,800)
Consolidated net income					127,200
Noncontrolling interest share			c 6,300		(6,300)
Controlling share of NI	**$120,900**	**$ 36,000**			**$ 120,900**
Retained Earnings Statement Retained earnings — Pan	$210,000				$ 210,000
Retained earnings — Sag		$100,000	b 100,000		
Controlling share of NI	120,900	36,000			120,900
Dividends	(80,000)	(20,000)		a 16,000 c 4,000	(80,000)
Retained earnings — Dec. 31	**$250,900**	**$116,000**			**$ 250,900**
Balance Sheet Other assets	$639,200	$350,000			$ 989,200
Investment in Sag	268,800			a 13,700 b 255,100	
Goodwill			b 20,000		20,000
	$908,000	$350,000			$1,009,200
Liabilities	$150,000	$ 34,000			$ 184,000
Capital stock	500,000	200,000	b 200,000		500,000
Other paid-in capital	7,100				7,100
Retained earnings	250,900	116,000			250,900
	$908,000	$350,000			
Noncontrolling interest — Jan. 1 April 1 December 31				b 32,000 b 32,900 c 2,300	67,200
					$1,009,200

The total equity effect of the two different assumptions is the same, but the effect on the consolidated financial statements differs. Both the controlling and noncontrolling interest shares of consolidated net income differ. Consolidation workpapers for a sale within an accounting period are illustrated in Exhibit 8-4.

We journalize workpaper entries to consolidate financial statements as follows:

a Income from Sag (−R, −SE)	29,700	
Dividends—Sag (+SE)		16,000
Investment in Sag (−A)		13,700

(continued)

b	Capital stock—Sag (−SE)	200,000	
	Retained earnings—Sag (−SE)	100,000	
	Goodwill (+A)	20,000	
	Investment in Sag (−A)		255,100
	Noncontrolling interest January 1 (+SE)		32,000
	Noncontrolling interest April 1 (+SE)		32,900
c	Noncontrolling interest share (−SE)	6,300	
	Dividends—Sag (+SE)		4,000
	Noncontrolling interest (+SE)		2,300

NONCONTROLLING INTEREST COMPUTATIONS We separate the noncontrolling interest amounts entered in entry b for illustrative purposes, but they do not have to be separated. We based one part of the noncontrolling interest calculation on the 10 percent noncontrolling interest at the beginning of the period [($300,000 equity of Sag at January 1 plus goodwill of $20,000) x 10%], and the other part reflects the book value of the 10 percent increase in noncontrolling interest from the April 1 sale [($309,000 equity of Sag at April 1 plus goodwill of $20,000) x 10%]. Note that we also need a dual calculation for noncontrolling interest share $6,300 [($36,000 x 10% x ¼ year) + ($36,000 x 20% x ¾ year)] for mid-year sale situations. The investment in Sag decreased when the interest was sold on April 1; therefore, the $255,100 credit in workpaper entry b reflects the $288,000 beginning investment balance less the $32,900 book value of the interest sold on April 1.

Except for the items discussed, the workpapers in Exhibits 8-3 and 8-4 are similar, and the resulting consolidated financial statements are equivalent in all material respects. Because of the additional complexity involved when recording a sale as of the actual sale date, it is more efficient to use the beginning-of-the-period sale assumption. Use of a beginning-of-the-period assumption is also practical because current earnings information is not always available during an accounting period.

Sale of an Interest Resulting in Deconsolidation

Whenever a parent ceases to have a controlling interest, the subsidiary should be deconsolidated (i.e., eliminated from the consolidated financial statements). Typically, this would result from a sale of an interest in the subsidiary, which reduces the parent share to less than 50 percent. In such cases, a gain or loss is calculated. The gain or loss is included in net income attributable to the parent. GAAP [5] measures the gain or loss as the difference between:

a. The aggregate of:
  1. The fair value of consideration received
  2. The fair value of any retained noncontrolling investment in the former subsidiary at the date the subsidiary is deconsolidated
  3. The carrying amount of the noncontrolling interest in the former subsidiary (including any accumulated other comprehensive income attributable to the noncontrolling interest) at the date the subsidiary is deconsolidated
b. The carrying amount of the former subsidiary's assets and liabilities.

Assume that Pet Corporation sells its entire 90 percent interest in Sod Corporation for $550,000 in cash. Pet looks to the carrying amount of its investment to determine the gain or loss on the sale. If the carrying value equals $530,000, then Pet deconsolidates Sod and records a gain of $20,000. Pet records the transaction as follows:

Cash (+A)	550,000	
Investment in Sod (−A)		530,000
Gain on sale (Ga, +SE)		20,000

LEARNING OBJECTIVE 3

CHANGES IN OWNERSHIP INTERESTS FROM SUBSIDIARY STOCK TRANSACTIONS

Subsidiary stock issuances provide a means of expanding the operations of a subsidiary through external financing. Both the expansion and the financing decisions are, of course, controlled by the parent. Parent management may decide to construct a new plant for the subsidiary and to finance the construction by advising the subsidiary to sell additional subsidiary stock to the parent.

Subsidiary operations may also be expanded through the issuance of subsidiary stock to the public. A parent may even issue shares of one subsidiary to acquire another. The following note appeared in the 2006 annual report of **Coca-Cola Company** (p. 84):

> *In 2003, one of our Company's equity method investees, Coca-Cola FEMSA, consummated a merger with another of the Company's equity method investees, Panamerican Beverages, Inc. At the time of the merger, the Company and Fomento Economico Mexicano, S.A.B. de C.V. ("FEMSA"), the major shareowner of Coca-Cola FEMSA, reached an understanding under which this shareowner could purchase from our Company an amount of Coca-Cola FEMSA shares sufficient for this shareowner to regain majority ownership interest in Coca-Cola FEMSA. That understanding expired in May 2006; however, in the third quarter of 2006, the Company and the shareowner reached an agreement under which the Company would sell a number of shares representing 8 percent of the capital stock of Coca-Cola FEMSA to FEMSA. As a result of this sale, which occurred in the fourth quarter of 2006, the Company received cash proceeds of approximately $427 million and realized a gain of approximately $175 million, which was recorded in the consolidated statement of income line item other income (loss)– net and impacted the Corporate operating segment. Also as a result of this sale, our ownership interest in Coca-Cola FEMSA was reduced from approximately 40 percent to approximately 32 percent. Refer to Note 18. (p. 84)*

In the case of a partially-owned subsidiary, noncontrolling stockholders may exercise their preemptive rights to subscribe to additional stock issuances in proportion to their holdings.

Subsidiary operations may be curtailed if the parent management decides to have the subsidiary reacquire its own shares.

A parent/investor's ownership in a subsidiary/investee may change as a result of subsidiary sales of additional shares or through subsidiary purchases of its own shares. The effect of such activities on the parent/investor depends on the price at which additional shares are sold or treasury stock is purchased and on whether the parent is directly involved in transactions with the subsidiary. In accounting for an equity investment under a one-line consolidation, GAAP [4] stipulates that transactions of an investee of a capital nature that affect the investor's share of stockholders' equity of the investee should be accounted for as if the investee were a consolidated subsidiary.

Sale of Additional Shares by a Subsidiary

Assume that Pun Corporation owns an 80 percent interest in Sit Corporation and that Pun's investment in Sit is $180,000 on January 1, 2012, equal to 80 percent of Sit's $200,000 stockholders' equity plus $20,000 of goodwill (total goodwill is $25,000). Sit's equity on this date consists of:

Capital stock, $10 par	$100,000
Additional paid-in capital	60,000
Retained earnings	40,000
Total stockholders' equity	$200,000

SUBSIDIARY SELLS SHARES TO PARENT If Sit sells an additional 2,000 shares of stock to Pun *at book value of $20 per share* on January 2, 2012, Pun's investment in Sit will increase by $40,000 to $220,000, and its interest in Sit will increase from 80 percent (8,000 ÷ 10,000 shares) to 83 1/3 percent (10,000 ÷ 12,000 shares). The amount paid for the 2,000 additional shares is equal to book value, so Pun's investment in Sit still reflects the $20,000 goodwill:

	January 1 Before Sale	January 2 After Sale
Sit's stockholders' equity	$200,000	$240,000
Pun's interest	80 %	83 1/3%
Pun's equity in Sit	160,000	200,000
Goodwill	20,000	20,000
Investment in Sit Balance	$180,000	$220,000

If Sit sells the 2,000 shares to Pun *at $35 per share*, Pun's investment in Sit will increase to $250,000 ($180,000 + $70,000 additional investment), and its ownership interest will increase from 80 percent to 83 1/3 percent. Now Pun's investment in Sit reflects a $25,000 excess of investment balance over underlying book value. The additional $5,000 excess is the result of Pun's $70,000 payment to increase its equity in Sit by $65,000, which we analyze as follows:

Price paid by Pun (2,000 shares × $35)		$70,000
Book value acquired:		
Underlying book value after purchase	$225,000	
($200,000 + $70,000) × 83 1/3%		
Underlying book value before purchase	160,000	
($200,000 × 80%)		
Book value acquired		65,000
Excess cost over book value acquired		$ 5,000

We assign the $5,000 excess to identifiable assets or goodwill as appropriate and amortize over the remaining life of undervalued assets.

Now assume that Sit sells the 2,000 shares to Pun at *$15 per share* (or $5 per share below book value). Pun's ownership interest increases from 80 percent to 83 1/3 percent as before, and its investment in Sit increases by $30,000 to $210,000. As a result of paying less than book value for the shares, however, book value acquired exceeds investment cost:

Price paid by Pun (2,000 shares × $15)		$30,000
Book value acquired:		
Underlying book value after purchase	$191,667	
($200,000 + $30,000) × 83 1/3%		
Underlying book value before purchase	160,000	
($200,000 × $80%)		
Book value acquired		31,667
Excess book value acquired over cost		$ 1,667

Conceptually, the $1,667 excess book value acquired over cost should be assigned to reduce overvalued identifiable net assets. The practical solution, however, is to charge the excess book value to goodwill from investments in the same company's stock. In this example, reduce goodwill from $20,000 to $18,333. (Total goodwill is reduced to $22,916.)

SUBSIDIARY SELLS SHARES TO OUTSIDE ENTITIES Assume that Sit sells the 2,000 additional shares to other entities (noncontrolling stockholders). Pun's ownership interest declines from 80% (8,000 ÷ 10,000 shares) to 66 2/3 percent (8,000 ÷ 12,000 shares), regardless of the selling price of the shares. But the effect on Pun's Investment in Sit account depends on the selling price. The effect of the sale on Pun's underlying book value in Sit under each of three issuance assumptions ($20, $35, and $15 per share) is:

	January 2, 2012, After Sale		
	Sale at $20	**Sale at $35**	**Sale at $15**
Sit's stockholders' equity	$240,000	$270,000	$230,000
Interest owned	66 2/3%	66 2/3%	66 2/3%
Pun's equity in Sit after issuance	160,000	180,000	153,333
Pun's equity in Sit before issuance	160,000	160,000	160,000
Increase (Decrease) in Pun's Equity in Sit	0	$ 20,000	$ (6,667)

Sale to outside entities at $20 per share does not affect Pun's equity in Sit because the selling price equals book value. If Sit sells the stock at $35 per share (above book value), Pun's equity in Sit will increase by $20,000, and if Sit sells at $15 per share (below book value), Pun's equity in Sit will decrease by $6,667.

GAAP [6] requires that we account for the effect of the decreased ownership percentage as an equity transaction. In other words, we adjust the parent's investment and additional paid-in capital account balances; we do not record a gain or loss on these types of transactions. Entries to record the changes in underlying equity on Pun's books under this method are:

Sale at $20 per Share (Book Value)
None
Sale at $35 per Share (Above Book Value)

Investment in Sit (+A)	20,000	
Additional paid-in capital (+SE)		20,000

Sale at $15 per Share (Below Book Value)

Additional paid-in capital[2] (−SE)	6,667	
Investment in Sit (−A)		6,667

Under this method, we do not adjust unamortized fair value/book value differentials for the decreased ownership percentage.

SUMMARY OF SUBSIDIARY STOCK SALES CONCEPTS Sales of stock by a subsidiary to its parent do not result in gain or loss recognition or adjustments to additional paid-in capital, but they do result in fair value/book value differentials equal to the difference between the cost of the additional shares and the parent's share of the difference in the subsidiary's stockholders' equity immediately before and after the stock sale.

GAAP considers sales of stock by a subsidiary to outside parties as capital transactions and requires adjustment of the parent's investment and additional paid-in capital accounts except when the shares are sold at book value. The amount of adjustment is the difference between the underlying book value of the interest in subsidiary's stockholders' equity held immediately before and after the additional shares are issued to outsiders.

If a parent and outside investors purchase shares of a subsidiary in relation to existing stock ownership (ratably), no adjustments to additional paid-in capital will be necessary, regardless of whether the stock is sold at book value, below book value, or above book value. Similarly, no excess or deficiency of investment cost over book value for the parent can result from this situation. This is true because the increased investment is necessarily equal to the parent's increase (decrease) in underlying book value from the ratable purchase of additional shares.

Treasury Stock Transactions by a Subsidiary

The acquisition of treasury stock by a subsidiary decreases subsidiary equity and shares outstanding. If the subsidiary acquires treasury stock from noncontrolling shareholders at book value, no change in the parent's share of subsidiary equity results even though the parent's percentage ownership increases. A subsidiary's purchase of its own shares from noncontrolling stockholders at an amount above or below book value decreases or increases the parent's share of subsidiary book value and at the same time increases the parent's ownership percentage. This latter situation requires an entry on the parent's books to adjust the investment in subsidiary balance and to debit or credit additional paid-in capital for the difference in the parent's share of subsidiary book value before and after the treasury stock transaction.

Assume that Sun Company is an 80 percent subsidiary of Pin and that Sun has 10,000 shares of common stock outstanding at December 31, 2012. On January 1, 2013, Sun purchases 400 shares of its stock from noncontrolling stockholders. Exhibit 8-5 summarizes the effect of this treasury stock acquisition on Pin's share of Sun's book value under three different assumptions regarding the purchase price of the treasury shares.

Pin's equity in Sun before the purchase of the 400 shares of treasury stock by Sun was $160,000, and its ownership interest was 80 percent, as shown in the first column of Exhibit 8-5. The purchase of the 400 treasury shares by Sun increases Pin's ownership percentage to 83 1/3 percent (or 8,000 of 9,600 outstanding shares), regardless of the price paid by Sun. If Sun purchases the 400 shares at their $20-per-share book value, Pin's share of Sun's equity remains at $160,000, as shown in the second column of Exhibit 8-5, even though its interest increases to 83 1/3 percent. This requires no adjustment.

---

[2] This debit is to retained earnings when the parent's additional paid-in capital is insufficient to stand the debit.

EXHIBIT 8-5

Purchase of Treasury
Stock by Subsidiary

EQUITY OF SUN COMPANY

	Column 1: Before Purchase of Treasury Stock	Column 2: After Purchase of 400 Shares at $20	Column 3: After Purchase of 400 Shares at $30	Column 4: After Purchase of 400 Shares at $15
Capital stock, $10 par	$100,000	$100,000	$100,000	$100,000
Retained earnings	100,000	100,000	100,000	100,000
	200,000	200,000	200,000	200,000
Less: Treasury stock (cost)	—	8,000	12,000	6,000
Total equity	$200,000	$192,000	$188,000	$194,000
Pin's interest	4/5*	5/6**	5/6**	5/6**
Pin's share of Sun's book value	$160,000	$160,000	$156,667	$161,667

*8,000 out of 10,000 outstanding shares.
**8,000 out of 9,600 outstanding shares.

If Sun purchases the 400 shares of treasury stock at $30 per share, Pin's equity decreases by $3,333 to $156,667, as shown in column 3 of Exhibit 8-5. Pin records the decrease with the following entry:

Additional paid-in capital (−SE)	3,333	
Investment in Sun (−A)		3,333
To record an investment decrease from Sun's purchase		
of treasury stock in excess of book value.		

This entry reduces Pin's Investment in Sun to its share of the underlying book value in Sun and also reduces additional paid-in capital. Treasury stock transactions are of a capital nature, so they do not affect gain or loss.

The third situation illustrated in Exhibit 8-5 (column 4) assumes that Sun purchases 400 shares of treasury stock at $15 per share ($5 per share below book value). As a result of Sun's acquisition of its own shares, Pin's share of Sun's equity increases from $160,000 to $161,667. This increase of $1,667 requires the following adjustment on Pin's books:

Investment in Sun (+A)	1,667	
Additional paid-in capital (+SE)		1,667
To record an investment increase from Sun's purchase		
of treasury shares below book value.		

Current GAAP supports the parent adjustments illustrated here for changes resulting from subsidiary treasury stock transactions. GAAP prohibits the recognition of gain or loss from treasury stock transactions but, at the same time, requires the equity method with amortization of any differences between the investment fair value and its underlying book value, unless the difference is due to an intangible asset with an indeterminate life, such as goodwill. The parent bases accounting from subsidiary treasury stock transactions on the book value of net assets. During the time treasury shares are held, the book value of net assets would change due to the subsidiary's operations. If the treasury shares are eventually resold, the parent would account for this change on the basis of the book value of the assets at the time of sale. It should be understood, however, that *frequent and insignificant treasury stock transactions by a subsidiary tend to be offsetting with respect to purchases and sales and do not require the adjustments illustrated.*

STOCK DIVIDENDS AND STOCK SPLITS BY A SUBSIDIARY

Stock dividends and splits by substantially owned subsidiaries are not common unless the noncontrolling interest actively trades in the security markets. This is because the parent controls such actions and there is ordinarily no advantage to the consolidated entity or the parent from increasing the number of subsidiary shares outstanding through stock splits or stock dividends. Even if a subsidiary splits its stock or issues a stock dividend, the effect of such actions on consolidation procedures is minimal.

A stock split by a subsidiary increases the number of shares outstanding, but it does not affect either the net assets of the subsidiary or the individual equity accounts. Also, parent and noncontrolling interest ownership percentages are unaffected by subsidiary stock splits; accordingly, parent accounting and consolidation procedures are unaffected.

These same observations apply to stock dividends by subsidiaries except that the individual subsidiary equity accounts are changed in the case of stock dividends. This change occurs because retained earnings equal to par or stated value or to the market price of the additional shares issued is transferred to paid-in capital. Although capitalization of retained earnings does not affect parent accounting, it does change the amounts of capital stock, additional paid-in capital, and retained earnings to be eliminated in consolidation.

Pit Corporation owns 80 percent of the outstanding stock of Sod Company acquired on January 1, 2011, for $160,000. Sod's stockholders' equity on that date was as follows:

Capital stock, $10 par	$100,000
Additional paid-in capital	20,000
Retained earnings	80,000
Total stockholders' equity	$200,000

During 2011, Sod had net income of $30,000 and paid cash dividends of $10,000. Pit increased its investment in Sod for its investment income of $24,000 ($30,000 × 80%) and decreased it for dividends received of $8,000 ($10,000 × 80%). Thus, Pit's Investment in Sod account at December 31, 2011, was $176,000.

On the basis of the information given, the consolidation workpaper for Pit Corporation and Subsidiary at December 31, 2011 would include the following adjustments and eliminations:

Income from Sod (−R, −SE)	**24,000**	
Dividends (+SE)		**8,000**
Investment in Sod (−A)		**16,000**
Capital stock—Sod (−SE)	**100,000**	
Additional paid-in capital—Sod (−SE)	**20,000**	
Retained earnings—Sod (−SE)	**80,000**	
Investment in Sod (−A)		**160,000**
Noncontrolling interest—beginning (+SE)		**40,000**

If Sod had also declared and issued a 10 percent stock dividend on December 31, 2011, when its stock was selling at $40 per share, Sod Corporation would record the stock dividend as follows:

Stock dividend on common (−SE)	40,000	
Capital stock, $10 par (+SE)		10,000
Additional paid-in capital (+SE)		30,000

This stock dividend does not affect Pit's accounting for its investment in Sod (although now there are more shares and a different cost per share), but it does affect the consolidation workpaper, because Sod's capital stock has increased to $110,000 ($100,000 + $10,000) and its additional paid-in capital has increased to $50,000 ($20,000 + $30,000). Consolidation workpaper adjustment and elimination entries at December 31, 2011, would be as follows:

Income from Sod (−R, −SE)	**24,000**	
Dividends (+SE)		**8,000**
Investment in Sod (−A)		**16,000**
Capital stock—Sod (−SE)	**110,000**	
Additional paid-in capital—Sod (−SE)	**50,000**	
Retained earnings—Sod (−SE)	**80,000**	
Investment in Sod (−A)		**160,000**
Noncontrolling interest—beginning (+SE)		**40,000**
Stock dividend on common (+SE)		**40,000**

We eliminate the $40,000 stock dividend account along with the reciprocal investment and equity balances because it is really an offset to $10,000 of the capital stock and $30,000 of the additional paid-in capital. In 2012 and subsequent years, retained earnings will reflect the $40,000 decrease from the stock dividend, and no further complications will result.

SUMMARY

When a parent purchases a subsidiary during an accounting period, we do not include pre-acquisition earnings in computing consolidated net income. Both the controlling share and consolidated net income should only reflect post-acquisition revenues and expenses. We also eliminate preacquisition dividends on an interest acquired during an accounting period in the consolidation process.

The acquisition of a controlling interest through a series of separate stock purchases over a period of time increases the detail involved in accounting for the total investment under the equity method. It also complicates the preparation of consolidated financial statements because the original investments must be adjusted to reflect the fair value on the date of the acquisition (i.e., when a controlling interest is achieved).

When a parent/investor sells an ownership interest in a subsidiary/investee, the gain or loss on sale is equal to the difference between the selling price and the book value of the investment interest sold. The gain or loss is recorded only when the parent no longer holds a controlling interest after the sale. If control is maintained by the parent after the sale, no gain or loss is recorded, and we adjust the additional paid-in capital instead. The sale of an interest during an accounting period increases the noncontrolling interest and necessitates changes in the computation of noncontrolling interest share.

The sale of additional shares by a subsidiary changes the parent's percentage ownership in the subsidiary unless the shares are sold to the parent and noncontrolling shareholders in proportion to their holdings. The direct sale of additional shares to the parent increases the parent's interest and decreases the noncontrolling shareholders' interest. The issuance of additional shares to noncontrolling stockholders or outside entities by the subsidiary decreases the parent's percentage interest and increases the noncontrolling shareholders' interests. Such changes require special care in accounting for a parent's investment under the equity method and in preparing consolidated financial statements.

Parent accounting and consolidation procedures are not affected by subsidiary stock splits. However, subsidiary stock dividends may lead to changes in the consolidation workpapers.

QUESTIONS

1. Explain the terms *preacquisition earnings* and *preacquisition dividends*.
2. How are preacquisition earnings accounted for by a parent under the equity method? How are they accounted for in the consolidated income statement?
3. Assume that an 80 percent investor of Sub Company acquires an additional 10 percent interest in Sub halfway through the current fiscal period. Explain the effect of the 10 percent acquisition by the parent on noncontrolling interest share for the period and on total noncontrolling interest at the end of the current period.
4. Isn't preacquisition income really noncontrolling interest share?
5. How is the gain or loss determined for the sale of part of an investment interest that is accounted for as a one-line consolidation? Is the amount of gain or loss affected by the accounting method used by the investor?
6. When a parent sells a part of its interest in a subsidiary during an accounting period, is the income applicable to the interest sold up to the time of sale included in consolidated net income and parent income under the equity method? Explain.
7. Assume that a subsidiary has 10,000 shares of stock outstanding, of which 8,000 shares are owned by the parent. What equity method adjustment will be necessary on the parent books if the subsidiary sells 2,000 additional shares of its own stock to outside interests at book value? At an amount in excess of book value?
8. Assume that a subsidiary has 10,000 shares of stock outstanding, of which 8,000 shares are owned by the parent. If the parent purchases an additional 2,000 shares of stock directly from the subsidiary at book value, how should the parent record its additional investment? Would your answer have been different if the purchase of the 2,000 shares had been made above book value? Explain.

9. How do the treasury stock transactions of a subsidiary affect the parent's accounting for its investment under the equity method?

10. Can gains or losses to a parent/investor result from a subsidiary's/investee's treasury stock transactions? Explain.

11. Do common stock dividends and stock splits by a subsidiary affect the amounts that appear in the consolidated financial statements? Explain, indicating the items, if any, that would be affected.

EXERCISES

E 8-1

Allocate income and dividends to controlling, noncontrolling, and preacquisition interests

Pie Corporation increases its ownership interest in its subsidiary, Set Corporation, from 70 percent on January 1, 2011, to 90 percent at July 1, 2011. Set's net income for 2011 is $100,000, and it declares $30,000 dividends on March 1 and $30,000 on September 1.

REQUIRED: Show the allocation of Set's net income and dividends among controlling interests, noncontrolling interests, and preacquisition interests.

E 8-2

Piecemeal acquisition of controlling interest with preacquisition income and dividends

On January 1, 2011, Pin Industries purchased a 40 percent interest in Sip Corporation for $800,000, when Sip's stockholders' equity consisted of $1,000,000 capital stock and $1,000,000 retained earnings. On September 1, 2011, Pin purchased an additional 20 percent interest in Sip for $420,000. Both purchases were made at book value equal to fair value.

Sip had income for 2011 of $240,000, earned evenly throughout the year, and it paid dividends of $60,000 in April and $60,000 in October.

REQUIRED: Compute the following:

1. Pin's income from Sip for 2011

2. Preacquisition income that will appear on the consolidated income statement for 2011

3. Noncontrolling interest share for 2011

E 8-3

Journal entries (sale of an interest—beginning-of-year assumption)

Pet Corporation owns 100 percent (300,000 shares) of the outstanding shares of Sap Corporation's common stock on January 1, 2011. Its Investment in Sap account on this date is $4,400,000, equal to Sap's $4,000,000 stockholders' equity plus $400,000 goodwill. During 2011, Sap reports net income of $600,000 and pays no dividends.

On April 1, 2011, Pet sells a 15 percent interest (45,000 shares) in Sap for $750,000, thereby reducing its holdings to 85 percent.

REQUIRED: Prepare the journal entries needed for Pet to account for its investment in Sap for 2011, using a beginning-of-the-period sales assumption.

E 8-4

Sale of equity interest—beginning-of-year or actual sale date assumption

The balance of Pal Corporation's investment in Sag Company account at December 31, 2010, was $436,000, consisting of 80 percent of Sag's $500,000 stockholders' equity on that date and $36,000 goodwill.

On May 1, 2011, Pal sold a 20 percent interest in Sag (one-fourth of its holdings) for $130,000. During 2011, Sag had net income of $150,000, and on July 1, 2011, Sag declared dividends of $80,000.

REQUIRED: (Solve using both the actual date of sale assumption and the beginning of the year sale assumption.)

1. Determine the gain or loss on sale of the 20 percent interest.

2. Calculate Pal's income from Sag for 2011.

3. Determine the balance of Pal's Investment in Sag account at December 31, 2011.

E 8-5

Computations and workpaper entries (mid-year acquisition)

Pig Corporation paid $1,274,000 cash for 70 percent of the common stock of Set Corporation on June 1, 2011. The assets and liabilities of Set were fairly valued, and any fair value/book value differential is goodwill. Data related to the stockholders' equity of Set are as follows:

Stockholders' Equity December 31, 2010

Common stock, $10 par	$1,000,000
Retained earnings	480,000
Total stockholders' equity	$1,480,000

Income and Dividends—2011

Net income (earned evenly throughout the year)	$ 240,000
Dividends (declared and paid in equal amounts in January, April, July, and October)	120,000

REQUIRED

1. Determine the following:
   a. Goodwill from the investment in Set
   b. Pig's income from Set for 2011
   c. The Investment in Set account balance at December 31, 2011

2. Prepare the workpaper entries needed to consolidate the financial statements for 2011. Add the preacquisition income to Retained Earnings—Set.

E 8-6

Additional stock issued by subsidiary directly to parent

The stockholders' equities of Pal Corporation and its 80 percent-owned subsidiary, Sow Corporation, on December 31, 2011, are as follows (in thousands):

	Pal	Sow
Common stock, $10 par	$10,000	$6,000
Retained earnings	4,000	3,000
Total Stockholders' Equity	$14,000	$9,000

Pal's Investment in Sow account balance on December 31, 2011, is equal to its underlying book value. On January 2, 2012, Sow issued 60,000 previously unissued common shares directly to Pal at $25 per share.

REQUIRED

1. Calculate the balance of Pal's Investment in Sow account on January 2, 2012, after the new investment is recorded.

2. Determine the goodwill, if any, from Pal's purchase of the 60,000 new shares.

E 8-7

Additional stock issued by subsidiary under different assumptions

The stockholders' equities of Pod Corporation and its 80 percent-owned subsidiary, Sod Corporation, on December 31, 2011, appear as follows (in thousands):

	Pod	Sod
Common stock, $10 par	$5,000	$2,200
Retained earnings	2,000	1,000
Total	$7,000	$3,200

Pod's Investment in Sod account on this date is equal to its underlying book value. On January 1, 2012, Sod issues 30,000 previously unissued common shares for $20 per share.

REQUIRED

1. If Pod purchases the 30,000 shares directly from Sod, what is Pod's percentage ownership in Sod after the new shares are acquired?

2. If Sod sells the 30,000 previously unissued common shares to the public, what is Pod's percentage ownership in Sod after the new issuance?

3. If Sod sells the 30,000 shares to the public, prepare the journal entry on Pod's books to account for the effect of the issuance on its Investment in Sod account assuming that *no* gain or loss is recognized.

E 8-8

Subsidiary issues additional stock under different assumptions

Pam Corporation owns two-thirds (600,000 shares) of the outstanding $1 par common stock of Sat Company on January 1, 2011. In order to raise cash to finance an expansion program, Sat issues an additional 100,000 shares of its common stock for $5 per share on January 3, 2011. Sat's stockholders' equity before and after the new stock issuance is as follows (in thousands):

	Before Issuance	After Issuance
Common stock, $1 par	$ 900	$1,000
Additional paid-in capital	600	1,000
Retained earnings	600	600
Total stockholders' equity	$2,100	$2,600

REQUIRED

1. Assume that Pam purchases all 100,000 shares of common stock directly from Sat.
   a. What is Pam's percentage ownership interest in Sat after the purchase?
   b. Calculate goodwill from Pam's acquisition of the 100,000 shares of Sat.

2. Assume that the 100,000 shares of common stock are sold to Van Company, one of Sat's noncontrolling stockholders.
   a. What is Pam's percentage ownership interest after the new shares are sold to Van?
   b. Calculate the change in underlying book value of Pam's investment after the sale.
   c. Prepare the journal entry on Pam's books to recognize the increase or decrease in underlying book value computed in b above assuming that gain or loss is *not* recognized.

E 8-9

Mid-year piecemeal acquisition with goodwill

The stockholder's equity of Sum Corporation at December 31, 2010, 2011, and 2012, is as follows (in thousands):

	December 31,		
	2010	2011	2012
Capital stock, $10 par	$200	$200	$200
Retained earnings	80	160	220
	$280	$360	$420

Sum reported income of $80,000 in 2011 and paid no dividends. In 2012, Sum reported net income of $80,000 and declared and paid dividends of $10,000 on May 1 and $10,000 on November 1. Income was earned evenly in both years.

Pin Corporation acquired 4,000 shares of Sum common stock on April 1, 2011, for $64,000 cash and another 8,000 shares on July 1, 2012, for $164,000. Any fair value/book value differential is goodwill.

REQUIRED: Determine the following:

1. Pin's income from Sum for 2011 and 2012

2. Noncontrolling interest at December 31, 2012

3. Preacquisition income in 2012

4. Balance of the Investment in Sum account at December 31, 2012

E 8-10

Computations for sale of an interest

Pit Corporation acquired a 90 percent interest in Sad on July 1, 2012, for $675,000. The stockholders' equity of Sad at December 31, 2011, was as follows (in thousands):

Capital stock	$500
Retained earnings	200
Total	$700

During 2012 and 2013, Sad reported income and declared dividends as follows:

	2012	2013
Net income	$100,000	$80,000
Dividends (December)	50,000	30,000

On July 1, 2013, Pit sold a 10 percent interest (or one-ninth of its investment) in Sad for $85,000.

REQUIRED

1. Determine Pit's investment income for 2012 and 2013, and its investment balance on December 31, 2012 and 2013.

2. Determine noncontrolling interest share for 2012 and 2013, and the total of noncontrolling interest on December 31, 2012 and 2013.

E 8-11

Changes in subsidiary's outstanding shares

Pan Corporation purchased a 75 percent interest in Soy Corporation in the open market on January 1, 2012, for $690,000. A summary of Soy's stockholders' equity on December 31, 2011 and 2012, is as follows (in thousands):

	December 31	
	2011	2012
Capital stock, $10 par	$400	$ 400
Additional paid-in capital	300	300
Retained earnings	100	300
Total stockholders' equity	$800	$1,000

On January 1, 2013, Soy sold an additional 10,000 shares of its own $10 par stock for $30 per share. Pan assigns any excess/deficiency of fair value over book value to goodwill.

REQUIRED: Compute the following:

1. The underlying book value of the interest in Soy held by Pan on December 31, 2012.

2. Pan's percentage ownership interest in Soy on January 3, 2013, assuming that Pan purchased the 10,000 additional shares directly from Soy.

3. Pan's investment in Soy on January 3, 2013, assuming that Pan purchased the additional shares directly from Soy.

4. Pan's percentage ownership interest in Soy on January 3, 2013, assuming that Soy sold the 10,000 additional shares to investors outside the consolidated entity.

5. Pan's investment in Soy on January 3, 2013, assuming that Soy sold the 10,000 additional shares to investors outside the consolidated entity and no gain or loss is recognized.

E 8-12

Journal entries when subsidiary issues additional shares directly to parent

Put Corporation's Investment in Son Company account had a balance of $475,000 at December 31, 2011. This balance consisted of goodwill of $35,000 and 80 percent of Son's $550,000 stockholders' equity.

On January 2, 2012, Son increased its outstanding shares from 10,000 to 12,000 shares by selling 2,000 additional shares directly to Put at $80 per share. Son's net income for 2012 was $90,000, and in December 2012 it paid $60,000 dividends.

REQUIRED: Prepare all journal entries other than closing entries to account for Put's investment in Son during 2012. Any difference between fair value and book value is goodwill.

E 8-13

Computations and entries (subsidiary issues additional shares to outside entities)

Pat Company paid $1,800,000 for 90,000 shares of Sir Company's 100,000 outstanding shares on January 1, 2011, when Sir's equity consisted of $1,000,000 of $10 par common stock and $500,000 retained earnings. The excess fair value over book value was goodwill. On January 2, 2013, Sir sold an additional 20,000 shares to the public for $600,000, and its equity before and after issuance of the additional 20,000 shares was as follows (in thousands):

	January 1, 2013 (Before Issuance)	January 2, 2013 (After Issuance)
$10 par common stock	$1,000	$1,200
Additional paid-in capital	—	400
Retained earnings	800	800
Total stockholders' equity	$1,800	$2,400

REQUIRED

1. Determine Pat's Investment in Sir account balance on January 1, 2013.

2. Prepare the entry on Pat's books to account for its decreased ownership interest if gain or loss is not recognized.

PROBLEMS

P8-1

Mid-year acquisition and purchase of additional shares

A summary of changes in the stockholders' equity of Sin Corporation from January 1, 2011, to December 31, 2012, appears as follows (in thousands):

	Capital Stock $10 Par	Additional Paid-in Capital	Retained Earnings	Total Equity
Balance January 1, 2011	$500	—	$ 50	$550
Dividends, December 2011	—	—	(50)	(50)
Income, 2011	—	—	100	100
Balance December 31, 2011	$500	—	$100	$600
Sale of stock January 1, 2012	100	$ 62	—	162
Dividends, December 2012	—	—	(60)	(60)
Income, 2012	—	—	150	150
Balance December 31, 2012	$600	$ 62	$190	$852

Par Corporation purchases 40,000 shares of Sin's outstanding stock on July 1, 2011, in the open market for $620,000 and an additional 10,000 shares directly from Sin for $162,000 on January 1, 2012. Any excess of investment fair value over book value is due to goodwill.

REQUIRED

1. Determine the balance of Par's Investment in Sin account on December 31, 2011.

2. Compute Par's investment income from Sin for 2012.

3. Determine the balance of Par's Investment in Sin account on December 31, 2012.

P 8-2

Computations and entries (subsidiary issues additional shares to public)

Pin Corporation purchased 960,000 shares of Sit Corporation's common stock (an 80 percent interest) for $21,200,000 on January 1, 2011. The $2,000,000 excess of investment fair value over book value acquired was goodwill.

On January 1, 2013, Sit sold 400,000 previously unissued shares of common stock to the public for $30 per share. Sit's stockholders' equity on January 1, 2011, when Pin acquired its interest, and on January 1, 2013, immediately before and after the issuance of additional shares, was as follows (in thousands):

	January 1, 2011	January 1, 2013 Before Issuance	January 1, 2013 After Issuance
Common stock, $10 par	$12,000	$12,000	$16,000
Other paid-in capital	4,000	4,000	12,000
Retained earnings	8,000	10,000	10,000
Total	$24,000	$26,000	$38,000

REQUIRED

1. Calculate the balance of Pin's Investment in Sit account on January 1, 2013, before the additional stock issuance.

2. Determine Pin's percentage interest in Sit on January 1, 2013, immediately after the additional stock issuance.

3. Prepare a journal entry on Pin's books to adjust for the additional share issuance on January 1, 2013, if gain or loss is not recognized.

P 8-3 Journal entries for sale of an interest

Pat Corporation owned a 90 percent interest in Saw Corporation, and during 2010 the following changes occurred in Saw's equity and Pat's investment in Saw (in thousands):

	Saw's Stockholders' Equity	Goodwill	Investment in Saw (90%)
Balance, January 1, 2010	$1,000	$49.5	$ 949.5
Income—2010	250	—	225
Dividends—2010	(150)	—	(135)
Balance, December 31, 2010	$1,100	$49.5	$1,039.5

During 2011, Saw's net income was $280,000, and it declared $40,000 dividends each quarter of the year.

Pat reduced its interest in Saw to 80 percent on July 1, 2011, by selling Saw shares for $120,000.

REQUIRED

1. Prepare the journal entry on Pat's books to record the sale of Saw shares as of the actual date of sale.

2. Prepare the journal entry on Pat's books to record the sale of shares as of January 1, 2011.

3. Prepare a schedule to reconcile the answers to parts 1 and 2.

P 8-4
Reduction of interest owned under three options

Pan Corporation owns 300,000 of 360,000 outstanding shares of Son Corporation, and its $8,700,000 Investment in Son account balance on December 31, 2011, is equal to the underlying equity interest in Son. Son's stockholders' equity at December 31, 2011, is as follows (in thousands):

Common stock, $10 par, 500,000 shares authorized, 400,000 shares issued, of which 40,000 are treasury shares	$ 4,000
Additional paid-in capital	2,500
Retained earnings	5,500
	12,000
Less: Treasury shares at cost	1,560
Total stockholder's equity	$10,440

Because of a cash shortage, Pan decided to reduce its ownership interest in Son from a 5/6 interest to a 3/4 interest and is considering the following options:

Option 1. Sell 30,000 of the 300,000 shares held in Son.
Option 2. Instruct Son to issue 40,000 shares of previously unissued stock.
Option 3. Instruct Son to reissue the 40,000 shares of treasury stock.

Assume that the shares can be sold at the current market price of $50 per share under each of the three options and that any tax consequences can be ignored. Pan's stockholders' equity at December 31, 2011, consists of $10,000,000 par value of common stock, $3,000,000 additional paid-in capital, and $7,000,000 retained earnings.

REQUIRED: Compare the consolidated stockholders' equity on January 1, 2012, under each of the three options. (*Hint:* Prepare journal entries on Pan's books as an initial step to your solution.)

P 8-5

Subsidiary issues additional shares

Pal Company purchased 9,000 shares of Sal Corporation's $50 par common stock at $90 per share on January 1, 2011, when Sal had capital stock of $500,000 and retained earnings of $300,000. During 2011, Sal Corporation had net income of $50,000 but declared no dividends.

On January 1, 2012, Sal Corporation sold an additional 5,000 shares of stock at $100 per share. Sal's net income for 2012 was $70,000, and no dividends were declared.

REQUIRED: Determine each of the following:

1. The balance of Pal Company's Investment in Sal account on December 31, 2011

2. The goodwill that should appear in the consolidated balance sheet at December 31, 2012, assuming that Pal Company purchased the 5,000 shares issued on January 1, 2012

3. Additional paid-in capital from consolidation at December 31, 2012, assuming that Sal sold the 5,000 shares issued on January 1, 2012, to outside entities

4. Noncontrolling interest at December 31, 2012, assuming that Sal sold the 5,000 shares issued on January 1, 2012, to outsiders

P 8-6

Mid-year purchase of additional interest, preacquisition income

Pot Corporation purchased a 70 percent interest in Sod Corporation on January 2, 2011, for $98,000, when Sod had capital stock of $100,000 and retained earnings of $20,000. On June 30, 2012, Pot purchased an additional 20 percent interest for $37,000.

Comparative financial statements for Pot and Sod Corporations at and for the year ended December 31, 2012, are as follows (in thousands):

	Pot	Sod
Combined Income and Retained Earnings Statement for the Year Ended December 31		
Sales	$400	$200
Income from Sod	24	—
Cost of sales	(250)	(150)
Expenses	(50)	(20)
Net income	124	30
Add: Beginning retained earnings	200	50
Less: Dividends, December 1	(64)	(10)
Retained earnings, December 31	$260	$ 70
Balance Sheet at December 31		
Other assets	$429	$200
Investment in Sod	171	—
Total assets	$600	$200
Liabilities	$ 40	$ 30
Common stock	300	100
Retained earnings	260	70
Total equities	$600	$200

REQUIRED

1. Prepare a schedule explaining the $171,000 balance in Pot's Investment in Sod account at December 31, 2012.

2. Compute goodwill that will appear in the December 31, 2012, consolidated balance sheet.

3. Prepare a schedule computing consolidated net income for 2012.

4. Compute consolidated retained earnings on December 31, 2012.

5. Compute noncontrolling interest on December 31, 2012.

P 8-7
Consolidated income statement (mid-year purchase of additional interest)

Comparative separate-company and consolidated balance sheets for Pod Corporation and its 70 percent-owned subsidiary, Saw Corporation, at year-end 2011 were as follows (in thousands):

	Pod	Saw	Consolidated
Cash	$ 100	$ 70	$ 170
Inventories	800	100	900
Other current assets	500	130	630
Plant assets—net	3,500	800	4,300
Investment in Saw	600	—	—
Goodwill	—	—	40
Total assets	$5,500	$1,100	$6,040
Current liabilities	$ 500	$ 300	$ 800
Capital stock, $10 par	3,000	500	3,000
Other paid-in capital	1,000	100	1,000
Retained earnings	1,000	200	1,000
Noncontrolling interest	—	—	240
Total equities	$5,500	$1,100	$6,040

Saw's net income for 2012 was $150,000, and its dividends for the year were $80,000 ($40,000 on March 1, and $40,000 on September 1). On April 1, 2012, Pod increased its interest in Saw to 80 percent by purchasing 5,000 shares in the market at $19 per share.

Separate incomes of Pod and Saw for 2012 are computed as follows:

	Pod	Saw
Sales	$2,000	$1,200
Cost of sales	(1,200)	(700)
Gross profit	800	500
Depreciation expense	(400)	(300)
Other expenses	(100)	(50)
Separate incomes	$ 300	$ 150

REQUIRED

1. Prepare a consolidated income statement for the year ended December 31, 2012.

2. Prepare a schedule to show how Saw's net income and dividends for 2012 are allocated among noncontrolling interests, controlling interests, and other interests.

P 8-8
Workpaper (mid-year acquisition of 80% interest, downstream inventory sales)

Pop Corporation acquired an 80 percent interest in Sat Corporation on October 1, 2011, for $82,400, equal to 80 percent of the underlying equity of Sat on that date plus $16,000 goodwill (total goodwill is $20,000). Financial statements for Pop and Sat Corporations for 2011 are as follows (in thousands):

	Pop	Sat
Combined Income and Retained Earnings Statement		
for the Year Ended December 31		
Sales	$112	$ 50
Income from Sat	3.8	—
Cost of sales	(60)	(20)
Operating expenses	(25.1)	(6)
Net income	30.7	24
Retained earnings January 1	30	20
Dividends	(20)	(10)
Retained earnings December 31	$ 40.7	$ 34

	Pop	Sat
Balance Sheet at December 31		
Cash	$ 5.1	$ 7
Accounts receivable	10.4	17
Note receivable	5	10
Inventories	30	16
Plant assets—net	88	60
Investment in Sat	82.2	—
Total assets	$220.7	$110
Accounts payable	$ 15	$ 16
Notes payable	25	10
Capital stock	140	50
Retained earnings	40.7	34
Total equities	$220.7	$110

ADDITIONAL INFORMATION

1. In November 2011, Pop sold inventory items to Sat for $12,000 at a gross profit of $3,000. One-third of these items remained in Sat's inventory at December 31, 2011, and $6,000 remained unpaid.

2. Sat's dividends were declared in equal amounts on March 15 and November 15, and its income was earned in proportionate amounts throughout each quarter of the year.

3. Pop applies the equity method such that its net income is equal to the controlling share of consolidated net income.

REQUIRED: Prepare a workpaper to consolidate the financial statements of Pop Corporation and Subsidiary for the year ended December 31, 2011.

P 8-9

Workpaper (noncontrolling interest, preacquisition income, downstream sale of equipment, upstream sale of land, subsidiary holds parent's bonds)

Pal Corporation paid $175,000 for a 70 percent interest in Sid Corporation's outstanding stock on April 1, 2011. Sid's stockholders' equity on January 1, 2011, consisted of $200,000 capital stock and $50,000 retained earnings.

Accounts and balances at and for the year ended December 31, 2011, follow (in thousands):

	Pal	Sid
Combined Income and Retained Earnings Statement for the Year Ended December 31		
Sales	$287.1	$150
Income from Sid	12.3	—
Gain	12	2
Interest income	—	5.85
Expenses (includes cost of goods sold)	(200)	(117.85)
Interest expense	(11.4)	—
Net income	100	40
Add: Beginning retained earnings	250	50
Less: Dividends	(50)	(20)
Retained earnings December 31	$300	$ 70
Balance Sheet at December 31		
Cash	$ 17	$ 4
Interest receivable	—	6
Inventories	140	60
Other current assets	110	20
Plant assets—net	502.7	107.3
Investment in Sid common	180.3	—
Investment in Pal bonds	—	102.7
Total assets	$950	$300

(continued)

	Pal	Sid
Interest payable	$ 6	$ —
Other current liabilities	38.6	30
12% bonds payable	105.4	—
Common stock	500	200
Retained earnings	300	70
Total equities	$950	$300

ADDITIONAL INFORMATION

1. Sid Corporation paid $102,850 for all of Pal's outstanding bonds on July 1, 2011. These bonds were issued on January 1, 2011, bear interest at 12 percent, have interest payment dates of July 1 and January 1, and mature 10 years from the date of issue. The $6,000 premium on the issue is being amortized under the straight-line method.

2. Other current liabilities of Sid Corporation on December 31, 2011, include $10,000 dividends declared on December 15 and unpaid at year-end. Sid also declared $10,000 dividends on March 15, 2011.

3. Pal Corporation sold equipment to Sid on July 1, 2011, for $30,000. This equipment was purchased by Pal on July 1, 2008, for $36,000 and is being depreciated over a six-year period using the straight-line method (no salvage value).

4. Sid sold land that cost $8,000 to Pal for $10,000 on October 15, 2011. Pal still owns the land.

5. Pal uses the equity method for its 70 percent interest in Sid.

REQUIRED: Prepare a consolidation workpaper for the year ended December 31, 2011.

P 8-10
Workpaper (mid-year purchase of 10% interest, downstream sales)

Pam Corporation acquired a 70 percent interest in Sam Corporation on January 1, 2011, for $420,000 cash, when Sam's equity of Sam consisted of $300,000 capital stock and $200,000 retained earnings. On July 1, 2012, Pam acquired an additional 10 percent interest in Sam for $67,500, to bring its interest in Sam to 80 percent. The financial statements of Pam and Sam Corporations at and for the year ended December 31, 2012, are as follows (in thousands):

	Pam	Sam
Combined Income and Retained Earnings Statement for the Year Ended December 31		
Sales	$ 900	$500
Income from Sam	38	—
Gain on machinery	40	—
Cost of sales	(400)	(300)
Depreciation expense	(90)	(60)
Other expenses	(160)	(40)
Net income	328	100
Add: Beginning retained earnings	155	250
Less: Dividends	(200)	(50)
Retained earnings December 31	$ 283	$300
Balance Sheet at December 31		
Cash	$ 20	$ 80
Accounts receivable	130	30
Dividends receivable	20	—
Inventories	90	70
Other current items	20	80
Land	50	40
Buildings—net	60	105
Machinery—net	100	320
Investment in Sam	510	—
Total assets	$1,000	$725
Accounts payable	$ 177	$ 40
Dividends payable	100	25
Other liabilities	140	60
Capital stock, $10 par	300	300
Retained earnings	283	300
Total equities	$1,000	$725

ADDITIONAL INFORMATION

1. The fair value/book value differential from Pam's two purchases of Sam was goodwill.

2. Pam Corporation sold inventory items to Sam during 2011 for $60,000, at a gross profit of $10,000. During 2012, Pam's sales to Sam were $48,000, at a gross profit of $8,000. Half of the 2011 intercompany sales were inventoried by Sam at year-end 2011, and three-fourths of the 2012 sales remained unsold by Sam at year-end 2012. Sam owes Pam $25,000 from 2012 purchases.

3. At year-end 2011, Sam purchased land from Pam for $20,000. The cost of this land to Pam was $12,000.

4. Pam sold machinery with a book value of $40,000 to Sam for $80,000 on July 8, 2012. The machinery had a five-year useful life at that time. Sam uses straight-line depreciation without considering salvage value on the machinery.

5. Pam uses a one-line consolidation in accounting for Sam. Both Pam and Sam Corporations declared dividends for 2012 in equal amounts in June and December.

REQUIRED: Prepare a workpaper to consolidate the financial statements of Pam Corporation and Subsidiary for the year ended December 31, 2012.

P 8-11

Workpaper (mid-year acquisition, preacquisition income and dividends, upstream sale of inventory, downstream sale of inventory item used by subsidiary as plant asset)

Pan Corporation acquired an 85 percent interest in Sly Corporation on August 1, 2011, for $522,750, equal to 85 percent of the underlying equity of Sly on that date.

In August 2011, Sly sold inventory items to Pan for $60,000 at a gross profit of $15,000. One-third of these items remained in Pan's inventory at December 31, 2011.

On September 30, 2011, Pan sold an inventory item (equipment) to Sly for $50,000 at a gross profit to Pan of $10,000. When this equipment was placed in service by Sly, it had a five-year remaining useful life and no expected salvage value.

Sly's dividends were declared in equal amounts on June 15 and December 15, and its income was earned in relatively-equal amounts throughout each quarter of the year. Pan applies the equity method, such that its net income is equal to the controlling share of consolidated net income. Financial statements for Pan and Sly are as follows (in thousands):

	Pan	Sly
Combined Income and Retained Earnings Statement		
for the Year Ended December 31, 2011		
Sales	$ 910	$400
Income from Sly	7.5	—
Cost of sales	(500)	(250)
Operating expenses	(200.0)	(90)
Net income	217.5	60
Add: Beginning retained earnings	192.5	100
Deduct: Dividends	(100)	(40)
Retained earnings December 31	$ 310	$120
Balance Sheet at December 31, 2011		
Cash	$ 33.75	$ 10
Dividends receivable	17	—
Accounts receivable—net	120	70
Inventories	300	150
Plant assets—net	880	500
Investment in Sly—85%	513.25	—
Total assets	$1,864	$730
Accounts payable	$ 154	$ 90
Dividends payable	—	20
Capital stock	1,400	500
Retained earnings	310	120
Total equities	$1,864	$730

REQUIRED: Prepare a consolidation workpaper for the year ended December 31, 2011.

P 8-12

Consolidated statement of cash flows–indirect method (sale of an interest)

Comparative consolidated financial statements for Pop Corporation and its subsidiary, Sat Corporation, at and for the years ended December 31, 2012 and 2011 follow (in thousands).

Pop Corporation and Subsidiary Comparative Consolidated Financial Statements at and for the Years Ended December 31, 2012 and 2011

	Year 2012	Year 2011	Year's Change 2012–2011
Income Statement			
Sales	$3,050.0	$2,850.0	$ 200.0
Gain on 10% interest	5.7		5.7
Cost of sales	(1,750.7)	(1,690.0)	(60.7)
Depreciation expense	(528.0)	(508.0)	(20.0)
Other expenses	(455.0)	(392.0)	(63.0)
Noncontrolling interest share	(22.0)	(10.0)	(12.0)
Net income	$ 300.0	$ 250.0	$ 50.0
Retained Earnings			
Retained earnings—beginning	$1,000.0	$ 950.0	$ 50.0
Net income	300.0	250.0	50.0
Dividends	(200.0)	(200.0)	.0
Retained earnings—ending	$1,100.0	$1,000.0	$ 100.0
Balance Sheet			
Cash	$ 46.5	$ 50.5	$ (4.0)
Accounts receivable—net	87.5	90.0	(2.5)
Inventories	377.5	247.5	130.0
Prepaid expenses	68.0	88.0	(20.0)
Equipment	2,970.0	2,880.0	90.0
Accumulated depreciation	(1,542.0)	(1,044.0)	(498.0)
Land and buildings	960.0	960.0	.0
Accumulated depreciation	(300.0)	(272.0)	(28.0)
Total assets	$2,667.5	$3,000.0	$(332.5)
Accounts payable	$ 140.0	$ 343.5	$(203.5)
Dividends payable	52.5	52.5	.0
Long-term notes payable	245.0	545.0	(300.0)
Capital stock, $10 par	1,000.0	1,000.0	.0
Retained earnings	1,100.0	1,000.0	100.0
Noncontrolling interest	130.0	59.0	71.0
Total equities	$2,667.5	$3,000.0	$(332.5)

REQUIRED: Prepare a consolidated statement of cash flows for the year ended December 31, 2012. The changes in equipment are due to a $100,000 equipment acquisition, current depreciation, and the sale of one-ninth of the fair value/book value differential allocated to equipment ($10,000) and related accumulated depreciation ($2,000). This reduction in the unamortized fair value/book value differential results from selling a 10 percent interest in Sat for $72,700 and thereby reducing its interest from 90 percent to 80 percent. Sat's net income and dividends for 2012 were $110,000 and $50,000, respectively. Use the indirect method.

INTERNET ASSIGNMENT

Visit the Web site of Google, Inc., and obtain a copy of the 2009 annual report. Prepare a brief summary of Google's acquisition activities during 2008 and 2009.

a. How many acquisitions were interim acquisitions?

b. How many combinations were recorded using acquisition method accounting?

c. Were acquisitions completed by exchanging shares or through cash payments?

REFERENCES TO THE AUTHORITATIVE LITERATURE

[1] FASB ASC 810-10-45-4. Originally Committee on Accounting Procedure. *Accounting Research Bulletin No. 51.* "Consolidated Financial Statements." New York: American Institute of Certified Public Accountants, 1959.

[2] FASB ASC 810-10-65-1. Originally *Statement of Financial Accounting Standards No. 160.* "Noncontrolling Interests in Consolidated Financial Statements (an amendment of ARB No. 51)." Norwalk, CT: Financial Accounting Standards Board, 2007.

[3] FASB ASC 810-10-65. Originally *Statement of Financial Accounting Standards No. 160.* "Noncontrolling Interests in Consolidated Financial Statements (an amendment of ARB No. 51)." Norwalk, CT: Financial Accounting Standards Board, 2007.

[4] FASB ASC 323-10-35. Originally *Accounting Principles Board Opinion No. 18.* "The Equity Method of Accounting for Investments in Common Stock." New York: American Institute of Certified Public Accountants, 1971.

[5] FASB ASC 810-10-65. Originally *Statement of Financial Accounting Standards No. 160.* "Noncontrolling Interests in Consolidated Financial Statements (an amendment of ARB No. 51)." Norwalk, CT: Financial Accounting Standards Board, 2007.

[6] FASB ASC 810-10-65-3. Originally *Statement of Financial Accounting Standards No. 160.* "Noncontrolling Interests in Consolidated Financial Statements (an amendment of ARB No. 51)." Norwalk, CT: Financial Accounting Standards Board, 2007.

9 CHAPTER

Indirect and Mutual Holdings

P revious chapters of this book presented stock ownership situations in which an investor or parent directly owned some or all of the voting stock of an investee. The equity method is appropriate in those situations and equally appropriate when an investor indirectly owns 20 percent or more of an investee's voting stock. Consolidation is appropriate when one corporation, directly or indirectly, owns a majority of the outstanding voting stock of another [1].

This chapter discusses parent accounting and consolidation procedures for indirect ownership situations under the heading of "Indirect Holdings." The chapter also considers additional complexities that arise when affiliates hold the voting stock of each other. Affiliation structures of this type are covered under the heading of "Mutual Holdings." Discussion of **mutual holding** relationships logically follows the coverage of indirect holdings because such relationships are a special type of indirect holdings in which affiliates indirectly own themselves.

Although consolidation procedures for indirectly and mutually-held affiliates are more complex than for directly held affiliates, the basic consolidation objectives remain the same. Most of the problems require measuring the realized income of the separate entities and allocating it between controlling and noncontrolling interests.

LEARNING OBJECTIVES

1 Prepare consolidated statements when the parent controls through indirect holdings.

2 Apply consolidation procedures to the special case of mutual holdings.

AFFILIATION STRUCTURES

PepsiCo's reports on its noncontrolled bottling affiliates *Pepsi Bottling Group* (PBG) and *PEPSIAMERICAS* (PAS). Note 8 to PepsiCo's 2009 annual report (p. 77) offers additional insight on the ownership status of PBG:

> *In addition to approximately 32% and 33% of PBG's outstanding common stock that we own at year-end 2009 and 2008, respectively, we own 100% of PBG's class B common stock and approximately 7% of the equity of Bottling Group, LLC, PBG's principal operating subsidiary.*

Note 8 also indicates that PepsiCo's consolidated financial statements reflect net revenue from related-party transactions with these bottling affiliates totaling $13.219 billion during 2009.

The 2009 annual report of *AT&T* summarizes some of its equity method investments in affiliates in Note 7 (p.73) as follows:

Other Equity Method Investments

Our investments in equity affiliates include primarily international investments. As of December 31, 2009, our investments in equity affiliates included a 9.8% interest in Teléfonos de México, S.A. de C.V. (Telmex), Mexico's national telecommunications company, and an 8.8% interest in América Móvil S.A. de C.V. (América Móvil), prima- rily a wireless provider in Mexico, with telecommunications investments in the United States and Latin America. ...

The potential complexity of corporate affiliation structures is limited only by one's imagina- tion. Even so, the general types of affiliations are not difficult to identify. Exhibit 9-1 illustrates the more basic types of affiliations.

Although Exhibit 9-1 illustrates affiliation structures for parent and subsidiary corporations, the diagrams also apply to investor and investee corporations associated through the direct or indirect

EXHIBIT 9-1

Affiliation Structures

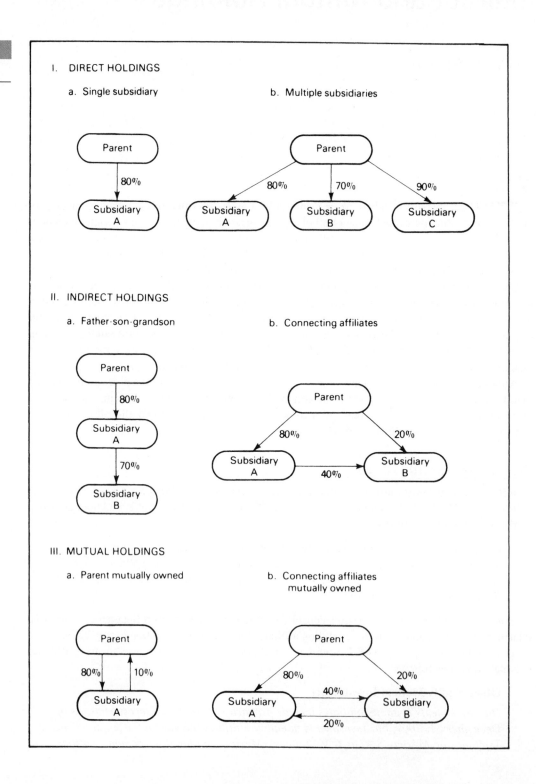

ownership of 20 percent or more of the voting stock of an investee. **Direct holdings** result from direct investments in the voting stock of one or more investees. **Indirect holdings** are investments that enable the investor to control or significantly influence the decisions of an investee not directly owned through an investee that is directly owned. Exhibit 9-1 illustrates two types of indirect ownership structures—the **father-son-grandson relationship** and the **connecting affiliates relationship**.

In the father-son-grandson diagram, the parent directly owns an 80 percent interest in Subsidiary A and indirectly owns a 56 percent interest (80% × 70%) in Subsidiary B. Noncontrolling shareholders own the other 44 percent of B—the 30 percent held directly by noncontrolling holders of B stock plus 14 percent held by the 20 percent noncontrolling holders of A stock (20% × 70%). The parent indirectly holds 56 percent of Subsidiary B stock, so consolidation of Subsidiary B is clearly appropriate. It is not the direct and indirect ownership of the parent, however, that determines whether an affiliate should be consolidated. The decision to consolidate is based on whether a controlling interest in an affiliate is held within the affiliation structure, thus giving the parent an ability to control the operations of the affiliate.

If Subsidiary A in the father-son-grandson diagram of Exhibit 9-1 had owned 60 percent of the stock of Subsidiary B, the parent's indirect ownership in Subsidiary B would have been 48 percent (80% × 60%), and the noncontrolling shareholders' interest would have been 52 percent [40% + (20% × 60%)]. Consolidation of Subsidiary B would still be appropriate, because 60 percent of B's stock would be held within the affiliation structure.

In the illustration of connecting affiliates, the parent holds 20 percent of Subsidiary B stock directly and 32 percent (80% × 40%) indirectly, for a total direct and indirect ownership of 52 percent. The other 48 percent of Subsidiary B is held 40 percent by B's noncontrolling shareholders and 8 percent (20% × 40%) indirectly by A's noncontrolling shareholders.

In the first affiliation diagram for mutual holdings, the parent owns 80 percent of the stock of Subsidiary A, and Subsidiary A owns 10 percent of the stock of the parent. Thus, 10 percent of the parent's stock is held within the affiliation structure and 90 percent is outstanding. In diagram b for mutual holdings, the parent is not a party to the mutual holding relationship, but Subsidiary A owns 40 percent of Subsidiary B, and Subsidiary B owns 20 percent of Subsidiary A. The complexity involved in this latter case requires the use of simultaneous equations or other appropriate mathematical procedures to allocate incomes and equities among the affiliates.

INDIRECT HOLDINGS—FATHER-SON-GRANDSON STRUCTURE

LEARNING OBJECTIVE **1**

The major problems encountered with indirect control situations are the determination of earnings and equities of the affiliates on an equity basis. Once we adjust the income and equity accounts of the affiliates to an equity basis, the consolidation procedures are the same for indirect as for direct ownership situations. The mechanics involved in the consolidation process may be cumbersome, however, because of the additional detail required to consolidate the operations of multiple entities.

Assume that Poe Corporation acquires 80 percent of the stock of Saw Corporation on January 1, 2011, and that Saw acquires 70 percent of the stock of Tub Corporation on January 1, 2012. Both Poe's investment in Saw and Saw's investment in Tub are made at fair value equal to book value. Trial balances for the three corporations on January 1, 2012, immediately after Saw acquires its 70 percent interest in Tub, are as follows (in thousands):

	Poe	Saw	Tub
Other assets	$400	$195	$190
Investment in Saw (80%)	200	—	—
Investment in Tub (70%)	—	105	—
	$600	$300	$190
Liabilities	$100	$ 50	$ 40
Capital stock	400	200	100
Retained earnings	100	50	50
	$600	$300	$190

Separate earnings of the three corporations (excluding investment income) and dividends for 2012 are (in thousands):

	Poe	Saw	Tub
Separate earnings	$100	$50	$40
Dividends	60	30	20

Equity Method of Accounting for Father-Son-Grandson Affiliates

In accounting for investment income for 2012 on an equity basis, Saw determines its investment income from Tub before Poe determines its investment income from Saw. Saw accounts for its investment in Tub for 2012 with the following entries:

SAW'S BOOKS

Cash (+A)	14,000	
Investment in Tub (−A)		14,000
To record dividends received from Tub		
(20,000 × 70%).		
Investment in Tub (+A)	28,000	
Income from Tub (R, +SE)		28,000
To record income from Tub ($40,000 × 70%).		

Saw's net income for 2012 is $78,000 ($50,000 separate income plus $28,000 income from Tub), and its Investment in Tub account balance at December 31, 2012, is $119,000 ($105,000 beginning balance, plus $28,000 income, less $14,000 dividends).

Poe's entries to account for its investment in Saw for 2012 are as follows:

POE'S BOOKS

Cash (+A)	24,000	
Investment in Saw (−A)		24,000
To record dividends received from Saw		
($30,000 × 80%).		
Investment in Saw (+A)	62,400	
Income from Saw (R, +SE)		62,400
To record income from Saw ($78,000 × 80%).		

Poe's net income for 2012 is $162,400 ($100,000 separate income plus $62,400 income from Saw), and its Investment in Saw account balance at December 31, 2012, is $238,400 ($200,000 beginning balance, plus $62,400 income, less $24,000 dividends). The controlling share of consolidated net income for 2012 is $162,400, equal to Poe's equity method income.

Computational Approaches for Consolidated Net Income

We determine Poe's income and consolidated net income independently by alternative methods. Computation in terms of the definition of consolidated net income is:

Poe's separate earnings	$100,000
Add: Poe's share of Saw's separate earnings ($50,000 × 80%)	40,000
Add: Poe's share of Tub's separate earnings ($40,000 × 80% × 70%)	22,400
Poe's net income and controlling share of consolidated net income	$162,400

We compute parent and controlling share of consolidated net income in terms of the consolidated income statement presentation by deducting noncontrolling interest share from combined separate earnings:

Combined separate earnings:		
Poe	$100,000	
Saw	50,000	
Tub	40,000	$190,000
Less: Noncontrolling interest shares:		
Direct noncontrolling interest in Tub's income		
($40,000 × 30%)	$ 12,000	
Indirect noncontrolling interest in Tub's income		
($40,000 × 70% × 20%)	5,600	
Direct noncontrolling interest in Saw's income		
($50,000 × 20%)	10,000	27,600
Poe's net income and controlling share of net income		$162,400

Still another computational approach uses a schedule such as the following:

	Poe	Saw	Tub
Separate earnings	$100,000	$ 50,000	$40,000
Allocate Tub's income to Saw			
($40,000 × 70%)	—	+28,000	−28,000
Allocate Saw's income to Poe			
($78,000 × 80%)	+62,400	−62,400	—
Controlling share of net income	$162,400		
Noncontrolling interest share		$ 15,600	$12,000

Schedules are often helpful in making allocations for complex affiliations. This is particularly true when there are intercompany profits and when the equity method is not used or is applied incorrectly. The schedule illustrated here shows parent and controlling share of consolidated net income, as well as noncontrolling interest share. It also shows Saw's investment income from Tub ($28,000) and Poe's investment income from Saw ($62,400).

Consolidation Workpaper—Equity Method

Exhibit 9-2 illustrates a consolidation workpaper for the year 2012. The workpaper shows that no new consolidation procedures have been introduced. Consolidation workpaper entries a and b eliminate investment income, dividends, and investment and equity balances for Saw's investment in Tub. Entries c and d eliminate investment income, dividends, and investment and equity balances for Poe's investment in Saw. Entry e records noncontrolling interests in the earnings and dividends of Tub and Saw.

e	Noncontrolling interest share—Saw (−SE)	15,600	
	Noncontrolling interest share—Tub (−SE)	12,000	
	Dividends (+SE)		12,000
	Noncontrolling interest—Saw (+SE)		9,600
	Noncontrolling interest—Tub (+SE)		6,000
	To enter noncontrolling interest shares of subsidiary income and dividends.		

Tub's $45,000 beginning noncontrolling interest is simply the 30 percent direct noncontrolling interest percentage times Tub's $150,000 equity at the beginning of 2012. Noncontrolling interest share of Tub is 30 percent of Tub's $40,000 reported income. Similarly, the

EXHIBIT 9-2

Indirect Holdings—
Father-Son-Grandson
Type (Equity Method)

POE CORPORATION AND SUBSIDIARIES CONSOLIDATION WORKPAPER FOR THE YEAR ENDED DECEMBER 31, 2012 (IN THOUSANDS)

	Poe	80% Saw	70% Tub	Adjustments and Eliminations Debits	Adjustments and Eliminations Credits	Consolidated Statements
Income Statement Sales	$ 200	$140	$100			$440
Income from Saw	62.4			c 62.4		
Income from Tub		28		a 28		
Expenses including cost of sales	(100)	(90)	(60)			(250)
Noncontrolling interest share—Saw				e 15.6		(15.6)
Noncontrolling interest share—Tub				e 12		(12)
Controlling share of Net income	**$ 162.4**	**$ 78**	**$ 40**			**$162.4**
Retained Earnings Statement Retained earnings—Poe	$ 100					$100
Retained earnings—Saw		$ 50		d 50		
Retained earnings—Tub			$ 50	b 50		
Dividends	(60)	(30)	(20)		a 14 c 24 e 12	(60)
Controlling share of Net income	162.4	78	40			162.4
Retained earnings—December 31	**$ 202.4**	**$ 98**	**$ 70**			**$202.4**
Balance Sheet Other assets	$ 461.6	$231	$200			$892.6
Investment in Saw	238.4				c 38.4 d 200	
Investment in Tub		119			a 14 b 105	
	$ 700	$350	$200			$892.6
Liabilities	$ 97.6	$ 52	$ 30			$179.6
Capital stock—Poe	400					400
Capital stock—Saw		200		d 200		
Capital stock—Tub			100	b 100		
Retained earnings	202.4	98	70			202.4
	$ 700	$350	$200			
Noncontrolling interest in Tub, January 1 Noncontrolling interest in Saw, January 1 Total noncontrolling interests, December 31					b 45 d 50 e 9.6 e 6	110.6
						$892.6

$50,000 beginning noncontrolling interest in Saw is 20 percent of Saw's $250,000 equity at January 1, 2012, and the $15,600 noncontrolling interest share of Saw is 20 percent of Saw's reported net income. The controlling share of net income and consolidated retained earnings of $162,400 and $202,400, respectively, are equal to Poe's net income and retained earnings.

INDIRECT HOLDINGS—CONNECTING AFFILIATES STRUCTURE

Pet Corporation owns a 70 percent interest in Sal Corporation and a 60 percent interest in Tie Corporation. In addition, Sal Corporation owns a 20 percent interest in Tie. We diagram the affiliation structure of Pet Corporation and Subsidiaries as follows:

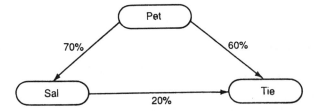

The following table summarizes data relevant to the investments of Pet and Sal.

	Pet's Investment in Sal (70%) Acquired January 1, 2012	Pet's Investment in Tie (60%) Acquired January 1, 2011	Sal's Investment in Tie (20%) Acquired January 1, 2008
Fair value / Cost	$176,400	$97,200	$22,400
Less: Book value	(164,400)	(85,200)	(22,400)
Goodwill	$ 12,000	$ 12,000	—
Investment Balance December 31, 2012			
Cost	$176,400	$97,200	$22,400
Add: Share of investees' pre-2013 income less dividends	7,000	18,000	16,000
Balance December 31, 2012	$183,400	$115,200	$38,400

During 2013, Pet, Sal, and Tie had earnings from their own operations of $70,000, $35,000, and $20,000 and declared dividends of $40,000, $20,000, and $10,000, respectively. Pet's separate earnings of $70,000 included an unrealized gain of $10,000 from the sale of land to Sal during 2013. Sal's separate earnings of $35,000 included unrealized profit of $5,000 on inventory items sold to Pet for $15,000 during 2013 that remained in Pet's December 31, 2013, inventory. A schedule computing controlling interest share and noncontrolling interest share of consolidated net income for the Pet-Sal-Tie affiliation for 2013 is shown in Exhibit 9-3.

Equity Method of Accounting for Connecting Affiliates

Before allocating the separate earnings of Sal and Tie to Pet, we eliminate any unrealized profits included in earnings. Exhibit 9-3 shows the allocation of Tie's income as 20 percent to Sal and 60 percent to Pet. This allocation must precede the allocation of Sal's income to Pet because Sal's income includes $4,000 investment income from Tie.

	Pet	Sal	Tie
Separate earnings	$ 70,000	$ 35,000	$20,000
Deduct: Unrealized profit	−10,000	−5,000	—
Separate realized earnings	60,000	30,000	20,000
Allocate Tie's income:			
20% to Sal	—	+4,000	−4,000
60% to Pet	+12,000	—	−12,000
Allocate Sal's income:			
70% to Pet	+23,800	−23,800	—
Pet's net income and controlling share of consolidated net income	$ 95,800		
Noncontrolling interest share		$ 10,200	$ 4,000

EXHIBIT 9-3

Income Allocation Schedule

In accounting for its investment in Tie for 2013, Sal makes the following entries:

Cash (+A)	2,000	
Investment in Tie (−A)		2,000
To record dividends received from Tie ($10,000 × 20%).		
Investment in Tie (+A)	4,000	
Income from Tie (R, + SE)		4,000
To record income from Tie ($20,000 × 20%).		

Sal's Investment in Tie account at December 31, 2013, has a balance of $40,400—the $38,400 balance at December 31, 2012, plus $4,000 investment income, less $2,000 dividends. We do not reduce Sal's income from Tie for the $5,000 unrealized profit on inventory items sold to Pet because Tie is not a party in the intercompany sale. Sal's $39,000 net income includes $5,000 unrealized profit, which we eliminate when allocating Sal's realized income to Pet and Sal's noncontrolling stockholders.

Pet makes the following entries to account for its investments during 2013:

Investment in Tie

Cash (+A)	6,000	
Investment in Tie (−A)		6,000
To record dividends received from Tie ($10,000 × 60%).		
Investment in Tie (+A)	12,000	
Income from Tie (R, +SE)		12,000
To record income from Tie.		

Investment in Sal

Cash (+A)	14,000	
Investment in Sal (−A)		14,000
To record dividends received from Sal ($20,000 × 70%).		
Investment in Sal (+A)	13,800	
Income from Sal (R, +SE)		13,800
To record income from Sal computed as follows:		
70% of Sal's reported income of $39,000		$27,300
Less: 70% of Sal's unrealized inventory profit of $5,000		−3,500
Less: 100% of unrealized gain on land		−10,000
		$13,800

Pet's investment accounts at December 31, 2013, show the following balances:

	Investment in Sal (70%)	Investment in Tie (60%)
Balance December 31, 2012	$183,400	$115,200
Add: Investment income	13,800	12,000
Deduct: Dividends	−14,000	−6,000
Balance December 31, 2013	$183,200	$121,200

Consolidation Workpaper—Equity Method

Exhibit 9-4 presents a consolidation workpaper for Pet Corporation and Subsidiaries for 2013.

EXHIBIT 9-4

Connecting Affiliates with Intercompany Profits

PET CORPORATION AND SUBSIDIARIES CONSOLIDATION WORKPAPER FOR THE YEAR ENDED DECEMBER 31, 2013 (IN THOUSANDS)

	Pet	Sal	Tie	Adjustments and Eliminations Debits	Credits	Consolidated Statements
Income Statement						
Sales	$200	$150	$100	a 15		$ 435
Income from Sal	13.8			g 13.8		

	Pet	Sal	Tie	Adjustments and Eliminations Debits	Adjustments and Eliminations Credits	Consolidated Statements
Income from Tie	12	4		d 16		
Gain on land	10			c 10		
Cost of sales	(100)	(80)	(50)	b 5	a 15	(220)
Other expenses	(40)	(35)	(30)			(105)
Noncontrolling interest share—Sal [($39 – $5) × 30%]				i 10.2		(10.2)
Noncontrolling interest share—Tie ($20 × 20%)				f 4		(4)
Controlling share of Net income	**$ 95.8**	**$ 39**	**$ 20**			**$ 95.8**
Retained Earnings Statement Retained earnings—Pet	$223					$223
Retained earnings—Sal		$ 50		h 50		
Retained earnings—Tie			$ 80	e 80		
Dividends	(40)	(20)	(10)		d 8 / f 2 / g 14 / i 6	(40)
Controlling share of net income	95.8	39	20			95.8
Retained earnings—December 31	**$278.8**	**$ 69**	**$ 90**			**$278.8**
Balance Sheet Other assets	$ 50.6	$ 19.6	$ 85			$155.2
Inventories	50	40	15		b 5	100
Plant assets—net	400	200	100		c 10	690
Investment in Sal (70%)	183.2			g .2	h 183.4	
Investment in Tie (60%)	121.2				d 6 / e 115.2	
Investment in Tie (20%)		40.4			d 2 / e 38.4	
Goodwill				e 12 / h 12		24
	$805	$300	$200			$969.2
Liabilities	$126.2	$ 31	$ 10			$167.2
Capital stock—Pet	400					400
Capital stock—Sal		200		h 200		
Capital stock—Tie			100	e 100		
Retained earnings	278.8	69	90			278.8
	$805	$300	$200			
Noncontrolling interest: Noncontrolling interest in Tie, January 1 Noncontrolling interest in Sal, January 1					e 38.4 / h 78.6 / f 2 / i 4.2	123.2
						$969.2

EXHIBIT 9-4

Connecting Affiliates with Intercompany Profits *(Continued)*

The adjustment and elimination entries are reproduced in journal form.

a	Sales (−R, −SE)	15,000	
	Cost of sales (−E, +SE)		15,000
	To eliminate reciprocal sales and cost of sales.		
b	Cost of sales (E, −SE)	5,000	
	Inventory (−A)		5,000
	To eliminate unrealized intercompany profit from inventory at December 31, 2013.		
c	Gain on land (−Ga, −SE)	10,000	
	Plant assets—net (−A)		10,000
	To eliminate unrealized profit from intercompany sale of land.		
d	Income from Tie (−R, −SE)	16,000	
	Dividends (Tie's) (+SE)		8,000
	Investment in Tie (60%) (−A)		6,000
	Investment in Tie (20%) (−A)		2,000
	To eliminate income from Tie and dividends from Tie and to adjust the Investment in Tie account.		
e	Retained earnings—Tie, January 1, 2013 (−SE)	80,000	
	Goodwill (+A)	12,000	
	Capital stock—Tie (−SE)	100,000	
	Investment in Tie (60%) (−A)		115,200
	Investment in Tie (20%) (−A)		38,400
	Noncontrolling interests—Tie (+SE)		38,400
	To eliminate reciprocal investment and equity amounts of Tie and to establish goodwill and noncontrolling interest at January 1, 2013.		
f	Noncontrolling interest share—Tie (−SE)	4,000	
	Dividends (+SE)		2,000
	Noncontrolling interest—Tie (+SE)		2,000
	To enter noncontrolling interest share of subsidiary income and dividends.		
g	Income from Sal (−R, −SE)	13,800	
	Investment in Sal (+A)	200	
	Dividends (Sal's) (+SE)		14,000
	To eliminate income from Sal and dividends from Sal and to adjust the Investment in Sal account.		
h	Retained earnings—Sal, January 1, 2013 (−SE)	50,000	
	Goodwill (+A)	12,000	
	Capital stock—Sal (−SE)	200,000	
	Investment in Sal (−A)		183,400
	Noncontrolling interest—Sal (+SE)		78,600
	To eliminate reciprocal investment and equity amounts in Sal and to establish goodwill and noncontrolling interest at January 1, 2013.		
i	Noncontrolling interest share—Sal (−SE)	10,200	
	Dividends (+SE)		6,000
	Noncontrolling interest—Sal (+SE)		4,200
	To enter noncontrolling interest share of subsidiary income and dividends.		

A check on the $123,200 noncontrolling interest at December 31, 2013, as shown in Exhibit 9-4 may be helpful at this point. We can confirm the noncontrolling interest as follows:

	Noncontrolling Interest in Sal (30%)	Noncontrolling Interest in Tie (20%)	Total Noncontrolling Interest
Fair value* at December 31, 2013:			
Sal (($269,000 + $12,000) × 30%)	$84,300	—	$ 84,300
Tie (($190,000 + $12,000) × 20%)	—	$40,400	40,400
Less: Unrealized profit of Sal ($5,000 × 30%)	(1,500)	—	(1,500)
Noncontrolling interest December 31, 2013	$82,800	$40,400	$123,200

* Book value plus implied total goodwill (i.e., goodwill associated with the 70% investment for Sal and the 60% investment for Tie).

Except for the deduction of 30 percent of the $5,000 unrealized inventory profit on Sal's sale to Pet, the noncontrolling interest is stated at its underlying fair value at December 31, 2013.

MUTUAL HOLDINGS—PARENT STOCK HELD BY SUBSIDIARY

LEARNING OBJECTIVE **2**

When affiliates hold ownership interests in each other, a mutual holding situation exists. Parent stock held by the subsidiary is not outstanding from the consolidated viewpoint and should not be reported as outstanding stock in a consolidated balance sheet [2].

For example, if Par Corporation owns a 90 percent interest in Sal and Sal owns a 10 percent interest in Par, the 10 percent interest held by Sal is not outstanding for consolidation purposes, nor is the 90 percent interest in Sal held by Par. Consolidation practice requires the exclusion of both the 10 percent and the 90 percent interests from consolidated statements, and the question is not whether the 10 percent interest in Par should be excluded, but rather how we eliminate it in the consolidation process. The elimination procedures depend on the method used in accounting for the investment.

There are two generally accepted methods of accounting for parent stock held by a subsidiary—the treasury stock approach and the conventional approach. The **treasury stock approach** considers parent stock held by a subsidiary to be treasury stock of the consolidated entity. Accordingly, we maintain the investment account on the books of the subsidiary on a cost basis and deduct it at cost from stockholders' equity in the consolidated balance sheet. The **conventional approach** is to account for the subsidiary investment in parent stock on an equity basis and to eliminate the subsidiary investment account against the parent equity accounts in the usual manner. Although both approaches are acceptable, they do not result in equivalent consolidated financial statements. In particular, the consolidated retained earnings and noncontrolling interest amounts usually differ under the two methods.

Treasury Stock Approach

Assume that Par Corporation acquired a 90 percent interest in Sal Corporation on January 1, 2011, for $270,000, when Sal's capital stock was $200,000 and its retained earnings $100,000. In addition, Sal purchased a 10 percent interest in Par on January 5, 2011, for $70,000, when Par's capital stock was $500,000 and its retained earnings $200,000. Trial balances for Par and Sal on December 31, 2011, before either company recorded its investment income, were as follows (in thousands):

	Par	Sal
Debits		
Other assets	$480	$260
Investment in Sal (90%)	270	—
Investment in Par (10%)	—	70
Expenses including cost of goods sold	70	50
	$820	$380
Credits		
Capital stock, $10 par	$500	$200
Retained earnings	200	100
Sales	120	80
	$820	$380

CONSOLIDATION IN YEAR OF ACQUISITION If we use the treasury stock approach, Sal Corporation has no investment income for 2011, and Par's share of Sal's $30,000 income ($80,000 sales − $50,000 expenses) is $27,000 ($30,000 × 90%). Exhibit 9-5 shows a consolidation workpaper for Par and Subsidiary for 2011. In examining the workpaper, notice that Sal's investment in Par is reclassified as treasury stock and deducted from stockholders' equity in the consolidated balance sheet.

CONSOLIDATION IN SUBSEQUENT YEARS The 2012 earnings and dividends are as follows:

	Par	Sal
Separate earnings	$60,000	$40,000
Dividends	30,000	20,000

Under the treasury stock approach, Sal records dividend income of $3,000 from Par (10% of Par's $30,000 dividends) and reports its net income for 2012 under the cost method in the amount of $43,000.

EXHIBIT 9-5

Parent Stock Held by Subsidiary—Treasury Stock Approach (Year of Acquisition)

PAR CORPORATION AND SUBSIDIARY CONSOLIDATION WORKPAPER FOR THE YEAR ENDED DECEMBER 31, 2011 (IN THOUSANDS)

	Par	90% Sal	Adjustments and Eliminations Debits	Credits	Consolidated Statements
Income Statement					
Sales	$120	$ 80			$200
Investment income	27		a 27		
Expenses including cost of sales	(70)	(50)			(120)
Noncontrolling interest share			d 3		(3)
Controlling share of Net income	**$ 77**	**$ 30**			**$ 77**
Retained Earnings Statement					
Retained earnings—Par	$200				$200
Retained earnings—Sal		$100	b 100		
Controlling share of net income	**77**	**30**			**77**
Retained earnings— December 31	**$277**	**$130**			**$277**
Balance Sheet					
Other assets	$480	$260			$740
Investment in Sal (90%)	297			a 27	
				b 270	
Investment in Par (10%)		70		c 70	
	$777	$330			$740
Capital stock—Par	$500				$500
Capital stock—Sal		$200	b 200		
Retained earnings	**277**	**130**			**277**
	$777	$330			
Treasury stock			c 70		(70)
Noncontrolling interest				b 30	
				d 3	33
					$740

Par Corporation accounts for its investment in Sal under the equity method as follows:

Cash (+A)	18,000	
Investment in Sal (−A)		18,000
To record 90% of $20,000 dividends paid by Sal		
Investment in Sal (+A)	38,700	
Income from Sal (R, +SE)		38,700
To record 90% of Sal's $43,000 income for 2012.		
Income from Sal (−R, −SE)	3,000	
Dividends (+SE)		3,000
To eliminate intercompany dividends of $3,000		
(10% of Par's $30,000 dividends paid to Sal) and		
to adjust investment income for Par's dividends		
that are included in Sal's income.		

Thus, Par records investment income from Sal of $35,700 ($38,700 − $3,000) and an investment account increase of $20,700 during 2012 ($38,700 − $18,000). The increase of $20,700 in Par's Investment in Sal account is equal to 90 percent of Sal's $40,000 separate earnings, plus 90 percent of the $3,000 dividends paid to Sal that accrued to the benefit of Par, less 90 percent of Sal's $20,000 dividends. Par's investment income from Sal consists of 90 percent of Sal's $40,000 separate earnings, less $300 (the part of the $3,000 dividends from Par that accrues to the benefit of Sal's noncontrolling stockholders).

Exhibit 9-6 shows a consolidation workpaper for Par and Subsidiary for 2012. We compute the $317,700 balance in Par's Investment in Sal account as follows:

Investment in Sal (90%) December 31, 2011	$297,000
Add: 90% of Sal's reported income	38,700
Deduct: 90% of Sal's dividends	(18,000)
Investment in Sal (90%) December 31, 2012	$317,700

Par's investment in Sal was acquired at fair value equal to book value, so we can also compute the Investment in Sal account balance as 90 percent of Sal's equity at December 31, 2012 ($353,000 × 90% = $317,700).

Entry a in the consolidation working paper shown in Exhibit 9-6 is affected by the $3,000 dividend adjustment under the equity method and is reproduced for convenient reference:

a	**Income from Sal (−R, −SE)**	**35,700**	
	Dividend income (−R, −SE)	**3,000**	
	Dividends (+SE)		**18,000**
	Investment in Sal (−A)		**20,700**

This entry is unusual because we eliminate both Par's investment income from Sal and Sal's dividend income from Par in adjusting the Investment in Sal account to its $297,000 beginning-of-the-period balance. Other workpaper adjustments are similar to those in Exhibit 9-5.

Although Par paid dividends of $30,000 during 2012, only $27,000 was paid to outside stockholders. Thus, Par's retained earnings statement and the consolidated retained earnings statement show $27,000 dividends rather than $30,000. The consolidated balance sheet shows a $70,000 equity deduction for the cost of Sal's investment in Par. This amount is the same as was shown in the workpaper in Exhibit 9-5.

Conventional Approach

The consolidated balance sheets in Exhibits 9-5 and 9-6 for the treasury stock approach consolidated 100 percent of Par Corporation's capital stock and retained earnings and deducted the cost of Sal's 10 percent investment in Par from the consolidated stockholders' equity. Under the conventional approach, we consider parent stock held by a subsidiary as constructively retired, and the capital stock and retained earnings applicable to the interest held by the subsidiary do not appear in the consolidated financial statements.

PAR CORPORATION AND SUBSIDIARY CONSOLIDATION WORKPAPER FOR THE YEAR ENDED DECEMBER 31, 2012 (IN THOUSANDS)

	Par	90% Sal	Adjustments and Eliminations Debits	Adjustments and Eliminations Credits	Consolidated Statements
Income Statement					
Sales	$140	$100			$240
Income from Sal	35.7		a 35.7		
Dividend income		3	a 3		
Expenses including cost of sales	(80)	(60)			(140)
Noncontrolling interest share			d 4.3		(4.3)
Controlling share of net income	**$ 95.7**	**$ 43**			**$ 95.7**
Retained Earnings Statement					
Retained earnings—Par	$277				$277
Retained earnings—Sal		$130	b 130		
Dividends	(27)	(20)		a 18	
				d 2	(27)
Controlling share of net income	95.7	43			95.7
Retained earnings—December 31	**$345.7**	**$153**			**$345.7**
Balance Sheet					
Other assets	$528	$283			$811
Investment in Sal (90%)	317.7			a 20.7	
				b 297	
Investment in Par (10%)		70		c 70	
	$845.7	$353			$811
Capital stock—Par	$500				$500
Capital stock—Sal		$200	b 200		
Retained earnings	345.7	153			345.7
	$845.7	$353			
Treasury stock			c 70		(70)
Noncontrolling interest				b 33	
				d 2.3	35.3
					$811

We consider Sal's acquisition of Par stock under the conventional procedure a constructive retirement of 10 percent of Par's capital stock. A consolidated balance sheet for Par and Subsidiary at acquisition shows capital stock and retained earnings applicable to the 90 percent of Par Corporation's equity held outside the consolidated entity as follows (in thousands):

	January 1, 2011	
	Par	**Consolidated**
Capital stock	$500	$450
Retained earnings	200	180
Total stockholders' equity	$700	$630

Accountants generally agree that the consolidated balance sheet should show the capital stock and retained earnings applicable to controlling stockholders outside the consolidated entity. However, this treatment raises a question concerning the applicability of the equity method to mutual holdings involving parent stock. Specifically, is the equity method applicable to affiliation structures that involve investments in the parent? If so, the parent's (investor's) share of consolidated net income for the period and its stockholders' equity at the end of the period are the same regardless of whether an investment in a subsidiary is accounted for under the equity method or the subsidiary is consolidated.

In spite of some reservations that have been expressed about the applicability of the equity method to mutually-held parent stock, the position taken in this book is that the equity method applies and is, in fact, required by GAAP [3]. Transactions of an investee of a capital nature that affect the investor's share of stockholders' equity of the investee should be accounted for as if the investee were a consolidated subsidiary. In accounting for Par's investment in Sal, we apply this requirement as follows:

January 1, 2011

Investment in Sal (90%) (+A)	270,000	
Cash (−A)		270,000

To record acquisition of a 90% interest in Sal at book value.

January 5, 2011

Capital stock, $10 par (−SE)	50,000	
Retained earnings (−SE)	20,000	
Investment in Sal (−A)		70,000

To record the constructive retirement of 10% of Par's outstanding stock as a result of Sal's purchase of Par stock.

These entries reduce parent capital stock and retained earnings to reflect amounts applicable to controlling stockholders outside the consolidated entity. We base the reduction of the Investment in Sal account on the theory that parent stock purchased by a subsidiary is, in effect, returned to the parent and constructively retired.

By recording the constructive retirement of the parent stock on the parent's books, parent equity reflects the equity of stockholders outside the consolidated entity. These are the shareholders for which the consolidated statements are intended. In addition, recording the constructive retirement as indicated establishes consistency between capital stock and retained earnings for the parent's outside stockholders (90%) and parent net income, dividends, and earnings per share, which also relate to the 90 percent outside stockholders of the parent. Financial statement notes should explain the details of the constructive retirement.

ALLOCATION OF MUTUAL INCOME When we use the conventional method of accounting for mutually-held stock, the income of the parent on an equity basis cannot be determined until the income of the subsidiary has been determined on an equity basis, and vice versa. This is because the incomes are mutually-related. The solution to the problem of determining parent and subsidiary incomes lies in the use of some mathematical procedure, the most common procedure being the use of simultaneous equations and substitution. We accomplish the allocation of income to the affiliates and to outside stockholders in two steps. First, we compute the incomes of Par and Sal on a consolidated basis, which includes the mutual income held by the affiliates. Next, we multiply these amounts by the percentage ownership held within the affiliated group and the noncontrolling interest percentage to determine consolidated net income on an equity basis and noncontrolling interest share.

In the first step, we determine the incomes of Par and Sal on a consolidated basis for 2011 mathematically as follows:

P = the income of Par on a consolidated basis (includes mutual income)

S = the income of Sal on a consolidated basis (includes mutual income)

Then,

$$P = \text{Par's separate earnings of } \$50,000 + 90\% \, S$$

$$S = \text{Sal's separate earnings of } \$30,000 + 10\% \, P$$

By substitution,

$$P = \$50,000 + 0.9(\$30,000 + 0.1P)$$

$$P = \$50,000 + \$27,000 + 0.09P$$

$$P = \underline{\$84,615}$$

$$S = \$30,000 + (\$84,615 \times 0.1)$$

$$S = \underline{\$38,462}$$

These are not final solutions because some of the income (mutual income) has been double-counted. The combined separate earnings of Par and Sal are only $80,000 ($50,000 + $30,000), but P plus S equals $123,077 ($84,615 + $38,462). In the next step, we determine Par's net income on an equity basis by multiplying the value determined for P in the equation by the 90 percent interest outstanding, and we determine noncontrolling interest share by multiplying the value determined for S by the noncontrolling interest percentage. In other words, *Par's net income on an equity basis is 90 percent of $84,615, or $76,154, and the noncontrolling interest share is 10 percent of $38,462, or $3,846.* Par's net income (and controlling share of consolidated net income) of $76,154, plus noncontrolling interest share of $3,846, is equal to the $80,000 separate earnings of Par and Sal.

ACCOUNTING FOR MUTUAL INCOME UNDER THE EQUITY METHOD Par Corporation records its investment income for 2011 on an equity basis as follows:

Investment in Sal (+A)	26,154	
Income from Sal (R, +SE)		26,154
To record income from Sal.		

The $26,154 income from Sal equals 90 percent of Sal's $38,462 income on a consolidated basis, less 10 percent of Par's $84,615 income on a consolidated basis [(38,462 × 90%) − (84,615 × 10%)]. This represents Par's 90 percent interest in Sal's income less Sal's 10 percent interest in Par's income. An alternative calculation that gives the same result deducts Par's separate earnings from its net income ($76,154 − $50,000).

Assume that Sal Corporation accounts for its investment in Par on a cost basis because its interest in Par is only 10 percent. Par did not declare dividends during 2011, so Sal would have no investment income for the year, and its investment account would remain at the $70,000 original cost of the 10 percent interest.

CONSOLIDATION UNDER THE EQUITY METHOD Exhibit 9-7 presents a consolidation workpaper for Par and Subsidiary under the conventional procedure for 2011. The workpaper shows the investment in Sal (90%) at $226,154 (the $270,000 initial investment, plus $26,154 investment income, less the $70,000 reduction for the constructive retirement of Par's stock). Entry a in the workpaper eliminates the $70,000 investment in Par (Sal's books) and increases Par's Investment in Sal account to $296,154. This entry reflects the constructive retirement of Par stock that was credited to Par's Investment in Sal account. Entry b eliminates investment income of $26,154 and reduces the investment account to its $270,000 cost at January 5, 2011. Entry c eliminates the reciprocal investment in Sal and equity of Sal amounts and establishes the noncontrolling interest in Sal at $30,000 (10% of $300,000) at the beginning of 2011.

In examining the workpaper in Exhibit 9-7, observe that the net income, capital stock, and retained earnings in the separate statements of Par Corporation are equal to the controlling share of consolidated net income, consolidated capital stock, and consolidated retained earnings. This equality would not have existed without the entry to record the constructive retirement of stock on Par's books.

CONSOLIDATION IN SUBSEQUENT YEARS The separate earnings and dividends of Par and Sal for 2012 are as follows:

	Par	Sal
Separate earnings	$60,000	$40,000
Dividends	30,000	20,000

EXHIBIT 9-7

Parent Stock Held
by Subsidiary—
Conventional Approach
(Year of Acquisition)

PAR CORPORATION AND SUBSIDIARY CONSOLIDATION WORKPAPER FOR THE YEAR ENDED DECEMBER 31, 2011

	Par	90% Sal	Adjustments and Eliminations Debits	Credits	Consolidated Statements
Income Statement					
Sales	$120,000	$ 80,000			$200,000
Investment income	26,154		b 26,154		
Expenses including cost of sales	(70,000)	(50,000)			(120,000)
Noncontrolling interest share			d 3,846		(3,846)
Controlling share of net income	**$ 76,154**	**$ 30,000**			**$ 76,154**
Retained Earnings Statement					
Retained earnings—Par	$180,000				$180,000
Retained earnings—Sal		$100,000	c 100,000		
Controlling share of net income	76,154	30,000			76,154
Retained earnings—December 31	**$256,154**	**$130,000**			**$256,154**
Balance Sheet					
Other assets	$480,000	$260,000			$740,000
Investment in Sal (90%)	226,154		a 70,000	b 26,154 c 270,000	
Investment in Par (10%)		70,000		a 70,000	
	$706,154	$330,000			$740,000
Capital stock—Par	$450,000				$450,000
Capital stock—Sal		$200,000	c 200,000		
Retained earnings	256,154	130,000			256,154
	$706,154	$330,000			
Noncontrolling interest				c 30,000 d 3,846	33,846
					$740,000

Application of the conventional method of accounting requires the following mathematical computations for Par and Sal for 2012:

P = Par's income on a consolidated basis (includes mutual income)

S = Sal's income on a consolidated basis (includes mutual income)

Basic equations:

$$P = \$60,000 + 0.9S$$
$$S = \$40,000 + 0.1P$$

Substitution:

$$P = \$60,000 + 0.9(\$40,000 + 0.1P)$$
$$0.91P = \$96,000$$
$$P = \underline{\$105,495}$$
$$S = \$40,000 + 0.1(\$105,495)$$
$$S = \underline{\$50,550}$$

These computed amounts for *P* and *S* include mutual income that we must then eliminate. We use these amounts to determine the controlling share of consolidated net income and noncontrolling interest share as follows:

Par's net income (and controlling share)	
($105,495 × 90% outside ownership)	$ 94,945
Noncontrolling interest share ($50,550 × 10%)	5,055
Total separate earnings of Par and Sal	$100,000

If Sal accounts for its investment in Par under the cost method, it will record dividend income from Par of $3,000 for 2012 (10% of Par's dividends). Alternatively, Sal will record income from Par of $10,550 ($105,495 × 10%) if it uses the equity method.

Par accounts for its investment in Sal on an equity basis as follows:

Cash (+A)	18,000	
Investment in Sal (−A)		18,000
To record 90% of Sal's $20,000 dividend for 2012.		
Investment in Sal (+A)	34,945	
Income from Sal (R, +SE)		34,945
To record investment income computed as follows:		
$94,945 Par's net income less $60,000 Par's separate		
earnings = $34,945. An alternative computation: 90% of		
Sal's income on a consolidated basis ($50,550 × 90%),		
less 10% of Par's income on a consolidated basis		
($105,495 × 10%) = $34,945.		
Investment in Sal (+A)	3,000	
Dividends (+SE)		3,000
To eliminate parent dividends paid to Sal and		
to adjust the investment in Sal account.		

Par's Investment in Sal account at December 31, 2012, will have a balance of $246,099 under the equity method. This balance is computed as follows:

Investment in Sal, December 31, 2011	$226,154
Add: Investment income	34,945
Add: Dividends paid to Sal	3,000
Deduct: Dividends received from Sal	−18,000
Investment in Sal, December 31, 2012	$246,099

Exhibit 9-8 presents a consolidation workpaper for Par and Subsidiary for 2012. We assume that Sal accounts for its investment in Par under the cost method. The equity method has been applied by Par. Therefore, parent net income of $94,945 is equal to the controlling share of consolidated net income. Parent capital stock and retained earnings amounts also equal their corresponding consolidated amounts. The workpaper adjustments in Exhibit 9-8 are procedurally equivalent to those shown earlier in the chapter.

CONVERSION TO EQUITY METHOD ON SEPARATE COMPANY BOOKS It is helpful at this point to consider the computations that would be necessary to correct consolidated retained earnings and noncontrolling interest if the equity method had not been used by Par. First, it would be necessary to determine the separate net asset increases of the mutually-held companies. We compute these increases from January 1, 2011, to December 31, 2012, as follows:

	Par	Sal	Total
Separate earnings—2011	$ 50,000	$ 30,000	$ 80,000
Separate earnings—2012	+60,000	+40,000	+100,000
Less: Dividends declared	−30,000	−20,000	−50,000
Add: Dividends received from affiliates	+18,000	+3,000	+21,000
Increase in net assets	$ 98,000	$ 53,000	$151,000

PAR CORPORATION AND SUBSIDIARY CONSOLIDATION WORKPAPER FOR THE YEAR ENDED DECEMBER 31, 2012 (IN THOUSANDS)

	Par	90% Sal	Adjustments and Eliminations Debits	Adjustments and Eliminations Credits	Consolidated Statements
Income Statement					
Sales	$140,000	$100,000			$240,000
Income from Sal	34,945		b 34,945		
Dividend income		3,000	b 3,000		
Expenses including cost of sales	(80,000)	(60,000)			(140,000)
Noncontrolling interest share			d 5,055		(5,055)
Controlling share of net income	**$ 94,945**	**$ 43,000**			**$ 94,945**
Retained Earnings Statement					
Retained earnings—Par	$256,154				$256,154
Retained earnings—Sal		$130,000	c 130,000		
Dividends	(27,000)	(20,000)		b 18,000	
				d 2,000	(27,000)
Controlling share of net income	**94,945**	**43,000**			**94,945**
Retained earnings—December 31	**$324,099**	**$153,000**			**$324,099**
Balance Sheet					
Other assets	$528,000	$283,000			$811,000
Investment in Sal (90%)	246,099		a 70,000	b 19,945 c 296,154	
Investment in Par (10%)		70,000		a 70,000	
	$774,099	$353,000			$811,000
Capital stock—Par	$450,000				$450,000
Capital stock—Sal		$200,000	c 200,000		
Retained earnings	**324,099**	**153,000**			**324,099**
	$774,099	$353,000			
Noncontrolling interest				c 33,846 d 3,055	36,901
					$811,000

Once we determine the net asset increases, the simultaneous equations used earlier for determining income allocations allocate the separate net asset increases to consolidated retained earnings and to noncontrolling interest. The computations for Par and Sal are:

P = increase in net assets of Par on a consolidated basis since acquisition by Sal

S = increase in net assets of Sal on a consolidated basis since acquisition by Par

Basic equations:

$$P = \$98,000 + 0.9S$$
$$S = \$53,000 + 0.1P$$

By substitution:

$$P = \$98,000 + 0.9(\$53,000 + 0.1P)$$
$$P = \$98,000 + \$47,700 + 0.09P$$
$$0.91P = \$145,700$$
$$P = \underline{\$160,110}$$
$$S = \$53,000 + (0.1 \times \$160,110)$$
$$S = \underline{\$69,011}$$

These computations (which still include mutual amounts) can be used to allocate the $151,000 net asset increase to consolidated retained earnings and noncontrolling interest as follows:

Par's retained earnings increase (or increase in consolidated retained earnings) = $160,110 × 90%	$144,099
Noncontrolling interest's retained earnings increase = $69,011 × 10%	6,901
Total net asset increase	$151,000

At acquisition, Par's retained earnings were $200,000, and they were adjusted downward to $180,000 for the constructive retirement of 10 percent of Par's stock. We compute the correct amount of consolidated retained earnings at December 31, 2012, as $180,000 + $144,099, or $324,099. This computation provides a convenient check on the $324,099 retained earnings shown in the consolidated balance sheet in Exhibit 9-8.

Noncontrolling interest in Sal Corporation at January 1, 2011, was $30,000 ($300,000 equity × 10%). We compute the noncontrolling interest at December 31, 2012, as $30,000 + $6,901, or $36,901. This computation confirms the $36,901 noncontrolling interest that appears in the consolidation workpaper of Exhibit 9-8.

SUBSIDIARY STOCK MUTUALLY-HELD

Parent stock held within an affiliation structure is not outstanding and is not reported as outstanding stock either in the parent statements under the equity method or in consolidated financial statements. Two generally-accepted approaches for eliminating the effect of mutually-held parent stock—the treasury stock approach and the conventional approach—were explained and illustrated in the previous section of this chapter. In this section, *the mutually-held stock involves subsidiaries holding the stock of each other, and the treasury stock approach is not applicable.*

Consider the following diagram of the affiliation structure of Pal, Set, and Ton. Pal owns an 80 percent interest in Set directly. Set has a 70 percent interest in Ton, and Ton has a 10 percent interest in Set. There is a 10 percent noncontrolling interest in Set and a 30 percent noncontrolling interest in Ton.

The acquisitions of Pal, Set, and Ton were as follows:

1. Pal acquired its 80 percent interest in Set Corporation on January 2, 2011, for $260,000, when the stockholders' equity of Set consisted of capital stock of $200,000 and retained earnings of $100,000 ($25,000 implied total goodwill).

2. Set acquired its 70 percent interest in Ton Corporation for $112,000 on January 3, 2012, when the stockholders' equity of Ton consisted of $100,000 capital stock and $50,000 retained earnings ($10,000 implied total goodwill).

3. Ton acquired its 10 percent interest in Set for $40,000 on December 31, 2012, when the stockholders' equity of Set consisted of $200,000 capital stock and $200,000 retained earnings (no goodwill).

Accounting Prior to Mutual Holding Relationship

Assume that the recorded net assets from the investments described were equal to their fair values at acquisition and that any excess was goodwill. Post-closing trial balances for Pal, Set, and Ton at December 31, 2012, are as follows (in thousands):

	Pal	Set	Ton
Cash	$ 64	$ 42	$ 20
Other current assets	200	85	80
Plant and equipment—net	500	240	110
Investment in Set (80%)	340	—	—
Investment in Ton (70%)	—	133	—
Investment in Set (10%)	—	—	40
	$1,104	$500	$250
Liabilities	$ 200	$100	$ 70
Capital stock	500	200	100
Retained earnings	404	200	80
	$1,104	$500	$250

The balance in Pal's Investment in Set account at December 31, 2012, is $340,000:

Cost	$260,000
Add: 80% of Set's $40,000 income less dividends—2011	32,000
80% of Set's $60,000 income less dividends—2012	48,000
	$340,000

The balance of Ton's 10 percent Investment in Set account at December 31, 2012, is equal to the $40,000 cost of the investment on that date. Assume that Ton accounts for this 10 percent investment in Set on a cost basis, even though the equity method might be used because absolute control lies with the parent.

We compute Set's $133,000 investment in Ton at December 31, 2012, as follows:

Investment in Ton January 3, 2012—cost	$112,000
Add: 70% of Ton's $30,000 income less dividends—2012	21,000
	$133,000

Accounting for Mutually-held Subsidiaries

During 2013, the affiliates had income from operations and dividends as follows (in thousands):

	Pal	Set	Ton	Total
Income from separate operations	$112	$51	$40	$203
Dividends declared	50	30	20	100

We allocate the incomes of the three companies under the conventional approach.

INCOME ALLOCATION COMPUTATIONS Income allocation computations for the affiliates follow:

$$P = \text{separate income of Pal} + 0.8S$$
$$S = \text{separate income of Set} + 0.7U$$
$$U = \text{separate income of Ton} + 0.1S$$
$$P = \$112,000 + 0.8S$$
$$S = \$51,000 + 0.7U$$
$$U = \$40,000 + 0.1S$$

Solve for S (amounts are rounded to nearest $1):

$$S = \$51,000 + 0.7(\$40,000 + 0.1S) = \$79,000 + 0.07S$$
$$0.93S = \$79,000$$
$$S = \underline{\$84,946}$$
$$U = \$40,000 + 0.1(\$84,946)$$
$$U = \underline{\$48,495}$$
$$P = \$112,000 + 0.8(\$84,946)$$
$$P = \underline{\$179,957}$$

We allocate total income for the affiliated group to:

Controlling share of consolidated net income (equal to Pal's net income)	$179,957
Noncontrolling interest share in Set's income ($84,946 × 10%)	8,495
Noncontrolling interest share in Ton's income ($48,495 × 30%)	14,548
Total separate income	$203,000

COMPUTATIONS OF INVESTMENT ACCOUNT BALANCES A summary of the investment account balances at December 31, 2013, is as follows:

	Pal (Equity Method)	Set (Equity Method)	Ton (Cost Method)*
Investment balances December 31, 2012	$340,000	$133,000	$40,000
Add: Investment income			
Pal ($84,946 × 0.8)	67,957	—	—
Set ($48,495 × 0.7)	—	33,946	—
Deduct: Dividends received:			
Pal ($30,000 × 0.8)	(24,000)	—	—
Set ($20,000 × 0.7)	—	(14,000)	—
Investment balance December 31, 2013	$383,957	$152,946	$40,000

> * $3,000 dividend income and dividends received amounts for Ton's 10 percent investment in Set do not affect the investment account because Ton uses the cost method.

CONSOLIDATION WORKPAPER—EQUITY METHOD Exhibit 9-9 reflects the investment incomes and balances in the consolidation workpaper. We show financial statements of Pal, Set, and Ton in the first three columns of the workpaper. Consolidation workpaper entries a, b, and c eliminate investment income (including dividend income of Ton) and intercompany dividends, and adjust the investment accounts to their beginning-of-the-period balances. Workpaper entry d eliminates reciprocal equity and investment balances for Ton, records the $10,000 beginning-of-the-period goodwill from Set's investment in Ton, and establishes the $57,000

EXHIBIT 9-9	
Consolidation Involving Mutually-held Subsidiary Stock	**PAL CORPORATION AND SUBSIDIARIES CONSOLIDATION WORKPAPER FOR THE YEAR ENDED DECEMBER 31, 2013**

	Pal	Set	Ton	Adjustments and Eliminations Debits	Credits	Consolidated Statements
Income Statement						
Sales	$412,000	$161,000	$100,000			$ 673,000
Income from Set (80%)	67,957			c 67,957		
Income from Ton (70%)		33,946		b 33,946		
Dividend income (10%)			3,000	a 3,000		
Cost of sales	(220,000)	(70,000)	(40,000)			(330,000)

	Pal	Set	Ton	Adjustments and Eliminations Debits	Adjustments and Eliminations Credits	Consolidated Statements
Expenses	(80,000)	(40,000)	(20,000)			(140,000)
Noncontrolling interest share—Set				f 8,495		(8,495)
Noncontrolling interest share—Ton				g 14,548		(14,548)
Controlling share of net Income	**$179,957**	**$ 84,946**	**$ 43,000**			**$ 179,957**
Retained Earnings Statement Retained earnings—Pal	$ 404,000					$ 404,000
Retained earnings—Set		$200,000		e200,000		
Retained earnings—Ton			$ 80,000	d 80,000		
Dividends	(50,000)	(30,000)	(20,000)		a 3,000	
					b 14,000	
					c 24,000	
					f 3,000	
					g 6,000	(50,000)
Controlling share of net income	179,957	84,946	43,000			179,957
Retained earnings— December 31	**$ 533,957**	**$254,946**	**$103,000**			**$ 533,957**
Balance Sheet Cash	$ 60,000	$ 33,000	$ 43,000			$ 136,000
Other current assets	250,000	80,000	70,000			400,000
Plant assets—net	550,000	300,000	130,000			980,000
Investment in Set (80%)	383,957				c 43,957 e 340,000	
Investment in Ton (70%)		152,946			b 19,946 d 133,000	
Investment in Set (10%)			40,000		e 40,000	
Goodwill—Pal				e 25,000		25,000
Goodwill—Set				d 10,000		10,000
	$1,243,957	$565,946	$283,000			$1,551,000
Liabilities	$ 210,000	$111,000	$ 80,000			$ 401,000
Capital stock—Pal	500,000					500,000
Capital stock—Set		200,000		e 200,000		
Capital stock—Ton			100,000	d 100,000		
Retained earnings	533,957	254,946	103,000			533,957
	$1,243,957	$565,946	$283,000			
Noncontrolling interest in Ton, January 1 Noncontrolling interest in Set, January 1					d 57,000 e 45,000 f 5,495 g 8,548	116,043
						$1,551,000

beginning noncontrolling interest in Ton (computed as $190,000 \times 30\%$). Entry e eliminates reciprocal equity and investment balances for Set (both Pal's 80% and Ton's 10%), records the $25,000 beginning-of-the-period goodwill from Pal's investment in Set, and establishes the $45,000 beginning noncontrolling interest in Set. Although there are two Investment in Set accounts and therefore two eliminations could have been made, *it is convenient to prepare one entry for each entity* (Set in this case) *rather than for each investment account.*

Pal accounts for its investment in Set as a one-line consolidation, so the controlling share of consolidated net income of $179,957 for 2013 and consolidated retained earnings of $533,957 at December 31, 2013, equal the corresponding amounts in the separate financial statements of Pal. We determine noncontrolling interest share by equation, as demonstrated earlier.

SUMMARY

One corporation may control another through direct or indirect ownership of its voting stock. Indirect holdings give the investor an ability to control or significantly influence the operations of the investee not directly owned through an investee that is directly owned. The major problem encountered in consolidating the financial statements of companies in indirect control situations lies in allocating income and equities among controlling and noncontrolling stockholders. Several computational approaches are available for such allocations, but the schedule approach is probably the best overall approach because of its simplicity and because it provides a step-by-step reference of all allocations made.

When affiliates hold the stock of each other, the stock is not outstanding from the viewpoint of the consolidated entity. We eliminate the effect of mutually-held parent stock from consolidated financial statements by either the treasury stock approach or the conventional approach. The treasury stock approach deducts the investment in parent stock on a cost basis from consolidated stockholders' equity. Under the conventional approach, we treat the investment in parent stock as constructively retired by adjusting the parent's investment in subsidiary and the parent's equity accounts to reflect a one-line consolidation. Then we eliminate the subsidiary's investment in parent account against the parent's investment in subsidiary account.

We account for mutual investments by subsidiaries in the stock of each other under the conventional method of eliminating reciprocal investment and equity balances. The treasury stock approach is not applicable to such mutually held investments because only parent stock and retained earnings appear in the consolidated financial statements. Under the conventional method, we use simultaneous equations to allocate income and equities among mutually held companies.

QUESTIONS

(Questions 1 through 7 cover indirect holdings, and 8 through 15 cover mutual holdings.)

1. What is an indirect holding of the stock of an affiliate?

2. P owns a 60 percent interest in S, and S owns a 40 percent interest in T. Should T be consolidated? If not, how should T be included in the consolidated statements of P and Subsidiaries?

3. Distinguish between indirect holding affiliation structures and mutual holding affiliation structures.

4. Parent Company owns 70 percent of the voting stock of Subsidiary A, and Subsidiary A owns 70 percent of the stock of Subsidiary B. Is the inside ownership of Subsidiary B more than 50 percent? Should Subsidiary B be included in the consolidated statements? Explain.

5. Pat Corporation owns 80 percent of the stock of Sam Corporation, and Sam owns 70 percent of the stock of Stan Corporation. Separate earnings of Pat, Sam, and Stan are $200,000, $160,000, and $100,000, respectively. Compute controlling and noncontrolling interest shares of consolidated net income under two different approaches.

6. In using the schedule approach for allocating income of subsidiaries to controlling and noncontrolling stockholders in an indirect holding affiliation structure, why is it necessary to begin with the lowest subsidiary in the affiliation tier?

7. P owns 80 percent of S1, and S1 owns 70 percent of S2. Separate incomes of P, S1, and S2 are $20,000, $10,000, and $5,000, respectively, for 2011. During 2011, S1 sold land to P at a gain of $1,000. Compute S1's income on an equity basis. Discuss why you did or did not adjust S1's investment in S2's account for the unrealized gain.

8. If a parent owns 80 percent of the voting stock of a subsidiary, and the subsidiary in turn owns 20 percent of the stock of the parent, what kind of affiliation structure is involved? Explain.

9. How is the treasury stock approach applied to the elimination of mutually-held stock?

10. Are the treasury stock and conventional approaches equally applicable to all mutual holdings? Explain.

11. Under the treasury stock approach, a mutually-held subsidiary accounts for its investment in the parent on a cost basis. Are dividends received by the subsidiary from the parent included in investment income of the parent under the equity method?

12. Describe the concept of a constructive retirement of parent stock. Should the parent adjust its equity accounts when its stock is constructively retired?

13. P's separate earnings are $50,000, and S's separate earnings are $20,000. P owns an 80 percent interest in S, and S owns a 10 percent interest in P. What is the controlling share of consolidated net income?

14. How do consolidation procedures for mutual holdings involving the father-son-grandson type of affiliation structure differ from those for mutually-held parent stock?

15. If companies in an affiliation structure account for investments on an equity basis, how can noncontrolling interests be determined without the use of simultaneous equations?

EXERCISES

(Exercises 9-1 through 9-8 cover indirect holdings, and 9-9 through 9-13 cover mutual holdings.)

E 9-1

Calculate consolidated net income

On January 1, 2011, Pen Corporation purchased a 60 percent interest in Sal Corporation at book value (equal to fair value). At that time, Sal owned a 60 percent interest in Tip Corporation (acquired at book value equal to fair value) and a 15 percent interest in Win Company. The four companies had the following separate incomes and dividends for 2011 (separate income does not include investment income or dividend income):

	Separate Income	Dividends
Pen Corporation	$1,600,000	$600,000
Sal Corporation	1,000,000	400,000
Tip Corporation	400,000	200,000
Win Company	600,000	200,000

REQUIRED: Determine the controlling and noncontrolling interest shares of consolidated net income.

E 9-2

Allocate investment income and loss

Pub Corporation owns 60 percent of Sam Corporation and 80 percent of Tim Corporation. Tim owns 20 percent of Sam. Separate income and loss data (not including investment income) for the three affiliates for 2011 are as follows:

Pub	$800,000 separate income
Sam	$300,000 separate income
Tim	($400,000) separate loss

There are no differentials or unrealized profits to consider in measuring 2011 income.

REQUIRED: Calculate the controlling share of consolidated net income for 2011.

E 9-3

Prepare an income allocation schedule (includes unrealized profit on land)

The affiliation structure for Place Corporation and its affiliates is as follows:

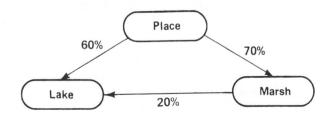

During 2011 the separate incomes of the affiliates were as follows:

Place	$200,000
Lake	$ 80,000
Marsh	$ 70,000

Lake's income includes $20,000 unrealized profit on land sold to Marsh during 2011.

REQUIRED: Prepare a schedule that shows the allocation of income among the affiliates and also shows controlling and noncontrolling interest shares of consolidated net income for 2011.

E 9-4

Determine equation to compute income from subsidiary, noncontrolling interest share, and controlling interest share of consolidated net income

The affiliation structure for Pin Corporation and its subsidiaries is as follows:

Separate incomes of Pin, Son, and Tan Corporations for 2011 are $360,000, $160,000, and $100,000, respectively.

1. The equation for determining Pin's income from Son on a one-line consolidation basis for 2011 is:
   a *$160,000 × 70%*
   b *($160,000 × 70%) + ($100,000 × 80%)*
   c *($160,000 × 70%) + ($100,000 × 56%)*
   d *70% × ($160,000 × $100,000)*

2. Noncontrolling interest share for Pin and Subsidiaries for 2011 is determined as follows:
   a *$30% × $160,000*
   b *(30% × $160,000) + (20% × $100,000)*
   c *(30% × $160,000) + (24% × $100,000)*
   d *(30% × $160,000) + (44% × $100,000)*

3. Controlling share of consolidated net income can be determined by the following equation:
   a *$620,000 − ($160,000 × 30%)*
   b *$620,000 − ($160,000 × 30%) − ($100,000 × 20%)*
   c *$620,000 − ($160,000 × 30%) − ($100,000 × 20%) − ($100,000 × 30% × 90%)*
   d *$620,000 − ($160,000 × 30%) − ($100,000 × 44%)*

E 9-5

Prepare income allocation schedule

Pal Corporation owns 80 percent each of the voting common stock of Sal and Tea Corporations. Sal owns 60 percent of the voting common stock of Won Corporation and 10 percent of the voting stock of Tea. Tea owns 70 percent of the voting stock of Val and 10 percent of the voting stock of Won.

The affiliates had separate incomes during 2011 as follows:

Pal Corporation	$50,000
Sal Corporation	$30,000
Tea Corporation	$35,000
Won Corporation	($20,000) loss
Val Corporation	$40,000

The only intercompany profits included in the separate incomes of the affiliates consisted of $5,000 on merchandise that Pal acquired from Tea and which remained in Pal's December 31, 2011, inventory.

REQUIRED: Compute controlling and noncontrolling interest shares of consolidated net income.

E 9-6

Calculate controlling interest share and noncontrolling interest share of consolidated net income

Pet Corporation owns 90 percent of the stock of Man Corporation and 70 percent of the stock of Nun Corporation. Man owns 70 percent of the stock of Oak Corporation and 10 percent of the stock of Nun Corporation. Nun Corporation owns 20 percent of the stock of Oak Corporation.

Separate incomes for the year ended December 31, 2011, are as follows:

Pet	$65,000
Man	$18,000
Nun	$28,000
Oak	$ 9,000

During 2011, Man sold land to Nun at a profit of $4,000. Oak sold inventory items to Pet at a profit of $8,000, half of which remains in Pet's inventory. Pet purchased for $15,000 Nun's bonds, which had a book value of $17,000 on December 31, 2011.

REQUIRED: Calculate controlling and noncontrolling interest shares of consolidated net income for 2011.

E 9-7

No intercompany profits

The affiliation structure for a group of interrelated companies is diagrammed as follows:

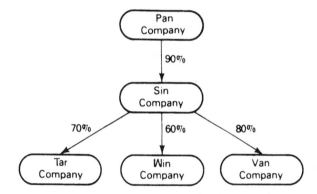

The investments were acquired at fair value equal to book value in 2011, and there are no unrealized or constructive profits or losses.

Separate incomes and dividends for the companies for 2011 are:

	Separate Income (Loss)	Dividends
Pan	$1,240,000	$400,000
Sin	350,000	200,000
Tar	400,000	160,000
Win	(100,000)	—
Van	240,000	120,000

1. The noncontrolling interest share of Tar Company's net income for 2011 is:

  a $120,000

  b $148,000

  c $252,000

  d $280,000

2. The noncontrolling interest share of Van Company's net income for 2011 is:

  a $48,000

  b $96,000

  c $110,400

  d $144,000

3. The total noncontrolling interest share that should appear in the consolidated income statement for 2011 is:
   a *$244,200*
   b *$210,200*
   c *$204,200*
   d *$76,200*

4. Controlling share of consolidated net income for Pan Company and Subsidiaries for 2011 is:
   a *$1,925,800*
   b *$1,881,800*
   c *$1,240,000*
   d *$685,800*

5. Pan's Investment in Sin account should reflect a net increase for 2011 in the amount of:
   a *$762,000*
   b *$685,800*
   c *$625,800*
   d *$505,800*

E 9-8
Correcting net income for unrealized profits

Pat Corporation owns an 80 percent interest in Sam Corporation and a 70 percent interest in Ten Corporation. Ten owns a 10 percent interest in Sam. These investment interests were acquired at fair value equal to book value.

The net incomes of the affiliates for 2011 were as follows:

Pat	$240,000
Sam	$ 80,000
Ten	$ 40,000

On December 31, 2011, Pat's inventory included $10,000 of unrealized profits on merchandise purchased from Sam during 2011, and Sam's land account reflected $15,000 unrealized profit on land purchased from Ten during 2011. These unrealized profits have not been eliminated from the net income amounts shown. Except for adjustments related to unrealized profits, the net income amounts were determined on a correct equity basis.

1. The separate incomes of Pat, Sam, and Ten for 2011 were:
   a *$240,000, $80,000, and $32,000, respectively*
   b *$148,000, $80,000, and $32,000, respectively*
   c *$148,000, $72,000, and $40,000, respectively*
   d *$240,000, $72,000, and $40,000, respectively*

2. The separate realized incomes of Pat, Sam, and Ten for 2011 were:
   a *$138,000, $80,000, and $25,000, respectively*
   b *$138,000, $70,000, and $25,000, respectively*
   c *$123,000, $80,000, and $17,000, respectively*
   d *$148,000, $70,000, and $17,000, respectively*

3. Controlling share of consolidated net income for Pat Corporation and Subsidiaries for 2011 was:
   a *$220,800*
   b *$215,900*
   c *$214,400*
   d *$212,400*

4. Noncontrolling interest share that should appear in the consolidated income statement for Pat Corporation and Subsidiaries for 2011 is:
   a *$23,600*
   b *$21,200*
   c *$19,100*
   d *$14,200*

E 9-9
Calculate consolidated net income (conventional method, no complications)

Pan Corporation owns an 80 percent interest in Sol Company and Sol owns a 30 percent interest in Pan, both acquired at a fair value equal to book value. Separate incomes (not including investment income) of the two affiliates for 2011 are:

Pan	$3,000,000
Sol	$1,500,000

REQUIRED: Compute controlling share of consolidated net income for 2011 using the conventional (equation) approach.

E 9-10
Prepare computations (subsidiary stock mutually-held, no unrealized profits)
Intercompany investment percentages and 2011 earnings for three affiliates are as follows:

	Percentage Interest in Sad	Percentage Interest in Two	Separate Earnings
Pad Corporation	70%	—	$200,000
Sad Corporation	—	80%	120,000
Two Corporation	10%	—	80,000

REQUIRED: Compute controlling share of consolidated net income and noncontrolling interest share for 2011.

E 9-11
[Based on AICPA] Mutually-held parent-company stock
Pin, Inc., owns 80 percent of the capital stock of Son Company and 70 percent of the capital stock of Tin, Inc. Son owns 15 percent of the capital stock of Tin. Tin owns 25 percent of the capital stock of Pin. These ownership interrelationships are illustrated in the following diagram:

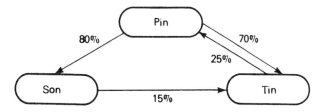

Income before adjusting for interests in intercompany income for each corporation follows:

Pin, Inc.	$190,000
Son Company	$170,000
Tin, Inc.	$230,000

The following notations relate to the questions below:

A = Pin's consolidated income—its separate income plus its share of the consolidated incomes of Son and Tin
B = Son's consolidated income—its separate income plus its share of the consolidated income of Tin
C = Tin's consolidated income—its separate income plus its share of the consolidated income of Pin

1. The equation, in a set of simultaneous equations, that computes A is:
 a $A = 0.75(190,000 + 0.8B + 0.7C)$
 b $A = 190,000 + 0.8B + 0.7C$
 c $A = 0.75(190,000) + 0.8(170,000) + 0.7(230,000)$
 d $A = 0.75(190,000) + 0.8B + 0.7C$

2. The equation, in a set of simultaneous equations, that computes B is:
 a $B = 170,000 + 0.15C + 0.75A$
 b $B = 170,000 + 0.15C$
 c $B = 0.2(170,000) + 0.15(230,000)$
 d $B = 0.2(170,000) + 0.15C$

3. Tin's noncontrolling interest share of consolidated income is:
 a $0.15(230,000)$
 b $230,000 + 0.25A$
 c $0.15(230,000) + 0.25A$
 d $0.15C$

4. Son's noncontrolling interest share of consolidated income is:

a *$34,316*

b *$25,500*

c *$45,755*

d *$30,675*

E 9-12

Mutually-held parent stock

Pet Corporation owns 90 percent of Sod Corporation's common stock and Sod owns 15 percent of Pet, both acquired at fair value equal to book value. Separate incomes and dividends of the affiliates for 2011 are as follows:

	Separate Incomes	**Dividends**
Pet Corporation	$100,000	$50,000
Sod Corporation	60,000	30,000

1. If the treasury stock approach is used, Pet's income and controlling share of consolidated net income for 2011 will be computed:

a *$100,000 + (90% × $60,000)*

b *$100,000 + (90% × $67,500)*

c *$100,000 + (90% × $67,500) − (90% × $30,000)*

d *($100,000 + $60,000) − (10% × $67,500)*

2. If the conventional approach is used, Pet's income on a consolidated basis is denoted $P = \$100,000 + 0.9S$, and Sod's income on a consolidated basis is denoted $S = \$60,000 + 0.15 P$. Given these equations, the controlling share of consolidated net income is equal to:

a *P*

b *0.85P*

c *P − 0.1S*

d *P + S − 0.15S*

E 9-13

Computations (treasury stock and conventional)

Pug Corporation acquired a 70 percent interest in Sat Corporation for $238,000 on January 2, 2010, when Sat's equity consisted of $200,000 capital stock and $50,000 retained earnings. The excess is due to a patent amortized over a 10-year period, at $9,000 per year. Pug accounted for its investment in Sat during 2010 as follows:

Investment cost January 2, 2010	$238,000
Income from Sat [($40,000 − $9,000) × 70%]	21,700
Dividends from Sat ($20,000 × 70%)	(14,000)
Investment balance December 31, 2010	$245,700

On January 3, 2011, Sat acquired a 10 percent interest in Pug at a $60,000 fair value equal to book value. No intercompany profit transactions have occurred. Incomes and dividends for 2011 were as follows:

	Pug	**Sat**
Separate income	$120,000	$50,000
Dividends	60,000	30,000

REQUIRED

1. Determine the balance of Pug's Investment in Sat account on December 31, 2011, if the treasury stock approach is used for Sat's investment in Pug.

2. Compute controlling and noncontrolling interest shares of consolidated net income if the conventional approach is used for Sat's investment in Pug. Also determine the amount of Pug's income from Sat and the balance in Pug's Investment in Sat account at December 31, 2011.

(Problems 9-1 through 9-3 cover indirect holdings, and 9-4 through 9-7 cover mutual holdings.)

P 9-1
Schedule for allocating income (unrealized profits and goodwill)

The affiliation structure for Pad Corporation and its subsidiaries is diagrammed as follows:

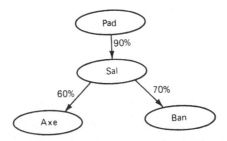

The incomes and dividends for the affiliates for 2011 are (in thousands):

	Pad	**Sal**	**Axe**	**Ban**
Separate income (loss)	$500	$300	$150	$(20)
Dividends	200	140	50	—

ADDITIONAL INFORMATION

1. Axe sold land to Sal during 2011 at a $20,000 gain. The land is still held by Sal.

2. Sal is amortizing a previously unrecorded patent of Axe at the rate of $12,000 per year. (Total amortization is $20,000.)

3. Pad is amortizing a previously unrecorded patent acquired from Sal with a book value of $360,000 over its remaining nine-year life.

REQUIRED: Prepare a schedule to compute controlling and noncontrolling interest shares of consolidated net income for each subsidiary for 2011.

P 9-2
Prepare journal entries, computations, and a financial position summary (unrealized profits)

A summary of the assets and equities of Pot Corporation and its 80 percent-owned subsidiary, Sea Corporation, at December 31, 2011, is given as follows (in thousands):

	Pot	**Sea**
Assets	$1,600	$700
Investment in Sea (80%)	400	—
Total assets	$2,000	$700
Liabilities	$ 300	$200
Capital stock	1,200	400
Retained earnings	500	100
Total equities	$2,000	$700

On January 2, 2012, Sea acquired a 70 percent interest in Toy Corporation for $294,000. Toy's net assets of $400,000 were recorded at fair values on this date. The equity of Toy on December 31, 2011, consisted of $300,000 capital stock and $100,000 retained earnings.

Data on operations of the affiliates for 2012 are as follows (in thousands):

	Separate Earnings	Dividends	Unrealized Profit Included in Separate Earnings
Pot	$300	$100	$20
Sea	100	60	—
Toy	60	20	10

Pot Corporation's $20,000 unrealized profit resulted from the sale of land to Toy. Toy's unrealized profit is from sales of merchandise items to Sea and is included in Sea's inventory at December 31, 2012.

REQUIRED

1. Prepare all journal entries required on the books of Pot and Sea to account for their investments for 2012 on an equity basis. The excess of fair value over book value is goodwill.

2. Compute the net incomes of Pot and Sea, and total noncontrolling interest share for 2012.

3. Prepare a schedule showing the assets and equities of Pot, Sea, and Toy on December 31, 2012, assuming liabilities of $300,000, $200,000, and $100,000 for Pot, Sea, and Toy, respectively.

P 9-3
Financial statement workpaper (goodwill and unrealized profits)

Comparative financial statements for Pen Corporation and its subsidiaries, Sir and Tip Corporations, for the year ended December 31, 2011, are as follows (in thousands):

	Pen	Sir	Tip
Income and Retained Earnings Statement for the Year Ended December 31			
Sales	$500	$300	$100
Income from Sir	72	—	—
Income from Tip	12.5	10	—
Cost of sales	(240)	(150)	(60)
Other expenses	(160)	(70)	(15)
Net income	184.5	90	25
Add: Beginning retained earnings	115.5	160	45
Deduct: Dividends	(80)	(40)	(10)
Ending retained earnings	$220	$210	$ 60
Balance Sheet at December 31			
Cash	$ 67	$ 36	$ 10
Accounts receivable—net	70	50	20
Inventories	110	75	35
Plant and equipment—net	140	425	115
Investment in Sir (80%)	508	—	—
Investment in Tip (50%)	95	—	—
Investment in Tip (40%)	—	74	—
Total assets	$990	$660	$180
Accounts payable	$ 70	$ 40	$ 15
Other liabilities	100	10	5
Capital stock	600	400	100
Retained earnings	220	210	60
Total equities	$990	$660	$180

ADDITIONAL INFORMATION

1. Pen acquired its 80 percent interest in Sir Corporation for $420,000 on January 2, 2009, when Sir had capital stock of $400,000 and retained earnings of $100,000. The excess fair value over book value acquired relates to equipment that had a remaining useful life of four years from January 1, 2009.

2. Pen acquired its 50 percent interest in Tip Corporation for $75,000 on July 1, 2009, when Tip's equity consisted of $100,000 capital stock and $20,000 retained earnings. Sir acquired its 40 percent interest in Tip on December 31, 2010, for $68,000, when Tip's capital stock was $100,000 and its retained earnings were $45,000. The difference between fair value and book value acquired is due to goodwill.

3. Although Pen and Sir use the equity method in accounting for their investments, they do not apply the method to intercompany profits or to differences between fair value and book value acquired.

4. At December 31, 2010, the inventory of Sir included inventory items acquired from Pen at a profit of $8,000. This merchandise was sold during 2011.

5. Tip sold merchandise that had cost $30,000 to Sir for $50,000 during 2011. All of this merchandise is held by Sir at December 31, 2011. Sir owes Tip $10,000 on this merchandise.

REQUIRED: Prepare a consolidation workpaper for the year ended December 31, 2011.

P 9-4
Computations for mutually-held subsidiaries

A schedule of intercompany investment interests and separate earnings for Par Corporation, Sit Corporation, and Tot Corporation is presented as follows:

	Percentage Interest in Sit	Percentage Interest in Tot	Separate Earnings Current Year
Par Corporation	80%	50%	$200,000
Sit Corporation	—	20	100,000
Tot Corporation	10	—	50,000

REQUIRED

1. Compute controlling interest share and noncontrolling interest share of consolidated net income assuming no investment differences between fair value and book value or unrealized profits.

2. Compute controlling interest share and noncontrolling interest share assuming $10,000 unrealized inventory profits on Tot's sales to Sit and a $20,000 gain on Par's sale of land to Sit.

P 9-5
Financial statement workpaper (treasury stock approach)

Pin Corporation acquired a 90 percent interest in Sun Corporation for $360,000 cash on January 2, 2009, when Sun had capital stock of $200,000 and retained earnings of $150,000. Sun purchased its 10 percent interest in Pin in 2010 for $80,000. The excess of Pin's investment fair value over book value acquired is due to goodwill.

Financial statements for the year ended December 31, 2013, are as follows (in thousands):

	Pin	Sun
Combined Income and Retained Earnings Statement for the Year Ended December 31		
Sales	$400	$100
Investment income	27	—
Dividend income	—	10
Cost of goods sold	(200)	(50)
Expenses	(50)	(30)
Net income	177	30
Add: Beginning retained earnings	300	200
Deduct: Dividends	(100)	(20)
Retained earnings December 31	$377	$210
Balance Sheet at December 31		
Other assets	$486	$420
Investment in Sun (90%)	414	—
Investment in Pin (10%)	—	80
Total assets	$900	$500
Liabilities	$123	$ 90
Capital stock	400	200
Retained earnings	377	210
Total equities	$900	$500

REQUIRED: Prepare a consolidation workpaper using the treasury stock approach.

P 9-6
Consolidation workpaper second year (conventional approach)

Par Corporation acquired an 80 percent interest in Sip Corporation for $180,000 cash on January 1, 2011, when Sip had capital stock of $50,000 and retained earnings of $150,000. The excess of fair value over book value acquired is due to a patent, which is being amortized over five years. Sip purchased its 20 percent interest in Par at book value on January 2, 2011, for $100,000.

Financial statements for the year ended December 31, 2012, are summarized as follows:

	Par	Sip
Combined Income and Retained Earnings Statement for the Year Ended December 31		
Sales	$140,000	$100,000
Income from Sip	28,000	—
Dividend income	—	4,000
Gain on sale of land	—	3,000
Expenses	(80,000)	(60,000)
Net income	88,000	47,000
Add: Beginning retained earnings	405,710	180,000
Deduct: Dividends	(16,000)	(20,000)
Retained earnings December 31	$477,710	$207,000
Balance Sheet at December 31		
Other assets	$448,000	$157,000
Investment in Sip (80%)	109,710	—
Investment in Par (20%)	—	100,000
Total assets	$557,710	$257,000
Capital stock	$ 80,000	$ 50,000
Retained earnings	477,710	207,000
Total equities	$557,710	$257,000

ADDITIONAL INFORMATION

1. Par's separate earnings and dividends for 2012 were $60,000 and $20,000, respectively. Sip's separate earnings and dividends in 2012 were $40,000 and $20,000, respectively.

2. Sip sold land to an outside interest for $7,000 on January 3, 2012, that it purchased from Par on January 3, 2011, for $4,000. The land had originally cost Par $2,000.

REQUIRED: Prepare consolidation workpaper entries and a consolidation workpaper for Par Corporation and Subsidiary at December 31, 2012, using the conventional approach for the mutual holding.

P 9-7
Computations and entries (parent stock mutually-held)

Pan Corporation purchased an 80 percent interest in Set for $340,000 on January 1, 2011, when Set's equity was $400,000. The excess of fair value over book value is due to goodwill.

At December 31, 2012, the balance of Pan's Investment in Set account is $416,000, and the stockholders' equity of the two corporations is as follows:

	Pan	Set
Capital stock	$1,200,000	$300,000
Retained earnings	400,000	200,000
Total	$1,600,000	$500,000

On January 2, 2013, Set acquires a 10 percent interest in Pan for $160,000. Earnings and dividends for 2013 are:

	Pan	Set
Separate earnings	$200,000	$80,000
Dividends	100,000	40,000

REQUIRED

1. Compute controlling and noncontrolling interest shares of consolidated net income for 2013 using the conventional approach.

2. Prepare journal entries to account for Pan's investment in Set for 2013 under the equity method (conventional approach).

3. Prepare journal entries on Set's books to account for its investment in Pan under the equity method (conventional approach).

4. Compute Pan's and Set's net incomes for 2013.

5. Determine the balances of Pan's and Set's investment accounts on December 31, 2013.

6. Determine the total stockholders' equity of Pan and Set on December 31, 2013.

7. Compute the noncontrolling interest in Set on December 31, 2013.

8. Prepare the adjusting and eliminating entries needed to consolidate the financial statements of Pan and Set for the year ended December 31, 2013.

INTERNET ASSIGNMENT

Pepsi-Cola and *Frito-Lay* Corporations merged in 1965 to form PepsiCo, Inc. Among PepsiCo's more recent merger and acquisition activity are deals with *Tropicana Products* and *Quaker Oats*. Visit the Web site of PepsiCo (*www.pepsico.com*) and review the corporate history file. Prepare a list of well-known companies controlled by PepsiCo in father-son-grandson type indirect holdings.

REFERENCES TO THE AUTHORITATIVE LITERATURE

[1] FASB ASC 325-20-35-4. Originally *Accounting Principles Board Opinion No. 18*. "The Equity Method of Accounting for Investments in Common Stock." New York: American Institute of Certified Public Accountants, 1971.

[2] FASB ASC 810-10-45-1. Originally AICPA Committee on Accounting Procedure. *Accounting Research Bulletin No. 51*. "Consolidated Financial Statements." New York: American Institute of Certified Public Accountants, 1959.

[3] FASB ASC 323-10-35-15. Originally *Accounting Principles Board Opinion No. 18*. "The Equity Method of Accounting for Investments in Common Stock." New York: American Institute of Certified Public Accountants, 1971.

10 CHAPTER

Subsidiary Preferred Stock, Consolidated Earnings per Share, and Consolidated Income Taxation

This chapter covers three miscellaneous topics related to consolidation: consolidation of a subsidiary with preferred stock in its capital structure, consolidated earnings per share, and accounting for income taxes of consolidated entities. These topics tend to be detailed and technical, and the illustrations often use simplifying assumptions to minimize details and emphasize significant concepts and relationships. An intermediate accounting background in all three areas is assumed.

SUBSIDIARIES WITH PREFERRED STOCK OUTSTANDING

LEARNING OBJECTIVE 1

Many modern corporations have complex capital structures, including various categories of preferred stock issued by the parent, a subsidiary, or both. For example, in its 2009 annual report, the **Dow Chemical Company** reports $1 billion in "Preferred Securities of Subsidiaries." Note U to the consolidated financial statements provides some additional detail (in millions):

Note U—Preferred Securities of Subsidiaries

The following transactions were entered into for the purpose of providing diversified sources of funds to the Company.

In July 1999, Tornado Finance V.O.F., a consolidated foreign subsidiary of the Company, issued $500 million of preferred securities in the form of preferred partnership units. The units provide a distribution of 7.965 percent, may be redeemed in 2009 or thereafter, and may be called at any time by the subsidiary. On June 4, 2009, the preferred partner notified Tornado Finance V.O.F. that the preferred partnership units would be redeemed in full on July 9, 2009, as permitted by the terms of the partnership agreement. On July 9, 2009, the preferred partnership units and accrued dividends were redeemed for a total of $520 million. Upon redemption, Tornado Finance V.O.F. was dissolved. The preferred partnership units were previously classified as "Preferred Securities of Subsidiaries" in the consolidated balance sheets. The distributions were included in "Net income attributable to noncontrolling interests" in the consolidated statements of income.

In September 2001, Hobbes Capital S.A., a consolidated foreign subsidiary of the Company, issued $500 million of preferred securities in the form of equity certificates. The certificates provide a floating rate of return (that could be reinvested) based on LIBOR. During the third quarter of 2008, the other partner of Hobbes redeemed its

$674 million ownership in Hobbes. The minority ownership was redeemed in a non-cash transaction in exchange for a three-year note payable with a floating rate based on LIBOR. Prior to redemption, the equity certificates of $500 million were classified as "Preferred Securities of Subsidiaries" and the reinvested preferred returns were included in "Noncontrolling interests" in the consolidated balance sheets. The preferred return was included in "Net income attributable to noncontrolling interests" in the consolidated statements of income.

The existence of preferred stock in the capital structure of a subsidiary complicates the consolidation process, but the basic procedures do not change. Parent/investor accounting under the equity method is also affected when an investee has preferred stock outstanding. The complications stem from the need to consider the contractual rights of preferred stockholders in allocating the investee's equity and income between preferred and common stock components.

Most preferred stock issues are cumulative, nonparticipating, and nonvoting. In addition, preferred stocks usually have preference rights in liquidation and frequently are callable at prices in excess of the par or liquidating values. We allocate net income of an investee with preferred stock outstanding first to preferred stockholders based on the preferred stock contract and then the remainder to common stockholders. Similarly, we first allocate the stockholders' equity of an investee to preferred stockholders based on the preferred stock contract, and then we allocate the remainder to common stockholders.

When preferred stock has a call or redemption price, we use this amount in allocating the investee's equity to preferred stockholders. In the absence of a redemption provision, we base the equity allocated to preferred stock on par value of the stock plus any liquidation premium. In addition, we include any dividends in arrears on cumulative preferred stock in the equity allocated to preferred stockholders. For nonparticipating preferred stock, we assign income to preferred stockholders on the basis of the preference rate or amount. If the preferred stock is cumulative and nonparticipating, the current year's income assigned to the preferred stockholders is the current year's dividend requirement, irrespective of whether the directors declare only current-year dividends, current-year dividends plus prior-year arrearages, or no dividends at all. We assign income to noncumulative, nonparticipating preferred stock only if dividends are declared and only in the amount declared.

Subsidiary with Preferred Stock Not Held by Parent

Assume that Poe Corporation purchases 90 percent of Sol Corporation's outstanding common stock for $396,000 on January 1, 2012, and that Sol Corporation's stockholders' equity on December 31, 2011, was as follows:

$10 preferred stock, $100 par, cumulative, nonparticipating, callable at $105 per share	$100,000
Common stock, $10 par	200,000
Other paid-in capital	40,000
Retained earnings	160,000
Total stockholders' equity	$500,000

There were no preferred dividends in arrears as of January 1, 2012. During 2012, Sol reported net income of $50,000 and paid dividends of $30,000 ($20,000 on common and $10,000 on preferred). Sol's assets and liabilities were stated at fair values equal to book values when Poe acquired its interest, so any excess of fair value over book value is goodwill.

In comparing the price paid for the 90 percent interest in Sol with the book value of the interest acquired, we separate Sol's December 31, 2011, equity into its preferred and common stock components:

Stockholders' equity of Sol	$500,000
Less: Preferred stockholders' equity (1,000 shares × $105 per share call price)	105,000
Common stockholders' equity	$395,000

We compare the price paid for 90 percent of the common equity of Sol with the book value (and fair value) acquired to determine goodwill. The implied total fair value is $440,000 ($396,000 ÷ 90%):

Fair value	$440,000
Less book value	395,000
Goodwill	$ 45,000

Sol's $50,000 net income for 2012 is allocated $10,000 to preferred stock (1,000 shares × $10 per share) and $40,000 to common stock. The entries to account for Poe's investment in Sol for 2012 are:

January 1

Investment in Sol common (+A)	396,000	
Cash (−A)		396,000
To record acquisition of 90% of Sol's common stock.		

During Year

Cash (+A)	18,000	
Investment in Sol common (−A)		18,000
To reduce Investment in Sol for dividends received		
($20,000 × 90%).		

December 31

Investment in Sol common (+A)	36,000	
Income from Sol (R, +SE)		36,000
To record equity in Sol's income.		

In consolidating the financial statements for 2012 (see Exhibit 10-1), we assign Sol's $520,000 equity at December 31, 2012, to preferred and common components as follows:

Total stockholders' equity	$520,000
Less: Preferred stockholders' equity (1,000 shares × $105	
call price per share)	105,000
Common stockholders' equity	$415,000

Noncontrolling Interest in Preferred Stock The *noncontrolling interest* in Sol at December 31, 2012, consists of 100 percent of the preferred stockholders' equity and 10 percent of the common stockholders' equity, or $151,000 [($105,000 × 100%) + ($415,000 × 10%)] plus 10 percent of the implied $45,000 goodwill. Similarly, *noncontrolling interest share* for 2012 consists of 100 percent of the income to preferred stockholders and 10 percent of the income to common stockholders, or $14,000 [($10,000 × 100%) + ($40,000 × 10%)]. This information is reflected in the consolidation workpaper for Poe Corporation and Subsidiary in Exhibit 10-1.

Except for workpaper entries a and e the entries are similar to those encountered in earlier chapters. Entry a is reproduced in journal form as follows:

a	Preferred stock—Sol (−SE)	100,000	
	Retained earnings—Sol (−SE)	5,000	
	Noncontrolling interest—preferred (+SE)		105,000

Entry a reclassifies the preferred stockholders' equity as a noncontrolling interest. The $105,000 preferred equity at the beginning of the period exceeded the $100,000 par value, so we debit the $5,000 excess to Sol's retained earnings. We make this debit to Sol's retained earnings because the preferred stockholders have a maximum claim on Sol's retained earnings for the $5,000 call premium.

The consolidated income statement of Exhibit 10-1 shows separate deductions for noncontrolling interest share applicable to preferred ($10,000) and common stock ($4,000). This division is helpful in preparing a workpaper, but a consolidated income statement prepared from the

EXHIBIT 10-1

Preferred and Common
Stock in the Affiliation
Structure

POE CORPORATION AND SUBSIDIARY CONSOLIDATION WORKPAPER FOR THE YEAR ENDED DECEMBER 31, 2012 (IN THOUSANDS)

	Poe	90% Sol	Adjustments and Eliminations Debits	Adjustments and Eliminations Credits	Consolidated Statements
Income Statement Sales	$ 618	$300			$ 918
Income from Sol (common)	36		b 36		
Expenses including cost of sales	(450)	(250)			(700)
Noncontrolling interest share (common) ($40 × 10%)			d 4		(4)
Noncontrolling interest share (preferred) ($10 × 100%)			e 10		(10)
Controlling share of net income	**$ 204**	**$ 50**			**$ 204**
Retained Earnings Statement Retained earnings—Poe	$ 300				$ 300
Retained earnings—Sol		$160	a 5 c 155		
Dividends (common)	(100)	(20)		b 18 d 2	(100)
Dividends (preferred)		(10)		e 10	
Controlling share of net income	**204**	**50**			**204**
Retained earnings—December 31	**$ 404**	**$180**			**$ 404**
Balance Sheet Other assets	$1,290	$600			$1,890
Investment in Sol (common)	414			b 18 c 396	
Goodwill			c 45		45
	$1,704	$600			$1,935
Liabilities	$ 200	$ 80			$ 280
Preferred stock—Sol		100	a 100		
Common stock	1,000	200	c 200		1,000
Other paid-in capital	100	40	c 40		100
Retained earnings	**404**	**180**			**404**
	$1,704	$600			
Noncontrolling interest: Preferred, January 1 Common, January 1				a 105 c 44 d 2	151
					$1,935

workpaper would ordinarily show noncontrolling interest share as one amount. Also, Exhibit 10-1 shows total noncontrolling interest in Sol at December 31, 2012, on one line of the consolidated balance sheet in the single amount of $151,000. Although the consolidation workpaper contains the information to separate this amount into preferred and common components, the separation is ordinarily not used for financial reporting, because we eliminate all individual subsidiary equity accounts in the consolidation process.[1] Consolidated financial statements are intended primarily for the stockholders and creditors of the parent, and we do not expect that the noncontrolling stockholders could benefit significantly from the information contained in them.

Subsidiary Preferred Stock Acquired by Parent

A parent's purchase of the outstanding preferred stock of a subsidiary results in a retirement of the stock purchased from the viewpoint of the consolidated entity. The stock is retired for consolidated statement purposes because its book value no longer appears as a noncontrolling interest in the consolidated balance sheet. However, the retirement is really a constructive retirement because we report the investment in preferred (parent) and the preferred stock equity (subsidiary) as outstanding in the financial statements of the parent and subsidiary.

We report the constructive retirement of subsidiary preferred stock through purchase by the parent as an actual retirement in the consolidated statements. That is, we eliminate the equity related to the preferred stock held by the parent and the investment in preferred stock, and we debit or credit any difference to the additional paid-in capital that would otherwise be reported in the consolidated balance sheet.[2] Parent stockholders' equity in a one-line consolidation is equal to consolidated stockholders' equity, so comparable accounting requires that the parent adjust its investment in subsidiary preferred stock to its book value at acquisition and debit or credit its additional paid-in capital for the difference between the price paid for the investment and its underlying book value. We account for the investment in preferred stock on the basis of its book value, not on the basis of the cost or equity method.

CONSTRUCTIVE RETIREMENT OF SUBSIDIARY PREFERRED STOCK Sol Corporation experiences a net loss of $40,000 in 2013 and pays no dividends. Its stockholders' equity decreases from $520,000 at December 31, 2012 (see Exhibit 10-1), to $480,000 at December 31, 2013. Poe's 90 percent investment in Sol decreases from $414,000 at year-end 2012 to $369,000 at year-end 2013. The $45,000 decrease in Poe's Investment in Sol common account is as follows:

Net loss of Sol	$40,000
Add: Income to preferred[3] (1,000 shares × $10)	10,000
Loss to common	50,000
Poe's ownership interest	90%
Loss from Sol for 2013	$45,000

We verify the $369,000 investment in Sol common at December 31, 2013, as follows:

Stockholders' equity of Sol, December 31, 2013	$480,000
Less: Preferred stockholders' equity [1,000 shares × ($105 per share call price + $10 per share dividend arrearage)]	115,000
Common stockholders' equity, December 31, 2013	365,000
Poe's ownership interest	90%
Share of Sol's common stockholders' equity	328,500
Add: Goodwill ($45,000 × 90%)	40,500
Investment in Sol common, December 31, 2013	$369,000

On January 1, 2014, Poe responded to the depressed price of Sol's preferred stock and purchased 800 shares (an 80% interest) at $100 per share. The $80,000 price paid is less than the

---

[1]Noncontrolling interest in a subsidiary's preferred stock is sometimes reported as outstanding stock of the consolidated entity with notation of the name of the issuing corporation. This reporting practice is usually confined to regulated companies.

[2]Parent's retained earnings are reduced when additional paid-in capital is insufficient to absorb an excess of purchase price over book value.

[3]A deduction of cumulative preferred dividends in computing income to common stockholders is required by GAAP [1], regardless of whether such dividends are declared.

$92,000 book value of the stock that is constructively retired ($115,000 × 80%), so Poe records the investment in Sol preferred as follows:

Investment in Sol preferred (+A)	80,000	
Cash (−A)		80,000
To record purchase of 80% of Sol's preferred stock.		
Investment in Sol preferred (+A)	12,000	
Other paid-in capital (+SE)		12,000
To adjust other paid-in capital to reflect the constructive retirement.		

Sol reports net income of $20,000 for 2014, but it again passes dividends for the year. Poe accounts for its investments during 2014 as follows:

Investment in Sol preferred (+A)	8,000	
Income from Sol preferred (R, +SE)		8,000
To record 80% of the $10,000 increase in Sol's preferred dividend arrearage.		
Investment in Sol common (+A)	9,000	
Income from Sol common (R, +SE)		9,000
To record equity in Sol's income to common [($20,000 net income − $10,000 preferred income) × 90%].		

A summary of Sol's preferred and common stockholders' equity and Poe's investment-account balances at the end of 2014 follows:

Sol's Stockholders' Equity, December 31, 2014	
Total stockholders' equity ($480,000 on January 1 plus $20,000 net income)	$500,000
Less: Preferred stockholders' equity [1,000 shares × ($105 call price + $20 dividends in arrears)]	125,000
Common stockholders' equity	$375,000
Poe's Investment Accounts, December 31, 2014	
Investment in Sol preferred ($125,000 preferred equity × 80% owned)	$100,000
Investment in Sol common [($375,000 common equity × 90%) + ($45,000 goodwill × 90%)]	$378,000

This information for 2014 is reflected in a consolidation workpaper for Poe and Sol Corporations in Exhibit 10-2.

The workpaper entries for 2014 are similar to those in Exhibit 10-1 for 2012, except for items related to the investment in Sol's preferred stock. Procedures to eliminate the preferred equity and investment accounts parallel those for common stock. First, we eliminate Poe's income from Sol preferred against the investment in Sol preferred. This workpaper entry (entry a) reduces the Investment in Sol preferred account to its $92,000 adjusted balance at January 1, 2014. Next, we eliminate the investment in Sol preferred and the preferred equity of Sol as of January 1, 2014, in workpaper entry b. This entry also enters the preferred noncontrolling interest as of the beginning of the year. Entries a and b in journal form follow:

a	Income from Sol preferred (−R, −SE)	8,000	
	Investment in Sol preferred (−A)		8,000
b	Preferred stock—Sol (−SE)	100,000	
	Retained earnings—Sol (−SE)	15,000	
	Investment in Sol preferred (−A)		92,000
	Noncontrolling interest in Sol preferred (+SE)		23,000

POE CORPORATION AND SUBSIDIARY CONSOLIDATION WORKPAPER FOR THE YEAR ENDED DECEMBER 31, 2014 (IN THOUSANDS)						EXHIBIT 10-2

EXHIBIT 10-2

Parent Company Holds
Subsidiary's Common
and Preferred Stock

	Poe	90% Sol	Adjustments and Eliminations		Consolidated Statements
			Debits	Credits	
Income Statement Sales	$ 690	$280			$ 970
Income from Sol (common)	9		c 9		
Income from Sol (preferred)	8		a 8		
Expenses including cost of sales	(583)	(260)			(843)
Noncontrolling interest share (common) ($10 × 10%)			e 1		(1)
Noncontrolling interest share (preferred) ($10 × 20%)			f 2		(2)
Controlling share of net income	**$ 124**	**$ 20**			**$ 124**
Retained Earnings Statement Retained earnings—Poe	$ 458				$ 458
Retained earnings—Sol		$140	b 15 d 125		
Dividends (common)	(70)	—			(70)
Controlling share of net income	**124**	**20**			**124**
Retained earnings—December 31	**$ 512**	**$160**			**$ 512**
Balance Sheet Other assets	$1,334	$600			$1,934
Investment in Sol (common)	378			c 9 d 369	
Investment in Sol (preferred)	100			a 8 b 92	
Goodwill (common)			d 45		45
	$1,812	$600			$1,979
Liabilities	$ 188	$100			$ 288
Preferred stock—Sol		100	b 100		
Common stock	1,000	200	d 200		1,000
Other paid-in capital	112	40	d 40		112
Retained earnings	**512**	**160**			**512**
	$1,812	$600			
Noncontrolling interest: Preferred, January 1 Common, January 1				b 23 d 41 e 1 f 2	67
					$1,979

The only difference is that we now have entries for preferred stock. The remaining entries (c through f) are similar to those for consolidations involving common stock only.

The workpaper in Exhibit 10-2 shows Poe Corporation's net income equal to the controlling share of consolidated net income and its stockholders' equity equal to consolidated stockholders' equity. These equalities result from parent entries to adjust the preferred stock investment account to its underlying equity at acquisition and to accrue dividend arrearages on cumulative preferred stock.

PREFERRED STOCK INVESTMENT MAINTAINED ON COST BASIS If the constructive retirement were *not* recorded by Poe at the time of purchase, the Investment in Sol preferred account would remain at its $80,000 cost throughout 2014, and we would recognize no preferred income. In this case, the consolidation workpaper entry to eliminate the preferred investment and equity amounts would be:

Retained earnings—Sol (−SE)	15,000	
Preferred stock—Sol (−SE)	100,000	
Investment in Sol preferred (−A)		80,000
Noncontrolling interest in Sol preferred (+SE)		23,000
Other paid-in capital—Poe (+SE)		12,000

To eliminate reciprocal preferred equity and investment amounts, establish noncontrolling interest at the beginning of the period (20% × $115,000 beginning book value of preferred), and adjust Poe's other paid-in capital account for the difference between the purchase price and underlying book value of the preferred stock.

COMPARISON OF COST METHOD AND CONSTRUCTIVE RETIREMENT The consolidated financial statements will be the same whether the investment in preferred stock remains at its original cost or is adjusted to book value in the parent's books. However, by adjusting the parent's additional paid-in capital for the constructive retirement of subsidiary preferred stock, we avoid further paid-in capital adjustments in the consolidation process. Under the cost method, we need a workpaper entry to adjust additional paid-in capital each time we consolidate parent and subsidiary statements.

PARENT AND CONSOLIDATED EARNINGS PER SHARE

LEARNING OBJECTIVE **2**

GAAP requires that all firms calculate and report basic and diluted (where applicable) earnings per share (EPS). Consolidated entities disclose EPS on a consolidated basis. For example, the consolidated statement of income included in the 2009 annual report of *The Hershey Company* reports:

The Hershey Company

Net income per share—Basic—Common stock	$ 1.97
Net income per share—Basic—Class B common stock	$ 1.77
Net income per share—Diluted—Common stock	$ 1.90
Net income per share—Diluted—Class B common stock	$ 1.77

Note 16 to the statements is titled "Capital Stock and Net Income per Share," and it describes the calculations in detail (pp. 86–89).

Similarly, the *PepsiCo* 2009 annual report discloses basic earnings per common share of $3.81 and earnings per common share assuming dilution of $3.77. Both amounts appear on the face of the income statement, and Pepsi reports these amounts on a consolidated basis.

A parent's net income and EPS under the equity method are equal to the controlling share of consolidated net income and controlling share of consolidated EPS. However, the computational differences in determining parent and consolidated net income (that is, one-line consolidation versus consolidation) do not extend to EPS calculations. Parent and controlling share of consolidated EPS calculations are identical. EPS procedures for equity investors who are able to exercise significant influence over investees are the same as those for parent investors.[4]

---

[4]The provisions of GAAP [2] on Earnings per Share that apply to subsidiaries also apply to investments accounted for by the equity method.

Parent procedures for computing EPS depend on the subsidiary's capital structure. When the subsidiary (or equity investee) has *no* potentially dilutive securities, the procedures applied in computing consolidated EPS are the same as for separate entities. When the subsidiary does have potentially dilutive securities outstanding, however, the potential dilution has to be considered in computing the parent's diluted EPS.

We compute basic EPS the same way for a consolidated entity as for separate entities (assuming the equity method is used). The nature of the adjustment to parent EPS calculations depends on whether the subsidiary's potentially dilutive securities are convertible into subsidiary or parent common stock. If convertible into subsidiary common stock, we reflect the potential dilution in subsidiary EPS computations, which are then used in determining parent (and consolidated) EPS. If the dilutive securities of the subsidiary are convertible into parent company common stock, we treat them as parent dilutive securities and include them directly in computing the parent EPS [3]. In this latter case, we do not need (or use) subsidiary EPS computations in parent EPS computations.

General formats for EPS calculations in these situations are summarized in Exhibit 10-3 for diluted EPS. The first column of Exhibit 10-3 shows parent computations for diluted EPS when the subsidiary has no potentially dilutive securities. In this case, EPS computations are the same as those for unrelated entities, and no adjustments are necessary for subsidiary income included in parent income, provided that the parent applies the equity method correctly.

Dilutive Securities of Subsidiary Convertible into Subsidiary Shares

The second column of Exhibit 10-3 summarizes parent EPS computations when subsidiary potentially dilutive securities are convertible into subsidiary common shares. We adjust diluted earnings

---

EXHIBIT 10-3

Parent-Company and Consolidated Diluted EPS Calculations

	Subsidiary Does Not Have Potentially Dilutive Securities Outstanding	Subsidiary Has Potentially Dilutive Securities Convertible into Subsidiary Common Stock	Subsidiary Has Potentially Dilutive Securities Convertible into Parent-Company Common Stock
Numerator in Dollars ($)			
Income to parent's common stockholders	$$$	$$$	$$$
Add: Adjustments for parent's dilutive securities	+$	+$	+$
Add: Adjustments for subsidiary's potentially dilutive securities convertible into parent-company stock	NA	NA	+$
Replacement calculation (must result in a net decrease)			
Deduct: Parent's equity in subsidiary's realized income	NA	−$	NA
Add: Parent's equity in subsidiary's diluted earnings	NA	+$	NA
Parent's diluted earnings = a	$$$	$$$	$$$
Denominator in Shares (Y)			
Parent's common shares outstanding	YYY	YYY	YYY
Add: Shares represented by parent's potentially dilutive securities	+Y	+Y	+Y
Add: Shares represented by subsidiary's potentially dilutive securities convertible into parent-company common shares	NA	NA	+Y
Parent's common shares and common share equivalents = b	YYY	YYY	YYY
Parent-Company and Consolidated Diluted EPS	a/b	a/b	a/b

NA—Not applicable.

of the parent (the numerators of the EPS calculations) by excluding the parent's **equity in subsidiary realized income** and replacing that equity with the parent's share of diluted earnings of the subsidiary.

Parent's equity in subsidiary realized income is the parent's percentage interest in reported income of the subsidiary adjusted for the effects of intercompany profits from upstream sales and constructive gains or losses of the subsidiary. This adjustment to remove the potential dilution from the parent's diluted earnings is based on separate EPS computations for the subsidiary. We make these computations of subsidiary EPS only for the purpose of calculating the parent's EPS, and they are not necessarily the same as those prepared by the subsidiary for its own external reporting.

Note that "parent's equity in subsidiary's realized income" in column 2 of Exhibit 10-3 differs from "parent's income from subsidiary," which includes amortization of valuation differentials and the income effects of all intercompany transactions. The parent's investment valuation differentials, unrealized profits from downstream sales, and constructive gains and losses assigned to the parent do not affect the equity of the subsidiary's security holders; therefore, we exclude these items from the replacement calculation.

We use the subsidiary's diluted EPS in determining diluted earnings of the parent (see column 2 of Exhibit 10-3), so EPS computations for the subsidiary (based on subsidiary realized income) are made as a first step in computing the parent's EPS. In computing the subsidiary's diluted earnings, we eliminate unrealized profits of the subsidiary and include constructive gains and losses of the subsidiary. We reflect the resulting EPS calculations of the subsidiary in the parent EPS calculation by replacing the "parent's equity in subsidiary's realized income" with the "parent's equity in subsidiary's diluted earnings." We determine the parent's equity in the subsidiary's diluted earnings by multiplying the subsidiary shares owned by the parent by the subsidiary's diluted EPS. This replacement allocates the subsidiary's realized income for EPS purposes to holders of the subsidiary's common stock and potentially dilutive securities, rather than only to the subsidiary's common stockholders.

Diluted Securities of Subsidiary Convertible into Parent Shares

Parent common shares (the denominators of EPSs) are identical in columns 1 and 2 of Exhibit 10-3 but increase in column 3 for subsidiary securities that are convertible into parent common stock. This adjustment in column 3 is necessary when the subsidiary's potentially dilutive securities are potentially dilutive securities of the parent rather than of the subsidiary. When potentially dilutive securities of a subsidiary are convertible into parent common stock, income attributable to these securities under the if-converted method must be added back in calculating the parent's diluted earnings. Thus, column 3 of Exhibit 10-3 includes the item "adjustment for subsidiary's dilutive securities convertible into parent common stock," which is not applicable when the subsidiary does not have potentially dilutive securities (column 1) or when such securities are convertible into subsidiary common stock (column 2).

SUBSIDIARY WITH CONVERTIBLE PREFERRED STOCK

Pan Corporation purchases 90 percent of Sad Corporation's outstanding voting common stock for $328,000 on January 1, 2011. On this date, the stockholders' equity of the two corporations consists of the following (in thousands):

	Pan	Sad
Common stock, $5 par, 200,000 shares issued and outstanding	$1,000	
Common stock, $10 par, 20,000 shares outstanding		$200
10% cumulative, convertible preferred stock, $100 par, 1,000 shares outstanding		100
Retained earnings	500	120
Total stockholders' equity	$1,500	$420

During 2011, Sad reports $50,000 net income and pays $25,000 dividends, $10,000 to preferred and $15,000 to common. Pan's net income for 2011 is $186,000, determined as follows:

Income from Pan's operations	$150,000
Income from Sad [(($50,000 net income − $10,000	
preferred income) × 90%]	36,000
Pan's net income	$186,000

Subsidiary Preferred Stock Convertible into Subsidiary Common Stock

Assume that Sad's preferred stock is convertible into 12,000 shares of Sad's common stock and that neither Pan nor Sad has other potentially dilutive securities outstanding. Sad's realized net income is $40,000. Sad's diluted EPS is $1.5625 [$50,000 earnings ÷ (20,000 common shares + 12,000 share dilution)], and Pan's diluted EPS is $0.89, computed as follows:

Net income of Pan (equal to income to common)	$186,000
Replacement of Pan's equity in Sad's realized	
income ($40,000 × 90%)	(36,000)
with Pan's equity in Sad's diluted earnings	
(18,000 shares of Sad × Sad's $1.5625 diluted EPS)	28,125
Pan's diluted earnings = a	$178,125
Pan's outstanding shares = b	200,000
Pan's diluted EPS = a ÷ b	$ 0.89

The $7,875 potential dilution reflected in Pan's diluted earnings results from replacing Pan's equity in Sad's realized income with Pan's equity in Sad's diluted earnings per share. Note that Pan's equity in Sad's realized income is $36,000, which is the same as Pan's income from Sad.

Subsidiary Preferred Stock Convertible into Parent Common Stock

Assume that Sad's preferred stock is convertible into 24,000 shares of Pan's common stock and that neither Pan nor Sad has other potentially dilutive securities outstanding. Sad's diluted EPS (not used in Pan's EPS computations) is $2 per share ($40,000 income to common ÷ 20,000 common shares outstanding) because the preferred stock is not a dilutive security of Sad Corporation. Pan's diluted EPS is computed as follows:

Net income of Pan (equal to income to common)	$186,000
Add: Income to preferred stockholders of Sad	
assumed to be converted (90 percent)	9,000
Pan's diluted earnings = a	$195,000
Pan's outstanding shares	200,000
Add: Sad's preferred shares assumed converted	24,000
Pan's common shares and common stock equivalents = b	224,000
Pan's diluted EPS = a ÷ b	$ 0.87

Preferred income is added to Pan's net income because we allocated no income to the preferred stock assumed to be converted.

SUBSIDIARY WITH OPTIONS AND CONVERTIBLE BONDS

Pad Corporation has $1,500,000 income from its own operations for 2011 and $300,000 income from Syd Corporation, its 80 percent-owned subsidiary. The $300,000 income from Syd consists of 80 percent of Syd's $450,000 net income for 2011, less 80 percent of a $50,000 unrealized gain on land purchased from Syd, less $20,000 (80%) amortization of the excess of fair value over the book value of Syd. The excess was assigned to a previously unrecognized patent. Assume the tax rate is 34 percent. Outstanding securities of the two corporations throughout 2011 are:

Pad: Common stock, 1,000,000 shares
Syd: Common stock, 400,000 shares
           Options to purchase 60,000 shares of stock at $10 per share (average
             market price is $15 per share)
           7% convertible bonds, $1,000,000 par outstanding, convertible into
             80,000 shares of common stock

Options and Bonds Convertible into Subsidiary Common Stock

Assume that the options are exercisable and the bonds are convertible into Syd's common stock. Exhibit 10-4 shows computations for Syd's diluted EPS. Under the treasury stock approach for options and warrants, the effect of options on EPS is dilutive when the average market price of the shares to which the options apply exceeds the exercise price. If holders of Syd's options had exercised rights to acquire 60,000 shares of Syd's common stock at $10 per share, Syd would have received $600,000 cash. Under the treasury stock approach, we assume Syd uses this cash to reacquire 40,000 shares of its own stock ($600,000 ÷ $15 average market price). This assumed exercise and repurchase of treasury shares increases Syd's outstanding common stock for EPS computations by 20,000 shares.

The convertible bonds must also be included in Syd's diluted EPS computations. Under the if-converted method, we include $46,200 net-of-tax interest in Syd's diluted earnings and include the 80,000 shares issuable upon conversion in calculating Syd's diluted common shares.

We use Syd's $0.89 diluted EPS in the EPS computations for Pad Corporation. Exhibit 10-5 shows computations for Pad's diluted EPS.

In the computation of Pad's diluted earnings, we replace Pad's equity in Syd's realized income ($320,000) with Pad's share of Syd's diluted earnings ($284,800). This replacement decreases Pad's diluted earnings by $35,200. This dilution results from allocating Syd's $400,000 realized income plus $46,200 net-of-tax interest effect from the convertible bonds to holders of Syd's common shares, options, and convertible bonds, rather than just to Syd's common stockholders.

Options and Convertible Bonds with Parent's Common Stock

Exhibit 10-6 presents computations for Pad's diluted EPS under the assumptions that Syd Corporation's options can be used to purchase 60,000 shares of Pad Corporation's common stock (a net new 20,000 shares under the Treasury Stock method as discussed above) and that Syd Corporation's bonds are convertible into 80,000 shares of Pad Corporation's common stock. Under these assumptions, we do not need Syd's diluted EPS in determining Pad's diluted EPS because we only use subsidiary EPS computations for replacement computations when subsidiary dilutive securities are convertible into subsidiary shares. The subsidiary dilutive securities are convertible into parent shares in this example, so we only need parent EPS computations.

LEARNING OBJECTIVE 3

INCOME TAXES OF CONSOLIDATED ENTITIES

This section of the chapter on accounting for income taxes of consolidated entities begins with a discussion of which companies may file consolidated tax returns, the advantages and disadvantages of filing consolidated tax returns, and the status of accounting pronouncements on income taxes. Temporary differences in consolidated and separate tax returns are discussed, and income tax allocation procedures are illustrated for a parent and subsidiary that file separate tax returns. Next, four cases compare consolidation procedures when a parent and subsidiary file separate tax returns with those necessary when filing a consolidated tax return. A final section looks at the tax basis of assets and liabilities acquired in an acquisition.

EXHIBIT 10-4

Subsidiary's Diluted EPS Computations

	Syd's Diluted EPS
Syd's income to common stockholders	$450,000
Less: Unrealized profit on sale of land	(50,000)
Add: Net-of-tax interest expense assuming subsidiary bonds converted into subsidiary shares ($1,000,000 × 7% × 66% assumed net-of-tax effect)	46,200
Subsidiary adjusted earnings = a	$446,200
Syd's common shares outstanding	400,000
Incremental shares assuming exercise of options [60,000 shares − ($600,000 proceeds from exercise of options ÷ $15 market price)]	20,000
Additional shares assuming bonds converted into subsidiary shares	80,000
Syd's adjusted shares = b	500,000
Syd's Diluted EPS = a ÷ b	$ 0.89

	Pad's Diluted EPS
Pad's income to common stockholders	$1,800,000
Replacement of Pad's $320,000 equity in Syd's realized income [($450,000 − $50,000 unrealized profit) × 80%]	(320,000)
with Pad's $284,800 equity in Syd's diluted EPS (320,000 shares × Syd's $0.89 diluted EPS)	284,800
Pad's adjusted earnings = a	$1,764,800
Pad's outstanding common shares = b	1,000,000
Pad's Diluted EPS = a ÷ b	$ 1.76

EXHIBIT 10-5

Parent's Diluted EPS Computations—Dilution Relates to Subsidiary Shares

Some consolidated entities prepare consolidated income tax returns and pay taxes on consolidated taxable income. Others prepare income tax returns for each affiliate and pay taxes on the taxable income included in the separate returns. The right of a consolidated entity to file a consolidated income tax return is contingent upon classification as an *affiliated group* under Sections 1501 through 1504 of the U.S. Internal Revenue Code (USIRC). An affiliated group exists when a common parent owns at least 80 percent of the voting power of all classes of stock and 80 percent or more of the total value of all outstanding stock of each of the includable corporations. The common parent must meet the 80 percent requirements directly for at least one includable corporation (USIRC 1504[a]).

A consolidated entity that is an affiliated group may elect to file consolidated income tax returns. All other consolidated entities *must* file separate income tax returns for each affiliate.

Note 1 to **Home Depot's** 2009 consolidated financial statements discusses its filing status as follows:

> *The Company and its eligible subsidiaries file a consolidated U.S. federal income tax return. Non-U.S. subsidiaries and certain U.S. subsidiaries, which are consolidated for financial reporting purposes, are not eligible to be included in the Company's consolidated U.S. federal income tax return. Separate provisions for income taxes have been determined for these entities. The Company intends to reinvest substantially all of the unremitted earnings of its non-U.S. subsidiaries and postpone their remittance indefinitely. Accordingly, no provision for U.S. income taxes for these non-U.S. subsidiaries was recorded in the accompanying Consolidated Statements of Earnings.*

Advantages of Filing Consolidated Tax Returns

The primary advantages of filing a consolidated return are as follows:

1. Losses of one affiliate are offset against income of other members of the group. However, loss carryforwards at the time of acquisition of an affiliate can be offset only against taxable income of the affiliate.

2. Intercorporate dividends are excluded from taxable income.

3. Intercompany profits are deferred from income until realized (but unrealized losses are also deferred until realized).

	Pad's Diluted EPS
Pad's income to common stockholders	$1,800,000
Add: Net-of-tax interest assuming subsidiary bonds converted into parent's common stock ($1,000,000 × 7% × 66% net-of-tax effect)	46,200
Pad's adjusted earnings = a	$1,846,200
Pad's outstanding shares	1,000,000
Incremental shares assuming options converted into Pad's shares [60,000 shares − ($600,000 proceeds from exercise of options ÷ $15 market price)]	20,000
Additional shares assuming subsidiary bonds are converted into Pad shares	80,000
Pad's adjusted shares = b	1,100,000
Pad's Diluted EPS = a ÷ b	$ 1.68

EXHIBIT 10-6

Parent's Diluted EPS Computations—Dilution Relates to Parent Shares

Exclusion of intercorporate dividends is not a unique advantage of filing a consolidated tax return, because a consolidated entity that is classified as an affiliated group is allowed a 100 percent exclusion on dividends received from members of the same group even if it elects not to file consolidated tax returns. In addition, corporate taxpayers can deduct 80 percent of the dividends received from domestic corporations that are 20 percent to 80 percent owned and can deduct 70 percent of the dividends received from domestic corporations that are less than 20 percent owned.

Disadvantages of Filing Consolidated Tax Returns

Consolidated entities that file consolidated tax returns lose some of the flexibility of entities that file separate returns. For example, each subsidiary included in a consolidated tax return must use the parent's taxable year. Different years can be used when filing separate returns. The election to file a consolidated return commits an entity to consolidated returns year after year. It is difficult to get permission to stop filing consolidated returns. Also, deconsolidated corporations cannot rejoin the affiliated group for five years.

INCOME TAX ALLOCATION

The objectives of accounting for income taxes under current GAAP [4] are to recognize the amount of taxes payable or refundable for the current year and to recognize deferred tax liabilities and assets for the future tax consequences of events that have been recognized in the financial statements or tax returns.

Events that have future tax consequences are designated *temporary differences* to separate them from events that do not have tax consequences, such as interest on municipal obligations. The tax consequences of temporary differences must be considered in the measurement of income for a period. Some accounting/income tax differences are the same, regardless of whether the affiliates file separate-entity or consolidated tax returns, whereas others depend on the kind of return filed. For example, unrealized and constructive gains and losses from intercompany transactions are temporary differences when filing separate returns because the individual entities are taxed on the income included in the separate returns. However, these items are *not* temporary differences when filing consolidated returns because adjustments to defer intercompany profits until realized are reflected in both the consolidation workpaper and the consolidated tax return.

Dividends received from members of an affiliated group are excluded from taxation regardless of whether affiliates file separate or consolidated returns, but dividends received from affiliates that are not members of an affiliated group are taxed currently, subject to the 80 percent dividends-received deduction.

Temporary Differences from Undistributed Earnings of Subsidiaries and Equity Investees

Accounting requirements under the equity method of accounting are generally the same for investments of 20 percent to 50 percent of the voting stock of an investee as for subsidiary investments. Investors pay income taxes currently on dividends received (distributed income) from equity investees and subsidiaries that are not members of an affiliated group, and GAAP requires investors to provide for deferred income taxes on their shares of undistributed income of their investees. That is, a temporary difference results when an investor's equity in its investees' income exceeds dividends received.

Under prior GAAP [5], the parent/investor could avoid the general presumption that all undistributed earnings will be transferred to the parent by showing that undistributed earnings of the subsidiary had been invested indefinitely. Current GAAP [6] amends prior standards to remove the exception and require the parent/investor to treat the undistributed income of their domestic subsidiaries as temporary differences unless the tax law provides a means by which the investment can be recovered tax free. An exception for undistributed earnings of foreign subsidiaries and foreign joint ventures remains.

In accounting for the *tax effect* of a temporary difference relating to income from equity investees, we do not use the one-line consolidation concept because we include investment income in the investor's income *before* income taxes—in other words, on a pretax basis. If undistributed earnings of an investee is the only temporary difference, a parent or equity investor provides for income taxes on its share of undistributed income by debiting income tax expense and crediting a deferred tax liability. The temporary difference related to undistributed earnings is, of course, only one of several possible differences that interact to produce the combined tax impact.

Accounting for Distributed and Undistributed Income

Assume that Par Corporation owns a 30 percent interest in Sea Corporation, a domestic corporation. Sea reports $600,000 net income for the current year and pays dividends of $200,000. An income tax rate of 34 percent applies. (The 34% tax rate is the *only* enacted tax rate applicable throughout this illustration.) We analyze Par's share of Sea's distributed and undistributed income as follows:

Share of distributed earnings (dividends) ($200,000 × 30%)	$ 60,000
Share of undistributed earnings (retained earnings increase) ($400,000 × 30%)	120,000
Equity in Sea's earnings ($600,000 × 30%)	$180,000

Par is taxed currently on 20 percent of the $60,000 dividends received because Sea is a domestic corporation that qualifies for the 80 percent dividends-received deduction. The income tax expense equals income tax liability for this part of Par's income from Sea. The current tax liability is $4,080 ($60,000 dividends received × 20% taxable × 34% tax rate).

No income tax is due currently on Par's share of Sea's undistributed earnings, but accounting standards require that we recognize income taxes attributable to that temporary difference as if the earnings had been remitted as dividends during the current period. Assuming that undistributed earnings is the only temporary difference, Par makes the following entry to provide for income taxes on its share of Sea's undistributed earnings:

December 31

Income tax expense (E, −SE)	8,160	
Deferred tax liability (+L)		8,160

To provide for taxes on undistributed earnings of
    Sea ($120,000 × 20% taxable × 34% rate).

The same procedures for income taxes on undistributed earnings apply to parent/investors, but not to dividends received from members of an affiliated group because we exclude 100 percent of those dividends from taxable income of the group.

Unrealized Gains and Losses from Intercompany Transactions

Unrealized and constructive gains and losses from intercompany transactions create temporary differences that may affect deferred tax calculations when filing separate income tax returns. (This is *not* true when filing consolidated tax returns.) In the case of an unrealized gain, the selling entity includes the gain in its separate tax return and pays the tax due on the transaction. We eliminate the unrealized gain in the consolidation process, so we defer the income taxes related to the gain. An unrealized loss is treated similarly.

We include the tax effects of temporary differences from unrealized gains and losses on intercompany transactions in measuring the income tax expense of the selling affiliate. Under this approach, the consolidated income tax expense is equal to the combined income tax expense of the consolidated entities, and we eliminate intercompany profit items on a gross basis. Similarly, this approach permits the parent/investor to eliminate intercompany profits on a gross, rather than a net-of-tax, basis. (When eliminating intercompany profits on a net-of-tax basis by the parent/ investor, we need a consolidation workpaper entry to convert the combined income tax expense of the affiliates into consolidated income tax expense and to adjust the deferred tax asset or liability amounts to a consolidated basis.)

Assume that Pet Corporation sells merchandise that cost $100,000 to Sal Corporation, its 75 percent-owned subsidiary, for $200,000, and that Sal still holds 70 percent of this merchandise at year-end. A 34 percent tax rate is applicable, and Pet pays $34,000 income tax on the transaction during the current year. Sal is a 75 percent-owned subsidiary, so we file separate tax returns. (Again, assume that the intercompany transaction is the only temporary difference and that the 34 percent tax rate is the only enacted rate.) Relevant consolidation and one-line consolidation entries are as follows:

Consolidation Workpaper Entries—Year of Sale		
Sales (−R, − SE)	**200,000**	
Cost of sales (−E, +SE)		**200,000**
To eliminate intercompany sales and cost of sales.		
Cost of sales (E, − SE)	**70,000**	
Inventory (−A)		**70,000**
To eliminate unrealized profit on intercompany merchandise remaining in inventory ($200,000 − $100,000) × 70%.		

Pet's One-Line Consolidation Entry—Year of Sale

Income from Sal (−R, −SE)	70,000	
Investment in Sal (−A)		70,000
To eliminate unrealized profit on sales to Sal ($70,000 unrealized profit × 100%).		

If Sal sells the merchandise in the next period, the consolidation and one-line consolidation entries in that year will be:

Consolidation Workpaper Entry—Year of Realization		
Investment in Sal (+A)	**70,000**	
Cost of sales (−E, +SE)		**70,000**
To recognize previously deferred profit on inventory and to adjust Pet's beginning Investment in Sal account to reflect realization.		

Pet's One-Line Consolidation Entry—Year of Realization

Investment in Sal (+A)	70,000	
Income from Sal (R, +SE)		70,000
To reinstate previously deferred profit on intercompany sales.		

If the sale had been upstream from Sal to Pet, the $34,000 tax on the intercompany profit would have been paid by Sal, but Sal would show $23,800 ($70,000 × 34%) of that amount as a deferred tax asset, rather than as income tax expense for the year. The consolidation workpaper entry to eliminate the intercompany profit in the year of sale would be for $70,000, the same amount as in the downstream example. Noncontrolling interest share in the year of sale would decrease by $17,500 (25% × $70,000 unrealized gain), and the amount of the one-line consolidation entry to eliminate the effect of the unrealized profit on Pet's books would be for $52,500 (75% × $70,000), rather than $70,000 as in the downstream example.

SEPARATE-COMPANY TAX RETURNS WITH INTERCOMPANY GAIN

This section provides an extended illustration of income tax allocation for a parent and its subsidiary that file separate tax returns. Pay Corporation paid $375,000 cash for a 75 percent interest in Sep Corporation on January 1, 2011, when Sep's equity consisted of

$300,000 capital stock and $200,000 retained earnings. At the time Pay acquired its interest in Sep, Pay had a deferred income tax liability of $10,200, consisting of $30,000 tax/book depreciation differences that reverse in equal ($7,500) amounts over the years 2012 through 2015.

On January 8, 2011, Pay sold equipment to Sep at a gain of $20,000. Sep is depreciating the equipment on a straight-line basis over five years. Comparative income and retained earnings data for 2011 are as follows:

	Pay	Sep
Sales	$380,000	$300,000
Gain on equipment sale	20,000	—
Income from Sep	23,600	—
Cost of sales	(200,000)	(180,000)
Operating expenses	(100,000)	(40,000)
Income tax expense	(31,253)	(27,200)
Net income	92,347	52,800
Add: Beginning retained earnings	357,653	200,000
Deduct: Dividends (December)	(50,000)	(28,000)
Retained earnings December 31	$400,000	$224,800

GAAP [7] requires Pay to provide for income taxes on its share of Sep's $24,800 undistributed earnings ($52,800 net income less $28,000 dividends). The 80 percent dividends-received deduction is applicable to dividends received from Sep. We assume a flat 34 percent income tax rate for Pay and Sep. Pay's deferred tax computation on the undistributed earnings is therefore $1,265 [($24,800 × 75% owned × 20% taxable) = $3,720 × 34% tax rate].

One-Line Consolidation

Pay makes the following journal entries to account for its investment in Sep during 2011:

January 1

Investment in Sep (+A)	375,000	
Cash (−A)		375,000

To record purchase of a 75% interest in Sep.

December

Cash (+A)	21,000	
Investment in Sep (−A)		21,000

To record dividends received from Sep ($28,000 × 75%).

December 31

Investment in Sep (+A)	23,600	
Income from Sep (R, +SE)		23,600

To record income from Sep computed as follows:

Pay's share of Sep's net income ($52,800 × 75%)	$ 39,600
Less: Unrealized profit on sale of equipment	(20,000)
Add: Piecemeal recognition of gain ($20,000 ÷ 5 years)	4,000
Income from Sep	$ 23,600

Note that in computing its investment income from Sep, Pay takes up its share of Sep's income on which taxes have been paid by Sep.

At December 31, 2011, Pay's Investment in Sep account has a balance of $377,600 ($375,000 beginning balance + $23,600 income from Sep − $21,000 dividends), and Pay's share of Sep's equity is $393,600 ($524,800 × 75%). The $16,000 difference ($377,600 − $393,600) is the $16,000 unrealized profit from downstream sale of equipment.

Income Tax Expense Based on Separate Returns

Sep's $27,200 income tax expense is simply 34 percent of Sep's $80,000 pretax accounting income, but Pay's income tax expense of $31,253 requires further analysis. In accordance with GAAP [8], we calculate Pay's income tax expense as follows:

Tax on Pay's operating income [(380,000 sales − $200,000 cost of sales − $100,000 operating expenses) × 34%]	$27,200
Tax on gain from sale of equipment ($20,000 × 34%)	6,800
Tax on dividends received [($21,000 × 20% taxable) × 34%]	1,428
Income taxes currently payable	35,428
Less: Decrease in deferred tax liability [($16,000 unrealized gain on equipment at year-end − $3,720 taxable share of Sep's undistributed earnings)] × 34%	(4,175)
Income tax expense	$31,253

Exhibit 10-7 provides a schedule to support the computation of Pay's income tax expense. Only one tax rate (34%) is applicable, so the schedule approach is not necessary, but it may be helpful. The calculation for future dividends in the schedule is $3,720 ($52,800 net income − $28,000 dividends) × 75% owned × 20% taxable portion, which reverses in 2016 when dividends are distributed.

Pay's interest in Sep is only 75 percent, so it must file separate tax returns and pay income taxes on the $20,000 intercompany gain on the equipment sold to Sep. Pay also pays income taxes on dividends received from Sep, less an 80 percent dividends-received deduction. The multiplication of dividends received and undistributed income by 20 percent in calculating Pay's income tax expense effectively takes the 80 percent dividends-received deduction into account without calculating the amount of the deduction and subtracting it from distributed dividends or undistributed earnings.

Sep's $27,200 income tax expense is equal to the tax liability indicated on its separate return because it has no temporary differences. Pay's income tax expense of $31,253 consists of $35,428 currently payable, less a $4,175 decrease in deferred tax liability for the year. The balance of Pay's deferred tax liability at December 31 is $6,025 ($10,200 beginning balance −$4,175 decrease for the year). Sep and Pay record income tax expenses as follows:

Sep's Books—December 31, 2011

Income tax expense (E, −SE)	27,200	
Income taxes currently payable (+L)		27,200
To accrue income taxes for 2011.		

Pay's Books—December 31, 2011

Income tax expense (E, −SE)	31,253	
Deferred tax liability (−L)	4,175	
Income taxes currently payable (+L)		35,428
To accrue income taxes for 2011.		

Consolidation Workpaper

Exhibit 10-8 presents a consolidation workpaper for Pay Corporation and Subsidiary. The workpaper entries are the same as those encountered in earlier chapters except for the inclusion of income tax considerations. Observe that Pay's income tax expense plus Sep's income tax expense equal the $58,453 consolidated income tax expense.

<table>
<tr><td>EXHIBIT 10-7

Schedule of Deferred Income Tax Liability at December 31, 2011</td><td colspan="7">

Temporary Difference	2011	2012	2013	2014	2015	Future Years
Depreciation		$7,500	$ 7,500	$ 7,500	$ 7,500	
Gain on equipment	$20,000					
Piecemeal recognition	(4,000)	(4,000)	(4,000)	(4,000)	(4,000)	
Future dividends	(3,720)	—	—	—	—	$3,720
Taxable in future years		3,500	3,500	3,500	3,500	3,720
Enacted tax rate		34%	34%	34%	34%	34%
Deferred tax liability		$1,190	$ 1,190	$ 1,190	$ 1,190	$1,265

</td></tr>
</table>

PAY CORPORATION AND SUBSIDIARY CONSOLIDATION WORKPAPER FOR THE YEAR ENDED DECEMBER 31, 2011					
			Adjustments and Eliminations		
	Pay	75% Sep	Debits	Credits	Consolidated Statements
Income Statement Sales	$380,000	$300,000			$680,000
Gain on equipment	20,000		a 20,000		
Income from Sep	23,600		c 23,600		
Cost of sales	(200,000)	(180,000)			(380,000)
Operating expense	(100,000)	(40,000)		b 4,000	(136,000)
Income tax expense	(31,253)	(27,200)			(58,453)
Noncontrolling interest share			e 13,200		(13,200)
Controlling share of net income	**$ 92,347**	**$ 52,800**			**$ 92,347**
Retained Earnings Statement Retained earnings—Pay	$357,653				$357,653
Retained earnings—Sep		$200,000	d 200,000		
Dividends	(50,000)	(28,000)		c 21,000 e 7,000	(50,000)
Controlling share of net income	92,347	52,800			92,347
Retained earnings— December 31	**$400,000**	**$224,800**			**$400,000**
Balance Sheet Other assets	$362,400	$432,000			$794,400
Equipment	120,000	200,000		a 20,000	300,000
Accumulated depreciation	(60,000)	(50,000)	b 4,000		(106,000)
Investment in Sep	377,600			c 2,600 d 375,000	
	$800,000	**$582,000**			**$988,400**
Deferred tax liability	$ 6,025				$ 6,025
Income tax liability	35,428	$ 27,200			62,628
Other liabilities	58,547	30,000			88,547
Capital stock	300,000	300,000	d 300,000		300,000
Retained earnings	**400,000**	**224,800**			**400,000**
	$800,000	**$582,000**			
Noncontrolling interest				d 125,000 e 6,200	131,200
					$988,400

EXHIBIT 10-8

Parent and Subsidiary Companies File Separate Tax Returns

Pay paid income taxes on the $20,000 gain on the intercompany sale of equipment. We do not recognize this gain for consolidated statement purposes, so a temporary difference exists for which we require income tax allocation procedures.

Workpaper Entry for 2012

The workpaper entry for 2012 to eliminate the effect of the unrealized profit from the intercompany sale of equipment is as follows:

Investment in Sep (+A)	16,000	
Accumulated depreciation (+A)	8,000	
Equipment (−A)		20,000
Depreciation expense (−E, +SE)		4,000
To eliminate unrealized profit from downstream sale of equipment.		

The income tax expense in 2012 will be equal to the income tax currently payable, adjusted for the change in the deferred tax asset or liability that occurs in 2012.

EFFECT OF CONSOLIDATED AND SEPARATE-COMPANY TAX RETURNS ON CONSOLIDATION PROCEDURES

This section compares consolidation procedures for a parent and its subsidiary when separate-company and consolidated tax returns are filed. Under GAAP [9], the income tax expense and the income from subsidiary are the same in both cases. When firms file consolidated tax returns, we allocate the tax liability among the parent and its subsidiaries.

Allocation of Consolidated Income Tax to Affiliates

A subsidiary that is part of a group filing a consolidated tax return is required to disclose its current and deferred income tax expense and any tax-related balances due to or from affiliates in its separate financial statements. Although GAAP provides no single method of allocating consolidated income tax expense among affiliates, firms must disclose the method used.

Four methods currently used in the allocation of consolidated income taxes to affiliates are as follows:

- **Separate return method.** Each subsidiary computes income taxes as if it were filing a separate return.
- **Agreement method.** Tax expense is allocated by agreement between parent and subsidiaries.
- **With-or-without method.** The income tax provision is computed for the group with and without the pretax income of the subsidiary. The subsidiary's income tax expense is the difference.
- **Percentage allocation method.** Consolidated income tax expense is allocated to a subsidiary on the basis of its pretax income as a percentage of consolidated pretax income.

The percentage allocation method is used for the illustrations in this book.

Background Information for Consolidated and Separate Tax Return Illustrations

The following illustrations for Pal Corporation and its 90 percent-owned subsidiary, Sal Corporation, compare consolidation procedures used when filing consolidated tax returns with consolidation procedures necessary when filing separate-company tax returns. Tax effects of intercompany profits from both upstream and downstream inventory sales are also illustrated.

On January 1, 2011, Pal acquired 90 percent of the outstanding voting stock of Sal for $432,000, when Sal had $300,000 capital stock and $100,000 retained earnings. The $432,000 purchase price implies that Sal's total fair value is $480,000 ($432,000/90%). Sal's book value is $400,000, implying goodwill of $80,000. Goodwill is not amortized for either financial reporting or tax purposes. Additional information follows:

1. A flat 34 percent enacted income tax rate applies to all years.
2. Pal and Sal are an affiliated group entitled to the 100 percent dividend exclusion.
3. Sal pays dividends of $20,000 during 2011.

4. Intercompany sales are $40,000, of which $10,000 represents unrealized profits at year-end 2011.

5. Pretax operating incomes for the two affiliates are:

	Pal	Sal
Sales	$900,000	$500,000
Cost of sales	(500,000)	(350,000)
Expenses	(250,000)	(100,000)
Pretax operating income	$150,000	$ 50,000

Cases 1 and 2 illustrate a temporary difference for unrealized profits from downstream sales that originates in the current year and reverses in the succeeding year. Subsequently, Cases 3 and 4 repeat illustrations 1 and 2 using an upstream-sale assumption as the only temporary difference.

CASE 1: CONSOLIDATED TAX RETURN WITH DOWNSTREAM SALES

Assume that a consolidated tax return is filed and that the intercompany sales are downstream. The consolidated tax return includes the $200,000 combined operating income (Pal's $150,000 operating income plus Sal's $50,000 operating income) less $10,000 unrealized profit. The consolidated tax expense will be $64,600 ($190,000 × 34%). The $64,600 income tax expense is equal to the $64,600 consolidated income tax liability because we eliminate the unrealized profits in the consolidation workpaper and in the consolidated tax return. In addition, no tax is assessed on the $18,000 dividends that Pal receives from Sal.

We allocate the $64,600 consolidated income tax liability to Pal and Sal based on the amounts of their income included in the $190,000 consolidated taxable income. The intercompany sales are downstream in this case, so the allocation is:

$$\text{Pal} = \frac{\$150,000 - \$10,000}{\$190,000} \times \$64,600 = \$47,600$$

$$\text{Sal} = \frac{\$50,000}{\$190,000} \times \$64,600 = \$17,000$$

Pal and Sal record the 2011 income tax expense amounts determined in this allocation as follows:

Pal's Books—December 31		
Income tax expense (E, −SE)	47,600	
Income taxes currently payable (+L)		47,600
To record share of the consolidated income tax liability.		
Sal's Books—December 31		
Income tax expense (E, −SE)	17,000	
Income taxes currently payable (+L)		17,000
To record share of the consolidated income tax liability.		

After entering this tax allocation, Sal's net income will be $33,000 ($50,000 − $17,000 income tax), and Pal records income from Sal as follows:

December 31		
Investment in Sal (+A)	19,700	
Income from Sal (R, +SE)		19,700
To record investment income from Sal computed as follows:		
Share of Sal's net income ($33,000 × 90%)		$29,700
Less: Unrealized profit in inventory		(10,000)
Income from Sal		$19,700

We deduct the full amount of the unrealized inventory profit because the sale is downstream and no tax is assessed on unrealized profits when filing consolidated income tax returns. Exhibit 10-9 presents a consolidation workpaper for Pal and Subsidiary.

EXHIBIT 10-9

Consolidated Tax
Return—Unrealized
Profit from Downstream
Sales

PAL CORPORATION AND SUBSIDIARY CONSOLIDATION WORKPAPER FOR THE YEAR ENDED DECEMBER 31, 2011 (IN THOUSANDS)

	Pal	Sal	Adjustments and Eliminations Debits	Adjustments and Eliminations Credits	Consolidated Statements
Income Statement Sales	$900	$500	a 40		$ 1,360
Income from Sal	19.7		c 19.7		
Cost of goods sold	(500)	(350)	b 10	a 40	(820)
Expenses (excluding income taxes)	(250)	(100)			(350)
Income tax expense	(47.6)	(17)			(64.6)
Noncontrolling interest share			e 3.3		(3.3)
Controlling share of net income	**$122.1**	**$ 33**			**$ 122.1**
Retained Earnings Statement Retained earnings—Pal	$352.9				$ 352.9
Retained earnings—Sal		$100	d 100		
Dividends	(80)	(20)		c 18 e 2	(80)
Controlling Share of net income	**122.1**	**33**			**122.1**
Retained earnings— December 31	**$395**	**$113**			**$ 395**
Balance Sheet Inventory	$183.3	$ 80		b 10	$ 253.3
Other assets	378	520			898
Investment in Sal	433.7			c 1.7 d 432	
Goodwill			d 80		80
	$995	$600			$ 1,231.3
Income tax payable	$ 47.6	$ 17			$ 64.6
Other liabilities	152.4	170			322.4
Capital stock	400	300	d 300		400
Retained earnings	**395**	**113**			**395**
	$995	$600			
Noncontrolling interest				d 48 e 1.3	49.3
					$ 1,231.3

Related workpaper entries, presented in general journal form, are:

a Sales (−R, −SE)	40,000	
Cost of goods sold (−E, +SE)		40,000
To eliminate intercompany sales and cost of sales.		
b Cost of goods sold (E, −SE)	10,000	
Inventory (−A)		10,000
To eliminate intercompany profits from downstream sale.		
c Income from Sal (−R, −SE)	19,700	
Investment in Sal (−A)		1,700
Dividends (+SE)		18,000
To eliminate investment income and dividends		
and adjust the Investment in Sal account to its		
beginning-of-the-period balance.		
d Capital stock—Sal (−SE)	300,000	
Retained earnings—Sal (−SE)	100,000	
Goodwill (+A)	80,000	
Investment in Sal (−A)		432,000
Noncontrolling interest—beginning (+SE)		48,000
To eliminate reciprocal beginning-of-the-period		
investment and equity amounts, establish		
beginning-of-the-period goodwill and noncontrolling interest.		
e Noncontrolling interest share (−SE)	3,300	
Dividends (+SE)		2,000
Noncontrolling interest (+SE)		1,300
To enter noncontrolling interest shares of subsidiary income and dividends.		

CASE 2: SEPARATE TAX RETURNS WITH DOWNSTREAM SALES

Assume that the intercompany sales are downstream and that they file separate tax returns. Sal has an income tax liability of $17,000 and reports net income of $33,000. Pal records income from Sal of $19,700, computed as follows:

Share of Sal's net income ($33,000 × 90%)	$29,700
Less: Unrealized profit	(10,000)
Income from Sal	$19,700

Pal's income tax currently payable is 34 percent of its $150,000 operating income, or $51,000. Pal's income tax expense is $47,600, computed as follows:

Income tax currently payable	$51,000
Less: Increase in deferred tax asset from	
temporary difference ($10,000 unrealized	
profit × 34% tax rate)	(3,400)
Income Tax Expense	$47,600

Exhibit 10-10 reflects these observations in the consolidation workpaper.

Income taxes currently payable that will appear in the consolidated balance sheet are $68,000 ($51,000 for Pal plus $17,000 for Sal). The difference between the consolidated income tax expense ($64,600) and income taxes currently payable ($68,000) is the $3,400 deferred tax asset

EXHIBIT 10-10

Separate Tax Returns—
Unrealized Profit from
Downstream Sales

PAL CORPORATION AND SUBSIDIARY CONSOLIDATION WORKPAPER FOR THE YEAR ENDED DECEMBER 31, 2011 (IN THOUSANDS)

	Pal	Sal	Adjustments and Eliminations Debits	Adjustments and Eliminations Credits	Consolidated Statements
Income Statement Sales	$900	$500	a 40		$1,360
Income from Sal	19.7		c 19.7		
Cost of goods sold	(500)	(350)	b 10	a 40	(820)
Expenses (excluding income taxes)	(250)	(100)			(350)
Income tax expense	(47.6)	(17)			(64.6)
Noncontrolling interest share			e 3.3		(3.3)
Controlling Share of net income	**$122.1**	**$ 33**			**$ 122.1**
Retained Earnings Statement Retained earnings—Pal	$352.9				$ 352.9
Retained earnings—Sal		$100	d 100		
Dividends	(80)	(20)		c 18 e 2	(80)
Controlling share of net income	**122.1**	**33**			**122.1**
Retained earnings— December 31	**$395**	**$113**			**$ 395**
Balance Sheet Inventory	$183.3	$ 80		b 10	$ 253.3
Deferred tax asset	3.4				3.4
Other assets	378	520			898
Investment in Sal	433.7			c 1.7 d 432	
Goodwill			d 80		80
	$998.4	$600			$1,234.7
Income tax payable	$ 51	$ 17			$ 68
Other liabilities	152.4	170			322.4
Capital stock	400	300	d 300		400
Retained earnings	**395**	**113**			**395**
	$998.4	$600			
Noncontrolling interest				d 48 e 1.3	49.3
					$1,234.7

for the $10,000 unrealized profit. The $64,600 income tax expense appearing in the consolidated income statement can be computed independently as follows:

Consolidated income before income taxes and noncontrolling interest expense ($1,360,000 sales − $820,000 cost of goods sold − $350,000 expenses)	$190,000
Tax rate	34%
Income tax expense	$ 64,600

Compare Exhibits 10-9 and 10-10. Income tax expense and income from subsidiary are the same whether we file separate tax returns or consolidated tax returns. However, there is a difference in income tax currently payable and in the deferred tax asset.

When filing a consolidated tax return, income tax expense is equal to income tax currently payable because no tax is assessed on the unrealized intercompany profit. Consolidated income tax expense is the same whether we file separate-company or consolidated income tax returns. However, with separate tax returns, Pal's income tax expense consists of $51,000 income tax currently payable, less the $3,400 deferred tax asset related to the $10,000 temporary difference.

CASE 3: CONSOLIDATED TAX RETURN WITH UPSTREAM SALES

Now assume that intercompany sales are upstream (from Sal to Pal). If we file a consolidated return, the consolidated tax expense will be $64,600, the same as in the downstream example, but the allocation to Pal and Sal changes because we exclude $10,000 of Sal's $50,000 pretax income from consolidated taxable income. The allocation is:

$$\text{Pal} = \frac{\$150,000}{\$190,000} \times \$64,600 = \$51,000$$

$$\text{Sal} = \frac{\$50,000 - \$10,000}{\$190,000} \times \$64,600 = \$13,600$$

We record these amounts in the separate company books as follows:

Pal's Books—December 31		
Income tax expense (E, −SE)	51,000	
Income taxes currently payable (+L)		51,000
To record share of consolidated income taxes		
Sal's Books—December 31		
Income tax expense (E, −SE)	13,600	
Income taxes currently payable (+L)		13,600
To record share of consolidated income taxes.		

Sal's net income is $36,400 ($50,000 pretax income less $13,600 income tax expense), and Pal determines income from Sal as follows:

Share of Sal's net income ($36,400 × 90%)	$32,760
Less: Unrealized profit from upstream sales ($10,000 × 90%)	(9,000)
Income from Sal	$23,760

Consolidation workpapers to illustrate the effect of the upstream-sales example appear in Exhibit 10-11. We compute noncontrolling interest share of $2,640 as 10 percent of Sal's realized income of $26,400 ($36,400 net income − $10,000 unrealized profit). The consolidated tax expense of $64,600 is the same as in the downstream-sale example, but controlling share of consolidated net income is $660 greater because we attribute the $10,000 unrealized gain and the related $3,400 tax allocation

EXHIBIT 10-11

Consolidated Tax
Return—Unrealized
Profit from Upstream
Sales

PAL CORPORATION AND SUBSIDIARY CONSOLIDATION WORKPAPER FOR THE YEAR ENDED DECEMBER 31, 2011 (IN THOUSANDS)

	Pal	90% Sal	Adjustments and Eliminations Debits	Credits	Consolidated Statements
Income Statement Sales	$ 900	$500	a 40		$1,360
Income from Sal	23.76		c 23.76		
Cost of goods sold	(500)	(350)	b 10	a 40	(820)
Expenses (excluding income taxes)	(250)	(100)			(350)
Income tax expense	(51)	(13.6)			(64.6)
Noncontrolling interest Share			e 2.64		(2.64)
Controlling share of net income	**$ 122.76**	**$ 36.4**			**$ 122.76**
Retained Earnings Statement Retained earnings—Pal	$ 352.9				$ 352.9
Retained earnings—Sal		$100	d 100		
Dividends	(80)	(20)		c 18 e 2	(80)
Controlling share of net income	**122.76**	**36.4**			**122.76**
Retained earnings— December 31	**$ 395.66**	**$116.4**			**$ 395.66**
Balance Sheet Inventory	$ 183.3	$ 80		b 10	$ 253.3
Other assets	378	520			898
Investment in Sal	437.76			c 5.76 d 432	
Goodwill			d 80		80
	$ 999.06	$600			$1,231.3
Income tax payable	$ 51	$ 13.6			$ 64.6
Other liabilities	152.4	170			322.4
Capital stock	400	300	d 300		400
Retained earnings	**395.66**	**116.4**			**395.66**
	$ 999.06	$600			
Noncontrolling interest				d 48 e 0.64	48.64
					$1,231.3

effect to subsidiary operations. Thus, noncontrolling interest share is $660 less than in the downstream-sale examples, and controlling share of consolidated net income is $660 more ($122,760 instead of $122,100 in Exhibits 10-9 and 10-10). The noncontrolling interest share computation in Exhibit 10-11 eliminates 100 percent of the $10,000 unrealized profit because no tax is paid on unrealized profits when filing consolidated returns.

CASE 4: SEPARATE TAX RETURNS WITH UPSTREAM SALES

Assume that intercompany sales are upstream and that they file separate tax returns. Sal's income tax currently payable, as determined from its separate tax return, is $17,000, because income taxes are assessed on Sal's $50,000 pretax income, which includes the $10,000 unrealized profit. However, Sal's income tax expense is only $13,600, computed as follows:

Income tax currently payable	$17,000
Less: Increase in deferred tax asset from temporary difference ($10,000 unrealized profit $\times$ 34% tax rate)	(3,400)
Income tax expense	$13,600

Sal's net income is $36,400, as in Case 3, and Pal records its income from Sal at $23,760, determined as follows:

Pal's share of Sal's net income ($36,400 $\times$ 90%)	$32,760
Less: Unrealized profit from upstream sales ($10,000 $\times$ 90% owned)	(9,000)
Pal's income from Sal	$23,760

Exhibit 10-12 shows a workpaper when separate returns are filed and unrealized inventory profit results from upstream sales.

In comparing Exhibits 10-11 and 10-12, note that the income tax expense and the income from the subsidiary are the same whether we file separate or consolidated tax returns. There is, however, a difference in income tax currently payable and in the deferred tax asset. When filing separate tax returns, consolidated tax expense consists of the following:

	Pal	Sal	Consolidated
Income taxes currently payable	$51,000	$17,000	$68,000
Deferred tax asset	—	(3,400)	(3,400)
Income tax expense	$51,000	$13,600	$64,600

Thus, the consolidated income statement will show income tax expense of $64,600, and the consolidated balance sheet will show a liability for income tax currently payable of $68,000 and a current asset for the $3,400 deferred tax asset.

BUSINESS COMBINATIONS

For income tax purposes, the term *reorganization* refers to certain corporate restructurings or combinations that are tax free under Internal Revenue Code Section 368. Reorganization transactions include mergers, recapitalizations, and divisions of corporations. Failure to meet any of the required conditions specified in the code may disqualify a reorganization so that the transaction loses its tax-free status. Although the code describes seven types of transactions (Type A through Type G) as reorganizations, only three are discussed here:

- **Merger or consolidation.** A merger occurs when one corporation acquires another corporation, primarily for the acquiring company's stock (but some other consideration may be given), and the acquired corporation is dissolved. Its assets and liabilities are taken over by the acquiring corporation. A consolidation occurs when two or more companies combine to form a new corporation and the original corporations are dissolved.[5]

---

[5]The accounting concepts of mergers and consolidations were discussed in Chapter 1.

EXHIBIT 10-12

Separate Tax Returns—
Unrealized Profit from
Upstream Sales

PAL CORPORATION AND SUBSIDIARY CONSOLIDATION WORKPAPER FOR THE YEAR ENDED DECEMBER 31, 2011 (IN THOUSANDS)

	Pal	Sal	Adjustments and Eliminations Debits	Adjustments and Eliminations Credits	Consolidated Statements
Income Statement Sales	$900	$500	a 40		$1,360
Income from Sal	23.76		c 23.76		
Cost of goods sold	(500)	(350)	b 10	a 40	(820)
Expenses (excluding income taxes)	(250)	(100)			(350)
Income tax expense	(51)	(13.6)			(64.6)
Noncontrolling interest share			e 2.64		(2.64)
Controlling share of net income	**$122.76**	**$ 36.4**			**$ 122.76**
Retained Earnings Statement Retained earnings—Pal	$352.9				$ 352.9
Retained earnings—Sal		$100	d 100		
Dividends	(80)	(20)		c 18 e 2	(80)
Controlling share of net income	**122.76**	**36.4**			**122.76**
Retained earnings—December 31	**$395.66**	**$116.4**			**$ 395.66**
Balance Sheet Inventory	$183.3	$ 80		b 10	$ 253.3
Deferred tax asset		3.4			3.4
Other assets	378	520			898
Investment in Sal	437.76			c 5.76 d 432	
Goodwill			d 80		80
	$999.06	$603.4			$1,234.7
Income tax payable	$ 51	$ 17			$ 68
Other liabilities	152.4	170			322.4
Capital stock	400	300	d 300		400
Retained earnings	**395.66**	**116.4**			**395.66**
	$999.06	$603.4			
Noncontrolling interest				d 48 e 0.64	48.64
					$1,234.7

- **Acquiring another corporation's stock.** If a corporation exchanges any of its voting stock *(and no other consideration is given)* for stock of another corporation and it controls the second corporation immediately after the exchange, the transaction is a reorganization. Control means ownership of at least 80 percent of the voting stock and at least 80 percent of all other classes of stock.
- **Acquiring another corporation's assets.** If a corporation exchanges any of its voting stock (and generally nothing else) for substantially all of another corporation's property, the transaction is a reorganization. The assumption of liabilities does not disqualify this transaction as a tax-free reorganization.

These summaries are brief and nontechnical. The point is, the qualifications under the tax code for an exchange of shares to be a tax-free reorganization are *not identical* to the qualifications under accounting principles for the former pooling of interests business combination. Purchase business combinations may be either taxable or tax free, and structuring a transaction to meet the goals of both buyer and seller is an important part of the negotiating process for any business combination.

As you would expect, firms often structure combinations to be tax free. A September 3, 2001, press release issued by ***Hewlett-Packard (HP)*** (obtained from HP's Web site) described terms of its proposed merger with ***Compaq Computer Corporation***:

> *Under terms of the agreement, unanimously approved by both Boards of Directors, Compaq shareowners will receive 0.6325 of a newly issued HP share for each share of Compaq, giving the merger a current value of approximately $25 billion. HP share-owners will own approximately 64 percent and Compaq shareowners 36 percent of the merged company. The transaction, which is expected to be tax-free to shareowners of both companies for U.S. federal income tax purposes, will be accounted for as a purchase.*

A December 3, 2005, press release (again from HP's Web site) discussed the structuring of its acquisition of Macromedia:

> *The acquisition has been structured to qualify as a tax-free reorganization within the meaning of Section 368(a) of the Internal Revenue Code of 1986, as amended. As a result, Macromedia stockholders will not recognize gain or loss for United States fed-eral income tax purposes upon the exchange of shares of Macromedia common stock for shares of Adobe common stock, except with respect to cash received in lieu of frac-tional shares of Adobe common stock. Tax matters are very complicated, and the tax consequences of the acquisition to a particular stockholder will depend in part on such stockholder's circumstances. Accordingly, you should consult your own tax adviser for a full understanding of the tax consequences of the acquisition to you, including the applicability and effect of federal, state, local, and foreign income and other tax laws.*

In a taxable business combination, we revalue the assets and liabilities of the acquired corpora-tion to reflect the fair value acquired. The seller recognizes gain or loss equal to the fair value of the consideration received, less the tax bases of the assets or stock sold. In a tax-free reorganiza-tion, the tax bases of the assets and liabilities are carried forward with no revaluation.

The Revenue Recognition Act of 1993 allows a tax deduction for amortization of goodwill (which is no longer amortized under GAAP [10]) and other intangible assets (called Section 197 intangible assets). This deduction is only allowed when taxes have been paid (gain or loss recog-nized) by the seller on the purchase transaction.[6] All Section 197 intangible assets are amortized for tax purposes over a 15-year period, regardless of their useful lives.

Purchase Business Combinations

GAAP [11] requires that firms recognize a deferred tax liability or deferred tax asset for the dif-ference between the book values (tax bases) and the assigned values of the assets and liabilities (except goodwill and leveraged leases) acquired in a purchase. In other words, we record the assets and liabilities acquired at their gross fair values and record a deferred tax asset or liability for the related tax effect.

A difference between book value and tax value only occurs when the assets are not written up to fair value for tax purposes as they are for book purposes. When the assets are written up for tax purposes, the only differences between written-up book value and tax basis should have already been accounted for in the purchaser's separate books as a deferred tax asset or liability (due to an original difference between book and tax value at the point of purchase).

The tax-free business combination of Pat and Sad is used to illustrate the computation of a deferred tax liability for the book value/fair value differentials and for the determination of

---

[6]The company's liabilities may or may not be assumed in the transaction.

goodwill. On January 1, 2011, Pat Corporation paid $400,000 for 60 percent of the outstanding voting stock of Sad Corporation, when Sad's stockholders' equity consisted of $300,000 capital stock and $200,000 retained earnings. Book values were equal to fair values of Sad's assets and liabilities, except for a building and land. The building had a book value of $80,000, a fair value of $120,000, and a remaining useful life of eight years. The land had a book value of $50,000 and a fair value of $150,000. Any goodwill is not amortized. The tax rate applicable to both companies is 34 percent, and an 80 percent dividends deduction applies.

We allocate the $100,000 excess of cost over book value acquired [$400,000 cost − ($500,000 book value of net assets × 60% interest)] as follows:

	Book Value	Pretax Fair Value	Difference	Pat's 60% Interest × The Difference
Building	$80,000	$120,000	$ 40,000	$ 24,000
Land	50,000	150,000	100,000	60,000
Revaluation of assets (gross amount)				84,000
Less: Deferred tax on revaluation ($84,000 × 34%)				(28,560)
Net differential from revaluation of assets				55,440
Goodwill				44,560
Excess cost over book value acquired				$100,000

The $24,000 assigned to the building and the $8,160 related deferred tax liability ($24,000 × 34%) will be written off over the building's remaining eight-year useful life at the annual amounts of $3,000 and $1,020, respectively. Thus, consolidated net income will be decreased by $1,980 each year on an after-tax basis. The $60,000 revaluation of the land and the $20,400 deferred tax liability on the revalued land will remain on the books until the land is sold to outside entities.

GAAP [12] does not assign a deferred tax liability to the goodwill account (when the goodwill is not deductible), due to the difficulty in the simultaneous calculation of the residual account, goodwill, and a deferred tax assignment to this residual account. The FASB decided that not much incremental information would be added by this calculation.

Equity Method of Accounting for Purchase Business Combinations

During 2011, Sad has net income of $100,000 and pays dividends of $40,000. Pat makes the following entries on its separate books to account for its investment in Sad:

Investment in Sad (+A)	400,000	
Cash (−A)		400,000
To record purchase of a 60% interest in Sad Corporation.		
Cash (+A)	24,000	
Investment in Sad (−A)		24,000
To record receipt of dividends from Sad ($40,000 × 60%). Note that Pat must also provide for income taxes on its share of the $60,000 undistributed earnings of Sad ($36,000 × 20% taxable × 34% tax rate = $2,448 deferred taxes).		
Investment in Sad (+A)	58,020	
Income from Sad (R, +SE)		58,020
To record income from Sad and the related amortization of deferred tax liability on the building computed as follows:		

Share of Sad's income ($100,000 × 60%)	$60,000
Less: Depreciation on excess allocated to building	(3,000)
Add: Amortization of deferred taxes on building	1,020
Income from Sad	$58,020

The stockholders' equity of Sad at December 31, 2011, consists of $300,000 capital stock and $260,000 retained earnings. The balance of Pat's Investment in Sad account at December 31, 2011 is $434,020. An analysis of the investment account balance shows the following:

	January 1, 2011	2011 Change	December 31, 2011
Book value of investment	$300,000	$36,000	$336,000
Unamortized excess:			
Building	24,000	(3,000)	21,000
Land	60,000		60,000
Deferred income taxes	(28,560)	1,020	(27,540)
Goodwill	44,560		44,560
Investment balance	$400,000	$34,020	$434,020

Workpaper Entries

When Pat prepares a consolidation workpaper at December 31, 2011, the Investment in Sad account will have a balance of $434,020 ($400,000 original investment + $58,020 income from Sad − $24,000 dividends). The workpaper entries in general journal form follow:

a	Income from Sad (−R, − SE)	58,020	
	Dividends (+SE)		24,000
	Investment in Sad (−A)		34,020
	To eliminate income and dividends from Sad and adjust the Investment in Sad account to its beginning-of-the-period balance.		
b	Capital stock—Sad (−SE)	300,000	
	Retained earnings—Sad (−SE)	200,000	
	Building (+A)	24,000	
	Land (+A)	60,000	
	Goodwill (+A)	44,560	
	Investment in Sad (−A)		400,000
	Deferred taxes on revaluation (+L)		28,560
	Noncontrolling interest—beginning (+SE)		200,000
	To eliminate reciprocal investment and equity balances, establish beginning noncontrolling interest, enter beginning-of-the-period cost/book value differentials, and enter deferred taxes on revaluation.		
c	Depreciation expense (E, −SE)	3,000	
	Accumulated depreciation—building (−A)		3,000
	To record depreciation on excess allocated to building.		
d	Deferred taxes on revaluation (−L)	1,020	
	Income tax expense (−E, +SE)		1,020
	To record amortization of deferred taxes.		
e	Noncontrolling interest share (−SE)	40,000	
	Dividends (+SE)		16,000
	Noncontrolling interest (+SE)		24,000
	To enter noncontrolling interest shares of subsidiary income and dividends.		

Income Tax Uncertainties

In June 2006, the FASB revised GAAP to clarify accounting for uncertainty in income taxes recognized in financial statements. GAAP prescribes both a recognition threshold and measurement attribute for tax positions taken in tax returns.

Evaluation of tax positions is a two-step process. The first step is recognition, where the reporting entity determines whether it is more likely than not that a tax position will be sustained upon examination. Entities should presume that the tax position will be examined by the appropriate taxing authority. The second step is measurement, where a tax position that meets the recognition threshold is measured to determine the amount to recognize in the financial statements. Per GAAP [13]:

> *A tax position that meets the more-likely-than-not recognition threshold shall initially and subsequently be measured as the largest amount of tax benefit that is greater than 50 percent likely of being realized upon settlement with a taxing authority that has full knowledge of all relevant information. Measurement of a tax position that meets the more-likely-than-not recognition threshold shall consider the amounts and probabilities of the outcomes that could be realized upon settlement using the facts, circumstances, and information available at the reporting date.*

Exhibit 10-13 provides an example of the measurement process.

Since the 2006 GAAP revision, more companies are now required to adjust and report a valuation allowance on recognized deferred tax assets. For example, **The Hershey Company** reported a $43.338 million valuation allowance for 2009 (see Exhibit 10-14).

FINANCIAL STATEMENT DISCLOSURES FOR INCOME TAXES

GAAP divides deferred tax assets or liabilities into two categories, a current amount and a noncurrent amount, for balance sheet presentation. GAAP [14] classifies deferred tax liabilities and assets as current or noncurrent based on the classification of the related asset or liability for financial reporting. If the deferred item is not related to an asset or liability for financial reporting, its classification depends on the reversal date of the temporary difference. In addition, the significant components of income tax expense or benefit are disclosed in the financial statements or notes to the financial statements.

GAAP also requires disclosures for income tax expense and benefits allocated to continuing operations, discontinued operations, extraordinary items, and prior-period adjustments.

The Hershey Company's 2009 annual report provides an example of required disclosures for income taxes. Note 13 offers a detailed description of its income tax calculations for the year. The note is reproduced in Exhibit 10-14.

EXHIBIT 10-13

Example: Measurement with Information About the Approach to Settlement

This example demonstrates an application of the measurement requirements of paragraph 740-10-30-7 for a tax position that meets the paragraph 740-10-25-6 requirements for recognition. Measurement in this example is based on identified information about settlement.

In applying the recognition criterion of this subtopic for tax positions, an entity has determined that a tax position resulting in a benefit of $100 qualifies for recognition and should be measured. The entity has considered the amounts and probabilities of the possible estimated outcomes as follows.

Possible Estimated Outcome	Individual Probability of Occurring (%)	Cumulative Probability of Occurring (%)
$100	5	5
80	25	30
60	25	55
50	20	75
40	10	85
20	10	95
0	5	100

Because $60 is the largest amount of benefit that is greater than 50 percent likely of being realized upon settlement, the entity would recognize a tax benefit of $60 in the financial statements.

Source: FASB Accounting Standards Codification 740-10-55-102–104.

EXHIBIT 10-14

The Hershey Company Corporation Income Tax Footnote

13. INCOME TAXES

Our income (loss) before income taxes was as follows:

For the Years Ended December 31,	2009	2008	2007
In thousands of dollars			
Domestic	$670,753	$568,282	$ 456,856
Foreign	378	(76,260)	(116,614)
Income before income taxes	$671,131	$492,022	$ 340,242

The 2008 and 2007 foreign losses before income taxes were due primarily to the business realignment and impairment charges recorded during each year.

Our provision for income taxes was as follows:

For the Years Ended December 31,	2009	2008	2007
In thousands of dollars			
Current:			
Federal	$235,282	$181,611	$ 208,754
State	42,206	13,839	26,082
Foreign	(1,773)	2,292	15,528
Current provision for income taxes	275,715	197,742	250,364
Deferred:			
Federal	(37,298)	(11,855)	(74,658)
State	(2,682)	1,843	(10,324)
Foreign	(598)	(7,113)	(39,294)
Deferred income tax benefit	(40,578)	(17,125)	(124,276)
Total provision for income taxes	$235,137	$180,617	$ 126,088

The income tax benefits associated with the exercise of non-qualified stock options reduced accrued income taxes on the Consolidated Balance Sheets by $4.5 million as of December 31, **2009** and by $1.4 million as of December 31, 2008. We credited additional paid-in capital to reflect these income tax benefits. The deferred income tax benefit in 2009, 2008 and 2007 primarily reflected the tax effect of the charges for the global supply chain transformation program recorded during the year.

Deferred taxes reflect temporary differences between the tax basis and financial statement carrying value of assets and liabilities. The tax effects of the significant temporary differences that comprised the deferred tax assets and liabilities were as follows:

December 31,	2009	2008
In thousands of dollars		
Deferred tax assets:		
Post-retirement benefit obligations	$122,815	$122,815
Accrued expenses and other reserves	108,633	103,694
Stock-based compensation	70,224	63,122
Accrued trade promotion reserves	5,041	4,819
Derivative Instruments	—	10,538
Pension	—	1,177
Net operating loss carryforwards	37,279	25,199
Other	16,354	15,133
Gross deferred tax assets	360,346	346,497
Valuation allowance	(43,388)	(30,814)
Total deferred tax assets	316,958	315,683
Deferred tax liabilities:		
Property, plant and equipment, net	161,150	164,629
Derivative instruments	37,014	—
Pension	14,028	—
Acquired intangibles	35,868	33,350
Inventories	17,805	31,404
Other	6,872	5,228
Total deferred tax liabilities	272,737	234,611
Net deferred tax assets	$ (44,221)	$ (81,072)
Included in:		
Current deferred tax assets, net	(39,868)	(70,903)
Non-current deferred tax assets, net	(4,353)	(13,815)
Non-current deferred tax liabilities, net	—	3,646
Net deferred tax assets	$ (44,221)	$ (81,072)

(continued)

We believe that it is more likely than not that the results of future operations will generate sufficient taxable income to realize the deferred tax assets. The valuation allowances as of December 31, 2009 and 2008, were primarily related to tax loss carryforwards from operations in various foreign tax jurisdictions. Additional information on income tax benefits and expenses related to components of accumulated other comprehensive income (loss) is provided in *Note 9, Comprehensive Income*.

The following table reconciles the Federal statutory income tax rate with our effective income tax rate:

For the Years Ended December 31,	2009	2008	2007
Federal statutory income tax rate	35.0%	35.0%	35.0%
Increase (reduction) resulting from:			
State income taxes, net of Federal income tax benefits	3.0	2.2	2.2
Qualified production income deduction	(1.7)	(1.7)	(1.7)
Business realignment initiatives	(.5)	.7	1.1
International operations	(.1)	1.3	.2
Other, net	(.7)	(.8)	.3
Effective income tax rate	35.0%	36.7%	37.1%

The effective income tax rate for 2009 was lower by 0.5 percentage points, the effective income tax rate for 2008 was higher by 0.7 percentage points and the effective income tax rate for 2007 was higher by 1.1 percentage points resulting from the impact of tax rates associated with business realignment and impairment charges. The effect of international operations varied based on the taxable income (loss) of our entities outside of the United States.

A reconciliation of the beginning and ending amount of unrecognized tax benefits is as follows:

December 31,	2009	2008
In thousands of dollars		
Balance at beginning of year	$58,000	$74,724
Additions for tax positions taken during prior years	13,399	1,436
Reductions for tax positions taken during prior years	(8,246)	(7,150)
Additions for tax positions taken during the current year	11,781	7,885
Settlements	(4,689)	(9,295)
Expiration of statutes of limitations	(7,240)	(9,600)
Balance at end of year	$63,005	$58,000

The total amount of unrecognized tax benefits that, if recognized, would affect the effective tax rate was $41.5 million as of December 31, 2009, and $39.2 million as of December 31, 2008. We report accrued interest and penalties related to unrecognized tax benefits in income tax expense. We recognized a benefit in the amount of $2.9 million in 2009 for interest and penalties. We recognized expense of $4.7 million during 2008 and $0.4 million during 2007 for interest and penalties. Accrued interest and penalties were $21.1 million as of December 31, 2009, and $27.1 million as of December 31, 2008. We file income tax returns in the U.S. federal jurisdiction and various state and foreign jurisdictions. A number of years may elapse before an uncertain tax position, for which we have unrecognized tax benefits, is audited and finally resolved. While it is often difficult to predict the final outcome or the timing of resolution of any particular uncertain tax position, we believe that our unrecognized tax benefits reflect the most likely outcome. We adjust these unrecognized tax benefits, as well as the related interest, in light of changing facts and circumstances. Settlement of any particular position could require the use of cash. Favorable resolution would be recognized as a reduction to our effective income tax rate in the period of resolution. The number of years with open tax audits varies depending on the tax jurisdiction. Our major taxing jurisdictions include the United States (federal and state), Canada and Mexico. During the second quarter of 2009, the U.S. Internal Revenue Service ("IRS") completed its audit of our U.S. income tax returns for 2005 and 2006 resulting in the resolution of tax contingencies associated with the 2004, 2005 and 2006 tax years. During the fourth quarter of 2009, the IRS commenced its audit of our U.S. income tax returns for 2007 and 2008. Tax examinations by various state taxing authorities could generally be conducted for years beginning in 2004. We are no longer subject to Canadian federal income tax examinations by the Canada Revenue Agency ("CRA") for years before 1999, and we are no longer subject to Mexican federal income tax examinations by Servicio de Administracion Tributaria ("SAT") for years before 2004. U.S., Canadian and Mexican federal audit issues typically involve the timing of deductions and transfer pricing adjustments. We work with the IRS, the CRA and SAT to resolve proposed audit adjustments and to minimize the amount of adjustments. We do not anticipate that any potential tax adjustments will have a significant impact on our financial position or results of operations.

We reasonably expect reductions in the liability for unrecognized tax benefits of approximately $16.5 million within the next 12 months because of the expiration of statutes of limitations and settlements of tax audits.

Source: The Hershey Company 2009 Form 10-K.

SUMMARY

When the capital structure of a subsidiary or equity investee includes outstanding preferred stock, we allocate the investee's equity and income to the preferred stockholders based on the preferred contract and then allocate to common stockholders. If the subsidiary's preferred stock is not held by the parent, we include the preferred income in noncontrolling interest share and the preferred equity in noncontrolling interest. The viewpoint of the consolidated entity considers any of the subsidiary's preferred stock held by the parent as retired for consolidated statement purposes.

Consolidated and parent earnings per share computations are identical, and the procedures used in computing parent earnings per share also apply to investor accounting under the equity method. Parent/investor relationships do not affect EPS computations unless the subsidiary/investee has outstanding potentially dilutive securities. When a subsidiary has potentially dilutive securities outstanding, the computational adjustments for EPS differ according to whether the subsidiary's potentially dilutive securities are convertible into subsidiary common stock or parent common stock.

A consolidated entity classified as an affiliated group may elect to file consolidated tax returns. All other consolidated entities file separate tax returns. In determining taxable income, consolidated entities that are members of an affiliated group can exclude all dividends received from group members. Affiliated groups that elect to file consolidated tax returns avoid paying taxes on unrealized profits and can offset losses of one group member against income of other group members.

Investors with equity investees and subsidiaries that are not members of an affiliated group pay income taxes currently on a portion of dividends received and provide for deferred income taxes on their share of undistributed income of their investees.

Unrealized and constructive gains and losses from intercompany transactions create temporary differences that may affect deferred tax calculations when filing separate-company tax returns.

An acquisition of another company for accounting purposes may be a taxable combination or a tax-free reorganization under the Internal Revenue Code. In a tax-free business combination, we allocate the fair value/book value differential to the assets and liabilities acquired at fair values and record a deferred tax asset or deferred tax liability for the related tax effect.

QUESTIONS

1. Sam Corporation has 100,000 outstanding shares of $10 par common stock and 5,000 outstanding shares of $100 par, cumulative, 10 percent preferred stock. Sam's net income for the year is $300,000, and its stockholders' equity at year end is as follows (in thousands):

10% cumulative preferred stock, $100 par	$ 500
Common stock, $10 par	1,000
Additional paid-in capital	600
Retained earnings	400
Total Stockholders' Equity	$2,500

Par Corporation owns 60 percent of the outstanding common stock of Sam, acquired at a fair value equal to book value several years ago. Compute Par's investment income for the year and the balance of its Investment in Sam account at the end of the year.

2. Refer to the information in question 1. Assume that Sam pays two years' preferred dividend requirements during the current year. Would this affect your computation of Par's investment income for the current year? If so, recompute Par's investment income.

3. How should preferred stock of a subsidiary be shown in a consolidated balance sheet in each case?
   a If it is held 100 percent by the parent
   b If it is held 50 percent by the parent and 50 percent by outside interests
   c If it is held 100 percent by outside interests

4. Describe the computation of noncontrolling interest share for an 80%-owned subsidiary with both preferred and common stock outstanding.

5. How does controlling share of consolidated earnings per share differ from parent earnings per share?

6. Do investments in nonconsolidated subsidiaries and 20%- to 50%-owned investees affect the nature of the investor's EPS calculations?

7. Under what conditions will the procedures used in computing a parent's EPS be the same as those for a company without equity investments?

8. It may be necessary to compute the earnings per share for subsidiaries and equity investees before parent (and consolidated) earnings per share can be determined. When are the subsidiary EPS computations used in calculating parent earnings per share?

9. Potentially dilutive securities of a subsidiary may be converted into parent common stock or subsidiary common stock. Describe how these situations affect the parent's EPS procedures.

10. In computing diluted earnings for a parent, it may be necessary to replace the parent's equity in subsidiary realized income with the parent's equity in the subsidiary's diluted earnings. Does this replacement calculation involve unrealized profits that are included in the parent's income from subsidiary.

11. Are consolidated income tax returns required for all consolidated entities? Discuss.

12. Can a consolidated entity that is classified as an "affiliated group" under the IRS code elect to file separate tax returns for each affiliate?

13. What are the primary advantages of filing a consolidated tax return?

14. Some or all of the dividends received by a corporation from domestic affiliates may be excluded from federal income taxation. When are all of the dividends excluded?

15. Describe the nature of the tax effect of temporary differences that arise from use of the equity method of accounting.

16. Does a parent/investor provide for income taxes on the undistributed earnings of a subsidiary by adjusting investment and investment income accounts? Explain.

17. When do unrealized and constructive gains and losses create temporary differences for a consolidated entity?

EXERCISES

E 10-1

[Based on AICPA] Preferred stock and income tax

1. [Preferred stock] Pin Corporation owns 20% of Sob Corporation's preferred stock and 80% of its common stock. Sob's stock outstanding on December 31, 2011, is as follows:

10% cumulative preferred stock	$ 200,000
Common stock	1,400,000

Sob reported net income of $120,000 for the year ended December 31, 2011. What amount should Pin record as equity in earnings of Sob for the year ended December 31, 2011?

a $84,000

b $96,000

c $96,800

d $100,000

2. [Tax] Pat Corporation uses the equity method to account for its 25% investment in Sam, Inc. During 2011, Pat received dividends of $30,000 from Sam and recorded $180,000 as its equity in the earnings of Sam. Additional information follows:

■ The dividends received from Sam are eligible for the 80% dividends-received deduction.

■ There are no other temporary differences.

■ Enacted income tax rates are 30% for 2011 and thereafter.

In its December 31, 2011, balance sheet, what amount should Pat report for deferred income tax liability?

a $9,000

b $10,800

c $45,000

d $54,000

3. [Tax] In 2011, Pal Corporation received $300,000 in dividends from Sal Corporation, its 80%-owned subsidiary. What net amount of dividend income should Pal include in its 2011 consolidated tax return?

a $300,000

b $240,000

c $210,000

d $0

4. [Tax] Pot Corporation and Sly Corporation filed consolidated tax returns. In January 2011, Pot sold land, with a basis of $60,000 and a fair value of $75,000, to Sly for $100,000. Sly sold the land in December 2012 for

$125,000. In its 2012 and 2011 tax returns, what amount of gain should be reported for these transactions in the consolidated return?

	2012	2011
a	$25,000	$40,000
b	$50,000	0
c	$50,000	$25,000
d	$65,000	0

E 10-2

[Preferred stock] Subsidiary preferred stock with dividends in arrears

The stockholders' equity of Sir Corporation at December 31, 2011, was as follows (in thousands):

10% cumulative preferred stock, $100 par, callable at $105, 20,000 shares issued and outstanding, with one year's dividends in arrears	$2,000
Common stock, $10 par, 200,000 shares issued and outstanding	2,000
Additional paid-in capital	4,000
Retained earnings	8,000
Total stockholders' equity	$16,000

On January 1, 2010, Pod Corporation purchased 90 percent of Sir Corporation's common stock at $90 per share. Sir's assets and liabilities were recorded at their fair values when Pod acquired its 90 percent interest. Any fair value/ book value differential is assigned to goodwill and is not amortized. During 2012, Sir reported net income of $2,400,000 and paid dividends of $1,200,000.

REQUIRED: Calculate the following:

1. The fair value/book value differential from Pod's investment in Sir.
2. Pod's income from Sir for 2012.
3. The balance of Pod's investment in Sir at December 31, 2012.
4. Total noncontrolling interest in Sir on December 31, 2012.

E 10-3

[Preferred stock] Goodwill and investment income—subsidiary preferred stock

The stockholders' equity of Sol Corporation at December 31, 2010, was as follows (in thousands):

12% preferred stock, cumulative, nonparticipating, $100 par, callable at $105	$ 600
Common stock, $10 par	1,000
Other paid-in capital	140
Retained earnings	760
Total stockholders' equity	$2,500

Par Corporation purchased 80 percent of Sol's common stock on January 2, 2011, for $1,536,000. During 2011, Sol reported a $100,000 net loss and paid no dividends. During 2012, Sol reported $500,000 net income and declared dividends of $344,000. Any excess fair value is allocated to goodwill.

REQUIRED

1. Compute the fair value/book value differential from Par's investment in Sol.
2. Determine Par's income (loss) from Sol for 2011.
3. Determine Par's income (loss) from Sol for 2012.
4. Compute the balance of Par's Investment in Sol account on December 31, 2012.

E 10-4

[Preferred stock] Investment cost and net income—subsidiary preferred stock

Pen Corporation owns 80 percent of San Corporation's common stock, having acquired the interest at a fair value equal to book value on December 31, 2011. During 2012, Pen's separate income is $3,000,000 and San's net income is $500,000. Pen and San declare dividends in 2012 of $1,000,000 and $300,000, respectively.

The stockholders' equity of San consists of the following (in thousands):

	December 31, 2011	December 31, 2012
12% cumulative preferred stock, $100 par, callable at $105 per share	$1,000	$1,000
Common stock, $10 par	2,000	2,000
Other paid-in capital	300	300
Retained earnings	700	900
Total stockholders' equity	$4,000	$4,200

REQUIRED

1. Determine the cost of Pen's investment in San on December 31, 2011, if San has one year's preferred dividends in arrears on that date.

2. Calculate Pen's net income and noncontrolling interest share for 2012.

3. Calculate the underlying book value of Pen's investment in San on December 31, 2012.

E 10-5

[Preferred stock] Journal entries—parent owns both common and preferred stock of subsidiary

The stockholders' equity of Son Corporation on December 31, 2011, was as follows (in thousands):

15% preferred stock, $100 par, cumulative, nonparticipating, with one year's dividends in arrears	$1,000
Common stock, $10 par	2,000
Other paid-in capital	200
Retained earnings	300
Total stockholders' equity	$3,500

Pam Corporation acquired 50 percent of Son's preferred stock for $600,000 and 80 percent of its common stock for $2,000,000 on January 1, 2012. Son reported net income of $400,000 and paid dividends of $300,000 in 2012.

REQUIRED

1. Prepare the journal entries to record Pam's 50% investment in Son preferred stock.

2. Calculate the excess fair value/book value differential from Pam's 80% investment in Son common. Assume the differential is goodwill.

3. Compute Pam's income from Son—preferred for 2012.

4. Compute Pam's income from Son—common for 2012 (assume a 10-year amortization period for the fair value/book value differential).

5. Calculate the noncontrolling interest in Son that will appear in the consolidated balance sheet of Pam Corporation and Subsidiary on December 31, 2012.

E 10-6

[Preferred stock] Fair value/book value differentials for preferred and common stock

Pay Corporation purchased 60 percent of Set Corporation's outstanding preferred stock for $6,500,000 and 70 percent of its outstanding common stock for $35,000,000 on January 1, 2012. Set's stockholders' equity on December 31, 2011, consisted of the following (in thousands):

10% cumulative, $100 par, preferred stock, callable at $105 (100,000 shares issued and outstanding with one year's dividends in arrears)	$10,000
Common stock, $10 par	30,000
Other paid-in capital	5,000
Retained earnings	15,000
Total stockholders' equity	$60,000

REQUIRED

1. Determine the fair value/book value differentials from Pay's investments in Set.

2. Without bias on your part, assume that the fair value/book value differential applicable to the preferred investment is a negative $400,000. Describe the accounting treatment of the preferred differential if the preferred investment is treated as a constructive retirement for consolidation purposes.

E 10-7
[EPS] General questions

1. A parent company and its 100%-owned subsidiary have only common stock outstanding (10,000 shares for the parent and 3,000 shares for the subsidiary), and neither company has issued other potentially dilutive securities. The equation to compute consolidated EPS for the parent company and its subsidiary is:

 a   *(Net income of parent + Net income of subsidiary) ÷ 13,000 shares*
 b   *(Net income of parent + Net income of subsidiary) ÷ 10,000 shares*
 c   *Net income of parent ÷ 13,000 shares*
 d   *Net income of parent ÷ 10,000 shares*

2. A parent company has a 90% interest in a subsidiary that has no potentially dilutive securities outstanding. In computing consolidated EPS:

 a   *Subsidiary common shares are added to parent common shares and common share equivalents*
 b   *Subsidiary EPS and parent EPS amounts are combined*
 c   *Subsidiary EPS computations are not needed*
 d   *Subsidiary EPS computations are used in computing basic earnings*

3. In computing a parent company's diluted EPS, it may be necessary to subtract the parent's equity in subsidiary realized income and replace it with the parent's equity in subsidiary diluted earnings. The subtraction in this replacement computation is affected by:

 a   *Constructive gain from purchase of parent bonds*
 b   *Current amortization from investment in the subsidiary*
 c   *Unrealized profits from downstream sales*
 d   *Unrealized profits from upstream sales*

E 10-8
[EPS] Consolidated EPS with goodwill, noncontrolling interest, and warrants

Pal Corporation's net income for 2011 is $316,000, including $160,000 income from Sod Corporation, its 80 percent-owned subsidiary. The income from Sod consists of $176,000 equity in income less $16,000 patent amortization. Pal has 300,000 shares of $10 par common stock outstanding, and Sod has 50,000 shares of $10 par common stock outstanding throughout 2011. In addition, Sod has 10,000 outstanding warrants to acquire 10,000 shares of Sod common stock at $10 per share. The average market price of Sod's common stock was $20 per share during 2011.

1. For purposes of calculating Pal Corporation's (and consolidated) diluted earnings per share, Sod's diluted earnings are:

 a   *$220,000*
 b   *$200,000*
 c   *$176,000*
 d   *$160,000*

2. For purposes of calculating Pal Corporation's (and consolidated) diluted earnings per share, Sod's outstanding common shares and common share equivalents are:

 a   *60,000 shares*
 b   *56,000 shares*
 c   *55,000 shares*
 d   *50,000 shares*

3. For purposes of calculating Pal Corporation's (and consolidated) earnings per share, assume that Sod's diluted EPS is $4 per share. Pal Corporation's (and consolidated) diluted earnings will be:

 a   *$316,000*
 b   *$300,000*
 c   *$156,000*
 d   *$140,000*

4. If Sod's diluted earnings for 2011 are $4 per share, Pal Corporation's (and consolidated) diluted earnings per share will be:

 a   *$1.64*
 b   *$1.59*
 c   *$1.04*
 d   *$1.00*

E 10-9

[EPS] Consolidated basic and diluted EPS

The following information is available regarding Put Corporation and its 80 percent-owned subsidiary, San Corporation, at and for the year ended December 31, 2011:

	Put	San
Outstanding common stock	8,000 shares	5,000 shares
Warrants to purchase 1,000 shares of San common stock at $9 per share (average market price is $15)		1,000 warrants
Net income (includes income from San)	$20,000	$18,000
Income from San ($14,400 − $2,400 amortization of excess cost over book value acquired)	$12,000	

REQUIRED: Determine consolidated earnings per share (both basic and diluted).

E 10-10

[EPS] Consolidated EPS with unrealized profit from upstream sale

The income statements of Pin Corporation and its 80 percent-owned subsidiary, Sal Corporation, for 2011 are as follows:

	Pin	Sal
Sales	$1,270,000	$ 740,000
Income from Sal (see note)	13,920	—
Cost of sales	(700,000)	(470,000)
Expenses	(462,000)	(230,000)
Income before taxes	121,920	40,000
Provision for income taxes	(41,453)	(13,600)
Net income	$ 80,467	$ 26,400

Note: Income from Sal is computed as [($26,400 reported income × 80%) − $2,000 patent amortization − $5,200 unrealized profit in Sal's inventory].

Pin had 10,000 shares of common stock and 1,200 shares of $100 par, 10 percent cumulative preferred stock outstanding throughout 2011. Sal had 20,000 shares of common stock and warrants to purchase 5,000 shares of Sal common stock at $24 outstanding throughout 2011. The average market price of Sal common stock was $30 per share.

REQUIRED: Compute Pin's (and consolidated) basic and diluted EPS.

E 10-11

[EPS] Subsidiary EPS and consolidated EPS with goodwill and warrants

Pow Corporation owns an 80 percent interest in Soy Corporation. Pow does not have common stock equivalents or other potentially dilutive securities outstanding, so it calculated its EPS for 2011 as follows:

$$\frac{\$1,000,000 \text{ separate income} + \$480,000 \text{ Income from Soy}}{1,000,000 \text{ outstanding common shares of Pow}} = \$1.48$$

An examination of Pow's income from Soy shows that it is determined correctly as 80 percent of Soy's $630,000 net income less $24,000 patent amortization. Pow's EPS computation is in error, however, because it fails to consider outstanding warrants of Soy that permit their holders to acquire 10,000 shares of Soy common stock at $24 per share and increase Soy's outstanding common stock to 60,000 shares. The average price of Soy common stock during 2011 was $40.

REQUIRED

1. Compute Soy Corporation's diluted EPS for use in determining consolidated EPS.

2. Compute consolidated EPS for 2011 (both basic and diluted).

E 10-12

[Tax] General questions

1. Income taxes are currently due on intercompany profits when:

 a   *Profits originate from upstream sales*

 b   *Separate-company tax returns are filed*

 c   *Consolidated tax returns are filed*

 d   *Affiliates are accounted for as consolidated subsidiaries*

2. The right of a consolidated entity to file a consolidated tax return is contingent upon:

 a   *Ownership by a common parent of all the voting stock of group members*

 b   *Ownership by a common parent of 90% of the voting stock of group members*

 c   *Classification as an affiliated group*

 d   *Direct or indirect ownership of a majority of the outstanding stock of all group members*

3. When affiliates are classified as an affiliated group for tax purposes, the group:

 a   *Excludes unrealized profits from intercompany transactions from taxable income*

 b   *Must file a consolidated income tax return*

 c   *May file separate income tax returns*

 d   *Pays lower income taxes*

4. Deferred income taxes are provided for unrealized profits from intercompany transactions when:

 a   *A consolidated tax return is filed*

 b   *Separate-company tax returns are filed*

 c   *The unrealized profits are from upstream sales*

 d   *The consolidated entity is an affiliated group*

E 10-13

[Tax] Asset allocation in business combination, tax effect from equity investees

1. When Pet Corporation acquired its 100% interest in Sin Corporation in a tax-free reorganization, Sin's equipment had a fair value of $6,000,000 and a book value and tax basis of $4,000,000. If Pet's effective tax rate is 34%, how much of the purchase price should be allocated to equipment and to deferred income taxes?

 a   *$4,000,000 and $0, respectively*

 b   *$5,320,000 and $680,000, respectively*

 c   *$6,000,000 and $680,000, respectively*

 d   *$6,000,000 and $2,040,000, respectively*

2. Car Corporation, whose effective income tax rate is 34%, received $200,000 dividends from its 30%-owned domestic equity investee during the current year and recorded $500,000 equity in the investee's income. Car's income tax expense for the year should include taxes on the investment of:

 a   *$13,600*

 b   *$20,400*

 c   *$34,000*

 d   *$68,000*

3. During 2011, Pal Corporation reported $60,000 investment income from Sap Corporation, its 30%-owned investee, and it received $30,000 dividends from Sap. Pal's effective income tax rate is 34%, and it is entitled to an 80% dividends-received deduction on dividends received from Sap. On the basis of this information, Pal should:

 a   *Report investment income from Sap of $57,960*

 b   *Increase its investment in Sap for 2011 in the amount of $27,960*

 c   *Credit its deferred income taxes in the net amount of $2,040 for 2011*

 d   *Debit its deferred income taxes in the net amount of $2,040 for 2011*

4. Pin Corporation owns 35% of the voting stock of Sis Corporation, a domestic corporation. During 2011, Sis reports net income of $100,000 and pays dividends of $50,000. Pin's effective income tax rate is 34%. What amounts should Pin record as income taxes currently payable and as deferred income taxes from its investment in Sis?

 a   *$17,000 and $0, respectively*

 b   *$5,950 and $5,950, respectively*

 c   *$3,400 and $3,400, respectively*

 d   *$1,190 and $1,190, respectively*

5. Pit Corporation and its 100%-owned domestic subsidiary, Sir Corporation, are classified as an affiliated group for tax purposes. During the current year, Sir pays $80,000 in cash dividends. Assuming a 34% income tax rate, how much income tax expense on this dividend should be reported in the consolidated income statement of Pit Corporation and Subsidiary?

a $0

b $27,200

c $5,440

d $2,720

E 10-14

[Tax] Compare separate and consolidated tax filings

The pretax accounting incomes of Pit Corporation and its 100 percent-owned subsidiary, Sol Company, for 2011 are as follows (in thousands):

	Pit	Sol
Sales	$1,000	$500
Gain on land	200	—
Total revenue	1,200	500
Cost of sales	500	300
Gross profit	700	200
Operating expenses	400	100
Pretax accounting income	$ 300	$100

The only intercompany transaction during 2011 was a gain on land sold to Sol. Assume a 34 percent flat income tax rate.

REQUIRED

1. What amount should be shown on the consolidated income statement as income tax expense if separate-company tax returns are filed?

2. Compute the consolidated income tax expense if a consolidated tax return is filed.

3. What will be the income taxes currently payable if separate income tax returns are filed? If a consolidated return is filed?

E 10-15

[Tax] Consolidated income statement (downstream gain on sale of equipment)

Pan Corporation and its 70 percent-owned subsidiary, Sum Corporation, have pretax operating incomes for 2011 as follows (in thousands):

	Pan	Sum
Sales	$8,000	$4,000
Gain on equipment	200	—
Cost of sales	(5,000)	(2,000)
Other expenses	(1,800)	(1,200)
Pretax income	$1,400	$ 800

Pan received $280,000 dividends from Sum during 2011. A previously unrecorded patent from Pan's investment in Sum is being amortized at a rate of $50,000 per year (the same time horizon is used for both book and tax purposes).

On January 1, 2011, Pan sold equipment to Sum at a $200,000 gain. Sum is depreciating the equipment at a rate of 20 percent per year. A flat 34 percent tax rate is applicable to both companies.

REQUIRED: Prepare a consolidated income statement for Pan Corporation and Subsidiary for 2011. (Assume no deferred tax balance on January 1, 2011.)

E 10-16

[Tax] Journal entries for unrealized profit with separate and consolidated tax returns

Sun Corporation is a 100 percent-owned subsidiary of Ped Corporation. During the current year, Ped sold merchandise that cost $50,000 to Sun for $100,000. A 34 percent income tax rate is applicable, and 80 percent of the merchandise remains unsold by Sun at year-end.

REQUIRED

1. Prepare comparative one-line consolidation entries relating to the unrealized profit when separate and consolidated income tax returns are filed.

2. Prepare comparative consolidation workpaper entries in general journal form relating to the intercompany sales transaction and the related income tax effect when separate and consolidated income tax returns are filed.

E 10-17

[Tax] Journal entries for unrealized profit from upstream sale and separate tax returns

Son Corporation, an 80 percent-owned subsidiary of Pin Corporation, sold equipment with a book value of $150,000 to Pin for $250,000 at December 31, 2011. Separate income tax returns are filed, and a 34 percent income tax rate is applicable to both Pin and Son.

REQUIRED

1. Prepare a one-line consolidation entry for Pin to eliminate the effect of the intercompany transaction.

2. Prepare workpaper entries in general journal form to eliminate the unrealized profit.

3. Assume that the reported net income of Son is $800,000 and that the sale of equipment is the only intercompany transaction between Pin and Son. What is the noncontrolling interest's share of total consolidated income?

E 10-18

[Tax] Valuation Allowance

Pax Corporation recognizes a deferred tax asset (benefit) of $500,000 related to its acquisition of Son Company. Pax has determined that the tax position qualifies for recognition and should be measured. Pax has determined the amounts and the probabilities of the possible outcomes, as follows:

Possible Estimated Outcome	Probability of Occurring (%)
$500,000	10
400,000	25
300,000	25
200,000	20
100,000	10
0	10

REQUIRED: Calculate the tax benefit to be recognized by Pax.

E 10-19

[Tax] Valuation Allowance

Pun Corporation recognizes a deferred tax asset (benefit) of $150,000 related to its acquisition of Sew Company. Pun has determined that the tax position qualifies for recognition and should be measured. Pun has determined the amounts and the probabilities of the possible outcomes, as follows:

Possible Estimated Outcome	Probability of Occurring (%)
$150,000	50
125,000	20
100,000	10
50,000	10
0	10

REQUIRED: Calculate the tax benefit to be recognized by Pun.

PROBLEMS

P 10-1

[Preferred stock] Investment in common stock (subsidiary preferred stock)

Par Corporation paid $7,200,000 for 360,000 shares of Sun Corporation's outstanding voting common stock on January 1, 2011, when the stockholders' equity of Sun consisted of (in thousands):

10% cumulative, preferred stock, $100 par. Liquidation preference is $105 per share, and 20,000 shares are issued and outstanding with one year's dividends in arrears	$2,000
Common stock, $10 par, 400,000 shares issued and outstanding	4,000
Other paid-in capital	1,000
Retained earnings	1,300
Total stockholders' equity	$8,300

During 2011, Sun reported net income of $1,000,000 and declared dividends of $800,000. Any excess of fair value over book value is goodwill, which is not amortized.

REQUIRED: Calculate the following:

1. Goodwill from Par's acquisition of Sun

2. Par's income from Sun for 2011

3. Noncontrolling interest share for 2011

4. Noncontrolling interest in Sun at December 31, 2011

5. Par's Investment in Sun account balance at December 31, 2011

P 10-2

[Preferred stock] Consolidation entries—investments in preferred and common stock—midyear purchases

Pun Corporation acquired 80 percent of Set Corporation's preferred stock for $175,000 and 90 percent of Set's common stock for $630,000 on July 1, 2011. Set's stockholders' equity on December 31, 2011, was as follows (in thousands):

Stockholders' Equity	
9% preferred stock, cumulative, nonparticipating, $100 par, call price $105	$200
Common stock, $10 par	500
Paid-in capital in excess of par	40
Retained earnings	160
Total stockholders' equity	$900

Set had net income of $24,000 in 2010 and $46,000 in 2011, but declared no dividends in either year. Assume that preferred dividends accrue ratably throughout each year and that Set's net assets were fairly valued on July 1, 2011.

REQUIRED

1. Determine the account balances of Pun Corporation's investments in Set's preferred and common stocks at December 31, 2011, on the basis of a one-line consolidation.

2. Prepare workpaper entries to consolidate the balance sheets of Pun and Set at December 31, 2011.

P 10-3

[Preferred stock] Consolidation workpaper (subsidiary preferred stock, equity method, mid-year purchase)

Financial statements for Pat and Sal Corporations for 2011 are summarized as follows (in thousands):

	Pat	Sal
Combined Income and Retained Earnings Statements for the Year Ended December 31		
Sales	$1,233	$700
Income from Sal	68	—
Cost of sales	(610)	(400)
Other expenses	(390)	(210)
Net income	301	90
Add: Retained earnings January 1	501	200
Less: Dividends	(200)	(50)
Retained earnings December 31	$ 602	$240
Balance Sheet at December 31		
Cash	$ 191	$ 50
Other current assets	200	300
Plant assets—net	900	600
Investment in Sal	711	—
Total assets	$2,002	$950
Current liabilities	$ 200	$ 60
$10 preferred stock	—	100
Common stock	1,200	500
Other paid-in capital	—	50
Retained earnings	602	240
Total equities	$2,002	$950

Pat owns 90,000 shares of Sal's outstanding voting common stock at December 31, 2011. These shares were acquired in two lots as follows:

	Date	Shares	Purchase Price
Lot 1	January 1, 2010	70,000	$490,000
Lot 2	April 1, 2011	20,000	152,000

The stockholders' equity of Sal at year-end 2009, 2010, and 2011 was as follows (in thousands):

	December 31,		
	2009	2010	2011
$10 preferred stock, $100 par, cumulative with no dividends in arrears	$100	$100	$100
Common stock, $5 par	500	500	500
Other paid-in capital	50	50	50
Retained earnings	150	200	240
Total stockholders' equity	$800	$850	$890

Sal's net income for 2011 is $90,000, earned proportionately throughout the year, and its quarterly dividends of $12,500 are declared on March 15, June 15, September 15, and December 15. (Quarterly dividends of $12,500 include dividends on common stock and preferred stock.) There are no intercompany receivables or payables at December 31, 2011, and there have been no intercompany transactions other than dividends.

REQUIRED: Prepare a consolidation workpaper for Pat and Subsidiary for 2011.

P 10-4

[Preferred stock] Consolidation workpaper (subsidiary preferred stock, downstream inventory sales, upstream sale of land, subsidiary bonds)

Par Corporation acquired an 80 percent interest in Sam Corporation common stock for $240,000 on January 1, 2010, when Sam's stockholders' equity consisted of $200,000 common stock, $100,000 preferred stock, and $25,000 retained earnings. The excess was due to goodwill.

Intercompany sales of inventory items from Par to Sam were $50,000 in 2010 and $60,000 in 2011. The cost of these items to Par was 60 percent of the selling price to Sam, and Sam inventoried $30,000 of the intercompany sales items at December 31, 2010, and $40,000 at December 31, 2011. Intercompany receivables and payables from these sales were $10,000 at December 31, 2010, and $5,000 at December 31, 2011.

Sam sold land that cost $10,000 to Par for $20,000 during 2010. During 2011, Par resold the land outside the consolidated entity for $30,000.

On July 1, 2011, Par purchased all of Sam's bonds payable in the open market for $91,000. These bonds were issued at par, have interest payment dates of June 30 and December 31, and mature on June 30, 2014.

Sam declared and paid dividends of $10,000 on its cumulative preferred stock and $10,000 on its common stock in each of the years 2010 and 2011.

Financial statements for Par and Sam Corporations at and for the year ended December 31, 2011, are summarized as follows (in thousands):

	Par	Sam
Combined Income and Retained Earnings Statement for the Year Ended December 31		
Sales	$ 900	$ 300
Gain on land	10	—
Interest income	6.5	—
Income from Sam	50	—
Cost of sales	(600)	(140)
Operating expenses	(208.5)	(90)
Interest expense	—	(10)
Net income	158	60
Add: Beginning retained earnings	132	50
Deduct: Dividends	(100)	(20)
Retained earnings December 31	$ 190	$ 90
Balance Sheet at December 31		
Cash	$ 5.5	$ 15
Accounts receivable	26	20
Inventories	80	60
Other current assets	100	5
Land	160	30
Plant and equipment—net	268	420
Investment in Sam—bonds	92.5	—
Investment in Sam—stock	282	—
Total assets	$1,014	$ 550
Accounts payable	$ 24	$ 15
10% bonds payable	—	100
Other liabilities	100	45
10% preferred stock	—	100
Common stock	700	200
Retained earnings	190	90
Total equities	$1,014	$ 550

REQUIRED: Prepare a consolidation workpaper for Par Corporation and Subsidiary for the year ended December 31, 2011.

P 10-5

[EPS] Computing EPS with convertible debentures

Pal Corporation has $108,000 income from its own operations for 2011, and $42,000 income from Sir Corporation, its 70 percent-owned subsidiary. Sir's net income of $60,000 consists of $66,000 operating income less $6,000 net-of-tax interest on its outstanding 10 percent convertible debentures. Throughout 2011, Pal has 100,000 shares of common stock outstanding, and Sir has 50,000 outstanding common shares.

REQUIRED

1. Compute Pal's diluted earnings per share for 2011, assuming that Sir's bonds are convertible into 10,000 shares of Sir's common stock.

2. Compute Pal's diluted earnings per share for 2011, assuming that Sir's bonds are convertible into 10,000 shares of Pal's common stock.

P 10-6

[EPS] Compute basic and diluted EPS (options; preferred stock)

Pen Corporation owns an 80 percent interest in She Company. Throughout 2011, Pen had 20,000 shares of common stock outstanding. She had the following securities outstanding:

- 10,000 shares of common stock
- Options to purchase 2,000 shares of She common at $15 per share
- 1,000 shares of 10%, $100 par, convertible, preferred stock that are convertible into 3,000 shares of She common stock

Income data for the affiliates for 2011 are as follows:

	Pen	She
Separate incomes	$120,000	$ 55,000
Income from She ($45,000 income to common × 80%) − $6,000 patent amortization	30,000	—
	$150,000	$ 55,000

REQUIRED: Compute basic and diluted earnings per share for Pen Corporation and Subsidiary for 2011, assuming an average market price for She common stock of $30 per share.

P 10-7

[EPS] Convertible preferred stock and amortization of excess

Pro Corporation owns 80 percent of Sit Corporation's outstanding common stock. The 80 percent interest was acquired in 2011 at $40,000 in excess of book value due to undervalued equipment with an eight-year remaining useful life. Outstanding securities of the two companies throughout 2012 and at December 31, 2012, are:

	Pro	Sit
Common stock, $5 par	20,000 shares	—
Common stock, $10 par	—	6,000 shares
14% Cumulative, Convertible, Preferred Stock, $100 Par	—	1,000 shares

Sit Corporation's net income is $50,000 for 2012, and Pro's net income consists of $70,000 separate income and $23,800 income from Sit.

REQUIRED

1. Compute consolidated basic and diluted earnings per share, assuming that the preferred stock is convertible into 4,000 shares of Sit Corporation's common stock.

2. Compute consolidated basic and diluted earnings per share, assuming that the preferred stock is convertible into 5,000 shares of Pro's common stock.

P 10-8

[EPS] Compute consolidated EPS; subsidiary diluted

Pin Company owns 40,000 of 50,000 outstanding shares of Sum Company, and during 2011, it recognizes income from Sum as follows:

Share of Sum net income ($500,000 × 80%)	$ 400,000
Patent amortization	(50,000)
Unrealized profit—downstream sales	(40,000)
Unrealized profit—upstream sales ($60,000 × 80%)	(48,000)
Income from Sum	$262,000

Pin's net income for 2011 is $1,262,000, consisting of separate income from Pin of $1,000,000 and $262,000 income from Sum. Pin has 100,000 shares of common stock outstanding, but no common stock equivalents or other potentially dilutive securities.

Sum has $100,000 par of 10 percent convertible bonds outstanding that are convertible into 10,000 shares of Sum common stock. The net-of-tax interest on the bonds is $6,400, and Sum's diluted earnings per share for purposes of computing consolidated earnings per share are determined as follows:

Net income	$500,000
Add: Net-of-tax interest on convertible bonds	6,400
Less: Unrealized profit on upstream sales	(60,000)
a Diluted earnings	$446,400
Common shares outstanding	50,000
Shares issuable upon conversion of bonds	10,000
b Common shares and equivalents	60,000
Diluted earnings per share (a ÷ b)	$ 7.44

REQUIRED: Compute Pin Company's and consolidated diluted earnings per share for 2011.

P 10-9

[EPS] Computations (subsidiary preferred stock and warrants)

Pit Corporation's net income for 2011 consists of the following:

Separate income		$320,000
Income from Sim Corporation:		
80% of Sim's income to common	$160,000	
Less: Patent amortization	(4,000)	
Less: Unrealized profits on equipment sold to Sim	(10,000)	
Less: 80% of unrealized profit on land purchased from Sim	(16,000)	130,000
Net income		$450,000

ADDITIONAL INFORMATION

1. Pit has 100,000 shares of common stock, and Sim has 50,000 shares of common and 10,000 shares of $10 cumulative, convertible, preferred stock outstanding throughout 2011. The preferred stock is convertible into 30,000 shares of Sim stock.

2. Sim has warrants outstanding that permit their holders to purchase 10,000 shares of Sim Corporation common stock at $15 per share (average market price $20).

3. Sim's reported net income for 2011 is $300,000, allocated $100,000 to preferred stockholders and $200,000 to common stockholders.

4. Pit owned 40,000 shares of Sim common stock throughout 2011.

REQUIRED: Compute Pit Corporation's (and consolidated) basic and diluted EPS.

P 10-10

[Tax] Comparative income statements (consolidated and separate tax returns)

Par Corporation and its 100 percent-owned subsidiary, Sam Corporation, are members of an affiliated group with pretax accounting incomes as follows (in thousands):

	Par	Sam
Sales	$2,400	$1,400
Gain on sale of land	100	—
Cost of sales	(1,200)	(600)
Operating expenses	(700)	(500)
Pretax accounting income	$ 600	$ 300

The gain reported by Par relates to land sold to Sam during the current year. A flat 34 percent income tax rate is applicable.

REQUIRED: Prepare income statements for Par Corporation assuming (a) that separate income tax returns are filed and (b) that a consolidated income tax return is filed. (*Note:* Par applies the equity method as a one-line consolidation.)

P 10-11

[Tax] Computations and income statement (upstream sales)

Pan Corporation paid $577,500 cash for a 70 percent interest in Sir Corporation's outstanding common stock on January 2, 2011, when the equity of Sir consisted of $500,000 common stock and $300,000 retained earnings. The excess fair value is due to goodwill.

In December 2011, Sir sold inventory items to Pan at a gross profit of $50,000 (selling price $120,000 and cost $70,000), and all these items were included in Pan's inventory at December 31, 2011.

Sir paid dividends of $50,000 in 2011, and an 80 percent dividends-received deduction is applicable. A flat 34 percent income tax rate is applicable to both companies.

Separate pretax incomes of Pan and Sir for 2011 are as follows (in thousands):

	Pan	Sir
Sales	$4,000	$1,000
Cost of sales	(2,000)	(550)
Operating expenses	(1,500)	(250)
Pretax income	$ 500	$ 200

REQUIRED

1. Determine 2011 income tax currently payable and income tax expense for Pan and Sir.

2. Calculate Pan's income from Sir for 2011.

3. Prepare a consolidated income statement for Pan and Sir for 2011.

P 10-12

[Tax] Consolidated income statement (downstream sales)

Taxable incomes for Pub Corporation and Sew Corporation, its 70 percent-owned subsidiary, for 2011 are as follows (in thousands):

	Pub	Sew
Sales	$500	$300
Dividends received from Sew	28	—
Total revenue	528	300
Cost of sales	250	120
Operating expenses	78	80
Total deductions	328	200
Taxable income	$200	$100

ADDITIONAL INFORMATION

1. Pub acquired its interest in Sew at a fair value equal to book value on December 31, 2010.

2. Sew paid dividends of $40,000 in 2011.

3. Pub sold $90,000 in merchandise to Sew during 2011, and there was $10,000 in unrealized profit from the sales at year end.

4. A flat 34% income tax rate is applicable.

5. Pub is eligible for the 80% dividends-received deduction.

REQUIRED: Prepare a consolidation income statement workpaper for Pub Corporation and Subsidiary for 2011.

P 10-13

[Tax] Reconstruct workpaper (separate and consolidated income statements)

Pen Corporation acquired a 90 percent interest in Soo Corporation in a taxable transaction on January 1, 2011, for $900,000, when Soo had $500,000 capital stock and $400,000 retained earnings. The $90,000 excess cost over book value is due to goodwill. Pen and Soo are an affiliated group for tax purposes.

During 2011, Pen sold land to Soo at a $20,000 profit. Soo still holds the land. Soo paid dividends of $50,000. A flat 34 percent tax rate applies to Pen and Soo. Income statements for Pen and Soo, and a consolidated income statement for Pen and Subsidiary, are summarized as follows:

	Pen	Soo	Consolidated
Sales	$ 800,000	$200,000	$1,000,000
Gain on sale of land	20,000	—	—
Income from Soo	36,430	—	—
Cost of sales	(400,000)	(75,000)	(475,000)
Other expenses	(150,000)	(30,000)	(180,000)
Income tax expense	(85,000)	(32,300)	(117,300)
Noncontrolling interest share	—	—	(6,270)
Net income	$ 221,430	$ 62,700	$ 221,430

REQUIRED: Reconstruct all the workpaper entries needed to consolidate the financial statements of Pen Corporation and Subsidiary for 2011.

P 10-14

[Tax] Allocate fair value/book value differentials in a taxable purchase combination

Par Corporation acquired all the stock of Sad Corporation on January 1, 2011, for $280,000 cash, when the book values and fair values of Sad's assets and liabilities were as follows (in thousands):

	Book Values (Tax Bases)	Fair Values
Current assets	$100	$100
Land	20	60
Buildings—net	80	110
Equipment—net	60	70
Assets	$260	$340
Liabilities	$ 90	$ 90
Capital stock	150	
Retained earnings	20	
Equities	$260	

Sad's buildings have a remaining life of 10 years, and the equipment has a useful life of 2 years from the date of the combination. During 2011, Sad had income of $50,000 and paid dividends of $20,000. Par and Sad are subject to a 35 percent tax rate.

REQUIRED

1. Prepare a schedule to allocate the excess fair value over book value to Sad's assets, liabilities, deferred taxes, and goodwill at January 1, 2011, assuming the purchase was a taxable transaction.

2. Prepare a schedule to allocate the excess fair value over book value to Sad's assets, liabilities, deferred taxes, and goodwill at January 1, 2011, assuming the purchase was a tax-free reorganization.

3. Compute Par's income from Sad for 2011 under both options.

P 10-15

[Tax] Consolidated income statement (separate returns and intercompany equipment)

The pretax operating incomes of Pop Corporation and Son Corporation, its 70 percent-owned subsidiary, for 2011 are as follows (in thousands):

	Pop	Son
Sales	$8,000	$4,000
Gain on equipment	500	—
Cost of sales	(5,000)	(2,000)
Other expenses	(2,100)	(1,200)
Pretax income (excluding Pop's income from Son)	$1,400	$ 800

ADDITIONAL INFORMATION

1. Pop received $280,000 dividends from Son during 2011.

2. Goodwill from Pop's investment in Son is not amortized.

3. Pop sold equipment to Son at a gain of $500,000 on January 1, 2011. Son is depreciating the equipment at a rate of 20% per year.

4. A flat 34% tax rate is applicable.

5. Pop provides for income taxes on undistributed income from Son.

REQUIRED

1. Determine the separate income tax expenses for Pop and Son.

2. Determine Pop's income from Son on an equity basis.

3. Prepare a consolidated income statement for Pop Corporation and Subsidiary for the year ended December 31, 2011.

P 10-16

[Tax] Computations (separate tax returns with goodwill, downstream inventory sales, and upstream land sale)

On January 3, 2011, Pix Corporation purchased a 90% interest in Sal Corporation at a price $120,000 in excess of book value and fair value. The excess is goodwill. During 2011, Pix sold inventory items to Sal for $100,000, and $15,000 in profit from the sale remained unrealized at year-end. Sal sold land to Pix during the year at a gain of $30,000.

ADDITIONAL INFORMATION

1. The companies are an affiliated group for tax purposes.
2. Sal declared and paid dividends of $100,000 in 2011.
3. Pix and Sal file separate income tax returns, and a 34% tax rate is applicable to both companies.
4. Pix uses a correct equity method to account for its investment in Sal.
5. Pretax accounting incomes, excluding Pix's income from Sal, are as follows (in thousands):

	Pix	Sal
Sales	$ 3,815	$ 2,000
Gain on land	—	30
Cost of sales	(2,200)	(1,200)
Other expenses	(1,000)	(400)
Pretax accounting income	$ 615	$ 430

REQUIRED: Calculate the following:

1. Sal's net income
2. Pix's income from Sal
3. Pix's net income

INTERNET ASSIGNMENT

Obtain a copy of the 2009 annual report of ***Dow Chemical Company (Dow)*** from the company's Web site. Prepare a brief summary of information you find related to the major topics covered in this chapter.

    a. Is there any disclosure of preferred stock or subsidiary preferred stock transactions?

    b. What amounts does Dow report for earnings per share? Summarize Dow's earnings per share calculations.

    c. Summarize Dow's reconciliation of its effective tax rate with the federal statutory rate for 2009 only.

REFERENCES TO THE AUTHORITATIVE LITERATURE

[1] FASB ASC 323-10-35-16. Originally *Accounting Principles Board Opinion No. 18.* "The Equity Method of Accounting for Investments in Common Stock." New York: American Institute of Certified Public Accountants, 1971.

[2] FASB ASC 260-10-05-1. Originally *Statement of Financial Accounting Standards No. 128.* "Earnings per Share." Norwalk, CT: Financial Accounting Standards Board, 1997.

[3] FASB ASC 260-10-55-20. Originally *Statement of Financial Accounting Standards No. 128.* "Earnings per Share." Norwalk, CT: Financial Accounting Standards Board, 1997.

[4] FASB ASC 740-10-05-1. Originally *Statement of Financial Accounting Standards No. 109.* "Accounting for Income Taxes." Norwalk, CT: Financial Accounting Standards Board, 1992.

[5] FASB ASC 740-30-25. Originally *Statement of Financial Accounting Standards No. 109*. "Accounting for Income Taxes." Norwalk, CT: Financial Accounting Standards Board, 1992 and *Accounting Principles Board Opinion No. 23*. "Accounting for Income Taxes – Special Areas." New York: American Institute of Certified Public Accountants, 1972.

[6] FASB ASC 740-10-05. Originally *Statement of Financial Accounting Standards No. 109*. "Accounting for Income Taxes." Norwalk, CT: Financial Accounting Standards Board, 1992.

[7] FASB ASC 740-10-05. Originally *Statement of Financial Accounting Standards No. 109*. "Accounting for Income Taxes." Norwalk, CT: Financial Accounting Standards Board, 1992.

[8] FASB ASC 740-10-05. Originally *Statement of Financial Accounting Standards No. 109*. "Accounting for Income Taxes." Norwalk, CT: Financial Accounting Standards Board, 1992.

[9] FASB ASC 740-10-05. Originally *Statement of Financial Accounting Standards No. 109*. "Accounting for Income Taxes." Norwalk, CT: Financial Accounting Standards Board, 1992.

[10] FASB ASC 350-20-35-1. Originally *Statement of Financial Accounting Standards No. 142*. "Goodwill and Other Intangible Assets." Stamford, CT: Financial Accounting Standards Board, 2001.

[11] FASB ASC 740-10-05-5. Originally *Statement of Financial Accounting Standards No. 109*. "Accounting for Income Taxes." Norwalk, CT: Financial Accounting Standards Board, 1992.

[12] FASB ASC 805-740-45-2. Originally *Statement of Financial Accounting Standards No. 109*. "Accounting for Income Taxes." Norwalk, CT: Financial Accounting Standards Board, 1992.

[13] FASB ASC 740-30-7. Originally *Financial Accounting Standards Board Interpretation No. 48*. "Accounting for Uncertainty in Income Taxes: An interpretation of FASB Statement No. 109." Norwalk, CT: Financial Accounting Standards Board, June 2006.

[14] FASB ASC 805-740-45. Originally *Statement of Financial Accounting Standards No. 109*. "Accounting for Income Taxes." Norwalk, CT: Financial Accounting Standards Board, 1992.

11 CHAPTER

Consolidation Theories, Push-Down Accounting, and Corporate Joint Ventures

P revious chapters have described practices used in the preparation of consolidated financial statements and have explained the rationale for those practices. The concepts and procedures discussed in earlier chapters reflect the **contemporary theory** of consolidated statements. Contemporary theory has evolved from accounting practice and is essentially an entity theory approach to the preparation of consolidated financial statements.

Traditional theory (GAAP prior to 2001 [1]) reflected parts of both parent-company theory and entity theory. **Parent-company theory** assumes that consolidated financial statements are an extension of parent statements and should be prepared from the viewpoint of parent stockholders. Under parent-company theory, we prepare consolidated statements for the benefit of the stockholders of the parent, and we do not expect that noncontrolling stockholders can benefit significantly from the statements. Consolidated net income under parent-company theory is a measurement of income to the parent stockholders.

Certain problems and inconsistencies in accounting procedures under parent-company theory arise in the case of less-than-100 percent-owned subsidiaries. For example, the noncontrolling interest is a liability from the viewpoint of parent stockholders, and published statements frequently reported the noncontrolling interest in the liability section of the consolidated balance sheet. Similarly, noncontrolling interest share is an expense from the viewpoint of controlling stockholders. However, shareholder interests, whether controlling or noncontrolling, are not liabilities under any of the accepted concepts of a liability, and income to shareholders does not meet the requirements for expense recognition. The problem lies in the controlling shareholder viewpoint.

Entity theory represents an alternative view of consolidation. It was developed by Professor Maurice Moonitz and published by the American Accounting Association in 1944 under the title *The Entity Theory of Consolidated Statements*. The focal point of entity theory is that the consolidated statements reflect the viewpoint of the total business entity, under which all resources controlled by the entity are valued consistently. Under entity theory, the income of noncontrolling interests is a distribution of the total income of the consolidated entity, and the interests of noncontrolling stockholders are a part of consolidated stockholders' equity.

Entity theory requires that the income and equity of a subsidiary be determined for all stockholders, so that the total amounts can be allocated between controlling and noncontrolling shareholders in a consistent manner. Entity theory accomplishes this by imputing a total fair value for the subsidiary on the basis of the price paid by the parent for its controlling interest. We assign the excess of total fair value of the subsidiary over the book value of subsidiary net assets 100 percent to identifiable assets

LEARNING OBJECTIVES

1 Compare and contrast the elements of consolidation approaches under traditional, parent-company, and contemporary/entity theory.

2 Adjust subsidiary assets and liabilities to fair values using push-down accounting.

3 Account for corporate and unincorporated joint ventures.

4 Identify variable interest entities.

5 Consolidate a variable interest entity.

and to goodwill. In this manner, entity theory consolidates subsidiary assets (including goodwill) and liabilities at fair values, which are applicable to both noncontrolling and controlling interests.

COMPARISON OF CONSOLIDATION THEORIES

Exhibit 11-1 compares the basic differences between parent-company, contemporary/entity, and traditional theories. Parent-company theory adopts the viewpoint of parent stockholders, and entity theory focuses on the total consolidated entity. By contrast, traditional theory identifies the primary users of consolidated financial statements as the stockholders and creditors of the parent, but it assumes the objective of reporting financial position and results of operations of a single business entity. Thus, the viewpoint of traditional theory [2] appears to be a compromise between the parent-company and entity theories.

Income Reporting

Consolidated net income is a measurement of income to parent stockholders under both the parent-company and traditional theories. Entity theory, however, requires a computation of income to all

EXHIBIT 11-1

COMPARISON OF CONSOLIDATION THEORIES

	Parent-Company Theory	Contemporary/Entity Theory	Traditional Theory
Basic purposes and users of consolidated financial statements	Consolidated statements are an extension of parent statements, prepared for the benefit and from the viewpoint of the stockholders of the parent.	Consolidated statements are prepared from the viewpoint of the total consolidated entity, intended for all parties having an interest in the entity.	Consolidated statements present the financial position and results of operations of a single business enterprise but are prepared primarily for the benefit of the stockholders and creditors of the parent.
Consolidated net income	Consolidated net income is income to the stockholders of the parent.	Total consolidated net income is income to all equity holders of the consolidated entity.	Consolidated net income is income to the stockholders of the parent.
Noncontrolling interest share	Noncontrolling interest share is an expense from the viewpoint of the parent stockholders measured on the basis of the subsidiary as a separate legal entity.	Noncontrolling interest share is an allocation of total consolidated net income to noncontrolling stockholders.	Noncontrolling interest share is a deduction in determining consolidated net income but not a true expense instead, it is an allocation of realized income of the entity between controlling and noncontrolling interests.
Equity of noncontrolling interests	Equity of noncontrolling stockholders is a liability from the viewpoint of the parent stockholders, measured based on the subsidiary's legal entity.	Equity of noncontrolling stockholders is a part of consolidated stockholders equity equivalent to the presentation accorded the equity of controlling stockholders.	Equity of noncontrolling stockholders is a part of consolidated stockholders equity presented as single amount because it is not expected that noncontrolling interest will benefit from the disclosure.
Consolidation of subsidiary net assets	Parent's share of subsidiary net assets is consolidated on the basis of the price paid by the parent for its interest. The noncontrolling interest's share is consolidated at book value.	All net assets of a subsidiary are consolidated at their fair values imputed on the basis of the price paid by the parent for its interest. Thus, controlling and noncontrolling interests in net assets are valued consistently.	Subsidiary net assets are consolidated at book value plus the excess of the parent company's investment cost over the book value of the interest acquired.
Unrealized gains and losses from intercompany transactions	100% elimination from consolidated net income for downstream sales and elimination of the parent's share for upstream sales.	100% elimination in determining total consolidated net income with allocation between controlling and noncontrolling interests for upstream sales.	100% elimination from revenue and expense accounts with allocation between controlling and noncontrolling interests for upstream sales.
Constructive gains and losses on debt retirement	100% recognition in consolidated net income on retirement of parent debt, and recognition of the parent's share for retirement of subsidiary debt.	100% recognition in total consolidated net income with allocation between controlling and noncontrolling interests for retirement of subsidiary debt.	100% recognition in revenue and expense accounts with allocation between controlling and noncontrolling interests for retirement of subsidiary debt.

equity holders, which we label "total consolidated net income." Entity theory then assigns total consolidated net income to noncontrolling and controlling stockholders, with appropriate disclosure on the face of the income statement. Consolidated net income under traditional theory reflected parent-company theory. This is evidenced by the practice of reporting noncontrolling interest share as an expense and the equity of noncontrolling stockholders as a liability. However, the preferred accounting practices under traditional theory show noncontrolling interest share as a separate deduction from consolidated net income, and report the equity of controlling and noncontrolling shareholders as a single amount within the consolidated stockholders' equity classification.

Under current GAAP [3] a noncontrolling interest in a subsidiary should be labeled and displayed as a separate component of equity in the consolidated balance sheet. Income attributable to the noncontrolling interest is not an expense or a loss, but it is a deduction from consolidated net income in computing income attributable to the controlling interest. The consolidated income statement should disclose the portions of consolidated net income attributable to the controlling interest and noncontrolling interests.

Asset Valuation

Perhaps the greatest difference between parent-company theory and entity theory lies in the valuation of subsidiary net assets. Parent-company theory initially consolidates subsidiary assets at their book values, plus the parent's share of any excess fair value over book values. In other words, we revalue subsidiary assets only to the extent of the net assets (including goodwill) acquired by the parent. We consolidate the noncontrolling interest in subsidiary net assets at book value. Although this approach reflects the cost principle from the viewpoint of the parent, it leads to inconsistent treatment of controlling and noncontrolling interests in the consolidated financial statements and to a balance sheet valuation that reflects neither historical cost nor fair value.

Entity theory consolidates subsidiary assets and liabilities at fair values, and accounts for the controlling and noncontrolling interests in those net assets consistently. However, this consistent treatment is obtained through the practice of imputing a total subsidiary valuation on the basis of the price paid by the parent for its controlling interest. Conceptually, this valuation approach has considerable appeal when the parent acquires essentially all of the subsidiary's stock for cash. It has less appeal when the parent acquires a slim majority of subsidiary outstanding stock for noncash assets or through an exchange of shares. An investor may be willing to pay a premium for the rights to *control* an investee (an investment of more than 50%), but not willing to purchase the remaining stock at the inflated price.

Additional problems with the imputed total valuation of a subsidiary under entity theory develop after the parent acquires its interest. *Once the parent is able to exercise absolute control over the subsidiary, the shares held by noncontrolling stockholders do not represent equity ownership in the usual sense.* Typically, the stock of a subsidiary will be "delisted" after an acquisition, leaving the parent as the only viable purchaser for noncontrolling shares. In this case, noncontrolling shareholders are at the mercy of the parent. A noncontrolling share does not have the same equity characteristics as a controlling share.

Traditional theory conforms to the practices of parent-company theory in the consolidation of subsidiary assets and liabilities. Although a conceptual superiority for entity theory in this area is frequently granted, there are practical disadvantages. Some believe the price paid by the parent for its controlling interest is not a valid basis for valuation of noncontrolling interests. Even the practice of measuring the equity of noncontrolling shareholders at book value is criticized because it tends to overstate the value of the noncontrolling interest (primarily due to the restricted marketability of noncontrolling shares).

Unrealized Gains and Losses

A difference between the parent-company and entity theories also exists in the treatment of unrealized gains and losses from intercompany transactions (see Exhibit 11-1). Although there is general agreement that 100 percent of all unrealized gains and losses from downstream sales should be eliminated, we accord gains and losses arising from upstream sales different treatment under parent-company and entity theories. Under parent-company theory, we eliminate unrealized gains and losses from upstream sales to the extent of the parent's ownership percentage in the subsidiary. The portion of unrealized gains and losses not eliminated relates to the noncontrolling interest and, from the parent viewpoint, is considered to be realized by noncontrolling shareholders.

We eliminate unrealized gains and losses in determining total consolidated net income under entity theory. In the case of upstream sales, however, we allocate the eliminated amounts between income to noncontrolling and controlling stockholders according to their respective ownership percentages.

The elimination of unrealized gains and losses under traditional theory follows the pattern and consistency of entity theory. GAAP [4] requires that all unrealized gains and losses be eliminated, but the elimination of the intercompany profit or loss may be allocated proportionately between the controlling and noncontrolling interests in the case of upstream sales. Presumably, the assignment of the full amount of unrealized gains and losses from upstream sales to controlling interests would also be acceptable. This latter approach was not used in earlier chapters because of its inherent inconsistency for consolidation purposes and because its use seems incompatible with requirements for the equity method of accounting. If unrealized gains and losses from upstream sales are not allocated between controlling and noncontrolling interests, the parent's income and equity will not equal the controlling share of consolidated net income and consolidated equity unless the same inconsistency is applied under the equity method.

Constructive Gains and Losses

The pattern of accounting for constructive gains and losses from intercompany debt acquisitions under the three theories parallels the pattern of accounting for unrealized gains and losses from intercompany transactions (see Exhibit 11-1). Gains and losses on the constructive retirement of debt under traditional theory are accounted for in the same manner as under entity theory.

Consolidated Stockholders' Equity

Current GAAP differs slightly from entity theory in reporting consolidated stockholders' equity. Under entity theory, both controlling and noncontrolling interests are components of consolidated equity. Further, entity theory would show the components of each interest, i.e., breaking the controlling and noncontrolling interests into their respective shares of contributed capital and retained earnings. Under GAAP [5], the noncontrolling interest is shown as a single, combined amount under consolidated stockholders' equity.

ILLUSTRATION—CONSOLIDATION UNDER PARENT-COMPANY AND ENTITY THEORIES

Differences among the various consolidation theories may be more comprehensible when shown in numerical examples. The following section relates to the acquisition of Sad by Ped Corporation on January 1, 2011. Assume that Ped Corporation acquires a 90 percent interest in Sad Corporation for $198,000 cash on January 1, 2011. Comparative balance sheets of the two companies immediately before the acquisition are as follows (in thousands):

	Ped		Sad	
	Book Value	**Fair Value**	**Book Value**	**Fair Value**
Cash	$220	$220	$ 5	$ 5
Accounts receivable—net	80	80	30	35
Inventories	90	100	40	50
Other current assets	20	20	10	10
Plant assets—net	220	300	60	80
Total assets	$630	$720	$145	$180
Liabilities	$ 80	$ 80	$ 25	$ 25
Capital stock, $10 par	400		100	
Retained earnings	150		20	
Total equities	$630		$145	

The $198,000 purchase price for the 90 percent interest implies a $220,000 total value for Sad's net assets ($198,000 ÷ 90%). Under entity theory, we revalue all subsidiary assets and liabilities and reflect these values in the consolidated statements on the basis of the $220,000 implied total valuation. Under parent-company theory, we do not reflect the total implied value of the subsidiary in the consolidated financial statements; therefore, only 90 percent of the subsidiary's net assets are revalued. Although *the different theories do not affect parent accounting under the equity method,* they do result in different amounts for consolidated assets, liabilities, and noncontrolling interests.

ENTITY THEORY In the Ped–Sad example, entity theory assigns the $100,000 excess of implied value over the $120,000 book value of Sad's net assets to identifiable net assets and goodwill as follows (in thousands):

	Fair Value		Book Value		Excess Fair Value
Accounts receivable—net	$35	–	$30	=	$ 5
Inventories	50	–	40	=	10
Plant assets—net	80	–	60	=	20
Goodwill (remainder)	—		—		65
Total implied fair value over book value					$100

PARENT-COMPANY THEORY Amounts assigned to identifiable net assets and goodwill under parent-company theory (and traditional theory) would be 90 percent of the foregoing amounts:

Accounts receivable—net	$ 5,000 × 90% = $ 4,500
Inventories	10,000 × 90% = 9,000
Plant assets—net	20,000 × 90% = 18,000
Goodwill	65,000 × 90% = 58,500
Total purchase price over book value acquired	$90,000

GOODWILL Goodwill under the two theories can be determined independently. Under entity theory, the $65,000 goodwill is equal to the total implied value of Sad's net assets over the fair value of Sad's identifiable net assets ($220,000 – $155,000). Under parent-company theory, the $58,500 goodwill is equal to the investment cost less 90 percent of the fair value of Sad's identifiable net assets ($198,000 – $139,500). Entity theory reflects the $10,000 additional amount assigned to identifiable assets and goodwill ($100,000 – $90,000) in the noncontrolling interest classification in a consolidated balance sheet.

Consolidation at Acquisition

Exhibit 11-2 compares consolidated balance sheet workpapers for Ped Corporation and Subsidiary under parent-company and entity theories. Recall that traditional theory is the same as parent-company theory in matters relating to the initial consolidation of a subsidiary.

The comparative workpapers in Exhibit 11-2 begin with separate balance sheets of the affiliates and use established procedures for consolidation. Although the workpapers could be modified under parent-company theory to reflect the noncontrolling interest among the liabilities, this modification does not seem necessary. Such classification differences can be reflected in the consolidated statements without changing workpaper procedures.

Parent-company theory allocates 90 percent of the excess of fair value over book value of identifiable net assets to identifiable assets and liabilities, and it allocates the $58,500 excess of investment cost over fair value of net assets acquired to goodwill. Noncontrolling interest of $12,000 for parent-company theory is equal to 10 percent of the $120,000 book value of Sad's net assets at the time of acquisition.

Entity theory assigns the full excess of fair value over book value to identifiable net assets, and it enters the excess of implied total value over fair value of net identifiable assets as goodwill. The $22,000 noncontrolling interest is 10 percent of the implied fair value of Sad's net assets (including goodwill).

Consolidated assets under parent-company theory consist of the book value of combined assets plus 90 percent of the excess of fair value of Sad's assets over their book value. Under entity theory, consolidated assets consist of the book value of Ped's assets plus the fair value of Sad's

EXHIBIT 11-2

Balance Sheet
Workpaper
Comparisons

PED CORPORATION AND SUBSIDIARY CONSOLIDATED BALANCE SHEET WORKPAPER AT JANUARY 1, 2011 (IN THOUSANDS)

	Ped	90% Sad	Adjustments and Eliminations		Consolidated Statements
			Debits	Credits	
Parent-Company Theory					
Assets					
Cash	$ 22	$ 5			$ 27
Accounts receivable—net	80	30	b 4.5		114.5
Inventories	90	40	b 9		139
Other current assets	20	10			30
Plant assets—net	220	60	b 18		298
Investment in Sad	198			a 198	
Goodwill			b 58.5		58.5
Unamortized excess			a 90	b 90	
Total assets	$630	$145			$667
Liabilities and Equity					
Liabilities	$ 80	$ 25			$105
Capital stock	400	100	a 100		400
Retained earnings	150	20	a 20		150
Noncontrolling interest				a 12	12
Total equities	$630	$145			$667
Entity Theory					
Assets					
Cash	$ 22	$ 5			$ 27
Accounts receivable—net	80	30	b 5		115
Inventories	90	40	b 10		140
Other current assets	20	10			30
Plant assets—net	220	60	b 20		300
Investment in Sad	198			a 198	
Goodwill			b 65		65
Unamortized excess			a 100	b 100	
Total assets	$630	$145			$677
Liabilities and Equity					
Liabilities	$ 80	$ 25			$105
Capital stock	400	100	a 100		400
Retained earnings	150	20	a 20		150
Noncontrolling interest				a 22	22
Total equities	$630	$145			$677

assets. Although entity theory consolidates all assets of Sad at their fair values, total consolidated assets do not reflect fair values under either theory because we never revalue the assets of the parent at the time of an acquisition.

Consolidation After Acquisition

Differences between parent-company theory and entity theory can be explained further by examining the operations of Ped Corporation and Sad Corporation for 2011. The following assumptions are made:

1. Sad's net income and dividends for 2011 are $35,000 and $10,000, respectively.

2. The excess of fair value over book value of Sad's accounts receivable and inventories at January 1, 2011, is realized during 2011.

3. Sad's plant assets are being depreciated over 20 years, using the straight-line method (i.e., at a 5% annual rate).

EQUITY METHOD Under these assumptions, Ped records $17,100 investment income from Sad for 2011, computed under the equity method as follows:

Share of Sad's net income ($35,000 × 90%)	$31,500
Less: Realization of excess allocated to receivables	
($5,000 × 90%)	(4,500)
Realization of excess allocated to inventories	
($10,000 × 90%)	(9,000)
Depreciation on excess allocated to plant assets	
($20,000 × 90%) ÷ 20 years	(900)
Income from Sad for 2011	$17,100

Ped's Investment in Sad account under the equity method has a balance of $206,100 at December 31, 2011. This consists of the $198,000 investment cost, plus $17,100 investment income for 2011, less $9,000 dividends received from Sad during 2011. Equity method accounting is not affected by the viewpoint adopted for consolidating the financial statements of affiliates; therefore, *the separate statements of Ped and Sad will be the same at December 31, 2011, regardless of the theory adopted.*

CONSOLIDATION PROCEDURES Consolidated net income under parent-company theory is the same as the income allocated to parent stockholders under entity theory. Therefore, the differences between the parent-company and entity theories lie solely in the manner of consolidating parent and subsidiary financial statements and in reporting the financial position and results of operations in the consolidated financial statements. Consolidation workpapers for Ped Corporation and Subsidiary under parent-company theory in Exhibit 11-3 and under entity theory in Exhibit 11-4 reflect these differences. Again, workpaper procedures have not been modified to reflect differences in financial statement classification. Exhibits 11-5 and 11-6 illustrate differences in financial statement presentation for Ped Corporation and Subsidiary and show financial statements prepared from the workpapers.

In comparing the consolidation workpapers under parent-company theory in Exhibit 11-3 with those under entity theory in Exhibit 11-4, note that the workpaper adjustment and elimination entries have the same debit and credit items, but the amounts differ for all workpaper entries other than entry a. Accounting for the subsidiary under the equity method is the same for both consolidation theories, so the entry to eliminate investment income and intercompany dividends and to adjust the investment account to its beginning-of-the-period balance (entry a) is exactly the same under parent-company theory as under entity theory.

The remaining adjustment and elimination entries in Exhibit 11-3 under parent-company theory differ from those under the contemporary theory used in earlier chapters. Entry b eliminates reciprocal subsidiary equity and investment amounts, establishes beginning noncontrolling interest at book value ($120,000 × 10%), and enters the unamortized excess. Entry c then allocates the excess of investment cost over book value acquired: $9,000 to cost of sales (for undervalued inventory items realized during 2011), $4,500 to operating expense (for undervalued receivables realized during 2011), $18,000

EXHIBIT 11-3

Parent-Company Theory

PED CORPORATION AND SUBSIDIARY CONSOLIDATION WORKPAPER FOR THE YEAR ENDED DECEMBER 31, 2011 (IN THOUSANDS)

	Ped	90% Sad	Adjustments and Eliminations Debits	Adjustments and Eliminations Credits	Consolidated Statements
Income Statement Sales	$600	$200			$800
Income from Sad	17.1		a 17.1		
Cost of sales	(300)	(120)	c 9		(429)
Operating expenses	(211.25)	(45)	c 4.5 d .9		(261.65)
Noncontrolling interest share ($35 × 10%)			e 3.5		(3.5)
Controlling share of net income	**$105.85**	**$ 35**			**$105.85**
Retained Earnings Statement Retained earnings	$150	$ 20	b 20		$150
Dividends	(80)	(10)		a 9 e 1	(80)
Controlling share of net income	105.85	35			105.85
Retained earnings— December 31	**$175.85**	**$ 45**			**$175.85**
Balance Sheet Cash	$ 29.75	$ 13			$ 42.75
Accounts receivable—net	90	32			122
Inventories	100	48			148
Other current assets	30	17			47
Plant assets—net	200	57	c 18	d .9	274.1
Investment in Sad	206.1			a 8.1 b 198	
Goodwill			c 58.5		58.5
Unamortized excess			b 90	c 90	
	$655.85	$167			$692.35
Liabilities	$ 80	$ 22			$102
Capital stock	400	100	b 100		400
Retained earnings	**175.85**	**45**			**175.85**
	$655.85	$167			
Noncontrolling interest				b 12 e 2.5	14.5
					$692.35

EXHIBIT 11-4

Entity Theory

PED CORPORATION AND SUBSIDIARY CONSOLIDATION WORKPAPER FOR THE YEAR ENDED DECEMBER 31, 2011 (IN THOUSANDS)

	Ped	90% Sad	Adjustments and Eliminations Debits	Credits	Consolidated Statements
Income Statement Sales	$600	$200			$800
Income from Sad	17.1		a 17.1		
Cost of sales	(300)	(120)	c 10		(430)
Operating expenses	(211.25)	(45)	c 5 d 1		(262.25)
Noncontrolling interest share*			e 1.9		(1.9)
Controlling share of net income	**$105.85**	**$ 35**			**$105.85**
Retained Earnings Statement Retained earnings	$150	$ 20	b 20		$150
Dividends	(80)	(10)		a 9 e 1	(80)
Controlling share of net income	105.85	35			105.85
Retained earnings— December 31	**$175.85**	**$ 45**			**$175.85**
Balance Sheet Cash	$ 29.75	$ 13			$ 42.75
Accounts receivable—net	90	32			122
Inventories	100	48			148
Other current assets	30	17			47
Plant assets—net	200	57	c 20	d 1	276
Investment in Sad	206.1			a 8.1 b 198	
Goodwill			c 65		65
Unamortized excess			b 100	c 100	
	$655.85	$167			$700.75
Liabilities	$ 80	$ 22			$102
Capital stock	400	100	b 100		400
Retained earnings	175.85	45			175.85
	$655.85	$167			
Noncontrolling interest				b 22 e .9	22.9
					$700.75

*Noncontrolling interest share ($35 − $16) × 10%.

EXHIBIT 11-5

Consolidated Income
Statements Under
Alternative Theories

PED CORPORATION AND SUBSIDIARY
CONSOLIDATED INCOME STATEMENTS
FOR THE YEAR ENDED DECEMBER 31, 2011
(IN THOUSANDS)

Parent-Company Theory		
Sales		$800.00
Less: Cost of sales	$429.00	
Operating expenses	261.65	
Noncontrolling interest share	3.50	
Total expenses		694.15
Consolidated net income		$105.85
Entity Theory		
Sales		$800.00
Less: Cost of sales	$430.00	
Operating expenses	262.25	
Total expenses		692.25
Total consolidated net income		$107.75
Attributable: to noncontrolling stockholders	$ 1.90	
to controlling stockholders	$105.85	
Traditional Theory		
Sales		$800.00
Less: Cost of sales	$429.00	
Operating expenses	261.65	
Total expenses		690.65
Total consolidated net income		109.35
Less: Noncontrolling interest share		3.50
Consolidated net income		$105.85

EXHIBIT 11-6

Consolidated Balance
Sheets Under
Alternative Theories

PED CORPORATION AND SUBSIDIARY
CONSOLIDATED BALANCE SHEETS
AT DECEMBER 31, 2011 (IN THOUSANDS)

	Parent-Company Theory	Entity Theory	Traditional Theory
Assets			
Cash	$ 42.75	$ 42.75	$ 42.75
Accounts receivable—net	122.00	122.00	122.00
Inventories	148.00	148.00	148.00
Other current assets	47.00	47.00	47.00
Total current assets	359.75	359.75	359.75
Plant assets—net	274.10	276.00	274.10
Goodwill	58.50	65.00	58.50
Total noncurrent assets	332.60	341.00	332.60
Total assets	$692.35	$700.75	$692.35
Liabilities and Equity			
Liabilities	$102.00	$102.00	$102.00
Noncontrolling interest	14.50	—	—
Total liabilities	116.50	102.00	102.00
Capital stock	400.00	400.00	400.00
Retained earnings	175.85	175.85	175.85
Noncontrolling interest	—	22.90	14.50
Total stockholders' equity	575.85	598.75	590.35
Total equities	$692.35	$700.75	$692.35

to plant assets (for undervalued plant assets at the beginning of 2011), and $58,500 to goodwill. Entries d and e reflect current depreciation on the excess allocated to plant assets ($18,000 × 5%) and the noncontrolling interest in subsidiary income and dividends, respectively. Noncontrolling interest share of $3,500 is simply 10 percent of Sad's $35,000 reported net income.

Entries b, c, d, and e in Exhibit 11-4 under entity theory have the same objective as those for the same items under parent-company theory, except for amounts that relate to the noncontrolling interest. Beginning noncontrolling interest under entity theory is $22,000, equal to 10 percent of the $220,000 implied total value of Sad Corporation at January 1, 2011. Beginning noncontrolling interest under entity theory is $10,000 greater than beginning noncontrolling interest of $12,000 under parent-company theory. The additional $10,000 relates to the allocation of 100 percent of the excess fair value over book value of Sad's net assets at acquisition under entity theory. In other words, workpaper entry b under entity theory is equivalent to entry b under parent-company theory, plus the additional $10,000 unamortized excess applicable to noncontrolling interest:

b	Unamortized excess (+A)	100,000	
	Capital stock (−SE)	100,000	
	Retained earnings January 1, 2011 (−SE)	20,000	
	Investment in Sad (−A)		198,000
	Noncontrolling interest January 1, 2011 (+SE)		22,000
	To eliminate reciprocal investment and equity balances, establish beginning noncontrolling interest, and enter the unamortized excess amount.		

Entry c under entity theory is equivalent to entry c under parent-company theory, plus the additional excess fair value over book value amounts:

c	Cost of sales (E, −SE)	10,000	
	Operating expenses (E, −SE)	5,000	
	Plant assets (+A)	20,000	
	Goodwill (+A)	65,000	
	Unamortized excess (−A)		100,000
	To allocate unamortized excess to identifiable assets and goodwill.		

Workpaper entry d for depreciation on the excess allocated to plant assets is $1,000 under entity theory, compared with $900 under parent-company theory. The $100 difference is simply the 5 percent depreciation rate applied to the additional $2,000 allocated to plant assets under entity theory.

Noncontrolling interest share under entity theory is $1,900, consisting of 10 percent of Sad's $35,000 income, less 10 percent of the $16,000 amortization on the $100,000 implied fair value/book value differential. Alternatively, noncontrolling interest share can be computed as follows:

Share of Sad's reported income ($35,000 × 10%)	$3,500
Less: Operating expenses for realization of excess allocated to receivables ($5,000 × 10%)	(500)
Cost of sales for realization of excess allocated to inventory ($10,000 × 10%)	(1,000)
Depreciation on excess allocated to plant assets ($20,000 ÷ 20 years × 10%)	(100)
Noncontrolling interest share	$1,900

COMPARISON OF CONSOLIDATED INCOME STATEMENTS   The additional expenses deducted in determining consolidated net income under entity theory can be summarized as follows:

	Parent-Company Theory	Entity Theory
Operating expenses (for receivables)	$ 4,500	$ 5,000
Cost of sales (for inventory)	9,000	10,000
Operating expenses (for depreciation)	900	1,000
	$14,400	$16,000

The $1,600 additional expenses ($16,000 − $14,400) under entity theory are exactly offset by the lower noncontrolling interest share ($3,500 − $1,900) under entity theory. Thus, income to the parent stockholders is the same under the two theories, even though there are differences in the amounts reported and in the way the amounts are disclosed in the consolidated income statements. These differences are shown in Exhibit 11-5, which compares consolidated income statements for Ped Corporation and Subsidiary under parent-company theory, entity theory, and traditional theory.

Consolidated net income under parent-company theory is the same as under traditional theory. The reporting of income under entity theory shows a final amount for "total consolidated net income" of $107,750 and attribution of that income to noncontrolling and controlling stockholders. Although the amounts shown for Ped Corporation and Subsidiary are identical under parent-company and traditional theories, this equivalence would not have existed if there had been unrealized profits from upstream sales or constructive gains or losses from intercompany purchases of subsidiary debt. Consolidation procedures for these items are the same under traditional theory as under entity theory.

The reporting formats under the three consolidation theories vary somewhat, but it may be helpful to note the following relationships:

1. If a subsidiary investment is made at book value and the book values of individual assets and liabilities are equal to their fair values, the income statement amounts should be the same under entity theory as under traditional theory.

2. In the absence of intercompany transactions, the income statement amounts should be the same under parent-company theory as under traditional theory.

3. In the absence of noncontrolling interests, the income statement amounts should be the same under all three theories.

COMPARISON OF CONSOLIDATED BALANCE SHEETS Comparative balance sheets for Ped Corporation and Subsidiary at December 31, 2011, are illustrated in Exhibit 11-6 under each of the three theories. The amount of total assets is the same under parent-company and traditional theories but is greater under entity theory. The difference in total assets is $8,400 ($700,750 − $692,350), and consists of the unamortized excess of implied fair value over book value of Sad's net assets. This difference relates to goodwill of $6,500 ($65,000 − $58,500) and plant assets of $1,900 ($276,000 − $274,100).

Total liabilities and equity are the same under parent-company theory and traditional theory, but liabilities are $14,500 greater under parent-company theory because noncontrolling interest is classified as a liability. Stockholders' equity is $14,500 greater under traditional theory because noncontrolling interest is classified as a part of stockholders' equity.

The difference between total liabilities and equity under the entity and traditional theories lies solely in the $8,400 ($22,900 − $14,500) greater noncontrolling interest under entity theory. As in the case of the income generalizations, balance sheet amounts under the parent-company and traditional theories will be the same in the absence of intercompany transactions, and they will be the same under entity and traditional theories in the absence of a difference between fair value and book value acquired. In the absence of noncontrolling interests, all balance sheet amounts should be identical under the three theories.

OTHER VIEWS OF NONCONTROLLING INTEREST Some accountants believe that noncontrolling interest should not appear as a separate line item in consolidated financial statements. One suggestion for eliminating noncontrolling interest from consolidated statements is to report total consolidated net income as the bottom line in the consolidated income statements, with separate *footnote disclosure* of controlling and noncontrolling interests. Consistent treatment in the consolidated balance sheet would require total consolidated equity to be reported as a single line item, with separate footnote disclosure of the equity of controlling and noncontrolling interests.

Another suggestion for excluding reference to noncontrolling interest in consolidated financial statements is to consolidate only the controlling interest portion of the revenues, expenses, assets, and liabilities of less-than-100 percent-owned subsidiaries. Proportional consolidation is discussed later in this chapter under accounting for corporate joint ventures.

PUSH-DOWN ACCOUNTING AND OTHER BASIS CONSIDERATIONS

LEARNING OBJECTIVE **2**

Under the theories discussed in the first section of this chapter, we assigned fair values to the individual identifiable assets and liabilities and goodwill of the subsidiary by workpaper entries in the process of consolidating the financial statements of the parent and subsidiary. The books of the subsidiary were not affected by the price paid by the parent for its ownership interest.

In certain situations, the SEC requires that the fair values of the acquired subsidiary's assets and liabilities, which represent the parent's fair value basis under GAAP [6], be recorded in the separate financial statements of the subsidiary. In other words, the values are "pushed down" to the subsidiary's statements.[1] The SEC requires the use of push-down accounting for SEC filings when a subsidiary is substantially wholly owned (usually 90%) with no substantial publicly-held debt or preferred stock outstanding.

The SEC's argument is that when the parent controls the form of ownership of an entity, the basis of accounting for purchased assets and liabilities should be the same regardless of whether the entity continues to exist or is merged into the parent's operations. However, when a subsidiary has outstanding public debt or preferred stock, or when a significant noncontrolling interest exists, the parent may not be able to control the form of ownership. The SEC encourages push-down accounting in these circumstances, but it does not require it.

The AICPA issues paper "Push-Down Accounting" (October 30, 1979) describes *push-down accounting* as:

> *The establishment of a new accounting and reporting basis for an entity in its separate financial statements, based on a purchase transaction in the voting stock of the entity that results in a substantial change of ownership of the outstanding voting stock of the entity.*

When we do not use push-down accounting in an acquisition, we assign the implied fair value/book value differential to identifiable net assets and goodwill in a consolidation workpaper. The consolidation process is simplified if the subsidiary records the fair values in its financial statements under push-down accounting.

Push-down accounting is controversial only in the separate-company statements of the subsidiary that are issued to noncontrolling interests, creditors, and other interested parties. Critics of push-down accounting argue that the transaction between the parent/investor and the subsidiary's old stockholders does not justify a new accounting basis for the subsidiary's assets and liabilities under historical cost principles. The subsidiary is not a party to the transaction—it receives no new funds; it sells no assets. Proponents counter that the price paid by the new owners provides the most relevant basis for measuring the subsidiary's assets, liabilities, and results of operations.

Push-down accounting is not consistently applied among the supporters of the concept, although, in practice, a subsidiary's assets are usually revalued on a proportional basis. What percentage of ownership constitutes a significant noncontrolling interest that would preclude the use of push-down accounting? Should the allocation be done on a proportional basis if less than a 100 percent change in ownership has occurred? These are questions in need of authoritative answers.

In the illustration that follows, the Ped–Sad example is extended using both a proportional allocation for the purchase of a 90 percent interest in Sad and a 100 percent allocation, in which we impute the entity's market value as a whole from the acquisition price of the 90 percent interest.

Push-Down Procedures in Year of Acquisition

Recall that Ped acquired its 90 percent interest for $198,000 cash on January 1, 2011. If we use push-down accounting and revalue only 90 percent of Sad's identifiable net assets

---

[1] *SEC Staff Accounting Bulletin, No. 54*, 1983. For further clarification of the SEC's position, see *Staff Accounting Bulletin, No. 73*, 1987.

(parent-company theory), we allocate the $90,000 fair value/book value differential as follows (in thousands):

	Book Value	Push-Down Adjustment	Book Value After Push-Down
Cash	$ 5	—	$ 5
Accounts receivable—net	30	$ 4.5	34.5
Inventory	40	9	49
Other current assets	10	—	10
Plant assets—net	60	18	78
Goodwill	—	58.5	58.5
	$145	$ 90	$235
Liabilities	$ 25	—	$ 25
Capital stock	100	—	100
Retained earnings	20	$(20)	—
Push-down capital	—	110	110
	$145	$ 90	$235

We record the push-down adjustment on Sad's separate books as follows:

Accounts receivable (+A)	4,500	
Inventory (+A)	9,000	
Plant assets (+A)	18,000	
Goodwill (+A)	58,500	
Retained earnings (−SE)	20,000	
Push-down capital (+SE)		110,000

If we impute a total value of $220,000 from the price of the 90 percent interest in Sad under entity theory ($198,000 cost ÷ 90%), we push down the $100,000 excess on Sad's books as follows (in thousands):

	Book Value	Push-Down Adjustment	Book Value After Push-Down
Cash	$ 5	—	$ 5
Accounts receivable—net	30	$ 5	35
Inventory	40	10	50
Other current assets	10	—	10
Plant assets—net	60	20	80
Goodwill	—	65	65
	$145	$100	$245
Liabilities	$ 25	—	$ 25
Capital stock	100	—	100
Retained earnings	20	$ (20)	—
Push-down capital	—	120	120
	$145	$100	$245

The entry to record the 100 percent push-down adjustment on Sad's separate books is:

Accounts receivable (+A)	5,000	
Inventory (+A)	10,000	
Plant assets (+A)	20,000	
Goodwill (+A)	65,000	
Retained earnings (−SE)	20,000	
Push-down capital (+SE)		120,000

Observe that we transfer the balance of Sad's Retained Earnings account to push-down capital regardless of whether the push down is for 90 percent or 100 percent of the fair value. This treatment is basic to push-down accounting, which requires a new accounting and reporting basis for the acquired entity. Push-down capital is an additional paid-in capital account. It includes the revaluation of subsidiary identifiable net assets and goodwill, based on the acquisition price, and the subsidiary's Retained Earnings account balance, which we eliminate under the new entity concept of push-down accounting.

Exhibit 11-7 presents a consolidated balance sheet workpaper to illustrate the effect of the push-down adjustments. The balance sheet worksheet at the top of the exhibit reflects the 90 percent push-down adjustment (with parent-company theory), and the worksheet at the bottom reflects the 100 percent push-down adjustment (entity theory). Including the push-down adjustments in Sad's separate balance sheets greatly simplifies consolidation procedures. The simplification results from not having to assign unamortized fair values in the workpaper under push-down accounting. The consolidated balance sheet amounts, however, are identical in Exhibit 11-7 under push-down accounting and in Exhibit 11-2, where we maintain the subsidiary balance sheets on an historical-cost basis.

Push-Down Procedures in Year After Acquisition

Exhibits 11-8 and 11-9 illustrate consolidated financial statement workpapers for Ped and Sad Corporations under push-down accounting procedures for the year ended December 31, 2011. Exhibit 11-8 reflects the 90 percent push-down adjustment (parent-company theory), and Exhibit 11-9 reflects the 100 percent push-down adjustment (entity theory). Both exhibits greatly simplify the consolidation procedures in relation to the comparable workpapers for Ped and Sad shown in Exhibits 11-3 and 11-4.

In the consolidation workpaper of Exhibit 11-9 (entity theory), the noncontrolling interest share of $1,900 is equal to 10 percent of Sad's $19,000 net income as measured under push-down accounting. Similarly, the $22,900 noncontrolling interest at December 31, 2011, is equal to 10 percent of Sad's $229,000 stockholders' equity on that date. We determine these noncontrolling interest items under standard consolidation procedures. By contrast, in Exhibit 11-8 (parent-company theory), the $3,500 noncontrolling interest share for 2011 and the $14,500 noncontrolling interest at December 31, 2011, do not have a direct reference to the $20,600 net income of Sad or the $220,600 stockholders' equity of Sad, as shown in Sad's separate income statement and balance sheet under 90 percent push-down accounting. This is a problem that arises in the use of push-down accounting for a less-than-100 percent-owned subsidiary, where only the parent's percentage interest is pushed down on the subsidiary's books. The noncontrolling interest amount in Exhibit 11-8 can be determined directly from Sad's separate cost-based statements as shown in Exhibit 11-3. Noncontrolling shareholders are not expected to get meaningful information from consolidated financial statements; therefore, the 100 percent push-down approach under entity theory may be preferable, especially when the affiliated group has multiple partially-owned subsidiaries.

Leveraged Buyouts

In a **leveraged buyout** (LBO), an investor group (often including company management, an investment banker, and financial institutions) acquires a company (Company A) from the public shareholders in a transaction financed with very little equity and very large amounts of debt. Usually, the investor group raises the money for the buyout by investing perhaps 10 percent of their own money and borrowing the rest. A holding company may be formed to acquire the shares of Company A.

Usually debt raised by the investors to finance the LBO is partially secured by Company A's own assets and is serviced with funds generated by Company A's operations and/or the sale of its assets. Because the loans are secured by Company A's assets, banks lending money to the investors often require that the debt appear on Company A's financial statements.

If the previous owners were paid a high premium for their stock, which is often the case, and book values, rather than fair values, of the assets and liabilities are carried forward to the balance sheet of the new company (the acquired Company A), the debt incurred in the LBO may cause the

EXHIBIT 11-7

Push-Down Accounting:
Parent-Company Versus
Entity Approach

PED CORPORATION AND SUBSIDIARY CONSOLIDATED BALANCE SHEET WORKPAPER AT JANUARY 1, 2011 (IN THOUSANDS)

	Ped	90% Sad	Adjustments and Eliminations Debits	Credits	Consolidated Statements
Parent-Company Theory					
Assets					
Cash	$ 22	$ 5			$ 27
Accounts receivable—net	80	34.5			114.5
Inventories	90	49			139
Other current assets	20	10			30
Plant assets—net	220	78			298
Investment in Sad	198			a 198	
Goodwill		58.5			58.5
Total assets	$ 630	$235			$667
Liabilities and Equity					
Liabilities	$ 80	$ 25			$105
Capital stock	400	100	a 100		400
Retained earnings	150	0			150
Push-down capital—Sad		110	a 110		
Noncontrolling interest				a 12	12
Total equities	$ 630	$235			$667
Entity Theory					
Assets					
Cash	$ 22	$ 5			$ 27
Accounts receivable—net	80	35			115
Inventories	90	50			140
Other current assets	20	10			30
Plant assets—net	220	80			300
Investment in Sad	198			a 198	
Goodwill		65			65
Total assets	$ 630	$245			$677
Liabilities and Equity					
Liabilities	$ 80	$ 25			$105
Capital stock	400	100	a 100		400
Retained earnings	150	0			150
Push-down capital—Sad		120	a 120		
Noncontrolling interest				a 22	22
Total equities	$ 630	$245			$677

EXHIBIT 11-8

Push-Down
Accounting—Parent-
Company Theory

PED CORPORATION AND SUBSIDIARY CONSOLIDATION WORKPAPER FOR THE YEAR ENDED DECEMBER 31, 2011 (IN THOUSANDS)

	Ped	90% Sad	Adjustments and Eliminations		Consolidated Statements
			Debits	Credits	
Income Statement Sales	$600	$200			$800
Income from Sad	17.1		a 17.1		
Cost of sales	(300)	(129)			(429)
Operating expenses	(211.25)	(50.4)			(261.65)
Noncontrolling interest share ($35 × 10%)			c 3.5		(3.5)
Controlling share of net income	**$105.85**	**$ 20.6**			**$105.85**
Retained Earnings Statement Retained earnings	$150	$ 0			$150
Dividends	(80)	(10)		a 9 c 1	(80)
Controlling share of net income	105.85	20.6			105.85
Retained earnings— December 31	**$175.85**	**$ 10.6**			**$175.85**
Balance Sheet Cash	$ 29.75	$ 13			$ 42.75
Accounts receivable—net	90	32			122
Inventories	100	48			148
Other current assets	30	17			47
Plant assets—net	200	74.1			274.1
Investment in Sad	206.1			a 8.1 b 198	
Goodwill		58.5			58.5
	$655.85	$242.6			$692.35
Liabilities	$ 80	$ 22			$102
Capital stock	400	100	b 100		400
Retained earnings	175.85	10.6			175.85
Push-down capital—Sad		110	b 110		
	$655.85	$242.6			
Noncontrolling interest				b 12 c 2.5	14.5
					$692.35

EXHIBIT 11-9

Push-Down
Accounting—Entity
Theory

PED CORPORATION AND SUBSIDIARY CONSOLIDATION WORKPAPER FOR THE YEAR ENDED DECEMBER 31, 2011 (IN THOUSANDS)

	Ped	90% Sad	Adjustments and Eliminations Debits	Adjustments and Eliminations Credits	Consolidated Statements
Income Statement Sales	$600	$200			$800
Income from Sad	17.1		a 17.1		
Cost of sales	(300)	(130)			(430)
Operating expenses	(211.25)	(51)			(262.25)
Noncontrolling interest share*			c 1.9		(1.9)
Controlling share of net income	**$105.85**	**$ 19**			**$105.85**
Retained Earnings Statement Retained earnings	$150	$ 0			$150
Dividends	(80)	(10)		a 9 c 1	(80)
Controlling share of net income	**105.85**	**19**			**105.85**
Retained earnings— December 31	**$175.85**	**$ 9**			**$175.85**
Balance Sheet Cash	$ 29.75	$ 13			$ 42.75
Accounts receivable—net	90	32			122
Inventories	100	48			148
Other current assets	30	17			47
Plant assets—net	200	76			276
Investment in Sad	206.1			a 8.1 b 198	
Goodwill		65			65
	$655.85	$251			$700.75
Liabilities	$ 80	$ 22			$102
Capital stock	400	100	b 100		400
Retained earnings	**175.85**	**9**			**175.85**
Push-down capital—Sad		120	b 120		
	$655.85	$251			
Noncontrolling interest				b 22 c .9	22.9
					$700.75

*Noncontrolling interest share = ($19 × 10%).

new company's financial condition to look worse than it is. The popularity of LBOs is one reason many accountants support a change to push-down accounting for acquisitions, including LBOs, that would allow the assets of the acquired firm to be written up on its financial statements to reflect the acquisition price.

Both the late 1980s and 1990s witnessed significant LBO activities in U.S. markets. ***Kohlberg, Kravis, Roberts and Company* (KKR)** has been a major acquirer, buying out ***Beatrice Foods*** for $6.25 billion and ***Safeway Stores*** for $4.24 billion, both in 1986, and taking over ***RJR Nabisco*** in 1989 at a cost of $24.72 billion. In 1986, ***Macy Acquisitions Corporation*** was formed to effect an LBO of ***R. H. Macy & Company,*** the department store chain, for $3.50 billion.

In 1997, ***Bain Capital*** acquired ***Sealy Corporation***. In 1998, ***Clayton, Dubilier, & Rice*** purchased ***North American Van Lines,*** and **KKR** combined with existing management in a buyout of ***Halley Performance Products***.

In 2000, ***Smithfield Foods*** bid to acquire rival food processor ***IBP,*** and ***Silver Lake Partners*** completed an LBO of ***Seagate***, the disk-drive maker, which was subsequently merged into ***Veritas Software*** in a deal valued at $2.1 billion. An April 10, 2001, press release by ***New Dresser*** revealed that a consortium of ***First Reserve Corporation, Odyssey Investment Partners,*** and members of Dresser management completed an LBO of Dresser from the ***Halliburton Company*** for $1.3 billion. LBO activity declined in the latter half of 2001, attributed by *The Wall Street Journal* to a lack of loans and bonds needed to fund such deals. There have been similar large LBOs in recent years, including ***Cerebrus Capital Management's*** acquisition of ***Chrysler*** in 2007 for $7.4 billion. However, such activity is cooling down once again due to problems in U.S. and worldwide credit markets.

The structure of a buyout influences the accounting basis for the new entity. For example, a holding company may be used to acquire the net assets of Company A, a holding company may be used to acquire the equity of Company A, or an investor group may acquire Company A without using a holding company.

If there has been a change in control, a change in accounting basis for the new entity is generally appropriate, because the new entity has new controlling stockholders and is similar to an acquisition.

Another Accounting Basis Solution

Corporations have tried to structure business combinations in ways to avoid recording goodwill. A corporation acquires a controlling interest in another company (the target), and, in the same transaction, the target issues additional shares to the parent in exchange for the parent's interest in a subsidiary. In substance, the parent sells its subsidiary to the target as part of the price of acquiring the target. The argument is that this is a combination of enterprises under common control. Therefore, the combination would not be an acquisition and the transaction would be accounted for using historical costs:

- The parent should account for the transfer of the subsidiary to the target as *an acquisition*. This would now be in accordance with GAAP [7]. Obtaining control of the target and the transfer of the subsidiary to the target cannot be separated and should be treated as one transaction.
- The parent should account for the transaction as a partial sale of the subsidiary (to the noncontrolling stockholders of the target) and a partial acquisition of the target. The parent should recognize gain or loss on the portion of the subsidiary sold.
- The parent should step up the target's assets and liabilities to the extent acquired by the parent and the subsidiary's assets and liabilities to the extent the ownership interest in the subsidiary was sold.

This structure for business combinations did not avoid acquisition accounting and the resulting goodwill. The pressure to search for ways to avoid recording goodwill diminished in 1993 because goodwill became tax deductible. The fact that goodwill will no longer be amortized (i.e., reducing reported earnings) under GAAP [8] eliminates the need to structure combinations to avoid recording goodwill.

LEARNING OBJECTIVE **3**

JOINT VENTURES

A *joint venture* is a form of partnership that originated with the maritime trading expeditions of the Greeks and Romans. The objective was to combine management participants and capital contributors in undertakings limited to the completion of specific trading projects. Today the joint venture takes many different forms, such as partnership and corporate, domestic and foreign, and temporary as well as relatively permanent.

A common type of temporary joint venture is the formation of syndicates of investment bankers to purchase securities from an issuing corporation and market them to the public. The joint venture enables several participants to share in the risks and rewards of undertakings that would be too large or too risky for a single venturer. It also enables them to combine technology, markets, and human resources to enhance the profit potential of all participants. Other areas in which joint ventures are common are land sales, oil exploration and drilling, and major construction projects.

New areas and uses for the joint venture form of organization continue to emerge. For example, nearly all major telecommunications companies use joint ventures to gain size and capital. The joint ventures amass capital in order to bid in the multi-billion-dollar auction for personal communications services licenses and to build nationwide wireless telephone networks. One advantage of these joint ventures is avoidance of expensive acquisitions.

Joint ventures by U.S. firms are common. An old and well-known example is *Dow Corning Corporation*, a corporate joint venture of the *Dow Chemical Company* and *Corning Incorporated.* The joint venture allows for a spreading of risk between or among the venturers, making this business form appealing in the oil and gas and chemical industries, and for international investing. The limited liability enjoyed by shareholders makes the corporate form of joint venture especially appealing. Joint ventures are also common in the pharmaceuticals industry.

Nature of Joint Ventures

A **joint venture** is a business entity that is owned, operated, and jointly controlled by a small group of investors (**venturers**) for the conduct of a specific business undertaking that provides mutual benefit for each of the venturers. It is common for each venturer to be active in management of the venture and to participate in important decisions that typically require the consent of each venturer irrespective of ownership interest. Ownership percentages vary widely, and unequal ownership interests in a specific venture are commonplace.

Organizational Structures of Joint Ventures

Joint ventures may be organized as corporations, partnerships, or undivided interests. These forms are defined in the AICPA's statement of position, "Accounting for Investment in Real Estate Ventures" *(SOP 78-9)*, as follows:

> **Corporate joint venture.** A corporation owned and operated by a small group of venturers to accomplish a mutually beneficial venture or project.
>
> **General partnership.** An association in which each partner has unlimited liability.
>
> **Limited partnership.** An association in which one or more general partners have unlimited liability and one or more partners have limited liability. A limited partnership is usually managed by the general partner or partners, subject to limitations, if any, imposed by the partnership agreement.
>
> **Undivided interest.** An ownership arrangement in which two or more parties jointly own property, and title is held individually to the extent of each party's interest.

Financial reporting requirements for the investors in ventures differ according to the organizational structures.

Accounting for Corporate Joint Ventures

Investors who can participate in the overall management of a *corporate joint venture* should report their investments as equity investments (one-line consolidations) under GAAP [9]. The approach for establishing significant influence in corporate joint ventures is quite different from that for most common stock investments because *each venturer* usually has to consent to *each significant venture decision*, thus establishing an ability to exercise significant influence regardless of ownership interest. Even so, when a venturer cannot exercise significant influence over its joint venture for whatever reason we account for its investment in the venture by the *cost method*.

An investment in the common stock of a corporate joint venture that exceeds 50 percent of the venture's outstanding shares is a *subsidiary investment*, for which parent–subsidiary accounting and reporting requirements apply. A corporate joint venture that is more than 50 percent owned by another entity is not considered a joint venture, even though it continues to be described as a joint venture in financial releases. GAAP [10] describes corporate joint ventures as follows:

> A corporation owned and operated by a small group of entities (the joint venturers) as a separate and specific business or project for the mutual benefit of the members of the group. A government may also be a member of the group. The purpose of a corporate joint venture frequently is to share risks and rewards in developing a new market, product or technology; to combine complementary technological knowledge; or to pool resources in developing production or other facilities. A corporate joint venture also usually provides an arrangement under which each joint venturer may participate, directly or indirectly, in the overall management of the joint venture. Joint venturers thus have an interest or relationship other than as passive investors. An entity that is a subsidiary of one of the joint venturers is not a corporate joint venture. The ownership of a corporate joint venture seldom changes, and its stock is usually not traded publicly. A noncontrolling interest held by public ownership, however, does not preclude a corporation from being a corporate joint venture.

Note that a subsidiary (more than 50 percent owned) of a joint venturer is *not* a corporate joint venture under GAAP [11]. Instead, we would consolidate it [12].

GAAP concludes that investors in the common stock of corporate joint ventures should account for investments by the equity method in consolidated financial statements. The equity method best enables the investors to reflect the underlying nature of the venture.

Investments in the common stock of joint venturers, or other investments accounted for by the equity method, may be material in relation to the financial position or results of operations of the joint venture investor. If so, it may be necessary for the investor to provide summarized information about the assets, liabilities, and results of operations of its investees in its own financial statements. The required disclosures should be presented *individually* for investments in joint ventures that are material in relation to the financial position or results of operations of the investor. Alternatively, the required disclosures can be *grouped* for investments that are material as a group but are not material individually.

Accounting for Unincorporated Joint Ventures

GAAP [13] also explains that many provisions of corporate joint venture accounting are appropriate in accounting for unincorporated entities. For example, partnership profits and losses accrued by investor-partners are generally reflected in the partners' financial statements. Elimination of intercompany profit in accounting for a partnership interest also seems appropriate, as does providing for deferred income tax liabilities on profits accrued by partner-investors. An example of this type of joint venture is the creation of a defense business partnership between **Harsco Corporation** and **FMC Corporation** in 1994. The new partnership was named **United Defense, L.P.**, and was formed by combining Harsco's BMY-Combat Systems Division with FMC's Defense Systems Group.

The previous discussion of the applicability of GAAP to partnerships also applies to undivided interests in joint ventures, where the investor-venturer owns an undivided interest in each asset and is proportionately liable for its share of each liability. However, the provisions do not apply in some industries that have specialized industry practices. For example, the established industry practice in oil and gas ventures is for the investor-venturer to account for its pro rata share of the assets, liabilities, revenues, and expenses of a joint venture in its own financial statements. This reporting procedure is referred to as ***pro rata*** or ***proportionate consolidation***. *Marathon Oil Corporation*

(All amounts in thousands)	Equity Method—Par Corporation	Sal Unincorporated	Proportionate Consolidation—Par and Sal
Income Statement			
Revenues			
Sales	$2,000	$ 500	$2,250
Income from Sal	100	—	—
Total revenue	2,100	500	2,250
Expenses			
Cost of sales	1,200	200	1,300
Other expenses	400	100	450
Total expenses	1,600	300	1,750
Net income	$ 500	$ 200	$ 500
Balance Sheet			
Cash	$ 200	$ 50	$ 225
Accounts receivable	300	150	375
Inventory	400	300	550
Plant assets	800	800	1,200
Investment in Sal	500	—	—
Total assets	$2,200	$1,300	$2,350
Accounts payable	$ 400	$ 200	$ 500
Other liabilities	500	100	550
Capital stock	1,000	—	1,000
Retained earnings	300	—	300
Venture capital	—	1,000	—
Total equities	$2,200	$1,300	$2,350

includes a note in its summary of principal accounting policies that "Investments in unincorporated joint ventures and undivided interests in certain operating assets are consolidated on a pro rata basis."[2]

Alternatively, the SEC [14] recommends against proportionate consolidation for undivided interests in real estate ventures subject to joint control by the investors. A venture is subject to joint control if decisions regarding the financing, development, or sale of property require the approval of two or more owner-venturers. A 1979 AICPA issues paper titled "Joint Venture Accounting" recommended that a venture that is not subject to joint control because its liabilities are several rather than joint be required to use proportionate consolidation.

One-Line Consolidation and Proportionate Consolidation

To illustrate the reporting alternatives for unincorporated joint ventures, assume that Par Corporation has a 50 percent undivided interest in Sal Company, a merchandising joint venture. Comparative financial statements under the two assumptions (accounting under the equity method and proportionate consolidation) appear in Exhibit 11-10. Column 1 presents a summary of Par's income statement and balance sheet, assuming that it uses the equity method of accounting for its investment in Sal, an unconsolidated joint venture company. Sal's income statement and balance sheet are summarized in column 2. In column 3, Par has consolidated its share (50 percent) of Sal's assets, liabilities, revenues, and expenses (from column 2)—in other words, a proportionate consolidation.

Note that we eliminate Sal's $1,000,000 venture capital in its entirety against the $500,000 Investment in Sal balance, the $100,000 Income from Sal and against half of Sal's asset, liability, revenue, and expense account balances in the proportionate consolidation.

---

[2] Marathon Oil Corporation annual report for the fiscal year ended December 31, 2009, p. 79.

The Accounting Standards Executive Committee of the AICPA is reviewing certain inconsistencies in reporting unincorporated joint ventures that have arisen from the lack of authoritative guidance. Likewise, the EITF of the FASB is currently reviewing joint venture accounting.

ACCOUNTING FOR VARIABLE INTEREST ENTITIES

LEARNING
OBJECTIVE **4**

Companies create special-purpose entities for a variety of valid business reasons. For example, companies separately account for employee benefit plans (pension funds or other postretirement-benefit plans) and do not include such plan accounting as a part of the consolidated financial statements. GAAP [15] sets accounting and disclosure rules for these plans.

These special-purpose entities are afforded off-balance-sheet treatment under GAAP. Companies record transactions with these entities, but they do not include the entities in the consolidated financial statements. For example, payments to a pension fund are recorded by the sponsor, but the assets and liabilities of the fund are not included in consolidated balance sheet asset and liability totals.

However, **Enron Corporation** provides an example in which exclusion of special-purpose entities from the consolidated financial statements gave investors a distorted picture of the company's financial health and business risks. The SEC has alleged financial reporting fraud against Enron in that many of the entities were created primarily to mislead investors, rather than to serve a legitimate business purpose. We will leave discussion of the alleged Enron fraud to other texts and courses on auditing, business law, and business ethics. Our goal here is to provide an introduction to accounting considerations for these special-purpose entities.

In 2003, GAAP [16] addressed perceived abuses in accounting for special-purpose entities, and continued to evolve the standard with an amendment in 2009. The process is ongoing. Both the FASB and IASB continue to work on consolidation policy for these entities.

The FASB coined the term *variable interest entities* (VIEs) to define those special-purpose entities that require consolidation. There are a few major issues and concepts to cover. First, does an entity meet the conditions for inclusion in consolidated financial statements? Second, if consolidation is required, how should consolidated amounts be determined? Prior rules for consolidation relied on voting control or percentage ownership of voting shares to decide both of the issues just noted. Current GAAP attempts to identify those entities in which financial control exists because of contractual and financial arrangements other than ownership of voting interests. Recall your early childhood. Your parents did not legally "own" you, but they clearly had financial control over your activities. GAAP now includes companies as VIEs in which the equity investors cannot provide financing for the entity's business risks and activities without additional financial support.

This change does not apply just to Enron. Many companies are required to consolidate variable interest entities under the new interpretation, even **Disney**. Note 7 to Disney's 2009 annual report indicates:

> *The Company has a 51 percent effective ownership interest in the operations of Euro Disney and a 47 percent ownership interest in the operations of Hong Kong Disneyland which are both variable interest entities and are consolidated in the Company's financial statements (p. 82).*

Note 7 also provides a condensed consolidating balance sheet and income statement summarizing amounts before and after consolidating these two entities as of October 3, 2009. A few items are notable. Consolidated net income is unaffected by the consolidations. Total assets increase from $58,718 million to $63,117 million, primarily due to the reported increase in fixed assets upon consolidation. Perhaps more important for investors evaluating the business and financial risks of Disney, total borrowings increase from $8,758 million to $11,495 million after consolidating these two entities.

Identifying Variable Interest Entities

A variable interest entity must be consolidated by the primary beneficiary. What is a variable interest? What is a variable interest entity? Our goal here is to provide an understanding of the concepts embodied in current GAAP, not to cover all of the details [17]. This is a very complex topic, and identification of a VIE requires considerable judgment.

"Variable interests are contractual, ownership, or other pecuniary interests in a legal entity that change with changes in the fair value of the legal entity's net assets exclusive of variable interests." [18] For example an at-risk equity investment is a variable interest.

GAAP looks at all forms of business entities to identify VIEs. Therefore, a VIE might be another corporation, partnership, limited liability company, or trust-type arrangement. A potential VIE must be a separate entity, not a subset, branch, or division of another entity. Certain entities, such as pension plans, are specifically excluded, as they are covered by other reporting standards. GAAP defines VIEs requiring consolidation. "The total equity investment at risk is not sufficient to permit the entity to finance its activities without additional subordinated financial support provided by any parties, including equity holders." For example, a company may own only a minimal voting equity interest in an entity, but be contractually required to provide additional financial support in the event of future operating losses.

"The investments or other interests that will absorb portions of a variable interest entity's expected losses or receive portions of the entity's expected residual returns are called variable interests."

> *A variable interest entity's expected losses are the expected negative variability in the fair value of its net assets exclusive of variable interests. A variable interest entity's expected residual returns are the expected positive variability in the fair value of its net assets exclusive of variable interests. Expected variability in the fair value of net assets includes expected variability resulting from operating results of the entity. [19]*

GAAP offers a general guideline of an equity investment at risk of less than 10 percent of total assets to be indicative of an entity unable to finance operations without additional subordinated financial support. GAAP also describes situations in which an even greater equity interest may be insufficient to indicate financial independence.

Having identified VIEs, entities that will require consolidation, GAAP turns its attention to who will be required to consolidate the VIE. GAAP uses the term ***primary beneficiary*** to indicate the company that will include the VIE in consolidated statements. There can be only one primary beneficiary. It is possible that no entity is a primary beneficiary (in which case the special purpose entity is not a VIE).

> *All enterprises holding a significant interest in a VIE are required to make disclosures under GAAP. The primary beneficiary must disclose:*
>
> **a.** The nature, purpose, size, and activities of the VIE.
> **b.** The carrying amount and classification of consolidated assets that are collateral for the VIE's obligations.
> **c.** Lack of recourse if creditors (or beneficial interest holders) of a consolidated VIE have no recourse to the general credit of the primary beneficiary.

Other enterprises, not the primary beneficiary, must disclose:

> **a.** The nature of the involvement with the VIE and when that involvement began.
> **b.** The nature, purpose, size, and activities of the VIE.
> **c.** The enterprise's maximum exposure to loss as a result of its involvement with the VIE.

The other entities (not the primary beneficiaries) account for their investment in the VIE under either the cost or equity methods of accounting.

Current GAAP provides two characteristics, which must both be met, to determine the primary beneficiary. The first is an economic power concept. Does the entity have power to direct the VIE activities that most significantly impact the VIE's economic performance? The second characteristic focuses on legal obligations. Does the entity have an obligation to absorb losses and/or a right to receive significant benefits from the VIE. If one or neither condition is met, the reporting entity is not the primary beneficiary.

Here is a simple example. Ten independent companies—Melanie, Troy, Matthew, Emily, Megan, Danielle, Ryan, Corinne, Tricia, and Lisa Corporations—decide to pool their financial resources for a new business venture investing in offshore oil leases, GetRichQuick Corporation.

There is no intent to publicly trade shares of the new company. If the concept is successful, Get-RichQuick will provide the investors with enormous future returns, but the venture is not without risk. Each investor contributes $1 million and each receives 10 percent of the voting common stock of GetRichQuick. Additionally, each investor will have one member on the board of directors of the new company. However, the other investors agree that Corinne will have veto power over any business decisions. Under the business plan, GetRichQuick will borrow an additional $20 million to help finance acquisition of leasing rights and subsequent exploration, research, and development. Corinne Corporation agrees to assume 75 percent of losses if the venture is unsuccessful. Corinne believes that the risk is minimal, but offshore oil leasing could produce significant environmental liabilities, well beyond the initial $10 million equity capitalization. In exchange for Corinne's generous offer to absorb a majority of the downside risks, the investors agree that Corinne will receive a 28 percent share of all future profits. The remaining nine investors will each receive an 8 percent profit share.

How should the investors account for their investments in GetRichQuick? At first glance, it appears that all 10 investors would apply the cost method of accounting under current GAAP. No company holds a significant influence or controlling voting interest in the new venture. Assume that the investors correctly determine that GetRichQuick is a VIE under GAAP. One of the investors will be required to consolidate the new venture.

Corinne's contractual agreement makes Corinne the primary beneficiary. Corinne's veto gives the power to direct economic activities of the VIE. Corinne also has an obligation to absorb losses and a right to share benefits from VIE operations. Because both conditions are met, Corinne is the primary beneficiary and is required to consolidate GetRichQuick. The remaining nine investors do not consolidate; however, because GetRichQuick has been identified as a VIE, they are required to make GAAP disclosures and account for their investments using the cost method. (The equity method is not appropriate, because the VIE shares are not publicly traded).

Consolidation of a Variable Interest Entity

LEARNING
OBJECTIVE **5**

We now consider the second issue: how the consolidation should be effected. The rules essentially follow those for any other consolidation. The primary beneficiary measures and consolidates based on the fair values of assets, liabilities, and noncontrolling interest at the date it becomes the primary beneficiary. If the primary beneficiary has transferred assets to the VIE, these should be transferred at the same amounts at which they were carried on the primary beneficiary's books (i.e., no gain or loss is recorded on the transfer). Thus, the primary beneficiary treats the initial valuation consistent with an application of GAAP for an acquisition.

After the initial measurement of fair values and consolidation, the primary beneficiary follows normal consolidation principles in subsequent accounting for the VIE. So the primary beneficiary uses voting interests to allocate future performance among the controlling and noncontrolling interests. All intercompany transactions and account balances must be eliminated. Income or expense due to fees between the primary beneficiary and the VIE must be eliminated against the net income of the VIE. None of these fees should be allocated to any noncontrolling interests.

Estimating the fair value of VIE assets will pose challenges for many firms. Often VIEs invest in unique assets for which fair market values cannot be found from simply looking up a current trading value on a stock exchange. Firms will often need to estimate expected future cash flows associated with VIE operations as a means of estimating fair values.

SUMMARY

This chapter covers several different theories related to consolidating the financial statements of a parent and its subsidiaries. It also examines "new basis accounting" for assets and liabilities in a subsidiary's separate financial statements under push-down accounting and describes accounting for corporate joint ventures.

We identify the concepts and procedures underlying current consolidation practices (i.e., current GAAP) to distinguish from accounting practices under parent-company and traditional theories. The basic differences among the three theories are compared in a matrix in Exhibit 11-1. Nearly all of the differences disappear when subsidiaries are wholly owned.

Under push-down accounting, we record the fair values determined in an acquisition in the separate books of the subsidiary. Push-down accounting is ordinarily required by the SEC for combinations in which all or substantially all of the ownership interests in the acquired company change hands. Some acquisitions can be structured to avoid push-down accounting.

A joint venture is a business entity that is owned, operated, and jointly controlled by a small group of investors for their mutual benefit. The joint venture investors are usually active in management of the venture, and each venturer usually has the ability to exercise significant influence over the joint venture investee. Investors account for investments in corporate joint ventures as one-line consolidations under the equity method. Similarly, investors account for investments in unincorporated joint ventures (partnerships and undivided interests) as one-line consolidations or proportionate consolidations, depending on the special accounting practices of the industries in which they operate.

Companies also create entities or relationships with other firms for a variety of special business purposes. Often these entities are structured such that an investor has effective economic control, even though the investor lacks voting control through a significant equity ownership interest. GAAP recognizes these situations and requires that the primary beneficiary consolidate these variable interest entities.

QUESTIONS

1. Compare the traditional, parent-company, and entity theories of consolidated financial statements.

2. Which, if any, of the consolidation theories would be changed by FASB pronouncements? (For example, assume that a new FASB statement requires noncontrolling interest share to be computed as the noncontrolling interest share of subsidiary dividends declared.)

3. Under the entity theory, a total valuation of the subsidiary is imputed on the basis of the price paid by the parent company for its controlling interest. Do you see any practical or conceptual problems with this approach?

4. Assume that Pat Corporation acquires 60% of the voting common stock of Sir Corporation for $6,000,000 and that a consolidated balance sheet is prepared immediately after the acquisition. Would total consolidated assets be equal to their fair values if the parent-company theory were applied? If the entity theory were applied?

5. Why might the traditional practice of valuing the equity of noncontrolling shareholders at book value overstate the value of the noncontrolling interest?

6. Cite the conditions under which consolidated net income under parent-company theory would equal income to controlling stockholders under entity theory.

7. If income from a subsidiary is measured under the equity method and the statements are consolidated under entity theory, will consolidated net income equal parent net income?

8. Why are the income statement amounts under entity theory and traditional theory the same if the subsidiary investment is made at book value? (Do not consider the different income statement presentations of controlling and noncontrolling interests in responding to this question.)

9. Does traditional theory correspond to parent-company or entity theory in matters related to unrealized and constructive gains and losses on intercompany transactions?

10. To what extent does push-down accounting facilitate the consolidation process?

11. What is a joint venture and how are joint ventures organized?

12. What accounting and reporting methods are used by investor-venturers in accounting for their joint venture investments?

EXERCISES

E 11-1
Parent-company and entity theories

1. The classification of noncontrolling interest share as an expense and noncontrolling interest as a liability is preferred under:
   a *Parent-company theory*
   b *Entity theory*
   c *Traditional theory*
   d *None of the above*

2. Traditional theory is most similar to parent-company theory in matters relating to:

  a Goodwill computations
  b Noncontrolling interest computations
  c Intercompany profit eliminations
  d Consolidated financial statement presentations

3. Traditional theory is most similar to entity theory in matters relating to:

  a Goodwill computations
  b Noncontrolling interest computations
  c Intercompany profit eliminations
  d Consolidated financial statement presentations

4. When "consolidated income allocated to controlling stockholders" under entity theory is compared to "consolidated net income" under traditional theory, one would expect consolidated net income under traditional theory to be:

  a Equal to consolidated income allocated to controlling stockholders under entity theory
  b Greater than consolidated income allocated to controlling stockholders under entity theory
  c Less than consolidated income allocated to controlling stockholders under entity theory
  d Greater or less depending on the relationship of investment fair value to book value

5. Consolidated financial statement amounts and classifications should be identical under the traditional, entity, and parent-company theories of consolidation if:

  a All subsidiaries are acquired at book value
  b Only 100%-owned subsidiaries are consolidated
  c There are no intercompany transactions
  d All subsidiaries are acquired at book value and there are no intercompany transactions

6. When the fair values of an acquired subsidiary's assets and liabilities are recorded in the subsidiary's accounts (push-down accounting), the subsidiary's retained earnings will be:

  a Adjusted for the difference between the push-down capital and goodwill from the acquisition
  b Credited for the amount of the push-down capital
  c Transferred in its entirety to push-down capital
  d Credited for the difference between the total imputed value of the entity and the purchase price of the interest acquired

7. The most consistent statement of assets in consolidated financial statements would result from applying:

  a Traditional theory
  b Parent-company theory
  c Entity theory
  d None of the above

E 11-2
Joint ventures

1. A joint venture would not be organized as a(an):

  a Corporation
  b Proprietorship
  c Partnership
  d Undivided interest

2. Corporate joint ventures should be accounted for by the equity method, provided that the joint venturer:

  a Cannot exercise significant influence over the joint venture
  b Can participate in the overall management of the venture
  c Owns more than 50% of the joint venture
  d All of the above

3. An investor in a corporate joint venture would be least likely to:

  a Be active in the management of the venture
  b Have an ability to exercise significant influence
  c Consent to each significant venture decision
  d Hold title to a pro rata share of joint venture assets

4. Investors account for investments in corporate joint ventures under the equity method if their individual ownership percentages are at least:

  a 10%
  b 20%
  c 50%
  d None of the above

5. Far, Get, and Hog Corporations own 60%, 25%, and 15%, respectively, of the common stock of Pod Corporation, a joint venture that they organized for wholesaling fruits. Which of the corporations should report their joint venture interests under the equity method?

 a *Far, Get, and Hog*
 b *Far and Get*
 c *Get and Hog*
 d *Far and Hog*

E 11-3

Parent-company and entity theories

1. Pet Company pays $1,440,000 for an 80% interest in Sit Corporation on December 31, 2011, when Sit's net assets at book value and fair value are $1,600,000. Under entity theory, the noncontrolling interest at acquisition is:

 a *$288,000*
 b *$320,000*
 c *$360,000*
 d *$400,000*

2. Sat Corporation sold inventory items to its parent company, Pan Corporation, during 2011, and at December 31, 2011, Pan's inventory included items acquired from Sat at a gross profit of $100,000. If Sat is an 80%-owned subsidiary of Pan, the amount of unrealized inventory profits to be eliminated in preparing the consolidated income statements of Pan and Subsidiary for 2011 is $80,000 under:

 a *Parent-company theory*
 b *Traditional theory*
 c *Entity theory*
 d *The equity method of accounting*

3. A parent company that applies the entity theory of consolidation in preparing its consolidated financial statements computed income from its 90%-owned subsidiary under the equity method of accounting as follows:

Equity in subsidiary income ($400,000 × 90%)	$360,000
Patent amortization ($140,000 ÷ 10 years × 90%)	(12,600)
Income from subsidiary	$347,400

Given the foregoing information, noncontrolling interest share is:

 a *$40,000*
 b *$38,600*
 c *$36,000*
 d *$34,600*

Use the following information in answering questions 4 and 5:

Pad Corporation acquired an 80% interest in Sun Corporation on January 1, 2011, when Sun's total stockholders' equity was $1,680,000. The book values and fair values of Sun's assets and liabilities were equal on this date.

At December 31, 2011, the consolidated balance sheet of Pad and Subsidiary shows unamortized patents from consolidation of $108,000, with a note that the patents are being amortized over a 10-year period.

4. If the entity theory of consolidation was used, the purchase price of the 80% interest in Sun must have been:

 a *$1,440,000*
 b *$1,464,000*
 c *$1,494,000*
 d *$1,800,000*

5. If the traditional theory of consolidation was used, the purchase price of the 80% interest in Sun must have been:

 a *$1,440,000*
 b *$1,464,000*
 c *$1,494,000*
 d *$1,800,000*

E 11-4

Computations (parent-company and entity theories)

Balance sheet information of Pod and Sad Corporations at December 31, 2011, is summarized as follows (in thousands):

	Pod Book Value	Sad Book Value	Sad Fair Value
Current assets	$ 520	$ 50	$ 90
Plant assets—net	480	250	360
	$1,000	$300	$450

	Pod Book Value	Sad Book Value	Sad Fair Value
Current liabilities	$ 80	$ 40	$ 50
Capital stock	800	200	
Retained earnings	120	60	
	$1,000	$300	

On January 2, 2011, Pod purchases 80 percent of Sad's outstanding shares for $500,000 cash.

REQUIRED

1. Determine goodwill from the acquisition under (a) parent-company theory and (b) entity theory.

2. Determine noncontrolling interest at January 2, 2011, under (a) parent-company theory and (b) entity theory.

3. Determine the amount of total assets that would appear on a consolidated balance sheet prepared at January 2, 2011, under (a) parent-company theory and (b) entity theory.

E 11-5

Computations under parent-company and entity theories (fair value/book value differentials)

On January 1, 2011, Par Corporation pays $300,000 for an 80 percent interest in Sal Company, when Sal's net assets have a book value of $275,000 and a fair value of $350,000. The $75,000 excess fair value is due to undervalued equipment with a five-year remaining useful life. Any goodwill is not written off.

Separate incomes of Par and Sal for 2011 are $500,000 and $50,000, respectively.

REQUIRED

1. Calculate consolidated net income and noncontrolling interest share under (a) parent-company theory and (b) entity theory.

2. Determine goodwill at December 31, 2011, under (a) parent-company theory and (b) entity theory.

E 11-6

Computations under parent-company, entity, and traditional theories (mid-year acquisition)

Sal Corporation's recorded assets and liabilities are equal to their fair values on July 1, 2011, when Pub Corporation purchases 72,000 shares of Sal common stock for $1,800,000. Identifiable net assets of Sal on this date are $1,710,000, and Sal's stockholders' equity consists of $800,000 of $10 par common stock and $910,000 retained earnings.

Sal has net income for 2011 of $80,000 earned evenly throughout the year and declares no dividends.

REQUIRED

1. Determine the total value of Sal's net assets at July 1, 2011, under entity theory.

2. Determine goodwill that would appear in a consolidated balance sheet of Pub Corporation and Subsidiary at July 1, 2011, under (a) entity theory, (b) parent-company theory, and (c) traditional theory.

3. Determine Pub's investment income from Sal on an equity basis for 2011.

4. Determine noncontrolling interest in Sal that will be reported in the consolidated balance sheet at December 31, 2011, under entity theory.

E 11-7

Computations under parent-company and entity theories (upstream sales)

Pal Company acquired an 80 percent interest in Sal Corporation at book value equal to fair value on January 1, 2011. During the year, Sal sold $100,000 inventory items to Pal, and at December 31, 2011, unrealized profits amounted to $30,000. Separate incomes of Pal and Sal for 2011 were $500,000 and $300,000, respectively.

REQUIRED

1. Determine consolidated net income for Pal Company and Subsidiary under the parent-company theory of consolidation.

2. Determine total consolidated income for Pal Company and Subsidiary, income to controlling stockholders, and income to noncontrolling stockholders under the entity theory of consolidation.

E 11-8

Compute consolidated net income under three theories (upstream and downstream sales)

Pad Corporation acquired an 80 percent interest in Sot Company at book value a number of years ago.

Separate incomes of Pad and Sot for 2011 were $120,000 and $60,000, respectively. The only transactions between Pad and Sot during 2011 were as follows:

1. Pad sold inventory items to Sot for $60,000. These items cost Pad $30,000, and half the items were inventoried at $30,000 by Sot at December 31, 2011.
2. Sot sold land that cost $70,000 to Pad for $96,000 during 2011. The land was held by Pad at December 31, 2011.
3. Sot paid $24,000 dividends to Pad during 2011.

REQUIRED: Compute consolidated net income for Pad Corporation and Subsidiary for 2011 under:

1. Traditional theory
2. Parent-company theory
3. Entity theory

E 11-9

Journal entries for push-down accounting

On January 1, 2011, Pin Corporation acquired a 90 percent interest in Set Corporation for $2,520,000. The book values and fair values of Set's assets and equities on this date are as follows (in thousands):

	Book Value	Fair Value
Cash	$ 200	$ 200
Accounts receivable—net	300	300
Inventories	500	600
Land	300	800
Buildings—net	700	1,000
Equipment—net	800	600
	$2,800	$3,500
Accounts payable	$ 550	$ 550
Other liabilities	450	550
Capital stock	1,000	
Retained earnings	800	
	$2,800	

REQUIRED

1. Prepare the journal entries on Set Corporation's books to push down the values reflected in the acquisition price under *parent-company theory.*
2. Prepare the journal entries on Set Corporation's books to push down the values reflected in the acquisition price under *entity theory.*

E 11-10

Determine investment income for corporate joint venturers

Sun Corporation is a corporate joint venture that is jointly controlled and operated by five investor-venturers, four with 15 percent interests each and one with a 40 percent interest. Each of the five venturers is active in venture management. Land sales and other important venture decisions require the consent of each venturer. All venturers paid $15 per share for their investments on January 1, 2011, and no changes in ownership interests have occurred since that time. During 2012, Sun reported net income of $500,000 and paid dividends of $100,000. The stockholders' equity of Sun at December 31, 2012, is as follows (in thousands):

Sun Corporation Stockholders' Equity at December 31, 2012

Common stock $10 par, 500,000 shares authorized, issued, and outstanding	$5,000
Additional paid-in capital	2,500
Total paid-in capital	7,500
Retained earnings	1,000
Total stockholders' equity	$8,500

REQUIRED: Determine the investment income for 2012 and the investment account balance at December 31, 2012, for the 40 percent venturer and for one of the 15 percent venturers.

E 11-11
Accounting for a VIE beyond the initial measurement date

Pat Corporation is the primary beneficiary in a VIE, even though Pat owns only 10 percent of the outstanding voting shares. In the year following the initial consolidation, the VIE earns net income of $1,000,000. Included in income is a fee paid by Pat for $80,000. What amount of noncontrolling interest share will appear in the consolidated income statement?

E 11-12
VIE reporting and disclosure requirements

Pal, Inc., holds an interest in Pot Corporation. Pal has determined that Pot qualifies as a VIE and that Pal's contractual position makes Pal the primary beneficiary. Den Corporation also holds a significant financial interest in Pot. What are the financial reporting and disclosure requirements for both Pal and Den?

E 11-13
Determining the primary beneficiary in a VIE

Jenn Corporation and Laura Company participate in a business classified as a VIE. Under terms of their contractual arrangement, Jenn and Laura share equally in expected residual returns of the VIE. However, expected losses are allocated 70 percent to Laura and 30 percent to Jenn. Laura serves as CEO and has the final decision on all operating and financing matters. Which of the investors is the primary beneficiary in this VIE?

PROBLEMS

P 11-1
Consolidated balance sheets (parent-company and entity theories)

The adjusted trial balances of Pin Corporation and its 80 percent-owned subsidiary, Son Corporation, at December 31, 2012, are as follows (in thousands):

	Pin	Son
Cash	$ 32	$ 20
Receivables—net	120	180
Inventories	300	150
Plant assets—net	1,200	750
Investment in Son	752	—
Cost of sales	1,300	600
Depreciation	225	75
Other expenses	271	175
Dividends	200	50
	$4,400	$2,000
Accounts payable	$ 204	$ 100
Other liabilities	300	200
Capital stock	1,000	500
Retained earnings	800	200
Sales	2,000	1,000
Income from Son	96	—
	$4,400	$2,000

Pin acquired its interest in Son for $640,000 on January 1, 2011, when Son's stockholders' equity consisted of $500,000 capital stock and $100,000 retained earnings. The excess cost was due to a $100,000 undervaluation of plant assets with a 5-year remaining useful life and to previously unrecorded patents with a 10-year amortization period. Pin uses a one-line consolidation in accounting for its investment in Son.

REQUIRED: Prepare comparative consolidated balance sheets at December 31, 2012, for Pin Corporation and Subsidiary under (a) parent-company theory and (b) entity theory.

P 11-2
Consolidated balance sheet and income statement under entity theory

Par Corporation acquires an 80 percent interest in Sip Company on January 3, 2011, for $320,000. On this date Sip's stockholders' equity consists of $200,000 capital stock and $140,000 retained earnings. The fair value/book value differential is assigned to undervalued equipment with a 6-year remaining life. Immediately after acquisition, Sip sells equipment with a 10-year remaining useful life to Par at a gain of $10,000.

Adjusted trial balances of Par and Sip at December 31, 2011, are as follows (in thousands):

	Par	Sip
Current assets	$ 303.2	$180
Plant and equipment	800	400
Investment in Sip	336.8	—
Cost of sales	500	260
Depreciation	100	50
Other expenses	120	40
Dividends	100	20
	$2,260	$950
Accumulated depreciation	$ 300	$100
Liabilities	200	100
Capital stock	600	200
Retained earnings	327.2	140
Sales	800	400
Gain on plant assets	—	10
Income from Sip	32.8	—
	$2,260	$950

REQUIRED

1. Prepare a consolidated income statement for 2011 using entity theory.

2. Prepare a consolidated balance sheet at December 31, 2011, using entity theory.

P 11-3
Computations (parent-company and entity theories)

Pal Corporation paid $595,000 cash for 70 percent of the outstanding voting stock of Sin Corporation on January 2, 2011, when Sin's stockholders' equity consisted of $500,000 of $10 par common stock and $250,000 retained earnings. The book values of Sin's assets and liabilities were equal to their fair values on this date.

During 2011, Pal Corporation had separate income of $300,000 and paid dividends of $150,000. Sin's net income for 2011 was $90,000 and its dividends were $50,000. At December 31, 2011, the stockholders' equities of Pal and Sin were as follows (in thousands):

	Pal	Sin
Common stock ($10 par)	$1,400	$500
Retained earnings	450	290
Total stockholders' equity	$1,850	$790

There were no intercompany transactions between Pal Corporation and Sin Corporation during 2011. Pal uses the equity method of accounting for its investment in Sin.

REQUIRED

1. Assume that Pal Corporation uses parent-company theory for preparing consolidated financial statements for 2011. Determine the following amounts:

a Pal Corporation's income from Sin for 2011
b Goodwill that will appear in the consolidated balance sheet at December 31, 2011
c Consolidated net income for 2011
d Noncontrolling interest expense for 2011
e Noncontrolling interest at December 31, 2011

2. Assume that Pal Corporation uses entity theory for preparing consolidated financial statements for 2011. Determine the following amounts:

a Pal Corporation's income from Sin for 2011
b Goodwill that will appear in the consolidated balance sheet at December 31, 2011
c Total consolidated income for 2011
d Noncontrolling interest share for 2011
e Noncontrolling interest at December 31, 2011

P 11-4
Comparative consolidated statements under alternative theories

At December 31, 2011, when the fair values of Sam Corporation's net assets were equal to their book values of $240,000, Pit Corporation acquired an 80 percent interest in Sam for $224,000. One year later, at December 31, 2012, the comparative adjusted trial balances of the two corporations appear as follows (in thousands):

	Pit Corporation	Sam Corporation
Cash	$ 40.8	$ 70
Accounts receivable	90	30
Inventory	160	40
Land	200	80
Buildings	900	200
Investment in Sam	240	—
Cost of sales	375	200
Expenses	150	50
Dividends	120	30
Total debits	$2,275.8	$700
Accumulated depreciation	$ 200	$ 60
Accounts payable	175.8	100
Capital stock	800	200
Retained earnings	360	40
Sales	700	300
Income from Sam	40	—
Total credits	$2,275.8	$700

ADDITIONAL INFORMATION: During 2012, Sam Corporation sold inventory items costing $15,000 to Pit for $23,000. Half of these inventory items remain unsold at December 31, 2012.

REQUIRED: Prepare comparative consolidated financial statements for Pit Corporation and Subsidiary at and for the year ended December 31, 2012, under

1. Traditional theory

2. Parent-company theory

3. Entity theory

P 11-5

Comparative balance sheets under traditional and entity theories

Balance sheets for Pad Corporation and its 80 percent-owned subsidiary, Sit Company, at December 31, 2012, are summarized as follows (in thousands):

	Pad	Sit
Assets		
Cash	$ 50	$ 20
Receivables—net	75	35
Inventories	110	30
Plant assets—net	215	85
Investment in Sit	144	—
Total assets	$594	$170
Liabilities and Stockholders' Equity		
Accounts payable	$ 80	$ 15
Other liabilities	20	5
Total liabilities	100	20
Capital stock	300	100
Retained earnings	194	50
Stockholders' equity	494	150
Total equities	$594	170

ADDITIONAL INFORMATION

1. Pad Corporation paid $128,000 for its 80% interest in Sit on January 1, 2011, when Sit had capital stock of $100,000 and retained earnings of $10,000.

2. At December 31, 2012, Pad's inventory included items on which Sit had recorded gross profit of $20,000.

REQUIRED: Prepare comparative consolidated balance sheets for Pad Corporation and Subsidiary at December 31, 2012, under the traditional and entity theories of consolidation.

P 11-6

[Based on AICPA] Separate and consolidated financial statements—entity theory

The individual and consolidated balance sheets and income statements of P and S Companies for the current year are presented in the accompanying table. The entity theory is used.

ADDITIONAL INFORMATION

1. P Company purchased its interest in S Company several years ago.

2. P Company sells products to S Company for further processing and also sells to firms outside the affiliated entity. The inventories of S Company include an intercompany profit at both the beginning and the end of the year.

3. At the beginning of the current year, S Company purchased bonds of P Company having a maturity value of $100,000. These bonds are being held as available-for-sale securities and are, correspondingly, carried at fair value. No change in fair value has occurred over the course of the year. S Company has agreed to offer P Company the option of reacquiring the bonds at S's cost before deciding to dispose of them on the open market.

P and S Companies' Individual and Consolidated Balance Sheets as of the End of the Current Year (in thousands)

	P Company	S Company	Consolidated
Assets			
Cash and receivables	$ 35	$108	$ 97.4
Inventories	40	90	122
Plant (net)	460	140	600
Patents	—	—	30
Investment in S	245	—	—
P bonds owned	—	103	—
Total assets	$780	$441	$849.40
Liabilities and Equity			
Current payables	$ 70	$ 23	$ 53
Dividends payable	10	8	12.4
Mortgage bonds (5%)	200	50	150
Capital stock	300	200	300
Retained earnings	200	160	217
Noncontrolling interest	—	—	117
Total liabilities and equity	$780	$441	$849.4

Individual and Consolidated Income Statements for the Current Year

Sales	$600	$400	$760
Cost of sales	(360)	(280)	(403)
Gross profit	240	120	357
Operating expenses	(130)	(54)	(189)
Operating profit	110	66	168
Interest revenue	1.8	5	1.8
Dividend revenue	11.2	—	—
	123	71	169.8
Interest expense	(10)	(3)	(8)
Provision for income tax	(56)	(34)	(90)
Nonrecurring loss	—	—	(3)
Noncontrolling share	—	—	60.1
Net income	$ 57	$ 34	$ (8.7)
Dividends	(20)	(16)	(24.8)
Transfer to retained earnings	$ 37	$ 18	$ 35.3

REQUIRED: Answer the following questions on the basis of the preceding information.

1. Does P Company carry its investment in S Company on the cost or the equity basis? Explain the basis of your answer.

2. If S Company's common stock has a stated value of $100 per share, how many shares does P Company own? How did you determine this?

3. When P acquired its interest in S Company, the assets and liabilities of S Company were recorded at their fair values. The $30,000 patents represents unamortized patents at the end of the current year. The unrecorded patents were $50,000 under entity theory, and the amortization is over a 10-year period. What was the amount of S's retained earnings at the date that P Company acquired its interest in S Company?

4. What is the nature of the nonrecurring loss appearing on the consolidated income statement? Reproduce the consolidating entry from which this figure originated and explain.

5. What is the amount of intercompany sales during the current year by P Company to S Company?

6. Are there any intercompany debts other than the intercompany bondholdings? Identify any such debts, and state which company is the debtor and which is the creditor in each case. Explain your reasoning.

7. What is the explanation for the difference between the consolidated cost of goods sold and the combined cost of goods sold of the two affiliated companies? Prepare a schedule reconciling combined and consolidated cost of goods sold, showing the amount of intercompany profit in the beginning and ending inventories of S Company and demonstrating how you determined the amount of intercompany profit. (*Hint:* A well-organized and labeled T-account for cost of goods sold will be an acceptable approach.)

8. Show how the $8,700 noncontrolling interest share in total consolidated net income was determined.

9. Show how the total noncontrolling interest on the balance sheet ($117,000) was determined.

10. Beginning with the $200,000 balance in P Company's retained earnings at the end of the current year, prepare a schedule in which you derive the $217,000 balance of consolidated retained earnings at the end of the current year.

P 11-7

Journal entry to record push-down, subsidiary balance sheet, and investment income

Pay Corporation paid $480,000 cash for a 100 percent interest in Sap Corporation on January 1, 2012, when Sap's stockholders' equity consisted of $200,000 capital stock and $80,000 retained earnings. Sap's balance sheet on December 31, 2011, is summarized as follows (in thousands):

	Book Value	**Fair Value**
Cash	$ 30	$ 30
Accounts receivable—net	70	70
Inventories	60	80
Land	50	75
Buildings—net	100	190
Equipment—net	90	75
Total assets	$400	$520
Accounts payable	$ 50	$ 50
Other liabilities	70	$ 60
Capital stock	200	
Retained earnings	80	
Total equities	$400	

Pay uses the equity method to account for its interest in Sap. The amortization periods for the fair value/book value differentials at the time of acquisition were as follows:

$20,000	Undervalued inventories (sold in 2012)
25,000	Undervalued land
90,000	Undervalued buildings (10-year useful life remaining)
(15,000)	Overvalued equipment (5-year useful life remaining)
10,000	Other liabilities (2 years before maturity)
70,000	Goodwill

REQUIRED

1. Prepare a journal entry on Sap's books to push down the values reflected in the purchase price.

2. Prepare a balance sheet for Sap Corporation on January 1, 2012.

3. Sap's net income for 2012 under the new push-down accounting system is $90,000. What is Pay's income from Sap for 2012?

P 11-8 Journal entries and calculations for push-down accounting

Par Corporation paid $3,000,000 for an 80 percent interest in Son Corporation on January 1, 2011, when the book values and fair values of Son's assets and liabilities were as follows (in thousands):

	Book Value	**Fair Value**
Cash	$ 300	$ 300
Accounts receivable—net	600	600
Inventories	800	2,400
Land	200	200
Buildings—net	600	600
Equipment—net	1,000	500
	$3,500	$4,600
Accounts payable	$ 500	$ 500
Long-term debt	1,000	1,000
Capital stock, $1 par	800	
Retained earnings	1,200	
	$3,500	

REQUIRED

1. Prepare a journal entry on Son's books to push down 80% of the values reflected in the purchase price (the parent-company-theory approach).

2. Prepare a journal entry on Son's books to push down 100% of the values reflected in the purchase price (the entity-theory approach).

3. Calculate the noncontrolling interest in Son on January 1, 2011, under parent-company theory.

4. Calculate the noncontrolling interest in Son on January 1, 2011, under entity theory.

P 11-9

Journal entries and comparative balance sheets at acquisition for push-down

Paw Corporation paid $180,000 cash for a 90 percent interest in Sun Corporation on January 1, 2012, when Sun's stockholders' equity consisted of $100,000 capital stock and $20,000 retained earnings. Sun Corporation's balance sheets at book value and fair value on December 31, 2011, are as follows (in thousands):

	Book Value	Fair Value
Cash	$ 20	$ 20
Accounts receivable—net	50	50
Inventories	40	30
Land	15	15
Buildings—net	30	50
Equipment—net	70	100
Total assets	$225	$265
Accounts payable	$ 45	$ 45
Other liabilities	60	60
Capital stock	100	
Retained earnings	20	
Total equities	$225	

ADDITIONAL INFORMATION

1. The amortization periods for the fair value/book value differentials at the time of acquisition are as follows:

Overvalued inventories (sold in 2012)	$10,000
Undervalued buildings (10-year useful lives)	20,000
Undervalued equipment (5-year useful lives)	30,000
Goodwill	Remainder

2. Paw uses the equity method to account for its interest in Sun.

REQUIRED

1. Prepare a journal entry on Sun Corporation's books to push down the values reflected in the purchase price under parent-company theory.

2. Prepare a journal entry on Sun Corporation's books to push down the values reflected in the purchase price under entity theory.

3. Prepare comparative balance sheets for Sun Corporation on January 1, 2012, under the approaches of (1) and (2).

P 11-10

Consolidation workpaper one year after acquisition under push-down accounting (both 90%- and 100%-ownership assumptions)

Use the information and assumptions from Problem P 11-9 for this problem. The accompanying financial statements are for Paw and Sun Corporations, one year after the acquisition. Note that Sun's statements are presented first under contemporary theory with no push-down accounting, then under 90 percent push-down accounting, and finally, under 100 percent push-down accounting.

Sun mailed a check to Paw on December 31, 2012, to settle an account payable of $8,000. Paw received the check in 2013. The $8,000 amount is included in Paw's December 31, 2012, accounts receivable.

Paw Corporation and Sun Corporation Comparative
Financial Statements With and Without Push-Down Accounting
at and for the Year Ended December 31, 2012 (in thousands)

	Basic Accounting Paw	Basic Accounting Sun	Push Down 90% Sun	Push Down 100% Sun
Income Statement				
Sales	$310.8	$110	$110	$110
Income from Sun	37.8	—	—	—
Cost of sales	(140)	(42)	(33)	(32)
Depreciation expense	(29)	(17)	(24.2)	(25)
Other operating expenses	(45)	(11)	(11)	(11)
Net income	$134.6	$ 40	$ 41.8	$ 42
Retained Earnings				
Retained earnings—beginning	$147	$ 20	$ —	$—
Add: Net income	134.6	40	41.8	42
Deduct: Dividends	(60)	(10)	(10)	(10)
Retained earnings—ending	$221.6	$ 50	$ 31.8	$ 32
Balance Sheet				
Cash	$ 63.8	$ 27	$ 27	$ 27
Accounts receivable	90	40	40	40
Dividends receivable	9	—	—	—
Inventories	20	35	35	35
Land	40	15	15	15
Buildings—net	140	27	43.2	45
Equipment—net	165	56	77.6	80
Investment in Sun	208.8	—	—	—
Goodwill	—	—	36	40
Total assets	$736.6	$200	$273.8	$282
Accounts payable	$125	$ 20	$ 20	$ 20
Dividends payable	15	10	10	10
Other liabilities	75	20	20	20
Capital stock	300	100	100	100
Push-down capital	—	—	92	100
Retained earnings	221.6	50	31.8	32
Total equities	$736.6	$200	$273.8	$282

REQUIRED: Prepare consolidation workpapers for Paw Corporation and Subsidiary for the year ended December 31, 2012, under (a) 90 percent push-down accounting and (b) 100 percent push-down accounting.

P 11-11
Workpaper for proportionate consolidation (joint venture)

Pep Corporation owns a 40 percent interest in Jay Company, a joint venture that is organized as an undivided interest. In its separate financial statements, Pep accounts for Jay under the equity method, but for reporting purposes, the proportionate consolidation method is used.

Separate financial statements of Pep and Jay at and for the year ended December 31, 2011, are summarized as follows (in thousands):

	Pep Corporation	Jay Company
Combined Income and Retained Earnings Statements for the Year Ended December 31, 2011		
Sales	$ 800	$300
Income from Jay	20	—
Cost of sales	(400)	(150)
Depreciation expense	(100)	(40)
Other expenses	(120)	(60)
Net income	200	50
Beginning retained earnings	300	—
Beginning venture equity	—	250
Dividends	(100)	—
Retained earnings/venture equity	$ 400	$300
Balance Sheets at December 31, 2011		
Cash	$ 100	$ 50
Receivables—net	130	30
Inventories	110	40
Land	140	60
Buildings—net	200	100
Equipment—net	300	180
Investment in Jay	120	—
Total assets	$1,100	$460
Accounts payable	$ 120	$100
Other liabilities	80	60
Common stock, $10 par	500	—
Retained earnings	400	—
Venture equity	—	300
Total equities	$1,100	$460

REQUIRED: Prepare a workpaper for a proportionate consolidation of the financial statements of Pep Corporation and Jay Company at and for the year ended December 31, 2011.

INTERNET ASSIGNMENT

Visit the Web site of *Dow Chemical Company* and obtain a copy of the 2009 annual report. Prepare a brief summary of the information you find regarding Dow's joint venture activities. Does Dow invest in variable interest entities (VIEs)? Is Dow the primary beneficiary in any VIEs? How does Dow account for VIE investments?

REFERENCES TO THE AUTHORITATIVE LITERATURE

[1] FASB ASC 810-10-05 and ASC 810-10-65. Originally *Statement of Financial Accounting Standards No. 141(R).* "Business Combinations." Norwalk, CT: Financial Accounting Standards Board, 2007 and *Statement of Financial Accounting Standards No. 160.* "Noncontrolling Interests in Consolidated Financial Statements—An amendment of *ARB No. 51.*" Norwalk, CT: Financial Accounting Standards Board, 2007.

[2] FASB ASC 810-10-15. Originally AICPA Committee on Accounting Procedure. *Accounting Research Bulletin No. 51.* "Consolidated Financial Statements." New York: American Institute of Certified Public Accountants, 1959.

[3] FASB ASC 805-10-65. Originally *Statement of Financial Accounting Standards No. 160.* "Noncontrolling Interests in Consolidated Financial Statements—An amendment of *ARB No. 51.*" Norwalk, CT: Financial Accounting Standards Board, 2007.

[4] FASB ASC 810-45-1. Originally AICPA Committee on Accounting Procedure. *Accounting Research Bulletin No. 51.* "Consolidated Financial Statements." New York: American Institute of Certified Public Accountants, 1959.

[5] FASB ASC 805-10-65-1. Originally *Statement of Financial Accounting Standards No. 160.* "Noncontrolling Interests in Consolidated Financial Statements—An amendment of *ARB No. 51.*" Norwalk, CT: Financial Accounting Standards Board, 2007.

[6] FASB ASC 810-10-25-10. Originally *Statement of Financial Accounting Standards No. 141(R).* "Business Combinations." Norwalk, CT: Financial Accounting Standards Board, 2007.

[7] FASB ASC 810-10-25-11. Originally *Statement of Financial Accounting Standards No. 141(R).* "Business Combinations." Norwalk, CT: Financial Accounting Standards Board, 2007.

[8] FASB ASC 350-20-35. Originally *Statement of Financial Accounting Standards No. 142.* "Goodwill and Other Intangible Assets." Stamford, CT: Financial Accounting Standards Board, 2001.

[9] FASB ASC 323-10-15. Originally *Accounting Principles Board Opinion No. 18.* "The Equity Method of Accounting for Investments in Common Stock." New York: American Institute of Certified Public Accountants, 1971.

[10] FASB ASC 323-10-15-3. Originally *Accounting Principles Board Opinion No. 18.* "The Equity Method of Accounting for Investments in Common Stock." New York: American Institute of Certified Public Accountants, 1971.

[11] FASB ASC 323-10-15. Originally *Accounting Principles Board Opinion No. 18.* "The Equity Method of Accounting for Investments in Common Stock." New York: American Institute of Certified Public Accountants, 1971.

[12] FASB ASC 840-10-45. Originally *Statement of Financial Accounting Standards No. 94.* "Consolidation of All Majority-Owned Subsidiaries." Stamford CT: Financial Accounting Standards Board, 1987.

[13] FASB ASC 323-10-15. Originally *Accounting Principles Board Opinion No. 18.* "The Equity Method of Accounting for Investments in Common Stock." New York: American Institute of Certified Public Accountants, 1971.

[14] FASB ASC 323-10-15. Originally *Accounting Principles Board Opinion No. 18.* "The Equity Method of Accounting for Investments in Common Stock." New York: American Institute of Certified Public Accountants, 1971.

[15] FASB ASC 860-10-05-5. Originally *Statement of Financial Accounting Standards No. 140.* "Accounting for Transfers and Servicing of Financial Assets and Extinguishment of Liabilities." Stamford, CT: Financial Accounting Standards Board, 2000.

[16] FASB ASC 860-10-60-2. Originally *FASB Interpretation No. 46 (Revised).* "Consolidation of Variable Interest Entities: An Interpretation of ARB No 51." Norwalk, CT: Financial Accounting Standards Board, December 2003.

[17] FASB ASC 810-10-15-13. Originally *FASB Interpretation No. 46 (Revised).* "Consolidation of Variable Interest Entities: An Interpretation of ARB No 51." Norwalk, CT: Financial Accounting Standards Board, December 2003.

[18] FASB ASC 810-10-15-14. Originally *Statement of Financial Accounting Standards No. 167.* "Amendments to FASB Interpretation No. 46(R)." Norwalk, CT: Financial Accounting Standards Board, June 2009.

[19] FASB ASC 810-10-15-14. Originally *Statement of Financial Accounting Standards No. 167.* "Amendments to FASB Interpretation No. 46(R)." Norwalk, CT: Financial Accounting Standards Board, June 2009.

12 CHAPTER

Derivatives and Foreign Currency: Concepts and Common Transactions

T his chapter covers the economics of derivatives and foreign currency transactions that are not being accounted for as part of a hedge transaction. The next chapter covers hedge accounting, which will include the accounting for derivatives that are used as a hedge. We first introduce some concepts about risk and how derivatives can manage various risks. Then different types of derivatives are described. Finally, we discuss concepts and transactions involving foreign currency–denominated transactions.

DERIVATIVES

LEARNING OBJECTIVE 1,2

Definitions

Derivative is the name given to a broad range of financial securities. Their common characteristic is that the derivative contract's value to the investor is directly related to fluctuations in price, rate, or some other variable that *underlies* it. Derivative contracts can be used to limit businesses' exposure to price or rate fluctuations. One party to the contract, in effect, bets that the underlying price or rate will move in the opposite direction to what the other party is expecting. The party trying to control its economic rate or price change risk is engaging in a derivative, or *hedge contract*. Contract structures and the accounting for such contracts vary across the types of risk being managed.

Interest rates, commodity prices, foreign currency exchange rates, and stock prices are the most common types of price and rate risks that companies hedge. For example, **Starbucks** faces a variety of risks including interest rate risk, commodity price fluctuation and foreign currency fluctuation. Because Starbucks forecasts future cash flows and earnings based on future rates and prices, it enters into derivative contracts to manage the risk of those future outcomes.[1] By entering into these types of agreements, Starbucks locks in exchange rates, interest rates, and commodity prices, reducing the effects of future changes in exchange rates, interest rates, and commodity prices, on its cash flow and income.

In 2000, the amusement park chain **Six Flags, Inc**., entered into interest rate swap agreements. These agreements, in effect, convert a $600,000,000 term loan from a variable-rate agreement to a fixed-rate agreement. Interest rate swap agreements are usually negotiated with financial institutions. Like Starbucks, Six Flags is reducing the variability of its future cash flow streams and income by entering into this type of agreement. By 2007 at least 2,000 public firms reported using some types of derivative to manage risks.

---

[1]*Source:* Starbucks' fiscal 2010 annual report.

LEARNING OBJECTIVES

1 Understand the definition of a derivative and the types of risks that derivatives can manage.

2 Understand the structure, benefits, and costs of options, futures, forward contracts, and swaps.

3 Understand key concepts related to foreign currency exchange rates, such as indirect and direct quotes; floating, fixed, and multiple exchange rates; and spot, current, and historical exchange rates.

4 Explain the difference between receivable or payable measurement and denomination.

5 Record foreign currency–denominated sales/receivables and purchases/payables at the initial transaction date, year-end, and the receivable or payable settlement date.

Companies enter into derivative contracts to reduce the vulnerability of their cash flows, market values of assets and liabilities, and earnings to changes in the prices of goods, commodities, and financial instruments that they purchase, sell, or invest in. Typical forms of derivative instruments are option contracts, forward contracts, futures contracts, and swaps.

LEARNING
OBJECTIVE **2**

Hedge Transactions

Hedge is the term we use to describe a combined transaction of an existing position and a derivative contract that is designed to manage the risks the firm faces by holding the existing position alone. Most hedges are accomplished by using one of a few basic types of derivatives: forward contracts, futures contracts, options, or swaps.

Forward contracts are negotiated contracts between two parties for the delivery or purchase of a commodity or foreign currency at a pre-agreed price, quantity, and delivery date. The agreement may require actual physical delivery of the goods or may allow a net settlement.

Net settlement allows the payment of money so that the parties are in the same economic condition as they would have been if delivery had occurred. For example, assume that BigOil wants to reduce its vulnerability to future oil price changes and contracts with an oil price speculator to buy 10,000 barrels of oil at $100 per barrel in three months. In three months, when the contract settles, oil is selling on the open market at $110 per barrel. Because BigOil has locked in a $100 per barrel price, the speculator could be required either to deliver 10,000 barrels of oil to BigOil in exchange for $100 per barrel or settle the contract net. In a net settlement situation, the speculator would not deliver 10,000 barrels of oil but would pay BigOil $100,000 [($110 − $100) × 10,000 barrels] to settle the contract. BigOil would then buy the oil in the open market at $110 per barrel ($100 from BigOil and $10 from the payment from the speculator). BigOil and the speculator are in the same position economically as they would have been if an actual exchange of oil had occurred between them. Many derivative transactions are designed in a similar fashion; the derivative's value mimics a physical transaction, and then settles in cash.

Futures contracts and forward contracts have essentially the same contracting characteristics, except futures differ from forward contracts in ways that allow them to be traded easily in markets. Futures contracts are very standardized. A futures exchange, not the trading parties, determines the contract termination date, the exact quality and quantity of the goods to be delivered, and the delivery location. The exchange guarantees the performance of both clearing firms engaged in the trade, who in turn guarantee the performance of the traders whom they represent.

To get out of a futures position, one can simply purchase or sell an identical contract in the opposite direction. The exchange will then cancel the two positions, so the net position is zero. One need not take delivery of the commodity. At the end of each day, the gain or loss on the futures position is computed. The clearing house representing the losing position for the day pays the exchange for the loss. The exchange then pays the winning position the gain for the day. In essence, the markets use a daily mark-to-market approach through these cash payments.

The cost of contracting in a futures market is generally lower than using a forward contract. In addition, the exchange and clearing houses guarantee performance or carrying out of the contract's terms. Firms must be careful about the possibility of nonperformance with forward contracts. Because individual companies contract with each other directly, if one company cannot pay when the contract settles, the other may be left absorbing the risk it was trying to hedge against. Futures contracts do not have this problem. However, forward contracts have their benefits also. Because the forward contract is a tailored contract, the exact quality of the goods to be delivered can be defined. Although this clearly is not crucial with currencies, it might be with respect to commodities such as oil, copper, and silver.

Forward contract delivery quantities, prices, product quality, and delivery dates can all be negotiated. Under a futures contract, the quantities, delivery dates, and product quality of each contract are defined by the exchange. The futures price is a market-determined amount.

For example, perhaps the only silver futures contracts available are for 25,000 troy ounces of silver to be delivered on January 6, 2011. If we wish to hedge a future purchase of 110,000 troy ounces of silver, either we underhedge by 10,000 [purchasing four contracts totaling 100,000] troy ounces or we overhedge by 15,000 [purchasing five contracts totaling 125,000] troy ounces. Either way, some of the hedge will be ineffective. In a forward contract, the exact amount can be negotiated. In a similar fashion, the delivery date can be negotiated.

Options are another commonly used hedging instrument structure. Option types are either call or put. A call gives the holder the right to buy an asset, and a put gives them the right to sell. The holder of an option has the right, but not the obligation to carry out the transaction at the strike price, a pre-determined amount. The writer or seller of an option is obligated to carry out the transaction, if the holder exercises their right to buy or sell. Only one side of the option contract is required to perform at the behest of the other. The other party to the option has the ability, but not the obligation, to perform.

Options are traded on equities, commodities, foreign currency, and interest rates. Option prices can be determined using a variety of option-pricing models. The most common is the Black-Scholes option pricing model. The Black-Scholes model uses probability parameters such as the variability of the underlying (the historical variability of the stock price, for an equity option), current price levels of the underlying (the stock's current market value), time to maturity, and the strike price to determine the price of the option. The option price will obviously be higher if the probability of exercise is higher. Two main classifications of options are American and European types, which differ in respect to exercise date. A European style can only be exercised on the maturity date, while the American style can be exercised anytime before the maturity date. If you compared two option contracts that were identical except for this distinction, the American style option would have a higher value. The American style option gives the holder many more chances to exercise at a profit.

Companies purchase options to manage risk—quite frequently, price risk. For example, a company may buy an option to purchase a commodity, say fuel, at a specified price. Assume that the option cost $1,000 and that the company can exercise its option to purchase 100,000 gallons of fuel at $1 per gallon. If the market fuel price is $1.10 at the time the company needs the fuel, then the company will exercise the option and purchase the fuel at the lower price. The total cost of the fuel is $1,000 + ($1 × 100,000), or $101,000. On the other hand, if the market fuel price is $0.90 per gallon, the company will allow the option to expire because it is cheaper to purchase the fuel at the market price. The company still incurs an expense of $1,000 related to the fuel option contract.

Swaps are contracts to exchange an ongoing stream of cash flows. The most common swap is an interest rate swap, but swaps can be designed around any underlying and corresponding price or rate. A common use for swaps is to lock in fixed rates on liabilities, as described in the above Six Flags example. Like forwards, swaps are commonly negotiated on an individual basis, although there are some standardized swaps that are exchange traded. A firm that holds variable rate debt might not want the risk of increases in future interest payments, and would enter into a receive-variable and pay-fixed swap. If the firm had $1M in debt currently at 8 percent, but subject to fluctuations in future rates, they could enter into a swap that would receive (pay) the increase (decrease) from the original 8 percent rate and a variable rate.

Date	Variable Rate	Interest payment on debt	Net settlement of swap pay (receive)	Net interest payment
At inception	8%			
Period 1	7%	70,000	10,000	80,000
Period 2	8%	80,000	0	80,000
Period 3	9%	90,000	(10,000)	80,000

The firm entering into a swap will have to pay a fee or premium to the counterparty of the swap. The counterparty for most interest rate swaps will be a large bank, which ideally has offsetting positions and is primarily acting as a market maker in interest rate hedging.

Economics Underlying Derivatives

To help you understand the economics underlying derivative contracting, the effects on income using both a forward contract and an option contract are examined. Recall that forward contracts and futures contracts are very similar so the economic effects will be similar. As a result futures will not be illustrated here.

Assume that Gre Company mines copper. It will mine and sell 100,000 pounds of copper during the next four quarters and will sell all the copper it produces at the end of that time. Gre's projected fixed costs are $25,000,000 and variable costs are $39 per pound. Based on these figures, Gre needs to cover $28,900,000 in costs in order to break even, $25,000,000 fixed plus $3,900,000 variable. The break-even revenue is $289 per pound.

The table below contains the profit and loss related to various per pound revenue points:

Per Pound Revenue	Profit (Loss)
$310	$2,100,000
$300	1,100,000
$289	—
$250	(3,900,000)
$200	(8,900,000)

Gre decides now to sell its future production by entering into a forward contract with Bro for delivery to Bro of 100,000 pounds of copper in one year at a price of $300 per pound.

Why would Gre decide to do this? If its projected costs are correct, Gre knows that the $300 price will generate a profit. In any event, the risk of fluctuations in sales price has been shifted to Bro. Bro might be a speculator who is willing to take the risk, hoping that the price will actually be higher in one year than $300, but willing to assume the risk that it could be lower than $300. Or Bro might use the copper in its own production and may be trying to manage its costs in the same way that Gre is trying to manage the risk on the revenue side.

Obviously, Gre is also giving up the possibility of making a larger profit, but there are several reasons that Gre might wish to manage its risk in this way. First, Gre might need to borrow money to finance its operation. By eliminating the selling price risk, Gre should be able to negotiate a lower interest rate and/or might now be able to find lenders from which to borrow, given the mitigation of this risk. Taxes are another reason that hedging might make sense. Losses are deductible to the extent of offsetting profits. However, losses must be carried forward to future years if there are insufficient profits to offset them. Thus the tax benefit of losses is smaller than the tax cost of profits because of time value of money concerns. As a result, because of the unequal treatment of income and losses, a company may be willing to forego some profit to avoid losses. Other reasons could include avoiding bankruptcy, or managerial bonus incentives.

The following table outlines what the impact on economic income—ignoring taxes—would be in an unhedged situation compared to if Gre hedges the transaction with a forward:

Market Price per Pound	Forward Price per Pound	Unhedged Gain/(Loss)	Economic Gain/(Loss) on Forward	Economic Income with Hedge
$310	$300	$2,100,000	$(1,000,000)	$ 1,100,000
$300	$300	1,100,000	—	1,100,000
$289	$300	—	1,100,000	1,100,000
$250	$300	(3,900,000)	5,000,000	1,100,000
$200	$300	(8,900,000)	10,000,000	1,100,000

Gre's reported income of $1,100,000 can be decomposed into the gain/(loss) related to the forward contract and the gain/(loss) if no hedging exists at each price. The column headed Economic Gain/(Loss) on Forward is computed by taking the difference in the market price per pound at the date the contract is settled and the forward price per pound multiplied by 100,000 pounds. For example, if the market price per pound is $310 and Gre receives $300 per pound from the forward contract, there is an economic loss from Gre's perspective related to the forward contract of $10 per pound, or $1,000,000. If Gre had not hedged, it would have earned revenue of $310 per pound and profit of $2,100,000. The difference between the gain if no hedging had occurred, $2,100,000, and the loss on the hedging contract, $1,000,000, results in reported income of $1,100,000.

This example demonstrates that the forward's gain/(loss) moves in the opposite direction of the unhedged gain/(loss) and effectively eliminates the revenue price risk at any level of price. This is a completely effective hedge. Notice that at every revenue price point, the reported income is $1,100,000.

In the next chapter, we discuss the accounting for this situation during the year that the forward contract is in place. We will see that the accounting is designed to reflect the economic impact of this strategy.

Another way that Gre might be able to manage its risk is through the use of options. Options can be thought of as a type of insurance. When an individual buys homeowners' insurance, the insurance company will cover the homeowner's losses in the event of theft, fire, or many other events. Of course, this is not costless, and the amount that the homeowner pays for insurance depends on the risk of loss. For example, high-property-crime areas typically have higher homeowners' insurance premiums than low-property-crime areas because the risk assumed by the insurance company is higher.

In a similar fashion, Gre might buy a put option. A put option requires that the seller (or writer) of the put option must buy the asset at a fixed price, while the buyer of the put option has the option to sell at market, and will if the price is higher at the option's exercise date. Gre would have a right to exercise the option and require the writer of the option to buy the copper at a set price, say $300. Gre would exercise its option if the market price of copper were below $300 at the option's exercise date. Gre would let the options expire if the price were above $300. In this way, Gre shifts the risk of lower market prices to the writer of the option but still can benefit from higher prices if the market price is higher than the option exercise price of $300.

In order for the option writer to agree to write the option, the writer must be compensated. Many different option pricing models exist. Many are based on the Black-Scholes option pricing model. The Black-Scholes model uses probability parameters such as the variability of the underlying (in this case, the historical copper price variability), current price levels of the underlying (in this case, copper), and time to maturity of the option to determine the price of the option. The option price will obviously be higher if the probability of exercise is higher.

Let's assume that the option price is $10.50 per pound and that the exercise price is $300. If the price of the copper is $300 or above at the exercise date, Gre will not exercise the option. Instead, Gre will sell the copper at the market price, say $340. But this is not a costless transaction, unlike the forward contract illustrated previously. The option cost to Gre is $10.50 per pound, so Gre will net only $329.50 revenue per pound after the option cost is considered. Gre's income is lower than it would have been if it had not hedged.

Using a table similar to the forward case, let's examine the impact on income of the option at various market prices:

Market Price per Pound	Option Exercise Price	Option Exercise, Yes or No	Unhedged Gain/(Loss)	Economic Gain/Loss on Option Exercise	Cost of Option	Economic Income (Loss)
$340	$300	No	$5,100,000	—	$1,050,000	$4,050,000
$300	$300	No	1,100,000	—	1,050,000	50,000
$289	$300	Yes	—	$ 1,100,000	1,050,000	50,000
$250	$300	Yes	(3,900,000)	5,000,000	1,050,000	50,000
$200	$300	Yes	(8,900,000)	10,000,000	1,050,000	50,000

From this table we can see the impact of the option exercise on income. If no option was purchased, the company's profit varies greatly, and the company may lose a large amount of money. The income distribution is transformed into a much less risky one after the option is purchased. At all price points $300 and below, the company earns $50,000. If no option had been purchased, Gre could have made $1,100,000 at $300 or could have lost $8,900,000 if the market price was $200.

If the copper price was above $300 per pound, the company would not exercise the option and would be able to sell the copper at the market price and make more than $50,000 but less than it would have if it had not purchased the option. For example, at $340 per pound, the unhedged gain would have been $5,100,000. Because the option cost $1,050,000, the actual income is only $4,050,000.

In the next chapter, we will illustrate the accounting for the Gre situation. Accounting under GAAP [1] is aimed at reflecting the underlying economic reality of the hedging relationship. Clearly, intent is important. The reason that Gre enters into the option contract is to mitigate risk, while the option writer is likely to be speculating. Should the accounting from both perspectives be identical? The answer is no.

FOREIGN EXCHANGE CONCEPTS AND DEFINITIONS

Foreign business activity by U.S. corporations has expanded rapidly over time. In 2009, exports of U.S. goods and services were $1.571 trillion, and imports of foreign goods and services totaled $1.946 trillion.[2] These figures were down slightly from the record-setting year of 2008 when combined imports and exports of goods and services in and out of the U.S. totaled $4.377 trillion.

The effect of international branch and subsidiary operations on U.S. companies' operating results is sizeable. Almost 70 percent of the *Coca-Cola Company's* operating revenues and 80 percent of its operating income came from operations outside of the United States in 2007. Also in 2007, 27 percent of *Apple's* net sales came from Europe and Japan, and 18 percent of *Starbucks'* revenues and 24 percent of *Wal-Mart's* were earned outside the United States. During 2004, nearly 63 percent of *Nike's* revenues came from non-U.S. sources.

In this section we discuss foreign currency concepts and foreign currency transaction accounting. Chapter 13 demonstrates the accounting for hedging foreign currency risks, while Chapter 14 discusses foreign currency financial statement translation.

Currencies provide a standard of value, a medium of exchange, and a unit of measure for economic transactions. Currencies of different countries perform the first two functions with varying degrees of efficiency, but essentially all currencies provide a unit of measure for the economic activities and resources of their respective countries.

For transactions to be included in financial records, they must be measured in a currency. Typically, the currency in which a transaction is recorded and the currency needed to settle the transaction are the same. For example, a Chicago pizza shop buys all its produce and other inputs and pays all of its employees and other bills using U.S. dollars. The pizza shop collects dollars from its customers. If a receivable or payable arises, it will require receiving or spending dollars for settlement. A receivable or payable is **denominated** in a currency when it must be paid in that currency. A receivable or payable is **measured** in a currency when it is recorded in the financial records in that currency. In this example, the pizza shop's receivables and payables are denominated and measured in the same currency, the U.S. dollar.

In the case of transactions between business entities of different countries, the amounts receivable and payable are ordinarily denominated in the local currency of either the buying entity or the selling entity.[3] For example, if a U.S. firm sells merchandise to a British firm, the transaction amount will be denominated (or paid) in either U.S. dollars or British pounds, even though the U.S. firm will measure and record its account receivable and sales in U.S. dollars and the British firm will measure and record its purchase and account payable in British pounds, regardless of the currency in which the transaction is denominated.

If the transaction is denominated in British pounds, the U.S. firm has to determine how many U.S. dollars the transaction represents in order to record it. If the transaction is denominated in U.S. dollars, the British firm has to determine how many British pounds the transaction represents. To measure transactions in their own currencies, businesses around the world rely on exchange rates negotiated on a continuous basis in world currency markets. Exchange rates are essentially prices for currencies expressed in units of other currencies.

Direct and Indirect Quotation of Exchange Rates

An **exchange rate** is the ratio between a unit of one currency and the amount of another currency for which that unit can be exchanged at a particular time. The exchange rate can be computed directly or indirectly. Assume that $1.60 can be exchanged for 1 British pound (£1).

Direct quotation (U.S. dollar per one foreign currency unit):

$$\frac{\$1.60}{1} = \$1.60$$

---

[2]U.S. Department of Commerce, Bureau of Economic Analysis. *U.S. International Trade in Goods and Services Report.* November 10, 2010.

[3]Sometimes the amounts are denominated in the currency of a third country whose currency is relatively more stable than the currency of either the buyer or the seller.

Indirect quotation (the number of foreign currency units per U.S. dollar):

$$\frac{1}{\$1.60} = £0.625$$

The first approach is a *direct quotation* (from a U.S. viewpoint) because the rate is expressed in U.S. dollars: $1.60 is equivalent to one British pound (one unit of the foreign currency). The second approach is an *indirect quotation* (from a U.S. viewpoint) because the rate is expressed in British pounds (the foreign currency): £0.625 is equivalent to one U.S. dollar. The Foreign Exchange section of *The Wall Street Journal* shows both direct (U.S. dollar equivalent) and indirect (currency per U.S. dollar) exchange rates on a daily basis.

Floating, Fixed, and Multiple Exchange Rates

Exchange rates may be fixed by a governmental unit or may be allowed to fluctuate (float) with changes in the currency markets. **Official**, or **fixed, exchange rates** are set by a government and do not change as a result of changes in world currency markets. **Free**, or **floating, exchange rates** are those that reflect fluctuating market prices for a currency based on supply and demand and other factors in the world currency markets.

FLOATING EXCHANGE RATES Theoretically, a currency's value should reflect its buying power in world markets. For example, an increase in a country's inflation rate indicates that its currency's purchasing power is decreasing. The currency's value should fall in relation to other currencies. The technical term for this movement in currency value is **weakening**. A currency falls, or *weakens*, relative to another currency if it takes more of the weakening currency to purchase one unit of the other currency.

A large trade surplus (when the amount of exports exceeds imports) usually results in an increased demand for a country's currency because many of those export sales must be paid in the exporting country's currency. The exporting country's currency becomes more valuable relative to the importing countries' currencies, or it **strengthens**. A currency strengthens relative to another currency if it takes fewer units of the strengthening currency to purchase one unit of the other currency.

A large trade deficit (when the amount of imports exceeds exports) should lead to a decrease, or weakening, of the currency's value. Although inflation and net trade position (trade surplus or trade deficit) are common causes of changes in floating exchange rates, other factors have occasionally been more influential. Interest rate differences across countries influence supply and demand for a country's currency because many investors buy securities in the international securities markets. Speculative trading to take advantage of currency movements also affects exchange rates.

To reduce its trade deficit, the U.S. government has occasionally asked other countries (Taiwan and South Korea, for example) to let their currencies strengthen against the U.S. dollar. A decline in value of the dollar in relation to other major currencies should increase the price of foreign products in the United States and lead to a reduction of imports to the United States. Similarly, U.S. goods can be sold in international markets for fewer foreign currency units when the dollar weakens against those currencies. Even so, a weakening U.S. dollar has often done little to abate U.S. consumers' demand for imported products, and changes in the exchange rates may have little effect on the trade deficit. Other factors that may affect a country's trade balance include interest rates and tax rates.

A mathematical example of strengthening and weakening of a currency relative to another currency follows. Initially, assume that one British pound can be purchased for $1.50. If the quote is indirect, $1 can be purchased for 0.6667 pounds.

If the dollar weakens relative to the pound, each pound is more expensive in dollar terms. If the dollar weakens by 10 percent, each pound will now cost $1.65. If the dollar weakens by 10 percent, it takes fewer pounds to buy $1, so now $1 can be purchased for 0.6061 pounds.

If the dollar strengthens relative to the pound, each pound is less expensive in dollar terms. If the dollar strengthens by 10 percent, each pound will now cost $1.35. If the quote is indirect, $1 can now be purchased for 0.7407 pounds.

FIXED AND MULTIPLE EXCHANGE RATES When exchange rates are fixed, the issuing government is able to set (fix) different rates for different kinds of transactions. For example, it may set a preferential rate for imports (or certain kinds of imports) and penalty rates for exports (or certain kinds of exports) in order to promote the economic objectives of the country. Such rates are referred to as **multiple exchange rates**.

Spot, Current, and Historical Exchange Rates

The exchange rates that are used in accounting for foreign operations and transactions (other than forward contracts) are spot rates, current exchange rates, and historical exchange rates. Spot rate is a *market* term; current and historical rates are *accounting* terms. These are defined as follows:

> **Spot rate.** The exchange rate for immediate delivery of currencies exchanged.
> **Current rate.** The rate at which one unit of currency can be exchanged for another currency at the balance sheet date or the transaction date.
> **Historical rate.** The rate in effect at the date a specific transaction or event occurred.

Spot, current, and historical rates may be either fixed or floating rates, depending on the particular currency involved. Spot rates for foreign transactions between the United States and a country with fixed exchange rates will normally change in that foreign country only as a result of government action (except for transactions in the black market in the foreign country's currency). For example, the Argentine government can control the exchange rate in Buenos Aires, but not in New York. Spot rates for foreign transactions with a country that has floating exchange rates may change daily, or several times in a single day, depending on factors that influence the currency markets. However, only one spot rate exists for a given transaction.

The foreign currency transaction's current rate is the spot rate in effect for immediate settlement of the amounts denominated in foreign currency at the transaction date or at the balance sheet date. Historical rates are the spot rates that were in effect on the date that a particular event or transaction occurred.

Foreign Exchange Quotations

Major U.S. banks facilitate international trade by maintaining departments that provide bank transfer services between U.S. and non-U.S. companies, as well as currency exchange services.

Selected interbank transaction exchange rates on November 28, 2010, were:[4]

	U.S. $ Equivalent	Currency per U.S. $
Britain (pound)	$1.5588	0.6413 pounds
Canada (dollars)	$0.9786	1.0219 Canadian dollars
Euro	$1.3242	0.7552 euros
Japan (yen)	$0.0119	84.095 yen
Mexico (peso)	$0.08	12.495 pesos

A payment of $1,558,800 to a U.S. banker at 4 P.M. EST on November 28, 2010, would have entitled a U.S. corporation to purchase British goods selling for £1,000,000 or to settle an account payable denominated at £1,000,000. Similarly, a U.S. company could have purchased merchandise selling for 1,000,000 Canadian dollars for $978,600 at that time.

The U.S. bankers that provide foreign exchange services are, of course, paid for their services. The payment is the difference between the amount that they receive from U.S. corporations and the amount they pay out for the foreign currencies, or vice versa. For example, a bank that trades foreign currency may offer to sell British pounds for $1.57 or to buy them for $1.55 when the quoted rate for British pounds is $1.56. Thus, a firm can buy 1,000,000 pounds from the bank for $1,570,000 or sell 1,000,000 pounds to the bank for $1,550,000, and the bank realizes a $10,000 gain in either case.

LEARNING OBJECTIVE **4**

FOREIGN CURRENCY TRANSACTIONS OTHER THAN FORWARD CONTRACTS

Transactions within a country that are measured and recorded in the currency of that country are **local transactions**. The transactions of a British subsidiary would be recorded in British pounds, and its financial statements would be stated in British pounds. However, its financial statements

---

[4]*Source:* Yahoo Finance Web site, November 29, 2010.

must be converted into U.S. dollars before consolidation with a U.S. parent company. Translation of foreign currency financial statements is covered in Chapter 14.

This discussion of foreign currency transactions assumes the point of view of a U.S. firm whose functional currency is the U.S. dollar (which is also its local currency). An entity's *functional currency* is the currency of its primary economic environment. Normally, the predominant currency received or expended to complete transactions is the functional currency. Chapter 14 contains a more extensive discussion of the functional currency concept. **Foreign transactions** are transactions between countries or between enterprises in different countries. **Foreign currency transactions** are transactions whose terms are stated (denominated) in a currency other than an entity's functional currency. Thus, a foreign transaction may or may not be a foreign currency transaction.

The most common types of foreign transactions are imports and exports of goods and services. Import and export transactions are foreign transactions, but they are not foreign currency transactions unless their terms are denominated in a foreign currency—that is, a currency other than the entity's functional currency. An export sale by a U.S. company to a Canadian company is a foreign currency transaction from the viewpoint of the U.S. company only if the invoice is denominated (fixed) in Canadian dollars. Translation is required if the transaction is denominated in a foreign currency, but not if it is denominated in the entity's functional currency.

FASB Requirements

Current GAAP [2] applies only to foreign currency transactions and to foreign currency financial statements. GAAP stipulates the following requirements for foreign currency transactions other than derivatives:

1. At the date the transaction is recognized, each asset, liability, revenue, expense, gain, or loss arising from the transaction shall be measured and recorded in the functional currency of the recording entity by use of the exchange rate in effect at that date.

2. At each balance sheet date, recorded balances that are denominated in a currency other than the functional currency of the recording entity shall be adjusted to reflect the current exchange rate.

TRANSLATION AT THE SPOT RATE   The first requirement for recording foreign currency transactions is that they must be translated into U.S. dollars at the spot rate in effect at the *transaction date*. Each asset, liability, revenue, and expense account arising from the transaction is translated into dollars before it is recorded. The unit of measurement is changed from the foreign currency to the U.S. dollar.

Assume that a U.S. corporation imports inventory from a Canadian firm when the spot rate for Canadian dollars is $0.7000. The invoice calls for payment of 10,000 Canadian dollars in 30 days. (*Note:* The $ sign used for the spot rate indicates direct quotation—the U.S. dollar equivalent of one unit of foreign currency.) The U.S. importer records the transaction as follows:

Inventory (+A)	$7,000	
Accounts payable (fc) (+L)		$7,000
(Translation: 10,000 Canadian dollars × $0.7000 spot rate.)		

Except for the foreign currency (fc) notation, the entry is recorded in the usual manner. The notation is used here to indicate that the account payable is denominated in foreign currency. The inventory is measured in U.S. dollars, and no subsequent adjustment is made to the inventory account for foreign currency rate fluctuations.

If the account payable is paid when the spot rate is $0.6900, the payment is recorded as follows:

Accounts payable (fc) (−L)	$7,000	
Exchange gain (+Ga, +SE)		$ 100
Cash (−A)		6,900
(Cash required equals 10,000 Canadian		
dollars × $0.6900 spot rate.)		

The $100 exchange gain results because a liability measured at $7,000 is settled for $6,900. This gain reflects a change in the exchange rate between the initial transaction date and the date of payment. If the exchange rate had changed to $0.7200, a $200 exchange loss would have resulted.

Exhibit 12-1 illustrates the accounting differences that arise when foreign transactions are denominated in an entity's functional currency (U.S. dollars) as opposed to a foreign currency. In examining the exhibit, keep in mind that a transaction must be denominated in a foreign currency to be a foreign currency transaction. When the billing for a U.S. company's sale or purchase is denominated in U.S. dollars, no translation is required.

EXHIBIT 12-1

Comparison of Purchase and Sale Transactions Denominated in U.S. Dollars Versus British Pounds

---

SALES TRANSACTION

Assumption: U.S. Foods sells merchandise to London Industries Ltd. for $16,500, or £10,000 when the exchange rate is $1.65, and receives payment when the exchange rate is $1.64.

IF BILLING IS IN U.S. DOLLARS

(Date of sale)		
Accounts receivable (+A)	$16,500	
Sales (+R, +SE)		$16,500
To record sale to London Industries; invoice is $16,500.		
(Date of receipt)		
Cash (+A)	$16,500	
Accounts receivable (−A)		$16,500
To record collection in full from London Industries.		

IF BILLING IS IN BRITISH POUNDS

Accounts receivable (fc) (+A)	$16,500	
Sales (+R, +SE)		$16,500
To record sale to London Industries; billing is for £10,000 (£10,000 × $1.65 = $16,500).		
Cash (fc) (+A)	$16,400	
Exchange loss (+Lo, −SE)	100	
Accounts receivable (fc) (−A)		$16,500
To record collection in full from London Industries (£10,000 × $1.64 = $16,400).		

PURCHASE TRANSACTION

Assumption: U.S. Foods purchases merchandise from London Industries Ltd. for $8,250, or £5,000 pounds when the exchange rate is $1.65 and pays the account when the exchange rate is $1.67.

IF BILLING IS IN U.S. DOLLARS

(Date of purchase)		
Inventory (+A)	$8,250	
Accounts payable (+L)		$8,250
To record purchase from London Industries; billing is $8,250.		
(Date of payment)		
Accounts payable (−L)	$8,250	
Cash (−A)		$8,250
To record payment in full to London Industries.		

IF BILLING IS IN BRITISH POUNDS

Inventory (+A)	$8,250	
Accounts payable (fc) (+L)		$8,250
To record purchase from London Industries; billing is for £5,000 (£5,000 × $1.65 = $8,250).		
Accounts payable (fc) (−L)	$8,250	
Exchange loss (+Lo, −SE)	100	
Cash (fc) (−A)		$8,350
To record payment in full to London Industries (£5,000 × $1.67 = $8,350).		

The potential for exchange gains and losses arises only when the receivable or payable is billed in the foreign currency. However, no gain or loss on translation is recorded at the initial recording.

BALANCE SHEET DATE ADJUSTMENTS Gains and losses on foreign currency transactions cannot be deferred until foreign currency is converted into U.S. dollars or until related receivables are collected or payables are settled. Instead, these amounts are adjusted to reflect current exchange rates at the balance sheet date, and any exchange gains or losses that result from the adjustments are included in current-year income.

Purchases Denominated in Foreign Currency

LEARNING OBJECTIVE **5**

ATC, a U.S. corporation, purchased merchandise from Paris Company on December 1, 2011, for 10,000 euros, when the spot rate for euros was $0.6600. ATC closed its books at December 31, 2011, when the spot rate for euros was $0.6550, and it settled the account on January 30, 2012, when the spot rate was $0.6650. These transactions and events are recorded by ATC as follows:

December 1, 2011
Inventory (+A) $6,600
    Accounts payable (fc) (+L) $6,600
    To record purchase of merchandise from
        Paris Company (10,000 euros × $0.6600 rate).

December 31, 2011
Accounts payable (fc) (−L) $ 50
    Exchange gain (+Ga, +SE) $ 50
    To adjust accounts payable to exchange rate at year-end
        [10,000 euros × ($0.6550 − $0.6600)].

January 30, 2012
Accounts payable (fc) (−L) $6,550
Exchange loss (+Lo, −SE)   100
    Cash (fc) (−A) $6,650
    To record payments in full to Paris Company
        (10,000 euros × 0.6650 spot rate).

Date	Spot Rate	Inventory	Accounts Payable (10,000 Euros)	Gain (Loss)
December 1, 2011 (initial transaction date)	$0.6600	$6,600	$6,600	—
December 31, 2011 (financial statement date)	$0.6550	$6,600	$6,550	$ 50
January 30, 2012 (settled accounts payable by purchasing and distributing euros)	$0.6650	$6,600	$6,650	($100)
Overall				($ 50)

The example shows that on December 1, 2011, ATC incurred a liability of $6,600 denominated in euros. On December 31, 2011, the liability was adjusted to reflect the current exchange rate, and a $50 exchange gain was included in ATC's 2011 income statement. The exchange gain is the product of multiplying 10,000 euros by the change in the spot rate for euros between December 1 and December 31, 2011. By January 30, 2012, when the liability was settled, the spot rate for euros had increased to $0.6650, and ATC recorded a $100 exchange loss. The actual total exchange loss is only $50 [10,000 euros × ($0.6650 − $0.6600)], but this loss is reported as a $50 exchange gain in 2011 and a $100 exchange loss in 2012.

In summary, foreign currency–denominated purchases must be measured in dollars at the purchase date using the foreign currency spot rate on that date.

If a balance sheet date occurs before the liability is paid, the accounts payable must be remeasured to reflect the spot rate at the financial statement date. A gain results if the dollar strengthens, because more euros can be purchased by one dollar than when the liability was first recorded. A loss results if the dollar weakens, because fewer euros can be purchased by one dollar than when the liability was first recorded.

When the liability is paid, a gain (when the liability is smaller since the last financial statement date) or loss (when the liability is larger than at the last financial statement date) is recorded because the liability is paid at the spot rate on the payment date. Typically, companies arrange with banks to handle the conversion. The bank charges the company's bank account in dollars (including a transaction fee) and transfers foreign currency to the payee's account.

Sales Denominated in Foreign Currency

On December 15, 2011, ATC sold merchandise to Rome Company for 20,000 euros, when the spot rate for euros was $0.6625. ATC closed its books on December 31, when the spot rate was $0.6550, collected the account on January 15, 2012, when the spot rate was $0.6700, and held the euros until January 20, when it converted the euros into U.S. dollars at the $0.6725 spot rate in effect on that date. ATC records the transactions as follows:

December 15, 2011
Accounts receivable (fc) (+A)	$13,250	
Sales (+R, +SE)		$13,250
To record sales to Rome		
(20,000 euros × $0.6625 spot rate).		

December 31, 2011
Exchange loss (+Lo, −SE)	$ 150	
Accounts receivable (fc) (−A)		$ 150
To adjust accounts receivable at year-end		
[20,000 euros × ($0.6550 − $0.6625)].		

January 15, 2012
Cash (fc) (+A)	$13,400	
Accounts receivable (fc) (−A)		$13,100
Exchange gain (+Ga, +SE)		300
To record collection in full from Rome (20,000		
euros × $0.6700) and recognize exchange gain		
for 2012 [20,000 euros × ($0.6700 − $0.6550)].		

January 20, 2012
Cash (+A)	$13,450	
Exchange gain (+Ga, +SE)		$ 50
Cash (fc) (−A)		13,400
To convert 20,000 euros into U.S. dollars		
(20,000 euros × $0.6725).		

Date	Spot Rate	Accounts Receivable 20,000 Euros	Sales	Gain (Loss)
12/15/11 (initial transaction date)	$0.6625	$13,250	$13,250	—
12/31/11* (financial statement date)	$0.6550	$13,100	Unchanged	($150)
1/15/12 (collection of accounts receivable in euros)	$0.6700	$13,400	Unchanged	$300
1/20/12 (conversion of euros to dollars)	$0.6725	$13,450	Unchanged	$ 50
Overall				$200

*Sales are closed at year-end into retained earnings. The term *unchanged* here means that no further adjustment of the sales amount is necessary because the sales amount was "locked in" when the accounts receivable and related sales were first recorded.

In summary, foreign currency–denominated sales must be measured in dollars at the sales date using the foreign currency spot rate on that date.

If a financial statement date occurs before the receivable is paid, the accounts receivable must be remeasured to reflect the spot rate at the financial statement date. A gain results when the dollar has weakened because the foreign currency to be received is worth more dollars than when initially recorded. A loss results when the dollar has strengthened because the foreign currency to be received is worth less in dollars than when it was originally recorded.

When the receivable is paid, a gain or loss is recorded because the receivable will be paid at the spot rate on the payment date. If a company holds foreign currency for a period of time for speculative purposes after a receivable is paid instead of converting it into dollars, gains and losses continue to be reported at each financial statement date until the foreign currency is converted into dollars.

SUMMARY OF DIRECT RATE CHANGES ($ PER CURRENCY UNIT) ON THE CARRYING VALUE OF FOREIGN CURRENCY–DENOMINATED ACCOUNTS RECEIVABLE AND ACCOUNTS PAYABLE

Spot Rate Change	Effect on the Dollar Relative to the Foreign Currency	Impact on Foreign Currency–Denominated Account	
Increases	Dollar weaker	Accounts receivable	Increases—Gain
Increases	Dollar weaker	Accounts payable	Increases—Loss
Decreases	Dollar stronger	Accounts receivable	Decreases—Loss
Decreases	Dollar stronger	Accounts payable	Decreases—Gain

International Accounting Standards

IFRS [3] addresses how to include foreign currency transactions and foreign operations in the financial statements. Like GAAP [2], IFRS requires that transactions be recorded initially at the rate of exchange at the date of the transaction. At each subsequent balance sheet date, foreign currency monetary amounts (such as foreign currency–denominated accounts receivables and payables) should be marked to the spot rate at the balance sheet date. Again, similar to GAAP, gains and losses from differences between the initial amount recorded and the year-end value for these monetary assets and liabilities are included in current year income.

SUMMARY

Derivatives are a widely-used mechanism to manage various risks. Because of their flexibility to isolate one type of risk, and manage risks with low costs, they have become very popular tools for hedging strategies. This chapter explains the types and uses of derivatives, while Chapter 13 covers the accounting for derivatives and hedging activity.

International accounting is concerned with accounting for foreign currency transactions and operations. An entity's functional currency is the currency of the primary environment in which the entity operates. Foreign currency transactions are denominated in a currency other than an entity's functional currency.

Foreign currency transactions (other than forward contracts) are measured and recorded in U.S. dollars at the spot rate in effect at the transaction date. A change in the exchange rate between the date of the transaction and the settlement date results in an exchange gain or loss that is reflected in income for the period. At the balance sheet date, any remaining balances that are denominated in a currency other than the functional currency are adjusted to reflect the current exchange rate, and the gain or loss is charged to income.

QUESTIONS

1. Define the term *derivative* and provide examples of risks that derivative contracts are designed to reduce.

2. Explain the differences between forward contracts and futures contracts and the potential benefits and potential costs of each type of contract.

3. Explain the differences between options and swaps and the potential benefits and potential costs of each type of contract.

4. What does "Net Settlement" mean?

5. Distinguish between *measurement* and *denomination* in a particular currency.

6. Assume that one euro can be exchanged for 1.20 U.S. dollars. What is the exchange rate if the exchange rate is quoted directly? Indirectly?

7. What is the difference between official and floating foreign exchange rates? Does the United States have floating exchange rates?

8. What is a spot rate with respect to foreign currency transactions? Could a spot rate ever be a historical rate? Could a spot rate ever be a fixed exchange rate? Discuss.

9. Assume that a U.S. corporation imports electronic equipment from Japan in a transaction denominated in U.S. dollars. Is this transaction a foreign currency transaction? A foreign transaction? Explain the difference between these two concepts and their application here.

10. How are assets and liabilities denominated in foreign currency measured and recorded at the transaction date? At the balance sheet date?

11. Criticize the following statement: "Exchange losses arise from foreign import activities, and exchange gains arise from foreign export activities."

12. When are exchange gains and losses reflected in a business's financial statements?

13. A U.S. corporation imported merchandise from a British company for £1,000 when the spot rate was $1.45. It issued financial statements when the current rate was $1.47, and it paid for the merchandise when the spot rate was $1.46. What amount of exchange gain or loss will be included in the U.S. corporation's income statements in the period of purchase and in the period of settlement?

EXERCISES

E 12-1

1. What is a characteristic of a forward?
   a *Traded on an exchange*
   b *Negotiated with a counterparty*
   c *Covers a stream of future payments*
   d *Must be settled daily*

2. What is a characteristic of a swap?
   a *Traded on an exchange*
   b *Only interest rates can be the underlying*
   c *Covers a stream of future payments*
   d *Must be settled daily*

3. What is a characteristic of a future?
   a *Gives the holder the right but not the obligation to buy or sell*
   b *Negotiated with a counterparty*
   c *Covers a stream of future payments*
   d *Must be settled daily*

4. What is a characteristic of a option?
   a *Gives the holder the right but not the obligation to buy or sell*
   b *Negotiated with a counterparty*
   c *Covers a stream of future payments*
   d *Must be settled daily*

E 12-2

1. Which is true about the seller of a put option?
   a *They have the right to buy the underlying*
   b *They have the right to sell the underlying*
   c *They have the obligation to buy the underlying*
   d *They have the obligation to sell the underlying*

2. Which is true about the holder of a call option?
   a *They have the right to buy the underlying*
   b *They have the right to sell the underlying*
   c *They have the obligation to buy the underlying*
   d *They have the obligation to sell the underlying*

3. Which is true about the seller of a call option?

　a *They have the right to buy the underlying*

　b *They have the right to sell the underlying*

　c *They have the obligation to buy the underlying*

　d *They have the obligation to sell the underlying*

4. Which is true about the holder of a put option?

　a *They have the right to buy the underlying*

　b *They have the right to sell the underlying*

　c *They have the obligation to buy the underlying*

　d *They have the obligation to sell the underlying*

E 12-3

Quotation conventions, measurement versus denomination

1. If $1.5625 can be exchanged for 1 British pound, the direct and indirect exchange rate quotations are:

　a *$1.5625 and 1 British pound, respectively*

　b *$1.5625 and 0.64 British pounds, respectively*

　c *$1.00 and 1.5625 British pounds, respectively*

　d *$1.00 and 0.64 British pounds, respectively*

2. A U.S. firm purchases merchandise from a Canadian firm with payment due in 60 days and denominated in Canadian dollars. The U.S. firm will report an exchange gain or loss on settlement if the transaction is:

　a *Recorded in U.S. dollars*

　b *Measured in U.S. dollars*

　c *Not hedged through a forward contract*

　d *Settled after an exchange rate change has occurred*

3. Exchange gains and losses on accounts receivable and payable that are denominated in a foreign currency are:

　a *Accumulated and reported upon settlement*

　b *Deferred and treated as transaction price adjustments*

　c *Reported as equity adjustments from translation*

　d *Recognized in the periods in which exchange rates change*

E 12-4

Accounting for foreign currency–denominated purchases

Zimmer Corporation, a U.S. firm, purchased merchandise from Taisho Company of Japan on November 1, 2011, for 10,000,000 yen, payable on December 1, 2011. The spot rate for yen on November 1 was $0.0075, and on December 1 the spot rate was $0.0076.

REQUIRED

1. Did the dollar weaken or strengthen against the yen between November 1 and December 1, 2011? Explain.

2. On November 1, 2011, at what amount did Zimmer record the account payable to Taisho?

3. On December 1, 2011, Zimmer paid the 10,000,000 yen to Taisho. Prepare the journal entry to record settlement of the account on Zimmer's books.

4. If Zimmer had chosen to hedge its exposed net liability position on November 1, would it have entered a forward contract to purchase yen for future receipt or to sell yen for future delivery? Explain.

E 12-5

Accounting for foreign currency–denominated purchases settled in subsequent year

On December 16, 2011, Aviator Corporation, a U.S. firm, purchased merchandise from Wing Company for 30,000 euros to be paid on January 15, 2012. Relevant exchange rates for euros are as follows:

December 16, 2011	$1.20
December 31, 2011	$1.25
January 15, 2012	$1.24

REQUIRED: Prepare all journal entries on Aviator Corporation's books to account for the purchase on December 16, adjustment of the books on December 31, and payment of the account payable on January 15.

E 12-6

Accounting for foreign currency–denominated sales settled in subsequent year

On November 16, 2011, Wick Corporation of the United States sold inventory items to Candle Ltd. of Canada for 90,000 Canadian dollars, to be paid on February 14, 2012. Exchange rates for Canadian dollars on selected dates are as follows:

November 16, 2011	$0.80
December 31, 2011	$0.84
February 14, 2012	$0.83

REQUIRED: Determine the exchange gain or loss on the sale to Candle Ltd. to be included in Wick's income statement for the years 2011 and 2012.

E 12-7

Accounting for foreign currency–denominated sales

Door Corporation, a U.S. company, sold inventory items to Royal Cabinets Ltd. of Great Britain for £200,000 on May 1, 2011, when the spot rate was 0.6000 pounds. The invoice was paid by Royal on May 30, 2011, when the spot rate was 0.6050 pounds.

REQUIRED: Prepare Door's journal entries for the sale to Royal on May 1 and receipt of the £200,000 on May 30.

E 12-8

[Based on AICPA] Various foreign currency–denominated transactions

1. On September 1, 2011, Bain Corporation received an order for equipment from a foreign customer for 300,000 euros, when the U.S. dollar equivalent was $400,000. Bain shipped the equipment on October 15, 2011, and billed the customer for 300,000 euros when the U.S. dollar equivalent was $420,000. Bain received the customer's remittance in full on November 16, 2011, and sold the 300,000 euros for $415,000. In its income statement for the year ended December 31, 2011, what should Bain report as a foreign exchange gain or loss?

2. On September 22, 2011, Yumi Corporation purchased merchandise from an unaffiliated foreign company for 10,000 euros. On that date, the spot rate was $1.20. Yumi paid the bill in full on March 20, 2012, when the spot rate was $1.30. The spot rate was $1.24 on December 31, 2011. What amount should Yumi report as a foreign currency transaction gain or loss in its income statement for the year ended December 31, 2011?

3. On July 1, 2011, Clark Company borrowed 1,680,000 pesos from a foreign lender by signing an interest-bearing note due on July 1, 2012, which is denominated in pesos. The U.S. dollar equivalent of the note principal was as follows:

July 1, 2011 (date borrowed)	$210,000
December 31, 2011 (Clark's year-end)	240,000
July 1, 2012 (date paid)	280,000

   In its income statement for 2012, what amount should Clark include as a foreign exchange gain or loss?

4. On July 1, 2011, Stone Company lent $120,000 to a foreign supplier by accepting an interest-bearing note due on July 1, 2012. The note is denominated in the currency of the borrower and was equivalent to 840,000 pesos on the loan date. The note principal was appropriately included at $140,000 in the receivables section of Stone's December 31, 2011, balance sheet. The note principal was repaid to Stone on the July 1, 2012, due date, when the exchange rate was 8 pesos to $1. In its income statement for the year ended December 31, 2012, what amount should Stone include as a foreign currency transaction gain or loss?

E 12-9

Various foreign currency–denominated transactions settled in subsequent year

Monroe Corporation imports merchandise from some Canadian companies and exports its own products to other Canadian companies. The *unadjusted* accounts denominated in Canadian dollars at December 31, 2011, are as follows:

Account receivable from the sale of merchandise on December 16 to Carver Corporation. Billing is for 150,000 Canadian dollars and due January 15, 2012	$103,500
Account payable to Forest Corporation for merchandise received December 2 and payable on January 30, 2012. Billing is for 275,000 Canadian dollars.	$195,250

Exchange rates on selected dates are as follows:

December 31, 2011	$0.68
January 15, 2012	$0.675
January 30, 2012	$0.685

REQUIRED

1. Determine the net exchange gain or loss from the two transactions that will be included in Monroe's income statement for 2011.

2. Determine the exchange gain or loss from settlement of the two transactions that will be included in Monroe's 2012 income statement.

E 12-10

Various foreign currency–denominated transactions settled in subsequent year

American TV Corporation had two foreign currency transactions during December 2011, as follows:

December 12	Purchased electronic parts from Toko Company of Japan at an invoice price of 50,000,000 yen when the spot rate for yen was $0.00750. Payment is due on January 11, 2012.
December 15	Sold television sets to British Products Ltd. for 40,000 pounds when the spot rate for British pounds was $1.65. The invoice is denominated in pounds and is due on January 14, 2012.

REQUIRED

1. Prepare journal entries to record the foregoing transactions.

2. Prepare journal entries to adjust the accounts of American TV Corporation at December 31, 2011, if the current exchange rates are $0.00760 and $1.60 for Japanese yen and British pounds, respectively.

3. Prepare journal entries to record payments to Toko Company on January 11, 2012, when the spot rate for Japanese yen is $0.00765, and to record receipt from British Products Ltd. on January 14, 2012, when the spot rate for British pounds is $1.63.

E 12-11

Accounting for speculative hedges

Martin Corporation, a U.S. import–export firm, enters into a forward contract on October 2, 2011, to speculate in euros. The contract requires Martin to deliver 1,000,000 euros to the exchange broker on March 31, 2012. Quoted exchange rates for euros are as follows:

	10/2/11	12/31/11	3/31/12
Spot rate	$0.6590	$0.6500	$0.6550
30-day forward rate	0.6580	0.6450	0.6500
90-day forward rate	0.6560	0.6410	0.6460
180-day forward rate	0.6530	0.6360	0.6400

REQUIRED: Prepare the journal entries on Martin's books to account for the speculation throughout the life of the contract.

PROBLEMS

P12-1

The Economics of derivatives

On June 1, 2011, TCO enters into a forward agreement with XYZ to buy 100,000 gallons of fuel oil at $2.40 on December 31, 2011. At the time of inception of the forward, the price of fuel oil is $2.45. On December 31, 2011 the price of fuel oil is $2.48. The contract allows for net settlement.

REQUIRED

1. What is the net settlement on the forward contract?

P12-2

The Economics of derivatives

In July of 2011, Sue enters into a forward agreement with Ann to lock in a sales price for wheat. Sue anticipates selling 300,000 bushels of wheat at the market in March of 2012. Ann agrees to a forward with Sue to buy 300,000 bushels at $6.20. Sue's cost for the wheat is $45.90 per bushel. The contract allows for net settlement.

REQUIRED

1. Determine the economic income of the sales transaction at various price levels at maturity for the forward. Consider market prices of $6.00, $6.10, $6.20, $6.30, and $6.40. Make a table similar to the Gre copper example found in the chapter.

P12-3

The economics of derivatives

Consider the same basic facts as in P12-2, but instead of a forward contract Sue purchases put options to sell 300,000 bushels at $6.20 per bushel. The options cost $0.05 a bushel.

REQUIRED

1. Determine the economic income of the sales transaction at various price levels at maturity for the forward. Consider market prices of $6.00, $6.10, $6.20, $6.30, and $6.40. Make a table similar to the Gre copper example.

P 12-4

Accounting for foreign currency–denominated receivables and payables—multiple years

The accounts of Lincoln International, a U.S. corporation, show $81,300 accounts receivable and $38,900 accounts payable at December 31, 2011, before adjusting entries are made. An analysis of the balances reveals the following:

Accounts Receivable	
Receivable denominated in U.S. dollars	$28,500
Receivable denominated in 20,000 Swedish krona	11,800
Receivable denominated in 25,000 British pounds	41,000
Total	$81,300
Accounts Payable	
Payable denominated in U.S. dollars	$ 6,850
Payable denominated in 10,000 Canadian dollars	7,600
Payable denominated in 15,000 British pounds	24,450
Total	$38,900

Current exchange rates for Swedish krona, British pounds, and Canadian dollars at December 31, 2011, are $0.66, $1.65, and $0.70, respectively.

REQUIRED

1. Determine the net exchange gain or loss that should be reflected in Lincoln's income statement for 2011 from year-end exchange adjustments.
2. Determine the amounts at which the accounts receivable and accounts payable should be included in Lincoln's December 31, 2011 balance sheet.
3. Prepare journal entries to record collection of the receivables in 2012 when the spot rates for Swedish krona and British pounds are $0.67 and $1.63, respectively.
4. Prepare journal entries to record settlement of accounts payable in 2012 when the spot rates for Canadian dollars and British pounds are $0.71 and $1.62, respectively.

P 12-5

Foreign currency–denominated receivables and payables—multiple years

Shelton Corporation of New York is an international dealer in jewelry and engages in numerous import and export activities. Shelton's receivables and payables in foreign currency units before year-end adjustments on December 31, 2011, are summarized as follows:

Foreign Currency	Currency Units	Rate on Date of Transaction	Per Books in U.S. Dollars	Current Rate on 12/31/11
Accounts Receivable Denominated in Foreign Currency				
British pounds	100,000	$1.6500	$165,000	$1.6600
Euros	250,000	0.6600	165,000	0.6700
Swedish krona	160,000	0.6600	105,600	0.6400
Japanese yen	2,000,000	0.0075	15,000	0.0076
			$450,600	
Accounts Payable Denominated in Foreign Currency				
Canadian dollars	150,000	$0.7000	$105,000	$0.6900
Mexican pesos	220,000	0.1300	28,600	0.1350
Japanese yen	4,500,000	0.0074	33,300	0.0076
			$166,900	

REQUIRED

1. Determine the amount at which the receivables and payables should be reported in Shelton's December 31, 2011, balance sheet.

2. Calculate individual gains and losses on each of the receivables and payables and the net exchange gain that should appear in Shelton's 2011 income statement.

3. Assume that Shelton wants to hedge its exposure to amounts denominated in euros. Should it buy or sell euros for future delivery? In what amount or amounts?

INTERNET EXERCISE

Go to the CNBC.com Web site and navigate to the commodities page. Click on a specific commodity link next to the "more contracts" label.

1. How many types of commodities are available for trading?

2. How far into the future can you trade on the prices of these commodities?

3. Which types of commodities are expected to have increasing (decreasing) prices in the future?

REFERENCES TO THE AUTHORITATIVE LITERATURE

[1] FASB ASC 815 "Derivatives and Hedging." Originally Statement of Financial Accounting Standards No. 133. *"Accounting for Derivative Instruments and Hedging Activities."* Stamford, CT: Financial Accounting Standards Board, 1998.

[2] FASB ASC 830 "Foreign Currency Matters." Originally Statement of Financial Accounting Standards No. 52. *"Foreign Currency Translation."* Stamford, CT: Financial Accounting Standards Board, 1981.

[3] IASC International Accounting Standard 21. "The Effects of Changes in Foreign Exchange Rates." International Accounting Standards Committee, 2003.

13 CHAPTER

Accounting for Derivatives and Hedging Activities

T his chapter describes in detail the accounting for derivatives used as hedges. There are three major types of hedge activity that we demonstrate the accounting for: cash-flow hedge, fair value hedge, and hedges of foreign currency–denominated transactions.

ACCOUNTING FOR DERIVATIVE INSTRUMENTS AND HEDGING ACTIVITIES

The FASB began to formally consider accounting for derivative instruments and hedges when it added the broad topic of accounting for financial instruments to its agenda in 1986. Financial accounting and reporting standards needed to address newly-created financial instruments. The FASB also needed to develop a set of broad, forward-thinking standards that would be able to properly report the impact on financial position of rapidly advancing innovations in financial instruments.

Since then, the FASB has issued many statements addressing aspects of accounting for financial instruments, including the following:

- *FASB Statement No. 105*, "Disclosure of Information About Financial Instruments with Off-Balance Sheet Risk and Financial Instruments with Concentrated Credit Risk" (March 1990)

- *FASB Statement No. 107*, "Disclosures About Fair Value of Financial Instruments" (December 1991), which superseded and amended *Statement No. 105*

- *FASB Statement No. 115*, "Accounting for Certain Investments in Debt and Equity Securities" (May 1993)

- *FASB Statement No. 119*, "Disclosure About Derivative Financial Instruments and Fair Value of Financial Instruments" (October 1994), which *Statement No. 133* supersedes

Many deliberations, public comments, field studies, and revisions occurred between the initial deliberations regarding derivative instruments and hedging activities in January 1992 and June 1998, when the final version of *FASB Statement No. 133*, "Accounting for Derivative Instruments and Hedging Activities," was issued.

Corporations had many implementation questions about a standard addressing as complex a topic as derivative instrument accounting. To address these concerns, the FASB formed the Derivatives Implementation Group (DIG) in 1998, which assists the FASB by advising them on how to resolve practical issues that arise when *Statement 133* is applied. The DIG functions in a similar way to the

LEARNING OBJECTIVES

1 Understand the definition of a cash flow hedge and the circumstances in which a derivative is accounted for as a cash flow hedge.

2 Understand the definition of a fair value hedge and the circumstances in which a derivative is accounted for as a fair value hedge.

3 Account for a cash-flow-hedge situation from inception through settlement and for a fair-value-hedge situation from inception through settlement.

4 Understand the special derivative accounting related to hedges of existing foreign currency–denominated receivables and payables.

5 Comprehend the footnote disclosure requirements for derivatives.

6 Understand the International Accounting Standards Board accounting for derivatives.

Emerging Issues Task Force (EITF) except that the DIG does not formally vote on issues to reach a consensus. Instead, the resolution from the group's deliberations is presented to the FASB for clearance. The DIG members include high-level executives from companies such as *Time Warner, Inc.*, *General Electric*, and *J. P. Morgan Chase, Inc.*, and partners from international accounting firms.

More than 150 issues have been forwarded to the FASB, and many of them have been cleared by the FASB. Once cleared, guidance is included in the FASB staff implementation guide (Q&A). Two major standards have amended parts of *Statement No. 133:*

> *In June 2000, FAS 138, "Accounting for Certain Derivative Instruments and Hedges," was issued. This standard addressed concerns about the accounting for foreign currency derivatives. This topic is discussed later in the chapter.*

> *In April 2003, FAS 149, "Amendment of Statement 133 on Derivative Instruments and Hedging Activities," was issued. This standard clarified the accounting and reporting for derivative instruments, including some types of derivative instruments embedded in other contracts. The latter topic is beyond the scope of our discussion.*

With the completion of the FASB ASC in 2009, all of the prior standards on derivatives and hedging are contained in Topic 815, "Derivatives and Hedging." For the remainder of this chapter when we refer to GAAP [1], we will be referencing ASC Topic 815, unless otherwise noted.

Hedge Accounting

GAAP's objective is to account for derivative instruments used to hedge risks so that the financial statements reflect their effectiveness in reducing the company's exposure to risk. For the financial statements to reflect the derivative contract's effectiveness, both changes in the hedged item's fair value and the hedging instrument's fair value resulting from the underlying change must be recorded in the same period. The investor can then clearly assess the effectiveness of the strategy. The term *hedge accounting* refers to accounting designed to record changes in the value of the hedged item, and in the value of the hedging instrument in the same accounting period.

ASC Topic 815 establishes three defining characteristics for a derivative:

1. It has one or more underlyings and one or more notional amounts or payment provisions, or both.

2. It requires no initial net investment or an initial net investment that is smaller than would be required for other types of contracts that would be expected to have a similar response to changes in market factors.

3. Its terms require or permit net settlement, so it can readily be settled net by a means outside the contract, or it provides for delivery of an asset that puts the recipient in a position not substantially different from net settlement.

The specific requirements of ASC Topic 815 are based on four fundamental or guiding decisions:

- Derivative instruments represent rights or obligations that meet the definitions of assets or liabilities and should be reported in the financial statements. At year-end, the derivative contract value is recorded on the books as an asset or liability.

- Fair value is the most relevant measure for financial instruments and the only relevant measure for derivative instruments. Derivative instruments should be measured at fair value, and adjustments to the carrying amounts of the hedged items should reflect changes in their fair value (that is, gains or losses) that are attributable to the risk being hedged and that arise while the hedge is in effect.

- Only items that are assets or liabilities should be reported as such in financial statements.

- Special accounting for items designated as being hedged should be provided only for qualifying items. One aspect of qualification should be an assessment of the expectation of effective offsetting changes in fair values or cash flows during the term of the hedge for the risk being hedged.

For hedged items and the derivative instruments designated to hedge them to qualify for hedge accounting, formal documentation must be prepared defining:

- The relationship between the hedged item and the derivative instrument
- The risk-management objective and the strategy that the company is achieving through this hedging relationship, including identification of:

> The hedging instrument
> The hedged item
> The nature of the risk being hedged
> For fair value hedges, how the hedging instrument's effectiveness in offsetting the exposure to changes in the hedged item's fair value will be assessed
> For cash flow hedges, how the hedging instrument's effectiveness in hedging the hedged transaction's variability in cash flows attributable to the hedged risk will be assessed

In order to qualify for hedge accounting, management must demonstrate that the derivative is considered highly effective in mitigating an identified risk.

Hedge Effectiveness

Once a type of risk is identified that qualifies for hedge accounting, the effectiveness of the hedge to offset gains or losses in the item being hedged must be assessed. This assessment is done when the hedge is first entered into and during the hedge's existence.

In order for a hedge to qualify for hedge accounting, the derivative instrument must be considered highly effective in offsetting gains or losses in the item being hedged. ASC Topic 815 requires statistical or other numerical tests to assess hedge effectiveness, unless a specific exception exists. Companies must choose a methodology to be applied to assess hedge effectiveness. Two common approaches are critical term analysis and statistical analysis.

Critical term analysis involves examining the nature of the underlying variable, the notional amount of the derivative and the item being hedged, the delivery date for the derivative, and the settlement date for the item being hedged. If the critical terms of the derivative and the hedged item are identical, then an effective hedge is assumed. For example, in the Gre Copper forward contract example used in chapter 12:

	Copper	Forward Contract Terms
Amount	100,000 pounds	100,000 pounds
Underlying variable	copper	
Hedge		copper

This situation would be considered a highly-effective hedge because the critical terms match exactly. Hedge accounting could be used for this situation.

If the critical terms don't match, a statistical approach can be used. For example, AMR enters into jet fuel, heating oil, and crude oil swap and option contracts to hedge the effect of jet-fuel price fluctuations on its operations. If AMR only used jet-fuel hedges, it might be able to use only critical term analysis to assess hedge effectiveness. But it uses heating oil and crude oil swaps and options also. Although we could assume that the prices of heating oil and crude oil might move in the same direction as jet fuel, the economics behind these prices are not exactly the same so we cannot conclude that their changes will be 100 percent correlated. A statistical approach such as correlation analysis or regression analysis can be used to show the relationship of jet-fuel prices to heating oil and crude oil prices over time. ASC Topic 815 does not define a specific benchmark correlation coefficient or an adjusted R^2; however, cash flow offsets of between 80 percent and 125 percent are considered to reflect highly-effective hedges.

In addition to an initial assessment of a hedge's effectiveness, an ongoing assessment must occur to ensure that the hedge continues to be highly-effective. Statistical methods again can be used to gauge ongoing effectiveness. AMR has used a regression model to determine the correlation of percentage changes in the prices of West Texas Intermediate (WTI) crude oil and New York

Mercantile Exchange (NYMEX) heating oil to the percentage change in jet fuel prices over 12 to 25 months to assess if its hedges continue to be highly effective.[1]

Another common method used to assess ongoing hedge effectiveness is called the *cumulative dollar-offset method*. This method compares the cumulative changes in the derivative's cash flow or fair value to cumulative changes in the hedged item's fair value. A ratio is computed by dividing the cumulative change in the derivative value by the cumulative change in the hedged item's fair value. Again, no benchmark ratio has been officially mandated, but a ratio in the range of 80 percent to 125 percent is generally considered to indicate a highly effective hedge.

If a derivative does not qualify as a highly-effective hedge, then the derivative is marked to market at the end of each year regardless of when the gain or loss on the item that management is attempting to hedge is recognized. No offsetting changes in the fair value of the item being hedged are recorded until they are realized.

Types of Hedge Accounting

LEARNING OBJECTIVE **1, 2**

One of three approaches must be used to account for the derivative and related hedged item that has qualified as a highly-effective hedge:

> **Fair value hedge accounting.** The item being hedged is an existing asset or liability position or firm purchase or sale commitment. In this case, both the item being hedged and the derivative are marked to fair value at the end of the quarter or year-end on the books. The gain or loss on these items is reflected immediately in earnings. The risk being hedged is the variability in the fair value of the asset or liability.

> **Cash flow hedge accounting.** The derivative hedges the exposure to the variability in expected future cash flows associated with a risk. The exposure may be related to a recognized asset or liability (such as a variable-rate financial instrument) or to a forecasted transaction such as a forecasted purchase or sale. The derivative is marked to fair value at year-end and is recorded as an asset or liability. The effective portion of the related gain or loss's recognition is deferred until the forecasted transaction affects income. The gain or loss is included as a component of accumulated other comprehensive income (AOCI) in the balance sheet's stockholders' equity section.

> **Hedge of net investment in a foreign subsidiary.** This will be discussed in Chapter 14.

GAAP allows the use of cash flow hedge accounting for certain types of hedges of existing foreign currency–denominated receivables or payables. We will discuss this accounting later.

We will begin exploring how to account for derivatives using the Gre copper forward contract that we began in Chapter 12. Recall that Gre anticipates producing and selling copper in one year. The expected cost of the 100,000-pound production was $28,900,000. Gre enters into a forward contract with Bro that locks in a $300 per pound price for the copper. Gre will sell the copper in the open market at the prevailing price and will then either receive or pay the difference between the market price and $300 so that Gre nets $300 per pound. All of the variability in income resulting from the revenue side is eliminated by this contract. This forward contract is a highly-effective hedge.

LEARNING OBJECTIVE **3**

The forward contract is signed on October 1, 2011. The contract will be settled in one year, on September 30, 2012. Gre prepares quarterly financial reports. Assume that the market price of copper is $300 on October 1, 2011. At this time, no entry would be recorded because the contract value is $0.

On December 31, 2011, the company would need to record the estimated value of the contract. Recall that the purpose of this contract is to mitigate the risk of revenue price fluctuations related to an anticipated or a forecasted transaction—the production and sale of copper. The company has entered into a **cash flow hedge** because it is attempting to control the impact of price fluctuations on its future cash flows and its sales. This is a hedge of an anticipated or a forecasted transaction. In order to reflect this strategy in the financial statements, the gain or loss on the contract will be recognized when the copper is actually sold, which is on September 30, 2012. We must defer recognition of the gain or loss of the contract until that time, and we use the other comprehensive income account to do so. Cash flow hedge accounting always uses other comprehensive income to defer recognition of gains or losses until the item being hedged actually is recognized in income.

---

[1]*Source:* AMR 2009 annual report.

Recall that other comprehensive income is a type of stockholders' equity account. While changes in it are reflected in the statement of comprehensive income, the income statement does not include those changes.

The entries to account for the forward contract are as follows:

October 1, 2011. No Entry

December 31, 2011. Assume that the market price of copper is $310 on this date. If the market price stays the same, Gre would pay Bro $10 × 100,000 = $1,000,000 at the expiration of the contract in nine months. We will use this information to estimate the value of the forward contract at December 31, 2011. Because the $1,000,000 is our estimate of a payment to be paid in nine months, we must use present value concepts to estimate its fair value on December 31, 2011. Assuming that a discount rate of 1 percent per month is reasonable, the estimated fair value of this contract is:

$$1,000,000/(1.01)^9 = \$914,340$$

Other comprehensive income (−SE)	914,340	
Forward contract (+L)		914,340

March 31, 2012. Assume that the market price of copper is $295. If this price remains constant, then the company can anticipate receiving $5 × 100,000 = $500,000 in six months. The estimated fair value of the forward contract is $500,000/(1.01)^6 = \$471,023$. We have moved from a liability situation to an asset situation. The entry to adjust the carrying value of the forward contract is:

Forward contract (+A)	471,023	
Forward contract (−L)	914,340	
Other comprehensive income (+SE)		1,385,363

Notice that the balance for other comprehensive income has moved from a debit balance of $914,340 to a credit balance of $471,023.

June 30, 2012. Assume that the market price of copper is $290. If this price remains constant, then the company can anticipate receiving $10 × 100,000 = $1,000,000 in three months. The estimated fair value of the forward contract is $1,000,000/(1.01)^3 = \$970,590$. We must increase the forward contract asset and other comprehensive income by $499,567 ($970,590 desired balance −$471,023 current balance). The entry to adjust the carrying value of the forward contract is:

Forward contract (+A)	499,567	
Other comprehensive income (+SE)		499,567

September 30, 2012. Assume that the company produced the copper this quarter and sold it on September 30, 2012. The cost was as expected at $28,900,000 for 100,000 pounds of copper. The market price of copper on this date is $310. Gre sells the copper in the market at $310 and will settle the forward contract by paying Bro $1,000,000 [($310 − $300) × 100,000].

The journal entries to record the sale are:

Cash (+A)	31,000,000	
Sales (+R, +SE)		31,000,000
Cost of goods sold (+E, −SE)	28,900,000	
Inventory (−A)		28,900,000

The journal entries to record the settlement of the forward contract are:

Sales (−R, −SE)	1,000,000	
Other comprehensive income (−SE)	970,590	
Cash (−A)		1,000,000
Forward contract (−A)		970,590

The effect of this strategy is to report net income of $1,100,000. Sales are $30,000,000, and cost of goods sold is $28,900,000. Recall that this is the economic income with hedge for every market price realization and agrees with our earlier discussion of this contract. On your own, prepare the journal entries for September 30, 2012 using different realizations of market price to prove to yourself that each realization will result in exactly the same income amount.

The preceding example was accounted as a cash flow hedge because the hedge was of an anticipated or forecasted transaction. The unrealized gain or loss on the forward contract was deferred until the transaction being hedged (the copper sale) was reflected in the income statement.

Later, we will explore other types of situations in which cash flow hedge accounting is appropriate, but now we turn to an example of a fair value hedge.

FAIR VALUE HEDGES Fair value hedge accounting is appropriate for highly-effective hedges of either existing assets or liabilities or firm sales/purchase commitments.

Wav Company refines oil. Wav purchases raw crude from various producers and, after the refinement process, sells it to gasoline wholesalers. The price that Wav receives from a gasoline wholesaler depends on the raw crude market price as well as other factors. Typically, Wav refines the oil almost immediately after purchase; however, because of some factory breakdowns, it has about 100,000 barrels of oil that will not be processed for six months. Wav is concerned about how to maintain the value of that oil. While it would be nice if the oil was worth more in six months than it currently is worth, there are no guarantees, and it might be worth less. As a result, Wav is considering entering into a derivative contract that will help it maintain its net investment value.

Wav enters into a forward contract to sell the crude for $90 per barrel in six months. The contract will be settled net. Wav won't actually sell the crude because it intends to refine it, but this type of contract will allow it to maintain the fair value of the crude on its books.

How does the contract work? If the price of crude is $95 per barrel in six months, then Wav will pay the counterparty to the forward $5 per barrel. However, Wav will also have crude that is worth $95 (and therefore will be able to sell it, processed, for more). If, on the other hand, the price of crude is $70 per barrel, Wav will receive $20 per barrel from the counterparty, which will help to compensate it for the lower value of its crude inventory (which will be sold for less when processed).

The accounting for such a situation will reflect the offsetting movement of the derivative and its underlying crude oil price fluctuation. Under fair value hedge accounting, Wav will write the derivative to market at each financial statement date and will be able to increase or decrease the value of the crude oil inventory by the change in its fair value from the date that the derivative contract is signed and the financial statement date. This is a significant departure from historical cost accounting; both the value of the derivative and the item it is hedging—the crude oil— will change over time.

Before we look at the journal entries to record this situation, we need to discuss one more aspect of hedging existing assets. The crude oil will not be marked to its fair value unless the fair value of the oil at the date the derivative contract is signed is equal to its original cost. If the values are different, the inventory will be changed only by the difference between its fair value and the fair value at the derivative contract signing date. This type of hybrid valuation is called a **mixed-attribute** model. The balance sheet value of the oil contains both historical cost and fair value elements.

Again, let us assume that the forward contract price of $90 equals the spot price at the contract date. Wav's book value of the oil is $86, its historical cost. Again, the present value model will be used to measure the forward value.

We will now also need a market value for the crude oil because under hedge accounting, we will change the carrying value by the difference between the market value at the date of the hedge contract and subsequent balance sheet dates until the date the forward contract settles. We need to determine which spot crude oil price to use. All crude oil prices, even for oil of the same quality, are not the same. Oil is costly to transport and is produced in many places in the world. As a result, crude oil (and many other commodities) has different spot prices, depending on where it is produced. We will assume that Wav is located in West Texas and that it is located next door to a major West Texas producer. The appropriate spot rate would be West Texas Crude.

On November 1, 2011, the forward contract is signed. No entries are required on this date because no cash payment or receipt exists.

On December 31, 2011, the market price of crude oil is $92. We must record the value of the forward contract at this date and adjust the inventory value for changes in its spot price since the contract was signed.

Forward Contract If the market price of crude stays at $92, then Wav will pay $2 × 100,000 = $200,000 to settle the contract. That payment will occur in four months, so the estimated value of the contract at December 31, 2011, assuming 1 percent per month interest, is $200,0000/(1.01)^4 = $192,196. The adjusting entry related to the forward is:

Loss on Forward contract (+Lo, −SE)	192,196	
Forward contract (+L)		192,196

Inventory The change in the inventory value from November 1, 2011 is also $2 ($92 − $90). So the inventory would be increased by $200,000:

Inventory (+A)	200,000	
Gain on Inventory (+Ga, +SE)		200,000

Notice that the inventory carrying value is now $8,600,000 + $200,000 = $8,800,000 compared to $9,200,000 for its market value. This is the result of using a mixed-attribute model.

On March 31, 2012, the spot price is $89. If the market price of crude remains at $89, then Wav will receive $100,000 in one month. The estimated value of the forward is $100,000/1.01 = $99,009.

The entry to record the forward contract is:

Forward contract (+A)	99,009	
Forward contract (−L)	192,196	
Gain on Forward contract (+Ga, +SE)		291,205

The inventory entry is ($92 − $89) × 100,000 = $300,000.

Loss on Inventory (+Lo, −SE)	300,000	
Inventory (−A)		300,000

The book value of the inventory is now $8,900,000 ($9,000,000 + $200,000 − $300,000).

On April 30, 2012 the contract settles. The spot price is $87.50. Wav will receive $250,000 [($90 − $87.50) × 100,000] to settle the contract.

Forward Contract

Cash (+A)	250,000	
Forward contract (−A)		99,009
Gain on Forward contract (+Ga, +SE)		150,991

Inventory

Loss on Inventory (+Lo, −SE)	150,000	
Inventory (−A)		150,000

Summary of Effect on Earnings

Date	Inventory Adjustment	Forward Contract Adjustment	Net Effect
December 31, 2011	+200,000	−192,196	+7,804
March 31, 2012	−300,000	+291,205	−8,795
April 30, 2012	−150,000	+150,991	+991
Total	−250,000	+250,000	+0

This forward contract works for Wav. Wav's inventory value went down by $250,000 over the time of the production delay. Wav received $250,000 cash on the forward contract, which compensated it for the decline in the value of its inventory. Wav's economic condition would have been worse if it had not entered into the contract.

Additional Cash Flow Hedge Examples

OPTION CONTRACTS Assume that a company signs a contract on January 15, 2011, the contract costs $1,000, the option price on that date is $1 per gallon on 100,000 gallons of fuel, and the option expires on May 31, 2011. Further assume that the option is a European one, in which the company can elect to exercise it only on the expiration date. The fuel option contract is a cash flow hedge because it is designed to limit the company's exposure to price changes in forecasted purchases of fuel. Because the purchase of the fuel will occur in the future and the company purchases the option contract now, it initially records the option contract price as an asset. The company records the option as follows:

January 15, 2011		
Fuel contract option (+A)	1,000	
Cash (−A)		1,000

The company prepares its quarterly report on March 31, 2011. Assume that the market price of fuel on March 31, 2011, is $1.25. If the company could exercise the option on this date, it would save $0.25 per gallon on the fuel, or $25,000 in total. The estimate of the option payment is $25,000 if it could be paid on March 31, 2011. But the actual payment will occur on May 31, 2011, two months later. The fair value of the option at March 31 needs to be estimated by computing the present value of the option payment. If we assume that the appropriate discount rate is 6 percent per year, or 0.5 percent per month, then we can compute the present value:

$$\$25,000 \div (1.005)^2 = \$24,752$$

The estimate of the value of the option to the company on March 31 is $24,752. The company needs to record an adjusting entry on March 31 because the option must be recorded at fair value according to Topic 815. The fuel contract option account already has a debit balance of $1,000, so the required adjustment is $23,752 to that account.

The purpose of the option contract is to control the cost that the company will pay when purchasing the fuel, so the increase in the option's value should be recorded in income in the same period that the fuel is used. The gain is deferred by including it as a component of other comprehensive income in the stockholders' equity section of the balance sheet. The gain bypasses that quarter's income statement. The entry is as follows:

March 31, 2011		
Fuel contract option (+A)	23,752	
Other comprehensive income—		
unrealized holding gain on fuel option		
contract (+SE)		23,752

On May 31, 2011, we assume that the fuel price is $1.30 per gallon. The fuel's market value is $130,000. The writer of the fuel price option must pay the company $0.30 per gallon, or $30,000. An additional gain of $5,248 occurs as a result of the change in market value. The company makes the following entries:

May 31, 2011		
Fuel inventory (+A)	130,000	
Cash (−A)		130,000
Cash (+A)	30,000	
Fuel contract option (−A)		24,752
Other comprehensive income (+SE)		5,248

Notice that the gain on the contract is still not recognized in income, because the fuel remains in inventory. Once the fuel is used, the gain on the contract will be recognized as a reduction in cost of goods sold, so the net impact on cost of goods sold is $100,000, not $130,000.

Assume that the fuel inventory is used on June 15, 2011. The entry to record expense is as follows:

June 15, 2011

Cost of goods sold (+E, −SE)	130,000	
Fuel inventory (−A)		130,000
Other comprehensive income (−SE)	30,000	
Cost of goods sold (−E, +SE)		30,000

FUTURES CONTRACTS—CASH FLOW HEDGE OF FORECASTED TRANSACTION Companies can also hedge forecasted transactions using futures contracts. Here is an illustration. On December 1, 2011, a utility enters into a futures contract to purchase 100,000 barrels of heating oil for delivery on January 31, 2012, at $1.4007 per gallon. Heating oil is traded on the New York Mercantile Exchange (NYMEX) exchange. Each contract is for 1,000 barrels (42,000 gallons). The utility must enter into 100 contracts. The exchange requires a margin of $100 per contract to be paid up front.

The utility enters into this contract so that it will have a supply of oil for delivery to customers in February and so it can lock in the $1.4007-per-gallon price. This is a forecasted purchase and therefore is accounted for as a cash flow hedge. The entries are:

December 1, 2011

Futures contract (+A)	10,000	
Cash (−A)		10,000

At year-end, the company must mark the futures contract to market. Unlike the option contract illustrated on page 436, which is not traded and which requires an estimate of its fair value, the futures contract has an observable market value at December 31, 2011. Assume that the NYMEX reported that the heating oil futures contract for delivery on January 31, 2012, is $1.4050 per gallon. This price already is adjusted for the time value of money because the market would have adjusted for it in the pricing. The contract's estimated value is $18,060 ([$1.4050 − $1.4007] × 4,200,000 gallons). We can now write the contracts to market:

December 31, 2011

Futures contract (+A)	18,060	
Other comprehensive income (+SE)		18,060

On January 31, 2012, the spot and futures rate are the same, $1.3995 per gallon. The company settles the futures contract and buys 100,000 barrels (4,200,000 gallons) of oil on the open market for $5,877,900 ($1.3995 per gallon × 4,200,000 gallons) for delivery to the utility's customers during the first week in February. The entry to mark the contract to market is:

January 31, 2012

Other comprehensive income (−SE)	23,100	
Futures contract (−A)		23,100
100 contracts × 42,000 gallons per contract × ($1.3995 − $1.4050) = $23,100 —		
Accumulated other comprehensive income account		

The balance in the Futures Contract account is a $4,960 debit ($10,000 margin + $18,060 December 31 adjustment − $23,100 January 31, 2012 adjustment). The company lost $5,040 ($23,100 − $18,060) on the contract, which is included in other comprehensive income as a debit balance. The entries to settle the futures contract and record the oil purchase are:

Cash (+A)	4,960	
Futures contract (−A)		4,960
Heating oil inventory (+A)	5,877,900	
Cash (−A)		5,877,900

Assume that the company sells the oil for $2.00 per gallon to its customers during the first week in February. The impact of the gain or loss on the futures contract on earnings is deferred until the hedged transaction actually affects income. The entries at the date of sale are:

Cash (+A)	8,400,000	
Sales (+R, +SE)		8,400,000
Cost of goods sold (+E, −SE)	5,877,900	
Heating oil inventory (−A)		5,877,900
Cost of goods sold (+E, −SE)	5,040	
Other comprehensive income (+SE)		5,040

The total cost of goods sold is $5,882,940 ($5,877,900 + $5,040), which is equal to 42,000 × 100 contracts × $1.4007(the contract rate).

Additional Fair Value Hedge Examples

A fair value hedge is a derivative contract that attempts to reduce the price risk of an existing asset or firm purchase commitment. Fair value hedge accounting is used when a highly-effective hedge is used to reduce the price risk of an existing asset or liability or a firm sale or purchase commitment contract. Both the item being hedged and the hedge contract are marked to market on an ongoing basis, and the gains and losses are recognized in income immediately. Even though firm sale and purchase commitments are usually not included on the balance sheet until they are executed, GAAP [1] requires the recognition of them on the balance sheet if they are the object of a hedging contract.

Assume that on January 1, 2011, a company agrees to take delivery of 100,000 liters of scotch whiskey from a manufacturer in six months—on June 30, 2011—at $15 per liter, the price of scotch on January 1. In order to take advantage of changes in the market price of whiskey over time, the company also enters into a pay variable/receive fixed forward contract with a speculator, with a fixed price of $15 per liter. The company has in essence unlocked the fixed element of the firm purchase commitment.

The following illustrates a pay variable/receive fixed forward contract from the company's perspective. The terminology pay variable/receive fixed pertains to the forward contract and not to the contract between the company and the supplier. The exposure being hedged is between the company and the supplier. The hedge of that exposure is the contract between the company and the speculator. If the market price is $14, the company receives $1 in net settlement ($100,000 in total). Then the company pays $14 ($1,400,000 in total) out of its own money and the $1 ($100,000 in total) received from the speculator to settle the fixed price contract with the supplier for $15 ($1,500,000).

If the market price is $17 per liter, the company must pay the speculator $2 per liter and then pay the whiskey supplier $15 per liter. In each case, the whiskey costs the company the market price after considering both the hedge settlement and any additional amounts that must be paid to the supplier out of the company's pocket.

Notice that the company has a *firm purchase commitment* with the whiskey distiller that is non-cancelable, and it has also entered into a forward contract with the speculator. This transaction qualifies as a fair value hedge because it is aimed at controlling the cost of an existing commitment, not a forecasted transaction.

As discussed earlier, a forward contract is negotiated between the parties, not through an exchange. This allows considerable flexibility in defining the quality, quantity, and delivery schedule.

On January 1, 2011, no entry would be required for either the firm purchase commitment or the forward contract.

On March 31, 2011, assume that the market price of scotch whiskey is $13 per liter. The company has experienced an unrealized gain of $200,000 on the forward contract [($15 − $13) × 100,000]. It has also experienced an unrealized loss on the purchase commitment because the market price of the whiskey is now below the fixed contract price. The change in the firm purchase commitment fair value and the offsetting change in the forward contract value are recorded immediately in income at present value, assuming a 0.5 percent per month interest rate:

March 31, 2011

Forward contract (+A)	197,030	
Unrealized gain on forward contract (+Ga, +SE)		197,030
To record the change in the fair value of the		
forward contract.		
Unrealized loss on firm purchase commitment (+Lo, −SE)	197,030	
Firm purchase commitment (+L)		197,030
To record the change in the firm purchase commitment.		

At June 30, 2011, both contracts are settled when the market price of whiskey is $14.50. The entries are as follows:

June 30, 2011

Cash (+A)	50,000	
Unrealized loss on forward contract (+Lo, −SE)	147,030	
Forward contract (−A)		197,030
Firm purchase commitment (−L)	197,030	
Whiskey inventory (+A)	1,450,000	
Cash (−A)		1,500,000
Unrealized gain on firm purchase commitment (+Ga, +SE)		147,030

ACCOUNTING FOR HEDGE CONTRACTS: ILLUSTRATIONS OF CASH FLOW AND FAIR VALUE HEDGE ACCOUNTING USING INTEREST RATE SWAPS

We will use interest rate swaps to illustrate the differences in accounting for derivatives as fair value and cash flow hedges.

Cash Flow Hedge Accounting

We will assume that on January 1, 2011, Jac Company borrows $200,000 from State Bank. The three-year loan with interest paid annually is a variable-rate loan. The initial interest rate is set at 9 percent for year 1. The subsequent years' interest-rate formula is the London Interbank Offer Rate (LIBOR) + 2%, determined at the end of each year for the next year. The LIBOR rate at December 31, 2011, is used to set the loan interest rate for 2012. The LIBOR rate at December 31, 2012, is used to set the loan interest rate for 2013.

Because Jac does not wish to assume the risk that the interest rate could increase and therefore the cash paid for interest could increase, Jac decides to hedge this risk.

On January 1, 2011, Jac enters into a **pay-fixed, receive-variable interest rate swap** with Watson for the latter two payments. Jac agrees to pay a set rate of 9 percent to Watson and will in return receive LIBOR + 2 percent. The hedge will be settled net. The notional amount is $200,000. Jac or Watson will pay the other the difference between the variable rate and the 9 percent fixed rate depending on which is higher. For example, if the LIBOR rate is 4 percent on December 31, 2011, then Watson will receive $6,000 on December 31, 2012. LIBOR + 2% is 6%. Jac has agreed to pay 9 percent, so Watson benefits from the lower interest rate and receives the difference multiplied by $200,000. Jac will still end up paying 9 percent in total—3 percent to Watson and 6 percent to State Bank.

If the LIBOR rate on December 31, 2012, is 8 percent, then Jac will receive $2,000 from Watson. LIBOR + 2% is 10%. Jac will again end up paying 9 percent net. It will pay 10 percent to State Bank and then receive 1 percent from Watson. As you can see, this hedge eliminates the cash flow variability related to this debt.

To determine the fair value of the interest rate swap to be recorded on Jac's books at December 31, 2011, Jac must make some assumptions about what the future LIBOR interest rates will be and, therefore, what its future cash receipts and future cash payments related to the hedge will be.

Assume that the LIBOR rate on December 31, 2011, is 6.5 percent. This means that Jac's interest payment on December 31, 2012, to State Bank will be 8.5% × $200,000, or $17,000. Jac has agreed to pay 9 percent to Watson. This means that, at this point in time, Jac knows it will pay $1,000 to Watson in one year. In order to measure the fair value of the swap arrangement, Jac will make an assumption about the payment that will be made on December 31, 2013. Assuming that a flat interest rate curve is expected, Jac will assume that the interest rate for 2013 will not change from the current rate, so it will expect to pay $1,000 at December 31, 2013, as well.

The interest rate swap fair-value computation at December 31, 2011 is:

Present value at December 31, 2011, of payment to be made to Watson on December 31, 2012:

$$\$1,000/(1.085) = \$922$$

Present value at December 31, 2011, of estimated payment to be paid to Watson on December 31, 2013:

$$\$1,000/(1.085)^2 = \$848$$

The total estimated value of the interest rate swap at December 31, 2011, is:

$$\$922 + \$848 = \$1,770$$

Because Jac anticipates paying this amount, the interest rate swap is recorded as a liability. Assume that at December 31, 2012, the LIBOR rate is 7.25 percent. Watson will now be required to pay Jac under the interest-rate-swap arrangement on December 31, 2013. Watson will pay $200,000 × (0.0925 − 0.0900) = $500. However, this payment will be received by Jac in one year. The fair value of the interest-rate-swap asset at December 31, 2012, is $500 ÷ (1.0925) = $458.

Because this hedge is designed to reduce the variability in the cash flows related to the debt, Jac designates it as a **cash flow hedge**. This hedge is also expected to be effective because its terms match the terms of the underlying debt interest payments it is hedging. The notional amount of both is $200,000, the term length matches exactly, and initially the fair value of the hedge is zero (the fixed rate of 9% equals the LIBOR + 2% at the inception of the hedge).

CASH FLOW HEDGE ACCOUNTING ENTRIES Jac's journal entries to account for the debt, the interest, and the derivative under cash flow hedge accounting follow:

January 1, 2011

Cash (+A)	200,000	
Loan payable (+L)		200,000
To record receipt of loan proceeds on Jac's books.		

December 31, 2011

Interest expense (+E, −SE)	18,000	
Cash (−A)		18,000
To record the payment of interest to State Bank.		
Other comprehensive income (−SE)	1,770	
Interest rate swap (+L)		1,770
To record the fair value of the interest rate swap.		

December 31, 2012

Interest expense (+E, −SE)	17,000	
Cash (−A)		17,000
To record interest payment to State Bank, $200,000 × 0.085 = $17,000; the variable interest rate was determined as of January 1, 2012, as LIBOR + 2%.		
Interest expense (+E, −SE)	1,000	
Cash (−A)		1,000
To record payment to Watson of interest-rate-swap settlement.		

Interest rate swap (−L)	1,770	
Interest rate swap (+A)	458	
Other comprehensive income (+SE)		2,228

To adjust the interest rate swap to fair value
at December 31, 2012; the other comprehensive
income account now has a balance of $458 credit.

December 31, 2013

Interest expense (+E, −SE)	18,500	
Cash (−A)		18,500

To record interest payment to State Bank,
$200,000 × 0.0925 = $18,500; the variable interest rate
was determined as of January 1, 2013, as LIBOR + 2%.

Cash (+A)	500	
Interest expense (−E, +SE)		500

To record receipt of interest-rate-swap settlement
from Watson.

Other comprehensive income (−SE)	458	
Interest rate swap (−A)		458

To adjust the interest rate swap to fair value
at December 31, 2013, which is zero; notice that the
other comprehensive income account is also zero.

Loan payable (−L)	200,000	
Cash (−A)		200,000

To record payment of loan agreement.

Fair Value Hedge Accounting

We will now assume that instead of initially borrowing $200,000 from State Bank using a variable-rate note, Jac borrows $200,000 for three years at a fixed rate of 9 percent on January 1, 2011. As a result, Jac enters into a **pay-variable, receive-fixed interest rate swap** with Watson. The notional amount is again $200,000, and the variable-rate formula is LIBOR + 2%. Assume that the LIBOR rate is 7 percent on January 1, 2011.

Jac designates this as a **fair value hedge**. This is a fair value hedge because the fair value of the fixed-rate loan fluctuates as a result of the changes in the market rate of interest. The hedge is designed to offset these changes in value.

In this case, both the loan and the interest rate swap will be marked to fair value at each year-end. Recording debt at fair value at year-end is a departure from the historical cost principle. Normally, a bond or loan is recorded initially at its fair value. In subsequent years, the interest expense is based on the market interest rate in effect at the initial borrowing date for the entire bond or loan's existence. Therefore, although amortization of a discount or premium may affect the loan's carrying value, the resulting carrying value is the present value of the cash flows using the original market rate, not the market rate in effect at each year-end.

In this case, the debt carrying value will be adjusted throughout its life for changes in the market interest rate.

Fair Value Hedge Accounting Entries

January 1, 2011

Cash (+A)	200,000	
Loan payable (+L)		200,000

To record the receipt of a loan from State Bank.

December 31, 2011

Interest expense (+E, −SE)	18,000	
Cash (−A)		18,000

To record fixed rate interest payment to State Bank.

Interest rate swap (+A)	1,770	
Loan payable (+L)		1,770

To mark both the swap and the loan to market to reflect
the market rate of interest on the swap agreement
at December 31, 2011, 8.5%. Because the market rate
is below the fixed interest rate of 9%, the loan's fair
value has increased. This is similar to a bond being
sold at a premium.

December 31, 2012

Interest expense (+E, −SE)	18,000	
Cash (−A)		18,000

To record fixed rate interest payment to State Bank.

Cash (+A)	1,000	
Interest expense (−E, +SE)		1,000

To record net settlement from Watson;
the variable rate is 8.5%, so Watson owes Jac
0.005 × $200,000 = $1,000.

Loan payable (−L)	2,228	
Interest rate swap (−A)		1,770
Interest rate swap (+L)		458

To mark both the swap and the loan to market; the
carrying value of the loan is now $200,000 − $458 =
$199,542, a discount. Remember that the variable rate,
LIBOR + 2%, on December 31, 2012, is 9.25%.

December 31, 2013

Interest Expense (+E, −SE)	18,000	
Cash (−A)		18,000

To record fixed-rate interest payment to State Bank.

Interest expense (+E, −SE)	500	
Cash (−A)		500

To record the payment of interest

Interest rate swap (−L)	458	
Loan payable (+L)		458

To mark the swap and the loan to market;
the carrying value of the loan is now $200,000,
which will now be paid.

Loan payable (−L)	200,000	
Cash (−A)		200,000

To record payment of the loan.

The following table summarizes the fair value hedge transactions.

Date	Interest Rate Swap Balance Sheet Debit—Asset; Credit—Liability	Loan Payable Balance Sheet	Interest Expense
January 1, 2011		$200,000	
December 31, 2011	$1,770 debit	$201,770	$18,000
December 31, 2012	$ 458 credit	$199,542	$17,000
December 31, 2013			$18,500

Notice that the fluctuation in the fair value of the loan is reflected in the liability. The company's strategy to hedge this risk is also reflected because the combination of the interest-rate-swap asset/liability value and the loan balance value at December 31, 2011, and December 31, 2012, is $200,000.

FOREIGN CURRENCY DERIVATIVES AND HEDGING ACTIVITIES

LEARNING OBJECTIVE 4

Foreign Currency–Denominated Receivables and Payables

In Chapter 12, we discussed the accounting for foreign currency–denominated receivables and payables. Companies frequently hedge their exposure to foreign currency exchange risk for existing foreign currency–denominated assets and liabilities and anticipated foreign currency–denominated transactions. In this section, we will focus on hedge accounting when foreign currency transactions are involved. The accounting for such foreign currency hedges is a bit different than for the derivatives discussed already.

FASB ASC Topic 830 requires marking to fair value (the current spot rate) foreign currency–denominated receivables and payables at year-end. The resulting gain or loss is recognized immediately in income. Under FASB ASC Topic 815, a company may be able to choose to account for hedges of such receivables and payables using either a fair value hedge model or a cash flow hedge model. The contract-term requirements for selecting a cash flow hedge model are stringent, as we will discuss later.

The forward premium or discount is the difference between the contracted forward rate and the spot rate prevailing when the contract is entered into. This premium or discount is amortized into income over the life of the contract if the hedge is designated a cash flow hedge. The effective interest method is appropriate.

CASH FLOW HEDGES   For a forward contract to qualify for cash flow hedge accounting, the contract must have the following characteristics:

1. Cash flow hedges can be used in recognized foreign currency–denominated asset and liability situations if the variability of the cash flows is completely eliminated by the hedge. This requirement is generally met if the settlement date, currency type, and currency amounts match the expected payment dates and amounts of the foreign currency–denominated receivable or payable. If any of these critical terms don't match between the hedged item and the hedging instrument, then the contract is designated a fair value hedge with current earnings recognition of changes in the value of the hedging derivative and the hedged item. (This is illustrated later.)

2. According to GAAP, the transaction gain or loss arising from the remeasurement of the foreign currency–denominated asset or liability is offset by a related amount reclassified from other comprehensive income to earnings each period. Thus, the foreign currency–denominated asset or liability is marked to fair value at year-end, and the gain or loss is recognized in income. The cash flow hedge is also marked to fair value at year-end. Like other cash flow hedges, the gain or loss is included in other comprehensive income. At year-end, a portion of the gain or loss included in other comprehensive income is then recognized in income to offset the gain or loss on the foreign currency–denominated asset or liability.

3. Finally, the premium or discount related to the hedge is amortized to income using an effective interest rate.

Example of Accounting for a Cash Flow Hedge of an Existing Foreign Currency–Denominated Accounts Receivable

Assume that Win Corporation, a U.S. firm, sold hospital equipment to Howard Ltd. of Britain on November 2, 2011, for 100,000 British pounds, payable in 90 days, on January 30, 2012. In addition, on November 2, Win enters into a 90-day forward contract with Ross Company to hedge its exposed net accounts receivable position. We will assume that the forward contract allows for net settlement. Assume that a reasonable incremental interest rate is 12 percent. Selected exchange rates of pounds are:

	November 2, 2011	December 31, 2011	January 30, 2012
Spot rate	$1.650	$1.660	$1.665
90-day forward rate	$1.638		
30-day forward rate		$1.655	

The entry on November 2, 2011, to record the sale is:

Accounts receivable (fc) (+A)	$165,000	
Sales (+R, +SE)		$165,000

To record the sale of equipment to Howard
Company, £100,000 × $1.6500, the spot rate at
November 2, 2011.

Because Win entered into a forward contract that is to be settled net, no entry is necessary at the date that contract is entered into. Recall that if this were a futures or option contract, an entry would be necessary because some cash would have been paid by Win at the inception of these types of contracts.

Both the foreign currency–denominated accounts receivable and the forward contract must be marked to fair value at year-end, December 31, 2011.

Accounts Receivable Adjustment

Accounts receivable (fc) (+A)	$1,000	
Exchange gain (+Ga, +SE)		$1,000

To adjust accounts receivable to spot rate at year-end [£100,000 × ($1.660 − $1.650)].

Forward Contract Adjustment Win's 90-day forward contract expires on January 30, 2012, with Win set to receive $1.638 per pound. At December 31, 2011, a 30-day forward contract rate is $1.655. A 30-day forward contract entered into on December 31, 2011 would be settled on January 30, 2012. Based on the change in the forward rate, the estimated loss on the forward contract is £100,000 × ($1.655 − $1.638) = $1,700. However, this is the estimated loss to be realized in one month. To estimate the fair value of the forward contract on December 31, 2011, we must compute the present value of this amount:

Date	Forward Contract Rate	Forward Contract Rate at This Date	Difference	×	100,000	Factor	Present Value at Date Below
December 31	1.638	1.655	0.017		1,700	1.01[1]	1,683

The approximate fair value of the forward contract is $1,683. The December 31, 2011, entry is:

Other comprehensive income (−SE)	$1,683	
Forward contract (+L)		$1,683

Entry to Offset Accounts Receivable Exchange Gain Thus far at December 31, 2011, an exchange gain of $1,000 has been recorded as a result of marking the accounts receivable to fair value. The related forward contract has also been marked to market with the resulting loss recorded in other comprehensive income. We must now record an entry to offset the exchange gain in order to properly account for this cash flow hedge. The entry is:

Exchange loss (+Lo, −SE)	$1,000	
Other comprehensive income (+SE)		$1,000

Discount or Premium Amortization This situation qualifies for cash flow hedge accounting because the forward contract completely eliminates the variability in cash flows related to the pound-denominated accounts receivable. Win has locked in a rate of $1.638. However, this is not a costless transaction. The spot rate on November 2, 2011, was $1.650. The company knows it will receive $1,200 less than the initial $165,000. This cost must be recognized in income over time. GAAP requires that an effective rate method be used to amortize the discount or premium. In this case, because the asset's ultimate amount to be received is less than the initial amount recorded, this is a discount. The formula to solve for the implicit interest rate is:

Hedged asset or liability fair value at the hedge date $\times (1 + r)^n$ = Hedge contract cash flow

Here the hedged accounts receivable fair value at November 2, 2011, is $165,000, the hedge contract cash flow is £100,000 $\times$ $1.638 = $163,800, and $n = 3$ because the contract will expire in 90 days, or three months. We will solve for r, the monthly implicit interest rate.

$$\$165,000(1 + r)^3 = \$163,800$$
$$(1 + r)^3 = 0.99273$$
$$\sqrt[3]{(1 + r)^3} = \sqrt[3]{(0.99273)}$$
$$(1 + r) = 0.99757$$
$$r = -0.00243, \text{ or } -0.243\% \text{ per month}$$

Here is the amortization table for this discount amortization:

	Discount Amortization: Balance $\times$ 0.00243	Balance
		165,000
November 30	401	164,599
December 31	400	164,199
January 30	399	163,800
Total discount amortization	1,200	

The journal entry at December 31, 2011, to record November and December amortization is:

Exchange loss (+Lo, −SE)	$801	
Other comprehensive income (+SE)		$801

At December 31, 2011, accounts receivable has a balance of $l66,000 (the fair value of the British pound denominated receivable), the forward contract balance is $1,683 credit (its fair value), and other comprehensive income is $118 credit. Income has been reduced by the amortization of the discount, $801.

ACCOUNTS RECEIVABLE FAIR VALUE ADJUSTMENT AND SETTLEMENT On January 30, 2012, five journal entries must be made. Assume that the spot rate at January 30, 2012, is $1.665 and that Win collects the £100,000 accounts receivable and immediately converts it into dollars.

Cash (+A)	$166,500	
Accounts receivable (fc) (−A)		$166,000
Exchange gain (+Ga, +SE)		$ 500

FORWARD CONTRACT FAIR VALUE ADJUSTMENT AND NET SETTLEMENT Win must pay Ross $166,500 − $163,800 = $2,700 because the spot rate on the date the contract expires is $1.665 and the forward contract rate is $1.638. We will first record the forward contract gain or loss from December 31 to January 30 and then record the net settlement payment to Ross.

Other comprehensive income (−SE)	$1,017	
Forward contract (+L)		$1,017

The contract loss is $2,700 (forward contract value at settlement date) − $1,683 (December 31, 2011, forward contract fair value estimate) = $1,017.

OFFSET GAIN ENTRY Next, we must record a loss to offset the exchange gain recorded related to the receivable:

Exchange loss (+Lo, −SE)	$ 500	
Other comprehensive income (+SE)		$ 500
Forward contract (−L)	$2,700	
Cash (−A)		$2,700

DISCOUNT OR PREMIUM AMORTIZATION ENTRY From the previous table, $399 of the discount must be amortized for the period December 31, 2011, to January 30, 2012:

Exchange loss (+Lo, −SE)	$399	
Other comprehensive income (+SE)		$399

Let's summarize what has happened to the accounts involved in this cash-flow-hedge situation:

Accounts Receivable (Asset)

November 2, 2011—initial sale date	+ $165,000
December 31, 2011—adjusted to spot rate	+ 1,000
Balance on December 31, 2011 (spot rate $1.66 × £100,000)	$166,000
January 30, 2012—adjusted to spot rate	+ 500
Balance on January 30, 2012, before settlement	$166,500

Forward Contract

November 2, 2011—initial contract date	No entry—net settlement
December 31, 2011—adjusted to fair value estimate	+ 1,683—liability
Balance on December 31, 2011	$1,683 credit—liability
January 30, 2012—adjusted to fair value	$1,017 credit
Balance before settlement	$2,700 credit
Settlement	$2,700 debit
Balance after settlement	$ 0

Other Comprehensive Income

November 2, 2011	No entry
December 31, 2011—adjust forward contract to fair value estimate	$1,683 debit
Offset gain on hedged item—accounts receivable	1,000 credit
Discount amortization for November and December	801 credit
Balance on December 31, 2011	$ 118 credit
January 30, 2012—adjust forward contract to fair value estimate	$1,017 debit
Offset gain on hedged item—accounts receivable	500 credit
Discount amortization for January	399 credit
Balance on January 30, 2012	$ 0

Income Effect

December 31, 2011

Gain on hedged item	$ 1,000
Offsetting amount from OCI due to forward contract and cash-flow-hedge accounting	−1,000
Discount amortization—exchange loss	− 801
Net exchange loss at December 31, 2011	−$ 801

January 30, 2012

Gain on hedged item	$ 500
Offsetting amount from OCI due to forward contract and cash-flow-hedge accounting	−500
Discount amortization-exchange loss	−399
Net exchange loss at January 30, 2012	−$399

What has this accounting accomplished? Notice that the company knew on November 2, 2011, that it was going to lose $1,200 related to the foreign currency–denominated accounts receivable and the related hedging contract. The accounting above reflects management's purpose in entering into this contract because the effect of changes in the exchange rate on the receivable value is exactly offset by reclassifying an offsetting amount from other comprehensive income. The actual cost of the cash flow hedge to the company, $1,200, is rationally and systematically amortized to income. Finally, both the item being hedged and the hedge contract are valued at fair value at year-end.

Also notice something else. Recall that the amortized value of the hedged item on December 31, 2011, from the discount amortization table on page 445 is $164,199. How is this number reflected on the balance sheet at December 31?

Accounts receivable—at fair value	$166,000 debit
Less: Forward contract—at estimated fair value	1,683 credit
Less: other comprehensive income	118 credit
Net balance sheet effect of the cash flow hedge	$164,199 debit

As illustrated previously, a company may incur losses (and garner gains) when the foreign exchange rate of foreign currency–denominated receivables or payables fluctuates between the date that the receivable (payable) is recorded and when it is ultimately received and converted into dollars (or dollars are used to buy the foreign currency used to settle the payable).

Fair Value Hedge Accounting: Foreign Currency–Denominated Receivable Example

ILLUSTRATION: HEDGE AGAINST EXPOSED NET ASSET (ACCOUNTS RECEIVABLE) POSITIONS U.S. Oil Company sells oil to Monato Company of Japan for 15,000,000 yen on December 1, 2011. The billing date for the sale is December 1, 2011, and payment is due in 60 days, on January 30, 2012. Concurrent with the sale, U.S. Oil enters into a forward contract to deliver 15,000,000 yen to its exchange broker in 60 days. This transaction will not be settled net. The yen will be delivered to the broker. Exchange rates for Japanese yen are as follows:

	December 1, 2011	December 31, 2011	January 30, 2012
Spot rate	**$0.007500**	**$0.007498**	**$0.007497**
30-day futures rate	$0.007490	**$0.007489**	$0.007488
60-day futures rate	**$0.007490**	$0.007488	$0.007486

The bold rates are the relevant rates for accounting purposes. The forward contract is carried at market value, which is the forward rate. Journal entries on the books of U.S. Oil are as follows:

December 1, 2011

Accounts receivable (fc) (+A)	$112,500	
Sales (+R, +SE)		$112,500
To record sales to Monato Company (15,000,000		
yen × $0.007500 spot rate).		
Contract receivable (+A)	$112,350	
Contract payable (fc) (+L)		$112,350
To record forward contract to deliver 15,000,000 yen in		
60 days. Receivable: 15,000,000 yen × $0.007490 forward rate.		

At the time that the forward contract is entered into, the company can compute its total gain or loss on the hedged item and the hedge contract. Fluctuations in exchange rates subsequent to this will not affect the magnitude of this gain or loss. The net gain or loss is the difference between the contracted forward rate and the spot rate on the date the contract is entered into:

$$(\$0.007490 - \$0.00750) \times 15{,}000{,}000 = -\$0.00001 \times 15{,}000{,}000 = -\$150$$

The company will lose $150, because it has contracted to receive $0.00001 less than the spot rate at the time the contract was entered into.

At December 31, 2011, the accounts receivable from the sale is adjusted to reflect the current exchange rate, and a $30 exchange loss is recorded. Calculating the exchange gain on the forward contract is a bit more complex. On the surface, the gain would appear to be the initial forward rate of $0.007490 × 15,000,000 less the current forward rate of $0.007489 × 15,000,000 ($112,350 − $112,335), which is $15. However, the FASB has elected to discount this amount from the contract termination date to the financial statement date. If we assume that 12 percent is a reasonable discount rate, this would be a discount of $0.15. The present value of $15 to be received one month is computed as $15 ÷ (1.01)^1 = $14.85.

December 31, 2011

Exchange loss (+Lo, −SE)	$ 30	
Accounts receivable (fc) (−A)		$ 30
To adjust accounts receivable to year-end spot exchange rate		
[15,000,000 yen × ($0.007500 − $0.007498) = $30].		
Contract payable (fc) (−L)	$14.85	
Exchange gain (+Ga, +SE)		$14.85
To adjust contract payable to exchange broker to		
the year-end forward exchange rate. Payable:		
15,000,000 yen × ($0.007490 − $0.007489)/(1.01)		

The exchange gain or loss on the hedged underlying asset is not the same as the exchange gain or loss on the forward contract because the underlying asset is carried at the spot rate and the forward contract is carried at the forward rate.

Over the contract period, the forward rate will approach the spot rate, exactly equaling it on the settlement date. In this example, the net change in the relative value was $15.15 ($30 loss − 14.85 gain) for 2011 and $135 ($15.15 loss + $119.85 loss) for 2012:

January 30, 2012

Cash (fc) (+A)	$ 112,455	
Exchange loss (+Lo, −SE)	15.15	
Accounts receivable (fc) (−A)		$112,470.15
To record collection of receivable from		
Monato Company. Cash: 15,000,000 yen × $0.007497.		
Contract payable (fc) (+L)	$112,335.15	
Exchange loss (−Lo, −SE)	119.85	
Cash (fc) (−A)		$112,455
To record delivery of 15,000,000 yen from Monato to		
foreign exchange broker in settlement of liability.		
Cash (+A)	$ 112,350	
Contract receivable (−A)		$112,350
To record receipt of cash from exchange broker.		

In the final analysis, U.S. Oil Company makes a sale in the amount of $112,500. It takes a $150 charge on the transaction in order to avoid the risks of foreign currency price fluctuations, and it collects $112,350 in final settlement of the sale transaction. The $150 is charged to income over the term of the forward contract.

HEDGE AGAINST EXPOSED NET LIABILITY POSITION Accounting procedures for hedging an exposed net liability position are comparable to those illustrated for U.S. Oil Company except that the objective is to hedge a liability denominated in foreign currency, rather than a receivable. Normally, the forward rate for buying foreign currency for future receipt is greater than the spot rate. For example, a forward contract to acquire 10,000 British pounds for receipt in 60 days might have a forward rate of $1.675 when the spot rate is $1.66. The forward contract is recorded as follows:

Contract receivable (fc) (+A)	$16,750	
Contract payable (+L)		$16,750

The contract hedges any effect of changes in the exchange rate so that the net cost over the life of the contract will be the $150 differential between the spot and forward rates.

RESULT OF HEDGING   Forward rates are ordinarily set so that a cost is incurred related to the hedge. Occasionally, the rates for futures contracts result in hedges that increase income.

In summary, a forward contract is recorded at the forward rate, while the underlying asset or liability is recorded at the spot rate (and adjusted to these respective rates and values at the financial statement date). Over the life of the contract, the initial difference between the spot and the forward rates is the cost of hedging the exchange rate risk. Because the gains and losses on both the hedge and the underlying asset or liability are recorded in current earnings, the net cost reported in the income statement is the change in the relative values of the spot and forward rates.

If a firm enters a forward contract for foreign currency units in excess of the foreign currency units reflected in its exposed net asset or net liability position (a speculation in the currency), the difference ends up as a gain or loss. This is due to the difference in the change in the value of the derivative and the change in the value of the underlying item hedged both being reported in the income statement.

Fair Value Hedge of an Identifiable Foreign Currency Commitment

A **foreign currency commitment** is a contract or agreement denominated in foreign currency that will result in a foreign currency transaction at a later date. For example, a U.S. firm may contract to buy equipment from a Canadian firm at a future date with the invoice price denominated in Canadian dollars. The U.S. firm has an exposure to exchange rate changes because the future price in U.S. dollars may increase or decrease before the transaction is consummated.

An identifiable foreign currency commitment differs from an exposed asset or liability position because the commitment does not meet the accounting tests for recording the related asset or liability in the accounts. The risk of the exposure still may be avoided by hedging. This situation is special because the underlying transaction being hedged is not recorded as an asset or liability. Therefore, some method must be established to record the change in the value of the underlying unrecorded commitment in order to record the derivative instrument as a hedge of the commitment. Once this mechanism has been created, the change in both the derivative instrument and the underlying commitment are recorded—in effect, offsetting each other. Because a forward contract that is a hedge of a firm commitment is based on the forward rate, not the spot rate, any gain or loss on the derivative and underlying contract is based on the forward rate.

The forward contract accounting begins when the forward contract is designated as a hedge of a foreign currency commitment.

ILLUSTRATION: HEDGE OF AN IDENTIFIABLE FOREIGN CURRENCY PURCHASE COMMITMENT   On October 2, 2011, American Stores Corporation contracts with Canadian Distillers for delivery of 1,000 cases of bourbon at a price of 60,000 Canadian dollars, when the spot rate for Canadian dollars is $0.70. The bourbon is to be delivered in March and payment made in Canadian dollars on March 31, 2012. In order to hedge this future commitment, American Stores enters into a forward contract to purchase 60,000 Canadian dollars for delivery to American Stores in 180 days at a forward exchange rate of $0.725. Applicable forward rates on December 31, 2011, and March 31, 2012 (because the maturity is March 31, this rate is also the spot rate) are $0.71 and $0.68, respectively.

Assume that the derivative instrument (the forward contract) is designated as a hedge of this identifiable foreign currency commitment (the bourbon purchase). The purchase of the forward contract on October 2, 2011, is recorded as follows:

October 2, 2011

Contract receivable (fc) (+A)	$43,500	
Contract payable (+L)		$43,500
To record forward contract to purchase 60,000		
Canadian dollars for delivery in 180 days at a		
forward rate of $0.725.		

By December 31, 2011, the forward exchange rate for Canadian dollars decreases to $0.71, and American Stores adjusts its receivable to reflect the 60,000 Canadian dollars at the 90-day forward exchange rate. This adjustment creates a $900 exchange loss on the forward contract as follows:

December 31, 2011

Exchange loss (+Lo, −SE)	$900	
Contract receivable (fc) (−A)		$900
To record exchange loss: 60,000		
Canadian dollars × ($0.725 − $0.71).		

However, this loss is offset by the increase in the value of the underlying firm commitment:

December 31, 2011

Change in value of firm commitment in	$900	
Canadian dollars (fc) (+A)		
Exchange gain (+Ga, +SE)		$900
To record exchange gain: 60,000 Canadian		
dollars × ($0.725 − $0.71). (Payment in Canadian		
dollars will cost fewer US$.)		

Journal entries on March 31, 2012, to account for the foreign currency transaction and related forward contract are as follows:

March 31, 2012

1. Contract payable (−L)	$43,500	
Cash (−A)		$43,500
To record settlement of forward contract with the		
exchange broker (denominated in U.S. dollars).		
2. Cash (fc) (+A)	$40,800	
Exchange loss (+Lo, −SE)	1,800	
Contract receivable (fc) (−A)		$42,600
To record receipt of 60,000 Canadian dollars from		
the exchange broker when the exchange rate is $0.68.		
3. Change in value of firm commitment in Canadian	$ 1,800	
dollars (+A)		
Exchange gain (+Ga, +SE)		$ 1,800
To record the change in the value of the underlying		
firm commitment.		
4. Inventory (+A)	$43,500	
Change in value of firm commitment in Canadian		$ 2,700
dollars (−A)		
Accounts payable (fc) (+L)		40,800
To record receipt of 1,000 cases of bourbon		
at a cost of 60,000 Canadian dollars × forward		
exchange rate of $0.725.		
5. Accounts payable (fc) (−L)	$40,800	
Cash (fc) (−A)		$40,800
To record payment of 60,000 Canadian dollars to		
Canadian Distillers.		

Entry 1 records payment to the exchange broker for the 60,000 Canadian dollars at the contracted forward rate of $0.725. The second entry reflects collection of the 60,000 Canadian dollars from the broker and records an additional exchange loss on the further decline of the exchange rate from the forward rate of $0.71 at December 31, 2011, to the $0.68 spot rate (this is also the forward rate for the date of settlement) at March 31, 2012. The third entry records the gain on the change in the dollar cost of the firm commitment to buy the bourbon since December 31, 2011.

The fourth entry on March 31 records receipt of the 1,000 cases of bourbon from Canadian Distillers and records the liability payable in Canadian dollars. It also incorporates the change in the firm commitment in the inventory value. In entry 5, Canadian Distillers is paid the 60,000 Canadian dollars in final settlement of the account payable.

HEDGE OF AN IDENTIFIABLE FOREIGN CURRENCY SALES COMMITMENT Accounting procedures for hedging an identifiable foreign currency sales commitment are comparable to those illustrated for hedging a purchase commitment, except that the sales, rather than the inventory, account is adjusted for any deferred exchange gains or losses.

Cash Flow Hedge of an Anticipated Foreign Currency Transaction

Win Corporation, a U.S. corporation, anticipates a contract based on December 2, 2011, discussions to purchase heavy equipment from Smith Ltd. of Scotland for 500,000 British pounds. The equipment is anticipated to be delivered to Win and the amount paid to Smith on March 1, 2012, but nothing has been signed.

In order to hedge its anticipated commitment, Win enters into a forward contract with Sea Company to buy 500,000 British pounds for delivery on March 1. The contract is to be settled net. Assume that this qualifies as an effective hedge under GAAP and should be accounted for as a cash flow hedge of an anticipated foreign currency commitment.

On December 2, 2011, the spot rate is $1.7000 and the 90-day forward rate is $1.6800 (for delivery on March 1, 2012). Because this is an anticipated commitment, there is no hedged item on the balance sheet that will be marked to fair value until the actual sale occurs, which will be in three months. However, the company has engaged in this forward contract. The contract must be recorded at estimated fair value at year-end. However because this is considered a cash flow hedge of an anticipated foreign currency commitment, the resulting gain or loss is deferred until the item being hedged actually affects income. The discount or premium related to the forward contract must be amortized to income over time.

FORWARD CONTRACT ADJUSTMENT AT DECEMBER 31, 2011 Assume that the 60-day forward rate at December 31, 2011, is $1.6900. We estimate the fair value of this forward contract as follows, assuming a 12 percent annual incremental borrowing rate:

Date	Forward Contract Rate	Forward Contract Rate at this Date	Difference × 500,000		Factor	Present Value at Date Below
December 31	1.68	1.69	0.01	5,000	1.01^2	4,901

The journal entry is:

Forward contract (+A)	$4,901	
Other comprehensive income (+SE)		$4,901

FORWARD DISCOUNT ADJUSTMENT The original forward discount was $1.70 − $1.68 = 0.02 × 500,000 = $10,000. Recall from our discussion of cash flow hedges of existing foreign currency–denominated receivables and payables that the discount or premium resulting from the hedge must be amortized to income over the life of the contract. If the spot rate and forward rate on December 2, 2011, had been the same, there would be no discount or premium to amortize. Win would have just recorded the forward contract fair value at year-end as illustrated above. Income would not have been affected. However, in this case, the spot and forward rates were different, resulting in a discount which must be amortized to income over the contract's life. A discount arises when the contracted forward rate is lower than the spot rate at that date. A premium arises when the contracted forward rate is higher than the spot rate at the contract date. We again solve for the monthly implicit rate to be used to amortize the $10,000 discount. The rate is .3937 percent or .003937. The amortization table is presented below:

	Discount Amortization	Balance
		850,000
December 31	3,347	846,653
January 31	3,333	843,320
February 28	3,320	840,000
Total discount amortization	10,000	

The journal entry to record the discount amortization and related gain at December 31 is:

Other comprehensive income (−SE)	$3,347	
Exchange gain (+Ga, +SE)		$3,347

There are four journal entries on March 1.

FORWARD CONTRACT ADJUSTMENT AND EQUIPMENT PURCHASE Assume that the spot rate on March 1 is $1.72. The forward contract value on this date is ($1.72 − $1.68) × 500,000 = $20,000. The balance on December 31, 2011, was $4,901 debit, so we must increase the forward contract to its fair value by increasing the account by $15,099. Win will receive $20,000 from Sea because the spot rate is higher than the forward contract rate:

Forward contract (+A)	$ 15,099	
Other comprehensive income (+SE)		$ 15,099
Equipment (+A)	$860,000	
Cash (−A)		$860,000
(1.72 × 500,000)		
Cash (+A)	$ 20,000	
Forward contract (−A)		$ 20,000

DISCOUNT AMORTIZATION ENTRY We must record the amortization of the discount for January and February. From the amortization table above, the amortization for those two months is $3,333 + $3,320 = $6,653:

Other comprehensive income (−SE)	$6,653	
Exchange gain (+Ga, +SE)		$6,653

This table presents a summary of account balances:

Forward contract

December 2, 2011—no entry required	$ 0
December 31, 2011	+ 4,901 debit
Balance on December 31, 2011	$ 4,901 debit—asset
Fair value adjustment at March 1, 2012	+15,099 debit
Balance before settlement on March 1, 2012	$20,000 debit—asset

Other Comprehensive Income

December 31, 2011, adjustment of forward contract to fair value	$ 4,901 credit
December 31, 2011, amortization of discount	3,347 debit
Balance on December 31, 2011	$ 1,554 credit
March 1, 2012, adjustment of forward contract to fair value	$15,099 credit
March 1, 2012, amortization of discount	$ 6,653 debit
Balance on March 1, 2012	$10,000 credit

Income

December 31, 2011—exchange gain resulting from amortizing discount	$3,347
March 1, 2012—exchange gain resulting from amortizing discount	$6,653

On March 1, 2012, the equipment is recorded at $860,000. As the equipment is depreciated, the $10,000 balance in the other comprehensive income account will be amortized to reduce depreciation expense.

Speculation

Exchange gains or losses on derivative instruments that speculate in foreign currency price movements are included in income in the periods in which the forward exchange rates change. Forward or future exchange rates for 30-, 90-, and 180-day delivery are quoted on a daily basis for the leading world currencies. A foreign currency derivative that is a speculation is valued at forward rates throughout the life of the contract (which is the fair value of the contract at that point in time). The basic accounting is illustrated in the following example.

On November 2, 2011, U.S. International enters into a 90-day forward contract (future) to purchase 10,000 euros when the current quotation for 90-day futures in euros is $0.5400. The spot rate for euros on November 2 is $0.5440. Exchange rates at December 31, 2011, and January 30, 2012, are as follows:

	December 31, 2011	**January 30, 2012**
30-day futures	$0.5450	$0.5480
Spot rate	0.5500	0.5530

Journal entries on the books of U.S. International to account for the speculation are as follows:

November 2, 2011

Contract receivable (fc) (+A)	$5,400	
Contract payable (+L)		$5,400
To record contract for 10,000 euros × $0.5400 exchange rate for 90-day futures.		

December 31, 2011

Contract receivable (fc) (+A)	$ 50	
Exchange gain (+Ga, +SE)		$ 50
To adjust receivable from exchange broker and recognize exchange gain (10,000 euros × $0.5450 forward exchange rate for 30-day futures − $5,400 per books).		

January 30, 2012

Cash (fc) (+A)	$5,530	
Exchange gain (+Ga, +SE)		$ 80
Contract receivable (fc) (−A)		$5,450
To record receipt of 10,000 euros. The current spot rate for euros is $0.5530.		
Contract payable (−L)	$5,400	
Cash (−A)		$5,400
To record payment of the liability to the exchange broker denominated in dollars.		

The entry on November 2 records U.S. International's right to receive 10,000 euros from the exchange broker in 90 days. It also records U.S. International's liability to pay $5,400 to the exchange broker in 90 days. Both the receivable and the liability are recorded at $5,400 (10,000 euros × $0.5400 forward rate), but only the receivable is denominated in euros and is subject to exchange rate fluctuations.

At December 31, 2011, the forward contract has 30 days until maturity. Under GAAP, the receivable denominated in euros is adjusted to reflect the exchange rate of $0.5450 for 30-day futures on December 31, 2011. This is the fair value of the contract. The amount of the adjustment is included in U.S. International's income for 2011.

On January 30, 2012, U.S. International receives 10,000 euros with a current value of $5,530 (10,000 euros × $0.5530 spot rate). The translated value of the foreign currency received is $80 more than the recorded amount of the receivable, so an additional exchange gain results. U.S. International also settles its liability with the exchange broker on January 30.

A speculation involving the sale of foreign currency for future delivery is accounted for in a similar fashion, except that the receivable is fixed in U.S. dollars and the liability is denominated in the foreign currency.

Derivative Accounting Summarized

The accounting required for a derivative depends primarily on management's intent when entering into the transaction. Exhibit 13-1 summarizes the types of derivatives and the purpose, required accounting, and effect on income of each.

Footnote-Disclosure Requirements

LEARNING OBJECTIVE 5

Disclosure requirements focus upon how its derivatives fit into a company's overall risk-management objectives and strategy. The company should be specific about the types of risks being hedged and how they are being hedged. In addition, the company should describe initially how it determines hedge effectiveness and how it assesses continuing hedge effectiveness.

The disclosures related to fair value hedges include reporting the net gain or loss included in earnings during the period and where in the financial statements the gain or loss is reported. This gain or loss is separated into the portion that represents the hedge's ineffectiveness and the portion of the gain or loss on the hedge instrument that was not included in the assessment of hedge effectiveness.

Cash flow hedging instrument disclosures include reporting the amount of any hedge ineffectiveness gain or loss and any gain or loss from the derivative excluded from the assessment of hedge effectiveness. In addition, location of these gains and losses in the financial statements should be disclosed.

EXHIBIT 13-1

SUMMARY OF TYPES OF DERIVATIVES AND THEIR ACCOUNTING

Classification	Purpose	Recognition	Expected Effect of Hedge and Related Item
Speculation	To speculate in exchange rate changes	Exchange gains and losses are recognized currently, based on forward exchange rate changes.	Income effect equals exchange gains and losses recognized.
Hedge of a net asset or liability position	To offset exposure to existing net asset or liability position	Exchange gains and losses are recognized currently, but they are offset by related gains or losses on net asset or liability position.	Income effect equals the amortization of premium or discount. (Gains and losses offset.)
Hedge of an identifiable commitment	To offset exposure to a future purchase or sale and thereby lock in the price of an existing contract in U.S. dollars	Exchange gains and losses are recognized currently, but they are offset by related gains or losses in the firm commitment.	Income effect equals the difference in the change in value of the hedge instrument versus the firm commitment.
Hedge of an anticipated transaction	To offset exposure of possible future purchase or sale	Exchange gains or losses on the hedge are counted in other comprehensive income until the underlying transaction is complete.	No immediate income effect. Adjusts underlying transaction.
Hedge of a net investment in a foreign entity (see Chapter 14)	To offset exposure to an existing net investment in a foreign entity	Exchange gains and losses are recognized as other comprehensive income and will offset translation adjustments recorded on the net investment.	Income effect equals the change in the future value of the hedge versus the value of the net investment.

The disclosures for cash flow hedges also include a description of the situations in which the gain or loss included in accumulated other comprehensive income is reclassified to income. An estimate of the amount of reclassification to occur within the next twelve months should also be reported.

Because cash flow hedge accounting can be used for forecasted transactions, the company should report the maximum length of time that the entity is hedging its exposure to these forecasted transactions. This disclosure excludes transaction hedges of variable interest on existing financial instruments.

Finally, the company should report the amount of gains and losses that could be reclassified to income if the cash flow hedges were discontinued because the original forecasted transactions did not occur.

Please attempt the Internet Assignment at the end of the chapter to examine an actual disclosure.

International Accounting Standards

LEARNING OBJECTIVE 6

International standards for accounting for hedging and derivatives are controlled by two companion standards. *International Accounting Standard No. 32*, "Financial Instruments: Disclosure and Presentation" [2] (revised in December 2003, originally issued in June 1995), and *International Accounting Standard No. 39*, "Financial Instruments: Recognition and Measurement" [3] (a significant revision in December 2003, but also revised in March 2004; originally issued in December 1998), are both related to the ASC Topic 815. *IAS No. 32's* major points include clarifying when a financial instrument issued by a company should be classified as a liability or as equity and requiring a wide range of disclosures regarding financial instruments, including their fair values. In addition, the statement defines and provides examples of many terms, such as financial assets, financial liability, equity instrument, and fair values.

IAS No. 39 addresses many of the same issues as ASC Topic 815, including defining and providing examples of derivatives as well as hedge accounting. In fact, the conditions that must be present to use hedge accounting, such as formally designating and documenting the corporation's risk-management objective and strategy for undertaking the hedge, as well as the need to assess hedge effectiveness initially and during the hedge's existence, are almost identical to GAAP. For example, the 80 percent to 125 percent range mentioned in ASC Topic 815 is also mentioned in *IAS 39* to assess effectiveness.

The definitions of fair value hedges and cash flow hedges and the general accounting are very similar. However, one difference between IAS and U.S. GAAP is how firm sale or purchase commitments are accounted for. Under U.S. GAAP, such firm sale or purchase commitments are accounted for as fair value hedges, but under IFRS [3] they can be accounted for as either fair value hedges or cash flow hedges. Despite some differences, U.S. GAAP and IFRS standards relating to derivatives are converging.

SUMMARY

Derivatives are a widely-used mechanism to mitigate various risks. Hedge accounting is designed so that companies' strategies to control risk are more transparently disclosed in the financial statements.

International accounting is concerned with accounting for foreign currency transactions and operations. An entity's functional currency is the currency of the primary environment in which the entity operates. Foreign currency transactions are denominated in a currency other than an entity's functional currency.

Foreign currency transactions (other than forward contracts) are measured and recorded in U.S. dollars at the spot rate in effect at the transaction date. A change in the exchange rate between the date of the transaction and the settlement date results in an exchange gain or loss that is reflected in income for the period. At the balance sheet date, any remaining balances that are denominated in a currency other than the functional currency are adjusted to reflect the current exchange rate, and the gain or loss is charged to income.

Corporations use forward exchange contracts and other derivatives to avoid the risks of exchange rate changes and to speculate on foreign currency exchange price movements. ASC Topic 815 prescribes different provisions for forward contracts (and other derivatives), depending on their nature and purposes.

QUESTIONS

1. Explain the objective of hedge accounting and how this objective should improve the transparency of financial statements.

2. Explain the differences between options, forward contracts, and futures contracts and the potential benefits and potential costs of each type of contract.

3. Hedge effectiveness must be documented before a particular hedge qualifies for hedge accounting. Describe the most common approaches used to determine hedge effectiveness and when they are appropriate. In each of the approaches, when would a particular hedge *not* be considered effective?

4. A hedged firm purchase or sale commitment typically qualifies for fair value hedge accounting if the hedge is documented to be effective. Compare the accounting for both the derivative and the firm purchase or sale commitment under each of these circumstances: (a) the hedge relationship is deemed to be effective and (b) the hedge relationship is *not* deemed to be effective.

5. Interest rate swaps were used in the chapter to highlight the differences between fair value and cash flow hedge accounting. Explain what type of risk is being hedged when a *pay-fixed, receive-variable swap* is used to hedge an existing variable-rate loan.

6. Interest rate swaps were used in the chapter to highlight the differences between fair value and cash flow hedge accounting. Explain what type of risk is being hedged when a *receive-fixed, pay-variable swap* is used to hedge an existing fixed-rate loan.

7. Explain the circumstances under which fair value hedge accounting should be used and when cash flow hedge accounting should be used.

8. *Statement No. 138* allows companies to account for certain hedges of existing foreign currency–denominated receivables and payables as cash flow hedges. Under *Statement No. 133*, hedges of existing assets and liabilities must be accounted for as fair value hedges. Explain the circumstances that must be present for a hedge of an existing foreign currency–denominated receivable or payable to be accounted for as a cash flow hedge and how the accounting differs from cash flow hedge accounting in more-general situations.

9. Briefly describe how derivatives are accounted for according to the International Accounting Standards Board. Is the accounting similar to U.S. GAAP? How is it different?

10. Describe how to account for a forward contract that is intended as a hedge of an identifiable foreign currency commitment.

EXERCISES

E 13-1

Hedge of an anticipated purchase

On December 1, 2011, Jol Company enters into a 90-day forward contract with a rice speculator to purchase 500 tons of rice at $1,000 per ton. Jol enters into this contract in order to hedge an anticipated rice purchase. The contract is to be settled net. The spot price of rice at December 1, 2011, is $950.

On December 31, 2011, the forward rate is $980 per ton. The contract is settled and rice is purchased on February 28, 2012. The spot and forward rates when the contract is settled are $1,005. Assume that Jol purchases 500 tons of rice on the date of the forward contract's expiration. Assume that this contract has been documented to be an effective hedge. Also assume an appropriate interest rate is 6 percent.

1. Prepare the required journal entries to account for this hedge situation and the subsequent rice purchase on:
   1. *December 1, 2011*
   2. *December 31, 2011*
   3. *The settlement date*

2. Assume that the rice is subsequently sold by Jol on June 1, 2012, for $1,200 per ton. What journal entries will Jol make on that date?

E 13-2

Hedge of a firm purchase commitment

Refer to Exercise E 13-1 and assume that Jol enters into the forward contract to hedge a firm purchase commitment. Repeat parts 1 and 2 under this assumption.

E 13-3

Firm sales commitment

Brk signs a firm sales commitment with Riv. The contract is to sell 100,000 widgets deliverable in three months, on January 31, 2012, at the prevailing market price of widgets at that date. On November 1, 2011, the current sales price of widgets is $5 each. Brk is concerned that the sales price could decrease by the time the delivery is to occur. On November 1, 2011, Brk contracts with Lyn to buy 100,000 widgets deliverable on January 31, 2012, for $5 each. The forward contract is to be settled net. Assume that 6 percent is a reasonable annual discount rate.

Prepare the journal entries to record the firm sales commitment and forward contract on the following dates:
1. *November 1, 2011, assuming a sales price of $5.00 per widget*
2. *December 31, 2011, assuming a sales price of $4.50 per widget*
3. *January 31, 2012, assuming a sales price of $6 per widget*

E 13-4

Hedging of an Existing Asset

Wil has 100,000 units of widgets in its inventory on October 1, 2011. Wil purchased them for $1 per unit one month ago. It hedges the value of the widgets by entering into a forward contract to sell 100,000 widgets on January 31, 2012, for $2 each. The contract is to be settled net. Assume that a discount rate of 6 percent is reasonable.

Prepare the journal entries to properly account for this hedge of an existing asset on the following dates:
1. *October 1, 2011, when the widget price is $1.50*
2. *December 31, 2011, when the widget price is $2.50*
3. *January 31, 2012, when the widget price is $2.30*

E 13-5

[Based on AICPA] Various foreign currency hedge situations

On December 12, 2011, Car entered into three forward exchange contracts, each to purchase 100,000 Canadian dollars in 90 days. Assume a 12 percent interest rate. The relevant exchange rates are as follows:

	Spot Rate	Forward Rate (for March 12, 2012)
December 12, 2011	$0.88	$0.90
December 31, 2011	0.98	0.93

1. Car entered into the first forward contract to hedge a purchase of inventory in November 2011, payable in March 2012. At December 31, 2011, what amount of foreign currency transaction gain should Car include in income from this forward contract? Explain.

2. Car entered into the second forward contract to hedge a commitment to purchase equipment being manufactured to Car's specifications. At December 31, 2011, what amount of net gain or loss on foreign currency transactions should Car include in income from this forward contract? Explain.

3. Car entered into a third forward contract for speculation. At December 31, 2011, what amount of foreign currency transaction gain should Car include in income from this forward contract? Explain.

E 13-6

Firm purchase commitment, foreign currency hedge

On April 1, 2011, Win of Canada ordered customized fittings from Ace, a U.S. firm, to be delivered on May 31, 2011, at a price of 50,000 Canadian dollars. The spot rate for Canadian dollars on April 1, 2011, was $0.71. Also on April 1, in order to fix the sale price of the fittings at $35,250, Ace entered into a 60-day forward contract with the exchange broker to hedge the Win contract. This derivative met the conditions set forth in ASC Topic 815 for a hedge of a foreign currency commitment. Exchange rates for Canadian dollars are as follows:

	April 1	May 31
Spot rate	$0.710	$0.725
60-day forward rate	0.705	0.715

REQUIRED: Prepare all journal entries on Ace's books to account for the commitment and related events on April 1 and May 31, 2011.

E 13-7

Firm purchase commitment, foreign currency hedge

On November 2, 2011, Baz, a U.S. retailer, ordered merchandise from Mat of Japan. The merchandise is to be delivered to Baz on January 30, 2012, at a price of 1,000,000 yen. Also on November 2, Import Baz hedged the foreign currency commitment with Mat by contracting with its exchange broker to buy 1,000,000 yen for delivery on January 30, 2012. Exchange rates for yen are:

	11/2/11	12/31/11	1/30/12
Spot rate	$0.0075	$0.0076	$0.0078
30-day forward rate	0.0076	0.0078	0.0079
90-day forward rate	0.0078	0.0079	0.0080

REQUIRED

1. Prepare the entry (or entries) on Baz's books on November 2, 2011.

2. Prepare the adjusting entry on December 31, 2011.

PROBLEMS

P 13-1
Cash flow hedge, futures contract

NGW, a consumer gas provider, estimates a rather cold winter. As a result it decides to enter into a futures contract on the NYMEX for natural gas on November 2, 2011. The trading unit is 10,000 million British thermal units (MMBtu). The three-month futures contract rate is $7.00 per MMBtu, so each contract will cost NGW $70,000. In addition, the exchange requires a $5,000 deposit on each contract. NGW enters into 20 such contracts.

REQUIRED

1. Why is this futures contract likely to be considered an effective hedge and therefore qualified for hedge accounting?

2. Why would this transaction be accounted for as a cash flow hedge?

3. Assume that the December 31, 2011, futures contract rate is $6.75 for delivery on February 2, 2012, and the spot rate on February 2, 2012, is $6.85. Assume that NGW sells all of the gas on February 3, 2012, for $8.00 per MMBtu. Prepare all the necessary journal entries from November 2, 2011, through February 3, 2012, to account for this hedge situation.

P 13-2
Fair value hedge, option

Ins makes sophisticated medical equipment. A key component of the equipment is Grade A silver. On May 1, 2011, Ins enters into a firm purchase agreement to buy 1,200,000 troy ounces (equal to 100,000 pounds) of Grade A silver from Sil, for delivery on February 1, 2012, at the market price on that date. To hedge against volatility in price, Ins also enters into an option contract with Cur to put 1,200,000 troy ounces on February 1, 2012, for $10 per troy ounce, the market price on May 1, 2011. If the market price of silver is below $10 per troy ounce on May 1, then Ins will let the option expire. If it is above $10 per troy ounce, then it will exercise the option. The option is to be settled net. Com will pay Instrument Works the difference between the market price and the exercise price. The option costs Ins $1,000 initially. Assume that a 6 percent annual incremental borrowing rate is reasonable.

1. Why would you expect this situation to qualify for hedge accounting?

2. Why should this hedge be accounted for as a fair value hedge instead of as a cash flow hedge?

3. What entries should be made on May 1, 2011, to account for the firm commitment and the option?

4. Assume that the market price for Grade A silver is $9 per troy ounce on December 31, 2011. What are the required entries?

5. Assume that the market price of Grade A silver is $9.50 per troy ounce on February 1, 2012, when Ins receives the silver from Silver Refiners. Prepare the appropriate journal entries on February 1, 2012.

P 13-3
Cash flow hedges, interest rate swap

On January 1, 2011, Cam borrows $400,000 from Ven. The five-year term note is a variable-rate one in which the 2011 interest rate is determined to be 8 percent, the LIBOR rate at January 1, 2011, + 2%. Subsequent years' interest rates are determined in a similar manner, with the rate set for a particular year equal to the beginning-of-the-year LIBOR rate + 2%. Interest payments are due on December 31 each year and are computed assuming annual compounding.

Also on January 1, 2011, Cam decides to enter into a pay-fixed, receive-variable interest rate swap arrangement with Gra. Cam will pay 8 percent.

Assume that the LIBOR rate on December 31, 2011, is 5 percent.

1. Why is this considered a cash flow hedge instead of a fair value hedge?

2. Do you think that this hedge would be considered effective and therefore would qualify for hedge accounting?

3. Assuming that this hedge relationship qualifies for hedge accounting:
   a. Determine the estimated fair value of the hedge at December 31, 2011. Recall that the hedge contract is in effect for the 2012, 2013, 2014, and 2015 interest payments.
   b. Prepare the entry at December 31, 2011, to account for this cash flow hedge as well as the December 31, 2011, interest payment.

4. Assuming that the LIBOR rate is 5.5% on December 31, 2012, prepare all the necessary entries to account for the interest rate swap at December 31, 2012, including the 2012 interest payment.

P 13-4
Fair value hedge, interest rate swap

Refer to Problem P 13-3 and assume that instead of initially signing a variable-rate loan, Cam receives a fixed rate of 8 percent on the loan on January 1, 2011. Instead of entering into a pay-fixed, receive-variable interest rate swap with Gra, Cam enters into a pay-variable, receive-fixed interest rate swap. The variable portion of the swap formula is LIBOR rate + 2%, determined at the end of the year to set the rate for the following year. The first year that the swap will be in effect is for interest payments in 2012.

Assume that the LIBOR rate on December 31, 2011, is 7 percent.

1. Why is this considered a fair value hedge instead of a cash flow hedge?

2. Do you think that this hedge would be considered effective and therefore would qualify for hedge accounting?

3. Assuming that this hedge relationship qualifies for hedge accounting:
   a. Determine the estimated fair value of the hedge at December 31, 2011. Recall that the hedge contract is in effect for the 2012, 2013, 2014, and 2015 interest payments.
   b. Prepare the entry at December 31, 2011, to account for this fair value hedge as well as the December 31, 2011, interest payment.

4. Assuming that the LIBOR rate is 6.5% on December 31, 2012, prepare all the necessary entries to account for the interest rate swap at December 31, 2012, including the 2012 interest payment.

P 13-5
Foreign currency hedge, existing receivable

On April 1, 2011, Bay delivers merchandise to Ram for 200,000 pesos when the spot rate for pesos is 6.0496 pesos. The receivable from Ram is due May 30. Also on April 1, Bay hedges its foreign currency asset and enters into a 60-day forward contract to sell 200,000 pesos at a forward rate of 6.019 pesos. The spot rate on May 30 was 5.992 pesos.

REQUIRED

1. Prepare journal entries to record the receivable from the sales transaction and the forward contract on April 1.

2. Prepare journal entries to record collection of the receivable and settlement of the forward contract on May 30.

P 13-6
Foreign currency hedge, firm purchase commitment

On October 2, 2011, Flx, a U.S. company, entered into a forward contract to purchase 50,000 euros for delivery in 180 days at a forward rate of $0.6350. The forward contract is a derivative instrument hedging an identifiable foreign currency commitment as defined in ASC Topic 815. The spot rate for euros on this date was $0.6250. Spot rates and forward rates for euros on December 31, 2011, and March 31, 2012, are as follows:

	December 31, 2011	March 31, 2012
Spot rate	$0.6390	$0.6560
Forward rates		
30-day futures	0.6410	0.6575
90-day futures	0.6420	0.6615
180-day futures	0.6450	0.6680

REQUIRED: Prepare journal entries to:

1. Record the forward contract on October 2, 2011

2. Adjust the accounts at December 31, 2011

3. Account for settlement of the forward contract and record and adjust the related cash purchase on March 31, 2012

P 13-7
Foreign currency hedge, anticipated sale

Bat, a U.S. corporation, anticipates a contract based on December 2, 2011 discussions to sell heavy equipment to Ram of Scotland for 500,000 British pounds. The equipment is likely to be delivered and the amount collected on March 1, 2012.

In order to hedge its anticipated commitment, Bat entered into a forward contract on December 2 to sell 500,000 British pounds for delivery on March 1. The forward contract meets all the conditions of ASC Topic 815 for a cash flow hedge of an anticipated foreign currency commitment. A 6 percent interest rate is appropriate.

Exchange rates for British pounds on selected dates are as follows:

British Pounds	12/2/11	12/31/11	3/1/12
Spot rate	$1.7000	$1.705	$1.7100
Forward rate for March 1, 2012, delivery	1.6800	1.6900	1.7100

REQUIRED: Prepare the necessary journal entries on Bat's books to account for:

1. The forward contract on December 2, 2011.

2. Year-end adjustments relating to the forward contract on December 31, 2011.

3. The delivery of the equipment and settlement of all accounts with Ram and the exchange broker on March 1, 2012.

P 13-8
Foreign currency hedge, existing payable

Mar, a U.S. firm, purchased equipment for 400,000 British pounds from Thc on December 16, 2011. The terms were n/30, payable in British pounds.

On December 16, 2011, Mar also entered into a 30-day forward contract to hedge the account payable to Thc. Exchange rates for British pounds on selected dates are as follows:

	12/16/11	12/31/11	1/15/12
Spot rate	$1.67	$1.65	$1.64
Forward rate for 1/15/12	1.68	1.66	1.64

REQUIRED

1. Assuming this situation qualifies as a cash flow hedge, prepare journal entries on December 16, 2011, to record Mar's purchase and the forward contract. A 6% interest rate is appropriate.

2. Prepare year-end journal entries for Mar as needed on December 31, 2011.

3. Prepare journal entries for Mar's settlement of its accounts payable and the forward contract on January 15, 2012.

INTERNET ASSIGNMENT

Go to *Xerox Corporation's* Web site and access their 2010 annual report. Answer the following questions regarding Xerox's derivative and foreign currency transactions.

1. Which categories of derivative transactions does Xerox engage in (cash flow hedges, fair value hedges, speculative hedges)? Describe the types of commodities that Xerox hedges. How do derivative transactions fit into Xerox's overall business strategy?

2. What was the 2010 income statement effect of each category? Give the total dollar amount, as well as the effect as a percentage of revenues and income before tax. Have these transactions materially affected the profitability of Xerox? Explain your answer.

3. Where does Xerox disclose the financial statement impact of the cash flow hedges it enters into? Do you consider these to have a material impact on its financial position? Explain.

REFERENCES TO THE AUTHORITATIVE LITERATURE

[1] FASB ASC 815 "Derivatives and Hedging." Originally Statement of Financial Accounting Standards No. 133. *Accounting for Derivative Instruments and Hedging Activities.*" Stamford, CT: Financial Accounting Standards Board, 1998.

[2] IASC International Accounting Standard 32 "Financial Instruments: Disclosure and Presentation." International Accounting Standards Committee, Revised 2003.

[3] IASC International Accounting Standard 39 "Financial Instruments: Disclosure and Presentation." International Accounting Standards Committee, Revised 2004.

14 CHAPTER

Foreign Currency Financial Statements

LEARNING OBJECTIVES

1 Identify the factors that should be considered when determining an entity's functional currency.

2 Understand how functional currency assignment determines the way the foreign entity's financial statements are converted into its parent's reporting currency.

3 Understand how a foreign subsidiary's economy is determined to be highly inflationary and how this affects the conversion of its financial statements to its parent's reporting currency.

4 Understand how the investment in a foreign subsidiary is accounted for at acquisition.

5 Understand which rates are used to translate balance sheet and income statement accounts under the current rate method and the temporal method on a translation/remeasurement worksheet.

6 Know how the translation gain or loss, or remeasurement gain or loss, is reported under the current rate and temporal methods.

7 Know how a parent accounts for its investment in a subsidiary using the equity method depending on the subsidiary's functional currency determination.

8 Understand consolidation under the temporal and current rate methods.

9 Understand how a hedge of the net investment in a subsidiary is accounted for under the current rate and temporal methods.

If a foreign subsidiary does not keep its records in its parent's currency, then the foreign subsidiary's financial statements must be *translated* or *remeasured* into its parent's currency prior to consolidation of the financial statements. U.S. multinational corporations apply the provisions of ASC Topic 830 "Foreign Currency Matters" to convert the financial statements of their foreign subsidiaries and branches into U.S. dollars. This chapter covers the mechanics of preparing translated and remeasured financial statements as required by GAAP.

OBJECTIVES OF TRANSLATION AND THE FUNCTIONAL CURRENCY CONCEPT

The objectives of translation are to (a) provide "information that is generally compatible with the expected economic effects of a rate change on an enterprise's cash flows and equity" and (b) reflect "in consolidated statements the financial results and relationships of the individual consolidated entities as measured in their *functional currencies* in conformity with U.S. generally accepted accounting principles"[1]. To decipher these objectives, one must first understand the functional currency concept.

LEARNING OBJECTIVE **1**

Functional Currency Concept

An entity's **functional currency** is the currency of the primary economic environment in which it operates. Normally, a foreign entity's functional currency is the currency it receives from its customers and spends to pay its liabilities. GAAP [1] only gives general guidance on determining the functional currency. Rather than a bright line rule, the topic of determining the functional currency is left up to management's judgment. GAAP identifies the following factors management should consider when determining the functional currency of a subsidiary.

1. If *cash flows* related to the foreign entity's assets and liabilities are denominated and settled in the foreign currency rather than parent's currency, then the foreign entity's local currency may be the functional currency.

2. If *sales prices* of the foreign entity's products are determined by local competition or local government regulation, rather than by short-run exchange rate changes or worldwide markets, then the foreign entity's local currency may be the functional currency.

3. A *sales market* that is primarily in the parent company's country, or sales contracts that are normally denominated in the parent's currency, may indicate that the parent's currency is the functional currency.

4. *Expenses* such as labor and materials that are primarily local costs provide some evidence that the foreign entity's local currency is the functional currency.

5. If *financing* is denominated primarily in the foreign entity's local currency and funds generated by its operations are sufficient to service existing and expected debt, then the foreign entity's local currency is likely to be the functional currency.

6. A high volume of *intercompany transactions and arrangements* indicates that the parent's currency may be the functional currency.

In the final analysis, the functional currency is based on management's judgment, including weighing the preceding factors.

Several definitions from ASC Topic 830 are related to the functional currency concept. A **foreign currency** is a currency other than the entity's functional currency. If the functional currency of a German subsidiary is the euro, the U.S. dollar is a foreign currency of the German subsidiary. If the functional currency of the German subsidiary is the U.S. dollar, the euro is a foreign currency to the German subsidiary.

The **local currency** is the currency of the country to which reference is made. Thus, the Canadian dollar is the local currency of a Canadian subsidiary of a U.S. firm. The subsidiary's books and financial statements will be prepared in the local currency in nearly all cases involving foreign currency financial statements, regardless of the determination of the functional currency.

The **reporting currency** is the currency in which the consolidated financial statements are prepared. The reporting currency for the consolidated statements of a U.S. firm with foreign subsidiaries is the U.S. dollar. **Foreign currency statements** are statements prepared in a currency that is *not* the reporting currency (the U.S. dollar) of the U.S. parent-investor.

LEARNING OBJECTIVE **2**

GAAP permits two different methods for converting the foreign subsidiary's financial statements into U.S. dollars, based on the foreign entity's functional currency. If the functional currency is the U.S. dollar, the foreign financial statements are remeasured into U.S. dollars using the **temporal method**. If the functional currency is the local currency of the foreign entity, the foreign financial statements are translated into U.S. dollars using the **current rate method**. A company should select the method that best reflects the nature of its foreign operations.

The designation of a functional currency for a foreign subsidiary is the criterion for choosing which method of foreign currency translation to use—the current rate method or the temporal method. Consolidated financial statement amounts, including net income, differ depending on which of these methods is used.

Recall that the purpose of translation or remeasurement of a foreign subsidiary's financial statements is to convert them to the parent's currency so that consolidation can occur. As a result, one must view the ultimate purpose behind the functional currency choice as being the generation of consolidated financial statements that will reflect the company's underlying economic condition.

Choosing the parent's currency as the functional currency means one should use the temporal method. Selecting this functional currency implies that the resulting consolidated financial statements will reflect the transactions engaged in by the subsidiary as if the parent had engaged in those transactions directly. For example, a company may choose to set up a sales subsidiary in a foreign country for legal or cultural convenience. The parent ships all of the goods to the subsidiary, which sells the goods in the foreign country. The subsidiary then remits the proceeds to the parent. If the foreign currency is remitted to the parent, the parent will report a foreign exchange gain or loss when the currency is converted to dollars. If the subsidiary remits the money to the parent, the final result is the same as if the parent had directly engaged in transactions in the foreign country. The method used to translate the subsidiary's financial statements should result in consolidated financial statements that reflect this underlying similarity. The temporal method is designed to accomplish this. The gain or loss on remeasurement is included in current year consolidated income because the transactions of the subsidiary are assumed to have immediate or almost immediate cash implications for the parent.

In contrast, if the foreign subsidiary functions as a freestanding enterprise that engages in manufacturing and/or providing services within the foreign country, pays for most of its costs in the local currency, receives proceeds from sales and services in the local currency, and rolls these amounts back into the subsidiary operations, economically the subsidiary does not function as a channel for the parent's operations. The functional currency in this case is the subsidiary's local currency, and the current rate method would be used to translate the financial statements.

Presumably, the parent receives most of its cash flow from the subsidiary in the form of dividends. As a result, the impact of exchange rate changes on parent cash flows is limited to the parent's net investment in the subsidiary when distributed. If the parent were to liquidate its entire investment, it would be subject to realized exchange rate gains and losses that would make their way into the income statement. The current rate method measures the effect of exchange rate changes on this net investment. Typically, liquidation is not imminent, so under the current rate method, the effect of changes in the net investment due to exchange rate fluctuations is not included on the income statement, but as part of stockholders' equity, under accumulated other comprehensive income.

APPLICATION OF THE FUNCTIONAL CURRENCY CONCEPT

A foreign subsidiary's foreign currency statements must be in conformity with U.S. generally accepted accounting principles before translation into U.S. dollars. Adjustments to the recorded amounts to convert them to U.S. GAAP are required before translation is performed. All account balances on the balance sheet date denominated in a foreign currency (from the foreign entity's point of view) are adjusted to reflect current exchange rates. For example a French subsidiary must adjust a British-pound-denominated receivable to reflect the pound-to-euro exchange rate on the financial statement date.

Under the objectives of the functional currency concept, a foreign entity's assets, liabilities, and operations must be measured in its functional currency. Subsequently, the foreign entity's balance sheet and income statement are consolidated with those of the parent company in the reporting enterprise's currency.

The accounting procedures required to convert a foreign entity's financial statements into the currency of the parent depend on the foreign subsidiary's functional currency. Because the foreign entity's books are maintained in its local currency, which may be its functional currency or a currency different from the functional currency, the combining or consolidating may require translation, remeasurement, or both.

Translation

When the foreign entity's books are maintained in its functional currency, the statements are *translated* into the reporting entity's currency. **Translation** involves expressing functional currency measurements in the reporting currency.

A basic provision of ASC Topic 830 is that all elements of financial statements, except for stockholders' equity accounts, are translated using a current exchange rate. This is referred to as the *current rate method*. The functional currency is not the parent's; therefore, no direct impact on the reporting entity's cash flows from exchange rate changes is expected. The effects of exchange rate changes are reported as stockholders' equity adjustments in other comprehensive income. The equity adjustments from translation are accumulated in this account until sale or liquidation of the foreign entity investment, at which time they are reported as adjustments of the gain or loss on sale.

Remeasurement

When the foreign entity's books are not maintained in its functional currency, the foreign currency financial statements must be **remeasured** into the functional currency. If the foreign currency financial statements are remeasured into a U.S. dollar functional currency, no translation is necessary because the reporting currency of the parent-investor is the U.S. dollar.

The objective of remeasurement is to produce the same financial statements as if the books had been maintained in the functional currency. To accomplish this objective, both historical and current exchange rates are used in the remeasurement process. Under this method (the *temporal method*), monetary assets and liabilities are remeasured at current exchange rates, and other assets and equities are remeasured at historical rates. **Monetary assets and liabilities** are those in which the amounts to be received or paid are fixed in particular currency units. Examples of monetary assets and liabilities are cash, accounts receivable and accounts payable. The remeasurement produces exchange rate adjustments that are included in income because a direct impact on the enterprise's cash flows is expected.

Translation and Remeasurement of Foreign Currency Financial Statements

Patriot Corporation, a U.S. company, has a wholly owned subsidiary, Regal Corporation, that operates in England. The translation/remeasurement possibilities for the accounts of Regal are as follows:

	Functional Currency	Currency of Accounting Records	Required Procedures for Consolidating or Combining
Case 1	British pounds	British pounds	Translation
Case 2	U.S. dollar	British pounds	Remeasurement
Case 3	Euro	British pounds	Remeasurement and translation

Under Case 1, Regal Corporation keeps its books in its local currency, pounds (£), which is also the functional currency, and no remeasurement is needed. The accounts require translation into U.S. dollars (the currency of the reporting enterprise). GAAP [1] requires translation using the current rate method. The current exchange rate at the balance sheet date is used to translate all assets and liabilities. Theoretically, the exchange rates in effect at each transaction date should be used to translate all revenues, expenses, gains, and losses. As a practical matter, revenues and expenses are generally translated at appropriate weighted average exchange rates for the period. The adjustments from translation are reported in other comprehensive income, as required by GAAP.

In Case 2, Regal's books are maintained in pounds, but the functional currency is the U.S. dollar. Under GAAP, the accounts of Regal are remeasured into the functional currency, the dollar. In this case, no translation is needed because the dollar is also the ultimate reporting currency. The objective of remeasurement is to obtain the results that would have been produced if Regal's books of record had been maintained in the functional currency. Thus, remeasurement requires the use of historical exchange rates for some items and current rates for others and recognition in income of exchange gains and losses from measurement of all monetary assets and liabilities not denominated in the functional currency (the U.S. dollar, in this case).

In Case 3, Regal's books are maintained in pounds although the functional currency is the euro. (This situation could arise if the subsidiary is a holding company for operations in France.) The consolidation requires a remeasurement of all assets, liabilities, revenues, expenses, gains, and losses into euros (the functional currency) and recognition in income of exchange gains and losses from remeasurement of the monetary assets and liabilities not denominated in euros. After the remeasurement is completed and Regal's financial statements are stated in euros, the statements are translated into U.S. dollars using the current rate method. This translation from the functional currency to the currency of the reporting entity will create translation adjustments, but such adjustments are not recognized in current income. Instead, they are reported in other comprehensive income, in stockholders' equity.

Exhibit 14-1 summarizes the exchange rates to be used for remeasurement and translation. Once the functional currency has been determined, it should be "used consistently unless significant changes in economic facts and circumstances" indicate that the functional currency has changed. A change in functional currency is not considered a change in an accounting principle [1].

Intercompany Foreign Currency Transactions

Intercompany transactions are foreign currency transactions if they produce receivable or payable balances denominated in a currency other than the entity's (parent's or subsidiary's) functional currency. Such intercompany foreign currency transactions result in exchange gains and losses that generally are included in income. An exception exists when these transactions produce intercompany balances of a long-term investment nature, when settlement is not expected in the foreseeable future. In these cases the translation adjustments are reported in other comprehensive income as an equity adjustment from translation.

EXHIBIT 14-1

Summary of Exchange Rates Used for Remeasurement and Translation

	Remeasurement to Functional Currency	Translation to Currency of Reporting Entity
Assets		
Cash, demand deposits, and time deposits	Current	Current
Marketable securities carried at cost		
Equity securities	Historical	Current
Debt securities	Historical	Current
Accounts and notes receivable and related unearned discounts	Current	Current
Accounts for uncollectible accounts and notes	Current	Current
Inventories		
Carried at cost	Historical	Current
Carried at lower of cost or market	*	Current
Prepaid insurance, advertising, and rent	Historical	Current
Refundable deposits	Current	Current
Property, plant, and equipment	Historical	Current
Accumulated depreciation on property, plant, and equipment	Historical	Current
Cash surrender value of life insurance	Current	Current
Deferred income tax assets	Current	Current
Patents, trademarks, licenses, and formulas	Historical	Current
Goodwill	Historical	Current
Other intangible assets	Historical	Current
Liabilities		
Accounts and notes payable and overdrafts	Current	Current
Accrued expenses	Current	Current
Deferred income tax liabilities	Current	Current
Deferred income	Historical	Current
Other deferred credits	Historical	Current
Bonds payable and other long-term debt	Current	Current
Stockholders' Equity		
Common stock	Historical	Historical
Preferred stock carried at issuance price	Historical	Historical
Other paid-in capital	Historical	Historical[†]
Retained earnings	Not remeasured	Not translated
Income Statement Items Related to Nonmonetary Items[‡]		
Cost of goods sold	Historical	Current
Depreciation on property, plant, and equipment	Historical	Current
Amortization of intangible items (patents, etc.)	Historical	Current
Amortization of deferred income taxes	Current	Current
Amortization of deferred charges and credits	Historical	Current

*When the books are not maintained in the functional currency and the lower-of-cost-or-market rule is applied to inventories, inventories at cost are remeasured using historical rates. Then the historical cost in the functional currency is compared to market in the functional currency.

[†]Translation at historical rates is necessary for elimination of reciprocal parent investment and subsidiary equity accounts. It should be noted that conversion of all asset, liability, and equity accounts at current exchange rates would obviate the "equity adjustment from translation" component.

[‡]Income statement items related to monetary items are translated or remeasured at weighted average exchange rates to approximate the exchange rates in existence at the time of the related transactions. Intercompany dividends are converted at the rate in effect at the time of payment under both the remeasurement and translation approaches. Translation of income statement items at current rates is implemented by using weighted average exchange rates.

An intercompany transaction requires analysis to see if it is a foreign currency transaction for one, both, or neither of the affiliates. To illustrate, assume that a U.S. parent company borrows $1,600,000 (£1,000,000) from its British subsidiary. The following analysis shows that either the parent or the subsidiary will have a foreign currency transaction if the subsidiary's local currency (the pound) is its functional currency.

	Currency in Which Loan Is Denominated	Functional Currency of Subsidiary	Foreign Currency Transaction of	
			Subsidiary?	Parent?
Case 1	British pound	British pound	No	Yes
Case 2	British pound	U.S. dollar	Yes	Yes
Case 3	U.S. dollar	British pound	Yes	No
Case 4	U.S. dollar	U.S. dollar	No	No

When the U.S. dollar is the functional currency of the subsidiary, either both affiliates have foreign currency transactions, which offset each other (Case 2), or the intercompany transaction is not a foreign currency transaction (Case 4). Only the cases in which the subsidiary's functional currency is its local currency (Cases 1 and 3) have the potential to affect consolidated income. In these cases, translation adjustments will be reported as equity adjustments from translation on the balance sheet if the loan is of a long-term investment nature; otherwise, they will be reported as exchange gains and losses on the income statement.

Foreign Entities Operating in Highly Inflationary Economies

LEARNING OBJECTIVE 3

In a highly inflationary economy, the local currency rapidly loses value, resulting in the escalation of goods and services' prices. Generally, the currency is weakening against other currencies as well. The lack of a stable measuring unit presents special problems for converting foreign currency statements into U.S. dollars.

For example, assume that at the end of year 1, $1 can be exchanged for 50 local currency units (LCU), a $0.02 exchange rate, but at the end of year 2, $1 can be exchanged for 200 LCU, a $0.005 exchange rate. An equity investment of 9,000,000 LCU at the end of year 1 is translated at $180,000 using the current exchange rate, but one year later the same investment of 9,000,000 LCU is translated at $45,000 using the current exchange rate. Under the current rate method, translation gains and losses are accumulated and reported in other comprehensive income. They are not recognized in income until the investment is sold.

The FASB recognized that the current rate method of translation would pose a problem for foreign entities operating in countries with high rates of inflation. Price-level-adjusted financial statements are not basic financial statements under GAAP, so the FASB prescribed a practical alternative. Recall that inflation is a major determinant of exchange rates. In order to reflect the impact of hyperinflation in the consolidated financial statements, the reporting currency (the U.S. dollar) is used to remeasure the financial statements of foreign entities in highly inflationary economies. Exchange gains and losses from remeasuring the financial statements of the foreign entity are recognized in the income for the period, thus reflecting the impact of hyperinflation on the consolidated entity.

GAAP [1] defines a "highly inflationary economy" as one with a cumulative three-year inflation rate of approximately 100 percent or more. Consider a foreign country with inflation data for a three-year period as follows:

	Index	Change in Index	Annual Rate of Inflation
January 1, 2011	120		
January 1, 2012	150	30	30 ÷ 120 (or 25%)
January 1, 2013	210	60	60 ÷ 150 (or 40%)
January 1, 2014	250	40	40 ÷ 210 (or 19%)

The three-year inflation rate is 108.3% [(250 − 120) ÷ 120], *not* 84% (25% + 40% + 19%). The three-year inflation rate in this example exceeds 100 percent, so the usual criteria for identifying the functional currency are ignored and the U.S. dollar (the functional currency of the reporting entity) is the functional currency for purposes of preparing consolidated financial statements.

Business Combinations

LEARNING OBJECTIVE 4

A foreign entity's assets and liabilities are translated into U.S. dollars using the current exchange rate in effect on the date of the business combination.

The identifiable assets and liabilities of the foreign operations are adjusted to their local currency fair values and are translated at the exchange rate in effect on the date of the business combination. Any difference between investment fair value and translated net assets acquired is accounted for as goodwill or as bargain purchase, as required by GAAP.

FAIR VALUE/BOOK VALUE DIFFERENTIAL When the foreign entity's books are maintained in the functional currency, the excess of fair value over book value acquired is assigned to assets, liabilities, and goodwill in local currency units and subsequently is *translated* at current exchange rates under the current rate method.

For example, assume that a 10,000 British-pound excess is allocated to equipment that has a five-year estimated life on January 1, 2011, when the exchange rate is $1.50. If the average exchange rate for 2011 is $1.45 and the year-end exchange rate is $1.40, depreciation on the excess for 2011 will be $2,900 (£2,000 × $1.45), and the undepreciated balance at December 31 will be $11,200 (£8,000 × $1.40). The unrealized translation loss of $900 [$15,000 − ($2,900 + $11,200)] will be recorded in comprehensive income as an equity adjustment from translation.

When the foreign entity's books are not maintained in the functional currency, *remeasurement* is required and the excess allocated to equipment is amortized at the historical exchange rate in effect at the time of the business combination. Thus, the depreciation expense would be $3,000 (£2,000 × $1.50), and the undepreciated balance would be $12,000 (£8,000 × $1.50).

NONCONTROLLING INTEREST The computation of the amount of a noncontrolling interest in a foreign subsidiary must be based on the translated or remeasured financial statements of the subsidiary adjusted for fair value/book value differences. Similarly, the financial statements of a foreign investee must be translated or remeasured before the equity method of accounting is applied.

ILLUSTRATION: TRANSLATION

Background Information

Pat Corporation, a U.S. firm, paid $525,000 cash to acquire all the stock of the British firm Star Company when the book value of Star's net assets was equal to fair value. This business combination was consummated on December 31, 2011, when the exchange rate for British pounds was $1.50. Star's assets and equities at acquisition on December 31, 2011, were as follows:

	British Pounds	Exchange Rate	U.S. Dollars
Assets			
Cash	£140,000	$1.50	$210,000
Accounts receivable	40,000	1.50	60,000
Inventories (cost)	120,000	1.50	180,000
Plant assets	100,000	1.50	150,000
Less: Accumulated depreciation	(20,000)	1.50	(30,000)
Total assets	£380,000		$570,000
Equities			
Accounts payable	£ 30,000	$1.50	$ 45,000
Bonds payable	100,000	1.50	150,000
Capital stock	200,000	1.50	300,000
Retained earnings	50,000	1.50	75,000
Total equities	£380,000		$570,000

During 2012, the British pound weakened against the U.S. dollar, resulting in a year-end current exchange rate of $1.40. Average exchange rates for 2012 were $1.45. Star paid £30,000 dividends on December 1, 2012, when the exchange rate was $1.42 (U.S.) per British pound.

Intercompany Transaction

The only intercompany transaction between the firms was an $84,000 (£56,000) non-interest-bearing advance by Star to Pat that was made on January 4, 2012, when the exchange rate was still $1.50. The advance is denominated in U.S. dollars. Under the assumption that Star's functional currency is determined to be the British pound, the advance to Pat is a foreign currency transaction from Star's perspective but not to Pat because it is denominated in dollars.

Star adjusts its Advance to Pat account at year-end 2012 to reflect the $1.40 current exchange rate. Star records an exchange gain because there is no evidence that the advance is of a long-term investment nature. The entry on Star's books is as follows:

Advance to Pat (+A)	£4,000	
Exchange gain (+Ga, +SE)		£4,000
To adjust receivable denominated in dollars		
[($84,000/$1.40) − £56,000 per books].		

Star's adjusted trial balance at December 31, 2012, reflects the advance to Pat, £60,000, and the exchange gain, £4,000.

LEARNING OBJECTIVE **5**

Translating the Foreign Subsidiary's Adjusted Trial Balance

Pat translates Star's adjusted trial balance at December 31, 2012, into U.S. dollars before it accounts for its investment under the equity method and consolidates its financial statements with those of Star. The translation of Star's accounts into U.S. dollars is shown in Exhibit 14-2, which illustrates translation working paper procedures.

The *current rate method* is required for foreign subsidiaries whose functional currency is not the parent's reporting currency, here the U.S. dollar. All assets and liabilities are translated at the balance sheet dates' exchange rates. All income statement items are translated at accounting-period average exchange rates. Average rates are applied to approximate the current exchange rates in effect when the revenue and expense transactions occurred during the period. The exchange rates in effect when dividends are paid are used to translate the foreign subsidiary's dividends.

The subsidiary's stockholders' equity accounts are not translated at current exchange rates. Capital stock and other paid-in capital accounts are translated at the exchange rate in effect when the subsidiary was acquired. The retained earnings ending balance is not translated after acquisition. The retained earnings account balance consists of retained earnings at acquisition, plus income, less dividends after acquisition, all in translated dollar amounts. In years subsequent to the year of acquisition, translated beginning retained earnings of one period is simply the prior year's ending translated retained earnings from the financial statements.

EXHIBIT 14-2

Translation of Foreign Subsidiary Accounts into U.S. Dollars

STAR COMPANY LTD. TRANSLATION WORKSHEET FOR 2012 (BRITISH POUNDS FUNCTIONAL CURRENCY)

	Trial Balance	Translation Rate	Trial Balance
Debits			
Cash	£110,000	$1.40	$ 154,000
Accounts receivable	80,000	1.40	112,000
Inventories (FIFO)	120,000	1.40	168,000
Plant assets	100,000	1.40	140,000
Advance to Pat	60,000	1.40	84,000
Cost of sales	270,000	1.45	391,500
Depreciation	10,000	1.45	14,500
Wages and salaries	120,000	1.45	174,000
Other expenses	60,000	1.45	87,000
Dividends	30,000	1.42	42,600
Accumulated other comprehensive income			28,600
	£960,000		$1,396,200
Credits			
Accumulated depreciation	£ 30,000	$1.40	$ 42,000
Accounts payable	36,000	1.40	50,400
Bonds payable	100,000	1.40	140,000
Capital stock	200,000	1.50	300,000
Retained earnings	50,000	Computed	75,000
Sales	540,000	1.45	783,000
Exchange gain (advance)	4,000	1.45	5,800
	£960,000		$1,396,200

After all financial statement items have been translated into dollars, the trial balance debits and credits are totaled and the amount needed to balance debits and credits is entered as an equity adjustment from translation and is included in other comprehensive income. For example, the $28,600 equity adjustment on translation in Exhibit 14-2 is measured by subtracting the $1,367,600 debits from the $1,396,200 credits in the U.S. dollar column. The resulting subsidiary reporting currency financial statements are illustrated in Exhibit 14-3 for Star Company.

Equity Method of Accounting

LEARNING OBJECTIVE **7**

Pat records the investment in Star at its $525,000 fair value on December 31, 2011, in order to track the total value of their investment in Star prior to the consolidation process. Pat subsequently uses the equity method to account for its foreign subsidiary. Star's translated financial statements are used by Pat when applying the equity method. The entry to record receipt of the £30,000, or $42,600, dividend from Star on December 1, 2012, follows:

Cash (+A)	$42,600	
Investment in Star (−A)		$42,600

Pat received this dividend when the exchange rate was $1.42, so the dividends paid by Star also have to be translated into dollars at the current exchange rate in effect when the dividends were paid, $1.42 (see Exhibit 14-2).

EXHIBIT 14-3

Translated Financial Statements—British Pounds Functional Currency

STAR COMPANY LTD.
INCOME AND RETAINED EARNINGS STATEMENTS
FOR THE YEAR ENDED DECEMBER 31, 2012
(IN U.S. DOLLARS)

Sales		$783,000
Less costs and expenses		
Cost of sales	$391,500	
Depreciation	14,500	
Wages and salaries	174,000	
Other expenses	87,000	
Total costs and expenses		667,000
Operating income		116,000
Exchange gain		5,800
Net income		121,800
Retained earnings January 1		75,000
		196,800
Less: Dividends		42,600
Retained earnings December 31, 2012		$154,200

STAR COMPANY LTD. BALANCE SHEET
AT DECEMBER 31, 2012
(IN U.S. DOLLARS)

Assets	
Cash	$154,000
Accounts receivable	112,000
Inventories	168,000
Plant assets	140,000
Less: Accumulated depreciation	(42,000)
Advance to Pat	84,000
	$616,000
Equities	
Accounts payable	$ 50,400
Bonds payable	140,000
Capital stock	300,000
Retained earnings	154,200
Accumulated other comprehensive income	(28,600)
	$616,000

Pat recognizes its equity in Star's income from 2012 in an entry that also recognizes Star's unrecognized loss on translation. The entry for 2012 is as follows:

Investment in Star (+A)	$93,200	
Other comprehensive income: equity adjustment		
on translation (−SE)	28,600	
Income from Star (R, +SE)		$121,800

This entry recognizes 100 percent of Star's 2012 net income in dollars, as investment income, and it also includes the $28,600 loss from translation on Pat's books in other comprehensive income. The reported income of $121,800 less the $28,600 loss on translation equals the $93,200 investment increase from Star's operations.

ILLUSTRATION OF AMORTIZATION WHEN EXCESS OF FAIR VALUE OVER BOOK VALUE IS ALLOCATED TO IDENTIFIABLE ASSETS AND LIABILITIES: PATENT AMORTIZATION

Pat paid $525,000 for its investment in Star. However, Star's book value and the fair value of its recorded net assets acquired were equal to $375,000. The $150,000 excess of cost over net asset book value is all allocable to a patent that has no book value on Star's books because it was internally developed with negligible legal costs. Under the current rate method, the patent-related calculations are based on local currency units (British pounds), rather than U.S. dollar amounts. The first step to calculate patent amortization for Pat's investment in Star is to convert the $150,000 allocated to the patent at acquisition into its pound equivalent. Because the exchange rate at December 31, 2011, the acquisition date, is $1.50, the pound equivalent of $150,000 is £100,000.

The 2012 amortization of the excess on Pat's books is £100,000 ÷ 10 years × $1.45 average exchange rate for 2012, or $14,500. Patent amortization for 2012 is recorded on Pat's books as follows:

Income from Star (−R, −SE)	$14,500	
Other comprehensive income:		
Equity adjustment from translation (−SE)	9,500	
Investment in Star (−A)		$24,000

The equity adjustment on translation of a patent that appears in the entry is the result of changes in exchange rates during 2012, and the $24,000 credit to the investment in Star reflects the decrease in unamortized patent during the year, $150,000 − (£90,000 × $1.40). These relationships are summarized as follows:

	In Pounds	Exchange Rate	In Dollars
Beginning patent	£100,000	$1.50	$150,000
Less: Amortization	10,000	1.45	14,500
	90,000		135,500
Equity adjustment	—		9,500
Ending patent	£ 90,000	1.40	$126,000

Alternatively, the $9,500 equity adjustment can be computed as follows:

£10,000 amortization × ($1.45 − $1.50) exchange rate decline to midyear	$ 500
£90,000 unamortized patent × ($1.40 − $1.50) exchange rate decline for the year	9,000
Equity adjustment	$9,500

Notice that this equity adjustment is *only* recorded on Pat's books because the patent is not recorded on Star's books.

Similar adjustments are required when an excess of fair value over book value is allocated to other identifiable assets and liabilities and the current rate method is used.

INVESTMENT IN FOREIGN SUBSIDIARY At this point, it may be helpful to summarize the changes in Pat's Investment in Star account during 2012:

Investment cost December 31, 2011	$525,000
Less: Dividends received 2012	(42,600)
Add: Equity in Star's net income	121,800
Less: Unrealized loss on translation	(28,600)
Less: Patent amortization	(14,500)
Less: Unrealized translation loss on patent	(9,500)
Investment balance December 31, 2012	$551,600

Consolidation

LEARNING OBJECTIVE **6, 8**

Exhibit 14-4 contains the financial statement consolidation worksheet for Pat Corporation and Star Company for the year ended December 31, 2012. Pat reports income from Star of $107,300. This is its share of Star's reported income ($121,800) less the amortization of the unrecorded patent, $14,500. The Investment in Star account balance of $551,600 agrees with the reconciliation presented above. Pat also has a $38,100 equity adjustment balance that equals Star's equity adjustment of $28,600, recorded by Pat when it applied the equity method to account for its investment in Star and also included in Star's translated financial statements. The remaining $9,500 equity adjustment is related to the unrecorded patent, which was only recorded by Pat.

The procedures to consolidate a foreign subsidiary are basically the same as the procedures needed to consolidate a domestic subsidiary. The sequence of working paper entries is the same also. Working paper entry a in Exhibit 14-4 is as follows:

a	Income from Star (−R, −SE)	$107,300	
	Dividends (+SE)		$42,600
	Investment in Star (−A)		64,700

Entry b eliminates reciprocal equity and investment balances at beginning-of-the-period amount and enters the beginning-of-the-period patent balance.

Entry c adjusts the Investment in Star account for unrealized translation losses, eliminates the unrealized translation loss for the patent, and eliminates Star's remaining stockholders' equity account—the equity adjustment from translation account:

b	Retained earnings—Star (−SE)	$ 75,000	
	Capital stock—Star (−SE)	300,000	
	Patent (+A)	150,000	
	Investment in Star (−A)		$525,000
c	Investment in Star (+A)	$ 38,100	
	Patent (−A)		$ 9,500
	Other comprehensive income: equity adjustment from translation—Star (+SE)		28,600

Working paper entry d in Exhibit 14-4 enters the current patent-amortization expense (£10,000 × $1.45 average exchange rate) and reduces the patent to $126,000, the unamortized amount at year-end (£90,000 × $1.40 exchange rate).

The final working paper entry eliminates the reciprocal balances of advance to Pat and advance from Star.

Under the current rate method, the change in the accumulated other comprehensive income account from the beginning to the end of the year represents the change in the dollar amount of the investment in the net assets of the company during the year due to exchange rate changes. The balance in the accumulated other comprehensive income account that represents the amount needed to balance the subsidiary's translated worksheet is the beginning AOCI plus the change in that account resulting from exchange rate changes during the year.

EXHIBIT 14-4

Working Papers Under
the British Pound
Functional Currency
Assumption

PAT CORPORATION AND SUBSIDIARY CONSOLIDATION WORKING PAPERS TRANSLATION—FUNCTIONAL CURRENCY BRITISH POUND FOR THE YEAR ENDED DECEMBER 31, 2012

	Pat	Star	Adjustments and Eliminations Debits	Credits	Consolidated Statements
Income Statement Sales	$1,218,300	$783,000			$2,001,300
Income from Star	107,300		a 107,300		
Cost of sales	(600,000)	(391,500)			(991,500)
Depreciation	(40,000)	(14,500)			(54,500)
Wages and salaries	(300,000)	(174,000)			(474,000)
Other expenses	(150,000)	(87,000)	d 14,500		(251,500)
Exchange gain		5,800			5,800
Net income	**$ 235,600**	**$121,800**			**$ 235,600**
Retained Earnings Retained earnings—Pat	$ 245,500				$ 245,500
Retained earnings—Star		$ 75,000	b 75,000		
Net income	**235,600**	**121,800**			**235,600**
Dividends	(100,000)	(42,600)		a 42,600	(100,000)
Retained earnings— December 31, 2012	**$ 381,100**	**$154,200**			**$ 381,100**
Balance Sheet Cash	$ 317,600	$154,000			$ 471,600
Accounts receivable	150,000	112,000			262,000
Inventories	300,000	168,000			468,000
Plant assets	400,000	140,000			540,000
Accumulated depreciation	(100,000)	(42,000)			(142,000)
Advance to Pat		84,000		e 84,000	
Investment in Star	551,600		c 38,100	a 64,700 b 525,000	
Patent			b 150,000	c 9,500 d 14,500	126,000
	$1,619,200	$616,000			$1,725,600
Accounts payable	$ 142,200	$ 50,400			$ 192,600
Advance from Star	84,000		e 84,000		
Bonds payable	250,000	140,000			390,000
Capital stock	800,000	300,000	b 300,000		800,000
Retained earnings	**381,100**	**154,200**			**381,100**
Accumulated other comprehensive income	(38,100)	(28,600)		c 28,600	(38,100)
	$1,619,200	$616,000			$1,725,600

To gain a better understanding of what the change in the accumulated other comprehensive income account balance represents, the change is computed directly for Star:

Star's beginning accumulated other comprehensive income-translation Loss	$ 0
Increase in AOCI—translation loss	$28,600
Ending AOCI—translation loss	$28,600

The impact of exchange rate changes on the book value of Star's net assets is shown here:

		Change in Exchange Rate	
Book value of beginning net assets	£250,000	−0.10 ($1.40 − $1.50)	($25,000)
Net income	£ 84,000	−0.05 ($1.40 − $1.45)	(4,200)
−Dividends	£−30,000	−0.02 ($1.40 − $1.42)	+600
Effect of exchange rate changes on net assets			($28,600)

On a consolidated basis, the change in the AOCI account is a loss of $38,100; the $9,500 loss in excess of the $28,600 computed here is due to changes in the value of the unamortized patent account during the year. The patent is not recorded on Star's books, but here it is a part of the Investment in Star account according to Pat's books.

The computation of the change in the AOCI provides insight into the nature of the loss and why it is included in other comprehensive income instead of being reflected immediately in income. Because the functional currency of the subsidiary is the local currency, the parent will realize a loss due to exchange rate changes when the earnings of the subsidiary are distributed to the parent or when the parent liquidates its investment in the company. The latter occurrence is not an immediate probability, so the gain or loss on translation is not included in current income but is reflected directly in the stockholders' equity section and in the statement of comprehensive income.

ILLUSTRATION: REMEASUREMENT

When the functional currency of a foreign entity is the U.S. dollar, the foreign entity's accounts are *remeasured* into its U.S. dollar functional currency, and the net exchange gains or losses that result from the remeasurement are recognized in current income. The objective of remeasurement is to produce the same results as if the books had been maintained in the U.S. dollar.

To enable you to compare the remeasurement (temporal method) and translation (current rate method) procedures, remeasurement procedures are applied to the Pat–Star example, assuming that Star's functional currency is the U.S. dollar and its books of record are maintained in British pounds.

Star's assets, liabilities, and stockholders' equity at acquisition on December 31, 2011, are all remeasured using the $1.50 exchange rate in effect on that date. The remeasurement at acquisition is exactly the same as translation at acquisition. The $525,000 investment cost to Pat over the $375,000 net assets acquired in Star results in $150,000 assigned to the patent. Unlike translation, under remeasurement procedures, the patent's value is not adjusted for subsequent changes in exchange rates. As a result, annual patent amortization over the 10-year period is $15,000.

The £56,000 ($84,000) advance to Pat is not a foreign currency transaction of either Pat or Star because the advance is denominated in dollars and the functional currency of both Pat and Star is the U.S. dollar. As a result, Star does not adjust its advance to Pat to reflect the £60,000 equivalent and does not report a £4,000 exchange gain. Instead, the £56,000 advance to Pat is remeasured at its $84,000 reciprocal amount on Pat's books. Exhibit 14-5 is a remeasurement worksheet for Star Company for 2012. Except for the advance to Pat and the resulting $5,800 exchange gain under translation, Star's December 31, 2012, trial balance in British pounds is the same as the one shown under the British-pound functional currency assumption in Exhibit 14-2.

Remeasurement of
Foreign Subsidiary
Accounts into U.S.
Dollars

STAR COMPANY LTD. REMEASUREMENT WORKSHEET FOR 2012 (U.S. DOLLAR FUNCTIONAL CURRENCY)

	Trial Balance in British Pounds	Exchange Rate		Trial Balance in U.S. Dollars
Debits				
Cash	£110,000	C	$1.40	$ 154,000
Accounts receivable	80,000	C	1.40	112,000
Inventories (FIFO)	120,000	H	1.42	170,400
Plant assets	100,000	H	1.50	150,000
Advance to Pat	56,000*	R		84,000
Cost of sales	270,000	H		401,100
Depreciation	10,000	H	1.50	15,000
Wages and salaries	120,000	A†	1.45	174,000
Other expenses	60,000	A†	1.45	87,000
Dividends	30,000	R		42,600
Exchange loss				3,300
	£956,000			$1,393,400
Credits				
Accumulated depreciation	£ 30,000	H	$1.50	45,000
Accounts payable	36,000	C	1.40	50,400
Bonds payable	100,000	C	1.40	140,000
Capital stock	200,000	H	1.50	300,000
Retained earnings	50,000	Computed		75,000
Sales	540,000	A	1.45	783,000
	£956,000			$1,393,400

A, average exchange rate; C, current exchange rate; H, historical exchange rate; R, reciprocal of U.S. dollar amounts.
*A translation gain might need to be reported under British GAAP to the British government. However, no gain or loss is reported under U.S. GAAP, and the reciprocal rate is used.
†Assumed to be paid in cash during 2012.

Except for the intercompany advance, all of Star's monetary items are remeasured at current exchange rates. These monetary items include cash, accounts receivable, accounts payable, and bonds payable. The remeasurement produces the same amounts as translation under the current rate method. The advance to Pat and the dividends paid are translated at the dollar amounts that Pat recorded on its own books.

The cost of sales and inventory remeasurements shown in the worksheet assume first-in, first-out procedures and acquisition of the ending inventory items on December 1, 2012, when the exchange rate was $1.42. Historical exchange rates are used in the computations as follows:

	Pounds	Exchange Rate	Dollars
Inventory December 31, 2011	£120,000	$1.50 H	$180,000
Purchases 2012	270,000	1.45 A	391,500
	390,000		571,500
Inventory December 31, 2012	(120,000)	1.42 H	(170,400)
Cost of sales	£270,000		$401,100

All of Star's plant assets were owned by Star when it became a subsidiary of Pat. Therefore, the plant assets, as well as the related depreciation expense and accumulated depreciation, are remeasured at the $1.50 exchange rate in effect at December 31, 2011. If Star had acquired additional plant assets during 2012, the additions and related depreciation would be remeasured at the exchange rates in effect when the additional assets were acquired.

Under GAAP [1], expenses are remeasured at average rates during the period if they relate to monetary items (cash, receivables, and payables), and at historical exchange rates if they relate to nonmonetary items (such as plant assets, deferred charges, or intangibles). The wages and salaries and other expense items in Exhibit 14-5 are remeasured at average exchange rates, assuming they are related to monetary items. When a single expense account includes amounts related to both monetary and nonmonetary items, the remeasurement involves more computations than application of a single average rate. The same reasoning applies to the remeasurement of sales, even though it would be rather unusual for sales to relate to nonmonetary items.

Capital stock and other paid-in capital items are remeasured at historical exchange rates. No difference exists between the amounts that result from remeasurement and translation for these items. As explained earlier, the retained earnings balance is computed but not remeasured or translated. (Ending retained earnings is equal to beginning retained earnings plus remeasured income less remeasured dividends.)

After all items in the remeasurement worksheet, other than the exchange loss, are remeasured into the U.S. dollar functional currency, the trial balance debits and credits are totaled and the difference between debits and credits is determined. If the credits are greater, the difference is entered in the remeasurement working papers as the exchange loss for the period. Thus, the $3,300 exchange loss in Exhibit 14-5 is computed by subtracting $1,390,100 debits, excluding the exchange loss, from $1,393,400 total credits.

ASC Topic 830 requires exchange gains and losses on remeasurement to be recognized in income. Exchange gains and losses on remeasurement and those arising from foreign currency transactions are combined for external reporting purposes. Separate disclosure of transaction and remeasurement gains and losses is provided in financial statement notes.

The Equity Method and Consolidation

LEARNING OBJECTIVE 7,8

Similar to the translation example, Pat tracks the value of the investment account using the equity method prior to the consolidation of the remeasured statements. All remeasurement gains and losses are recognized in current income. The entries on Pat's books to account for its investment in Star are as follows:

Investment in Star (+A)	$525,000	
Cash (−A)		$525,000
To record acquisition on December 31, 2011.		
Cash (+A)	$ 42,600	
Investment in Star (−A)		$ 42,600
To record dividends received on December 1, 2012.		
Investment in Star (+A)	$ 87,600	
Income from Star (R, +SE)		$ 87,600
To record investment income for 2012 equal to Star's $102,600 net income less $15,000 patent amortization.		

Pat's Investment in Star account at December 31, 2012, has a balance of $570,000 and is equal to Star's $435,000 net assets on that date plus $135,000 unamortized patent. These amounts are shown in the consolidation working papers of Exhibit 14-6.

The consolidation worksheet entries under remeasurement are listed here in journal entry form:

a	Income from Star (−R, −SE)	$87,600	
	Dividends (+SE)		$42,600
	Investment in Star (−A)		45,000
b	Capital stock—Star (−SE)	300,000	
	Retained earnings—Star (−SE)	75,000	
	Patent (+A)	150,000	
	Investment in Star (−A)		525,000
c	Other expenses (+E, −SE)	15,000	
	Patent (−A)		15,000
d	Advance from Star (−L)	84,000	
	Advance to Pat (−A)		84,000

EXHIBIT 14-6

Working Papers
Under the U.S. Dollar
Functional Currency
Assumption

PAT CORPORATION AND SUBSIDIARY CONSOLIDATION WORKING PAPERS REMEASUREMENT—FUNCTIONAL CURRENCY U.S. DOLLAR FOR THE YEAR ENDED DECEMBER 31, 2012

	Pat	Star	Adjustments and Eliminations Debits	Adjustments and Eliminations Credits	Consolidated Statements
Income Statement Sales	$1,218,300	$783,000			$2,001,300
Income from Star	87,600		a 87,600		
Cost of sales	(600,000)	(401,100)			(1,001,100)
Depreciation	(40,000)	(15,000)			(55,000)
Wages and salaries	(300,000)	(174,000)			(474,000)
Other expenses	(150,000)	(87,000)	c 15,000		(252,000)
Exchange loss		(3,300)			(3,300)
Net income	**$ 215,900**	**$102,600**			**$ 215,900**
Retained Earnings Retained earnings—Pat	$ 245,500				$ 245,500
Retained earnings—Star		$ 75,000	b 75,000		
Net income	**215,900**	**102,600**			**215,900**
Dividends	(100,000)	(42,600)		a 42,600	(100,000)
Retained earnings— December 31, 2012	**$ 361,400**	**$135,000**			**$ 361,400**
Balance Sheet Cash	$ 317,600	$154,000			$ 471,600
Accounts receivable	150,000	112,000			262,000
Inventories	300,000	170,400			470,400
Plant assets	400,000	150,000			550,000
Accumulated depreciation	(100,000)	(45,000)			(145,000)
Advance to Pat		84,000		d 84,000	
Investment in Star	570,000			a 45,000 b 525,000	
Patent			b 150,000	c 15,000	135,000
Total assets	$1,637,600	$625,400			$1,744,000
Accounts payable	$ 142,200	$ 50,400			$ 192,600
Advance from Star	84,000		d 84,000		
Bonds payable	250,000	140,000			390,000
Capital stock	800,000	300,000	b 300,000		800,000
Retained earnings	**361,400**	**135,000**			**361,400**
Total equities	$1,637,600	$625,400			$1,744,000

Consolidation of a foreign subsidiary with a U.S. dollar functional currency is essentially the same as for a domestic subsidiary, once the foreign entity's financial statements have been remeasured in U.S. dollars. Although the remeasurement process is more complex than translation, the consolidation process is less complex because remeasurement does not produce unrealized translation gains and losses or equity adjustments from translation.

In a manner similar to the translation proof illustrated earlier, the gain or loss on remeasurement can also be computed directly. However, as one might expect given the complexity of the remeasurement procedure, the proof is more complicated than under the current rate method. All monetary assets and liabilities are remeasured using the year-end current exchange rate, whereas all non-monetary assets and liabilities are remeasured using the historical exchange rate.

As previously disclosed on page 469, Star's December 31, 2011, net monetary assets in pounds were cash, 140,000; accounts receivable, 40,000; accounts payable, 30,000; and bonds payable, 100,000. Thus, a beginning net monetary asset (Monetary assets − Monetary liabilities) exists equal to 180,000 pounds − 130,000 pounds, or 50,000 pounds.

		Change in Exchange rate	
Beginning net monetary asset position	£ 50,000	$1.40 − $1.50	($5,000)
Sales (increases cash or accounts receivable during the year)	£540,000	$1.40 − $1.45	(27,000)
Purchases (decreases cash or accounts receivable or increases accounts payable)	£270,000	$1.40 − $1.45	13,500
Wages and salaries (assumed to be in cash)	£120,000	$1.40 − $1.45	6,000
Other expenses (assumed to be in cash)	£ 60,000	$1.40 − $1.45	3,000
Advance to Pat	£ 56,000	$1.40 − $1.50	5,600
Dividends	£ 30,000	$1.40 − $1.42	600
Total exchange loss			$(3,300)

The exchange loss results from the effect of exchange rate changes on the monetary position of the firm during the year.

Translation and Remeasurement Differences in Consolidated Statements

The consolidated financial statements of Pat Corporation and Subsidiary under the translation (current rate) and remeasurement (temporal) procedures are presented in comparative form in Exhibit 14-7.

DISCLOSURE FOR CHANGES IN TRANSLATION ADJUSTMENTS The Pat–Star illustration involves consolidation in the year of acquisition, so the impact of translation and remeasurement differences is relatively small. For many firms it can be substantial, however. For example, Ford reported a pre-tax $1,780 million gain, a $5,576 million loss, and a $2,236 gain in 2007, 2008 and 2009, respectively.

HEDGING A NET INVESTMENT IN A FOREIGN ENTITY

LEARNING OBJECTIVE **9**

U.S. firms with foreign investees may enter into forward exchange contracts or other foreign currency transactions to offset the effects of foreign currency fluctuations on their net investments in the foreign investee. Gains and losses that arise from foreign currency transactions designated as, and effective as, economic hedges of a net investment in a foreign entity are recorded as translation adjustments of stockholders' equity.

Classification as a **translation adjustment** means that these transaction gains and losses are included in comprehensive income [2] and are excluded from the determination of net income. This treatment is necessary because translation of the financial statements of a foreign subsidiary *with a functional currency other than the U.S. dollar* also produces translation adjustments, which are included in comprehensive income, rather than deductions or credits to net income. Thus, the adjustment from hedging a net investment in a foreign entity offsets the adjustment from translating the foreign investees' financial statements into U.S. dollars.

Procedures to hedge a net investment in a foreign entity are not applicable to investees with a U.S. dollar functional currency. Hedges of these investments are accounted for as speculations. Gains and losses from remeasuring foreign-investee financial statements into U.S. dollars are included in net income for the period if the U.S. dollar is the investee's functional currency. Therefore, the gains and losses resulting from the hedge of the net investment must be included in net income for the period. This means that the gain or loss on the hedge will offset the recognized gain or loss from the remeasurement.

EXHIBIT 14-7

Comparative
Consolidated Financial
Statements

PAT CORPORATION AND BRITISH SUBSIDIARY
CONSOLIDATED INCOME AND RETAINED EARNINGS STATEMENTS
FOR THE YEAR ENDED DECEMBER 31, 2012

	Translation (Current Rate Method)	Remeasurement (Temporal Method)
Sales	$2,001,300	$2,001,300
Less: Costs and expenses		
Cost of sales	991,500	1,001,100
Wages and salaries	474,000	474,000
Other expenses	237,000	237,000
Depreciation	54,500	55,000
Patent amortization	14,500	15,000
Total costs and expenses	1,771,500	1,782,100
Operating income	229,800	219,200
Exchange gain (loss)	5,800	(3,300)
Net income	235,600	215,900
Retained earnings January 1, 2012	245,500	245,500
	481,100	461,400
Less: Dividends	100,000	100,000
Retained earnings December 31, 2012	$ 381,100	$ 361,400

PAT CORPORATION AND BRITISH SUBSIDIARY
CONSOLIDATED BALANCE SHEETS AT DECEMBER 31, 2012

	Translation (Current Rate Method)	Remeasurement (Temporal Method)
Assets		
Cash	$ 471,600	$ 471,600
Accounts receivable	262,000	262,000
Inventories	468,000	470,400
Plant assets	540,000	550,000
Less: Accumulated depreciation	(142,000)	(145,000)
Patent	126,000	135,000
Total assets	$1,725,600	$1,744,000
Liabilities		
Accounts payable	$ 192,600	$ 192,600
Bonds payable	390,000	390,000
Total liabilities	582,600	582,600
Stockholders' Equity		
Capital stock	800,000	800,000
Retained earnings	381,100	361,400
Other comprehensive income: equity adjustment on translation	(38,100)	
Total stockholders' equity	1,143,000	1,161,400
Total liabilities and stockholders' equity	$1,725,600	$1,744,000

Illustration

To illustrate the hedge of a net investment of a foreign entity, assume that Pin, a U.S. company, has a 100 percent equity investment in a British company, Ben, acquired at book value equal to fair value. Ben's functional currency is the British pound. An investee's assets and liabilities hedge each other, so only the net assets are exposed to the risk of exchange rate fluctuations.

To hedge the foreign currency exposure, the translation adjustment from the hedging transaction must move in a direction opposite to the translation adjustment from the net assets of the investee. Thus, Pin borrows British pounds to hedge the equity investment. Any translation losses on the equity investment will be fully or partially offset by the translation gains on the loan, and vice versa.

The balance in Pin's Investment in Ben account at December 31, 2011, is $1,280,000, 100 percent of Ben's £800,000 times a $1.60 year-end current exchange rate. On this date, Pin has no translation adjustment balance relative to its investment in Ben. In order to hedge its net investment in Ben, Pin borrows £800,000 for one year at 12 percent interest on January 1, 2012, at a spot rate of $1.60. The loan is denominated in pounds, with principal and interest payable on January 1, 2013. Pin records its loan as follows:

January 1, 2012

Cash (+A)	$1,280,000	
Loan payable (fc) (+L)		$1,280,000
To record loan denominated in British pounds		
(£800,000 × $1.60 spot rate).		

On November 1, 2012, Ben declares and pays a £40,000 dividend. Pin records receipt of the dividend at the $1.75 spot rate on this date.

November 1, 2012

Cash (+A)	$70,000	
Investment in Ben (−A)		$70,000
To record receipt of dividends from Ben		
(£40,000 × $1.75 spot rate).		

For 2012, Ben reports net income of £160,000. The weighted average exchange rate for translation of Ben's revenue and expense items for the year is $1.70, and the current exchange rate at December 31, 2012, is $1.80. These changes in Ben's net assets are included in the following summary:

	British Pounds		U.S. Dollars
Net assets on January 1, 2012	£800,000	× $1.60	$1,280,000
Add: Net income for 2012	160,000	× $1.70	272,000
Less: Dividends	(40,000)	× $1.75	(70,000)
Equity adjustment—change			174,000
Net assets on December 31, 2012	£920,000	× $1.80	$1,656,000

Pin makes the following entry at December 31, 2012, to record its share of Ben's income:

December 31, 2012

Investment in Ben (+A)	$446,000	
Income from Ben (R, +SE)		$ 272,000
Other comprehensive income (+SE)		174,000
To record 100% share of Ben's income (£160,000 ×		
$1.70 weighted average exchange rate) and to record		
100% share of translation adjustment.		

Also, Pin adjusts the loan payable and the equity investment to the current rate at December 31, 2012, and accrues interest on the loan:

Other comprehensive income (−SE)	$160,000	
Loan payable (fc) (+L)		$160,000
To adjust loan payable denominated in British pounds to		
the current rate at year-end [£800,000 × ($1.80 − $1.60)].		
Interest expense (+E, −SE)	$163,200	
Exchange loss (+Lo, −SE)	9,600	
Interest payable (fc) (+L)		$172,800
To record interest expense (at weighted average exchange		
rates) and accrue interest payable denominated in pounds		
at the year-end current rate as follows:		
Interest payable (£800,000 × 12% interest × 1 year ×		
$1.80 current exchange rate)		$172,800
Less: Interest expense (£800,000 × 12% interest × 1 year ×		
1.70 weighted average exchange rate)		163,200
Exchange loss		$ 9,600

On January 1, 2013, Pin pays the loan and interest at the $1.80 spot rate as follows:

January 1, 2013

Interest payable (fc) (−L)	$ 172,800	
Loan payable (fc) (−L)	1,440,000	
Cash (−A)		$1,612,800

    To record payment of loan and interest denominated in
      British pounds when the spot rate is $1.80.

As a result of the hedging operation, the changes in Pin's investment in Ben that were due to changing exchange rates were partially offset by its loan in British pounds. The equity adjustment from translation balance that appears in the stockholders' equity section of Pin's December 31, 2012, balance sheet is a $14,000 credit ($174,000 credit from the equity investment from translation, less $160,000 debit from adjustment of the loan denominated in British pounds).

Limit on Gain or Loss from Translation Adjustment

The gain or loss on an after-tax basis from the hedging operations that can be considered a translation adjustment is limited in amount to the *current* translation adjustment from the equity investment [1].

SUMMARY

Before the results of foreign operations can be included in the financial statements of U.S. corporations, they have to be converted into U.S. dollars using procedures specified in ASC Topic 830 that are based on the foreign entity's functional currency.

    If the U.S. dollar is determined to be the functional currency, the foreign entity's financial statements are remeasured into U.S. dollar financial statements using the temporal method, and the resulting exchange gain or loss is included in consolidated net income for the period.

    If the functional currency is determined to be the local currency of the foreign entity, the financial statements of that entity must be translated into U.S. dollars using the current rate method. The effects of the exchange rate changes from translation are accumulated in an equity adjustment from translation account and are reported in other comprehensive income.

    Foreign currency financial statements of subsidiaries operating in highly inflationary economies are remeasured as if the functional currency were the U.S. dollar.

    Intercompany transactions between affiliated companies will result in a foreign currency transaction for either the parent or the subsidiary if the subsidiary's local currency is its functional currency. Alternatively, if the subsidiary's functional currency is the U.S. dollar, the intercompany transaction will be a foreign currency transaction to both affiliates or to neither affiliate.

    On the date of a business combination, assets and liabilities are translated into U.S. dollars using current exchange rates.

QUESTIONS

1. Define the functional currency concept and briefly describe how a foreign entity's functional currency is determined. Why is this definition critical from a financial reporting perspective?

2. How does ASC Topic 830 define a highly inflationary economy? If the economy is deemed to be highly inflationary, which method for converting the financial statements to the reporting currency is used? How does the use of this method improve the economic representational faithfulness of the financial statements?

3. What procedure is used to allocate the investment purchase price at the date of acquisition of a foreign subsidiary?

4. Describe what the current rate method is and under what circumstances it should be used.

5. Describe what the temporal method is and under what circumstances it should be used.

6. If the current rate method is used, the gain or loss on translation is included under other comprehensive income. Explain why this makes sense economically.

7. The gain or loss on remeasurement is included in net income each year if the temporal method is used. Explain why this makes sense economically.

8. Under what circumstances would a foreign entity's financials statements need to be both remeasured and translated? Would this process have an effect on both the income statement and other comprehensive income? Explain.

9. If a company's sales were very seasonal—for example, a holiday-tree grower—would it be appropriate to use the annual average exchange rate to translate and remeasure sales and other expenses? Why or why not?

10. In the current-rate-method example in the chapter, the parent's other comprehensive income adjustment related to its investment in the subsidiary was larger than the other comprehensive income adjustment on the subsidiary's translated financial statements. Why?

11. Under the current rate method, all the expenses are translated using some form of current-period exchange rate. Under the temporal method, some expenses such as salaries and utilities are translated using current rates but others, such as cost of goods sold and depreciation expense, use historical rates. Why are different rates used between the two methods? After all, they are all expenses.

12. How does the choice of functional currency affect how the gain or loss on a hedge of a net investment in a foreign subsidiary is reported in the financial statements?

EXERCISES

E 14-1
Translation/remeasurement differences

1. A German subsidiary of a U.S. firm has the British pound as its functional currency. Under the provisions of ASC Topic 830, the U.S. dollar from the subsidiary's viewpoint would be:
   a *Its local currency*
   b *Its recording currency*
   c *A foreign currency*
   d *None of the above*

2. Which of the following foreign subsidiary accounts will be converted into the same number of U.S. dollars, regardless of whether translation or remeasurement is used?
   a *Accounts receivable*
   b *Inventories*
   c *Machinery*
   d *Prepaid insurance*

3. Which one of the following items from the financial statements of a foreign subsidiary would be translated into dollars using the historical exchange rate?
   a *Accounts payable*
   b *Amortization of bond premium*
   c *Common stock*
   d *Inventories*

4. Average exchange rates are used to translate certain items from foreign income statements into U.S. dollars. Such averages are used to:
   a *Approximate the effects of using the current exchange rates in effect on the transaction dates*
   b *Avoid using different exchange rates for some revenue and expense accounts*
   c *Eliminate large and temporary fluctuations in exchange rates that may reverse in the near future*
   d *Smooth out large exchange gains and losses*

5. Pal, a U.S. Corporation, made a long-term, dollar-denominated loan of $600,000 to its British subsidiary on January 1, 2011, when the exchange rate for British pounds was $1.73. If the subsidiary's functional currency is its local currency, this transaction is a foreign currency transaction of:
   a *The parent company but not the subsidiary*
   b *The subsidiary company but not the parent*
   c *Both the subsidiary and the parent*
   d *Neither the subsidiary nor the parent*

6. Sum is a 100%-owned subsidiary of a U.S. corporation. The country in which Sum is located has been determined to have a highly inflationary economy. Given this information, the functional currency of Sum is:
   a *Its local currency*
   b *The U.S. dollar*
   c *Its recording currency*
   d *None of the above*

7. An exchange gain on a long-term loan of a U.S. parent company to its British subsidiary whose functional currency is the British pound is:

 a   Recognized in consolidated income currently
 b   Deferred until the loan is settled
 c   Treated as an equity adjustment from translation
 d   Treated as an equity adjustment from remeasurement

8. A U.S. firm has a $10,000,000 investment in a foreign subsidiary, and the U.S. dollar is weakening against the currency of the country in which the foreign entity is located, which is also the subsidiary's functional currency. On the basis of this information, one would expect the consolidated financial statements to show:

 a   Translation gains
 b   Translation losses
 c   Stockholders' equity increase from remeasurement adjustments
 d   Stockholders' equity decrease from remeasurement adjustments

9. Which one of the following would not give rise to changes in a parent company's equity adjustment from translation account?

 a   Remeasurement of a foreign subsidiary's statements
 b   Hedge of a net investment in a foreign subsidiary
 c   Long-term intercompany loans to its foreign subsidiary
 d   Translation of a foreign subsidiary's statements

E 14-2

[Based on AICPA] Translation/remeasurement differences

1. When consolidated financial statements for a U.S. parent and its foreign subsidiary are prepared, the account balances expressed in foreign currency must be converted into the currency of the reporting entity. One objective of the translation process is to provide information that:

 a   Reflects current exchange rates
 b   Reflects current monetary equivalents
 c   Is compatible with the economic effects of rate changes on the firm's cash flows
 d   Reflects each translated account at its unexpired historical cost

2. A company is translating account balances from another currency into dollars for its December 31, 2011, statement of financial position and its calendar year 2011 earnings statement and statement of cash flows. The average exchange rate for 2011 should be used to translate:

 a   Cash at December 31, 2011
 b   Land purchased in 2011
 c   Retained earnings at January 1, 2011
 d   Sales for 2011

3. A subsidiary's functional currency is the local currency, which has not experienced significant inflation. The appropriate exchange rate for translating the depreciation on plant assets in the income statement of the foreign subsidiary is the:

 a   Exit rate
 b   Historical exchange rate
 c   Weighted average exchange rate over the economic life of each plant asset
 d   Weighted average exchange rate for the current year

4. The year-end balance of accounts receivable on the books of a foreign subsidiary should be translated by the parent company for consolidation purposes at the:

 a   Historical rate
 b   Current rate
 c   Negotiated rate
 d   Average rate

5. When remeasuring foreign currency financial statements into the functional currency, which of the following items would be remeasured using historical exchange rates?

 a   Inventories carried at cost
 b   Marketable equity securities reported at market values
 c   Bonds payable
 d   Accrued liabilities

E 14-3

Acquisition date effects

On January 1, 2011, Pai, a U.S. firm, purchases all the outstanding capital stock of Sta, a British firm, for $990,000, when the exchange rate for British pounds is $1.65. The book values of Sta's assets and liabilities are equal to fair values on this date, except for land that has a fair value of £200,000 and equipment with a fair value of £100,000.

Summarized balance sheet information for Pai in U.S. dollars and for Sta in pounds just before the business combination is as follows:

	Pai	Sta
Current assets	$3,000,000	£100,000
Land	800,000	100,000
Buildings—net	1,200,000	250,000
Equipment—net	1,000,000	50,000
	$6,000,000	£500,000
Current liabilities	$ 600,000	£ 50,000
Notes payable	1,000,000	150,000
Capital stock	3,000,000	200,000
Retained earnings	1,400,000	100,000
	$6,000,000	£500,000

REQUIRED: Prepare a consolidated balance sheet for Pai and Subsidiary at January 1, 2011, immediately after the business combination.

E 14-4

Inventory remeasurement effect

Stadt Corporation of the Netherlands is a 100 percent-owned subsidiary of Port Corporation, a U.S. firm, and its functional currency is the U.S. dollar. Stadt's books of record are maintained in euros and its inventory is carried at cost.

The current exchange rate for euros at December 31, 2011, is $0.60.
The historical cost of the inventory is 10,000 euros.
The historical exchange rate is $0.53.

REQUIRED: Determine the amount at which the inventory will be carried on (a) the foreign currency statements, (b) the remeasured statements, and (c) the translated statements.

E 14-5

Acquisition—Excess allocation and amortization effect

On January 1, 2011, Pan acquired all the stock of Sim of Belgium for $1,200,000, when Sim had 20,000,000 euros (Eu) capital stock and Eu 15,000,000 retained earnings. Sim's net assets were fairly valued on this date and any cost/ book value differential is due to a patent with a 10-year amortization period. Sim's functional currency is the euro. The exchange rates for euros for 2011 were as follows:

January 1, 2011	$.030
Average for 2011	$.032
December 31, 2011	$.035

REQUIRED

1. Calculate the patent value from the business combination on January 1, 2011.

2. Determine patent amortization in U.S. dollars for 2011.

3. Prepare a journal entry on Pan's books to record the patent amortization for 2011.

E 14-6

Acquisition—Excess allocation and amortization effect

Pal acquired all the stock of Sta of Britain on January 1, 2011, for $163,800, when Sta had capital stock of £60,000 and retained earnings of £30,000. Sta's assets and liabilities were fairly valued, except for equipment with a three-year life that was undervalued by £6,000. Any remaining excess is due to a patent with a useful life of 10 years.

Sta's functional currency is the pound. Exchange rates for British pounds are as follows:

January 1, 2011	$1.66
Average for the year 2011	1.65
December 31, 2011	1.64

REQUIRED

1. Determine the unrealized translation gain or loss at December 31, 2011, related to the cost/book value differential assigned to equipment.

2. Determine the unrealized translation gain or loss at December 31, 2011, related to the patent.

E 14-7

Acquisition—excess allocation

Pac of the United States purchased all the outstanding stock of Swi of Switzerland for $1,350,000 cash on January 1, 2011. The book values of Swi's assets and liabilities were equal to fair values on this date except for land, which was valued at 1,000,000 euros. Summarized balance sheet information in euros at January 1, 2011, is as follows:

Current assets	Eu 800,000	Current liabilities	Eu 400,000
Land	600,000	Bonds payable	500,000
Buildings—net	400,000	Capital stock	1,000,000
Equipment—net	500,000	Retained earnings	400,000
	Eu 2,300,000		Eu 2,300,000

The functional currency of Swi is the euro. Exchange rates for euros for 2011 are as follows:

Spot rate January 1, 2011	$0.75
Average rate 2011	0.76
Current rate December 31, 2011	0.77

REQUIRED: Determine the unrealized translation gain or loss at December 31, 2011, relating to the excess allocated to the undervalued land.

E 14-8

[Based on AICPA] Acquisition excess allocation effects, specific account translation and remeasurement

1. Fay had a realized foreign exchange loss of $15,000 for the year ended December 31, 2011, and must also determine whether the following items will require year-end adjustment:

    Fay had an $8,000 equity adjustment resulting from the translation of the accounts of its wholly owned foreign subsidiary for the year ended December 31, 2011.

    Fay had an account payable to an unrelated foreign supplier payable in the supplier's local currency. The U.S. dollar equivalent of the payable was $64,000 on the October 31, 2011, invoice date, and it was $60,000 on December 31, 2011. The invoice is payable on January 30, 2012.

    In Fay's 2011 consolidated income statement, what amount should be included as foreign exchange loss?

    a $11,000
    b $15,000
    c $19,000
    d $23,000

2. On January 1, 2011, the Ben Company formed a foreign subsidiary. On February 15, 2011, Ben's subsidiary purchased 100,000 local currency units (LCU) of inventory; 25,000 LCU of the original inventory made up the entire inventory on December 31, 2011. The subsidiary's functional currency is the U.S. dollar. The exchange rates were 2.2 LCU to $1 from January 1, 2011, to June 30, 2011, and 2 LCU to $1 from July 1, 2011, to December 31, 2011. The December 31, 2011, inventory balance for Ben's foreign subsidiary should be remeasured into U.S. dollars in the amount of:

    a $10,500
    b $11,364
    c $11,905
    d $12,500

3. The Dee Company owns a foreign subsidiary with 3,600,000 local currency units of property, plant, and equipment before accumulated depreciation at December 31, 2013. Of this amount, 2,400,000 LCU were acquired in 2011, when the rate of exchange was 1.6 LCU to $1, and 1,200,000 LCU were acquired in 2012, when the rate of exchange was 1.8 LCU to $1.

The rate of exchange in effect at December 31, 2013, was 2 LCU to $1. The weighted average of exchange rates in effect during 2013 was 1.92 LCU to $1. The subsidiary's functional currency is the U.S. dollar.

Assuming that the property, plant, and equipment are depreciated using the straight-line method over a 10-year period with no salvage value, how much depreciation expense relating to the foreign subsidiary's property, plant, and equipment should be charged in Dee's income statement for 2013?

a $180,000

b $187,500

c $200,000

d $216,667

4. The Clark Company owns a foreign subsidiary that had net income for the year ended December 31, 2011, of 4,800,000 local currency units, which was appropriately translated into $800,000.

On October 15, 2011, when the rate of exchange was 5.7 LCU to $1, the foreign subsidiary paid a dividend to Clark of 2,400,000 LCU. The dividend represented the net income of the foreign subsidiary for the six months ended June 30, 2011, during which time the weighted average exchange rate was 5.8 LCU to $1.

The rate of exchange in effect at December 31, 2011, was 5.9 LCU to $1. What rate of exchange should be used to translate the dividend for the December 31, 2011, financial statements?

a 5.7 LCU to $1

b 5.8 LCU to $1

c 5.9 LCU to $1

d 6.0 LCU to $1

5. The Jem Company used the current rate method when translating foreign currency amounts at December 31, 2011. At that time, Jem had foreign subsidiaries with 1,500,000 local currency units in long-term receivables and 2,400,000 LCU in long-term debt. The rate of exchange in effect when the specific transactions occurred involving those foreign currency amounts was 2 LCU to $1. The rate of exchange in effect at December 31, 2011, was 1.5 LCU to $1. The translation of these foreign currency amounts into U.S. dollars would result in long-term receivables and long-term debt, respectively, of:

a $750,000 and $1,200,000

b $750,000 and $1,600,000

c $1,000,000 and $1,200,000

d $1,000,000 and $1,600,000

6. Certain balance sheet accounts of a foreign subsidiary of Row at December 31, 2011, have been translated into U.S. dollars as follows:

	Translated at	
	Current Rates	Historical Rates
Note receivable, long-term	$240,000	$200,000
Prepaid rent	85,000	80,000
Patent	150,000	170,000
	$475,000	$450,000

The subsidiary's functional currency is the currency of the country in which it is located. What total amount should be included in Row's December 31, 2011, consolidated balance sheet for the three accounts?

a $450,000

b $455,000

c $475,000

d $495,000

7. Inflation data of a foreign country for three years are as follows:

	Index	Change in Index	Annual Rate of Inflation
January 1, 2010	150	—	
January 1, 2011	200	50	$50 \div 150 = 33\%$
January 1, 2012	250	50	$50 \div 200 = 25\%$
January 1, 2013	330	80	$80 \div 250 = 32\%$

The cumulative three-year inflation rate is:

a 45%

b 90%

c 120%

d 180%

PROBLEMS

P 14-1
Parent accounting under the equity method

Pak purchased a 40 percent interest in Sco of Germany for $1,080,000 on January 1, 2011. The excess cost over book value is due to a patent with a 10-year amortization period. A summary of Sco's net assets at December 31, 2010, and at December 31, 2011, after translation into U.S. dollars, is as follows:

	Capital Stock	Retained Earnings	Equity Adjustment	Net Assets
December 31, 2010	$2,000,000	$400,000		$2,400,000
Net income		310,000		310,000
Dividends		(192,000)		(192,000)
Translation adjustment			$212,000	212,000
December 31, 2011	$2,000,000	$518,000	$212,000	$2,730,000

Exchange rates for euros were $0.60 on January 1, 2011; $0.62 average for 2011; $0.64 when dividends were declared; and $0.65 at December 31, 2011. Sco had net assets of Eu 4,000,000 at January 1, 2011; net income of Eu 500,000 for 2011; and dividends of Eu 300,000. It ended the year with net assets of Eu 4,200,000. Sco's functional currency is the euro.

REQUIRED

1. Calculate Pak's income from Sco for 2011.

2. Determine the balance of Pak's Investment in Sco account at December 31, 2011.

3. Develop a proof of your calculation of the Investment in Sco account balance at December 31, 2011.

P 14-2
Parent accounting under the equity method

Pla purchased a 40 percent interest in Sor, a foreign company, on January 1, 2011, for $342,000, when Sor's stockholders' equity consisted of 3,000,000 LCU capital stock and 1,000,000 LCU retained earnings. Sor's functional currency is its local currency unit. The exchange rate at this time was $0.15 per LCU. Any excess allocated to patents is to be amortized over 10 years.

A summary of changes in the stockholders' equity of Sor during 2011 (including relevant exchange rates) is as follows:

	LCUs	Exchange Rate	U.S. Dollars
Stockholders' equity January 1, 2011	4,000,000	$0.15 C	$600,000
Net income	800,000	0.14 A	112,000
Dividends	(400,000)	0.14 C	(56,000)
Equity adjustment			(84,000)
Stockholders' equity December 31, 2011	4,400,000	0.13 C	$572,000

REQUIRED: Determine the following:

1. Excess patent from Pla's Investment in Sor on January 1, 2011

2. Excess patent amortization for 2011

3. Unamortized excess patent at December 31, 2011

4. Equity adjustment from patents for 2011

5. Income from Sor for 2011

6. Investment in Sor balance at December 31, 2011

P 14-3
Translation worksheet, parent accounting

Pyl acquired all the outstanding capital stock of Soo of London on January 1, 2011, for $800,000, when the exchange rate for British pounds was $1.60 and Soo's stockholders' equity consisted of £400,000 capital stock and £100,000 retained earnings. Soo's functional currency is the British pound. Balance sheet accounts for Sooth at January 1, 2011, in British pounds and U.S. dollars are summarized as follows:

	British Pounds	Exchange Rate	U.S. Dollars
Cash	£ 50,000	$1.60	$ 80,000
Accounts receivable—net	60,000	1.60	96,000
Inventories	40,000	1.60	64,000
Equipment	750,000	1.60	1,200,000
	£900,000		$1,440,000
Accumulated depreciation	£250,000	$1.60	$ 400,000
Accounts payable	150,000	1.60	240,000
Capital stock	400,000	1.60	640,000
Retained earnings	100,000	1.60	160,000
	£900,000		$1,440,000

Exchange rates for 2011 are as follows:

Current exchange rate January 1, 2011	$1.60
Average exchange rate for 2011	1.63
Rate for cash dividends	1.62
Current exchange rate December 31, 2011	1.65

Soo's adjusted trial balance in British pounds at December 31, 2011, is as follows:

Debits	
Cash	£ 20,000
Accounts receivable—net	70,000
Inventories	50,000
Equipment	800,000
Cost of sales	350,000
Depreciation expense	80,000
Operating expenses	100,000
Dividends	30,000
	£1,500,000
Credits	
Accumulated depreciation	£ 330,000
Accounts payable	70,000
Capital stock	400,000
Retained earnings	100,000
Sales	600,000
	£1,500,000

REQUIRED

1. Prepare a translation worksheet to convert Soo's December 31, 2011, adjusted trial balance into U.S. dollars.

2. Prepare journal entries on Pyl's books to account for the investment in Soo for 2011.

3. Directly compute the translation gain or loss.

P 14-4
Translation worksheet, parent accounting

Pet acquired 80 percent of the common stock of Sul for $4,000,000 on January 2, 2011, when the stockholders' equity of Sul consisted of 5,000,000 euros capital stock and 2,000,000 euros retained earnings. The spot rate for euros on this date was $0.50. Any cost/book value difference attributable to a patent is to be amortized over a 10-year period, and Sul's functional currency is the euro.

Accounts from Sul's adjusted trial balance in euros at December 31, 2011, are as follows:

Debits	
Cash	€ 1,000,000
Accounts receivable	2,000,000
Inventories	4,000,000
Equipment	8,000,000
Cost of sales	4,000,000
Depreciation expense	800,000
Operating expenses	2,700,000
Dividends	500,000
	€ 23,000,000
Credits	
Accumulated depreciation—equipment	€ 2,400,000
Accounts payable	3,600,000
Capital stock	5,000,000
Retained earnings January 1	2,000,000
Sales	10,000,000
	€ 23,000,000

Relevant exchange rates in U.S. dollars for euros are as follows:

Current exchange rate December 31, 2011	$0.60
Average exchange rate 2011	0.55
Exchange rate applicable to dividends	0.54

REQUIRED

1. Prepare a translation worksheet for Sul at December 31, 2011.

2. Calculate Pet's income from Sul for 2011 on the basis of a one-line consolidation.

3. Determine the correct balance of Pet's investment in Sul at December 31, 2011.

P 14-5
Remeasurement worksheet

Par of Chicago acquired all the outstanding capital stock of Sar of London on January 1, 2011, for $1,200,000. The exchange rate for British pounds was $1.60 and Sar's stockholders' equity was £800,000, consisting of £500,000 capital stock and £300,000 retained earnings. The functional currency of Sar is the U.S. dollar.

Exchange rates for British pounds for 2011 are as follows:

Current rate December 31, 2010	$1.60
Current rate December 31, 2011	1.70
Average exchange rate for 2011	1.65
Exchange rate for dividends	1.64

Sar's cost of goods sold consists of £200,000 inventory on hand at January 1, 2011, and purchases of £600,000 less £150,000 inventory on hand at December 31, 2011, that was acquired at an exchange rate of $1.68.

All of Sar's plant assets were on hand when Par acquired Sar, and Sar's other expenses were paid in cash or relate to accounts payable.

Sar's adjusted trial balance at December 31, 2011, in British pounds is as follows:

Debits		
Cash	£	50,000
Accounts receivable		200,000
Short-term note receivable		50,000
Inventories		150,000
Land		300,000
Buildings—net		400,000
Equipment—net		500,000
Cost of sales		650,000
Depreciation expense		200,000
Other expenses		400,000
Dividends		100,000
		£ 3,000,000
Credits		
Accounts payable	£	180,000
Bonds payable—10%		500,000
Bond interest payable		20,000
Capital stock		500,000
Retained earnings		300,000
Sales		1,500,000
		£ 3,000,000

REQUIRED: Prepare a remeasurement worksheet to restate Sar's adjusted trial balance at December 31, 2011, in U.S. dollars.

P 14-6
Remeasurement worksheet

Phi, a U.S. firm, acquired 100 percent of Stu's outstanding stock at book value on January 1, 2011, for $112,000. Stu is a New Zealand company, and its functional currency is the U.S. dollar. The exchange rate for New Zealand dollars (NZ$) was $0.70 when Phi acquired its interest. Stu's stockholders' equity on January 1, 2011, consisted of NZ$150,000 capital stock and NZ$10,000 retained earnings. The adjusted trial balance for Stu at December 31, 2011, is as follows:

Debits	
Cash	NZ$ 15,000
Accounts receivable—net	60,000
Inventories	30,000
Prepaid expenses	10,000
Land	45,000
Equipment	60,000
Cost of sales	120,000
Depreciation expense	12,000
Other operating expenses	28,000
Dividends	20,000
	NZ$400,000
Credits	
Accumulated depreciation	NZ$ 22,000
Accounts payable	18,000
Capital stock	150,000
Retained earnings	10,000
Sales	200,000
	NZ$400,000

ADDITIONAL INFORMATION

1. Prepaid expenses (supplies) of NZ$18,000 were on hand when Phi acquired Stu. Other operating expenses include NZ$8,000 of these supplies that were used in 2011. The remaining NZ$10,000 of supplies is on hand at year-end.

2. The NZ$120,000 cost of sales consists of NZ$50,000 inventory on hand at January 1, 2011, and NZ$100,000 in purchases during the year, less NZ$30,000 ending inventory that was acquired when the exchange rate was $0.66.

3. The NZ$60,000 of equipment consists of NZ$50,000 included in the business combination and NZ$10,000 purchased during 2011, when the exchange rate was $0.68. A depreciation rate of 20 percent is applicable to all equipment for 2011.

4. Exchange rates for 2011 are summarized as follows:

Current exchange rate January 1, 2011	$0.70
Exchange rate when new equipment was acquired	0.68
Average exchange rate for 2011	0.67
Exchange rate for December 31, 2011, inventory	0.66
Exchange rate for dividends	0.66
Current exchange rate December 31, 2011	0.65

REQUIRED: Prepare a worksheet to remeasure the adjusted trial balance of Stu Corporation into U.S. dollars at December 31, 2011.

P 14-7
Translation worksheet, parent accounting

Pel, a U.S. firm, paid $308,000 for all the common stock of Sar of Israel on January 1, 2011, when the exchange rate for sheqels was $0.35. Sar's equity on this date consisted of 500,000 sheqels common stock and 300,000 sheqels retained earnings. The $28,000 (80,000 sheqels) excess is attributable to a patent with a 10-year amortization period. Sar's functional currency is the sheqel.

Sar's adjusted trial balance at December 31, 2011, in sheqels is as follows:

Debits	**Sheqels**	*Credits*	**Sheqels**
Cash	40,000	Accounts payable	120,000
Receivables—net	50,000	Other liabilities	60,000
Inventories	150,000	Advance from Pel	140,000
Land	160,000	Common stock	500,000
Equipment—net	300,000	Retained earnings 1/1	300,000
Buildings—net	500,000	Sales	600,000
Expenses	400,000		
Exchange loss (advance)	20,000		
Dividends	100,000		
	1,720,000		1,720,000

On January 2, 2011, Pel advanced $42,000 (120,000 sheqels) to Sar. This advance was short-term, denominated in U.S. dollars, and made when the exchange rate for sheqels was $0.35. In June 2011, Sar paid a 100,000-sheqel dividend when the exchange rate was $0.33. The average and year-end exchange rates for sheqels are $0.32 and $0.30, respectively.

REQUIRED

1. Prepare a worksheet to translate Sar's adjusted trial balance at December 31, 2011, into U.S. dollars.

2. Prepare the necessary journal entries for Pel to account for its investment in Sar for 2011.

P 14-8
Parent accounting and consolidation under translation

PWA Corporation paid $1,710,000 for 100 percent of the stock of SAA Corporation on January 1, 2011, when the stockholders' equity of SAA consisted of 5,000,000 LCU capital stock and 3,000,000 LCU retained earnings. SAA's functional currency is the local currency unit, and any cost/book value differential is attributable to a patent with a 10-year amortization period.

On July 1, 2011, PWA advanced $333,000 (1,800,000 LCU) to SAA when the exchange rate was $0.185. The advance is short-term and denominated in U.S. dollars.

Relevant exchange rates for LCUs for 2011 are as follows:

Rate at acquisition on January 1	$0.190
Rate applicable to the advance on July 1	0.185
Rate applicable to dividends on September 1	0.185
Average rate for the year	0.185
Current rate at December 31	0.180

A translation worksheet for SAA's adjusted trial balance at December 31, 2011, is as follows:

	LCUs	Exchange Rate	U.S. Dollars
Debits			
Cash	550,000	$0.180 C	$ 99,000
Accounts receivable—net	500,000	0.180 C	90,000
Inventories	1,500,000	0.180 C	270,000
Land	1,600,000	0.180 C	288,000
Equipment—net	3,000,000	0.180 C	540,000
Buildings—net	5,000,000	0.180 C	900,000
Expenses	4,000,000	0.185 A	740,000
Exchange loss (advance)	50,000	0.185 A	9,250
Dividends	1,000,000	0.185 R	185,000
Equity adjustment from translation	—		84,750
	17,200,000		$3,206,000
Credits			
Accounts payable	750,000	$0.180 C	$ 135,000
Other liabilities	600,000	0.180 C	108,000
Advance from PWA (short-term)	1,850,000	0.180 C	333,000
Capital stock	5,000,000	0.190 H	950,000
Retained earnings January 1	3,000,000	0.190 H	570,000
Sales	6,000,000	0.185 A	1,110,000
	17,200,000		$3,206,000

Financial statements for PWA and SAA at and for the year ended December 31, 2011, are summarized as follows:

	PWA	SAA
Combined Income and Retained Earnings Statement for the Year Ended December 31, 2011		
Sales	$ 569,500	$1,110,000
Income from SAA	342,250	—
Expenses	(400,000)	(740,000)
Exchange loss	—	(9,250)
Net income	511,750	360,750
Add: Beginning retained earnings	856,500	570,000
Less: Dividends	(300,000)	(185,000)
Retained earnings December 31	$1,068,250	$ 745,750
Balance Sheet at December 31, 2011		
Cash	$ 90,720	$ 99,000
Accounts receivable—net	128,500	90,000
Advance to SAA	333,000	—
Inventories	120,000	270,000
Land	100,000	288,000
Equipment—net	600,000	540,000
Buildings—net	300,000	900,000
Investment in SAA	1,773,000	—
	$3,445,220	$2,187,000

(*continued*)

	PWA	SAA
Accounts payable	$ 162,720	$ 135,000
Advance from PWA	—	333,000
Other liabilities	308,500	108,000
Common stock	2,000,000	950,000
Retained earnings	1,068,250	745,750
Equity adjustment from translation	(94,250)	(84,750)
	$3,445,220	$2,187,000

REQUIRED

1. Prepare journal entries on PWA's books to account for its investment in SAA for 2011.

2. Prepare consolidation working papers for PWA Corporation and Subsidiary for the year ended December 31, 2011.

P 14-9
Translation worksheet, parent accounting, consolidation

San is a 90 percent-owned foreign subsidiary of Par, acquired by Par on January 1, 2011, at book value equal to fair value, when the exchange rate for LCUs of San's home country was $0.24. Sans functional currency is the LCU. Par made a 200,000 LCU loan to San on May 1, 2011, when the exchange rate for LCUs was $0.23. The loan is short-term and is denominated at $46,000. Adjusted trial balances of the affiliated companies at year-end 2011 are as follows:

	Par in U.S. Dollars	San in LCU
Debits		
Cash	$ 25,100	150,000
Accounts receivable	90,000	180,000
Short-term loan to San	46,000	—
Inventories	110,000	230,000
Land	150,000	250,000
Buildings	300,000	600,000
Equipment	220,000	800,000
Investment in San (100%)	230,000	—
Cost of sales	400,000	200,000
Depreciation expense	81,000	100,000
Other expenses	200,000	120,000
Exchange loss	—	30,000
Dividends	100,000	100,000
Equity adjustment	44,000	—
	$1,996,100	2,760,000
Credits		
Accumulated depreciation—buildings	$ 120,000	300,000
Accumulated depreciation—equipment	60,000	400,000
Accounts payable	241,100	130,000
Short-term loan from Par	—	230,000
Capital stock	500,000	800,000
Retained earnings January 1	220,000	200,000
Sales	800,000	700,000
Income from San	55,000	—
	$1,996,100	2,760,000

San paid dividends in September, when the exchange rate was $0.21. The exchange rate for LCUs was $0.20 at December 31, 2011, and the average exchange rate for 2011 was $0.22.

REQUIRED

1. Prepare a worksheet to translate San's adjusted trial balance into U.S. dollars at December 31, 2011.

2. Prepare the necessary journal entries for Par to account for its investment in San for 2011 under the equity method.

3. Prepare consolidation working papers for Par Corporation and Subsidiary for the year ended December 31, 2011.

INTERNET ASSIGNMENT

Go to *Ford Motor Company's* Web site and access its 2009 annual report. Answer the following questions:

1. What are the functional currencies of Ford's subsidiaries?

2. How much and where did Ford report the gain or loss on remeasurement of its subsidiaries' financial statements? From what currencies were the subsidiaries' financial statements remeasured into dollars? How material are these gains or losses with respect to Ford's overall profitability? In examining the comparative financial statements, do these gains and losses appear to change dramatically over time? Does this appear to affect the volatility (and apparent riskiness) of Ford's cash flow stream?

3. How much and where did Ford report the gain or loss on translation of its subsidiaries' financial statements? From what currencies were the subsidiaries' financial statements translated into dollars? How material are these cumulative gains or losses to Ford's overall financial position? Do these cumulative gains or losses appear to fluctuate over time, and what impact would this have on the apparent riskiness of Ford's cash flow stream?

4. Does Ford enter into any cash flow hedges in an attempt to hedge its net investment in these subsidiaries? How are these reported in Ford's financial statements? What is Ford's reasoning for entering into such investments?

REFERENCES TO THE AUTHORITATIVE LITERATURE

[1] FASB ASC 830 "Foreign Currency Matters", Originally Statement of Financial Accounting Standards No. 52. "*Foreign Currency Translation*" Stamford, CT: Financial Accounting Standards Board, 1981.

[2] FASB ASC 220 "Comprehensive Income", Originally Statement of Financial Accounting Standards No. 130. "*Reporting Comprehensive Income*" Stamford, CT: Financial Accounting Standards Board, 1997.

15 CHAPTER

Segment and Interim Financial Reporting

Consolidated financial statements enable investors to assess management's overall effectiveness in managing company resources by providing useful information for computing overall measures of profitability, liquidity, and efficiency. To help investors evaluate a company's business segments' performance, supplemental footnote disclosures are required. The first part of this chapter discusses business segment reporting.

Financial accounting courses typically focus on reporting company performance for a year—the annual report. Many companies are also required to issue financial reports covering shorter periods of time during the year, most notably on a quarterly basis. The second part of this chapter focuses on reporting guidelines for such interim reports.

LEARNING OBJECTIVES

1 Understand how the management approach is used to identify potentially reportable operating segments.

2 Apply the threshold tests to identify reportable operating segments: the revenue test, the asset test, and the operating-profit test.

3 Apply the 75 percent external-revenue test to determine whether additional segments must be reported.

4 Understand the types of information that may be disclosed for segments and the reasons that the levels of disclosure may vary across companies.

5 Understand what segment disclosures are reconciled to the consolidated amounts.

6 Know the types of enterprise-wide disclosures related to products and services, geographic areas of operation, and major customers that are required to be disclosed.

7 Understand the similarities and differences in the reporting of operations in an interim versus an annual reporting period.

8 Compute interim-period income tax expense.

SEGMENT REPORTING

LEARNING OBJECTIVE 1

Segment reporting under GAAP [1] applies to public business enterprises, which are defined as enterprises that have issued debt or equity securities that are traded in a public market, that are required to file financial statements with the SEC, or that provide financial statements for the purpose of issuing securities in a public market. Enterprises must report segment information in the same way that management organizes the enterprise into units for internal decision-making and performance-evaluation purposes. GAAP [2] refers to this approach as the *management approach* to segmentation. The management approach relies on the concept of a *chief operating decision maker* (CODM). The CODM identifies a function rather than a specific person or title. That function is allocating resources and assessing the performance of the segments of the firm. For some firms the CODM is the chief executive officer or chief operating officer, but it could be any combination of executives or other managers.

If internal reporting and evaluation are geographically based, segment reporting should be geographically based; if internal reporting and evaluation are product-line or industry based, segment reporting should be similarly based.

For example, **Intel Corporation's** CODM is its president and chief executive officer. The CODM allocated resources to, and evaluated the performance of, its operating segments using revenue and operating income before interest and taxes. According to its 2009 annual report, Intel's operating segments are the PC Client Group (which focuses on microprocessors and related chipsets for desktop and notebook computers), Data Center Group, and Other Intel Architecture operating segments. Intel also reports as segments the Other operating and Corporate groups.

The PC Client and Other Intel Architecture groups are reportable segments because they meet one or more of the quantitative threshold tests (revenue, asset, and operating-profit tests) described later in the chapter. Intel has chosen to also report the Other operating and Corporate groups, even though they do not meet one of the threshold tests, because management believes that such disclosure is useful for the reader.

In contrast, *Apple, Inc.,* manages its business primarily on a geographic basis. According to its 2009 annual report, its reported segments were the Americas, Europe, Japan, and Retail Operations. The other operating segments were reported together as "other."

<table>
<tr><td>LEARNING OBJECTIVE 2</td></tr>
</table>

Identifying Reportable Segments

Management-approach-based segments are called **operating segments**. GAAP [3] characterizes an operating segment as a component of an enterprise (1) that engages in business activities from which it may earn revenues and incur expenses, including intersegment revenues and expenses; (2) whose operating results are regularly reviewed by the enterprise's chief operating decision maker; and (3) for which discrete financial information is available.

Some parts of an enterprise are not included in operating segments. Pension and other postretirement benefit plans are not operating segments. Likewise, corporate headquarters or functional departments that do not earn revenues are not operating segments. Intel reports that in addition to its reported operating segments, it also has sales and marketing, manufacturing, finance, and administration groups. The costs of these groups are allocated to the operating segments.

AGGREGATION CRITERIA An enterprise may combine similar operating segments if aggregation is consistent with the objectives of the CODM and if the segments have similar economic characteristics. The segments also must be similar in each of the following areas: (1) the nature of the products and services, (2) the nature of the production processes, (3) the type or class of customer for their products and services, (4) the distribution method for products and services, and (5) if applicable, the nature of the regulatory environment (public utilities, for example).

QUANTITATIVE THRESHOLDS Operating segments are reportable if they meet materiality thresholds. A segment is considered material and separately reportable if one of the following three criteria is met:

1. Its reported revenue, including intersegment revenues, is 10 percent or more of the combined revenue of all operating segments.

2. The absolute value of its reported profit or loss is 10 percent or more of the greater of (a) the combined reported profit of all operating segments that reported a profit or (b) the absolute value of the combined reported loss of all operating segments that reported a loss.

3. Its assets are 10 percent or more of the combined assets of all operating segments.

Once reportable segments are identified, all other operating segments are combined with other business activities in an "all other" category for reporting purposes.

<table>
<tr><td>LEARNING OBJECTIVE 3</td></tr>
</table>

RECONSIDERATION OF REPORTABLE SEGMENTS Reported segments must include 75 percent of all external revenue. External revenue excludes intersegment revenue. If reportable segments do not meet this criterion, additional segments must be identified as reportable, even if they do not meet the quantitative thresholds. Two or more of the smaller segments that were not reportable on their own may be aggregated to form a reportable operating segment *only if* they meet a majority of the aggregation criteria.

GAAP [4] does not specify the number of segments that must be reported. However, too many segments would be considered overly detailed and therefore counterproductive. Although no firm limit was established, the standard encourages enterprises that identify more than 10 reportable segments to consider additional aggregation of their segments.

For some firms, GAAP [5] determines directly which operating segments will be reported. A firm whose CODM reviews multiple overlapping cross sections of their operations must present segments based on products and services. For example, a manufacturer who managed using geography, product line, and marketing channels, at both the unit and global level, is described as a matrix style of organizational management. A firm such as this would be required to present segments based on products.

Illustration of the Tests for Reportable Operating Segments

Acme Corporation's chief operating decision maker, Mr. Roadrunner, evaluates the company operating results, organized by industry. We apply the three materiality tests to determine which of Acme's operating segments (Transportation, Oil Refining, Insurance, and Finance) are reportable segments.

REVENUE TEST We apply the revenue test by comparing each operating segment's revenue (revenue to external customers plus intersegment revenue) with 10 percent of the combined revenue (both internal and external) of all operating segments. Acme's revenue test is as follows:

Segment	Operating Segment Revenue	Intersegment Revenue	Total Segment Revenue		Test Value	Reportable Segment Under Revenue Test?
Transportation	$ 360,000	$ 0	$ 360,000	≥	$150,000	Yes
Oil refining	405,000	480,000	885,000	≥	150,000	Yes
Insurance	95,000	20,000	115,000	≤	150,000	No
Finance	140,000	0	140,000	≤	150,000	No
Total	$1,000,000	$500,000	$1,500,000			

The revenue test value is $150,000 because the total revenue for all operating segments is $1,500,000. The transportation ($360,000) and oil refining ($885,000) segments are reportable segments under the revenue test because each of these segments' total revenue exceeds $150,000. The insurance and finance segments are not reportable segments under this criterion.

ASSET TEST The asset test involves comparing the total amount of each operating segment's assets with 10 percent of the total assets of all operating segments. A segment's assets are defined as those assets included in the measure of the segment's assets that are reviewed by the chief operating decision maker. General corporate assets may be included or excluded in the asset measurement, depending on the way management has organized the assets for operating decision-making purposes.

Assume that all assets of Acme Corporation are assigned to operating segments except those maintained for general corporate purposes:

Segment	Operating Segment's Identifiable Assets		Test Value	Reportable Segment Under Asset Test?
Transportation	$ 700,000	≥	$300,000	Yes
Oil refining	950,000	≥	300,000	Yes
Insurance	180,000	≤	300,000	No
Finance	1,170,000	≥	300,000	Yes
Total	$3,000,000			

The finance segment is added to the reportable-segment list because its identifiable assets exceed the $300,000 threshold.

OPERATING PROFIT TEST No uniform definition of operating profit is required in applying this test. An operating segment's operating profit or loss depends on the revenues and expenses that management includes in the measurement reviewed by the chief operating decision maker.

In applying the operating-profit test, the absolute amount of each segment's operating profit or loss is compared with 10 percent of the greater of the combined operating profits of all profitable operating segments or the absolute value of the combined operating losses of all unprofitable operating segments. Acme's test is as follows:

Segment	Operating Segment's Operating Profit	Operating Segment's Operating Loss		Test Value	Reportable Segment Under Operating Profit Test?
Transportation		$(100,000)	≥	$27,000	Yes
Oil refining	$200,000		≥	27,000	Yes
Insurance	20,000		≤	27,000	No
Finance	50,000		≥	27,000	Yes
Total	$270,000	$(100,000)			

Because the profitable segments' operating profit total of $270,000 exceeds the absolute value of the $100,000 total operating loss for loss segments, the test value is based on $270,000. After the $27,000 test value is determined, the test is applied to the absolute amounts of operating profit or loss for each segment. The transportation, oil refining, and finance segments are reportable segments under the 10 percent operating-profit test.

REEVALUATION OF REPORTABLE SEGMENTS The insurance segment failed to meet any of the 10 percent tests for a reportable segment. The reportable segments are thus transportation, oil refining, and finance. In the revenue test, the test value is based on 10 percent of the total external and intersegment revenue. If intersegment revenue is very large, some segments that make up a large percentage of consolidated (or external) revenue may not qualify for reporting under the revenue test. If these segments do not qualify for reporting under either of the other two tests, then investors will not be provided with potentially relevant information. GAAP [6] requires that total external revenue from the reportable operating segments be equal to at least 75 percent of total consolidated revenue.

In the Acme example, total revenue of all segments is $1,500,000; $500,000 of this amount is intersegment, so $1,000,000 is revenue from external customers or consolidated revenue. The external revenue of the transportation, oil refining, and finance operating segments of $905,000 is greater than 75 percent of consolidated revenue, and thus no additional segments need to be reported. If the 75 percent test is not met, additional operating segments are added until the 75 percent criterion is met.

If the insurance segment had been a reportable segment in the previous period and Acme's management considered it still to be significant, Acme would report the insurance segment separately as a reportable operating segment, even though it failed all of the 10 percent tests for this period.

LEARNING OBJECTIVE **4**

Segment Disclosures

The basis of organization used by the chief operating decision maker to determine operating segments (for example, products and services, geographic areas, regulatory environments, or some combination of these factors) must be disclosed, as well as any aggregation of operating segments used in arriving at these reportable segments. Each reportable segment's types of products and services are disclosed. Required disclosures are made for each year for which financial statements are presented.

PROFIT/LOSS AND ASSET INFORMATION A measure of *profit or loss* and *total assets* is reported for each reportable operating segment. In addition, GAAP [7] requires the following information for each reportable segment "if the specified amounts are included in the measure of segment profit or loss reviewed by the chief operating decision maker":

1. Amount of revenue from external customers
2. Amount of revenue from other operating segments of the same enterprise
3. Interest revenue
4. Interest expense (If a segment's revenues are primarily interest and the chief operating decision maker relies on net interest revenue to evaluate performance, the segment may report interest revenue net of interest expense.)
5. Depreciation, depletion, and amortization expense
6. Unusual items [8]
7. Equity in the net income of investees accounted for by the equity method
8. Income tax expense or benefit
9. Extraordinary items
10. Significant noncash items other than depreciation, depletion, and amortization expense

Other disclosures about assets are required if the specified amounts are included for review by the chief operating decision maker. These include the amount of investment in equity investees, the total expenditures for additions to long-lived assets other than financial instruments and certain other items, and deferred tax assets.

MEASUREMENT The amounts reported in segment information disclosures depend on the amounts reported to the chief operating decision maker. If allocations of revenues, expenses, gains, or losses are made to operating segments in determining the profit or loss measures used by the chief operating decision maker, the allocations are also a part of the reported segment data. If assets are allocated to segments in internal reports, assets are allocated to segments for external reporting.

The enterprise also reports the accounting basis of intersegment transactions (cost or market, for example). Any differences between segment profit or loss, asset measurements and the consolidated amounts that are not apparent from the required reconciliation (described below) are disclosed. Changes in measurement methods from prior periods are also disclosed.

RECONCILIATION REQUIREMENTS In addition to the information provided for each segment, a reconciliation between the segment data and consolidated information must be provided for the following items:

> LEARNING OBJECTIVE **5**

1. The total of the reportable segments' revenues and the reported consolidated revenues

2. The total reportable segments' profit or loss and consolidated income before taxes (However, if items such as taxes and extraordinary items are included in segment profit or loss, segment profit or loss can be reconciled to consolidated income after these items are included)

3. The total reportable segments' assets to consolidated assets

4. The total reportable segments' amounts for every other significant item of information disclosed, with their corresponding consolidated amount

Enterprisewide Disclosures

> LEARNING OBJECTIVE **6**

Enterprises report limited information about products and services, geographic areas of operation, and major customers, regardless of the operating segmentation used. This additional information is only required if it is not provided as part of the reportable operating-segment information.

PRODUCTS AND SERVICES Enterprises disclose either revenues from each product or service or group of similar products or services or the fact that it is impractical to provide this information.

GEOGRAPHIC INFORMATION If practicable, enterprises disclose geographic information, including revenues from external customers attributed to the enterprise's home country and revenues attributed to all foreign countries in total. If revenue from one country is material (generally considered 10 percent), it is disclosed separately. Similarly, enterprises disclose long-lived assets by country of domicile and by all other foreign countries in total. Plus, they make separate disclosures for any individual country where the assets are material.

MAJOR CUSTOMERS Enterprises are required to disclose the existence of major customers. The fact that a single customer accounts for 10 percent or more of the enterprise's revenue must be disclosed, as well as the amount of revenue from each such customer and the segments reporting the revenue. Disclosure of the identity of the customer is not required. In calculating the 10 percent rule, a group of entities under common control count as a single customer. However, federal, state, and local governments count as different entities. In its 2009 annual report, for example, *Intel* reported that one customer accounted for 21 percent of the company's revenue and another customer 17 percent. The majority of sales to these customers were from the sale of microprocessors, chipsets, and other components by PC Client Group and the Data Center Group operating segments.

Exhibit 15-1 presents segment disclosures *Archer Daniels Midland Company* included in its 2009 annual report. The disclosures are required for each year for which a complete set of financial statements is presented.

EXHIBIT 15-1

Archer Daniels
Midland 2009 Annual
Report Segment and
Geographic Information

ARCHER DANIELS MIDLAND COMPANY NOTE 15. SEGMENT AND GEOGRAPHIC INFORMATION

	2009	2008	2007
(In millions)			
Sales to external customers			
Oilseeds Processing	$ 24,518	$ 23,279	$ 13,943
Corn Processing	7,723	7,137	5,825
Agricultural Services	31,584	33,968	20,419
Other	5,382	5,432	3,831
Total	$ 69,207	$ 69,816	$ 44,018
Intersegment sales			
Oilseeds Processing	$ 109	$ 535	$ 328
Corn Processing	80	99	50
Agricultural Services	2,767	2,965	1,833
Other	153	140	125
Total	$ 3,109	$ 3,739	$ 2,336
Net sales			
Oilseeds Processing	$ 24,627	$ 23,814	$ 14,271
Corn Processing	7,803	7,236	5,875
Agricultural Services	34,351	36,933	22,252
Other	5,535	5,572	3,956
Intersegment elimination	(3,109)	(3,739)	(2,336)
Total	$ 69,207	$ 69,816	$ 44,018
Depreciation			
Oilseeds Processing	$ 190	$ 202	$ 190
Corn Processing	319	293	285
Agricultural Services	96	92	91
Other	101	114	112
Corporate	24	20	23
Total	$ 730	$ 721	$ 701
Asset abandonments and write-downs			
Oilseeds Processing	$ 4	$ 28	$ 6
Corn Processing	–	2	15
Other	9	2	–
Total	$ 13	$ 32	$ 21
Interest expense			
Oilseeds Processing	$ 89	$ 186	$ 136
Corn Processing	17	49	46
Agricultural Services	80	170	133
Other	86	119	134
Corporate	158	(47)	(15)
Total	$ 430	$ 477	$ 434
Investment income			
Oilseeds Processing	$ 36	$ 24	$ 17
Agricultural Services	29	48	29
Other	79	136	137
Corporate	37	61	74
Total	$ 181	$ 269	$ 257
Equity in earnings of affiliates			
Oilseeds Processing	$ 283	$ 156	$ 88
Corn Processing	44	53	54
Agricultural Services	76	105	29
Other	(253)	113	105
Corporate	(5)	(12)	18
Total	$ 145	$ 415	$ 294

ARCHER DANIELS MIDLAND COMPANY NOTE 15. SEGMENT AND GEOGRAPHIC INFORMATION

	2009	2008	2007
Operating profit			
Oilseeds Processing	$ 1,280	$ 1,040	$ 1,139
Corn Processing	185	961	1,105
Agricultural Services	994	1,017	538
Other	(6)	423	379
Total operating profit	2,453	3,441	3,161
Corporate	81	(817)	(7)
Earnings before income taxes	$ 2,534	$ 2,624	$ 3,154
Investments in and advances to affiliates			
Oilseeds Processing	$ 1,202	$ 1,059	
Corn Processing	402	431	
Agricultural Services	201	242	
Other	256	593	
Corporate	398	448	
Total	$ 2,459	$ 2,773	
Identifiable assets			
Oilseeds Processing	$ 10,266	$ 12,906	
Corn Processing	6,333	5,779	
Agricultural Services	5,657	9,876	
Other	7,965	7,922	
Corporate	1,364	573	
Total	$ 31,585	$ 37,056	
Gross additions to property, plant, and equipment			
Oilseeds Processing	$ 258	$ 190	
Corn Processing	1,018	979	
Agricultural Services	254	166	
Other	471	405	
Corporate	58	49	
Total	$ 2,059	$ 1,789	

Geographic information: The following geographic area data include net sales and other operating income attributed to the countries based on the location of the subsidiary making the sale and long-lived assets based on physical location. Long-lived assets represent the sum of the net book value of property, plant, and equipment plus goodwill related to consolidated businesses.

	2009	2008	2007
(*In millions*)			
Net sales and other operating income			
United States	$ 35,485	$ 37,466	$ 24,244
Germany	7,431	8,335	6,569
Other Foreign	26,291	24,015	13,205
	$ 69,207	$ 69,816	$ 44,018
Long-lived assets			
United States	$ 6,452	$ 5,554	
Foreign	1,754	1,817	
	$ 8,206	$ 7,371	

Segment Disclosure

Archer Daniels Midland (ADM) is primarily engaged in procuring, transporting, storing, processing, and merchandising agricultural commodities and products. ADM reports three business segments: Oilseeds Processing, Corn Processing, and Agricultural Services. The segments are organized by the nature of the products and services offered. This company also has sizable intersegment sales.

According to the disclosure, about $3,109 million out of total sales of about $72,316 million were intersegment in 2009. These amounts are eliminated in consolidation but included in the segment disclosure resulting in net sales of $69,207 million reported in its consolidated income statement.

ADM reports the following information for each of its segments:

Sales to external customers

Intersegment sales

A reconciliation of segment sales to consolidated sales, which is included under the caption Net Sales

Depreciation

Asset abandonments and write-downs

Interest expense

Investment income

Equity in earnings of affiliates

Operating profit, which is again reconciled to consolidated operating profit

Investments in and advances to affiliates

Identifiable assets

Gross additions to property, plant, and equipment

The CODM evaluates these segments on many of the dimensions listed on page 500. It appears that income taxes, unusual items, extraordinary items, and interest revenue are not allocated to the individual segments when internal financial statements are prepared for review by the chief operating decision maker. In contrast to ADM, Intel reports only net revenue and operating income or loss for its segments. As we can observe from these two companies, considerable variety exists in the type of information reviewed by the chief operating decision maker when evaluating segments.

Segment Disclosures for Interim Reports

GAAP [9] requires limited segment information to be included in interim reports. These requirements are covered in the next section of this chapter.

LEARNING OBJECTIVE **7**

INTERIM FINANCIAL REPORTING

Interim financial reports provide information about a firm's operations for less than a full year. They are commonly issued on a quarterly basis and typically include cumulative, year-to-date information, as well as comparative information for corresponding periods of the prior year. Before 1973, little uniformity existed in the content of interim financial reports issued to shareholders. To correct this, the APB issued *Opinion No. 28*, "Interim Financial Reporting," in May 1973. Today, these reporting requirements are codified in FASB ASC Topic 270 "Interim Reporting."

The guidelines for interim reporting are particularly applicable to publicly traded companies that are required to prepare quarterly reports according to SEC and New York Stock Exchange requirements. Even so, GAAP [10] guidelines apply whenever publicly traded companies issue interim financial information to their security holders.

Nature of Interim Reports

Interim financial reports provide more timely, but less complete, information than annual financial reports. Interim reports reflect a trade-off between timeliness and reliability because estimates must replace many of the extensive reviews of receivables, payables, inventory, and the related income effects that support the measurements presented in annual financial reports, which have to meet audit requirements. Under current GAAP [11], interim financial statements only require a minimum level of disclosure. Therefore, interim financial statements are usually labeled *unaudited*.

Under GAAP, each interim period is considered an integral part of each annual period, rather than a basic accounting period unto itself. Generally, interim-period results should be based on the accounting principles and practices used in the latest annual financial statements. Some modifications may be needed, however, to relate the interim-period to annual-period results in a meaningful manner. For example, interim statements may modify the procedures used in annual statements for product costs and other expenses, as discussed below.

Product Costs

GROSS PROFIT METHOD The gross profit method of estimating inventory and cost of goods sold was discussed in your intermediate accounting course. As you may recall, this method is not acceptable for annual financial statement purposes. However, a company can use the gross profit method for interim reporting purposes when it does not use the perpetual inventory method and it is too costly to perform an inventory count to price out the inventory. Obviously, the gross profit method must yield a reasonable estimate of the inventory and cost of goods sold in order to be used.

LIFO INVENTORIES One reason companies use the LIFO method is to reduce taxable income, and therefore taxes paid, when prices are rising. The IRS requires the LIFO method's use for financial reporting purposes if it is used for tax purposes. To avoid paying taxes previously avoided, companies attempt to avoid LIFO layer liquidation that results in lower cost of goods sold, higher net income, and a higher tax bill.

LIFO inventory layers may be liquidated during an interim period but could be expected to be replaced by year-end. Cost of sales can include the replacement cost of the liquidated LIFO layer if the reduction is determined to be temporary. For example, a firm experiencing a temporary 100-unit LIFO inventory liquidation would expense the current cost of the 100 units, rather than the historical LIFO cost. The amount of current cost in excess of the historical cost is shown as a current liability on the interim balance sheet.

INVENTORY MARKET DECLINES Permanent inventory market declines are recognized in the interim period unless they are considered temporary (i.e., no loss is expected for the fiscal year as a whole).

STANDARD COST SYSTEM Planned variances under a standard cost system that are expected to be absorbed by year-end are usually deferred at the interim date.

Expenses Other Than Product Costs

ANNUAL EXPENSES IN INTERIM REPORTS Annual expenses are allocated to the interim periods to which they relate. Major annual repair allowances are an example of this kind of allocation. Expenses arising in an interim period are not deferred unless they would be deferred at year-end. For example, property taxes accrued or deferred for annual purposes are also accrued or deferred for interim periods.

ADVERTISING COSTS Advertising costs are expensed in the interim period in which they are incurred unless the benefits clearly apply to subsequent interim periods.

INCOME TAXES Income taxes for interim reporting are divided into (1) those applicable to income from continuing operations before income taxes, excluding unusual or infrequently occurring items, and (2) those applicable to significant, unusual, or infrequently occurring items, discontinued items, and extraordinary items.

Income tax expense for an interim period is based on an estimated effective annual tax rate that is applied to taxable income from continuing operations, excluding unusual and infrequently occurring items. The year-to-date tax expense, less the tax expense recognized in earlier interim periods, is the tax expense for the current interim period. The tax effects of unusual and infrequently occurring items are calculated separately and added to the tax expense of the interim period in which these items are reported. Gains and losses on discontinued operations and extraordinary items are reported on a net-of-tax basis, as in annual reports.

LEARNING
OBJECTIVE **8**

Computation of the Estimated Annual Effective Tax Rate

The following example shows how Small Corporation estimates its annual effective tax rate for the purpose of preparing quarterly financial reports. Small Corporation bases its estimate on the following *assumed* tax-rate schedule for corporations for the current year:

If Taxable Income Is:		The Tax Is:			
Over	But Not Over	Pay	+	Excess	Of the Amount Over
$ 0	$ 50,000			15%	$ 0
50,000	75,000	$ 7,500	+	25	50,000
75,000	100,000	13,750	+	34	75,000
100,000	335,000	22,250	+	39	100,000
335,000	—			34	0

Small Corporation estimates quarterly income for the calendar year 2010 as follows:

Quarter	Estimated Income		Rate	Estimated Tax
First	$ 20,000	×	15%	$ 3,000
Second	30,000	×	15	4,500
Third	25,000	×	25	6,250
Fourth	25,000	×	34	8,500
Totals	$100,000			$22,250

The estimated quarterly income and income tax estimates assume that Small anticipates no accounting changes, discontinued operations, or extraordinary items for the year. Thus, the estimated annual effective tax rate is 22.25 percent, equal to the estimated tax divided by the estimated income for the year. This computation reflects the *integral theory*, such that each interim period is an essential part of an annual period, and not the *discrete theory* that each interim period is a basic, independent accounting period. The integral theory is required by GAAP. If no changes in the estimates occur during the year, the income by quarter would be estimated as follows:

	First Quarter	Second Quarter	Third Quarter	Fourth Quarter	Fiscal
Income year-to-date	$20,000	$50,000	$75,000	$100,000	$100,000
Quarterly period income	$20,000	$30,000	$25,000	$ 25,000	$100,000
Tax expense (22.25%)	(4,450)	(6,675)	(5,563)	(5,563)	(22,250)
Net income	$15,550	$23,325	$19,437	$ 19,437	$ 77,750

The estimated annual effective tax rate is applied to year-to-date income, and prior-quarter income taxes are deducted to compute the current quarterly income tax expense. For example, the third-quarter tax expense is calculated as follows: $(($75,000 \times 0.2225) - ($4,450 + $6,675)) = $5,563$. This procedure provides for revision of the estimated annual effective tax rate to reflect changes in estimated income levels during the year. For example, if the $100,000 estimated income for the year had included $5,000 dividend income subject to an 80 percent dividend-received deduction, the annual effective tax rate would have been 20.89 percent. The calculation entails a $1,360 deduction for the tax savings on the dividends-received deduction: The estimated annual effective tax rate would have been calculated as follows: $($22,250 - $1,360)/$100,000$.

GUIDELINES FOR PREPARING INTERIM STATEMENTS

Current GAAP [12] summarizes both the consolidated and segment financial information to be disclosed in interim reports. At a minimum, publicly traded companies should report:

a. Sales or gross revenues, provision for income taxes, extraordinary items (including related income tax effects), net income, and comprehensive income

b. Basic and diluted earnings per share data for each period presented

c. Seasonal revenue, costs or expenses

d. Significant changes in estimates or provisions for income taxes

e. Disposal of a component of an entity and extraordinary, unusual or infrequently occurring items

f. Contingent items

g. Changes in accounting principles or estimates

h. Significant changes in financial position

i. All of the following information about reportable operating segments

1. Revenues from external customers
2. Intersegment revenues
3. A measure of segment profit or loss
4. Total assets for which there has been a material change from the amount disclosed in the last annual report
5. A description of differences from the last annual report in the basis of segmentation or in the measurement of segment profit or loss
6. A reconciliation of the total of the reportable segments' measures of profit or loss to the entity's consolidated income before income taxes, extraordinary items, and discontinued operations. However, if, for example, an entity allocates items such as income taxes and extraordinary items to segments, the entity may choose to reconcile the total of the segments' measures of profit or loss to consolidated income after those items. Significant reconciling items shall be separately identified and described in that reconciliation.

j. All of the following information about defined benefit pension plans and other defined benefit postretirement benefit plans, disclosed for all periods presented:

1. The amount of net periodic benefit cost recognized, for each period for which a statement of income is presented, showing separately the service cost component, the interest cost component, the expected return on plan assets for the period, the gain or loss component, the prior service cost or credit component, the transition asset or obligation component, and the gain or loss recognized due to a settlement or curtailment

2. The total amount of the employer's contributions paid, and expected to be paid, during the current fiscal year, if significantly different from amounts previously disclosed. Estimated contributions may be presented in the aggregate combining all of the following:

   i. Contributions required by funding regulations or laws
   ii. Discretionary contributions
   iii. Noncash contributions

k. The information about the use of fair value to measure assets and liabilities recognized in the statement of financial position

l. The information about derivative instruments

m. The information about fair value of financial instruments

n. The information about certain investments in debt and equity securities

o. The information about other-than-temporary impairments

Exhibit 15-2 displays the third fiscal quarterly report for *Colgate-Palmolive,* including their segment report. The Income Statement reports comparative information for both the prior year's quarter, and for the prior year's cumulative 9-month period. The Statement of Cash Flows reports only the prior year's cumulative 9-month period. The segment footnote disclosure displays the same time periods as the Income Statement.

COLGATE-PALMOLIVE COMPANY CONDENSED CONSOLIDATED STATEMENTS OF INCOME (DOLLARS IN MILLIONS EXCEPT PER SHARE AMOUNTS) (UNAUDITED)

	Three Months Ended September 30,		Nine Months Ended September 30,	
	2010	2009	2010	2009
Net sales	$ 3,943	$ 3,998	$ 11,586	$ 11,246
Cost of sales	1,599	1,631	4,732	4,665
Gross profit	2,344	2,367	6,854	6,581
Selling, general and administrative expenses	1,391	1,403	4,038	3,885
Other (income) expense, net	(5)	38	232	72
Operating profit	958	926	2,584	2,624
Interest expense, net	13	17	43	59
Income before income taxes	945	909	2,541	2,565
Provision for income taxes	300	292	879	824
Net income including noncontrolling interests	645	617	1,662	1,741
Less: Net income attributable to noncontrolling interests	26	27	83	81
Net income attributable to Colgate-Palmolive Company	$ 619	$ 590	$ 1,579	$ 1,660
Earnings per common share, basic	$ 1.26	$ 1.17	$ 3.17	$ 3.27
Earnings per common share, diluted	$ 1.21	$ 1.12	$ 3.07	$ 3.16
Dividends declared per common share	$ 0.53	$ 0.44	$ 1.50	$ 1.28

COLGATE-PALMOLIVE COMPANY CONDENSED CONSOLIDATED BALANCE SHEETS (DOLLARS IN MILLIONS) (UNAUDITED)

	September 30, 2010	December 31, 2009
Assets		
Current Assets		
Cash and cash equivalents	$ 654	$ 600
Receivables (net of allowances of $53 and $50, respectively)	1,690	1,626
Inventories	1,278	1,209
Other current assets	469	375
Total current assets	4,091	3,810
Property, plant and equipment:		
Cost	6,998	6,700
Less: Accumulated depreciation	(3,426)	(3,184)
	3,572	3,516
Goodwill, net	2,336	2,302
Other intangible assets, net	818	821
Other assets	573	685
Total assets	$ 11,390	$ 11,134
Liabilities and Shareholders' Equity		
Current Liabilities		
Notes and loans payable	$ 51	$ 35
Current portion of long-term debt	8	326
Accounts payable	1,096	1,172
Accrued income taxes	307	387
Other accruals	1,714	1,679
Total current liabilities	3,176	3,599
Long-term debt	3,329	2,821
Deferred income taxes	112	82
Other liabilities	1,927	1,375
Shareholders' Equity		
Preference stock	159	169
Common stock	733	733
Additional paid-in capital	1,826	1,764

COLGATE-PALMOLIVE COMPANY CONDENSED CONSOLIDATED BALANCE SHEETS (DOLLARS IN MILLIONS) (UNAUDITED)

	September 30, 2010	December 31, 2009
Retained earnings	13,980	13,157
Accumulated other comprehensive income (loss)	(2,308)	(2,096)
	14,390	13,727
Unearned compensation	(100)	(133)
Treasury stock, at cost	(11,618)	(10,478)
Total Colgate-Palmolive Company shareholders' equity	2,672	3,116
Noncontrolling interests	174	141
Total shareholders' equity	2,846	3,257
Total liabilities and shareholders' equity	$ 11,390	$ 11,134

COLGATE-PALMOLIVE COMPANY CONDENSED CONSOLIDATED STATEMENTS OF CASH FLOWS (DOLLARS IN MILLIONS) (UNAUDITED)

	Nine Months Ended September 30,	
	2010	2009
Operating Activities		
Net income including noncontrolling interests	$ 1,662	$ 1,741
Adjustments to reconcile net income including noncontrolling interests to net cash provided by operations:		
Venezuela hyperinflationary transition charge	271	—
Restructuring, net of cash	—	(14)
Depreciation and amortization	278	262
Stock-based compensation expense	101	97
Deferred income taxes	91	16
Cash effects of changes in:		
Receivables	(56)	(104)
Inventories	(63)	10
Accounts payable and other accruals	(95)	355
Other non-current assets and liabilities	54	12
Net cash provided by operations	2,243	2,375
Investing Activities		
Capital expenditures	(318)	(347)
Purchases of marketable securities and investments	(211)	(147)
Proceeds from sales of marketable securities and investments	94	—
Other	(3)	10
Net cash used in investing activities	(438)	(484)
Financing Activities		
Principal payments on debt	(3,469)	(3,011)
Proceeds from issuance of debt	3,709	2,561
Dividends paid	(804)	(702)
Purchases of treasury shares	(1,385)	(664)
Proceeds from exercise of stock options and excess tax benefits	204	196
Net cash used in financing activities	(1,745)	(1,620)
Effect of exchange rate changes in cash and cash equivalents	(6)	21
Net increase (decrease) in cash and cash equivalents	54	292
Cash and cash equivalents at beginning of period	600	555
Cash and cash equivalents at end of period	$ 654	$ 847
Supplemental Cash Flow Information		
Income taxes paid	$ 854	$ 853

(*continued*)

EXHIBIT 15-2

Colgate-Palmolive Third
Quarter 2010 Financial
Statements (*Continued*)

COLGATE-PALMOLIVE COMPANY NOTES TO CONDENSED CONSOLIDATED FINANCIAL STATEMENTS (DOLLARS IN MILLIONS EXCEPT SHARE AND PER SHARE AMOUNTS) (UNAUDITED)

Net sales and Operating profit by segment were as follows:

	Three Months Ended September 30,		Nine Months Ended September 30,	
	2010	2009	2010	2009
Net sales				
Oral, Personal and Home Care				
North America	$ 753	$ 740	$ 2,274	$ 2,204
Latin America	1,069	1,136	3,130	3,097
Europe/South Pacific	821	896	2,415	2,406
Greater Asia/Africa	779	695	2,239	1,972
Total Oral, Personal and Home Care	3,422	3,467	10,058	9,679
Pet Nutrition	521	531	1,528	1,567
Total Net sales	$ 3,943	$ 3,998	$ 11,586	$ 11,246
Operating profit				
Oral, Personal and Home Care				
North America	$ 224	$ 217	$ 668	$ 608
Latin America	332	346	975	987
Europe/South Pacific	197	219	572	539
Greater Asia/Africa	195	161	573	457
Total Oral, Personal and Home Care	948	943	2,788	2,591
Pet Nutrition	138	136	413	407
Corporate	(128)	(153)	(617)	(374)
Total operating profit	$ 958	$ 926	$ 2,584	$ 2,624

SEC Interim Financial Disclosures

The SEC requires that quarterly reports be prepared for the company's stockholders and for filing with the SEC. These reports are to be prepared using GAAP and are filed on Form 10-Q within 45 days after the end of a quarter. Fourth-quarter reports are not required, but SEC Rule 14a-3 requires inclusion of selected quarterly data in the annual report to shareholders. Quarterly reports are not audited, so the CPA's report states that a *review*, rather than an audit, has been performed.

A company's Form 10-Q report to the SEC includes additional information beyond the minimum reporting requirements under GAAP. SEC quarterly and annual reporting requirements are similar. For example, Part I of Form 10-Q contains the following summary contents:

> Part 1—Financial Information
> Item 1—Consolidated Balance Sheet
>   Consolidated Statement of Income
>   Consolidated Statement of Cash Flows
>   Notes to Consolidated Financial Statements
> Item 2—Management's Discussion of Financial Condition and Results of Operations

Companies present comparative consolidated balance sheets as of the end of the current quarter and at the prior year-end. They present the comparative consolidated income statements for the current quarter and the same quarter of the prior year. Companies also present the current year-to-date and the prior year-to-date results. Comparative consolidated statements of cash flows are presented for the current year-to-date and the prior year-to-date activity.

International Accounting Standards

The current IFRS [13] for reporting operating segments was adopted in November 2006 and became effective on January 1, 2009. This recent update is a good example of the convergence process. The prior IFRS dates to 1997, and had a number of differences from GAAP. The current IFRS is similar to GAAP in most respects, with few differences. The major similarities include using a management approach in defining reportable segments, and the same types and level of quantitative thresholds. Additionally, the 75 percent consolidated-revenue test is also applied to determine if additional segments must be disclosed.

IFRS [14] for interim reporting has one major difference with GAAP for interim reporting. IFRS uses the discrete theory, treating each interim period as an independent period.

SUMMARY

Current GAAP requires disclosures about operating segments. The operating segments of a public business enterprise are determined by the structure of the enterprise's internal organization. This method of identifying segments is called the management approach. Aggregation criteria and materiality tests determine which operating segments are reportable.

Disclosures required for each reportable operating segment include a description of the types of products and services sold, a profit or loss measure used internally to evaluate the segment, and total assets. Other disclosures on revenues, expenses, gains, losses, and assets may be made if these amounts are included in the profit or loss and segment-assets measures reviewed by the chief operating decision maker. Reportable segment data are reconciled with the enterprise's consolidated amounts. Limited segment information is also disclosed in quarterly reports.

GAAP also requires disclosures on an enterprisewide basis. A company must disclose information about its products and services, geographic areas, and major customers unless the information is included as part of the segment disclosures.

Segment information is important for effective analysis of financial statements because the opportunities for expansion and capital requirements differ by industry and geographic area.

GAAP for interim financial report disclosures helps to assure that interim financial reports provide timely information. However, much of the information is based on estimates, and the reports are unaudited. Each interim period is considered an integral part of the annual period. As a result, interim-period information is based on the accounting principles used in the last annual report. However, some modifications at the interim reporting date may be necessary so that the interim-period results complement the annual results of operations.

QUESTIONS

1. What is an operating segment?

2. What is a reportable segment according to *FASB ASC Topic 280*? What criteria are used in determining what operating segments are also reportable segments?

3. How are the segments that are not reportable segments handled in the required disclosures of *FASB ASC Topic 280*?

4. Revenue information for Mahoney Corporation is as follows:

Consolidated revenue (from the income statement)	$400,000
Intersegment sales and transfers	80,000
Combined revenues of all industry segments	$480,000

Does the 10% revenue test for a reportable segment apply to 10% of the $400,000 or 10% of the $480,000?

5. Describe the 10% operating-profit test for determining reportable segments.

6. Describe the 10% asset test for determining reportable segments.

7. Describe the 10% revenue test for determining reportable segments.

8. Assume that an enterprise has ten operating segments. Of these, five segments qualify as reportable segments by passing one of the 10% tests. However, their combined revenues from sales to unaffiliated customers total only 70% of the combined unaffiliated revenues from all operating segments. Should the remaining five operating segments be aggregated and shown as an "other segments" category? Explain.

9. What disclosures are required for the reportable segments and all remaining segments in the aggregate?

10. When is an enterprise required to include information in its financial statements about its foreign and domestic operations?

11. Must a major customer be identified by name?

12. Do the requirements of *FASB ASC Topic 280* apply to financial statements for interim periods? If so, how?

13. Explain how a company estimates its annual effective tax rate for interim reporting purposes.

14. What is the difference between the integral theory and the discrete theory with respect to interim financial reporting?

15. Describe the minimum financial information to be disclosed in interim reports under the provisions of *FASB ASC Topic 270.*

EXERCISES

E 15-1
Segment disclosures

1. The disclosure requirements for an operating segment do not include:
   a *Unusual items*
   b *Income tax expense or benefit*
   c *Extraordinary items*
   d *Cost of goods or services sold*

2. A reconciliation between the numbers disclosed in operating segments and consolidated numbers need not be provided for:
   a *Cost of goods sold*
   b *Profit or loss*
   c *Net assets*
   d *Revenues*

3. Each reportable segment is required to disclose the following information except for:
   a *Extraordinary items*
   b *Depreciation, depletion, and amortization*
   c *Capital expenditures*
   d *Gross profit or loss*

4. An enterprise is required to disclose information about its major customers if 10% or more of its revenue is derived from any single customer. This disclosure must include:
   a *The products or services generating the revenue from such sales*
   b *The operating segment or segments making such sales and the total revenue from the customer*
   c *The name of the customer to whom the sales were made*
   d *The dollar amounts of revenue and any profit or loss on the sales*

5. Which of the following is not a criterion for aggregating two or more operating segments?
   a *The segments should have similar products or services.*
   b *The segments should have similar production processes.*
   c *The distribution of products should be similar.*
   d *The segments should have similar amounts of revenue.*

6. Required segment disclosures in interim-period statements do not include:
   a *A measure of segment profit or loss*
   b *Net interest revenue*
   c *A description of a change in segmentation from the last annual report*
   d *Intersegment revenue*

E 15-2
Apply threshold tests—disclosure

Vic Corporation operates entirely in the United States but in different industries. It segments the business based on industry. Total sales of the segments, including intersegment sales, are as follows:

Concrete and stone products	$ 400,000
Construction	1,000,000
Lumber and wood products	1,800,000
Building materials	1,000,000
Other	100,000

Further analysis reveals sales from one segment to another as follows:

Lumber and wood products	$800,000
Building materials	400,000

REQUIRED

1. Determine which segments are reportable segments under both the 10 percent and the 75 percent revenue tests.

2. Prepare a schedule suitable for disclosing revenue by industry segment for external reporting.

3. Prepare a reconciliation of segment revenue with corporate revenue.

E 15-3
Apply threshold tests

Sur Corporation's internal divisions are based on industry. The revenues, operating profits, and assets of the operating segments of Sur are presented in thousands of dollars as follows:

	Sales to Nonaffiliates	Inter-segment Sales	Total Sales	Operating Profit (Loss)	Assets
Food service industry	$150,000	$20,000	$170,000	$ 20,000	$100,000
Copper mine	40,000	—	40,000	(5,000)	30,000
Information systems	10,000	7,500	17,500	2,500	20,000
Chemical industry	65,000	10,000	75,000	15,250	108,500
Agricultural products	24,000	—	24,000	(7,750)	25,000
Pharmaceutical products	10,000	—	10,000	4,000	9,000
Foreign operations	7,500	—	7,500	2,500	10,000
Corporate assets*					16,500
	$306,500	$37,500	$344,000	$ 31,500	$319,000

*Corporate assets include equity investees of $5,000 and general assets of $11,500.

REQUIRED: Determine the reportable segments of Sur Corporation.

E 15-4
Segment and enterprisewide disclosures

The sales in thousands of dollars of the segments of Wow Corporation (Wow is organized on a geographic basis) for 2011 are as follows:

	Unaffiliated Sales	Intersegment Sales	Total
United States	$100,000	$30,000	$ 130,000
Canada	36,000	16,000	52,000
Europe	20,000	2,000	22,000
Latin America	14,000	6,000	20,000
Japan	6,000	—	6,000
Korea	2,000	—	2,000
	$178,000	$54,000	$ 232,000

The $178,000 sales to unaffiliated customers is the amount of revenue reported in Wow's consolidated income statement.

REQUIRED: Illustrate the disclosure of Wow's domestic and foreign revenue in a form acceptable for external reporting, including reconciliation with consolidated revenue.

E 15-5
Apply threshold tests

1. Coy Corporation and its divisions are engaged solely in manufacturing operations. The following data (consistent with prior years' data) pertain to the industries in which operations were conducted for the year ended December 31, 2011 (in thousands):

Industry	Total Revenue	Operating Profit	Assets at December 31, 2011
A	$10,000	$1,750	$20,000
B	8,000	1,400	17,500
C	6,000	1,200	12,500
D	3,000	550	7,500
E	4,250	675	7,000
F	1,500	225	3,000
	$32,750	$5,800	$67,500

In its segment information for 2011, how many reportable segments does Coy have?

a   *Three*
b   *Four*
c   *Five*
d   *Six*

2. Hen Corporation's revenues for the year ended December 31, 2011, are as follows (in thousands):

Consolidated revenue per income statement	$1,200
Intersegment sales	180
Intersegment transfers	60
Combined revenues of all segments	$1,440

Hen has a reportable segment if that segment's revenues exceed:

a   *$6*
b   *$24*
c   *$120*
d   *$144*

3. The following information pertains to Ari Corporation and its divisions for the year ended December 31, 2011 (in thousands):

Sales to unaffiliated customers	$4,000
Intersegment sales of products similar to those sold to unaffiliated customers	1,200
Interest earned on loans to other industry segments	80

The intersegment interest is not reported by the divisions on internal reports reviewed by the chief operating officer. Ari and all of its divisions are engaged solely in manufacturing operations. Ari has a reportable segment if that segment's revenue exceeds:

a   *$528*
b   *$520*
c   *$408*
d   *$400*

4. The following information pertains to revenue earned by Wig Company's operating segments for the year ended December 31, 2011:

Segment	Sales to Unaffiliated Customers	Intersegment Sales	Total Revenues
Ames	$ 10,000	$ 6,000	$ 16,000
Beck	16,000	8,000	24,000
Cyns	8,000	—	8,000
DG	86,000	32,000	118,000
Combined	120,000	46,000	166,000
Elimination	—	(46,000)	(46,000)
Consolidated	$120,000	—	$120,000

In conformity with the revenue test, Wig reportable segments were:

a   *Only DG*
b   *Beck and DG*
c   *Ames, Beck, and DG*
d   *Ames, Beck, Cyns, and DG*

Use the following information in answering questions 5 and 6: Gum Corporation, a publicly owned corporation, is subject to the requirements for segment reporting. In its income statement for the year ended December 31, 2011, Gum reported revenues of $50,000,000, operating expenses of $47,000,000, and net payroll costs of $15,000,000. Gum's combined identifiable assets of all industry segments at December 31, 2011, were $40,000,000.

5. In its 2011 financial statements, Gum should disclose major customer data if sales to any single customer amount to at least:

a   *$300,000*
b   *$1,500,000*
c   *$4,000,000*
d   *$5,000,000*

6. In its 2011 financial statements, if Gum is organized on an industry basis, it should disclose foreign operations data on a specific country if revenues from that country's operations are at least:

a   *$5,000,000*
b   *$4,700,000*
c   *$4,000,000*
d   *$1,500,000*

7. Selected data for a segment of a business enterprise are to be separately reported in accordance with GAAP when the revenues of the segment exceed 10% of the:

a   *Combined net income of all segments reporting profits*
b   *Total revenues obtained in transactions with outsiders*
c   *Total revenues of all the enterprise's operating segments*
d   *Total combined revenues for all segments reporting profits*

8. In financial reporting of segment data, which of the following items is used in determining a segment's operating income?

a   *Income tax expense*
b   *Sales to other segments*
c   *General corporate expense*
d   *Gain or loss on discontinued operations*

E 15-6
Apply threshold tests

A summary of the segment operations of the Nog Corporation for the year ended December 31, 2011, follows:

	United States	Canada	Germany	Japan	Mexico	Other Foreign	Consolidated
Sales to unaffiliated customers	$ 35,000	$ 6,000	$ 3,000	$ 3,500	$1,500	$1,000	$ 50,000
Interarea transfers	10,000	—	—	$ 3,000	—	—	13,000
Total revenue	$ 45,000	$ 6,000	$ 3,000	$ 6,500	$1,500	$1,000	$ 63,000
Operating profits	$ 8,000	$ 1,000	$ 1,500	$ 1,000	$ 500	$ 500	$ 12,500
Segment assets	$ 50,000	$ 7,500	$8,500	$ 9,000	$2,000	$1,500	$ 78,500

1. For which of the following geographic areas will separate disclosures be required if only the 10% revenue test is considered?

a   *United States, Canada, and Japan*
b   *United States and Canada*
c   *United States and Japan*
d   *United States, Canada, Germany, and Japan*

2. For which of the following geographic areas will separate disclosures be required if only the 10% asset test is considered?

a   *United States*
b   *United States and Canada*
c   *United States, Japan, and Germany*
d   *United States, Canada, Germany, and Japan*

3. For which of the following geographic areas will separate disclosures be required if all relevant tests are considered?

  a   United States, Canada, Germany, and Japan
  b   United States, Germany, and Japan
  c   United States, Canada, and Japan
  d   United States and Canada

E 15-7

Interim accounting for various situations—tax

1. Interim reporting under *FASB ASC Topic 270* guidelines refers to financial reporting:

  a   On a monthly basis
  b   On a quarterly basis
  c   On a regular basis
  d   For periods less than a year

2. A liquidation of LIFO inventories for interim reporting purposes may create a problem in measuring cost of sales. Accordingly, cost of sales in interim periods should:

  a   Be determined using the gross profit method
  b   Include the income effect of the LIFO liquidation
  c   Include the expected cost of replacing the liquidated LIFO base
  d   None of the above

3. Bar Company's effective annual income tax rates for the first two quarters of 2011 are 34% and 30% for the first and second quarter, respectively. Assume that Bar's pretax income is $240,000 for the first quarter and $180,000 for the second quarter. Income tax expense for the second quarter is computed:

  a $54,000
  b $126,000
  c $135,600
  d $44,400

4. Assume corporate tax rates of 15% on the first $50,000 of taxable income, 25% on taxable income between $50,000 and $75,000, 34% on taxable income between $75,000 and $100,000, and 39% on taxable income between $100,000 and $335,000. If a corporation estimates its pretax income at $20,000 for the first quarter, $25,000 for the second quarter, $30,000 for the third quarter, and $35,000 for the fourth quarter, its estimated annual effective tax rate is:

  a   23.77%
  b   25%
  c   24.67%
  d   34%

E 15-8

Interim tax

The estimated and actual pretax incomes of Ent Corporation by quarter for 2011 were as follows:

	1st Quarter	2nd Quarter	3rd Quarter	4th Quarter
Estimated pretax income	$30,000	$30,000	$40,000	$50,000
Actual pretax income	30,000	40,000	40,000	40,000

Ent calculated its estimated annual effective income tax rate to be 27.8333 percent, based on estimated pretax income and existing income tax rates.

REQUIRED: Prepare a schedule to calculate Ent Corporation's net income by quarter.

E 15-9

Interim accounting for various situations—tax

1. An inventory loss from a market price decline occurred in the first quarter, and the decline was not expected to reverse during the fiscal year. However, in the third quarter, the inventory's market price recovery exceeded the market decline that occurred in the first quarter. For interim financial reporting, the dollar amount of net inventory should:

a *Decrease in the first quarter by the amount of the market price decline and increase in the third quarter by the amount of the decrease in the first quarter*

b *Decrease in the first quarter by the amount of the market price decline and increase in the third quarter by the amount of the market price recovery*

c *Decrease in the first quarter by the amount of the market price decline and not be affected in the third quarter*

d *Not be affected in either the first quarter or the third quarter*

2. Far Corporation had the following transactions during the quarter ended March 31, 2011:

Loss on early extinguishment of debt	$ 70,000
Payment of fire insurance premium for calendar year 2011	100,000

What amount should be included in Far's income statement for the quarter ended March 31, 2011?

	Extraordinary Loss	Insurance Expense
a	$70,000	$100,000
b	$70,000	$ 25,000
c	$17,500	$ 25,000
d	0	$100,000

3. An inventory loss from a permanent market decline of $360,000 occurred in May 2011. Cox Company appropriately recorded this loss in May 2011, after its March 31, 2011, quarterly report was issued. What amount of inventory loss should be reported in Cox's quarterly income statement for the three months ended June 30, 2011?

a *$0*

b *$90,000*

c *$180,000*

d *$360,000*

4. On July 1, 2011, Dol Corporation incurred an extraordinary loss of $300,000, net of income tax saving. Dol's operating income for the full year ending December 31, 2011, is expected to be $500,000. In Dol's income statement for the quarter ended September 30, 2011, how much of this extraordinary loss should be disclosed?

a *$300,000*

b *$150,000*

c *$75,000*

d *$0*

5. In January 2011, Pin Company paid property taxes of $80,000 covering the calendar year 2011. Also in January 2011, Pin estimated that its year-end bonuses to executives would amount to $320,000 for 2011. What is the total amount of expense relating to these two items that should be reflected in Pin's quarterly income statement for the three months ended June 30, 2011?

a *$100,000*

b *$80,000*

c *$20,000*

d *$0*

E 15-10

Interim accounting under LIFO

Tap Manufacturing Company records sales of $1,000,000 and cost of sales of $550,000 during the first quarter of 2011. Tap uses the LIFO inventory method, and its inventories are computed as follows:

Beginning LIFO inventory at January 1	10,000 units at $5	$50,000
Ending LIFO inventory at March 31	6,000 units at $5	$30,000

Before year-end, Tap expects to replace the 4,000 units liquidated in the first quarter. The current cost of the inventory units is $7each.

REQUIRED: At what amount will Tap report cost of sales in its first-quarter interim report?

PROBLEMS

P 15-1
Apply threshold tests

The following information has been accumulated for use in preparing segment disclosures for Wod Corporation (in thousands):

	Sales to Unaffiliated Customers	Sales to Affiliated Customers	Total Sales
Apparel	$164	—	$ 164
Construction	112	—	112
Furniture	208	$ 6	214
Lumber and wood products	175	90	265
Paper	90	—	90
Textiles	50	170	220
Tobacco	93	—	93
Total	$892	$266	$1,158

REQUIRED

1. Determine Wod's reportable segments under the 10 percent revenue test.

2. Are additional reportable segments required under the 75 percent revenue test?

3. Prepare a schedule to disclose revenue by operating segment for external reporting. Assume that the paper and tobacco segments, both sold in grocery stores, share similar operating characteristics on four of the five aggregation criteria.

P 15-2
Apply threshold tests

The following data for 2011 relate to Hay Industries, a worldwide conglomerate:

	Sales to Unaffiliated Customers	Intersegment Sales	Operating Profit (Loss)	Assets
Food	$300,000	$ 50,000	$45,000	$310,000
Chemical	110,000	40,000	23,000	150,000
Textiles	65,000	5,000	(8,000)	60,000
Furniture	48,000	—	9,000	40,000
Beverage	62,000	10,000	18,000	60,000
Oil	15,000	—	(2,000)	25,000
Segment	600,000	105,000	85,000	645,000
Corporate	—	—	(7,000)	15,000
Consolidated	$600,000	0	$78,000	$660,000

REQUIRED: Answer the following questions related to Hay's required segment disclosures and show computations:

1. Which segments are reportable segments under (a) the revenue test, (b) the operating-profit test, and (c) the asset test?

2. Do additional reportable segments have to be identified?

P 15-3
Apply threshold tests—Disclosure

DaP Corporation's home country is the United States, but it also has operations in Canada, Mexico, Brazil, and South Africa and reports internally on a geographic basis. Information relevant to DaP's operating-segment disclosure requirement for the year ended December 31, 2011, is presented in summary form as follows:

	United States	Canada	Mexico	Brazil	South Africa	Consolidated
Sales to unaffiliated customers	$120,000	$13,000	$20,000	$22,000	$15,000	$190,000
Intersegment transfers	29,000	11,000	—	—	10,000	$ 50,000
Total revenue	$149,000	$24,000	$20,000	$22,000	$25,000	$240,000
Operating profit	$ 24,000	$ 6,000	$ 8,000	$ 5,000	$ 7,000	$ 50,000
Identifiable assets	$150,000	$30,000	$19,000	$20,000	$31,000	$250,000

REQUIRED

1. Prepare schedules to show which of DaP's operating segments require separate disclosure under (a) the 10% revenue test, (b) the 10% asset test, and (c) the 10% profit test.

2. Which of DaP's operating segments meet at least one of the tests for segment reporting?

3. Prepare a schedule to disclose DaP's segment operations from the information given.

P 15-4
Apply threshold tests—Segment and enterprisewide disclosure

Mer Corporation has five major operating segments and operates in both domestic and foreign markets. Mer is organized internally on an industry basis. Information about its revenue from operating segments and foreign operations for 2011 is as follows (in thousands):

SALES TO UNAFFILIATED CUSTOMERS

	Domestic	Foreign	Total
Foods	$ 150	$ 30	$ 180
Soft drinks	650	250	900
Distilled spirits	500	50	550
Cosmetics	200	—	200
Packaging	110	—	110
Other (four minor segments)	240	—	240
	$1,850	$330	$2,180

SALES TO AFFILIATED CUSTOMERS

	Domestic	Foreign	Total
Foods	$ 30	—	$ 30
Soft drinks	160	—	160
Distilled spirits	—	$20	20
Cosmetics	—	—	—
Packaging	10	—	10
Other (four minor segments)	—	—	—
	$200	$20	$220

A Japanese subsidiary of Mer operates exclusively in the soft drink market. All other foreign operations are carried out through Canadian subsidiaries, none of which are included in the soft drink business.

Only the soft drink and distilled spirits segments are reportable segments under the asset and operating-profit tests for segments.

REQUIRED

1. Determine which industry segments are reportable segments under the revenue test for segment reporting. Assume no further aggregation is possible. Would the possible aggregation of smaller segments change your response?

2. Prepare a schedule suitable for disclosing Mer's revenue by segment for 2011, assuming no further aggregation is possible.

3. Prepare a schedule suitable for disclosing Mer's revenue by geographic area for 2011.

P 15-5
Apply threshold tests—Disclosure

Selected information, which is reported to the chief operating officer, for the five segments of Rad Company for the year ended December 31, 2011, is as follows:

	Food	Tobacco	Lumber	Textiles	Furniture	General Corporate	Consolidated
Revenue Data							
Sales to unaffiliated customers	$12,000	$10,000	$7,000	$18,000	$7,000		$ 54,000
Sales to affiliated customers	5,000	7,000		8,000			20,000
Income from equity investees				3,000		$ 6,000	9,000
Total revenue	$17,000	$17,000	$ 7,000	$29,000	$7,000	$ 6,000	$ 83,000
Expense Data							
Cost of sales	$10,000	$ 9,000	$4,000	$16,000	$4,000		$ 43,000
Depreciation expense	1,000	2,000	2,500	3,000	500		9,000
Other operating expenses	2,000	2,000	1,000	2,000	1,000		8,000
Interest expense	2,000			2,000		$ 3,000	7,000
Income taxes	1,000	2,000	(250)	3,000	750	1,500	8,000
Net income	$ 1,000	$ 2,000	$ (250)	$ 3,000	$ 750	$ 1,500	$ 8,000
Asset Data							
Segment assets	$18,000	$19,000	$ 6,000	$22,000	$7,000		$ 72,000
Investment in affiliates				20,000		$40,000	60,000
General corporate assets						4,000	4,000
Intersegment advances	1,000	2,000					
Total assets	$19,000	$21,000	$6,000	$42,000	$7,000	$44,000	$136,000

The lumber segment has not been a reportable segment in prior years and is not expected to be a reportable segment in future years.

REQUIRED

1. Prepare schedules to show which of the segments are reportable segments under:
   a   The 10% revenue test
   b   The 10% operating-profit test
   c   The 10% asset test

2. Which of the segments meet at least one of the tests for reportable segments?

3. Must additional reportable segments be identified?

4. Prepare a schedule for appropriate disclosure of the above segmented data in the financial report of Rad Company for the year ended December 31, 2011.

P 15-6
Apply threshold tests—Disclosure

The consolidated income statement of Tut Company for 2011 is as follows (in thousands):

TUT CONSOLIDATED INCOME STATEMENT
FOR THE YEAR ENDED DECEMBER 31, 2011

Sales	$360
Interest income	10
Income from equity investee	30
Total revenue	400
Cost of sales	$180
General expenses	40
Selling expenses	50
Interest expense	10
Noncontrolling interest expense	15
Income taxes	45
Total expenses	340
Income before extraordinary loss	$ 60
Extraordinary loss (net of income taxes)	10
Consolidated net income	$ 50

Tut's operations are conducted through three domestic operating segments with sales, expenses, and assets as follows (in thousands):

	Chemical	Food	Drug	Corporate
Sales (including intersegment sales)	$160	$140	$120	
Cost of sales (including intersegment cost of sales)	80	70	60	
General expenses	15	10	10	$ 5
Selling expenses	20	15	15	
Interest expense (unaffiliated)	5		5	
Identifiable assets	200	180	150	200
Investment in equity investee				300

The $10,000 interest income is not related to any industry segment. Consolidated total assets are $1,000,000. The chemical and food segments had intersegment sales of $35,000 and $25,000, respectively.

REQUIRED: Prepare a schedule of required disclosures for Tut's industry segments in a form acceptable for reporting purposes.

P 15-7
Apply threshold tests—Disclosure

The information that follows is for Cob Company at and for the year ended December 31, 2011. Cob's operating segments are cost centers currently used for internal planning and control purposes. Amounts shown in the Total Consolidated column are amounts prepared under GAAP for external reporting. (Data are in thousands of dollars.)

	Food Industry	Packing Industry	Textile Industry	Foreign Operations	All Other Industries	Corporate	Total Consolidated
Income Statement							
Sales to unaffiliated customers	$950	$500	$300	$250	$400		$2,400
Income from equity investees							100
Cost of sales to unaffiliated customers	(600)	(350)	(175)	(125)	(250)		(1,500)
Operating expense	(200)	(75)	(150)	(75)	(75)	$ (25)	(600)
Interest expense							(20)
Income taxes							(150)
Noncontrolling interest expense							(30)
Income (loss)	$150	$ 75	$(25)	$ 50	$ 75	$ (25)	$ 200

(continued)

	Food Industry	Packing Industry	Textile Industry	Foreign Operations	All Other Industries	Corporate	Total Consolidated
Assets							
Current assets	$300	$100	$ 75	$100	$225	$ 25	$ 825
Plant assets—net	400	400	250	100	175	25	1,350
Advances	50		25			50	
Equity investments						1,000	1,000
Total assets	$750	$500	$350	$200	$400	$1,100	$3,175
Intersegment Transfers							
Sales*	$ 60	$ 60	$ 30	$ 50			
Purchases*	$100	$ 25		$ 75			

*Amounts have been eliminated from the income data given.

REQUIRED

1. Prepare a schedule to determine which of Cob's operating segments are reportable segments under (a) the 10% revenue test, (b) the 10% operating-profit test, and (c) the 10% asset test.

2. Prepare a schedule to show how Cob's segment information would be disclosed under the provisions of *FASB ASC Topic 280.*

P 15-8
Interim reporting—tax

Tor Corporation is subject to income tax rates of 20 percent on its first $50,000 pretax income and 34 percent on amounts in excess of $50,000. Quarterly pretax accounting income for the calendar year is estimated by Tor to be as follows:

Quarter	Estimated Pretax Income
First	$ 20,000
Second	30,000
Third	60,000
Fourth	50,000
Total	$160,000

No changes in accounting principles, discontinued items, unusual or infrequently occurring items, or extraordinary items are anticipated for the year. The fourth quarter's pretax income is, however, expected to include $20,000 in dividends from domestic corporations, for which an 80 percent dividend-received deduction is available.

REQUIRED

1. Calculate the estimated annual effective tax rate for Tor Corporation for 2011.

2. Prepare a schedule showing Tor's estimated net income for each quarter and the calendar year 2011.

INTERNET ASSIGNMENT

Go to **H. J. Heinz's** Web site and obtain a copy of its most recent annual report.

a. What are Heinz's business segments? Are Heinz's operating segments based on product/industry or geographic groupings?

b. Examine the segment-disclosure totals for revenues, profits, and assets. Do they agree with the totals reported in the consolidated financial statements?

c. How significant is intersegment revenue? From this analysis, is Heinz primarily horizontally or vertically integrated, or a conglomerate?

d. What geographical area provides most of Heinz's revenues? Would you consider Heinz a multinational corporation? Why or why not?

e. Qualitatively, do you consider Heinz's segmental reporting to be adequate? What additional information or details would you like to see disclosed regarding its segments?

REFERENCES TO THE AUTHORITATIVE LITERATURE

[1] FASB ASC 280. Originally *Statement of Financial Accounting Standards No. 131.* "Disclosures about Segments of an Enterprise and Related Information." Stamford, CT: Financial Accounting Standards Board, 1997.

[2] FASB ASC 280-10-50-5. Originally *Statement of Financial Accounting Standards No. 131.* "Disclosures about Segments of an Enterprise and Related Information." Stamford, CT: Financial Accounting Standards Board, 1997. (paragraph 12)

[3] FASB ASC 280-10-50-1. Originally *Statement of Financial Accounting Standards No. 131.* "Disclosures about Segments of an Enterprise and Related Information." Stamford, CT: Financial Accounting Standards Board, 1997. (paragraph 10)

[4] FASB ASC 280-10-50-18. Originally *Statement of Financial Accounting Standards No. 131.* "Disclosures about Segments of an Enterprise and Related Information." Stamford, CT: Financial Accounting Standards Board, 1997. (paragraph 24)

[5] FASB ASC 280-10-50-9. Originally *Statement of Financial Accounting Standards No. 131.* "Disclosures about Segments of an Enterprise and Related Information." Stamford, CT: Financial Accounting Standards Board, 1997. (paragraph 15)

[6] FASB ASC 280-10-50-14. Originally *Statement of Financial Accounting Standards No. 131.* "Disclosures about Segments of an Enterprise and Related Information." Stamford, CT: Financial Accounting Standards Board, 1997. (paragraph 20)

[7] FASB ASC 280-10-50-22. Originally *Statement of Financial Accounting Standards No. 131.* "Disclosures about Segments of an Enterprise and Related Information." Stamford, CT: Financial Accounting Standards Board, 1997. (paragraph 27)

[8] FASB ASC 225-20-45-16. Originally APB 30. "Reporting the Results of Operations—Reporting the Effects of Disposal of a Segment of a Business, and Extraordinary, Unusual and Infrequently Occurring Events and Transactions." AICPA Accounting Standards Executive Committee (AcSEC). 1973. (paragraph 26)

[9] FASB ASC 280-10-50-32. Originally *Statement of Financial Accounting Standards No. 131.* "Disclosures about Segments of an Enterprise and Related Information." Stamford, CT: Financial Accounting Standards Board, 1997. (paragraph 33)

[10] FASB ASC 270-10-05-1. Originally APB Opinion 28. *"Interim Financial Reporting."* Accounting Principles Board, 1973. (paragraph 1)

[11] FASB ASC 270-10-45-1. Originally APB Opinion 28. *"Interim Financial Reporting."* Accounting Principles Board, 1973. (paragraph 9)

[12] FASB ASC 270-10-50-1. Originally APB Opinion 28. *"Interim Financial Reporting."* Accounting Principles Board, 1973. (paragraph 30)

[13] IASB International Financial Reporting Standard 8. "Operating Segments." International Accounting Standards Board, 2006.

[14] IASC International Accounting Standard 34. "Interim Financial Reporting." International Accounting Standards Committee, 1998.

16 CHAPTER

Partnerships—Formation, Operations, and Changes in Ownership Interests

This chapter and Chapter 17 focus on accounting for partnership entities. This chapter describes general matters involving the partnership form of business organization, including partnership formation, accounting for partnership operations, and accounting for changes in ownership interests. The limited partnership, a special kind of partnership frequently used in professional partnerships such as CPA firms, is described at the end of this chapter. Chapter 17 covers the dissolution and liquidation of partnerships.

Although accounting for partnerships differs from that of other types of business organizations, asset, liability, and income accounting usually follow GAAP.

NATURE OF PARTNERSHIPS

Partnerships allow a business venture's required investment and its risk to be shared by two or more people. Partners can contribute their expertise to the venture. Partnerships are found in many areas of business, including service industries, retail trade, wholesale and manufacturing operations, and the professions, particularly the legal, medical, and public accounting professions.

Partnership formation, operation, and dissolution are governed by state statutes. In 1914, the National Conference of Commissioners on Uniform State Laws developed the Uniform Partnership Act (1914), that was eventually adopted, with some variations, by all states except Louisiana. In 1992 and 1997, the Uniform Partnership Act (1914) was revised by the National Conference and has been adopted, with revision, by several states. The original Uniform Partnership Act still provides legal guidance for general partnerships in most states, and its provisions generally apply to the formation, operation, and dissolution of partnerships in the United States. The change in the Uniform Partnership Act (1997) (UPA) that is relevant to our discussion here is the adoption of the entity theory to define the nature of partnerships. Under the entity theory, partners own their share of the partnership but do not have ownership shares in the individual assets of the entity. The Uniform Partnership Act (1914) applied an aggregate theory approach in which partners not only had an ownership interest in the partnership but also in the individual assets of the entity. Under UPA, in most circumstances, partners can dissociate themselves from a partnership without an accompanying winding up of the business. Winding up the business requires selling off all assets, settling liabilities, and distributing the proceeds to the partners. This process is called dissolution of a partnership. Dissociation allows the other partners or other people to buy out the dissociating partner's share of the business without interrupting the business itself. This is similar to the way in which a corporation's stock can be traded.

We discuss dissociation in this chapter and dissolution with resulting winding up of the business in Chapter 17. The 1997 UPA is included on this book's Web site. Remember, however, that each state has its own variation of partnership law.

LEARNING OBJECTIVES

1 Comprehend the legal characteristics of partnerships.

2 Understand initial investment valuation and record keeping.

3 Grasp the diverse nature of profit and loss sharing agreements and their computation.

4 Value a new partner's investment in an existing partnership.

5 Value a partner's share upon retirement or death.

6 Understand limited liability partnership characteristics.

LEARNING
OBJECTIVE 1

Partnership Characteristics

Partnership is defined in Section 101(6) of the UPA as "an association of two or more persons to carry on as co-owners a business for profit." Partnership business operations frequently continue to run smoothly when partners are admitted or withdraw.

Under the legal concept of **mutual agency**, each partner is an agent for all partnership activities, with the power to bind all other partners by his or her actions on behalf of the partnership. The implications of mutual agency are particularly significant when considered in conjunction with the **unlimited liability** feature of partnerships. Each partner is liable for all partnership debts and, in case of insolvency, may be required to use personal assets to pay partnership debts authorized by any other partner.

Articles of Partnership

A partnership may be formed by a simple oral agreement among two or more people to operate a business for profit. Even though oral agreements may be legal and binding, written **partnership agreements** are a sound business practice. Such agreements should specify:

1. The types of products and services to be provided and other details of the business's operations
2. Each partner's rights and responsibilities in conducting the business
3. Each partner's initial investment including the value assigned to noncash asset investments
4. Additional investment conditions
5. Asset withdrawal provisions
6. Profit and loss sharing formulas
7. Procedures for dissolving the partnership

When no specific agreement for dividing profits and losses exists, all partners share equally, irrespective of investments made or time devoted to the business (UPA Section 401(b)).

Partnership Financial Reporting

The accounting reports of partnerships are designed to meet the needs of three user groups—the partners, the partnership creditors, and the Internal Revenue Service (IRS). Partners need accounting information for planning and controlling partnership assets and activities and for making personal investment decisions with respect to their partnership investments. In the absence of an agreement to the contrary, every partner has access to the partnership books at all times (Section 403(b)). Credit grantors such as banks and other financial institutions frequently require financial reports in support of loan applications and other credit matters relating to partnerships.

Although partnerships do not pay federal income taxes, partnerships are required to submit financial information to the IRS. This allows the IRS to verify that each partner pays income taxes on his or her share of partnership income. Partnerships are not required to prepare annual reports for public inspection.

LEARNING
OBJECTIVE 2

INITIAL INVESTMENTS IN A PARTNERSHIP

All property brought into the partnership or acquired by the partnership is partnership property (UPA Section 203). Initial investments in a partnership are recorded in capital accounts maintained for each partner. If Ash and Bec each invest $20,000 cash in a new partnership, they record the investments as follows:

Cash (+A)	20,000	
Ash capital (+OE)*		20,000
To record Ash's original investment of cash.		
Cash (+A)	20,000	
Bec capital (+OE)		20,000
To record Bec's original investment of cash.		

---

*Our journal entry notation in chapters 16 and 17 uses OE to represent partnership equity instead of SE to represent shareholder equity.

Noncash Investments

When property other than cash is invested in a partnership, the noncash property is recorded at the fair value of the property at the time of the investment. Conceptually, the fair value should be determined by independent valuations, but as a practical matter, the fair value of noncash property is determined by agreement of all partners. The amounts involved should be specified in the written partnership agreement.

Assume, for example, that Col and Cro enter into a partnership with the following investments:

	Col (Fair Value)	Cro (Fair Value)
Cash	—	$ 7,000
Land (cost to Col, $5,000)	$10,000	—
Building (cost to Col, $30,000)	40,000	—
Inventory items (cost to Cro, $28,000)	—	35,000
Total	$50,000	$42,000

After Col and Cro agree to the values assigned to the assets, they record the investments as follows:

Land (+A)	10,000	
Building (+A)	40,000	
Col capital (+OE)		50,000
To record Col's original investment of land		
and building at fair value.		
Cash (+A)	7,000	
Inventory (+A)	35,000	
Cro capital (+OE)		42,000
To record Cro's original investment of cash		
and inventory items at fair value.		

Bonus or Goodwill on Initial Investments

A valuation problem arises when partners agree on relative capital interests that are not aligned with their investments of identifiable assets. For example, Col and Cro could agree to divide initial partnership capital equally, even though Col contributed $50,000 in identifiable assets and Cro contributed $42,000. Such an agreement implies that Cro is contributing an unidentifiable asset such as individual talent, established clientele, or banking connections to the partnership. The dollar amount of the implied unidentifiable asset can be inferred from Col's fair value contribution. Col invested $50,000 of assets measured at fair value for a 50 percent interest in the partnership. One can infer from Col's investment that the fair value of the partnership is $100,000 ($50,000 ÷ 50%). The implied fair value of the unidentifiable asset contributed by Cro is $8,000 because Cro also has a 50 percent interest in the partnership but only contributed identifiable assets with a fair value of $42,000.

The partnership agreement specifies equal capital interests, so we should adjust the capital account balances of Col and Cro to meet the agreement's conditions. Either of two approaches may be used to adjust the capital accounts—the bonus approach or the goodwill approach. Under the **bonus approach**, the unidentifiable asset is not recorded on the partnership books.

Because the total identifiable contributed capital is $92,000, each partner will start with $46,000 if the unidentifiable asset is not recorded. As a result, Col's capital will be reduced by $4,000, and Cro's will be increased by $4,000. This is recorded as follows:

Col capital (−OE)	4,000	
Cro capital (+OE)		4,000
To establish equal capital interests of $46,000 by recording		
a $4,000 bonus from Col to Cro.		

When the **goodwill approach** is used, the unidentifiable asset contributed by Cro is measured on the basis of Col's $50,000 investment for a 50 percent interest. Col's investment implies total partnership capital of $100,000 ($50,000 ÷ 50%) and goodwill of $8,000 ($100,000 total capital −$92,000 identifiable assets). We record the unidentifiable asset as follows:

Goodwill (+A)	8,000	
Cro capital (+OE)		8,000

    To establish equal capital interests of $50,000 by recognizing
      Cro's investment of an $8,000 unidentifiable asset.

Both approaches are equally effective in aligning the capital accounts with the agreement and are equitable in assigning capital interests to individual partners. A decision to use one approach over the other will depend on partner attitudes toward recording the $8,000 unidentifiable asset under the goodwill method and on Col's willingness to receive a $46,000 capital credit for a $50,000 investment under the bonus approach.

ADDITIONAL INVESTMENTS AND WITHDRAWALS

The partnership agreement should establish guidelines for additional investments and withdrawals made after partnership operations have begun. Additional investments are credited to the investing partner's capital account at fair value at the time of the investment. Withdrawals of large and irregular amounts are ordinarily recorded directly in the withdrawing partner's capital account. The entry for such a withdrawal is:

Smith capital (−OE)	20,000	
Cash (−A)		20,000

    To record the withdrawal of cash.

Drawings

Partnership profits are the business rewards for partners, so partners do not have take-home pay as do the employees of the partnership business. Instead, active partners commonly withdraw regular amounts of money on a weekly or monthly basis in anticipation of their share of partnership profits. Such withdrawals are called **drawings**, **drawing allowances**, or sometimes **salary allowances**, and they are usually recorded in the partners' drawing accounts rather than directly in the capital accounts. For example, if Tow and Lee withdraw $1,000 from the partnership each month, they would record the monthly withdrawals as follows:

Tow drawing (−OE)	1,000	
Cash (−A)		1,000

    To record Tow's drawing allowance for January.

Lee drawing (−OE)	1,000	
Cash (−A)		1,000

    To record Lee's drawing allowance for January.

Drawing accounts provide a record of each partner's drawings during an accounting period. This record may be compared with drawings allowed in the partnership agreement in order to establish an accounting control over excessive drawings. Drawings balances are also a factor in many profit and loss sharing agreements and are discussed later in the chapter.

If Tow draws $1,000 each month during the year, his drawing account balance at year-end is $12,000, and his drawing account is closed by the following entry:

Tow capital (−OE)	12,000	
Tow drawing (+OE)		12,000

    To close Tow's drawing account.

Regardless of the name given to regular withdrawals by partners, such withdrawals are disinvestments of essentially the same nature as large and irregular withdrawals. Drawing accounts are closed to capital accounts before a partnership balance sheet is prepared.

Loans and Advances

A partner may make a personal loan to the partnership. UPA section 401(d) specifies that "a partner, who in the aid of the partnership makes any payment or advance beyond the amount of capital which he agreed to contribute, shall be paid interest from the date of the payment or advance." Such loans or advances and related accrued interest are regarded as liabilities of the partnership. Similarly, partnership loans and advances to an individual partner are considered partnership assets. Matters concerning loans and advances to or from partners should be covered in the partnership agreement.

PARTNERSHIP OPERATIONS

LEARNING OBJECTIVE **3**

The operations of a partnership are similar in most respects to those of other forms of organizations operating in the same line of business. In measuring partnership income for a period, however, the expenses should be scrutinized to make sure that partners' personal expenses are excluded from the partnership's business expenses. If a partner's personal expenses are paid with partnership assets, the payment is charged to the drawing or capital account of that partner. Drawings and salary allowances are closed to the capital accounts of the partners rather than to an income summary account.

Partnership general-purpose financial statements include an income statement, a balance sheet, a statement of partnership capital, and a statement of cash flows. The statement of partnership capital is unique to the partnership form of organization and is illustrated here.

Assume that Rat and Yan are partners sharing profits in a 60:40 ratio, respectively. Data relevant to the partnership's equity accounts for 2011 are:

Partnership net income 2011	$34,500
Rat capital January 1, 2011	40,000
Rat additional investment 2011	5,000
Rat drawing 2011	6,000
Yan capital January 1, 2011	35,000
Yan drawing 2011	9,000
Yan withdrawal 2011	3,000

The statement of partners' capital that appears in Exhibit 16-1 reflects this information. Although other forms of presentation can be used, the format illustrated in Exhibit 16-1 provides a comparison of capital changes before and after the division of partnership net income. An ability to compare beginning capital balances and net contributed capital is helpful to the partners in setting investment and withdrawal policies and in controlling abuses of the established policies.

The additional investment by Rat and withdrawal by Yan have been directly recorded in their respective capital accounts. Partnership income and drawings are closed to each partner's capital accounts at year-end.

RAT AND YAN STATEMENT OF PARTNERS' CAPITAL FOR THE YEAR ENDED DECEMBER 31, 2011

	60% Rat	40% Yan	Total
Capital balances January 1, 2011	$40,000	$35,000	$75,000
Add: Additional investments	5,000	—	5,000
Deduct: Withdrawals	—	(3,000)	(3,000)
Deduct: Drawings	(6,000)	(9,000)	(15,000)
Net contributed capital	39,000	23,000	62,000
Add: Net income for 2011	20,700	13,800	34,500
Capital balances December 31, 2011	$59,700	$36,800	$96,500

EXHIBIT 16-1

Format for a Statement of Partners' Capital

Closing entries for the Rat and Yan partnership at December 31, 2011, are as follows:

December 31, 2011

Revenue and expense summary (−OE)	34,500	
Rat capital (+OE)		20,700
Yan capital (+OE)		13,800
To divide net income 60% to Rat and 40% to Yan.		

December 31, 2011

Rat capital (−OE)	6,000	
Yan capital (−OE)	9,000	
Rat drawing (+OE)		6,000
Yan drawing (+OE)		9,000
To close partner drawing accounts to capital accounts.		

PROFIT AND LOSS SHARING AGREEMENTS

Equal division of partnership income is required in the absence of a profit and loss sharing agreement. However, partners generally agree to share profits in a specified ratio, such as the 60:40 division illustrated for the Rat and Yan partnership. Profit sharing agreements also apply to the division of losses unless the agreement specifies otherwise.

Although agreements to share profits and losses equally or in specified ratios are common, more-complex profit sharing agreements are also encountered in practice. The time that partners devote to the partnership business and the capital invested in the business by individual partners are frequently considered in determining the profit sharing agreement. If one partner manages the partnership, the partnership agreement may allow that partner a salary allowance equal to the amount he or she could earn in an alternative employment opportunity before remaining profits are allocated. Similarly, if one partner invests significantly more than another in a partnership venture, the agreement may provide an interest allowance on capital investments before remaining profits are divided. As in the case of salary allowances, interest allowances are provisions of the partnership agreement and have no effect on the measurement of partnership income but do affect how much of that income is assignable to each partner.

Service Considerations in Profit and Loss Sharing Agreements

As mentioned earlier, a partner who devotes time to the partnership business while other partners work elsewhere may receive a salary allowance. Salary allowances are also used to compensate for differences in the fair value of the talents of partners, all of whom devote their time to the partnership. Another variation in profit and loss sharing agreements provides salary allowances to active partners and a bonus to the managing partner to encourage profit maximization. These alternatives are illustrated for the partnership of Ann, Gary, and Kate. Ann is the managing partner, Gary is the sales manager, and Kate works outside the partnership.

Salary Allowances in Profit Sharing Agreements

Assume that Ann, Gary, and Kate's partnership agreement provides that Ann and Gary receive salary allowances of $12,000 each, with the remaining income allocated equally among the three partners. If partnership net income is $60,000 for 2011 and $12,000 for 2012, the income allocations are as shown in Exhibit 16-2. The total 2011 allocation is $24,000 each to Ann and Gary and $12,000 to Kate. The 2012 allocation is $8,000 income to Ann and Gary and a $4,000 loss to Kate. Note that the partnership agreement was followed in 2012 even though the salary allowances of $24,000 exceeded partnership net income of $12,000. The income allocation schedule follows the order of the profit sharing agreement even when the partnership has a loss. Salary allowances increase the loss to be divided equally.

EXHIBIT 16-2

**Salary Allowances
in Profit Sharing
Agreements**

INCOME ALLOCATION SCHEDULE—2011

		Ann	Gary	Kate	Total
Net income		$60,000			
Salary allowances to Ann and Gary		(24,000)	$12,000	$12,000		$24,000
Remainder to divide		36,000			
Divided equally		(36,000)	12,000	12,000	$12,000	36,000
Remainder to divide		0			
Net income allocation			$24,000	$24,000	$12,000	$60,000

INCOME ALLOCATION SCHEDULE—2012

		Ann	Gary	Kate	Total
Net income		$12,000			
Salary allowances to Ann and Gary		(24,000)	12,000	12,000		$24,000
Remainder to divide		(12,000)			
Divided equally		$12,000	(4,000)	(4,000)	$ (4,000)	(12,000)
Remainder to divide		0			
Net income allocation			$ 8,000	$ 8,000	$ (4,000)	$12,000

Journal entries to distribute partnership income to individual capital accounts for 2011 and 2012 follow:

December 31, 2011

Revenue and expense summary (−OE)	60,000	
Ann capital (+OE)		24,000
Gary capital (+OE)		24,000
Kate capital (+OE)		12,000
Partnership income allocation for 2011.		

December 31, 2012

Revenue and expense summary (−OE)	12,000	
Kate capital (−OE)	4,000	
Ann capital (+OE)		8,000
Gary capital (+OE)		8,000
Partnership income allocation for 2012.		

In partnership accounting, partner salary allowances are not expenses in the determination of partnership net income. They are a means of achieving a fair division of income among the partners based on the time and talents devoted to partnership business.

Calculating partnership income after salary allowances is appropriate when comparing the performance of a partnership business with similar businesses operated under the corporate organizational form. Stockholders who devote their time to corporate affairs are employees, and their salaries are deducted in measuring corporate net income. Failure to adjust partnership income for salary allowances may result in inaccurate comparisons of a corporation's performance to a partnership's performance. Other adjustments, such as for corporate income taxes, also need to be made for accurate comparisons.

Calculation of partnership income after salary allowances is also appropriate in assessing the success of a business. The financial success of a partnership business lies in its earning a fair return for the services performed by partners, for capital invested in the business, and for the risks taken. If partnership income is not greater than the combined amounts that active partners could earn by working outside of the partnership, then the business is not a financial success. Income after salary allowances (or imputed salaries) should be sufficient to compensate for capital invested and risks undertaken.

BONUS AND SALARY ALLOWANCES Assume that the partnership agreement of Ann, Gary, and Kate provides that Ann receive a bonus of 10 percent of partnership net income for managing the business; that Ann and Gary receive salary allowances of $10,000 and $8,000, respectively, for services rendered; and that the remaining partnership income be divided equally among the three partners. If partnership net income is $60,000 in 2011 and $12,000 in 2012, the partnership income is allocated as shown in Exhibit 16-3.

The allocation schedules follow the order of the profit sharing agreement in allocating the bonus first, then the salary allowances, and finally the remainder to individual partners. The bonus is computed on the basis of partnership net income as the concept of "partnership net income" is generally understood in accounting practice (i.e., before salary allowances are deducted).

Partners may, however, require salary allowances to be deducted in determining the base for computing the bonus. If this had been the case here, the bonus illustrated for 2011 would have been $4,200 [($60,000 − $18,000) × 10%] rather than $6,000, and the final net income allocation would have been $26,800, $20,600, and $12,600 for Ann, Gary, and Kate, respectively.

Sometimes the partners may want the bonus, as well as salary allowances, to be deducted in determining the base for the bonus computation. Had this been the case in the Ann, Gary, and Kate partnership agreement, the bonus would have been $3,818, computed as follows:

$$\text{Let } B = \text{bonus}$$
$$B = 0.1 \ (\$60,000 - \$18,000 - B)$$
$$B = \$6,000 - \$1,800 - 0.1B$$
$$1.1B = \$4,200$$
$$\underline{B = 3,818} \text{ (rounded)}$$
$$Check: \$60,000 - \$18,000 - 3,818 = \$38,182 \text{ bonus base}$$
$$\$38,182 \times 10\% = \$3,818 \text{ bonus}$$

In this scenario, the final net allocation would be $26,545, $20,727, and $12,728 for Ann, Gary, and Kate respectively. The partnership agreement should be precise in specifying the measurement procedures to be used in determining the amount of a bonus.

EXHIBIT 16-3

Bonus and Salary Allowances in Profit Sharing Agreements

INCOME ALLOCATION SCHEDULE—2011

		Ann	Gary	Kate	Total
Net income	$60,000				
Bonus to Ann	(6,000)	$ 6,000			$ 6,000
Remainder to divide	54,000				
Salary allowances to					
Ann and Gary	(18,000)	10,000	$ 8,000		18,000
Remainder to divide	36,000				
Divided equally	(36,000)	12,000	12,000	$12,000	36,000
Remainder to divide	0				
Net income allocation		$28,000	$20,000	$12,000	$60,000

INCOME ALLOCATION SCHEDULE—2012

		Ann	Gary	Kate	Total
Net income	$12,000				
Bonus to Ann	(1,200)	$ 1,200			$ 1,200
Remainder to divide	10,800				
Salary allowances to					
Ann and Gary	(18,000)	10,000	$ 8,000		18,000
Remainder to divide	(7,200)				
Divide equally	7,200	(2,400)	(2,400)	$ (2,400)	(7,200)
Remainder to divide	0				
Net income allocation		$ 8,800	$ 5,600	$ (2,400)	$12,000

Capital as a Factor in Profit Sharing Agreements

The capital contributions of partners are frequently considered in profit and loss sharing agreements. If capital is to be considered in the division of partnership income, the profit sharing agreement should be specific with respect to which concept of capital is to be applied. For example, *capital* may refer to beginning capital balances, ending capital balances, or average capital balances. In addition, several interpretations of *average capital balances* are possible, and capital balances may be determined before or after drawing accounts are closed to the partners' capital accounts.

When beginning capital balances are used in allocating partnership income, additional investments during the accounting period may be discouraged because the partners making such investments are not compensated in the division of income until a later period. A similar problem exists when ending capital balances are used. Year-end investments are encouraged by their inclusion in determining each partner's share of income, but no incentive exists for a partner to make any investments before year end. Also, no penalty exists for withdrawals if the amounts withdrawn are reinvested before the period's end. Weighted average capital balances provide the fairest basis for allocating partnership income. A weighted average interpretation of capital should be assumed in the absence of evidence to the contrary.

Typically, the drawing allowances specified in a partnership agreement may be withdrawn without affecting the capital balances used in dividing partnership income. Drawing account balances up to the amounts specified in the agreement would not be deducted in determining the partners' average or year-end capital balances. For purposes of dividing partnership income, drawings in excess of allowable amounts are deducted from the partner's capital accounts in computing average or ending capital balances.

INCOME ALLOCATED IN RELATION TO PARTNERSHIP CAPITAL The partnership of Ace and Soy was formed on January 1, 2011, with each partner investing $20,000 cash. Changes in the capital accounts during 2011 are summarized as follows:

	Ace	Soy
Capital balances January 1, 2011	$20,000	$20,000
Investment April 1	2,000	—
Withdrawal July 1	—	(5,000)
Investment September 1	3,000	—
Withdrawal October 1	—	(4,000)
Investment December 31	—	8,000
Capital balances December 31, 2011	$25,000	$19,000

The beginning, ending, and average capital amounts for Ace and Soy for 2011 are as follows (in thousands):

COMPARISON OF CAPITAL BASES

	Beginning Capital Investment	Ending Capital Investment	Weighted Average Capital Investment
Ace	$20	$25	$22.5
Soy	20	19	16.5
Total	$40	$44	$39.0

Exhibit 16-4 shows computations of the weighted average capital investments of Ace and Soy. Actual investments are multiplied by the number of months outstanding to get dollar-month investment computations. Total dollar-month investments are divided by 12 to get weighted average annual capital balances.

EXHIBIT 16-4

Computations of
Weighted Average
Capital Investment

WEIGHTED AVERAGE CAPITAL CALCULATIONS

	Dollar-Month Investment	
Weighted-Average Capital Investment of Ace		
$20,000 × 3 months (January 1 to April 1)	$ 60,000	
$22,000 × 5 months (April 1 to September 1)	110,000	
$25,000 × 4 months (September 1 to December 31)	100,000	
12 months	$270,000	
Ace's weighted-average capital investment $270,000 ÷ 12 months)		$22,500
Weighted-Average Capital Investment of Soy		
$20,000 × 6 months (January 1 to July 1)	$120,000	
$15,000 × 3 months (July 1 to October 1)	45,000	
$11,000 × 3 months (October 1 to December 31)	33,000	
12 months	$198,000	
Soy's weighted-average capital investment $198,000 ÷ 12 months)		$16,500

Let's extend the Ace and Soy example by assuming that partnership net income is allocated on the basis of capital balances and that net income for 2011 is $100,000. Allocation of partnership income to Ace and Soy under each of the three capital bases is as follows:

Beginning Capital Balances	
Ace ($100,000 × 20/40)	$ 50,000.00
Soy ($100,000 × 20/40)	50,000.00
Total income	$100,000.00
Ending Capital Balances	
Ace ($100,000 × 25/44)	$ 56,818.18
Soy ($100,000 × 19/44)	43,181.82
Total income	$100,000.00
Weighted-Average Capital Balances	
Ace ($100,000 × 22.5/39)	$ 57,692.00
Soy ($100,000 × 16.5/39)	42,308.00
Total income	$100,000.00

If the partnership agreement of Ace and Soy specifies that income is to be divided based on capital balances but fails to specify how capital balances are to be computed, the weighted average computation is used.

INTEREST ALLOWANCES ON PARTNERSHIP CAPITAL An agreement may provide for interest allowances on partnership capital in order to encourage capital investments, as well as salary allowances to recognize time devoted to the business. Remaining profits are then divided equally or in any other ratio specified in the profit sharing agreement.

Consider the following information relating to the capital and drawing accounts of the Rus and Nag partnership for the calendar year 2011 (amounts in thousands):

	Rus	**Nag**
Capital Accounts		
Capital balances January 1, 2011	$186	$114
Additional investments June 1, 2011	24	36
Withdrawal July 1, 2011	—	(10)
Capital balances December 31, 2011 (before drawings)	$210	$140
Drawing Accounts		
Drawing account balances* December 31, 2011	$ 10	$ 12

*Account titles may be labeled partner salaries rather than partner drawings. In either case, the balances should be closed to partner capital accounts and not to the income summary.

The average capital balances for Rus and Nag are computed as follows (amounts in thousands):

	Dollar-Month Investment	
Weighted-Average Capital Investment of Rus		
$186 × 5 months	$ 930	
$210 × 7 months	1,470	
12 months	$2,400	
Weighted-Average capital ($2,400 ÷ 12 months)		$200
Weighted-Average Capital Investment of Nag		
$114 × 5 months	$ 570	
$150 × 1 month	150	
$140 × 6 months	840	
12 months	$1,560	
Weighted-Average capital ($1,560 ÷ 12 months)		$130

The partnership agreement provides that the partnership income is divided equally after salary allowances of $12,000 per year for each partner and after interest allowances at a 10 percent annual rate on average capital balances. Exhibit 16-5 shows the income allocations for 2011 under this agreement. Part A assumes that partnership net income for 2011 is $91,000, and Part B assumes a partnership loss for 2011 of $3,000.

Exhibit 16-5 shows that all provisions of the profit sharing agreement are used in allocating partnership income, regardless of whether the partnership has net income or net loss. The full amount of salary allowances as provided in the agreement is included in the income division, even though Rus withdrew only $10,000 of the $12,000 allowable amount.

PART A—PARTNERSHIP INCOME ASSUMED TO BE $91,000
INCOME ALLOCATION SCHEDULE

		Rus	Nag	Total
Net income	$91,000			
Salary allowances	(24,000)	$12,000	$12,000	$24,000
Remainder to divide	67,000			
Interest allowances				
$200,000 × 10%	(20,000)	20,000		20,000
$130,000 × 10%	(13,000)		13,000	13,000
Remainder to divide	34,000			
Divided equally	(34,000)	17,000	17,000	34,000
Remainder to divide	0			
Net income allocation		$49,000	$42,000	$91,000

PART B—PARTNERSHIP LOSS ASSUMED TO BE $3,000
INCOME ALLOCATION SCHEDULE

		Rus	Nag	Total
Net loss	$ (3,000)			
Salary allowances	(24,000)	$12,000	$ 12,000	$ 24,000
Remainder to divide	(27,000)			
Interest allowances				
$200,000 × 10%	(20,000)	20,000		20,000
$130,000 × 10%	(13,000)		13,000	13,000
Remainder to divide	(60,000)			
Divided equally	60,000	(30,000)	(30,000)	(60,000)
Remainder to divide	0			
Net income (loss) allocation		$ 2,000	$ (5,000)	$ (3,000)

EXHIBIT 16-5

Interest and Salary Allowances in Profit Sharing Agreements

In Part A of Exhibit 16-5, partnership income of $91,000 was divided $49,000 to Rus and $42,000 to Nag. The division of the $3,000 net loss in Part B was allocated as $2,000 income to Rus and a $5,000 loss to Nag. In both cases, the partnership agreement resulted in a $7,000 income difference between the two partners because of the difference in their weighted average capital balances. The amount of this difference was the same for the income and loss situations because the residual income amount was divided equally. A 60:40 division of income after salary and interest allowances would have resulted in a larger difference in Part A of ($13,800). Rus's income would be $52,400 and Nag's $38,600. For Part B, Rus's allocation would be a loss of $4,000, and Nag's income would be $1,000. Thus, one must be careful in making generalizations about the effect of various profit sharing provisions on final income allocations.

CHANGES IN PARTNERSHIP INTERESTS

Dissociation

Under UPA Section 601, a partner has the power to dissociate from the partnership at any time. Dissociation is the change in relationship caused by a partner's ceasing to be associated with the carrying on of the business. Under UPA, the dissociation of the partner always results in either a buyout of the dissociated partner's interest or a dissolution and winding up of the business.

In addition to a partner providing notice to withdraw as a partner, other events that can give rise to dissociation include expulsion of the partner according to the terms of the partnership agreement by the vote of the other partners as well as expulsion by judicial decision because the partner engaged in wrongful conduct that adversely and materially affected the partnership business and breached the partnership agreement.

Here we discuss the dissociation of a partner that results in a buyout of the partner's interest. Chapter 17 discusses the dissolution and winding up of a business.

Dissociation does not necessarily result in the termination of the partnership operations or of the partnership as a separate business and accounting entity. **Partnership dissociation** under the UPA is "the change in the relation of the partners caused by any partner ceasing to be associated in the carrying on as distinguished from the winding up of the business."

A question arises regarding whether the assets of the continuing partnership business should be revalued. Some argue that because legal dissolution terminates the old partnership, all assets transferred to the new partnership should be revalued in the same manner as if the assets had been sold to a corporate entity. Others argue that changes in partnership interests are not unlike changes in the stockholders of a corporation, and that private sales of ownership interests provide no basis for revaluation of the business entity. These alternative views reflect the concepts of the legal and business entities, respectively. Both views have merit, and this text does not emphasize either view. Instead, both views are discussed and illustrated in the following sections on changes in partnership interests. The revaluation approach is generally referred to as the *goodwill procedure*, and the absence of revaluation is referred to as the *bonus procedure*.

Assignment of an Interest to a Third Party

A partnership is not dissolved when a partner assigns his or her interest in the partnership to a third party, because such an assignment does not in itself change the relationship of the partners. Such assignment only entitles the assignee to receive the assigning partner's interest in future partnership profits and in partnership assets in the event of liquidation. The assignee does not become a partner and does not obtain the right to share in management of the partnership (UPA Section 503). Because the assignee does not become a partner, the only change required on the partnership books is to transfer the capital interest of the assignor partner to his or her assignee.

We record the assignment by Mark to Sutton of his 25 percent interest in the Hall–Mark partnership as follows:

Mark capital (−OE)	50,000	
Sutton capital (+OE)		50,000

The amount of the capital transfer is equal to the recorded amount of Mark's capital at the time of the assignment, and it is independent of the consideration received by Mark for his 25 percent interest. If the recorded amount of Mark's capital is $200,000, then the amount of the transfer entry is $50,000 ($200,000 × 0.25), regardless of whether Sutton pays Mark $50,000 or some other amount.

Admission of a New Partner

A new partner can be admitted with the consent of all continuing partners in the business. In the absence of a new profit sharing agreement, all profits and losses in the new partnership are divided equally under UPA.

A person may become a partner in an existing partnership with the consent of all continuing partners by purchasing an interest from one or more of the existing partners, or by investing money or other resources in the partnership.

PURCHASE OF AN INTEREST FROM EXISTING PARTNERS

LEARNING OBJECTIVE **4**

With the consent of all continuing partners, a new partner may be admitted into an existing partnership by purchasing an interest directly from the existing partners. The old partnership is dissolved, its books are closed, and a new partnership agreement governs the continuing business operations.

For example, Alf and Bal are partners with capital balances of $50,000 each, and they share profits and losses equally. Cob purchases one-half of Alf's interest from Alf for $25,000, and a new partnership of Alf, Bal, and Cob is formed such that Alf and Cob each have a 25 percent interest in the capital and profits of the new partnership. Bal's 50 percent interest is unchanged. The only entry required to record Alf's transfer to Cob is:

Alf capital (−OE)	25,000	
Cob capital (+OE)		25,000
To record Cob's admission into the partnership with the		
purchase of one-half of Alf's interest.		

In this case, the capital and income interests are aligned before and after the admission of Cob, and the net assets of the old partnership were correctly valued on the books. Cob's payment of $25,000 for a 25 percent interest in the capital and future income of the partnership implies a total valuation for the partnership of $100,000 ($25,000 ÷ 0.25). The net assets of the old partnership were recorded at $100,000, so no basis for revaluation arises.

Now assume that Alf and Bal have capital balances of $50,000 and $40,000, respectively, that they share profits equally, and that they agree to take Cob into the partnership with a payment of $25,000 directly to Alf. The partners may agree that half of Alf's capital balance is to be transferred to Cob (as in the previous example), that the net assets are not to be revalued, and that future profits will be shared 25 percent, 50 percent, and 25 percent to Alf, Bal, and Cob, respectively. Although it seems equitable, there is no compelling reason for such an agreement, because the capital and income interests were not aligned either before or after the admission of Cob.

	Old Partnership			New Partnership		
	Capital Investment		Income Interest	Capital Investment		Income Interest
Alf	$50,000	5/9	50%	$25,000	5/18	25%
Bal	40,000	4/9	50%	40,000	8/18	50%
Cob				25,000	5/18	25%
	$90,000			$90,000		

The $25,000 payment of Cob to Alf does not provide evidence regarding the correct valuation of partnership net assets, because the payment was for five-eighteenths of the partnership net assets but 25 percent of future partnership profits. If revaluation is desirable, the asset value should be based on appraisals or evidence other than the amount of Cob's payment to Alf.

Revaluation: Goodwill Approach

A third possibility is that Alf and Bal have capital balances of $50,000 and $40,000, respectively, that they share profits equally, and that Cob is admitted to the partnership with a total payment of $50,000 directly to the partners. Cob is to have a 50 percent interest in the capital and income of the new partnership. Alf and Bal will each have a 25 percent interest in future income of the partnership.

Several additional questions of fairness arise concerning the valuation of total partnership assets, the capital transfers to Cob, and the division of the $50,000 payment between Alf and Bal. Cob's $50,000 payment for a 50 percent interest in both capital and future income implies a $100,000 valuation for total partnership assets. If assets are to be revalued, the revaluation should be recorded prior to Cob's admission to the partnership. The partnership would record the revaluation as follows:

Goodwill (or identifiable net assets) (+A)	10,000	
Alf capital (+OE)		5,000
Bal capital (+OE)		5,000

If the assets are revalued and identifiable asset accounts are adjusted, the amount of the adjustments are amortized or depreciated over the remaining asset lives. Although the revaluation procedure is commonly referred to as the goodwill approach, goodwill should not be recorded until all identifiable assets have been adjusted to their fair values. The approach is comparable to the approach used to record business combinations under the acquisition method or the acquisition of operating divisions or groups of assets.

The previous entry recording goodwill of $10,000 gives Alf and Bal capital balances of $55,000 and $45,000, respectively. If equal amounts of capital are to be transferred to Cob, the entry to record Cob's admission to the partnership is:

Alf capital (−OE)	25,000	
Bal capital (−OE)	25,000	
Cob capital (+OE)		50,000

The capital balances are summarized as follows:

CAPITAL BALANCES

	Before Revaluation	Revaluation	After Revaluation	Capital Transferred	Capital After Transfer	
Alf	$50,000	$ 5,000	$ 55,000	$−25,000	$ 30,000	(30%)
Bal	40,000	5,000	45,000	−25,000	20,000	(20%)
Cob				50,000	50,000	(50%)
	$90,000	$10,000	$100,000	$ 0	$100,000	

Alternatively, it may be desirable to realign the capital balances of Alf and Bal in the new partnership such that each will have a 25 percent interest in the capital and income of the new partnership. In this case, the partnership would record the admission of Cob as follows:

Alf capital (−OE)	30,000	
Bal capital (−OE)	20,000	
Cob capital (+OE)		50,000

In this case, the capital changes are as follows:

CAPITAL BALANCES

	Before Revaluation	Revaluation	After Revaluation	Capital Transferred	Capital After Transfer	
Alf	$50,000	$ 5,000	$ 55,000	$−30,000	$ 25,000	(25%)
Bal	40,000	5,000	45,000	−20,000	25,000	(25%)
Cob				50,000	50,000	(50%)
	$90,000	$10,000	$100,000	$ 0	$100,000	

Nonrevaluation: Bonus Approach

If the assets of the new partnership are not to be revalued, but equal amounts of capital are to be transferred to Cob, the entry to record the transfer is:

Alf capital (−OE)	22,500	
Bal capital (−OE)	22,500	
Cob capital (+OE)		45,000

Alf and Bal transfer equal amounts of capital and equal rights to future income to Cob, so each receiving $25,000 cash from Cob seems equitable. Each of the old partners receives $2,500 in excess of the amount of book capital transferred ($25,000 received less $22,500 capital transferred). The capital accounts before and after the admission of Cob are as follows:

CAPITAL BALANCES

	Per Books	Capital Transferred	Capital After Transfer	
Alf	$50,000	$−22,500	$27,500	(30.6%)
Bal	40,000	−22,500	17,500	(19.4%)
Cob		45,000	45,000	(50.0%)
	$90,000	$ 0	$90,000	

Should Alf and Bal desire that their recorded capital and income interests in the new partnership be equal (that is 25%), Alf would receive $30,000 of the amount paid by Cob, and Bal would receive $20,000. The entry to record the capital transfer in that case would be:

Alf capital (−OE)	27,500	
Bal capital (−OE)	17,500	
Cob capital (+OE)		45,000

A summary of the capital balances follows:

CAPITAL BALANCES

	Per Books	Capital Transferred	Capital After Transfer	
Alf	$50,000	$−27,500	$22,500	(25%)
Bal	40,000	−17,500	22,500	(25%)
Cob		45,000	45,000	(50%)
	$90,000	$ 0	$90,000	

Although the evidence supporting revaluation is not always convincing, a revaluation based on the price paid by an incoming partner does have the advantage of establishing a capital balance for that partner equal to the amount of his or her investment. For example, Cob's capital credit was equal to his $50,000 payment to Alf and Bal when the assets were revalued. It was only $45,000 when the assets were not revalued. Also, the amounts of capital transfer and cash allocations are easier to determine when assets are revalued because gains and losses relating to the old partnership are formally recorded in the accounts.

INVESTING IN AN EXISTING PARTNERSHIP

A new partner may be admitted into an existing partnership by investing cash or other assets in the business or by bringing clients or abilities into the business that will contribute to future profitability. As in the case of a purchase of an interest from existing partners, the net assets contributed by the old partners' partnership may or may not be revalued. Because new assets are being invested in the business, the basis for a revaluation is not necessarily determined by the investment of the new partner. If the amount invested by the new partner implies that the old partnership has unrecorded asset values, a total revaluation of the new business based on the investment of the new partner seems appropriate. On the other hand, if the capital interest granted to the new partner is greater than the amount of his or her investment and the identifiable assets of the old partnership are recorded at their fair values, there is an implication that the new partner is bringing goodwill into the business. In this case, the valuation of the new business is determined by referring to the capital of the old partnership.

The evidence provided by the amount of an investment only relates to the total value of the business. Values for identifiable assets are determined on an individual asset basis by appraisal or other valuation techniques. The identifiable assets of the old partnership are recorded at their fair values, in the absence of evidence to the contrary. If identifiable assets of a partnership are to be revalued, the revaluation must be based on appraisals or other evidence relating to specific assets.

Partnership Investment at Book Value

Dre and Boy have capital balances of $40,000 each and share profits equally. They agree to admit Cry to a one-third interest in capital and profits of a new Dre, Boy, and Cry partnership for a $40,000 cash investment. Cry's $40,000 investment is equal to the capital interest that she receives [($80,000 + $40,000)/3], so the issue of revaluation does not arise. Cry's investment is recorded on the partnership books as follows:

Cash (+A)	40,000	
Cry capital (+OE)		40,000
To record Cry's $40,000 cash investment for a one-third interest in partnership capital and income.		

Partnership Assets Revalued (Goodwill to Old Partners)

Now assume that Dre and Boy, who have capital balances of $40,000 each and share profits equally, agree to admit Cry to a one-third interest in the capital and profits of a new partnership for a cash investment of $50,000. Because Cry is willing to invest $50,000 for a one-third interest in the $80,000 recorded assets plus her $50,000 investment ($130,000 assets), the implication is that the old partnership had unrecorded asset values. The fair value of unrecorded assets is determined by referring to Cry's investment. By implication, the fair value of the new partnership's assets is $150,000 ($50,000 ÷ 1/3). The fair value of unrecorded assets is $20,000, the excess of the $150,000 total value less the $80,000 recorded assets plus the $50,000 new investment. If the assets contributed by the old partnership are revalued, the following entries are made:

Goodwill (+A)	20,000	
Dre capital (+OE)		10,000
Boy capital (+OE)		10,000
To revalue the assets contributed by the old partnership based on the value of Cry's investment.		
Cash (+A)	50,000	
Cry capital (+OE)		50,000
To record Cry's investment in the partnership for a one-third interest in capital and income.		

The $20,000 recorded as goodwill in the first entry is credited to the old partners in their old profit and loss sharing ratios. Conceptually, the revaluation constitutes a final act of the old partnership, and all subsequent entries are those of the new partnership. The second entry records Cry's $50,000 cash investment and capital account in equal amounts. A summary of the capital balances before and after the $20,000 revaluation and the investment of Cry is as follows:

CAPITAL BALANCES

	Before Revaluation	Revaluation	After Revaluation	New Investment	Capital After Investment	
Dre	$40,000	$10,000	$ 50,000		$ 50,000	1/3
Boy	40,000	10,000	50,000		50,000	1/3
Cry				$50,000	50,000	1/3
	$80,000	$20,000	$100,000	$50,000	$150,000	

Partnership Assets Not Revalued (Bonus to Old Partners)

If the partners decide against revaluation, the entry required to record Cry's admittance into the partnership is as follows:

Cash (+A)	50,000	
Dre capital (+OE)		3,333
Boy capital (+OE)		3,333
Cry capital (+OE)		43,334

To record Cry's investment in the partnership and to
allow Dre and Boy a bonus due to unrecorded asset values.

In this case, partnership net assets are increased only by the amount of the new investment. The new partner's capital account is credited for her one-third interest in the $130,000 ($80,000 book value of old partnership plus $50,000 contributed by Cry) capital of the new partnership. The difference between the investment ($50,000 contributed by Cry) and capital account ($43,334) of the new partner is allocated to the capital accounts of the old partners in relation to the old profit sharing agreement.

This situation is referred to as a *bonus to old partners* because the old partners receive capital credits for a part of the new partner's investment. The capital balances before and after the admission of Cry are as follows:

CAPITAL BALANCES

	Per Books	Investment	Capital After Investment	
Dre	$40,000	$ 3,333	$ 43,333	1/3
Boy	40,000	3,333	43,333	1/3
Cry		43,334	43,334	1/3
	$80,000	$50,000	$130,000	

Partnership Assets Revalued (Goodwill to New Partner)

Suppose that Dre and Boy agreed to admit Cry into the partnership *for a 40 percent interest* in the capital and profit with an investment of $50,000. In this case, the implication is that Cry is bringing goodwill into the partnership. That is, Dre and Boy must be willing to admit Cry to a 40 percent interest in the $80,000 recorded assets plus her $50,000 investment ($40\% \times \$130,000 = \$52,000$) because they expect Cry's total contribution to exceed her cash investment. Accordingly, the total value of the partnership is determined by reference to the 60 percent interest retained in the new partnership capital and profits by Dre and Boy. Total capital of the new partnership is $133,333 ($80,000 old capital assumed to be fairly valued $\div$ 60%), and the partnership records the admission of Cry as follows:

Cash (+A)	50,000	
Goodwill (+A)	3,333	
Cry capital (+OE)		53,333

To admit Cry to a 40 percent interest in capital and profits.

A summary of the capital balances before and after the admittance of Cry is as follows:

CAPITAL BALANCES

	Per Books	Investment Plus Goodwill	Capital After Investment	
Dre	$40,000		$ 40,000	30%
Boy	40,000		40,000	30%
Cry		$53,333	53,333	40%
	$80,000	$53,333	$133,333	

Partnership Assets Not Revalued (Bonus to New Partner)

Instead of recording goodwill attributable to the incoming partner, the bonus procedure can be used to ensure that the beginning partnership capital balances reflect the profit sharing arrangement percentages. Under this procedure, the total assets of the new partnership are $130,000 ($80,000 contributed by Dre and Boy plus $50,000 contributed by Cry). Cry's share is $52,000 ($130,000 × .40), but she contributed only $50,000. The $2,000 difference between Cry's capital credit of $52,000 and her $50,000 investment is considered a bonus to Cry. Partnership assets are not revalued, so the excess $2,000 credited to Cry's account must be charged against the capital accounts of Dre and Boy in relation to their old profit and loss sharing ratios. The partnership records Cry's admittance under the bonus procedure as follows:

Cash (+A)	50,000	
Dre capital (−OE)	1,000	
Boy capital (−OE)	1,000	
Cry capital (+OE)		52,000

    To record Cry's investment of $50,000 for a 40%
       interest in the partnership and allow her a $2,000 bonus.

The capital accounts of the partnership before and after admitting Cry are as follows:

CAPITAL BALANCES

	Per Books	Investment	Capital After Investment	
Dre	$40,000	$ (1,000)	$ 39,000	30%
Boy	40,000	(1,000)	39,000	30%
Cry		52,000	52,000	40%
	$80,000	$ 50,000	$130,000	

LEARNING OBJECTIVE **5**

DISSOCIATION OF A CONTINUING PARTNERSHIP THROUGH DEATH OR RETIREMENT

The retirement or death of a partner from a continuing partnership business results in a dissociation and requires a settlement with the retiring partner or with the estate of the deceased partner. In the absence of a partnership agreement to the contrary, the settlement is in accordance with UPA Section 701.

According to UPA Section 701, "the buyout price of a dissociated partner's interest is the amount that would have been distributable to the dissociating partner under Section 807(b) if, on the date of dissociation, the assets of the partnership were sold at a price equal to the greater of the liquidation value or the value based on a sale of the entire business as a going concern without the dissociated partner and the partnership were wound up as of that date. Interest must be paid from the date of dissociation to the date of payment." Notice that fair value is not included in the definition. However, valuation models could be used to determine the value of the entire business.

The valuation is at the date of dissolution, so partnership books are closed as of the date of death or retirement. When a time lag exists between death or retirement and final settlement, the capital balance of the deceased or retiring partner is reclassified as a liability. Any interest (or other return) accruing on the liability up to the date of final settlement is considered an expense of the continuing partnership entity.

If the retiring partner (or the estate of a deceased partner) is paid an amount equal to the final balance of his or her capital account, the only entry necessary is a charge to his or her capital account and a credit to cash for the amount paid. When the settlement with a retiring partner is more or less than the final capital account balance, the revaluation (goodwill) and nonrevaluation (bonus) procedures provide alternate methods of accounting for the settlement.

To illustrate, assume that Ann, Mic, and Jus are partners with profit sharing percentages of 40 percent, 20 percent, and 40 percent, respectively, and that Jus decides to retire. The capital and income interests of the three partners on the date of Jus's retirement are as follows:

	Capital Balances	Percentage of Capital	Profit and Loss Percentage
Ann	$ 70,000	35%	40%
Mic	50,000	25	20
Jus	80,000	40	40
Total capital	$200,000	100%	100%

Excess Payment to Retiring Partner

The partners agree that the business is undervalued on the partnership books and that Jus will be paid $92,000 in final settlement of his partnership interest. The excess payment to Jus can be recorded by three methods: (1) Jus may be granted a bonus, (2) partnership capital may be revalued to the extent of the excess payment to Jus, or (3) partnership capital may be revalued based on the amount implied by the excess payment.

BONUS TO RETIRING PARTNER The partnership would record Jus's withdrawal as follows under the bonus procedure:

Jus capital (−OE)	80,000	
Ann capital (−OE)	8,000	
Mic capital (−OE)	4,000	
Cash (−A)		92,000

Because Ann and Mic granted a $12,000 bonus to Jus, that amount reduces their capital accounts using their 40:20 relative profit sharing ratios.

GOODWILL EQUAL TO EXCESS PAYMENT IS RECORDED A second method of recording Jus's withdrawal is to record the $12,000 excess of cash paid to Jus over his capital account balance as goodwill:

Jus capital (−OE)	80,000	
Goodwill (+A)	12,000	
Cash (−A)		92,000

Under this approach, goodwill is recorded only to the extent paid by the continuing partnership to Jus. This approach only provides a revaluation of Jus's share of partnership assets; it does not provide a revaluation of Ann and Mic's capital interests.

REVALUATION OF TOTAL PARTNERSHIP CAPITAL BASED ON EXCESS PAYMENT A third approach for recording Jus's retirement is to revalue total partnership capital on the basis of the $12,000 excess payment. Under this method, total partnership capital is revalued as follows:

Goodwill (other assets) (+A)	30,000	
Ann capital (+OE)		12,000
Mic capital (+OE)		6,000
Jus capital (+OE)		12,000

The total undervaluation of the partnership is measured by the amount implied by the excess payment. In this case, the $30,000 is computed by dividing the $12,000 excess payment by Jus's 40% profit sharing percentage. The partnership then records Jus's retirement as follows:

Jus capital (−OE)	92,000	
Cash (−A)		92,000

Payment to Retiring Partner Less than Capital Balance

Suppose that Jus is paid $72,000 in final settlement of his capital interest. In this case, the three partners may have agreed that the business is worth less than its book value.

OVERVALUED ASSETS WRITTEN DOWN A retirement payment to Jus of $8,000 less than his final capital balance implies that existing partnership capital is overvalued by $20,000 [($80,000 − $72,000) ÷ 40%]. If the evidence available supports this implication, the overvalued assets should be identified and reduced to their fair values. The partnership records the revaluation and payment to Jus as follows:

Ann capital (−OE)	8,000	
Mic capital (−OE)	4,000	
Jus capital (−OE)	8,000	
Net assets (−A)		20,000
Jus capital (−OE)	72,000	
Cash (−A)		72,000

This method of recording Jus's withdrawal is appropriate if the $72,000 paid to Jus is the result of a valuation provided for under UPA. However, it would not be appropriate if the $72,000 were determined by prior agreement of the partners without regard to total partnership capital at the time of withdrawal.

BONUS TO CONTINUING PARTNERS If evidence indicates that partnership capital is fairly valued, the partnership would record the retirement of Jus under the bonus procedure as follows:

Jus capital (−OE)	80,000	
Ann capital (+OE)		5,333
Mic capital (+OE)		2,667
Cash (−A)		72,000

This method of recording provides a bonus to Ann and Mic. The bonus is measured by the excess of Jus's capital balance over the cash paid by the partnership for his 40 percent interest.

LEARNING OBJECTIVE 6

LIMITED PARTNERSHIPS

Under some circumstances, the unlimited liability characteristic of general partnerships may be circumvented by creating a special kind of partnership called a *limited partnership*. The Uniform Limited Partnership Act provides legal guidance for limited partnerships. The limited partnership consists of at least one general partner and one or more limited partners. The general partner is like any partner in a general partnership, and he or she has unlimited liability for partnership debt. The limited partner is basically an investor whose risk is limited to his or her equity investment in the partnership. The limited partner is *excluded* from the management of the business. If he or she takes part in management, he or she loses the limited partner status and becomes a general partner with unlimited liability.

A limited partnership is more difficult to form than a general partnership. The limited partnership agreement *must be written*, signed by the partners, and filed with the appropriate public official in the state where the partnership is created. If the statute is not carefully followed, the courts may find the partnership to be a general partnership rather than a limited partnership.

Joint Ventures

Joint ventures have the characteristics of partnerships, except that the joint venture is usually set up for a specific limited purpose. When the activity is complete, the venture is terminated. For this reason, the agency power of joint ventures is limited. Joint ventures are covered in Chapter 11 of this book.

SUMMARY

Partnership accounting procedures are similar to those for other forms of business organization, except for procedures relating to the measurement of partnership capital interests. Accounting measurements relating to the capital and income interests of partners are based on the partnership agreement or, in the absence of an agreement, on the Uniform Partnership Act, except for partnerships in states that have not adopted the act. The partnership agreement should be in writing and should cover matters relating to the amount and valuation of capital contributions, additional investments with withdrawals, loans to partners, profit sharing arrangements, changes in partnership interests, and various other matters.

QUESTIONS

1. Explain why the noncash investments of partners should be recorded at their fair values.
2. Is there a conceptual difference between partner drawings and withdrawals? Is there a practical difference?
3. In the absence of an agreement for the division of profits, how are they divided under UPA? Does your answer also apply to losses? Does it apply if one partner invests three times as much as the other partners?
4. Why do some profit sharing agreements provide for salary and interest allowances?
5. Are partner salary allowances expenses of the partnership?
6. When a profit sharing agreement specifies that profits should be divided using the ratio of capital balances, how should capital balances be computed?
7. Explain how a partner could have a loss from partnership operations for a period even though the partnership had net income.
8. The concept of partnership dissociation has a technical meaning under the provisions of UPA. Explain the concept.
9. If a partner sells his or her partnership interest directly to a third party, the partnership may or may not be dissolved. Under what conditions is the partnership dissolved?
10. How does the purchase of an interest from existing partners differ from the acquisition of an interest by investment in a partnership?
11. What alternative approaches can be used in recording the admission of a new partner?
12. Why is the goodwill procedure best described as a revaluation procedure?
13. Explain the bonus procedure for recording an investment in a partnership. When is the bonus applicable to old partners, and when is it applicable to new partners?
14. The goodwill procedure was used to record the investment of a new partner in the XYZ Partnership, but immediately thereafter, the entire business was sold for an amount equal to the recorded capital of the partnership. Under what conditions would the amounts received in final liquidation of the partnership have been the same as if the bonus procedure had been used?
15. Bob invests $10,000 cash for a 25 percent interest in the capital and earnings of the BOP Partnership. Explain how this investment could give rise to (a) recording goodwill, (b) the write-down of the partnership assets, (c) a bonus to old partners, and (d) a bonus to Bob.

E 16-1

Computing initial partner investments

Car and Lam establish an equal partnership in both equity and profits to operate a used-furniture business under the name of C&L Furniture. Car contributes furniture inventory that cost $120,000 and has fair value of $160,000. Lam contributes $60,000 cash and delivery equipment that cost $80,000 and has a fair value of $60,000.

REQUIRED: Assume that the initial noncash contributions of the partners are recorded at fair market value. Compute the ending balance of each capital account under the bonus and goodwill approaches.

E 16-2

Partnership income allocation—Bonus

Arnold, Beverly, and Carolyn are partners who share profits and losses 40:40:20, respectively, after Beverly, who manages the partnership, receives a bonus of 10 percent of income, net of the bonus. Partnership income for the year is $198,000.

REQUIRED: Prepare a schedule to allocate partnership income to Arnold, Beverly, and Carolyn.

E 16-3

Partnership income allocation—Salary allowance

Mel and Dav created a partnership to own and operate a health-food store. The partnership agreement provided that Mel receive a salary of $10,000 and Dav a salary of $5,000 to recognize their relative time spent in operating the store. Remaining profits and losses were divided 60:40 to Mel and Dav, respectively. Income of $13,000 for 2011, the first year of operations, was allocated $8,800 to Mel and $4,200 to Dav.

On January 1, 2012, the partnership agreement was changed to reflect the fact that Dav could no longer devote any time to the store's operations. The new agreement allows Mel a salary of $18,000, and the remaining profits and losses are divided equally. In 2012 an error was discovered such that the 2011 reported income was understated by $4,000. The partnership income of $25,000 for 2012 included this $4,000 related to 2011.

REQUIRED: Prepare a schedule to allocate the $25,000 reported 2012 partnership income to Mel and Dav.

E 16-4

Partnership income allocation—Salary allowance and interest

The partnership agreement of Dan, Hen, and Bai provides that profits are to be divided as follows:

- Bai receives a salary of $24,000, and Hen receives a salary of $18,000 for time spent in the business.
- All partners receive 10 percent interest on average capital balances.
- Remaining profits and losses are divided equally among the three partners.

On January 1, 2011, the capital balances were Dan, $200,000; Hen, $160,000; and Bai, $150,000. Dan invested an additional $40,000 on July 1 and withdrew $40,000 on October 1. Hen and Bai had drawings of $18,000 each during the year.

REQUIRED: Prepare a schedule to allocate partnership net income of $28,000 for 2011.

E 16-5

Partnership income allocation—Partnership capital statement

On December 31, 2011, the total partnership capital (assets less liabilities) for the Bird, Cage, and Dean partnership is $186,000. Selected information related to the **preclosing** capital balances as follows:

	Bird Capital	Cage Capital	Dean Capital	Total Capital
Balance January 1	$ 60,000	$ 45,000	$70,000	$175,000
Investments 2011		10,000	10,000	20,000
Withdrawals 2011	(15,000)		(15,000)	(30,000)
Drawings 2011	(5,000)	(5,000)	(5,000)	(15,000)
	$ 40,000	$ 50,000	$60,000	$150,000

REQUIRED: Prepare a statement of partnership capital for the Bird, Cage, and Dean partnership at year-end 2011, assuming that no specific profit or loss sharing agreement exists.

E 16-6

Partnership income allocation—Assignment of interest to a third party

Capital balances and profit and loss sharing ratios of the partners in the BIG Entertainment Galley are as follows:

Ben capital (50%)	$ 700,000
Irv capital (30%)	480,000
Geo capital (20%)	300,000
Total	$1,480,000

Ben needs money and agrees to assign half of his interest in the partnership to Pet for $180,000 cash. Pet pays $180,000 directly to Ben.

REQUIRED

1. Prepare a journal entry to record the assignment of half of Ben's interest in the partnership to Pet.

2. What is the total capital of the BIG partnership immediately after the assignment of the interest to Pet?

E 16-7

Recording new partner investment

The capital accounts of the Fax and Bel partnership on September 30, 2011, were:

Fax capital (75% profit percentage)	$140,000
Bel capital (25% profit percentage)	60,000
Total capital	$200,000

On October 1, Rob was admitted to a 40 percent interest in the partnership when he purchased 40 percent of each existing partner's capital for $120,000, paid directly to Fax and Bel.

REQUIRED

1. Determine the capital balances of Fax, Bel, and Rob after Rob's admission to the partnership if goodwill is *not* recorded.

2. Determine the capital balances of Fax, Bel, and Rob after Rob's admission to the partnership if goodwill is recorded, assuming that the book value and fair value of recorded assets are equal.

E 16-8

Recording new partner investment—Revaluation case

Bow and Mon are partners in a retail business and divide profits 60 percent to Bow and 40 percent to Mon. Their capital balances at December 31, 2011, are as follows:

Bow capital	$90,000
Mon capital	90,000
Total capital	$180,000

Partnership assets and liabilities have book values equal to fair values. The partners agree to admit Joh into the partnership. Joh purchases a one-third interest in partnership capital and profits directly from Bow and Mon (one-third of each of their capital accounts) for $75,000.

REQUIRED: Prepare journal entries for the admission of Joh into the partnership, assuming that partnership assets are revalued.

E 16-9

Recording new partner investment—Revaluation and nonrevaluation cases

The capital balances and profits and loss sharing percentages for the Sprint, Jog, and Run partnership at December 31, 2011, are as follows:

Sprint capital (30%)	$160,000
Jog capital (50%)	$180,000
Run capital (20%)	$140,000

The partners agree to admit Walk into the partnership on January 1, 2012, for a 20 percent interest in the capital and income of the business.

REQUIRED

1. Prepare the journal entry or entries to record Walk's admission to the partnership assuming that he invests $100,000 in the partnership for the 20% interest and that partnership capital is *revalued*. Assume that the book value of partnership assets equals the fair value.

2. Prepare the journal entry or entries to record Walk's admission to the partnership assuming that he invests $140,000 in the partnership for the 20% interest and that partnership capital is *revalued*.

E 16-10

Recording new partner investment—Nonrevaluation case

Capital balances and profit sharing percentages for the partnership of Man, Eme, and Fot on January 1, 2011, are as follows:

Man (36%)	$140,000
Eme (24%)	100,000
Fot (40%)	160,000
	$400,000

On January 3, 2011, the partners agree to admit Box into the partnership for a 25 percent interest in capital and earnings for his investment in the partnership of $120,000. Partnership assets are not to be revalued.

REQUIRED

1. Determine the capital balances of the four partners immediately after the admission of Box.

2. What is the profit and loss sharing ratio for Man, Eme, Fot, and Box?

E 16-11

Partner retirement entries

Capital balances and profit and loss sharing ratios for the Nix, Man, and Per partnership on December 31, 2011, just before the retirement of Nix, are as follows:

Nix capital (30%)	$128,000
Man capital (30%)	$140,000
Per capital (40%)	$160,000

On January 2, 2012, Nix is paid $170,000 cash upon his retirement.

REQUIRED: Prepare the journal entry or entries to record Nix's retirement assuming that goodwill, as implied by the payment to Nix, is recorded on the partnership books.

E 16-12

Partner retirement entries—Fair value adjustment

A balance sheet at December 31, 2011, for the Beck, Dee, and Lynn partnership is summarized as follows:

Assets	$800,000	Liabilities	$200,000
Loan to Dee	100,000	Beck capital (50%)	300,000
	$900,000	Dee capital (40%)	300,000
		Lynn capital (10%)	100,000
			$900,000

Dee is retiring from the partnership. The partners agree that partnership assets, excluding Dee's loan, should be adjusted to their fair value of $1,000,000 and that Dee should receive $310,000 for her capital balance net of the $100,000 loan. The bonus approach is used; therefore, no goodwill is recorded.

REQUIRED: Determine the capital balances of Beck and Lynn immediately after Dee's retirement.

E 16-13

Partnership income allocation—Salary allowance, bonus, and additional contributions during the year

Kathy and Eddie formed the K & E partnership several years ago. Capital account balances on January 1, 2011, were as follows:

Kathy	$496,750
Eddie	$268,250

The partnership agreement provides Kathy with an annual salary of $10,000 plus a bonus of 5 percent of partnership net income for managing the business. Eddie is provided an annual salary of $15,000 with no bonus. The remainder is shared evenly. Partnership net income for 2011 was $30,000. Eddie and Kathy each invested an additional $5,000 during the year to finance a special purchase. Year-end drawing account balances were $15,000 for Kathy and $10,000 for Eddie.

REQUIRED

1. Prepare an income allocation schedule.

2. Create the journal entries to update the equity accounts at the end of the year.

3. Determine the capital balances as of December 31, 2011.

E 16-14

Partnership retirement—Revaluation and bonus approaches

The capital account balances and profit and loss sharing ratios of the Byd, Box, Dar, and Fus partnership on December 31, 2011, after closing entries are as follows:

Byd (30%)	$ 30,000
Box (20%)	25,000
Dar (40%)	25,000
Fus (10%)	20,000
Total capital	$100,000

Box is retiring from the partnership, and the partners agree that he will receive a cash payment of $35,000 in final settlement of his interest. The book values of partnership assets and liabilities are equal to fair values, except for a building with a book value of $15,000 and a fair value of $25,000.

REQUIRED

1. Prepare the journal entry or entries to record Box's retirement assuming that assets are revalued to the basis implied by the excess payment to Box.

2. Prepare the journal entry or entries to record Box's retirement assuming the bonus approach is used.

E 16-15

Recording new partner investment and partner retirements—Various situations

1. Bill and Ken enter into a partnership agreement in which Bill is to have a 60% interest in capital and profits and Ken is to have a 40% interest in capital and profits. Bill contributes the following:

	Cost	Fair Value
Land	$ 10,000	$20,000
Building	100,000	60,000
Equipment	20,000	15,000

There is a $30,000 mortgage on the building that the partnership agrees to assume. Ken contributes $50,000 cash to the partnership. Bill and Ken agree that Ken's capital account should equal Ken's $50,000 cash contribution and that goodwill should be recorded. Goodwill should be recorded in the amount of:

a $10,000

b $15,000

c $16,667

d $20,000

2. Thomas and Mark are partners having capital balances of $50,000 and $60,000, respectively. They admit Jay to a one-third interest in partnership capital and profits for an investment of $65,000. If the goodwill procedure is used in recording Jay's admission to the partnership:

a Jay's capital will be $58,333

b Total capital will be $175,000

c Mark's capital will be $70,000

d Goodwill will be recorded at $15,000

3. On December 31, 2011, Tina and Webb, who share profits and losses equally, have capital balances of $170,000 and $200,000, respectively. They agree to admit Zen for a one-third interest in capital and profits for his investment of $200,000. Partnership net assets are not to be revalued. Capital accounts of Tina, Webb, and Zen, respectively, immediately after Zen's admission to the partnership are:

a $170,000, $200,000, and $200,000

b $165,000, $195,000, and $200,000

c $175,000, $205,000, and $190,000

d $185,000, $215,000, and $200,000

4. Finney and Rhoads have capital balances of $100,000 and $80,000, respectively, and they share profits equally. The partners agree to accept Chesterfield for a 25 percent interest in capital and profits for her investment of $90,000. If goodwill is recorded, the capital account balances of Finney and Rhoads immediately after Chesterfield's admittance to the partnership will be:

a Finney, $100,000; Rhoads, $120,000

b Finney, $111,250; Rhoads, $91,250

c Finney, $145,000; Rhoads, $125,000

d Finney, $120,000; Rhoads, $120,000

5. The balance sheet of the Fred, Gini, and Peggy partnership on December 31, 2011, together with profit sharing ratios, revealed the following:

Cash	$240,000	Fred capital (30%)	$ 200,000
Other assets	360,000	Gini capital (30%)	170,000
		Peggy capital (40%)	230,000
	$600,000		$ 600,000

Gini is retiring from the partnership, and the partners agreed that she should receive $200,000 cash as payment in full for her share of partnership assets. If the goodwill implied by the settlement with Gini is recorded on the partnership books, total partnership assets after Gini's withdrawal should be:

a $566,667

b $500,000

c $430,000

d $400,000

E 16-16

Recording new partner investment and partner retirements—Various situations

1. Shirley purchased an interest in the Tony and Olga partnership by paying Tony $40,000 for half of his capital and half of his 50 percent profit sharing interest. At the time, Tony's capital balance was $30,000 and Olga's capital balance was $70,000. Shirley should receive a credit to her capital account of:

a $15,000

b $20,000

c $25,000

d $33,333

2. Lin and Que are partners with capital balances of $50,000 and $70,000, respectively, and they share profits and losses equally. The partners agree to take Dun into the partnership for a 40% interest in capital and profits, while Lin and Que each retain a 30% interest. Dun pays $60,000 cash directly to Lin and Que for his 40% interest, and

goodwill implied by Dun's payment is recognized on the partnership books. If Lin and Que transfer equal amounts of capital to Dun, the capital balances after Dun's admittance will be:

a Lin, $35,000; Que, $55,000; Dun, $60,000
b Lin, $45,000; Que, $45,000; Dun, $60,000
c Lin, $36,000; Que, $36,000; Dun, $48,000
d Lin, $26,000; Que, $46,000; Dun, $48,000

Use the following information in answering questions 3 and 4: McC and New are partners with capital balances of $70,000 and $50,000, respectively, and they share profit and losses equally. Oak is admitted to the partnership with a contribution to the partnership of $50,000 cash for a one-third interest in the partnership capital and in future profits and losses.

3. If the goodwill is recognized in accounting for the admission of Oak, what amount of goodwill will be recorded?
   a $60,000
   b $20,000
   c $10,000
   d $6,667

4. If no goodwill is recognized, the capital balances of McC and New immediately after the admission of Oak will be:
   a McC, $65,000; New, $45,000
   b McC, $66,667; New, $46,666
   c McC, $67,500; New, $47,500
   d McC, $70,000; New, $50,000

5. The December 31, 2011, balance sheet of the Ben, Car, and Das partnership is summarized as follows:

Cash	$100,000	Car loan	$100,000
Other assets, at cost	500,000	Ben capital	100,000
		Car capital	200,000
		Das capital	200,000
	$600,000		$600,000

The partners share profits and losses as follows: Ben, 20 percent; Car 30 percent; and Das, 50 percent. Car is retiring from the partnership, and the partners have agreed that "other assets" should be adjusted to their fair value of $600,000 at December 31, 2011. They further agree that Car will receive $244,000 cash for his partnership interest exclusive of his loan, which is to be paid in full, and that no goodwill implied by Car's payment will be recorded.

   After Car's retirement, the capital balances of Ben and Das, respectively, will be:
   a $116,000 and $240,000
   b $101,714 and $254,286
   c $100,000 and $200,000
   d $73,143 and $182,857

E 16-17
[Based on AICPA] Partnership income allocation and new partner investment—Various situations

1. Cob, Inc., a partner in TLC Partnership, assigns its partnership interest to Bean, who is not made a partner. After the assignment, Bean asserts the rights to:
   I   Participate in the management of TLC
   II Cob's share of TLC's partnership profits

   Bean is correct as to which of these rights?
   a I only
   b II only
   c I and II
   d Neither I nor II

2. When property other than cash is invested in a partnership, at what amount should the noncash property be credited to the contributing partner's capital account?
   a Fair value at the date of contribution
   b Contributing partner's original cost
   c Assessed valuation for property tax purposes
   d Contributing partner's tax basis

3. Arthur Plack, a partner in the Brite Partnership, has a 30% participation in partnership profits and losses. Plack's capital account had a net decrease of $60,000 during the calendar year 2011. During 2011, Plack withdrew $130,000 (charged against his capital account) and contributed property valued at $25,000 to the partnership. What was the net income of the Brite Partnership for 2011?

   a $150,000

   b $233,333

   c $350,000

   d $550,000

4. Fox, Greg, and Howe are partners with average capital balances during 2011 of $120,000, $60,000, and $40,000, respectively. Partners receive 10% interest on their average capital balances. After deducting salaries of $30,000 to Fox and $20,000 to Howe, the residual profit or loss is divided equally. In 2011 the partnership sustained a $33,000 loss before interest and salaries to partners. By what amount should Fox's capital account change?

   a $7,000 increase

   b $11,000 decrease

   c $35,000 decrease

   d $42,000 increase

5. Beck, an active partner in the Beck and Cris partnership, receives an annual bonus of 25% of partnership net income after deducting the bonus. For the year ended December 31, 2011, partnership net income before the bonus amounted to $300,000. Beck's 2011 bonus should be:

   a $56,250

   b $60,000

   c $62,500

   d $75,000

E 16-18

[Based on AICPA] Partnership retirement—Various situations

1. Partners Allen, Baker, and Coe share profits and losses 50:30:20, respectively. The balance sheet at April 30, 2011, follows:

Assets		Equities	
Cash	$ 40,000	Accounts payable	$100,000
Other assets	360,000	Allen capital	74,000
		Baker capital	130,000
		Coe capital	96,000
	$400,000		$400,000

The assets and liabilities are recorded and presented at their respective fair values. Jones is to be admitted as a new partner with a 20% capital interest and a 20% share of profits and losses in exchange for a cash contribution. No goodwill or bonus is to be recorded. How much cash should Jones contribute?

   a $60,000

   b $72,000

   c $75,000

   d $80,000

2. Elton and Don are partners who share profits and losses in the ratio of 7:3, respectively. On November 5, 2011, their respective capital accounts were as follows:

Elton	$ 70,000
Don	60,000
	$130,000

On that date they agreed to admit Kravitz as a partner with a one-third interest in the capital and profits and losses upon his investment of $50,000. The new partnership will begin with a total capital of $180,000. Immediately after Kravitz's admission, what are the capital balances of Elton, Don, and Kravitz, respectively?

   a $60,000, $60,000, $60,000

   b $63,000, $57,000, $60,000

   c $63,333, $56,667, $60,000

   d $70,000, $60,000, $50,000

3. William desires to purchase a one-fourth capital and profit and loss interest in the partnership of Eli, George, and Dick. The three partners agree to sell William one-fourth of their respective capital and profit and loss interests in

exchange for a total payment of $40,000. The capital accounts and the respective percentage interests in profits and losses immediately before the sale to William are as follows:

Eli capital (60%)	$ 80,000
George capital (30%)	40,000
Dick capital (10%)	20,000
	$140,000

All other assets and liabilities are fairly valued, and implied goodwill is to be recorded prior to the acquisition by William. Immediately after William's acquisition, what should be the capital balances of Eli, George, and Dick, respectively?

a *$60,000, $30,000, $15,000*
b *$69,000, $34,500, $16,500*
c *$77,000, $38,500, $19,500*
d *$92,000, $46,000, $22,000*

4. The capital accounts of the partnership of Newton, Sharman, and Jackson on June 1, 2011, are presented, along with their respective profit and loss ratios:

Newton	$139,200	1/2
Sharman	208,800	1/3
Jackson	96,000	1/6
	$444,000	

On June 1, 2011, Sidney was admitted to the partnership when he purchased, for $132,000, a proportionate interest from Newton and Sharman in the net assets and profits of the partnership. As a result of this transaction, Sidney acquired a one-fifth interest in the net assets and profits of the firm. Assuming that implied goodwill is *not* to be recorded, what is the combined gain realized by Newton and Sharman upon the sale of a portion of their interests in the partnership to Sidney?

a *$0*
b *$43,200*
c *$62,400*
d *$82,000*

5. Kern and Pate are partners with capital balances of $60,000 and $20,000, respectively. Profits and losses are divided in the ratio of 60:40. Kern and Pate decide to admit Grant, who invested land valued at $15,000 for a 20% capital interest in the partnership. Grant's capital account should be credited for:

a *$12,000*
b *$15,000*
c *$16,000*
d *$19,000*

6. James Dixon, a partner in an accounting firm, decided to withdraw from the partnership. Dixon's share of the partnership profits and losses was 20%. Upon withdrawing from the partnership, he was paid $74,000 in final settlement for his partnership interest. The total of the partners' capital accounts *before* recognition of partnership goodwill prior to Dixon's withdrawal was $210,000. After his withdrawal, the remaining partners' capital accounts, excluding their share of goodwill, totaled $160,000. The total agreed-upon goodwill of the firm was:

a *$120,000*
b *$140,000*
c *$160,000*
d *$250,000*

7. On June 30, 2011, the balance sheet for the partnership of Williams, Brown, and Lowe, together with their respective profit and loss ratios, is summarized as follows:

Assets, at cost	$300,000	Williams loan	$ 15,000
		Williams capital (20%)	70,000
		Brown capital (20%)	65,000
		Lowe capital (60%)	150,000
			$300,000

Williams has decided to retire from the partnership, and by mutual agreement the assets are to be adjusted to their fair value of $360,000 at June 30, 2011. It is agreed that the partnership will pay Williams $102,000 cash for his partnership interest exclusive of his loan, which is to be repaid in full. Goodwill is to be recorded in this transaction, as implied by the excess payment to Williams. After Williams's retirement, what are the capital account balances of Brown and Lowe, respectively?

a *$65,000 and $150,000*
b *$97,000 and $246,000*
c *$73,000 and $174,000*
d *$77,000 and $186,000*

E 16-19

Partnership income allocation—Salary allowance and interest

The partnership agreement of Kray, Lam, and Mann provides for the division of net income as follows:

1. Lam, who manages the partnership, is to receive a salary of $11,000 per year.
2. Each partner is to be allowed interest at 10% on beginning capital.
3. Remaining profits are to be divided equally.

During 2011, Kray invested an additional $4,000 in the partnership. Lam withdrew $5,000, and Mann withdrew $4,000. No other investments or withdrawals were made during 2011. On January 1, 2011, the capital balances were Kray, $65,000; Lam, $75,000; and Mann, $70,000. Total capital at year end was $252,000.

REQUIRED: Prepare a statement of partners' capital for the year ended December 31, 2011.

E 16-20

Recording new partner investment

After operating as partners for several years, Gro and Ham decided to sell one-half of each of their partnership interests to lot for a total of $70,000, paid directly to Gro and Ham.

At the time of lot's admittance to the partnership, Gro and Ham had capital balances of $45,000 and $65,000, respectively, and shared profits 45 percent to Gro and 55 percent to Ham.

REQUIRED

1. Calculate the capital balances of each of the partners immediately after Iot is admitted as a partner assuming that the assets are not revalued, and prepare a second calculation of the capital balances assuming that the assets are revalued at the time Iot is admitted.

2. In designing a new partnership agreement, how should profits and losses be divided?

3. If a new partnership agreement is not established, how will profits and losses be divided?

E 16-21

Partnership retirement—Various situations

The Cas, Don, and Ear partnership balance sheet and profit and loss percentages at June 30, 2011, are summarized as follows:

Assets	$500,000	Cas capital (30%)	$140,000
		Don capital (30%)	175,000
		Ear capital (40%)	185,000
	$500,000		$500,000

On July 1, 2011, the partners agree that Cas is to retire immediately and receive $161,000 for her partnership interest.

REQUIRED: Prepare journal entries to illustrate *three* possible methods of accounting for the retirement of Cas.

PROBLEMS

P 16-1

Partnership income allocation—Statement of partnership capital

Ellen, Fargo, and Gary are partners who share profits and losses 20 percent, 20 percent, and 60 percent, respectively, after Ellen and Fargo each receive a $12,000 salary allowance. Capital balances on January 1, 2011, are as follows:

Ellen (20%)	$ 69,000
Fargo (20%)	85,500
Gary (60%)	245,500

During 2011, Gary invested an additional $20,000 in the partnership, and Ellen and Fargo each withdrew $12,000, equal to their salary allowances as provided by the profit and loss sharing agreement. The partnership net assets at December 31, 2011, were $481,000.

REQUIRED: Prepare a statement of partnership capital for the year ended December 31, 2011.

P 16-2
Recording new partner investment—Revaluation and nonrevaluation cases

The partnership of Mortin and Oscar is being dissolved, and the assets and equities at book value and fair value and the profit and loss sharing ratios at January 1, 2011, are as follows:

	Book Value	Fair Value
Cash	$ 20,000	$ 20,000
Accounts receivable—net	100,000	100,000
Inventories	50,000	200,000
Plant assets—net	100,000	120,000
	$270,000	$440,000
Accounts payable	$ 50,000	$ 50,000
Mortin capital (50%)	120,000	
Oscar capital (50%)	100,000	
	$270,000	

Mortin and Oscar agree to admit Trent into the partnership for a one-third interest. Trent invests $95,000 cash and a building to be used in the business with a book value to Trent of $100,000 and a fair value of $120,000.

REQUIRED

1. Prepare a balance sheet for the Mortin, Oscar, and Trent partnership on January 2, 2011, just after the admission of Trent, assuming that the assets are revalued and goodwill is recognized.

2. Prepare a balance sheet for the Mortin, Oscar, and Trent partnership on January 2, 2011, after the admission of Trent, assuming that the assets are not revalued.

P 16-3
Partnership income allocation

Ashe and Barbour are partners with capital balances on January 1, 2011, of $40,000 and $50,000, respectively. The partnership agreement provides that each partner is allowed 10 percent interest on beginning capital balances; that Ashe receives a salary allowance of $12,000 per year and a 20 percent bonus of partnership income after interest, salary allowance, and bonus; and that remaining income is divided equally.

REQUIRED: Prepare an income distribution schedule to show how the $105,000 partnership net income for 2011 should be divided.

P 16-4
Partnership income allocation—Complex, net loss

The partnership agreement of Alex, Carl, and Erika provides that profits are to be divided as follows:

1. Alex is to receive a salary allowance of $10,000 for managing the partnership business.

2. Partners are to receive 10% interest on average capital balances. Drawings are excluded from computing these averages.

3. Remaining profits are to be divided 30%, 30%, and 40% to Alex, Carl, and Erika, respectively.

Alex had a capital balance of $60,000 at January 1, 2011, and had drawings of $8,000 on July 1, 2011. Carl's capital balance on January 1, 2011, was $90,000, and he invested an additional $30,000 on September 1, 2011. Erika's beginning capital balance was $110,000, and she withdrew $10,000 on July 1 but invested an additional $20,000 on October 1, 2011.

The partnership has a net loss of $12,000 during 2011, and the accountant in charge allocated the net loss as follows: $200 profit to Alex, $4,800 loss to Carl, and $7,400 loss to Erika.

REQUIRED

1. A schedule to show the correct allocation of the partnership net loss for 2011

2. A statement of partnership capital for the year ended December 31, 2011

3. Journal entries to correct the books of the partnership at December 31, 2011, assuming that all closing entries for the year have been recorded.

P 16-5
Partnership income allocation—Profit sharing based on beginning, ending, and average capital balances

A summary of changes in the capital accounts of the Katie, Lynda, and Molly partnership for 2011, before closing partnership net income to the capital accounts, is as follows:

	Katie Capital	Lynda Capital	Molly Capital	Total Capital
Balance January 1, 2011	$80,000	$80,000	$90,000	$250,000
Investment April 1	20,000			20,000
Withdrawal May 1		(15,000)		(15,000)
Withdrawal July 1	(10,000)			(10,000)
Withdrawal September 1			(30,000)	(30,000)
	$90,000	$65,000	$60,000	$215,000

REQUIRED: Determine the allocation of the 2011 net income to the partners under each of the following sets of independent assumptions:

1. Partnership net income is $60,000, and profit is divided on the basis of average capital balances during the year.

2. Partnership net income is $50,000, Katie gets a bonus of 10% of income for managing the business, and the remaining profits are divided on the basis of beginning capital balances.

3. Partnership net loss is $35,000, Molly receives a $12,000 salary, each partner is allowed 10% interest on beginning capital balances, and the remaining profits are divided equally.

P 16-6
Partner income allocation—Correction of error

The partnership of Jones, Keller, and Glade was created on January 2, 2011, with each of the partners contributing cash of $30,000. Reported profits, withdrawals, and additional investments were as follows:

	Reported Net Income	Withdrawals	Additional Investments
2011	$19,000	$4,000 Keller 5,000 Jones	$5,000 Glade
2012	22,000	8,000 Glade 3,000 Keller	5,000 Jones
2013	29,000	2,000 Glade 4,000 Keller	6,000 Glade

The partnership agreement provides that partners are to be allowed 10 percent interest on the beginning-of-the-year capital balances, that Jones is to receive a $7,000 salary allowance, and that remaining profits are to be divided equally.

After the books were closed on December 31, 2013, it was discovered that depreciation had been understated by $2,000 each year and that the inventory taken at December 31, 2013, was understated by $8,000.

REQUIRED

1. Calculate the balances in the three capital accounts on January 1, 2014.

2. Calculate the balances that should be in the three capital accounts on January 1, 2014, taking into account the corrections that must be made for errors made in the calculation of income in the prior years.

3. Give the journal entry (one entry) to correct the books on January 1, 2014.

P 16-7
Recording new partner investment and subsequent balance sheet

The partnership of Addie and Bal is adding a new partner, Cathy, and its assets and equities at book value and fair value just prior to her admission to the partnership on January 1, 2011, are as follows:

	Book Value	Fair Value
Assets		
Cash	$ 15,000	$ 15,000
Accounts receivable—net	45,000	40,000
Inventories	50,000	60,000
Plant assets—net	90,000	105,000
	$200,000	$220,000
Equities		
Accounts payable	$ 30,000	$ 30,000
15% note payable	50,000	40,000
Addie capital (60%)	64,000	
Bal capital (40%)	56,000	
	$200,000	

On January 2, 2011, Addie and Bal take Cathy into the partnership of Addie, Bal, and Cathy for a 40 percent interest in capital and profits.

REQUIRED

1. Prepare journal entries for the admission of Cathy into the partnership for an investment of $150,000 assuming that assets (including any goodwill) are revalued.

2. Prepare a balance sheet for the Addie, Bal, and Cathy partnership on January 2, 2011, just after the admission of Cathy.

P 16-8
Recording new partner investment—Various situations

The capital accounts of the Ann, Bob, and Carrie partnership at December 31, 2011, together with profit and loss sharing ratios, are as follows:

Ann (25%)	$ 75,000
Bob (25%)	100,000
Carrie (50%)	125,000

The partners agree to admit Darling into the partnership.

REQUIRED: Prepare the journal entry or entries to admit Darling into the partnership and calculate the partners' capital balances immediately after his admission under each of the following independent assumptions:

1. Carrie sells half of her interest to Darling for $90,000, and the partners agree to admit Darling into the partnership.

2. Darling invests $75,000 cash in the partnership for a 25% interest in the partnership capital and profits, and partnership assets are revalued.

3. Darling invests $80,000 cash in the partnership for a 20% interest in the capital and profits, and partnership assets are revalued.

4. Darling invests $90,000 cash in the partnership for a 30% interest in the capital and profits, and partnership assets are *not* revalued.

P 16-9
Recording new partner investment—Various situations

Three partners, Pat, Mic, and Hay, have capital balances and profit sharing ratios at December 31, 2011, as follows:

Pat	$144,000	profit ratio 2/5
Mic	216,000	profit ratio 1/2
Hay	90,000	profit ratio 1/10

On January 1, 2012, Con invests $85,080 in the business for a one-sixth interest in capital and income.

REQUIRED

1. Prepare journal entries giving *two* alternative solutions for recording Con's admission to the partnership.

2. Prepare journal entries giving *two* alternative solutions for recording Con's admission to the partnership if she purchased a one-sixth interest from each of the partners, rather than paying the $85,080 into the business.

P 16-10
Recording new partner investment—Various situations

The AT Partnership was organized several years ago, and on January 1, 2011, the partners agree to admit Carmen for a 40 percent interest in capital and earnings. Capital account balances and profit and loss sharing ratios at January 1, 2011, before the admission of Carmen, are as follows:

Aida (50%)	$500,000
Thais (50%)	280,000

REQUIRED: Prepare journal entries to record the admission of Carmen for a 40 percent interest in the capital and rights to future profits under the following independent assumptions.

1. Carmen pays $450,000 directly to Aida and Thais for 40% of each of their interests, and the bonus procedure is used.

2. Carmen pays $600,000 directly to Aida and Thais for 40% of each of their interests, and goodwill is recorded.

3. Carmen invests $450,000 in the partnership for her 40% interest, and goodwill is recorded.

4. Carmen invests $600,000 in the partnership for her 40% interest, and goodwill is recorded.

P 16-11
Partnership income allocation—Multiple years

Harry, Iona, and Jerry formed a partnership on January 1, 2011, with each partner contributing $20,000 cash. Although the partnership agreement provided that Jerry receive a salary of $1,000 per month for managing the partnership business, Jerry has never withdrawn any money from the partnership. Harry withdrew $4,000 in each of the years 2011 and 2012, and Iona invested an additional $8,000 in 2011 and withdrew $8,000 during 2012. Due to an oversight, the partnership has not maintained formal accounting records, but the following information as of December 31, 2012, is available:

Cash on hand	$ 28,500
Due from customers	20,000
Merchandise on hand (at cost)	40,000
Delivery equipment—net of depreciation	37,000
Prepaid expenses	4,000
Assets	$129,500
Due to suppliers	$ 14,600
Wages payable	4,400
Note payable	10,000
Interest payable	500
Liabilities	$ 29,500

ADDITIONAL INFORMATION

1. The partners agree that income for 2012 was about half of the total income for the first two years of operations.

2. Although profits were not divided until 2012, the partnership agreement provides that profits, after allowance for Jerry's salary, are to be divided each year on the basis of beginning-of-the-year capital balances.

REQUIRED: Prepare statements of partnership capital for the years ended December 31, 2011, and December 31, 2012.

P 16-12
Partnership income allocation

The partnership of Parker and Boone was formed and commenced operations on March 1, 2011, with Parker contributing $30,000 cash and Boone investing cash of $10,000 and equipment with an agreed-upon valuation of $20,000. On July 1, 2011, Boone invested an additional $10,000 in the partnership. Parker made a capital withdrawal of $4,000 on May 2, 2011, but reinvested the $4,000 on October 1, 2011. During 2011, Parker withdrew $800 per month, and Boone, the managing partner, withdrew $1,000 per month. These drawings were charged to salary expense. A preclosing trial balance taken at December 31, 2011, is as follows:

	Debit	Credit
Cash	$ 9,000	
Receivables—net	15,000	
Equipment—net	50,000	
Other assets	19,000	
Liabilities		$ 17,000
Parker capital		30,000
Boone capital		40,000
Service revenue		50,000
Supplies expense	17,000	
Utilities expense	4,000	
Salaries to partners	18,000	
Other miscellaneous expenses	5,000	
Total	$137,000	$137,000

REQUIRED

1. Journalize the entries necessary to close the partnership books assuming that there is no agreement regarding profit distribution.

2. Prepare a statement of partnership capital assuming that the partnership agreement provides for monthly salary allowances of $800 and $1,000 for Parker and Boone, respectively, and for the division of remaining profits in relation to average capital balances.

3. Prepare a profit distribution schedule for the Parker and Boone partnership assuming monthly salary allowances of $800 and $1,000 for Parker and Boone, respectively; interest allowances at a 12 percent annual rate on average capital balances; and remaining profits divided equally.

P 16-13
Recording new partner investment—Complex nonrevaluation and revaluation cases

A condensed balance sheet for the Peter, Quarry, and Sherel partnership at December 31, 2011, and their profit and loss sharing percentages on that date are as follows:

Condensed Balance Sheet at December 31, 2011

Cash	$ 15,000	Liabilities	$ 50,000
Other assets	185,000	Peter capital (50%)	75,000
Total assets	$200,000	Quarry capital (30%)	50,000
		Sherel capital (20%)	25,000
		Total liabilities and capital	$200,000

On January 1, 2012, the partners decided to bring Tom into the partnership for a one-fourth interest in the capital and profits of the partnership. The following proposals for Tom's admittance into the partnership were considered:

1. Tom would purchase one-half of Peter's capital and right to future profits directly from Peter for $60,000.

2. Tom would purchase one-fourth of each partner's capital and rights to future profits by paying a total of $45,000 directly to the partners.

3. Tom would invest $55,000 cash in the partnership for a 25% interest in capital. Future profits would be divided 37.5 percent, 22.5 percent, 15 percent, and 25 percent for Peter, Quarry, Sherel, and Tom, respectively.

REQUIRED: Prepare journal entries with supporting computations to show Tom's admittance into the partnership under each of the above proposals assuming that:

1. Partnership net assets are not to be revalued
2. Partnership net assets are to be revalued

P 16-14
Partnership income allocation

Timmy and Lassie have been operating an accounting firm as partners for a number of years, and at the beginning of 2011, their capital balances were $60,000 and $75,000, respectively. During 2011, Timmy invested an additional $10,000 on April 1 and withdrew $6,000 on August 30. Lassie withdrew $12,000 on May 1 and withdrew another $6,000 on November 1. In addition, Timmy and Lassie withdrew their salary allowances of $18,000 and $24,000, respectively. At year-end 2011, total capital of the Timmy and Lassie partnership was $182,000. Timmy and Lassie share income after salary allowances in a 60:40 ratio.

REQUIRED

1. Determine average capital balances for Timmy and Lassie for 2011.
2. Allocate 2011 partnership income to Timmy and Lassie.

INTERNET ASSIGNMENT

Cedar Fair, L.P., is a publicly traded limited partnership that owns and operates six amusement parks, including Cedar Point in Sandusky, Ohio, and Knotts Berry Farm in Buena Park, California. Cedar Fair trades on the New York Stock Exchange, under the ticker symbol FUN.

1. Go to Cedar Fair's Web site, *www.cedarfair.com*, and access its most recent annual report. Use the annual report to complete the following questions.
2. a. What is a publicly traded limited partnership?
   b. Instead of common stock, what security represents ownership?
   c. What rights do the partnership security owners have? Are they similar to common stockholders?
   d. Do the owners of trading limited partnerships receive dividends? If not, what types of "dividend"-like distributions do they receive?
3. A partnership needs at least one general partner. In the case of Cedar Fair,
   a. Who is (are) the general partner(s)?
   b. What role does the general partner have in running Cedar Fair?
   c. What is this partner's legal liability for the partnership's liabilities?
   d. What is the percentage of ownership for the general partner?
   e. How is the general partner compensated by the partnership? Does this seem reasonable given the risk and work performed for the partnership?
4. What is the major reason(s) that Cedar Fair was organized as a partnership instead of as a stock corporation?
5. In reviewing the financial statements of Cedar Fair, how are they different from a traditional stock corporation's statements?

17 CHAPTER

Partnership Liquidation

This chapter covers the situation in which a partnership is dissolved and the business ceases to operate. In this case, the business must be liquidated. The liquidation process—or winding up the business—includes paying liabilities, selling assets, and distributing monies to the partners.

THE LIQUIDATION PROCESS

Usually, **partnership liquidation** involves the following:

- Converting noncash assets into cash
- Recognizing gains and losses and expenses incurred during the liquidation period
- Settling all liabilities
- Distributing cash to the partners according to the final balances in their capital accounts

This general description of the liquidation process assumes the following:

- The partnership is solvent (i.e., partnership assets exceed partnership liabilities).
- All partners have equity in partnership net assets.
- No outstanding loan balances to any partner exist.
- All assets are converted into cash before any cash is distributed to the partners.

As these assumptions are relaxed, the liquidation process becomes more complex. Accordingly, this chapter begins with simple liquidations for solvent partnerships and proceeds to installment liquidations and liquidations of insolvent partnerships.

The rules for distributing assets in the liquidation of a partnership are covered in Section 807 of the Uniform Partnership Act of 1997 (UPA). The rank order of payment is as follows:

1. Amounts owed to creditors other than partners and amounts owed to partners other than for capital and profits
2. Amounts due to partners liquidating their capital balance upon conclusion of the liquidation of partnership assets and liabilities

Simple Partnership Liquidation

A simple partnership liquidation is a conversion of all partnership assets into cash with a single distribution of cash to partners in final settlement of the partnership's affairs. To illustrate a simple liquidation, assume that the balance sheet of Hol and Kir at December 31, 2011, is as follows (amounts in thousands):

HOL AND KIR
BALANCE SHEET
AT DECEMBER 31, 2011

Assets		Liabilities and Equity	
Cash	$ 10	Accounts payable	$ 40
Accounts receivable—net	30	Loan from Hol	10
Inventory	30	Hol capital	25
Plant assets—net	40	Kir capital	35
	$110		$110

Hol and Kir share profits and losses 70 percent and 30 percent, respectively, and agree to liquidate their partnership as soon as possible after January 1, 2012. Assume that on January 5, 2012, the inventory items are sold for $25,000, plant assets are sold for $30,000, and $22,000 is collected in final settlement of the accounts receivable.

The balance sheet after these transactions are recorded (see Exhibit 17-1, Part A, for the journal entries) is as follows (amounts in thousands):

HOL AND KIR
BALANCE SHEET
JANUARY 5, 2012
(IMMEDIATELY AFTER ASSET SALE AND RECEIVABLE COLLECTION)

Assets		Liabilities and Equity	
Cash	$87	Accounts payable	$40
		Loan from Hol	10
		Hol capital	8.9
		Kir capital	28.1
	$87		$87

As the final step in the partnership liquidation, the cash is distributed to the creditors and partners as follows (see Exhibit 17-1, Part B, for the journal entries):

Order of Payment		
I To creditors for accounts payable	$40,000	
To Hol for his loan balance	10,000	
II To Hol for his capital balance	8,900	
To Kir for his capital balance	28,100	
Total distribution	$87,000	

The established profit and loss sharing ratios (in this example, 70% and 30%) are used during the liquidation period unless the partnership agreement specifies a different division of profits and losses during liquidation. In the case of partnership agreements that provide for salary and interest allowances, only the residual profit and loss sharing ratios would be applied during the liquidation period. This is because the gains and losses at liquidation are essentially adjustments of prior profits that would have been shared using the residual profit sharing ratios if they had been recognized prior to dissolution.

A liquidating partnership should maintain a summary of transactions and balances during the liquidation stage. This summary of transactions and balances, called a partnership liquidation statement, is presented for the Hol and Kir partnership in Exhibit 17-2.

Debit Capital Balances in a Solvent Partnership

If liquidating partnerships are solvent, sufficient resources exist to pay creditors and distribute some cash to the partners. However, the process of liquidation may result in losses that force the capital accounts of some partners into debit balances. When this happens, those partners with debit

JOURNAL ENTRIES TO RECORD THE LIQUIDATION

PART A: JOURNAL ENTRIES TO RECORD ASSET SALE AND ACCOUNTS RECEIVABLE COLLECTION

Cash (+A)	25,000	
Hol capital (−OE)	3,500	
Kir capital (−OE)	1,500	
Inventory (−A)		30,000

   To record sale of inventory items and allocation
      of the $5,000 loss to the partners' capital accounts
      in their residual profit and loss sharing ratios.

Cash (+A)	30,000	
Hol capital (−OE)	7,000	
Kir capital (−OE)	3,000	
Plant assets—net (−A)		40,000

   To record sale of plant assets and allocation
      of the $10,000 loss to the partners' capital accounts
      in their residual profit and loss sharing ratios.

Cash (+A)	22,000	
Hol capital (−OE)	5,600	
Kir capital (−OE)	2,400	
Accounts receivable—net (−A)		30,000

   To record collection of $22,000 of accounts receivable
      and to write off the remaining $8,000 receivables as
      a loss charged to the partners' capital accounts in their
      residual profit and loss sharing ratios.

PART B: TO RECORD LIABILITY PAYMENT AND FINAL DISTRIBUTION TO PARTNERS

Accounts payable (−L)	40,000	
Cash (−A)		40,000

   To record payment of nonpartner liabilities.

Loan from Hol (−L)	10,000	
Cash (−A)		10,000

   To pay loan from Hol.

Hol capital (−OE)	8,900	
Kir capital (−OE)	28,100	
Cash (−A)		37,000

   To distribute cash to partners in final liquidation of the
     partnership.

---

balances have an obligation to partners with credit balances, and they can be required to use their personal assets to settle their partnership obligations. If the partners with debit balances are without personal resources, the partners with positive equity absorb losses equal to the debit balances. Such losses are shared in the relative profit and loss sharing ratios of the partners with positive equity balances.

The partnership of Jay, Jim, and Joe is in the process of liquidation. The partnership accounts have the following balances after all assets have been converted into cash and all liabilities have been paid (amounts in thousands):

	Debit	Credit
Cash	$25	
Jay capital (40%)	3	
Jim capital (40%)		$16
Joe capital (20%)		12
Total	$28	$28

EXHIBIT 17-2

Statement of Partnership Liquidation

HOL AND KIR PARTNERSHIP STATEMENT OF PARTNERSHIP LIQUIDATION FOR THE PERIOD JANUARY 1, 2012, TO JANUARY 31, 2012 (IN THOUSANDS)

	Cash	Noncash Assets	Priority Liabilities	Hol Loan	Hol Capital (70%)	Kir Capital (30%)
Balances January 1, 2012	$10	$100	$40	$10	$25	$35
Sale of inventory	25	(30)			(3.5)	(1.5)
	35	70	40	10	21.5	33.5
Sale of plant assets	30	(40)			(7)	(3)
	65	30	40	10	14.5	30.5
Collection of receivables	22	(30)			(5.6)	(2.4)
	87	$ 0	40	10	8.9	28.1
Payment of liabilities	(40)		(40)			
	47		$ 0	10	8.9	28.1
Payment of Hol loan	(10)			(10)		
	37			$ 0	8.9	28.1
Final distribution to partners	(37)				(8.9)	(28.1)
	$ 0				$ 0	$ 0

If Jay is personally solvent, he should pay $3,000 into the partnership to eliminate his debit capital account balance. His payment of $3,000 will bring the partnership cash up to $28,000, which can then be distributed to Jim and Joe in final liquidation of the partnership.

If Jay is unable to pay the debit balance, the debit balance represents a $3,000 loss to be absorbed by Jim and Joe according to their relative profit and loss sharing ratios. Jim's share of the loss is $2,000 ($3,000 × 0.4/0.6), and Joe's share is $1,000 ($3,000 × 0.2/0.6). In this case, the $25,000 is distributed $14,000 to Jim and $11,000 to Joe, and the partnership business is terminated.

UPA assigns higher payment priority in liquidation to amounts owed to partners other than their capital balances. This priority is usually abandoned and the legal doctrine of *right of offset* is applied when the partner has a debit capital balance. In this situation, the amount owed to the partner offsets up to the debit capital balance amount.

For example, assume that the partnership of Jay, Jim, and Joe had the following account balances (in thousands):

	Debit	Credit
Cash	$25	
Loan From Jay		$ 5
Jay capital (40%)	8	
Jim capital (40%)		16
Joe capital (20%)		12
Total	$33	$33

Under the right of offset rule, the loan from Jay would not be paid even though it has a higher-priority ranking in liquidation than the capital interests of Jim and Joe. Instead, it would be offset against Jay's debit capital balance, leaving Jay with a $3,000 obligation to Jim and Joe. If Jay is personally solvent, he pays $3,000 to the partnership so that Jim and Joe can receive the balances in their capital accounts in final liquidation.

If Jay is personally insolvent, however, the situation is changed considerably. In this case, Jay's personal creditors would have a prior claim on any money paid to Jay because personal creditors have a prior claim on personal assets. If the right of offset is applied by the partnership, $25,000 cash would be paid: $14,000 to Jim and $11,000 to Joe.

If the right of offset is not applied, Jay's personal creditors would be paid the amount of their claims up to $5,000, leaving less than $25,000 for distribution to Jim and Joe. If the entire $5,000 is paid to Jay's creditors, only $20,000 would be distributed to Jim and Joe.

Because of insufficient evidence that the right of offset rule is generally accepted by the courts, it has been recommended that the rule not be applied without agreement from the partners when a partner-creditor is personally insolvent.[1] Upon dissolution and subject to the rights of creditors, partners can agree to different property distributions than provided for under UPA.[2]

SAFE PAYMENTS TO PARTNERS

LEARNING OBJECTIVE **3**

Ordinarily, the process of liquidating a business takes considerable time. Some cash may become available for distribution to partners after all liabilities are paid but before all noncash assets are converted into cash. If the partners decide to distribute available cash before all noncash assets are sold (and before all gains or losses are recognized), the question arises as to how much cash can be safely distributed to the individual partners. *Safe payments* are distributions that can be made to partners with assurance that the amounts distributed will not need to be returned to the partnership at some later date to cover known liabilities or realign partner capital.

The calculation of safe payments is based on the following assumptions: (1) All partners are personally insolvent (that is, partners could not make any payments into the partnership), and (2) all noncash assets represent possible losses (that is, noncash assets should be considered losses for purposes of determining safe payments). In addition, when calculating safe payments, the partnership may withhold specific amounts of cash on hand to cover liquidation expenses, unrecorded liabilities, and general contingencies. The amounts of cash withheld are contingent losses to the partners and are considered losses for purposes of determining safe payments.

Application of a Safe Payments Schedule

Assume that the partnership of Buz, Max, and Nan is in the process of liquidation and that its account balances are as follows (in thousands):

Debits		**Credits**	
Cash	$ 80	Loan payable to Nan	$ 20
Loan due from Max	10	Buz capital (50%)	50
Land	20	Max capital (30%)	70
Buildings—Net	140	Nan capital (20%)	110
	$250		$250

All liabilities other than to partners have been paid, and the partners expect the sale of the land and buildings to take several months. Therefore, they agree that all cash on hand other than $10,000 to cover expenses and contingencies should be distributed immediately. Given this information, a schedule of safe payments (Exhibit 17-3) is prepared to determine the amount of cash that can be safely distributed to each partner.

The safe payments schedule begins with the equity of each partner shown on the top line. Partner equity is determined by combining the capital and loan balances for each of the partners. Possible losses are allocated to the partners in their profit and loss sharing ratios and are deducted from partner equity balances in the safe payments schedule in the same manner that actual losses would be deducted.

The possible losses shown in Exhibit 17-3 include the $160,000 book value of the land and buildings (the only noncash assets) and the $10,000 cash withheld from distribution. After possible losses are deducted from the equity of each partner for purposes of safe payment calculations, some partners may show negative equity. The negative amounts must be allocated to the partners with positive equity balances using their relative profit and loss sharing ratios. Allocations are

[1]Stephen A. Zeff, "Right of Offset vs. Partnership Act in Winding-up Process," *Accounting Review* (January 1957), pp. 68–70.

[2]*Anderson v. Anderson*, 1958, 138 A.2d 880, 215 Md.-483.

EXHIBIT 17-3

Safe Payments
Schedule

BUZ, MAX, AND NAN PARTNERSHIP
SCHEDULE OF SAFE PAYMENTS (AMOUNTS IN THOUSANDS)

	Possible Losses	Buz Equity (50%)	Max Equity (30%)	Nan Equity (20%)
Partners' equities (capital ± loan balances)		$50	$60	$130
Possible loss on noncash assets				
Book value of land and buildings	$160	(80)	(48)	(32)
		(30)	12	98
Possible loss on contingencies				
Cash withheld for contingencies	10	(5)	(3)	(2)
		(35)	9	96
Possible loss from Buz				
Buz's debit balance allocated 60:40 to Max and Nan		35	(21)	(14)
		$ 0	(12)	82
Possible loss from Max				
Max's debit balance assigned to Nan			12	(12)
			$ 0	$ 70

continued until none of the partners shows negative equity. At that point, the amount shown for partners with equity balances will be equal to the cash available for distribution. In Exhibit 17-3, the allocations are continued until Nan's equity shows a $70,000 balance and the equity of Buz and Max is zero. Thus, the $70,000 can be safely distributed to Nan, but nothing can be safely distributed to either Buz or Max.

Note that the safe payments schedule is used *only* to determine the amount of advance distribution. The safe payments schedule does not affect account balances or the statement of partnership liquidation. Actual cash distributed to Nan is recorded in the usual fashion, with Nan's loan balance being reduced to zero before her capital account is charged. The journal entry is as follows (in thousands):

Loan payable to Nan (−L)	20	
Nan capital (−OE)	50	
Cash (−A)		70

After this entry is recorded, the account balances of the Buz, Max, and Nan partnership are as follows (in thousands):

Debits		**Credits**	
Cash	$ 10	Buz capital (50%)	$ 50
Loan due from Max	10	Max capital (30%)	70
Land	20	Nan capital (20%)	60
Buildings—net	140		
	$180		$180

The partnership loan to Max can be charged to the capital balance of Max at any time, subject to the approval of the partners. Observe that the $10,000 loan to Max does not affect the determination of safe payments because the computations are based on the equity rather than the capital balances of the partners. Ordinarily, partnership loans to partners should be charged against partner capital balances at the beginning of the liquidation process.

Advance Distribution Requires Partner Approval

Any distribution to partners before all gains and losses have been realized and recognized requires approval of all partners. Assume that Vax, Yoo, and Zeb are partners sharing profits and losses equally and that the partnership is in the process of liquidation with the following account balances after all nonpartner liabilities have been paid (amounts in thousands):

Debits		Credits	
Cash	$30	Vax loan	$15
Equipment	45	Yoo capital	30
Vax capital	10	Zeb capital	40
	$85		$85

If available cash is to be distributed, $10,000 should be paid to Yoo and $20,000 to Zeb according to the following safe payments computations (in thousands):

	Possible Losses	Vax Equity	Yoo Equity	Zeb Equity
Partners' equities		$ 5	$30	$40
Possible loss on noncash asset:				
equipment	$45	(15)	(15)	(15)
		(10)	15	25
Possible loss on Vax's debit		10	(5)	(5)
balance shared 50:50				
Safe payments		—	$10	$20

Vax may object to the immediate distribution of the $30,000 cash to Yoo and Zeb because his $15,000 loan to the partnership has a higher priority in liquidation than the capital balances of Yoo and Zeb. The objection means that the partners do not agree to the advance distribution of cash, and accordingly, all distributions to partners are delayed until all assets are converted into cash and a final settlement can be made.

INSTALLMENT LIQUIDATIONS

LEARNING OBJECTIVE **4**

An **installment liquidation** involves the distribution of cash to partners as it becomes available during the liquidation period and before all liquidation gains and losses have been realized. The alternative is a simple liquidation, in which no cash is distributed to partners until all gains and losses on liquidation are realized and reflected in the partners' capital account balances.

General Principles of Installment Liquidation

An orderly liquidation of a solvent partnership may be carried out with distributions of available cash on a regular basis until all noncash assets are converted into cash. Liabilities other than those to the partners must be paid before any distributions are made to the partners.

Once cash is available for distribution to partners, the amounts to be distributed to individual partners can be determined by preparing a schedule of safe payments for each installment distribution. A safe payments schedule will not be necessary, however, when the capital accounts at the start of the liquidation process are in the relative profit and loss sharing ratios of the partners and there are no partner loan or advance balances. In this case, all distributions to partners will be made in the relative profit and loss sharing ratios.

When installment payments to partners are determined using safe payments schedules, the order of distributions will be such that the remaining capital balances (equity balances if there are loans with partners) after each distribution will be ever closer to alignment with the profit and loss sharing ratios of the partners. Once all partners are included in an installment distribution, the remaining capital balances (equities) will be aligned, and further installment payments will be in the profit sharing ratios. Thus, even though the capital accounts (equities) are not aligned at the start of the liquidation process, if all partners are included in the first installment, future installment payments to partners will be in the profit sharing ratios, and additional safe payments schedules are not necessary.

Installment Liquidation Illustration

The partnership of Duro, Kemp, and Roth is to be liquidated as soon as possible after December 31, 2011. All cash on hand except for a $20,000 contingency balance is to be distributed at the end of each month until the liquidation is completed. Profits and losses are shared 50 percent, 30 percent, and 20 percent by Duro, Kemp, and Roth, respectively. The partnership balance sheet at December 31, 2011, contains the following (in thousands):

DURO, KEMP, AND ROTH
BALANCE SHEET
AT DECEMBER 31, 2011

Assets		Liabilities and Capital	
Cash	$ 240	Accounts payable	$ 300
Accounts receivable—net	280	Note payable	200
Loan to Roth	40	Loan from Kemp	20
Inventories	400	Duro capital (50%)	340
Land	100	Kemp capital (30%)	340
Equipment—net	300	Roth capital (20%)	200
Goodwill	40		
	$1,400		$1,400

A summary of liquidation events is as follows:

January 2012	The loan to Roth is offset against his capital balance, the goodwill is written off, $200,000 is collected on account, inventory items that cost $160,000 are sold for $200,000, non-owner liabilities are settled at recorded values, and cash is distributed.
February 2012	Equipment with a book value of $80,000 is sold for $60,000, the remaining inventory items are sold for $180,000, liquidation expenses of $4,000 are paid, a liability of $8,000 is discovered and paid, and cash is distributed.
March 2012	The land is sold for $150,000, liquidation expenses of $5,000 are paid, and cash is distributed.
April 2012	Additional equipment is sold for $150,000, the remaining equipment and receivables are written off, and all cash on hand is distributed in final liquidation of the partnership.

JANUARY LIQUIDATION EVENTS   The events of the Duro, Kemp, and Roth partnership during the month of January 2012 are recorded as follows (in thousands):

Roth capital (−OE)	40	
Loan to Roth (−A)		40
To offset loan against capital.		
Duro capital (−OE)	20	
Kemp capital (−OE)	12	
Roth capital (−OE)	8	
Goodwill (−A)		40
To write off goodwill.		
Cash (+A)	200	
Accounts receivable (−A)		200
To record collection of receivables.		
Cash (+A)	200	
Inventories (−A)		160
Duro capital (+OE)		20
Kemp capital (+OE)		12
Roth capital (+OE)		8
To record sale of inventory items at a gain.		

(continued)

Accounts payable (−L)	300
Note payable (−L)	200
Cash (−A)	500

To record payment of nonpartner liabilities.

Loan from Kemp (−L)	20
Kemp capital (−OE)	100
Cash (−A)	120

To record distribution of cash to Kemp.

In addition to being recorded in the accounts, each of the foregoing entries should be reflected in a statement of partnership liquidation, such as the one shown in Exhibit 17-4. A liquidation statement is a continuous record that summarizes all transactions and events during the liquidation period, and it will not be complete until the liquidation is finalized. The statement shown in Exhibit 17-4 for January events is really an interim statement. However, interim liquidation statements are probably more important than the final liquidation statement because interim statements show the progress that has been made toward liquidation to date and can provide a basis for current decisions as well as future planning. The completed liquidation statement can do little more than provide interested parties with an ability to check what has been done. The partnership liquidation statement may be an acceptable legal document for partnerships that are liquidated through a bankruptcy court.[3]

In the cash distribution that is made on January 31, 2012 (see Exhibit 17-4), the partnership has $140,000 in cash remaining after all nonpartner debts have been paid. Of this amount, $20,000 is retained by the partnership for contingencies, and $120,000 is available for distribution to the partners. The safe payments schedule that appears in Exhibit 17-5 shows that the full $120,000 should be distributed to Kemp. The partnership has a $20,000 loan payable to Kemp, so the first $20,000 distributed to Kemp is applied to the loan, and the remaining $100,000 is charged to Kemp's capital account.

EXHIBIT 17-4

Interim Statement of Partnership Liquidation

DURO, KEMP, AND ROTH STATEMENT OF PARTNERSHIP LIQUIDATION FOR THE PERIOD JANUARY 1, 2012, TO FEBRUARY 1, 2012 (AMOUNTS IN THOUSANDS)

	Cash	Noncash Assets	Priority Liabilities	50% Duro Capital	Kemp Loan	30% Kemp Capital	20% Roth Capital
Balances January 1	$240	$1,160	$500	$340	$20	$340	$200
Offset Roth loan		(40)					(40)
Write-off of goodwill		(40)		(20)		(12)	(8)
Collection of receivables	200	(200)					
Sale of inventory items	200	(160)		20		12	8
Predistribution balances January 31	640	720	500	340	20	340	160
January distribution (see Exhibit 17-5)							
Creditors	(500)		(500)				
Kemp	(120)				(20)	(100)	
Balances February 1	$ 20	$ 720	$ 0	$340	$ 0	$240	$160

[3]When a partnership is liquidated under Chapter 7 of the Bankruptcy Act, court approval is required for all distributions.

EXHIBIT 17-5

First Installment—Safe
Payments Schedule

DURO, KEMP, AND ROTH SCHEDULE OF SAFE PAYMENTS
JANUARY 31, 2012

	Possible Losses	50% Duro Capital	30% Kemp Capital and Loan	20% Roth Capital
Partners' equities January 31, 2012 (see statement of liquidation)		$340	$360	$160
Possible loss on noncash assets (see statement of liquidation)	$720	(360)	(216)	(144)
		(20)	144	16
Possible loss on contingencies: cash withheld	20	(10)	(6)	(4)
		(30)	138	12
Possible loss from Duro: debit balance allocated 60:40		30	(18)	(12)
		$0	$120	$0

FEBRUARY LIQUIDATION EVENTS Journal entries to record the February 2012 events of the Duro, Kemp, and Roth liquidation are as follows (in thousands):

Cash (+A)	60	
Duro capital (−OE)	10	
Kemp capital (−OE)	6	
Roth capital (−OE)	4	
Equipment—Net (−A)		80

To record sale of equipment at a $20,000 loss.

Cash (+A)	180	
Duro capital (−OE)	30	
Kemp capital (−OE)	18	
Roth capital (−OE)	12	
Inventories (−A)		240

To record sale of remaining inventory items at a $60,000 loss.

Duro capital (−OE)	2	
Kemp capital (−OE)	1.2	
Roth capital (−OE)	.8	
Cash (−A)		4

To record payment of liquidation expenses.

Duro capital (−OE)	4	
Kemp capital (−OE)	2.4	
Roth capital (−OE)	1.6	
Accounts payable (+L)		8

To record identification of an unrecorded liability.

Accounts payable (−L)	8	
Cash (−A)		8

To record payment of accounts payable.

Duro capital (−OE)	84	
Kemp capital (−OE)	86.4	
Roth capital (−OE)	57.6	
Cash (−A)		228

To record distribution of cash to partners.

Exhibit 17-6 reflects these entries in a liquidation statement for the period January 1, 2012, to March 1, 2012. Exhibit 17-7 shows computations for the amount of cash distributed to partners on February 29, 2012. All the partners are included in the February 29 distribution, so all future distributions will be in the profit and loss sharing ratios, provided that the liquidation proceeds as planned.

The plan of distribution can be upset by events such as the distribution of noncash assets to specific partners. In the liquidation of a medical practice partnership, for example, doctors might withdraw equipment early in the liquidation process in order to continue their own practices. When noncash assets are distributed to partners, the fair value of such assets should be determined, and any difference between fair value and book value should be recognized as a partnership gain or loss. The distribution of noncash assets to specific partners and the valuation of the property distributed must be approved by all partners.

MARCH AND APRIL LIQUIDATION EVENTS By March 2012 the liquidation of the Duro, Kemp, and Roth partnership has progressed to a point at which partner capital balances are in their relative profit and loss sharing ratios. Journal entries for the events of March and April are as follows (in thousands):

Entries for March

Cash (+A)	150	
Duro capital (+OE)		25
Kemp capital (+OE)		15
Roth capital (+OE)		10
Land (−A)		100

To record sale of land at a $50,000 gain.

Duro capital (−OE)	2.5	
Kemp capital (−OE)	1.5	
Roth capital (−OE)	1	
Cash (−A)		5

To record payment of liquidation expenses.

Duro capital (−OE)	72.5	
Kemp capital (−OE)	43.5	
Roth capital (−OE)	29	
Cash (−A)		145

To record the March distribution of cash to partners.

Entries for April

Cash (+A)	150	
Duro capital (−OE)	35	
Kemp capital (−OE)	21	
Roth capital (−OE)	14	
Equipment—net (−A)		220

To record sale of the remaining equipment at a $70,000 loss.

Duro capital (−OE)	40	
Kemp capital (−OE)	24	
Roth capital (−OE)	16	
Accounts receivable (−A)		80

To record write-off of remaining receivables.

Duro capital (−OE)	85	
Kemp capital (−OE)	51	
Roth capital (−OE)	34	
Cash (−A)		170

To record distribution of cash to partners in final liquidation.

EXHIBIT 17-6

Interim Statement of Partnership Liquidation

DURO, KEMP, AND ROTH
STATEMENT OF PARTNERSHIP LIQUIDATION
FOR THE PERIOD JANUARY 1, 2012, TO MARCH 1, 2012 (AMOUNTS IN THOUSANDS)

	Cash	Noncash Assets	Priority Liabilities	Duro Capital (50%)	Kemp Loan	Kemp Capital (30%)	Roth Capital (20%)
Balances January 1	$240	$1,160	$500	$340	$20	$340	$200
Offset Roth loan		(40)					(40)
Write-off of goodwill		(40)		(20)		(12)	(8)
Collection of receivables	200	(200)					
Sale of inventory items	200	(160)		20		12	8
Predistribution balances							
January 31	640	720	500	340	20	340	160
January distribution (see Exhibit 17-5)							
Creditors	(500)		(500)				
Kemp	(120)				(20)	(100)	
Balances February 1	20	720	0	340	$ 0	240	160
Equipment sale	60	(80)		(10)		(6)	(4)
Sale of inventory items	180	(240)		(30)		(18)	(12)
Liquidation expenses	(4)			(2)		(1.2)	(.8)
Liability discovered			8	(4)		(2.4)	(1.6)
Predistribution balances							
February 29	256	400	8	294		212.4	141.6
February distribution (see Exhibit 17-7)							
Creditors	(8)		(8)				
Partners	(228)			(84)		(86.4)	(57.6)
Balances March 1	$ 20	$ 400	$ 0	$210		$126	$ 84

EXHIBIT 17-7

Second Installment—
Safe Payments Schedule

DURO, KEMP, AND ROTH
SCHEDULE OF SAFE PAYMENTS
FEBRUARY 29, 2012 (AMOUNTS IN THOUSANDS)

	Possible Losses	Duro Capital (50%)	Kemp Capital (30%)	Roth Capital (20%)
Partners' equities February 29, 2012 (see statement of liquidation)		$ 294	$212.4	$141.6
Possible loss on noncash assets (see statement of liquidation)	$400	(200)	(120)	(80)
		94	92.4	61.6
Possible loss on contingencies: cash withheld	20	(10)	(6)	(4)
		$ 84	$ 86.4	$ 57.6

Exhibit 17-8 reflects these entries in a complete liquidation statement for the partnership. The complete liquidation statement covers the period January 1 to April 30, 2012. The March and April cash distributions to partners are in the relative profit and loss sharing ratios, so safe payments computations are not necessary. The $145,000 distributed to partners on March 31 is determined by subtracting the $20,000 cash reserve from the $165,000 cash balance immediately before the distribution. All remaining cash is remitted to the partners in the final installment distribution on April 30, 2012.

EXHIBIT 17-8

Final Statement of Partnership Liquidation

DURO, KEMP, AND ROTH
STATEMENT OF PARTNERSHIP LIQUIDATION
FOR THE PERIOD JANUARY 1, 2012, TO APRIL 30, 2012 (AMOUNTS IN THOUSANDS)

	Cash	Noncash Assets	Priority Liabilities	Duro Capital (50%)	Kemp Loan	Kemp Capital (30%)	Roth Capital (20%)
Balances January 1	$240	$1,160	$500	$340	$20	$340	$200
Offset Roth loan		(40)					(40)
Write-off of goodwill		(40)		(20)		(12)	(8)
Collection of receivables	200	(200)					
Sale of inventory items	200	(160)		20		12	8
Predistribution balances							
January 31	640	720	500	340	20	340	160
January distribution (see Exhibit 17-5)							
Creditors	(500)		(500)				
Kemp	(120)				(20)	(100)	
Balances February 1	20	720	0	340	$ 0	240	160
Equipment sale	60	(80)		(10)		(6)	(4)
Sale of inventory items	180	(240)		(30)		(18)	(12)
Liquidation expenses	(4)			(2)		(1.2)	(.8)
Liability discovered			8	(4)		(2.4)	(1.6)
Predistribution balances							
February 29	256	400	8	294		212.4	141.6
February distribution (see Exhibit 17-7)							
Creditors	(8)		(8)				
Partners	(228)			(84)		(86.4)	(57.6)
Balances March 1	20	400	$ 0	210		126	84
Sale of land	150	(100)		25		15	10
Liquidation expenses	(5)			(2.5)		(1.5)	(1)
Predistribution							
balances March 31	165	300		232.5		139.5	93
March distribution							
(50:30:20)	(145)			(72.5)		(43.5)	(29)
Balances April 1	20	300		160		96	64
Sale of equipment	150	(220)		(35)		(21)	(14)
Write-off of receivables		(80)		(40)		(24)	(16)
Predistribution							
balances April 30	170	$ 0		85		51	34
April distribution							
(50:30:20)	(170)			(85)		(51)	(34)
Liquidation completed							
April 30	$ 0			$ 0		$ 0	$ 0

CASH DISTRIBUTION PLANS

LEARNING OBJECTIVE 5

Safe payments schedules are an effective method of computing the amount of safe payments to partners and of preventing excessive payments to any partner. However, the approach is inefficient if numerous installment distributions are made to partners, because a safe payments schedule must be prepared for each distribution until the capital balances are aligned with the profit and loss sharing ratios. The safe payments schedule approach is also deficient as a planning device because it does not provide information that will help the partners project when they can expect to be included in cash distributions. These deficiencies of the safe payments approach can be overcome by preparing a cash distribution plan at the start of the liquidation process.

The development of a ***cash distribution plan*** (also referred to as a *cash predistribution plan*) for the liquidation of a partnership involves ranking the partners in terms of their vulnerability to possible losses, using the vulnerability ranking to prepare a schedule of assumed loss absorption, and developing a cash distribution plan from the assumed-loss-absorption schedule. In illustrating the preparation of a cash distribution plan, the Duro, Kemp, and Roth example is used again.

Vulnerability Ranking

At the inception of the liquidation process, Duro, Kemp, and Roth had capital balances of $340,000, $340,000, and $200,000, respectively, but their equities (capital ± loan balances) were $340,000, $360,000, and $160,000, respectively. In determining their vulnerability to possible losses, the equity of each partner is divided by his or her profit sharing ratio to identify the maximum loss that the partner could absorb without reducing his or her equity below zero. ***Vulnerability rankings*** for Duro, Kemp, and Roth are determined as follows:

DURO, KEMP, AND ROTH VULNERABILITY RANKING

	Partner's Equity		Profit Sharing Ratio		Loss Absorption Potential	Vulnerability Ranking (1 most vulnerable)
Duro	$340,000	÷	0.5	=	$ 680,000	1
Kemp	360,000	÷	0.3	=	1,200,000	3
Roth	160,000	÷	0.2	=	800,000	2

The vulnerability ranks indicate that Duro is most vulnerable to losses because his equity would be reduced to zero with a total partnership loss on liquidation of $680,000. Kemp, on the other hand, is least vulnerable because his equity is sufficient to absorb his share of liquidation losses up to $1,200,000. This interpretation helps explain why Kemp received all the cash distributed to partners in the first installment distribution in the previous illustration.

Assumed Loss Absorption

A **schedule of assumed loss absorption** is prepared as a second step in developing the cash distribution plan. This schedule starts with the preliquidation equities and charges each partner's equity with its share of the loss that would exactly eliminate the equity of the most vulnerable partner. The next step is to charge each remaining partner's equity with its share of the loss that would exactly eliminate the equity of the next most vulnerable partner. This process is continued until the equities of all but the least vulnerable partner have been reduced to zero. A schedule of assumed loss absorption for the Duro, Kemp, and Roth partnership is as follows (amounts in thousands):

DURO, KEMP, AND ROTH SCHEDULE OF ASSUMED LOSS ABSORPTION

	Duro (50%)	Kemp (30%)	Roth (20%)	Total
Preliquidation equities	$340	$360	$160	$860
Assumed loss to absorb Duro's equity (allocated 50:30:20)	(340)	(204)	(136)	(680)
Balances	—	156	24	180
Assumed loss to absorb Roth's equity (allocated 60:40)		(36)	(24)	(60)
Balances		$120	—	$120

The partnership loss that exactly eliminates Duro's equity is $680,000, an amount computed in preparing the vulnerability ranks. After Duro's equity is reduced to zero in the first step, losses are divided 60 percent to Kemp and 40 percent to Roth until Roth's equity is reduced to zero. The additional partnership loss that reduces Roth's equity to zero is $60,000—Roth's $24,000 equity divided by his 40 percent profit sharing ratio after Duro is eliminated from consideration (in other words, it is assumed that Duro is personally insolvent). After Roth's equity has been reduced to zero, the equity of Kemp, the least vulnerable partner, stands at $120,000.

Cash Distribution Plan

Kemp should receive the first $120,000 distributed to the partners. A cash distribution plan for the Duro, Kemp, and Roth partnership is prepared from the schedule of assumed loss absorption as follows:

DURO, KEMP, AND ROTH CASH DISTRIBUTION PLAN

	Priority Liabilities	Kemp Loan	Duro	Kemp	Roth
First $500,000	100%				
Next $20,000		100%			
Next $100,000				100%	
Next $60,000				60	40%
Remainder			50%	30	20

In developing the cash distribution plan, the first cash available for distribution goes to nonpartner creditors. These consist of the $300,000 accounts payable and the $200,000 note payable of the Duro, Kemp, and Roth partnership at December 31, 2011. The next $20,000 goes to Kemp to settle his loan to the partnership, because partner loans have a higher priority than partner capital balances. The next $100,000 available is distributed to Kemp in consideration of his capital balance. This distribution aligns the capital and profit sharing ratios of Kemp and Roth. The next $60,000 is shared 60 percent and 40 percent between Kemp and Roth. This distribution completes the alignment of all capital balances and profit sharing ratios, and the remaining distributions are in accordance with the profit sharing ratios.

Kemp can analyze the cash distribution plan on January 1, 2012, and determine that he will begin to receive cash after $500,000 has been paid to priority creditors. Similarly, Roth and Duro can use the plan to determine their chances of recovering some or all of their partnership equities. For example, if Duro expects $800,000 to be realized from all partnership assets, he can easily compute the amount he would receive [($800,000 −$680,000) × 50% = $60,000].

Cash Distribution Schedule

Further application of the cash distribution plan can be illustrated by assuming that the Duro, Kemp, and Roth partnership is liquidated in two installments, with $550,000 cash being distributed in the first installment and $250,000 in the second and final installment. Under these assumptions, the cash distribution plan would be used in preparing a ***cash distribution schedule***, such as the following one (amounts in thousands):

DURO, KEMP, AND ROTH CASH DISTRIBUTION SCHEDULE

	Cash Distributed	Priority Liabilities	Kemp Loan	Duro Capital	Kemp Capital	Roth Capital
First Installment						
Priority creditors	$500	$500				
Kemp loan	20		$20			
Kemp capital (remainder)	30				$ 30	
	$550	$500	$20		$ 30	
Second Installment						
Kemp capital	$ 70				$ 70	
Kemp and Roth (60:40)	60				36	$24
Remainder (50:30:20)	120			$60	36	24
	$250			$60	$142	$48

The $550,000 cash distributed in the first installment is allocated $500,000 to nonpartner liabilities and $20,000 to repay the loan from Kemp. The remaining $30,000 is paid to Kemp to reduce the balance of his capital account. In the second installment distribution, as shown in the cash distribution schedule, Kemp receives the first $70,000 in order to align his capital balance with that of Roth. The next $60,000 is allocated to Kemp and Roth in accordance with their 60:40 relative profit and loss sharing ratios, and the final $120,000 is allocated to Duro, Kemp, and Roth in their 50:30:20 relative profit and loss sharing ratios.

The information from the cash distribution schedule is used in the same manner as information from safe payments schedules. The cash payments indicated by the cash distribution schedules are entered in the statement of partnership liquidation and in the partnership records as cash distributions are actually made.

The preparation of a cash distribution plan is more time-consuming than the preparation of a single safe payments schedule. However, as shown here, the cash distribution plan provides a flexible and efficient means of determining safe payments to partners. In addition, the cash distribution plan aids in planning.

LEARNING OBJECTIVE **6**

INSOLVENT PARTNERS AND PARTNERSHIPS

The order for distributing assets in the liquidation of a partnership was listed earlier in this chapter as:

I. Amounts owed to creditors and amounts owed to partners other than for capital and profits

II. Amounts due to partners after liquidation

This order of distribution is specified in UPA section 807.

Insolvent Partnership

When a partnership is insolvent, the cash available after all noncash assets have been converted into cash is not enough to pay partnership creditors.[4] Partnership creditors will obtain partial recovery from partnership assets and will call upon individual partners to use their personal resources to satisfy remaining claims.

Partnership creditors can seek recovery of their claims from the personal assets of any partner who is personally solvent. Partners are required to contribute the amounts necessary to satisfy partnership liabilities. UPA is specific in stating that a partner must contribute his or her share of the payment to satisfy the liabilities, as well as his or her relative share of the liabilities of any partners who are insolvent or who cannot or will not contribute their share of the liabilities (see UPA Sections 807(a) and (c)). A partner who pays more than his or her share of partnership liabilities does, of course, have a claim against partners with debit capital balances.

Rose, Faye, and Kate are partners sharing profits equally. Their partnership is in the process of liquidation. After all assets have been converted into cash and all available cash applied to payment of partnership liabilities, the following account balances remain on the partnership books (amounts in thousands):

Liabilities	$90 CR
Rose capital (1/3)	30 DR
Faye capital (1/3)	30 DR
Kate capital (1/3)	30 DR

Provided that all partners have personal resources of at least $30,000, each partner should pay $30,000 into the partnership in full satisfaction of partnership liabilities. However, the creditors may collect the full $90,000 deficiency from any one of the partners. For example, creditors may collect the $90,000 from Rose, in which case the remaining partnership balances would be as follows (in thousands):

Rose capital	$60 CR
Faye capital	30 DR
Kate capital	30 DR

---

[4]In this chapter, *insolvent partnership* means that partnership liabilities exceed the fair value of partnership assets. Under the Bankruptcy Act of 1978, a partnership is insolvent if partnership liabilities exceed the fair value of partnership assets plus the excess of each general partner's personal assets over personal debts (11 *USC*, paragraph 101[26]B).

If Faye and Kate can each pay $30,000 into the partnership, the fact that the creditors proceeded against Rose is of no great concern. However, if the creditors proceeded against Rose because Kate is personally insolvent and Faye's net personal assets are only $35,000, the situation is changed considerably. In this case, Rose and Faye share equally the $30,000 loss on Kate's insolvency, after which Rose will have a $45,000 credit capital balance and Faye will have a $45,000 debit capital balance. Faye's personal assets are only $35,000, so Rose proceeds to collect the $35,000 from Faye, and the remaining $10,000 debit balance in Faye's capital account is written off as a loss to Rose.

The examples in this section illustrate some of the common problems that can arise in liquidations of partnerships that are insolvent or in which there are insolvent partners.

SUMMARY

The liquidation of a partnership involves converting noncash assets into cash, recognizing gains and losses during the liquidation period, paying liabilities, and distributing cash to partners in final termination of the business entity. A simple liquidation refers to the conversion of all assets into cash before any distributions are made to partners.

A primary financial statement of a liquidating partnership is the statement of partnership liquidation, which summarizes all financial transactions and events during the liquidation period. This statement may also be used as a legal document for liquidations carried out under the jurisdiction of a court.

When partnerships are liquidated through installment distributions to partners, cash is distributed to partners after liabilities have been paid but before all gains and losses on liquidation are recognized in the accounts. To prevent excessive payments to any partner, the amount of cash to be distributed is computed on the basis of two assumptions—that all partners are personally insolvent and that all noncash assets are actual losses. Two approaches exist for computing the amounts that can be safely paid to partners in each installment distribution. A safe payments schedule may be prepared for each installment distribution, or a cash distribution plan may be prepared that can be used throughout the liquidation process.

The Uniform Partnership Act of 1997 (UPA) specifies priorities for the distribution of partnership assets in liquidations and for the distribution of the personal assets of insolvent partners. Partnership creditors rank first in recovering their claims from partnership property. Priorities for other claims depend on whether the partnership or the individual partners are insolvent, and each case requires separate analysis.

QUESTIONS

1. How does partnership liquidation differ from partnership dissolution?
2. What is a simple partnership liquidation, and how are distributions to partners computed?
3. UPA specifies a priority ranking for distribution of partnership assets in liquidation. What is the ranking?
4. What is the right of offset rule? How does it affect the amount to be distributed to partners in a liquidation?
5. What assumptions are made in determining the amount of distributions (or safe payments) to individual partners prior to the recognition of all gains and losses on liquidation?
6. What are partner equities? Why are partner equities rather than partner capital balances used in the preparation of safe payments schedules?
7. How do safe payments computations affect partnership ledger account balances?
8. What is a statement of partnership liquidation, and how is the statement helpful to partners and other parties involved in partnership liquidation?
9. A partnership in liquidation has satisfied all of its nonpartner liabilities and has cash available for distribution to partners. Under what circumstances would it be permissible to divide available cash in the profit and loss sharing ratios of the partners?
10. What are vulnerability ranks? How are they used in the preparation of cash distribution plans for partnership liquidations?
11. If a partnership is insolvent, how is the amount of cash distributed to individual partners determined?
12. When all partnership assets have been distributed in the liquidation of a partnership, some partners may have debit capital balances and others may have credit capital balances. How are such balances eliminated if the partners with debit balances are personally solvent? If they are personally insolvent?

EXERCISES

E 17-1

Simple liquidation—Schedule of cash available

The partnership of Folly and Frill is in the process of liquidation. On January 1, 2011, the ledger shows account balances as follows:

Cash	$10,000	Accounts payable	$15,000
Accounts receivable	25,000	Folly capital	40,000
Lumber inventory	40,000	Frill capital	20,000

On January 10, 2011, the lumber inventory is sold for $25,000, and during January, accounts receivable of $21,000 are collected. No further collections on the receivables are expected. Profits are shared 60 percent to Folly and 40 percent to Frill.

REQUIRED: Prepare a schedule showing how the cash available on February 1, 2011, should be distributed.

E 17-2

Liquidation—Journal entries

After closing entries were made on December 31, 2011, the ledger of Mike, Nan, and Okey contained the following balances:

Cash	$39,000	Accounts payable	$ 5,000
Inventory	16,000	Mike capital (40%)	15,000
		Nan capital (30%)	8,000
		Okey capital (30%)	27,000

Due to unsuccessful operations, the partners decide to liquidate the business. During January some of the inventory is sold at cost for $10,000, and on January 31, 2012, all available cash is distributed. It is not known if the remaining inventory items can be sold.

REQUIRED: Prepare all journal entries necessary to account for the transactions of the partnership during January 2012.

E 17-3

Liquidation—Cash distribution computation, safe payments schedule

Fred, Ethel, and Lucy have decided to liquidate their partnership. Account balances on January 1, 2011, are as follows:

Cash	$120,000	Accounts payable	$ 40,000
Other assets	120,000	Fred capital (30%)	85,000
	$240,000	Ethel capital (30%)	25,000
		Lucy capital (40%)	90,000
			$240,000

The partners agree to keep a $10,000 contingency fund and to distribute available cash immediately.

REQUIRED: Determine the amount of cash that should be paid to each partner.

E 17-4

Liquidation—Cash distribution computation, safe payments schedule

Jan, Kim, and Lee announce plans to liquidate their partnership immediately. The assets, equities, and profit and loss sharing ratios are summarized as follows.

Loan to Kim	$ 20,000	Accounts payable	$ 60,000
Other assets	180,000	Jan capital (50%)	59,000
	$200,000	Kim capital (30%)	29,000
		Lee capital (20%)	52,000
			$200,000

The other assets are sold for $120,000, and an overlooked bill for landscaping services of $5,000 is discovered. Kim cannot pay her partnership debt at the present time, but she expects to have the money in a month or two.

REQUIRED: Determine how cash should be distributed to creditors and partners.

E 17-5

Liquidation—Capital balance computation correcting an error

The profit and loss sharing agreement of the partnership of Ali, Bart, and Carrie provides a salary allowance for Ali and Carrie of $10,000 each. Partners receive a 10 percent interest allowance on their average capital balances for the year. The remainder is divided 40 percent to Ali, 20 percent to Bart, and 40 percent to Carrie. The December 31, 2011, after-closing balances are as follows:

Net assets	$150,000	Ali capital	$ 60,000
		Bart capital	25,000
		Carrie capital	65,000
			$150,000

In January 2012 the partners are preparing to liquidate the business and discover that the year-end inventory was erroneously undervalued by $15,000, resulting in an error in calculating the 2011 net income.

REQUIRED: Determine the correct capital balances of Ali, Bart, and Carrie.

E 17-6

Safe payments schedule

A condensed balance sheet with profit sharing percentages for the Evers, Freda, and Grace partnership on January 1, 2011, shows the following:

Cash	$100,000	Liabilities	$ 80,000
Other assets	500,000	Evers capital (40%)	100,000
		Freda capital (40%)	250,000
		Grace capital (20%)	170,000
	$600,000		$600,000

On January 2, 2011, the partners decide to liquidate the business, and during January they sell assets with a book value of $300,000 for $170,000.

REQUIRED: Prepare a safe payments schedule to show the amount of cash to be distributed to each partner if all available cash, except for a $10,000 contingency fund, is distributed immediately after the sale.

E 17-7

Statement of partnership liquidation

The partnership of Alice, Betty, and Carle became insolvent during 2011, and the partnership ledger shows the following balances after all partnership assets have been converted into cash and all available cash distributed:

	Debit	Credit
Accounts payable		$ 30,000
Alice capital		20,000
Betty capital	$120,000	
Carle capital		70,000
	$120,000	$120,000

Profit and loss sharing percentages for the three partners are Alice, 30 percent; Betty, 40 percent; and Carle, 30 percent. The personal assets and liabilities of the partners are as follows:

	Alice	Betty	Carle
Personal assets	$60,000	$110,000	$60,000
Personal liabilities	50,000	60,000	40,000

REQUIRED: Prepare a schedule to show the phaseout of the partnership and final closing of the books if the partnership creditors recover $30,000 from Betty.

E 17-8

Statement of partnership liquidation—Partner insolvency case

After all partnership assets were converted into cash and all available cash distributed to creditors, the ledger of the Daniel, Eric, and Fred partnership showed the following balances:

	Debit	Credit
Accounts payable		$20,000
Daniel capital (40%)		10,000
Eric capital (30%)		60,000
Fred capital (30%)	$90,000	
	$90,000	$90,000

The percentages indicated are residual profit and loss sharing ratios. Personal assets and liabilities of the partners are as follows:

	Daniel	Eric	Fred
Personal assets	$50,000	$50,000	$100,000
Personal liabilities	45,000	40,000	40,000

The partnership creditors proceed against Fred for recovery of their claims, and the partners settle their claims against each other in accordance with UPA.

REQUIRED: Prepare a schedule to show the phaseout of the partnership and final closing of the books.

E 17-9

Statement of partnership liquidation—Partner insolvency case

The partnership of Ace, Ben, Cid, and Don is dissolved on January 5, 2011, and the account balances at June 30, 2011, after all noncash assets are converted into cash, are as follows:

	Debits	Credits
Cash	$200,000	
Cid capital (20%)	170,000	
Don capital (10%)	80,000	
Accounts payable		$400,000
Ace capital (50%)		40,000
Ben capital (20%)		10,000
	$450,000	$450,000

ADDITIONAL INFORMATION

1. The percentages indicated represent the relevant profit and loss sharing ratios.
2. Personal assets and liabilities of the partners at June 30, 2011, are as follows:

	Personal Assets	Personal Liabilities
Ace	$600,000	$300,000
Ben	100,000	150,000
Cid	400,000	300,000
Don	100,000	20,000

3. Ace pays $200,000 into the partnership, and partnership liabilities are paid on July 1, 2011.
4. On July 15, 2011, Cid pays $100,000 into the partnership and Don pays $80,000. No further contributions from either Cid or Don are possible.
5. Losses from the bankruptcy of Cid are divided among the solvent partners on July 15, 2011.
6. Available cash is distributed and the partnership books are closed on July 31, 2011.

REQUIRED: Prepare a liquidation statement for the Ace, Ben, Cid, and Don partnership for the period June 30, 2011, to July 31, 2011.

E 17-10

Safe payments schedule

The partnership of Denver, Elsie, Fannie, and George is being liquidated over the first few months of 2011. The trial balance at January 1, 2011, is as follows:

	Debits	Credits
Cash	$200,000	
Accounts receivable	56,000	
Inventory	142,000	
Equipment (net)	300,000	
Land	150,000	
Loan to Denver	20,000	
Accounts payable		$400,000
Denver capital (20%)		170,000
Elsie capital (10%)		80,000
Fannie capital (50%)		140,000
George capital (20%)		78,000
	$868,000	$868,000

ADDITIONAL INFORMATION

1. The partners agree to retain $20,000 cash on hand for contingencies and to distribute the rest of the available cash at the end of each month.

2. In January, half of the receivables were collected. Inventory that cost $75,000 was liquidated for $45,000. The land was sold for $250,000.

REQUIRED: Prepare a schedule of safe payments for the Denver, Elsie, Fannie, and George partnership for January 31, 2011.

E 17-11

Installment liquidation—Various situations

The assets and equities of the Quen, Reed, and Stacy partnership at the end of its fiscal year on October 31, 2011, are as follows:

Assets		Equities	
Cash	$ 15,000	Liabilities	$ 50,000
Receivables—net	20,000	Loan from Stacy	10,000
Inventory	40,000	Quen capital (30%)	45,000
Plant assets—net	70,000	Reed capital (50%)	30,000
Loan to Reed	5,000	Stacy capital (20%)	15,000
	$150,000		$150,000

The partners decide to liquidate the partnership. They estimate that the noncash assets, other than the loan to Reed, can be converted into $100,000 cash over the two-month period ending December 31, 2011. Cash is to be distributed to the appropriate parties as it becomes available during the liquidation process.

1. The partner most vulnerable to partnership losses on liquidation is:
   a Quen
   b Reed
   c Reed and Quen equally
   d Stacy

2. If $90,000 is available for the first distribution, it should be paid to:

	Creditors, Including Stacy	Quen	Reed	Stacy (Capital)
a	$60,000	$ 18,000	$ 0	$ 12,000
b	60,000	9,000	15,000	6,000
c	50,000	12,000	20,000	8,000
d	60,000	27,000	0	3,000

3. If a total amount of $7,500 is available for distribution to partners after all nonpartner liabilities are paid, it should be paid as follows:

	Quen	Reed	Stacy
a	$7,500	$ 0	$ 0
b	0	3,750	3,750
c	2,250	3,750	1,500
d	2,500	2,500	2,500

E 17-12

Liquidation—Various situations

1. In a partnership liquidation, the final cash distribution to the partners should be made in accordance with the:
   a *Partner profit and loss sharing ratios*
   b *Balances of partner capital accounts*
   c *Ratio of the capital contributions by partners*
   d *Safe payments computations*

2. In accounting for the liquidation of a partnership, cash payments to partners after all nonpartner creditors' claims have been satisfied, but before final cash distribution, should be according to:
   a *Relative profit and loss sharing ratios*
   b *The final balances in partner capital accounts*
   c *The relative share of gain or loss on liquidation*
   d *Safe payments computations*

3. After all noncash assets have been converted into cash in the liquidation of the Maris and DeMarco partnership, the ledger contains the following account balances:

	Debit	Credit
Cash	$34,000	—
Accounts payable	—	$25,000
Loan payable to Maris	—	9,000
Maris capital	8,000	—
DeMarco capital	—	8,000

Available cash should be distributed as follows: $25,000 to accounts payable and:
   a *$9,000 for loan payable to Maris*
   b *$4,500 each to Maris and DeMarco*
   c *$1,000 to Maris and $8,000 to DeMarco*
   d *$8,000 to Maris and $1,000 to DeMarco*

4. The partnership of Gwen, Bill, and Sissy is liquidating and the ledger shows the following:

Cash	$ 80,000
Inventories	100,000
Accounts payable	60,000
Gwen capital (50%)	40,000
Bill capital (25%)	45,000
Sissy capital (25%)	35,000

If all available cash is distributed immediately:
   a *Gwen, Bill, and Sissy should get $26,667 each*
   b *Gwen, Bill, and Sissy should get $6,667 each*
   c *Gwen should get $10,000, and Bill and Sissy should get $5,000 each*
   d *Bill should get $15,000, and Sissy $5,000*

5. The following balance sheet summary, together with residual profit sharing ratios, was developed on April 1, 2011, when the Dick, Frank, and Helen partnership began its liquidation:

Cash	$140,000	Liabilities	$ 60,000
Accounts receivable	60,000	Loan from Frank	20,000
Inventories	85,000	Dick capital (20%)	75,000
Plant assets—net	200,000	Frank capital (40%)	200,000
Loan to Dick	25,000	Helen capital (40%)	155,000
	$510,000		$510,000

If available cash except for a $5,000 contingency fund is distributed immediately, Dick, Frank, and Helen, respectively, should receive:

a   *$0, $60,000, and $15,000*
b   *$11,000, $22,000, and $22,000*
c   *$0, $70,000, and $5,000*
d   *$0, $27,500, and $27,500*

6. The partnership of Unsel, Vance, and Wayne was dissolved on June 30, 2011, and account balances after noncash assets were converted into cash on September 1, 2011, are:

Cash	$50,000	Accounts payable	$120,000
		Unsel capital (30%)	90,000
		Vance capital (30%)	(60,000)
		Wayne capital (40%)	(100,000)

Personal assets and liabilities of the partners at September 1, 2011, are:

	Personal Assets	**Personal Liabilities**
Unsel	$ 80,000	$90,000
Vance	100,000	61,000
Wayne	190,000	80,000

If Wayne contributes $70,000 to the partnership to provide cash to pay the creditors, what amount of Unsel's $90,000 partnership equity would appear to be recoverable?

a   *$90,000*
b   *$81,000*
c   *$79,000*
d   *None of the above*

PROBLEMS

P 17-1
Cash distribution plan and entries—Installment

Barney, Betty, and Rubble are partners in a business that is in the process of liquidation. On January 1, 2011, the ledger accounts show the balances indicated:

Cash	$25,000	Barney capital	$72,000
Inventory	72,000	Betty capital	28,000
Supplies	18,000	Rubble capital	15,000

The cash is distributed to partners on January 1, 2011. Inventory and supplies are sold for a lump-sum price of $81,000 on February 9, 2011, and on February 10, 2011, cash on hand is distributed to the partners in final liquidation of the business.

REQUIRED

1. Prepare the journal entry to distribute available cash on January 1, 2011. Include a safe payments schedule as proper explanation of who should receive cash.

2. Prepare journal entries necessary on February 9, 2011, to record the sale of assets and distribution of the gain or loss to the partners' capital accounts.

3. Prepare the journal entry to distribute cash on February 10, 2011, in final liquidation of the business.

P 17-2
Cash distribution plan

The December 31, 2011, balance sheet of the Chan, Dickerson, and Grunther partnership, along with the partners' residual profit and loss sharing ratios, is summarized as follows:

Assets		Equities	
Cash	$ 60,000	Accounts payable	$ 90,000
Receivables	120,000	Loan from Dickerson	50,000
Inventories	150,000	Chan capital (20%)	95,000
Due from Chan	15,000	Dickerson capital (30%)	160,000
Other assets	255,000	Grunther capital (50%)	205,000
	$600,000		$600,000

The partners agree to liquidate their partnership as soon as possible after January 1, 2012, and to distribute all cash as it becomes available.

REQUIRED: Prepare a cash distribution plan to show how cash will be distributed as it becomes available.

P 17-3
Cash distribution plan

Fred, Flint, and Wilma announced the liquidation of their partnership beginning on January 1, 2011. Profits and losses are divided 30 percent to Fred, 20 percent to Flint, and 50 percent to Wilma. Balance sheet items are summarized as follows:

Cash	$ 45,000	Accounts payable	$ 20,000
Accounts receivable—net	25,000	Fred capital (30%)	75,000
Inventories	25,000	Flint capital (20%)	30,000
Plant assets—net	80,000	Wilma capital (50%)	60,000
Flint loan	10,000		
	$185,000		$185,000

REQUIRED: Prepare a cash distribution plan as of January 1, 2011, for the Fred, Flint, and Wilma partnership.

P 17-4
Installment liquidation

The partnership of Gary, Henry, Ian, and Joseph is preparing to liquidate. Profit and loss sharing ratios are shown in the summarized balance sheet at December 31, 2011, as follows:

Cash	$200,000	Other liabilities	$100,000
Inventories	200,000	Gary capital (40%)	300,000
Loan to Henry	20,000	Henry capital (30%)	320,000
Other assets	510,000	Ian capital (20%)	100,000
		Joseph capital (10%)	110,000
	$930,000		$930,000

REQUIRED

1. The partners anticipate an installment liquidation. Prepare a cash distribution plan as of January 1, 2012, that includes a $50,000 contingency fund to help the partners predict when they will be included in cash distributions.

2. During January 2012, the inventories are sold for $100,000, the other liabilities are paid, and $50,000 is set aside for contingencies. The partners agree that loan balances should be closed to capital accounts and that remaining cash (less the contingency fund) should be distributed to partners. How much cash should each partner receive?

P 17-5
Statement of partnership liquidation

Eli, Joe, and Ned agree to liquidate their consulting practice as soon as possible after the close of business on July 31, 2011. The trial balance on that date shows the following account balances:

	Debits	Credits
Cash	$13,000	
Accounts receivable	12,000	
Furniture and fixtures	35,000	
Accounts payable		$ 6,000
Eli capital		24,000
Joe capital		15,000
Ned capital		15,000
	$60,000	$60,000

The partners share profits and losses 20 percent, 30 percent, and 50 percent to Eli, Joe, and Ned, respectively, after Ned is allowed a monthly salary of $4,000.

August transactions and events are as follows:

1. The accounts payable are paid.

2. Accounts receivable of $8,000 are collected in full. Ned accepts accounts receivable with a face value and fair value of $3,000 in partial satisfaction of his capital balance. The remaining accounts receivable are written off as uncollectible.

3. Furniture with a book value of $25,000 is sold for $15,000.

4. Furniture with a book value of $4,000 and an agreed-upon fair value of $1,000 is taken by Joe in partial settlement of his capital balance. The remaining furniture and fixtures are donated to Goodwill Industries.

5. Liquidation expenses of $3,000 are paid.

6. Available cash is distributed to partners on August 31.

REQUIRED: Prepare a statement of partnership liquidation for the Eli, Joe, and Ned partnership for August.

P 17-6
Installment liquidation

Jones, Smith, and Tandy are partners in a furniture store that began liquidation on January 1, 2011, when the ledger contained the following account balances:

	Debit	Credit
Cash	$ 15,000	
Accounts receivable	20,000	
Inventories	65,000	
Land	50,000	
Buildings	100,000	
Accumulated depreciation—buildings		$ 40,000
Furniture and fixtures	50,000	
Accumulated depreciation—furniture and fixtures		30,000
Accounts payable		80,000
Jones capital (20%)		40,000
Smith capital (30%)		60,000
Tandy capital (50%)		50,000
	$300,000	$300,000

The following transactions and events occurred during the liquidation process:

January	Inventories were sold for $20,000 cash, collections on account totaled $14,000, and half of the amount due to creditors was paid.
February	Land costing $40,000 was sold for $60,000, the remaining land and buildings were sold for $40,000, half of the remaining receivables were collected, and the remainder were uncollectible.
March	The remaining liabilities were paid, and available cash was distributed to the partners in final liquidation.

REQUIRED: Prepare a statement of liquidation for the Jones, Smith, and Tandy partnership.

P 17-7
Installment liquidation
The after-closing trial balance of the Lin, Mary, and Nell partnership at December 31, 2011, was as follows:

	Debit	Credit
Cash	$ 47,000	
Receivables—net	25,000	
Inventories	20,000	
Plant assets—net	50,000	
Accounts payable		$ 55,000
Lin capital (50%)		55,000
Mary capital (30%)		12,000
Nell capital (20%)		20,000
Total	$142,000	$142,000

ADDITIONAL INFORMATION
1. The partnership is to be liquidated as soon as the assets can be converted into cash. Cash realized on conversion of assets is to be distributed as it becomes available, except that $10,000 is to be held to provide for contingencies during the liquidation period.
2. Profits and losses on liquidation are to be divided in the percentages indicated in the trial balance.

REQUIRED
1. Prepare a cash distribution plan for the Lin, Mary, and Nell partnership.
2. If $25,000 cash is realized from the receivables and inventories during January 2012, how should the cash be distributed at the end of January? (Assume that this is the first distribution of cash during the liquidation period.)

P 17-8
Installment liquidation—Safe payments schedule
Jason, Kelly, and Becky, who share partnership profits 50 percent, 30 percent, and 20 percent, respectively, decide to liquidate their partnership. They need the cash from the partnership as soon as possible but do not want to sell the assets at fire-sale prices, so they agree to an installment liquidation. A summary balance sheet on January 1, 2011, is as follows:

Cash	$ 16,500	Accounts payable	$ 21,000
Accounts receivable	28,000	Jason capital	69,000
Inventory	20,500	Kelly capital	47,000
Equipment—net	101,000	Becky capital	43,000
Loan to Jason	14,000		
	$180,000		$180,000

Cash is distributed to the partners at the end of each month, with $5,000 retained for possible contingencies in the liquidation process.

During January 2011, Jason agreed to offset his capital balance with his loan from the partnership, $25,000 was collected on the accounts receivable, and the balance is determined to be uncollectible. Liquidation expenses of $2,000 were paid.

During February 2011, $18,000 was collected from the sale of inventories and $90,000 collected from the sale of equipment. Additional liabilities of $3,000 were discovered, and $2,000 of liquidation expenses were paid. All cash was then distributed in a final liquidation.

REQUIRED: Prepare a statement of partnership liquidation with supporting safe payments schedules for each cash distribution.

P 17-9
Installment liquidation—Safe payments schedules

The balance sheet of Roger, Susan, and Tom, who share partnership profits 30 percent, 30 percent, and 40 percent, respectively, included the following balances on January 1, 2011, the date of dissolution:

Cash	$ 20,000	Liabilities	$ 40,100
Other assets	130,000	Loan from Roger	5,000
Loan to Susan	10,000	Roger capital	9,900
		Susan capital	45,000
		Tom capital	60,000
	$160,000		$160,000

During January 2011, part of the firm's assets are sold for $40,000. In February the remaining assets are sold for $21,000. Assume that available cash is distributed to the proper parties at the end of January and at the end of February.

REQUIRED: Prepare a statement of partnership liquidation with supporting safe payments schedules for each cash distribution. (It will not be possible to determine the actual gains and losses in January.)

P 17-10
Installment liquidation

Account balances for the Rob, Tom, and Val partnership on October 1, 2011, are as follows:

Cash	$ 21,000	Accounts payable	$ 80,000
Accounts receivable	63,000	Note payable	50,000
Inventory	120,000	Rob capital (30%)	43,600
Equipment	150,000	Tom capital (50%)	150,000
Rob loan	15,000	Val capital (20%)	45,400
	$369,000		$369,000

The partners have decided to liquidate the business. Activities for October and November are as follows:

October

1 Rob is short of funds, and the partners agree to charge her loan to her capital account.
2 $40,000 is collected on the accounts receivable; $4,000 is written off as uncollectible.
3 Half the inventory is sold for $50,000.
4 Equipment with a book value of $55,000 is sold for $60,000.
5 The $50,000 bank note plus $600 accrued interest is paid in full.
6 The accounts payable are paid.
7 Liquidation expenses of $2,000 are paid.
8 Except for a $5,000 contingency fund, all available cash is distributed to partners at the end of October.

November

   9 The remaining equipment is sold for $38,000.

   10 Val accepts inventory with a book value of $20,000 and a fair value of $10,000 as payment for part of her capital balance. The rest of the inventory is written off.

   11 Accounts receivable of $10,000 are collected. The remaining receivables are written off.

   12 Liquidation expenses of $800 are paid.

   13 Remaining cash, including the contingency fund, is distributed to the partners.

REQUIRED: Prepare a statement of partnership liquidation for the period October 1 through November 30.

P 17-11
Installment liquidation

The adjusted trial balance of the Jee, Moore, and Olsen partnership at December 31, 2011, is as follows:

Cash	$ 50,000
Accounts receivable—net	100,000
Nonmonetary assets	800,000
Expenses	400,000
Total debits	$1,350,000
Accounts payable	$ 80,000
Jee capital	250,000
Moore capital	450,000
Olsen capital	370,000
Revenue	200,000
Total credits	$1,350,000

ADDITIONAL INFORMATION

1. Partnership profits are divided 20%, 40%, and 40% to Jee, Moore, and Olsen, respectively, after salary allowances of $25,000 each to Jee and Moore for time devoted to the business.

2. Due to the disastrous results of 2011, the partners agreed to liquidate the business as soon as possible after January 1, 2012, and to distribute available cash on a weekly basis.

3. During the first week in January, $85,500 was collected on the accounts receivable, and cash was distributed on January 8, 2012.

REQUIRED

1. Prepare the journal entries to close the partnership books at December 31, 2011.

2. Develop a cash distribution plan for the partnership as of January 1, 2012.

3. Prepare a cash distribution schedule for the January 8, 2012, distribution of available cash.

P 17-12
Installment liquidation

The after-closing trial balances of the Beams, Plank, and Timbers partnership at December 31, 2011, included the following accounts and balances:

Cash	$120,000
Accounts receivable—net	140,000
Inventory	200,000
Plant assets—net	200,000
Trademarks	20,000
Total debits	$680,000
Accounts payable	$150,000
Notes payable	100,000
Beams capital (profit sharing ratio, 50%)	170,000
Plank capital (profit sharing ratio, 30%)	180,000
Timbers capital (profit sharing ratio, 20%)	80,000
Total credits	$680,000

The partnership is to be liquidated as soon as possible, and all available cash except for a $10,000 contingency balance is to be distributed at the end of each month prior to the time that all assets are converted into cash.

During January 2012, $100,000 was collected from accounts receivable, inventory items with a book value of $80,000 were sold for $100,000, and available cash was distributed.

During February 2012, Beams received plant assets with a book value of $60,000 and a fair value of $50,000 in partial settlement of her equity in the partnership. Also during February, the remaining inventory items were sold for $60,000, liquidation expenses of $2,000 were paid, and a liability of $8,000 was discovered. Cash was distributed on February 28.

During March 2012, the plant assets were sold for $110,000, the remaining noncash assets were written off, final liquidation expenses of $5,000 were paid, and cash was distributed. The dissolution of the partnership was completed on March 31, 2012.

REQUIRED: Prepare a statement of partnership liquidation for the Beams, Plank, and Timbers partnership for the period January 1 to March 31, 2012.

INTERNET ASSIGNMENT

Many investment clubs are organized as partnerships. Perform an Internet search and find a club that is organized as a partnership. Review the partnership's bylaws. What provisions has the club made for the death or retirement of a partner and the ultimate liquidation of the partnership?

18 CHAPTER

Corporate Liquidations and Reorganizations

This chapter examines accounting and legal matters related to financially distressed corporations.[1] Some corporations are able to recover from financial adversity through internal operating and policy changes, whereas others with more serious financial problems are forced to seek external remedies. These remedies are classified as direct agreements with creditors, reorganizations, and liquidations.

If a company is unable to meet its debt payments on time, direct negotiations with its creditors can result in a debt restructuring agreement or a debt settlement agreement. You probably covered accounting for troubled debt restructuring in an intermediate accounting class. The *Advanced Accounting* Web site includes a review of this subject.

This chapter focuses on bankruptcies that result either in corporate liquidation or reorganization. We first provide an overview of U.S. bankruptcy law. We then discuss the requirements and procedures related to liquidations and reorganizations.

BANKRUPTCY REFORM ACT OF 1978

LEARNING OBJECTIVE 1

A debtor corporation is considered insolvent when it is unable to pay its debts as they come due, or when its total debts exceed the fair value of its assets. The inability to make payment on time is referred to as **equity insolvency**. Having total debts that exceed the fair value of total assets is referred to as **bankruptcy insolvency**. Debtor corporations that are insolvent in the equity sense may be able to avoid bankruptcy proceedings by negotiating an agreement directly with creditors. Debtor corporations that are insolvent in the bankruptcy sense ordinarily will be reorganized or liquidated under the supervision of a bankruptcy court.

Prior to 1898, state government legislation governed bankruptcy proceedings. The 1898 Bankruptcy Act, a federal law, preempted the state legislation. The 1898 Bankruptcy Act and its numerous amendments were repealed when Congress enacted Title 11 of the *United States Code*, the Bankruptcy Reform Act of 1978, which reflects the entire bankruptcy law and became effective October 1, 1979. The 1978 Act established comprehensive bankruptcy law as well as new bankruptcy judges and new bankruptcy courts. The Act has been amended several times since it was enacted, most recently in 2005.

Effective in October 2005, the Bankruptcy Abuse Prevention and Consumer Protection Act (BAPCPA) received a great deal of attention for its provisions, which made it more difficult for individual debtors to abuse the spirit behind bankruptcy provisions. BAPCPA also has ramifications for businesses, primarily through its limitations on the time frames allowed for plan exclusivity in Chapter 11 bankruptcies and real estate leases.

---

[1]Municipalities, railroads, stockbrokers, and commodity brokers are excluded from the discussion in this chapter. Bankruptcies of these entities are covered by special provisions of Title 11 of the *United States Code*.

	Type	Description
EXHIBIT 18-1 **Types of Bankruptcies**	Chapter 7: Liquidation	A trustee is appointed to sell off the assets of the individual or company and pay claims to creditors.
	Chapter 9: Adjustments of debts of a municipality	Municipalities (not covered here).
	Chapter 11: Reorganization	The debtor corporation is expected to be rehabilitated, and the reorganization of the corporation is anticipated. ■ Either a trustee is appointed or the company performs the duties of a trustee (debtor in possession). ■ A plan of reorganization is negotiated with creditors, stockholders, employees, and others so that claims are settled and the company can continue to operate during bankruptcy proceedings and emerge from bankruptcy. ■ Although Chapter 11 also applies to individuals, Chapter 13 bankruptcy is usually easier.
	Chapter 12: Farmers	Family farmers with regular income (not covered here).
	Chapter 13: Adjustments of debts of an individual with regular income	Exclusively applies to individuals, including sole proprietorships. Unsecured debts less than $307,675 and secured debts less than $922,975 (not covered here).

Under the current rules a debtor company that files for bankruptcy is given 120 days initially to submit a plan of reorganization to the court for approval. During this time, no other parties, such as creditors, can submit plans to the court. Before the enactment of BAPCPA, debtor companies could repeatedly ask for extensions of the exclusivity period, but BAPCPA limits the exclusivity period to a maximum of 18 months. This could speed up the process and allow creditors to recover more of their money since the plan-writing process cannot be dragged out indefinitely.

Another change is that retail debtors now have only 120 days to assume or reject unexpired leases on nonresidential real property with a maximum 90-day extension. Only with the written consent of landlords are businesses able to extend this.

The bankruptcy law facilitates debt relief to individuals and corporations under various provisions, called chapters. Exhibit 18-1 summarizes the major bankruptcy-code chapters. The purposes of the bankruptcy law are to protect the interests of creditors, to ensure an equitable distribution of assets in settlement of liabilities, and to give debtors a "fresh start." Once the debtor has settled its debts through the bankruptcy process, the debtor can start anew without the constant threat of legal actions and collection agencies.

Chapter 11 reorganizations provide businesses and individuals with the time needed to put together a business plan. It is hoped that the plan will ensure the future survival of the corporation once it emerges from bankruptcy proceedings, as well as provide for the settlement of its existing debts. The bankruptcy court and creditors' committees must approve of the plan.

If a corporation cannot produce a plan the court approves, the corporation may be forced into Chapter 7 bankruptcy, or liquidation. Some companies (such as **Montgomery Ward**, **LTV Steel** and **US Airways**) emerge from Chapter 11 bankruptcy and subsequently file for bankruptcy again because their business plan does not work.

Occasionally, corporations may file for bankruptcy protection even though they have sufficient fair value of assets to cover their debts, because they have liquidity problems and cannot meet debt payments as they come due. A few times in history, the bankruptcy court has allowed companies to file for bankruptcy even though they had sufficient liquidity to meet current debts, because they were parties to potentially large lawsuit findings. For example, **Dow Chemical** filed for bankruptcy as a result of silicon-breast-implant lawsuits; in 1985, **AH Robins** filed for bankruptcy as a result of Dalkon Shield IUD lawsuits; and **Johns Manville** filed for bankruptcy in 1982 as a result of threatened asbestos lawsuits. Unfortunately in recent years, corporate accounting scandals have emerged as another reason firms file for bankruptcy. Some examples include **Enron**, **WorldCom**, and **Adelphia**. The most recent events in the world of corporate bankruptcy are also some of the most dramatic. The real estate and banking collapse of 2007 and 2008 led to half of the twenty largest U.S. public company bankruptcies taking place in 2007–2009.

The large firms filing for protection in this period include seven banking and real estate firms, two of the world's largest car manufacturers, and one Chemical company. Some of the firms are familiar, like **Lehman Brothers** and **General Motors**; some, like **Thornburg Mortgage** and **Lyondell Chemical Company**, are less well known. They all have in common that they listed at least $26B in total assets when they filed for protection. The great recession of 2008–2009 took its toll on smaller business as well. In 2006 there were 17,730 commercial Chapter 7 cases, which had more than tripled to 59,768 by 2009. The Chapter 11 petitions had also seen a similar increase from 4,227 in 2006 to 12,495 in 2009. This increase is seen quite clearly in the following chart (source: http://bdp.law.harvard.edu).

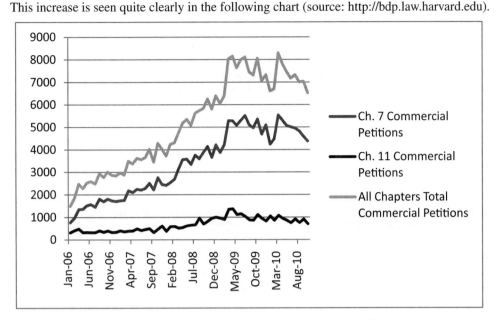

When a firm files for bankruptcy protection, the court must decide if it has a role. If the court issues an **order of relief**, the debtor company is protected from further litigation during the time the reorganization plan is being developed. Under court supervision, the creditors and the debtor work out a plan to settle the creditors' claims. The court is the final arbiter in such cases.

Sometimes companies are acquired by other companies as part of the reorganization plan. For example, Montgomery Ward filed for bankruptcy protection in 1997 and was acquired by *General Electric* (GE Capital) in 1999, bringing it out of bankruptcy. Despite an active plan to return the firm to profitability, Montgomery Ward again filed for bankruptcy in 2001, shuttered all of its stores, and set about liquidating its assets. Lehman Brothers, which filed for protection in 2008 with almost $700B in assets recorded, was sold to Barclays and Nomura Holdings for less than $2B.

Other well-known companies have recently filed for bankruptcy protection—for example, *Chiquita Brands* ($1,788 million in liabilities) in January 2001, *Fruit of the Loom* ($1,741 million in liabilities) in December 1999, *Loews Cineplex* ($1,506 million in liabilities) in February 2001, and *Circuit City* in November of 2008 ($2,320 million in liabilities). Even a large accounting firm has filed for bankruptcy—*Laventhol and Horwath* ($2,000 million in liabilities) in November 1990. As you can see from these examples, bankruptcy is a tool that companies use to help them in difficult situations.

The jurisdiction of the bankruptcy court covers all cases under Title 11 of the *U.S. Code*. A case begins with the filing of a petition under which a debtor is initially brought into bankruptcy court. Usually, the petition is filed in the U.S. bankruptcy court district where the debtor's principal place of business or principal assets have been located for at least 180 days. Either the debtor corporation or its creditors may file the petition. If the debtor corporation files the petition, the proceeding is termed a **voluntary bankruptcy proceeding**; if creditors file, it is an **involuntary bankruptcy proceeding**. Most bankruptcy filings are voluntary.

A petition commencing a case by or against a corporate debtor may be filed under either Chapter 7 or Chapter 11 of the bankruptcy act. **Chapter 7 of the Bankruptcy Reform Act** covers straight bankruptcy, under which liquidation of the debtor corporation is expected, and **Chapter 11 of the Bankruptcy Reform Act** covers rehabilitation of the debtor and anticipates reorganization of the debtor corporation.[2] The bankruptcy court has the power (subject to various requests and

---

[2]Not all liquidations result from financial adversity. Voluntary liquidations are often based on the belief that the market value of the company's stock is less than the amount that could be realized by selling the company's assets. This type of liquidation does not involve restructurings or judicial remedies, and established accounting principles are applicable to winding up the company's affairs through liquidating dividends. For a discussion of voluntary liquidations, see Ronald J. Kudle, *Voluntary Corporate Liquidations* (Westport, CT: Quorum Books, Greenwood Press, 1988), or George E. Nogler and Kenneth B. Schwartz, "Financial Reporting and Auditors' Opinions on Voluntary Liquidations," *Accounting Horizons* (September 1989), pp. 12–20.

conditions) to dismiss a case, to enter the order for relief (in other words, accept the petition), or to convert a Chapter 11 reorganization case into a Chapter 7 liquidation case or vice versa.

LEARNING
OBJECTIVE 2

The Office of U.S. Trustee

The Bankruptcy Reform Act created the Office of U.S. Trustee, a branch of the Department of Justice, to be responsible for the administrative duties of bankruptcy cases. The U.S. Attorney General appoints U.S. trustees for seven-year terms. The duties of the U.S. trustee are to maintain and supervise a panel of private trustees eligible to serve in Chapter 7 cases, to serve as trustee or interim trustee in some bankruptcy cases (such as in a Chapter 7 case in which a qualified private trustee is not available), to supervise the administration of bankruptcy cases, to monitor appointed creditors' committees, and to preside over creditor meetings.

Duties of the Debtor Corporation

In both Chapter 7 liquidation cases and Chapter 11 reorganization cases, the debtor corporation is required to do the following:

- File a list of creditors, a schedule of assets and liabilities, and a statement of debtor's financial affairs
- Cooperate with the trustee as necessary to enable the trustee to perform his or her duties
- Surrender all property to the trustee, including books, documents, records, and papers relating to the estate in cases involving a trustee
- Appear at hearings of the court as required

Identifying creditors and filing documents may take several months. It is an important task because creditors who have been notified of the bankruptcy proceedings may receive only a percentage of their claims. Those creditors not notified are entitled to the full amount.

Duties of the Bankruptcy Judge

The bankruptcy judge settles disputes that occur during the case and approves all payments of debts incurred before the bankruptcy filing, as well as other payments that are considered extraordinary.

LIQUIDATION

The Administrative Office of the U.S. Courts reported that of the 61,148 business bankruptcy filings for the 12 months ended March 31, 2010, 42,346, or about 69 percent, were filed under Chapter 7 of the bankruptcy act. Chapter 7 liquidations are cheaper and faster than Chapter 11 reorganizations. A Chapter 7 liquidation case begins voluntarily when a debtor corporation files a petition with the bankruptcy court, or involuntarily through filing by three or more entities holding non-contingent, unsecured claims totaling at least $12,300.[3] A single creditor with an unsecured claim of $12,300 or more may also file a petition if there are fewer than 12 unsecured creditors.

The court will grant the order for relief (accept the petition) under Chapter 7 if the creditors prove their claims or if the debtor fails to contest the petition on a timely basis. The order for relief prevents creditors from seeking payment of their claims directly from the debtor. If the creditors fail to prove their alleged claims, the court will dismiss the case. The debtor may respond to the petition by filing for protection from creditors under Chapter 11, under which, instead of being liquidated, it can reorganize.

If an order for relief under Chapter 7 is granted, the U.S. trustee (or the court) appoints an interim trustee to take possession of the debtor corporation's estate until a trustee is elected. (An interim trustee may be appointed at any time after commencement of a case if the court considers it necessary to preserve the property of the estate or prevent losses.)

The election for trustee takes place at a meeting of creditors, and only unsecured creditors with undisputed claims are eligible to vote. A trustee is elected if creditors holding a minimum of 20

---

[3]An *entity* under Title 11 means a person, an estate, a trustee, or a government unit. *Person* means an individual, a partnership, or a corporation, but not a government unit.

percent of the dollar amount of claims request an election and one candidate obtains the votes of creditors holding a majority in the dollar amount of claims actually voting. If a trustee is not elected, the interim trustee serves as trustee. The unsecured creditors eligible to vote may also elect a creditors' committee of 3 to 11 members to consult with the trustee and to submit questions regarding the debtor's estate to the court.

Duties of the Trustee in Liquidation Cases

The filing of a case creates an estate. The trustee takes possession of the estate, converts the estate assets into cash, and distributes the proceeds according to the priority of claims, as directed by the bankruptcy court. Other duties of the trustee in a liquidation case are as follows:

- To investigate the financial affairs of the debtor
- To provide information about the debtor's estate and its administration to interested parties
- To examine creditor claims and object to claims that appear to be improper
- To provide periodic reports and summaries of operations, a statement of receipts and disbursements, and other information as the court specifies, if they are authorized to operate the debtor's business,
- To file final reports on trusteeship as required by the court

Payment of Claims

Claims in a Chapter 7 liquidation case are paid in the order shown in Exhibit 18-2. Claims secured by valid liens are paid to the extent of the proceeds from property pledged as security. If the proceeds are insufficient to satisfy the claims of secured creditors, the amounts not satisfied are classified as unsecured nonpriority claims (or general unsecured claims). Unsecured claims are divided into priority and nonpriority classes for Chapter 7 liquidation cases (see Exhibit 18-2). Unsecured priority claims are paid in full before any distributions are made to unsecured nonpriority claims.

Claims within the unsecured priority claims class are ranked 1 through 6, such that claims in the first rank (administrative expenses) are paid in full before any distribution is made for claims in the second rank, and so forth. Within each of the six priority ranks, however, distributions are made on a pro rata basis when available cash is insufficient to pay all claims of that rank. Equivalent procedures apply to cash distributions in the four ranks included within the unsecured nonpriority class. Stockholders under a Chapter 7 liquidation case are included in distributions only when all valid creditor claims have been fully satisfied.

I Secured Claims
Claims secured by valid liens.

II Unsecured Priority Claims
1. Administrative expenses incurred in preserving and liquidating the estate, including trustee's fees and legal and accounting fees.
2. Claims incurred between the date of filing an involuntary petition and the date an interim trustee is appointed.
3. Claims for wages, salaries, and commissions earned within 90 days of filing the petition and not exceeding $10,000 per individual.
4. Claims for contributions to employee benefit plans arising from services rendered within 180 days of filing the petition and limited to $10,000 per employee.
5. Claims of individuals, not to exceed $1,800, arising from the purchase, lease, or rental of property that was not delivered or the purchase of services that were not provided by the debtor.
6. Claims of governmental units for income or gross receipts taxes, property taxes, employment taxes, excise taxes, and customs duties that originated within one to four years before filing (periods vary for different claims). Taxes collected or withheld for which the debtor is liable and penalties related to the foregoing are also included.

III Unsecured Nonpriority Claims
1. Allowed claims that were timely filed.
2. Allowed claims whose proof of claim was filed late.
3. Allowed claims (secured and unsecured) for any fine, penalty, or forfeiture, or for multiple, exemplary, or punitive charges arising to the order for relief or appointment of trustee.
4. Claims for interest on the unsecured priority claims or the unsecured nonpriority claims.

IV Stockholders' Claims
Remaining assets are returned to the debtor corporation or its stockholders.

EXHIBIT 18-2

Ranking of Claims in Chapter 7 Liquidation Cases

ILLUSTRATION OF A LIQUIDATION CASE

Cam Corporation experienced a large operating loss in 2011 and the first half of 2012. By July 2012 its accounts payable were overdue, and its accounts receivable had been pledged to support a bank loan that was in default. Cam's creditors were unwilling to extend additional credit or to amend the terms of any of their loans, and on August 1, 2012, Cam filed a voluntary petition for relief under Chapter 7 of the bankruptcy act.

Exhibit 18-3 presents a balance sheet prepared at the filing date. Although the balance sheet shows stockholders' equity of $13,000, historical cost valuations are not good indicators of financial condition for a liquidating company. An accounting statement that does provide relevant information for a liquidating company is the *statement of affairs*.

Statement of Affairs

A trustee's duties may include filing a statement of financial affairs with the bankruptcy court. This statement is a legal document prepared for the bankruptcy court. The **statement of affairs** is a financial statement that emphasizes liquidation values and provides relevant information for the trustee in liquidating the debtor corporation. It also provides information that may be useful to creditors and to the bankruptcy court.

A statement of affairs is prepared at a specific date and shows balance sheet information. Assets are measured at expected net realizable values and are classified on the basis of availability for fully secured, partially secured, priority, and unsecured creditors. Liabilities are classified as priority, fully secured, partially secured, and unsecured. Historical cost valuations are included in the statement for reference purposes.

EXHIBIT 18-3

Debtor Corporation's Balance Sheet at the Bankruptcy Filing Date

---

CAM CORPORATION BALANCE SHEET, AUGUST 1, 2012

Assets		
Current Assets		
Cash	$ 3,000	
Marketable securities (at market)	7,000	
Accounts receivable (net of estimated uncollectible accounts)	25,000	
Inventories	50,000	
Prepaid expenses	4,000	$ 89,000
Long-Term Assets		
Land	$ 15,000	
Building—net	40,000	
Equipment—net	30,000	
Intangible assets	6,000	91,000
Total assets		$180,000

Liabilities and Stockholders' Equity		
Current Liabilities		
Accounts payable	$ 65,000	
Wages payable	13,000	
Property taxes payable	2,000	
Note payable—bank	25,000	
Notes payable—suppliers	5,000	
Interest payable	7,000	$117,000
Long-Term Liabilities		
Mortgage payable		50,000
Total liabilities		167,000
Stockholders' Equity		
Capital stock	$200,000	
Retained earnings	(187,000)	
Total stockholders' equity		13,000
Total liabilities and stockholders' equity		$180,000

Exhibit 18-4 presents the statement of affairs for Cam Corporation. Information for the statement is derived from the balance sheet (see Exhibit 18-3) at the filing date and other sources, such as appraisals of the assets' expected liquidation values and contractual agree-

EXHIBIT 18-4

Statement of Affairs

CAM CORPORATION STATEMENT OF AFFAIRS ON AUGUST 1, 2012

Assets

Book Value		Estimated Realizable Values Less Secured Creditor Liabilities		Estimated Realizable Value Available for Unsecured Creditors
	Pledged for Fully Secured Creditors			
$ 55,000	Land and buildings—net		$60,000	
	Less: Mortgage payable	$50,000		
	Interest payable	5,000	55,000	$ 5,000
	Pledged for Partially Secured Creditors			
25,000	Accounts receivable		$22,000	
	Less: Note payable to bank	$25,000		
	Interest payable	2,000	27,000	0
	Available for Priority and Unsecured Creditors			
3,000	Cash			3,000
7,000	Marketable securities			7,000
50,000	Inventories			55,000
4,000	Prepaid expenses			0
30,000	Equipment—net			12,000
6,000	Intangible assets			0
	Total available for priority and unsecured creditors			82,000
	Less: Priority liabilities			15,000
	Total available for unsecured creditors			67,000
	Estimated deficiency			8,000
$180,000				$75,000

Liabilities and Stockholders' Equity

Book Value		Secured and Priority Claims	Unsecured Nonpriority Claims
	Fully Secured Creditors		
50,000	Mortgage payable	50,000	
5,000	Interest payable	5,000	
		55,000	
	Partially Secured Creditors		
25,000	Note payable—bank	25,000	
2,000	Interest payable	2,000	
		27,000	
	Less: Accounts receivable pledged	22,000	$ 5,000
	Priority Liabilities		
$ 13,000	Wages payable	$13,000	
2,000	Property taxes payable	2,000	
		15,000	
	Unsecured Creditors		
65,000	Accounts payable		65,000
5,000	Notes payable to suppliers		5,000
	Stockholders' Equity		
200,000	Capital stock		
(187,000)	Retained earnings		
$180,000			$75,000

ments with creditors. The mortgage payable, together with $5,000 interest payable, is secured by the land and building. All accounts receivable are pledged as security for the bank loan and $2,000 interest payable.

It is expected that Cam's assets can be converted into cash within three months. The estimated realizable values are as follows:

Cash	$ 3,000
Marketable securities	7,000
Accounts receivable	22,000
Inventories (net of selling expenses)	55,000
Prepaid expenses	—
Land and building	60,000
Equipment	12,000
Intangible assets	—
	$159,000

Assets pledged as security for creditor claims are offset against the estimated claims of secured creditors in the asset section of the statement of affairs. Any excess of the realizable value of assets pledged over related claims is carried to the right-hand column of the statement to indicate the amount available for unsecured creditors. An excess of secured creditor claims over the estimated value of assets pledged as security indicates that these claims are only partially secured. The unsecured portion is shown in the liability section of the statement as an unsecured nonpriority claim. The value of total assets available to pay unsecured creditors is estimated to fall short by $8,000.

Trustee Accounting

A trustee in a Chapter 7 bankruptcy case stewards the assets of the debtor corporation until being released by the bankruptcy court. The bankruptcy act does not cover procedural accounting details such as whether the trustee should create a new set of accounting records to establish accountability for the estate and show the eventual discharge of responsibility, or whether the corporation's existing accounting records should be continued under the direction of the trustee.

The trustee for Cam Corporation creates a new set of accounting records. The assets are recorded on the trustee's books at book values, rather than at expected realizable values, because of the subjectivity involved in estimating realizable amounts at the time of filing. Contra asset accounts are omitted from the trustee's books because they are not meaningful in a liquidation case and because it is desirable to keep the trustee accounts as simple as possible. The following entry could be prepared to open the trustee's books for Cam:

Cash (+A)	3,000	
Marketable securities (+A)	7,000	
Accounts receivable (+A)	25,000	
Inventories (+A)	50,000	
Prepaid expenses (+A)	4,000	
Land (+A)	15,000	
Building (+A)	40,000	
Equipment (+A)	30,000	
Intangible assets (+A)	6,000	
Accounts payable (+L)		65,000
Wages payable (+L)		13,000
Property taxes payable (+L)		2,000
Note payable—bank (+L)		25,000
Notes payable—suppliers (+L)		5,000
Interest payable (+L)		7,000
Mortgage payable (+L)		50,000
Estate equity (+EE)		13,000

To record custody of Cam Corporation in liquidation.

After assuming custody of the estate, the trustee records gains, losses, and liquidation expenses directly in the estate equity account. This account represents the residual equity that shareholders can claim after the liquidation of assets and settlement of liabilities. Any unrecorded assets or liabilities that the trustee discovers are also entered in the estate equity account. To distinguish assets and liabilities included in the initial estate and those acquired or incurred by the trustee, the assets and liabilities recorded after the trustee takes charge of the estate are identified as "new."

Transactions and events during the first month of Cam's trusteeship are described and journal entries to record them in the trustee's books are illustrated as follows:

1. A previously unrecorded utility bill for $500 is received.

Estate equity (−EE)	500	
Utilities payable—new (+L)		500

2. Intangible assets are deemed worthless and are written off.

Estate equity (−EE)	6,000	
Intangible assets (−A)		6,000

3. All inventory items are sold for $48,000, of which $18,000 is on account and $30,000 is in cash.

Cash (+A)	30,000	
Accounts receivable—new (+A)	18,000	
Estate equity (−EE)	2,000	
Inventories (−A)		50,000

4. The equipment is sold for $14,200 cash.

Cash (+A)	14,200	
Estate equity (−EE)	15,800	
Equipment (−A)		30,000

5. Wages and property taxes owed on August 1 (priority liabilities) are paid.

Wages payable (−L)	13,000	
Property taxes payable (−L)	2,000	
Cash (−A)		15,000

6. Land and building are sold for $64,000 cash, and the mortgage payable and related interest are paid.

Cash (+A)	64,000	
Land (−A)		15,000
Building (−A)		40,000
Estate equity (+EE)		9,000
Mortgage payable (−L)	50,000	
Interest payable (−L)	5,000	
Cash (−A)		55,000

7. Insurance policies (included in prepaid expenses) are canceled, and a $1,000 cash refund is received.

Cash (+A)	1,000	
Prepaid expenses (−A)		1,000

8. Accounts receivable of $21,000 are collected from the amounts owed to Cam at August 1. The remaining $4,000 is uncollectible.

Cash (+A)	21,000	
Estate equity (−EE)	4,000	
Accounts receivable (−A)		25,000

9. The $21,000 received on account is applied to the bank note payable and related interest.

Interest payable (−L)	2,000	
Note payable—bank (−L)	19,000	
Cash (−A)		21,000

10. Estate administration expenses of $3,000 are paid.

Estate equity (−EE)	3,000	
Cash (−A)		3,000

11. Trustee fees of $2,000 are accrued.

Estate equity (−EE)	2,000	
Trustee's fee payable—new (+L)		2,000

After the transactions and events occurring through August 31 are entered on the trustee's books, financial statements can be prepared as needed to show progress toward liquidation and financial position at that date.

STATEMENT OF CASH RECEIPTS AND DISBURSEMENTS The statement of cash receipts and disbursements is prepared directly from entries in the cash account. It appears in summary form here.

CASH

Balance, August 1, 2012	$ 3,000	Wages and property taxes	$ 15,000
Inventory items sold	30,000	Mortgage and interest payment	55,000
Equipment sold	14,200	Bank notes and interest	21,000
Land and building sold	64,000	Administrative expenses	3,000
Insurance refund	1,000	**Balance forward**	**39,200**
Accounts receivable	21,000		$133,200
	$133,200		
Balance, August 31, 2012	$ 39,200		

Exhibit 18-5 illustrates the trustee's interim statement of cash receipts and cash disbursements for the period August 1 to August 31, 2012. All disbursements require approval of the court, so the statement should be a useful financial summary.

STATEMENT OF CHANGES IN ESTATE EQUITY The estate equity account in summary form is as follows:

ESTATE EQUITY (DEFICIT)

Utility bill discovered	$ 500	August 1, 2012, balance	$13,000
Intangibles written off	6,000	Land and building gain	9,000
Inventory loss	2,000		
Equipment loss	15,800		
Accounts receivable written off	4,000		
Administrative expenses	3,000		
Trustee's fee	2,000	**Balance forward (deficit)**	**11,300**
	$33,300		$33,300
August 31, 2012	$11,300		

EXHIBIT 18-5 Trustee's Interim Statement of Cash Receipts and Cash Disbursements	**CAM CORPORATION IN TRUSTEESHIP STATEMENT OF CASH RECEIPTS AND DISBURSEMENTS FROM AUGUST 1 TO AUGUST 31, 2012**

Cash balance, August 1, 2012		$ 3,000
Add: Cash receipts		
Sale of inventory items	$30,000	
Sale of equipment	14,200	
Sale of land and building	64,000	
Refund from insurance policy	1,000	
Collection of receivables	21,000	
Total cash receipts		130,200
		133,200
Deduct: Cash disbursements		
Wages payable (priority claim)	$13,000	
Property taxes payable (priority claim)	2,000	
Mortgage payable and interest (fully secured)	55,000	
Bank note payable and interest (for secured portion)	21,000	
Administrative expenses (priority item)	3,000	
Total cash disbursements		94,000
Cash balance, August 31, 2012		$ 39,200

CAM CORPORATION IN TRUSTEESHIP STATEMENT OF CHANGES IN ESTATE EQUITY FROM AUGUST 1 TO AUGUST 31, 2012

Estate equity August 1, 2012		$ 13,000
Less: Net loss on asset liquidation		
(see schedule below)	$18,800	
Liability for utilities discovered	500	
Administrative expenses	3,000	
Trustee's fee	2,000	
Net decrease for the period		(24,300)
Estate deficit August 31, 2012		$ 11,300

SCHEDULE OF NET LOSSES ON ASSET LIQUIDATION

	Book Value August 1	−	Proceeds on Realization	=	Gain (Loss)
Accounts receivable	$25,000		$21,000		$ (4,000)
Inventories	50,000		48,000		(2,000)
Land and building	55,000		64,000		9,000
Equipment	30,000		14,200		(15,800)
Intangible assets	6,000		0		(6,000)
Net loss on liquidation of assets					$(18,800)

Exhibit 18-6 illustrates the statement of changes in estate equity for Cam Corporation from August 1 to August 31, 2012. Observe that the statement separates gains and losses on asset realization from expenses involved in liquidating the corporation.

BALANCE SHEET A balance sheet is prepared directly from the ledger account balances of the trustee and is presented in Exhibit 18-7. Two key amounts that appear in the balance sheet—cash and estate deficit—are supported by amounts from the statements of cash receipts and disbursements (Exhibit 18-5) and changes in estate equity (Exhibit 18-6). The statements presented in Exhibits 18-5, 18-6, and 18-7 are in a format familiar to accountants, but you will want to compare these financial statements with the traditional statement of realization and liquidation that is presented in Exhibit 18-8.

STATEMENT OF REALIZATION AND LIQUIDATION A statement of realization and liquidation is an activity statement that shows progress toward the liquidation of a debtor's estate. It also informs the bankruptcy court and interested creditors of the accomplishments of the trustee. The bankruptcy act does not require such a statement; instead, the act allows the judge in a bankruptcy case to prescribe the form in which information is presented to the court.

CAM CORPORATION IN TRUSTEESHIP BALANCE SHEET ON AUGUST 31, 2012

Assets	
Cash	$39,200
Marketable securities	7,000
Accounts receivable—net	18,000
Prepaid expenses	3,000
Total assets	$67,200
Liabilities and Deficit	
Accounts payable	$65,000
Utilities payable—discovered	500
Trustee's fee payable—new	2,000
Note payable—bank (unsecured portion)	6,000
Notes payable—suppliers	5,000
Total liabilities	78,500
Less: Estate deficit	11,300
Total liabilities less deficit	$67,200

EXHIBIT 18-8

Statement of Realization and Liquidation

CAM CORPORATION IN TRUSTEESHIP
STATEMENT OF REALIZATION AND LIQUIDATION
AUGUST 1, 2012, TO AUGUST 31, 2012

Assets

Assets to Be Realized [Noncash assets at August 1]			*Assets Realized* [Proceeds from sale, disposal, or write-off]			
Marketable securities	$ 7,000		Accounts receivable	$21,000		
Accounts receivable	25,000		Inventories	48,000		
Inventories	50,000		Prepaid expenses	1,000		
Prepaid expenses	4,000		Land and building	64,000		
Land	15,000		Equipment	14,200		
Building	40,000		Intangible assets	none	$148,200	
Equipment	30,000					
Intangible assets	6,000	$177,000				
Assets Acquired [New noncash assets received]			*Assets Not Realized* [Noncash assets at August 31]			
Accounts receivable—new		18,000	Marketable securities	$ 7,000		
			Prepaid expenses	3,000		
			Accounts receivable—new	18,000	28,000	

Liabilities

Liabilities to Be Liquidated [Liabilities at August 1]			*Liabilities Liquidated* [Amounts paid on liabilities]			
Accounts payable	$65,000		Wages payable	13,000		
Wages payable	13,000		Property taxes payable	2,000		
Property taxes payable	2,000		Note payable—bank	19,000		
Note payable—bank	25,000		Interest payable	7,000		
Notes payable—suppliers	5,000		Mortgage payable	50,000	91,000	
Interest payable	7,000					
Mortgage payable	50,000	167,000	*Liabilities Not Liquidated* [Liabilities at August 31]			
			Accounts payable	$65,000		
Liabilities Incurred or Discovered			Note payable—bank	6,000		
[Amounts incurred or discovered but unpaid at August 31]			Notes payable—suppliers	5,000		
			Liability discovered for utilities	500		
Liability discovered for utilities	$ 500					
Trustee's fee payable—new	2,000	2,500	Trustee's fee payable— new	2,000	78,500	

Income or Loss and Supplemental Items

Supplementary Expenses [Expenses excluding asset losses and write-offs]			*Supplementary Revenues* [Revenues excluding gains on assets or liability settlements]		
Liability discovered for utilities	$ 500		None		
Trustee's fee	2,000		*Net Loss*	24,300	
Administrative expenses— new	3,000	5,500			
		$370,000		$370,000	

Exhibit 18-8 presents a statement of realization and liquidation for Cam Corporation. The statement is presented in its traditional format except for bracketed explanations of the various categories. An examination of Cam's statement of realization and liquidation shows that the statement is complex and that its format is unusual. In addition, the logic of the statement's construction is not immediately apparent. Although a number of alternative formats for the statement have been proposed, many accountants feel that basic financial statements with supporting schedules provide more relevant information about liquidation activity than the statement of realization and liquidation.

Winding Up the Case

During September 2012 the trustee for Cam Corporation collected the $18,000 accounts receivable, sold the marketable securities for $7,300, sold supplies (included in prepaid expenses) for $995, wrote off the remaining prepaid expenses, and distributed cash in final liquidation of the estate. Journal entries to record these transactions and events are as follows:

Cash (+A)	18,000	
Accounts receivable—new (−A)		18,000
Collection of receivable in full.		
Cash (+A)	7,300	
Marketable securities (−A)		7,000
Estate equity (+EE)		300
Sale of marketable securities for cash.		
Cash (+A)	995	
Estate equity (−EE)	2,005	
Prepaid expenses (−A)		3,000
Sale of supplies and write-off of prepaid expenses.		

Account balances after these entries are entered in the trustee's records are as follows:

	Debit	Credit
Cash	$65,495	
Accounts payable		$65,000
Utilities payable—new		500
Trustee's fee payable—new		2,000
Note payable—bank (unsecured portion)		6,000
Notes payable—suppliers		5,000
Estate equity	13,005	
	$78,500	$78,500

The trustee's fee is a priority claim, so it is paid in full. The remaining claims of $76,500 (all first-rank unsecured creditors) receive 83¢ on the dollar (63,495 ÷ $76,500) in final settlement of their claims. Entries to record the cash distributions are as follows:

Trustee's fee payable—new (−L)	2,000	
Cash (−A)		2,000
To record payment of trustee's fee.		
Accounts payable (−L)	53,950	
Utilities payable—new (−L)	415	
Note payable—bank (−L)	4,980	
Notes payable—suppliers (−L)	4,150	
Cash (−A)		63,495
To record payment of 83¢ on the dollar to the general unsecured creditors.		

A case involving a corporation is closed when the estate is fully administered and the trustee is dismissed. The trustee makes the following entry in closing out the Cam Corporation case:

Accounts payable (−L)	11,050	
Utilities payable—new (−L)	85	
Note payable—bank (−L)	1,020	
Notes payable—suppliers (−L)	850	
Estate equity (+EE)		13,005
To close the trustee's records.		

REORGANIZATION

Fewer than 25 percent of business bankruptcy cases are filed each year under Chapter 11. For example, for the 12 months ended March 31, 2010, 13,553 Chapter 11 business cases were filed out of 61,148 total business bankruptcy cases (22%). Chapter 11 reorganization cases usually involve very large organizations.

A Chapter 11 reorganization case is initiated voluntarily when a debtor corporation files a petition with the bankruptcy court or involuntarily when creditors file a petition. The same $12,300 claim limitations applicable to Chapter 7 filings apply here.

The act of filing commences the case and initiates a hearing before the bankruptcy court. As mentioned earlier, the court may enter an order for relief under Chapter 11, convert the case to a Chapter 7 liquidation, or dismiss the case (for example, the case will be dismissed if the bankruptcy court believes that the filing was an act of bad faith). A U.S. trustee is appointed by the bankruptcy judge to be responsible for the administration of the Chapter 11 case.

Trustee or Debtor in Possession

In a Chapter 11 case, a private trustee may be appointed for cause, but otherwise the debtor corporation is continued in possession of the estate and is referred to as a **debtor in possession**. A trustee may be appointed in cases involving fraud, dishonesty, or gross mismanagement, or if the court rules that appointment of a trustee is in the best interest of creditors, equity holders, and other parties with an interest in the estate. For the most part, bankruptcy judges have been reluctant to appoint private trustees to operate businesses in reorganization cases because company management is usually more qualified to operate and reorganize insolvent companies. However, trustees are occasionally appointed. In 2003, at the behest of a major creditor, a subsidiary of *Boeing*, a trustee was appointed to operate *Hawaiian Airlines*, which filed for bankruptcy on March 21, 2003.

If the court orders the appointment of a private trustee, one is appointed by the U.S. trustee or by the bankruptcy court in non–U.S. trustee districts. Within 30 days of the order to appoint a private trustee, any party in interest in the case may request the election of a disinterested person to serve as trustee, and the U.S. trustee will call a meeting of creditors for that purpose. The option to elect a trustee is an important change provided by the 1994 Bankruptcy Reform Act.

The duties of a trustee or debtor in possession include the following:

- Being accountable for the debtor's property, including operations of the debtor's business
- Filing a list of creditors, a schedule of assets and liabilities, and a statement of financial affairs (if not filed by the debtor)
- Furnishing information to the court about the debtor's estate and its administration
- Examining creditor claims and objecting to claims that appear to be improper (normally, only the trustee can object)
- Filing a reorganization plan or reporting why a plan will not be filed
- Filing final reports on the trusteeship as required by the court

Trustees and debtors in possession negotiate with the creditors, stockholders, and others in creating a plan of reorganization that will be approved by the bankruptcy court.

If a debtor in possession is appointed, an examiner will be appointed if loans to outsiders other than for goods and services exceed $5,000,000 or if the court concludes that such appointment is in the interests of the creditors, equity holders, or other parties with an interest in the estate. A primary function of the examiner is to value the debtor's assets and report such valuations to the court.

Committee Representation

Creditors' committees are responsible for protecting the interests of the creditors they represent and preserving the debtor's assets. The committees may review debtor transactions proposed to the court during bankruptcy, such as debtor-in-possession financing and disposal of assets. Committees can bring their objections to the court for consideration. All negotiations between prepetition creditors and the debtor in possession must take place through the creditors' committees.

Unlike in Chapter 7 cases, creditors' committees are not elected in Chapter 11 cases. A creditors' committee is appointed by the U.S. trustee as soon as practicable after the bankruptcy court grants an order for relief under Chapter 11. The creditors' committee (usually seven members) is selected from the largest unsecured creditors. Subsequently, the composition of that committee may be changed and other committees of creditors or equity holders may be appointed. The selection of creditors' committees can be extremely important to the final disposition of a reorganization case. If creditors' committees begin fighting each other, a simple and timely reorganization is nearly impossible.

Governmental units are generally not eligible to serve on creditors' committees. Prior to 1994, the Pension Benefit Guaranty Corporation (PBGC) sat on creditors' committees, but only as a nonvoting member. However, the 1994 Bankruptcy Reform Act gave the PBGC voting rights on creditors' committees.

Operating Under Chapter 11

Reorganization may take from six months to several years. In the meantime, subject to restrictions of the Bankruptcy Code and the bankruptcy court, the debtor in possession continues operating the business while working out a reorganization plan that is acceptable to all parties concerned. On the day of the bankruptcy filing, the company's existing bank accounts and books are closed and new accounts and books opened.

Usually, the company will arrange a new line of credit with its banks to enable it to continue to operate. This is often referred to as *debtor-in-possession financing*. The bankruptcy court must approve new financing agreements.

POSSIBLE BENEFITS OF CHAPTER 11 PROTECTION TO THE DEBTOR IN POSSESSION With the bankruptcy court's approval, the company may be able to reduce its labor costs through layoffs or wage reductions, or by terminating its pension plans. With the bankruptcy court's approval, the company can reject certain executory contracts and unexpired leases. (**Executory contracts** are those that have not been completely performed by both parties, such as purchase commitments.) Any claims for damages resulting from the cancellation of unfavorable contracts are treated as unsecured debt. Interest accrual on unsecured debt stops at the time of filing. This can be a big factor for some companies. Interest of nearly $3 million a day was accruing on *Pennzoil's* $10.3 billion award from *Texaco* until the date of Texaco's Chapter 11 filing.

Creditors subject to the jurisdiction of the bankruptcy court may not commence or continue a lawsuit to take possession of the debtor's property without permission of the bankruptcy court; however, secured creditors may receive payments to protect their interest in collateral that the debtor continues to use in its operations. This is particularly applicable when the debtor continues to use collateralized property subject to depreciation, depletion, or amortization. Payments to the secured creditor may reduce the loan balance as the value of the collateral declines.

Financially distressed companies that find it necessary to restructure or swap debt may have difficulty gaining the necessary support from bondholders without filing for bankruptcy. A debt-restructuring plan typically requires approval of 95 percent of each class of bondholders and a majority of stockholders. However, a debt restructuring under the bankruptcy court requires only two-thirds approval of each class of bondholders.

DISADVANTAGES OF A CHAPTER 11 FILING A Chapter 11 filing creates the obvious disadvantage for the debtor corporation of losing the confidence of its lenders, suppliers, customers, and employees. Beyond this stigma of bankruptcy, there is the additional disadvantage of operating a business in competitive markets when capital expenditures, acquisitions, disposals of assets, borrowing money, and so on, require prior approval of the court. Depending on the circumstances of a particular case, the bankruptcy court may impose so many restrictions on company management that even day-to-day operations of the business become difficult. The company may have to sell off its profitable units to meet creditor demands for emerging from Chapter 11.

The biggest disadvantage to the debtor is the cost of the bankruptcy proceedings.[4] Lawyers and other advisers are hired by the creditors' committees and the stockholders' committees, as well as

---

[4]*Finley Kumble* is a good example of how costly and drawn out bankruptcy cases can be. The company filed for bankruptcy in 1988. During the next six years while in Chapter 11, the trustee collected $60 million in cash for creditors. However, 80 percent of the money went for operating and administering the bankruptcy case, including $37 million for lawyers, trustees, and accountants. (*The Wall Street Journal*, April 8, 1994, pp. B1 and B5).

by the debtor, but they are all paid from the debtor's assets. Expenses of the creditors' committees may also be reimbursed. Soaring fees in bankruptcy cases prompted some judges to cut fees that they considered unreasonable. The 1994 amendments to the bankruptcy act specifically granted the court the authority to award compensation less than the compensation requested when the fees seem unreasonable.

The Plan of Reorganization

Confirmation of a **reorganization plan** that is "fair and equitable" to all interests concerned is the final objective of Chapter 11. Only the debtor corporation may file a plan during the first 120 days after the order for relief is granted. Subsequently, the debtor, the trustee, the creditors' committees, an equity security holders' committee, or other parties in interest may file plans.

To reduce bankruptcy expenses and reduce the time a debtor must operate under bankruptcy court restrictions, some firms file preapproved reorganization plans with the court at the same time as they file under Chapter 11 (often called a *prepackaged bankruptcy*). In other words, the terms of the debt restructuring have been worked out with creditors, and some or all creditors have agreed to the plan before the bankruptcy filing. In 2001, ***Chiquita Brands International*** filed for bankruptcy under a prearranged plan. Before filing for bankruptcy, Chiquita negotiated with its bondholders to reduce debt and issue new common stock and debt. The prearrangement with creditors was intended to shorten the time before Chiquita emerged from bankruptcy.

Chapter 11 provisions stipulate that the plan of reorganization must:

- Identify classes of claims (except for the administrative expenses, claims arising after an involuntary filing but before the order for relief or appointment of a trustee, and certain tax claims that are given priority)
- Specify any class of claims that is not impaired (a class of claims is *impaired* unless the plan leaves unaltered the legal rights of each claim in the class)
- Specify any class of claims that is impaired
- Treat all claims within a particular class alike
- Provide adequate means for the plan's execution (such as retention of property by the debtor, merger, modification of a lien, and extension of maturity dates)
- Prohibit the issuance of nonvoting equity securities
- Contain provisions for selection of officers and directors that are consistent with the interests of creditors, equity holders, and public policy

A reorganization plan may provide for sale of the debtor's property and distribution of the proceeds. A debtor corporation may prefer to liquidate under Chapter 11 instead of Chapter 7 because it expects that an orderly sale by company management will raise more money than a liquidating sale by a trustee. ***Montgomery Ward*** and ***Service Merchandise*** are examples of filing for Chapter 11 bankruptcy with the intent to liquidate.

The court may confirm a reorganization plan if it is accepted by each class of creditors and stockholders whose claims or interests will be impaired. Alternatively, the plan may be confirmed even if some impaired classes reject it, a "cramdown," if the bankruptcy judge determines the plan is fair and equitable.

Acceptance of a plan by a class of claims requires approval by at least two-thirds of those claim holders in dollar amount and more than half in number of claims. Classes of claims that are unimpaired are assumed to have accepted the plan, and classes that receive nothing are assumed to have rejected it without the necessity of a vote. In order for the bankruptcy court to confirm a plan, each class of claims must have accepted the plan or not be impaired under it. Within each class, each holder of a claim must either have accepted the plan or must receive (or retain an interest) not less than that holder would receive if the debtor corporation were liquidated.

After the necessary approval has been obtained, the court holds a confirmation hearing to entertain objections to confirmation and to confirm that the plan is "fair and equitable." Confirmation by the court constitutes discharge of the debtor except for claims provided for in the reorganization plan.

The ranking of unsecured creditors in a large reorganization case is seldom simple and is often the result of negotiation rather than rules. Professional investors who buy debt claims from the original holders at deep discounts and then push for settlements to turn a quick profit from their investment complicate many reorganizations.

Two years after **R. H. Macy & Company** filed for Chapter 11, **Federated Department Stores** purchased half of Macy's billion-dollar secured creditor claims held by **Prudential Insurance Company of America** for $449.3 million and took an option to buy the rest. This gave Federated the ability to block any takeover attempt by another retailer while it negotiated its own Macy takeover with the eight major creditors' committees.

Shareholders have also become more aggressive in bankruptcies. One reason for the increased shareholder activism is the increase in investors who speculate in the stock of companies in Chapter 11. Another reason is the rise of lawyers and financial advisers who specialize in leading equity committees against creditors and management. When solvent companies seek bankruptcy reorganization (AH Robins and Texaco, for example), shareholders have equity to protect.

FINANCIAL REPORTING DURING REORGANIZATION

LEARNING
OBJECTIVE **3**

The reorganization process can take several years. The corporation must still prepare financial statements and filings for the SEC during this time period and after it emerges from reorganization.

Current GAAP [1] provides guidance for financial reporting by firms during Chapter 11 reorganization and when they emerge from Chapter 11. Accounting practices were diverse prior to this standard because no prescribed accounting for reorganization existed.

The objective of financial statements prepared for a company operating under Chapter 11 is to reflect the financial evolution during the bankruptcy proceedings. Therefore, the financial statements should distinguish the transactions and events directly related to the reorganization from the ongoing operations of the business.

Effects of Chapter 11 Proceedings on the Balance Sheet

Unsecured liabilities (no collateral) and undersecured liabilities incurred before the company entered Chapter 11 proceedings are **prepetition liabilities subject to compromise**. The debtor corporation and creditors' committees negotiate payment of these liabilities, which may result in payment of less than the claimed amount. The total of these liabilities is reported as a separate line item on the balance sheet. The remainder of a company's liabilities is reported in the usual manner. These represent secured prepetition liabilities and postpetition liabilities. Recall that liabilities incurred after entering Chapter 11 must be preapproved by the bankruptcy court.

On its June 3, 2006, balance sheet, debtor in possession **Interstate Bakeries Corporation**, maker of Hostess Twinkies and Wonder Bread, reported liabilities subject to compromise of $287,080,000, which represented 19 percent of its total liabilities at that date.

Prepetition claims discovered after the Chapter 11 filing are included in the balance sheet at the court-allowed amount of the claims, rather than the amount at which they may be settled. Claims that cannot be reasonably estimated should be disclosed in notes to the financial statements according to GAAP [2].

Effects of Chapter 11 Proceedings on the Income Statement and the Statement of Cash Flows

Professional fees and similar expenses related directly to the Chapter 11 proceedings are expensed as incurred. "Income, expenses, realized gains and losses, and provisions for losses that result from the restructuring of the business should be reported separately in the income statement as *reorganization items*, except for those required to be reported as discontinued operations" [1].

Hawaiian Airlines reported $115,063,000 of reorganization costs for the year ended December 31, 2003. Without these charges, Hawaiian's pretax operating income was $77,478,000. Over $14,000,000 of the reorganization costs were attributable to professional fees.

Recorded interest expense is the amount that will be paid during the proceedings, or the probable amount to be allowed as a priority, secured, or unsecured claim. Amounts by which reported interest expense differs from contractual interest should be disclosed. For example, Interstate Bakeries suspended accrual of interest on $100 million of pre-petition liabilities. As a result, it parenthetically disclosed on its 2006 income statement that $6.0 million and $4.1 million of contractual interest expense was not accrued in 2006 and 2005, respectively.

Earnings per share for Chapter 11 companies should be reported as usual. Probable issuance of common stock or common stock equivalents under a reorganization plan should be disclosed.

Cash flow items relating to reorganization are disclosed separately from cash flow items relating to the ongoing operations of the business in the statement of cash flows. *SOP 90-7* recommends the direct method of presenting cash flows.

Supplementary Combined Financial Statements

The AcSEC concluded that consolidated financial statements that include one or more companies operating under Chapter 11 do not provide adequate information about the bankruptcy proceedings. Therefore, GAAP requires the presentation of *condensed combined financial statements* for all entities in reorganization proceedings, as supplementary information. Intercompany receivables and payables are disclosed, with receivables written down if necessary. Consolidation may be inappropriate for some subsidiaries in bankruptcy, particularly if a trustee is appointed to operate the company in bankruptcy.

FINANCIAL REPORTING FOR THE EMERGING COMPANY

LEARNING OBJECTIVE **4**

Ordinarily, a corporate reorganization involves a restructuring of liabilities and capital accounts and a revaluation of assets. Participation of stockholders in the reorganized company depends upon whether they are deemed to have an equitable interest by the bankruptcy court. Many companies cannot emerge from bankruptcy as independent companies, and their reorganization plans include sale of the company. To aid in the plan's execution, the debtor corporation typically amends its charter to provide for the issuance of new securities for cash or in exchange for creditor claims.

The financial condition of companies filing for bankruptcy court protection varies drastically. Occasionally, profitable corporations file for protection under Chapter 11. Settlements under a reorganization plan are influenced by the ability of the interested parties to negotiate and manipulate their relative positions through creditors' and equity holders' committees. Bankruptcy judges also have broad discretionary powers in bankruptcy settlements. A provision of the Bankruptcy Code known as the *doctrine of equitable subordination* allows judges to move unsecured creditors ahead of secured creditors in certain situations in the interest of "fairness."

Reorganization Value

Determining the reorganization value of the entity emerging from bankruptcy is an important part of the reorganization plan. The emerging entity's **reorganization value** approximates fair value of the entity without considering liabilities. Generally, the reorganization value is determined by discounting future cash flows for the reconstituted business, plus the expected proceeds from sale of assets not required in the new business. The discount rates should reflect the business and financial risks involved [1].

The reorganization value determines how much creditors will recover and how much stock of the reorganized company each class of creditors will receive when the company emerges from bankruptcy. For example, in the Macy bankruptcy case, senior creditors were owed $3.1 billion, and public bondholders were owed $1.2 billion. Macy's board of directors debated a $3.5 billion reorganization value under one plan and a $3.8 billion value under another. Senior creditors would receive a smaller stake in the reorganized company under the higher reorganization value, and bondholders would receive almost nothing under the lower value. The unsecured bondholders' committee pushed for a reorganization value of $4 billion, and another plan put forth by Federated Department Stores, a major creditor, was based on a $3.35 billion reorganization value. After months of negotiation, Federated and Macy filed a joint plan that called for the merger of the two companies and a reorganization value of $4.1 billion.

Financial reporting by a company whose reorganization plan has been confirmed by the court is determined by whether the reorganized entity is essentially a new company that qualifies for fresh-start reporting. GAAP [1] provides two conditions that must be met for **fresh-start reporting**:

1. The reorganization value of the emerging entity's assets immediately before the date of confirmation of the reorganization plan must be less than the total of all postpetition liabilities and allowed claims.

2. Holders of existing voting shares immediately before confirmation of the reorganization plan must receive less than 50 percent of the emerging entity. This loss of control must be substantive and not temporary.

When both of these conditions are met, the emerging entity is in effect a new company and should adopt fresh-start reporting.

Fresh-Start Reporting

Fresh-start reporting results in a new reporting entity with no retained earnings or deficit balance.

ALLOCATING THE REORGANIZATION VALUE TO IDENTIFIABLE ASSETS The reorganization value of the company should be allocated to tangible and identifiable intangible assets according to the acquisition method of accounting for transactions under GAAP [3]. Any amount of reorganization value not attributed to the tangible and identifiable intangible assets is reported as an unidentifiable intangible asset, "reorganization value in excess of amounts allocable to identifiable assets."

REPORTING LIABILITIES Liabilities, other than deferred income taxes, should be reported at their current value at the confirmation date of the reorganization plan. GAAP [4] requires that deferred tax benefits realized from prior net operating loss carryforwards are applied first to reduction of the reorganization value in excess of amounts allocable to identifiable assets and to other intangibles until exhausted and, finally, as a reduction of income tax expense.

FINAL STATEMENTS OF OLD ENTITY The final statements of the old entity as of and for the period ending on the date of confirmation of the plan disclose the effects of the adjustments on the individual asset and liability accounts resulting from adopting fresh-start reporting. The statements also show the effect of debt forgiveness. The ending balance sheet of the old entity is the same as the opening balance sheet of the new entity, including a zero retained earnings balance.

DISCLOSURES IN INITIAL FINANCIAL STATEMENTS OF NEW ENTITY GAAP [1] requires the following disclosures to be included in notes to the initial financial statements of the new entity:

- Adjustments to the historical amounts of individual assets and liabilities
- The amount of debt forgiveness
- The amount of prior retained earnings or deficit eliminated
- Significant factors relating to the determination of reorganization value

COMPARATIVE FINANCIAL STATEMENTS The new entity's fresh-start financial statements are not comparable with those prepared by the predecessor company before confirmation of the reorganization plan. If the SEC or another regulatory agency requires predecessor statements, a clear distinction is made between the fresh-start statements of the new entity and the statements of the predecessor company.

Reporting by Entities That Do Not Qualify for Fresh-Start Reporting

Companies emerging from reorganization that do not meet the criteria for fresh-start reporting report liabilities at present values using appropriate interest rates under GAAP [5]. Forgiveness of debt should be reported as an extraordinary item. Quasi-reorganization accounting is *not* used for any entities emerging from bankruptcy court protection.

ILLUSTRATION OF A REORGANIZATION CASE

Tig Corporation files for protection from creditors under Chapter 11 of the bankruptcy act on January 5, 2011. Tig is a debtor in possession and, at the time of filing, its balance sheet includes the following (amounts in thousands):

Current assets		
Cash	$ 50	
Accounts receivable—net	500	
Inventory	300	
Other current assets	50	$ 900
Plant assets		
Land	$200	
Building—net	500	
Equipment—net	300	
Patent	200	1,200
		$2,100
Current liabilities		
Accounts payable	$600	
Taxes payable	150	
Accrued interest on 15% bonds	90	
Note payable to bank	260	$1,100
15% bonds payable (partially secured with land and building)		1,200
Stockholders' deficit		
Capital stock	$500	
Deficit	(700)	(200)
		$2,100

On the filing date, Tig's bank accounts and books are closed, and a new set of books is opened. The company arranges short-term financing with a bank (with the bankruptcy court's approval) in order to continue operations while working out a reorganization plan.

During 2011, no prepetition liabilities are paid and no interest is accrued on the bank note or the bonds payable. The bankruptcy court allows Tig Corporation to invest $100,000 in new equipment in August 2011. This new equipment has a useful life of five years, and Tig uses straight-line depreciation calculated to the nearest half-year. The building's depreciation expense is $50,000 per year, and the old equipment's rate is $60,000 per year. Patent amortization is $50,000 per year.

Costs related to the bankruptcy, including all expenses of the creditors' committees and the equity holder committee, are expensed as incurred and paid in cash.

Reclassification of Liabilities Subject to Compromise

At the beginning of 2011, Tig reclassifies the liabilities subject to compromise into a separate account. The entry to record the reclassification is as follows (in thousands):

Accounts payable (−L)	600	
Taxes payable (−L)	150	
Accrued interest payable on 15% bonds (−L)	90	
Note payable to bank (−L)	260	
15% bonds payable (partially secured) (−L)	1,200	
Liabilities subject to compromise (+L)		2,300
To reclassify liabilities subject to compromise.		

The $2,300,000 prepetition claims are included in the December 31, 2011, balance sheet separately. A supplemental schedule shows details of these claims.

TIG CORPORATION
INCOME AND RETAINED EARNINGS STATEMENT
FOR THE YEAR 2011

Sales	$ 1,000,000
Cost of sales	(430,000)
Wages and salaries	(250,000)
Depreciation and amortization	(170,000)
Other expenses	(50,000)
Earnings before reorganization items	100,000
Professional fees related to bankruptcy proceedings	(450,000)
Net loss	(350,000)
Beginning deficit	(700,000)
Deficit December 31, 2011	$(1,050,000)

BALANCE SHEET AT DECEMBER 31, 2011

Current assets		
Cash	$ 150,000	
Accounts receivable—net	350,000	
Inventory	370,000	
Other current assets	50,000	$ 920,000
Plant assets		
Land	$ 200,000	
Building—net	450,000	
Equipment—net	330,000	
Patent	150,000	1,130,000
		$2,050,000
Current liabilities		
Short-term borrowings	$ 150,000	
Accounts payable	100,000	
Wages and salaries payable	50,000	300,000
Liabilities subject to compromise*		2,300,000
Stockholders' deficit		
Capital stock	$ 500,000	
Deficit	(1,050,000)	(550,000)
		$2,050,000

---

*Liabilities subject to compromise:	
Partially secured 15% bonds payable plus $90,000 interest,	
secured by first mortgage on land and building	$1,290,000
Priority tax claim	150,000
Accounts payable and unsecured note to bank	860,000
	$2,300,000

DISCLOSING RECLASSIFIED LIABILITIES IN THE FINANCIAL STATEMENTS Exhibit 18-9 presents a combined income and retained earnings statement for 2011, as well as a balance sheet at December 31, 2011.

Although the reclassification of liabilities subject to compromise poses no difficulties in preparing balance sheets and income statements, it does complicate the preparation of the cash flow statement. The year's changes in the account balances that are reclassified must be separated from changes that affect operations and cash flows for the period. Exhibit 18-10 presents the cash flows statement. Only the direct method of presenting the cash flows statement is illustrated because GAAP [1] recommends this format.

One item unique to firms in reorganization is professional fees relating to bankruptcy proceedings. Cash paid for these items is classified as cash flows from operating activities, but separate disclosure of operating cash flows *before* and *after* the bankruptcy proceedings is recommended.

EXHIBIT 18-10

Statement of Cash
Flows During Chapter 11
Reorganization

TIG CORPORATION
STATEMENT OF CASH FLOWS
FOR THE YEAR ENDED DECEMBER 31, 2011 (IN THOUSANDS)

Cash Flows from Operating Activities		
Cash received from customers		$1,150
Cash paid to suppliers		(400)
Cash paid to employees		(200)
Cash paid for other expenses		(50)
Net cash flows provided by operating activities		
before reorganization items		500
Operating cash flows from reorganization		
Professional fees paid for services relating		
to bankruptcy proceedings		(450)
Net cash provided by operating activities		50
Cash Flows from Investing Activities		
Capital expenditures	$(100)	
Net cash used in investing activities		(100)
Cash Flows from Financing Activities		
Net short-term borrowings	$ 150	
Net cash provided by financing activities		150
Net increase in cash		$ 100
Reconciliation of net income to net cash provided		
by operating activities		
Net loss		$ (350)
Adjustments to reconcile net loss to net cash		
provided by operations:		
Depreciation and amortization		170
Increase in postpetition payables (operating activities)		150
Decreases in accounts receivable		150
Increase in inventory		(70)
Cash provided by operating activities		$ 50

Operations Under Chapter 11

During the next six months, Tig continues to operate under Chapter 11 of the Bankruptcy Code while it works out a reorganization plan, and by June 30, 2012, Tig has a plan. Balance sheet and income statement amounts reflecting operations for the first six months of 2012 are summarized as follows (in thousands):

COMPARATIVE BALANCE SHEETS 2012

	January 1	June 30	Change
Cash	$ 150	$ 300	$150
Accounts receivable	350	335	(15)
Inventory	370	350	(20)
Other current assets	50	30	(20)
Land	200	200	—
Building—net	450	425	(25)
Equipment—net	330	290	(40)
Patent	150	125	(25)
Assets	$2,050	$2,055	$ 5
Liabilities subject to compromise	$2,300	$2,300	—
Short-term loan	150	75	$ (75)
Accounts payable	100	125	25
Wages and salaries	50	55	5
Liabilities	2,600	2,555	(45)
Common stock	500	500	—
Deficit	(1,050)	(1,000)	50
Equities	$2,050	$2,055	$ 5

INCOME STATEMENT FOR SIX MONTHS ENDING JUNE 30, 2012

Sales		$ 600
Cost of sales		(200)
Wages and salaries expense		(100)
Depreciation and amortization		
Building	$25	
Old equipment	30	
New equipment	10	
Patent	25	(90)
Other expenses		(30)
Earnings before reorganization items		180
Professional fees related to bankruptcy proceedings		(130)
Net income		50
Beginning deficit		(1,050)
Ending deficit		$(1,000)

The Reorganization Plan

After extensive negotiations among the parties of interest, a reorganization value of $2,200,000 is agreed upon, and a plan of reorganization is filed with the court. The terms of Tig's proposed reorganization plan include the following:

1. Tig's 15% bonds payable were secured with the land and building. The bondholders agree to accept $500,000 new common stock, $500,000 senior debt of 12% bonds, and $100,000 cash payable December 31, 2012.

2. The priority tax claims of $150,000 will be paid in cash as soon as the bankruptcy court confirms the reorganization plan.

3. The remaining unsecured, nonpriority, prepetition claims of $950,000 will be settled as follows:
   a. Creditors represented by the accounts payable will receive $275,000 subordinated debt and $140,000 common stock.
   b. The $90,000 accrued interest on the 15% bonds will be forgiven.
   c. The $260,000 note payable to the bank will be exchanged for $120,000 subordinated debt and $60,000 common stock.

4. Equity holders will exchange their stock for $100,000 common stock of the emerging company.

Fresh-Start Reporting

The reorganization value is compared with the total postpetition liabilities and court-allowed claims at June 30 to determine if fresh-start reporting is appropriate (amounts in thousands):

Postpetition liabilities	$ 255
Allowed claims subject to compromise	2,300
Total liabilities on June 30, 2012	2,555
Less: Reorganization value	(2,200)
Excess liabilities over reorganization value	$ 355

The excess liabilities over reorganization value indicates that the first condition for fresh-start reporting is met. The reorganization plan calls for the old equity holders to retain less than a 50 percent interest in the emerging company, so the second condition also is met, and fresh-start reporting is appropriate. A summary of the proposed reorganized capital structure is as follows (in thousands):

Postpetition liabilities	$ 255
Taxes payable	150
Current portion of senior debt, due December 31, 2012	100
Senior debt, 12% bonds	500
Subordinated debt	395
Common stock	800
	$2,200

The plan is approved by each class of claims and confirmed by the bankruptcy court on June 30, 2012. Tig Corporation records the provisions of the reorganization plan and the adoption of fresh-start reporting in the books of the old entity as follows (in thousands):

Accounts payable (prepetition) (−L)	600	
Interest payable (prepetition) (−L)	90	
Note payable to bank (prepetition) (−L)	260	
15% bonds payable (prepetition) (−L)	1,200	
12% senior debt (+L)		500
12% senior debt—current (+L)		100
Subordinated debt (+L)		395
Common stock (new) (+SE)		700
Gain on debt discharge (+Ga, +SE)		455
To record settlement of the prepetition claims.		
(The summary account "prepetition claims		
subject to compromise" could have been used.)		
Common stock (old) (−SE)	500	
Common stock (new) (+SE)		100
Additional paid-in capital (+SE)		400
To record exchange of stock by equity holders.		

Tig's assets that have fair values different from their recorded book values on June 30, 2012, are summarized as follows (in thousands):

	Fair Value	Book Value	Difference
Inventory	$ 375	$ 350	$ 25
Land	300	200	100
Buildings—net	350	425	(75)
Equipment—net	260	290	(30)
Patent	0	125	(125)
	$1,285	$1,390	$(105)

The entries to adjust Tig's assets for the fair value/book value differences and record the fresh-start are as follows (in thousands):

Inventory (+A)	25	
Land (+A)	100	
Loss on asset revaluation (+Lo, −SE)	105	
Buildings—net (−A)		75
Equipment—net (−A)		30
Patent (−A)		125
To adjust Tig's assets to their fair values.		
Reorganization value in excess of identifiable assets (+A)	250	
Gain on debt discharge (−Ga, −SE)	455	
Additional paid-in capital (−SE)	400	
Loss on asset revaluation (−Lo, +SE)		105
Deficit (+SE)		1,000
To eliminate the deficit and additional paid-in capital		
and to record the excess reorganization value and		
the fresh start.		

Exhibit 18-11 presents working papers to show the effect of the reorganization plan on Tig's balance sheet.

EXHIBIT 18-11

Working Papers to Show Confirmation of Reorganization Plan with Fresh-Start Reporting

TIG CORPORATION COMPARATIVE BALANCE SHEETS AT JUNE 30, 2012 (IN THOUSANDS)

	Preconfirmation Balance Sheet	Adjustments to Record Confirmation of Plan		Reorganized Balance Sheet
		Debits	Credits	
Assets				
Cash	$ 300			$ 300
Accounts receivable	335			335
Inventory	350	a 25		375
Other current assets	30			30
Land	200	b 100		300
Building	425		c 75	350
Equipment	290		d 30	260
Patent	125		e 125	—
Reorganization excess	—	f 250		250
	$2,055			$2,200
Equities				
Postpetition Claims				
Short-term bank loan	$ 75			$ 75
Accounts payable	125			125
Wages payable	55			55
Prepetition Claims				
Accounts payable—old	600	h 600		—
Taxes payable	150			150
Interest	90	i 90		—
Bank note	260	j 260		—
15% bonds payable	1,200	g 1,200		—
Stockholders' Equity				
Capital stock—old	500	k 500		—
Deficit	(1,000)	c 75 d 30 e 125	a 25 b 100 f 250 g 100 h 185 i 90 j 80 k 400	—
New Equities: Current portion—bonds	—		g 100	100
12% senior debt	—		g 500	500
Subordinated debt	—		h 275 j 120	395
Common stock—new	—		g 500 h 140 j 60 k 100	800
Retained earnings—new	—			0
	$2,055			$2,200

The first column of the working papers reflects the balance sheet at June 30, 2012, immediately before recognizing the terms of the reorganization plan and establishing fresh-start reporting. Entries a through f in the adjustment columns adjust the identifiable assets to their reorganization value, which approximates fair value. The excess reorganization value over the fair value of identifiable assets is entered. Working paper entries g through k impose the terms of the reorganization plan.

Note that the last column, Reorganized Balance Sheet, is both the final balance sheet of the old entity and the opening balance sheet of the emerging entity. Although the opening balance sheet of the new entity reflects the reorganization values of the assets, GAAP [1] provides that the adjustments to historical cost should be disclosed in notes to the initial financial statements. The new Tig Corporation should also disclose the amount of debt forgiveness, the deficit eliminated, and key factors used in the determination of the reorganization value.

SUMMARY

A debtor corporation that cannot solve its financial problems internally may be able to obtain relief by direct negotiation with creditors. Failing this, the debtor may seek protection from creditors by filing a petition for bankruptcy under Title 11 of the *United States Code*. Either the debtor or the creditors can file a petition. A petition filed under Chapter 11 of the bankruptcy act covers reorganization of the debtor; a Chapter 7 filing covers liquidation of the debtor.

In a Chapter 7 liquidation case, a trustee and creditors' committee are elected by the unsecured creditors. The trustee takes possession of the debtor's estate, converts the assets into cash, and distributes the proceeds according to the priority of claims, as directed by the bankruptcy court.

In a Chapter 11 reorganization case, the U.S. trustee appoints a creditors' committee as soon as practicable after the filing. A trustee may be appointed for cause, but generally the debtor continues in possession. The debtor corporation continues operations while it works out a reorganization plan that is fair and equitable.

GAAP [1] prescribes financial reporting for companies operating under Chapter 11. Some companies emerging from Chapter 11 are essentially new companies and qualify for fresh-start reporting. Emerging companies that do not meet the criteria for fresh-start reporting account for their liabilities in accordance with GAAP [5].

QUESTIONS

1. What is the distinction between *equity insolvency* and *bankruptcy insolvency*?
2. Bankruptcy proceedings may be designated as *voluntary* or *involuntary*. Distinguish between the two types, including the requirements for filing of an involuntary petition.
3. What are the duties of the U.S. trustee under BAPCPA? Do U.S. trustees supervise the administration of all bankruptcy cases?
4. What obligations does a debtor corporation have in a bankruptcy case?
5. Is a trustee appointed in Title 11 cases? In all Chapter 7 cases? Discuss.
6. Describe the duties of a trustee in a liquidation case under the BAPCPA 1978.
7. Which unsecured claims have priority in a Chapter 7 liquidation case? Discuss in terms of priority ranks.
8. Does the BAPCPA establish priorities for holders of unsecured nonpriority claims (that is, general unsecured claims)?
9. What is the purpose of a statement of affairs, and how are assets valued in this statement?
10. Does filing a case under Chapter 11 of the bankruptcy act mean that the company will not be liquidated? Discuss.
11. What is a debtor-in-possession reorganization case?
12. When can a creditors' committee file a plan of reorganization under a Chapter 11 case?
13. Discuss the requirements for approval of a plan of reorganization.
14. Describe *prepetition liabilities subject to compromise* on the balance sheet of a company operating under Chapter 11 of the bankruptcy act.
15. The *reorganization value* of a firm emerging from Chapter 11 bankruptcy is used to determine the accounting of the reorganized company. Explain reorganization value as used in FASB ASC 852.

16. FASB ASC 852 provides two conditions that must be met for an emerging firm to use fresh-start reporting. What are these two conditions?

17. A firm emerging from Chapter 11 bankruptcy that does not qualify for fresh-start reporting must still report the effect of the reorganization plan on its financial position and results of operations. How is debt forgiveness reported in the reorganized company's financial statements?

EXERCISES

E 18-1

Differences among types of bankruptcy filings and other terminology related to bankruptcy law

1. Bankruptcy *Insolvency* means:
 a   *Book value of assets is greater than liabilities*
 b   *Fair value of assets is less than liabilities*
 c   *Inability to meet financial obligations as they come due*
 d   *Liabilities are greater than book value of assets*

2. Aside from liability discharge provided for in the reorganization plan, the discharge of a debtor corporation's liabilities occurs when:
 a   *The plan is accepted by a majority of unsecured creditors*
 b   *Each class of claims has accepted the plan or is not impaired under it*
 c   *Each holder of a claim has accepted the plan or will receive at least as much as if the company were liquidated*
 d   *The court confirms that the plan is fair and equitable*

3. A trustee's election in a Chapter 7 case requires:
 a   *Approval by a majority of creditors*
 b   *Approval by a majority of claims represented*
 c   *Approval by a majority in dollar amount of voting creditors, and at least 20% of claims must vote*
 d   *Approval of two-thirds in dollar amount and a majority of holders of all claims*

4. A corporation may *not* be a debtor in possession if:
 a   *The case is initiated in a voluntary filing*
 b   *The case is initiated in an involuntary filing*
 c   *Loans other than for goods and services exceed $5,000,000*
 d   *The court concludes that appointment of a trustee is in the best interests of creditors*

E 18-2

Financial reporting during bankruptcy

Use the following information in answering questions 1 and 2:

Hal Company filed for protection from creditors under Chapter 11 of the bankruptcy act on July 1, 2011. Hal had the following liabilities at the time of filing:

10% mortgage bonds payable, secured by a building with a book value and fair value of $100,000	$200,000
Accrued interest on mortgage (January 1–July 1)	10,000
Accounts payable	80,000
Priority tax claims	50,000
	$340,000

1. The December 31, 2011, balance sheet will show prepetition liabilities of:
 a   *$340,000 (the claims at filing)*
 b   *$240,000 (the original claims less the secured portion of the mortgage bonds)*
 c   *$350,000 (the original claims plus six months' interest on the bonds)*
 d   *$290,000 (the original claims less the priority tax claims)*

2. Two and a half years after filing the petition for bankruptcy, Hal's management, its creditors, the equity holders, and other parties in interest agree on a reorganization value of $500,000. Which of the following statements is most likely?
 a   *The reorganization value approximates the appraised value of the firm as a going concern less the prepetition liabilities.*
 b   *The reorganization value approximates the fair value of the assets less the fair value of the prepetition and postpetition liabilities.*

c The reorganization value approximates the fair value of the assets less the book value of the postpetition liabilities and the estimated settlement value of the prepetition liabilities.

d The reorganization value approximates the fair value of the entity without considering the liabilities.

3. Uni, a parent company with five wholly owned operating subsidiaries, is in the process of preparing consolidated financial statements for the year. Two of Uni's subsidiaries are operating as debtors in possession under Chapter 11 of the bankruptcy act. Which of the following statements is correct?

   a ASC Topic 810, "Consolidation," prohibits Uni from consolidating the financial statements of the two subsidiaries in bankruptcy with those of the other affiliated companies.

   b ASC Topic 810, "Consolidation," requires that the financial statements of all five of the subsidiaries be consolidated with those of the parent company.

   c If Uni's consolidated financial statements include the operations of the two subsidiaries in bankruptcy, ASC Topic 852 requires that condensed combined financial statements for all entities in reorganization be presented as supplementary financial statements.

   d If Uni's consolidated financial statements do not include the operations of the two subsidiaries in bankruptcy, those subsidiaries must be accounted for under the cost method.

4. When fresh-start reporting is used, the initial financial statement disclosures should not include:

   a Adjustments made in the amounts of individual assets and liabilities

   b The amount of debt forgiven

   c The amount of prior retained earnings or deficit eliminated

   d Current and prior-year EPS amounts

E 18-3

Financial reporting during bankruptcy—Distributions to creditors

Ram holds a $200,000 note receivable from Pat. It has been learned that Pat filed for Chapter 7 bankruptcy and that the expected recovery of nonsecured claims is 35¢ on the dollar. Inventory items with an estimated recoverable value of $50,000 secure Pat's note payable to Ram.

REQUIRED: Determine Ram's expected recovery on the note.

E 18-4

Fresh-start reporting requirements

Bax has been operating under Chapter 11 of the Bankruptcy Code for the past 15 months. On March 31, 2011, just before confirmation of its reorganization plan, Bax's reorganization value is estimated at $2,000,000. A balance sheet for Bax prepared on the same date is summarized as follows:

Current assets	$ 750,000
Plant assets	3,000,000
	$3,750,000
Postpetition liabilities	$1,200,000
Prepetition liabilities subject to compromise*	1,500,000
Fully secured debt	900,000
Capital stock	900,000
Deficit	(750,000)
	$3,750,000

*Represents allowed claims. The reorganization plan calls for payment of $150,000 and issuance of $300,000 notes and $375,000 common stock in settlement of the prepetition liabilities.

REQUIRED

1. Does Bax qualify for fresh-start reporting on the basis of the reorganization value?

2. What other conditions must be met for fresh-start reporting? Show calculations.

E 18-5

Financial reporting during bankruptcy—Distributions to creditors

Hol is in bankruptcy and is being liquidated by a court-appointed trustee. The financial report that follows was prepared by the trustee just before the final cash distribution:

Assets

Cash	$ 200,000

Approved Claims

Mortgage payable (secured by property that was sold for $100,000)	$ 160,000
Accounts payable, unsecured	100,000
Administrative expenses payable, unsecured	16,000
Salaries payable, unsecured	4,000
Interest payable, unsecured	20,000
Total approved claims	$ 300,000

The administrative expenses are for trustee fees and other costs of administering the debtor corporation's estate.

REQUIRED: Show how the $200,000 cash will be distributed to holders of each of the claims.

PROBLEMS

P 18-1
Financial reporting during bankruptcy

The balance sheet of Sco appeared as follows on March 1, 2011, when an interim trustee was appointed by the U.S. trustee to assume control of Sco's estate in a Chapter 7 case.

Assets		Liabilities and Stockholders' Equity	
Cash	$ 4,000	Accounts payable	$ 50,000
Accounts receivable—net	8,000	Note payable—unsecured	40,000
Inventories	36,000	Revenue received in advance	1,000
Land	20,000	Wages payable	3,000
Buildings—net	100,000	Mortgage payable	80,000
Intangible assets	26,000	Capital stock	40,000
		Retained earnings deficit	(20,000)
Assets	$194,000	Liabilities and equity	$194,000

ADDITIONAL INFORMATION

1. Creditors failed to elect a trustee; accordingly, the interim trustee became trustee for the case.

2. The land and buildings are pledged as security for the mortgage payable.

3. In January 2011, Sco received $1,000 from a customer as a payment in advance for merchandise that is no longer marketed.

4. Activities of the trustee during March are summarized as follows:
   a. $7,200 is collected on the receivables, and the balance is determined to be uncollectible.
   b. All inventories are sold for $19,400.
   c. Land and buildings bring a total of $90,000.
   d. Nothing is realized from the intangible assets.
   e. Administrative expenses of $8,200 are incurred by the trustee.

REQUIRED

1. Prepare a separate set of books for the trustee to assume possession of the estate and convert its assets into cash.

2. Prepare financial statements on March 31 for Sco in trusteeship (balance sheet, cash receipts and disbursements, and changes in estate equity).

3. Prepare journal entries on the trustee's books to distribute available cash to creditors and close the case.

P 18-2

Financial reporting during bankruptcy

Justin Corporation filed a petition under Chapter 7 of the bankruptcy act in January 2011. On March 15, 2011, the trustee provided the following information about the corporation's financial affairs.

	Book Values	Estimated Realizable Values
Assets		
Cash	$ 20,000	$ 20,000
Accounts receivable—net	100,000	75,000
Inventories	150,000	70,000
Plant assets—net	250,000	280,000
Total assets	$520,000	
Liabilities		
Liability for priority claims	$ 80,000	
Accounts payable—unsecured	150,000	
Note payable, secured by accounts receivable	100,000	
Mortgage payable, secured by all plant assets	220,000	
Total liabilities	$550,000	

REQUIRED

1. Determine the amount expected to be available for unsecured claims.

2. Determine the expected recovery per dollar of unsecured claims.

3. Estimate the amount of recovery for each class of creditors.

P 18-3

Claims rankings and cash distribution upon liquidation

Fabulous Fakes Corporation is being liquidated under Chapter 7 of the bankruptcy act. All assets have been converted into cash, and $374,500 cash is available to pay the following claims:

1.	Administrative expenses of preserving and liquidating the debtor corporation's estate	$ 12,500
2.	Merchandise creditors	99,000
3.	Local government for property taxes	4,000
4.	Local bank for unsecured loan (principal is $30,000 and interest is $4,500)	34,500
5.	State government for gross receipts taxes	3,000
6.	Employees for unpaid wages during the month before filing (includes $5,000 for the company president and less than $4,000 for each of the other employees)	48,000
7.	Customers for prepaid merchandise that was not delivered	1,500
8.	Holders of the first mortgage on the company's real estate that was sold for $240,000 (includes $220,000 principal and $8,500 interest)	228,500

Assume that all the claims are allowed and that they were timely filed.

REQUIRED

1. Rank the claims according to priority under the bankruptcy act.

2. Show how the available cash will be distributed in final liquidation of the corporation.

P 18-4
Financial reporting during bankruptcy—Statement of affairs

Hanna Corporation filed a petition under Chapter 7 of the bankruptcy act on June 30, 2011. Data relevant to its financial position as of this date are:

	Book Value	Estimated Net Realizable Values
Cash	$ 2,200	$ 2,200
Accounts receivable—net	15,000	13,500
Inventories	20,000	22,500
Equipment—net	55,000	28,000
Total assets	$92,200	$66,200
Accounts payable	$26,400	
Rent payable	7,600	
Wages payable	12,000	
Note payable plus accrued interest	31,000	
Capital stock	55,000	
Retained earnings (deficit)	(39,800)	
Total liabilities and equity	$92,200	

REQUIRED

1. Prepare a statement of affairs assuming that the note payable and interest are secured by a mortgage on the equipment and that wages are less than $4,000 per employee.

2. Estimate the amount that will be paid to each class of claims if priority liquidation expenses, including trustee fees, are $4,000 and estimated net realizable values are actually realized.

P 18-5
Financial reporting during bankruptcy

The unsecured creditors of Dawn Corporation filed a petition under Chapter 7 of the bankruptcy act on July 1, 2011, to force Dawn into bankruptcy. The court order for relief was granted on July 10, at which time an interim trustee was appointed to supervise liquidation of the estate. A listing of assets and liabilities of Dawn Corporation as of July 10, 2011, along with estimated realizable values, is as follows:

	Book Values	Estimated Realizable Values
Assets		
Cash	$ 80,000	$ 80,000
Accounts receivable—net	210,000	160,000
Inventories	200,000	210,000
Equipment—net	150,000	60,000
Land and buildings—net	250,000	140,000
Intangible assets	10,000	—
	$900,000	$650,000
Accounts payable	$400,000	
Note payable	100,000	
Wages payable (from June and July)	24,000	
Taxes payable	76,000	
Mortgage payable $200,000, plus $5,000 unpaid interest to July 10	205,000	
Capital stock	300,000	
Retained earnings deficit	(205,000)	
	$900,000	

ADDITIONAL INFORMATION

1. Accounts receivable are pledged as security for the note payable.

2. No more than $1,000 is owed to any employee.

3. Taxes payable is a priority item.

4. Inventory items include $50,000 acquired on July 5, 2011; the unpaid invoice is included in accounts payable.

5. The mortgage payable and interest are secured by the land and buildings.

6. Trustee fees and other costs of liquidating the estate are expected to be $11,000.

REQUIRED

1. Prepare a statement of affairs for Dawn Corporation on July 10, 2011.

2. Develop a schedule showing how available cash will be distributed to each class of claims, assuming that (a) the estimated realizable values are actually received and (b) the trustee and other fees of liquidating the estate are $11,000.

P 18-6
Financial reporting during bankruptcy

The balance sheet of Everlast Window Corporation at June 30, 2011, contains the following items:

Assets	
Cash	$ 40,000
Accounts receivable—net	70,000
Inventories	50,000
Land	30,000
Building—net	200,000
Machinery—net	60,000
Goodwill	50,000
	$500,000

Equities	
Accounts payable	$110,000
Wages payable	60,000
Property taxes payable	10,000
Mortgage payable	150,000
Interest on mortgage payable	15,000
Note payable—unsecured	50,000
Interest payable—unsecured	5,000
Capital stock	200,000
Retained earnings deficit	(100,000)
	$500,000

The company is in financial difficulty, and its stockholders and creditors have requested a statement of affairs for planning purposes. The following information is available:

1. The company estimates that $63,000 is the maximum amount collectible for the accounts receivable.

2. Except for 20% of the inventory items that are damaged and worth only $2,000, the cost of the other items is expected to be recovered in full.

3. The land and building have a combined appraisal value of $170,000 and are subject to the $150,000 mortgage and related accrued interest.

4. The appraised value of the machinery is $20,000.

5. Wages payable and property taxes payable are unsecured priority items that do not exceed any limitations of the bankruptcy act.

REQUIRED

1. Prepare a statement of affairs for Everlast Window Corporation as of June 30, 2011.

2. Compute the estimated settlement per dollar of unsecured liabilities.

P 18-7
Installment liquidation

Lowstep Corporation filed for relief under Chapter 11 of the bankruptcy act on January 2, 2011. A summary of Lowstep's assets and equities on this date, and at June 30, 2011, follows. Estimated fair values of Lowstep's assets at June 30 are also shown.

	January 2, 2011	June 30, 2011	
	Per Books	Per Books	Estimated Fair Value
Assets			
Cash	$ 200	$ 6,700	$ 6,700
Trade receivables—net	800	1,000	1,000
Inventories	2,000	1,600	2,000
Prepaid items	500	—	—
Land	1,000	1,000	2,000
Buildings—net	3,000	2,900	1,500
Equipment—net	2,000	1,800	1,800
Patent	4,500	4,000	0
	$14,000	$19,000	$15,000
Equities			
Accounts payable	$ 1,000	$ 3,000	
Wages payable	500	1,000	
Bank note payable (includes $500 interest)	5,000		
Long-term note payable (secured with equipment)	6,000		
Prepetition liabilities allowed		12,500	
Common stock	7,000	7,000	
Deficit	(5,500)	(4,500)	
	$14,000	$19,000	

The parties in interest agree to a reorganization plan on July 1, 2011, and a hearing to confirm that the plan is fair and equitable is scheduled for July 8. Under the reorganization plan, the reorganization value is set at $16,000, and the debt and equity holders will receive value as follows:

	To Receive Cash Consideration	To Receive Noncash Consideration	
Postpetition Claims			
Accounts payable (in full)	$3,000		
Wages payable (in full)	1,000		
Prepetition Claims			
Accounts payable (80%)	800		
Wages payable (80%)	400		
Bank note payable and interest (80%)		$ 2,000	note payable
		2,000	common stock
Long-term note payable (80%)		1,800	note payable
		3,000	common stock
Common stockholders*		2,000	common stock
	$5,200	$10,800	

*Reorganization value over consideration allocated to creditors.

The reorganization plan is confirmed on July 8, 2011, under the new name of Highstep Corporation. There are no asset or liability changes between July 1 and July 8.

REQUIRED

1. Is the reorganization of Lowstep eligible for fresh-start accounting? Show calculations.

2. Prepare journal entries to adjust Lowstep's accounts for the reorganization plan.

3. Prepare a fresh-start balance sheet as of July 8, 2011.

INTERNET EXERCISE

Access **Delta Air Lines's** September 30, 2007, Form 10-Q (filed in October 2007) on the SEC Edgar Web site. Using the 10-Q, answer the following questions:

1. When and why did Delta apply for Chapter 11 bankruptcy protection?
2. When did the court approve Delta's plan of reorganization?
3. What were the terms of the reorganization with respect to its debt and stockholders?
4. Did the company qualify for fresh-start reporting?
5. In reviewing the consolidated financial statements, how do the financial statements differ from what you would typically observe for a non-bankrupt company?
6. How much money did the reorganization cost in litigation, reorganization, and restructuring charges? Was this a material amount relative to income and assets?
7. How much debt was forgiven? Was this a material amount?
8. How was fresh-start reporting presented in the financial statements?
9. Overall, do you believe that Delta's presentation of its bankruptcy process is informative to investors? What additional information would you like to know?

REFERENCES TO THE AUTHORITATIVE LITERATURE

[1] FASB ASC 852. "Reorganizations." Originally *Statement of Position 90-7.* "Financial Reporting by Entities in Reorganization Under the Bankruptcy Code." Accounting Standards Executive Committee of the AICPA, 1990.

[2] FASB ASC 450. "Contingencies." Originally *Statement of Financial Accounting Standards No. 5.* "Accounting for Contingencies." Stamford, CT: Financial Accounting Standards Board, 1975.

[3] FASB ASC 805. "Business Combinations." Originally *Statement of Financial Accounting Standards No. 141R.* "Business Combinations." Stamford, CT: Financial Accounting Standards Board, 2007.

[4] FASB ASC 740. "Income Taxes." Originally *Statement of Financial Accounting Standards No. 109.* "Accounting For Income Taxes." Stamford, CT: Financial Accounting Standards Board, 1992.

[5] FASB ASC 835. "Interest." Originally APB Opinion 21. "Interest on Receivables and Payables." New York: American Institute of Certified Public Accountants, 1971.

19 CHAPTER

An Introduction to Accounting for State and Local Governmental Units

Have you ever examined a set of financial statements for the city where you live, or have you wondered how your donation to the Red Cross is accounted for? The preceding 18 chapters of this book have highlighted issues affecting the accounting and financial reporting practices of commercial business organizations. Other organizations exist whose composition or operations differ to some extent from those of the commercial business organizations with which you have become most familiar as an accounting student. For example, governmental units, not-for-profit organizations, colleges and universities, and some health care entities are deemed different enough to warrant the establishment of accounting standards for their specific use. In fact, generally-accepted accounting principles of state and local governments are established by the **Governmental Accounting Standards Board (GASB)** under the auspices of the Financial Accounting Foundation. As you will recall, GAAP for businesses and other nongovernment (essentially, private not-for-profit) organizations are established by the GASB's sister organization, the Financial Accounting Standards Board.

This chapter provides an overview of fund accounting and financial reporting for state and local governmental units. Chapters 20 and 21 illustrate fund accounting practices for specific funds of a local governmental entity. Chapter 22 provides an introduction to accounting principles and reporting practices for not-for-profit organizations.

HISTORICAL DEVELOPMENT OF ACCOUNTING PRINCIPLES FOR STATE AND LOCAL GOVERNMENTAL UNITS

> LEARNING OBJECTIVE 1

According to the U.S. Census Bureau's 2007 *Census of Governments*, there are more than 89,000 general and special-purpose governmental entities in the United States. A governmental entity is generally created for the administration of public affairs and has one or more of the following characteristics:[1]

- Popular election of officers or appointment (or approval) of a controlling majority of the members of the organization's governing body by officials of one or more state or local governments
- The potential for unilateral dissolution by a government with the net assets reverting to a government
- The power to enact and enforce a tax

---

[1]*AICPA Audit and Accounting Guide; Audits of State and Local Governments* 2010, sec. 1.01

LEARNING OBJECTIVES

1 Learn about the historical development of accounting principles for state and local governmental units.

2 Understand the need for fund accounting and its basic premises.

3 Perform transaction analysis using proprietary and governmental accounting models.

4 Recognize various fund categories, as well as their measurement focus and basis of accounting.

5 Review basic governmental accounting principles.

6 Learn about the contents of a governmental entity's comprehensive annual financial report.

625

An organization may also be classified as a governmental entity if it possesses the ability to directly issue debt that is exempt from federal taxation.

With the exception of the federal government, state and local governmental units such as the State of Maine, New York City, and the City of Golden, Colorado, constitute the largest single category of nonprofit organizations in terms of the dollar volume of annual expenditures. Since 1984, the primary source of accounting principles for states, cities, counties, towns, villages, school districts, special districts and authorities, and other local governmental entities has been the statements and interpretations of the GASB. Before 1984, the most important continuous source of accounting principles for state and local governmental units was the Municipal Finance Officers Association (MFOA) and its committees on governmental accounting.[2] The MFOA's National Committee on Governmental Accounting issued *Municipal Accounting and Auditing* in 1951 and *Governmental Accounting, Auditing, and Financial Reporting* (*GAAFR*) in 1968. These resources constituted the most complete frameworks of accounting principles specific to governmental units, and they provided standards for preparing and evaluating the financial reports of governmental units. In 1974 the AICPA issued its industry audit guide, *Audits of State and Local Governmental Units*, in which it noted that *GAAFR*'s accounting and reporting principles constituted GAAP except when they were modified by the audit guide. The AICPA's endorsement was important to the *GAAFR*'s authority and general acceptance by preparers, auditors, and users of governmental financial statements.

The AICPA's audit guide prompted the 1980 revision of *GAAFR* to update and clarify governmental accounting and financial reporting principles and to incorporate pertinent aspects of the audit guide. The MFOA established a new committee, the National Council on Governmental Accounting (NCGA), to develop the *GAAFR* restatement. As part of this project, the NCGA issued *Governmental Accounting and Financial Reporting Principles, Statement No. 1* (NCGA1) in 1979. The following year, a new *GAAFR* was issued as a comprehensive volume to explain and illustrate the principles of NCGA1. Shortly thereafter, the AICPA issued *Statement of Position 80-2*, which amended *Audits of State and Local Governmental Units* to recognize the principles of NCGA1 as generally-accepted accounting principles. GAAFRs and AICPA audit guides are updated periodically.

The Governmental Accounting Standards Board

Although the NCGA was successful in developing and documenting governmental accounting principles, it was criticized for its lack of independence (due to its MFOA sponsorship) and slow progress. Thus, in 1984, the Financial Accounting Foundation (which also oversees the FASB) formed the Governmental Accounting Standards Board to establish and improve standards for governmental accounting and financial reporting. Financial Accounting Foundation trustees appoint one full-time chair and six part-time members to serve on the board.

In July 1984, GASB issued *GASB Statement No. 1*, "Authoritative Status of NCGA Pronouncements and AICPA Industry Audit Guide," designating all NCGA statements and interpretations issued and currently in effect as "generally-accepted accounting principles" until changed or superseded.

The GASB in 1985 integrated all effective accounting and reporting standards into one publication called *Codification of Governmental Accounting and Financial Reporting Standards*. The *Codification* is revised annually to reflect all current GASB official pronouncements. In 1986, the AICPA council declared that Rule 203 of its Rules of Conduct applies to the GASB's pronouncements. Therefore, those pronouncements constitute GAAP for governments. At this writing, the GASB has issued 59 statements of standards, 5 concept statements, and 6 interpretations that set forth governmental accounting and reporting requirements. The GASB issues technical bulletins, implementation guides, and user guides as well.

GAAP Hierarchy for State and Local Governmental Entities

During the first five years of the GASB's existence, discussions arose about the jurisdiction of the GASB and FASB. In 1990 the Financial Accounting Foundation and constituents of the two boards agreed on a jurisdictional formula. The resulting agreement, which is reflected in the AICPA's

---

[2]The Municipal Finance Officers Association was renamed the Government Finance Officers Association in 1985.

1991 *Statement on Auditing Standards No. 69*, addressed the potential overlap between the two bodies by identifying the relative authoritative strength of available resources. In March of 2009, GASB issued Statement No. 55, *The Hierarchy of Generally Accepted Accounting Principles for State and Local Governments.* The GASB largely kept the hierarchy that had been in place for 20 years, but incorporated that guidance formally in the GASB authoritative literature rather than the auditing literature where it had resided. GAAP guidelines for state and local governments include the following, listed in descending order of authority:

a. *GASB statements and interpretations.* The statements and interpretations are semi-annually incorporated into the *Codification of Governmental Accounting and Financial Reporting Standards.*

b. *GASB technical bulletins.* This category also includes AICPA industry audit and accounting guides and statements of position if specifically made applicable to state and local governments by the AICPA and cleared by the GASB.

c. *Consensus positions* of GASB's Emerging Issues Task Force (EITF) and AICPA practice bulletins if specifically made applicable to state and local governments by the AICPA and cleared by the GASB. (No GASB EITF exists currently.)

d. *Implementation guides* published by the GASB staff and industry practices that are widely recognized and prevalent in state and local governments.

If none of the above provides adequate guidance, governmental entities should consider *other accounting literature* (including GASB Concepts Statements, Standards of the International Public Sector Accounting Standards Board, FASB standards not made applicable to governments by a GASB standard,[3] and textbooks). Thus, when addressing an accounting issue, governmental financial statement preparers should first look to GASB statements and interpretations, followed by GASB technical bulletins, and so on. From a practical standpoint, *SAS 69* requires independent auditors who audit governmental entities to express an opinion about whether the auditee has complied with GASB pronouncements. Bond rating agencies consider the audit opinion when assessing a governmental entity's rating for a municipal bond offering, which provides further incentive for compliance with GASB standards.

OVERVIEW OF BASIC GOVERNMENTAL ACCOUNTING MODELS AND PRINCIPLES

LEARNING OBJECTIVE **2**

Governmental accounting and financial reporting differ from corporate accounting and financial reporting. The primary reasons for the differences are that governments lack a profit motive and must focus on demonstrating accountability to the public and governmental authorities.[4] Governments focus on their continuing ability to provide and fund goods and services, rather than on measures of income. In doing so, they must simultaneously utilize two bases of accounting and two measurement focuses. In this section, you will be introduced to some of the unique aspects of governmental accounting. This discussion continues in Chapters 20 and 21.

State and local governmental units engage in both business-type activities and general governmental activities. **Business-type activities** provide services to users for fees that are intended to recover all, or at least the primary portion, of the costs of providing the services. Some of these activities provide services to the constituency, such as water and sewer services, electric service, golf courses, public docks and wharves, and transit systems. Others provide services to departments or agencies within the government, such as central motor pools, self-insurance activities, and central printing and data processing services.

---

[3]The GASB has a current project on incorporating FASB and AICPA guidance explicitly into the GASB authoritative literature. This project is motivated in part by the FASB no longer issuing individual Standards but using instead the ASC (Accounting Standards Codification), http://asc.fasb.org.

[4]GASB White Paper "Why Governmental Accounting and Financial Reporting Is—and Should Be—Different." Norwalk, CT. 2006.

General governmental activities provide goods and services to citizens without regard to their ability to pay. The level of goods and services provided is mandated by the citizens through their elected officials or is determined by persuasion from a higher level of government. General governmental activities (police and fire protection, road maintenance) are usually financed by taxes or intergovernmental grants and subsidies, and there may be no relationship between the people receiving the services and those paying for them (for example, free immunizations provided to children of low-income families). Limited governmental resources are allocated by establishing fixed dollar budgets and legally restricting the use of resources to various general governmental projects and programs. For example, the City of Portland, Maine, may levy taxes to finance the construction of a new school, the State of Montana may provide monies to finance a drug prevention program at local levels, or Orange County, California, may borrow resources to finance a convention center addition. In each of these cases, the resources collected are formally restricted for a specific purpose. The appropriate governmental bodies must approve expenditures beyond the allocated limits.

Because general governmental activities and business-type activities constitute two different models of financing and providing services, governments are said to have a dual nature. Furthermore, the existence of restrictions on most governmental resources is the primary reason for fund accounting, a major feature of governmental accounting that helps governments demonstrate compliance with resource restrictions.

Fund accounting supports the practice of restricting financial resource usage to specific purposes as a means of controlling governmental operations, and it also accommodates the differing accounting bases that general governmental activities and business-type activities use for resource allocation. It is a system that requires multiple accounting entities, called funds, for a single government. Governments use an individual fund to account for a certain business-type activity or a certain subset of general governmental financial resources that are set-aside for a certain purpose or purposes. Indeed, not only are funds separate accounting entities, but they also use different accounting models for business-type activities and general governmental activities. Thus, just as governments have a dual nature, they also have dual accounting models.

Fund Definition and Categories

GASB defines a fund as

> *a fiscal and accounting entity with a self-balancing set of accounts recording cash and other financial resources, together with all related liabilities and residual equities or balances, and changes therein, which are segregated for the purpose of carrying on specific activities or attaining certain objectives in accordance with special regulations, restrictions, or limitations.*[5]

Note that because a fund is an accounting entity, each fund has the following:

- Its own accounting equation
- Its own journals, ledgers, and other accounting records needed to account for the effects of external transactions or interfund activities on the net assets/activities accounted for in the fund
- Financial statements that report on the fund itself

Business-type activities are accounted for in a category of funds called **proprietary funds**. General governmental activities are accounted for in **governmental funds**. There are two types of proprietary funds and five types of governmental funds. Fortunately, accounting for each of the two types of proprietary funds is quite similar, and accounting for each of the five types of governmental funds is also quite similar. Thus, once you learn to account for one type of proprietary fund, you will know most of what is needed to account for all other proprietary funds. Likewise, once you can account for one type of governmental fund, you know most of what is needed to account for all governmental funds.

---

[5]*GASB Codification* Section 1100. 102.

A third category of funds is the **fiduciary** or **trust and agency funds**. Most transactions or interfund activities within funds in this category are accounted for like proprietary funds. Hence, learning how to account for proprietary funds enables one to account for most fiduciary funds as well. The following sections focus on accounting for proprietary funds and governmental funds, and they begin to discuss the various models of accounting.

The Proprietary Fund Accounting Model

The most effective way to understand the nature and working of funds is to understand the basic accounting model or accounting equation. Proprietary funds are explained first because accounting for a proprietary fund is very similar to accounting for a commercial business. In fact, the GASB requires governments to apply a substantial portion of the FASB's standards to proprietary funds.

The accounting equation for a proprietary fund is:

$$\text{Current assets} + \text{Noncurrent assets} - \text{Current liabilities} - \text{Noncurrent liabilities} = \text{Net assets}$$

With the exception of the term *net assets*, which is used to represent fund equity, the same accounting equation is used for businesses and proprietary funds. Proprietary funds report revenues and expenses using the accrual basis of accounting, and they use the **economic resources** measurement focus. Because most proprietary fund transactions are accounted for and reported in the same manner as commercial businesses, your business accounting background is directly applicable to proprietary fund accounting. The transactions and events that are unique to governments or that are accounted for differently from a commercial business enterprise are the focus of much of the discussion of proprietary funds in Chapter 21.

The Governmental Fund Accounting Model

Accounting for general governmental activities (for example, public safety, general administration, and the judicial system) differs from the accounting for business-type activities. Governmental funds, in their purest and simplest form, are essentially working capital entities. The accounting equation for a governmental fund is:

$$\text{Current assets} - \text{Current liabilities} = \text{Fund balance}$$

The measurement focus of governmental funds is **current financial resources**. Although this equation becomes complicated by practical considerations, it is important to continue to think of governmental funds as working capital entities, which focus on current assets and current liabilities, even as you address more advanced issues. In fact, governmental funds generally record **expenditures** to reflect the use of governmental fund working capital, instead of traditional "expenses." Expenditures normally represent the disbursement of working capital funds during a period, whether or not consumption of resources occurs.

Obviously, the governmental funds are not adequate to account for all the assets and liabilities of general governmental activities. When comparing the proprietary and governmental fund models, note that noncurrent assets (for example, fixed assets) and long-term liabilities are excluded from the governmental fund equation. General governmental activities, however, require significant investments in fixed assets, and governments commonly incur large debt obligations associated with general governmental operations. General governmental fixed assets (that is, all fixed assets except those of specific proprietary or similar fiduciary funds) are referred to as *general fixed assets*. Although governments do not account for and record these fixed assets and their depreciation within the governmental funds or governmental fund statements, they do maintain fixed asset records. The general fixed assets and related depreciation are reflected in government-wide financial statements, which are discussed later in the chapter.

General governmental long-term liabilities (that is, all governmental long-term liabilities except those of specific proprietary or similar fiduciary funds) are referred to as *general long-term debt*. These long-term liabilities include bonds, notes, warrants, claims and judgments, unfunded pension obligations, and accumulated vacation and sick leave that will be paid with general governmental resources. As in the accounting for general fixed assets, governments do not account for and record long-term liabilities within the governmental funds or governmental fund statements. Again, debt records are maintained, and general long-term debt is reflected in government-wide financial statements, which are discussed later in the chapter.

Although the governmental fund model has never included noncurrent assets and liabilities, general fixed assets and general long-term debt have been historically reported in governmental-entity financial statements within account groups called the *general fixed asset account group* and the *general long-term debt account group. GASB Statement No. 34*, issued in 1999, eliminated these account groups, but it requires inclusion of these noncurrent items in government-wide financial statements. Many governmental entities may accomplish the recordkeeping requirements associated with the noncurrent items through maintenance of the account groups; however, in name, they no longer exist.

LEARNING
OBJECTIVE **3**

Applying the Models—Transaction Analysis

To solidify your understanding of the proprietary (or business-type activity) fund accounting model and the governmental fund accounting model, consider the effects of several transactions on each of those models. The various types of governmental and proprietary funds are discussed later.

Some transactions have essentially the same impact on a proprietary fund as they would on a governmental fund. This is true for most events that affect only working capital accounts. Consider the analysis of the following four transactions from Exhibit 19-1:

Transactions

1. Incurred salary cost of $5,000.
2. Charges for services rendered, $2,500, were billed and collected immediately.
3. Borrowed $30,000 on a one-year, 6% note six months before year-end.
4. Year-end accrual of interest on the note.

Note that the analysis is identical except that net increases and decreases in proprietary fund asset and liability accounts affect net assets, whereas net increases and decreases in governmental fund assets and liabilities affect fund balance. We would report transaction 1 as an *expense* of $5,000 in a proprietary fund and as an *expenditure* of $5,000 in a governmental fund. We would report transaction 2 as revenue of $2,500 in each case. Transaction 3 does not affect the operating statement of either a proprietary fund or a governmental fund. We would report transaction 4 as interest expense of $900 in a proprietary fund and as $900 of interest expenditures in a governmental fund.

In many other cases, identical transactions impact proprietary and governmental funds differently. This is particularly true for transactions that relate to long-term liabilities or fixed assets. The full effects of such transactions related to business-type activities are accounted for completely within a proprietary fund. The same transaction involving general governmental activity is handled quite differently, because governmental funds focus on current financial resources and are not equipped to record noncurrent assets and liabilities. Therefore, we make memorandum entries in fixed asset or long-term debt records to accommodate subsequent reporting of these

EXHIBIT 19-1

Transaction Analysis—Only Working Capital Accounts Affected

Proprietary Fund	Business-Type Activity				Governmental Fund	General Governmental Activity			
	No. 1	No. 2	No. 3	No. 4		No. 1	No. 2	No. 3	No. 4
Current assets		+2,500	+30,000		Current assets		+2,500	+30,000	
Noncurrent assets									
Current liabilities	+5,000		+30,000	+900	Current liabilities	+5,000		+30,000	+900
Noncurrent liabilities									
Net assets	−5,000	+2,500		−900	Fund balance	−5,000	+2,500		−900

EXHIBIT 19-2

Transaction Analysis—Non-Working Capital Accounts Affected

Proprietary Fund	Business-Type Activity				Governmental Fund	General Governmental Activity			
	No. 5	No. 6	No. 7	No. 8		No. 5	No. 6	No. 7	No. 8
Current assets	+15,000	−2,800	+1,000		Current assets	+15,000	−2,800	+1,000	
Noncurrent assets		+2,800	−1,200	−875					
Current liabilities					Current liabilities				
Noncurrent liabilities	+15,000								
Net assets			−200	−875	Fund balance	+15,000	−2,800	+1,000	

items as appropriate within the financial statements. Consider the analysis of the following four transactions from Exhibit 19-2:

Transactions

5. Borrowed $15,000 by issuing a three-year note.

6. Purchased computer equipment costing $2,800 for cash.

7. Sold a truck for $1,000. It was originally purchased five years ago for $18,000, has an estimated residual value of $1,200, and is fully depreciated.

8. Computed depreciation on the computer equipment for the year, $875.

Notice the dramatic difference in the accounting and reporting of these transactions under the two models. Transactions 5 and 6 do not affect a proprietary fund's net assets. However, both of these transactions do affect working capital. Therefore, the fund balance of a governmental fund is affected by both transactions. We report fund balance increases resulting from issuance of general long-term debt as other financing sources in governmental funds and refer to them as "long-term note proceeds, $15,000." Transaction 6 is reported as expenditures for capital outlay in the governmental fund and is capitalized as computer equipment in the proprietary fund.

Transaction 7 affects the proprietary fund net assets and the fund balance in very different ways. A proprietary fund would report a $200 loss on disposal of fixed assets (book value less cash received) for transaction 7, whereas a governmental fund would report the $1,000 of "proceeds from the sale of fixed assets" as an other financing source, because it has experienced a cash inflow and carried no fixed assets in its fund balance sheet.

Transaction 8 requires that we report $875 of depreciation expense in the proprietary fund operating statement. However, if the computers are general fixed assets, we do not report depreciation in the governmental fund because depreciation is not a use of working capital, and we do not recognize the fixed asset within the fund.

After you have mastered the transaction analysis for a generic proprietary fund and that for a generic governmental fund, two primary elements remain to establish a good understanding of the basic governmental accounting model. The first is to know and distinguish the specific types of funds. The second is to understand the basis of accounting used for each type of fund. In addition, it is helpful to be able to identify and classify interfund transactions, which are simply transactions between two funds.

Proprietary Fund Types

LEARNING OBJECTIVE **4**

Governments account for their business-type activities in one of two types of proprietary funds: enterprise funds and internal service funds. Some governments do not have any enterprise or internal service funds; other governments have several of each type. The primary distinction between the two types of proprietary funds is that governmental units use **internal service funds** to account for activities operated and financed on a business-type basis that provide goods or services either solely or almost solely to *internal customers*, that is, other departments or agencies of the government. Governments use **enterprise funds** to account for business-type

EXHIBIT 19-3 **Fund Type Definitions***	**Governmental Fund Types** ■ *General fund.* Accounts for all financial resources except those accounted for in another fund. ■ *Special revenue funds.* Account for the proceeds of specific revenue sources that are restricted or committed to expenditure for specified purposes other than debt service or capital projects. Is not used for resources held in trust for individuals, private organizations, or other governments. ■ *Capital projects funds.* Account for financial resources that are restricted, committed or assigned to expenditure for capital outlays, including the acquisition or construction of capital facilities and other capital assets (excluding those financed by proprietary funds or in trust funds for individuals, private organizations, or other governments). ■ *Debt service funds.* Account for financial resources that are restricted, committed or assigned to expenditure for principal and interest (including financial resources accumulating for future principal and interest payments). ■ *Permanent funds.* Report resources that are legally restricted to the extent that only earnings, and not principal, may be used for purposes that support the reporting government's programs—that is, for the benefit of the government or its citizenry. **Proprietary Fund Types** ■ *Enterprise funds.* Report any activity for which a fee is charged to external users for goods and services. Activities are required to be reported as enterprise funds if any of the following criteria are met: (a) the activity is financed with debt that is secured solely by a pledge of the net revenues from fees and charges of the activity; (b) laws and regulations require that the activity's costs of providing services, including capital costs (such as depreciation or debt service), be recovered with fees and charges, rather than with taxes or similar revenues; or (c) the pricing policies of the activity establish fees and charges designed to recover its costs, including capital costs (such as depreciation or debt service). ■ *Internal service funds.* Report any activity that provides goods or services to other funds, departments, or agencies of the primary government and its component units, or to other governments, on a cost-reimbursement basis. Internal service funds should be used only if the reporting government is the predominant participant in the activity. **Fiduciary Fund Types** ■ *Trust and agency funds.* Report assets held in a trustee capacity for others that therefore cannot be used to support the government's own programs. The fiduciary fund category includes (a) pension (and other employee benefit) trust funds, (b) investment trust funds, (c) private-purpose trust funds, and (d) agency funds. *GASB Codification, sec 1300* --- *The governmental fund definitions were updated in GASB 54 *Fund Balance Reporting and Governmental Fund Definitions* issued in February of 2009 and effective for fiscal years ending after June 15, 2010.

activities that serve primarily *outside customers*, typically the public. Enterprise fund activities often provide services to internal customers as well, but those customers are not the predominant customers.

Exhibit 19-3 contains the formal definitions of the specific fund types. Common examples of activities accounted for in internal service funds include centralized data processing services, central motor pools and garages, centralized risk financing activities, and central inventory stores. Activities commonly accounted for in enterprise funds include public (government-owned) gas and electric utilities, water and sewer departments, government trash and garbage services, parking garages, civic centers, toll roads, mass transit services, and golf courses.

Notice how the internal service fund definition requires departments or agencies that provide goods or services to other departments or agencies on a cost-reimbursement basis to use these funds for accounting. A cost-reimbursement basis means that the fee charged is intended to cover the costs (expenses) of providing the good or service, rather than to produce net income. Proprietary funds, which provide goods and services to external parties, are more apt to produce net income. As noted earlier, the key distinction between the two types of proprietary funds is whether they primarily serve the public or external entities or they predominantly serve internal departments and agencies.

Governmental Fund Types

Five types of governmental funds are used to account for general governmental activities. Each is a working capital entity that accounts for only a portion of the general governmental working capital. The difference between these funds, then, is the purpose or purposes for which the working capital accounted for in each of them may or must be used. **Special revenue funds** account for general governmental financial resources restricted for specific purposes. **Permanent funds** report resources whose use is permanently restricted, but whose earnings are expendable for the benefit of the government or its citizens. A **capital projects fund** accounts for resources to be used to construct or acquire a major general governmental fixed asset and the related current liabilities. A **debt service fund** accounts for resources to be used to pay principal, interest, and related charges on general long-term debt. Finally, the **general fund** accounts for working capital available for general use. A government has only one general fund, but it may have any number of each of the other fund types. Recall that each of these governmental funds has the same accounting equation that was discussed and illustrated earlier for a generic governmental fund. The only added complexity is that we must understand which governmental fund is affected in order to account for general governmental activities properly.

Fiduciary (Trust and Agency) Fund Types

As indicated in Exhibit 19-3, trust and agency funds include three types of trust funds as well as agency funds. Note that all fiduciary funds contain resources held for the benefit of parties other than the government itself. **Pension trust funds** account for government pension plans, if the government acts as a trustee. **Investment trust funds** account for the external portion of investment pools reported by the sponsoring government. **Private-purpose trust funds** report all other trust arrangements whose resources provide benefits to parties outside the government.

Agency funds are essentially "receive-hold-remit" or "bill-collect-hold-remit" accountability devices, which account for resources a government is holding as an agent on behalf of parties outside the government. For example, an agency fund may be used to record payroll taxes withheld and remitted to a higher government. The accounting equation for an agency fund is:

$$\text{Assets} = \text{Liabilities}$$

Every asset received by an agency fund results in a corresponding increase in liabilities or a decrease in another asset. Agency funds have no equity or fund balance and, therefore, have no operations to report. No revenues, expenditures or expenses, or transfers are reported in an agency fund.

Applying the Model Using Specific Funds

A useful way to solidify your understanding of the funds and the model at this point is to expand your knowledge using transactions. Exhibit 19-4 analyzes the following general governmental transactions:

Transactions

1. Issued general obligation bonds, par value of $3,000,000, at 101 to finance construction of a government office building.

2. Transferred the premium on the bonds to the fund used to account for payment of principal and interest on the bonds.

3. Incurred and paid construction costs of $12,500 on the building.

4. Levied and collected sales taxes restricted to use for economic development, $6,000.

Governmental Fund		Accounting Equation		
No.	Fund	Current Assets	Current Liabilities	Fund Balance
1	Capital projects	+3,030,000		+3,030,000
2a	Capital projects	−30,000		−30,000
2b	Debt service	+30,000		+30,000
3	Capital projects	−12,500		−12,500
4	Special revenue	+6,000		+6,000
5	General	−4,500	+500	−5,000
6	General	+7,500	+7,500	

EXHIBIT 19-4

General Governmental Transaction Analysis Using Specific Funds

5. Paid general governmental employees' salaries, $4,500. Another $500 of salaries accrued but not paid.

6. Borrowed $7,500 on a six-month note to finance general operating costs of the government.

Note that the transaction analysis is the same as for general governmental activities in the previous section on applying the model, except that the exhibit identifies the specific governmental fund affected by each transaction. Transaction 1 represents a long-term debt issuance. Because governmental funds do not record long-term liabilities, fund balance is increased by the amount of bond proceeds. Transaction 2 illustrates a transfer of resources between funds. The premium amount transferred from the capital projects fund to the debt service fund will be held for the purpose of debt repayment. The premium amount, which represents an increase to fund balance in the debt service fund is recognized as an "other financing source—nonreciprocal transfer from the capital projects fund." The premium is termed an "other financing source" to distinguish it from a revenue, and it is nonreciprocal because it will not be repaid to the capital projects fund. The transfer is reflected as "other financial use—nonreciprocal transfer to the debt service fund" in the capital projects fund. The remaining transactions affect current assets, current liabilities, and fund balance as you might anticipate.

Bases of Accounting

Key aspects of the proprietary fund and governmental fund models are the *basis of accounting* and *measurement focus* used for each. Consistent with having fundamentally different accounting equations and models, governmental and proprietary funds use different bases of accounting in measuring financial position and operating results. The GASB specifies when the accrual and modified accrual bases of accounting are to be used.

In essence, the *accrual basis* refers to recognition of revenues and expenses as in business accounting. It follows an "economic resources" measurement focus, whereby all economic resources, whether current or noncurrent, are reported. We report proprietary funds using the accrual basis of accounting.

The *modified accrual basis* refers to recognition of revenues when resources become available to meet current obligations and recognition of expenditures when incurred. The modified accrual basis of accounting is consistent with a "flow of current financial resources" measurement focus, whereby funds report on current resources and current obligations. In general, we report governmental funds using the modified accrual basis of accounting, which is consistent with the governmental model introduced earlier in the chapter. In addition, governments prepare government-wide financial statements, which present governmental and proprietary funds together on the accrual basis of accounting.

It is important to understand the differences between the accrual basis of accounting and the modified accrual basis of accounting. We always report proprietary (or business-type) funds on the accrual basis of accounting, whereas we report governmental funds using the modified accrual basis of accounting in the fund statements and the accrual basis of accounting in the government-wide statements. Chapter 20 focuses on governmental funds and governmental fund financial statements. We record governmental fund transactions using the modified accrual basis of accounting. Later, when we prepare the government-wide statements, we make adjustments to reflect governmental fund activities under the accrual basis of accounting.[6] Chapter 21 discusses the accounting and financial reporting for proprietary and fiduciary funds in detail.

LEARNING OBJECTIVE **5**

Revenue Recognition

Governmental revenue sources are varied and include taxes, grant receipts, and collections of user fees and fines. Revenue recognition within governmental entities is determined by the nature of the underlying transaction. *GASB Statement No. 33*, "Accounting and Financial Reporting for

---

[6]Governments have three options for original entries in the governmental funds: 1) record using modified accrual during the year and make year-end adjustments to accrual for the government-wide statements, 2) record using accrual during the year and make year-end adjustments to modified accrual for the fund statements, or 3) record each event under both modified accrual and full accrual during the year. Due to its prevalence in practice, we present the first approach.

EXHIBIT 19-5

Recognition Criteria for Nonexchange Transactions

Class of Revenue	Recognition
Derived Tax Revenues Examples: sales taxes, personal and corporate income taxes, motor fuel taxes, and similar taxes on earnings and consumption	*Assets* Period when underlying exchange has occurred or when resources are received, whichever is first. *Revenues* Period when underlying exchange has occurred. (Report advance receipts as deferred revenues.) When modified accrual accounting is used, resources should be "available."
Imposed Nonexchange Revenues Examples: property taxes, most fines and forfeitures	*Assets* Period when an enforceable legal claim has arisen or when resources are received, whichever is first. *Revenues* Period when resources are required to be used or first period that use is permitted (for example, for property taxes, the period for which levied). When modified accrual accounting is used, resources should be "available."
Government-Mandated Nonexchange Transactions Examples: federal government mandates on state and local governments *Voluntary Nonexchange Transactions* Examples: certain grants and entitlements, most donations	*Assets and Liabilities* Period when all eligibility requirements have been met or (for asset recognition) when resources are received, whichever is first. *Revenues and Expenses or Expenditures* Period when all eligibility requirements have been met. (Report advance receipts or payments for use in the following period as deferred revenues or advances, respectively.) However, when a provider precludes the sale, disbursement, or consumption of resources for a specified number of years, until a specified event has occurred, or permanently (for example, permanent and term endowments), report revenues and expenses or expenditures when the resources are received or paid, respectively, and report resulting net assets, equity, or fund balance as restricted. When modified accrual accounting is used, resources should be "available."

Source: GASB Statement 33, p. 48.

Nonexchange Transactions," characterizes revenue transactions as (1) exchange (and exchange-like) transactions or (2) nonexchange transactions. *Exchange transactions* are those "in which each party receives and gives up essentially equal values."[7] *Nonexchange transactions* are those "in which a government gives (or receives) value without directly receiving (or giving) equal value in exchange." Many of the transactions in governmental funds are nonexchange in nature, because general governmental activities often address the needs of the public and are funded by taxpayers who generally do not receive benefits in direct relation to their tax payments.

Exhibit 19-5 provides an overview of the four classifications of nonexchange transactions identified in *GASB Statement No. 33* (derived tax revenues, imposed nonexchange revenues, government-mandated nonexchange transactions, and voluntary nonexchange transactions) and the criteria that must be met prior to revenue and asset recognition. Derived tax revenues include sales and income taxes, because they are assessed based on a value that a taxpayer spends or earns. Imposed nonexchange revenues include property taxes. Although the tax is assessed based on property value, the governmental resources available to the taxpayer (police and fire protection) are not necessarily relative to the amount paid. Government-mandated and voluntary nonexchange transactions, which include grant funds and donations, do not require an equal exchange by the governmental entity.

In general, a transaction should be substantially complete prior to revenue recognition. However, the modified accrual basis of accounting used for governmental funds also requires that revenues be objectively measurable and "available" in order to be recognized. To be available, the revenues

---

[7]*GASB Statement No. 33.*

must be "collectible within the current period or soon enough thereafter to pay liabilities of the current period."[8] Recognition of revenues that do not meet these "available" criteria must be *deferred* (recorded as "deferred revenues," a liability) initially. Then revenues are recognized when "available." (Thus, revenues may be recognized later in governmental funds than in proprietary funds.)

The criterion of being collected "soon enough" after the current period to pay liabilities for current expenditures is not defined in the *GASB Codification*. However, with respect to property tax revenue recognition, the *Codification* limits this period to not more than 60 days after the end of the fiscal year. Most government accountants extend this "not more than 60 days" limitation to all other governmental fund revenues as well. Governments are required to disclose their revenue recognition policies in the notes to the financial statements.

The GASB established an exception to the 60-day rule of thumb in *GASB Statement No. 31*, "Accounting and Financial Reporting for Certain Investments and for External Investment Pools." This statement requires most investments to be reported at their fair value. Investment income of each fund of a government, therefore, is increased or decreased by the net change in the fair value of investments. Governments report income as a single line item in the financial statements, with the effect of the change in fair value disclosed in the notes, or they present details in the financial statements as follows:

Interest income	XXX
Net increase (decrease) in fair value of investments	YYY
Total investment income	ZZZ

A final point is that governmental funds recognize revenues on the net revenue approach. These funds recognize revenues net of allowances for uncollectible accounts, rather than at gross amounts earned or levied. Therefore, whereas a proprietary fund that levied charges on customers of $1,000 but expected $10 to prove uncollectible would report revenues of $1,000 and expenses of $10, a governmental fund in a similar scenario would report only the net realizable value, or $990, as revenues.

Expense and Expenditure Recognition

The expenses of a governmental unit are similar to those of a commercial business enterprise. Expenses essentially reflect the cost of assets or services used by an entity, and they are recognized in the period incurred. Expenditures, unique to government accounting, typically reflect the use of governmental fund working capital. Thus, expenditures normally reflect the cost of goods or services acquired during a period, whether or not consumed, and the maturing of general long-term debt principal. With limited exceptions, governmental funds recognize expenditures in the period that the fund liability is incurred.

Recall that under fund accounting, proprietary funds recognize expenses using the accrual basis of accounting, whereas governmental funds recognize expenditures, based on the modified accrual basis. However, *GASB Statement No. 34* requires both proprietary funds and governmental funds to report expenses within the government-wide statements. In fund statements, governmental funds report expenditures, whereas proprietary funds report expenses. Although this may sound confusing, examples in Chapters 20 and 21 should help clarify the difference between expenses and expenditures, as well as their treatment within the financial statements.

Many operating expenses and expenditures occur simultaneously. For instance, the use of electricity results in both an expense and an expenditure in the same amount at the same point in time. The same is true for salaries and wages of government employees. For other items, the timing of expense and expenditure recognition differs dramatically. The purchase of a fixed asset that is to be used by a governmental fund over a 10-year period results in a capital outlay *expenditure* in the year of acquisition and no additional expenditures over the next 9 years. The same purchase within a proprietary fund results in a depreciation *expense* each year over the 10-year period of its use, however. Note that a fixed asset acquired by a governmental fund is treated differently within a set of financial statements. In the fund statements, a governmental fund records an expenditure for the full cost of the asset in the year purchased. In the government-wide statements, an adjustment is

---

[8]*GASB Codification*, Section 1600.106.

made to capitalize and depreciate the same fixed asset. This occurs because of the unique bases of accounting used in the government-wide and fund financial statements.

Likewise, the government as a whole sometimes incurs liabilities that do not result in governmental fund liabilities being incurred at the same point in time. This may be true for general government claims and judgments, compensated absences, or pension contributions. For example, proceeds of general long-term debt issuances increase both the fund balance and the current assets of the governmental funds, but the liability is not recorded in the fund statements. In the fund statements, the recipient governmental fund will report the fund balance increase as bond issue proceeds, or a similar title, and show it as an other financing source in the statement of revenues, expenditures, and changes in fund balance (a fund statement). Long-term debt appears as a long-term liability within the government-wide statement of net assets.

The primary exception to recognizing expenditures when a governmental fund incurs a liability relates to interest and principal expenditures on general long-term debt. Governmental funds record these amounts "when due"; however, although they are never required to be reported before the legal due date, it is permissible to accrue such expenditures if (1) they are due early in the next year and (2) the financial resources for their payment have been provided in the current year.

Interfund Activity

Governments use several funds to account for their activities, and numerous transactions between funds, or interfund transactions, occur annually. Examples include sales of services from an enterprise or internal service fund department to other departments, shifts of general fund resources to capital projects funds to cover part of the cost of a capital project, and interfund loans. *GASB Codification*, Section 1800.102, classifies interfund transactions into several types, each of which is reported differently in the financial statements.

Interfund loans are loans that are made by one fund to another and must be repaid. The receivable and payable resulting from an interfund loan appear in the lender and borrower funds. If prompt payment is not expected, the activity may require reclassification as a transfer. Interfund transfers occur when one fund provides resources to another for legally authorized purposes (an operating transfer) or when one fund helps to establish or enhance another (a residual equity transfer). Transfers are either reciprocal or nonreciprocal, depending on whether or not repayment is expected. Governmental funds record transfers as other financing sources/uses, whereas proprietary funds record transfers in a category following nonoperating revenues/expenses. Interfund services provided and used include sales and purchases between funds at approximate external market value. The seller fund records these activities as revenues, whereas the purchasing fund recognizes an expense or expenditure; however, unpaid amounts should be reported as interfund receivables and payables in the fund financial statements. An interfund reimbursement is necessary when an expenditure applicable to one fund is made by a different fund. Reimbursements are not reported in the financial statements.

The Role of the Budget

Because resource use within governments typically must be authorized by laws or ordinances, the role and impact of the budget is dramatically more significant in governments than in business accounting.[9] In fact, every governmental unit is required to adopt a budget document, which is often considered more significant than the financial reports.[10] Governmental accounting systems are required to provide appropriate budgetary control either formally through the use of budgetary accounts (typical in the general fund, special revenue funds, and other governmental funds) or informally through the maintenance of separate budgetary records and comparisons. In addition, a comparison of actual and budgetary amounts is required to be included in the annual operating statements (or in required supplementary information) of all governmental funds for which an annual budget has been adopted. (We will illustrate how budgets are used within fund accounting in Chapter 20.)

---

[9]GASB White Paper 2006.

[10]*GASB Codification*, Section 1100.111.

A **budget** is a plan of financial operation consisting of an estimate of proposed expenditures for a given period and the proposed means of financing them. Ordinarily, the preparation of a budget is the responsibility of the executive branch of government—the mayor, city manager, governor, and so on. Approval of a budget, however, is a legislative responsibility. A legislative body may approve a proposed budget as submitted by the chief executive, or it may amend the executive budget prior to approval. *When approved by the legislative body, the budget for expenditures becomes a spending ordinance that has the force of law. An approved revenue plan also has the force of law*, because it provides the governmental unit with the power to levy taxes, to sell licenses, to charge for services, and so on, in the amount or at the rate approved.

Appropriations are approved or authorized expenditures. They provide legislative control over the expenditure budget prepared by the executive branch. Such control may be in detail, such as when the legislative body makes appropriations for each item included in the budget. The legislative body, however, may approve expenditures (make appropriations) by category (by department, for example) or in total. Line-item approval provides maximum control over the management by the legislative branch because the legislative body must approve any change in the budget. If a department makes appropriations, however, managers could allocate more resources to some items within a department (supplies, for example) and less to others (salaries, for example) without legislative approval of the change.

If an appropriation is allocated to a specific time period, it is termed an **allotment**. In other words, the yearly appropriations may be allotted to months or quarters to prevent expenditure of the appropriation too early in the year. Furthermore, allotments may be necessary for coordinating revenues collected with payments for expenditures (that is, managing cash flows).

A current budget is normally for a one-year period, and it includes the operating budget as well as the capital budget for the current period. A **capital budget**, as used here, represents the current portion of a **capital program** (a plan of capital expenditures to be incurred each year over a fixed period of years).

THE FINANCIAL REPORTING ENTITY

Many governments are closely associated with other entities or governmental units, which may or may not be economically dependent on the government. For example, Genesee County, New York, houses a local community college, and your hometown has probably established a public housing authority to provide low-cost housing to residents. When a government has such relationships, the question arises about how (or if) these entities should be reported in the financial statements of the government. *GASB Statement No. 14*, "The Financial Reporting Entity," explains that the financial reporting entity is made up of the primary government and its component units. Each state government and each general-purpose local government (city, town, county, and so on) is a **primary government**, whereas a special-purpose government (a water district, hospital, or transit authority, for example) is a primary government if it has a separately elected governing body, is legally separate, and is fiscally independent of other state or local governments. **Component units** are legally separate organizations for which the primary government is financially accountable. They can also be other organizations for which the nature and significance of their relationship with the primary government are such that their exclusion would result in the reporting entity's statements being misleading or incomplete.

Governments have two main options on how to report component units in their financial statements. The component units can be combined (a.k.a. blended) into the primary government, or they can be discretely presented in a separate column depending on how closely related the component is to the primary government. Component units that provide services primarily to the public or to other entities use blending only if a voting majority of the primary-government governing body serves on the component-unit governing board and also constitutes a voting majority of that board (for example, the component unit has substantively the same governing body as the primary government). If this strict criterion is not met, the component unit is discretely presented in the reporting entity's financial statements. Discrete presentation requires the presentation of the component unit's financial data in a column or columns separate from the primary government's financial data in the government-wide statements. Supporting information for the individual component units should be provided in combining statements that follow the fund financial statements or in condensed financial statements included in the notes to the financial statements of the primary government.

GASB Statement No. 39, "Determining Whether Certain Organizations Are Component Units,"[11] provides criteria for deciding whether organizations for which the primary government is not financially accountable but with which it maintains significant relationships should be reported as component units. *Statement 39* primarily refers to organizations that raise and hold economic resources for the direct benefit of a governmental unit.

COMPREHENSIVE ANNUAL FINANCIAL REPORT

LEARNING OBJECTIVE **6**

All state and local governmental units must report their activities to residents and other interested parties. *GASB Codification*, Section 2200.101, states that "Every governmental entity should prepare and publish, as a matter of public record, a *comprehensive annual financial report* (CAFR) that encompasses all funds of the primary government (including its blended component units). The CAFR should also encompass all discretely presented component units of the reporting entity."

In 1999, the GASB issued *GASB Statement No. 34*, "Basic Financial Statement—and Management's Discussion and Analysis—for State and Local Governments" (*GASB 34*), which instituted major changes to the manner in which governmental entities prepare and present their financial statements. *GASB 34* retains traditional fund accounting and fund financial statements; however, it also introduces *government-wide financial statements*, which are prepared using accrual accounting for all of a government's activities—both governmental and business-type. Prior to *GASB 34*, each of the basic financial statements (referred to as general-purpose financial statements) was prepared using the appropriate fund basis of accounting. For example, governmental fund statements were prepared on the modified accrual basis of accounting, and proprietary fund statements were prepared on the accrual basis of accounting. The combined balance sheet included columns for each fund type, and governmental funds used modified accrual accounting, whereas proprietary funds followed accrual accounting. Under *GASB 34*, the two bases of accounting no longer appear on the same financial statement. Instead, governmental fund activity is converted to the accrual basis of accounting on the combined *government-wide* financial statements.

CAFRs contain three major sections (introductory, financial, and statistical) and are considered an entity's "official annual report." Exhibit 19-6 lists the contents of a *GASB 34* CAFR, which are described in detail here.

Introductory Section of a CAFR

The introductory section of a CAFR includes a table of contents, a letter of transmittal, a list of principal officers, and an organizational chart. It might also include copies of awards that were received for financial reporting. The transmittal letter provides an introduction to the financial report, describes management's responsibility for the statements, and outlines significant developments within the entity during the fiscal year. Prior to GASB 34 implementation, transmittal letters were quite extensive, but *GASB 34* requires an in-depth analysis of the entity's economic condition in management's discussion and analysis, which is found in the financial section. Thus, transmittal letters are now relatively brief in comparison.

Financial Section

The financial section includes the management's discussion and analysis, the auditor's report, the government-wide financial statements, and the fund financial statements.

MANAGEMENT'S DISCUSSION AND ANALYSIS (MD&A) The MD&A is a new requirement under *GASB 34*. Considered *required supplementary information*, the MD&A precedes the financial statements and is comparable to the MD&A of a corporate financial statement. Intended to "provide an objective

---

[11]GASB has a current project to reexamine Statement 14 and has conducted research on existing patterns. As of this writing GASB has not published a document for public comment. Project updates are available at the GASB Web site www.gasb.org.

EXHIBIT 19-6

GASB 34 **CAFR Contents**

CAFR CONTENTS REQUIRED UNDER *GASB 34*

Introductory Section

Table of contents
Letter of transmittal
List of principal officers
Organization chart

Financial Section

Management's discussion and analysis (MD&A)
Auditor's report
Basic financial statements
  Government-wide statements
    Statement of net assets (accrual basis)
    Statement of activities (accrual basis)
  Fund financial statements
    Balance sheet—governmental funds (modified accrual basis)
    Statement of revenues, expenditures, and changes in fund balance—governmental funds
      (modified accrual basis)
    Statement of net assets—proprietary funds (accrual basis)
    Statement of revenues, expenses, and changes in net assets—all proprietary and similar trust fund types
      (accrual basis)
    Statement of cash flows—all proprietary and similar trust fund types (accrual basis)
    Statement of fiduciary net assets—fiduciary funds (accrual basis)
    Statement of changes in fiduciary net assets—fiduciary funds (accrual basis)
Notes to the financial statements
Required supplementary information other than MD&A
Combining statements and individual fund statements and schedules
Statistical Section

and easily readable analysis of the government's financial activities based on the currently known facts, decisions, or conditions,"[12] the MD&A should include the following:

1. A brief discussion of the basic financial statements, including the relationships of the statements to each other, and the significant differences in the information they provide. This discussion should include analyses that assist readers in understanding why measurements and results reported in fund financial statements either reinforce information in government-wide statements or provide additional information.

2. Condensed financial information derived from government-wide financial statements comparing the current year to the prior year. At a minimum, governments should present the information needed to support their analysis of financial position and results of operations required in 3, below, including these elements:
   a. Total assets, distinguishing between capital and other assets
   b. Total liabilities, distinguishing between long-term liabilities and other liabilities
   c. Total net assets, distinguishing among amounts invested in capital assets, net of related debt; restricted amounts; and unrestricted amounts
   d. Program revenues, by major source
   e. General revenues, by major source
   f. Total revenues
   g. Program expenses, at a minimum by function
   h. Total expenses
   i. Excess (deficiency) before contributions to term and permanent endowments or permanent fund principal, special and extraordinary items, and transfers
   j. Contributions
   k. Special and extraordinary items

---

[12]*GASB Statement 34*, paragraph 11.

    l. Transfers

    m. Change in net assets

    n. Ending net assets

3. An analysis of the government's overall financial position and results of operations to assist users in assessing whether financial position has improved or deteriorated as a result of the year's operations. The analysis should address both governmental and business-type activities as reported in the government-wide financial statements and should include *reasons* for significant changes from the prior year, not simply the amounts or percentages of change. In addition, important economic factors, such as changes in the tax or employment bases, that significantly affected operating results for the year should be discussed.

4. An analysis of balances and transactions of individual funds. The analysis should address the reasons for significant changes in fund balances or fund net assets and whether restrictions, commitments, or other limitations significantly affect the availability of fund resources for future use.

5. An analysis of significant variations between original and final budget amounts and between final budget amounts and actual results for the general fund (or its equivalent). The analysis should include any currently known reasons for those variations that are expected to have a significant effect on future services or liquidity.

6. A description of significant capital asset and long-term debt activity during the year, including a discussion of commitments made for capital expenditures, changes in credit ratings, and debt limitations that may affect the financing of planned facilities or services.

7. A discussion by governments that use the modified approach to report some or all of their infrastructure assets.

8. A description of currently known facts, decisions, or conditions that are expected to have a significant effect on financial position (net assets) or results of operations (revenues, expenses, and other changes in net assets).

A sample MD&A appears in the appendix to *GASB Statement No. 34*.

AUDITOR'S REPORT The auditor's report within the financial section of a CAFR indicates that the financial statements are the responsibility of the government's management. It identifies the financial statements that have been audited and expresses an opinion about whether the financial statements are presented in conformity with generally-accepted accounting principles. It should also specify the information included within the CAFR that was unaudited.

GOVERNMENT-WIDE FINANCIAL STATEMENTS Government-wide statements which consist of the statement of net assets and the statement of activities, provide consolidated information for the government as a whole and introduce the concept of operational accountability to governmental financial reporting. **Operational accountability** measures the extent of a government's success at meeting operating objectives efficiently and effectively and its ability to meet operating objectives in the future.[13]

The government-wide statements report governmental activities, business-type activities, and discretely presented component units; however, they do not include fiduciary funds. All data are reported on the accrual basis of accounting. Thus, it may be necessary to convert governmental fund balances to the accrual basis of accounting. Chapter 20 examines this conversion process.

The **statement of net assets** reports the difference between assets and liabilities as *net assets*, preferably in the format of assets less liabilities equal net assets.[14] The statement lists both assets and liabilities in terms of liquidity and categorizes net assets as either: 1) invested in capital assets, net of related debt, 2) restricted, or 3) unrestricted.[15] The statement of net assets

---

[13]*GASB Statement No. 34*, p. 78.

[14]*GASB Statement No. 34*, p. 199.

[15]*GASB Statement No. 46* provides additional guidance regarding restricted net asset classification. *GASB Statement No. 54* provides new guidance for reporting fund balance in the governmental fund statements for fiscal years beginning after June 15, 2010. *GASB Statement 54* does not change the reporting of net assets and is illustrated in the next chapter.

contains columns for governmental activities, business-type activities, totals of the primary government, and component unit totals, if applicable. Columns for reporting entity totals and prior-year comparative data are optional. The governmental activity column aggregates all general governmental assets and liabilities, including fixed assets and general long-term debt, from the general, special revenue, permanent, debt service, and capital projects funds. This column also includes most internal service fund assets and liabilities, because general governmental departments are typically the largest customers of internal service funds. Exhibit 19-7 presents the statement of net assets for the City of Golden, Colorado.

The **statement of activities** presents governmental and proprietary fund revenues and expenses on the same statement using full accrual accounting. The format, which appears quite complex at first glance, can be viewed as two distinct parts. The upper portion focuses on costs of services and reports to taxpayers both the total expenses and the net expenses of the government by functional area or program. The lower portion of the statement displays

EXHIBIT 19-7

Statement of Net Assets

CITY OF GOLDEN, COLORADO STATEMENT OF NET ASSETS DECEMBER 31, 2009

| | Primary Government | | | | |
	Governmental Activities	Business-Type Activities	Totals 2009	Totals 2008	Component Unit
Assets					
Cash and investments	$14,102,028	$ 4,685,071	$ 18,787,099	$ 20,475,843	$ 481,051
Property taxes receivable	5,084,000	—	5,084,000	4,531,800	1,413,941
Accounts receivable	3,278,290	936,469	4,214,759	3,519,023	89,067
Internal balances	(1,519,197)	1,519,197	—	—	—
Inventory and prepaid expenses	77,043	92,139	169,182	97,871	3,355
Restricted cash and investments	—	640,683	640,683	467,500	500,000
Bond issuance costs (net of amortization)	265,174	291,630	556,804	589,394	63,493
Capital assets not being depreciated	13,683,591	22,349,548	36,033,139	37,333,718	1,009,149
Capital assets (net of accumulated depreciation)	63,740,386	76,901,520	140,641,906	138,824,816	5,880,156
Total assets	$98,711,315	$107,416,257	$206,127,572	$205,839,965	$ 9,440,212
Liabilities					
Accounts payable	813,774	410,167	1,223,941	2,475,961	92,228
Accrued liabilities	7,464	217,726	225,190	682,728	—
Claims payable	677,236	—	677,236	342,880	—
Deferred property taxes	5,084,000	—	5,084,000	4,531,800	1,413,941
Deferred revenue	623,466	149,786	773,252	608,061	—
Noncurrent liabilities					
Due within one year	1,960,000	1,103,883	3,063,883	2,879,168	939,064
Due in more than one year	32,194,020	11,376,228	43,570,248	46,360,572	5,214,884
Total liabilities	41,359,960	13,257,790	54,617,750	57,881,170	7,660,117
Net Assets					
Invested in capital assets, net of related debt	44,353,119	87,045,968	131,399,087	128,250,214	735,357
Restricted for					
Parks & recreation	896,093	—	896,093	792,055	—
Capital projects	1,415,624	—	1,415,624	2,531,955	—
Cemetery perpetual care (nonexpendable)	1,104,115	—	1,104,115	1,060,299	—
Cemetery perpetual care (expendable)	433,984	—	433,984	406,740	—
Debt service reserve	—	640,683	640,683	467,500	500,000
Emergency reserves	820,000	—	820,000	820,000	—
Unrestricted	8,328,420	6,471,816	14,800,236	13,630,032	544,738
Total net assets	$57,351,355	$ 94,158,467	$151,509,822	$147,958,795	$ 1,780,095

Source: City of Golden, Colorado, Comprehensive annual financial report, 2009.

how the net program expenses incurred during the year compared with general revenues. The complete format of the statement of activities for the City of Golden, Colorado, appears in Exhibit 19-8.

For example, during 2009, $543,739 of expenses were incurred by the "business-activity" Splash Aquatic Park in Golden, while only $356,646 in revenues were recognized ($348,031 Charges for Services + $8,615 Capital grants and Contributions). Thus, this functional area (the Splash Park) was not totally self-financed and had a net expense of ($187,093) for the year. The ($187,093) net expense is subsidized by general governmental revenues, such as taxes or grant receipts. Note that this does not necessarily reflect negatively on the Splash Park or its operations, because a partial subsidy might be the city policy or goal. The financial statement simply informs taxpayers of the functions or activities that are partially supported by taxes.

Program revenues are defined as being "directly from the program itself or from parties outside the reporting government's constituency." They are categorized as charges for services, (program-specific) operating grants and contributions, or (program-specific) capital grants and contributions within the statement's columns. For example, revenues from the water and wastewater facilities or grants for the cemetery are program revenues. All revenues other than program revenues are considered *general revenues*. General revenues, which include all taxes (even those restricted to programs), grants and investment income not considered program revenue, contributions to endowments, special and extraordinary items, and transfers, are reported in the lower section. Note that governmental activities and business-type activities are distinguished both in the presentation of functional classifications (the rows) and in the presentation of net expenses or revenues and changes in net assets (the columns).

FUND FINANCIAL STATEMENTS Fund financial statements focus on fiscal accountability rather than operational accountability. **Fiscal accountability** is the responsibility of a government to demonstrate compliance with public decisions regarding the use of financial resources.[16] The individual fund statements include the following: balance sheet—governmental funds; statement of revenues, expenditures, and changes in fund balance—governmental funds; statement of net assets—proprietary funds; statement of revenues, expenses, and changes in net assets—all proprietary and similar trust fund types (if applicable); statement of cash flows—all proprietary and similar trust fund types (if applicable); statement of fiduciary net assets—fiduciary funds; and statement of fund changes in fiduciary net assets—fiduciary funds. Exhibits 19-9 through 19-13 present illustrative statements for the City of Golden, Colorado. (Fiduciary fund statements are shown in Chapter 21.)

A significant change that *GASB Statement No. 34* made to fund financial statements was introduction of the concept of a *major fund*. The general fund is always a major fund. Other funds are considered major funds if they meet both of the following criteria:

1. Total assets, liabilities, revenues, or expenditures/expenses (excluding extraordinary items) of that individual governmental or enterprise fund are at least 10 percent of the *corresponding* total (assets, liabilities, and so forth) for *all* funds of that *category* or *type* (that is, total governmental or total enterprise funds).

2. Total assets, liabilities, revenues, or expenditures/expenses (excluding extraordinary items) of that individual governmental or enterprise fund are at least 5 percent of the *corresponding* total for all governmental and enterprise funds *combined*.

Using the concept of major fund reporting, the required governmental fund statements will include a separate column for each major governmental fund and a column with aggregated information for all other governmental funds, as well as a total column for all governmental funds. Proprietary fund statements will include a separate column for each major enterprise fund, a column with aggregated information for all other enterprise funds, a total column for all enterprise funds, and a column with aggregated information for *all* internal service funds. (The City of

---

[16]*GASB Statement No. 34*, page 78.

CITY OF GOLDEN, COLORADO,
STATEMENT OF ACTIVITIES
FOR THE YEAR ENDED DECEMBER 31, 2009

Functions/Programs	Expenses	Program Revenues		
		Charges for Services	Operating Grants and Contributions	Capital Grants and Contributions
Primary Government				
Governmental activities				
General government	$ 5,177,505	$ 1,200,019	$ 13,180	$ —
Planning & economic development	1,369,737	193,281	—	—
Police	6,708,952	487,604	167,062	—
Fire	1,641,196	90,423	48,995	—
Public works	5,904,355	24,475	455,178	40,828
Parks and recreation	2,862,860	574,066	—	743,994
Unallocated interest on long-term debt	1,662,301	—	—	—
Total governmental activities	25,326,906	2,569,868	684,415	784,822
Business type activities				
Water	5,015,706	5,120,162	—	1,122,454
Wastewater	1,800,782	1,370,846	—	238,133
Drainage	688,114	875,074	—	182,404
Fossil trace golf course	2,777,396	2,851,431	—	2,361
Community center	2,242,511	1,542,138	—	153,619
Splash aquatic park	543,739	348,031	—	8,615
Cemetery operations	405,231	360,008	—	31,143
Rooney road sports complex	429,611	71,841	—	19,802
Total business-type activities	13,903,090	12,539,531	—	1,758,531
Total Primary Government	$39,229,996	$15,109,399	$684,415	$2,543,353
Component Unit				
Golden urban renewal authority	$ 1,333,238	$ —	$ —	$ —
General Revenues				
Taxes				
Property				
Sales and use				
Other				
Grants and contributions not restricted to specific programs				
Investment income				
Miscellaneous				
Gain on disposal of capital assets				
Transfers				
Total general revenues and transfers				
Change in net assets				
Net assets, beginning, restated				
Net assets, ending				

Source: City of Golden, Colorado, Comprehensive annual financial report, 2009.

Golden has one major governmental fund—Sales and use tax capital improvement—and five major proprietary funds: Water, Wastewater, Drainage, Fossil Trace Golf Course and Community Center Fund.) Governmental officials may also present a separate column for any nonmajor fund that they feel is particularly important and therefore should be presented to financial statement users. For both governmental and proprietary fund statements, whenever a nonmajor total column is used, a combining statement must be presented.

Because governmental funds are accounted for using the accrual basis of accounting in the government-wide statements and using the modified accrual basis of accounting in the fund

EXHIBIT 19-8

Statement of Activities
(*Continued*)

		Net (Expense) Revenue and Changes in Net Assets		
			Totals	
Governmental Activities	Business-Type Activities	2009	2008	Component Unit
$ (3,964,306)	$ —	$ (3,964,306)	$ (3,253,642)	$ —
(1,176,456)	—	(1,176,456)	(1,215,338)	—
(6,054,286)	—	(6,054,286)	(6,199,939)	—
(1,501,778)	—	(1,501,778)	(1,421,057)	—
(5,383,874)	—	(5,383,874)	(4,532,621)	—
(1,544,800)	—	(1,544,800)	(2,001,049)	—
(1,662,301)	—	(1,662,301)	(1,783,158)	—
(21,287,801)	—	(21,287,801)	(20,406,804)	—
—	1,226,910	1,226,910	344,788	—
—	(191,803)	(191,803)	(176,245)	—
—	369,364	369,364	42,055	—
—	76,396	76,396	320,861	—
—	(546,754)	(546,754)	(709,756)	—
—	(187,093)	(187,093)	(195,292)	—
—	(14,080)	(14,080)	(151,974)	—
—	(337,968)	(337,968)	(33,714)	—
—	394,972	394,972	(559,277)	—
(21,287,801)	394,972	(20,892,829)	(20,966,081)	—
—	—	—	—	(1,333,238)
4,507,619	—	4,507,619	3,933,004	1,174,344
15,751,182	—	15,751,182	15,470,174	487,978
1,333,663	—	1,333,663	1,483,706	—
1,274,517	—	1,274,517	312,501	17,005
371,821	174,057	545,878	811,322	22,263
751,527	279,470	1,030,997	1,463,256	5,488
—	—	—	1,494,223	—
876,000	(876,000)	—	—	—
24,866,329	(422,473)	24,443,856	24,968,186	1,707,078
3,578,528	(27,501)	3,551,027	4,002,105	373,840
53,772,827	94,185,968	147,958,795	143,956,690	1,406,255
$57,351,355	$94,158,467	$151,509,822	$147,958,795	$ 1,780,095

statements, a reconciliation between the government-wide statements of net assets and activities and the fund balance sheet and statement of revenues, expenditures, and changes in fund balance is required either on the face of the fund financial statements or in an accompanying schedule. (See Golden's reconciliations at the bottom of Exhibits 19-9[17] and 19-10.)

---

[17]Note that Golden's 2009 CAFR does not include the impact of *GASB Statement No. 54* regarding fund balance classifications because it is not required until fiscal periods beginning after June 15, 2010. Chapter 20 illustrates the new classifications.

EXHIBIT 19-9

Balance Sheet—Governmental Funds

CITY OF GOLDEN, COLORADO, BALANCE SHEET—GOVERNMENTAL FUNDS
DECEMBER 31, 2009

	General	Sales and Use Tax Capital Improvement	Other Governmental Funds	Total Governmental Funds 2009	2008
Assets					
Cash and investments	$ 4,775,111	$2,886,398	$2,395,087	$10,056,596	$12,103,453
Property taxes receivable	5,057,800	—	26,200	5,084,000	4,531,800
Accounts and taxes receivable	2,230,630	106,688	54,291	2,391,609	2,119,521
Inventories	40,964	—	—	40,964	—
Due from other governments	116,823	—	92,245	209,068	257,785
Total assets	12,221,328	2,993,086	2,567,823	17,782,237	19,012,559
Liabilities and fund balance					
Liabilities					
Accounts payable	632,992	58,265	48,156	739,413	1,399,231
Accrued liabilities	7,464	—	—	7,464	403,484
Interfund payable	—	1,519,197	—	1,519,197	1,519,197
Deferred property taxes	5,057,800	—	26,200	5,084,000	4,531,800
Deferred revenue	623,466	—	—	623,466	458,074
Total liabilities	6,321,722	1,577,462	74,356	7,973,540	8,311,786
Fund balance					
Reserved for parks & recreation	—	—	896,093	896,093	792,055
Reserved for capital projects	—	1,415,624	—	1,415,624	2,531,955
Reserved for cemetery perpetual care (nonexpendable)	—	—	1,104,115	1,104,115	1,060,299
Reserved for cemetery perpetual care (expendable)	—	—	433,984	433,984	406,740
Reserved for inventories	40,964	—	—	40,964	—
Emergency reserves	820,000	—	—	820,000	820,000
Unreserved, reported in General fund	5,038,642	—	—	5,038,642	5,043,365
Special revenue funds	—	—	10,589	10,589	1,719
Capital projects funds	—	—	48,686	48,686	44,640
Total fund balance	5,899,606	1,415,624	2,493,467	9,808,697	10,700,773
Total liabilities and fund balance	$12,221,328	$2,993,086	$2,567,823		

Amounts reported for governmental activities in the Statement of Net Assets are different because:

Capital assets used in governmental activities are not financial resources and therefore are not reported in the funds. Capital assets for internal service funds of $4,227,444 have been deducted from total governmental net capital assets of $77,423,977.	73,196,533	70,797,029
Internal service funds are used by management to charge the costs of certain activities to individual funds, such as insurance, fleet and information technology management. The assets and liabilities of the internal service funds are included in governmental activities in the statement of net assets.	8,164,586	7,958,797
Long-term liabilities, including bonds payable ($19,915,000), bond premium ($270,858), capital leases ($12,885,000), compensated absences ($1,012,777), and bond issuance costs $265,174 are not due and payable in the current period and therefore are not reported in the funds.	(33,818,461)	(35,683,772)
Net Assets of Governmental Activities	$57,351,355	$53,772,827

Source: City of Golden, Colorado, Comprehensive annual financial report, 2009.

The information in the business-type activities column is basically the same as that provided by the enterprise fund columns within the fund financial statements.

BUDGETARY COMPARISONS Governments must present budgetary comparison information for the general fund and each special revenue fund that has a legally adopted annual budget. The comparison may be presented as a comparison statement within the basic financial statements or as a schedule

EXHIBIT 19-10

Statement of Revenues, Expenditures, and Changes in Fund Balances—Governmental Funds

CITY OF GOLDEN, COLORADO, STATEMENT OF REVENUES, EXPENDITURES, AND CHANGES IN FUND BALANCES—GOVERNMENTAL FUNDS FOR THE YEAR ENDED DECEMBER 31, 2009

	General	Sales and Use Tax Capital Improvement	Other Governmental Funds	Total Governmental Funds 2009	Total Governmental Funds 2008
Revenues					
Taxes	$16,395,054	$ 5,173,539	$ 23,871	$ 21,592,464	$ 20,886,884
Licenses and permits	408,720	—	—	408,720	497,159
Intergovernmental	944,584	600,000	1,199,172	2,743,756	1,993,520
Charges for services	1,646,078	—	43,815	1,689,893	1,882,222
Fines and forfeitures	471,253	—	—	471,253	512,488
Investment income	138,671	76,112	62,947	277,730	372,418
Miscellaneous	667,994	44,979	38,554	751,527	1,294,886
Total revenues	20,672,354	5,894,630	1,368,359	27,935,343	27,439,577
Expenditures					
Current					
General government	4,474,053	—	19,736	4,493,789	4,297,011
Planning & economic development	1,372,685	—	—	1,372,685	1,390,685
Police	6,540,684	—	—	6,540,684	6,595,491
Fire	1,391,733	—	—	1,391,733	1,300,760
Public works	3,786,083	—	—	3,786,083	3,615,899
Parks and recreation	2,028,967	—	—	2,028,967	2,435,339
Debt service					
Principal	—	1,855,000	—	1,855,000	1,775,000
Interest and other charges	—	1,683,333	—	1,683,333	1,783,158
Capital outlay	—	4,630,246	1,489,499	6,119,745	7,457,230
Total expenditures	19,594,205	8,168,579	1,509,235	29,272,019	30,650,573
Excess (deficiency) of revenues over expenditures	1,078,149	(2,273,949)	(140,876)	(1,336,676)	(3,210,996)
Other Financing Sources (Uses)					
Transfers in	108,300	1,516,508	493,890	2,118,698	2,872,194
Transfers (out)	(1,150,208)	(358,890)	(165,000)	(1,674,098)	(2,186,990)
Total other financing sources (uses)	(1,041,908)	1,157,618	328,890	444,600	685,204
Net change in fund balances	36,241	(1,116,331)	188,014	(892,076)	(2,525,792)
Fund balances, beginning	5,863,365	2,531,955	2,305,453	10,700,773	13,226,565
Fund balances, ending	$ 5,899,606	$ 1,415,624	$ 2,493,467	$ 9,808,697	$ 10,700,773

Net Change in Fund Balances—Total Governmental Funds	$ (892,076)
Amounts reported for governmental activities in the Statement of Activities are different because:	
Governmental funds report capital outlays as expenditures. However, in the statement of activities, the cost of those assets is allocated over their estimated useful lives as depreciation expense. This is the amount by which capital outlays $7,277,943 less dispositions ($2,063,507) and internal service fund capital outlays ($347,474) exceed depreciation ($3,330,299) less internal service fund depreciation $862,842 in the current period.	2,399,505
Repayment of bond principal is an expenditure in the governmental funds, but the repayment reduces long-term debt liabilities in the statement of net assets. Bond proceeds provide current financial resources to governmental funds, but issuing debt increases long-term liabilities in the statement of net assets. These include bond payments $1,345,000, capital lease payments $510,000, amortization of bond premium $21,032 amortization of bond issuance costs ($22,098), and a decrease in accrued compensated absences of $11,375.	1,865,309
Internal service funds are used by management to charge the costs of certain activities to individual funds, such as insurance, fleet and information technology management. The net revenue (expense) of the internal service funds is reported with governmental activities.	205,790
Change in Net Assets of Governmental Activities	$3,578,528

Source: City of Golden, Colorado, Comprehensive annual financial report, 2009

EXHIBIT 19-11

Statement of Net
Assets—Proprietary
Funds

CITY OF GOLDEN, COLORADO, STATEMENT OF NET ASSETS—PROPRIETARY FUNDS DECEMBER 31, 2009

	Business-Type Activities—Enterprise Funds		
	Water Fund	Wastewater Fund	Drainage Fund
Assets			
Current assets			
Cash and investments	$ 2,906,820	$ 703,780	$ 17,796
Accounts receivable	551,847	194,045	131,913
Inventory and prepaid expenses	19,239	—	—
Interfund receivable	500,000	1,519,197	—
Restricted cash and investments	464,500	—	176,183
Total current assets	4,442,406	2,417,022	325,892
Non-current assets			
Bond issuance costs (net of amortization)	234,215	—	57,415
Capital assets not being depreciated	19,471,594	—	461,649
Capital assets (net of accumulated depreciation)	31,605,107	5,739,712	13,166,854
Total non-current assets	51,310,916	5,739,712	13,685,918
Total assets	55,753,322	8,156,734	14,011,810
Liabilities			
Current liabilities			
Accounts payable	195,506	123,202	3,277
Accrued liabilities	56,516	9,094	1,173
Accrued interest payable	53,852	—	3,948
Interfund payable	—	—	500,000
Claims payable	—	—	—
Deferred revenue	—	—	—
Compensated absences, current portion	29,168	5,226	1,042
Bonds payable, current portion	805,000	—	250,000
Total current liabilities	1,140,042	137,522	759,440
Non-current liabilities			
Accrued compensated absences	87,243	47,030	9,375
Bonds payable, long-term portion (net of unamortized premium)	8,739,943	—	2,410,157
Total non-current liabilities	8,827,186	47,030	2,419,532
Total liabilities	9,967,228	184,552	3,178,972
Net Assets			
Invested in capital assets, net of related debt	41,531,758	5,739,712	10,968,346
Reserved for debt service	464,500	—	176,183
Unrestricted	3,789,836	2,232,470	(311,691)
Total net assets	$45,786,094	$7,972,182	$10,832,838

Source: City of Golden, Colorado, Comprehensive annual financial report, 2009.

within CAFR-required supplementary information. The statement or schedule must disclose the budgetary basis of accounting and include columns presenting the original budget, the final appropriated budget, and actual balances (on the budgetary basis) for the fiscal year. Variance columns are optional. Exhibit 19-14 presents the budgetary comparison statement for Golden, Colorado.

REQUIRED SUPPLEMENTARY INFORMATION Governments are required to supply supplementary information, including schedule(s) of funding progress of pension plans, schedule(s) of employer contributions to pension plans, budgetary comparison schedules for the general and special revenue funds, and information about infrastructure assets reported using the modified approach (if applicable).

EXHIBIT 19-11

Statement of Net Assets—Proprietary Funds (Continued)

	Fossil Trace Golf Course Fund	Community Center Fund	Total Non major Proprietary Funds	Totals 2009	Totals 2008	Governmental Activities—Internal Service Funds
	$ 215,323	$ 246,324	$ 595,028	$ 4,685,071	$ 4,713,015	$4,045,432
	15,666	28,271	14,727	936,469	1,126,334	677,612
	72,900	—	—	92,139	97,871	36,079
	—	—	—	2,019,197	2,119,197	—
	—	—	—	640,683	467,500	—
	303,889	274,595	609,755	8,373,559	8,523,917	4,759,123
	—	—	—	291,630	302,122	—
	2,024,661	182,890	208,754	22,349,548	22,108,551	—
	10,229,252	8,004,874	8,155,721	76,901,520	78,416,475	4,227,444
	12,253,913	8,187,764	8,364,475	99,542,698	100,827,148	4,227,444
	12,557,802	8,462,359	8,974,230	107,916,257	109,351,065	8,986,567
	28,305	54,833	5,044	410,167	939,113	74,359
	1,104	87,604	4,435	159,926	209,906	—
	—	—	—	57,800	69,338	—
	—	—	—	500,000	600,000	—
	—	—	—	—	—	677,236
	149,786	—	—	149,786	149,987	—
	5,190	6,394	1,863	48,883	29,168	—
	—	—	—	1,055,000	970,000	—
	184,385	148,831	11,342	2,381,562	2,967,512	751,595
	46,715	25,575	10,190	226,128	206,158	70,385
	—	—	—	11,150,100	11,991,427	—
	46,715	25,575	10,190	11,376,228	12,197,585	70,385
	231,100	174,406	21,532	13,757,790	15,165,097	821,980
	12,253,913	8,187,764	8,364,475	87,045,968	87,563,599	4,227,444
	—	—	—	640,683	467,500	—
	72,789	100,189	588,223	6,471,816	6,154,869	3,937,143
	$12,326,702	$8,287,953	$8,952,698	$94,158,467	$94,185,968	$8,164,587

NOTES TO THE FINANCIAL STATEMENTS The basic financial statements also include notes to the financial statements. The *GASB Codification* provides details regarding required CAFR note disclosure.[18] The purpose of the notes is to communicate information essential for fair presentation of the financial statements that is not displayed on the face of the financial statements. Given this, the notes are an integral part of the basic financial statements. The notes should focus on the primary

[18]*GASB Codification* Section 2300.103.

Statement of Revenues,
Expenses, and Changes
in Fund Net Assets—
Proprietary Funds

CITY OF GOLDEN, COLORADO, STATEMENT OF REVENUES, EXPENSES AND CHANGES IN FUND NET ASSETS PROPRIETARY FUNDS FOR THE YEAR ENDED DECEMBER 31, 2009

| | Business-Type Activities—Enterprise Funds | | |
	Water Fund	Wastewater Fund	Drainage Fund
Operating revenues			
Charges for services	$ 5,120,162	$1,370,846	$ 875,074
Miscellaneous	24,736	—	—
Total operating revenues	5,144,898	1,370,846	875,074
Operating Expenses			
Personnel services	1,296,071	452,393	82,117
Operating	2,121,063	1,137,181	149,657
Depreciation and amortization	1,096,978	211,208	365,903
Claims	—	—	—
Premiums	—	—	—
Total operating expenses	4,514,112	1,800,782	597,677
Operating income (loss)	630,786	(429,936)	277,397
Nonoperating revenues (expenses)			
Investment income	81,711	52,641	—
Investment expense	(499,760)	—	(90,437)
Gain (loss) on sale of capital assets	(1,834)	—	—
Total nonoperating revenues (expenses)	(419,883)	52,641	(90,437)
Income (loss) before transfers and capital contributions	210,903	(377,295)	186,960
Transfers in	6,100	4,000	—
Transfers (out)	(418,100)	(12,800)	(51,200)
Capital contributions	1,122,454	238,133	182,404
Change in net assets	921,357	(147,962)	318,164
Net assets, beginning	44,864,737	8,120,144	10,514,674
Net assets, ending	$45,786,094	$7,972,182	$10,832,838

Source: City of Golden, Colorado, Comprehensive financial report, 2009.

government—specifically, its governmental activities, business-type activities, major funds, and nonmajor funds in the aggregate.

INFRASTRUCTURE   The most controversial portion of *GASB Statement No. 34* regards capital assets, particularly infrastructure assets. Prior to the issuance of *GASB 34*, capital assets acquired by governmental funds (general governmental assets) were not capitalized and recorded as assets in governmental funds. They were treated as expenditures in the period of acquisition and also were recorded in a general fixed asset account group. (*GASB Statement No. 34* eliminated account groups.) Infrastructure assets, which are long-lived capital assets that are normally stationary in nature and include roads, bridges, drainage systems, and other public-domain capital assets, were not required to be reported in governmental financial statements. Depreciation was also optional. Under *GASB 34*, general governmental assets, including infrastructure assets, are capitalized and depreciated within the government-wide statements.

For many governments, the historical costs of infrastructure assets, such as roads and sidewalks, may be somewhat difficult to ascertain. Expenditures may not have been closely traced to infrastructure projects, because financial statement reporting of these assets was not required. Many infrastructure assets, such as sidewalks and streets, were constructed long ago, and costs are not readily available or may have little current economic meaning. Understandably, finance directors and preparers of governmental financial statements strongly opposed *GASB 34*'s infrastructure

EXHIBIT 19-12

Statement of Revenues, Expenses, and Changes in Fund Net Assets— Proprietary Funds (*Continued*)

Fossil Trace Golf Course Fund	Community Center Fund	Total Nonmajor Proprietary Funds	Totals		Governmental Activities— Internal Service Funds
			2009	2008	
$ 2,851,431	$1,542,138	$ 779,880	$12,539,531	$13,103,651	$5,241,811
85,848	663	168,223	279,470	168,370	280,842
2,937,279	1,542,801	948,103	12,819,001	13,272,021	5,522,653
1,130,194	1,068,491	367,114	4,396,380	4,325,301	801,714
920,008	832,383	407,879	5,568,171	5,962,536	1,160,766
722,583	318,855	603,588	3,319,115	2,918,404	862,841
—	—	—	—	—	2,055,441
—	—	—	—	—	972,329
2,772,785	2,219,729	1,378,581	13,283,666	13,206,241	5,853,091
164,494	(676,928)	(430,478)	(464,665)	65,780	(330,438)
21,098	5,466	13,141	174,057	346,310	94,091
—	—	—	(590,197)	(709,279)	—
(4,611)	(22,782)	—	(29,227)	1,494,223	(4,263)
16,487	(17,316)	13,141	(445,367)	1,131,254	89,828
180,981	(694,244)	(417,337)	(910,032)	1,197,034	(240,610)
500	445,400	98,500	554,500	565,996	477,600
(927,800)	(16,500)	(4,100)	(1,430,500)	(1,305,500)	(46,200)
2,361	153,619	59,560	1,758,531	524,434	15,000
(743,958)	(111,725)	(263,377)	(27,501)	981,964	205,790
13,070,660	8,399,678	9,216,075	94,185,968	93,204,004	7,958,797
$12,326,702	$8,287,953	$8,952,698	$94,158,467	$94,185,968	$8,164,587

reporting requirements. To alleviate the difficulty of complying with the new infrastructure requirements, the GASB allowed prospective reporting of general infrastructure assets during a transition period ending in 2005. From now on, governments with total assets in excess of $10 million will be required to retroactively report the estimated historical cost of infrastructure assets acquired or significantly improved or reconstructed in fiscal years ending after June 30, 1980.

GASB 34 also allows adoption of a modified approach for handling infrastructure assets that are part of a network. Under the modified approach, a government must maintain an up-to-date inventory of eligible infrastructure assets, perform condition assessments of the assets a minimum of every three years using a measurement scale, and estimate the annual amount necessary to maintain and preserve the eligible assets at a condition established by the government. If the infrastructure assets are shown to be preserved at the condition level determined by the government, all expenditures for these assets (except for additions and improvements, which should be capitalized) should be expensed in the period incurred, and depreciation will not be necessary.

COMBINING AND INDIVIDUAL FUND STATEMENTS In each of the government-wide and fund financial statements, column data often include the activity of several individual funds. Combining financial statements aggregate individual fund account balances and produce relevant totals by classification or activity (for example, governmental, business-type, type of program revenue). The combining statement total data correspond to an aggregated column on an associated financial statement. For

EXHIBIT 19-13

Statement of Cash
Flows—Proprietary
Funds

CITY OF GOLDEN, COLORADO, STATEMENT OF CASH FLOWS— PROPRIETARY FUNDS FOR THE YEAR ENDED DECEMBER 31, 2009

	Business-Type Activities—Enterprise Funds		
	Water Fund	Wastewater Fund	Drainage Fund
Cash Flows from Operating Activities			
Cash received from customers/users	$5,266,435	$1,417,224	$905,769
Cash paid to suppliers	(2,422,653)	(1,251,808)	(236,253)
Cash paid to employees	(1,255,340)	(447,093)	(82,204)
Cash paid to providers	—	—	—
Cash paid to claimants	—	—	—
Net cash provided (used) by operating activities	1,588,442	(281,677)	587,312
Cash Flows from Noncapital Financing Activities			
Transfers (to) other funds	(418,100)	(12,800)	(51,200)
Transfers (to) other funds	6,100	4,000	—
Interfund loan made	(500,000)	—	500,000
Repayment of interfund loan	600,000	—	(600,000)
Net cash provided (used) by noncapital financing activities	(312,000)	(8,800)	(151,200)
Cash Flows from Capital Financing Activities			
Purchase of capital assets	(1,109,925)	(325,080)	(148,155)
Proceeds from sale of capital assets	—	—	—
Proceeds from issuance of debt	—	—	3,024,291
Interest paid	(454,161)	—	(94,574)
Principal payments	(755,000)	—	(255,000)
Payments for bond issuance costs	—	—	(63,157)
Payments to escrow agent	—	—	(2,779,525)
Contributed capital	1,128,079	243,758	—
Net cash provided (used) by capital financing activities	(1,191,007)	(81,322)	(316,120)
Cash flows from investing activities			
Interest received	81,711	52,641	—
Net cash provided (used) by investing activities	81,711	52,641	—
Net increase (decrease) in cash and cash equivalents	167,146	(319,158)	119,992
Cash and cash equivalents, beginning	3,204,174	1,022,938	73,987
Cash and cash equivalents, ending	$3,371,320	$ 703,780	$ 193,979
Reconciliation of Operating Income (Loss) to Net Cash Provided (Used) by Operating Activities			
Operating income (loss)	630,786	$ (429,936)	$ 277,397
Adjustments to reconcile operating income (loss) to net cash provided (used) by operating activities			
Depreciation expense	1,073,165	211,208	360,161
Amortization expense	23,813	—	5,742
Changes in assets and liabilities			
Accounts receivable	121,537	46,378	30,695
Inventory and prepaid expenses	(5,911)	—	—
Accounts payable	(323,030)	(100,654)	(87,769)
Accrued liabilities	27,351	(13,973)	1,173
Claims payable	—	—	—
Deferred revenue	—	—	—
Accrued compensated absences	40,731	5,300	(87)
Total adjustments	957,656	148,259	309,915
Net cash provided (used) by operating activities	$1,588,442	$ (281,677)	$ 587,312
Non-cash Transactions			
Capital assets contributed by (to) other funds	$ (5,625)	$ (5,625)	$ 182,404

Source: City of Golden, Colorado, Comprehensive annual financial report, 2009.

EXHIBIT 19-13

Statement of Cash
Flows—Proprietary
Funds (*Continued*)

	Fossil Trace Golf Course Fund	Community Center Fund	Total Nonmajor Proprietary Funds	Totals 2009	Totals 2008	Governmental Activities—Internal Service Funds
	$2,929,379	$1,537,888	$ 951,970	$13,008,665	$13,070,365	$4,860,426
	(945,241)	(849,106)	(411,366)	(6,116,427)	(5,848,915)	(1,275,903)
	(1,119,877)	(1,069,359)	(407,757)	(4,381,630)	(4,264,226)	(803,271)
	—	—	—	—	—	(956,529)
	—	—	—	—	—	(1,721,085)
	864,261	(380,577)	132,847	2,510,608	2,957,224	103,638
	(927,800)	(16,500)	(4,100)	(1,430,500)	(1,305,500)	(46,200)
	500	445,400	98,500	554,500	565,996	477,600
	—	—	—	—	—	—
	—	—	—	—	—	—
	(927,300)	428,900	94,400	(876,000)	(739,504)	431,400
	(28,777)	—	(49,200)	(1,661,137)	(2,206,704)	(271,565)
	3,000	—	—	3,000	1,495,721	28,495
	—	—	—	3,024,291	—	—
	—	—	—	(548,735)	(639,319)	—
	—	—	—	(1,010,000)	(940,000)	—
	—	—	—	(63,157)	—	—
	—	—	—	(2,779,525)	—	—
	—	—	—	1,371,837	252,592	—
	(25,777)	—	(49,200)	(1,663,426)	(2,037,710)	(243,070)
	21,098	5,466	13,141	174,057	346,310	94,091
	21,098	5,466	13,141	174,057	346,310	94,091
	(67,718)	53,789	191,188	145,239	526,320	386,059
	283,041	192,535	403,840	5,180,515	4,654,195	3,659,373
	$ 215,323	$ 246,324	$ 595,028	$ 5,325,754	$ 5,180,515	$4,045,432
	$ 164,494	$ (676,928)	$(430,478)	$ (464,665)	$ 65,780	$ (330,438)
	722,583	318,855	603,588	3,289,560	2,890,182	862,841
	—	—	—	29,555	28,222	—
	(7,699)	(4,913)	3,867	189,865	(190,611)	(662,227)
	11,643	—	—	5,732	(13,628)	(99,337)
	(34,389)	20,387	(3,487)	(528,942)	122,104	—
	(2,487)	(37,110)	(24,935)	(49,981)	61,729	—
	—	—	—	—	—	334,356
	(201)	—	—	(201)	(11,045)	—
	10,317	(868)	(15,708)	39,685	4,491	(1,557)
	699,767	296,351	563,325	2,975,273	2,891,444	434,076
	$ 864,261	$ (380,577)	$ 132,847	$ 2,510,608	$ 2,957,224	$ 103,638
	$ 2,361	$ 153,619	$ 59,560	$ 386,694	$ 271,842	$ 15,000

EXHIBIT 19-14

Budgetary Comparison Statement

CITY OF GOLDEN, COLORADO, BUDGETARY COMPARISON STATEMENT, GENERAL FUND, FOR THE YEAR ENDED DECEMBER 31, 2009

	Budgeted Amounts			Variance with Final Budget Positive (Negative)	Actual 2008
	Original	Final	Actual		
Budgetary fund balance, beginning	$ 5,997,630	$ 5,997,630	$ 5,863,365	$ (134,265)	$ 5,585,200
Resources (inflows)					
Taxes	16,340,986	16,253,386	16,395,054	141,668	15,683,070
Licenses and permits	403,500	403,500	408,720	5,220	497,159
Intergovernmental	893,093	965,693	944,584	(21,109)	894,276
Charges for services	1,841,474	1,841,474	1,646,078	(195,396)	1,842,442
Fines and forfeitures	507,295	507,295	471,253	(36,042)	512,488
Investment income	138,411	138,411	138,671	260	177,917
Miscellaneous	618,598	605,348	667,994	62,646	771,286
Transfers in	80,050	108,300	108,300	—	78,296
Amounts available for appropriation	$26,821,037	$26,821,037	$26,644,019	$ (177,018)	$26,042,134
Charges to Appropriations (outflows)					
Current					
General government	4,952,840	5,287,140	4,474,053	813,087	4,192,895
Planning & economic development	1,473,113	1,249,263	1,372,685	(123,422)	1,390,685
Police	6,904,180	6,810,780	6,540,684	270,096	6,595,491
Fire	1,472,560	1,462,810	1,391,733	71,077	1,300,760
Public works	3,507,229	3,734,229	3,786,083	(51,854)	3,615,899
Parks and recreation	2,338,042	2,206,242	2,028,967	177,275	2,435,339
Transfers out	894,400	791,900	1,150,208	(358,308)	647,700
Total charges to appropriations	21,542,364	21,542,364	20,744,413	797,951	20,178,769
Budgetary fund balance, ending	5,278,673	5,278,673	5,899,606	620,933	5,863,365
Total Appropriations	$26,821,037	$26,821,037	$26,644,019	$ (177,018)	$26,042,134

Budget-to-GAAP Reconciliation

Resources (Inflows)

Actual amounts (budgetary basis) available for appropriation			$26,644,019		$26,042,134
Differences—budget to GAAP					
The fund balance at the beginning of the year is a budgetary resource but is not a current-year revenue for financial reporting purposes			(5,863,365)		(5,585,200)
Transfers from other funds are inflows of budgetary resources but are not revenue for financial reporting purchase			(108,300)		(78,296)
Total revenues as reported on the statement of revenues, expenditures, and changes in fund balances—governmental funds			$20,672,354		$20,378,638

Charges to Appropriations (Outflows)

Actual amount (budgetary basis) of total charges to appropriations			20,744,413		20,178,769
Differences—budget to GAAP					
Transfers to other funds are outflows of budgetary resources but are not expenditures for financial reporting purposes			(1,150,208)		(647,700)
Total expenditures as reported on the statement of revenues, expenditures and changes in fund balances—governmental funds			$19,594,205		$19,531,069

Source: City of Golden, Colorado, Comprehensive annual financial report, 2009.

example, see Exhibit 19-15 for the nonmajor enterprise funds of the City of Golden, Colorado. Individual fund balances are combined to arrive at totals that agree with the appropriate columns on the proprietary fund statement of net assets shown in Exhibit 19-11. The *GASB Codification* requires that comprehensive annual financial reports include combining financial statements; however, combining statements that detail the aggregation of nonmajor funds is optional.

EXHIBIT 19-15

Combining Statement—Nonmajor Enterprise Funds

CITY OF GOLDEN, COLORADO, COMBINING STATEMENT OF NET ASSETS NONMAJOR ENTERPRISE FUNDS DECEMBER 31, 2009

	Splash Aquatic Fund	Cemetery Operations Fund	Rooney Road Sports Complex Fund	Totals 2009
Assets				
Current Assets				
Cash and investments	$ 29,203	$ 48,159	$ 517,666	$ 595,028
Accounts receivable	344	7,068	7,315	14,727
Total current assets	29,547	55,227	524,981	609,755
Non-current assets				
Capital assets				
Capital assets (net of accumulated depreciation)	4,816,299	383,095	3,165,081	8,364,475
Total assets	4,845,846	438,322	3,690,062	8,974,230
Liabilities				
Current liabilities				
Accounts payable	3,460	1,559	25	5,044
Accrued liabilities	660	3,610	165	4,435
Compensated absences—current portion	—	1,863	—	1,863
Total current liabilities	4,120	7,032	190	11,342
Non-current liabilities				
Accrued compensated absences	1,807	7,452	931	10,190
Total liabilities	5,927	14,484	1,121	21,532
Net assets				
Invested in capital assets	4,816,299	383,095	3,165,081	8,364,475
Unrestricted	23,620	40,743	523,860	588,223
Total net assets	$4,839,919	$423,838	$ 3,688,941	$8,952,698

Source: City of Golden, Colorado, Comprehensive annual financial report, 2009.

Statistical Section

The final required section of a CAFR contains statistical tables with comparative data from several periods of time. The tables, which focus on social and economic data, financial trends, and the fiscal capacity of the government, include both accounting and nonaccounting information.

As you can well imagine, the CAFR of a large metropolitan government amounts to hundreds of pages of information. Although the preceding discussion has provided a brief description of CAFR contents, each CAFR is unique, especially in terms of its transmittal letter and MD&A presentation. Although it is not required, many governments also publish other information, such as Single Audit reports, with their annual CAFR.

Additional Reporting

In recent years, the GASB has suggested that governments supplement CAFR reporting with nonfinancial information that is deemed important to their citizens.[19] *Service efforts and accomplishment (SEA)* reporting is a form of performance measurement that provides more-complete information about an entity's performance than is found in the CAFR. SEA indicators are concerned with the *results* of services delivered by the government and the assessment of whether an entity is progressing toward stated goals. Governments gather information about the *outputs* and *outcomes* of the services they provide and the relationship between the use of resources of those outputs and outcomes. SEA indicators enable management and citizens to evaluate the manner and effectiveness with which a branch or agency of a political system functions, operates, or behaves in carrying out a given task.

---

[19]GASB *Suggested Guidelines for Voluntary Reporting SEA Performance Information.* Norwalk, CT 2010. See also the GASB SEA Web site at http://www.seagov.org.

SUMMARY

Accounting principles for state and local governmental units have been developed through the efforts of the Municipal Finance Officers Association and its committees and, more recently, the Governmental Accounting Standards Board. The *GASB Codification of Governmental Accounting and Financial Reporting Standards* provides GAAP for the financial statements of state and local governmental units. Twelve basic accounting principles from *Governmental Accounting and Financial Reporting Principles, Statement No. 1*, which are included in the *GASB Codification*, establish the objectives and underlying support for the accounting and reporting practices of state and local governments.

Governmental entities utilize fund accounting as a means of ensuring and demonstrating compliance with formal budgetary constraints. There are five governmental fund types, which generally follow the modified accrual basis of accounting and maintain a focus on current financial resources, and two proprietary fund types, which follow the accrual basis of accounting and maintain an economic resources measurement focus. Fiduciary fund types are also reported in governmental financial statements.

The formal financial report of a governmental unit is called a comprehensive annual financial report. A CAFR under *GASB Statement No. 34*, a statement that initiated major changes to governmental financial reporting, contains three major sections: introductory, financial, and statistical.

QUESTIONS

1. What organization provides accounting standards for state and local governmental units? What organization or organizations preceded this group?
2. What is the *GAAFR*? Who creates the *GAAFR*?
3. What are the characteristics of a government?
4. Why do governmental entities use fund accounting? How many funds might be used by a single governmental unit? How many fund types?
5. Distinguish between governmental funds, proprietary funds, and fiduciary funds. Which funds are classified as governmental funds?
6. List the five types of governmental funds. What are the primary distinctions among them?
7. What is the accounting equation for a governmental fund?
8. List the two types of proprietary funds. What distinguishes them from each other?
9. What is the accounting equation for a proprietary fund?
10. Why aren't fixed assets recorded in the accounts of a general fund? Where are they recorded?
11. What is the modified accrual basis of accounting? Which funds utilize the modified accrual basis of accounting?
12. What does *measurement focus* mean? What two focuses are used in governmental accounting? Which fund types use each?
13. What types of revenue do governments have? How do nonexchange transactions differ from exchange transactions?
14. How does the accounting treatment of a nine-month note payable differ from the accounting treatment of a five-year note payable within a governmental fund? Why?
15. Are interfund transfers expenditures? Expenses? Explain.
16. What is an appropriation? How can budgetary approval be arranged to give the legislative body maximum control over the budget? How can it be arranged to give the executive maximum flexibility?
17. List the required governmental fund and proprietary fund financial statements under *GASB 34*. On what basis of accounting are these statements prepared?
18. How do nonreciprocal transfers differ from reciprocal transfers?
19. List the authoritative documents available to financial statement preparers and auditors related to governmental accounting and financial reporting. Which is the most authoritative according to *GASB 55*?
20. Distinguish between the various types of interfund activity.
21. How does an expenditure differ from an expense? Identify the funds that report expenditures and those that report expenses.
22. What are the three sections of a CAFR? Briefly identify the contents of each section.
23. How do operational accountability and fiscal accountability differ? In what context are they used?

EXERCISES

E 19-1
Multiple choice

1. Which of the following items has the greatest GAAP authority under *SAS 69?*
   a *GASB implementation guides*
   b *Consensus positions of GASB's Emerging Issues Task Force*
   c *GASB statements and interpretations*
   d *FASB statements and interpretations*

2. The primary emphasis in accounting and reporting for governmental funds is on:
   a *Flow of current financial resources*
   b *Income determination*
   c *Capital transfers*
   d *Transfers relating to proprietary activities*

3. The term *appropriation,* as used in governmental accounting, is:
   a *A budget request*
   b *A commitment*
   c *An authorization to spend*
   d *An allotment*

4. Which of the following will not appear in financial statements prepared under *GASB 34?*
   a *Government-wide statements*
   b *Fund financial statements*
   c *Management's discussion and analysis*
   d *General long-term debt account group*

5. Ketchum County issues general obligation serial bonds to finance construction of a new high school. Which of the following funds are affected by the transaction?
   a *Special revenue fund*
   b *Capital projects fund and general fund*
   c *Capital projects fund, general fund, and debt service fund*
   d *Capital projects fund and debt service fund*

E 19-2
Multiple choice [AICPA adapted]

1. Depreciation expense accounts would likely be found in the
   a *General fund*
   b *Capital projects fund*
   c *Debt service fund*
   d *Enterprise fund*

2. The government-wide statements of a state government
   a *May not be issued separately from the comprehensive annual financial report*
   b *Are prepared on both the accrual and modified accrual bases of accounting*
   c *Include both governmental and proprietary funds*
   d *Contain more-detailed information regarding the state government's finances than is contained in the comprehensive annual financial report*

3. Under the modified accrual basis of accounting for a governmental unit, revenues should be recognized in the accounting period in which they
   a *Are earned and become measurable*
   b *Are collected*
   c *Become available and measurable*
   d *Become available and earned*

4. Authority granted by a legislative body to make expenditures and to incur obligations is the definition of an
   a *Appropriation*
   b *Allowance*
   c *Encumbrance*
   d *Expenditure*

5. An expense would be reported in which of the following funds?

  a   Special revenue funds
  b   Capital projects funds
  c   Enterprise funds
  d   Permanent funds

E 19-3
Multiple choice

1. Which of the following is considered an exchange transaction under *GASB 33?*

  a   A city receives a federal grant
  b   A bus driver collects bus fare from a rider
  c   Property taxes are collected from a homeowner
  d   An employer withholds state income tax from employee paychecks

2. One would not expect to find fixed asset accounts in the

  a   Governmental fund financial statements
  b   Proprietary fund financial statements
  c   Government-wide financial statements
  d   Financial statements of a governmental entity

3. The cash received from the sale of vehicles used by the sheriff's office should be recorded in

  a   The general fund
  b   The general fixed assets account group
  c   A capital projects fund
  d   A debt service fund

4. Which fund follows the modified accrual basis of accounting?

  a   General fund
  b   Special revenue fund
  c   Debt service fund
  d   All of the above

5. The governmental fund accounting model is as follows:

  a   Assets = Liabilities + Fund Balance
  b   Current Assets – Current Liabilities = Fund Balance
  c   Current Assets + Noncurrent Assets – Current Liabilities – Noncurrent Liabilities = Fund Balance
  d   Current Assets + Noncurrent Assets – Current Liabilities – Noncurrent Liabilities = Net Assets

E 19-4
Multiple choice

1. Which of the following is not a governmental fund?

  a   Special revenue fund
  b   Debt service fund
  c   Trust fund
  d   General fund

2. Which of these funds generally follows the accrual basis of accounting?

  a   General fund
  b   Internal service fund
  c   Debt service fund
  d   Special revenue fund

3 Which of the following funds will report fixed assets in the fund financial statements?

  a   General fund
  b   Special revenue fund
  c   Debt service fund
  d   None of the above

4. Which of the following funds would not be included in governmental fund financial statements?

  a   Debt service fund
  b   General fund
  c   Pension trust fund
  d   Permanent fund

5. Which of the following funds would be used to account for an activity that provides goods or services to other funds?

  a *General fund*
  b *Enterprise fund*
  c *Debt service fund*
  d *Internal service fund*

E 19-5
Multiple choice

1. Which of the following are eliminated from the financial statements under *GASB 34?*

  a *General long-term debt account group*
  b *General fixed asset account group*
  c *Both a and b*
  d *None of the above*

2. An expense would be reported in which of the following funds?

  a *General fund*
  b *Internal service fund*
  c *Debt service fund*
  d *Special revenue fund*

3. A component unit

  a *Is financially accountable to the primary government*
  b *Must be discretely presented in a primary government's CAFR*
  c *Is excluded from a primary government's CAFR*
  d *Is a legally separate organization for which the primary government is financially accountable*

4. Budgetary comparison information must be presented for the

  a *Debt service fund*
  b *General fund*
  c *Pension fund*
  d *Permanent trust fund*

5. Required supplementary information includes

  a *Schedule(s) of funding progress of pension plans*
  b *Schedule(s) of employer contributions to pension plans*
  c *Budgetary comparison schedules for the general and special revenue funds*
  d *All of the above*

E 19-6
Identification of fund type

Identify each of the fund types described.

1. A fund that is used to report assets held in a trustee capacity for others and that cannot be used to support the government's own programs.

2. A fund used to report any activity for which a fee is charged to external users for goods and services.

3. A fund used to account for all financial resources except those required to be accounted for in another fund.

4. A fund used to account for the accumulation of resources for, and the payment of, general long-term debt principal and interest.

5. A fund used to report resources that are legally restricted to the extent that only earnings, and not principal, may be used for purposes that support the reporting government's programs—that is, for the benefit of the government or its citizenry.

6. A fund used to account for the proceeds of specific revenue sources (other than trusts for individuals, private organizations, or other governments or for major capital projects) that are legally restricted to expenditures for specified purposes.

7. A fund used to report any activity that provides goods or services to other funds, departments, or agencies of the primary government and its component units, or to other governments, on a cost-reimbursement basis.

8. A fund used to account for financial resources to be used for the acquisition or construction of major capital facilities (other than those financed by proprietary funds or in trust funds for individuals, private organizations, or other governments).

E 19-7

Transaction analysis—governmental funds

Use transaction analysis to determine the effects of each of the following transactions in the general fund.

1. Salaries paid totaled $30,000. Additional salaries incurred, but not paid, totaled $2,500.

2. Levied property taxes of $100,000; $98,000 was collected during the year. The balance is expected to be uncollectible.

3. Borrowed $60,000 by issuing a nine-month note bearing interest at 7%.

4. Repaid the note plus interest when due.

5. Borrowed $600,000 by issuing bonds at par. The bonds mature in 10 years.

6. Purchased equipment costing $25,000 with cash.

7. Sold equipment at the end of its expected useful life. The equipment had no expected residual value when acquired (at a cost of $13,000), but it sold for $1,200.

8. Determined that it is probable that a lawsuit involving a claim against a department will result in a settlement of at least $50,000. However, it is not expected that any payments will be required for two years or more.

E 19-8

Transaction analysis—proprietary funds

Repeat Exercise 19-7, this time assuming that the transactions involve a proprietary activity instead of a general governmental activity.

E 19-9

Identification of fund type

For each of the following events or transactions, identify the fund or funds that will be affected.

1. The principal, interest, and related charges from a city's general long-term debt bond issue will be handled in a fund established for that purpose.

2. A wealthy citizen donates $10,000,000 for city park maintenance. The principal cannot be spent.

3. A wealthy citizen donates $10,000,000 for city park maintenance. The principal may be spent as needed.

4. A village collects cigarette taxes from vendors. The tax funds must be remitted to the state.

5. The city issued general obligation bonds at par to finance construction of a government office building.

E 19-10

Identification of fund type

For each of the following events or transactions, identify the fund or funds that will be affected.

1. The Board of County Commissioners approved the construction of a new town band shell.

2. A central computing center was established to handle the data processing needs of a municipality.

3. A local municipality provides water and sewer services to residents of nearby communities for a fee.

4. A village receives a grant from the state government. The funds are to be used solely for preserving wetlands.

5. Property taxes are levied by a city government.

E 19-11

Identification of fund type

For each of the following events or transactions, identify the fund or funds that will be affected.

1. A new city government establishes an employee pension program.

2. A utility department constructs a new building.

3. A truck is purchased for use at the centralized storage center.

4. A new fleet of police cars is purchased.

5. Property taxes are collected by a city government.

E 19-12

Identification of fund type and transaction analysis

The City of Sioux Falls entered into a number of transactions for the current fiscal year. Identify the fund or funds affected by each transaction and determine how each transaction will affect the accounting equation of the particular fund.

1. Sioux Falls paid salaries to general government employees, $95,000.

2. Sioux Falls purchased an automobile by issuing a $25,000, 8% note to the vendor. The purchase occurred at mid-year, and the note is a one-year note.

3. The city sold general fixed assets with an original cost of $300,000 for $30,000 at the end of their useful life. The use of the resources received is not restricted.

4. In the second fiscal year, the city repaid the principal and interest on the note issued in transaction 2 at the due date of the note.

5. "Profits" of $500,000 from the airport enterprise fund were transferred to the general fund of the city to subsidize general fund operations.

6. Interest income collected on Sioux Falls's general fund investments totaled $70,000 for the year.

E 19-13

Identification of fund type and transaction analysis

Perez County entered into a number of transactions for the current fiscal year. Identify the fund or funds affected by each transaction and determine how each transaction will affect the accounting equation of the particular fund.

1. Perez County issued $10 million of general obligation bonds at par to finance construction of a new county office building.

2. The county purchased a truck for a general governmental department. The cost of the truck, $22,000, was paid in cash.

3. The county-owned and -operated electric utility billed residents and businesses $500,000 for electricity sales.

4. The county paid $2 million to High Rise Construction Company during 2008 for work completed during the year.

5. The county paid general governmental employee salaries of $4,500. Another $500 of salaries accrued but has not been paid.

6. The county borrowed $7,500 on a six-month note to finance general operating costs of the government.

INTERNET ASSIGNMENT

1. Visit the GASB's Web site at *www.GASB.org*. Click on the Technical Issues icon and select Summaries/Status. What is the title of the most recently issued GASB standard? When was it issued? What is its effective date?

2. Locate the Web site for the municipality in which your college or university is located. Is the municipality's financial report available on the Web site? If so, review the CAFR and answer the following questions:

   a. How many governmental funds does the government have? List the name of one special revenue fund.

   b. Does the government have a capital projects fund? For what purpose was it created?

   c. How many enterprise funds does the government have? List the name of one enterprise fund.

   d. How many trust and agency funds does the government have? List the name of one such fund.

SELECTED READINGS

[1] *AICPA. State and Local Governmental, Audit and Accounting Guide*. New York: American Institute of Certified Public Accountants, 2007.

[2] Freeman, Robert J., Craig D. Shoulders and Gregory Allison. *Governmental and Non-Profit Accounting* (8th ed.). New York: Prentice Hall, 2006.

[3] Governmental Accounting Standards Board. *Codification of Governmental Accounting and Financial Reporting Standards*. Norwalk, CT: Governmental Accounting Standards Board, 2004.

[4] Governmental Accounting Standards Board. *SEA Performance Information*. Norwalk, CT: Governmental Accounting Standards Board, 2010.

[5] Governmental Accounting Standards Board. *Statement No. 34*, "Basic Financial Statements— and Management's Discussion and Analysis—for State and Local Governments." Norwalk, CT: Governmental Accounting Standards Board, 1999.

[6] Government Finance Officers Association of the United States and Canada. *Governmental Accounting, Auditing, and Financial Reporting*. Chicago: Municipal Finance Officers Association of the United States and Canada, 2005.

[7] National Council on Government Accounting. *Governmental Accounting and Financial Reporting Principles, Statement 1*. Chicago: Municipal Finance Officers Association of the United States and Canada, 1979.

[8] U.S. General Accounting Office. *Government Auditing Standards*. Washington, D.C.: Government Printing Office, 2007.

20 CHAPTER

Accounting for State and Local Governmental Units—Governmental Funds

LEARNING OBJECTIVES

1 Prepare journal entries to record transactions in governmental funds, including the new fund balance classifications.

2 Learn about accounting methods unique to government accounting: budgetary issues, encumbrance accounting, and interfund transactions.

3 Determine the appropriate governmental fund to be used.

4 Prepare governmental fund financial statements.

5 Convert governmental fund financial statements to government-wide financial statements.

Chapter 19 introduced accounting and financial reporting practices applicable to state and local governments. This chapter begins with a summary of recent changes to how we report fund balances and define governmental funds. It then continues the discussion of fund accounting by illustrating the proper accounting for governmental funds. It also provides examples of fund statements for governmental funds and outlines the process of converting the modified-accrual-basis financial information in the governmental fund statements into the accrual-basis information presented in the government-wide statements.

Recall that governmental funds include the general fund as well as special revenue, permanent, capital projects, and debt service funds. Every governmental entity has one general fund and may have zero, one, or many of each of the other four governmental funds. The general governmental activities included within governmental funds are accounted for in the same manner, regardless of specific fund type. This chapter reviews transactions in the general fund and each of the other four governmental funds so that you may recognize the different purpose of each governmental fund.

RECENT CHANGES TO GOVERNMENTAL FUND ACCOUNTING

LEARNING OBJECTIVES 1,2

As noted in the previous chapter, GASB Statement No. 34 (GASB 34) was a major change in governmental accounting and reporting. Perhaps the most significant change was that governmental funds essentially report financial statements on two bases of accounting with different goals for each reporting basis. The modified accrual basis focusing on current resources helps users assess budgetary compliance and fiscal accountability. The accrual basis focusing on all economic resources helps users assess long-term financial and operational accountability.

One area of inconsistent application of the GASB 34 reporting model was reporting of Fund Balance. There was also confusion about reserved vs. restricted fund balances in the governmental funds and government-wide statements, respectively. Issued in March 2009, *GASB Statement No. 54*, "Fund Balance Reporting and Government Fund Type Definitions" establishes five classifications of governmental fund balance listed in decreasing order of spending constraints:

- *Nonspendable fund balance*—amounts not in spendable form, such as inventories, or amounts that must be maintained, such as the principal of an endowment.

- *Restricted fund balance*—amounts can only be spent for the specific purposes stipulated by constitution, external resource providers, or through enabling legislation.

- *Committed fund balance*—amounts can only be spent for the specific purposes determined by a formal action of the government's highest level of decision-making authority.

- *Assigned fund balance*—amounts intended to be used by the government for specific purposes but do not meet the criteria to be classified as restricted or committed. In governmental funds other than the general fund, assigned fund balance represents the remaining amount that is not restricted or committed.

- *Unassigned fund balance*—the residual classification for the government's general fund and includes all spendable amounts not contained in the other classifications. In other funds, the unassigned classification should be used only to report a deficit balance resulting from overspending for specific purposes for which amounts had been restricted, committed, or assigned.

Governments are required to disclose information about the processes through which constraints are imposed on amounts in the committed and assigned classifications. They also must disclose their policies regarding how they determine the amounts in each classification that have been spent. The use of "reserved" and "unreserved" fund balance is no longer permitted for governmental funds. The new classifications are required for fiscal periods starting after June 15, 2010. GASB Statement No. 54 (GASB 54) also refined the definitions of the governmental funds as listed in Exhibit 19-3.

THE GENERAL FUND

Governments use the *general fund (GF)* to account for all unrestricted resources except those accounted for in a specific fund. In more descriptive terms, the general fund is the governmental fund used to account for the general operations of government, including the revenue received and the expenditures made in providing public goods and services to citizens. If a general-purpose government has only one fund accounting entity, that fund is a general fund. Recall that the general fund follows the modified accrual basis of accounting.[1]

ACCOUNTING FOR THE GENERAL FUND

This chapter uses the small town of Grantville to demonstrate accounting for the general fund. The postclosing trial balance of the Town of Grantville general fund at September 30, 2010, shows the following ledger account balances:

Debits	
Cash	$310,000
Taxes receivable—delinquent	150,000
Accounts receivable	30,000
Supplies inventory	60,000
Total debits	$550,000
Credits	
Allowances for uncollectible taxes—delinquent	$ 10,000
Vouchers payable	140,000
Note payable (short-term)	150,000
Fund balance – reserved	90,000
Fund balance – unreserved	160,000
Total credits	$550,000

---

[1]Governments may choose to record governmental fund transactions under the accrual basis of accounting and later adjust balances to the modified accrual basis for presentation in fund financial statements. This book presents the traditional fund accounting approach to accounting for governmental funds, whereby transactions in governmental funds are initially recorded on the modified accrual basis of accounting. Governments also may record transactions under both methods, thus having two sets of books throughout the year—one on the accrual basis and the other on the modified accrual basis. GAAP does not require a method for the internal record-keeping, but it does require both methods in a complete financial report.

Events for the town during the year October 1, 2010, to September 30, 2011, that involve the general fund include reclassifying fund balance to comply with GASB 54, recording an approved budget, accounting for revenues from various sources, accounting for expenditures with encumbrance controls, preparing year-end adjusting and closing entries, and preparing the fund financial statements.

Fund Balance Reclassification

This is the first year that The Town of Grantville implements the new fund balance classifications of GASB 54. Grantville determines that $60,000 is *unspendable* because it is tied up in inventory; $90,000 is *committed* because the town council voted at the September 15, 2010 council meeting to make the appropriation binding for next period;[2] and $100,000 is *unassigned*.

> *General Fund—Beginning Fund Balance Reclassification Entry*

Fund balance – unreserved	160,000	
Fund balance – reserved	90,000	
Fund balance – nonspendable		60,000
Fund balance – committed		90,000
Fund balance – unassigned		100,000

> To reclassify opening fund balances to comply with GASB 54.

The Budget

The Town of Grantville approved the following general fund budget for the fiscal year October 1, 2010, to September 30, 2011:

TOWN OF GRANTVILLE GENERAL
FUND BUDGET SUMMARY FOR THE YEAR
OCTOBER 1, 2010, TO SEPTEMBER 30, 2011

Revenue Sources	
Taxes	$2,075,000
Licenses and permits	205,000
Intergovernmental revenue	400,000
Charges for services	557,000
Fines and forfeitures	118,000
Investment income	100,000
Miscellaneous revenues	45,000
Total budgeted revenues	$3,500,000
Expenditures	
Current services	
General government	$ 477,500
Public safety	897,750
Highways and streets	825,000
Sanitation	525,000
Health and welfare	175,000
Recreation	270,000
Capital outlays	150,000
Total appropriations	$3,320,250
Other Financing Sources (Uses)	
Transfers out	115,000
Budgeted increase in fund balance	$ 64,750

The budgeted general fund activity includes revenue from various sources, expenditures, and a category of "other sources and uses" of working capital funds. Section 1100.112 of the *GASB Codification* addresses classification requirements for revenue and expenditure accounts.

---

[2]The government's policies will determine the classification of fund balance for prior period encumbrances, though it is possible they could be any three of the four expendable classes: restricted, committed, or assigned. Encumbrance accounting is illustrated later in this chapter.

As required, the town classifies budgeted general fund revenue items by source (taxes, licenses and permits, and so on). Budgeted expenditures are organized by character class (current services, capital outlays) and by function within each character category (general government, public safety). If desired, the town could further classify expenditures for each of the functions by specific departments or units within the organization (such as police department and fire department). It could also present expenditures in each of the organizational units in terms of the object of expenditure (such as personal services, supplies, and other services and charges). The classification scheme is an important part of operational control over expenditures, because most governmental entities limit expenditures within a functional or object category to the amount of the formal budget approval. Any excess requires administrative approval.

RECORDING THE BUDGET At the beginning of the fiscal year, the approved budget of Grantville is recorded. Although many business entities adopt and approve budgets, only governmental entities formally prepare journal entries to record the budget within the accounting records. The town makes the following general journal entry to record the budget in the accounts of the general fund.

General Fund—Budgetary Entry		
Estimated revenues	3,500,000	
Appropriations		3,320,250
Estimated other financing uses—transfers out		115,000
Fund balance – unassigned		64,750
To record the budget for the year October 1, 2010, to September 30, 2011.		

The entry records total estimated revenues, total appropriations, and estimated other financing uses in the general ledger and credits the budgeted excess to the fund balance-unassigned account. Some governments require budgeted revenues to exceed appropriations, resulting in a balanced budget.

T-accounts for all general fund transactions appear in Exhibit 20-1. Journal entry numbers correspond to entries in the T-accounts. The beginning balances in the T-accounts are obtained from the postclosing trial balance at September 30, 2010 on page 664.

SUBSIDIARY LEDGERS Although budgets may be approved in terms of broad categories, governments record details of the planned revenues (such as property taxes, sales taxes, and license revenue) and appropriations (such as police supplies, mayor's office expenses, and maintenance of the town hall) in subsidiary revenue and expenditure ledgers. Recording estimated revenues for individual items as debits in the subsidiary revenue ledger and recording actual revenue items as credits allows the outstanding subsidiary account balances during the year to reveal differences between actual and budgeted revenue for each item to date, as well as the final excess or deficiency at year-end. Similarly, recording appropriations as credits and recording actual expenditures or commitments for expenditures (encumbrances) as debits helps a government monitor expenditures. The account balances shown in the individual accounts of the subsidiary expenditure ledger represent unencumbered, unexpended appropriations (or amounts that remain to be spent) for each expenditure item. These subsidiary ledger techniques provide the means of achieving formal budgetary control over the items included in the approved budget. The financial statements or their notes will report budget compliance for the general and budgeted special revenue funds, as illustrated in Chapter 19.

Transactions and Interfund Activities for the Year

ACCOUNTING FOR PROPERTY TAXES Recall that under the modified accrual basis of accounting, revenues are generally recognized in the period in which they become measurable and available to finance expenditures of the period. Governments recognize property tax revenues, which are considered imposed nonexchange revenues under *GASB Statement No. 33*,[3] when taxpayers are billed for the amount of taxes levied, if the resources collected can be used in that period.

---

[3]The classifications from GASB 33 are summarized in Exhibit 19-5.

EXHIBIT 20-1

General Fund Transactions

Cash

Debit		Credit	
beg.	310,000	5,000	14)
2)	1,900,000	164,250	15)
5)	200,000	150,000	16)
6)	1,240,000	3,143,500	18)
Adj. bal.	3,650,000	3,462,750	
bal.	187,250		

Accounts receivable

Debit		Credit	
beg.	30,000	150,000	4)
4)	150,000		
Adj. bal.	180,000	180,000	
bal.	180,000		

Fund balance—unassigned

Debit		Credit	
	0	beg.	
	100,000	reclass-beg	
	64,750	bud.	
	10,000	reclass-end	
	174,750	Adj. bal.	
close 1	64,750	52,250	close 2
	64,750	227,000	bal.
		162,250	bal.

Revenues

Debit		Credit	
	0	beg	
	1,980,000	1)	
	100,000	4)	
	200,000	5)	
	1,240,000	6)	
	3,520,000	Adj. bal.	
close 2	3,520,000	3,520,000	

Estimated revenues

Debit		Credit	
beg.	0		
bud.	3,500,000	3,500,000	close 1
Adj. bal.	3,500,000		
bal.	0		

Taxes receivable—delinquent

Debit		Credit	
beg.	150,000	140,000	2)
Adj. 2	240,000	10,000	3)
Adj. bal.	390,000	150,000	
bal.	240,000		

Supplies inventory

Debit		Credit	
beg.	60,000	30,000	Adj. 1
13c)	60,000		
Adj. bal.	120,000	30,000	
bal.	90,000		

Fund balance—nonspendable

Debit		Credit	
	0	beg.	
	60,000	reclass-beg	
	30,000	reclass-end	
	90,000	Adj. bal.	
		90,000	bal.

Expenditures

Debit		Credit	
beg.	0		
7)	200,000		
10)	140,000		
14)	50,000		
17)	2,843,500		
Adj. 1	30,000		
Adj. bal.	3,263,500		
		3,263,500	close 2
		0	bal.

Appropriations

Debit		Credit	
	0	beg.	
	3,320,250	bud.	
close 1	3,320,250	3,320,250	Adj. bal.
		0	bal.

Allowance for u/c taxes—delinquent

Debit		Credit	
3)	10,000	10,000	beg.
		20,000	Adj. 2
		30,000	Adj. bal.
	10,000	20,000	bal.

Vouchers payable

Debit		Credit	
18)	3,143,500	140,000	beg.
		200,000	7)
		140,000	10)
		85,000	12b)
		60,000	13c)
		2,843,500	17)
	3,143,500	3,468,500	Adj. bal.
		325,000	bal.

Fund balance—committed

Debit		Credit	
	0	beg.	
reclass-end	40,000	90,000	reclass-beg
	40,000	90,000	Adj. bal.
		50,000	bal.

Expenditures—PY

Debit		Credit	
beg.	0		
12b)	85,000	85,000	Adj. bal.
		0	bal.

Estimated other financing uses

Debit		Credit	
	0	beg.	
	115,000	bud.	
close 1	115,000	115,000	Adj. bal.
		0	bal.

Allowance for u/c taxes—current

Debit		Credit	
		0	beg.
		20,000	1)
Adj. 2	20,000	20,000	Adj. bal.
		0	bal.

Taxes receivable—current

Debit		Credit	
beg.	0	1,760,000	2)
1)	2,000,000	240,000	Adj. 2
	2,000,000	2,000,000	Adj. bal.
		0	bal.

Deferred revenue

Debit		Credit	
		0	beg.
		50,000	4)
		50,000	Adj. bal.
		50,000	bal.

Reserve for encumbrances

Debit		Credit	
		0	beg.
9)	150,000	150,000	8)
12a)	90,000	90,000	11)
13b)	60,000	60,000	13a)
	50,000	50,000	13d)
	350,000	350,000	Adj. bal.
reclass-end	0	0	bal.

Other financing sources

Debit		Credit	
		0	beg
		45,000	14)
close 2	45,000	45,000	Adj. bal.
		0	bal.

Fund balance—unreserved

Debit		Credit	
reclass-beg	160,000	160,000	beg.
	160,000	160,000	Adj. bal.
		0	bal.

Notes payable

Debit		Credit	
16)	150,000	150,000	beg.
	150,000	150,000	Adj. bal.
		0	bal.

Encumbrances

Debit		Credit	
beg.	0		
8)	150,000	150,000	9)
11)	90,000	90,000	12a)
13a)	60,000	60,000	13b)
13d)	50,000	50,000	reclass-end
Adj. bal.	350,000	350,000	

Other financing uses

Debit		Credit	
beg.	0		
15)	164,250	164,250	close 2
Adj. bal.	164,250		
		0	bal.

Fund balance—reserved

Debit		Credit	
reclass-beg	90,000	90,000	beg.
	90,000	90,000	Adj. bal.
		0	bal.

The treasurer of Grantville records the following entry when property tax bills of $2,000,000 are mailed:

> *General Fund—Entry 1*
> Taxes receivable—current   2,000,000
>   Allowance for uncollectible taxes—current   20,000
>   Revenue   1,980,000
>   To record the property tax levy.

This entry assumes that 1 percent of property tax levies are not collectible and that the rest of the taxes will be collected either during the current year or within not more than 60 days thereafter. Therefore, it recognizes revenue for 99 percent of the amount billed. However, governments must record a liability, instead of revenue, for taxes not collected by year-end or within 60 days thereafter, because they are not "available." Likewise, governments record taxes collected in a period before they become legally available to finance expenditures as deferred taxes (or taxes collected in advance). Governments cannot recognize revenue until the period when it becomes legally available to cover expenditures.

Uncollectible taxes are not expenditures in governmental accounting; instead, they are revenue adjustments. Like accounts receivable, taxes receivable is a control account for individual amounts owed. The current designation for taxes receivable distinguishes current taxes receivable from taxes that are past due. Governments also reclassify any balances remaining in the "taxes receivable—current" and "allowance for uncollectible taxes—current" accounts after the due date for payment as "taxes receivable—delinquent" and "allowance for uncollectible taxes—delinquent." Note that the postclosing trial balance for the Town of Grantville's general fund at September 30, 2010, includes a debit account, "taxes receivable—delinquent," of $150,000 and a credit account, "allowance for uncollectible taxes—delinquent," of $10,000.

The town records collection of current property taxes of $1,760,000 and past-due taxes of $140,000 in the usual manner for receivables as follows:

> *General Fund—Entry 2*
> Cash   1,900,000
>   Taxes receivable—current   1,760,000
>   Taxes receivable—delinquent   140,000
>   To record collection of property taxes.

When specific delinquent property tax bills totaling $10,000 are determined to be uncollectible, the town writes them off with the following entry:

> *General Fund—Entry 3*
> Allowance for uncollectible taxes—delinquent   10,000
>   Taxes receivable—delinquent   10,000
>   To record write-off of uncollectible accounts.

DERIVED TAX REVENUES Derived tax revenues, such as sales and income taxes, require the merchant or taxpayer to determine the tax base. Under *GASB Statement No. 33*, governments recognize derived tax revenues when the underlying exchange (e.g., the sale) has occurred; however, within governmental funds, the resources must also be measurable and available. Thus, the taxing authority should accrue sales taxes collected and held by merchants at the end of the fiscal year if they will be remitted in time to pay liabilities of the current period.[4]

Governments recognize sales tax revenue when tax returns are received from merchants, and the taxes are expected to be remitted to the government by year-end (or within 60 days thereafter). The entry to record $150,000 in sales taxes reported on tax returns, of which three equal payments

---

[4]Although the 60-day rule applies to property tax revenue collections only, many governments choose to use the same criterion for other revenues. Thus, revenues collected within 60 days of year-end are considered available to meet the liabilities of the current period. *GASB 38* requires governments to disclose the length of time used to define "available" in the financial statement note that summarizes significant accounting principles.

are required to be remitted by the fifteenth day of October 2011, November 2011, and December 2011, is as follows:

General Fund—Entry 4

Accounts receivable	150,000	
Revenue		100,000
Deferred revenue		50,000

To record sales tax activity.

Because October 15, 2011 and November 15, 2011 fall within 60 days of the September 30, 2011 fiscal year-end, two of the payment amounts will be available to meet current obligations and thus should be recognized as income under the modified accrual basis of accounting. The amount scheduled to be received in December is recorded as deferred revenue.

REVENUE FROM OTHER SOURCES Unlike levied or derived taxes, other imposed nonexchange revenues, such as revenues from licenses, permits, fines, and the like, cannot be measured objectively until cash is actually received. Therefore, revenues from these sources are usually recognized when cash is collected. Thus, the town records the collection of fees ($200,000) from business licenses as follows:

General Fund—Entry 5

Cash	200,000	
Revenue		200,000

To record collection of business license fees.

Other revenues for the 2010–2011 fiscal year are recognized as cash is received. The amount in the following entry includes all revenue items not listed individually:

General Fund—Entry 6

Cash	1,240,000	
Revenue		1,240,000

To summarize other revenue items for the year.

Although the general ledger ordinarily includes only one revenue account, remember that a government has to record the detailed revenue sources individually in a subsidiary revenue ledger.

RECORDING EXPENDITURES Expenditures are decreases in the net financial resources of a governmental fund, as noted earlier. Under modified accrual accounting, we normally record expenditures when the related fund liability is incurred. Do not confuse this concept with the expense concept, in which proprietary funds recognize expenses when the funds use the related goods or services. Under modified accrual accounting, governmental funds recognize salaries, supplies, utilities, and fixed assets alike as expenditures when they incur the related liabilities.

When salaries ($200,000) are vouchered for payment (that is, a payroll document is prepared and approved), the town records the following general fund entry:

General Fund—Entry 7

Expenditures	200,000	
Vouchers payable		200,000

To record accrual of salaries.

ACCOUNTING FOR ENCUMBRANCES The law limits expenditures for each period, as measured on a government's budgetary basis, to those for which appropriations have been made. Thus, it is extremely important to keep expenditures within authorized levels. Approving expenditures without considering outstanding purchase orders or unperformed contracts could result in overspending appropriations. For example, assume that total appropriations for the year exceed actual expenditures to date by $4,000 and that an unknowing employee approves an additional equipment purchase for $3,000. If $2,000 worth of supplies are already on order and expenditures are made for both the equipment and the supplies, actual expenditures for the period will exceed appropriations by $1,000. Encumbrance accounting helps prevent this type of situation by maintaining a running total of outstanding purchase commitments. *Encumbrance* means "commitment," and encumbrance accounting records commitments made for goods on order and for unperformed contracts in order to provide additional control over expenditures.

During the year, the town orders snow-removal equipment expected to cost $150,000. Grantville makes the following encumbrance entry *at the time the purchase order is placed* to recognize a commitment to pay for the equipment when it is received:

> *General Fund—Entry 8*
> Encumbrances   150,000
>   Reserve for encumbrances   150,000
>   To record a purchase order for $150,000 of snow-removal
>   equipment.

This information helps prevent overspending because encumbrances can be deducted from unexpended appropriations to determine unencumbered appropriations (that is, maximum additional authorizations):

Appropriations (authorized expenditures)	$ X
Less: Expenditures to date	Y
Unexpended appropriations	X–Y
Less: Encumbrances (commitments for expenditures)	Z
Unencumbered appropriations	$X–Y–Z

The remaining expenditure authority for the budgetary period appears in the amount of unencumbered appropriations.

When the snow-removal equipment is received, Grantville reverses the entry recording the encumbrance:

> *General Fund—Entry 9*
> Reserve for encumbrances   150,000
>   Encumbrances   150,000
>   To reverse the encumbrance entry for snow-removal equipment.

The entry to record the receipt of the equipment is unaffected by the encumbrance entries and reflects the actual amount of the invoice. Assuming that the actual cost of the equipment purchased is $140,000, the town records the expenditure as follows:

> *General Fund—Entry 10*
> Expenditures   140,000
>   Vouchers payable   140,000
>   To record the purchase of snow-removal equipment.

As noted in the transaction analysis in the previous chapter, the acquisition of fixed assets (such as the snow-removal equipment) by a governmental fund decreases net assets (working capital) and the fund balance. Therefore, under the modified accrual basis of accounting, we do not record fixed assets as assets in the general fund, and they will not appear in the fund statements; however, we maintain fixed asset records and include governmental fund fixed assets in the government-wide statements, which we prepare on the accrual basis of accounting. Thus, fixed assets are one of the reconciling items between the fund financial statements and the government-wide financial statements.

Note that the amount of the encumbrance was an estimate of the actual cost, which was $10,000 less than the estimate. Like formal budgetary accounting, encumbrance accounting does not affect the recording of actual transactions and events.

If a governmental unit does not spend the full amount of an appropriation during the period covered by an appropriation, a question arises about whether the unexpended portion can be carried over as authorization for expenditures in the succeeding year. Although laws of the governmental unit will cover this matter, a common position is that all appropriations lapse at the end of the year for which they are made, with the exception of committed appropriations (that is, encumbrances outstanding), which can continue to serve as authorizations for items on order or under contract.

Prior to GASB 54, total expenditures for the period and outstanding encumbrance amounts at fiscal year end were closed to fund balance at year-end while reserve for encumbrance credits remained in the accounting records as reservations of fund balance within the governmental fund statements. Note that the 2010 postclosing trial balance for the Town of Grantville at the beginning of the chapter includes a credit account, "Fund balance—reserved," of $90,000. This account represents a commitment of fund balance to appropriations from a prior fiscal period. The new classifications from GASB 54 require the government to be more specific about the level of constraints and the end of period reports must move the amounts from reserved and unreserved fund balance to fund balance classified as either nonspendable, restricted, committed, assigned or unassigned.

Grantville has a long tradition of using encumbrance accounting and decides to keep its record-keeping entries as similar to pre-GASB 54 methods as possible. Thus, it decides to continue recording all initial encumbrances as in entry 8 with a debit to Encumbrances and a credit to Reserve for encumbrances. At year-end, any encumbrances still open will be closed with a reversing entry debiting Reserve for encumbrances and crediting Encumbrances. A final reclassification entry will be done for all fund balance categories based on an analysis of the spending constraints at year end. This bookkeeping method retains the useful internal control aspects of encumbrance accounting while also improving external reporting to outsiders.[5]

For those encumbrances that were closed at the end of the year and for which the legal and accounting policies allow them to be paid in the subsequent year, such as the $90,000 in the opening trial balance, Grantville reinstates the encumbrance:

> *General Fund—Entry 11*
> | | | |
> |---|---|---|
> | Encumbrances | 90,000 | |
> | Reserve for encumbrances | | 90,000 |
> | To reinstate the prior period encumbrance. | | |

The above entry would be done at the beginning of every fiscal period.

In October 2010, Grantville receives the equipment that was ordered in the previous fiscal year and for which an encumbrance of $90,000 had been reinstated. If the actual invoice is $85,000, the entry to record receipt of the equipment is as follows:

> *General Fund—Entry 12a*
> | | | |
> |---|---|---|
> | Reserve for Encumbrances | 90,000 | |
> | Encumbrances | | 90,000 |
> | To reverse the encumbrance upon receipt of equipment. | | |

> *General Fund—Entry 12b*
> | | | |
> |---|---|---|
> | Expenditures—prior year | 85,000 | |
> | Vouchers payable | | 85,000 |
> | To record receipt of equipment ordered during the prior year and chargeable against the prior year's budget. | | |

---

[5]As of this writing, few governments have implemented GASB 54 so it is unclear what the prevailing record-keeping approach will become. Governments that wish to use the new fund balance categories during the fiscal period might quit using "reserve for encumbrances" altogether and instead directly credit and debit the appropriate classes of fund balance depending on the level of spending constraints.

SUPPLIES Within governmental funds, a government may treat supply acquisitions as expenditures either when purchased (purchases method) or when used (consumption method), as long as it reports *significant* amounts of inventory in the balance sheet.[6] Although the consumption method is similar to the manner in which commercial businesses record supplies, the purchases method better allows for comparison of expenditures and appropriations. Thus, if a government's annual appropriations include all inventory acquisitions for the period, the government will likely select the purchases method. Under the purchases method, a government with significant inventory balances at year-end will recognize the balances as assets in the fund balance sheet and establish an accompanying increase in fund balance-nonspendable to reflect the fact that the supply amount is not an available financial asset.

Under the consumption method, which is preferred by the GASB, we record the process of acquiring supplies as follows:

General Fund—Entry 13a		
Encumbrances	60,000	
Reserve for encumbrances		60,000
To record the purchase order for operating supplies.		
General Fund—Entry 13b		
Reserve for encumbrances	60,000	
Encumbrances		60,000
To reverse the encumbrance entry upon receipt of the supplies.		
General Fund—Entry 13c		
Supplies inventory	60,000	
Vouchers payable		60,000
To record receipt of operating supplies.		

Depending on their policies, governments may make an entry in the middle of the period to increase fund balance-nonspendable when supplies are acquired and reduce fund balance-nonspendable when supplies are consumed. Grantville chooses instead to make year-end reclassification entries to fund balance when it adjusts inventory and expenditures for the amount consumed.

When an additional $50,000 of supplies is ordered, the entry is:

General Fund—Entry 13d		
Encumbrances	50,000	
Reserve for encumbrances		50,000
To record encumbrances for a purchase order for supplies.		

These supplies have not been received at year-end, September 30, 2011.

CAPITAL LEASE Lease agreements of state and local governments fall under the provisions of *FASB Statement No. 13*, "Accounting for Leases," as amended and interpreted by *NCGA Statement No. 5*, "Accounting and Financial Reporting Principles for Lease Agreements of State and Local Governments," and by *GASB No. 13*, "Accounting for Operating Leases with Scheduled Rent Increases." A lease agreement that is financed from general government resources must be accounted for under governmental fund accounting principles. (See *GASB Codification*, Section L20.)

When governments use capital leases to acquire general fixed assets, the governmental fund acquiring the general fixed asset records an expenditure and an other financing source, as if long-term debt had been issued (*GASB Codification*, Section L20.115).

---

[6]*GASB Codification* Section 1600.123.

The Town of Grantville enters into a general government capital lease for a fixed asset with an initial down payment of $5,000 and a present value of minimum lease payments of $50,000 and records the following entry:

> *General Fund—Entry 14*
>
> | Expenditures | 50,000 | |
> |---|---|---|
> | Cash | | 5,000 |
> | Other financing sources—capital lease | | 45,000 |

At the same time, the town notes a liability (capital lease payable) in the general long-term debt account records for the amount remaining due ($45,000) and adds an asset to the general fixed asset account records at the present value of the minimum lease payments determined by *FASB 13* criteria ($50,000). The asset and liability, as well as associated depreciation, will appear in the government-wide financial statements; however, only an expenditure and other financing source appear in the governmental fund statements. The town may record future capital lease payments as expenditures of principal and interest in the general fund or transfer resources to the debt service fund, which will recognize the expenditures. The notes to the financial statements disclose minimum lease payments for each of the following five years and in five-year increments thereafter.

INTERFUND TRANSACTIONS During the year, the general fund transfers funds to three other governmental funds. (The transactions are covered from the perspectives of the other funds later in this chapter.) The town transfers a total of $50,000 to establish a special revenue fund balance, $100,000 to help finance a capital project, and $14,250 to the debt service fund to finance general long-term debt payments. (Note that the $50,000 transfer was not appropriated in the general fund budget and therefore will require administrative approval.) A summary entry for these transfers is as follows:

> *General Fund—Entry 15*
>
> | Other financing uses—nonreciprocal transfer to town hall capital project fund (CPF) | 100,000 | |
> |---|---|---|
> | Other financing uses—reciprocal transfer to special revenue fund (SRF) | 50,000 | |
> | Other financing uses—nonreciprocal transfer to debt service fund (DSF) | 14,250 | |
> | Cash | | 164,250 |
> | To record transfers to town hall CPF, the SRF, and the DSF. | | |

This entry recognizes slight differences between the interfund transfers. *GASB 34* distinguishes between reciprocal and nonreciprocal transfers. **Reciprocal transfers** are loans for which a fund expects repayment, whereas **nonreciprocal transfers** represent flows of assets that do not require repayment. Furthermore, *GASB Statement No. 38,* "Certain Financial Statement Note Disclosures," requires note disclosure of significant transfers that are considered nonroutine or are inconsistent with the activities of the fund making the transfer.[7] The transfers in the previous entry include nonreciprocal transfers to the capital projects and debt service funds and a reciprocal transfer (loan) to a special revenue fund. Each of these transfers is considered routine and consistent with the activities of the general fund.

OTHER TRANSACTIONS FOR THE YEAR The short-term note payable that was outstanding at September 30, 2010, becomes due and is paid:

> *General Fund—Entry 16*
>
> | Note payable | 150,000 | |
> |---|---|---|
> | Cash | | 150,000 |

---

[7]*GASB Codification*, Section 2300.120–121.

Here is a summary entry for the remainder of the various expenditures throughout the year:

General Fund—Entry 17

Expenditures	2,843,500	
Vouchers payable		2,843,500

Summary entry for accrual of salaries, purchase of supplies, and other expenditures.

General Fund—Entry 18

Vouchers payable	3,143,500	
Cash		3,143,500

To record payment of vouchers during the year in summary form.

Year-End Procedures

ADJUSTING ENTRIES   If supplies with a historical cost of $90,000 are on hand at the balance sheet date, the town needs to make a $30,000 adjusting entry under the consumption method of accounting for inventory balances as follows: $60,000 beginning balance + $60,000 purchased − $90,000 remaining. (Under the purchases method, the town would adjust supplies inventory and fund balance-nonspendable.)

General Fund—Adjusting Entry 1

Expenditures	30,000	
Supplies inventory		30,000

To adjust the supplies inventory and supplies expenditures accounts using consumption method.

Assume that uncollected taxes on September 30, 2011, are past due but will be collected within 60 days of year-end.[8] Accordingly, the $240,000 taxes receivable—current and the $20,000 allowance for uncollectible taxes—current are reclassified as delinquent. The entry for this reclassification is as follows:

General Fund—Adjusting Entry 2

Taxes receivable—delinquent	240,000	
Allowance for uncollectible taxes—current	20,000	
Taxes receivable—current		240,000
Allowance for uncollectible taxes—delinquent		20,000

To reclassify past-due taxes receivable as delinquent.

By year-end, Grantville created accounting policies related to fund balance classifications that were approved by the Council. First, all open encumbrances and the related reserves are closed via reversal. Second, all of the open encumbrances are analyzed for the level of spending constraints. The Council approved a default policy where end of period encumbrances constitute "commitments" unless otherwise acted upon by the Council. Finally, all of the fund balance accounts are reviewed for possible adjustments and a reclassification entry is made to adjust the fund balance accounts to the proper classification—the unassigned category is the plug account.

Grantville needs to make two fund balance adjustments. The first is to update the nonspendable category for the $30,000 increase in inventory. The second is to update the committed category for the $40,000 decrease in open encumbrances at the end of the period (remember the

---

[8]If the taxes are not expected to be collected within 60 days of year-end, the revenue would be reclassified as deferred revenue because it would not be available to meet current obligations.

outstanding encumbrances at the beginning of the fiscal year are $90,000 and the outstanding encumbrances at the end of the fiscal year are $50,000). Note the open encumbrance for $50,000 at the end of the year is represented by the post-closing balance of $50,000 in fund balance—committed from the commitment to purchase supplies in entry 13d. This amount will be classified as committed rather than nonspendable because the supplies have not yet been delivered.

General Fund—Ending Fund Balance Reclassification Entry

Reserve for encumbrances	50,000	
Fund balance—committed	40,000	
Encumbrances		50,000
Fund balance—nonspendable		30,000
Fund balance—unassigned		10,000

To reverse end of year encumbrances and adjust related fund balance classifications.

Grantville's adjusted general fund trial balance at September 30, 2011, includes the following accounts and balances:

Debits	
Cash	$ 187,250
Taxes receivable—delinquent	240,000
Accounts receivable	180,000
Supplies inventory	90,000
Estimated revenues	3,500,000
Expenditures	3,263,500
Expenditures—prior year	85,000
Other financing uses	164,250
Total debits	$7,710,000
Credits	
Allowance for uncollectible taxes—delinquent	$ 20,000
Vouchers payable	325,000
Deferred revenue	50,000
Fund balance—nonspendable	90,000
Fund balance—committed	50,000
Fund balance—unassigned	174,750
Appropriations	3,320,250
Revenues	3,520,000
Estimated other financing uses—transfers out	115,000
Other financing sources	45,000
Total credits	$7,710,000

CLOSING ENTRIES By year-end, the budgetary accounts will have served their purpose and must be closed. The most direct method of closing budgetary accounts is to reverse the original entry used to record the budget. At September 30, 2011, Grantville could close its accounts as follows:

General Fund—Closing Entry 1

Appropriations	3,320,250	
Estimated other financing uses—transfers out	115,000	
Fund balance—unassigned	64,750	
Estimated revenues		3,500,000

To close the budgetary accounts.

The town closes actual revenues and expenditures directly to the fund balance-unassigned account. The adjusted trial balance shows that Grantville had revenue of $3,520,000, expenditures of

$3,263,500 for the current year and $85,000 for the prior year, other financing sources of $45,000, and other financing uses of $164,250 at September 30, 2011. The entry to close these accounts is as follows:

General Fund—Closing Entry 2		
Revenues	3,520,000	
Other financing sources—capital lease (OFS)	45,000	
Expenditures		3,263,500
Expenditures-prior year		85,000
Other financing uses (OFU)—nonreciprocal transfer to town hall CPF		100,000
Other financing uses—reciprocal transfer to SRF		50,000
Other financing uses—nonreciprocal transfer to DSF		14,250
Fund balance—unassigned		52,250
To close revenues, expenditures, and OFS/OFU accounts.		

This entry reveals that actual revenues and other financing sources exceeded expenditures and other financing uses by $52,250, which is the change in fund balance shown later in Exhibit 20-3.

LEARNING OBJECTIVE **3**

Special Revenue Funds

A *special revenue fund (SRF)* is the entity that a government uses to account for the proceeds of specific revenue sources (other than resources for permanent funds, major capital projects, or debt service on general long-term debt) that are restricted by law or administrative action to expenditures for specified purposes. Although a government has only one general fund, it can have many special revenue funds, or none at all. If specific revenue sources are earmarked for education, the government may use a special revenue education fund to account for the earmarked resources.[9] Similarly, if a city receives state or federal funds specifically designated for highway maintenance, the government may create an SRF to account for such fund resources.

Governments account for earmarked revenues in separate special revenue funds to show compliance with legal or administrative requirements. GASB 54 requires that a SRF fund balance is classified as nonspendable, restricted, committed or assigned. The fund balance cannot be classified as unassigned in an SRF, unless there is a deficit. Outside of the need to separate earmarked revenue sources and the limited use of unassigned fund balance, there is no essential difference between an SRF and a general fund. Indeed, if a special revenue fund is not legally or contractually required, governments have the option of accounting for a special revenue source in the general fund. Both types of funds are governmental funds, use the modified accrual basis for fund statements, and typically integrate their budgets into their accounting systems. Because the accounting requirements for special revenue funds are essentially the same as for a general fund, this chapter illustrates only special revenue fund entries used to record grant proceeds.

GRANTS Governments often receive grants from other governments or private sources. For example, the federal government provides grant funds for public safety at the local level, and private organizations donate grant funds for senior citizen activities. If the grant funds are restricted to a specific purpose other than a capital acquisition, they will usually be accounted for in a special revenue fund. Grant revenues can be recognized when all eligibility requirements set forth in the grant contract have been met, if the funds are available to meet current liabilities. If the grant funds are disbursed to the government prior to the eligibility requirements having been met, they must be accounted for as deferred revenue.

In July 2011, the state awards a highway beautification grant of up to $50,000 to the Town of Grantville for the purchase and placement of trees on the major highway within town jurisdiction. Because the grant funds are not paid to the town until after approved expenditures have been incurred, the general fund "loans" cash of $50,000 to the special revenue fund. (Recall the interfund

---

[9]GASB 54 clarifies that GAAP does not require the use of specific funds for specific activities or specific revenues (paragraph 110). Thus, some governments may record specific revenues in the General Fund and some governments may record multiple revenue sources in a single SRF. GAAP provides flexibility for preparers to best communicate their financial activities and position.

transfer entry in the general fund.) During July and August, the town incurs $38,000 in approved expenditures and records the following entries in a special revenue fund:

Special Revenue Fund—Highway Beautification
Cash	50,000	
Other financing sources—reciprocal transfer from GF		50,000
To record a transfer of cash from the general fund.		

Special Revenue Fund—Highway Beautification
Expenditures	38,000	
Vouchers payable		38,000
To record expenditures related to highway beautification.		

Special Revenue Fund—Highway Beautification
Accounts receivable—grant	38,000	
Grant revenue		38,000
To recognize grant revenue related to approved grant expenditures.		

Note that the town recognizes revenue and a receivable equal to the amount of acceptable expenditures, because the state will reimburse Grantville the $38,000 of approved expenditures. This amount is now measurable and should be available soon enough to meet current obligations.

In July 2011, the Town of Grantville receives $20,000 from the state to be used for police and fire officer training sessions on the proper installation of child car seats. The town records the following entry:

Special Revenue Fund—Officer Training
Cash	20,000	
Deferred revenue		20,000
To record the receipt of grant funds from the state.		

When expenditures have been incurred for the training sessions in the amount of $18,500, the entry is as follows:

Special Revenue Fund—Officer Training
Expenditures	18,500	
Vouchers payable		18,500
To record expenditures for an officer training program.		

Special Revenue Fund—Officer Training
Deferred revenue	18,500	
Grant revenue		18,500
To recognize grant revenue.		

If additional training will take place in the time span identified in the grant agreement (if any), then the special revenue fund can remain open. If the town has completed all training related to the grant's purpose and will not spend the remaining $1,500, the town will return the money to the state and close the special revenue fund.

At the end of the year, the town will prepare closing entries for special revenue fund revenues and expenditures (including encumbrances, if any), as well as budgetary funds, in the same manner as was illustrated for the general fund earlier in the chapter.

PERMANENT FUNDS

GASB 34 created a new governmental fund category, permanent funds, for nonexpendable resources set aside for support of a government's programs or citizenry. *Permanent funds (PF)* typically account for contributions for which the grantor specifies that a principal amount must be maintained but for which interest accumulation or asset appreciation, or both, are to be used for a specified purpose. (Such resources were previously referred to as nonexpendable trust funds.) In contrast, if funds are expendable (that is, they can be spent), a government accounts for them in a special revenue fund; or, if the contribution benefits parties external to the government, it should be accounted for in a private-purpose trust fund.

In April 2011, the Town of Grantville receives a gift of $500,000 in bonds. The 5 percent bonds pay interest semiannually in September and March. The contributor wants to ensure that the seal exhibit at the town zoo is maintained for years to come. He instructs that the principal shall be maintained, but all interest income and asset appreciation may be used for the benefit of the seal exhibit. During the year, the town receives an interest installment and incurs $3,000 in approved expenditures. The town makes the following entries in a permanent fund:

Permanent Fund—Seal Exhibit		
Investments—bonds	500,000	
Revenues—additions to permanent		
endowments		500,000
To record the receipt of a permanent endowment.		
Permanent Fund—Seal Exhibit		
Cash	12,500	
Revenues—investment income—interest		12,500
To record the receipt of interest ($500,000 × 5% × ½ year)		
Permanent Fund—Seal Exhibit		
Expenditures	3,000	
Cash		3,000
To record allowable expenditures.		

The town may constrain the spending of the expendable interest in the permanent fund until the funds are used for the seal exhibit, or it may transfer the expendable funds to a special revenue fund (or the general fund); however, the interest must be earmarked for the seal exhibit with an appropriate classification of fund balance as restricted due to the external resource provider.

According to *GASB Statement No. 31*, "Accounting and Financial Reporting for Certain Investments and for External Investment Pools," governments should record investments with determinable fair values at fair value. Thus, if the fair value of the bonds, excluding accrued interest, had changed, the town would have made an entry to reflect the fair market value of the bonds. The value of the bonds in this example remained unchanged.

At the end of the year, the town will close the permanent fund's revenues and expenditures (including encumbrances, if any), as well as budgetary funds, in the same manner as was illustrated for the general fund earlier in the chapter.

CAPITAL PROJECTS FUNDS

Governments account for the acquisition of most general fixed assets from expenditures of annual appropriations in the general fund or special revenue funds; however, *major*[10] general fixed assets are seldom financed through appropriations of these funds. The purpose of *capital projects funds (CPF)* is to account for resources segregated for the acquisition or construction of capital facilities or other capital assets other than those financed by trust and proprietary funds. Typical sources of financing include the proceeds of bond issues, grants and shared revenues, transfers from other funds, and contributions from property owners.

Capital projects funds are governmental funds that account for working capital to be used for general governmental capital projects. Capital projects funds use modified accrual accounting and revenue and expenditure accounts. Governments use encumbrance accounting procedures to account for commitments made to contractors and for material and supply orders. Ordinarily, a governmental unit will create a separate CPF to account for each significant capital project that has been legally authorized. Once created, a CPF exists for the life of the project. Capital projects funds typically do not use formal budgetary accounting unless numerous capital projects are financed through the same fund or facilities are being constructed with the governmental unit as the primary contractor.

The next section illustrates the accounting and reporting for a CPF during a two-year construction period.

---

[10]GASB 54 changed the definition of capital projects funds and removed the requirement that the capital expenditures be for "major" projects. Capital projects funds may now be used for any capital facilities or other capital assets.

Accounting for a Capital Projects Fund

The Town of Grantville authorizes an addition to the town hall on December 15, 2010, in the amount of $1,000,000. Financing for the project consists of $500,000 from a 6.5 percent serial bond issue, $400,000 from a federal grant, and $100,000 from the general fund. Transactions and events during the life of the project are as follows:

2010–2011 Fiscal Year

1. The town transfers $100,000 from the general fund to the town hall addition capital projects fund (a CPF created to account for the town hall construction).
2. Planning and architect's fees are paid in the amount of $40,000.
3. The contract is awarded to the lowest bidder for $950,000.
4. The bonds are sold for $502,000 (at a premium of $2,000).
5. The amount of the premium is transferred to the debt service fund.
6. The construction is certified to be 50% complete, and a bill for $475,000 is received from the contractor.
7. Contract payable, less a 10% retained percentage, is paid.
8. The books are closed and financial statements are prepared.

2011–2012 Fiscal Year

9. The amount due from the federal grant is received.
10. Construction is completed and the contractor is paid.
11. Closing entries are recorded.
12. Remaining cash is transferred to the GF.

CREATION OF THE CPF When the town hall addition CPF is created, the town makes a memorandum entry in the CPF noting the $1,000,000 authorization.

> *Capital Projects Fund*
> Memorandum—town hall project authorization $1,000,000

INTERFUND TRANSFER (1) Transaction 1 increases CPF current assets and fund balance. As discussed earlier, the town classifies this interfund transaction as a nonreciprocal transfer, because it does not expect it to be repaid. The town reports fund balance increases from transfers as other financing sources, not as revenues, in the fund receiving the transfer. Likewise, it records this transaction, which decreases general fund current assets and fund balance, as an other financing use, not an expenditure, in the fund transferring the cash. The $100,000 transfer requires an entry in both funds. Recall the interfund transfer entry in the general fund. The corresponding entry in the capital projects fund to receive the $100,000 is as follows:

> *Capital Projects Fund*
> Cash   100,000
>   Other financing sources—nonreciprocal transfer   100,000
>   from general fund
>   To record receipt of funds from the GF.

RECORDING EXPENDITURES (2) The town records payments for planning and architect's fees as follows:

> *Capital Projects Fund*
> Expenditures   40,000
>   Cash   40,000
>   To record payments for planning and architect's fees.

RECORDING ENCUMBRANCES (3) When the contract is awarded to a contractor, the town makes an encumbrance entry for the full amount of the contract:

Capital Projects Fund

Encumbrances	950,000	
Reserve for encumbrances		950,000
To record encumbrances for the amount of the contract.		

ACCOUNTING FOR THE BOND PROCEEDS (4 AND 5) Governments recognize the proceeds of bond issues in the CPF at the time the bonds are sold. The sale of the bonds increases CPF current assets (cash). The bond liability is long-term, so the town does not account for it in the CPF; rather, it includes it in long-term debt records. As in the general fund treatment of the capital lease, this debt will appear on the government-wide statements; however, within the CPF, the fund balance increases by the amount of the bond proceeds ($502,000). The increase is classified as an other financing source (bond issue proceeds), not as revenue.

The town sold the bonds at a premium. Although the following entry places the full amount of the proceeds in the CPF, the premium is not available to finance the project; however, premiums often are set aside to service the debt. Thus, a second entry transfers the premium to the debt service fund through which the bond liability will be serviced. (The corresponding entry for the debt service fund is illustrated later in this chapter.) Journal entries for the sale of bonds and transfer of the premium are as follows:

Capital Projects Fund

Cash	502,000	
Other financing sources—proceeds from bond issue		502,000
To record sale of bonds.		
Other financing uses—nonreciprocal transfer to debt service fund	2,000	
Cash		2,000
To transfer the premium to the town hall addition debt service fund.		

When bonds sell at a discount, bond proceeds equal the amount received. Governments selling bonds at a discount must reduce the project authorization or transfer additional resources to the CPF.

PROGRESS PAYMENTS AND RETAINED PERCENTAGES (6 AND 7) A construction contract often stipulates that a portion of the contractor's remuneration be withheld until completion of the construction project and final inspection. Note that the fixed asset (construction in progress) is not recorded in the CPF, because it is a governmental fund. The fixed asset does not represent CPF working capital. Instead, the incurrence of the contract payable liability increases CPF liabilities and decreases CPF fund balance. Governments report this fund balance decrease as an expenditure. Accounting entries for the amount owed on partial completion of the contract and the first progress payment on the contract appear as follows:

Capital Projects Fund

Reserve for encumbrances	475,000	
Encumbrances		475,000
To reverse half of the amount encumbered.		
Expenditures	475,000	
Contracts payable		427,500
Contracts payable—retained percentage		47,500
To record expenditures and a 10% retained percentage on the town hall construction.		
Contracts payable	427,500	
Cash		427,500
To record partial payment to the contractor.		

Adjusting and Closing Entries (8)

At the end of the fiscal year, the town closes the CPF books and prepares financial statements. The town hall construction project has not been completed, and the statements for the CPF are interim statements from the standpoint of the project.

INTERGOVERNMENTAL REVENUE The grant from the federal government is intergovernmental revenue. Under modified accrual accounting, a governmental fund recognizes revenue on restricted grants when qualifying costs have been incurred (and other significant conditions, if any, have been met), assuming that the funds are measurable and available.

Because the CPF did not receive the federal grant proceeds for the town hall project at the time the books were closed, the town will prepare an accrual entry, provided that the commitment is firm. Just as previously discussed in the section on special revenue funds, governments recognize revenue if the receivable will be collected and available to meet current obligations. Otherwise, they must credit deferred revenue. Failure to recognize revenue from the grant could make the CPF appear to be in financial difficulty for interim reporting purposes when, in fact, it has progressed as planned.

Capital Projects Fund (Adjusting Entry)		
Due from federal government	400,000	
Grant revenue		400,000
To recognize revenue from the federal grant.		

This entry assumes that the federal government has agreed to contribute $400,000 to the project regardless of the total cost. Therefore, because more than $400,000 of costs were incurred in 2011, the town records the full $400,000 as revenue. If the grant had specified that the federal government would pay a percentage of the cost of the project up to $400,000, the town would prorate the amounts in the entry.

CLOSING ENTRY—SEPTEMBER 30, 2011 To determine the classification of the fund balance, the accounting staff reviewed the documentation accompanying all of the funding sources and determined that all of them made a legally binding restriction on the use of the funds only for the capital project. The town records a closing entry for the CPF as follows:

Capital Projects Fund (Closing Entry)		
Grant revenue	400,000	
Other financing sources—nonreciprocal transfer		
from general fund	100,000	
Other financing sources—proceeds from bond issue	502,000	
Reserve for encumbrances	475,000	
Expenditures		515,000
Other financing uses—nonreciprocal transfer to debt		
service fund		2,000
Encumbrances		475,000
Fund balance—restricted		485,000
To close the books at the end of fiscal year 2011.		

UNISSUED BONDS AT AN INTERIM STATEMENT DATE The bonds to finance the town hall capital project have been issued by September 30, 2011, but in some cases there will be authorized but unissued bonds at an interim reporting date. The existence of the unissued bonds would be disclosed only in a statement note. The authorization of the bonds does not represent a CPF asset. Assets are received only upon bond issuance.

Entries for 2011 to 2012

The following entries illustrate the proper accounting treatment for the completion of a capital project; however, they will not be reflected in the October 1, 2010, to September 30, 2011, financial statements at the end of the chapter.

REINSTATEMENT OF ENCUMBRANCES At the start of the 2011–2012 fiscal year, the $475,000 encumbrance that was closed at the end of the prior fiscal year is reinstated in the accounts as follows:

Capital Projects Fund

Encumbrances	475,000	
Reserve for encumbrances		475,000
To reinstate the encumbrances.		

It is not necessary to denote the encumbrance in the CPF as related to the prior year, because capital projects are budgeted by project rather than on an annual basis.

RECEIPT OF GRANT (9) When the federal grant is received, it is recorded:

Capital Projects Fund

Cash	400,000	
Due from federal government		400,000
To record receipt of the federal grant.		

COMPLETION OF THE PROJECT (10) The journal entries to record completion of construction and payment to the contractor are as follows:

Capital Projects Fund

Reserve for encumbrances	475,000	
Encumbrances		475,000
To remove encumbrances when construction is complete.		
Expenditures	475,000	
Contracts payable		475,000
To record expenditures on town hall construction.		
Contracts payable	475,000	
Contracts payable—retained percentage	47,500	
Cash		522,500
To record final payment to contractor.		

CLOSING ENTRIES—SEPTEMBER 30, 2012 (11) The town makes an entry to close expenditures:

Capital Projects Fund

Fund balance—restricted	475,000	
Expenditures		475,000
To close the expenditures to fund balance.		

NONRECIPROCAL TRANSFER (12) The town records the transfer of the remaining fund balance to the general fund in final termination of the town hall addition CPF as follows:

Capital Projects Fund

Other financing uses—nonreciprocal transfer to GF	10,000	
Cash		10,000
To record transfer of cash to the general fund.		
Fund balance—restricted	10,000	
Other financing uses—nonreciprocal transfer to GF		10,000
To close town hall addition CPF ledger.		

A corresponding entry is required in the general fund to receive the cash transferred. That entry is as follows:

General Fund

Cash	10,000	
Other financing sources—nonreciprocal transfer from CPF		10,000
To record receipt of cash from town hall addition CPF.		

The $10,000 transfer to the general fund is a nonreciprocal transfer because the fund is being terminated. It should be presented separately as an increase or decrease in fund balance in the financial statements. Also, the appropriate fund balance classification will need to be used when the General Fund closes the Other Financing Sources—whether it is unassigned or in some way constrained per the terms of the financing providers.

SPECIAL ASSESSMENT ACTIVITIES

Governments sometimes finance public improvements that benefit a limited group of property owners through special taxes levied against these residents. These special tax levies are known as *special assessment levies,* or just *special assessments.* The more common types of special assessment projects include street paving, the construction of sidewalks, and the installation of sewer lines. Ordinarily, a special assessment project originates when property owners in an area petition the government to construct the improvements desired. If the project is authorized, the government obtains the financing, makes the improvement, and levies special assessments on the property owners for some or all of the cost incurred. If the project will benefit the general citizenry, the government may pay a portion of the cost.

The property owners may pay the special assessments immediately, in which case the governmental unit is repaid for the resources it uses in constructing the improvement, and the special assessment project is terminated. In many cases, however, the government issues special assessment bonds to pay the construction costs and collects the assessment in installments over the term of the special assessment bond issue. Interest charged on the unpaid balances of special assessment receivables covers the interest on the special assessment bonds. If special assessments are not paid as they come due, the governmental unit has the power to enforce collection through seizure of the real property against which special assessments are levied.

The GASB requires that governments account for capital improvements related to special assessment projects in capital projects funds. If the special assessment involves general obligation debt that will be repaid, in part, from special assessments, or if *the government is obligated in some manner* for debt repayment, the government should report the debt in the governmental activities column of the government-wide statement of net assets. If, however, *the governmental unit is not obligated in any manner,* it should not report the special assessment obligation in its financial statements.[11] In this case, special assessment receipts can be accounted for in an agency fund, and the related special assessment obligation is only disclosed in notes to the financial statements.

DEBT SERVICE FUNDS

Debt service funds (DSF) are governmental funds that account for the receipt of resources from designated sources (such as taxes or transfers from the general fund) and for the use of these resources to make principal and interest payments on general long-term debt obligations. Ordinarily, governments create a separate DSF to account for servicing each general long-term debt issue, but some use one DSF for all governmental fund debt. Although debt service funds make interest and principal payments on general long-term debt, they do not record the liability for general long-term debt. You will recall that governments maintain internal records of general long-term debt, which coordinate with the records of debt service. When long-term debt matures, governments record the appropriate expenditures in debt service funds and reduce the liability for the debt in the internal debt records and the appropriate financial statements.

Debt service funds generally follow the modified accrual basis of accounting. *GASB Codification,* Section 1600.122, identifies a major exception for DSF expenditures. Because resources for debt service are often appropriated in other funds and transferred to a DSF, the DSF may recognize principal and interest expenditures on general long-term debt when due (i.e., in the year of payment). This exception is made to avoid showing an expenditure and a liability for debt service in one period and the transfer of resources from the general fund or other sources to pay the liability in the following period.[12]

---

[11]*GASB Codification*, Section S40.

[12]Accrual is permitted, but not required, if two conditions are met. First, the resources to be used for payment must be available in the DSF by year-end. Second, the payment must be due early (the first few weeks) in the next year.

The operations of debt service funds for serial bond issues differ from those for term bond issues. In the case of a serial bond issue, in which bonds are retired at regular intervals, resources typically are received as needed to service the debt, and no significant balances are carried over from one period to the next. However, debt service funds for term bond issues accumulate resources over time to retire all of the debt at maturity as well as make periodic interest payments. Debt service funds for term bond issues accommodate both sinking fund operations and operations for current debt service. Thus, they are much more complex than those for serial bond issues. Formal budgetary accounting is ordinarily needed for term bond issues but not for serial bond issues. This chapter illustrates only debt service fund operations for serial bond issues.

Accounting for the Debt Service Fund

Assume that the $500,000, 6.5 percent serial bond issue of the Town of Grantville that was issued for $502,000 on April 3, 2011, has interest payment dates of April 1 and October 1 of each year. Principal amounts of $50,000 are due each year starting on April 1, 2012, and cash for all debt service is to be provided by transfers from the general fund. The town transfers amounts needed for debt service payments from the general fund during the month before the due date. Under these assumptions, the required journal entries for the town hall addition debt service fund for the 2010–2011 and 2011–2012 fiscal years are as follows:

Debt Service Fund—April 3, 2011

Cash	2,000	
Other financing sources—nonreciprocal transfer		
from town hall CPF		2,000
To record receipt of issue premium from town hall		
addition CPF.		

Debt Service Fund—September 2011

Cash	14,250	
Other financing sources—nonreciprocal transfer from		
general fund		14,250
To record receipt of resources for the October 1, 2011,		
interest payment from the general fund, less the $2,000		
already accumulated.		
($500,000 × 6.5% × 1/2 year) − 2,000 = $14,250.		

Debt Service Fund—Adjusting Entry—September 30, 2011

Expenditures—interest payment	16,250	
Matured interest payable		16,250
To accrue payment of interest due on 6.5% serial bond issue,		
due October 1.		

Debt Service Fund Closing Entries—September 30, 2011

Other financing sources—nonreciprocal transfer from		
town hall CPF	2,000	
Other financing sources—nonreciprocal transfer from		
general fund	14,250	
Expenditures—interest payment		16,250
To close the accounts.		

The following entries illustrate the proper accounting treatment for debt service transactions; however, they will not be reflected in the October 1, 2010, to September 30, 2011, financial statements at the end of the chapter.

Debt Service Fund—October 1, 2011

Matured interest payable	16,250	
Cash		16,250
To record payment of interest on the serial bond issue.		

Debt Service Fund—March 2012

Cash	66,250	
Other financing sources—nonreciprocal transfer from		
general fund		66,250

To record receipt of $16,250 for interest payment plus
$50,000 for the first serial payment due April 1, 2012.

Debt Service Fund—April 1, 2012

Expenditures—principal payment	50,000	
Expenditures—interest payment	16,250	
Cash		66,250

To record payment of principal and interest on the serial
bond issue.

Debt Service Fund—September 2012

Cash	14,625	
Other financing sources—nonreciprocal transfer from		
general fund		14,625

To record receipt of cash from GF for the October 1, 2012,
interest payment ($450,000 × 6.5% × 1/2 year).

Debt Service Fund—Adjusting Entry—September 30, 2012

Expenditures—interest payment	14,625	
Matured interest payable		14,625

To accrue payment of interest due.

Debt Service Fund Closing Entries—September 30, 2012

Other financing sources—nonreciprocal transfer from		
general fund	80,875	
Expenditures—principal payment		50,000
Expenditures—interest payment		30,875

To close the accounts.

NONRECIPROCAL, ROUTINE TRANSFERS The receipts of cash from the general fund in September 2011, March 2012, and September 2012 are nonreciprocal, routine transfers made in connection with the normal operations of government. Such recurring transfers are not revenues or expenditures of either fund in the transaction. Instead, governments report recurring transfers as "other financing sources (uses)." In this case, the town reports the $2,000 transfer of the bond premium on April 3, 2011, the $14,250 nonreciprocal, routine transfer in September 2011 for the payment of interest; the $66,250 recurring transfer in March 2012 for interest and the first principal payment; and the $14,625 nonreciprocal, routine transfer in September 2012 for interest as other financing sources in the DSF and as other financing uses in the GF or in the CPF.

Note that interest payable was accrued on September 30, 2011 and 2012, for interest payments due on October 1, 2011 and 2012. The interest could be accrued because the amounts payable are due on October 1 and resources are available in the DSF at year-end to cover the interest payments due early in the next fiscal year. Interest could not be accrued at September 30 if the general fund nonreciprocal, routine transfers were made on October 1 to pay interest on October 1.

GOVERNMENTAL FUND FINANCIAL STATEMENTS

LEARNING OBJECTIVE **4**

As noted in discussing the new *GASB 34* financial reporting model, the required governmental fund financial statements include a statement of net assets or balance sheet and a statement of revenues, expenditures, and changes in fund balance. Exhibits 20-2 and 20-3 present examples of these statements for Grantville's 2010–2011 fiscal year governmental activities. In addition, governments must present budgetary comparison information for the general fund and each special revenue fund that has a legally adopted annual budget. Exhibit 20-4 illustrates one accepted method of presenting this information for the Town of Grantville general fund.

EXHIBIT 20-2

Balance Sheet—Governmental Funds

TOWN OF GRANTVILLE BALANCE SHEET—GOVERNMENTAL FUNDS SEPTEMBER 30, 2011

	General Fund	Seal Exhibit Permanent Fund	Debt Service Fund	Town Hall Capital Projects Fund	Other Governmental Funds	Total Governmental Funds
Assets						
Cash and cash equivalents	$187,250	$ 9,500	$ 16,250	$132,500	$ 95,605	$ 441,105
Investments	—	500,000	—	—	11,435	511,435
Receivables						
Taxes receivable—delinquent (net of $20,000 estimated uncollectible taxes)	220,000	—	—	—	—	220,000
Accounts receivable	180,000	—	—	—	14,950	194,950
Due from other governments	—	—	—	400,000	53,225	453,225
Supplies inventory	90,000	—	—	—	—	90,000
Total assets	$677,250	$509,500	$ 16,250	$532,500	$175,215	$1,910,715
Liabilities and Fund Balances						
Liabilities						
Vouchers payable	$325,000	—	—	—	$ 58,000	$ 383,000
Matured interest payable	—	—	$ 16,250	—	—	16,250
Contracts payable	—	—	—	$ 47,500	—	47,500
Deferred revenue	50,000	—	—	—	5,000	55,000
Total liabilities	375,000	—	16,250	47,500	63,000	501,750
Fund balances						
Nonspendable	90,000	500,000	—	—	—	590,000
Restricted	—	9,500	—	485,000	—	494,500
Committed	50,000	—	—	—	112,215	162,215
Assigned	—	—	—	—	—	0
Unassigned	162,250	—	—	—	—	162,250
Total fund balance	302,250	509,500	0	485,000	112,215	1,408,965
Total liabilities and fund balance	$677,250	$509,500	$ 16,250	$532,500	$175,215	$1,910,715

The balance sheet in Exhibit 20-2 contains separate columns for the general fund, the seal exhibit permanent fund, and the town hall capital projects fund. Each of these funds meets the criteria of a *major fund* outlined in Chapter 19. The balance sheet also has a column for the debt service fund, which was not considered a major fund in this example; however, the town's management opted to disclose the fund because they felt it was important to financial statement users. Also, just prior to a totals column, there is a column for other governmental funds, where all nonmajor governmental fund balances are presented in aggregate. The special revenue funds within the chapter example that the town used to account for the highway beautification grant and the state grant for police and fire officer training are included in this column, because they are relatively small in dollar amount and their separate presentation on the face of the balance sheet is not essential. Note that the balance sheet does not include fixed assets or long-term debt. This is consistent with the governmental fund accounting model and makes governmental fund balance sheets relatively straightforward.

The total fund balance reported on the balance sheet is the same as the ending fund balance reported in the statement of revenues, expenditures, and changes in fund balance in Exhibit 20-3. This governmental fund operating statement has the same columns as the balance sheet and lists revenues, expenditures, and other financing sources (uses) to illustrate changes in fund balance (working capital) for the governmental funds.

Finally, Exhibit 20-4 presents a budgetary comparison schedule for the general fund. This statement, which is required supplementary information for the general fund and for all special revenue funds with legally adopted budgets, includes columns for the original budget, the final budget, actual amounts and variances (optional). It typically includes the same classifications as the GAAP

EXHIBIT 20-3

Statement of Revenues, Expenditures, and Changes in Fund Balance

TOWN OF GRANTVILLE GOVERNMENTAL FUNDS STATEMENT OF REVENUES, EXPENDITURES, AND CHANGES IN FUND BALANCE FOR THE FISCAL YEAR ENDED SEPTEMBER 30, 2011

	General Fund	Seal Exhibit Permanent Fund	Debt Service Fund	Town Hall Capital Projects Fund	Other Governmental Funds	Total Governmental Funds
Revenues						
Taxes	$2,080,000	—	—	—	$ 5,250	$2,085,250
Licenses and permits	203,000	—	—	—	—	203,000
Intergovernmental revenues	400,000	—	—	$400,000	61,500	861,500
Charges for services	563,000	—	—	—	—	563,000
Fines and forfeitures	122,000	—	—	—	—	122,000
Addition to permanent endowments	0	$500,000	—	—	—	500,000
Investment income	110,000	12,500	—	—	—	122,500
Miscellaneous revenue	42,000	—	—	—	8,200	50,200
Total revenues	$3,520,000	$512,500	—	$400,000	$ 74,950	$4,507,450
Expenditures						
Current services						
General government	896,000	—	—	—	6,150	902,150
Public safety	927,750	—	—	—	23,500	951,250
Highways and streets	528,750	—	—	—	38,000	566,750
Sanitation	427,000	—	—	—	—	427,000
Health and welfare	175,000	—	—	—	4,200	179,200
Recreation	204,000	3,000	—	—	—	207,000
Capital outlays	190,000	—	—	515,000	—	705,000
Debt service	—	—	$ 16,250	—	—	16,250
Total expenditure	3,348,500	3,000	16,250	515,000	71,850	3,954,600
Excess of revenues over expenditures	171,500	509,500	(16,250)	(115,000)	3,100	552,850
Other Financing Sources (Uses)						
Bond proceeds	—	—	—	502,000	—	502,000
Capital lease	45,000	—	—	—	—	45,000
Transfers in	—	—	16,250	100,000	50,000	166,250
Transfers out	(164,250)	—	—	(2,000)	—	(166,250)
Excess of revenues and other financing sources over expenditures and other financing uses	52,250	509,500	0	485,000	53,100	1,099,850
Fund balance at October 1, 2010	250,000	0	0	0	59,115	309,115
Fund balance at September 30, 2011	$ 302,250	$509,500	$ 0	$485,000	$112,215	$1,408,965

operating statement. Often, however, the amounts reported for revenues, expenditures, and fund balance differ between the two statements. Differences exist when a government uses a non-GAAP basis of accounting for budgeting purposes, as Grantville does because of its use of encumbrance accounting. The budget and actual comparison statement must be presented on the budgetary basis of accounting even if it differs from GAAP. The differences between the two statements must be reconciled on the face of the statements, as done here, or in the notes to the financial statements. The reconciliation can explain differences between GAAP-basis and budgetary-basis fund balance amounts or differences between the excess of revenues and other financing sources over expenditures and other financing uses reported in the two statements.

The exhibits do not present budgetary data for the special revenue funds, because it appears that they did not have legally adopted budgets. You can see that the $50,000 transfer of cash from the general fund to the special revenue fund was not originally budgeted. Transfers of $115,000 were originally budgeted for debt service and capital projects only. Note, however, that the town's elected officials must have

EXHIBIT 20-4

General Fund Budgetary
Comparison Schedule

TOWN OF GRANTVILLE BUDGETARY COMPARISON SCHEDULE—GENERAL FUND FOR THE YEAR ENDED SEPTEMBER 30, 2011

	Original Budget	Final Budget	Actual Amounts (Budgetary Basis)	Variance with Final Budget, Positive (Negative)
Revenues				
Taxes	$2,075,000	$2,075,000	$2,080,000	$ 5,000
Licenses and permits	205,000	205,000	203,000	(2,000)
Intergovernmental revenues	400,000	400,000	400,000	—
Charges for services	557,000	557,000	563,000	6,000
Fines and forfeitures	118,000	118,000	122,000	4,000
Investment income	100,000	105,000	110,000	5,000
Miscellaneous revenue	45,000	45,000	42,000	(3,000)
Total revenues	$3,500,000	$3,505,000	$3,520,000	$15,000
Expenditures and Encumbrances				
Current services				
General government	$ 477,500	$ 477,500	$ 475,000	$ 2,500
Public safety	897,750	897,750	892,750	5,000
Highways and streets	825,000	830,000	828,750	1,250
Sanitation	525,000	527,000	527,000	—
Health and welfare	175,000	175,000	175,000	—
Recreation	270,000	275,000	275,000	—
Capital outlays	150,000	150,000	140,000	10,000
Total expenditures and encumbrances	3,320,250	3,332,250	3,313,500*	18,750
Excess of revenues over expenditures and encumbrances	179,750	172,750	206,500	33,750
Other Financing Sources (Uses)				
Capital lease	—	45,000	45,000	—
Transfers out	(115,000)	(164,250)	(164,250)	—
Net change in fund balance	64,750	53,500	87,250	33,750
Budgetary fund balance—beginning	160,000	160,000	160,000	—
Add: Excess prior year encumbrance over actual expenditure	—	—	5,000	5,000
Budgetary fund balance—ending	$ 224,750	$ 213,500	$ 252,250	$38,750
Encumbrances outstanding at September 30, 2011			50,000	
Fund balance—ending			$ 302,250	

*Actual expenditures on a budgetary basis include the $50,000 supplies purchase commitment chargeable against the 2011 appropriations, but exclude the $85,000 expenditure chargeable against the prior year's carryover appropriation.

approved the transfers and amendments to the budget during the year. In fact, each time the actual expenditures or outflows of the general fund exceeded budget, approvals had to be sought and the budget had to be amended. This demonstrates the legal level of control that a governmental entity's budget has over spending. *GASB 34* requires disclosure of the original and final budget information, along with actual figures, in budgetary comparison disclosures. Thus a user of the financial statements can examine the extent of budgetary amendments that were necessary during the financial statement period.

LEARNING
OBJECTIVE **5**

PREPARING THE GOVERNMENT-WIDE FINANCIAL STATEMENTS

In addition to the fund financial statements illustrated previously, a government must include governmental fund activities in the government-wide statements. You may recall, however, that the government-wide statements are prepared on the accrual basis of accounting, whereas the fund financial statements for the governmental funds are prepared on the modified accrual basis of accounting. Thus, governments must convert governmental fund financial information to the accrual basis of accounting for inclusion in the government-wide statements of activities and net assets. This conversion, illustrated for the Town of Grantville in Exhibit 20-5, includes the following actions. (The letters in the list correspond with those in the exhibit.)

a. Governments must capitalize governmental fund fixed assets, which were recorded as expenditures in the fund statements, at cost in the government-wide statements. During the year, Grantville purchased $190,000 in equipment. For simplicity, we treat the equipment purchases as the only fixed assets in this example; however, most governmental entities possess extensive general fixed asset balances, which must be reinstated in total each year as part of the conversion process.

b. Grantville must also record depreciation associated with the governmental fixed assets in the government-wide statements. If the equipment has a 10-year estimated useful life and the town uses straight-line depreciation, depreciation expense and accumulated depreciation amount to $19,000. Until the equipment is retired or sold, this $19,000, as well as annual depreciation expense, will be reinstated as accumulated depreciation in the conversion process.

c. Grantville should recognize capital projects fund construction expenditures as "construction in progress" in the government-wide statements. These expenditures will later be reclassified as "buildings" once construction of the town hall addition is completed.

d. Governments must report governmental fund long-term liabilities, where applicable, in the government-wide statements. Thus, Grantville's capital lease, which was recorded as an "other financing source," should be recognized as a long-term liability, "capital lease payable."

e. Similar to the capital lease in (d), Grantville recorded bond proceeds as an "other financing source" and must reclassify them as a long-term liability, "bonds payable," on the government-wide statements.

f. Governments must also adjust for instances when revenue recognition differs between the modified accrual and accrual bases of accounting. The sales tax revenue in Grantville's general fund that was deferred because it would not be collected within 60 days of year-end was earned within the fiscal year, so it should be recognized under the accrual basis of accounting. Thus, for Grantville, the $50,000 general fund deferred revenue will be treated as government-wide revenue.

g. Because the government-wide statement is, in essence, a combined financial statement, it is necessary to eliminate interfund balances within the governmental funds. For Grantville, the $166,250 transfers between funds are eliminated.

h. Internal service funds primarily provide goods and services within a governmental entity. Therefore, internal service funds are reported with the governmental activities in the government-wide statements. In the statement of net assets, internal service fund balance sheet accounts are included in the governmental activity column; however, the statement of activities will include only those internal service fund transactions involving entities other than the primary reporting entity. Thus, internal service fund revenues (and expenditures) resulting from transactions with parties external to the government are added to the statement of activities, and internal governmental transactions are excluded from government-wide statements.

This chapter did not review the accounting for internal service funds for Grantville, so internal service balances are noted as zero, but the column is included to show how internal service funds would be treated in the conversion worksheet.

Note that the conversion worksheet is an internal, optional document that will never be presented in the financial statements. It is simply helpful for use in preparing the government-wide statement of net assets and statement of activities, as well as required reconciliations.

EXHIBIT 20-5

Conversion Worksheet

	Fund Financial Statement Balances—Governmental Funds		Adjustments/Eliminations		(h) Internal Service Funds	Total Governmental Activities			
	DR	CR	DR	CR		Statement of Activities DR	Statement of Activities CR	Statement of Net Assets DR	Statement of Net Assets CR
Cash and cash equivalents	441,105				X			441,105	
Investments	511,435				X			511,435	
Taxes receivable	220,000				X			220,000	
Accounts receivable	194,950				X			194,950	
Due from other governments	453,225				X			453,225	
Supplies inventory	90,000				X			90,000	
Vouchers payable		383,000			X				383,000
Matured interest payable		16,250			X				16,250
Contracts payable		47,500			X				47,500
Deferred revenue		55,000	(f) 50,000		X				5,000
Fund balances/Net assets, beg.		309,115			X				309,115
Revenues		4,507,450		(f) 50,000	X		4,557,450		

EXHIBIT 20-5

Conversion Worksheet (*Continued*)

Expenditures	3,954,600		(b) 19,000	(a) 190,000 / (c) 515,000	X	3,268,600		
OFS—Bond proceeds		502,000	(e) 502,000		X			
OFS—Capital lease		45,000	(d) 45,000		X			
OFS—Transfers in		166,250	(g) 166,250		X			
OFU—Transfers out	166,250			(g) 166,250	X			
Construction in progress			(c) 515,000		X		515,000	
Equipment			(a) 190,000		X		190,000	
Accumulated depreciation				(b) 19,000	X			19,000
Capital leases payable				(d) 45,000	X			45,000
Bonds payable				(e) 500,000	X			500,000
Premium on bonds payable				(e) 2,000	X			2,000
	6,031,565		1,487,250	1,487,250		3,268,600	4,557,450	1,326,865
Change in net assets						1,288,850		1,288,850
	6,031,565					4,557,450	4,557,450	2,615,715

CR, credit; DR, debit; OFS, other financing source; OFU, other financing use.

STATEMENT OF NET ASSETS We can prepare the governmental activities column of the government-wide statement of net assets by transferring the converted balance sheet numbers from the conversion worksheet to the statement of net assets. Exhibit 20-6 presents a sample statement of net assets.

GASB 34 requires a reconciliation between the fund and government-wide financial statements to be presented either at the bottom of the fund financial statements or in an accompanying schedule. We can easily prepare the reconciliation by referencing adjustments on the conversion schedule. An acceptable format for the reconciliation follows:

Total fund balance—governmental funds	$1,408,965
Amounts reported for *governmental activities* in the statement of net assets differ from those in the governmental fund balance sheet because:	
Capital assets (net) used in governmental activities are not financial resources and therefore are not reported in the fund balance sheet	686,000
Revenues reported as deferred on the fund balance sheet using the 60-day criteria are recognized as revenue in the government-wide statement	50,000
Long-term liabilities (bonds and capital lease payable) are not due and payable in the current period and therefore are not reported in the governmental fund balance sheet	(547,000)
Net assets—governmental funds	$1,597,965

STATEMENT OF ACTIVITIES Governmental activities reported on the government-wide statement of activities correspond to figures on the conversion worksheet. Exhibit 20-7 presents the

---

EXHIBIT 20-6

Government-wide
Statement of Net Assets

**TOWN OF GRANTVILLE STATEMENT OF NET ASSETS
SEPTEMBER 30, 2011**

	Governmental Activities	Business Type Activities	Total
Assets			
Cash and cash equivalents	$ 441,105	$ xxx,xxx	$ x,xxx,xxx
Investments	511,435	xxx,xxx	x,xxx,xxx
Receivables			
Taxes receivable—delinquent (net of $20,000 estimated uncollectible taxes)	220,000	xx,xxx	xxx,xxx
Accounts receivable	194,950	xxx,xxx	xxx,xxx
Due from other governments	453,225	xx,xxx	xxx,xxx
Supplies inventory	90,000	xx,xxx	xxx,xxx
Capital assets, net	686,000	xxx,xxx	x,xxx,xxx
Total assets	$2,596,715	$ x,xxx,xxx	$ x,xxx,xxx
Liabilities and Fund Balances			
Liabilities			
Vouchers payable	$ 383,000	$ xxx,xxx	$ xxx,xxx
Matured interest payable	16,250	xx,xxx	xx,xxx
Contracts payable	47,500	xx,xxx	xx,xxx
Deferred revenue	5,000	xx,xxx	xx,xxx
Capital leases payable	45,000	xx,xxx	xxx,xxx
Bonds payable	500,000	xxx,xxx	x,xxx,xxx
Premium on bonds payable	2,000	x,xxx	x,xxx
Total liabilities	998,750	xxx,xxx	x,xxx,xxx
Net assets			
Invested in capital assets, net of related debt	139,000	x,xxx,xxx	x,xxx,xxx
Restricted for debt service	—	xxx,xxx	xxx,xxx
Restricted for capital projects	485,000	xxx,xxx	xxx,xxx
Restricted for other purposes	9,500	xx,xxx	xxx,xxx
Unrestricted	964,465	x,xxx,xxx	x,xxx,xxx
Total net assets	$1,597,965	$x,xxx,xxx	$xx,xxx,xxx

EXHIBIT 20-7

Government-wide Statement of Activities

TOWN OF GRANTVILLE
STATEMENT OF ACTIVITIES
FOR THE FISCAL YEAR ENDED SEPTEMBER 30, 2011

Functions/Programs	Expenses	Charges for Services	Operating Grants and Contributions	Capital Gains and Contributions	Governmental Activities	Business-Type Activities	Total
Governmental Activities							
General government	$ 921,150	$ 138,250	—	$ 405,000	($377,900)	—	$ (377,900)
Public safety	951,250	129,650	—	18,500	(803,100)	—	(803,100)
Highways and streets	566,750	25,350	$400,000	38,000	(103,400)	—	(103,400)
Sanitation	427,000	390,750	—	—	(36,250)	—	(36,250)
Health and welfare	179,200	102,200	—	—	(77,000)	—	(77,000)
Recreation	207,000	152,000	12,500	—	(42,500)	—	(42,500)
Debt service	16,250	—	—	—	(16,250)	—	(16,250)
Total governmental activities	3,268,600	938,200	412,500	461,500	(1,456,400)	—	(1,456,400)
Business-type activities							
Utilities	x,xxx,xxx	x,xxx,xxx	—	xxx,xxx	—	xx,xxx	xx,xxx
Parking facilities	xx,xxx	xx,xxx	x,xxx	—	—	x,xxx	x,xxx
Total business-type activities	x,xxx,xxx	x,xxx,xxx	—	—	—	—	xx,xxx
Total government	$x,xxx,xxx	$x,xxx,xxx	$ xxx,xxx	$x,xxx,xxx	($1,456,400)	$ xx,xxx	$x,xxx,xxx

	Governmental Activities	Business-Type Activities	Total
General Revenues			
Property taxes	$1,980,000		
Sales taxes	155,250		
Investment Earnings	110,000		
Special item—permanent fund contribution	500,000		
Total general revenues and special items	2,745,250		
Change in net assets	1,288,850		
Net assets—beginning	309,115		
Net assets—ending	$1,597,965		

statement of activities for the Town of Grantville. You can trace the total expenses of $3,268,600 to the conversion worksheet. Also, the various revenues ($938,200 + $412,500 + $461,500 + $2,745,250) agree with the $4,557,450 on the conversion worksheet.[13]

GASB 34 also requires a reconciliation between the change in fund balance reported on the fund statement of revenues, expenditures, and changes in fund balance and the change in net assets reported on the statement of activities. This reconciliation may be presented either on the face of the fund financial statements or in an accompanying schedule. Again, the conversion worksheet is helpful. An acceptable format for the reconciliation follows:

Net change in fund balance—total governmental funds	$1,099,850
Amounts reported for *governmental activities* in the statement of activities differ from those in the governmental fund statement of revenues, expenditures and changes in fund balance because:	
Governmental funds report capital outlays as expenditures; the assets are capitalized and depreciated in the government-wide statements	686,000
Revenues in the statement of activities that do not provide current financial resources are not reported as revenues in the governmental funds	50,000
Bond proceeds provide current financial resources in the fund statement, but issuing debt increases long-term liabilities in the statement of net assets	(502,000)
A capital lease is treated as an expenditure in the governmental funds in the year that the lease agreement is entered into; however, it increases long-term liabilities in the statement of net assets	(45,000)
Change in net assets of governmental activities	$1,288,850

Although the two reconciliations between governmental fund financial statements and government-wide statements will include many of the same items, they will not be identical, and reconciling items will often differ between the two schedules.

SUMMARY

Governmental funds are used to account for general governmental activities affecting a governmental entity. They generally follow the modified accrual basis for accounting and reporting within the fund financial statements. This chapter included a review of appropriate accounting for the general fund, as well as special revenue, permanent, capital projects, and debt service funds using the governmental fund model introduced in Chapter 19.

Accounting for each of the governmental funds is the same, but the purpose of each fund type differs. The essential difference between a general fund and a special revenue fund lies in the fact that a general fund includes revenues available to finance the general needs of government, whereas the revenues of special revenue funds are restricted to specific uses. Permanent funds are used to account for nonexpendable resources set aside for support of a government's programs or citizenry. Capital projects funds are used to account for the acquisition of capital assets, and debt service funds are used to account for the receipt and use of resources to service general long-term debt obligations.

General and special revenue activities normally are controlled with formal budgetary procedures and accounting practices. Compliance with the budget is demonstrated by presenting budgetary comparison statements comparing actual and budgeted revenues and expenditures. Required fund financial statements for governmental funds include a statement of net assets or balance sheet and a statement of revenues, expenditures, and changes in fund balance. Those governments that record governmental fund transactions in the accounting records on the modified accrual basis of accounting must convert governmental fund statement data into their government-wide statement counterparts.

---

[13]Criteria for classification of the "converted" revenues and expenses into the program and function categories are provided in *GASB Statement No. 34,* paragraphs 38–56.

QUESTIONS

1. What is the accounting equation for a governmental fund?
2. What classifications of fund balance are currently allowed and which ones are no longer allowed?
3. If property tax bills totaling $200,000 are mailed to taxpayers and 97% are deemed collectible, what amount should be recorded as revenue?
4. What are encumbrances, and how does encumbrance accounting help control expenditures?
5. List the required governmental fund financial statements under *GASB 34*. On what basis of accounting are these statements prepared?
6. What is the purpose of a capital projects fund? Are all general fixed assets of a governmental unit acquired through capital projects funds? Explain.
7. How are capital projects funds financed, and when would a capital projects fund be terminated?
8. How do the purchases and consumption methods of accounting for inventory differ?
9. Are debt service funds used to account for debt service on all long-term obligations of a governmental unit? If not, which long-term debt obligations are excluded?
10. Describe a transaction that would affect the general fund and the debt service fund at the same time.
11. How do special assessment levies differ from general tax levies?
12. Which funds may be used to account for the activities of a general governmental special assessment construction project with long-term financing? Explain.
13. How are capital leases recorded in governmental funds?
14. Assume that supplies on hand at the beginning of the year amount to $60,000 and that supply purchases during the year are $400,000. Supplies on hand at year-end are $40,000, and the consumption basis of accounting for supplies is used. What adjusting entry for supplies should be made at year-end?
15. What is the role of a subsidiary ledger in a governmental entity?
16. The Village of Lester had appropriations of $250,000 for the current fiscal year. If $175,000 worth of items has been ordered but only $150,000 of the $175,000 has been received, what amount can city officials order prior to year-end? What happens if they have not spent the full $250,000 prior to year-end?
17. How does a permanent fund differ from a special revenue fund? A private-purpose trust fund?
18. How can you determine whether or not a governmental fund should be considered major?
19. What is included on a budgetary comparison schedule? Is such a schedule required to be included in a CAFR?
20. How is a conversion worksheet used? Why is it necessary?
21. List three items that might appear on the reconciliation between the governmental fund balance sheet and the government-wide statement of net assets. List three items that might appear on the reconciliation between the governmental fund operating statement and the government-wide statement of activities.

EXERCISES

E 20-1
Multiple choice

1. Which of the following statements regarding budgetary accounting is true?
   a *When the budget is recorded, estimated revenues are debited.*
   b *Budgetary accounts are never closed.*
   c *Encumbrance is another term for appropriation.*
   d *Budgeted revenues can be classified by source or character class.*

2. The encumbrance account of a governmental unit is debited when:
   a *The budget is recorded*
   b *A purchase order is approved*
   c *Goods are received*
   d *A voucher payable is recorded*

3. Encumbrance outstanding at year end in a state's general fund could be reported as a:
   a *Liability in the general fund*
   b *Fund balance—committed in the general fund*
   c *Liability in the general long-term debt account group*
   d *Expenditure in the general fund*

4. For the budgetary year ending December 31, 2011. Emerald City's general fund expects the following inflows of resources:

Property taxes, licenses, and fees	$9,000,000
Proceeds of debt issue	5,000,000
Interfund transfers for debt service	1,000,000

In the budgetary entry, what amount should Emerald record for estimated revenues?

a   *$9,000,000*
b   *$10,000,000*
c   *$14,000,000*
d   *$15,000,000*

5. During its fiscal year ended June 30, 2011, the City of Ingalls issued purchase orders totaling $5,000,000, which were properly charged to encumbrances at that time. Ingalls received goods and related invoices at the encumbered amounts totaling $4,500,000 before year end. The remaining goods of $500,000 were not received until after year end. Ingalls paid $4,200,000 of the invoices received during the year. What amount of Ingalls's encumbrances was outstanding at June 30, 2011?

a   *$0*
b   *$300,000*
c   *$500,000*
d   *$800,000*

E 20-2

Multiple choice

1. The accounts "estimated revenues" and "appropriations" appear in the trial balance of the general fund. These accounts indicate:

a   *The use of cash basis accounting*
b   *The use of accrual basis accounting*
c   *The formal use of budgetary accounts*
d   *The informal use of budgetary accounts*

2. When a complete system of encumbrance accounting is used, the authorizations remaining available for expenditures at any interim date will be equal to:

a   *Appropriations less encumbrances*
b   *Appropriations less expenditures*
c   *Appropriations plus encumbrances less expenditures*
d   *Appropriations less expenditures and encumbrances*

3. Encumbrance accounting is designed to:

a   *Prevent overspending of amounts appropriated*
b   *Replace expenditure accounting for governmental organizations*
c   *Prevent excessive appropriations*
d   *Prevent or reduce waste in governmental spending*

4. Reserve for encumbrance accounts in general fund balance sheets at year-end indicate:

a   *The amount of net assets required to complete the transaction(s) in the succeeding period*
b   *Noncompliance with GAAP*
c   *Cash on hand*
d   *Valuation reserves*

5. The reserve for encumbrances—past year account typically represents amounts recorded by a governmental unit for:

a   *Anticipated expenditures in the next year*
b   *Expenditures for which purchase orders were made in the prior year but for which expenditure and disbursement will be in the current year*
c   *Excess expenditures in the prior year that will be offset against the current-year budgeted amounts*
d   *Unanticipated expenditures of the prior year that become evident in the current year*

E 20-3

Multiple choice

1. When equipment was purchased with general fund resources, which of the following accounts would have been increased in the general fund?

a   *Due from general fixed assets account group*
b   *Expenditures*
c   *Appropriations*
d   *No entry should be made in the general fund*

2. Which of the following funds would not be included in governmental fund financial statements?

a *Debt service fund*

b *General fund*

c *Permanent fund*

d *Pension trust fund*

3. When the purchases method of accounting for supplies is used, the financial statements of the related fund entity:

a *Need not show material amounts of supplies on hand as an asset*

b *Must disclose the cost of supplies used during the period*

c *Are substantially the same as they would be under the consumption method*

d *Must disclose a fund balance reserve for material amounts of supplies on hand*

4. When the consumption basis of accounting for supplies is used, the financial statements of the related fund entity must:

a *Show supply purchases as expenditures of the period*

b *Show a fund balance restriction for material amounts of supplies on hand*

c *Reflect the fact that perpetual inventory procedures have been used in accounting for supplies*

d *Show supplies on hand as an asset*

5. The receipts from a special tax levy to retire and pay interest on general obligation bonds should be recorded in a:

a *Debt service fund*

b *Capital projects fund*

c *Revolving interests fund*

d *Special revenue fund*

E 20-4

Multiple choice

1. Howard City should use a capital projects fund to account for:

a *Proceeds of a capital grant to finance a new civic center that will not provide services primarily on a user-charge basis*

b *Construction of sewer lines by the water and sewer utility to be financed by user costs*

c *The accumulation of resources to retire bonds issued to construct the town hall*

d *Construction of an addition to the airport terminal owned by the Howard City Municipal Airport, an enterprise fund*

2. When a capital projects fund is dissolved by paying any remaining assets to another fund, the decrease in fund balance is a (an):

a *Expenditure*

b *Operating transfer*

c *Residual equity transfer*

d *Reimbursement*

3. Which of the following items would be least likely to appear in the account titles of a capital projects fund?

a *Due from federal government (for grant)*

b *Due from general fund*

c *Proceeds from bond issue*

d *Construction in progress*

4. Three financial statements may be required to present the results of operations and financial position of a special revenue fund. Which of the following is not one of these required statements?

a *Statement of cash flows*

b *Statement of revenues, expenditures, and changes in fund balance*

c *Statement of revenues, expenditures, and changes in fund balance—budget and actual*

d *Balance sheet*

5. Assets financed through a capital projects fund should be capitalized in the government-wide financial statements:

a *Only when construction is completed*

b *On the basis of expenditures to date in Construction in Progress*

c *On the basis of expenditures and encumbrances to date in Construction in Progress*

d *On the basis of amounts paid to date in Construction in Progress*

E 20-5

Multiple choice [Based on AICPA]

1. If numerous funds are maintained, which of the following transactions would typically not be reported in a municipality's general fund?

a *The collection of property taxes*

b *The purchase of office equipment*

c *The receipt of grant funds for local youth programs*

d *The payment of salaries to municipal employees*

2. Proceeds of general obligation bonds is an account of a governmental unit that typically would be included in the:
   a *Enterprise fund*
   b *Special revenue fund*
   c *Capital projects fund*
   d *Government-wide financial statements*

3. Equipment in general governmental service that had been constructed 10 years before by a capital projects fund was sold. The receipts were accounted for as an other financing source. Entries are necessary in the:
   a *General fund and capital projects fund*
   b *General fund only*
   c *General fund, capital projects fund, and enterprise fund*
   d *General fund, capital projects fund, and general fixed assets account group*

4. Martha County issues general obligation serial bonds at a premium to finance construction of a sheriff's office. Which of the following are affected by the transaction?
   a *Special revenue*
   b *Capital projects fund and general fund*
   c *Capital projects fund, general fund, and debt service fund*
   d *Capital projects fund and debt service fund*

5. Property taxes are considered:
   a *Derived tax revenues*
   b *Imposed nonexchange revenues*
   c *Government-mandated nonexchange transactions*
   d *Voluntary nonexchange transactions*

E 20-6

Multiple choice [AICPA adapted]

1. The following information pertains to Walnut Corners:

2011 governmental fund revenues that became measurable and available in time to be used for payment of 2011 liabilities	$16,000,000
Revenues earned in 2009 and 2010 and included in the $16,000,000 indicated	2,000,000
Sales taxes collected by merchants in 2011 but not required to be remitted to Walnut Corners until January 2012	3,000,000

   For the year ended December 31, 2011, Walnut Corners should recognize revenues of:
   a *$14,000,000*
   b *$16,000,000*
   c *$17,000,000*
   d *$19,000,000*

2. Capital City was awarded a $3,000,000 grant from the state. Of this grant, $1,500,000 was sent to the city and recorded in a special revenue fund. Qualified expenditures of that fund totaled $900,000 in the year that the grant was received. What amount of revenues should the city recognize with respect to the grant?
   a *$0*
   b *$900,000*
   c *$1,500,000*
   d *$3,000,000*

3. The following information pertains to property taxes levied by Coral City for the calendar year 2011:

Collections during 2011	$500,000
Expected collections during the first 60 days of 2012	100,000
Expected collections during the balance of 2012	60,000
Expected collections during January 2013	30,000
Estimated to be uncollectible	10,000
Total levy	$700,000

   What amount should Coral City report for 2011 net property tax revenues?
   a *$700,000*
   b *$690,000*
   c *$600,000*
   d *$500,000*

4. The following information pertains to Tedfred's general fund for 2012:

Appropriations	$6,500,000
Expenditures	5,000,000
Other financing sources	1,500,000
Other financing uses	2,000,000
Revenues	8,000,000

In 2012, Tedfred's total fund balance increased by:

a *$3,000,000*
b *$2,500,000*
c *$1,500,000*
d *$1,000,000*

5. The following information pertains to Amber Township's general fund at December 31, 2011:

Total assets, including $200,000 of cash	$1,000,000
Total liabilities	600,000
Fund balance—restricted	100,000

Appropriations do not lapse at year-end. At December 31, 2011, what amount should Amber report as fund balance—unassigned in its general fund balance sheet?

a *$800,000*
b *$400,000*
c *$300,000*
d *$100,000*

E 20-7

General fund journal entries (property taxes)

The following events and transactions relate to the levy and collection of property taxes for Jedville Township:

March 21, 2011—Property tax bills for $2,500,000 are sent to property owners. An estimated 2% of the property tax levies are uncollectible. The taxes are due on May 1.
May 4, 2011—$1,900,000 in taxes have been collected. The remaining receivables are reclassified as delinquent.
May 5 to December 31, 2011—An additional $150,000 of taxes are collected.
November 1, 2011—A $5,000 tax receivable account is determined to be uncollectible and is written off.
January 1, 2012, to February 28, 2012—An additional $87,750 of 2011 taxes are collected.

REQUIRED

1. Prepare summary journal entries for the events and transactions described for the Jedville general fund.

2. How will property taxes be presented in the December 31, 2011, balance sheet?

3. What amount of property tax revenues should be reported for 2011?

E 20-8

Governmental fund closing entries

A general ledger trial balance for Any City contained the following balances at June 30, 2011, just before closing entries were made:

Due from other funds	$ 600
Fund balance—unassigned	3,000
Estimated revenues	18,000
Revenues	17,380
Appropriations	17,500
Expenditures—current year	16,450
Expenditures—prior year	1,900
Encumbrances	1,000
Nonreciprocal transfer in	3,200
Reserve for encumbrances	1,000
Reserve for encumbrances—prior year	2,000

REQUIRED: Prepare the necessary closing entries.

E 20-9

Preparation of fund balance sheet

A general ledger trial balance at June 30, 2011, for Millar City is as follows:

	Debits	Credits
Cash	$ 12,000	—
Taxes receivable	30,000	—
Allowance for uncollectible taxes	—	$ 2,000
Due from other funds	3,000	—
Supplies inventory, June 30, 2011	4,000	—
Estimated revenues	300,000	—
Expenditures	290,000	—
Expenditures—prior year	5,000	—
Encumbrances	6,000	—
Vouchers payable	—	13,000
Due to other funds	—	5,000
Reserve for encumbrances	—	6,000
Reserve for encumbrances—prior year	—	5,000
Fund balance—nonspendable	—	4,000
Fund balance—unassigned	—	10,000
Appropriations	—	300,000
Revenues	—	305,000
	$650,000	$650,000

Millar City uses a purchases basis in accounting for supplies. Open encumbrances are considered constrained by the highest decision-making level of the city.

REQUIRED: Prepare a fund balance sheet as of June 30, 2011.

E 20-10

Preparation of a fund statement of revenues, expenditures, and changes in fund balance

The trial balance of the general fund of Madelyn City before closing at December 31, 2011, contained the following accounts and balances:

Fund balance—unassigned	$ 25,000
Estimated revenues	100,000
Appropriations	95,000
Encumbrances	4,000
Reserve for encumbrances	4,000
Reserve for encumbrances—prior year	5,000
Revenues	101,000
Expenditures	94,000
Expenditures—prior year	4,800
Nonreciprocal transfers out	18,000
Reciprocal transfers in	27,000

REQUIRED: Prepare a statement of revenues, expenditures, and changes in (total) fund balance for Madelyn City's general fund in 2011. (Details of revenue and expenditure accounts are omitted to simplify the requirement.)

E 20-11

General fund journal entries

Prepare entries in the general fund to record the following transactions and events:

1. Estimated revenues for the fiscal year were $250,000 and appropriations were $248,000.

2. The tax levy for the fiscal year, of which 99% is believed to be collectible, was $200,000.

3. Taxes collected were $150,000.

4. A short-term loan of $15,000 was made to the special revenue fund.

5. Orders for supplies were placed in the amount of $18,000.

6. The items ordered in transaction 5 were received. Actual cost was $18,150, and vouchers for that amount were prepared.

7. Materials were acquired from the stores fund (an internal service fund) in the amount of $800 (without encumbrance).

8. A $5,000 payment (transfer) was made to the debt service fund.

9. A cash payment of $15,000 was made for the purchase of equipment.

10. Licenses were collected in the amount of $3,000.

11. The balance of taxes receivable became delinquent.

12. Delinquent taxes of $30,000 were collected before year-end. The remaining net realizable value of delinquent taxes is expected to be collected uniformly over the first four months of the next fiscal year.

E 20-12
General fund journal entries
Prepare the journal entries required to record the following transactions in the general fund of Rochester Township.

1. Borrowed $75,000 by issuing six-month tax anticipation notes.

2. Ordered equipment with an estimated cost of $33,000.

3. Received the equipment along with an invoice for its actual cost, $33,250.

4. Transferred $200,000 of general fund resources to a debt service fund.

5. On January 1, the township levied property taxes of $1,000,000. The township expects to collect all except $100,000 by the end of the fiscal year or within not more than 60 days thereafter. Of the remaining $100,000, half is expected to prove uncollectible.

6. The township received a $100,000 restricted grant for certain library programs from another unit of government. The grant will be accounted for in the general fund.

7. The township incurred $75,000 of expenditures for the programs covered by the library grant.

E 20-13
Governmental fund journal entries
For each of the following transactions, note the fund(s) affected, and prepare appropriate journal entries.

1. General obligation bonds with a par value of $750,000 are issued at $769,000 to finance construction of a government office building.

2. A Community Block Development Grant in the amount of $450,000 is awarded for residential services within a city.

3. Upon approval of a new town band shell, the general fund transfers $500,000 to create a new fund.

4. A wealthy citizen donates $10,000,000 for city park maintenance. The principal cannot be spent.

5. Automobiles and vans for general governmental use are purchased for $375,000.

6. General fixed assets with an original cost of $300,000 sold for $30,000 at the end of their useful life.

7. Sold equipment at the end of its expected useful life. The equipment had no expected residual value when acquired (at a cost of $13,000), but it sold for $1,200.

8. The general fund transfers $50,000 for an interest payment on debt. The interest payment is made.

E 20-14
Governmental fund reconciliation to total net assets
The postclosing trial balance for the Village of Alantown general fund at June 30, 2011, shows the following ledger account balances:

Debits	
Cash	$410,000
Investments	300,000
Tax receivable—delinquent	150,000
Accounts receivable	30,000
Supplies inventory	60,000
Total debits	$950,000
Credits	
Allowances for uncollectible taxes—delinquent	$ 10,000
Vouchers payable	140,000
Deferred revenue	40,000
Note payable (short-term)	150,000
Fund balance—committed	90,000
Fund balance—unassigned	520,000
Total credits	$950,000

ADDITIONAL INFORMATION

1. The village owns general fixed assets with a historical cost of $100,000 and accumulated depreciation totaling $65,000.

2. General long-term debt recorded in the internal debt records is $100,000. This was recorded as an other financing source in the general fund.

3. A capital lease payable in the amount of $75,000 is noted in the internal debt records. This was recorded as an other financing source in the general fund.

4. Revenues reported as deferred on the fund balance sheet using the 60-day criteria are recognized as revenue in the government-wide statement.

REQUIRED: Determine the village's general fund net assets that will appear on the government-wide statement of net assets.

E 20-15
Governmental fund reconciliation to total net assets

The following data are available from the City of Boulder's financial records on September 30, 2011:

a. The net change in fund balance—total governmental funds for the city is $1,408,950.

b. The city purchased general fixed assets at a historical cost of $225,000 during the year. No depreciation is recorded in the year of purchase.

c. Grants receivable in the amount of $165,000 are recorded as deferred revenue in the fund statements but would be recognized as revenue under accrual accounting.

d. A capital lease payable in the amount of $75,000 has been recorded as an expenditure in the general fund. The related long-term debt at year-end is $55,000.

e. General long-term debt in the amount of $350,000 has been issued and recorded in the general fund.

REQUIRED: Determine the city's change in net assets of governmental activities that will appear in the government-wide statements.

PROBLEMS

P 20-1
Preparation of a general fund balance sheet

The unadjusted trial balance for the general fund of the City of Orchard Park at December 31, 2011, is as follows:

	Debit	Credit
Accounts receivable	$ 25,000	—
Allowance for bad debts	—	$ 2,000
Allowance for uncollectible taxes	—	30,000
Appropriations	—	900,000
Cash	40,000	—
Due from agency fund	10,000	—
Due to utility fund	—	20,000
Encumbrances	50,000	—
Estimated revenues	910,000	—
Expenditures	858,000	—
Fund balance—unassigned	—	26,000
Reserve for encumbrances	—	50,000
Revenues	—	910,000
Taxes receivable—delinquent	210,000	—
Taxes received in advance	—	10,000
Vouchers payable	—	155,000
	$2,103,000	$2,103,000

Supplies on hand at December 31, 2011, are $3,000. The $50,000 encumbrance relates to equipment ordered November 28 for the Department of Public Works but not received by year-end. The equipment purchase was approved by the City Council.

REQUIRED: Prepare a balance sheet for the general fund of the City of Orchard Park at December 31, 2011.

P 20-2
Preparation of general fund statements

The preclosing account balances of the general fund of the City of Batavia on June 30, 2012, were as follows:

Debits	
Cash	$ 80,000
Taxes receivable—delinquent	160,000
Due from County	18,000
Estimated revenues	1,000,000
Expenditures	940,000
Nonreciprocal transfers out	10,000
Encumbrances	20,000
	$2,228,000
Credits	
Allowance for uncollectible taxes—delinquent	$ 30,000
Vouchers payable	58,000
Notes payable	60,000
Reserve for encumbrances	20,000
Fund balance—unassigned	120,000
Revenues	980,000
Appropriations	960,000
	$2,228,000

The fund balance—unassigned at the beginning of the year was $80,000, and there were no carryover encumbrances at the beginning of the fiscal year. The end of year encumbrances are a result of enabling legislation.

REQUIRED

1. Prepare a statement of revenues, expenditures, and changes in total fund balance for the year ended June 30, 2012.

2. Prepare a general fund balance sheet at June 30, 2012.

P 20-3
Governmental fund journal entries, budgetary comparison, and reconciling items

The Town of Tyler approved the following general fund budget for the fiscal year July 1, 2011, to June 30, 2012:

TOWN OF TYLER GENERAL FUND BUDGET SUMMARY
FOR THE YEAR JULY 1, 2011 TO JUNE 30, 2012

Revenue Sources	
Taxes	$ 250,000
Licenses and permits	20,000
Intergovernmental revenue	40,000
Charges for services	60,000
Fines and forfeits	15,000
Rents and royalties	10,000
Miscellaneous revenues	5,000
Total budgeted revenues	$ 400,000

**TOWN OF TYLER GENERAL FUND BUDGET SUMMARY
FOR THE YEAR JULY 1, 2011 TO JUNE 30, 2012**

Expenditures	
Current services	
General government	$ 45,000
Public safety	140,000
Highways and streets	90,000
Sanitation	55,000
Health and welfare	20,000
Recreation	30,000
Capital outlays	15,000
Total appropriations	$395,000
Budgeted increase in fund balance	$ 5,000

The after-closing trial balance of the Town of Tyler general fund at June 30, 2011, shows the following ledger account balances:

Debits	
Cash	$31,000
Tax receivable—delinquent	15,000
Accounts receivable	3,000
Supplies inventory	6,000
Total debits	$55,000
Credits	
Allowances for uncollectible taxes—delinquent	$ 1,000
Vouchers payable	14,000
Note payable (short-term)	15,000
Fund balance—committed	9,000
Fund balance—nonspendable	6,000
Fund balance—unassigned	10,000
Total credits	$55,000

1. Prepare journal entries to record the budget and each of the following transactions:
   a. The treasurer of Tyler sends out property tax bills of $200,000; 1% is considered uncollectible.
   b. Current property taxes of $176,000 and past-due taxes of $14,000 were collected.
   c. A specific property tax bill ($1,000) is determined to be uncollectible.
   d. Fees in the amount of $20,000 are collected for hunting licenses.
   e. Other revenues in the amount of $200,000 are collected.
   f. The payroll for salaries of $20,000 is vouchered for payment.
   g. Playground equipment expected to cost $15,000 is ordered.
   h. The playground equipment is received and has an actual cost of $14,000.
   i. Tyler received equipment that had been ordered in the previous fiscal year. The actual cost was $9,500.
   j. Supplies in the amount of $11,000 were ordered. By year-end, only $5,000 worth of these supplies has been received. The consumption method is used.
   k. The note payable that was outstanding at June 30, 2011, becomes due and is paid.
   l. Various expenditures are paid throughout the year totaling $348,040.
   m. Supplies in the amount of $3,000 are on hand at year-end.
   n. Assume that uncollected taxes on June 30, 2011, are past due.
   o. Closing entries are made.

2. Prepare a budgetary comparison statement for the Tyler general fund.

3. Identify the transactions above that will be reconciling items between the fund financial statements and the government-wide financial statements.

P 20-4
Governmental fund conversion worksheet

The post-closing trial balance for the City of Fort Collins governmental funds at June 30, 2011, shows the following ledger account balances:

	DR	CR
Cash and cash equivalents	$ 541,100	
Investments	520,000	
Taxes receivable	520,000	
Accounts receivable	187,500	
Due from other governments	364,970	
Supplies inventory	290,000	
Vouchers payable		$ 379,500
Contracts payable		47,500
Deferred revenue		55,000
Fund balance/net assets, beginning		912,720
Revenues		3,507,450
Expenditures	3,043,600	
OFS—Bond proceeds		500,000
OFS—Capital lease		65,000
OFS—Transfers in		75,250
OFU—Transfers out	75,250	
	$5,542,420	$5,542,420

ADDITIONAL INFORMATION

1. During the year, Fort Collins purchased $9,000 in equipment, which was not depreciated.

2. Fort Collins also has other fixed assets with a historical cost of $95,000 and accumulated depreciation of $65,000.

3. Fort Collins has capital project fund construction expenditures totaling $20,000.

4. During the year, the city issued a bond at $500,000 par value.

5. During the year, the city entered into a lease agreement. The entire amount should be recognized as general long-term debt.

6. The city's deferred revenue would be treated as revenue under accrual accounting.

7. The transfers in and out were made between governmental funds.

8. The city does not report internal service funds.

REQUIRED: Prepare a conversion worksheet to determine the change in net assets and the net asset balance for the city's governmental funds.

P 20-5
Reconstruct general fund journal entries [AICPA adapted]

The following summary of transactions was taken from the accounts of the Oslo School District general fund before the books had been closed for the fiscal year ended June 30, 2011:

	Postclosing Balances June 30, 2010	Preclosing Balances June 30, 2011
Cash	$400,000	$ 700,000
Taxes receivable	150,000	170,000
Estimated uncollectible taxes	(40,000)	(70,000)
Estimated revenues	—	3,000,000
Expenditures	—	2,842,000
Expenditures—prior years	—	—
Encumbrances	—	91,000
	$510,000	$6,733,000

	Postclosing Balances June 30, 2010	Preclosing Balances June 30, 2011
Vouchers payable	$ 80,000	$ 408,000
Due to other funds	210,000	142,000
Fund balance—committed	60,000	91,000
Fund balance—unassigned	160,000	182,000
Revenues from taxes	—	2,800,000
Miscellaneous revenues	—	130,000
Appropriations	—	2,980,000
	$510,000	$6,733,000

ADDITIONAL INFORMATION

1. The estimated taxes receivable for the year ended June 30, 2011, were $2,870,000, and current-year taxes collected during the year totaled $2,810,000.

2. Estimated uncollectible taxes from the prior year were written off.

3. An analysis of the transactions in the vouchers payable for the year ended June 30, 2011, follows:

	Debit (Credit)
Current expenditures	$(2,700,000)
Expenditures for prior years	(58,000)
Vouchers for payment to other funds	(210,000)
Cash payments during the year	2,640,000
Net change	$ (328,000)

4. During the year the general fund was billed $142,000 for services performed on its behalf by other city funds.

5. On May 2, 2011, commitment documents were issued for the purchase of new textbooks at a cost of $91,000.

REQUIRED: Based on the data presented, reconstruct the original detailed journal entries that were required to record all transactions for the fiscal year ended June 30, 2011, including the recording of the current year's budget. Do not prepare closing entries at June 30, 2011.

P 20-6
Journal entries from trial balance [AICPA adapted]

The following information was abstracted from the accounts of the general fund of the City of Lahti after the books had been closed for the fiscal year ended June 30, 2011:

	Trial Balance June 30, 2010	Transactions July 1, 2010 to June 30, 2011 Debit	Transactions July 1, 2010 to June 30, 2011 Credit	Postclosing Trial Balance June 30, 2011
Cash	$700,000	$1,820,000	$1,852,000	$668,000
Taxes receivable	40,000	1,870,000	1,828,000	82,000
	$740,000			$750,000
Allowances for uncollectible taxes	$ 8,000	8,000	10,000	$ 10,000
Vouchers payable	132,000	1,852,000	1,840,000	120,000
Fund balance:				
Committed	—	1,000,000	1,070,000	70,000
Unassigned	600,000	140,000	60,000	
			30,000	550,000
	$740,000			$750,000

ADDITIONAL INFORMATION: The budget for the fiscal year ended June 30, 2011, provided for estimated revenues of $2,000,000 and appropriations of $1,940,000.

REQUIRED: Prepare journal entries to record the budgeted and actual transactions for the fiscal year ended June 30, 2011.

P 20-7
Preparation of a fund statement of revenues, expenditures and changes in fund balance

The following information regarding the fiscal year ended December 31, 2011, was drawn from the accounts and records of the Volendam County general fund:

Revenues and Other Asset Inflows	
Taxes	$10,000,000
Licenses and permits	2,000,000
Intergovernmental grants	300,000
Proceeds of short-term note issuances	1,000,000
Collection of interfund advance to other fund	450,000
Receipt of net assets of terminated fund	2,000,000
Expenditures and Other Asset Outflows	
General government expenditures	8,000,000
Public safety expenditures	1,500,000
Judicial system expenditures	1,000,000
Health and welfare expenditures	1,200,000
Equipment purchases	600,000
Payment to debt service fund to cover future debt	
service on general government bonds	320,000
Fund balance—unassigned, January 1, 2011	$ 3,130,000

REQUIRED: Prepare a statement of revenues, expenditures, and changes in fund balance for the Volendam County general fund for the year ended December 31, 2011.

P 20-8
Debt service fund journal entries

The Town of Lilehammar has $3,000,000 of 6 percent bonds outstanding. Interest on the general obligation, general government indebtedness is payable semiannually each March 31 and September 30. December 31 is the fiscal year-end. Record the following transactions in the town's debt service fund.

1. Received a transfer from the general fund to provide financing for the March 31, interest payment.

2. Paid the interest due on March 31.

3. Received a transfer from the general fund to provide financing for the September 30, interest payment and retirement of $1,000,000 of the bonds.

4. Paid the interest on September 31, and repaid $1,000,000 of the bonds.

5. December 31 is the fiscal year-end. Record any appropriate adjustments.

6. Received a transfer from the general fund to provide financing for the March 31 interest payment for year two of the bond.

7. Paid the interest due on March 31 for year two of the bond.

REQUIRED: Prepare a statement of revenues, expenditures, and changes in fund balance for the Town of Lilehammar debt service fund for the year ended December 31, 2011.

P 20-9
Capital projects fund journal entries

The City of Stockholm authorized construction of a $600,000 addition to the municipal building in September 2011. The addition will be financed by $200,000 from the general fund and a $400,000 serial bond issue to be sold in April 2012.

REQUIRED: Prepare journal entries for the capital projects fund and any other fund involved to the extent of requiring journal entries to record the transactions described.

1. On October 1, 2011, the general fund transferred $200,000 to the capital projects fund.

2. On November 1, 2011, a contract for the addition was awarded to Crooked Construction for $580,000.

3. On April 15, 2012, the $400,000, 7% bonds were sold for $401,000 and the premium was transferred to the debt service fund.

4. On May 2, 2012, construction was completed and Crooked Construction submitted a bill for $580,000.

5. On May 12, 2012, the bill to Crooked Construction was paid in full. The CPF was closed, and the remaining cash was transferred to the general fund.

P 20-10
Journal entries associated with a capital project

On June 15, 2011, Malmo City authorizes the issuance of $500,000 par of 6 percent serial bonds to be issued on July 1, 2011, and to mature in annual serials of $100,000 beginning on July 1, 2012. The proceeds of the bond issue are to be used to finance a new tourist rest area.

During the fiscal year ended June 30, 2012, the following events and transactions occurred:

> July 1—A contract for construction of the rest area is awarded to Gunnarsson Construction Company for $480,000.
>
> July 1—$250,000 par value of 6 percent serial bonds are sold at a premium of 2 percent.
>
> December 20—A bill is received from Gunnarsson Construction Company for one-third of the contract price.
>
> January 1—Gunnarsson Construction Company is paid for work completed to date, less a 10 percent retained percentage to ensure performance.
>
> January 1—Bond interest due is paid with funds transferred from the general fund and from the premium that was made available for interest payments.
>
> June 30—A bill is received from Gunnarsson Construction Company for one-third of the contract price.

REQUIRED

1. Prepare journal entries in each of the affected funds to account for the transactions and events described. Identify the fund for each journal entry.

2. Prepare a closing journal entry for the capital projects fund at June 30, 2012.

P 20-11
Capital projects fund journal entries and balance sheet [AICPA adapted]

In a special election held on May 1, 2011, the voters of the City of Cerone approved a $10,000,000 issue of 6 percent general obligation bonds maturing in 20 years. The proceeds of this sale will be used to help finance the construction of a new civic center. The total cost of the project was estimated at $15,000,000. The remaining $5,000,000 will be financed by a state grant, which has been awarded. A capital projects fund was established to account for this project and was designated the civic center construction fund. The formal project authorization was appropriately recorded in a memorandum entry.

The following transactions occurred during the fiscal year beginning July 1, 2011, and ending June 30, 2012.

1. On July 1 the general fund loaned $500,000 to the civic center construction fund for defraying engineering and other expenses.

2. Preliminary engineering and planning costs of $320,000 were paid to Eminem Engineering Company. There had been no encumbrance for this cost.

3. On December 1 the bonds were sold at 101. The premium on the bonds was transferred to the debt service fund.

4. On March 15 a contract for $12,000,000 was entered into with Candu Construction Company for the major part of the project.

5. Orders were placed for materials estimated to cost $55,000.

6. On April 1 a partial payment of $2,500,000 was received from the state.

7. The materials that were previously ordered were received at a cost of $51,000 and paid.

8. On June 15 a progress billing of $2,000,000 was received from Candu Construction for work done on the project. As per the terms of the contract, the city will withhold 6 percent of any billing until the project is completed.

9. The general fund was repaid the $500,000 previously loaned.

REQUIRED

1. Prepare journal entries to record the transactions in the civic center construction fund for the period July 1, 2011, through June 30, 2012, and the appropriate closing entries at June 30, 2012.

2. Prepare a balance sheet for the civic center construction fund on June 30, 2012.

P 20-12
Capital projects fund journal entries and financial statements

The City of Catalina authorized the construction of a new recreation center at a total cost of $1,000,000 on June 15, 2011. On the same date, the city approved a $1,000,000, 8 percent, 10-year general obligation serial bond issue to finance the project. During the year July 1, 2011, to June 30, 2012, the following transactions and events occurred relative to the recreation center project:

1. On July 1, 2011, the city sold $500,000 par of the authorized bonds, with interest payment dates on December 31 and June 30 and the first serial retirement to be made on June 30, 2009. The bonds were sold at 102.

2. On July 5, 2011, a construction contract for the recreation center was created in the amount of $960,000.

3. On December 15, 2011, the contractor's bill for $320,000 was received based on certification that the work was one-third completed.

4. The contractor was paid for one-third of the contract less a 10% retained percentage to ensure performance.

5. On December 30, 2011, the GF transferred $30,000 to the fund responsible for servicing the serial bonds.

6. Interest on the serial bonds was paid on December 31, 2011, with the money transferred from the GF and the CPF.

7. On June 15, 2012, the contractor's bill for $320,000 was received based on certification that the work was two-thirds completed.

8. On June 28, 2012, the GF transferred $90,000 to the fund responsible for servicing the serial bonds: $40,000 for interest and $50,000 for principal.

9. Interest and principal on the serial bonds were paid on June 30, 2012.

10. On June 30, 2012, the city sold the remaining $500,000 par of authorized bonds at par.

REQUIRED

1. Prepare all journal entries in the funds necessary to account for the transactions and events given. (If amounts are not known, use xxx.)

2. Prepare financial statements for the CPF for the year ended June 30, 2012.

INTERNET ASSIGNMENT

1. Choose a CAFR from a city, county, or other local government. Review the CAFR and answer the following questions:

   a. How many governmental funds does the government have? List the name of one special revenue fund.

   b. Does the government have a capital projects fund? For what purpose was it created? Is it a major fund?

   c. Does the government use a debt service fund?

   d. Does the government use encumbrance accounting? How can you tell?

   e. Has the government implemented GASB Statement No. 54? How can you tell?

   f. Locate the reconciliations between the fund and government-wide statements. List two reconciling items.

   g. Locate the budgetary comparison statement or schedule for the general fund. Comment on the extent of the differences between the original and final budgets.

2. Locate the Web site for the municipality in which your college or university is located. List one major event that has occurred recently and will be recorded in the accounting records. What fund or funds will be affected by this event?

3. Locate the Web site for the county in which your college or university is located. Has the county recorded any new debt this year in its governmental funds? How much? How can you tell?

21 CHAPTER

Accounting for State and Local Governmental Units—Proprietary and Fiduciary Funds

This chapter concludes coverage of state and local governmental accounting practices with a review of accounting and reporting procedures applicable to proprietary funds (internal service funds and enterprise funds) and fiduciary funds (trust funds and agency funds). Recall that governments use proprietary funds to account for business-type activities, while they use fiduciary funds to account for resources that are held for the benefit of others.

LEARNING OBJECTIVES

1 Review the appropriate accounting and financial reporting for proprietary funds.

2 Recognize the proper treatment of internal service funds in the government-wide statements.

3 Introduce the differences between a proprietary fund statement of cash flows and its commercial business counterpart.

4 Prepare journal entries and fund financial statements for fiduciary funds.

5 Learn about GASB guidance for pension fund accounting.

PROPRIETARY FUNDS

Governmental units use *proprietary funds* to account for business-type activities that provide goods and services to users and that finance those services largely from user charges. The objective of proprietary funds is to maintain capital or to produce income, or both, and full accrual accounting procedures apply. Thus, proprietary funds have revenue and expense, not expenditure, accounts. Within proprietary funds, governments recognize revenues in the accounting period in which they are earned (or in which similar recognition criteria have been met) and become measurable, and they recognize expenses in the period incurred, if measurable. The availability criterion for governmental fund revenue recognition does not apply to proprietary fund and similar trust fund revenue recognition.

Recall that the accounting equation for proprietary funds is:

$$\text{Current assets} + \text{Noncurrent assets} - \text{Current liabilities} - \text{Noncurrent liabilities} = \text{Net assets}$$

Unlike governmental funds, the fixed assets of proprietary funds and long-term liabilities expected to be serviced by proprietary fund revenues are both reported in proprietary fund financial statements. Long-term liabilities incurred by a proprietary fund and expected to be serviced from its revenues are fund liabilities, rather than general long-term debt. Lease agreements of proprietary funds are accounted for entirely within the fund under the provisions of *FASB Statement No. 13*, "Accounting for Leases," except for operating leases with scheduled rent increases. When governments report operating leases with scheduled rent increases in proprietary funds and similar trust funds, they recognize rental revenue as it accrues over the lease term.

As noted in Chapter 19, *GASB Statement No. 34* requires the preparation of three fund financial statements for proprietary funds. The required statements are a statement of net assets; a statement of revenues, expenses, and changes in net assets; and a statement of cash flows.

Because proprietary funds account for transactions in much the same manner as commercial business organizations, the GASB allows some reference to FASB statements. *GASB Statement No. 20*, "Accounting and Financial Reporting for Proprietary Activities," governs

LEARNING OBJECTIVE 1

accounting and reporting standards that apply to proprietary activities.[1] Governmental proprietary activities *must apply*:

- All applicable GASB statements *and*
- All FASB and predecessor standards issued before November 30, 1989, that do not conflict with GASB standards.[2]

Governmental proprietary activities *may either apply*:

- All FASB standards issued after November 30, 1989, as long as they do not conflict with GASB standards, *or*
- No FASB standards issued after November 30, 1989, even if they modify or rescind earlier issued FASB statements. (This election does not completely prohibit applying an FASB standard. In essence, they are in the lowest level of the GAAP hierarchy.)

Governments must disclose the option selected in the notes to the financial statements.

The two types of funds within the proprietary fund classification are internal service funds and enterprise funds. The key difference between an internal service fund and an enterprise fund lies in the user group for which the goods and services are intended. Enterprise funds provide goods and services primarily to the general public, whereas internal service funds provide their goods and services primarily to other departments or agencies within the same governmental unit (or, on a limited basis, to other governmental units). Even though the user groups for enterprise and internal service funds differ, the accounting treatment is similar. Under *GASB Statement No. 34*, however, presentation within both the government-wide and fund financial statements differs for internal service and enterprise funds. This chapter discusses and illustrates these differences.

INTERNAL SERVICE FUNDS

Internal service funds (ISF) are proprietary funds that a government uses to account for governmental activities that provide goods and services to other departments or agencies of the governmental unit, or to other governmental units, on a cost-reimbursement basis. The account classifications used by an ISF are those that would be used in accounting for similar operations of a private business enterprise.

Centralized purchasing, motor pools, printing shops, and self-insurance are examples of internal service fund operations. Each activity offers potential efficiencies through economies of scale, improved services, and better control.

In many cases, governmental units provide the initial financing of an ISF through a contribution of cash or operating facilities, while expecting the ISF to be self-sustaining in future periods. Alternatively, the governmental unit may provide a loan to an ISF to be repaid from future operating flows of the fund. A contribution is classified as a nonreciprocal transfer, which flows through the statement of revenues, expenses, and changes in fund net assets; whereas a loan is recorded as a liability of the ISF in the statement of net assets.

Accounting for an Internal Service Fund

The Village of Tara creates a central motor pool fund with a cash contribution of $200,000 from the general fund and a contribution of existing motor vehicles with a book value of $120,000. Because the cash is not expected to be repaid, the village will record the cash contribution as a $200,000 nonreciprocal transfer. The village will also remove the transferred equipment from the records

---

[1] GASB issued a 600 page exposure draft on January 29, 2010, on codifying pre-November 30, 1989, FASB pronouncements. The exposure draft is motivated by the FASB move to a single source of standards in the ASC (Accounting Standard Codification) but was not issued as of this writing.

[2] November 30, 1989, is the date that the Financial Accounting Foundation reaffirmed that the GASB was responsible for setting standards for state and local governments.

of general fixed assets at its original cost, or at book value if accumulated depreciation has been recorded. In the records of the central motor pool fund, the appropriate journal entry is as follows:

Internal Service Fund		
Cash	200,000	
Motor vehicles	120,000	
Nonreciprocal transfer from GF		200,000
Contributed capital from municipality		120,000
To record establishment of the fund.		

The village also records the transfer in the general fund:

General Fund		
Other financing use—nonreciprocal transfer to ISF	200,000	
Cash		200,000
To record the transfer of resources to establish an ISF.		

Note that there is no need to reflect the fixed asset contribution in the general fund accounting system; however, we will remove the assets from the general fixed asset *records* and record them as internal service fund fixed assets. Because internal service funds are reported as governmental activities on the government-wide statement of net assets, this interfund activity will not affect the amount of fixed assets reported in the governmental activity column of the government-wide statement of net assets.

The village obtains a maintenance facility at a cost of $100,000, purchases equipment for $50,000, and acquires operating supplies for $20,000. The village records these cash expenditures, in summary form, as follows:

Internal Service Fund		
Building	100,000	
Equipment	50,000	
Supplies on hand	20,000	
Cash		170,000
To record purchase of building, equipment, and supplies.		

Notice how the building and equipment are recorded in the ISF, as it is a proprietary fund. Depreciation expense will also be recognized.

During the first year of operation, the central motor pool fund provides motor pool vehicles to municipal departments and bills these departments at a predetermined rate based on miles driven. The rate is set to cover all costs of operating the motor pool and servicing the vehicles, including the cost of replacing worn-out vehicles. Note the similarity to business accounting entries.

When the internal service fund bills user funds, individual funds will record entries at the amount charged. Governments record short-term interfund receivables/payables as "Due to" in the fund that gets billed and "Due from" in the fund that sends the bill.

Internal Service Fund		
Due from general fund	100,000	
Due from special revenue fund	30,000	
Service revenue		130,000
To charge user funds for vehicle services.		
General Fund		
Expenditures	100,000	
Due to internal service fund		100,000
To record user charges for vehicle services.		
Special Revenue Fund		
Expenditures	30,000	
Due to internal service fund		30,000
To record user charges for vehicle services.		

Similarly, collection of the user charges triggers entries in the funds involved:

Internal Service Fund

Cash	100,000	
Due from general fund		100,000
To record collections from user funds.		

General Fund

Due to internal service fund	100,000	
Cash		100,000
To record payment of user charges for vehicle services.		

If revenue is received from external parties, the village will record ISF revenue in the following manner:

Internal Service Fund

Cash	1,000	
Interest revenue		1,000
To record interest revenue.		

Internal service funds record expenses as they are incurred. The predetermined billing rate was designed to cover such expenses:

Internal Service Fund

Salaries expense	40,000	
Utilities expense	18,000	
Insurance expense	16,000	
Cash		74,000
To record payments for expense items.		

Adjusting and closing entries are similar to those noted in a commercial enterprise:

Internal Service Fund—Adjusting Entries

Supplies expense	15,000	
Supplies on hand		15,000
To adjust supplies expense and supplies on hand accounts at year-end.		
Salaries expense	4,000	
Accrued salaries payable		4,000
To accrue salaries.		
Depreciation expense—building	5,000	
Accumulated depreciation—building		5,000
To record depreciation on building ($100,000 ÷ 20 years).		
Depreciation expense—motor vehicles	20,000	
Accumulated depreciation—motor vehicles		20,000
To record depreciation on vehicles (200,000 miles driven × 10 cents per mile).		
Depreciation expense—equipment	10,000	
Accumulated depreciation—equipment		10,000
To record depreciation on equipment ($50,000 ÷ 5 years).		

Internal Service Fund—Closing Entries

Nonreciprocal transfer from GF	200,000	
Net assets		200,000
To close transfer to net assets.		
Contributed capital from municipality	120,000	
Net assets		120,000
To close contributed capital to net assets.		

Service revenue	130,000	
Interest revenue	1,000	
Supplies expense		15,000
Insurance expense		16,000
Salaries expense		44,000
Utilities expense		18,000
Depreciation expense—building		5,000
Depreciation expense—motor vehicles		20,000
Depreciation expense—equipment		10,000
Net assets, unrestricted		3,000
To close revenue and expense accounts to net assets.		

Notice that the internal service fund had revenue in excess of expenses in the amount of $3,000. This slight income figure indicates that the predetermined rate charged to users was appropriate.

Reporting Internal Service Funds in the Financial Statements

LEARNING OBJECTIVE **2**

Internal service funds are officially designated as proprietary funds; however, their intended purpose is to provide goods and services to governmental and enterprise funds of the governmental entity. Thus, they possess a unique nature, and, under *GASB Statement No. 34*, governments report them in a unique manner. In the fund financial statements, governments include internal service funds with the proprietary funds. Due to their nature, though, they are never considered major funds, and all internal service funds are aggregated into a single column within the proprietary fund statement of net assets, the statement of revenues, expenses, and changes in net assets, and the statement of cash flows. The column containing internal service fund activities is captioned Governmental Activities. Exhibits 21-1, 21-2, and 21-3 use this format for the sample proprietary fund financial statements for the Village of Tara.

Within the government-wide statements, governments report internal service funds with the governmental activities. The internal service fund balance sheet accounts are included in the governmental activity column of the statement of net assets. However, the statement of activities will include only those internal service fund transactions involving entities other than the primary reporting entity. Thus, governments add external internal service fund revenues (and expenses) to the statement of activities, while they exclude internal governmental transactions. For example, Tara includes only the $1,000 of ISF interest in the governmental activities totals in the government-wide statement of activities. This, in essence, eliminates double counting of interfund transactions, much like consolidated entities eliminate intercompany transactions. This process is reviewed later in the chapter.

ENTERPRISE FUNDS

Enterprise funds (EF) are proprietary funds that a government uses to account for activities that are financed and operated similarly to those of private business enterprises. Typically, enterprise funds provide goods and services to the general public on a continuing basis, with the costs being financed primarily through user charges. Governments may use enterprise funds to record any business activities for which a user fee is charged. However, they are required to use an enterprise fund for activities that (1) are financed with debt secured solely by net revenue from fees and charges to external users; (2) operate under laws or regulations requiring that the activity's costs of providing services, including capital costs, be recovered with fees and charges; or (3) have prices established by management to cover the costs (including capital costs) of providing services.[3] As you can imagine, enterprise fund operations are about as diverse as those found in private enterprise. They range from the operation of electric and water utilities, which are intended to produce income, to swimming pool and golf course operations, in which costs are intended to be recovered primarily

---

[3]*GASB Statement No. 34*, paragraph 387.

from user charges, to activities such as mass transit authorities and civic centers, which are often heavily subsidized from general governmental revenues.

The objective of an enterprise fund is to maintain capital or to generate net income, or both; thus, full accrual accounting procedures are applicable. Like internal service funds, enterprise funds are proprietary funds that use revenue and expense accounts and accrual accounting practices similar to those of private business enterprises. Enterprise fund fixed assets and long-term liabilities are fund fixed assets and fund long-term liabilities. Therefore, governments record them in the enterprise fund. Often, the long-term debt obligations are in the form of revenue bonds secured only by enterprise fund operations. If such bonds are also secured by the "full faith and credit" of the governmental unit, the enterprise fund still records the liability in the fund, but the notes to the financial statements will also disclose a contingent liability, indicating the extent of general government responsibility for repayment.

Initial financing of many enterprise funds is typically the same as for an internal service fund. The governmental unit makes a capital contribution (a transfer from the general fund) or provides a long-term interfund loan to the enterprise fund. Future operations are expected to cover all costs, including depreciation on fund fixed assets, so operations can continue indefinitely without further capital contributions.

The following section presents sample entries related to a utility department's operations. Because the accounting for enterprise funds is quite similar to accounting for commercial business enterprises, the discussion and examples are abbreviated.

Accounting for an Enterprise Fund

Utility-type enterprise funds often require customer deposits to assure timely payment for services. The utility normally collects the deposit before service starts and refunds the money after a minimum holding period has elapsed or when service is terminated. Land developers may also be required to make good-faith deposits to finance the cost of extending utility service lines. Governments segregate such assets and report them as restricted assets in the enterprise fund balance sheet. Customer deposits remain in current liabilities until they are applied against unpaid billings or refunded to customers. Entries related to customer deposits are as follows:

Enterprise Fund		
Restricted cash	10,000	
Customer deposits		10,000
To record customer deposits collected.		
Enterprise Fund		
Customer deposits	3,000	
Restricted cash		3,000
To record customer deposit refunds.		

An enterprise fund records customer billings and receipts as follows:

Enterprise Fund		
Accounts receivable	680,000	
Charges for services		680,000
To record customer charges for utility services.		
Enterprise Fund		
Cash	640,000	
Accounts receivable		640,000
To record collection from customers for utility services.		

Enterprise funds often receive intergovernmental grants that are designated for operations (operating grants) or capital asset acquisition (capital grants). For example, the Gator County Waste Management Facility may receive grant funds from the Environmental Protection Agency designated for pollution control. Governments report operating grants as nonoperating revenues in proprietary funds, whereas they recognize capital grants as contributed capital, not as revenues. Under *GASB Statement No. 33*, enterprise funds recognize grant revenues and capital contributions in the period in which qualifying expenses are incurred, assuming any other significant conditions have been met. If funds are received before qualifying expenses are incurred, deferred revenue is recorded. The entry to record an intergovernmental capital grant once qualified expenses have been made is as follows:

Enterprise Fund

Due from other governments	50,000	
Contributed capital—grant		50,000
To recognize capital grant revenue for qualified expenses.		

If a new generator is purchased by issuing a note payable, the enterprise fund entry will be as follows:

Enterprise Fund

Equipment	35,000	
Notes payable		35,000
To record the purchase of equipment.		

Using accrual accounting, enterprise funds record other operating expenses as they are incurred:

Enterprise Fund

Salaries expense	150,000	
Repairs and maintenance expense	78,000	
Supplies expense	132,000	
Utilities expense	60,000	
Insurance expense	15,000	
Cash		435,000
To record payments for expense items.		

Adjusting and closing entries are similar to those recorded in internal service funds:

Enterprise Fund—Adjusting Entries

Salaries expense	17,000	
Accrued salaries payable		17,000
To accrue salaries.		
Interest expense	2,000	
Interest payable		2,000
To accrue interest on note payable.		
Depreciation expense	42,000	
Accumulated depreciation		42,000
To record depreciation for the year.		

Enterprise Fund—Closing Entries

Charges for services	680,000	
Salaries expense		167,000
Repairs and maintenance expense		78,000
Supplies expense		132,000
Depreciation expense		42,000
Interest expense		2,000
Utilities expense		60,000
Insurance expense		15,000
Net assets, unrestricted		184,000
To close revenue and expense accounts to net assets.		
Contributed capital—grant	50,000	
Net assets, restricted		50,000
To close contributed capital to net assets.		

PROPRIETARY FUND FINANCIAL STATEMENTS

Required fund financial statements for proprietary funds consist of a statement of net assets; a statement of revenues, expenses, and changes in net assets; and a statement of cash flows. Each of these statements includes a column for each enterprise fund that is considered a major fund, as well as a column totaling all nonmajor enterprise fund activity.[4] As noted earlier, proprietary fund statements report internal service funds with the enterprise funds. The fund financial statements aggregate all internal service funds in a single column. Exhibits 21-1, 21-2, and 21-3 illustrate this format for the sample proprietary fund financial statements for the Village of Tara.

The financial statements of proprietary funds are similar to those of a business enterprise, with a few exceptions. Internal service and enterprise funds do not pay property taxes or income taxes, and thus these items are noticeably absent from the operating statement. The funds may exhibit interfund activity; therefore, governmental entity financial statements may include interfund account titles such as due from general fund (for utility charges or supply acquisitions), advance from general fund (for long-term financing), and transfers.

In addition, proprietary funds do not have capital stock or paid-in capital. In place of stockholders' equity, their statement of net assets (balance sheet) shows a net assets section, such as the following:

Net Assets	
Invested in capital assets, net of related debt	$500,000
Restricted	150,000
Unrestricted	300,000
Total fund equity	$950,000

Net assets *invested in capital (fixed) assets, net of related debt* are equal to the fixed assets of the fund less all fixed-asset-related debt, whether current or long-term. *Restricted net assets* are equal to the difference between (1) assets externally restricted by creditors, grantors, donors, or laws and regulations of other governments, or internally by constitutional provisions or enabling legislation and (2) liabilities payable from those restricted assets. The restrictions must be narrower than the purposes of the fund being reported. *Unrestricted net assets* are equal to the difference between the remaining assets and liabilities of the fund. Restricted net assets must be reclassified as unrestricted when the government satisfies the restriction.

LEARNING OBJECTIVE 3

Statement of Cash Flows for Proprietary Funds

The statement of cash flows for proprietary funds also differs slightly from its commercial business counterpart. First of all, *GASB Statement No. 34* makes the direct method mandatory for statement presentation. Also, cash flow classifications have been modified. You may recall that *FASB Statement No. 95* specifies a three-section format for cash flow statements of business enterprises: operating activities, investing activities, and financing activities. *GASB Statement No. 9*, "Reporting Cash Flows of Proprietary and Nonexpendable Trust Funds and Governmental Entities That Use Proprietary Fund Accounting," which establishes standards for cash flow reporting for proprietary funds, separates financing activities into noncapital and capital related. Therefore, a proprietary fund cash flow statement has four separate sections: cash flows from operating activities, cash flows from noncapital financing activities, cash flows from capital and related financing activities, and cash flows from investing activities. The following sections review the content of the four separate sections of the statement of cash flows for proprietary funds and government entities that

---

[4]Recall from Chapter 19 that a fund is considered a major fund if it meets both of the following criteria: (a) Total assets, liabilities, revenues, or expenditures/expenses (excluding extraordinary items) of that individual governmental or enterprise fund are at least 10% of the *corresponding* total (assets, liabilities, and so forth) for *all* funds of that *category* or *type* (that is, total governmental or total enterprise funds), and (b) total assets, liabilities, revenues, or expenditures/expenses (excluding extraordinary items) of that individual governmental or enterprise fund are at least 5% of the *corresponding total* for all governmental *and* enterprise funds *combined*.

EXHIBIT 21-1

Proprietary Fund
Statement of Net Assets

VILLAGE OF TARA STATEMENT OF NET ASSETS—PROPRIETARY FUNDS
JUNE 30, 2011

| | Business-Type Activities—Enterprise Funds | | | | Governmental Activities |
	Utilities	Parking Facilities	Other Enterprise Funds	Totals	Internal Service Funds
Assets					
Current assets					
Cash and cash equivalents	$ 614,635	$ 75,000	$ 30,000	$ 719,635	$ 57,000
Receivables, net	235,915	20,000	5,000	260,915	—
Due from other funds	—	—	—	—	30,000
Due from other governments	32,112	—	—	32,112	—
Supplies	61,443	1,000	—	62,443	5,000
Total current assets	944,105	96,000	35,000	1,075,105	92,000
Noncurrent assets					
Restricted cash and cash equivalents	185,000	—	—	185,000	—
Land	45,000	50,000	—	95,000	—
Buildings and equipment	1,000,000	850,000	140,000	1,990,000	150,000
Vehicles	220,000	—	—	220,000	120,000
Less accumulated depreciation	(520,000)	(450,000)	(35,000)	(1,005,000)	(35,000)
Total noncurrent assets	930,000	450,000	105,000	1,485,000	235,000
Total assets	$1,874,105	$546,000	$140,000	$2,560,105	$327,000
Liabilities					
Current liabilities					
Accounts payable	$ 45,000	$ 20,000	$ 3,000	$ 68,000	—
Accrued liabilities	19,000	20,000	5,000	44,000	$ 4,000
Due to other funds	—	—	4,000	4,000	—
Compensated absences	3,000	2,000	—	5,000	—
Bonds and notes payable	20,000	50,000	10,000	80,000	—
Total current liabilities	87,000	92,000	22,000	201,000	4,000
Noncurrent liabilities					
Customer deposits	185,000	—	—	185,000	—
Compensated absences	230,000	65,000	—	295,000	—
Bonds and notes payable	275,000	100,000	90,000	465,000	—
Total noncurrent liabilities	690,000	165,000	90,000	945,000	—
Total liabilities	$ 777,000	$257,000	$112,000	$1,146,000	$ 4,000
Net Assets					
Invested in capital assets, net of related debt	$ 450,000	$300,000	$ 5,000	$ 755,000	$235,000
Restricted	185,000	—	—	185,000	—
Unrestricted	462,105	11,000	23,000	474,105	88,000
Total net assets	$1,097,105	$289,000	$ 28,000	$1,414,105	$323,000

use proprietary fund accounting. A proprietary fund cash flow statement for the Village of Tara is presented in Exhibit 21-3.

CASH FLOWS FROM OPERATING ACTIVITIES Cash inflows of the operating activities section include the following:

Receipts from sales of goods or services

Receipts from interfund services provided

Receipts from interfund reimbursements

All other receipts not included in one of the other three sections

Cash outflows of the operating activities section include the following:

Payments for materials used in providing services or manufacturing goods for resale

Principal payments to suppliers of those materials or goods on account or under short-term or long-term notes payable

VILLAGE OF TARA STATEMENT OF REVENUES, EXPENSES, AND CHANGES IN FUND NET ASSETS—PROPRIETARY FUNDS FOR THE YEAR ENDED JUNE 30, 2011

	Business-Type Activities—Enterprise Funds				Governmental Activities
	Utilities	Parking Facilities	Other Enterprise Funds	Totals	Internal Service Funds
Operating Revenues					
Charges for services	$ 680,000	$500,000	$40,000	$1,220,000	$130,000
Miscellaneous	—	—	—	—	—
Total operating revenues	680,000	500,000	40,000	1,220,000	130,000
Operating Expenses					
Salaries	167,000	25,000	12,000	204,000	44,000
Contractual services	—	275,000	—	275,000	—
Utilities	60,000	24,000	—	84,000	18,000
Repairs and maintenance	78,000	11,000	—	89,000	—
Insurance expense	15,000	8,000	—	23,000	16,000
Supplies and other expenses	132,000	1,200	3,000	136,200	15,000
Depreciation	42,000	65,000	18,000	125,000	35,000
Total operating expenses	494,000	409,200	33,000	936,200	128,000
Operating income (loss)	186,000	90,800	7,000	283,800	2,000
Nonoperating Revenues (Expenses)					
Interest	—	—	—	—	1,000
Miscellaneous revenue (expense)	—	—	—	—	—
Interest expense	2,000	12,000	5,000	19,000	—
Total nonoperating revenue (expense)	(2,000)	(12,000)	(5,000)	(19,000)	1,000
Income (loss) before contributions and transfers	184,000	78,800	2,000	264,800	3,000
Capital contributions	50,000	—	—	50,000	120,000
Transfers in	—	—	—	—	200,000
Transfers out	—	—	—	—	—
Change in net assets	234,000	78,800	2,000	314,800	323,000
Total net assets—beginning	863,105	210,200	26,000	1,099,305	—
Total net assets—ending	$1,097,105	$289,000	$28,000	$1,414,105	$323,000

Payments to suppliers for other goods and services

Payments to employees for salaries

Payments to other governments as grants for operating activities

Payments for taxes and in lieu of taxes

All other cash payments not included in one of the other three sections

CASH FLOWS FROM NONCAPITAL FINANCING ACTIVITIES Items to be considered cash inflows for the non-capital financing activities section include the following:

Proceeds from bonds and notes not clearly issued specifically for the acquisition, construction, or improvement of capital assets

Receipts from grants and subsidies and receipts from other funds (except those restricted for capital purposes or operating activities)

Receipts from property taxes and other taxes collected for the governmental enterprise and not restricted for capital purposes

VILLAGE OF TARA STATEMENT OF CASH FLOWS—PROPRIETARY FUNDS FOR THE YEAR ENDED JUNE 30, 2011

EXHIBIT 21-3

Proprietary Fund Cash Flow Statement

	Business-Type Activities—Enterprise Funds				Governmental Activities
	Utilities	Parking Facilities	Other Enterprise Funds	Totals	Internal Service Funds
Cash Flows from Operating Activities					
Cash received from customers	$640,000	$489,000	$32,000	$1,161,000	$100,000
Cash paid to suppliers	(132,000)	(2,000)	(6,000)	(140,000)	(20,000)
Cash paid for salaries	(150,000)	(25,000)	(11,000)	(186,000)	(40,000)
Cash paid for utilities	(60,000)	(24,000)	—	(84,000)	(18,000)
Cash paid for contractual services	—	(275,000)	—	(275,000)	—
Cash paid for insurance	(15,000)	(8,000)	—	(23,000)	(16,000)
Cash paid for repairs and maintenance	(78,000)	(11,000)	—	(89,000)	—
Net cash provided (used) by operating activities	205,000	144,000	15,000	364,000	6,000
Cash Flows from Noncapital Financing Activities					
Cash received from general fund (noncapital loan)	—	—	3,000	3,000	200,000
Net cash provided (used) by noncapital financing activities	—	—	3,000	3,000	200,000
Cash Flows from Capital and Related Financing Activities					
Purchase of building	—	—	—	—	(100,000)
Purchase of equipment	—	(12,000)	(6,000)	(18,000)	(50,000)
Principal paid on capital debt	—	(75,000)	—	(75,000)	—
Interest paid on capital debt	—	(12,000)	—	(12,000)	—
Net cash provided(used) by capital and related financing activities	—	(99,000)	(6,000)	(105,000)	(150,000)
Cash Flows from Investing Activities					
Interest and dividends	—	—	—	—	1,000
Net cash provided by investing activities	—	—	—	—	1,000
Net (decrease) increase in unrestricted cash and cash equivalents	205,000	45,000	12,000	262,000	57,000
Balances—beginning	409,635	30,000	18,000	457,635	—
Balances—ending	$614,635	$ 75,000	$30,000	$ 719,635	$ 57,000

Cash outflows for this section include the following:

Repayments of amounts borrowed (including interest payments) other than those related to acquiring or constructing capital assets

Amounts paid for grants and subsidies (except those for specific operating activities of the grantor government)

Cash paid to other funds, except for interfund services used

CASH FLOWS FROM CAPITAL (FIXED ASSET) AND RELATED FINANCING ACTIVITIES Capital and related activities include acquiring and disposing of capital assets used in providing goods and services, including borrowing money to finance fixed asset construction or acquisition and repaying it with interest. Cash inflows include amounts from capital grants (i.e., grants for the sole purpose of acquiring, constructing, or improving a fixed asset), contributions, special assessments, insurance proceeds, and so on, as long as they are received specifically to defray the cost of acquiring, constructing, or improving capital assets. Cash received from sale or disposal of fixed assets is included in this section also.

Cash outflows include amounts to acquire, construct, or improve capital assets, and to repay amounts borrowed (including interest), as long as the purpose of the borrowing was directly related to acquiring, constructing, or improving capital assets.

Cash Flows from Investing Activities Investing activities include making and collecting loans and acquiring and disposing of investments in debt or equity instruments. Cash inflows include collections of loans and sales of investment securities (other than from cash equivalents) and the receipt of interest and dividends. Cash outflows include making loans and payments to acquire investment securities (other than for cash equivalents).

<table>
<tr><td>LEARNING
OBJECTIVE **4**</td></tr>
</table>

FIDUCIARY FUNDS

Governmental units use *fiduciary funds* to account for assets held in a trustee or agency capacity on behalf of others external to the governmental entity. Such resources cannot be used for the benefit of the government's own programs. The fiduciary grouping includes trust funds (private-purpose, investment, and pension) and agency funds, which are similar in the sense that the governmental unit acts in a fiduciary capacity for both types of funds. The accounting emphasis for trust and agency funds lies in demonstrating how the government's fiduciary responsibilities have been met. The basic difference between the two fund types is that a trust agreement, which mandates the degree of management involvement and the duration of the trust, typically exists for trust fund resources. Furthermore, agency funds are more temporary in nature.

Accounting for fiduciary funds follows the accrual basis of accounting; however, agency funds do not have revenues or expenses because their operations are of a custodial nature. Governments report fiduciary funds in the fund financial statements on a statement of fiduciary net assets and a statement of changes in fiduciary net assets. Fiduciary funds are not included in the government-wide statements.

Agency Funds

Agency funds are fiduciary funds used to account for resources that governments hold in a custodial or agency capacity. For example, a local government acts as an agent for the federal government when it withholds income and Social Security taxes, which will later be remitted to other government agencies, from employee payrolls. Also, an agency fund reports the debt service transactions of a special assessment bond issue for which the government is not obligated in any manner in order to reflect the fact that the government's duties are limited to acting as an agent for the assessed property owners and bondholders. Thus, the government acts as an agent for the property owners in collecting special assessments and remitting the amounts collected to bondholders.

Governments utilize agency funds when their agency responsibilities involve numerous transactions, include several different governmental units, or do not arise from normal and recurring operations of any other fund. For example, if a county unit of government serves as a tax collection agency for all towns and cities located within the county, the county will create an agency fund to demonstrate acceptance of responsibility for collecting and remitting taxes for other governmental units. To use an agency fund, however, the governmental entity should only act as a cash conduit, collecting and dispersing cash. If the governmental entity undertakes any administrative duties, such as determining who will receive the cash or monitoring recipient eligibility, it cannot use an agency fund.

The accounting treatment for agency funds is quite simple, as reflected in the following accounting equation:

$$\text{Assets} = \text{Liabilities}$$

There is no fund balance or equity. Assets and liabilities are recognized at the time that the government becomes responsible for the assets.

Accounting for an Agency Fund

Assume that Morris County collects property taxes for its own purposes as well as for the cities of Howard Lake, Brownsville, and Clute, and that total property tax levies for the 2010–2011 fiscal year are as follows:

Morris County	$100,000	50%
Howard Lake	50,000	25
Brownsville	20,000	10
Clute	30,000	15
Total	$200,000	100%

When the tax levies are certified to the county for collection, a tax agency fund records the county's custodial responsibility for collecting the taxes:

Agency Fund

Taxes receivable for local governmental units	200,000	
Liability to Morris County		100,000
Liability to Howard Lake		50,000
Liability to Brownsville		20,000
Liability to Clute		30,000
To record tax levy.		

The county collects $180,000 of the levy for remittance to the respective units of government during the year. Ninety percent of the taxes are collected for Morris County and each of the three cities. The following entry is made to record the collection:

Agency Fund

Cash	180,000	
Taxes receivable for local governmental units		180,000
To record collection of taxes receivable.		

If Morris County charges Howard Lake, Brownsville, and Clute a fee of 1 percent of taxes collected, the total charges would be $900 ($90,000 collected for these three cities multiplied by 1%), recorded as follows:

Agency Fund

Liability to Howard Lake	450	
Liability to Brownsville	180	
Liability to Clute	270	
Due to general fund (of Morris County)		900
To charge cities a 1% fee for taxes collected for them.		

General Fund

Due from other governments	900	
Miscellaneous revenues		900
To record fees charged to cities.		

The following entries reflect the remittance:

Agency Fund

Due to general fund	900	
Liability to Morris County	90,000	
Liability to Howard Lake	44,550	
Liability to Brownsville	17,820	
Liability to Clute	26,730	
Cash		180,000
To record remittance of taxes collected net of 1% fee.		

EXHIBIT 21-4

Statement of Fiduciary
Net Assets

MORRIS COUNTY STATEMENT OF FIDUCIARY NET ASSETS—FIDUCIARY FUNDS JUNE 30, 2011

	Tax Collection Agency Fund	School Library Trust Fund
Assets		
Cash and cash equivalents	0	0
Investments	0	$100,000
Taxes receivable	$20,000	0
Interest receivable	0	1,667
Total assets	$20,000	$101,667
Liabilities		
Liability to Morris County	10,000	0
Liability to Howard Lake	5,000	0
Liability to Brownsville	2,000	0
Liability to Clute	3,000	0
Total liabilities	$20,000	$ 0
Net Assets		
Available for distribution to school libraries	0	1,667
Held in trust for endowment	0	100,000
Total net assets	$ 0	$101,667

General Fund		
Cash	900	
Due from other governments		900
To record collection of fees.		

Financial Statements for the Agency Fund

Morris County includes the tax collection agency fund in the statement of fiduciary net assets shown in Exhibit 21-4. Because agency funds do not have revenues and expenses, they need not be included in the statement of changes in fiduciary net assets. Agency funds are not included in the government-wide statements.

Trust Funds

Investment trust funds are fiduciary funds used to account for multigovernment external investment pools sponsored by the governmental entity. For example, a county government may offer to pool the cash available for investment from cities located within its boundaries. Because the cash is not an asset of the county government and cannot be used for its benefit, the resources should be accounted for in a fiduciary fund. Furthermore, if a formal agreement exists and income will be recognized in the fund, it would be appropriate to establish a trust. *GASB Statement No. 31* describes the accounting for investment trust funds. Accounting for investment trust funds is beyond the scope of this chapter, so the following discussion focuses on private-purpose and pension trust funds.

Private-purpose trust funds are fiduciary funds used to account for resources (other than investment pools and employee benefits) that are held for the benefit of parties outside the governmental entity.[5] *Pension trust funds* are fiduciary funds used when a government acts as trustee for defined benefit and defined contribution pension plans of a government or for other employee benefit programs.

---

[5]Recall that permanent funds are used to account for restricted resources that will benefit the government or its citizens.

Accounting for a Private-Purpose Trust Fund

Assume that on July 2, 2011, Morris County receives a $100,000 contribution from the Hurricane Valley Historical Society. A trust agreement specifying that the income from the contribution must be distributed each May 15 to the three school libraries in Morris County accompanies the contribution. The principal amount is intended to remain intact indefinitely. The county establishes a private-purpose trust fund to account for the contribution and associated activities, because the county itself will not benefit from these resources. The entry is as follows:

Trust Fund

Cash	100,000	
Contributions—foundations		100,000
To record a contribution received.		

This principal amount is not expendable and will remain in the trust fund. Expendable income amounts may be either accounted for within the same trust fund or transferred to a separate expendable trust fund.

On September 1, the county invests the contribution in bonds, which yield 5 percent annually (payable on March 1 and September 1):

Trust Fund

Investments	100,000	
Cash		100,000
To record an investment in bonds.		

On March 1, the county receives the first interest payment:

Trust Fund

Cash	2,500	
Interest income		2,500
To record the collection of interest.		

On May 15, Morris County distributes the interest to local school libraries:

Trust Fund

Distribution to school libraries	2,500	
Cash		2,500
To record the distribution of interest.		

On June 30, the county adjusts and closes its accounts:

Trust Fund—Adjusting Entry

Interest receivable	1,667	
Interest income		1,667
To accrue interest income ($100,000 \times .05 \times 4/12$).		

Trust Fund—Closing Entry

Interest income	4,167	
Contributions—foundations	100,000	
Distribution to school libraries		2,500
Net assets held in trust for school libraries—nonexpendable		100,000
Net assets held in trust for school libraries—expendable		1,667
To close accounts.		

Financial Statements for the Trust Fund

Morris County includes the school library trust fund in the statement of fiduciary net assets (Exhibit 21-4) and the statement of changes in fiduciary net assets (Exhibit 21-5). Note how a statement of changes in fiduciary net assets reports fund additions and deductions to reflect funds held on behalf of others and distributed to parties outside the government. Trust funds are not included in the government-wide statements.

EXHIBIT 21-5

Statement of Changes in
Fiduciary Net Assets

MORRIS COUNTY STATEMENT OF CHANGES IN FIDUCIARY NET ASSETS—TRUST FUND FOR THE YEAR ENDED JUNE 30, 2011	
Additions	
Contributions	
Foundations	$100,000
Total contributions	100,000
Investment earnings	
Interest	4,167
Total investment earnings	4,167
Total additions	104,167
Deductions	
Distributions to school libraries	2,500
Total deductions	2,500
Change in net assets	101,667
Net assets—beginning of the year	0
Net assets—end of the year	$101,667

LEARNING OBJECTIVE **5**

Accounting for a Pension Trust Fund

Governments account and report for public employee retirement systems (PERS) through pension trust funds. There are two primary types of pension plans: defined benefit and defined contribution. A defined benefit plan specifies the amount of benefits that will be provided to the employee after retirement, and a defined contribution plan specifies the amount of resources that the government will invest on behalf of employee retirement during the employee's employment. Pension plans are further classified as single-employer plans if they involve only one government or multiple-employer if they include more than one government. Finally, for multiple-employer plans, a cost-sharing plan pools the cost of financing pensions, while an agent plan maintains separate actuarial calculations for each participating government.

PERS are not subject to the regulations of ERISA (the federal government's Employee Retirement Income Security Act); consequently, some governmental pension plans are fully funded, others are partially funded, and still others make all pension payments from current revenue. Pension trust fund accounting and financial reporting requirements are set forth primarily in *GASB Statement No. 25,* "Financial Reporting for Defined Benefit Pension Plans and Note Disclosures for Defined Contribution Plans," and *GASB Statement No. 27,* "Accounting for Pensions by State and Local Governmental Employers," as amended by *GASB Statement No. 50,* "Pension Disclosures." FASB pension accounting guidance is never to be applied by governments.

GASB pension standards require governments to present a schedule of funding progress for defined benefit, single-employer, and multiple-employer pension plans. The schedule of funding progress allows financial statement users to determine whether a government's aggregate payments for retirement benefits are adequate and whether the funding status has improved or diminished over time. While various actuarial methods are allowed, GASB Statement No. 50 requires funding status information to be disclosed regardless of the method used.

Accounting and reporting for pension trust funds is quite complex, and, as noted earlier, differs by pension fund classification. Thus, pension trust fund accounting is not examined in detail here.

In addition to pensions, many state and local governmental employers provide other postemployment benefits (OPEB) to qualified employees. OPEB includes postemployment health care as well as other forms of postemployment benefits (for example, life insurance) provided separately from a pension plan. *GASB Statement No. 43,* "Financial Reporting for Postemployment Benefit Plans Other Than Pension Plans," and *GASB Statement No. 45,* "Accounting and Financial Reporting by Employers for Postemployment Benefits Other Than Pensions," establish standards for the reporting, measurement, recognition, and display of OPEB expense/expenditures and related liabilities (assets), note disclosures, and, if applicable, required supplementary information (RSI) in the financial reports of state and local governmental employers.

PREPARING THE GOVERNMENT-WIDE FINANCIAL STATEMENTS

The government-wide statements include a column for business-type activities. This column includes enterprise fund amounts only. Because the government-wide statement of activities and statement of net assets report all items using the accrual basis of accounting, conversion between the enterprise fund and government-wide statements is not necessary. Governments can simply transfer enterprise fund figures from the proprietary fund statements to the government-wide statements, *with one exception*: Governments must either eliminate internal balances or report them as interfund balances in the asset section of the statement of net assets. For example, in the Village of Tara illustration, $4,000 is due to other funds from an enterprise fund. Because the enterprise fund owes this interfund payable to a governmental fund, the village will report the amount as an "internal balance." It appears in the asset section of the statement of net assets as a debit in the governmental activities column (for the governmental fund receivable) and as a credit in the business-type activity column (for the enterprise fund payable). Internal balances account for the only difference between enterprise balances on the fund statements and the government-wide statements, so no reconciliations are necessary.

Recall that government-wide statements report internal service funds with governmental activities. When preparing the government-wide statements, governments add internal service fund assets and liabilities to governmental fund assets and liabilities, as was indicated in the conversion worksheet in Exhibit 20-5; however, note that internal balances among governmental activities are eliminated. For example, in the Village of Tara illustration, Tara will eliminate the $30,000 due to the internal service fund from the special revenue fund in the governmental activities column. Also, Tara will eliminate the $200,000 transfer in from the general fund. Any revenues from external parties, such as the $1,000 interest revenue recognized earlier in the chapter, will be included in governmental totals reported on the statement of activities. However, because the internal service fund benefited the governmental funds only, debiting internal service fund net assets and crediting governmental fund expenditures eliminate the intra-governmental operating revenue and expenses for the internal service fund. This adjustment ensures that figures in the governmental activity column are not "grossed up."

REQUIRED PROPRIETARY FUND NOTE DISCLOSURES

Enterprise funds follow the accrual basis of accounting and are therefore able to report long-term debt within their funds. If an enterprise fund issues debt that is backed by its revenue-generating activity (i.e., revenue-backed debt instruments), the government must present certain detailed segment information in the notes to the financial statements.[6] The information helps creditors and financial statement users to determine if the segment that has issued the debt is generating the proceeds to fund the debt. The segment disclosure includes a description of the type of goods and services provided by the segment, as well as condensed statements of net assets; revenues, expenses, and changes in net assets; and cash flows.

SUMMARY

Governmental units use proprietary funds to account for business-type activities and use fiduciary funds to account for assets held in a trustee or agency capacity on behalf of others external to the governmental entity. This chapter reviewed the appropriate accounting and financial reporting for proprietary and fiduciary funds, which generally follow the accrual basis for accounting and reporting.

Accounting for each of the proprietary funds is the same; however, financial statement presentation differs. Within the proprietary fund financial statements, each major enterprise fund appears in a separate column, whereas nonmajor enterprise fund activities are totaled and reported in a single column. A separate column reports the total of all internal service fund balances. Within the government-wide statements, however, enterprise funds appear in a column labeled Business-Type Activities, whereas internal service funds are included with governmental activities. Governmental funds financial statements report fiduciary funds in fund statements, but government-wide statements do not include these funds.

---

[6]*GASB statement No. 34*, paragraph 122.

QUESTIONS

1. How are enterprise and internal service funds similar? How are they different?

2. Cite some governmental operations that might be accounted for through an internal service fund.

3. What fund financial statements are needed for an enterprise fund to meet the requirements for fair presentation in accordance with GAAP? Which government-wide statements include enterprise fund data?

4. Which fund financial statements include internal service fund data? Which government-wide statements include internal service fund data?

5. How does the presentation of an enterprise *major* fund differ from the presentation of an internal service *major* fund?

6. Because proprietary funds are accounted for in much the same manner as commercial business organizations, is it appropriate for FASB pronouncements to be used for their accounting?

7. Why is it important for internal service funds to differentiate between revenues generated by interfund transactions and transactions with external parties?

8. How does a proprietary fund statement of cash flows differ from a commercial enterprise's statement of cash flows?

9. What fund types are included in the fiduciary fund category? Where are they reported in the financial statements?

10. How might an internal service fund be financed initially? How will the financing appear in the fund financial statements?

11. How does a private-purpose trust fund differ from a permanent fund?

12. How many columns (not including total columns) are needed for a government-wide statement of net assets of a governmental unit with a general fund, two special revenue funds, three internal service funds, four enterprise funds, and a component unit? Explain.

13. Do governmental financial statements indicate whether a pension plan is fully funded? Explain.

14. What is the accounting equation for an agency fund?

15. Under what circumstances will a proprietary fund be required to report segment information?

16. How might the enterprise fund amounts on the proprietary fund statement of net assets differ from the amounts reported as "business-type activities" on the government-wide statement of net assets?

EXERCISES

E 21-1

Multiple choice

1. Internal service funds are reported:
   a *With governmental funds on the fund financial statements*
   b *With governmental funds on the government-wide statement of net assets*
   c *With proprietary funds on the government-wide statement of net assets*
   d *All of the above*

2. Which of the following is not a fiduciary fund?
   a *Agency fund*
   b *Trust fund*
   c *Permanent fund*
   d *All of the above are fiduciary funds*

3. The proprietary fund statement of cash flows includes all of the following sections except:
   a *Cash flows from operating activities*
   b *Cash flows from investing activities*
   c *Cash flows from capital and related financing activities*
   d *Cash flows from noncapital investing activities*

4. The accounting equation for proprietary funds is:
   a *Current assets − Noncurrent assets − All liabilities = Fund balance*
   b *Current assets − Noncurrent assets − All liabilities = Net assets*
   c *Current assets + Noncurrent assets − All liabilities = Net assets*
   d *Assets = Liabilities*

5. The accounting equation for agency funds is:

 a *Current assets* − *Noncurrent assets* − *All liabilities* = *Fund balance*

 b *Current assets* − *Noncurrent assets* − *All liabilities* = *Net assets*

 c *Current assets* + *Noncurrent assets* − *All liabilities* = *Net assets*

 d *Assets* = *Liabilities*

E 21-2
Multiple choice [Based on AICPA]

1. The billings for transportation services provided to other governmental units are recorded by the internal service fund as:

 a *Interfund exchanges*

 b *Intergovernmental transfers*

 c *Transportation appropriations*

 d *Operating revenues*

2. Which of the following transactions would be *not* allowed in an internal service fund?

 a *The purchase of capital items*

 b *Borrowing from another fund*

 c *Transfers from other funds*

 d *None of the above*

3. Initial financing for internal service fund activities may be obtained from

 a *Advances from another fund*

 b *Transfers from another fund*

 c *Transfer of related materials held by governmental departments*

 d *All of the above*

4. Carlton City serves as a collecting agency for the local independent school district and for a local water district. For this purpose, Carlton has created a single agency fund and charges the other entities a fee of 1 percent of the gross amounts collected. (The service fee is treated as a general fund revenue.) During the latest fiscal year, a gross amount of $268,000 was collected for the independent school district and $80,000 for the water district. As a consequence of the forgoing, Carlton's general fund should:

 a *Recognize receipts of $348,000*

 b *Recognize receipts of $344,520*

 c *Record revenue of $3,480*

 d *Record encumbrances of $344,520*

5. Through an internal service fund, Floyd County operates a centralized data processing center to provide services to Floyd's other departments. In 2012, this internal service fund billed Floyd's parks and recreation fund $75,000 for data processing services. What account should Floyd's internal service fund credit to record this $75,000 billing to the parks and recreation fund?

 a *Operating revenues*

 b *Interfund exchanges*

 c *Intergovernmental transfers*

 d *Data processing department expenses*

E 21-3
Multiple choice

1. Charges for services are a major source of revenue for:

 a *A debt service fund*

 b *A trust fund*

 c *An enterprise fund*

 d *A capital projects fund*

2. A city provides initial financing for its enterprise fund with the stipulation that the amount advanced be returned to the general fund within five years. The general fund expects prompt repayment. In recording the payment to the enterprise fund, the general fund should:

 a *Debit the contribution to enterprise fund account*

 b *Debit the expenditures account*

 c *Debit a reserve for advance to enterprise fund account*

 d *Debit a due from enterprise fund account*

3. If enterprise fund assets are financed through general obligation bonds, rather than revenue bonds, the debt:

    a *Is not an enterprise fund liability*

    b *Must be serviced through a debt service fund*

    c *Is an enterprise fund liability if enterprise fund revenues are intended to service the debt*

    d *Is reported both as a long-term fund liability and a general obligation liability*

4. An internal service fund would most likely be created to provide:

    a *Debt service*

    b *Centralized purchasing*

    c *Perpetual care of cemeteries*

    d *Tax collection and recording services*

5. Enterprise funds should be used in accounting for governmental activities that involve:

    a *Providing goods and services to the public*

    b *Providing goods and services to other departments of the government*

    c *Providing goods and services to the public if a substantial amount of revenue is derived from user charges*

    d *Collection of money from the public*

E 21-4

Multiple choice

1. Fiduciary funds include four different types of funds. Which of the following is *not* one of these types?

    a *Agency funds*

    b *Tax collection funds*

    c *Private-purpose trust funds*

    d *Pension trust funds*

2. Agency funds maintain accounts for:

    a *Liabilities*

    b *Revenues*

    c *Fund balance*

    d *Expenditures*

3. Funds for which a government entity has fiduciary responsibilities:

    a *Must be accounted for in trust and agency funds according to GAAP*

    b *May be accounted for as liabilities of the general fund*

    c *Are infrequently encountered in accounting for governments*

    d *Arise whenever assets are placed in trust for particular purposes*

4. If Hudack County established a separate fund entity to account for state income taxes collected and remitted to the state, the fund would likely be:

    a *An agency fund*

    b *An internal service fund*

    c *An endowment fund*

    d *A trust fund*

5. The accounting and financial reporting concepts are virtually the same for which of the following fund types?

    a *Private-purpose trust funds and permanent funds*

    b *Permanent funds and pension trust funds*

    c *Pension trust funds and investment trust funds*

    d *Permanent funds and agency funds*

E 21-5

Multiple choice [AICPA adapted]

1. The following revenues were among those reported by Arvida Township in 2012:

Net rental revenue (after depreciation) from a parking garage owned by Arvida	$ 40,000
Interest earned on investments held for employees' retirement benefits	100,000
Property taxes	6,000,000

What amount of the forgoing revenues should be accounted for in Arvida's governmental funds?

a   *$6,140,000*
b   *$6,100,000*
c   *$6,040,000*
d   *$6,000,000*

2. Taylor City issued the following long-term obligations:

Revenue bonds to be repaid from admission fees collected from users of the city swimming pool	$1,000,000
General obligation bonds issued for the city water and sewer fund that will service the debt	$1,800,000

Although these bonds are expected to be paid from enterprise funds, the full faith and credit of the city has been pledged as further assurance that the obligations will be paid. What amount of these bonds should be accounted for in the proprietary funds?

a   *$0*
b   *$1,000,000*
c   *$1,800,000*
d   *$2,800,000*

3. The following proceeds received by Glad City in 2011 are legally restricted to expenditure for specified purposes:

Donation by a benefactor mandated to provide meals for the needy	$200,000
Sales taxes to finance the maintenance of tourist facilities owned by the city	800,000

What amount should be accounted for in Glad's fiduciary funds?

a   *$0*
b   *$200,000*
c   *$800,000*
d   *$1,000,000*

4. In connection with Thurman Township's long-term debt, the following cash accumulations are available to cover payment of principal and interest on:

Bonds for financing of water treatment plant construction	$1,000,000
General long-term obligations	400,000

The amount of these cash accumulations that should be accounted for in Thurman's debt service funds is:

a   *$0*
b   *$400,000*
c   *$1,000,000*
d   *$1,400,000*

Use the following information in answering questions 5 and 6:
On December 31, 2011, Cane City paid a contractor $3,000,000 for the total cost of a new municipal annex built in 2011 on city-owned land. Financing was provided by a $2,000,000 general obligation bond issue sold at face amount on December 31, 2011, with the remaining $1,000,000 transferred from the general fund.

5. What account and amount should be reported in Cane's 2011 financial statements for the general fund?

a   *Other financing uses, $1,000,000*
b   *Other financing sources, $2,000,000*
c   *Expenditures, $3,000,000*
d   *Other financing sources, $3,000,000*

6. What accounts and amounts should be reported in Cane's 2011 financial statements for the capital projects fund?

a   *Other financing sources, $2,000,000; general long-term debt, $2,000,000*
b   *Revenues, $2,000,000; expenditures, $2,000,000*
c   *Other financing sources, $3,000,000; expenditures, $3,000,000*
d   *Revenue, $3,000,000; expenditures, $3,000,000*

E 21-6

Agency fund statement of net assets

The City of Laramee established a tax agency fund to collect property taxes for the City of Laramee, Bloomer County, and Bloomer School District. Total tax levies of the three governmental units were $200,000 for 2011, of which $60,000 was for the City of Laramee, $40,000 for Bloomer County, and $100,000 for Bloomer School District.

The tax agency fund charges Bloomer County and Bloomer School District a 2 percent collection fee that it transfers to the general fund of the City of Laramee in order to cover costs incurred for agency fund operations.

During 2011 the tax agency fund collected and remitted $150,000 of the 2011 levies to the various governmental units. The collection fees associated with the $150,000 were remitted to Laramee's general fund before year-end.

REQUIRED: Prepare a statement of fiduciary net assets for the City of Laramee Tax Agency Fund at December 31, 2011.

E 21-7
Enterprise fund journal entries and reporting

Prepare journal entries to record the following grant-related transactions of an enterprise fund activity. Explain how these transactions should be reported in the enterprise fund's financial statements, including the statement of cash flows.

1. Received an operating grant in cash from the state, $3,000,000.

2. Incurred qualifying expenses on the grant program, $1,200,000.

3. Received a federal grant to finance construction of a processing plant, $7,000,000. (The cash was received in advance.)

4. Incurred and paid construction costs on the processing plant, $4,000,000.

E 21-8
Identification of fund type

For each of the following events or transactions, identify the fund or funds that will be affected.

1. A governmental unit operates a municipal pool. Costs are intended to be recovered primarily from user charges.

2. A bond offering was issued at par to subsidize the construction of a new convention center.

3. A bond offering was issued at a premium to subsidize the construction of a new convention center.

4. A town receives a donation of cash that must be used for the benefit of the town's bird sanctuary, which is not operated by the town.

5. A central computing center was established to handle the data processing needs of a municipality.

6. A local municipality provides water and sewer services to residents of nearby communities for a fee.

7. A village receives a grant from the state government. The funds are to be used solely for preserving wetlands.

8. Property taxes are levied by a city government.

9. A county government serves as a tax collection agency for all towns and cities located within the county.

10. A county government offers to pool the cash available for investment from cities located within its boundaries. A formal agreement exists, and income will be recognized in the fund.

E 21-9
Journal entries—various funds

For each of the following events or transactions, prepare the necessary journal entry or entries and identify the fund or funds that will be affected.

1. A governmental unit collects fees totaling $4,500 at the municipal pool. The fees are charged to recover costs of pool operation and maintenance.

2. A county government that serves as a tax collection agency for all towns and cities located within the county collects county sales taxes totaling $125,000 for the month.

3. A $1,000,000 bond offering was issued, with a premium of $50,000, to subsidize the construction of a city visitor center.

4. A town receives a donation of $50,000 in bonds. The bonds should be held indefinitely, but bond income is to be donated to the local zoo. The zoo is not associated with the town.

5. A central printing shop is established with a $150,000 nonreciprocal transfer from the general fund.

6. A $1,000,000 revenue bond offering was issued at par by a fund that provides water and sewer services to residents of nearby communities for a fee. The funds are to be used for facility expansion.

7. A village is awarded a grant of $250,000 from the state government for highway beautification. The general fund provides a $50,000 loan, because grant funds will be disbursed after valid expenditures are documented.

8. Property taxes of $5,000,000 are levied by a city government. One percent is considered uncollectible, and the taxes will be used to fund current obligations.

E 21-10
Net asset classification

Note how each of the following transactions affects (a) net assets invested in capital assets, net of related debt, (b) restricted net assets, and (c) unrestricted net assets. (Record N/A if there is no effect on the net asset section.)

1. The sale of a building for a gain
2. Depreciation of an asset
3. The issuance of capital asset-related debt
4. The payment of capital asset-related debt
5. Property taxes are levied and collected
6. Supplies are purchased and used

PROBLEMS

P 21-1
Internal service fund journal entries

The City of Thomasville established an internal service fund to provide printing services to all city offices and departments. The following transactions related to the fund took place in 2011:

1. On January 15 the general fund transferred equipment valued at $550,000 and provided a $500,000 loan to the internal service fund.

2. On February 1 the internal service fund acquired $200,000 worth of printing equipment and computers. The assets have a five-year life with no salvage, and the city uses straight-line depreciation. Assume half-year depreciation in the year of acquisition.

3. Throughout the year, the internal service fund billed various departments $345,000 for service rendered and collected $300,000 of the amount billed.

4. Various expenses for the year were as follows: wages and salaries, $180,000; payroll taxes, $37,800; repayment to the general fund, $50,000; and other operating expenses, $120,000.

REQUIRED: Prepare all necessary journal entries for the printing services internal service fund for the year ended December 31, 2011.

P 21-2
Enterprise fund journal entries and trial balance

The following transactions relate to the Fiedler County Utility Plant, a newly established municipal facility financed with debt secured solely by net revenue from fees and charges to external users.

1. The general fund made a $30,000,000 contribution to establish the working capital of the new utility enterprise fund.

2. The utility fund purchased a utility plant for $25,250,000.

3. The utility fund issued a $5,000,000 revenue bond for renovations to the facility.

4. Utility bills of $4,500,000 were mailed to customers.

5. Utility collections totaled $4,400,000.

6. Renovations of $3,500,000 were completed during the year and recorded as building improvements.

7. Salaries of $700,000 were paid to employees.

8. Interest expense of $300,000 related to the revenue bonds was paid during the year, and $100,000 was accrued at year-end.

9. Operating expenses totaling $1,000,000 were paid during the year, and an additional $100,000 of operating expenses was accrued at year-end.

10. Depreciation of $1,050,000 was recorded.

REQUIRED: Prepare all necessary journal entries and an adjusted trial balance for the utility enterprise fund for the year.

P 21-3
Preparation of internal service fund statements

Comparative adjusted trial balances for the motor pool of Douwe County at June 30, 2011, and June 30, 2012, are as follows:

	June 30, 2012	June 30, 2011
Cash	$ 37,000	$ 44,000
Due from general fund	—	8,000
Due from electric fund	4,000	3,000
Supplies on hand	14,000	12,000
Autos	99,000	80,000
Supplies used	68,000	60,000
Salaries expense	25,000	20,000
Utilities expense	9,000	8,000
Depreciation expense	16,000	15,000
Operating transfer to general fund	12,000	—
	$284,000	$250,000
Accumulated depreciation—autos	$ 56,000	$ 40,000
Accounts payable	11,000	10,000
Advance from general fund (current)	5,000	5,000
Contribution from general fund	50,000	50,000
Net assets (beginning)	42,000	35,000
Revenue from billings	120,000	110,000
	$284,000	$250,000

REQUIRED: Prepare fund financial statements for the motor pool for the year ended June 30, 2012. (The statement of cash flows is to be included.)

P 21-4
Preparation of trust fund statements

On January 1, 2011, J. G. Monee created a student aid trust fund to which he donated a building valued at $400,000 (his cost was $250,000), bonds having a market value of $500,000, and $100,000 cash. The trust agreement stipulated that principal was to be maintained intact and earnings were to be used to support needy students. Consider gains on investments and depreciation as adjustments of earnings rather than of trust fund principal.

Activities for 2011

1. During the year, net rentals of $40,000 were collected for building rental.

2. The bonds were sold for $550,000 on June 30, 2011. Of the proceeds, $30,000 represented interest accrued from January 1 to June 30.

3. Stocks were purchased for $600,000 cash.

4. Depreciation on the building was calculated at $20,000 for the year.

5. Dividends receivable of $60,000 were recorded at December 31, 2011.

REQUIRED: Prepare a statement of fiduciary net assets and a statement of changes in fiduciary net assets for this private-purpose trust fund at December 31, 2011.

P 21-5
Preparation of trust fund statements

On July 1, 2011, Duchy County receives a $500,000 contribution from the local chapter of Homeless No More. A trust agreement specifying that the income from the contribution be distributed each May 15 to the downtown homeless shelter accompanies the contribution. The principal amount is intended to remain intact indefinitely. The following transactions related to the contribution occur during the fiscal year:

1. On September 1, the county invests the contribution in bonds, which yield 4.5% annually (payable on March 1 and September 1).

2. On March 1, the county receives the first interest payment.

3. On May 15, the county distributes the interest to the homeless shelter.

4. On June 30, the county closes its accounts.

REQUIRED: Prepare a statement of fiduciary net assets and a statement of changes in fiduciary net assets for this private-purpose trust fund at June 30, 2012.

P 21-6
Internal service fund journal entries [AICPA adapted]

The City of Meringen operates a central garage through an internal service fund to provide garage space and repairs for all city-owned and -operated vehicles. The central garage fund was established by a contribution of $200,000 from the general fund, when the building was acquired several years ago. The postclosing trial balance at June 30, 2011, was as follows:

	Debit	Credit
Cash	$150,000	
Due from general fund	20,000	
Inventory of materials and supplies	80,000	
Land	60,000	
Building	200,000	
Accumulated depreciation—building		$ 10,000
Machinery and equipment	56,000	
Accumulated depreciation—machinery and equipment		12,000
Vouchers payable		38,000
Contribution from general fund		200,000
Retained earnings		306,000
	$566,000	$566,000

The following information applies to the fiscal year ended June 30, 2012:

1. Materials and supplies were purchased on account for $74,000.

2. The inventory of materials and supplies at June 30, 2012, was $58,000, which agreed with the physical count taken.

3. Salaries and wages paid to employees totaled $230,000, including related costs.

4. A billing was received from the enterprise fund for utility charges totaling $30,000, and it was paid.

5. Depreciation of the building was recorded in the amount of $5,000. Depreciation of the machinery and equipment totaled $8,000.

6. Billings to other departments for services rendered to them were as follows:

General fund	$262,000
Water and sewer fund	84,000
Special revenue fund	32,000

7. Unpaid interfund receivable balances at June 30, 2012, were as follows:

General fund	$ 6,000
Special Revenue Fund	16,000

8. Vouchers payable at June 30, 2012, were $14,000.

REQUIRED

1. For the period July 1, 2011, through June 30, 2012, prepare journal entries to record all the transactions in the central garage fund accounts.

2. Prepare closing entries for the central garage fund at June 30, 2012.

P 21-7
Enterprise fund statement of cash flows

Caleb County had a beginning cash balance in its enterprise fund of $714,525. During the year, the following transactions affecting cash flows occurred:

1. Acquired equity investments totaling $165,000

2. Receipts from sales of goods or services totaled $3,276,500

3. Payments for materials used in providing services were made in the amount of $2,694,500

4. A capital grant, whose proceeds of $750,000 are restricted for the acquisition of constructing or improving a fixed asset, was awarded (cash was received during the year).

5. Payments to employees for salaries amounted to $479,300

6. The fund's allocated portion of property taxes was $217,000

7. Other cash expenses for operations were $819,200

8. Capital assets used in providing goods and services were sold for $522,000. They had a book value of $550,000

9. Long-term debt payments totaled $515,000

REQUIRED: Prepare a statement of cash flows for the Caleb County enterprise fund.

INTERNET ASSIGNMENT

1. Choose a CAFR from a city, county, or other local government. Review the CAFR and answer the following questions:

a. How many proprietary funds does the government have? List the name of one enterprise fund.

b. Does the government have an internal service fund? What product or service does it provide?

c. Does the government have an agency fund? What is its title?

d. What type of pension fund is reported in the financial statements? Are the required disclosures contained in the CAFR?

2. Locate the Web site for the municipality in which your college or university is located. Does this municipality provide utilities, sewer, or water to its residents? Are these activities accounted for in the appropriate fund?

3. Locate the Web site for your hometown. Does this municipality provide local transit service (i.e., bus, subway, etc.)? If so, how is it funded? Did the government receive any capital or operating grants during the year?

22 CHAPTER

Accounting for Not-for-Profit Organizations

This chapter provides an introduction to accounting principles and reporting practices of not-for-profit (NFP) entities, which include voluntary health and welfare organizations, other not-for-profit organizations (such as churches and museums), health care entities, and colleges and universities. Each of these organizational types is important for the resources it controls and for its impact on society.

Although these four NFP organizational types often share a focus on service objectives, their sources of financing and degree of autonomy vary significantly. Also, some NFP organizations are governments required to follow the pronouncements of the GASB, whereas others are nongovernmental not-for-profit organizations, whose standards are established by the FASB. This chapter describes not-for-profit organizations, introduces the *FASB Accounting Standards Codification* sections applicable to nongovernmental not-for-profits, and provides detailed examples of journal entries and financial statements for nongovernmental not-for-profit organizations.

THE NATURE OF NOT-FOR-PROFIT ORGANIZATIONS

LEARNING OBJECTIVE 1

You can distinguish a not-for-profit entity from a commercial business enterprise by examining its underlying characteristics. A not-for-profit entity (1) receives contributions of significant amounts of resources from resource providers who do not expect commensurate or proportionate pecuniary return, (2) operates for purposes other than to provide goods or services at a profit, and (3) does not possess ownership interests like those of business enterprises [1].

Once designated as such, a not-for-profit organization finds itself in a quite diverse sector of entities whose members are public and private, charitable and self-promoting, and tax-exempt and taxable. Although the term *not-for-profit* conjures up thoughts of the Salvation Army or your local church, NFP entities can fall into one of four categories: voluntary health and welfare organizations (such as the Salvation Army), other not-for-profit organizations (such as churches and museums), health care entities, and colleges and universities. The accounting and financial reporting methods of each type of NFP vary. Not-for-profit entities are first designated as governmental or nongovernmental to determine whether they should follow GASB or FASB standards.

A governmental not-for-profit organization meets the aforementioned not-for-profit criteria and also possesses one of the following characteristics: officers are elected by popular vote or appointment by a state or local government; a government can unilaterally dissolve the entity, with the assets reverting back to the government; or the entity has the power to enact and enforce a tax levy.[1] Unlike

LEARNING OBJECTIVES

1 Learn about the four main categories of not-for-profit organizations.

2 Differentiate between governmental and non-governmental not-for-profit organizations.

3 Introduce FASB not-for-profit accounting principles.

4 Apply not-for-profit accounting principles to voluntary health and welfare organizations.

5 Apply not-for-profit accounting principles to hospitals and other health care organizations.

6 Apply not-for-profit accounting principles to private not-for-profit colleges and universities.

---

[1]An organization may also be considered a government if it has the ability to issue tax-exempt debt directly; however, if this is the only governmental characteristic that it possesses, the organization can dispute the presumption that it is governmental in nature.

general-purpose governments, such as the state and local municipalities discussed in Chapters 19 to 21, the GASB defines other legally-separate governmental entities as *special-purpose governments*. Governmental not-for-profit organizations are therefore special-purpose governments and are generally required to follow GASB standards; however, their reporting requirements are often less than those of general-purpose governments. *GASB Statements No. 34* and *35* require special-purpose governments with more than one governmental program or both governmental and business-type activities to present both government-wide and fund financial statements, as well as the MD&A, notes, and required supplementary information. Special-purpose governments with only one governmental program may combine fund and government-wide statements, whereas those with only business-type activities should report only the financial statements required for enterprise funds, as well as the MD&A, notes, and required supplementary information. Because accounting and financial reporting under *GASB 34* was covered extensively in previous chapters, the remainder of this chapter is devoted to the accounting and financial reporting required for nongovernmental not-for-profit entities, and mention of governmental not-for-profits is limited.

LEARNING OBJECTIVE **2**

Nongovernmental not-for-profit organizations are NFP entities that lack the governmental element. All nongovernmental, not-for-profit organizations—whether voluntary health and welfare organizations (VHWOs), health care organizations, colleges and universities, or other—use essentially the same basic guidance, although the nature of their transactions differs. The *FASB Accounting Standards Codification* (FASB ASC) became the sole source of authoritative GAAP for interim and annual periods ending after September 15, 2009. FASB ASC 958 incorporates the prior FASB standards that provided guidance for NFP's, primarily *FASB Statement No. 116*, "Accounting for Contributions Received and Contributions Made," which established accounting standards for contributions, and *Statement No. 117*, "Financial Statements of Not-for-Profit Organizations," which identified the required statements to be presented by nongovernmental, not-for-profit organizations.

LEARNING OBJECTIVE **3**

NOT-FOR-PROFIT ACCOUNTING PRINCIPLES

Until 1993, not-for-profit organizations looked primarily to the AICPA for accounting principles and financial reporting guidance. The AICPA published four industry audit guides related to voluntary health and welfare organizations, health care entities, colleges and universities, and other not-for-profit organizations. (This is the reason for the four categories of NFP organizations.) In the early 1990s, the FASB took a more active role in setting NFP standards with its issuance of *Statements No. 116* and *117*.[2] These standards, applicable to all nongovernmental not-for-profit entities, served to standardize accounting and financial reporting in the not-for-profit sector.

The model for developing and disseminating accounting guidance changed in 2009 with FASB's publication of the Codification. FASB will now issue ASU (Accounting Standard Updates) that will be pending until formally incorporated into the Codification.[3] The FASB also created a Not-for-Profit Advisory Committee (NAC) in October of 2009 to provide advice on existing guidance, current projects and future issues. Concurrently, the AICPA continues its Not-for-Profit Organization Committee, which updated the *AICPA Audit and Accounting Guide: Not-for-Profit Organizations* in 2010. The AICPA guide incorporates three of the prior audit guides (VHWOs, colleges and universities, and "other" NFP organizations), includes FASB NFP standards, and contains additional guidance for such organizations. The AICPA also updated its Audit and Accounting guide for health care entities in 2010.

Financial Statements

GAAP [2] requires not-for-profit organizations to provide a set of financial statements that includes a statement of financial position, statement of activities, statement of cash flows, and accompanying notes. Voluntary health and welfare organizations must also provide a statement of functional expenses.

Within the financial statements, not-for-profit organizations classify net assets, revenues, expenses, gains, and losses according to three classes of net assets—unrestricted, temporarily

---

[2]Other FASB Statements with substantial content for NFP's include 124, 136, 157, 159, and 164.

[3]FASB published a notice to constituents that explains the scope, structure, and usage of FASB ASC. Constituents can read the notice and the full ASC at http://asc.fasb.org/home at no charge in a basic view.

restricted, and permanently restricted—based on the existence or absence of donor-imposed restrictions. The three classes of net assets are defined as follows:

- **Permanently restricted net assets** are the portion of net assets whose use is limited by donor-imposed stipulations that do not expire by time and cannot be removed by action of the not-for-profit entity.
- **Temporarily restricted net assets** are the portion of net assets whose use is limited by donor-imposed stipulations that either expire (time restrictions) or can be removed by the organization fulfilling the stipulations (purpose restrictions).
- **Unrestricted net assets** are the portion of net assets that carry no donor-imposed stipulations.

Organizations can report revenues, gains, and losses in each net asset class, but expenses are reported only in the unrestricted net assets class.

STATEMENT OF FINANCIAL POSITION The statement of financial position or balance sheet reports assets, liabilities, and net assets. It reports net assets in total and by the three classes of net assets—unrestricted, temporarily restricted, and permanently restricted. Permanently and temporarily restricted amounts appear on the face of the balance sheet or in notes. Assets received with donor-imposed restrictions that limit their use to long-term purposes should be separated from assets available for current use. Comparative statements from the prior period are not required.

STATEMENT OF ACTIVITIES The statement of activities provides information about the change in amount and nature of net assets and reports how resources are used to provide various programs or services. Not-for-profit organizations account for revenues and expenses using the accrual basis of accounting. Not-for-profit organizations that issue GAAP-basis financial statements must recognize depreciation expense on long-lived assets. NFP organizations should record depreciation even if the assets are gifts; however, certain works of art and certain historical treasures that meet the definition of "collections" need not be capitalized or depreciated.

The statement of activities focuses on the organization as a whole. It reports the amount of change in net assets, ending with a net asset figure that is the same as net assets on the balance sheet. The statement presents revenues, expenses, gains, and losses by net asset class; thus, there are columns or sections reporting the amount of change in permanently restricted net assets, temporarily restricted net assets, and unrestricted net assets.

Not-for-profit revenues, described in detail later, increase unrestricted net assets unless use of the assets received is limited by donor-imposed restrictions. Gains and losses on investments are increases or decreases in unrestricted net assets unless their use is restricted by explicit donor stipulations or by law. Expenses always decrease unrestricted net assets; thus, they cannot appear in the temporarily restricted or permanently restricted net asset classes. Temporarily restricted or permanently restricted net assets consist of donor-restricted contributions whose restrictions have not yet been met. If restrictions placed on donor-restricted contributions are met in the same reporting period in which the contribution is made, the organization may report the contribution as unrestricted as long as the organization follows a consistent policy. Reclassifications between net asset classes are reported separately.

Generally, NFP organizations report revenues and expenses at gross amounts. Gains and losses from peripheral or incidental transactions or events beyond the control of the organization may be reported at net amounts, and investment income is reported net of related expenses. Further classifications of revenues, expenses, gains, and losses (such as operating or nonoperating, recurring or nonrecurring, and so on) are optional.

NFP organizations report expenses by functional classification—major classes of program services and supporting services—in the statement or notes. *Program services* are the activities that distribute goods and services that fulfill the purpose or mission of the organization to beneficiaries, customers, or members. *Supporting services* are all activities other than program services. Supporting services include the following:

- **Management and general.** Oversight, business management, general record-keeping, budgeting, financing, and related administrative activities
- **Fund-raising.** Publicizing and conducting fund-raising campaigns; maintaining donor mailing lists; conducting special fund-raising events; preparing and

distributing fund-raising manuals, instructions, and other materials; and other activities to solicit contributions

- ■ **Membership-development activities.** Soliciting for prospective members and membership dues, membership relations, and so on

STATEMENT OF FUNCTIONAL EXPENSES Voluntary health and welfare organizations must report expenses classified by function and by natural classification (salaries, rent, etc.) in a matrix format as a separate statement. Other not-for-profit organizations are encouraged, but not required, to provide this additional expense information.

STATEMENT OF CASH FLOWS Not-for-profit organizations use the same cash flow classifications and definitions as business enterprises, except that the description of financing activities is expanded to include resources that are donor restricted for long-term purposes. The NFP statement of cash flows reports investing activities of permanent endowments as cash flows of investing activities.

When preparing the balance sheet, organizations cannot aggregate cash restricted for long-term purposes with cash available for current uses in the balance sheet. Similarly, they should exclude cash and cash equivalents that are restricted for long-term purposes from cash in the cash flows statement.

NFP organizations are encouraged to use the direct method for presenting cash flows, but are allowed to use the indirect method. Organizations that select the direct method must provide a schedule to reconcile the change in net assets in the statement of activities to net cash flows from operating activities.

Contributions

For some not-for-profit entities, contributions are a major source of revenue. GAAP defines a **contribution** as "an unconditional transfer of cash or other assets to an entity or a settlement or cancellation of its liabilities in a voluntary, nonreciprocal transfer by another entity acting other than as an owner." Examples of other assets include buildings, securities, the use of facilities or services, and unconditional promises to give. GAAP describes a *promise to give* as a written or oral agreement to contribute cash or other assets to another entity. The promise should be verifiable by evidence such as pledge cards or tape recordings of oral promises. A promise to give may be conditional or unconditional.

A *conditional promise to give* depends on the occurrence of a specified future and uncertain event to bind the promisor. For example, a church parishioner may pledge to contribute a sum of money if a local government approves a proposed church renovation. Organizations recognize conditional promises to give as contribution revenue and receivables when the conditions are substantially met (in other words, when the conditional promise to give becomes unconditional); however, they account for a conditional gift of cash or other asset that may have to be returned to the donor if the condition is not met as a refundable advance (liability). Disclosures in notes to the financial statements for conditional promises to give include the total amounts promised and a description and amount for any group of promises having similar characteristics (i.e., a specific project or goal).

An *unconditional promise to give* depends only on the passage of time or demand by the promisee for performance. Promises to give are unconditional if the possibility that a condition will not be met is remote. Organizations recognize unconditional promises to give as contribution revenue and receivables in the period in which the promise is received. They report such promises as restricted support (in other words, as contribution revenues in temporarily restricted net assets, based on the time restriction), even if the resources are not restricted for specific purposes, until cash is received and available for expenditure.[4] Not-for-profit entities should disclose both anticipated time frame for receipt (amounts of unconditional promises receivable in less than one year, in one to five years, and in more than five years) and the allowance for uncollectible promises receivable.

Generally, NFP organizations measure restricted and unrestricted contributions at fair value and recognize them as revenues or gains in the period in which they are received. As previously noted,

---

[4]An exception is provided when the donor explicitly stipulates that the contribution is intended to support current-period activities, in which case it is reported as unrestricted support.

contributions are separated into the three classes of net assets on the statement of activities: those that increase unrestricted net assets, those that increase temporarily restricted net assets, and those that increase permanently restricted net assets.

DONOR-IMPOSED RESTRICTIONS OR CONDITIONS A *donor-imposed condition* provides that the donor's money be returned or the donor be released from the promise to give if the condition is not met. *Donor-imposed restrictions* simply limit the use of contributed assets. If it is unclear whether donor stipulations are conditions or restrictions, the organization should presume that the promise is conditional. A donor-imposed restriction expires in the period in which the restriction is satisfied (i.e., when a time restriction is met or a purpose restriction satisfied). If a given contribution is subject to more than one restriction, the restrictions expire in the period in which the last restriction is satisfied.

When a temporary restriction is met (either by the passage of time or by the incurrence of expenses for the restricted purpose), organizations reclassify resources from the temporarily restricted net assets category to the unrestricted net assets category. On the statement of activities, they report the reclassified amount as net assets released from restrictions. These assets increase unrestricted net assets and decrease temporarily restricted net assets. If donor-imposed restrictions are met in the same period in which the contributions are received, organizations may report the contributions as unrestricted if the following conditions are met: (1) the policy must be disclosed in the notes and followed consistently, and (2) the organization must have the same policy for temporarily restricted investment income whose restrictions are met in the same period as income is recognized.

GIFTS OF LONG-LIVED ASSETS Gifts of long-lived assets may be restricted or unrestricted, depending on the organization's accounting policy or the donor's restriction. If the donor restricts contributed long-lived assets for use over a certain period of time, recipients report the assets as restricted support in temporarily restricted net assets. Later, the recipient organization recognizes depreciation by reclassifying the amount of the depreciation from temporarily restricted to unrestricted net assets and recording an expense in unrestricted net assets.

If the donor contributes the long-lived assets with no restrictions or if the assets are purchased with contributions restricted to the acquisition of long-lived assets, the organization can choose either of two accounting methods, which should be used consistently. The accounting policy must be disclosed in notes to the financial statements. The two acceptable methods are as follows:

1. The organization may adopt an accounting policy that implies a time restriction that expires over the useful life of the donated asset. As in the case of contributed long-lived assets with an explicit donor-imposed time restriction, the gift is reported as restricted support in temporarily restricted net assets. Depreciation is recorded as an expense in unrestricted net assets, and a reclassification for the amount of the depreciation from temporarily restricted to unrestricted net assets. (This also applies to assets purchased with cash that was restricted to the purchase of long-lived assets.)

2. If no policy implying a time restriction exists and there are no donor-imposed restrictions, the gifts are unrestricted support.

INVESTMENTS AND INVESTMENT INCOME Not-for-profit organizations initially record purchased investments at their cost and contributed investments at fair value in the appropriate net asset classification. They recognize investment income as earned and report the income as an increase in unrestricted, temporarily restricted, or permanently restricted net assets, depending on donor-imposed restrictions on the use of the investment income. GAAP [3] requires organizations to report investments in debt securities at their fair values. Investments in equity securities that have readily determinable fair values also must be reported at fair values. Changes in fair values are reported in the statement of activities. The fair value accounting requirement does not apply to equity investments that are accounted for by the equity method or investments in consolidated subsidiaries.

Transfers That Are Not Contributions

Contributions do not include several items: transfers that are exchange transactions; transfers in which the not-for-profit enterprise is acting as an agent, trustee, or intermediary for the donor; or possibly gifts in kind.

EXCHANGE TRANSACTIONS Exchange transactions are reciprocal transfers in which both parties give and receive approximately equal value. Sales of products and services are exchange transactions. Exchange transactions are sometimes difficult to distinguish from contributions. Assume that a not-for-profit organization sends calendars (premiums) to potential donors in a fund-raising appeal. The recipients keep the premium whether or not they make a donation. In this case the donations that result from the calendar mailing are contributions, and the cost of premiums is a fund-raising expense. The same is true if the not-for-profit organization gives the premiums only to donors, but the premiums are nominal in relation to the donations. If donors receive gifts that approximate the value of their donations, however, the transaction is an exchange.

Dues charged to members of not-for-profit entities may have characteristics of both contributions and exchange transactions. The portion of the dues representing contributions will be recognized as revenue when received, but the portion representing an exchange transaction will be recognized as revenue as it is earned.

Resources received in exchange transactions are classified as unrestricted revenues and unrestricted net assets even if the resource provider limits use of the resources.

AGENCY TRANSACTIONS An agency transaction is one in which assets are transferred to the not-for-profit organization, but the not-for-profit organization has little or no discretion over the use of those assets, and the assets are passed on to a third party. The resource provider is using the not-for-profit entity as an agent or intermediary to transfer assets to a third-party donee. For example, the United Way often acts as an agent by collecting contributions for distribution to a number of local organizations. Under GAAP [4], the receipt of assets in an agency transaction increases the assets and liabilities of the not-for-profit agent, and disbursement of those assets decreases assets and liabilities. No contribution is recorded by the agent. The NFP agent reports the cash received and paid as cash flows from operating activities in the statement of cash flows.

GIFTS IN KIND Gifts in kind are noncash contributions, such as clothing, furniture, and services. They are contributions if the not-for-profit entity has discretion over the disposition of the resources. Otherwise, the entity will account for the gifts as agency transactions. Organizations measure gifts in kind that are contributions at fair value, if practicable. When fair value cannot be reasonably determined, NFP entities should not record the gifts as contributions. Instead, they record the items as sales revenue when they are sold. Cost of sales is the cost of getting the inventory ready for sale. GAAP [5] limits the recognition of contributed services to those that (1) create or enhance nonfinancial assets of the organization or (2) require specialized skills, are provided by individuals possessing those skills, and would typically need to be purchased if not provided by donation. If contributed services do not meet these criteria, they should not be recognized; however, information about services contributed to the organization's programs and activities should be described in the financial statement notes.

Measurement Principles

Not-for-profit organizations measure contributions at fair value. Quoted market prices are the best estimate of fair values for both monetary and nonmonetary assets. Other valuation methods that might be used include quoted market prices for similar assets or independent appraisals. If a reasonable estimate for fair value cannot be made, the contribution should not be recognized.

Recall that not-for-profit organizations record unconditional promises to give when pledges are made. If the fair value of the contributed asset changes significantly between the pledge date and the date the asset is received, the not-for-profit entity accounts for the contribution as follows:

■ No additional revenue is recognized if the fair value increases.
■ If the fair value decreases, the difference is recognized in the period the decrease occurred and is reported as a change in the net asset class in which the revenue was originally reported or in the class where the net assets are represented.

A not-for-profit entity may record unconditional promises to give that it expects to collect within one year of the financial statement date at their net realizable value (gross amount less an allowance for uncollectible accounts). However, the entity should measure unconditional promises to give that are not expected to be collected within the year at the present value of the amounts expected to be collected (estimated future cash flows).[5]

Collections

Collections of works of art, historical treasures, and similar items may be capitalized but are not required to be so long as the following conditions are satisfied:

- They are held for public exhibition, education, or research in furtherance of public service rather than financial gain.
- They are protected, kept encumbered, cared for, and preserved.
- They are subject to an organizational policy that requires proceeds from sales of collection items to be used to acquire other items for collections.[6]

Organizations that choose not to capitalize collections should describe the collections in the notes to the financial statements. Contributed collection items are recognized as revenues or gains if the collection is capitalized.

When collection items are not recognized, the costs of collection items, proceeds from sales, and proceeds from insurance recoveries appear as increases or decreases of the appropriate net asset class on the activities statement, separately from revenues, expenses, gains, and losses.

Fund Accounting

Not-for-profit entities receive resources from contributions, charges for services, grants, appropriations, and so on, and the use of some of these resources is restricted for specific activities or purposes. Fund accounting principles provide a convenient method for segregating the accounting records of resources restricted for specific purposes. Many not-for-profit organizations choose to use fund accounting for internal accounting, although FASB issuances and the AICPA guide do not require fund accounting. Although GAAP allows fund reporting as additional information, fund information is rarely presented in financial statements of nongovernmental not-for-profit organizations. Therefore, this chapter does not discuss or illustrate fund accounting for nongovernmental organizations.

VOLUNTARY HEALTH AND WELFARE ORGANIZATIONS

LEARNING OBJECTIVE 4

Voluntary health and welfare organizations encompass a diverse group of not-for-profit entities that are supported by and provide voluntary services to the public. They may expend their resources to solve basic social problems in the areas of health or welfare either globally, nationally, at the community level, or on an individual basis. Examples include charities such as the March of Dimes or the American Cancer Society, Girl Scouts of the USA, Boy Scouts of America, and Meals on Wheels. VHWOs follow FASB standards, and the 2010 *AICPA Audit and Accounting Guide: Not-for-Profit Organizations* provides additional, but no longer authoritative, guidance.

Accounting for a VHWO

A group of concerned citizens organized a voluntary health and welfare organization called Neighbors Helping Neighbors (NHN). The following journal entries provide examples of some typical accounting procedures for this organization.

CONTRIBUTIONS As part of its fund-raising effort in 2011, NHN distributed decals to all residents in the community. The decals cost NHN $145. As a result of the campaign, the organization received unrestricted cash contributions of $4,000 and unconditional promises to give totaling $6,000. Of this $6,000 contribution receivable, $2,000 is not collectible until 2012. A

---

[5]See FASB ASC 820 for general coverage of fair value and FASB ASC 985.605.30 for specific guidance related to not-for-profits.

[6]FASB ASC 958.360.25.

presumption exists that the $2,000 due in 2012 is restricted for use in 2012. NHN estimates that 10 percent of the pledges will be uncollectible and makes the following entries in 2011:

Expenses—supporting services—fund-raising	145	
Cash		145
To record payment for decals used in fund-raising.		
Cash	4,000	
Unrestricted support—contributions		4,000
To record cash contributions.		
Contributions receivable	6,000	
Allowance for uncollectible contributions		600
Unrestricted support—contributions		3,600
Temporarily restricted support—contributions		1,800
To record unrestricted promises to give, promises restricted for use in 2012, and estimated uncollectibles.		

NHN collected $3,600 of the contributions receivable due in 2011 and wrote off the remaining $400 as uncollectible:

Cash	3,600	
Allowance for uncollectible contributions	400	
Contributions receivable		4,000
To record collection of contributions receivable.		

The following two journal entries do NOT pertain to 2011, and thus are not utilized in the closing entries on page 748. Assume NHN collects the full $2,000 due in 2012 during that year. When the receivables are collected, NHN reports any difference between the estimated amount of uncollectibles and the actual amount as a gain or loss in the appropriate net asset class. The implied time restriction is met, so NHN reclassifies $1,800 of temporarily restricted net assets as unrestricted net assets:

Cash	2,000	
Allowance for uncollectible contributions	200	
Contributions receivable		2,000
Unrestricted support—contributions		200
To record collection of receivables and recognize support for the difference between the estimated and actual allowance for uncollectible amounts.		
Temporarily restricted net assets—reclassifications out	1,800	
Unrestricted net assets—reclassifications in		1,800
To reclassify net assets for which the restriction has been met.		

A donor gives NHN $1,000 that is restricted for a playground project. NHN purchases supplies for the playground project for $900 and reports the expenses as changes in unrestricted net assets. The organization makes an entry to reclassify $900 of temporarily restricted net assets. The reclassification is entered even though unrestricted resources were used to pay for the playground supplies:

Cash	1,000	
Temporarily restricted support—contributions		1,000
To record a gift restricted for a special project.		
Expenses—program services—community service	900	
Cash		900
To record purchase of supplies used in the playground project.		
Temporarily restricted net assets—reclassifications out	900	
Unrestricted net assets—reclassifications in		900
To reclassify net assets restricted for the playground project for which the restriction has been met.		

As shown earlier, a VHWO classifies its expenses as program services or supporting services and reports them on a functional basis under these classifications (for example, community service, recreation programs, fund-raising). Program services relate to the expenses incurred in providing the organization's social service activities. Supporting services consist of administrative expenses and fund-raising costs.

DONATED LONG-LIVED ASSETS   NHN has a policy of implying a time restriction on donated fixed assets over the life of each asset. On January 1, 2011, Martin Construction donated a used van to the organization. The fair value of the van is $1,500, and it has a three-year remaining useful life. The van will be used in the organization's community service program.

NHN initially records the donated van as temporarily restricted support. Later, NHN records depreciation expense on the van as a program expense. The amount of depreciation expense is reclassified from temporarily restricted net assets to unrestricted net assets, because all expenses decrease unrestricted net assets.

Equipment	1,500	
Temporarily restricted support—contributions		1,500
To record receipt of donated van.		
Depreciation expense—program services—community service	500	
Accumulated depreciation—equipment		500
To record depreciation.		
Temporarily restricted net assets—reclassifications out	500	
Unrestricted net assets—reclassifications in		500
To record reclassification of net assets for which the temporary restriction is satisfied.		

SPECIAL EVENT FUND-RAISERS   A fund-raising event for NHN featured a dinner and dance. Ticket sales for the dinner totaled $950, and expenses of the fund-raiser amounted to $650. VHWOs generally report gross revenues and expenses for special events related to the major ongoing activities of the organization in which attendees receive a benefit. If the special event is incidental to the activities of the organization, the organization may report the proceeds of the special event as gains net of direct costs:

Cash	950	
Unrestricted gains—special event		950
To record proceeds from a fund-raising event.		
Unrestricted gains—special event	650	
Cash		650
To charge costs of fund-raising event against support from the event.		

GIFTS IN KIND   Throughout the summer, NHN receives donations of used housewares and furniture that are then sold at a rummage sale held in August. Fair values for the donated items cannot be reasonably determined, but the cost of storing and moving the items to the rummage sale location is $550. Proceeds from the sale are $6,595. Because the fair value cannot be determined, NHN cannot record the items as contributions:

Cost of goods sold	550	
Cash		550
To pay costs of storing and moving rummage sale items.		
Cash	6,595	
Unrestricted revenues—sales		6,595
To record proceeds from rummage sale.		

Alternatively, if the fair value of donated items can be reasonably determined, the gifts in kind are recorded as contributions. Office-Mate Company donates office supplies with a fair value of $390 to NHN. Office-Mate puts no restrictions on the use of the donated items. The organization records the gift as follows:

Materials and supplies inventory	390	
Unrestricted support—contributions		390
To record receipt of office supplies.		

MEMBERSHIP FEES Memberships give members certain benefits, such as the right to receive the organization's newsletters. Dues from members may represent exchange transactions, contributions, or both, depending on the benefits provided to members. Revenues from exchange transactions are classified as unrestricted and are recognized as revenue as benefits are provided. Dues received when member benefits are negligible are recognized as contributions when received with a credit to "unrestricted support—contributions."

In cases in which the fair value of member benefits is less than the amount of dues, VHWOs divide the transfers between contributions and revenues. An organization may have different levels of memberships, but the more-expensive memberships do not necessarily entitle the members to additional benefits. The excess payments are classified as contributions. NHN offers regular memberships for $10 and sustaining memberships for $50 and over. All members are entitled to the same newsletter and local discount coupons that are distributed when the dues are received. NHN received 500 regular memberships ($5,000) and 130 sustaining memberships ($6,500), which it records as follows:

Cash	11,500	
Unrestricted revenues—dues		6,300
Unrestricted support—contributions		5,200
To record revenue and support from the sale of		
memberships.		

DONATED SECURITIES AND INVESTMENT INCOME NHN receives securities (fair value of $5,000) with a stipulation that they permanently endow a park enhancement project. Income earned on the securities is restricted to use for the park enhancement project. Dividend income is $475:

Securities	5,000	
Permanently restricted support—contribution		5,000
To record receipt of securities permanently restricted		
for a park enhancement project.		
Cash	475	
Temporarily restricted revenue—investment income		475
To record investment income restricted for a park		
enhancement project.		

SUPPLIES NHN had supplies on hand of $1,600 at January 1, 2011. The organization purchased supplies for $1,500 during the year and received donations of supplies that had a fair value of $2,050 in addition to the $390 already received. At the end of 2011, the inventory on hand was $750. The supplies used were allocated to recreation programs, $2,000; community service programs, $1,400; fund-raising expenses, $600; and management and general $790:

Materials and supplies inventory	3,550	
Unrestricted support—contributions		2,050
Cash		1,500
To record donated materials and supplies and to		
record purchase of supplies.		

Expenses—supporting services—management and general	790	
Expenses—program services—recreation programs	2,000	
Expenses—program services—community service	1,400	
Expenses—supporting services—fund-raising	600	
Materials and supplies inventory		4,790
To record allocation of supplies expense.		

DONATED SERVICES AND PAYMENT OF SALARIES An accounting firm donated its services to audit the books of NHN. The audit would have cost the association $1,200 if the services had not been donated. NHN also paid salaries allocated to program services and supporting services as follows: recreation programs, $6,000; community services, $4,000; management and general, $1,500; and fund-raising $500:

Expenses—supporting services—management and general	1,200	
Unrestricted support—donated services		1,200
To record donated services allocated to management and general expenses.		
Expenses—program services—recreation programs	6,000	
Expenses—program services—community service	4,000	
Expenses—supporting services—management and general	1,500	
Expenses—supporting services—fund-raising	500	
Cash		12,000
To record salaries allocated to program services and supporting services.		

DEPRECIATION Equipment owned by NHN is used to travel through the neighborhood and provide park programs. There are no explicit or implicit donor-imposed restrictions on the fixed assets, so the equipment has been recorded as an unrestricted asset. The organization allocates the $8,000 depreciation expense on the equipment to its program services and supporting services as follows:

Depreciation expense—program services— recreation programs	3,000	
Depreciation expense—program services— community service	4,000	
Depreciation expense—supporting services— management and general	1,000	
Accumulated depreciation		8,000
To record depreciation allocated to program services and supporting services.		

FIXED ASSET PURCHASE WITH RESTRICTED RESOURCES NHN purchased equipment costing $4,000. The equipment was financed by $3,000 from contributions with donor-imposed restrictions that were accumulated for purchase of the equipment and $1,000 from general resources:

Equipment	4,000	
Cash		4,000
To record payment for the purchase of equipment.		
Temporarily restricted net assets—reclassifications out	3,000	
Unrestricted net assets—reclassifications in		3,000
To record reclassification of temporarily restricted net assets.		

CLOSING ENTRIES NHN's closing entries for 2011 are as follows:

Unrestricted support—contributions	15,240	
Unrestricted revenues—dues	6,300	
Unrestricted support—donated services	1,200	
Unrestricted revenues—sales	6,595	
Unrestricted gains—special event	300	
Unrestricted net assets—reclassifications in	4,400	
Expenses—program services—community service		10,800
Expenses—program services—recreation programs		11,000
Expenses—supporting services—fund-raising		1,245
Expenses—supporting services—management and general		4,490
Cost of goods sold		550
Unrestricted net assets		5,950
Temporarily restricted support—contributions	4,300	
Temporarily restricted revenue—investment income	475	
Temporarily restricted net assets—reclassifications out		4,400
Temporarily restricted net assets		375
Permanently restricted support—contribution	5,000	
Permanently restricted net assets		5,000

Financial Reporting

Exhibits 22-1 to 22-4 present sample financial statements for NHN. The basic financial statements of nongovernmental voluntary health and welfare organizations include the same statements required for other not-for-profit organizations (a statement of financial position, a statement of activities, and a statement of cash flows). The statement of activities reports revenues in the net asset class to which they relate, using the accrual basis of accounting. Revenues with no donor-imposed restrictions

EXHIBIT 22-1

Balance Sheet for
Nongovernmental
Voluntary Health and
Welfare Organization

NEIGHBORS HELPING NEIGHBORS (A VHWO) STATEMENTS OF FINANCIAL POSITION—DECEMBER 31, 2011 AND 2010

	2011	2010
Assets		
Cash and cash equivalents	$22,375	$14,000
Inventories	750	1,600
Contributions receivable (less allowance of $300 in 2011 and $100 in 2010)	2,200	400
Short-term investments	1,000	1,000
Land, buildings, and equipment (less accumulated depreciation of $16,500 in 2011 and $8,000 in 2010)	34,000	37,000
Assets restricted for endowment	10,000	5,000
Total assets	$70,325	$59,000
Liabilities and Net Assets		
Liabilities		
Accounts payable	$ 2,300	$ 2,300
Grants payable	1,550	1,550
Mortgage payable	3,000	3,000
Interest payable	50	50
Total liabilities	$ 6,900	$ 6,900
Net assets		
Unrestricted	$24,350	$18,400
Temporarily restricted	29,075	28,700
Permanently restricted	10,000	5,000
Total net assets	63,425	52,100
Total liabilities and net assets	$70,325	$59,000

EXHIBIT 22-2

Statement of Activities

NEIGHBORS HELPING NEIGHBORS (A VHWO) STATEMENT OF ACTIVITIES FOR THE YEAR ENDED DECEMBER 31, 2011

Changes in Unrestricted Net Assets			
Revenues and gains			
Contributions		$15,240	
Membership dues		6,300	
Donated services		1,200	
Sales, net		6,045	
Special event	$950		
Less: Direct costs	650	300	
Total unrestricted revenues and gains			$29,085
Net assets released from restrictions			
Satisfaction of program restriction		900	
Expiration of time restriction		3,500	
Total net assets released from restrictions			4,400
Total unrestricted revenues, gains, and			
other support			33,485
Expenses and losses			
Program services			
Community service		10,800	
Recreation programs		11,000	21,800
Supporting services			
Fund-raising		1,245	
Management and general		4,490	5,735
Total expenses and losses			27,535
Increase in unrestricted net assets			5,950
Changes in Temporarily Restricted Net Assets			
Contributions		4,300	
Income on investments		475	
Net assets released from restrictions		(4,400)	
Increase in temporarily restricted net assets			375
Changes in Permanently Restricted Net Assets			
Contributions			5,000
Increase in net assets			11,325
Net assets at the beginning of the year			52,100
Net assets at the end of the year			$63,425

increase unrestricted net assets; revenues with donor-imposed restrictions increase temporarily restricted or permanently restricted net assets. Expenses decrease unrestricted net assets only. Note that expenses are classified as either program services or supporting services and are reported on a functional basis under these classifications (for example, community service, recreation programs). The functional basis of reporting expenses results in an informative but highly aggregated form of statement presentation. To overcome the limitations of aggregation, voluntary health and welfare organizations prepare an additional, separate statement of functional expenses, as shown in Exhibit 22-4. This statement reconciles the functional classifications with basic object-of-expense classifications such as salaries, supplies, professional fees and depreciation

A national VHWO may have financially interrelated local affiliates. Unless the local organizations are independent of the national organization, with separate purposes and separate governing boards, the financial statements of the national and local organizations are combined for reporting in accordance with GAAP.

"OTHER" NOT-FOR-PROFIT ORGANIZATIONS

As noted earlier, not-for-profit classifications include four categories corresponding to four previously published AICPA audit and accounting guides: voluntary health and welfare organizations, health care entities, colleges and universities, and other not-for-profit organizations. The "other" category encompasses a variety of organizations, such as cemetery associations, civic organizations, libraries, museums, social organizations, political organizations, and religious organizations. The accounting and financial reporting for each of these entities is quite similar to that for the VHWO illustrated

EXHIBIT 22-3

Statement of Cash
Flows (Indirect Method)

NEIGHBORS HELPING NEIGHBORS (A VHWO) STATEMENT OF CASH FLOWS—INDIRECT METHOD YEAR ENDED DECEMBER 31, 2011

Cash Flows from Operating Activities		
Change in net assets		$11,325
Adjustments to reconcile change in net assets to net cash provided by operating activities		
Depreciation	$ 8,500	
Increase in net contributions receivable	(1,800)	
Decrease in inventories	850	
Noncash contribution of equipment	(1,500)	
Noncash contribution of securities	(5,000)	1,050
Net cash provided by operating activities		12,375
Cash Flows from Investing Activities		
Cash paid for equipment	(4,000)	
Net cash used for investing activities		(4,000)
Cash Flows from Financing Activities		
Net cash used in financing activities		—
Increase in cash and cash equivalents		8,375
Cash and cash equivalents at beginning of year		14,000
Cash and cash equivalents at end of year		$22,375

previously, although the statement of functional expenses would be optional. In fact, "other" not-for-profits follow the same FASB ASC and are discussed in the 2010 umbrella *AICPA Audit and Accounting Guide: Not-for-Profit Organizations*, which supersedes and consolidates the AICPA guides for voluntary health and welfare organizations, colleges and universities, and other not-for-profit organizations. Because the accounting for other not-for-profit organizations is similar to the previous example provided, this book does not provide further illustrations.

LEARNING
OBJECTIVE **5**

NONGOVERNMENTAL NOT-FOR-PROFIT HOSPITALS AND OTHER HEALTH CARE ORGANIZATIONS

Hospitals and other health care providers constitute a significant area of accounting, both in terms of the entities represented and the cost of services provided. Health care providers include clinics, ambulatory care organizations, continuing-care retirement communities, health maintenance organizations, home health agencies, hospitals, government-owned health care entities, and nursing homes that provide health care. Health care entities may be organized as not-for-profit entities, governmental entities, or private business enterprises owned by investors (stockholders, partners, or sole proprietors).

As of 2009, the authoritative source of GAAP for non-governmental not-for-profit health care organizations is FASB ASC 958 on not-for-profit organizations (discussed above) and FASB ASC 954[7] on health-care organizations (discussed below). Topic Code 954 relates to both for-profit and not-for-profit health care organizations, while GASB is the source of GAAP for governmental health

EXHIBIT 22-4

Statement of Functional
Expenses

NEIGHBORS HELPING NEIGHBORS (A VHWO) STATEMENT OF FUNCTIONAL EXPENSES FOR THE YEAR ENDED DECEMBER 31, 2011

	Total	Community Service	Recreation Programs	Fund-Raising	Management and General
Salaries	$12,000	$ 4,000	$ 6,000	$ 500	$1,500
Supplies	5,835	2,300	2,000	745	790
Professional fees	1,200	—	—	—	1,200
Depreciation	8,500	4,500	3,000	—	1,000
	$27,535	$10,800	$11,000	$1,245	$4,490

[7]As noted earlier, the FASB created a not-for-profit advisory group in 2009. Some of the members of the advisory group are health care experts.

care organizations. As with not-for-profit organizations, the AICPA maintains an industry "audit and accounting guide," revised in June 2010 to reflect the FASB ASC. The AICPA guide provides guidance (not authoritative since 2009) on accounting and reporting for both governmental and nongovernmental health care organizations, even though there are significant differences between the two. Although the FASB and GASB have responsibility for setting accounting standards, the AICPA guide is likely to continue as a useful resource for both accounting and auditing professionals.

The discussion in this chapter generally refers to hospitals as a matter of convenience, but the principles apply to other health care organizations as well. Accounting and reporting for a nongovernmental not-for-profit hospital are based on the same standards and principles as for any other nongovernmental not-for-profit organization. However, there are unique characteristics of a health care entity that warrant specific discussion. First, health care entities have unique revenue sources, such as patient service revenues and premium fees, and their expense classifications are relatively specialized. Also, health care organizations present a statement of financial position, a statement of operations, a statement of changes in net assets, and a statement of cash flows. The health care audit guide requires that the statement of operations, which replaces the statement of activities reported by other not-for-profit organizations, report a performance measurement (such as excess of revenues over expenses or earned income) and the change in unrestricted net assets. These differences are covered in detail here.

Accounting for a Nongovernmental Not-for-Profit Hospital

The following situations review typical activities often unique to a health care entity. The sample journal entries demonstrate how the activities are reflected in the accounting system of a nongovernmental, not-for-profit hospital.

PATIENT SERVICE REVENUE Patient service revenues include room and board, nursing services, and other professional services. Patient revenues are recorded at full established rates when service has been provided. However, because a hospital's objective is to report the amount of revenues that it will ultimately collect, adjustments are made for deductions from revenues, such as the following:

- **Courtesy allowances.** Discounts for doctors and employees
- **Contractual adjustments.** Discounts arranged with third-party payors (Medicare and Blue Cross, for example) that frequently have agreements to reimburse at less-than-established rates

Courtesy allowances and contractual adjustments are not expenses. They are revenue deductions that are subtracted from gross patient service revenues to arrive at the net patient service revenue reported in the statement of operations. In addition, bad debt expense is recorded and allowance accounts are used to reduce net receivables for estimated bad debts. Charity care services—those provided free of charge to patients who qualify under a hospital's charity care policy—are excluded from both gross and net patient service revenues, because they are not expected to generate cash flow.

Community General Hospital is a nongovernmental not-for-profit hospital. Gross charges at established rates for services rendered to patients amounted to $1,300,000 during 2011. The hospital had contractual adjustments with insurers and Medicare of $300,000. Hospital staff and their dependents received courtesy discounts of $9,000. Bad debts are estimated at 2 percent of gross patient revenues. Community General records these transactions as follows:

Patient accounts receivable	1,300,000	
Patient service revenues—unrestricted		1,300,000
To record patient service charges at established rates.		
Courtesy discounts	9,000	
Contractual adjustments	300,000	
Patient accounts receivable		309,000
To record courtesy discounts and contractual		
adjustments.		
Bad debt expense	26,000	
Allowance for uncollectible patient accounts receivable		26,000
To establish an allowance for uncollectible receivables.		

PREMIUM FEES Premium fees, also known as subscriber fees or capitation fees, are revenues from agreements under which a hospital provides any necessary patient services (perhaps from a contractually established list of services) for a specific fee. The fee is usually a specific fee per member per month. Hospitals earn the agreed-upon fee whether the standard charges for services actually rendered are more or less than the amount of the fee—that is, without regard to services actually provided in the period. Therefore, hospitals report premium fees, which constitute a growing portion of revenues in many hospitals, separately from patient service revenues.

Community General Hospital receives premium revenue from capitation agreements totaling $454,000. The revenues are recognized as follows:

Cash	454,000	
Premium revenue—unrestricted		454,000
To record premium revenue from capitation agreements.		

OTHER OPERATING REVENUES The "other operating revenue" classification includes revenue from services to patients other than for health care and revenues from sales and services provided to nonpatients. This classification might include tuition from schools operated by the hospital, rentals of hospital space, charges for preparing and reproducing medical records, and proceeds from cafeterias, gift shops, and snack bars.

Throughout the year, Community General Hospital offers several health care courses, for which it charges tuition. Revenue for hospital space rental was $72,000 for the year, and the tuition charges for courses were $24,000. The hospital also receives revenue from the gift shop ($85,000) and cafeteria ($135,000). Community General records these other revenues as follows:

Cash (or accounts receivable)	316,000	
Other operating revenue—unrestricted		316,000
To record revenue from rentals, fees charged for courses,		
and gift shop and cafeteria proceeds.		

GIFTS AND BEQUESTS[8] Community General Hospital received unrestricted cash donations of $25,000 and a $250,000 donation for a pediatric care room:

Cash	275,000	
Unrestricted support—nonoperating gains		25,000
Temporarily restricted support		250,000
To record receipt of contributions.		

DONATED ASSETS Community General Hospital received marketable equity securities valued at $500,000 that were donor restricted for the purchase of diagnostic equipment. (Income from the securities is also restricted.) Community General records the donation in a restricted fund until the funds are used to purchase the equipment:

Investments	500,000	
Temporarily restricted support		500,000
To record donation of securities.		

At year-end, Community General determined that the market value of the investment increased by $40,000:

Investments	40,000	
Net realized and unrealized gains on investments—		
temporarily restricted		40,000
To record receipt of investment appreciation restricted		
to the acquisition of diagnostic equipment.		

---

[8]Many hospitals have a separate fund-raising entity typically called a Foundation, regardless of whether the hospital is governmental, not-for-profit or investor-owned. Foundations collect unrestricted, temporarily restricted, and permanently restricted endowments. The results and condition of foundations can be reported separately, discretely presented with the hospital, or blended (i.e., combined) into the parent hospital depending upon the circumstances.

Assume that these securities, which now have a book value of $540,000, are sold for $600,000. The hospital uses the proceeds to purchase the diagnostic equipment, which costs $560,000, and records the following entries:

Cash	600,000	
Investments		540,000
Temporarily restricted support—gain on the sale		
of investments		60,000
To record sale of securities.		
Equipment	560,000	
Cash		560,000
To record purchase of diagnostic equipment.		
Temporarily restricted net assets—reclassifications out	560,000	
Unrestricted net assets—reclassifications in		560,000
To record reclassification of net assets for which the		
temporary restriction is satisfied.		

OPERATING EXPENSES Hospitals record operating expenses on an accrual basis and normally specify functional categories for nursing services (medical and surgical, intensive care, nurseries, operating rooms), other professional services (laboratories, radiology, anesthesiology, pharmacy), general services (housekeeping, maintenance, laundry), fiscal services (accounting, admissions, credits and collections, data processing), administrative services (personnel, purchasing, insurance, governing board), interest, and depreciation provisions.

The hospital accrues salaries and wages allocated to functional categories as follows: nursing services, $355,000; other professional services, $115,000; fiscal services, $112,000; and administrative services, $120,000:

Nursing services expense	355,000	
Other professional services	115,000	
Fiscal services	112,000	
Administrative services	120,000	
Wages and salaries payable		702,000
To record accrual of payroll.		

The hospital purchases materials and supplies for $110,000. The supplies usage by the major functional categories during the year is as follows: nursing services, $50,000; other professional services, $40,000; fiscal services, $5,000; and administrative services, $8,000:

Inventory of materials and supplies	110,000	
Cash (or accounts payable)		110,000
To record purchase of supplies.		
Nursing services expense	50,000	
Other professional services expense	40,000	
Fiscal services expense	5,000	
Administrative services expense	8,000	
Inventory of materials and supplies		103,000
To record usage of materials and supplies.		

Community General Hospital recognizes depreciation on its equipment ($50,000) and building ($20,000):

Depreciation expense	70,000	
Accumulated depreciation—equipment		50,000
Accumulated depreciation—building		20,000
To record depreciation on major equipment and building.		

Statement of Operations and Other Hospital Financial Statements

Basic statements for nongovernmental not-for-profit health care entities consist of a balance sheet, or statement of financial position, a statement of operations, a statement of changes in net assets, and a statement of cash flows. Exhibits 22-5 to 22-8 illustrate these basic statements for a fictitious nongovernmental not-for-profit hospital unrelated to the preceding journal entries. Note that the statement of operations and the statement of changes in net assets taken together present essentially the same information as a statement of activities. Also, in Exhibit 22-6, Care Hospital reports the excess of revenues, gains, and other support over expenses and losses, as well as the increase in unrestricted net assets. The statement of cash flows illustrated in Exhibit 22-8 is prepared using the indirect method.

EXHIBIT 22-5

Nongovernmental Not-for-Profit Hospital Statement of Financial Position

---

CARE HOSPITAL STATEMENT OF FINANCIAL POSITION
DECEMBER 31, 2011

Current Assets			
Cash and cash equivalents			$ 60,000
Investments			540,000
Accounts receivable—patients, less $120,000			
estimated uncollectible receivables			1,080,000
Accounts receivable—Medicare			400,000
Receivable from limited-use assets			100,000
Inventories and prepaid items			170,000
Total current assets			2,350,000
Noncurrent Assets			
Assets whose use is limited			
by board for capital improvements			230,000
Property, plant, and equipment:			
Land		650,000	
Buildings	$5,000,000		
Fixed equipment	2,000,000		
Movable equipment	1,500,000		
	8,500,000		
Less: Accumulated depreciation	2,800,000	5,700,000	
Total property, plant, and equipment			6,350,000
Assets restricted for plant purposes			300,000
Assets restricted for endowment			1,420,000
Total assets			$10,650,000
Current Liabilities			
Accounts payable			$ 300,000
Accrued interest			150,000
Accrued salaries			210,000
Payroll taxes payable			140,000
Accrued pension expense			50,000
Current portion of long-term debt			100,000
Total current liabilities			950,000
Long-Term Debt			
Notes payable			500,000
Bonds payable (net of current portion)			900,000
Mortgage payable			3,000,000
Total long-term liabilities			4,400,000
Total liabilities			5,350,000
Net Assets			
Unrestricted			$ 3,220,000
Temporarily restricted			660,000
Permanently restricted			1,420,000
Total net assets			5,300,000
Total liabilities and net assets			$10,650,000

EXHIBIT 22-6

Nongovernmental Not-for-Profit Hospital Statement of Operations

CARE HOSPITAL STATEMENT OF OPERATIONS FOR THE YEAR ENDED DECEMBER 31, 2011

Unrestricted Revenues, Gains, and Other Support		
Net patient service revenues	$7,740,000	
Other operating revenues	950,000	
Unrestricted donations	150,000	
Unrestricted income from endowments	120,000	
Income from board-designated funds	20,000	
Net assets released from restrictions upon satisfaction of program restrictions	50,000	
Total unrestricted revenues, gains, and other support		$9,030,000
Expenses and Losses		
Nursing services	$2,700,000	
Other professional services	1,800,000	
General services	1,500,000	
Fiscal services	500,000	
Administrative services	300,000	
Medical malpractice costs	180,000	
Provision for uncollectible accounts	600,000	
Provision for depreciation	400,000	
Total expenses and losses		7,980,000
Excess (deficiency) of revenues, gains, and other support over expenses and losses		1,050,000
Net assets released from restrictions for plant-asset purposes		20,000
Increase in unrestricted net assets		$1,070,000

PRIVATE NOT-FOR-PROFIT COLLEGES AND UNIVERSITIES

LEARNING OBJECTIVE **6**

The primary objective of a college or university is to provide educational services to its constituents. Like governmental entities, colleges and universities often provide their services on the basis of social desirability and finance them, at least in part, without reference to those receiving the benefits. For example, very bright students may receive a full academic scholarship, or needy students might receive federal subsidies and financial aid to cover the costs of their education. The objectives of college and university accounting are to show the sources from which resources have been received and to demonstrate how those resources have been utilized in meeting educational objectives.

The primary authority over accounting principles for private (nongovernmental) colleges and universities is the FASB ASC. FASB standards have been incorporated into the *AICPA Audit and Accounting Guide: Not-for-Profit Organizations*, which provides accounting and reporting guidance (non-authoritative since 2009) for private colleges and universities as well as voluntary health and welfare organizations and other not-for-profit organizations. In addition to the audit guide,

EXHIBIT 22-7

Nongovernmental Not-for-Profit Hospital Statement of Changes in Net Assets

CARE HOSPITAL STATEMENT OF CHANGES IN NET ASSETS FOR THE YEAR ENDED DECEMBER 31, 2011

	Unrestricted	Temporarily Restricted	Permanently Restricted	Total
Balance, January 1, 2011	$2,150,000	$450,000	$1,010,000	$3,610,000
Excess of revenues, gains, and other support over expenses and losses	1,050,000	—	—	1,050,000
Contributions	—	270,000	300,000	570,000
Restricted investment income	—	10,000	110,000	120,000
Net assets released from restrictions	20,000	(70,000)	—	(50,000)
Changes in net assets	1,070,000	210,000	410,000	1,690,000
Balance, December 31, 2011	$3,220,000	$660,000	$1,420,000	$5,300,000

CARE HOSPITAL STATEMENT OF CASH FLOWS (INDIRECT METHOD) FOR THE YEAR ENDED DECEMBER 31, 2011

Cash Flows from Operating Activities and Gains and Losses		
Change in net assets		$1,690,000
Adjustments to reconcile change in net assets to net cash provided by operating activities		
Provision for depreciation	$ 400,000	
Provision for uncollectible accounts	600,000	
Decrease in Medicare accounts receivable	40,000	
Decrease in unearned interest (limited-use assets)	15,000	
Increase in accounts payable and accrued expenses	60,000	
Increase in patient accounts receivable	(195,000)	
Increase in inventories and supplies	(40,000)	880,000
Net cash provided by operating activities and gains and losses		2,570,000
Cash Flows from Investing Activities		
Purchase of property, plant, and equipment	(2,280,000)	
Purchase of investments	(300,000)	
Cash invested in limited-use assets	(350,000)	
Net cash used by investing activities		(2,930,000)
Cash Flows from Financing Activities		
Proceeds from contributions restricted for investment in endowment	300,000	
Other financing activities		
Proceeds from long-term note payable	500,000	
Repayment of bonds payable	(100,000)	
Repayment of mortgage note payable	(800,000)	
Net cash used by financing activities		(100,000)
Net decrease in cash for 2011		(460,000)
Cash and cash equivalents at beginning of year		520,000
Cash and cash equivalents at end of year		$ 60,000

much college and university implementation guidance comes from the *Financial Accounting and Reporting Manual*, an accounting manual prepared by the National Association of College and University Business Officers (NACUBO). The required financial statements of private not-for-profit colleges and universities are the same as those for voluntary health and welfare organizations, except for the statement of functional expenses.

Colleges and universities maintain accounts and reports on an accrual basis; thus, revenues are recognized when earned and expenses are recognized when the related materials or services are received. They report expenses by function, either on the face of the financial statements or in the notes. As with other NFP organizations, private institutions classify net assets, revenues, expenses, gains, and losses based on the existence or absence of donor-imposed restrictions (unrestricted, temporarily restricted, or permanently restricted), in accordance with the FASB ASC.

Accounting for a Private Not-for-Profit College or University

This section presents several journal entries to illustrate the recording of typical events and transactions that would occur in a private not-for-profit college or university.

TUITION AND FEES Private colleges and universities recognize the full amount of tuition and fees (net of refunds) assessed against students for educational purposes as revenue. Tuition waivers for scholarships appear in a contra revenue account, while estimated bad debts are recorded as institutional support expenses.

Student tuition and fees for Cane College total $1,000,000. Student tuition and fees also include $50,000 of tuition reductions provided under a fellowship program that requires no services on the part of the student. The college estimates bad debts at 3 percent of gross revenue from student tuition and fees, or $30,000. The following entries, recorded in the unrestricted category, reflect these events:

Accounts receivable	1,000,000	
Unrestricted revenues—tuition and fees		1,000,000
To record tuition and fees.		
Tuition reduction: unrestricted—student aid	50,000	
Accounts receivable		50,000
To record tuition reductions.		
Expenses—educational and general—institutional support	30,000	
Allowance for uncollectible accounts		30,000
To record allowance for uncollectible accounts.		

APPROPRIATIONS FROM FEDERAL, STATE, AND LOCAL GOVERNMENTS Appropriations include unrestricted amounts for current operations that are received, or made available, from legislative acts or from a local taxing authority. Institutions may classify restricted appropriations as unrestricted if the governing board can change a restriction without going through a legislative process. Cane College receives appropriations on a per-student basis from the state totaling $700,000. The funds are unrestricted:

Cash	700,000	
Unrestricted revenues—state appropriation		700,000
To record appropriations from the state government.		

STUDENT FINANCIAL AID Universities often receive financial aid funds from third parties that are intended to be used by students to cover educational costs. For example, Cane College receives federal grants through the Pell Grant program in the amount of $150,000 for its students. Cane College plays an agency role by holding the funds until they are disbursed to the students. The funds are not considered revenue for the college:

Cash	150,000	
Grant funds held for students		150,000
To record the receipt of Pell Grant funds.		
Grant funds held for students	150,000	
Cash		150,000
To record the distribution of Pell Grant funds.		

CONTRIBUTIONS Universities record contributions that carry no specifications regarding the time period or purpose of use as unrestricted revenue, whereas they must record contributions that may only be expended after a point in time or for a specific purpose as temporarily restricted. Cane College received contributions totaling $300,000; $225,000 were unrestricted, and $75,000 were for alumni center renovations. An additional $12,000 was pledged for the center:

Cash	300,000	
Contributions receivable	12,000	
Unrestricted revenues—contributions		225,000
Temporarily restricted revenues—contributions		87,000
To record contributions received and pledged.		

ENDOWMENTS Universities record contributions of principal that must be held indefinitely but whose income is available for restricted or unrestricted purposes as special contributions termed *endowments*. At Cane College, an elderly alumnus established a $50,000 endowment to provide book scholarships for athletes. During the year, investment income on the endowment was $4,000 and book scholarships for Cane athletes totaled $2,500:

Cash	50,000	
Permanently restricted revenues—endowment contribution		50,000
To record receipt of an endowment.		
Cash	4,000	
Temporarily restricted revenues—endowment income		4,000
To record endowment income.		
Expenses: Unrestricted—student aid	2,500	
Cash		2,500
To record payment of scholarships.		
Temporarily restricted net assets—reclassifications out	2,500	
Unrestricted net assets—reclassifications in		2,500
To record reclassification of net assets for which the temporary restriction is satisfied.		

SALES AND SERVICES OF AUXILIARY ENTERPRISES The revenue of auxiliary enterprises includes amounts earned in providing facilities and services to faculty, staff, and students. It includes amounts charged for residence halls, food services, intercollegiate athletics, and college student unions, as well as sales and receipts from college stores, barber shops, movie houses, and so on. Colleges and universities classify all revenue and expenses directly related to the operations of auxiliary enterprises as "auxiliary" and report them as unrestricted.

The dining hall at Cane College had sales of $60,800 and purchased $30,000 worth of supplies during May. The supplies used by the auxiliary enterprise during the period amounted to $28,000. Salaries paid to auxiliary employees were $31,000. Summary entries are as follows:

Cash	60,800	
Revenues—auxiliary enterprises		60,800
To record sales and services related to auxiliary enterprises.		
Supplies inventory	30,000	
Cash (or accounts payable)		30,000
To record purchase of supplies.		
Expenses—auxiliary enterprises—supplies	28,000	
Supplies inventory		28,000
To record utilization of supplies related to auxiliary enterprises.		
Expenses—auxiliary enterprises	31,000	
Cash		31,000
To record expenses for salaries of auxiliary enterprises.		

SALES AND SERVICES OF EDUCATIONAL ACTIVITIES The sale of goods and services that are related incidentally to educational activities of the university can generate unrestricted revenue. Often, the goods and services sold are a by-product of training or instruction. An example of this revenue category is the dairy creamery of Cane College, which has $550 revenue from sales of its products.

Cash	550	
Revenue—educational and general		550
To record sales related to educational activities.		

EXPENSES For reporting purposes, colleges and universities classify unrestricted expenses broadly, as either educational and general or as auxiliary enterprises. Expenses are further classified on a functional basis in the statement of activities. Functional classifications include the following:

- **Instruction.** Expenses for educational programs
- **Research.** Expenses to produce research outcome
- **Public service.** Expenses for activities to provide noninstructional services to external groups
- **Academic support.** Expenses to provide support for instruction, research, and publications (i.e., computing, libraries)
- **Student services.** Amounts expended for admissions and registrar, and amounts expended for students' emotional, social, and physical well-being
- **Institutional support.** Amounts expended for administration and the long-range planning of the university
- **Operation and maintenance of plant.** Expenses of operating and maintaining the physical plant (net of amounts to auxiliary enterprises and university hospitals)
- **Student aid.** Expenses from restricted or unrestricted funds in the form of grants, scholarships, or fellowships to students

Cane College incurred the following expenses in June: instruction, $45,000; research, $22,000; student services, $12,000; and institutional support, $3,500:

Expenses—educational and general—instruction	45,000	
Expenses—educational and general—research	22,000	
Expenses—educational and general—student services	12,000	
Expenses—educational and general—institutional support	3,500	
Cash (or payables)		82,500
To record expenses for June.		

PURCHASE OF PLANT ASSETS Recall that property, plant, and equipment acquired by a not-for-profit organization with unrestricted or restricted resources may be recorded at acquisition as unrestricted or temporarily restricted. If temporarily restricted, the assets are reclassified when depreciation is recognized.

Cane College purchases equipment with unrestricted assets in the amount of $35,000. Depreciation expense for the year is $3,500, and the equipment is allocated to each of the functional categories as shown here. The entries for the year are as follows:

Equipment	35,000	
Cash		35,000
To record purchase of equipment with unrestricted funds.		
Expenses—educational and general—instruction	1,300	
Expenses—educational and general—research	800	
Expenses—educational and general—student services	1,000	
Expenses—educational and general—institutional support	400	
Accumulated depreciation		3,500
To record depreciation of equipment.		

Cane College purchases land adjacent to the campus. The land costs $200,000, and financial resources were previously restricted for the purchase. The entries to record this transaction are as follows:

Land	200,000	
Cash		200,000
To record payment for the purchase of land.		

	Temporarily restricted net assets—reclassifications out	200,000	
	Unrestricted net assets—reclassifications in		200,000
	To record reclassification of temporarily restricted net assets.		

Financial Statements of Private Not-for-Profit Colleges and Universities

The required financial statements of private not-for-profit colleges and universities include a statement of financial position, a statement of activities, and a statement of cash flows. There are several acceptable alternatives for the statement of activities, so long as revenues, expenses, and reclassifications are clearly shown and changes in net assets are presented by classification (unrestricted, temporarily restricted, and permanently restricted). One popular, acceptable alternative to the statement of activities is to present two other statements: a statement of unrestricted revenues, expenses, and other changes in unrestricted net assets; and a statement of changes in net assets. The statement of financial position need not be classified, but assets are generally shown in order of liquidity. The statement of cash flows may be prepared using either the direct or the indirect method.

Exhibits 22-9 to 22-11 illustrate sample statements for a fictitious university. (The statements are for illustrative purposes only. They have no relationship to the preceding sample journal entries for Cane College.)

Internal Accounting and Control—The AICPA Model

Traditionally, colleges and universities used fund accounting practices within their accounting systems. Many adopted a fund structure referred to as the *AICPA model*. Although not-for-profit colleges and universities are now only required to report their resources based on restrictions rather than funds, the fund structure is often used for internal accounting and control. For this reason, the current AICPA NFP guide includes the AICPA fund structure. The structure includes the following fund classifications: current operating, loan, endowment, annuity and life income, plant, and agency.

The *current operating funds* grouping includes resources that are expendable for operating purposes. The current operating funds grouping contains two subgroups—one for unrestricted current funds and the other for restricted current funds.

The *loan funds* group accounts for resources held by colleges and universities under agreements to provide loans to students (and possibly faculty and staff). The *endowment fund* group consists of gifts with specifications about the manner in which the cash or donated item should be maintained and distributed. A separate fund is used for each endowment. *Annuity and life income funds* account for special types of endowment funds whereby the donor or a specified beneficiary receives a return from the gift for a specified period of time. After that time, the remainder of the gift belongs to the educational institution.

The *plant funds* group comprises four subgroups: unexpended plant funds, renewal and replacement funds, retirement of indebtedness funds, and investment in plant accounts. Colleges and universities use the first three funds to account for their financial resources, and the last subgroup (the investment in plant accounts) to account for the physical plant and related long-term debt. Institutions use unexpended plant funds to account for resources held for additions and improvements to the physical plant, whereas they use renewal and replacement funds for resources held for renewal and replacements of the existing plant. Fund assets of a retirement of indebtedness fund consist of liquid resources for current debt service and investments held for future debt retirement, including sinking fund investments. The assets of the investment in plant accounts consist of the physical plant (land, buildings, improvements other than buildings, and equipment, which includes library books).

Agency funds are used to account for assets held by the college or university for individual students and faculty members and for their organizations. As with the agency funds of governmental entities, transactions of college and university agency funds only affect asset and liability accounts and do not result in revenues and expenses.

ALMA MATER UNIVERSITY
STATEMENT OF ACTIVITIES
FOR THE YEAR ENDED JUNE 30, 2011

Revenues	
Tuition and fees (net of allowances of $150,000)	$1,000,000
State appropriations	1,200,000
Federal grants and contracts	50,000
Private grants and gifts	400,000
Endowment income	75,000
Sales and services of educational departments	60,000
Sales and services of auxiliary enterprises	800,000
Total current revenues	3,585,000
Total net assets released from	
restrictions for operations	370,000
Total revenues and reclassifications	3,955,000
Expenses	
Educational and general	
Instruction	1,640,000
Research	850,000
Public service and extension	100,000
Academic support	50,000
Student services	40,000
Institutional support	90,000
Operation and maintenance	
of plant	80,000
Student aid	150,000
Educational and general expenditures	3,000,000
Auxiliary enterprises	
Expenses	865,000
Total operating expenses	3,865,000
Net increase in unrestricted net assets	90,000
Changes in temporarily restricted net assets:	
Federal grants and contracts	100,000
Private grants and gifts	250,000
Endowment income	20,000
Net assets released from restrictions	(370,000)
Increase in temporarily restricted net assets	0
Changes in permanently restricted net assets:	
Private grants and gifts	100,000
Increase in permanently restricted net assets	100,000
Change in net assets	190,000
Net assets, July 1, 2010	535,000
Net assets, June 30, 2011	$ 725,000

SUMMARY

Not-for-profit organizations include a diverse group of governmental and private entities. Governmental not-for-profit organizations must follow the GASB standards covered in prior chapters, whereas private not-for-profit organizations look to the FASB for primary accounting guidance and the AICPA for supplemental accounting guidance. In recent years, the FASB has issued several statements aimed at improving comparability in the financial statements of all nongovernmental not-for-profit entities that issue statements in accordance with GAAP. Thus, nongovernmental voluntary health and welfare organizations, health care entities, and colleges and universities prepare a set of financial statements that present unrestricted net assets, temporarily restricted net assets, permanently restricted net assets, and total net assets, as well as changes in each class of net assets and in total.

EXHIBIT 22-10

Private Not-for-Profit
College or University
Statement of Financial
Position

ALMA MATER UNIVERSITY
STATEMENT OF FINANCIAL POSITION
FOR THE YEAR ENDED JUNE 30, 2011

	2011	2010
Assets		
Cash and cash equivalents	$ 95,000	$ 25,000
Investments	500,000	400,000
Accounts receivable (net of allowances)	70,000	44,500
Accrued interest receivable	5,000	—
Contributions receivable (net of allowances)	20,000	15,000
Loans to students	7,500	5,000
Inventories	12,000	5,000
Property, plant, and equipment (net of accumulated depreciation)	175,500	190,500
Total assets	$885,000	$685,000
Liabilities		
Accounts payable	$ 90,000	$ 75,000
Students' deposits	25,000	25,000
Bonds payable	45,000	50,000
Total liabilities	160,000	150,000
Net Assets		
Unrestricted	190,000	100,000
Temporarily restricted	35,000	35,000
Permanently restricted	500,000	400,000
Total net assets	725,000	535,000
Total liabilities and net assets	$885,000	$685,000

EXHIBIT 22-11

Private Not-for-Profit
College or University
Statement of Cash
Flows

ALMA MATER UNIVERSITY
STATEMENT OF CASH FLOWS—INDIRECT METHOD
FOR THE YEAR ENDED JUNE 30, 2011

Cash Flows from Operating Activities		
Change in net assets		$190,000
Adjustments to reconcile change in net assets to net cash provided by operating activities		
Depreciation	$ 15,000	
Increase in investments	(100,000)	
Increase in net accounts receivable	(25,500)	
Increase in accrued interest receivable	(5,000)	
Increase in net contributions receivable	(5,000)	
Increase in inventories	(7,000)	
Increase in accounts payable	15,000	(112,500)
Net cash provided by operating activities		77,500
Cash Flows from Investing Activities		
Increase in loans to students	(2,500)	
Net cash used by investing activities		(2,500)
Cash Flows from Financing Activities		
Payment of bonds payable	(5,000)	
Net cash used by financing activities		(5,000)
Increase in cash and cash equivalents		70,000
Cash and cash equivalents at beginning of year		25,000
Cash and cash equivalents at end of year		$ 95,000

Financial statements of nongovernmental not-for-profit entities include the statement of financial position, statement of activities, and statement of cash flows. Voluntary health and welfare organizations also prepare a statement of functional expenses. The financial statements and notes include all information required by GAAP and from which not-for-profit entities are not specifically exempt, as well as information required by applicable specialized accounting and reporting principles and practices. The focus of the financial statements is on the entity as a whole.

QUESTIONS

1. What statements are included in a set of financial statements for nongovernmental not-for-profit entities?
2. How does one determine whether a hospital, college, or voluntary health and welfare organization should be reported in accordance with FASB standards or GASB standards?
3. What is the authoritative status of *AICPA Audit and Accounting Guides* for not-for-profit and health care organizations as of 2010?
4. Explain the difference between a conditional promise to give and an unconditional promise to give.
5. Explain the difference between donor-imposed conditions and donor-imposed restrictions.
6. How are unconditional promises to give with collections due in the next period accounted for?
7. How is the expiration of a time restriction recognized?
8. Are gifts in kind always reported as unrestricted support that increases unrestricted net assets?
9. Expenses of voluntary health and welfare organizations include classifications for program services and supporting services. Explain these classifications.
10. What is the purpose of the statement of functional expenses of voluntary health and welfare organizations?
11. Are contributed services reported in the statement of activities of a nongovernmental voluntary health and welfare organization?
12. Health care entities frequently provide charity care to qualified individuals. How is charity care reported in the financial statements of a hospital?
13. How are net patient service revenues of hospitals measured, and in which hospital financial statement are they reported?
14. What are the major revenue groupings of hospitals? Give an example of a revenue item that would be included in each grouping.
15. Are provisions for bad debts and depreciation of hospitals reported as expenses? Explain.
16. Describe the difference in a set of financial statements for a governmental university and a private not-for-profit university.
17. When is the AICPA college guide model used?
18. Other than FASB standards and the AICPA guide, where can you find guidance on accounting and reporting issues for colleges and universities?
19. Describe the reporting requirements for a governmental not-for-profit entity with both governmental and business-type activities.
20. Identify the functional expense classifications for a university. Provide an example of each.
21. Discuss the two options that not-for-profit organizations have for recording donated fixed assets.

EXERCISES

E 22-1
Multiple choice

1. Contributions that are restricted by a donor to a nongovernmental not-for-profit organization are reported as a part of:
   a *Permanently restricted net assets*
   b *Temporarily restricted net assets*
   c *Unrestricted net assets*
   d *Either permanently restricted or temporarily restricted net assets, depending on the terms of the restriction*

2. Unconditional promises to give are recognized as contribution revenue under GAAP when:
   a *The promise is received*
   b *The related receivable is collected*
   c *The time or purpose restriction is satisfied*
   d *The future event that binds the promisor occurs*

3. Which of the following is not a characteristic of a conditional promise to give?
   a *It depends on the occurrence of a specified future and uncertain event to bind the promisor.*
   b *The gift may have to be returned to the donor if the condition is not met.*
   c *It is recognized as contribution revenue when the conditions are substantially met.*
   d *It depends on demand by the promisee for performance.*

4. Contributed long-lived assets that are donor restricted for a certain time period are reported by a nongovernmental not-for-profit entity as:

a *Unrestricted support in unrestricted net assets*

b *Restricted support in permanently restricted net assets*

c *Restricted support in temporarily restricted net assets*

d *Unrestricted support in temporarily restricted net assets*

5. Long-lived assets are purchased by a nongovernmental not-for-profit entity with cash that was restricted for that purpose. The assets are reported in temporarily restricted net assets. Depreciation expense is reported in unrestricted net assets.

a *The depreciation expense is incorrectly reported.*

b *An amount equal to the depreciation is reclassified from temporarily restricted to unrestricted net assets.*

c *An amount equal to the depreciation is reclassified from unrestricted to temporarily restricted net assets.*

d *An amount equal to the depreciation is reported as revenues.*

E 22-2

Multiple choice

1. When a temporary restriction on resources of a nongovernmental not-for-profit entity is met by the incurrence of an expense for the restricted purpose:

a *The expense is reported in the statement of activities as an increase in unrestricted net assets*

b *Amounts reported in the temporarily restricted net assets are reclassified as unrestricted net assets*

c *The entry is a debit to expense and a credit to the program services*

d *The expense is reported in restricted net assets*

2. A nongovernmental not-for-profit entity gives donors a sweatshirt imprinted with its logo when they pay $25 dues. The value of the sweatshirt is approximately $25. This transaction is most likely reported as:

a *An exchange transaction*

b *An agency transaction*

c *A contribution*

d *A gift in kind*

3. How will a nongovernmental not-for-profit entity record an agency transaction in which it receives resources?

a *No entry is made in the accounts.*

b *Debit the asset account and credit contribution revenue.*

c *Debit the asset account and credit temporarily restricted net assets.*

d *Debit the asset account and credit a liability account.*

4. Unconditional promises to give that are collectible within one year of the financial statement date:

a *Should be reported at their gross amount*

b *Should be reported at the gross amount less an allowance for uncollectible accounts*

c *Should be reported at the present value of the amounts expected to be collected, using the donor's incremental borrowing rate*

d *Should not be reported until collected*

5. In preparing the statement of cash flows for a nongovernmental not-for-profit entity, cash contributions that are restricted for long-term purposes are classified as:

a *Operating activities*

b *Investing activities*

c *Financing activities*

d *None of the above*

E 22-3

Multiple choice

1. Which of the following statements is not required for nongovernmental voluntary health and welfare organizations that issue financial statements in accordance with GAAP?

a *Balance sheet*

b *Statement of support, revenues, and expenses, and changes in retained earnings*

c *Statement of functional expenses*

d *Statement of cash flows*

2. Voluntary health and welfare organizations:

   a *Are required to use fund accounting principles to segregate unrestricted and restricted net assets*

   b *May report fund accounting information as additional information*

   c *Must report by funds if fund accounting principles are used for internal accounting purposes*

   d *Are prohibited from reporting by funds, even if fund accounting is used for internal accounting purposes*

3. Fund-raising costs of voluntary health and welfare organizations are classified as:

   a *Functional expenses*

   b *Program services*

   c *Supporting services*

   d *Management and general expenses*

4. Volunteers collect money and nonperishable food for the Food Pantry, a nongovernmental VHWO, by going house to house once each year for donations. The services of the volunteers should be accounted for as follows:

   a *The fair value of the service is estimated and recorded as contributions that increase unrestricted net assets.*

   b *The fair value of the service is estimated and recorded as contributions that increase either unrestricted net assets or temporarily restricted net assets, depending on donor-imposed restrictions on the resources collected.*

   c *The per diem wage rates of the donors are recorded in unrestricted net assets.*

   d *None of the above*

5. Unconditional promises to give (pledges) of nongovernmental voluntary health and welfare organizations are recognized as revenue and support in the period in which:

   a *The pledges are received*

   b *Cash is received from the pledges*

   c *All restrictions on pledged resources have been removed*

   d *Pledged resources are expended*

E 22-4

Multiple choice

  1. A university that is considered a special-purpose government:

   a *Is generally required to follow GASB standards*

   b *Is generally required to follow FASB standards*

   c *Should refer to the* **AICPA Audit and Accounting Guide** *for governmental colleges and universities*

   d *May choose whether to follow FASB, GASB, or AICPA guidelines*

  2. The operations of dormitories and dining halls for colleges and universities are reported as:

   a *Operating income*

   b *Auxiliary operations*

   c *Restricted income*

   d *Specific-purpose income*

  3. A university that follows the AICPA college model for internal control may have all of the following funds, *except*:

   a *Property, plant, and equipment*

   b *Loan*

   c *Life income*

   d *Endowment*

  4. Required financial statements for a private, nongovernmental not-for-profit college include which of the following?

   a *A statement of cash flows*

   b *A statement of functional expenses*

   c *A statement of changes in fund balances*

   d *A statement of revenues, expenses, and other changes*

  5. Grant funds received from the federal government and remitted directly to students provide an example of:

   a *An exchange transaction*

   b *An endowment*

   c *An agency transaction*

   d *A restricted contribution*

E 22-5

Multiple choice

1. Tuition waivers for scholarships are:
   - a   *Not reflected in the accounting records*
   - b   *Recorded in a contra revenue account*
   - c   *Recorded as institutional support expenses*
   - d   *None of the above*

2. Auxiliary enterprises in a college and university include all of the following, *except*:
   - a   *Bookstore*
   - b   *Research*
   - c   *Cafeteria*
   - d   *Dormitories*

3. Under *GASB Statement No. 35*, a state university (governmental) with only business-type activities may present:
   - a   *Fund financial statements*
   - b   *Government-wide financial statements*
   - c   *Only the financial statements required of enterprise funds*
   - d   *Condensed financial information*

4. Contributions of principal that must be held indefinitely but whose income is available for restricted or unrestricted purposes are termed:
   - a   *Bequests*
   - b   *Annuities*
   - c   *Endowments*
   - d   *Support*

5. Scholarships are classified as:
   - a   *Academic support*
   - b   *Student services*
   - c   *Institutional support*
   - d   *Student aid*

E 22-6

Multiple choice

1. A principal source of revenue for hospitals is from patient services. Patient services revenue for hospitals is recorded at:
   - a   *Amounts actually billed to patients*
   - b   *The hospital's full established rates for services provided*
   - c   *Amounts actually received from patients*
   - d   *Amounts actually billed to patients less discounts granted*

2. Premium fees:
   - a   *Are earned whether the standard charges for services actually rendered are more or less than the amount of the fee*
   - b   *Are earned only to the extent of services actually provided in the period*
   - c   *Must be returned to the subscriber if services are not provided*
   - d   *Are initially recorded as deferred revenues*

3. Oliver Hardwick, a roofing contractor, repaired the roof on the Mosely Clinic, a nongovernmental health care entity, at no charge to the clinic. The estimate for the job was $3,000.
   - a   *The donated services meet the criteria in FASB ASC and should be reported in the statement of operations as unrestricted support—donated services.*
   - b   *The donated services should be described in notes to the financial statements, but not included in the statement of operations.*
   - c   *Only donated services that directly provide health care to patients can be recognized in the financial statements.*
   - d   *The donated services are a direct addition to the current fund.*

4. Charity care provided by a not-for-profit hospital:
   - a   *Is reported as an operating expense in the statement of operations of unrestricted funds*
   - b   *Is reported as a deduction from gross patient service revenues in the statement of operations of unrestricted funds*

    c Is excluded from both gross patient service revenue and expense
    d Is reported in the statement of functional expenses

5. Discounts allowed to third-party payors in hospital accounting are recorded as:
    a Charity care
    b Contractual adjustments
    c Courtesy allowances
    d Mandatory discounts

E 22-7
Multiple choice

1. Hospital room charges for telephone and television rentals should be classified as:
    a Patient service revenues
    b Other operating revenues
    c Nonoperating gains
    d Premium fees

2. A hospital bills patients at gross rates and provides for courtesy allowances for employees when they settle their accounts at less than gross rates. In accordance with this system, the journal entry to record courtesy allowances would appear as:
    a Debit—cash; debit—courtesy allowance; credit—accounts receivable
    b Debit—courtesy discount; credit—allowance for courtesy discounts
    c Debit—cash; debit—patient service revenue; credit—accounts receivable
    d Debit—accounts receivable; credit—courtesy allowances; credit—patient service revenue

3. Unrestricted income from a nongovernmental health care entity's permanent endowment investments should be reported:
    a In the permanently restricted net assets as unrestricted support—nonoperating gains
    b In the statement of operations as unrestricted support—operating gains
    c In the statement of operations as unrestricted revenues—investment income
    d In the permanently restricted net assets as restricted revenues—investment income

4. Depreciation and amortization of hospital property and equipment:
    a Are required for both governmental and nongovernmental hospitals
    b Are not recorded in the statement of operations, but accumulated depreciation is disclosed in the statement of financial position
    c Are reported in the plant replacement and expansion fund of hospitals that use fund accounting
    d Are optional on donated property

5. A nongovernmental health care entity receives a gift of cash that is specified by the donor to be used for cancer research. The contribution will most likely be reported in:
    a Unrestricted net assets
    b Temporarily restricted net assets
    c Permanently restricted net assets
    d Either a or b, depending on the mission and activities of the health care entity

E 22-8
Not-for-profit expense classifications

A voluntary health and welfare organization summarizes its expenses by function, as follows:

Education	$20,400
Fund-raising	11,400
Management and general	5,500
Public health	15,700
Research	12,000

REQUIRED: Determine the expenses for program services and for supporting services.

E 22-9
Journal entries—Various not-for-profit organizations

1. A nongovernmental VHWO receives $20,000 of unconditional promises to give with no donor-imposed restrictions. Of this amount $14,000 is due during the current period and $6,000 is due in the next period. The organization estimates that 3% of the pledges will be uncollectible.

2. A nongovernmental VHWO receives a $200 cash gift that is restricted for use in a project to provide immediate assistance to qualified people with temporary hardships. Money is given to a qualified individual during the same period.

3. The Uptown Restaurant donated restaurant equipment to the Food Kitchen, a nongovernmental VHWO. The equipment had a fair value of $6,000 and a remaining useful life of four years, with no scrap value. No restrictions were imposed on the use of the equipment, either by the Uptown Restaurant or the Food Kitchen.

4. A donor contributed $8,000 to a homeless shelter that was restricted to the purchase of a new truck. The money was invested in a CD that pays 5% interest. Accrued interest on the investment totaled $215 at year-end. The income from the investment was also restricted for the purchase of a truck.

5. Orleans Community College assessed its students $750,000 tuition for the 2011 fall term. The college estimates bad debts will be 1% of the gross assessed tuition. Orleans's scholarship program provides for tuition waivers totaling $65,000. Because of class cancellations, $15,000 is refunded to the students.

6. Your State University received donations of $3 million in 2011 that were restricted to certain research projects on the feasibility of growing tobacco for pharmaceutical uses. The university incurred $1.2 million of expenses on this research in 2011.

REQUIRED: Prepare journal entries to account for these transactions. Include net asset classifications, where applicable.

PROBLEMS

P 22-1
Journal entries—Various not-for-profit organizations

Three wealthy friends, Tom, Grant, and Karen, each decided to donate $5,000,000 to the not-for-profit organization of their choice. Each donation was made on May 21, 2011. Prepare the entries required for each of the recipient organizations under the following scenarios.

1. Tom chose to contribute to a local voluntary health and welfare organization, and no restrictions were placed on the use of the donated resources.
   a Prepare the May 21, 2011, entry.
   b Prepare any entries necessary in 2012 if $2,300,000 of the gift is used to finance operating expenses.

2. Grant contributed to a local private university, and the donation was restricted to research.
   a Prepare the May 21, 2011, entry.
   b Prepare any entries necessary in 2012 if $2,300,000 of the gift is used to finance research expenses.

3. Karen gave to the local hospital, and the donation was restricted for construction of a fixed asset.
   a Prepare the May 21, 2011, entry.
   b Prepare any entries necessary in 2012 if $2,300,000 of the gift is used to finance construction costs.

P 22-2
Journal entries—Voluntary health and welfare organization

At the beginning of 2011, the citizens of North Ptarmigan created Share Shop, a voluntary health and welfare organization. Share receives donations of money, nonperishable groceries, and household items from contributors. The food and household items are distributed free of charge to families on the basis of need. Share allocates expenses 80 percent to community services and 20 percent to management and general services, unless otherwise noted.

Share has one paid administrator with a yearly salary of $14,600. An accountant donates accounting services to Share that have a fair value of $900 and are allocated to management and general. Work is also performed by regular volunteers whose services cannot be measured.

A local transit company has provided free warehouse space for the operations of Share Shop. Fair value of rent for the warehouse is $3,000 a year. Utilities of $1,800 are paid by Share for 2011.

During the year, Share purchased supplies for $300. At December 31, 2011, the supplies inventory was insignificant. Expenses incurred in determining which families were eligible for Share's services and other accounting and reporting expenses totaled $6,000.

Donated assets for 2011 included nonperishable groceries with a fair value of $60,000 and household items with a fair value of $40,000. During the year, Share Shop distributed three-fourths of the groceries and half of the household items. No portion of these distributions was allocated to management and general services.

In addition to the donated assets, Share received cash donations of $10,000 and pledges of $20,000. Share estimated that 10 percent of the pledges would be uncollectible. At year-end 2011, $15,000 of the pledges had been collected. Share estimates that only $1,000 of the remaining pledges will be uncollectible.

The town council of North Ptarmigan made a $25,000 grant to Share Shop that will be paid in January 2012.

REQUIRED: Prepare summary entries for Share Shop for 2011.

P 22-3
Statement of operations—Nongovernmental not-for-profit health care organization

The following selected items were taken from the accounts of Hometown Memorial Hospital, a not-for-profit hospital, at December 31, 2011:

Debits	
Administrative services	$ 310,000
Contractual allowances	400,000
Depreciation	200,000
Employee discounts	100,000
General services	290,000
Loss on sale of assets	50,000
Nursing services	1,000,000
Other professional services	500,000
Provision for bad debts	150,000
Credits	
Donated medicine	300,000
Income from investment in affiliate	80,000
Patient service revenues	2,500,000
Television rentals to patients	50,000
Unrestricted donations	200,000
Unrestricted income from investments of endowment funds	270,000
Restricted donations for fixed asset purchases	300,000
Restricted donations for specific operating purposes	100,000

REQUIRED: Use the information given to prepare a statement of operations for Hometown Memorial Hospital at December 31, 2011. Assume that $80,000 of expenses were for purposes for which restricted donations were available and that fixed assets costing $97,000 were purchased from donations restricted for their purchase.

P 22-4

Journal entries and statement of activities—Nongovernmental not-for-profit college

The following information relates to revenues and expenses for a private not-for-profit college:

Tuition and Fees	
Total assessed	$2,000,000
Tuition waivers	120,000
Appropriations	
State	800,000
Local	300,000
Auxiliary Enterprises	
Sales	500,000
Expenses	480,000
Endowment Income	
Restricted to research	70,000
Unrestricted	20,000
Private Gifts and Grants	
Restricted to student scholarships	300,000
Unrestricted	80,000
Expenses	
Instruction	2,100,000
Research	100,000
Student services	120,000
Operation of plant	180,000
Scholarships (does not include tuition waivers)	200,000

REQUIRED: Prepare journal entries and a statement of activities for the college.

P 22-5

Statement of activities—Nongovernmental not-for-profit organization

The following information was taken from the accounts and records of the Community Society, a nongovernmental not-for-profit organization. The balances are as of December 31, 2011, unless otherwise stated:

Unrestricted support—contributions	$3,000,000
Unrestricted support—membership dues	400,000
Unrestricted revenues—investment income	83,000
Temporarily restricted gain on sale of investments	5,000
Expenses—education	300,000
Expenses—research	2,300,000
Expenses—fund-raising	223,000
Expenses—management and general	117,000
Restricted support—contributions	438,000
Restricted revenues—investment income	22,500
Permanently restricted support—contributions	37,000
Unrestricted net assets, January 1, 2011	435,000
Temporarily restricted net assets, January 1, 2011	5,000,000
Permanently restricted net assets, January 1, 2011	40,000

The unrestricted support from contributions was all received in cash during the year. Additionally, the society received pledges totaling $425,000. The pledges should be collected during 2012, except for the estimated uncollectible portion of $16,000. The society spent $3,789,000 of restricted resources on construction of a major capital facility during 2011, and $500,000 of research expenses were for research financed from restricted donations.

REQUIRED: Prepare the statement of activities for the Community Society for 2011.

P 22-6
Journal entries—Nongovernmental not-for-profit university

Prepare journal entries to record the following transactions in the appropriate funds of a nongovernmental not-for-profit university:

1. Tuition and fees assessed total $6,000,000. Eighty percent is collected by year-end, scholarships are granted for $200,000, and $100,000 is expected to be uncollectible.

2. Revenues collected from sales and services of the university bookstore, an auxiliary enterprise, were $800,000.

3. Salaries and wages were paid, $2,600,000. Of this amount, $170,000 was for employees of the university bookstore.

4. Unrestricted resources were used to service the long-term mortgage on the university's buildings, $1,000,000.

5. Mortgage payments totaled $960,000, of which $600,000 was for interest.

6. Restricted contributions for a specific academic program were received, $440,000.

7. Expenses for the restricted program were incurred and paid, $237,000.

8. Equipment was purchased from resources previously set aside for that purpose, $44,000.

P 22-7
Journal entries—Voluntary health and welfare organization

The Good Grubb Food for the Hungry Institute is a nongovernmental not-for-profit organization that provides free meals for the destitute in a large metropolitan area. Record the following transactions in the accounts of Good Grubb.

1. Cash gifts that were received last year, but designated for use in the current year, totaled $20,000.

2. Unrestricted pledges of $65,000 were received. Five percent of pledges typically prove uncollectible. Additional cash contributions during the year totaled $35,000.

3. Donations of food totaled $150,000. The inventory of food on hand decreased by $1,200 during the year.

4. Expenses were incurred as follows: salary of director, $10,000; facility rental, $8,000; purchases of food, $70,000; and supplies, $27,000. Supplies inventory increased by $5,000 during the year.

5. Restricted pledges of $300,000 were received during the year. The pledges are restricted for use in constructing a new kitchen and dining hall. Of the pledges received, 5% is expected to be uncollectible.

P 22-8
Journal entries—Nongovernmental not-for-profit health care organization

The Fort Collins Health Center is a nongovernmental not-for-profit health care organization. During the current year, the following occurred:

1. Gross charges at established rates for services rendered to patients amounted to $102,300. The clinic had contractual adjustments with insurers and Medicare of $30,000. Bad debts are estimated at 2% of gross charges.

2. The health center receives premium revenue from capitation agreements totaling $54,000.

3. The center also receives revenue of $16,000 from the pharmacy housed in its building.

4. The center paid salaries and wages allocated to functional categories as follows: nursing services, $35,000; other professional services, $11,000; general services, $10,000; fiscal services, $2,000; and administrative services, $20,000.

5. The health center receives a federal grant for $12,000. The money must be used for medical equipment.

6. Supplies costing $13,000 were purchased during the month, and $6,700 in nursing supplies were used.

REQUIRED: Prepare journal entries to account for these transactions. Include net asset classifications, where applicable.

INTERNET ASSIGNMENT

1. Search the Internet for the financial statements of the United Way (*www.unitedway.org* or *www.uwint.org*) or a charity of your choice.

   a. Print a copy of the financial statements and bring them to class for discussion.

   b. Is the charity a VHWO? How can you tell?

   c. Are net assets properly classified into three categories?

   d. Are expenses classified into function categories on the face of the financial statements or in the notes?

   e. Were any temporarily restricted net assets reclassified as unrestricted? Can you determine the nature of the restrictions that were met?

2. Visit the AICPA's Web site, at *www.AICPA.org*. Select Publications and then select *Journal of Accountancy*. Find an article related to Not-for-Profits. Read the article and prepare a one-page summary.

3. Visit NACUBO's Web site, at *www.nacubo.org*. Locate the Accounting Advisory Reports. Select Business and Policy Areas and then choose Accounting. Under Accounting select Advisory Reports. View the most recent advisory report related to institutions of higher learning, and prepare a one-paragraph summary of its purpose.

4. Visit *www.guidestar.org* and obtain the Form 990 for a local not-for-profit organization.

   a. Examine Part VIII of the 990 to determine gross receipts of the organization.

   b. Examine Part IX of the 990. What category contained the majority of the organization's expenses?

   c. From Part VII, note the salaries of officers.

   d. After examining Parts VII–IX, look at the mission in Part III. Do you think spending is in line with the organization's mission?

REFERENCES TO THE AUTHORITATIVE LITERATURE

[1] FASB ASC Master Glossary and FASB ASC 985. Originally *Statement of Financial Accounting Standards No. 116.* "Accounting for Contributions Received and Contributions Made." Norwalk, CT: Financial Accounting Standards Board, 1993.

[2] FASB ASC 985-205. Originally *Statement of Financial Accounting Standard No. 117.* "Financial Statements of Not-for-Profit Organizations." Norwalk, CT: Financial Accounting Standards Board, 1993.

[3] FASB ASC 985-320. Originally *Statement of Financial Accounting Standards No. 124.* "Accounting for Certain Investments Held by Not-for-Profit Organizations." Norwalk, CT: Financial Accounting Standards Board, 1995.

[4] FASB ASC 985-605. Originally *Statement of Financial Accounting Standards No. 136.* "Transfers of Assets to a Not-for-Profit Organization or Charitable Trust that Raises or Holds Contributions for Others." Norwalk, CT: Financial Accounting Standards Board, 1999.

[5] FASB ASC 985-605-25-16.

SELECTED READINGS

American Institute of Certified Public Accountants. *AICPA Audit and Accounting Guide: Health Care Organizations.* New York: AICPA, 2010.

American Institute of Certified Public Accountants. *AICPA Audit and Accounting Guide: Not-for-Profit Organizations.* New York: AICPA, 2010.

Benson, Martha L., Alan S. Glazer, and Henry R. Jaenicke. "Coping with NPO Standards—It's Not Difficult." *Journal of Accountancy* (September 1998), pp. 67–74.

Booker, Quinton. "Accounting for Transfers to Non-Profits That Raise or Hold Contributions for Others: An Overview of *SFAS No. 136.*" *National Public Accountant* (February/March 2001), p. 14.

Financial Accounting and Reporting Manual for Higher Education. Washington, DC: National Association of College and University Business Officers, 2003. (Now available only as an online subscription service.)

Governmental Accounting Standards Board. *Statement No. 29.* "The Use of Not-for-Profit Accounting Principles by Governmental Entities." Norwalk, CT: Governmental Accounting Standards Board, 1995.

Governmental Accounting Standards Board. *Statement No. 34.* "Basic Financial Statements—and Management's Discussion and Analysis—for State and Local Governments." Norwalk, CT: Governmental Accounting Standards Board, 1999.

Governmental Accounting Standards Board. *Statement No. 35.* "Basic Financial Statements—and Management's Discussion and Analysis—for Public Colleges and Universities." Norwalk, CT: Governmental Accounting Standards Board, 1999.

Henry, Elaine, Oscar J. Holzmann, and YA-Wen Yang. "Fair Value Measurements, The Next Step." *The Journal of Corporate Finance & Accounting* (September/October 2007), pp. 89–94.

Statement of Financial Accounting Standards No. 93. "Recognition of Depreciation by Not-for-Profit Organizations." Stamford, CT: Financial Accounting Standards Board, 1987.

Statement of Financial Accounting Standards No. 116. "Accounting for Contributions Received and Contributions Made." Norwalk, CT: Financial Accounting Standards Board, 1993.

Statement of Financial Accounting Standards No. 117. "Financial Statements of Not-for-Profit Organizations." Norwalk, CT: Financial Accounting Standards Board, 1993.

Statement of Financial Accounting Standards No. 124. "Accounting for Certain Investments Held by Not-for-Profit Organizations." Norwalk, CT: Financial Accounting Standards Board, 1995.

Statement of Financial Accounting Standards No. 136. "Transfers of Assets to a Not-for-Profit Organization or Charitable Trust That Raises or Holds Contributions for Others." Norwalk, CT: Financial Accounting Standards Board, 1999.

Statement of Financial Accounting Standards No. 157. "Fair Value Measurements." Norwalk, CT: Financial Accounting Standards Board, 2006.

Statement of Financial Accounting Standards No. 159. "The Fair Value Option for Financial Assets and Financial Liabilities—Including an amendment of FASB Statement No. 115." Norwalk, CT: Financial Accounting Standards Board, 2007.

Statement of Financial Accounting Standards No. 164. "Not-for-Profit Entities: Mergers and Acquisitions—Including an amendment of FASB Statement No. 142." Norwalk, CT: Financial Accounting Standards Board, 2009.

23 CHAPTER

Estates and Trusts

ccountants frequently refer to estate and trust accounting as **fiduciary accounting** because estate and trust managers operate in a good-faith custodial or stewardship relationship with beneficiaries of the estate or trust property. A *fiduciary* is a person who is held in particular confidence by other people. Fiduciaries may be executors, trustees, administrators, and guardians, depending on the nature of their duties and the demands of custom.

In legal terms, a **fiduciary** is an individual or an entity authorized to take possession of the property of others. Upon taking possession of estate or trust property, the fiduciary (trustee of a trust, for example) has an obligation to administer it in the best interest of all beneficiaries. Although similar practices are used in accounting for estates and trusts, there are a number of differences between the two types of entities. These include the manner in which the entities are created, the objectives of their activities, and the life of their existence. This chapter discusses these differences and reviews and illustrates accounting practices for estates and trusts.

Our goal in this chapter is to provide an overview of accounting for estates and trusts. You should recognize that these are very complex areas, from both accounting and legal viewpoints. Estates are subject to probate laws, which vary widely across the 50 states. Estates and trusts may also be subject to taxation. There are potentially taxes on the value of estate assets (often referred to as *inheritance taxes*) at both the federal and state levels. Estates and trusts may also be subject to income taxes, once again at both the state and federal levels. Calculations of inheritance and income taxes may differ at the state and federal levels, and across the 50 states. More detailed coverage of these topics is left to courses in law and tax accounting.

EARNING OBJECTIVES

1 Understand basic accounting for the estate of a decedent.

2 Understand the principal versus income issues in estate and trust accounting.

3 Understand basic accounting for a trust.

4 Understand how estates are taxed.

CREATION OF AN ESTATE

An estate comes into existence at the death of an individual. If the deceased (**decedent**) had a valid will in force at the time of death, he or she is said to have died **testate**.[1] In the absence of a valid will, the decedent is said to have died **intestate**. The estate consists of the property of the decedent at the time of death. Ordinarily, a probate court appoints a **personal representative** of the decedent to take control of the property, but flexibility is provided if a valid will is in force. In this case, the personal representative may leave real or tangible personal property under the control of the person entitled to it under the terms of the will.

---

[1]People with sizable estates usually have lawyers draw up their wills. The lawyer can provide for the eventual validation of the will and also help with estate planning so that property is distributed according to the client's wishes and taxes are minimized.

75

PROBATE PROCEEDINGS

The personal representative of the deceased files a petition with the appropriate probate court requesting that an existing will be **probated**, that is, for the will to be validated. The hearing of the probate court to establish validity is called a **testacy proceeding** because it determines whether the deceased died testate or intestate. Under the **Uniform Probate Code (UPC)**, the term *personal representative* includes both executor and administrator, as well as other designations for persons who perform the same functions.

Confirmation

A confirmation by a probate court that a will is valid means that the decedent died testate. Ordinarily, this leads to appointment of the personal representative named in the will as **executor** of the will. It also leads to the presumption that estate property will be distributed in accordance with the provisions of the will, in the absence of extenuating circumstances.

A person dies intestate when he or she dies without leaving a will. Failure of the probate court to validate a will submitted for probate also means that the decedent died intestate. In either case, the court appoints an **administrator** to take control of the estate and supervise the distribution of estate assets in accordance with applicable state laws.

Uniform Probate Code

The state laws governing probate and distribution of estate property vary considerably and do not provide a uniform basis for classifying the legal and accounting characteristics of estates. Therefore, this chapter bases its discussion and illustrations on the UPC, which was approved by the National Conference of Commissioners on Uniform State Laws. The UPC has been approved by the American Bar Association, even though most states have not adopted it.

ADMINISTRATION OF THE ESTATE

The executor or administrator of the estate is a fiduciary who is expected to observe the standards of care applicable to trustees. Appointment by a probate court gives the executor authority to carry out the written instructions of the decedent, including settlement and distribution of the estate. The executor is expected to perform this duty as expeditiously and efficiently as possible.

Within 30 days after appointment, the executor or administrator must inform the heirs and devisees of his or her appointment and provide selected information about certain other matters. **Heirs** are the persons entitled to the property of the decedent under the statutes of intestate succession. **Intestate succession** is the order in which estate property is distributed to the surviving spouse, parents, children, and so on, if any estate property is not effectively distributed by will. **Devisees** are those persons designated in a will to receive a *devise* (a testamentary disposition of real or personal property). Under the UPC, "to devise" means to dispose of real or personal property by will. A *specific devise* is the gift of an object, and a *general devise* is a gift of money.

Intestate Succession

Under the UPC, as amended, the entire estate of a person who dies intestate passes to the spouse if (1) the decedent has no living descendants or (2) all surviving descendants are also descendants of the surviving spouse. If there are descendants from a prior marriage or relationship, the surviving spouse receives the first $100,000 (the amount varies by state) and one-half of the remaining intestate estate. The remaining part of the estate not passing to the spouse (or the entire estate if there is no surviving spouse) passes to the descendants as directed in the state code.

Inventory of Estate Property

The executor or administrator is required to prepare and file an inventory of property owned by the deceased within three months of appointment. This inventory must list the property in reasonable detail and show the fair market value on the date of death for each item of property. Any encumbrance on the property (such as a lien or other claim) must also be disclosed for each item. This inventory is filed with the probate court, and additional copies must be provided to interested persons on request. If appraisers are employed to assist in valuing the property, their names and addresses must accompany the inventory. Subsequent discovery of property omitted from the inventory, or errors in valuing certain items, are corrected by preparing and filing a new or supplementary inventory. Personal items of limited value are usually excluded from the inventory.

Exempt Property and Allowances

The UPC entitles the surviving spouse to a **homestead allowance** that is exempt from, and has priority over, all claims against the estate. The amount of the allowance varies, but in some states it is $15,000. In the absence of a surviving spouse, the minor children would share the allowance equally. The surviving spouse also has an entitlement of up to $10,000 (varies by state) in household furniture, automobiles, and personal effects from the estate, depending on whether or not the property has been used to secure a loan. In the absence of a surviving spouse, the minor children share this property jointly.

The surviving spouse and minor children who were dependent on the deceased are also entitled to a reasonable family allowance to be paid out of the estate property during the period in which the estate is being administered. This family allowance is exempt from and has priority over all claims except the homestead allowance.

Claims Against the Estate

Under the UPC, the personal representative publishes a notice in a newspaper of general circulation in the county for three consecutive weeks. The purpose is to announce his or her appointment and to notify creditors to present their claims within four months of the date of first publication of the notice.

Claims against the estate *that arose before death* and were not presented within four months (or three years, if the required notice to creditors was not published) are barred forever against the estate, the personal representative, the heirs, and the devisees.

All claims against the decedent's estate *that arose after death* are barred as claims against the estate, the personal representative, the heirs, and the devisees unless presented as:

1. A claim based on a contract with the personal representative within four months after performance is due and discharged
2. Any other claim within four months after it arises

CLASSIFICATION OF CLAIMS When estate assets are insufficient to pay all claims in full, the UPC provides that payments are made as follows:

1. Costs and expenses of administration of the estate
2. Reasonable funeral expenses and reasonable and necessary medical and hospital expenses of the last illness of the decedent
3. Debts and taxes with preference under federal or state law
4. All other claims

No preference is given for payment within a given class of claims.

SECURED CLAIMS Payment of secured claims against the estate depends on the amount allowed if the creditor surrenders his or her security. However, if the assets of the estate are encumbered by mortgage, pledge, lien, or other security interest, the personal representative may pay the encumbrance if it appears to be in the best interests of the estate.

ACCOUNTING FOR THE ESTATE

LEARNING OBJECTIVE **1**

The executor records the inventory of estate property in a self-balancing set of accounts that show:

1. The property for which responsibility has been assumed
2. The manner in which that responsibility is subsequently discharged

The executor does not accept responsibility for obligations of the decedent (testator), so the liabilities of the estate are not recorded until paid.

LEARNING
OBJECTIVE 2

Estate Principal and Income

The focus of fiduciary accounting lies in distinguishing between principal and income. That focus applies to accounting for both estates and trusts. Estates frequently realize income from investments between the time that the property inventory is filed by the executor and the time the estate is fully administered. A primary reason for dividing estate principal and income is that the beneficiaries are likely to be different. For example, some devises specified in the will are distributed from estate principal, but the income may accrue to the residual beneficiaries. **Residual beneficiaries** are those entitled to the remainder of the estate after all other rightful claims on the estate have been satisfied.

The National Conference of Commissioners on Uniform State Laws approved a Revised Uniform Principal and Income Act to provide guidance in distinguishing between estate principal and income. That act provides that expenses incurred in settling a decedent's estate be charged against the principal of the estate. These expenses include debts, funeral expenses, estate taxes, interest and penalties, family allowances, attorney's fees, personal representative's fees, and court costs.

Alternatively, income (less expenses) earned after death on assets included in the decedent's estate is distributed to the specific devisee to whom the property was devised. Any remaining income that accrues during the period of estate administration is distributed to the devisees in proportion to their interests in the undivided (residual) assets of the estate.

ESTATE INCOME, GAINS, AND LOSSES In accounting for the decedent's estate, the receipts due but unpaid at the date of death are a part of the estate principal. These include items such as interest, dividends, rents, royalties, and annuities due at the time of death. After death, earnings from income-producing property are estate income, unless the will specifically provides otherwise. That is, amounts earned for the items listed would be classified as income, rather than principal, if they came due during the period of estate administration. In accounting for interest income on bond investments included in the estate, no provision is made for amortization of bond premiums and discounts. This is because bonds (and other securities) are included in the inventory at fair market value, and any gains or losses on disposal are adjustments of estate principal.

Depreciation is a related matter that requires interpretation under the Uniform Principal and Income Act. The act provides that a reasonable allowance for depreciation be made on depreciable property of the estate, except that no depreciation is to be made on real property used by a beneficiary as a residence or on personal property held by a trustee who is not then making a depreciation allowance.

ILLUSTRATION OF ESTATE ACCOUNTING

On April 1, 2011, Harry Olds entered the hospital with a terminal illness. He died on May 1, 2011, at the age of 70. Laura Hunt, Harry's daughter, was appointed executor of the estate by the probate court, which also confirmed that Harry had died testate. The will provided specific devises at estimated values to be awarded as follows:

Summer home to his daughter, Laura Hunt	$145,000
2008 Ford Taurus to his grandson, Gary Hunt	12,000
200 shares of FFF stock to his friend, Michael Wallace	10,000
All other personal effects to Harry's widow, Gloria Olds	

The following general devises of cash were also provided:

Laura Hunt, in lieu of fees as executor	$20,000
Sara Tyson, Harry's housekeeper	10,000
First Methodist Church	10,000
Humane Society	10,000
Gloria Olds is to receive the income in excess of expenses during the administration of the estate.	
The residue of the estate is to be placed in trust, with the income used to support Harry's widow during her lifetime. Upon her mother's death, Laura gets the remainder of the estate.	

EXHIBIT 23-1

Inventory of Estate
Assets

HARRY OLDS, TESTATOR
INVENTORY OF ESTATE ASSETS
AS OF THE DATE OF DEATH ON MAY 1, 2011

Description of Property	Fair Value
Cash in Commercial National Bank	$ 30,000
Cash in savings account at First National Bank, 6% annual interest	93,000
Certificate of deposit, 8 percent, 18 months, due August 1, 2011 (includes $10,000 accrued interest)	110,000
Certificate of deposit, 9 percent, one year, due July 1, 2011 (includes $7,500 interest)	107,500
Note receivable plus $1,500 accrued interest from George Stein, 10 percent, due June 1, 2011	21,500
Rocky Mountain Power common stock, 1,000 shares	40,000
Southern Natural Gas common stock, 2,000 shares	30,000
Danville City 9 percent, $50,000 par municipal bonds	58,000
Interest on Danville City bonds, due June 1, 2011	1,875
Dividends receivable—utility stocks	1,500
Summer home	145,000
FFF common stock, 200 shares	10,000
2008 Ford Taurus	12,000
Personal effects*	—
	$660,375

*The probate court permitted Laura to exclude Harry's personal effects other than specific devises from the inventory. Submitted by Laura Hunt, executor on June 15, 2011.

Laura informed the heirs and devisees of her appointment as executor of Harry's estate on May 19, 2011, and at the same time, placed the required notice to creditors in the newspaper. On June 15, 2011, she filed the estate inventory that appears in Exhibit 23-1 with the probate court.

Laura subsequently prepared the following entries to record transactions and events during the period of estate administration (all during 2011):[2]

MAY 19 Memorandum: Placed a notice in the *Montgomery News Messenger* that creditors of the estate of Harry Olds should present claims against the estate within four months.

JUNE 15 Recorded the inventory of estate assets as of May 1:

Cash—principal (+A)	30,000	
Savings account (+A)	93,000	
Certificate of deposit, due August 1, 2011 (+A)	100,000	
Certificate of deposit, due July 1, 2011 (+A)	100,000	
Note receivable—George Stein (+A)	20,000	
Rocky Mountain Power common stock (+A)	40,000	
Southern Natural Gas common stock (+A)	30,000	
FFF Company common stock (+A)	10,000	
Danville municipal bonds (+A)	58,000	
Summer home (+A)	145,000	
2008 Ford Taurus (+A)	12,000	
Interest receivable on CDs (+A)	17,500	
Interest receivable—George Stein (+A)	1,500	
Interest receivable—municipal bonds (+A)	1,875	
Dividends receivable—common stock (+A)	1,500	
Estate principal (+SE)		660,375

JUNE 16 Cashed dividend checks received May 5 on utility stock:

Cash—principal (+A)	1,500	
Dividends receivable—common stock (−A)		1,500

---

[2]This chapter treats the estate principal as a stockholders' equity–type account, to be consistent with other topics in the text.

JUNE 18 Collected interest of $2,250 on Danville City bonds. Interest of $375 was earned after the date of death:

Cash—principal (+A)	1,875	
Cash—income (+A)	375	
Interest receivable—municipal bonds (−A)		1,875
Estate income (R, +SE)		375

JUNE 23 Funeral expenses of $4,500 were paid:

Funeral expenses (E, −SE)	4,500	
Cash—principal (−A)		4,500

JUNE 24 Collected the $20,000 George Stein note and $1,650 interest. Interest of $150 was earned after the date of death:

Cash—principal (+A)	21,500	
Cash—income (+A)	150	
Note receivable—George Stein (−A)		20,000
Interest receivable—George Stein (−A)		1,500
Estate income (R, +SE)		150

JUNE 25 Discovered and cashed a certificate of deposit that matured on April 15 and was excluded from the estate inventory. The proceeds were $10,800:

Cash—principal (+A)	10,800	
Assets subsequently discovered (−A)		10,800

JUNE 28 Paid hospital and medical bills in excess of amounts paid by Medicare and private health insurance policies:

Hospital and medical expenses (E, −SE)	19,000	
Cash—principal (−A)		19,000

JULY 1 Cashed the certificate of deposit that was due on July 1:

Cash—principal (+A)	107,500	
Cash—income (+A)	1,500	
Certificate of deposit (−A)		100,000
Interest receivable on CDs (−A)		7,500
Estate income (R, +SE)		1,500

JULY 12 Paid cash to general devisees as provided in the will:

Devise—Laura Hunt (E, −SE)	20,000	
Devise—Sara Tyson (E, −SE)	10,000	
Devise—First Methodist Church (E, −SE)	10,000	
Devise—Humane Society (E, −SE)	10,000	
Cash—principal (−A)		50,000

AUGUST 1 Received interest from savings account for the quarter ending July 31:

Cash—income (+A)	1,395	
Estate income (R, +SE)		1,395

AUGUST 1 Cashed in the certificate of deposit due August 1:

Cash—principal (+A)	110,000	
Cash—income (+A)	2,000	
Certificate of deposit (−A)		100,000
Interest receivable on CDs (−A)		10,000
Estate Income (R, +SE)		2,000

AUGUST 5 Received dividend checks on utilities stock:

Cash—income (+A)	1,500	
Estate income (R, +SE)		1,500

AUGUST 15 Paid a $500 mechanics bill on the Ford that was incurred on April 10, and submitted for payment on August 10:

Debts of decedent paid (E, −SE)	500	
Cash—principal (−A)		500

AUGUST 15 Delivered specific devises as provided in the will. Personal effects not included in the estate inventory were left with the widow, Gloria Olds:

Devise—Laura Hunt (E, −SE)	145,000	
Devise to Gary Hunt (E, −SE)	12,000	
Devise to Michael Wallace (E, −SE)	10,000	
Summer home (−A)		145,000
2008 Ford Taurus (−A)		12,000
FFF Company common stock (−A)		10,000

AUGUST 28 Payment of attorney fees and court costs:

Attorney fees paid (E, −SE)	4,500	
Court costs paid (E, −SE)	500	
Cash—principal (−A)		5,000

AUGUST 31 Distribution of estate income to Gloria Olds:

Distribution to Gloria Olds (E, −SE)	6,920	
Cash—income (−A)		6,920

Closing Entries

Entries to close the nominal accounts to estate income and estate principal on August 31 are as follows:

Estate principal (−SE)	246,000	
Funeral expenses (−E, +SE)		4,500
Hospital and medical expenses (−E, +SE)		19,000
Devise—Laura Hunt (−E, +SE)		165,000
Devise—Sara Tyson (−E, +SE)		10,000
Devise—First Methodist Church (−E, +SE)		10,000
Devise—Humane Society (−E, +SE)		10,000
Debts of decedent paid (−E, +SE)		500
Devise to Gary Hunt (−E, +SE)		12,000
Devise to Michael Wallace (−E, +SE)		10,000
Attorney fees paid (−E, +SE)		4,500
Court costs paid (−E, +SE)		500
Estate income (−R, −SE)	6,920	
Distribution to Gloria Olds (−E, +SE)		6,920
Assets subsequently discovered (+A)	10,800	
Estate Principal (+SE)		10,800

After these closing entries are made, the remaining account balances are as follows:

Cash—principal	$204,175
Savings account	93,000
Rocky Mountain Power common stock	40,000
Southern Natural Gas common stock	30,000
Danville municipal bonds	58,000
Estate principal	$425,175

August 31 Laura Hunt transfers estate property to Ed Jones, trustee for Gloria Olds, in accordance with the income trust established by Harry Olds's will:

Estate principal (−SE)	425,175	
Cash—principal (−A)		204,175
Savings account (−A)		93,000
Rocky Mountain Power common stock (−A)		40,000
Southern Natural Gas common stock (−A)		30,000
Danville municipal bonds (−A)		58,000

Charge–Discharge Statement

The **charge–discharge statement** is a document prepared by the personal representative (executor or administrator) to show accountability for estate property received and maintained or disbursed in accordance with the will (or the probate court in intestate cases). A charge–discharge statement shows progress in the administration of the estate and termination of responsibility when the will has been fully administered. Exhibit 23-2 shows a final charge–discharge statement by Laura Hunt for her father's estate. The statement consists of two major parts: one for estate principal and one for estate income. The extent of detail is determined by the complexity of the estate, number of devises, and instructions from the probate court.

LEARNING OBJECTIVE **3**

ACCOUNTING FOR TRUSTS

The will of Harry Olds resulted in the creation of an income trust for Gloria Olds. A trust created pursuant to a will is referred to as a **testamentary trust.** The fiduciary that administers a trust is the **trustee.** A trustee may be a business entity or a natural person. As in the case of estates, guidance in accounting for trusts comes from state laws, the Uniform Trusts Act, the UPC, and the Revised Uniform Principal and Income Act.

The entry made by Ed Jones, the trustee, to open the books for the creation of the Gloria Olds Trust is as follows:

Cash (+A)	204,175	
Savings account (+A)	93,000	
Rocky Mountain Power common stock (+A)	40,000	
Southern Natural Gas common stock (+A)	30,000	
Danville municipal bonds (+A)	58,000	
Trust fund principal (+SE)		425,175
To record receipt of property transferred from Laura Hunt, executor.		

A primary concern in accounting for trust entities is distinguishing between principal and income. This is especially true of income trusts such as the one created for Gloria Olds because the principal amount of the trust is to be maintained intact to provide income for Mrs. Olds's care until her death. Separate trust fund principal and trust fund income accounts are used to separate principal and income balances for accounting purposes. The use of separate principal and income cash accounts, however, is of limited value, and is usually unnecessary.

After the original entry to record the creation of the trust, trust accounting essentially parallels accounting for an estate. Income and distributions are recorded following the terms of the trust

EXHIBIT 23-2

Charge–Discharge
Statement

ESTATE OF HARRY OLDS
CHARGE—DISCHARGE STATEMENT
FOR THE PERIOD OF ESTATE ADMINISTRATION
MAY 1 TO AUGUST 31, 2011

Estate Principal

I charge myself for:

Assets included in estate inventory	$660,375	
Assets discovered after inventory	10,800	671,175
Total estate principal charge		$671,175

I credit myself for:

Funeral expenses paid	$ 4,500	
Hospital and medical expenses paid	19,000	
Mechanic's bill paid	500	
Attorney fees and court costs	5,000	$ 29,000
Devises paid in cash to:		
Laura Hunt	$ 20,000	
Sara Tyson	10,000	
First Methodist Church	10,000	
Humane Society	10,000	50,000
Devises distributed in kind to:		
Laura Hunt (Summer home)	$ 145,000	
Gary Hunt (2008 Ford)	12,000	
Michael Wallace (FFF stock)	10,000	167,000
Transferred to Ed Jones, trustee for Gloria Olds:		
Cash—principal	$ 204,175	
Savings account	93,000	
Rocky Mountain Power Company stock	40,000	
Southern Natural Gas Company stock	30,000	
Danville municipal bonds	58,000	425,175
Total estate principal discharge		$671,175

Estate Income
I charge myself for:

Estate income received during estate administration	$ 6,920

I credit myself for:

Payment of estate income to Gloria Olds as directed by the will	$ 6,920

Respectfully submitted: Laura Hunt, Estate Executor, August 31, 2011.

agreement. A trustee may also be responsible for supervising the investment trust assets, once again in accordance with the original trust agreement. If the trust has a termination date, the trustee must prepare a charge and discharge statement indicating the final disposition of all trust assets.

ESTATE TAXATION

LEARNING
OBJECTIVE 4

An estate may be subject to taxation (referred to as estate, or inheritance, taxes) at both the state and federal levels. Accountants and attorneys play a vital role in estate planning to minimize these tax burdens for their clients and heirs. State taxes vary considerably across the 50 states and will not be discussed further here. Even if the federal tax is permanently repealed (as discussed in the following section), estate planning services will remain critical for larger estates subject to state-level taxation.

Estate Taxes

Federal taxation of estates is currently in a period of flux. The Economic Growth and Tax Relief Reconciliation Act of 2001 proposed reduction of the tax, and a total repeal in 2010. However, the tax returned in 2011 because Congress did not vote to make the repeal permanent. Exhibit 23-3 summarizes the current federal estate tax provisions.

The taxable amount of an estate is based on fair values of all estate assets at the date of death. Assets include real and personal property, as well as life insurance policies. The estate value is reduced by

EXHIBIT 23-3

Federal Estate
Provisions of the
2001 Economic
Growth and Tax Relief
Reconciliation Act

Year of Death	Tax Exempt Estate	Maximum Tax Rate
2005	$1,500,000	47%
2006	2,000,000	46
2007	2,000,000	45
2008	2,000,000	45
2009	3,500,000	45
*2010	5,000,000	35
2011	5,000,000	35
2012	5,000,000	35
**2013	1,000,000	55

*In 2010, decedent estates were given the option of using the $5,000,000 exemption limit and 35 percent excess estate tax rate or $0 limit/0 percent tax rate together with modified carryover basis rules.
** The Tax Relief, Unemployment Insurance Reauthorization, and Job Creation Act that was signed into law on December 17, 2010, which provided the federal estate tax exemption and tax rate for 2010-2012 is only good until December 31, 2012. Effective 2013, the exemption and rate will revert to 2002 levels unless Congress acts prior to that time.

funeral expenses, settlement of estate liabilities, bequests to qualified charities, a marital deduction/exemption for properties given to a spouse, state-level taxes, expenses of estate administration (e.g., executor's fees) and a tax-exempt amount (current levels are shown in Exhibit 23-3).

Michael Dennyson dies on August 1, 2008, leaving taxable estate assets valued at $4,200,000. Michael is survived by his widow, Danielle. Details of the estate are as follows:

Fair value of gross estate	$4,200,000
Funeral expenses	(10,000)
Executor's fees	(25,000)
Estate liabilities	(250,000)
Bequest to local symphony	(200,000)
Bequest to church	(100,000)
Bequest to State University	(200,000)
Marital deduction	(3,415,000)
Taxable value of estate	$ 0
Estate tax due	$ 0

Under this scenario, no federal estate tax is due. However, the $3,415,000 marital deduction becomes a part of Danielle's estate, subject to taxation upon her demise.

Suppose instead that Michael's sole heir is his niece Jennifer. The marital deduction is no longer available, leaving a taxable estate value of $3,415,000. The estate tax is calculated as follows:

Taxable value of estate	$3,415,000
Estate tax exemption	(2,000,000)
Estate subject to tax	$1,415,000
Estate tax due (assuming 45% maximum rate)	$ 636,750
Jennifer's net inheritance	$2,778,250

Notice that with proper planning, Michael could have provided a $636,750 combined greater benefit to his favorite charities and his niece. If Michael had bequeathed an additional $1,415,000 to the three charities, the remaining $2,000,000 would have been exempt from federal estate tax. Jennifer's net inheritance would have been reduced to $2,000,000.

The taxable estate can also be reduced through gifts to an unlimited number of donees. However, these may be subject to federal gift taxes beyond a certain level. Annual gift amounts are indexed to inflation, currently standing at $13,000 per donee ($26,000 for a married couple). The exclusion from gift taxation is further subject to a $1,000,000 lifetime maximum. Bequests to qualified charities are not considered gifts. The 2001 Economic Growth and Tax Relief Reconciliation Act does not eliminate gift taxes.

Income Taxes on Estate Income

In addition to federal and state estate and inheritance taxes, trusts and estates are also subject to federal (and possibly state) income taxes. An estate is a taxable entity and is subject to tax on income earned from the date of death until final settlement of the estate. The tax may be paid by the estate or by the beneficiary if estate property has already been distributed to the beneficiary.

Estates and trusts file federal income tax returns on Form 1041, U.S. Fiduciary Income Tax Return. The beneficiary's share of income is reported on Schedule K-1 of Form 1041. Income for estates and trusts and applicable tax rates are defined in essentially the same manner as for individuals. Income includes interest and dividends, rent, etc. Deductions and/or exemptions for estate administration fees, charitable donations and distributions to beneficiaries reduce taxable income. Distributions to beneficiaries may be taxable income amounts in their personal tax returns. There is also a tax exemption for estates and trusts with taxable income less than $600. The fiduciary of the estate must provide applicable information to the beneficiary on Schedule K-1.

SUMMARY

When a person dies without a valid will, he or she dies intestate. The deceased person's estate is distributed under the statutes of intestate succession. When the decedent has a valid will in force, he or she dies testate. The probate court normally names the personal representative named in the will as executor of the estate. The executor is a fiduciary charged with carrying out the provisions of the will, including the settlement and distribution of the estate.

The executor records an inventory of the estate in a self-balancing set of accounts; however, obligations of the decedent are not recorded until paid. The executor must distinguish estate principal and income in accounting for the estate. Guidance for distinguishing estate principal and estate income is found in the Uniform Principal and Income Act. The executor prepares a charge–discharge statement to show accountability for estate property and progress in the administration of the estate. A final charge–discharge statement is prepared when the estate has been fully administered.

QUESTIONS

1. Does accounting for a trust follow GAAP?
2. Briefly summarize differences between principal and income transactions for estates and trusts. Why is the classification important in estate and trust accounting?
3. What is the meaning of a devise in estate accounting?
4. What does it mean to die intestate?
5. What is meant by a homestead, or family, allowance?
6. Does the calculation of the federal estate tax permit any deductions?
7. How should assets and liabilities be measured in the accounting records of an estate?
8. Is it possible to avoid estate taxation by giving assets as gifts prior to death?
9. Briefly summarize how income earned on estate property should be treated by a beneficiary for purposes of filing a federal tax return. Where should the beneficiary look to provide this information?
10. Under current law, the federal estate tax will revert to 2002 levels in 2013. Even if the federal estate tax is repealed at that time, offer advice to your client as to why estate planning and tax planning are still important.
11. Summarize reasons why it may be important to have a will.
12. Are estate income taxes the responsibility of the estate or its beneficiaries?

EXERCISES

E 23-1
Prepare journal entries for an estate

You serve as the executor for the estate of Willy Rock. The following transactions occur during June 2011:

a *Willy's estate included a municipal bond with a value of $500,000. On the date of Willy's death, there was $4,400 of accrued but unpaid interest. On June 5, you received a check in the amount of $9,000, representing the normal semiannual interest payment.*

b   *Included in the specific devises of Willy's will was a bequest to the Atlanta Animal Shelter in the amount of $100,000. You decide that estate assets will be more than adequate to meet all obligations of the estate and to pay all specific devises, and you issue a check for $100,000 to the animal shelter on June 10.*

c   *On June 20, you pay funeral expenses for Willy, in the amount of $16,400.*

d   *You receive an interest check in the amount of $3,000 from First Atlanta National Bank on June 24 and realize that an unknown investment in a certificate of deposit in the amount of $50,000 was omitted in the original inventory of estate assets, along with $1,200 of accrued interest.*

REQUIRED: Prepare journal entries for the listed transactions. You can ignore estate and income taxes.

E 23-2

Prepare journal entries for an estate

You serve as the executor for the estate of Maribeth Rainy. The following transactions occur during July 2011:

a   *The Rainy estate included a certificate of deposit in the amount of $600,000. On the date of death, there was $11,600 of accrued but unpaid interest. On July 15, you received a check in the amount of $15,000, representing the normal semiannual interest payment.*

b   *Included in the specific devises of Maribeth's will was a bequest to the local symphony orchestra in the amount of $150,000. You decide that estate assets will be more than adequate to meet all obligations of the estate and to pay all specific devises, and you issue a check for $150,000 to the orchestra on July 18.*

c   *You pay a probate court fee of $2,800 on July 24.*

d   *On July 20, you pay funeral expenses in the amount of $12,800.*

e   *On July 28, you receive a bill from the local hospital for costs not covered by Maribeth's insurance in the amount of $44,000. The liability was unknown and not included in your initial estate inventory.*

REQUIRED: Prepare journal entries for the listed transactions. You can ignore estate and income taxes.

E 23-3

Prepare journal entries for an estate

You serve as the executor for the estate of Virginia Troy. Virginia's will provides that all remaining assets other than specific items in the will pass to her longtime friend Melanie Matthews. The following transactions occur during October and November 2011:

a   *The Troy estate included 100,000 shares of common stock of the Board of Water & Light, valued at $62 per share. On the date of death, there were no outstanding dividends receivable. On October 15, you note that a dividend of $3 per share has been declared, payable on October 25.*

b   *Included in the specific devises of Virginia's will was a bequest to the Philadelphia Art Museum in the amount of $150,000.*

c   *You pay a probate court fee of $3,800 on October 24.*

d   *On October 29, you pay funeral expenses in the amount of $11,600.*

e   *On October 28, you receive and pay a bill from the local hospital for costs not covered by Virginia's insurance in the amount of $37,000. The liability was unknown and not included in your initial estate inventory.*

f   *On October 29, you receive a dividend check from the Board of Water & Light in the amount of $300,000.*

REQUIRED: Prepare journal entries for the listed transactions. You may ignore estate and income taxes.

E 23-4

Accounting for an estate

K.T. Tim has been appointed to serve as executor for the estate of Ms. Melanie Triciao, who passed away on August 15, 2011. Ms. Triciao's assets consisted of the following:

Asset	Book Value	Fair Value
Cash	$118,225	$ 118,225
Savings accounts	250,000	250,000
ViaReggio common stock	67,500	225,000
City of Roma municipal bonds	381,500	412,000
Mercedes sports car	57,500	41,000
Condominium on Italian Riviera	399,700	1,265,500
Atlanta personal residence	225,700	430,000
Collection of rare hand puppets	11,145	85,000
Fully restored Model T Ford	1,750	125,000

The probate court has ruled that other personal effects may be excluded from the estate inventory.

REQUIRED: Prepare the estate inventory as of August 15, 2011.

E 23-5 Journal entries and accounting for an estate

You serve as the executor for the estate of Jeff Carpenter, who passed away on August 25, 2011, at the age of 102. Jeff's estate consisted of two certificates of deposit totaling $800,000 and a $15,000 balance in his checking account. Total accrued interest on the CDs at the date of death amounted to $7,000. Jeff left a valid will, which provided that most of the estate be inherited by his sole surviving nephew, J.J. Kara. The will further provided that $100,000 be transferred to a trust account for his faithful dog, Sooner XXV. Income from the trust would be used to care for Sooner. Upon Sooner's demise, the trust would end, and remaining trust principal would transfer to J.J. Kara. Jeff's personal effects were minimal and excluded from the estate. Ms. Colleen Ryan, a trust officer at the Oxford National Bank, serves as estate executrix and as fiduciary for the trust. Ms. Ryan determines that no federal or state inheritance taxes are due. The limited estate income is also free from any federal or state income tax. The following transactions occur during September 2011:

  a *On September 12, received a check in the amount of $11,500, representing the normal semiannual interest payment on the certificates of deposit.*
  b *On September 13, cashed out the certificates of deposit for $800,000.*
  c *On September 15, transferred $100,000 to a trust account at Oxford National Bank to provide care for Sooner XXV. Also, on the way to the bank, Sooner was dropped off at Puppy Paradise, his new home.*
  d *On September 18, paid funeral expenses for Jeff in the amount of $7,200.*
  e *On September 20, paid herself the $2,500 executor's fee specified in Jeff's will.*
  f *On September 28, finalized the estate and transferred the balance of the estate assets to Jeff's nephew, J.J. Kara.*

REQUIRED

1. Prepare an estate inventory at the date of death.

2. Prepare journal entries to record the estate transactions during September.

3. Prepare the estate closing entries on September 28.

4. Prepare the charge–discharge statement for the estate of Jeff Carpenter for the period August 25 through September 28, 2011.

E 23-6
Prepare journal entries for a trust

You serve as the trustee for the Sooner XXV trust. The following transactions occur during 2011:

September 15	Open the Sooner XXV trust account, depositing the $100,000 transferred from the estate of Jeff Carpenter.
September 16	Deposit the $100,000 into an insured money market fund earning 5 percent annually, in accordance with the trust agreement.
October 16	Deposit $417 interest received from the money market fund into the trust checking account.
October 19	Write a $300 check to Puppy Paradise to cover Sooner's November room and board costs. Costs to November 1 had been prepaid by the estate.
October 27	Write a check for $22 to cover chew toys for Sooner.
November 16	Deposit $417 interest received from the money market fund into the trust checking account.
November 22	Write a $300 check to Puppy Paradise to cover Sooner's December room and board costs.
December 16	Deposit $417 interest received from the money market fund into the trust checking account.
December 28	Puppy Paradise informs you of Sooner's passing. Pay $700 for Sooner's funeral and burial costs.
December 31	Pay yourself the agreed $100 trust administration fee.
December 31	Distribute all remaining trust principal by transferring the title to the money market fund and cash to J.J. Kara.

REQUIRED: Prepare journal entries for the listed transactions. You may ignore taxes.

E 23-7

Prepare charge and discharge statement for the Sooner XXV trust

Use information from E 23-6 to prepare a charge and discharge statement for the trust for the period September 15, 2011 through December 31, 2011.

E 23-8

Prepare journal entries for a trust

You serve as the trustee for the Lisa Ann Trust. The following transactions occur during June and July 2011:

June 1	Open the trust account, depositing the $1,000,000 transferred from the estate of Cheri James into a non-interest-bearing checking account to be used for trust investment and administration and for accumulation of interest and dividends received from trust investments.
June 2	Deposit $500,000 into a two-year certificate of deposit earning 6 percent annually, with interest paid monthly.
June 3	Invest the remaining $500,000 in a stock mutual fund.
July 2	Record deposit of one month's interest from the certificate of deposit to the trust checking account.
July 3	Pay bank's trust administration monthly fee of $41.

REQUIRED: Prepare journal entries for the listed transactions. You may ignore taxes.

E 23-9

Prepare journal entries for a trust

You serve as the trustee for the Josephine Frederick testamentary income trust. The trust was created by the will of her late husband, John. Under the terms of John's will, all assets are transferred to the trust to cover living expenses for his spouse. Upon her demise, trust assets will be sold, with the proceeds distributed to their six children. Each is to receive an equal share.

The probate court ruled that household furnishings and John's personal effects could be excluded from the estate. The executor has paid all inheritance and income taxes on estate income for the period of estate administration. The estate inventory prepared by John's estate executor showed the following assets:

Asset	Cost	Fair Value
Cash	$218,220	$218,220
Savings accounts	300,000	300,000
Microsystems common stock	163,400	400,000
Big Casino common stock	181,500	120,000
Vintage sports car	17,500	31,000
Mountain cottage	39,700	114,500
Personal residence	209,900	457,500

REQUIRED: Prepare the journal entries for the creation of the trust.

E 23-10

Estate tax calculation

Mr. Dogbert dies on March 1, 2009, and leaves his entire estate, valued at $5,300,000 (after settlement of all estate expenses and liabilities) to his sole surviving family member, his daughter Emily.

REQUIRED

1. Calculate the federal tax on Mr. Dogbert's estate. (You may ignore any state-level inheritance taxes and assume that federal taxes are paid at the 45 percent rate.)

2. Offer suggestions as to how the estate tax might be avoided, leaving Dogbert's daughter Emily better off financially.

E 23-11

Estate tax calculation

Mr. Chuck Rainy dies on May 21, 2009, and leaves his entire estate, valued at $3,600,000 (after settlement of all estate expenses and liabilities) to be equally divided among his sole surviving family members, his daughters Emily and Laura, and his son Tom.

REQUIRED: Calculate the federal tax on Mr. Rainy's estate. (You may ignore any state-level inheritance taxes and assume that federal taxes are paid at the 45 percent rate.)

E 23-12
Estate tax calculation

Ms. Jacki Jerome, a famous rock superstar, dies on November 28, 2009, and leaves her entire estate, valued at $23,400,000 (after settling all estate expenses and liabilities) to her cousin Maggie.

REQUIRED: Calculate the federal tax on Ms. Jerome's estate. (You may ignore any state-level inheritance taxes and assume that federal taxes are paid at the 45 percent rate.)

PROBLEMS

P 23-1
Estate accounting

Jimmy Olson died on June 15, 2011, at the age of 75, after a brief illness. Jimmy is survived by his wife, Lois, and two adult sons, Clark and Kent. Jimmy left a valid will, requesting that Clark serve as executor of his estate. Jimmy's widow will maintain the family residence, which was owned jointly.

Jimmy's will provided the following specific devises:

2005 Corvette to his son, Clark	$ 35,000
Summer cottage on Lake Michigan to his son Kent	40,000
Stock investments to be shared equally between his two sons	400,000
Miscellaneous personal effects to his widow, Lois	—

Jimmy's will also provided the following general devises of cash:

Clark—to cover executor's services	$ 5,000
Ms. Lana Lang, Jimmy's personal trainer	200,000
Jimmy's church	50,000
The local symphony orchestra	50,000

Jimmy's will further provides that Lois should receive any excess of income over expenses during the administration of his estate. All remaining assets are to be placed in a trust to support Lois for the remainder of her lifetime. Upon Lois's death, the remainder of the estate is to be divided equally between Clark and Kent.

Clark filed notice of his appointment as executor on June 25 and placed the required notice to potential creditors in *The Daily Planet*, the local newspaper. Clark prepared and filed the following estate inventory with the probate court on July 15:

Jimmy Olson, Testator
Inventory of Estate Assets
As of the date of Death on June 15, 2011
Submitted by Clark Olson, executor, on July 15

Property Description	Fair Value
Cash checking and savings accounts in Metropolis FNB	$ 750,000
Certificate of deposit (6 percent, 36 months, matures December 31) (includes $5,000 accrued interest)	505,000
Stocks held by Perry White brokerage	460,000
Dividends receivable on stocks	12,000
Lake Michigan cottage	40,000
2005 Corvette	35,000
Personal effects*	—
	$1,802,000

*The probate court permitted Clark to exclude Jimmy's personal effects from the inventory.

The following events occurred during June and July 2011:

June 22	Received a check in the amount of $15,000, representing interest on the certificates of deposit, including the amount accrued at the date of death.
June 24	Received a dividend check in the amount of $12,000.
June 30	Paid $250 to repair a roof leak on the Lake Michigan cottage.
July 4	Paid $4,900 in funeral expenses for Jimmy.
July 12	Cashed out the certificate of deposit for $501,300. The additional $1,300 represented interest income from June 23 through July 12. The bank waived the fees for early withdrawal because Jimmy had been a loyal, long-term customer.
July 15	Filed the estate inventory with the probate court.
July 20	Distributed the general property devises as provided in Jimmy's will.
July 21	Distributed the general cash devises as provided in Jimmy's will.
July 22	Closed the accounts, finalizing the estate administration, paid remaining estate income to Lois, and transferred remaining estate assets to Lois Olson testamentary income trust.

REQUIRED

1. Prepare journal entries for the transactions related to the estate during 2011.

2. Prepare entries to terminate the estate and transfer remaining assets to the trust.

3. Prepare the final charge–discharge statement for the estate of Jimmy Olson for the period June 15, 2011 through July 22, 2011.

P 23-2
Creation of a trust

You have been hired as trustee for the testamentary trust created by the will of Jimmy Olson. The trust is created on July 22, 2011. (Use the information provided in P 23-1.)

The trust initially invests the proceeds from the estate in a checking account that pays 3 percent per year. Interest is paid monthly. On July 23, the trust invests $300,000 in a certificate of deposit at Metropolis National Bank. The certificate earns 6 percent interest per year, paid monthly. On July 25, the trust invests $500,000 in the Super Stock Mutual Fund. On July 31, the trust invests $100,000 in 10-year 10 percent Smallville Municipal Bonds, which mature on July 31, 2018. The bonds pay interest semiannually on January 31 and July 31. On August 22, you receive a check for $1,500, representing one month's interest on the certificate of deposit. On August 23, you receive the statement on the checking account indicating a deposit of $405 for one month's interest on the checking account. The statement also indicates the bank's monthly fee of $100 for maintaining the trust. On August 31, you send a check to Lois Olson for $3,700 to cover her monthly living expenses.

REQUIRED: Prepare the entry to record the creation of the Olson trust on July 22. Prepare all additional required entries to account for trust activities through August 31.

P 23-3
Estate accounting

George Wilson dies on March 1, 2011, leaving a valid will. The will reads as follows:

I leave my home, furnishings, remaining bank account balances and personal possessions to my wife Helen. I leave my automobile to my nephew, Dennis. I leave my stock investment accounts to my niece, Denise. I leave income on my estate to be divided equally between Dennis and Denise. Estate expenses are to be paid from principal, not from estate income. All remaining property is to be placed in a trust for my four children. I name my nephew, Dennis, as executor of my estate.

Dennis prepares an estate inventory for all assets discovered and files the appropriate notice to potential creditors on March 15:

George Wilson, Testator
Inventory of Estate Assets
As of March 1, 2011

Assets	Fair Value
Cash—checking	$ 16,500
Cash—savings	50,000
Dividends receivable on stocks	400
Interest receivable on bonds	2,400
Life insurance—payable to the estate	500,000
Personal residence	325,000
Household furnishings and personal effects	76,000
2000 Thunderbird Convertible	21,000
Investments in stocks	25,000
Investments in bonds	200,000
	$1,216,300

The following transactions occurred during March and April:

March 25	Dennis pays funeral expenses of $2,800.
March 30	Dennis receives a check from the life insurance company for $500,000.
April 9	Dennis discovers title to a small parcel of lakefront property in George's safe deposit box. The title indicates that George purchased the land for $10,000.
April 15	A check for $3,000 in bond interest is received.
April 19	Dennis receives an appraiser's report on the lakefront property, valuing it for $28,000.
April 28	Dennis pays $13,250 to settle all liabilities of the estate, including property taxes and George's medical bills.
April 29	A check for $500 in stock dividends is received.
April 30	Dennis makes all remaining payments and property transfers and closes the estate.

REQUIRED: Prepare all journal entries required to account for the estate of George Wilson. You may ignore taxes.

P 23-4
Charge and discharge statement for an estate

Use the information in P 23-3 to prepare a charge–discharge statement for the estate of George Wilson for the period March 1, 2011 through April 30, 2011.

P 23-5
Creation of a trust

You have been hired as trustee for the testamentary trust created by the will of George Wilson. The trust is created on April 30, 2011. (Use the information provided in P 23-3 and P 23-4.) The trust initially invests the proceeds from the estate in a checking account, which pays 3 percent per year. Interest is paid quarterly. On May 3, the trust invests $450,000 in a certificate of deposit at the local bank. The certificate earns 6 percent interest per year, paid monthly. On May 25, the trust sells the land for $31,300 in cash. On May 31 and June 30, you pay the $165 monthly service fees to the bank. On June 3, you receive a check for $2,250, representing the first month's interest on the certificate of deposit. On June 15, you send a check to Jimmy Wilson (George's oldest son) for $8,700 to cover his fall semester tuition, room, and board at Big State University.

REQUIRED: Prepare the entry to record the creation of the Wilson Family Trust on April 30. Prepare all required entries to account for trust activities through June 30.

P 23-6
Estate accounting

Tom Josephson dies on May 16, 2011, leaving a valid will. The will reads as follows:

I leave my automobile to my niece, Pat. I leave my stock investment accounts to my niece, Sue. I leave income on my estate to the local humane society. Estate expenses *are to be paid from principal, not from estate income. All remaining property is to be placed in a trust for my two children, Megan and Ryan. I name my niece, Prima, as executrix of my estate, for which she should be paid a fee of $2,500.*

Prima prepares an estate inventory for all assets discovered and files the appropriate notice to potential creditors on May 31. Prima excludes the personal residence, furnishings, and bank accounts from the inventory, as these were jointly owned by Tom and his wife, Corinne.

Tom Josephson, Testator
Inventory of Estate Assets
As of May 16, 2011

Assets*	Fair Value
Dividends receivable on stocks	$ 1,200
Interest receivable on bonds	6,750
Life insurance—payable to the estate	750,000
2000 Volkswagen	2,600
Investments in stocks	52,000
Investments in bonds	400,000
	$1,212,550

*The probate court allowed exclusion of Tom's personal effects.

The following transactions occurred during May and June:

June 5   Prima discovers government bonds with a face value of $200,000 in Tom's safe deposit box. The box also contains an additional life insurance policy in the amount of $50,000.

June 15 Prima receives a check from the life insurance company for $750,000.

June 16 A check for $8,000 in bond interest is received.

June 18 Prima pays funeral expenses of $4,300.

June 22 Prima cashes in the government bonds for $215,000, which includes accrued interest at the date of death. The bonds matured several years earlier and were no longer accruing interest.

June 23 Prima receives a check from the insurance company on the subsequently discovered policy for $50,000.

June 24 Prima pays $18,250 to settle all liabilities of the estate, including property taxes and Tom's medical bills.

June 28 A check for $1,600 in stock dividends is received.

June 30 Prima makes all remaining payments (including her fee as executrix) and property transfers and closes the estate.

REQUIRED: Prepare all journal entries required to account for the estate of Tom Josephson. You may ignore taxes.

P 23-7
Charge and discharge statement for an estate

Use the information in P 23-6 to prepare a charge—discharge statement for the estate of Tom Josephson for the period May 16, 2011 through June 30, 2011.

P 23-8
Creation of a trust

You have been hired as trustee for the testamentary trust created by the will of Tom Josephson. The trust is created on June 30, 2011. (Use the information provided in P 23-6 and P 23-7.) The trust initially invests the proceeds from the estate in a checking account, which pays 3 percent per year. Interest is paid quarterly. On July 5, the trust invests $750,000 in a certificate of deposit at the local bank. The certificate earns 6 percent interest per year, paid monthly. On July 31, you pay the $275 quarterly trust service fees to the bank. On August 5, you receive a check for $3,750, representing the first month's interest on the certificate of deposit. On August 19, you send a $15,000 check to Superprivate Academy to cover fall semester tuition, room, and board for Megan and Ryan.

REQUIRED: Prepare the entry to record the creation of the Josephson Family Trust on June 30, 2011. Prepare all required entries to account for trust activities through August 31.

INTERNET ASSIGNMENT

1. Does your state have an inheritance/estate tax? If so, provide a brief summary indicating the tax rates and levels at which an estate/inheritance is taxed.

2. Has your state adopted the Revised Uniform Principal and Income Act? If so, has your state adopted the act in its entirety? If not, briefly summarize the major modifications made.

3. Johnny dies intestate. Johnny's entire estate is valued at an estimated $2 million. Johnny is survived by his spouse and three adult children. Review probate laws for your state and summarize the distribution of Johnny's estate. You may ignore state and federal estate tax considerations.

GLOSSARY

Acquisition: a business combination in which one corporation acquires control over the operations of another entity. Acquisitions are recorded based on the fair value of net assets.

Actual Retirement of Bonds: the repurchase and retirement of bonds by the issuing affiliate.

Additions (Governmental Colleges and Universities): increases to the fund balance of fund groupings other than current unrestricted funds and current restricted funds to the extent that expenditures have not been made.

Administrator: the court-appointed representative who takes control of the estate of a person who died intestate and supervises the estate's distribution.

Affiliate: a subsidiary in a technical sense, although the term is sometimes used to refer to 20%- to 50%-owned equity investees.

Agency Funds (Governmental Accounting): used to account for resources held by the governmental unit as agent for other funds, other governmental units, or individuals.

Agency Theory: a theory of intercompany bond holdings that allocates constructive gains and losses to the issuing affiliate.

Allotments: divisions of the appropriation authority by time period.

Annuity Funds: a college and university fund type to account for resources acquired under the condition that stipulated periodic payments be made to individuals as directed by the donor of the resources.

Appropriations: budget authorizations of expenditures.

Assigned fund balance (governmental): amounts intended to be used by the government for specific purposes but do not meet the criteria to be classified as restricted or committed.

Auxiliary Enterprises: a college and university activity encompassing student unions, dormitories, resident halls, and intercollegiate athletics that are intended to be self-sustaining.

Bankruptcy Insolvency: a condition in which an entity has total debts in excess of the fair market value of its assets.

Bonus Approach (Partnerships): the adjustment of partner capital balances as an alternative to revaluing partnership assets or recording goodwill.

Branch Operation: a company outlet that stocks goods, makes sales, maintains accounting records, and functions much like a separate business enterprise.

Budget: a plan of financial operations including proposed expenditures for a period and the means of financing them.

Business Combination: a uniting of previously separate business entities through acquisition by one entity of another entity's net assets or a majority of its outstanding voting common stock, or through an exchange of common stock.

Capital Budget (Governmental Accounting): the current portion of a capital program.

Capital Program (Governmental Accounting): a plan of capital expenditures by year over a fixed period of years.

Capital Projects Funds (Governmental Accounting): used to account for resources to be used for acquisition or construction of major general government capital facilities.

Cash Distribution Plan (Partnerships): a plan developed at the beginning of the liquidation period that shows how cash will be distributed throughout the phase-out period.

Cash Distribution Schedule (Partnerships): a schedule of cash distributions made to creditors and partners in a partnership liquidation.

Chapter 11 of the Bankruptcy Reform Act: Chapter 11 covers rehabilitation of the debtor and anticipates a reorganization of the debtor corporation.

Chapter 7 of the Bankruptcy Reform Act: Chapter 7 covers straight bankruptcy under which the debtor entity is expected to be liquidated.

Charge-Discharge Statement (Estates and Trusts): a document prepared by the executor or administrator of an estate to show accountability for property received and disbursed.

Charity Care: hospital terminology for services provided free of charge to qualifying patients.

Committed fund balance (governmental): amounts can only be spent for the specific purposes determined by a formal action of the government's highest level of decision-making authority.

Conditional Promise to Give (Not-for-Profit Accounting): a pledge that is dependent upon the occurrence or failure to occur of an uncertain future event.

Conglomeration: the combination of firms in unrelated and diverse product lines and/or service functions.

Connecting Affiliates Relationship: a type of affiliation structure involving indirect or mutual holdings between a parent company and its subsidiaries.

Consolidation: (1) a business combination in which a new corporation is formed to take over two or more business entities that then go out of existence; (2) in a generic sense, it means the same as acquisition or merger; (3) the process of combining parent-company and subsidiary financial statements.

Constructive Retirement of Bonds: the repurchase of bonds of one affiliate by another so that the bonds are held within the parent–subsidiary affiliation and, in effect, retired.

Constructive Retirement of Preferred Stock: the purchase of a subsidiary's preferred stock by the parent company results in a retirement of the preferred stock from the viewpoint of the consolidated entity.

Contemporary Theory: the current theory underlying consolidated financial statements; it reflects certain aspects of both entity and parent-company theory.

Contribution (Not-for-Profit Accounting): a transfer of cash or other assets to an entity or a settlement or cancellation of its liabilities from a voluntary nonreciprocal transfer.

Conventional Approach of Accounting for Mutually Held Common Stock: parent-company stock held by a subsidiary is accounted for as being constructively retired for consolidation purposes.

Conversion to Equity Method Approach: an approach used in the preparation of consolidation working papers when the parent company has used an incomplete equity or cost method in accounting for its subsidiaries: the parent company's accounts are converted to the equity method as the first working paper entry.

Corporate Joint Venture: a joint venture organized under the corporate form of business organization.

Current Funds: a college and university fund grouping to account for resources expendable for operating purposes; includes unrestricted current funds and restricted current funds.

Current Rate: the exchange rate in effect at the balance sheet date or the transaction date.

Current Rate Method: translation of all assets, liabilities, revenues, and expenses at current exchange rates.

Debtor in Possession: a Chapter 11 case in which the debtor corporation keeps control of the business and performs the duties of a trustee.

Debt Service Funds (Governmental Accounting): used to account for the accumulation of resources for payment of principal and interest on general long-term debt.

Decedent: a person that is deceased.

Defeasance of Debt: occurs when the debt is legally satisfied even though the debt is not actually paid (legal defeasance) or when the debtor irrevocably places cash or certain other assets with an escrow agent in a trust for the payment of the debt (in substance defeasance).

Denominated: to denominate in a currency is to fix the amount in units of that currency.

Devisees: those persons designated in a will to receive real or personal property.

Direct Holdings: direct investments in voting stock of one or more investee companies.

Direct Quotation: the expression of an exchange rate in U.S. dollars (U.S. dollar equivalent).

Donor-Imposed Conditions (Not-for-Profit Accounting): the occurrence or failure to occur of an uncertain future event that releases the donor from its obligation.

Donor-Imposed Restrictions (Not-for-Profit Accounting): specifications of how or when the assets promised or received must be used.

Downstream Sale: sales or other intercompany transactions from parent company to subsidiary.

Drawings (Partnerships): regular partner withdrawals as provided in the partnership agreement and closed to partner capital at year-end.

EDGAR System: the SEC's electronic data gathering, analysis, and retrieval system. Forms filed with the SEC can be downloaded from the EDGAR system at http://www.sec.gov/edaux/formlynx.htm by providing the form desired and company name.

Encumbrance Accounting: recording commitments made for goods on order and for unperformed contracts to prevent overspending of amounts appropriated.

Endowment Funds (Not-for-Profit Accounting): used to account for gifts and bequests received from donors under endowment agreements (hospitals); a fund type for colleges and universities to account for resources received from donors or outside agencies with the stipulation that the principal be maintained in perpetuity and income be used as directed.

Endowment Trust Funds (Governmental Accounting): a trust fund in which the principal must remain intact but the earnings may be expended for authorized purposes.

Enterprise Funds (Governmental Accounting): used to account for operations that are financed and operated in a manner similar to private enterprise.

Entitlements (Governmental Accounting): payments to which state and local governmental units are entitled based on an allocation formula.

Entity Theory: a theory under which consolidated financial statements are prepared from the view of the total business entity.

Equity Adjustment on Translation: an exchange gain or loss that is reported as a stockholders' equity adjustment (and in other comprehensive income).

Equity Insolvency: the inability of an entity to pay its debts as they come due.

Equity in Subsidiary Realized Income: the parent company's or noncontrolling interest's share of subsidiary income adjusted for intercompany gains and losses and amortization of fair value/book value differentials.

Equity Method: accounting for a common stock investment on an accrual basis; earnings increase the investment and dividends decrease it.

Exchange Rate: the ratio between a unit of one currency and the amount of another currency for which it can be exchanged.

Executor: the court-appointed representative who takes control of the estate of a decedent who died testate and supervises its distribution.

Executory Contracts: contracts that have not been completely performed by the parties to the contract (purchase commitments and leases, for example).

Expendable Funds: those in which resources can be expended to meet the objective of the fund.

Expendable Trust Funds: a trust fund in which the assets can be expended as needed to meet the fund's objectives.

Expenditures: decreases in the net financial resources of a governmental type fund other than those caused by transfers or similar other financing uses.

Fair Value/Cost Method (for Equity Investments): If the stock is not marketable, a common stock investment is accounted for at its original cost. If the stock is marketable, the investment is carried at fair market value with an associated adjunct/contra equity account for the change in value from original cost (assuming an available-for-sale security). In both cases, dividends received are recorded as income from the investment.

Family Allowance: an allowance to a surviving spouse and minor children to be paid out of estate property during the period of estate administration.

Father-Son-Grandson Relationship: a type of affiliation structure involving indirect or mutual holdings between a parent company and its subsidiaries.

Fiduciary: an individual or entity authorized to take possession of the property of others.

Fiduciary Accounting: a term used to describe accounting for estates and trusts whose managers have a custodial or stewardship relationship with the trust or estate beneficiaries.

Fiduciary Funds: a category of funds to account for assets held by the government as trustee or agent; includes expendable, nonexpendable, and pension trust funds and agency funds.

Fixed Exchange Rates: exchange rates set by a government and subject to change only by that government. (Also *official exchange rates*.)

Floating Exchange Rates: exchange rates that are market driven and reflect supply and demand factors, inflation, and so on. (Also *free exchange rates*.)

Foreign Currency: a currency other than the entity's functional currency.

Foreign Currency Commitment: a contract or agreement that will result in a foreign currency transaction at a later date.

Foreign Currency Cash Flow Hedge: a derivative instrument that hedges against the effect of the change in the relative value of two currencies due to the inherent exposure in forecasted transactions denominated in the foreign currency.

Foreign Currency Fair Value Hedge: a derivative instrument that hedges against the effect of the change in the relative value of two currencies due to the inherent exposure of holding an asset, liability, or firm commitment denominated in a foreign currency.

Foreign Currency Statements: the financial statements of a foreign subsidiary or other foreign entity and expressed in its local currency.

Foreign Currency Transactions: transactions whose terms are denominated in a currency other than the entity's functional currency.

Foreign Transactions: transactions between entities in different countries.

Form 8-K: form to disclose significant changes in firm policies, financial condition, etc., to the SEC.

Form 10-K: basic form for the annual report that firms file with the SEC.

Form 10-Q: form for quarterly reports that firms file with the SEC.

Fraudulent Transfer: a transfer of an interest or an obligation incurred by the debtor within one year prior to the date of filing a bankruptcy petition with the intent to defraud creditors.

Free Exchange Rates: exchange rates that are market driven and reflect supply and demand factors, inflation, and so on. (Also *floating exchange rates*.)

Fresh-Start Reporting: accounting under a reorganization plan that meets prescribed conditions and enables the new entity to eliminate its prior deficit and report zero retained earnings.

Functional Currency: the currency of the primary environment in which an entity operates.

Fund: a fiscal and accounting entity with a self-balancing set of accounts that records cash and other assets together with related liabilities and residual balances.

Fund Accounting or Fund Basis: financial systems that are segmented into separate accounting and reporting entities (funds) on the basis of their objectives and restrictions on their operations and resources.

Fund Balance: assets less liabilities of a governmental fund; often is essentially the working capital of a governmental fund.

Fund Equity: an amount equal to assets less liabilities of a fund.

Fund Fixed Assets (Governmental Accounting): fixed assets related to specific proprietary or trust funds and accounted for in those funds.

Fund Long-Term Liabilities (Governmental Accounting): longterm liabilities of proprietary and trust funds are designated fund long-term liabilities and are accounted for in those funds.

General Fixed Assets (Governmental Accounting): all fixed assets not classified as fund fixed assets; general fixed assets are reported for in the government-wide financial statements.

General Fund (Governmental Accounting): used to account for all financial resources not accounted for in another fund.

General Governmental Activities: in a simple situation, they are essentially taxpayer financed activities made available to all members of a government's constituency without charges for use. These activities commonly include general administration, public safety, education, the judicial system, and so on.

General Long-Term Debt (Governmental Accounting): all unmatured long-term liabilities other than fund long-term liabilities; reported in the government-wide financial statements.

General Partnership: an association in which each partner has unlimited liability.

Goodwill Approach (Partnerships): the adjustment of assets and liabilities to fair values and recording goodwill as an alternative to adjusting partner equity balances (also, a partnership revaluation approach).

Governmental Accounting Standards Board (GASB): the standards-setting body for state and local governmental accounting and financial reporting in the United States.

Governmental Fund Expenditures: decreases in fund financial resources other than from interfund transfers and other financing uses.

Governmental Fund Revenues: increases in fund financial resources other than from transfers, debt issue proceeds, and interfund reimbursement transactions.

Governmental Funds: a category of funds used to account for most governmental functions that are basically different from private enterprise; they include the general fund, special revenue funds, capital projects funds, debt service funds and permanent funds.

Grants: contributions from other governmental units to be used for specific purposes.

Hedging Operations: purchase or sale of a foreign currency contract to offset the risks of holding receivables or payables denominated in a foreign currency.

Heirs: the persons entitled to the property of the decedent under the statutes of intestate succession.

Historical Rate: the exchange rate in effect at the time a specific transaction or event occurred.

Homestead Allowance: an allowance to a surviving spouse that has priority over all other claims against the estate.

Horizontal Integration: the combination of firms in the same business lines or markets.

IASC: International Accounting Standards Committee.

Incomplete Application of the Equity Method: accounting for an equity investee without considering amortization of cost-book value differentials or intercompany profits (also called the simple equity method).

Indirect Holdings: investments that enable an investor company to control an investee that is not directly owned through an investee that is directly owned.

Indirect Quotation: the expression of an exchange rate in foreign currency units (foreign currency per U.S. dollar).

Installment Liquidation (Partnerships): distribution of cash as it becomes available during the liquidation period.

Interfund Loans: loans made by one fund to another and that must be repaid.

Intergovernmental Revenue: revenues received from other governmental units.

Interim Financial Reports: unaudited financial reports that are issued for periods of less than a full year and frequently are called quarterly reports.

Internal Service Funds (Governmental Accounting): used to account for financing goods and services provided by one department to other departments on a cost-reimbursement basis.

Intestate: having died without a valid will.

Intestate Succession: the order in which intestate estate property is distributed to the surviving spouse, descendants, parents, and so on.

Investment in Plant Accounts: used by colleges and universities to account for the physical plant, which includes land, buildings, improvements other than buildings, and equipment including library books, and for related debt.

Involuntary Bankruptcy Proceedings: the filing is involuntary if the creditors file the bankruptcy petition.

Joint Venture: a business entity that is owned, operated, and jointly controlled by a small group of investors (venturers) for a specific undertaking; it may be temporary or relatively permanent, and it may be corporate or partnership.

Leveraged Buyout: acquisition of a public-held company directly from its shareholders in a transaction financed primarily by debt.

Liabilities Not Subject to Compromise: the fully secured liabilities incurred before a Chapter 11 bankruptcy filing and all postpetition claims.

Life Income Funds: a college and university fund type to account for resources acquired under the condition that the income be paid to a designated individual until death.

Limited Life: the legal life of partnerships terminates with the admission of a new partner, death or retirement of an old partner, etc.

Limited Partnership: an association in which one or more partners have limited liability and at least one partner has unlimited liability.

Loan Funds: a college and university fund grouping to account for resources available for student and faculty loans.

Local Currency: the currency of the country being referred to.

Local Transactions: transactions within a country that are measured in the currency of that country.

Mandatory Transfers (Colleges and Universities): transfers of resources under binding agreements with outside agencies or donors; a matching gift to a student loan fund, for example.

Measurement Focus (Governmental Accounting): that which is expressed in reporting an entity's financial performance and position.

Merger: a business combination in which one corporation takes over the operations of another entity and that entity goes out of existence; also, a business combination or an acquisition in a generic sense.

Monetary Assets and Liabilities: are assets and liabilities in which the amounts are fixed in currency units. If the value of the currency unit changes, it is still settled with the same number of units.

Monetary–Nonmonetary Method: translation of monetary items at current exchange rates and nonmonetary items at historical rates.

Multiple Exchange Rates: fixed exchange rates with preferential rates set for different kinds of transactions.

Mutual Agency (Partnerships): each partner has the power to bind all other partners, in the absence of notification to the contrary.

Mutual Holdings: two or more affiliated companies that hold stock in each other.

Negative Goodwill: the excess of the fair market value of assets acquired in a purchase business combination over the investment cost. Under new FASB guidance, this is termed a bargain purchase, recognized as a gain to the acquirer.

Noncontrolling Interest: the stockholder interest in a subsidiary not owned by the parent company.

Nonexpendable Trust Funds: principal is maintained intact but income may or may not be expendable.

Nonmandatory Transfers (Colleges and Universities):   funds transferred back to unrestricted current funds or transfers at the discretion of the governing board.

Nonmonetary Items: are items that would change with changes in market price or changes in the value of the currency.

Nonprofit or Not-for-Profit Entities: nonbusiness organizations that have neither individual ownership nor private-profit objectives.

Nonspendable fund balance (governmental): represents amounts not in spendable form, such as inventories, or amounts that must be maintained, such as the principal of an endowment.

Offering Circular: similar to a prospectus, but with fewer disclosure requirements.

Official Exchange Rates: exchange rates set by a government and subject to change only by that government. (Also *fixed exchange rates*.)

One-Line Consolidation: another name for the equity method of accounting; under the equity method the investor's income and the controlling interest share of consolidated net income are equal.

Operating Profit Test: a test to determine if an operating segment is a reportable segment of the enterprise.

Operating Segment: a component of an enterprise engaged in providing goods and services to unaffiliated or affiliated customers for a profit.

Operating Transfers (Governmental Accounting):   legally authorized shifts of resources from one fund to another that are not revenues, expenditures or expenses, or residual equity transfers.

Parent-Company Theory: a theory under which consolidated financial statements are prepared from the view of parent-company stockholders.

Parent–Subsidiary Relationship: a relationship that gives one corporation the power to control another corporation through its majority common stock ownership.

Partnership: an association of two or more persons to carry on as co-owners in a business for profit.

Partnership Agreement: a contract between partners covering duties of partners, investments, withdrawals, profit sharing, and so on. Without this agreement, these issues are settled by the Uniform Partnership Act.

Partnership Dissolution: the change in the relation of partners when any partner is no longer involved in carrying on the business. The business may continue as an operating business despite the dissolution of the partnership.

Partnership Liquidation: the process of converting assets into cash, settling all liabilities, and distributing any remaining cash to partners.

Par Value Theory: a theory of intercompany bond holdings that allocates constructive gains or losses between the purchasing and issuing affiliates on the basis of the par value of the bonds.

Patient Service Revenue (Hospitals):   revenue from board and room, nursing services, and other professional services, and recorded on an accrual basis.

Payments in Lieu of Taxes: payments by one governmental unit to another for revenues lost because governments cannot tax each other. Also, similar payments from a government's enterprise fund to its other tax-supported funds.

Performance Budget: a budget that emphasizes measurable performance of work programs and activities.

Permanently Restricted Net Assets (Not-for-Profit Accounting):   the portion of a not-for-profit entity's net assets whose use is limited by donor-imposed stipulations that do not expire and cannot be removed by action of the entity.

Personal Representative: a person named by the probate court to take control of a decedent's estate.

Piecemeal Acquisition: a corporation gains control of a subsidiary through a series of separate stock purchases.

Plant Funds: a college and university fund grouping to account for unexpended plant funds, renewal and replacement funds, retirement of indebtedness funds, and investment in plant funds.

Plant Replacement and Expansion Funds (Hospitals):   a hospital fund group to account for donor-restricted resources for plant, property and equipment.

Pledge (Nonprofit Accounting):   a written or oral promise to contribute cash or other assets to the organization.

Postpetition Liabilities: liabilities incurred after a Chapter 11 filing and not associated with prebankruptcy events.

Preacquisition Dividends: dividends paid on an equity investment prior to the date the investment was acquired during the year.

Preferences: certain transfers of property of a debtor or certain obligations incurred by a debtor prior to filing a bankruptcy petition.

Preliminary Prospectus: a preliminary communication about securities to be issued that also explains how to get a copy of the prospectus filed with the SEC.

Prepetition Liabilities: liabilities of the debtor corporation at the time of a bankruptcy filing.

Prepetition Liabilities Subject to Compromise: unsecured and undersecured liabilities incurred before a Chapter 11 bankruptcy filing.

Probate: to probate a will is to validate a will.

Program Budget: an expenditure budget of the total cost of programs to be carried out or functions to be performed.

Proportionate or Pro Rata Consolidation: a practice in accounting for joint ventures in which each investor-venturer accounts for its share of assets, equities, revenues, and expenses.

Proprietary Funds (Governmental Accounting):   a category of funds to account for operations that are similar to those of private business enterprises; including enterprise funds and internal service funds.

Prospectus: information about an SEC registrant firm that includes its type of business, company background, and financial statements; it is a part of the SEC registration statement.

Pure Endowments: endowments for which the principal is permanently restricted. (*Quasi-endowments* can be changed by the governing board.)

Push-Down Accounting: establishment of a new basis of subsidiary accounting based on the price paid by the parent company.

Quasi-Endowment Funds: a college and university fund type to account for resources designated by the governing board to be invested indefinitely, with income being expended as directed.

Quasi-External Transactions: those that would be revenues and expenses or expenditures for organizations external to the governmental unit.

Registration Statements: statements required to be filed with the SEC for firms that issue securities to the public, and for firms whose shares are traded on national stock exchanges.

Regulation S: a 1990 regulation to clarify the applicability of security laws across national boundaries.

Reimbursements: transactions between two funds of a government that constitute reimbursements of a fund for expenditures or expenses initially made from it that are properly applicable to another fund. Reimbursements are recorded as expenditures or expenses in the reimbursing fund and as reductions of expenditures or expenses in the reimbursed fund.

Remeasurement: the conversion of a foreign entity's financial statements from another currency into its own functional currency.

Renewal and Replacement Funds (Colleges and Universities): used to account for the resources held by colleges and universities for renewal and replacement of the physical plant.

Reorganization Items: income, expenses, realized gains and losses, and provisions for losses that result from restructuring a business under Chapter 11 of the Bankruptcy Act.

Reorganization Plan: a plan for rehabilitation of the debtor corporation in a Chapter 11 case; to be confirmed, the plan must be fair and equitable to all interests concerned.

Reorganization Value: an approximation of the amount a willing buyer would pay for the assets of the corporation at the time of restructuring.

Reportable Operating Segment: an operating segment for which information is required to be reported.

Reporting Currency: the currency in which consolidated financial statements are prepared.

Residual Beneficiaries: those entitled to the remainder of an estate after all other rightful claims have been satisfied.

Residual Equity Transfer (Governmental Accounting): nonrecurring or nonroutine transfers of equity between funds.

Restricted Current Funds (Colleges and Universities): encompasses resources expendable currently but restricted to expenditures for specified operating purposes.

Restricted Funds (Hospitals): a hospital fund grouping that includes specific purpose funds, plant replacement and expansion funds, and endowment funds.

Restricted fund balance (governmental): amounts can only be spent for the specific purposes stipulated by constitution, external resource providers, or through enabling legislation.

Retirement of Indebtedness Fund: used in college and university accounting for liquid resources held for current debt service, and investments held for future debt retirement.

Safe Payments (Partnerships): distributions that can be made to partners with assurance that the amounts are not excessive.

Salary Allowances (Partnerships): partner salary allowances are drawings authorized in lieu of salaries because partner rewards come from sharing in partnership earnings.

Sales Agency: a business office established to display merchandise and take customer orders, but not to fill orders or grant credit.

Schedule of Assumed Loss Absorption: used in developing the cash distribution plan in a partnership liquidation. Each partner's equity is charged with a loss amount to eliminate the equity of the most vulnerable partner, and so on.

Shared Revenues (Governmental Accounting): specific revenue sources shared with other governmental units; sales taxes and gasoline taxes are examples.

Special Assessments: special tax levies against benefited property owners for improvements that benefit the owner's property.

Special Revenue Funds (Governmental Accounting): used to account for proceeds from specific revenue sources that are legally restricted to specified purposes.

Specific Purpose Funds (Hospitals): a hospital fund group to account for resources restricted by donors for specific operating purposes.

Spot Rate: the exchange rate in effect for immediate delivery of the currencies exchanged.

Statement of Affairs: a financial statement that shows liquidation values of a bankrupt entity and provides estimates of possible recovery for unsecured creditors.

Statement of Functional Expenses (Voluntary Health and Welfare Organizations): a financial statement that shows the costs associated with the program services or other activities of the organization.

Statement of Realization and Liquidation: statement showing progress toward liquidation in a bankruptcy case.

Step-by-Step Acquisitions: acquiring an equity interest in a series of separate stock purchases.

Subsidiary: a corporation in which the controlling stockholders' interest lies with a parent company that controls its decisions and operations.

Temporal Method: translation of items carried at past, current, and future prices in a manner that retains their measurement bases.

Temporarily Restricted Net Assets (Not-for-Profit Accounting): the portion of a not-for-profit entity's net assets whose use is limited by donor-imposed stipulations that either expire or can be removed by fulfilling the stipulations.

Temporary Differences: differences in taxable income and accounting income that originate in one accounting period and reverse in a later period.

Term Endowment Funds: a college and university fund type to account for resources received from donors or outside agencies with the stipulation that the principal may be expended after a period of time or the occurrence of some event.

Term Endowments: endowments for which the principal is temporarily restricted.

Testacy Proceeding: a hearing of a probate court to determine if the deceased died testate or intestate (that is, with or without a will).

Testate: having died with a valid will in force.

Testamentary Trust: a trust that is created pursuant to a will.

Translation: expressing functional currency measurements in the reporting currency.

Translation Adjustment (also *Equity Adjustment on Translation*): an exchange gain or loss that is reported as an equity adjustment in other comprehensive income.

Treasury Stock Approach: accounting for parent-company stock held by a subsidiary as treasury stock in consolidated statements.

Troubled Debt Restructuring: occurs when a creditor grants a concession to a debtor because of the debtor's financial difficulties.

Trust and Agency Funds: used to account for assets held in a trustee capacity or as agent for individuals, private organizations, and other governmental units.

Trustee: a lawyer appointed by the U.S. trustee or by the bankruptcy court to assume control of the debtor's estate and coordinate its administration with the court.

Unassigned fund balance (governmental): the residual classification for the government's general fund and includes all spendable amounts not contained in the other classifications. In other funds, the unassigned classification should be used only to report a deficit balance resulting from overspending for specific purposes for which amounts had been restricted, committed, or assigned.

Unconditional Promises to Give (Nonprofit Accounting): a pledge without conditions.

Undivided Interest (Joint Ventures): an ownership arrangement in which two or more parties own property and title is held individually to the extent of each party's interest.

Unexpended Plant Funds: used by colleges and universities to account for resources held for additions and improvements to the physical plant.

Uniform Probate Code: a document prepared by the National Conference of Commissioners on Uniform State Laws that provides guidelines for estate and trust administration.

Unlimited Liability: each partner is liable for all partnership debts. Limited partners in a limited partnership, which is allowed in some states, do not have unlimited liability.

Unrestricted Current Funds (Colleges and Universities): encompasses resources received and expended for instruction, research, extension, and public services, as well as auxiliary enterprises.

Unrestricted Funds (Hospitals): used to account for all resources of a hospital not restricted by donors or grantors.

Unrestricted Net Assets (Not-for-Profit Accounting): the portion of net assets of a not-for-profit entity that carries no donor-imposed restrictions.

Upstream Sale: sales or other intercompany transactions from subsidiary to parent company.

U.S. Trustee: an administrative officer of the bankruptcy court; appointed by the attorney general for five-year terms.

Venturers: the owner participants in a joint venture.

Vertical Integration: the combination of firms with operations in different but successive stages of production and/or distribution.

Voidable Preferences: preferences that can be voided by a trustee in a bankruptcy case.

Voluntary Bankruptcy Proceedings: the filing is voluntary if the debtor files the bankruptcy petition.

Voluntary Health and Welfare Organizations: a diverse group of nonprofit entities that is supported by donations and seeks to solve basic social problems of health and welfare.

Vulnerability Ranking (Partnerships): a ranking of partners on the basis of the amount of partnership losses they could absorb without reducing their capital accounts below zero.

Zero-Base Budgeting: making budgetary appropriations without direct reference to prior years' programs or expenditure budgets.

INDEX

A

Abbott Laboratories, 65
accountability, fiscal, 643
accounting, 723–724
  for agency funds, 633
  bases of, 634
  for business combinations, 6–15
  cash flow hedge, 432, 439–441
  for corporate joint ventures
  for encubrances, 669–671
  equity method of, 27–28
  for estates, 777–781
  for excess of invetment cost over
      book value, 31–33
  fair value (cost) method of, 25–29
  fair value hedge, 432, 434, 441–442
  fiduciary, 775
  fund, 628
  hedge, 430–431
  for internal service funds, 712–713
  international, for goodwill, 13
  for nongovernmental not-for-profit
      hospitals/health care organiza-
      tions, 751–753
  pension trust funds, 726
  for private not-for-profit colleges/
      universities, 756–760
  for private-purpose trust funds, 725
  for property taxes, 666–668
  push-down, 79–81
  for stock investments, 25–29
  for trusts, 782–783
  for variable interest entities, 391–393
  voluntary health and welfare organi-
      zations, 743–748
Accounting Series Releases (ASRs),
      181–182
acquisition method, for business
      combinations, 6
acquisitions, 4
  during accounting period, 247–251
  consolidated balance sheet after,
      70–71
  consolidated balance sheet
      at, 66–69

contingent consideration in, 9–10
equity investments at, 29–30
  financing, 65
  illustration, 11
  piecemeal, 251–253
  recording fair values in, 8–10
activities, statement of, 642–643
actual retirement, of bonds, 220
Adelphia, 592
administrator, 776
affiliates, 42, 62–63
affiliation structure, 62–64
affiliation structures, 279–281
agency funds, 633, 722–724, 760
  accounting equation for, 633, 722
  accounting for, 723–724
  defined, 722
  financial statements for, 724
agency theory, 221
agency transactions, 742
AH Robins, 592
*AICPA Audit and Accounting Guide
  Not-for-Profit Organizations,* 755
AICPA model, 760
allocation, income tax, 328–330
allotment, 638
amortization, *versus* nonamortization,
      15
AMR, 431–432
Anheuser-Busch Companies, 63–64
Aon, 1
Apple, 414
Apple, Inc., 498
appropriations, 638
  private not-for-profit colleges/univer-
      sities accounting for, 757
Archer Daniels Midland Company,
      501–503
Arthur Andersen and Company, 17
ASC Topic 815, 430–431, 443
ASC Topic 830, 443
assets
  donated long-lived, 745
  general fixed, 629
  gifts of long-lived, 741

  intangible, 8–14
  intercompany profit transactions–
      plant, 185–203
  net, 641–642
  partnership, 540–542
  permanently restricted net, 739
  plant, 759–760
  temporarily restricted net, 739
  total, 1118
  unrestricted net, 739
asset valuation, 371
assigned fund balance, 664
assumed loss absorption, schedule
      of, 574
AT&T, 2, 16, 27, 279
*Audits of State and Local Governmental
      Units* (AICPA), 626
Aventis SA, 3
average capital balances, 533

B

Baby Superstore, 3
Bain Capital, 387
Bank of America, 1
Bank Reform Act (1978), 591–594
bankruptcy. *See also* liquidation
  bankruptcy judge, duties of, 594
  chapters, 592–594
  debtor corporation, duties of, 594
  involuntary, 593
  Office of U.S. Trustee, 594
  types of, 592
  voluntary, 593
Bankruptcy Abuse Prevention and
      Consumer Protect Act
      (BAPCPA), 591–592
Bankruptcy Act (1898), 591
bankruptcy insolvency, 591
Bankruptcy Reform Act (1994), 605
bargain purchase, 34–35
bases of accounting, 634
Beatrice Foods, 387
Bell Atlantic Corporation, 3
Black-Scholes option pricing
      model, 411

Boeing, 604
bonus
    on initial investments in partnerships, 527
    to retiring partner, 543
bonus approach, 539
book value
    excess investment cost over underlying, 30–31
    excess of, over cost, 33–34
    excess of investment cost over, 31–33
Briggs & Stratton Corporation, 2
budget, general fund (GF), 665–666
    recording, 666
    subsidiary ledgers, 666
budgets
    capital, 638
    role of, 637–638
business combinations, 1, 341–346
    accounting concept of, 4–6
    accounting for, 6–15
    antitrust considerations, 3
    consummated through stock acquisitions, 61–65
    disclosure requirements, 15–17
    foreign currency financial statements and, 468–469
    income tax uncertainties, 345–346
    legal form, 4
    purchase, 343–345
        equity method of accounting for, 344–345
        workpaper entries for, 345
    reasons for, 2–3
business-type activities, 627

C
call options, 411
Canadian GAAP, 13
capital, as factor in profit sharing agreements, 533–536
capital budgets, 638
capital lease, state and local government, 672–673
capital programs, 638
capital projects fund, 633
Caremark Rx, Inc., 2
CARGOTEC, 220
cash distribution plans, 573–576
    cash distribution schedule, 575–576
cash flow hedge, 432, 440
    of anticipated foreign currency transaction, 451–453
cash flow hedge accounting, 432, 439–441
    examples of, 436–437

Centennial, 17
Cerebrus Capital Management, 387
Chapter 7 bankruptcy, 593
Chapter 11 reorganizations, 592–594, 603–605
    operating under, 605–606
charge-discharge statement, 782
Chevron Corporation, 1, 42, 146
chief operating decision maker (CODM), 497
Chiquita Brands International, 593, 606
Chrysler, 387
Circuit City, 593
Citigroup Inc., 43
claims
    classification of, 777
    against estates, 777
    secured, 777
Clayton, Dubilier, & Rice, 387
Coca-Cola Company, 62, 146, 253, 414
Codification of Governmental Accounting and Financial Reporting Standards (GASB), 626
combinations. See business combinations
committed fund balance, 664
Compaq Computer Corporation, 65, 343
component units, 638–639
comprehensive annual financial report (CAFR), 639–655
    auditor's report, 641
    budgetary comparisons, 646–649
    combining and individual fund statements, 651–655
    financial section, 639–655
    fund financial statements, 643–646
    general revenues, 643
    government-wide financial statements, 641
    introductory section, 639
    management's discussion and analysis (MD&A), 639–641
    program revenues, 643
    required supplementary information, 648
    service efforts and accomplishment (SEA) reporting, 655
    statistical section, 655
confirmation, 776
conglomeration, defined, 2
connecting affiliates relationships, 281
consolidated balance sheet
    at acquisition, 66–69
        noncontrolling interest, 68–69

parent acquires 90 percent of subsidiary—with goodwill, 67–68
parent acquires 100 percent of subsidiary at book value, 66
parent acquires 100 percent of subsidiary—with goodwill, 67
    after acquisition, 70–71
consolidated balance sheet worksheets, preparing, 81–83
consolidated financial statements, 29
    combinations consummated through stock acquisitions, 63–65
consolidated income statements, 78–79
consolidated statement of cash flows (SCF), 112–117
    direct method, 115–117
    income/dividends from investees under indirect and direct methods, 115
    indirect method, 114
consolidated tax returns
    advantages of filing, 327–328
    disadvantages of filing, 328
consolidated working papers
    entry sequence for, 103
    locating errors in, 106
consolidation
    business combinations, 341–346
    defined, 4, 341
    effect of consolidated and separate-company tax returns on procedures of, 334–341
        allocation of consolidated income tax to affiliates, 334
        background information for consolidated and separate tax return illustration, 334–341
    equity method
        workpaper entry sequence, 103
        year of acquisition, 99–103
        year subsequent to acquisition, 104–106
    income tax allocation, 328–330
        accounting for distributed and undistributed income, 329
        temporary differences from undistributed earnings of subsidiaries and equity investees, 328–329
        unrealized gains and losses from intercompany transactions, 329–330
    income taxes of consolidated entities, 326–328
    one-line, 390–391
    ownership interests
        sale, 253–262

parent-company theory, 369
  at acquisition, 373–375
  after acquisition, 375–381
  equity method, 375
  goodwill, 373
  pooling of interest method, 5–6
  procedures, 249–251
  proportionate, 389–391
  separate-company tax returns with intercompany gain, 330–334
    consolidation workpaper, 332–333
    income tax expense based on separate returns, 332
    one-line consolidation, 331
    workpaper entry for 2012, 334
consolidation policies, 63–65
consolidation theories, 369–372
  asset valuation, 371
  consolidated stockholders' equity, 372
  constructive gains and losses, 372
  income reporting, 370–371
  unrealized gains and losses, 371–372
consolidation worksheets, preparing, 117–121
constructive retirement, of bonds, 220
contemporary theory of consolidated statements, 369
contingent consideration, 9–10
contractual adjustments, 751
contributions
  not-for-profit organization, 740–741
    accounting for, 757–758
    conditional promise to give, 740
    donor-imposed conditions or restrictions, 741
    gifts of long-lived assets, 741
    investments and investment income, 741
    unconditonal promise to give, 740
  voluntary health and welfare organization, 743–745
conventional approach, 289, 291–298
convertible bonds, subsidiaries with, 325
converting foreign, 464
Corning Incorporated, 43, 388
corporate joint ventures. *See also* joint ventures
  accounting for, 388–389
  defined, 388
corporate liquidations and reorganizations, 591–624
  Bank Reform Act (1978), 591–594
  financial reporting during reorganization, 607–608

financial reporting for emerging company, 608–616
  illustration of liquidation case, 596–603
  liquidation, 594–595
  reorganization, 603–607
corporation liquidation and reorganization
  bankruptcy judge, duties of, 594
  Bankruptcy Reform Act (1978), 591–594
  office of U.S. Trustee, 594
cost, fair value *vs.*, 10
courtesy allowances, 751
Creditors' committees, 604–605
cumulative dollar-offset method, 432
currency
  foreign (*See* foreign currency)
  local, 464
  reporting, 464
current exchange rates, 416
current financial resources, 629
current operating funds, 760
current rate method, of converting foreign financial statements, 464, 470
CVS Corporation, 2

D
death, partnership dissociation due to excess payment to retiring partner, 543–544
  overvalued assets written down, 544
  payment to retiring partner less than capital balance, 544
debtor corporation, duties of, 594
debtor in possession, 604
debt service fund accounts, 633
decedent, defined, 775
Delta Air Lines, 2
denominated receivables/payables, 414, 443
depreciation
  estates, 745
  voluntary health and welfare organizations (VHWOs), 745
derivatives
  accounting summation for, 454
  defined, 409–410
  economics underlying, 411–413
  footnote disclosure requirements, 454–455
  hedge transactions, 410–411
Derivatives Implementation Group (DIG), 429–430
devise, 776

devisees, 776
Dillard's, Inc., 43
direct holdings
  affiliated structures, 279–281
  defined, 281
disclosures
  enterprise, 501–503
  for equity investees, 40–42
  footnote, for derivatives, 454–455
  proprietary fund, 727
  SEC, 510
  segment, 500–501, 503–505
Disney. *See* Walt Disney Company
dissociation, partnership, 536
dissolution. *See* liquidation
donor-imposed conditions or restrictions, contributions, 741
Dow Chemical Company, 27, 40, 315, 388, 592
  disclosure for equity investees, 40–41
Dow Corning Corporation, 388
downstream sales, 150–153
  intercompany profits from equity method, 158–161
  unrealized profits from
    deferral of intercompany profit in period of intercompany sale, 153–154
    recognition of intercompany profit upon sale to outside entities, 154–155
drawing allowances, 528–529
drawings, 528–529

E
economic resources, 629
EDGAR system (Electronic Data Gathering Analysis and Retrieval System), 184
E.I. Du Pont De Nemours, 43
Emerging Issues Task Force (EITF), 430
encumbrances, accounting for, 669–671
ending inventory of purchasing affiliate, 147
endowments, private not-for-profit colleges/universities accounting for, 757–758
Enron Corporation, 17, 102, 179, 391, 592
enterprise disclosures, 501–503
enterprise funds (EFs), 631–632, 715–717
entity theory, 369–370

equitable subordination, doctrine of, 608
equity insolvency, 591
equity in subsidiary realized income, 324
equity interest, sale of, 37–38, 45
equity method, consolidation at acquisition, 375
equity method investments, fair value option for, 45
equity method of accounting, 25
  accounting procedures under, 27–28
  concepts underlying, 26–27
  economic consequences of using, 28–29
  illustration of translation and, 471–473
  one-line consolidation, 29–37
estates
  accounting for, 777–778
    illustration of, 778–781
  administration of, 776–777
  administrator, 776
  charge-discharge statement, 782
  claims against the estate, 777
  classification of claims, 777
  closing entries, 781–782
  confirmation, 776
  creation of, 755
  divisees, 776
  estate income, gains, and losses, 778
  exempt property and allowances, 777
  heirs, 776
  homestead allowance, 777
  income taxes on estate income, 785
  intestate succession, 776
  inventory of estate property, 776–777
  principal and income, 778
  probate proceedings, 776
  residual beneficiaries, 778
  secured claims, 777
  taxes, 783–784
  Uniform Probate Code, 776
excess, assigned to identifiable net assets, 106–111
excess, assigning, to identifiable net assets and goodwill, 72–78
excess of book value over cost, 33–34
excess of investment cost over book value, accounting for, 31–33
exchange rates. *See also* foreign exchange
  current, 416
  defined, 414
  direct quotations of, 414–415
  fixed, 415–416

floating, 415
free, 415
historical, 416
indirect quotations of, 415
multiple, 415–416
official, 415
spot, 416
exchange transactions, 634, 742
executory contracts, 605, 776
exempt property and allowances, 777
expenditures, 629
  recording, 669
expenses, recognition of, 636–637
extraordinary items, stock investments, 39–40
Exxon Mobil Corporation, 1

F
fair value
  cost *vs.,* 10
  implied, of good will, 43–44
  option, for equity method investments, 45
  recording, 8–10
  of reporting unit, determining, 44
fair value (cost) method of accounting, 25
  accounting procedures under, 27–28
  concepts underlying, 26–27
  economic consequences of using, 28–29
fair value hedge, 441
  of identifiable foreign currency commitment, 449–451
fair value hedge accounting, 432, 434, 441–442
  examples of, 438–439
fair value hedges, 434
FASB. *See* Financial Accounting Standards Board (FASB)
FASB ASC 954, 750–751
father-son-grandson relationship, 281
  computational approaches for consolidated net income, 282–283
  consolidation workpaper—equity method, 283–284
  equity method of accounting for, 282
  indirect holdings, 281–282
Federated Department Stores, 607
fiduciary, defined, 775
fiduciary accounting, 775
fiduciary funds, 629
  accounting for, 722
  agency funds, 722–724
  defined, 722

government-wide financial statements, preparing, 727
  trust funds, 724–727
  types, 632, 633
Financial Accounting and Reporting Manual, 756
Financial Accounting Standards Board (FASB), 13, 626
  Accounting Standards Codification (FASB ASC), 738
  foreign currency transaction requirements, 417–419
  pooling, 5
  Statement No. 105, 429
  Statement No. 107, 429
  Statement No. 115, 429
  Statement No. 116, 738
  Statement No. 117, 738
  Statement No. 119, 429
  Statement No. 133, 429–430
financial statements
  for agency funds, 724
  comprehensive annual, 643–646
  converting foreign, 470
  foreign currency, 466, 468–469
  government funds, 685–688
  government-wide, 641, 727
  methods for converting foreign, 464
  nongovernmental not-for-profit hospitals/health care organizations, 754–755
  not-for-profit organizations, 738–740
  private not-for-profit colleges/universities, 760
  proprietary funds, 718–722
  reporting internal service funds in, 715
  standardization of audited, 182–183
  supplementary combined, 608
  trust funds, 725
Finley Kumble, 605n4
First Reserve Corporation, 387
fiscal accountability, 643
fixed exchange rates, 415
FleetBoston Financial Corporation, 1
floating exchange rates, 415
FMC Corporation, 389
footnote disclosures, 380
  for derivatives, 454–455
Ford Motor Company, 185
foreign currency, 463–465
  defined, 464
  denominated receivables/payables, 414, 443
    cash flow hedge accounting, 443–447

fair value hedge accounting, 447–449
FASB requirements, 417–419
footnote-disclosure requirements, 454–455
highly inflationary economies and, 468
intercompany transactions, 466–468
international accounting standards, 421, 455
local transactions, 416–417
methods for converting, 464
purchases denominated in, 419–420
remeasurement, 465–466
sales denominated in, 420–421
speculation, 453–454
transactions, 417
translation, 465
foreign currency commitment, defined, 449
foreign currency statements, defined, 464
foreign exchange quotations, 416
Form 8-K (SEC), 182–183
Form 10-K (SEC), 182
Form S-1 (SEC), 181
Form S-2 (SEC), 181
Form S-3 (SEC), 181
Form S-4 (SEC), 181
forward contracts, 410–411, 434–435
forward premium/discount, 443
free exchange rates, 415
Freeport-McMoRan Copper & Gold, 1
fresh-start reporting, 609, 613–616
Fruit of the Loom, 593
functional currency, 417
  application of, 465–469
  defined, 463–464
  intercompany foreign currency transactions, 466–467
  remeasurement, 465–466
  translation, 465–466
fund accounting
  government organizations, 628
  not-for-profit organizations, 738
futures contracts, 410–411, 437–438

G
GAAP, 13
GASB. *See* Governmental Accounting Standards Board (GASB)
general devise, 776
General Electric (GE), 106, 430, 593
  segment reporting, 2
general fixed asset account group, 630

general fixed assets, 629
general fund accounts, 633
general governmental activities, 628
general long-term debt, 629
general long-term debt account group, 630
generally accepted accounting principles (GAAP), pooling, 5–6
General Motors (GM), 1, 592
general partnerships, 388
general-purpose governments, 738
general revenues, 643
gifts and bequests, 752
gifts in kind, 742, 745–746
gifts of long-lived assets, contributions, 741
goodwill, 12–13
  combinations to avoid recording, 387
  current GAAP for, 13–14
  impairment test, 14–15
  on initial investments in partnerships, 528
  international accounting for, 13
  partnerships, equal to excess payment, recording, 543
  stock investments
    determining fair value of reporting unit, 44
    equity method investments, 45
    fair value option for equity method investments, 45
    implied fair value of, 43–44
    potential problems, 45
    recognizing and measuring impairment losses, 43
    reporting and disclosures, 45
    testing for impairment, 43–445
goodwill approach, 538
Goodyear, 62
Governmental Accounting, Auditing, and Financial Reporting (GAAFR), 626
Governmental Accounting and Financial Reporting Principles, Statement No. 1 (NCGA), 626
Governmental Accounting Standards Board (GASB), 625, 626
  basic governmental accounting models and principles, 627–638
  fund definition and categories, 628–629
  hierarchy for state and local entities, 626–627
  Statement No. 1, 626
  Statement No. 3, 666
  Statement No. 13, 672

  Statement No. 14, 638
  Statement No. 27, 726
  Statement No. 33, 634–635
  Statement No. 34, 630, 636, 643, 650–651, 663, 677, 688, 712, 718–722, 738
  Statement No. 35, 738
  Statement No. 38, 673
  Statement No. 39, 639
  Statement No. 43, 726
  Statement No. 45, 726
  Statement No. 50, 726
  Statement No. 54, 664
  Statement No. 55, 627
governmental funds, 628
  recent changes in accounting for, 663–664
  types, 632–633
Government Finance Officers Association, 626n2
government funds
  capital projects funds (CPFs), 678
    accounting for, 679–680
    adjusting and closing entries, 681
    entries for 2011 to 2012, 681–683
  debt service funds (DSFs), 683
    accounting for, 684–685
    and modified accrual basis of accounting, 683
    nonreciprocal routing transfers, 685
    operations of, 685
  financial statements, 685–688
  general fund
    accounting for, 664–677
    budget, 665–666
    defined, 664
    fund balance reclassification, 665
    transactions and interfund activities for year, 666–674
  general fund (GF)
    capital lease, 672–673
    derived tax revenues, 668–669
    encumbrances, accounting for, 669–671
    expenditures, recording, 669
    interfund transactions, 673
    property taxes, 666–668
    revenues from other sources, 669
    supplies, 672
  government-wide financial statements, preparing, 688–694
  permanent funds (PFs), 677–678
  special assessment activities, 683
  special revenue funds (SRFs)
    defined, 676

grants, 676–677
year-end procedures
    adjusting entries, 674–675
    closing entries, 675–676
grants, 676–677
Guidant, 1

H

Halliburton Company, 387
Handy & Harman, 3
Harsco Corporation, 389
Hawaiian Airlines, 604, 608
hedge
  defined, 410
  of net investment in a foreign subsidiary, 432
  net investment in foreign entity, 479–482
hedge accounting, 430–431
  cash flow hedge accounting, 432, 439–441
  fair value hedge accounting, 424, 434, 441–442
  types of, 432–435
hedge contracts, 409
hedge effectiveness, 431–432
hedge transactions, 410–411
heirs, 776
The Hershey Company, 322, 346
Hewitt Associates, 1
Hewlett-Packard (HP), 343
Hierarchy of Generally Accepted Accounting Principles for State and Local Governments (GASB), 627
highly inflationary economies, defined, 468
historical exchange rates, 416
homestead allowance, 777
horizontal integration, 1–2

I

IASB (iInternational Accounting Standards Board), 13
IASC (International Accounting Standards Committee), 13
IAS (International Accounting Standard) No. 39, 455
IBM, 3
IBP, 387
IFRS (International Financial Reporting Standards), 6, 13
impairment test, goodwill, 14–15
income statement, effects of Chapter 11 proceedings on, 607–608
income taxes, financial statement disclosures for, 346–348

indirect holdings, 281
  connecting affiliates structure
    consolidation workpaper–equity method, 286–289
    equity method of account for, 285–286
insolvent partnership, 576–577
installment liquidations, 567–573
  cash distribution plans, 573–576
    schedule of assumed loss absorption, 574
    vulnerability ranking, 574
  general principles, 567
  illustration, 568–573
intangible assets
  current GAAP for, 13–14
  identifiable, 10
  recognition and measurement, 8–9
Intel Corporation, 43, 497–500, 501
intercompany bonds, 219–232
  constructive gains and lessons on, 220–222
  parent
    acquisition of subsidiary bonds by, 222
    purchased by subsidiary, 22–227, 221
intercompany profit transactions–inventory, 145–164
  elimination of intercompany purchases and sales, 146–147
  elimination of unrealized profit in ending inventory, 147–149
    equity method, 149
    workpaper entries, 148–149
  recognition of unrealized profit in beginning inventory, 149–150
intercompany profit transactions—plant assets, 185–203
  depreciable, 190–198
    downstream sales, 190–193
    upstream sales, 193–198
  example of upstream and downstream sales of, 199–202
  inventory purchased for use as operating assets, 202–203
  nondepreciable, 185–190
    downstream sale of land, 186–188
    upstream sale of land, 188–190
  sold at other than fair value, 198–199
intercompany transactions
  of foreign currency, 466–468
  illustration, 469–475
interfund loans, 637

interfund transactions, 673
interim acquisitions of investment interest, 35–37
interim financial reports, 504–511, 505
  estimated annual effective tax rate, computing, 506
  expenses other than product costs, 505
  guidelines for preparing, 506–510
  international accounting standards, 510–511
  nature of, 504–505
  product costs, 505
  SEC disclosures, 510
internal service funds, 631, 712
  accounting for, 712–715
  reporting, in financial statements, 715
International Accounting standards Board (IASB), 6
intestate, defined, 775
intestate succession, 776
inventory
  ending, of purchasing affiliate, 147
  of estate property, 776–777
  intercompany profit transactions, 145–165
  purchased for use as operating assets, 202–203
  recognition of unrealized profit in beginning, 149–150
investee corporation with preferred stock, 38–39
investments, not-for-profits recording of, 741
investment trust funds, 633
involuntary bankruptcy proceeding, 593

J

Johns Manville, 592
Johnson & Johnson, 1
joint ventures, 388–391, 545
  corporate
    accounting for, 388–389
    defined, 388
  general partnerships, 388
  limited partnerships, 388
  nature of, 388
  organizational structures of, 388
  undivided interest, 388
J.P. Morgan Chase, Inc., 430

K

Kimberly-Clark, 2
Kohlberg, Kravis, Roberts and Company (KKR), 387

Kraft Corporation, 2
Krispy Kreme Doughnuts, Inc., 17, 180

L
Laventhol and Horwath, 593
lease agreements, state and local
    government, 672–673
Lehman Brothers, 592
leveraged buyouts (LBOs),
    383–387
limited partnerships, 388,
    544–545
liquidation, 594–603. *See also*
    bankruptcy
  case illustration, 596–603
  Chapter 7 bankruptcy, 594–595
  payment of claims, 595
  statement of affairs, 596–598
  trustee, duties of, 595
  trustee accounting, 598–602
  winding up the case, 603
loan funds, 760
local currency, 464
Loews Cineplex, 593
Lotus Development Corporation, 3
LTV Steel, 592
Lufkin-Conroe Communications
    Company, 2
Lyondell Chemical Company, 592

M
major funds, 643
management approach, 497
Marathon Oil Corporation,
    389–390
MBNA Corporation, 1
MCI, Inc., 43
measured receivables/payables, 414
mergers
  consolidation *vs.*, 4
  defined, 4, 341
  rise in, 1
Microsoft Corporation, 27
mixed-attribute model, 434
Mobile, 1
Montgomery Ward, 592, 606
Moonitz, Maurice, 369
multiple exchange rates, 415–416
Municipal Accounting and Auditing
    (MFOA), 626
Municipal Finance Officers Association
    (MFOA), 626, 626n2. *See also*
    Government Finance Officers
    Association
mutual agency, 526
mutual holdings, 279

parent stock held by subsidiary,
    289–298
subsidiary stock mutually-held,
    298–302

N
National Association of College and
    University Business Officers
    (NACUBO), 756
National Council on Governmental
    Accounting (NCGA), 626
NCR, 2
net assets, statement of, 641–642
net income, 118
net settlement, 410
Nike, 414
noncontrolling interest, 102
noncontrolling interest share, 102
nonexchange transactions, 635
nongovernmental not-for-profit hospi-
    tals/health care organizations,
    750–755
  accounting for, 751–753
  contractual adjustments, 751
  courtesy allowances, 751
  donated assets, 752–753
  gifts and bequests, 752
  operating expenses, 753
  other operating revenues, 752
  patient service revenue, 751
  premium fees, 752
  statement of operations and other
      hospital financial statements,
      754–755
nongovernmental not-for-profit
    organizations, 738
nonreciprocal transfers, 673
nonspendable fund balance, 663
North American Free Trade Agreement
    (NAFTA), 13
North American Van Lines, 387
Northwest Air Lines, 2
not-for-profit (NFP) organization
    "other," 749–750
  voluntary health and welfare
      organizations (VHWOs),
      743–749
    accounting for, 743–748
    closing entries, 748
    contributions, 743–745
    depreciation, 747
    donated long-lived assets, 745
    donated securities and investment
        income, 746–747
    donated services and payment of
        salaries, 747

financial reporting, 748–749
    fixed asset purchase with restricted
        resources, 747
    gifts in kind, 745–746
    membership fees, 746
    special event fund-raisers, 745
    supplies, 746–747
not-for-profit (NFP) organizations
  accounting principles, 738–743
  collections, 743
  contributions, 740–741
    conditional promise to give, 740
    donor-imposed conditions or
        restrictions, 741
    gifts of long-lived assets, 741
    investments and investment
        income, 741
    unconditional promise to
        give, 740
  financial statements, 738–740
    permanently restricted net
        assets, 739
    statement of activities, 739–740
    statement of cash flows, 740
    statement of financial
        position, 739
    statement of functional
        expenses, 740
    temporarily restricted net
        assets, 739
    unrestricted net assets, 739
  fund accounting, 743
  measurement principles, 742–743
  nature of, 737–738
  program services, 739
  supporting services, 739–740
  transfers, 741–742
    agency transactions, 742
    exchange transactions, 742
    gifts in kind, 742
Nynex Corporation, 3

O
Odyssey Investment Partners, 387
offering circular, 80
Office Depot, 3
Office of U.S. Trustee, 594
official exchange rates, 415
one-line consolidation, 29–37,
    390–391
operating segments, 498
operational accountability, 641
option contracts, 436–437
options, 411
Oracle Corporation, 1
order or relief, 593

other postemployment benefits (OPEB), 726
outside customers, 632
ownership interests
    sale of, 253–262
        at beginning of the period, 254
        noncontrolling interest computation, 258
        resulting in deconsolidation, 258–259
        sale of additional shares by a subsidiary, 259–261
        subsidiary sells shares to outside entities, 260–261
        subsidiary sells shares to parent, 259–260
        summary of subsidiary stock sales concepts, 261
        treasury stock transactions by a subsidiary, 261–262

P
parent bonds
    purchased by subsidiary, 222–227
        effect on consolidate statements in subsequently years, 227
        equity method, 223–227
        subsidiary acquisition of, 221
parent-company and consolidated earnings per share, 322–323
    diluted securities of subsidiary convertible into parent shares, 324
    dilutive securities of subsidiary convertible into subsidiary shares, 323–324
parent company theory, 369
parent-subsidiary relationship, 62–63
partnership agreements, 526
    insolvent partners and partnerships, 576–577
partnership liquidation, 561–589
    debt capital balances in solvent partnership, 562–565
    installment liquidation, 567–573
    interim statement of, example of, 569
    process, 561–565
    safe payment to partners, 565–567
    simple, 561–562
partnership liquidations, cash distribution schedule, 575–576
partnerships, 525–560
    additional investments and withdrawals, 528–529
    admission of new partner, 537

articles of, 526
assignment of interest to third party, 536–537
defined, 526
dissociation, 536
dissociation of, through death or retirement, 542–544
    excess payment to retiring partner, 543–544
    overvalued assets written down, 544
    payment to retiring partner less than capital balance, 544
financial reporting, 526
goodwill on, 528
initial investments in, 526–528
    bonus on, 527
    noncash investments, 527
investing in existing, 539–542
    basis for revaluation, 538–539
    at book value, 540
    partnership assets not revalued (bonus to new partner), 542
    partnership assets not revalued (bonus to old partners), 541
    partnership assets revalued (goodwill to new partner), 541–542
    partnership assets revalued (goodwill to old partners), 540–541
limited, 544–545
loans and advances, 529
nature of, 525–526
operations, 529–530
partnership agreements, 526
profit and loss sharing agreements, 530–536
purchase of interest from existing partner, 537–539, 539
    goodwill approach, 538
par value theory, 220
patient service revenue, 751
pay-fixed, receive-variable interest swamp, 439
pay-variable, receive-fixed swamp, 441
Pennzoil, 605
Pension Benefit Guaranty Corporation (PBGC), 605
pension trust funds, 633, 724
    accounting for, 726
PeopleSoft, Inc., 1
PepsiCo, 62, 253, 279, 322
permanent funds (PFs), 632–633, 677–678

permanently restricted net assets, 739
personal representative, defined, 775, 776
Phelps Dodge, 1
Phillip Morris Company, 2
piecemeal acquisitions, 251–253
Pixelworks, Inc., 220
plant assets
    intercompany profit transactions, 185–203
    purchase of, private not-for-profit colleges/universities accounting for, 759–760
plant funds, 760
pooling of interests method, 5–6
Pratt and Lambert, 2
preacquisition dividends, 247, 249
preacquisition earnings, 247
preferred stock, investee corporation with, 38–39
preliminary prospectus, 180
primary beneficiary, 392
primary government, 638
private not-for-profit colleges/universities, 755–761
    accounting for, 756–760
        appropriations from federal, state, and local governments, 757
        contributions, 757
        endowments, 757–758
        expenses, 759
        purchases of plant assets, 759–760
        sales and services of auxiliary enterprises, 758
        sales and services of educational activities, 758
        student financial aid, 757
        tuition and fees, 756–757
    agency funds, 760
    AICPA model (fund structure), 760–761
    current operating funds, 760
    financial statements, 760
    loan funds, 760
    plant funds, 760
private-purpose trust funds, 633, 724
    accounting for, 725
probated, 776
probate proceedings, 776
profit and loss sharing agreements, 530–536
program revenues, 643
program services, not-for-profit organizations, 739

promise to give, defined, 740
property taxes, accounting for, 666–668
proportionate consolidation, 389–390, 389–391
proprietary funds, 628, 711–712
    accounting equation for, 629
    enterprise funds, 631–632
    enterprise funds (EFs), 715–717
    financial statements, 718–722
    government-wide financial statements, preparing, 727
    internal service funds, 631, 712–715
    required note disclosures, 727
    statement of cash flows, 718–722
    types, 631–632
pro rata, 389–390
prospectus, 180
Prudential Insurance Company of America, 607
purchase business combinations, 343–345
    equity method of accounting for, 344–345
    workpaper entries for, 344–345
push-down accounting, 79–81
    defined, 381
    leveraged buyouts (LBOs), 383–387
    nature of, 381
    in year after, 383
    in year of acquisition, 381–383
put options, 411

R
R. H. Macy & Company, 607
reacquisition earnings, 248–249
reciprocal transfers, 673
red herring prospectus, 180
registration statements, 180
Regulation A, Securities Act of 1933, 180
Regulation S-K (SEC), 181
Regulation S (SEC), 183
Regulation S-X (SEC), 181
related-party transactions, 42
remeasurement
    of foreign currency financial statements, 466
    functional currency and, 465–466
    illustration, 475–479
reorganization
    case illustration, 610–616
        fresh-start reporting, 613–616
        operations under Chapter 11, 612–613

reclassification of liabilities subject to compromise, 610–612
    reorganization plan, 613
Chapter 11 bankruptcy, 603–605
    committee representation, 604–605
    defined, 341
    doctrine of equitable subordination, 608
    effects of Chapter 11 proceedings
        on balance sheet, 607
        on income statement and statement of cash flows, 607–608
    financial reporting during, 607–608
    operating under Chapter 11, 605–606
    reorganization value, 608–609
    supplementary combined financial statements, 608
    trustee or debtor in possession, 604
reorganization plan, 606–607, 613
reorganization value, 608–609
    fresh-start reporting, 609
reportable segments
    aggregation criteria, 498
    operating, illustration of
        asset test, 499
        operating profit test, 499–500
        revenue test, 499
    quantitative thresholds, 498
    reconciliation requirements, 501
    reconsideration of, 498
    reevaluation, 500
    segment disclosures, 500–501
reporting currency, 464
reporting entity, 62
residual beneficiaries, 778
restricted fund balance, 663
retained earnings (ending), 118
revenue recognition, 634–636
revenues
    general, 643
    program, 643
R.H. Macy & Company, 387
RJR Nabisco, 387

S
safe payments, to partners, 565–567
Safeway Stores, 387
salary allowances, 528–529
Sanofi-Synthelabo SA, 3
Sarbanes-Oxley Act of 2002 (SOX), 17–18, 180–181
schedule of assumed loss absorption, 574

Scott Paper, 2
Seagate, 387
Sealy Corporation, 387
Securities Act of 1933, 179–180
    exempt securities issues, 180
    issuance of securities in public offerings, 179–180
    prospectus, 180
    registering securities and, 181
    Regulation A, 180
Securities Act of 1934, 17
Securities and Exchange Commission (SEC), 17
    Accounting Series Releases (ASRs), 181–182
    developments
        EDGAR system, 184
        international registration and, 183
        Regulation S, 183
        small business, 183
    Form 8-K, 182–183
    Form 10-K, 182
    Form S-1, 181
    Form S-2, 181
    Form S-3, 181
    Form S-4, 181
    influence on accounting, 179–184
    integrated disclosure system, 181–182
        codification of SABs and ASRs, 182
        Form 10-1, 183
        Form 8-K, 182
        objective of, 182
        standardization of audited financial statements, 182–183
    national exchanges and, 180
    Regulation S-K, 181
    Regulation S-X, 181
    responsibilities of, 181
    and SOX violations, 17
    Staff Accounting Bulletins (SABs), 181–182
Securities Exchange Act of 1934
    creation of, 180
segment disclosures, 500–501, 503–504
segment reporting, 497–504
service efforts and accomplishment (SEA) reporting, 655
Service Merchandise, 606
Sherwin-Williams, 2
Silver Lake Partners, 387
simple partnership liquidation, 561–562

Simplicity Manufacturing, Inc., 2
Six Flags, Inc., 409, 411
Smithfield Foods, 387
SOP 90-7, 608
special assessment levies, 683
special purpose entities (SPEs), 102
special-purpose governments, 738
special revenue funds, 632
special revenue funds (SRFs)
  defined, 676
  grants, 676–677
specific devise, 776
speculation, foreign currency, 453–454
spot exchange rates, 416
Staff Accounting Bulletin (SAB) No. 101, Revenue Recognition in Financial Statements, 180–181
Staples, 3
Starbucks, 409, 414
state and local governmental units, historical development of accounting principles for, 625–627
statement of activities, 642–643
statement of affairs, 596–598
statement of cash flows, effects of Chapter 11 proceedings on, 607–608
statement of net assets, 641–642
Statement of Position 80-2 (AICPA), 626
Statement on Auditing Standards No. 69, 627
step-by-step acquisition, investment in, 37
stock dividends, by a subsidiary, 262–264
stock investments, accounting for, 25–29
stock splits, by a subsidiary, 262–264
strengthening currency, 415
student financial aid, private not-for-profit colleges/universities accounting for, 757
subsidiaries, 5
  with convertible preferred stock, 324–325
    convertible into parent-company common stock, 325
    convertible into subsidiary common stock, 325

with options and convertible bonds, 325
    options and bonds convertible into subsidiary common stock, 326
    options and convertible bonds with parent's common stock, 326
subsidiary bonds
  acquisition of, 222
  constructive gains and losses, 220–222
  purchased by parent
    effect on consolidated statements in subsequent years, 231
    equity method, 228–230
subsidiary ledgers, 666
subsidiary preferred stock, 315–322
  held by parent, 319–322
    comparison cost method and constructive retirement, 322
    constructive retirement of, 319–322
    preferred stock investment maintained on cost basis, 322
  not held by parent, 316–319
supplies, accounting for, 672
supporting services, not-for-profit organizations, 739–740
swaps, 411
Symantec, 1

T
Telecommunications Act of 1996, 2
temporal method, of converting foreign financial statements, 464
temporarily restricted net assets, 739
testacy proceeding, 776
testate, defined, 775
Texaco, 1, 605
Texas Utilities Company, 2
Thornburg Mortgage, 592
Time Warner, Inc., 42, 430
total assets, 118
total equities, 118
Toys R Us, 3
traditional theory of consolidation, 369
transaction analysis, 630–631
  using specific funds, 633–634
transactions
  exchange, 635
  nonexchange, 635
translation
  foreign currency, 465
  of foreign currency financial statements, 466

illustration, 469–475
translation adjustment, 479
  illustration, 480–482
  limit on gain/loss from, 482
treasury stock approach, 289–291
trust and agency funds, 629. *see also* fiduciary funds
trust funds, 724–727
  defined, 724
  financial statements for, 725
  pension, 724
  private-purpose, 724
trusts
  accounting for, 782–783
  testamentary, 782
  trustee, 782
tuition and fees/ private not-for-profit colleges/universities accounting for, 756–757
Tweedie, Sir David, 6

U
unassigned fund balance, 64
undivided interest, 388
Uniform Partnership Act (1914), 525
Uniform Partnership Act (1997) (UPA), 525
Uniform Probate Code (UPC), 776
United Defense, L.P., 389
unlimited liability, 526
unrestricted net assets, 739
upstream sales, 150–153
  intercompany profits from equity method, 158–161, 161–164
  unrealized profits from
    deferral of intercompany profit in period of intercompany sale, 156–157
    recognition of intercompany profit upon sale to outside entities, 157–158
US Airways, 592
USX Corporation, 251

V
variable interest entities (VIEs), 102
  accounting for, 391–393
  consolidation of, 393
  defined, 391
  identifying, 391–393
Venturers, 388
Veritas Software, 1, 387
voluntary bankruptcy proceeding, 593

voluntary health and welfare
      organizations (VHWOs),
      743–749
   accounting for, 743–748
   closing entries, 748
   contributions, 743–745
   depreciation, 747
   donated long-lived a
      ssets, 745
   donated securities and investment
      income, 746–747
   donated services and payment of
      salaries, 747
   financial reporting, 748–749
   fixed asset purchase with restricted
      resources, 747
   gifts in kind, 745–746
   membership fees, 746
   special event fund-raisers, 745
   supplies, 746–747
vulnerability rankings, 574

W
Wachovia Corporation, 1
Wal-Mart, 414
Walt Disney Company, 106, 146,
      247–248
weakening currency, 415
Wells Fargo, 1
Wheeling-Pittsburgh Steel, 3
WHX, 3
WorldCom, 17, 592